PREFACE

This Supplement is designed to provide students, instructors and practitioners with a convenient one-volume compilation of statutes, regulations, and forms governing nonprofit organizations. Both state and federal materials are included. The state materials include selected provisions from the nonprofit corporation acts of California, Illinois, and New York. Excerpts from the Restatement of Nonprofit Charitable Organizations, the Restatement (Third) of Trusts, and several other pertinent uniform acts also are included.

The federal materials consist of extensive provisions of the Internal Revenue Code of 1986 and the Treasury Regulations, and more selective excerpts from the federal antitrust laws. Some of the tax regulations have been edited more heavily than others to winnow out arcane minutia and transitional rules, but considerable detail remains for those with the time or inclination for more technical coverage, particularly in the area of private foundations. We have done our best to include sufficiently precise header references to enable users to navigate successfully through the various sub-sections of the Code and regulations.

To give students some exposure to the tools with which the legal and accounting profession must work in this area, we also have included selected tax forms and other materials, such as a sample conflict of interest policy. Particularly instructive are the application for tax-exempt status under § 501(c)(3) (Form 1023) and the Form 990 information return. The Supplement also includes a list of useful Internet sites.

This edition is current through March 1, 2026. We will provide new editions as developments warrant and always welcome comments and suggestions for improvement.

JAMES J. FISHMAN
STEPHEN SCHWARZ
LLOYD HITOSHI MAYER
ROGER COLINVAUX

March 2026

ACKNOWLEDGMENTS

We gratefully acknowledge the publishers and copyright holders who gave permission to reprint excerpts from the following works:

Revised Model Nonprofit Corporation Act (1988) and Model Nonprofit Corporation Act (1964). Reprinted with permission of Panel Publishers, a division of Aspen Publishers, Inc., 36 W. 44th St., Suite 1316, New York, N.Y. 10036. All rights reserved.

Restatement of the Law, Charitable Nonprofit Organizations. Copyright © 2021 by The American Law Institute. All rights reserved. Reprinted with the permission of The American Law Institute.

Restatement Second Trusts; Restatement Third Trusts. Copyright © 1959, 2003, 2007, 2012 by The American Law Institute. All rights reserved. Reprinted with the permission of The American Law Institute.

Uniform Prudent Management of Institutional Funds Act; Uniform Prudent Investor Act; Uniform Unincorporated Nonprofit Association Act. Copyright © 2006 by the National Conference of Commissioners on Uniform State Laws. Reproduced with permission.

By-Laws of XYZ, Inc. from Getting Organized. Reprinted with permission of Lawyers Alliance for New York.

Model Protection of Charitable Assets Act. Copyright © 2011 by the National Conference of Commissioners on Uniform State Laws. Reproduced with permission.

TABLE OF CONTENTS

APPENDIX

SELECTED SECTIONS

NONPROFIT ORGANIZATIONS

STATUTES, REGULATIONS, AND FORMS

2026 Edition

CALIFORNIA CORPORATIONS CODE (SELECTED PROVISIONS)

TITLE 1. CORPORATIONS

DIVISION 2. NONPROFIT CORPORATION LAW

PART 1

GENERAL PROVISIONS AND DEFINITIONS GOVERNING PARTS 1 THROUGH 5

PART 2

NONPROFIT PUBLIC BENEFIT CORPORATIONS

CHAPTER 1. ORGANIZATION AND BYLAWS

Article 1. Title and Purposes

Article 3. Articles of Incorporation

Article 4. Powers

CHAPTER 2. DIRECTORS AND MANAGEMENT

Article 1. General Provisions

Article 2. Selection, Removal and Resignation of Directors

Article 3. Standards of Conduct

Article 4. Investments

Article 5. Examination by Attorney General

Article 6. Compliance with Internal Revenue Code

CHAPTER 3. MEMBERS

Article 4. Termination of Membership

CHAPTER 4. DISTRIBUTIONS

Article 1. Limitations

Article 2. Liability of Members

CHAPTER 10. MERGERS

CHAPTER 12. REQUIRED FILINGS BY CORPORATION OR ITS AGENT

CHAPTER 13. RECORDS, REPORTS, AND RIGHTS OF INSPECTION

Article 2. Required Records, Reports to Directors and Members

Article 3. Rights of Inspection

CHAPTER 15. INVOLUNTARY DISSOLUTION

CHAPTER 18. CRIMES AND PENALTIES

PART 3

NONPROFIT MUTUAL BENEFIT CORPORATIONS

CHAPTER 1. ORGANIZATION AND BYLAWS

Article 1. Title and Purposes

CHAPTER 2. DIRECTORS AND MANAGEMENT

Article 3. Standards of Conduct

CHAPTER 3. MEMBERS

Article 4. Termination of Memberships

CHAPTER 4. DISTRIBUTIONS

Article 1. Limitations

CHAPTER 13. RECORDS, REPORTS AND RIGHTS OF INSPECTION

Article 2. Required Records, Reports to Directors and Members

CHAPTER 15. INVOLUNTARY DISSOLUTION

CHAPTER 17. GENERAL PROVISIONS RELATING TO DISSOLUTION

PART 4

NONPROFIT RELIGIOUS CORPORATIONS

CHAPTER 2. DIRECTORS AND MANAGEMENT

Article 3. Examination by Attorney General

TITLE 1. CORPORATIONS

DIVISION 2. NONPROFIT CORPORATION LAW

PART 1

GENERAL PROVISIONS AND DEFINITIONS

GOVERNING PARTS 1 THROUGH 5

§ 5047.5. Actions for damages against directors and officers; legislative findings; liability; applicability

(a) The Legislature finds and declares that the services of directors and officers of nonprofit corporations who serve without compensation are critical to the efficient conduct and management of the public service and charitable affairs of the people of California. The willingness of volunteers to offer their services has been deterred by a perception that their personal assets are at risk for these activities. The unavailability and unaffordability of appropriate liability insurance makes it difficult for these corporations to protect the personal assets of their volunteer decisionmakers with adequate insurance. It is the public policy of this state to provide incentive and protection to the individuals who perform these important functions.

(b) Except as provided in this section, no cause of action for monetary damages shall arise against any person serving without compensation as a director or officer of a nonprofit corporation subject to Part 2 (commencing with Section 5110), Part 3 (commencing with Section 7110), or Part 4 (commencing with Section 9110) of this division on account of any negligent act or omission occurring (1) within the scope of that person's duties as a director acting as a board member, or within the scope of that person's duties as an officer acting in an official capacity; (2) in good faith; (3) in a manner that the person believes to be in the best interest of the corporation; and (4) is in the exercise of his or her policymaking judgment.

(c) This section shall not limit the liability of a director or officer for any of the following:

(1) Self-dealing transactions, as described in Sections 5233 and 9243.

(2) Conflicts of interest, as described in Section 7233.

(3) Actions described in Sections 5237, 7236, and 9245.

(4) In the case of a charitable trust, an action or proceeding against a trustee brought by a beneficiary of that trust.

(5) Any action or proceeding brought by the Attorney General.

(6) Intentional, wanton, or reckless acts, gross negligence, or an action based on fraud, oppression, or malice.

(7) Any action brought under Chapter 2 (commencing with Section 16700) of Part 2 of Division 7 of the Business and Professions Code.

(d) This section only applies to nonprofit corporations organized to provide religious, charitable, literary, educational, scientific, social, or other forms of public service that are exempt from federal income taxation under Section 501(c)(3) or 501(c)(6) of the Internal Revenue Code.

(e) This section applies only if the nonprofit corporation maintains a general liability insurance policy with an amount of coverage of at least the following amounts:

(1) If the corporation's annual budget is less than fifty thousand dollars ($50,000), the minimum required amount is five hundred thousand dollars ($500,000).

(2) If the corporation's annual budget equals or exceeds fifty thousand dollars ($50,000), the minimum required amount is one million dollars ($1,000,000).

This section applies only if the claim against the director or officer may also be made directly against the corporation and a general liability insurance policy is in force both at the time of injury and at the time the claim against the corporation is made, so that a policy is applicable to the claim. If a general liability policy is found to cover the damages caused by the director or officer, no cause of action as provided in this section shall be maintained against the director or officer.

(f) For the purposes of this section, the payment of actual expenses incurred in attending meetings or otherwise in the execution of the duties of a director or officer shall not constitute compensation.

(g) Nothing in this section shall be construed to limit the liability of a nonprofit corporation for any negligent act or omission of a director, officer, employee, agent, or servant occurring within the scope of his or her duties.

(h) This section does not apply to any corporation that unlawfully restricts membership, services, or benefits conferred on the basis of race, religious creed, color, national origin, ancestry, sex, marital status, disability, political affiliation, or age.

(i) This section does not apply to any volunteer director or officer who receives compensation from the corporation in any other capacity, including, but not limited to, as an employee.

§ 5056. Member

(a) "Member" means any person who, pursuant to a specific provision of a corporation's articles or bylaws, has the right to vote for the election of a director or directors or on a disposition of all or substantially all of the assets of a corporation or on a merger or on a dissolution unless the provision granting such right to vote is only effective as a result of paragraph (2) of subdivision (a) of Section 7132. "Member" also means any person who is designated in the articles or bylaws as a member and, pursuant to a specific provision of a corporation's articles or bylaws, has the right to vote on changes to the articles or bylaws.

(b) The articles or bylaws may confer some or all of the rights of a member, set forth in this part and in Parts 2 through 5 of this division.

* * *

§ 5057. Membership

A "membership" refers to the rights a member has pursuant to a corporation's articles, bylaws and this division.

§ 5059. Nonprofit mutual benefit corporation; mutual benefit corporation

"Nonprofit mutual benefit corporation" or "mutual benefit corporation" means a corporation which is organized under Part 3 (commencing with Section 7110), or subject to Part 3 under the provisions of subdivision (a) of Section 5003.

§ 5060. Nonprofit public benefit corporation; public benefit corporation

"Nonprofit public benefit corporation" or "public benefit corporation" means a corporation which is organized under Part 2 (commencing with Section 5110) or subject to Part 2 under the provisions of subdivision (a) of Section 5003.

§ 5061. Nonprofit religious corporation; religious corporation

"Nonprofit religious corporation" or "religious corporation" means a corporation which is organized under Part 4 (commencing with Section 9110) or subject to Part 4 pursuant to subdivision (a) of Section 5003.

Part 2

NONPROFIT PUBLIC BENEFIT CORPORATIONS

Chapter 1

ORGANIZATION AND BYLAWS

Article 1. Title and Purposes

§ 5111. Public or charitable purposes

Subject to any other provisions of law of this state applying to the particular class of corporation or line of activity, a corporation may be formed under this part for any public or charitable purposes.

Article 3. Articles of Incorporation

§ 5130. Name; statement of purposes; agent for service of process; addresses

The articles of incorporation formed under this part shall set forth:

(a) The name of the corporation.

(b)(1) Except as provided in paragraph (2), the following statement:

"This corporation is a nonprofit public benefit corporation and is not organized for the private gain of any person. It is organized under the Nonprofit Public Benefit Corporation Law for (public or charitable [insert one or both]) purposes."

[If the purposes include "public" purposes, the articles shall, and in all other cases the articles may, include a further description of the corporation's purposes.]

(2) If the corporation is a public bank, as defined in Section 57600 of the Government Code, the articles shall set forth a statement of purpose that is prescribed in subdivision (b) of Section 57601 of the Government Code.

(c) The name and street address in this state of the corporation's initial agent for service of process in accordance with subdivision (b) of Section 6210.

(d) The initial street address of the corporation.

(e) The initial mailing address of the corporation, if different from the initial street address.

Article 4. Powers

§ 5142. Breach of charitable trust; actions; standing; notice to and intervention of attorney general; rescission or injunction of contractual performance

(a) Notwithstanding Section 5141, any of the following may bring an action to enjoin, correct, obtain damages for or to otherwise remedy a breach of a charitable trust:

(1) The corporation, or a member in the name of the corporation pursuant to Section 5710.

(2) An officer of the corporation.

(3) A director of the corporation.

(4) A person with a reversionary, contractual, or property interest in the assets subject to such charitable trust.

(5) The Attorney General, or any person granted relator status by the Attorney General.

The Attorney General shall be given notice of any action brought by the persons specified in paragraphs (1) through (4), and may intervene.

(b) In an action under this section, the court may not rescind or enjoin the performance of a contract unless:

(1) All of the parties to the contract are parties to the action;

(2) No party to the contract has, in good faith, and without actual notice of the trust restriction, parted with value under the contract or in reliance upon it; and

(3) It is equitable to do so.

Chapter 2

DIRECTORS AND MANAGEMENT

Article 1. General Provisions

§ 5210. Board of directors; conduct and exercise of corporate activities, affairs and powers; delegation

Each corporation shall have a board of directors. Subject to the provisions of this part and any limitations in the articles or bylaws relating to action required to be approved by the members (Section 5034), or by a majority of all members (Section 5033), the activities and affairs of a corporation shall be conducted and all corporate powers shall be exercised by or under the direction of the board. The board may delegate the management of the activities of the corporation to any person or persons, management company, or committee however composed, provided that the activities and affairs of the corporation shall be managed and all corporate powers shall be exercised under the ultimate direction of the board.

§ 5211. Board meetings; regular meetings; notice; time and place; participation through use of conference telephones, electronic transmissions, or electronic video screen communications; quorum; waiver of meeting requirement; voting

(a) Unless otherwise provided in the articles or in the bylaws, all of the following apply:

(1) Meetings of the board may be called by the chair of the board or the president or any vice president or the secretary or any two directors.

(2) Regular meetings of the board may be held without notice if the time and place of the meetings are fixed by the bylaws or the board. Special meetings of the board shall be held upon four days' notice by first-class mail or 48 hours' notice delivered personally or by telephone, including a voice messaging system or by electronic transmission by the corporation (Section 20). The articles or bylaws may not dispense with notice of a special meeting. A notice, or waiver of notice, need not specify the purpose of any regular or special meeting of the board.

(3) Notice of a meeting need not be given to a director who provides a waiver of notice or consent to holding the meeting or an approval of the minutes thereof in writing, whether before or after the meeting, or who attends the meeting without protesting, prior thereto or at its commencement, the lack of notice to that director. These waivers, consents, and approvals shall be filed with the corporate records or made a part of the minutes of the meetings.

(4) A majority of the directors present, whether or not a quorum is present, may adjourn any meeting to another time and place. If the meeting is adjourned for more than 24 hours, notice of an adjournment to another time or place shall be given prior to the time of the adjourned meeting to the directors who were not present at the time of the adjournment.

(5) Meetings of the board may be held at a place within or without the state that has been designated in the notice of the meeting or, if not stated in the notice or there is no notice, designated in the bylaws or by resolution of the board.

(6) Directors may participate in a meeting through use of conference telephone, electronic video screen communication, or electronic transmission by and to the corporation (Sections 20 and 21). Participation in a meeting through use of conference telephone or electronic video screen communication pursuant to this subdivision constitutes presence in person at that meeting as long as all directors participating in the meeting are able to hear one another. Participation in a meeting through use of electronic transmission by

and to the corporation, other than conference telephone and electronic video screen communication, pursuant to this subdivision constitutes presence in person at that meeting if both of the following apply:

(A) Each director participating in the meeting can communicate with all of the other directors concurrently.

(B) Each director is provided the means of participating in all matters before the board, including, without limitation, the capacity to propose, or to interpose an objection to, a specific action to be taken by the corporation.

(7) A majority of the number of directors authorized in or pursuant to the articles or bylaws constitutes a quorum of the board for the transaction of business. The articles or bylaws may require the presence of one or more specified directors in order to constitute a quorum of the board to transact business, as long as the death or nonexistence of a specified director or the death or nonexistence of the person or persons otherwise authorized to appoint or designate that director does not prevent the corporation from transacting business in the normal course of events. The articles or bylaws may not provide that a quorum shall be less than one-fifth the number of directors authorized in or pursuant to the articles or bylaws, or less than two, whichever is larger, unless the number of directors authorized in or pursuant to the articles or bylaws is one, in which case one director constitutes a quorum.

(8) Subject to the provisions of Sections 5212, 5233, 5234, 5235, and subdivision (e) of Section 5238, an act or decision done or made by a majority of the directors present at a meeting duly held at which a quorum is present is the act of the board. The articles or bylaws may not provide that a lesser vote than a majority of the directors present at a meeting is the act of the board. A meeting at which a quorum is initially present may continue to transact business notwithstanding the withdrawal of directors, if any action taken is approved by at least a majority of the required quorum for that meeting, or a greater number required by this division, the articles, or the bylaws.

(b) An action required or permitted to be taken by the board may be taken without a meeting if all directors individually or collectively consent in writing to that action and if, subject to subdivision (a) of Section 5224, the number of directors then in office constitutes a quorum. The written consent or consents shall be filed with the minutes of the proceedings of the board. The action by written consent shall have the same force and effect as a unanimous vote of the directors. For purposes of this subdivision only, "all directors" does not include an "interested director" as defined in subdivision (a) of Section 5233 or a "common director" as described in Section 5234 who abstains in writing from providing consent, if (1) the facts described in paragraph (2) or (3) of subdivision (d) of Section 5233 are established or the provisions of paragraph (1) or (2) of subdivision (a) of Section 5234 are satisfied, as appropriate, at or prior to execution of the written consent or consents; (2) the establishment of those facts or satisfaction of those provisions, as applicable, is included in the written consent or consents executed by the noninterested or noncommon directors or in other records of the corporation;

and (3) the noninterested or noncommon directors, as applicable, approve the action by a vote that is sufficient without counting the votes of the interested directors or common directors.

(c) Each director shall have one vote on each matter presented to the board of directors for action. A director shall not vote by proxy.

(d) The provisions of this section apply also to incorporators, to committees of the board, and to action by those incorporators or committees mutatis mutandis.

§ 5213. Officers; titles; duties; selections; resignation

(a) A corporation shall have (1) a chair of the board, who may be given the title chair, chairperson, chair of the board, or chairperson of the board, or a president or both, (2) a secretary, (3) a treasurer or a chief financial officer or both, and (4) any other officers with any titles and duties as shall be stated in the bylaws or determined by the board and as may be necessary to enable it to sign instruments. The president, or if there is no president the chair of the board, is the general manager and chief executive officer of the corporation, unless otherwise provided in the articles or bylaws. Unless otherwise specified in the articles or the bylaws, if there is no chief financial officer, the treasurer is the chief financial officer of the corporation. Any number of offices may be held by the same person unless the articles or bylaws provide otherwise, except that no person serving as the secretary, the treasurer, or the chief financial officer may serve concurrently as the president or chair of the board. Any compensation of the president or chief executive officer and the chief financial officer or treasurer shall be determined in accordance with subdivision (g) of Section 12586 of the Government Code, if applicable.

(b) Except as otherwise provided by the articles or bylaws, officers shall be chosen by the board and serve at the pleasure of the board, subject to the rights, if any, of an officer under any contract of employment. Any officer may resign at any time upon written notice to the corporation without prejudice to the rights, if any, of the corporation under any contract to which the officer is a party.

(c) If the articles or bylaws provide for the election of any officers by the members, the term of office of the elected officer shall be one year unless the articles or bylaws provide for a different term which shall not exceed three years.

Article 2. Selection, Removal and Resignation of Directors

§ 5227. Interested persons; limitation

(a) Any other provision of this part notwithstanding, not more than 49 percent of the persons serving on the board of any corporation may be interested persons.

(b) For the purpose of this section, "interested persons" means either:

(1) Any person currently being compensated by the corporation for services rendered to it within the previous 12 months, whether as a full or part-time employee, independent contractor, or otherwise, excluding any reasonable compensation paid to a director as director; or

(2) Any brother, sister, ancestor, descendant, spouse, brother-in-law, sister-in-law, son-in-law, daughter-in-law, mother-in-law, or father-in-law of any such person.

(c) A person with standing under Section 5142 may bring an action to correct any violation of this section. The court may enter any order which shall provide an equitable and fair remedy to the corporation, including, but not limited to, an order for the election of additional directors, an order to enlarge the size of the board, or an order for the removal of directors.

(d) The provisions of this section shall not affect the validity or enforceability of any transaction entered into by a corporation.

Article 3. Standards of Conduct

§ 5230. Duties and liabilities; compensation; obligations of trustees

(a) Any duties and liabilities set forth in this article shall apply without regard to whether a director is compensated by the corporation.

(b) Part 4 (commencing with Section 16000) of Division 9 of the Probate Code does not apply to the directors of any corporation.

§ 5231. Good faith; standard of care; reliance on information presented by others; liability

(a) A director shall perform the duties of a director, including duties as a member of any committee of the board upon which the director may serve, in good faith, in a manner such director believes to be in the best interests of the corporation and with such care, including reasonable inquiry, as an ordinarily prudent person in a like position would use under similar circumstances.

(b) In performing the duties of a director, a director shall be entitled to rely on information, opinions, reports or statements, including financial statements and other financial data, in each case prepared or presented by:

(1) One or more officers or employees of the corporation whom the director believes to be reliable and competent in the matters presented;

(2) Counsel, independent accountants or other persons as to matters which the director believes to be within such person's professional or expert competence; or

(3) A committee upon which the director does not serve that is composed exclusively of any or any combination of directors, or persons described in paragraph (2), as to matters

within the committee's designated authority, which committee the director believes to merit confidence, so long as, in any case, the director acts in good faith, after reasonable inquiry when the need therefor[e] is indicated by the circumstances and without knowledge that would cause that reliance to be unwarranted.

(c) Except as provided in Section 5233, a person who performs the duties of a director in accordance with subdivisions (a) and (b) shall have no liability based upon any alleged failure to discharge the person's obligations as a director, including, without limiting the generality of the foregoing, any actions or omissions which exceed or defeat a public or charitable purpose to which a corporation, or assets held by it, and dedicated.

§ 5233. Self-dealing transactions; interested director; exceptions; actions; burden of proof; limitations; remedies

(a) Except as provided in subdivision (b), for the purpose of this section, a self-dealing transaction means a transaction to which the corporation is a party and in which one or more of its directors has a material financial interest and which does not meet the requirements of paragraph (1), (2), or (3) of subdivision (d). Such a director is an "interested director" for the purpose of this section.

(b) The provisions of this section do not apply to any of the following:

(1) An action of the board fixing the compensation of a director as a director or officer of the corporation.

(2) A transaction which is part of a public or charitable program of the corporation if it:

(i) is approved or authorized by the corporation in good faith and without unjustified favoritism; and

(ii) results in a benefit to one or more directors or their families because they are in the class of persons intended to be benefited by the public or charitable program.

(3) A transaction, of which the interested director or directors have no actual knowledge, and which does not exceed the lesser of 1 percent of the gross receipts of the corporation for the preceding fiscal year or one hundred thousand dollars ($100,000).

(c) The Attorney General or, if the Attorney General is joined as an indispensable party, any of the following may bring an action in the superior court of the proper county for the remedies specified in subdivision (h):

(1) The corporation, or a member asserting the right in the name of the corporation pursuant to Section 5710.

(2) A director of the corporation.

(3) An officer of the corporation.

(4) Any person granted relator status by the Attorney General.

(d) In any action brought under subdivision (c) the remedies specified in subdivision (h) shall not be granted if:

(1) The Attorney General, or the court in an action in which the Attorney General in an indispensable party, has approved the transaction before or after it was consummated; or

(2) The following facts are established:

(A) The corporation entered into the transaction for its own benefit;

(B) The transaction was fair and reasonable as to the corporation at the time the corporation entered into the transaction;

(C) Prior to consummating the transaction or any part thereof the board authorized or approved the transaction in good faith by a vote of a majority of the directors then in office without counting the vote of the interested director or directors, and with knowledge of the material facts concerning the transaction and the director's interest in the transaction. Except as provided in paragraph (3) of this subdivision, action by a committee of the board shall not satisfy this paragraph; and

(D)(i) Prior to authorizing or approving the transaction the board considered and in good faith determined after reasonable investigation under the circumstances that the corporation could not have obtained a more advantageous arrangement with reasonable effort under the circumstances or (ii) the corporation in fact could not have obtained a more advantageous arrangement with reasonable effort under the circumstances; or

(3) The following facts are established:

(A) A committee or person authorized by the board approved the transaction in a manner consistent with the standards set forth in paragraph (2) of this subdivision;

(B) It was not reasonably practicable to obtain approval of the board prior to entering into the transaction; and

(C) The board, after determining in good faith that the conditions of subparagraphs (A) and (B) of this paragraph were satisfied, ratified the transaction at its next meeting by a vote of the majority of the directors then in office without counting the vote of the interested director or directors.

(e) Except as provided in subdivision (f), an action under subdivision (c) must be filed within two years after written notice setting forth the material facts of the transaction and the director's interest in the transaction is filed with the Attorney General in accordance with such regulations, if any, as the Attorney General may adopt or, if no such notice is filed, within three years after the transaction occurred, except for the Attorney General, who shall have 10 years after the transaction occurred within which to file an action.

(f) In any action for breach of an obligation of the corporation owed to an interested director, where the obligation arises from a self-dealing transaction which has not been approved as provided in subdivision (d), the court may, by way of offset only, make any order authorized by subdivision (h), notwithstanding the expiration of the applicable period specified in subdivision (e).

(g) Interested directors may be counted in determining the presence of a quorum at a meeting of the board which authorizes, approves or ratifies a contract or transaction.

(h) If a self-dealing transaction has taken place, the interested director or directors shall do such things and pay such damages as in the discretion of the court will provide an equitable and fair remedy to the corporation, taking into account any benefit received by the corporation and whether the interested director or directors acted in good faith and with intent to further the best interest of the corporation. Without limiting the generality of the foregoing, the court may order the director to do any or all of the following:

(1) Account for any profits made from such transaction, and pay them to the corporation;

(2) Pay the corporation the value of the use of any of its property used in such transaction; and

(3) Return or replace any property lost to the corporation as a result of such transaction, together with any income or appreciation lost to the corporation by reason of such transaction, or account for any proceeds of sale of such property, and pay the proceeds to the corporation together with interest at the legal rate. The court may award prejudgment interest to the extent allowed in Section 3287 or 3288 of the Civil Code. In addition, the court may, in its discretion, grant exemplary damages for a fraudulent or malicious violation of this section.

§ 5234. Mutual directors; voidability of contracts or transactions

(a) No contract or other transaction between a corporation and any domestic or foreign corporation, firm or association of which one or more of its directors are directors is either void or voidable because such director or directors are present at the meeting of the board or a committee thereof which authorizes, approves or ratifies the contract or transaction, if:

(1) The material facts as to the transaction and as to such director's other directorship are fully disclosed or known to the board or committee, and the board or committee authorizes, approves or ratifies the contract or transaction in good faith by a vote sufficient without counting the vote of the common director or directors; or

(2) As to contracts or transactions not approved as provided in paragraph (1) of this subdivision, the contract or transaction is just and reasonable as to the corporation at the time it is authorized, approved or ratified.

(b) This section does not apply to transactions covered by Section 5233.

§ 5235. Compensation; liability for unreasonable amount

(a) The board may fix the compensation of a director, as director or officer, and no obligation, otherwise valid, to pay such compensation shall be voidable merely because the persons receiving the compensation participated in the decision to pay it, unless it was not just and reasonable as to the corporation at the time it was authorized, ratified or approved. The board shall take other actions that are required by subdivision (g) of Section 12586 of the Government Code, if applicable.

(b) In the absence of fraud, any liability under this section shall be limited to the amount by which the compensation exceeded what was just and reasonable, plus interest from the date of payment.

§ 5236. Loans, guarantees, advancements; life insurance; financing residence of officer

(a) A corporation shall not make any loan of money or property to or guarantee the obligation of any director or officer, unless approved by the Attorney General; provided, however, that a corporation may advance money to a director or officer of the corporation or of its parent or any subsidiary for expenses reasonably anticipated to be incurred in the performance of the duties of such officer or director, provided that in the absence of such advance, such director or officer would be entitled to be reimbursed for such expenses by such corporation, its parent, or any subsidiary.

(b) The provisions of subdivision (a) do not apply to the payment of premiums in whole or in part by a corporation on a life insurance policy on the life of a director or officer so long as repayment to the corporation of the amount paid by it is secured by either the policy's death benefit proceeds or its cash surrender value, or both.

(c) When repayment of a loan, entered into under subdivision (b), to a corporation is secured by only the policy's death benefit, the contract between the corporation and director or officer that secures the loan shall include terms sufficient to ensure that any policy fees and charges, withdrawals of the cash value, or loans taken against it do not impair the value of the death benefit to repay the cost of the loan, for the life of the policy.

(d) When repayment of a loan, entered into under subdivision (b), to a corporation is secured by only the policy's cash surrender value, the contract between the corporation and the director or officer that secures the loan shall include terms sufficient to ensure that the cash surrender value is sufficient to repay the cost of the loan, for the life of the policy.

(e) The provisions of subdivision (a) do not apply to a loan of money to or for the benefit of an officer in circumstances where the loan is necessary, in the judgment of the board, to provide financing for the purchase of the principal residence of the officer in order to secure the services or continued services of the officer and the loan is secured by real property located in the state.

§ 5237. Distributions, loans or guarantees; liability; actions; damages

(a) Subject to the provisions of Section 5231, directors of a corporation who approve any of the following corporate actions shall be jointly and severally liable to the corporation for:

(1) The making of any distribution.

(2) The distribution of assets after institution of dissolution proceedings of the corporation, without paying or adequately providing for all known liabilities of the corporation, excluding any claims not filed by creditors within the time limit set by the court in a notice given to creditors under Chapters 15 (commencing with Section 6510), 16 (commencing with Section 6610) and 17 (commencing with Section 6710).

(3) The making of any loan or guaranty contrary to Section 5236.

(b) A director who is present at a meeting of the board, or any committee thereof, at which action specified in subdivision (a) is taken and who abstains from voting shall be considered to have approved the action.

(c) Suit may be brought in the name of the corporation to enforce the liability:

(1) Under paragraph (1) of subdivision (a) against any or all directors liable by the persons entitled to sue under subdivision (b) of Section 5420;

(2) Under paragraph (2) or (3) of subdivision (a) against any or all directors liable by any one or more creditors of the corporation whose debts or claims arose prior to the time of the corporate action who have not consented to the corporate action, whether or not they have reduced their claims to judgment;

(3) Under paragraph (1), (2) or (3) of subdivision (a), by the Attorney General.

(d) The damages recoverable from a director under this section shall be the amount of the illegal distribution, or if the illegal distribution consists of property, the fair market value of that property at the time of the illegal distribution, plus interest thereon from the date of the distribution at the legal rate on judgments until paid, together with all reasonably incurred costs of appraisal or other valuation, if any, of that property, or the loss suffered by the corporation as a result of the illegal loan or guaranty.

(e) Any director sued under this section may implead all other directors liable and may compel contribution, either in that action or in an independent action against directors not joined in that action.

(f) Directors liable under this section shall also be entitled to be subrogated to the rights of the corporation:

(1) With respect to paragraph (1) of subdivision (a), against the persons who received the distribution.

(2) With respect to paragraph (2) of subdivision (a), against the persons who received the distribution.

(3) With respect to paragraph (3) of subdivision (a), against the person who received the loan or guaranty.

Any director sued under this section may file a cross-complaint against the person or persons who are liable to the director as a result of the subrogation provided for in this subdivision or may proceed against them in an independent action.

§ 5238. Indemnification of corporate agents; grounds; approval; advancement of expenses; liability insurance

(a) For the purposes of this section, "agent" means any person who is or was a director, officer, employee or other agent of the corporation, or is or was serving at the request of the corporation as a director, officer, employee or agent of another foreign or domestic corporation, partnership, joint venture, trust or other enterprise, or was a director, officer, employee or agent of a foreign or domestic corporation that was a predecessor corporation of the corporation or of another enterprise at the request of the predecessor corporation; "proceeding" means any threatened, pending or completed action or proceeding, whether civil, criminal, administrative or investigative; and "expenses" includes without limitation attorneys' fees and any expenses of establishing a right to indemnification under subdivision (d) or paragraph (3) of subdivision (e).

(b) A corporation shall have power to indemnify any person who was or is a party or is threatened to be made a party to any proceeding (other than an action by or in the right of the corporation to procure a judgment in its favor, an action brought under Section 5233, or an action brought by the Attorney General or a person granted relator status by the Attorney General for any breach of duty relating to assets held in charitable trust) by reason of the fact that the person is or was an agent of the corporation, against expenses, judgments, fines, settlements and other amounts actually and reasonably incurred in connection with such proceeding if the person acted in good faith and in a manner the person reasonably believed to be in the best interests of the corporation and, in the case of a criminal proceeding, had no reasonable cause to believe the conduct of the person was unlawful. The termination of any proceeding by judgment, order, settlement, conviction or upon a plea of nolo contendere or its equivalent shall not, of itself, create a presumption that the person did not act in good faith and in a manner which the person reasonably believed to be in the best interests of the corporation or that the person had reasonable cause to believe that the person's conduct was unlawful.

(c) A corporation shall have power to indemnify any person who was or is a party or is threatened to be made a party to any threatened, pending or completed action by or in the right of the corporation, or brought under Section 5233, or brought by the Attorney General or a person granted relator status by the Attorney General for breach of duty relating to assets held in charitable trust, to procure a judgment in its favor by reason of the fact that the person is or was an agent of the corporation, against expenses actually and reasonably incurred by the person in connection with the defense or settlement of the action if the person acted in good faith, in a manner the person believed to be in the best interests of the corporation and with such care, including reasonable inquiry, as an ordinarily prudent person in a like position would use under similar circumstances. No indemnification shall be made under this subdivision:

(1) In respect of any claim, issue or matter as to which the person shall have been adjudged to be liable to the corporation in the performance of the person's duty to the corporation, unless and only to the extent that the court in which the proceeding is or was pending shall determine upon application that, in view of all the circumstances of the case, the person is fairly and reasonably entitled to indemnity for the expenses which the court shall determine;

(2) Of amounts paid in settling or otherwise disposing of a threatened or pending action, with or without court approval; or

(3) Of expenses incurred in defending a threatened or pending action which is settled or otherwise disposed of without court approval unless it is settled with the approval of the Attorney General.

(d) To the extent that an agent of a corporation has been successful on the merits in defense of any proceeding referred to in subdivision (b) or (c) or in defense of any claim, issue or matter therein, the agent shall be indemnified against expenses actually and reasonably incurred by the agent in connection therewith.

(e) Except as provided in subdivision (d), any indemnification under this section shall be made by the corporation only if authorized in the specific case, upon a determination that indemnification of the agent is proper in the circumstances because the agent has met the applicable standard of conduct set forth in subdivision (b) or (c), by:

(1) A majority vote of a quorum consisting of directors who are not parties to the proceeding;

(2) Approval of the members (Section 5034), with the persons to be indemnified not being entitled to vote thereon; or

(3) The court in which the proceeding is or was pending upon application made by the corporation or the agent or the attorney or other person rendering services in connection with the defense, whether or not the application by the agent, attorney or other person is opposed by the corporation.

(f) Expenses incurred in defending any proceeding may be advanced by the corporation prior to the final disposition of the proceeding upon receipt of an undertaking by or on behalf of the agent to repay the amount unless it shall be determined ultimately that the agent is entitled to be indemnified as authorized in this section. The provisions of subdivision (a) of Section 5236 do not apply to advances made pursuant to this section.

(g) No provision made by a corporation to indemnify its or its subsidiary's directors or officers for the defense of any proceeding, whether contained in the articles, bylaws, a resolution of members or directors, an agreement or otherwise, shall be valid unless consistent with this section. Nothing contained in this section shall affect any right to indemnification to which persons other than the directors and officers may be entitled by contract or otherwise.

(h) No indemnification or advance shall be made under this section, except as provided in subdivision (d) or paragraph (3) of subdivision (e), in any circumstance where it appears:

(1) That it would be inconsistent with a provision of the articles, bylaws, a resolution of the members or an agreement in effect at the time of the accrual of the alleged cause of action asserted in the proceeding in which the expenses were incurred or other amounts were paid, which prohibits or otherwise limits indemnification; or

(2) That it would be inconsistent with any condition expressly imposed by a court in approving a settlement.

(i) A corporation shall have power to purchase and maintain insurance on behalf of any agent of the corporation against any liability asserted against or incurred by the agent in such capacity or arising out of the agent's status as such whether or not the corporation would have the power to indemnify the agent against that liability under the provisions of this section; provided, however, that a corporation shall have no power to purchase and maintain that insurance to indemnify any agent of the corporation for a violation of Section 5233.

(j) This section does not apply to any proceeding against any trustee, investment manager, or other fiduciary of a pension, deferred compensation, saving, thrift, or other retirement, incentive, or benefit plan, trust, or provision for any or all of the corporation's directors, officers, employees, and persons providing services to the corporation or any of its subsidiary or related or affiliated corporations, in that person's capacity as such, even though the person may also be an agent as defined in subdivision (a) of the employer corporation. A corporation shall have power to indemnify the trustee, investment manager or other fiduciary to the extent permitted by subdivision (f) of Section 5140.

§ 5239. Personal liability of volunteer director or officer for negligence

(a) There shall be no personal liability to a third party for monetary damages on the part of a volunteer director or volunteer executive officer of a nonprofit corporation subject to this part, caused by the director's or officer's negligent act or omission in the performance of that person's duties as a director or officer, if all of the following conditions are met:

(1) The act or omission was within the scope of the director's or executive officer's duties.

(2) The act or omission was performed in good faith.

(3) The act or omission was not reckless, wanton, intentional, or grossly negligent.

(4) Damages caused by the act or omission are covered pursuant to a liability insurance policy issued to the corporation, either in the form of a general liability policy or a director's and officer's liability policy, or personally to the director or executive officer. In the event that the damages are not covered by a liability insurance policy, the volunteer director or volunteer executive officer shall not be personally liable for the damages if the board of directors of the corporation and the person had made all reasonable efforts in good faith to obtain available liability insurance.

(b) "Volunteer" means the rendering of services without compensation. "Compensation" means remuneration whether by way of salary, fee, or other consideration for services rendered. However, the payment of per diem, mileage, or other reimbursement expenses to a director or executive officer does not affect that person's status as a volunteer within the meaning of this section.

(c) "Executive officer" means the president, vice president, secretary, or treasurer of a corporation, or such other individual who serves in like capacity, who assists in establishing the policy of the corporation.

(d) Nothing in this section shall limit the liability of the corporation for any damages caused by acts or omissions of the volunteer director or volunteer executive officer.

(e) This section does not eliminate or limit the liability of a director or officer for any of the following:

(1) As provided in Section 5233 or 5237.

(2) In any action or proceeding brought by the Attorney General.

(f) Nothing in this section creates a duty of care or basis of liability for damage or injury caused by the acts or omissions of a director or officer.

(g) This section is only applicable to causes of action based upon acts or omissions occurring on or after January 1, 1988.

(h) As used in this section as applied to nonprofit public benefit corporations which have an annual budget of less than twenty-five thousand dollars ($25,000) and that are exempt from federal income taxation under Section 501(c)(3) of the Internal Revenue Code, the condition of making "all reasonable efforts in good faith to obtain available liability insurance" shall be satisfied by the corporation if it makes at least one inquiry per year to purchase a general liability insurance policy and that insurance was not available at a cost of less than

5 percent of the previous year's annual budget of the corporation. If the corporation is in its first year of operation, this subdivision shall apply for as long as the budget of the corporation does not exceed twenty-five thousand dollars ($25,000) in its first year of operation.

An inquiry pursuant to this subdivision shall obtain premium costs for a general liability policy with an amount of coverage of at least five hundred thousand dollars ($500,000).

Article 4. Investments

§ 5240. Application; standards; conformity to instruments

(a) This section applies to all assets held by the corporation for investment. Assets which are directly related to the corporation's public or charitable programs are not subject to this section.

(b) Except as provided in subdivision (c), in investing, reinvesting, purchasing, acquiring, exchanging, selling and managing the corporation's investments, the board shall do the following:

(1) Avoid speculation, looking instead to the permanent disposition of the funds, considering the probable income, as well as the probable safety of the corporation's capital.

(2) Comply with additional standards, if any, imposed by the articles, bylaws or express terms of an instrument or agreement pursuant to which the assets were contributed to the corporation.

(c) No investment violates this section where it conforms to provisions authorizing the investment contained in an instrument or agreement pursuant to which the assets were contributed to the corporation. No investment violates this section or Section 5231 where it conforms to provisions requiring the investment contained in an instrument or agreement pursuant to which the assets were contributed to the corporation.

(d) In carrying out duties under this section, each director shall act as required by subdivision (a) of Section 5231, may rely upon others as permitted by subdivision (b) of Section 5231, and shall have the benefit of subdivision (c) of Section 5231, and the board may delegate its investment powers as permitted by Section 5210.

(e) Compliance with the Uniform Prudent Management of Institutional Funds Act, Part 7 (commencing with Section 18501) of Division 9 of the Probate Code, if that act would be applicable, will be deemed to be in compliance with subsection (b).

§ 5241. Trusts or agreements; deviation from terms

Nothing in Section 5240 shall abrogate or restrict the power of the appropriate court in proper cases to direct or permit a corporation to deviate from the terms of a trust or agreement regarding the making or retention of investments. Notice of such action or proceeding shall be given to the Attorney General who may intervene.

Article 5. Examination by Attorney General

§ 5250. Purposes; proceedings to correct noncompliance

A corporation is subject at all times to examination by the Attorney General, on behalf of the state, to ascertain the condition of its affairs and to what extent, if at all, it fails to comply with trusts which it has assumed or has departed from the purposes for which it is formed. In case of any such failure or departure the Attorney General may institute, in the name of the state, the proceeding necessary to correct the noncompliance or departure.

Article 6. Compliance with Internal Revenue Code

§ 5260. Distributions; self-dealing; excess business holdings; investments; taxable expenditures

Notwithstanding any other provision of law notwithstanding, every corporation, during any period or periods that corporation is deemed to be a "private foundation" as defined in Section 509 of the Internal Revenue Code of 1986 shall distribute its income for each taxable year (and principal, if necessary) at the time and in a manner so as not to subject that corporation to tax under Section 4942 of that code, and the corporation shall not engage in any act of self-dealing as defined in subsection (d) of Section 4941 of that code, retain any excess business holdings as defined in subsection (c) of Section 4943 of that code, make any investments in a manner that subjects the corporation to tax under Section 4944 of that code, or make any taxable expenditure as defined in subsection (d) of Section 4945 of that code.

This section shall apply to any corporation and any provision contained in its articles of incorporation or other governing instrument inconsistent with, or contrary to, this section shall be without effect.

Chapter 3

MEMBERS

Article 4. Termination of Membership

§ 5341. Expulsion, suspension or termination; procedure; limitation of actions

(a) No member may be expelled or suspended, and no membership or membership rights may be terminated or suspended, except according to procedures satisfying the requirements of this section. An expulsion, termination or suspension not in accord with this section shall be void and without effect.

(b) Any expulsion, suspension or termination must be done in good faith and in a fair and reasonable manner. Any procedure which conforms to the requirements of subdivision (c) is fair and reasonable, but a court may also find other procedures to be fair and reasonable when the full circumstances of the suspension, termination, or expulsion are considered.

(c) A procedure is fair and reasonable when:

(1) The provisions of the procedure have been set forth in the articles or bylaws, or copies of such provisions are sent annually to all the members as required by the articles or bylaws;

(2) It provides the giving of 15 days prior notice of the expulsion, suspension or termination and the reasons therefor[e]; and

(3) It provides an opportunity for the member to be heard, orally or in writing, not less than five days before the effective date of the expulsion, suspension or termination by a person or body authorized to decide that the proposed expulsion, termination or suspension not take place.

(d) Any notice required under this section may be given by any method reasonably calculated to provide actual notice. Any notice given by mail must be given by first-class or registered mail sent to the last address of the member shown on the corporation's records.

(e) Any action challenging an expulsion, suspension or termination of membership, including any claim alleging defective notice, must be commenced within one year after the date of the expulsion, suspension or termination. In the event such an action is successful the court may order any relief, including reinstatement, it finds equitable under the circumstances, but no vote of the members or of the board may be set aside solely because a person was at the time of the vote wrongfully excluded by virtue of the challenged expulsion, suspension or termination, unless the court finds further that the wrongful expulsion, suspension or termination was in bad faith and for the purpose, and with the effect, of wrongfully excluding the member from the vote or from the meeting at which the vote took place, so as to affect the outcome of the vote.

(f) This section governs only the procedures for expulsion, suspension or termination and not the substantive grounds therefor[e]. An expulsion, suspension or termination based upon substantive grounds which violate contractual or other rights of the member or are otherwise unlawful, is not made valid by compliance with this section.

(g) A member who is expelled or suspended or whose membership is terminated shall be liable for any charges incurred, services or benefits actually rendered, dues, assessments or fees incurred before the expulsion, suspension or termination or arising from contract or otherwise.

Chapter 4

DISTRIBUTIONS

Article 1. Limitations

§ 5410. Prohibition; limited-equity housing cooperatives excepted

No corporation shall make any distribution. This section shall not apply to the purchase of a membership in a limited-equity housing cooperative, as defined in Section 33007.5 of the Health and Safety Code, which is organized as a public benefit corporation.

Article 2. Liability of Members

§ 5420. Action to recover distribution

(a) Any person who receives any distribution is liable to the corporation for the amount so received by such person with interest thereon at the legal rate on judgments until paid.

(b) Suit may be brought in the name of a corporation by a creditor, a director, the Attorney General, or, subject to meeting the requirements of Section 5710, a member. In any such action in addition to the remedy provided in subdivision (a), the court may award punitive damages for the benefit of the corporation against any director, officer, member or other person who with intent to defraud the corporation caused, received or aided and abetted in the making of any distribution.

(c) Any person sued under this section may implead all other persons liable under this section and may in the absence of fraud by such moving party compel contribution, either in that action or in an independent action against persons not joined in the action.

(d) This section shall not affect any liability which any person may have under The Uniform Voidable Transactions Act (Chapter 1 (commencing with Section 3439) of Title 2 of Part 2 of Division 4 of the Civil Code).

Chapter 10

MERGERS

§ 6010. Restrictions as to types of corporations; attorney general; membership in surviving corporation

(a) A public benefit corporation may merge with any domestic corporation, foreign corporation (Section 171) or other business entity (Section 5063.5). However, without the prior written consent of the Attorney General, a public benefit corporation may only merge with another public benefit corporation or a religious corporation or a foreign nonprofit corporation the articles of which provide that its assets are irrevocably dedicated to charitable, religious, or public purposes.

(b) At least 20 days prior to consummation of any merger allowed by subdivision (a), the Attorney General must be provided with a copy of the proposed agreement of merger.

(c) Without the prior written consent of the Attorney General, when a merger occurs pursuant to subdivision (a), each member of a constituent corporation may only receive or keep a membership in the surviving corporation for or as a result of the member's membership in the constituent corporation.

Chapter 12

REQUIRED FILINGS BY CORPORATION OR ITS AGENT

§ 6215. Liability for falsification of or tampering with reports, records, etc.

Any officers, directors, employees or agents of a corporation who do any of the following are liable jointly and severally for all the damages resulting therefrom to the corporation or any person injured thereby who relied thereupon or to both:

(a) Make, issue, deliver or publish any report, circular, certificate, financial, statement, balance sheet, public notice or document respecting the corporation or its memberships, assets, liabilities, business, earnings or accounts which is false in any material respect, knowing it to be false, or participate in the making, issuance, delivery or publication thereof with knowledge that the same is false in a material respect.

(b) Make or cause to be made in the books, minutes, records or accounts of a corporation any entry which is false in any material particular knowing such entry is false.

(c) Remove, erase, alter or cancel any entry in any books or records of the corporation, with intent to deceive.

§ 6216. Enforcement

(a) The Attorney General, upon complaint of a member, director or officer, that a corporation is failing to comply with the provisions of this chapter, Chapter 5 (commencing with Section 5510), Chapter 6 (commencing with Section 5610) or Chapter 13 (commencing with Section 6310), may, in the name of the people of the State of California, send to the principal office of such corporation, (or, if there is no such office, to the office or residence of the chief executive officer or secretary, of the corporation, as set forth in the most recent statement filed pursuant to Section 6210) notice of the complaint. If the answer is not satisfactory, or if there is no answer within 30 days, the Attorney General may institute, maintain or intervene in such suits, actions, or proceedings of any type in any court or tribunal of competent jurisdiction or before any administrative agency for such relief by way of injunction, the dissolution of entities, the appointment of receivers or any other temporary, preliminary, provisional or final remedies as may be appropriate to protect the rights of members or to undo the consequences of failure to comply with such requirements. In any such action, suit or proceeding there may be joined as parties all persons and entities responsible for or affected by such activity.

(b) The Attorney General may bring an action under subdivision (a) without having received a complaint, and without first giving notice of a complaint.

Chapter 13

RECORDS, REPORTS, AND RIGHTS OF INSPECTION

Article 2. Required Records, Reports to Directors and Members

§ 6320. Books and records

(a) Each corporation shall keep:

(1) Adequate and correct books and records of account;

(2) Minutes of the proceedings of its members, board and committees of the board; and

(3) A record of its members giving their names and addresses and the class of membership held by each.

(b) Those minutes and other books and records shall be kept either in written form or in any other form capable of being converted into clearly legible tangible form or in any combination of the foregoing. When minutes and other books and records are kept in a form capable of being converted into clearly legible paper form, the clearly legible paper form into which those minutes and other books and records are converted shall be admissible in evidence, and accepted for all other purposes, to the same extent as an original paper record of the same information would have been, provided that the paper form accurately portrays the record.

§ 6321. Annual report

(a) Except as provided in subdivision (c), (d), or (f), the board shall cause an annual report to be sent to the members not later than 120 days after the close of the corporation's fiscal year. Unless otherwise provided by the articles or bylaws and if approved by the board of directors, that report and any accompanying material sent pursuant to this section may be sent by electronic transmission by the corporation (Section 20).That report shall contain in appropriate detail the following:

(1) The assets and liabilities, including the trust funds, of the corporation as of the end of the fiscal year.

(2) The principal changes in assets and liabilities, including trust funds, during the fiscal year.

(3) The revenue or receipts of the corporation, both unrestricted and restricted to particular purposes, for the fiscal year.

(4) The expenses or disbursements of the corporation, for both general and restricted purposes, during the fiscal year.

(5) Any information required by Section 6322.

(b) The report required by subdivision (a) shall be accompanied by any report thereon of independent accountants, or, if there is no such report, the certificate of an authorized officer of the corporation that such statements were prepared without audit from the books and records of the corporation. The report shall be prepared, audited, and made available in the manner required by paragraph (1) of subdivision (e) of Section 12586 of the Government Code, if applicable.

(c) Subdivision (a) does not apply to any corporation which receives less than twenty-five thousand dollars ($25,000) in gross revenues or receipts during the fiscal year.

(d) Where a corporation has provided, pursuant to Section 5510, for regular meetings of members less often than annually, then the report required by subdivision (a) need be made to members only with the frequency with which regular membership meetings are required, unless the articles or bylaws require a report more often.

(e) Subdivisions (c) and (d) notwithstanding, a report with the information required by subdivision (a) shall be furnished annually to:

(1) All directors of the corporation; and

(2) Any member who requests it in writing.

(f) A corporation which in writing solicits contributions from 500 or more persons need not send the report otherwise required by subdivision (a) if it does all of the following:

(1) Includes with any written material used to solicit contributions a written statement that its latest annual report will be mailed upon request and that such request may be sent to the corporation at a name and address which is set forth in the statement. The term "annual report" as used in this subdivision refers to the report required by subdivision (a).

(2) Promptly mails a copy of its latest annual report to any person who requests a copy thereof; and

(3) Causes its annual report to be published not later than 120 days after the close of its fiscal year in a newspaper of general circulation in the county in which its principal office is located.

§ 6322. Annual statement of transactions with interested persons and of indemnifications

(a) Any provision of the articles or bylaws notwithstanding, every corporation shall furnish annually to its members and directors a statement of any transaction or indemnification of a kind described in subdivision (d) or (e), if any such transaction or indemnification took place. If the corporation issues an annual report to all members, this subdivision shall be satisfied by including the required information in the annual report. A corporation which does not issue an annual report to all members, pursuant to subdivision (c) or (d) of Section 6321, shall satisfy this section by mailing or delivering to its members the required statement within 120 days after the close of the corporation's fiscal year. Unless otherwise provided by the articles or bylaws and if approved by the board of directors, that statement may be sent by electronic transmission by the corporation (Section 20).

(b) Except as provided in subdivision (c), a covered transaction under this section is a transaction in which the corporation, its parent, or its subsidiary was a party, and in which either of the following had a direct or indirect material financial interest:

(1) Any director or officer of the corporation, or its parent or subsidiary.

(2) Any holder of more than 10 percent of the voting power of the corporation, its parent or its subsidiary.

For the purpose of subdivision (d), an "interested person" is any person described in paragraph (1) or (2) of this subdivision.

(c) For the purpose of subdivision (b), a mere common directorship is not a material financial interest.

(d) The statement required by subdivision (a) shall describe briefly:

(1) Any covered transaction during the previous fiscal year involving more than fifty thousand dollars ($50,000), or which was one of a number of covered transactions in which the same interested person had a direct or indirect material financial interest, and which transactions in the aggregate involved more than fifty thousand dollars ($50,000).

(2) The names of the interested persons involved in such transactions, stating such person's relationship to the corporation, the nature of such person's interest in the transaction and, where practicable, the amount of such interest; provided, that in the case of a transaction with a partnership of which such person is a partner, only the interest of the partnership need be stated.

(e) The statement required by subdivision (a) shall describe briefly the amount and circumstances of any indemnifications or advances aggregating more than ten thousand dollars ($10,000) paid during the fiscal year to any officer or director of the corporation pursuant to Section 5238; provided that no such report need be made in the case of indemnification approved by the members (Section 5034) under paragraph (2) of subdivision (e) of Section 5238.

§ 6323. Judicial enforcement; award of expenses and attorney fees

(a) The superior court of the proper county shall enforce the duty of making and mailing or delivering the information and financial statements required by this article and, for good cause shown, may extend the time therefor.

(b) In any action or proceeding under this section, if the court finds the failure of the corporation to comply with the requirements of this article to have been without justification, the court may award the member reasonable expenses, including attorneys' fees, in connection with such action or proceeding.

Article 3. Rights of Inspection

§ 6330. Demand; persons authorized; reason; alternative proposal

(a) Subject to Sections 6331 and 6332, and unless the corporation provides a reasonable alternative pursuant to subdivision (c), a member may do either or both of the following as permitted by subdivision (b):

(1) Inspect and copy the record of all the members' names, addresses and voting rights, at reasonable times, upon five business days' prior written demand upon the corporation which demand shall state the purpose for which the inspection rights are requested; or

(2) Obtain from the secretary of the corporation, upon written demand and tender of a reasonable charge, an alphabetized list of the names, addresses, and voting rights of those members entitled to vote for the election of directors, as of the most recent record date for which it has been compiled or as of a date specified by the member subsequent to the date of demand. The demand shall state the purpose for which the list is requested. The membership list shall be made available on or before the later of 10 business days after the demand is received or after the date specified therein as the date as of which the list is to be compiled.

(b) The rights set forth in subdivision (a) may be exercised by:

(1) Any member, for a purpose reasonably related to the person's interest as a member. Where the corporation reasonably believes that the information will be used for another purpose, or where it provides a reasonable alternative pursuant to subdivision (c), it may deny the member access to the list. In any subsequent action brought by the member under Section 6336, the court shall enforce the rights set forth in subdivision (a) unless the corporation proves that the member will allow use of the information for purposes

unrelated to the person's interest as a member or that the alternative method offered reasonably achieves the proper purpose set forth in the demand.

(2) The authorized number of members for a purpose reasonably related to the members' interest as members.

(c) The corporation may, within 10 business days after receiving a demand under subdivision (a), deliver to the person or persons making the demand a written offer of an alternative method of achieving the purpose identified in the demand without providing access to or a copy of the membership list. An alternative method which reasonably and in a timely manner accomplishes the proper purpose set forth in a demand made under subdivision (a) shall be deemed a reasonable alternative, unless within a reasonable time after acceptance of the offer the corporation fails to do those things which it offered to do. Any rejection of the offer shall be in writing and shall indicate the reasons the alternative proposed by the corporation does not meet the proper purpose of the demand made pursuant to subdivision (a).

§ 6333. Accounting books; minutes of meetings; demand; purpose

The accounting books and records and minutes of proceedings of the members and the board and committees of the board shall be open to inspection upon the written demand on the corporation of any member at any reasonable time, for a purpose reasonably related to such person's interests as a member.

§ 6334. Directors' rights

Every director shall have the absolute right at any reasonable time to inspect and copy all books, records and documents of every kind and to inspect the physical properties of the corporation of which such person is a director.

Chapter 15

INVOLUNTARY DISSOLUTION

§ 6510. Complaint, persons authorized to file; grounds; intervention; attorney general as party

(a) A complaint for involuntary dissolution of a corporation on any one or more of the grounds specified in subdivision (b) may be filed in the superior court of the proper county by any of the following persons:

(1) One-half or more of the directors in office.

(2) A person or persons holding or authorized in writing by persons holding not less than 33 1/3 percent of the voting power exclusive of memberships held by persons who have personally participated in any of the transactions enumerated in paragraph (5) of subdivision (b).

(3) Any member if the ground for dissolution is that the period for which the corporation was formed has terminated without extension thereof.

(4) Any other person expressly authorized to do so in the articles.

(5) The Attorney General.

(6) The head organization under whose authority the corporation was created, where the corporation's articles include the provision authorized by subdivision (a), paragraph (2), clause (i), of Section 5132.

(b) The grounds for involuntary dissolution are that:

(1) The corporation has abandoned its activity for more than one year.

(2) The corporation has an even number of directors who are equally divided and cannot agree as to the management of its affairs, so that its activities can no longer be conducted to advantage or so that there is danger that its property will be impaired or lost or its activities impaired and the members are so divided into factions that they cannot elect a board consisting of an uneven number.

(3) There is internal dissension and two or more factions of members in the corporation are so deadlocked that its activities can no longer be conducted with advantage.

(4) When during any four-year period or when all voting power has been exercised at two consecutive meetings or in two written ballots for the election of directors, whichever period is shorter, the members have failed to elect successors to directors whose terms have expired or would have expired upon election of their successors.

(5) Those in control of the corporation have been guilty of or have knowingly countenanced persistent and pervasive fraud, mismanagement or abuse of authority or the corporation's property is being misapplied or wasted by its directors or officers.

(6) Liquidation is reasonably necessary as the corporation is failing and has continuously failed to carry out its purposes.

(7) The period for which the corporation was formed has terminated without extension of such period.

(8) The corporation is required to dissolve under the terms of any article provision adopted pursuant to subdivision (a), paragraph (2), clause (i), of Section 5132.

(c) At any time prior to the trial of the action any creditor or the authorized number (Section 5036) of members may intervene therein.

(d) In any action brought pursuant to subdivision (a), the Attorney General shall be an indispensable party.

§ 6511. Action by attorney general; purpose and grounds; powers of court; process

(a) The Attorney General may bring an action against any corporation or purported corporation in the name of the people of this state, upon the Attorney General's own information or upon complaint of a private party, to procure a judgment dissolving the corporation and annulling, vacating or forfeiting its corporate existence upon any of the following grounds:

(1) The corporation has seriously offended against any provision of the statutes regulating corporations or charitable organizations.

(2) The corporation has fraudulently abused or usurped corporate privileges or powers.

(3) The corporation has violated any provision of law by any act or default which under the law is a ground for forfeiture of corporate existence.

(4) The corporation has failed to pay to the Franchise Tax Board for a period of five years any tax imposed upon it by the Bank and Corporation Tax Law.

(b) If the ground of the action is a matter or act which the corporation has done or omitted to do that can be corrected by amendment of its articles or by other corporate action, such suit shall not be maintained unless:

(1) the Attorney General, at least 30 days prior to the institution of suit, has given the corporation written notice of the matter or act done or omitted to be done; and (2) the corporation has failed to institute proceedings to correct it within the 30-day period or thereafter fails to duly and properly make such amendment or take the corrective corporate action.

(c) In any such action the court may order dissolution or such other or partial relief as it deems just and expedient. The court also may appoint a receiver for winding up the affairs of the corporation or may order that the corporation be wound up by its board subject to the supervision of the court.

(d) Service of process on the corporation may be made pursuant to Chapter 17 (commencing with Section 1700) of Division 1 or by written notice to the president or secretary of the corporation at the address indicated in the corporation's last tax return filed pursuant to the Bank and Corporation Tax Law. The Attorney General shall also publish one time in a newspaper of general circulation in the proper county a notice to the members of the corporation.

Chapter 18

CRIMES AND PENALTIES

§ 6811. Fraudulent distributions

Any director of any corporation who concurs in any vote or act of the directors of the corporation or any of them, knowingly and with dishonest or fraudulent purpose, to make any distribution with the design of defrauding creditors, members, or the corporation, is guilty of a crime. Each such crime is punishable by imprisonment pursuant to subdivision (b) of Section 1170 of the Penal Code or by a fine of not more than one thousand dollars ($1,000) or imprisonment in a county jail for not more than one year, or both such fine and imprisonment.

§ 6812. False financial reports or statements; failure to make book entries or post notices

(a) Every director or officer of any corporation is guilty of a crime if such director or officer knowingly concurs in making or publishing, either generally or privately, to members or other persons:

(1) Any materially false report or statement as to the financial condition of the corporation, or

(2) Any willfully or fraudulently exaggerated report, account or statement of operations or financial condition, intended to induce and having a tendency to induce, contributions or donations to the corporation by members or other persons.

(b) Every director or officer of any corporation is guilty of a crime who refuses to make or direct to be made any book entry or the posting of any notice required by law in the manner required by law.

(c) A violation of subdivision (a) or (b) of this section shall be punishable by imprisonment in state prison or by a fine of not more than one thousand dollars ($1,000) or imprisonment in the county jail for not more than one year or both such fine and imprisonment.

§ 6813. Fraudulent acquisition of corporate property; falsification of books, records or documents

(a) Every director, officer or agent of any corporation, who knowingly receives or acquires possession of any property of the corporation, otherwise than in payment of a just demand, and, with intent to defraud, omits to make, or to cause or direct to be made, a full and true entry thereof in the books or accounts of the corporation is guilty of a crime.

(b) Every director, officer, agent or member of any corporation who, with intent to defraud, destroys, alters, mutilates or falsifies any of the books, papers, writings or securities belonging to the corporation or makes or concurs in omitting to make any material entry in any book of accounts or other record or document kept by the corporation is guilty of a crime.

(c) Each crime specified in this section is punishable by imprisonment in state prison, or by imprisonment in a county jail for not exceeding one year, or a fine not exceeding one thousand dollars ($1,000), or by both such fine and imprisonment.

§ 6814. Deception of public officer examining organization of corporation

Every director, officer or agent of any corporation, or any person proposing to organize such a corporation, who knowingly exhibits any false, forged or altered book, paper, voucher, security or other instrument of evidence to any public officer or board authorized by law to examine the organization of such corporation or to investigate its affairs, with intent to deceive such officer or board in respect thereto, is punishable by imprisonment pursuant to subdivision (h) of Section 1170 of the Penal Code, or by imprisonment in a county jail for not more than one year.

Part 3

NONPROFIT MUTUAL BENEFIT CORPORATIONS

Chapter 1

ORGANIZATION AND BYLAWS

Article 1. Title and Purposes

§ 7111. Corporate purposes; exclusion of corporations for certain purposes

Subject to any other provision of law of this state applying to the particular class of corporation or line of activity, a corporation may be formed under this part for any lawful purpose; provided that a corporation all of the assets of which are irrevocably dedicated to charitable, religious, or public purposes and which as a matter of law or according to its articles or bylaws must, upon dissolution, distribute its assets to a person or persons carrying on a charitable, religious, or public purpose or purposes may not be formed under this part.

Chapter 2

DIRECTORS AND MANAGEMENT

Article 3. Standards of Conduct

§ 7231.5. Liability of volunteer director or officer; failure to discharge duties

(a) Except as provided in Section 7233 or 7236, there is no monetary liability on the part of, and no cause of action for damages shall arise against, any volunteer director or volunteer executive officer of a nonprofit corporation subject to this part based upon any alleged failure to discharge the person's duties as a director or officer if the duties are performed in a manner that meets all of the following criteria:

(1) The duties are performed in good faith.

(2) The duties are performed in a manner such director or officer believes to be in the best interests of the corporation.

(3) The duties are performed with such care, including reasonable inquiry, as an ordinarily prudent person in a like position would use under similar circumstances.

(b) "Volunteer" means the rendering of services without compensation. "Compensation" means remuneration whether by way of salary, fee, or other consideration for services rendered. However, the payment of per diem, mileage, or other reimbursement expenses to a director or executive officer does not affect that person's status as a volunteer within the meaning of this section.

(c) "Executive officer" means the president, vice president, secretary, or treasurer of a corporation or other individual serving in like capacity who assists in establishing the policy of the corporation.

(d) This section shall apply only to trade, professional, and labor organizations incorporated pursuant to this part which operate exclusively for fraternal, educational, and other nonprofit purposes, and under the provisions of Section 501(c) of the United States Internal Revenue Code.

(e) This section shall not be construed to limit the provisions of Section 7231.

§ 7233. Conflicts of interest; disclosure; common directorships; just and reasonable contracts

(a) No contract or other transaction between a corporation and one or more of its directors, or between a corporation and any domestic or foreign corporation, firm or association in which one or more of its directors has a material financial interest, is either void or voidable because such director or directors or such other corporation, business corporation, firm or association are parties or because such director or directors are present at the meeting of the board or a committee thereof which authorizes, approves or ratifies the contract or transaction, if:

(1) The material facts as to the transaction and as to such director's interest are fully disclosed or known to the members and such contract or transaction is approved by the members (Section 5034) in good faith, with any membership owned by any interested director not being entitled to vote thereon;

(2) The material facts as to the transaction and as to such director's interest are fully disclosed or known to the board or committee, and the board or committee authorizes, approves or ratifies the contract or transaction in good faith by a vote sufficient without counting the vote of the interested director or directors and the contract or transaction is just and reasonable as to the corporation at the time it is authorized, approved or ratified; or

(3) As to contracts or transactions not approved as provided in paragraph (1) or (2) of this subdivision, the person asserting the validity of the contract or transaction sustains the burden of proving that the contract or transaction was just and reasonable as to the corporation at the time it was authorized, approved or ratified. A mere common directorship does not constitute a material financial interest within the meaning of this subdivision. A director is not interested within the meaning of this subdivision in a resolution fixing the compensation of another director as a director, officer or employee of the corporation, notwithstanding the fact that the first director is also receiving compensation from the corporation.

(b) No contract or other transaction between a corporation and any corporation, business corporation or association of which one or more of its directors are directors is either void or voidable because such director or directors are present at the meeting of the board or a committee thereof which authorizes, approves or ratifies the contract or transaction, if:

(1) The material facts as to the transaction and as to such director's other directorship are fully disclosed or known to the board or committee, and the board or committee authorizes, approves or ratifies the contract or transaction in good faith by a vote sufficient without counting the vote of the common director or directors or the contract or transaction is approved by the members (Section 5034) in good faith; or

(2) As to contracts or transactions not approved as provided in paragraph (1) of this subdivision, the contract or transaction is just and reasonable as to the corporation at the time it is authorized, approved or ratified. This subdivision does not apply to contracts or transactions covered by subdivision (a).

§ 7236. Liability for illegal loans and distributions; suits; damages; contribution; subrogation; cross-complaint

(a) Subject to the provisions of Section 7231, directors of a corporation who approve any of the following corporate actions shall be jointly and severally liable to the corporation for the benefit of all of the creditors entitled to institute an action under paragraph (1) or (2) of subdivision (c) or to the corporation in an action by the head organization or members under paragraph (1) or (3) of subdivision (c):

(1) The making of any distribution contrary to Chapter 4 (commencing with Section 7410).

(2) The distribution of assets after institution of dissolution proceedings of the corporation, without paying or adequately providing for all known liabilities of the corporation, excluding any claims not filed by creditors within the time limit set by the court in a notice given to creditors under Chapter 15 (commencing with Section 8510), Chapter 16 (commencing with Section 8610), and Chapter 17 (commencing with Section 8710).

(3) The making of any loan or guaranty contrary to Section 7235.

(b) A director who is present at a meeting of the board, or any committee thereof, at which an action specified in subdivision (a) is taken and who abstains from voting shall be considered to have approved the action.

(c) Suit may be brought in the name of the corporation to enforce the liability:

(1) Under paragraph (1) of subdivision (a) against any or all directors liable by the persons entitled to sue under subdivision (c) of Section 7420.

(2) Under paragraph (2) or (3) of subdivision (a) against any or all directors liable by any one or more creditors of the corporation whose debts or claims arose prior to the time of the corporate action who have not consented to the corporate action, whether or not they have reduced their claims to judgment.

(3) Under paragraph (3) of subdivision (a) against any or all directors liable by any one or more members at the time of any corporate action specified in paragraph (3) of subdivision (a) who have not consented to the corporate action, without regard to the provisions of Section 7710.

(d) The damages recoverable from a director under this section shall be the amount of the illegal distribution, or if the illegal distribution consists of property, the fair market value of that property at the time of the illegal distribution, plus interest thereon from the date of the distribution at the legal rate on judgments until paid, together with all reasonably incurred costs of appraisal or other valuation, if any, of that property, or the loss suffered by the corporation as a result of the illegal loan or guaranty, but not exceeding, in the case of an action for the benefit of creditors, the liabilities of the corporation owed to nonconsenting creditors at the time of the violation.

(e) Any director sued under this section may implead all other directors liable and may compel contribution, either in that action or in an independent action against directors not joined in that action.

(f) Directors liable under this section shall also be entitled to be subrogated to the rights of the corporation:

(1) With respect to paragraph (1) of subdivision (a), against the persons who received the distribution.

(2) With respect to paragraph (2) of subdivision (a), against the persons who received the distribution.

(3) With respect to paragraph (3) of subdivision (a), against the person who received the loan or guaranty.

Any director sued under this section may file a cross-complaint against the person or persons who are liable to the director as a result of the subrogation provided for in this subdivision or may proceed against them in an independent action.

Chapter 3

MEMBERS

Article 4. Termination of Membership

§ 7341. Expulsion, suspension or termination; fairness and reasonableness; procedure

(a) No member may be expelled or suspended, and no membership or memberships may be terminated or suspended, except according to procedures satisfying the requirements of this section. An expulsion, termination or suspension not in accord with this section shall be void and without effect.

(b) Any expulsion, suspension, or termination must be done in good faith and in a fair and reasonable manner. Any procedure which conforms to the requirements of subdivision (c) is fair and reasonable, but a court may also find other procedures to be fair and reasonable when the full circumstances of the suspension, termination, or expulsion are considered.

(c) A procedure is fair and reasonable when:

(1) The provisions of the procedure have been set forth in the articles or bylaws, or copies of such provisions are sent annually to all the members as required by the articles or bylaws;

(2) It provides the giving of 15 days' prior notice of the expulsion, suspension or termination and the reasons therefor; and

(3) It provides an opportunity for the member to be heard, orally or in writing, not less than five days before the effective date of the expulsion, suspension or termination by a person or body authorized to decide that the proposed expulsion, termination or suspension not take place.

(d) Any notice required under this section may be given by any method reasonably calculated to provide actual notice. Any notice given by mail must be given by first-class or registered mail sent to the last address of the members shown on the corporation's records.

(e) Any action challenging an expulsion, suspension or termination of membership, including any claim alleging defective notice, must be commenced within one year after the date of the expulsion, suspension or termination. In the event such an action is successful the court may order any relief, including reinstatement, it finds equitable under the circumstances, but no vote of the members or of the board may be set aside solely because a person was at the time of the vote wrongfully excluded by virtue of the challenged expulsion, suspension or termination, unless the court finds further that the wrongful expulsion, suspension or termination was in bad faith and for the purpose, and with the effect, of wrongfully excluding the member from the vote or from the meeting at which the vote took place, so as to affect the outcome of the vote.

(f) This section governs only the procedures for expulsion, suspension or termination and not the substantive grounds therefor. An expulsion, suspension or termination based upon substantive grounds which violate contractual or other rights of the member or are otherwise unlawful is not made valid by compliance with this section.

(g) A member who is expelled or suspended or whose membership is terminated shall be liable for any charges incurred, services or benefits actually rendered, dues, assessments or fees incurred before the expulsion, suspension or termination or arising from contract or otherwise.

Chapter 4

DISTRIBUTIONS

Article 1. Limitations

§ 7411. Prohibited distributions; exception; purchase or redemption of memberships

(a) Except as provided in subdivision (b), no corporation shall make any distribution except upon dissolution.

(b) A corporation may, subject to meeting the requirements of Sections 7412 and 7413 and any additional restrictions authorized by Section 7414, purchase or redeem memberships.

Chapter 13

RECORDS, REPORTS AND RIGHTS OF INSPECTION

Article 2. Required Records, Reports to Directors and Members

§ 8320. Books and records

(a) Each corporation shall keep:

(1) Adequate and correct books and records of account;

(2) Minutes of the proceedings of its members, board and committees of the board; and

(3) A record of its members giving their names and addresses and the class of membership held by each.

(b) Those minutes and other books and records shall be kept either in written form or in any other form capable of being converted into clearly legible tangible form or in any combination of the foregoing. When minutes and other books and records are kept in a form capable of being converted into clearly legible paper form, the clearly legible paper form into which those minutes and other books and records are converted shall be admissible in evidence, and accepted for all other purposes, to the same extent as an original paper record of the same information would have been, provided that the paper form accurately portrays the record.

Chapter 15

INVOLUNTARY DISSOLUTION

§ 8510. Complaint; persons authorized to file; grounds; intervention; exemptions; service on Attorney General

(a) A complaint for involuntary dissolution of a corporation on any one or more of the grounds specified in subdivision (b) may be filed in the superior court of the proper county by any of the following persons:

(1) One-half or more of the directors in office.

(2) A person or persons holding or authorized in writing by persons holding not less than 33⅓ percent of the voting power exclusive of memberships held by persons who have personally participated in any of the transactions enumerated in paragraph (5) of subdivision (b).

(3) Any member if the ground for dissolution is that the period for which the corporation was formed has terminated without extension thereof.

(4) Any other person expressly authorized to do so in the articles.

(5) In the case of a corporation holding assets in charitable trust, the Attorney General.

(6) The head organization under whose authority the corporation was created, where the corporation's articles include the provision authorized by subdivision (a), paragraph (4), clause (i), of Section 7132.

(b) The grounds for involuntary dissolution are that:

(1) The corporation has abandoned its activity for more than one year.

(2) The corporation has an even number of directors who are equally divided and cannot agree as to the management of its affairs, so that its activities can no longer be conducted to advantage or so that there is danger that its property will be impaired or lost or its activities impaired and the members are so divided into factions that they cannot elect a board consisting of an uneven number.

(3) There is internal dissension and two or more factions of members in the corporation are so deadlocked that its activities can no longer be conducted with advantage.

(4) When during any four-year period or when all voting power has been exercised at two consecutive meetings or in two written ballots for the election of directors, whichever period is shorter, the members have failed to elect successors to directors whose terms have expired or would have expired upon election of their successors.

(5) Those in control of the corporation have been guilty of or have knowingly countenanced persistent and pervasive fraud, mismanagement or abuse of authority or persistent unfairness toward any member or the corporation's property is being misapplied or wasted by its directors or officers.

(6) In the case of any corporation with 35 or fewer members, liquidation is reasonably necessary for the protection of the rights or interests of a complaining member or members.

(7) The period for which the corporation was formed has terminated without extension of such period.

(8) The corporation is required to dissolve under the terms of any article provision adopted pursuant to subdivision (a), paragraph (4), clause (i) of Section 7132.

(c) At any time prior to the trial of the action any member or creditor may intervene therein.

(d) This section does not apply to any corporation subject to:

(1) The Public Utilities Act (Part 1 (commencing with Section 201) of Division 1 of the Public Utilities Code) unless an order is obtained from the Public Utilities Commission authorizing the corporation either (a) to dispose of its assets as provided in Section 851 of the Public Utilities Code or (b) to dissolve.

(2) The provisions of Article 14 (commencing with Section 1010) of Chapter 1 of Part 2 of Division 1 of the Insurance Code when the application authorized by Section 1011 of the Insurance Code has been filed by the Insurance Commissioner unless the consent of the Insurance Commissioner has been obtained.

(3) The California Credit Union Law (Chapter 1 (commencing with Section 14000) of Division 5 of the Financial Code).

(e) In the case of a corporation holding assets in charitable trust at the time of the filing of the complaint pursuant to subdivision (a), a copy thereof shall be served on the Attorney General who may intervene.

Chapter 17

GENERAL PROVISIONS RELATION TO DISSOLUTION

§ 8716. Disposition; trust assets; court decree; waiver of objections

After complying with the provisions of Section 8713 [payment or provision for debts and liabilities, Eds.]:

(a) Except as provided in Section 8715 [return or transfer of distributable assets held upon condition, Eds.] those assets held by a corporation in a charitable trust shall be disposed of on dissolution in conformity with its articles or bylaws subject to complying with the provisions of any trust under which such assets are held.

(b) Except as provided in subdivision (c), the disposition required in subdivision (a) shall be made by decree of the superior court of the proper county in proceedings to which the Attorney General is a party. The decree shall be made upon petition therefor by the Attorney General or, upon 30 days' notice to the Attorney General, by any person concerned in the dissolution.

(c) The disposition required in subdivision (a) may be made without the decree of the superior court, subject to the rights of persons concerned in the dissolution, if the Attorney General makes a written waiver of objections to the disposition.

§ 8717. Method of distribution

After complying with the provisions of Section 8713 and except as otherwise provided in Sections 8715 and 8716, assets held by a corporation shall be disposed of on dissolution as follows:

(a) If the articles or bylaws provide the manner of disposition, the assets shall be disposed of in that manner.

(b) If the articles or bylaws do not provide the manner of disposition, the assets shall be distributed among the members in accordance with their respective rights therein.

§ 8718. Distribution in money, property or securities; installments

Subject to the provisions of any trust under which assets to be distributed are held, distribution may be made either in money or in property or securities and either in installments from time to time or as a whole, if this can be done fairly and ratably and in conformity with the provisions of the articles and bylaws and shall be made as soon as reasonably consistent with the beneficial liquidation of the corporation assets.

§ 8719. Different classes of membership; plan of distribution of assets of another corporation

(a) If a corporation in process of winding up has more than one class of memberships outstanding, a plan of distribution of the memberships, obligations or securities of any other corporation, domestic or foreign, or assets other than money which is not in accordance with the liquidation rights of any class or classes as specified in the articles or bylaws may nevertheless be adopted if approved by:

(1) The board and

(2) By approval by the members (Section 5034) of each class.

The plan may provide that such distribution is in complete or partial satisfaction of the rights of any of such members upon distribution and liquidation of the assets.

(b) A plan of distribution so approved shall be binding upon all the members. The board shall cause notice of the adoption of the plan to be given by mail within 20 days after its adoption to all holders of memberships having a liquidation preference.

Part 4

NONPROFIT RELIGIOUS CORPORATIONS

Chapter 2

DIRECTORS AND MANAGEMENT

Article 3. Examination by Attorney General

§ 9230. Religious corporations; attorney general; powers and restrictions

(a) Except as the Attorney General is empowered to act in the enforcement of the criminal laws of this state, and except as the Attorney General is expressly empowered by subdivisions (b), (c) and (d), the Attorney General shall have no powers with respect to any corporation incorporated or classified as a religious corporation under or pursuant to this code.

(b) The Attorney General shall have authority to institute an action or proceeding under Section 803 of the Code of Civil Procedure, to obtain judicial determination that a corporation is not properly qualified or classified as a religious corporation under the provisions of this part.

(c) The Attorney General shall have the authority:

(1) Expressly granted with respect to any subject or matter covered by Sections 9660 to 9690, inclusive;

(2) To initiate criminal procedures to prosecute violations of the criminal laws, and upon conviction seek restitution as punishment; and

(3) To represent as legal counsel any other agency or department of the State of California expressly empowered to act with respect to the status of religious corporations, or expressly empowered to regulate activities in which religious corporations, as well as other entities, may engage.

(d) Where property has been solicited and received from the general public, based on a representation that it would be used for a specific charitable purpose other than general support of the corporation's activities, and has been used in a manner contrary to that specific charitable purpose for which the property was solicited, the Attorney General may institute an action to enforce the specific charitable purpose for which the property was solicited; provided

(1) that before bringing such action the Attorney General shall notify the corporation that an action will be brought unless the corporation takes immediate steps to correct the improper diversion of funds, and

(2) that in the event it becomes impractical or impossible for the corporation to devote the property to the specified charitable purpose, or that the directors or members of the corporation in good faith expressly conclude and record in writing that the stated purpose for which the property was contributed is no longer in accord with the policies of the corporation, then the directors or members of the corporation may approve or ratify in good faith the use of such property for the general purposes of the corporation rather than for the specific purpose for which it was contributed.

As used in this section, "solicited from the general public" means solicitations directed to the general public, or to any individual or group of individuals who are not directly affiliated with the soliciting organization and includes, but is not limited to, instances where property has been solicited on an individual basis, such as door to door, direct mail, face to face, or similar solicitations, as well as solicitations on a more general level to the general public, or a portion thereof, such as through the media, including newspapers, television, radio, or similar solicitations.

(e) Nothing in this section shall be construed to affect any individual rights of action which were accorded under law in existence prior to the enactment of Chapter 1324 of the Statutes of 1980.

As used in this section, "individual rights of action" include only rights enforceable by private individuals and do not include any right of action of a public officer in an official capacity regardless of whether the officer brings the action on behalf of a private individual.

(f) Nothing in this section shall be construed to require express statutory authorization by the California Legislature of any otherwise lawful and duly authorized action by any agency of local government.

CALIFORNIA NONPROFIT INTEGRITY ACT

(Cal. Govt. Code §§ 12581–12586)

State of California, Office of Attorney General

SUMMARY OF KEY PROVISIONS

1. Charitable Organizations Have 30 Days, Instead Of Six Months, To Register And File Articles Of Incorporation With The Attorney General's Registry Of Charitable Trusts [Government Code section 12585]

Charitable corporations, unincorporated associations and trusts must file with the Attorney General articles of incorporation, or other documents governing the organization's operations, (e.g., articles of association or trust instrument) within 30 days after initial receipt of property.

2. Independent Audit Of Annual Financial Statements Now Required For Charities With Gross Revenues Of $2 Million Or More [Government Code section 12586(e)(1)]

Charitable corporations with gross revenues of $2 million or more must prepare annual financial statements audited by an independent certified public accountant (CPA). The statements must use generally accepted accounting principles. The independent CPA must follow generally accepted auditing standards.

If the accounting firm and CPA performing the audit also provides non-audit services to the nonprofit, the accounting firm and CPA must follow the independence standards in the Yellow Book issued by the U.S. Comptroller General.

The audited financial statements must be made available for inspection by the Attorney General and the public no later than nine months after the close of the fiscal year covered by the financial statement.

The audit requirement applies to charitable corporations, unincorporated associations and trustees required to register and file reports with the Attorney General, whenever such organizations accrue $2 million or more in gross revenue in any fiscal year.

The $2 million-threshold excludes grants received from governmental entities, if the nonprofit must provide an accounting of how it used the grant funds.

3. Charities With Gross Revenues Of $2 Million Or More Must Establish And Maintain An Audit Committee [Government Code section 12586(e)(2)]

Requirements for an audit committee apply only to charitable corporations that must register and file reports with the Attorney General, whenever such organizations accrue $2 million or more in gross revenue in any fiscal year. $2 million-threshold excludes grants received from governmental entities, if the nonprofit must provide an accounting of how it uses the grant funds.

Governing boards must appoint an audit committee. The audit committee may include persons who are not members of the governing board.

The audit committee cannot include staff members, the president or chief executive officer, the treasurer or chief financial officer of the organization. If an organization has a finance committee, members of that committee may serve on the audit committee, but cannot comprise 50 percent or more of the audit committee.

The audit committee, under the governing board's supervision, is responsible for making recommendations to the board on the hiring and firing of independent certified public accountants (CPAs). The audit committee can negotiate the independent CPA's compensation, on behalf of the governing board.

The audit committee must:

- Confer with the auditor to satisfy committee members that the financial affairs of the nonprofit organization are in order;
- Review the audit and decide whether to accept it; and
- Approve non-audit services by the independent CPAs accounting firm, and ensure such services conform to standards in the Yellow Book issued by the U.S. Comptroller General.

4. Executive Compensation By Charitable Corporations, Unincorporated Associations And Charitable Trusts Must Be Reviewed And Approved [Government Code section 12586(g)]

Charitable corporations and unincorporated associations must have their governing board or authorized board committee review and approve the compensation of the Chief Executive Officer or President, and the compensation of the Chief Financial Officer or treasurer, to ensure that the payment is "just and reasonable."

All trustees of a charitable trust must review and approve any executive compensation to ensure it is "just and reasonable."

The review and approval must occur at the time of initial hiring, when the term is renewed or extended, and when the compensation is modified.

Compensation includes benefits.

5. Commercial Fundraisers Must Notify Attorney General Before Starting A Solicitation Campaign [Government Code section 12599(h)]

Commercial fundraisers for charitable purposes must report to the Attorney General's Registry of Charitable Trusts the start of a solicitation campaign or event. This notice must be filed not less than 10 working days prior to the start of a solicitation campaign or event.

If proceeds are intended for victims of disasters or emergencies, the commercial fundraiser must file the required disclosure report no later than the date on which the campaign begins. The report must include:

- The identity of the commercial fundraiser;
- The name of the organization for whom donations are being solicited;
- The name of the person directing and supervising the fundraiser's work within the commercial fundraising company; and
- Projected start and end dates for the commercial fundraiser's work.

6. Commercial Fundraisers Must Have Written Contracts With The Charitable Organizations For Whom They Are Working [Government Code section 12599(i)]

For every solicitation campaign or event produced by a commercial fundraiser for a charitable organization, there must be a written contract between the fundraiser and the charitable organization.

The written contract must contain or state:

- The charitable purpose for which the solicitation campaign or event is being conducted.
- The respective obligations of the commercial fundraiser and charitable organization.
- If the commercial fundraiser will be paid a fixed fee, the amount of the fee and a good faith estimate of what percentage of the total contributions the fee will comprise. The contract must clearly set forth the assumptions on which the good faith estimate is based.
- If the commercial fundraiser will be paid a percentage fee, the percentage of total contributions the charitable organization will retain. If the solicitation involves the sale of goods or services, or sale of admission to an event, the contract must state the percentage of the purchase price the charitable organization will retain. The percentage must be calculated by subtracting from total contributions and sales receipts not only the commercial fundraiser's fee, but also any additional fundraising costs the charitable organization must pay.
- The effective date and terminate date of the contract, and the date the solicitation will start in the state.

- A provision setting forth the requirement that all contributions received by the commercial fundraiser must, within five working days of receipt, either be deposited in a bank account controlled by the charitable organization or delivered in person to the charitable organization. The charitable organization controls and approves the content and frequency of any solicitation.

- The maximum amount the commercial fundraiser plans to pay individuals or entities to secure any person's attendance at, or approval, sponsorship or endorsement of, a fundraising event.

- Provisions specifying that the charitable organization has a right to cancel the contract without liability for 10 days following the date the contract is executed. The organization may cancel the contract with 30-days notice and payment for services provided by the commercial fundraiser for up to 30 days after the notice is served.

- Provisions specifying that after the initial 10-day period, the charitable organization has a right to cancel the contract for any reason without liability if the commercial fundraiser or its agents make material misrepresentations, harm the charitable organization's reputation or are found to have been convicted of a crime arising from charitable solicitations.

- Any other information required by regulations adopted by the Attorney General.

- The contract must be signed by the commercial fundraiser's authorized contracting officer and an official of the charitable organization authorized to sign by the governing board.

7. Charitable Organizations Can Void Contracts With Unregistered Commercial Fundraisers [Government Code section 12599.3(a)]

Contracts between commercial fundraisers for charitable purposes and charitable organizations are voidable unless the commercial fundraiser is registered with the Attorney General's Registry of Charitable Trusts prior to the start of the solicitation campaign or event.

8. Fundraising Counsel Must Notify Attorney General Before Starting Solicitation Campaign [Government Code section 12599.1(e)]

Fundraising counsel must file a notice with the Attorney General's Registry of Charitable Trusts not less than 10 working days prior to the start of a solicitation campaign or event; or if the purpose is to raise funds for victims of disasters or emergencies, no later than the date on which the campaign begins.

The form of notice will be specified by the Attorney General's Registry of Charitable Trusts.

The information that must be reported includes: the commercial fundraiser's name, address and telephone number; the name, address and telephone number of the organization with whom the fundraising counsel has contracted; the name, address and telephone number of the person who will direct and supervise the work of the fundraising counsel; and the projected dates when the contract will begin and end.

9. Fundraising Counsel Must Have Written Contracts With Charitable Organizations [Government Code section 12599]

For every solicitation campaign or event, there must be a written contract between the fundraising counsel and the charitable organization. The contract must be signed by the fundraising counsel's authorized contracting officer and an official of the charitable organization authorized to sign by the governing board.

The written contract must contain or state:

- The charitable purpose for which the solicitation campaign or event is being conducted.
- The respective obligations of the fundraising counsel and charitable organization.
- A statement that the fundraising counsel will neither solicit, receive nor control donated funds, assets and property, or employ any other person to do so.
- A statement that the charitable organization exercises control and approval over the content and frequency of solicitation.
- A clear statement of the fees and any other forms of compensation that will be paid to the fundraising counsel.
- The effective date and terminate date of the contract, and the date the solicitation will start in the state.
- Provisions specifying the charitable organization's right to cancel the contract without liability for 10 days following the date the contract is executed; and right to cancel the contract after the initial period by giving 30-days notice and payment for services provided by the fundraising counsel up to the effective date of the notice.
- Any other information required by regulations adopted by the Attorney General.

10. Charitable Organizations Can Cancel Contracts With Commercial Fundraisers [Government Code sections 12599.3(b)(f)(g)]

Charitable organizations have the right to cancel a contract with a commercial fundraiser without liability for 10 days following the date the contract is executed.

Following the initial 10-day period, charitable organizations have the right to cancel a contract with a commercial fundraiser by providing 30-day notice. The charitable organization is liable for services provided by the commercial fundraiser up to 30 days after the notice is served.

Following the initial 10-day period, a charitable organization has the right to cancel a contract with a commercial fundraiser without liability if the commercial fundraiser or its agents make material misrepresentations during a solicitation, harm the charitable organization's reputation during a solicitation, or are found to have been convicted of a crime arising from fundraising activities.

11. Charitable Organizations And Commercial Fundraisers For Charitable Purposes Have Specific Obligations When Fundraising [Government Code sections 12599.6(a)(b)(c)(d)(e)]

Charitable organizations and commercials fundraisers cannot misrepresent the purpose of a charitable organization, or the nature or purpose of the beneficiary of a solicitation.

Charitable organizations must establish and exercise control over fundraising activities conducted for their benefit. This obligation includes approving all written contracts and agreements, and assuring fundraising activities are conducted without coercion.

Charitable organizations cannot enter into any contract or agreement with a commercial fundraiser that is not registered with the Attorney Generals Registry of Charitable Trusts.

Charitable organizations cannot raise funds for any charitable organization required to be registered with the Attorney Generals Registry of Charitable Trusts unless the charitable organization is so registered or, if not, agrees to register prior to the start of a solicitation.

Commercial fundraisers must, within five working days, either deposit in a bank account controlled by the charitable organization or deliver personally to the charitable organization all contributions received on behalf of the charitable organization.

12. Charitable Organizations And Commercial Fundraisers For Charitable Purposes Are Prohibited From Engaging In Misrepresentation And Certain Other Acts When Soliciting Donations [Government Code section 12599.6(f)]

The following acts are prohibited in the planning, conduct or execution of solicitation campaigns:

- Operating in violation of the Supervision of Trustees and Fundraisers for Charitable Purposes Act [Govt. Code sec. 12580 et seq.], regulations and orders issued by the Attorney General.
- Committing unfair or deceptive acts, or engaging in fraudulent conduct.
- Using any name, symbol, emblem or other information that falsely suggests or implies a contribution is for a particular charitable organization.
- Falsely telling donors that a contribution is for a charitable organization or will be used for a charitable purpose.

- Telling donors that a person sponsors, endorses or approves a charitable solicitation when that person has not agreed in writing to have their name used for such a purpose.
- Misrepresenting that goods or services have endorsements, sponsorships, approvals, characteristics or qualities they do not have.
- Misrepresenting that a person has endorsements, approvals, sponsorships,status or affiliations they do not have.
- Misrepresenting that registration with the Attorney Generals Registry of Charitable Trusts constitutes an endorsement or approval by the Attorney General.
- Representing that a charitable organization will receive an amount greater than the reasonably estimated net proceeds from a solicitation campaign or event.
- Issuing cards, stickers, emblems, plates or other items that can be used for display on a motor vehicle, and which suggest an affiliation with, or endorsement by, public safety personnel or a group of public safety personnel.
- Representing that any portion of contributions solicited by a charitable organization will be given to another charitable organization unless the second charitable organization provides prior written consent for such use of its name.
- Representing that tickets to events will be donated for use by another person or entity unless: the charitable organization or commercial fundraiser has obtained written commitments from charitable organizations that they will accept a specific number of donated tickets; and the donated tickets, when combined with other ticket donations, do exceed either the ticket donations received from charitable organizations or the total capacity of the event site.

13. Commercial Fundraisers Must Keep Records Of Solicitation Campaigns For At Least 10 Years [Government Code section 12599.7(a)]

Commercials must maintain for at least 10 years following each solicitation campaign records that contain:

- The date and amount of each cash contribution.
- The date, amount, name and address of each non-cash contributor.
- The name and address of each employee or agent involved.
- Documentation of all revenue received and expenses incurred.
- For each account into which the fundraiser deposited revenue, the account number and name and location of the bank or other financial institution in which the account was maintained.

ILLINOIS GENERAL NOT FOR PROFIT CORPORATION ACT (SELECTED PROVISIONS)

805 ILLINOIS COMPILED STATUTES, CHAPTER 105

§ 103.05. Purposes and authority of corporations; particular purposes; exemptions

(a) Not-for-profit corporations may be organized under this Act for any one or more of the following or similar purposes:

(1) Charitable.

(2) Benevolent.

(3) Eleemosynary.

(4) Educational.

(5) Civic.

(6) Patriotic.

(7) Political.

(8) Religious.

(9) Social.

(10) Literary.

(11) Athletic.

(12) Scientific.

(13) Research.

(14) Agricultural.

(15) Horticultural.

(16) Soil improvement.

(17) Crop improvement.

(18) Livestock or poultry improvement.

(19) Professional, commercial, industrial, or trade association.

(20) Promoting the development, establishment, or expansion of industries.

(21) Electrification on a cooperative basis.

(22) Telephone service on a mutual or cooperative basis.

(23) Ownership and operation of water supply facilities for drinking and general domestic use on a mutual or cooperative basis.

(24) Ownership or administration of residential property on a cooperative basis.

(25) Administration and operation of property owned on a condominium basis or by a homeowner association.

(26) Administration and operation of an organization on a cooperative basis producing or furnishing goods, services, or facilities primarily for the benefit of its members who are consumers of those goods, services, or facilities.

(27) Operation of a community mental health board or center organized pursuant to the Community Mental Health Act for the purpose of providing direct patient services.

(28) Provision of debt management services as authorized by the Debt Management Service Act.

(29) Promotion, operation, and administration of a ridesharing arrangement as defined in Section 1–176.1 of the Illinois Vehicle Code.

(30) The administration and operation of an organization for the purpose of assisting low-income consumers in the acquisition of utility and telephone services.

(31) Any purpose permitted to be exempt from taxation under Sections 501(c) or 501(d) of the United States Internal Revenue Code [26 U.S.C. §§ 501], as now in or hereafter amended.

(32) Any purpose that would qualify for tax-deductible gifts under the Section 170(c) of the United States Internal Revenue Code [26 U.S.C. §§ 170(c)], as now or hereafter amended. Any such purpose is deemed to be charitable under subsection (a)(1) of this Section.

(33) Furnishing of natural gas on a cooperative basis.

(34) Ownership and operation of agriculture-based biogas (an aerobic digester) systems on a cooperative basis including the marketing and sale of products produced from these, including but not limited to methane gas, electricity and compost.

(35) Ownership and operation of a hemophilia program, including comprehensive hemophilia diagnostic treatment centers, under Section 501(a)(2) of the Social Security Act. The hemophilia program may employ physicians, other health care professionals, and staff. The program and the corporate board may not exercise control over, direct, or interfere with a physician's exercise and execution of his or her professional judgment in the provision of care or treatment.

(36) Engineering for conservation services associated with wetland restoration or mitigation, flood mitigation, groundwater recharge, and natural infrastructure. Non-profit engineering for conservation services may not be procured by qualifications based selection criteria for contracts with the Department of Transportation, Illinois State Highway Authority, or Cook County, except as a subcontractor or subconsultant.

(b) A corporation may be organized hereunder to serve in an area that adjoins or borders (except for any intervening natural watercourse) an area located in an adjoining state intended to be similarly served, and the corporation may join any corporation created by the adjoining state having an identical purpose and organized as a not-for-profit corporation. Whenever any corporation organized under this Act so joins with a foreign corporation having an identical purpose, the corporation shall be permitted to do business in Illinois as one corporation; provided:

(1) that the name, bylaw provisions, officers, and directors of each corporation are identical,

(2) that the foreign corporation complies with the provisions of this Act relating to the admission of foreign corporation, and

(3) that the Illinois corporation files a statement with the Secretary of State indicating that it has joined with a foreign corporation setting forth the name thereof and the state of its incorporation.

§ 108.60. Director conflict of interest

(a) If a transaction is fair to a corporation at the time it is authorized, approved, or ratified, the fact that a director of the corporation is directly or indirectly a party to the transaction is not grounds for invalidating the transaction.

(b) In a proceeding contesting the validity of a transaction described in subsection (a), the person asserting validity has the burden of proving fairness unless:

(1) The material facts of the transaction and the director's interest or relationship were disclosed or known to the board of directors or a committee consisting entirely of directors and the board or committee authorized, approved or ratified the transaction by the affirmative votes of a majority of disinterested directors, even though the disinterested directors be less than a quorum; or

(2) The material facts of the transaction and the director's interest or relationship were disclosed or known to the members entitled to vote, if any, and they autho-

rized, approved or ratified the transaction without counting the vote of any member who is an interested director.

(c) The presence of the director, who is directly or indirectly a party to the transaction described in subsection (a), or a director who is otherwise not disinterested, may be counted in determining whether a quorum is present but may not be counted when the board of directors or a committee of the board takes action on the transaction.

(d) For purposes of this Section, a director is "indirectly" a party to a transaction if the other party to the transaction is an entity in which the director has a material financial interest or of which the director is an officer, director or general partner; except if a director is an officer or director of both parties to a transaction involving a grant or contribution, without consideration, from one entity to the other, that director is not "indirectly" a party to the transaction provided the director does not have a material financial interest in the entity that receives the grant or contribution.

§ 108.65. Liability of directors in certain cases

(a) In addition to any other liabilities imposed by law upon directors of a corporation, they are liable as follows:

(1) The directors of a corporation who vote for or assent to any distribution authorized by Section 109.10 or Article 12 of this Act shall be jointly and severally liable to the corporation for the amount of such distribution.

(2) If a dissolved corporation shall proceed to bar any known claims against it under Section 112.75 of this Act, the directors of such corporation who fail to take reasonable steps to cause the notice required by Section 112.75 of this Act to be given to any known creditor of such corporation shall be jointly and severally liable to such creditor for all loss and damage occasioned thereby.

(3) Unless dissolution is subsequently revoked pursuant to Section 112.25 of this Act, the directors of a corporation that conducts its affairs after the filing by the Secretary of State of articles of dissolution with respect to a voluntary dissolution authorized as provided by this Act, otherwise than as necessary or appropriate to wind up and liquidate its affairs, shall be jointly and severally liable to the creditors of such corporation for all debts and liabilities of the corporation incurred in so conducting its affairs. Directors of a corporation that conduct its affairs during a period of administrative dissolution shall not be liable under this paragraph (a)(3) if the Secretary of State subsequently files an application for reinstatement under subsection (c) of Section 112.45, which reinstatement shall have the effect described in subsection (d) of Section 112.45.

(b) A director of a corporation who is present at a meeting of its board of directors at which action on any corporate matter is taken is conclusively presumed to have assented to the action taken unless his or her dissent or abstention is entered in the minutes of the meeting or unless he or she files his or her written dissent or abstention to such action with the person acting as the secretary of the meeting before the adjournment thereof or forwards such dissent or abstention by registered or certified mail to the secretary of the corporation immediately after the adjournment of the meeting. Such right to dissent or abstain does not apply to a director who voted in favor of such action.

(c) A director shall not be liable for a distribution of assets to any person in excess of the amount authorized by Section 109.10 or Article 12 of this Act if he or she relied and acted in good faith upon a balance sheet and profit and loss statement of the corporation represented to him or her to be correct by the president or the officer of such corporation having charge of its books of account, or certified by an independent public or certified public accountant or firm of such accountants to fairly reflect the financial condition of such corporation, nor shall he or she be so liable if in good faith in determining the amount available for any such distribution he or she considered the assets to be of their book value.

(d) Any director against whom a claim is asserted under this Section and who is held liable thereon, is entitled to contribution from the other directors who are likewise liable thereon. Any director against whom a claim is asserted for the improper distribution of assets of a corporation, and who is held liable thereon, is entitled to contribution from the persons who knowingly accepted or received any such distribution in proportion to the amounts received by them respectively.

§ 108.70. Limited liability of directors, officers and persons who serve without compensation

(a) No director or officer serving without compensation, other than reimbursement for actual expenses, of a corporation organized under this Act or any predecessor Act and exempt, or qualified for exemption, from taxation pursuant to Section 501(c) of the Internal Revenue Code of 1986 [26 U.S.C. §§ 501(c)], as amended, shall be liable, and no cause of action may be brought, for damages resulting from the exercise of judgment or discretion in connection with the duties or responsibilities of such director or officer unless the act or omission involved willful or wanton conduct.

(b) No director of a corporation organized under this Act or any predecessor Act for the purposes identified in items (14), (19), (21) and (22) of subsection (a) of Section 103.05 of this Act, and exempt or qualified for exemption from taxation pursuant to Section 501(c) of the Internal Revenue Code of 1986 [26 U.S.C. §§ 501(c)], as amended, shall be liable, and no cause of action may be brought for damages resulting from the exercise of judgment or discretion in connection with the duties or responsibilities of such director, unless:

(1) Such director earns in excess of $25,000 per year from his duties as director, other than reimbursement for actual expenses; or

(2) The act or omission involved willful or wanton conduct.

(b–5) Except for willful and wanton conduct, no volunteer board member serving without compensation, other than reimbursement for actual expenses, of a corporation organized under this Act or any predecessor Act and exempt, or qualified for exemption, from taxation pursuant to Section 501(c)(3) of the Internal Revenue Code of 1986, as amended, shall be liable, and no action may be brought, for damages resulting from any action of the executive director concerning the false reporting of or intentional tampering with financial records of the organization, where the actions of the executive director result in legal action.

This subsection (b–5) shall not apply to any action taken by the Attorney General (i) in the exercise of his or her common law or statutory power and duty to protect charitable assets or (ii) in the exercise of his or her authority to enforce the laws of this State that apply to trustees of a charity, as that term is defined in the Charitable Trust Act and the Solicitation for Charity Act.

(c) No person who, without compensation other than reimbursement for actual expenses, renders service to or for a corporation organized under this Act or any predecessor Act and exempt or qualified for exemption from taxation pursuant to Section 501(c)(3) of the Internal Revenue Code of 1986 [26 U.S.C. §§ 501(c)(3)] as amended, shall be liable, and no cause of action may be brought, for damages resulting from an act or omission in rendering such services, unless the act or omission involved willful or wanton conduct.

(d) (Blank)

(e) Nothing in this Section is intended to bar any cause of action against the corporation or change the liability of the corporation arising out of an act or omission of any director, officer or person exempt from liability for negligence under this Section.

§ 108.80. Prohibited loans to directors and officers

Except as permitted by subsection (e) of Section 108.75, no loan shall be made by a corporation to a director or officer except that a loan may be made to a director or officer who is employed by the corporation if authorized by a majority of the non-employed directors and either:

(a) in the case of a corporation organized for and holding property for any charitable, religious, eleemosynary, benevolent, educational or similar purpose, the purpose of such loan is to provide financing for the principal residence of the employed director or officer upon receipt of adequate collateral consisting of marketable real estate or securities readily capable of valuation or

(b) the loan is otherwise in furtherance of the purposes of the corporation and in the ordinary course of its affairs.

The directors of a corporation who vote for or assent to the making of loan to any non-employed director or non-employed officer of the corporation, otherwise prohibited by this Section, and any other person knowingly participating in the making of such loan, shall be jointly and severally liable the corporation for the amount of such loan until the repayment thereof.

§ 112.16. Distribution of assets

The assets of a corporation in the process of dissolution shall be applied and distributed as follows:

(a) All liabilities and obligations of the corporation shall be paid, satisfied and discharged, or adequate provision shall be made therefor;

(b) Assets held by the corporation upon condition requiring return, transfer or conveyance, which condition occurs by reason of the dissolution, shall be returned, transferred or conveyed in accordance with such requirements;

(c) Assets held for a charitable, religious, eleemosynary, benevolent, educational or similar use, but not held upon a condition requiring return, transfer or conveyance by reason of the dissolution, shall be transferred or conveyed to one or more domestic or foreign corporations, societies or organizations engaged in activities substantially similar to those of the dissolving corporation, pursuant to a plan of distribution adopted as provided in this Act;

(d) To the extent that the articles of incorporation or bylaws determine the distributive rights of members, or any class or classes of members, or provide distribution to others, other assets, if any, shall be distributed in accordance with such provisions;

(e) Any remaining assets may be distributed to such societies, organizations domestic or foreign corporations, whether for profit or not for profit, as may be specified in a plan of distribution adopted as provided in Section 112.17 of this Act.

NEW YORK NOT-FOR-PROFIT CORPORATION LAW (SELECTED PROVISIONS)

§ 102. Definitions

(a) As used in this chapter, unless the context otherqise requires, the team:

* * *

(3–a) "Charitable corporation" means any corporation formed, or for the purposes of this chapter, deemed to be formed, for charitable purposes.

(3–b) "Charitable purposes" of a corporation means one or more of the following purposes: charitable, educational, religious, scientific, literary, cultural or for the prevention of cruelty to children or animals.

* * *

(6–a) "Entire board" means the total number of directors entitled to vote which the corporation would have if there were no vacancies. If the by-laws of the corporation provide that the board shall consist of a fixed number of directors, then the "entire board" shall consist of that number of directors. If the by-laws of any corporation provide that the board may consist of a range between a minimum and maximum number of directors, and the number within that range has not been fixed in accordance with paragraph (a) of section seven hundred two of this chapter, then the "entire board" shall consist of the number of directors within such range that were elected or appointed as of the most recently held election of directors, as well as any directors whose terms have not yet expired.

(9–a) "Non-charitable corporation" means any corporation formed under this chapter, other than a charitable corporation, including but not limited to one formed for any one or more of the following non-pecuniary purposes: civic, patriotic, political, social, fraternal, athletic, agricultural, horticultural, or animal husbandry, or for the purpose of operating a professional, commercial, industrial, trade or service association.

* * *

(21) "Independent director" means a director who: (i) is not, and has not been within the last three years, an employee or a key person of the corporation or an affiliate of the corporation, and does not have a relative who is, or has been within the last three years, a key person of the corporation or an affiliate of the corporation; (ii) has not received, and does not have a relative who has received, in any of the last three fiscal years, more than ten thousand dollars in direct compensation from the corporation or an affiliate of the corporation (iii) is not a current employee of or does not have a substantial financial interest in, and does not have a relative who is a current officer of or has a substantial financial interest in, any entity that has provided payments, property or services to, or received payments property or services from, the corporation or an affiliate of the corporation for if the amount paid by the corporation to the entity or received by the corporation from the entity for such property or services in any of the last three fiscal years, exceeded the lesser of ten thousand dollars or two percent of such entity's consolidated gross revenues if the entity's consolidated gross revenue was less than five hundred thousand dollars; twenty-five thousand dollars if the entity's consolidated gross revenue was five hundred thousand dollars or more but less than ten million dollars; one hundred thousand dollars if the entity's consolidated gross revenue was ten million dollars or more; or (iv) is not and does not have a relative who is a current owner, whether wholly or partially, director, officer or employee of the corporation's outside auditor or who has worked on the corporation's audit at any time during the past three years. For

purposes of this subparagraph, the terms: "compensation" does not include reimbursement for expenses reasonably incurred as a director or reasonable compensation for service as a director as permitted by paragraph (a) of section 202 (General and special powers) of this chapter; and "payment" does not include charitable contributions, dues or fees paid to the corporation for services which the corporation performs as part of its nonprofit purposes, or payments made by the corporation at fixed or non-negotiable rates or amounts for services received, provided that such services by and to the corporation are available to individual members of the public on the same terms, and such services received by the corporation are not available from another source.

* * *

(23) "Related party" means (i) any director, officer or key person of the corporation or any affiliate of the corporation; (ii) any relative of any individual described in clause (i) of this subparagraph; or (iii) any entity in which any individual described in clauses (i) and (ii) of this subparagraph has a thirty-five percent or greater ownership or beneficial interest or, in the case of a partnership or professional corporation, a direct or indirect ownership interest in excess of five percent.

(24) "Related party transaction" means any transaction, agreement or any other arrangement in which a related party has a financial interest and in which the corporation or any affiliate of the corporation is a participant, except that a transaction shall not be a related party transaction if: (i) the transaction or the related party's financial interest in the transaction is de minimis, (ii) the transaction would not customarily be reviewed by the board or boards of similar organizations in the ordinary course of business and is available to others on the same or similar terms, or (iii) the transaction constitutes a benefit provided to a related party solely as a member of a class of the beneficiaries that the corporation intends to benefit as part of the accomplishment of its mission which benefit is available to all similarly situated members of the same class on the same terms.

(25) "Key person" means any person, other than a director or officer, whether or not an employee of the corporation, who (i) has responsibilities, or exercises powers or influence over the corporation as a whole similar to the responsibilities, powers, or influence of directors and officers; (ii) manages the corporation, or a segment of the corporation that represents a substantial portion of the activities, assets, income or expenses of the corporation; or (iii) alone or with others controls or determines a substantial portion of the corporation's capital expenditures or operating budget.

§ 112. Actions or special proceedings by attorney-general

(a) The attorney-general may maintain an action or special proceeding:

(1) To annul the corporate existence or dissolve a corporation that has acted beyond its capacity or power or to restrain it from carrying on unauthorized activities;

(2) To annul the corporate existence or dissolve any corporation that has not been duly formed;

(3) To restrain any person or persons from acting as a domestic or foreign corporation within this state without being duly incorporated or from exercising in this state any corporate rights, privileges or franchises not granted to them by the law of the state;

(4) To procure a judgment removing a director of a corporation for cause under section 706 (Removal of directors);

(5) To dissolve a corporation under article 11 (Judicial dissolution);

(6) To restrain a foreign corporation or to annul its authority to carry on activities in this state under section 1303 (Violations).

(7) To enforce any right given under this chapter to members, a director or an officer of a charitable corporation. The attorney-general shall have the same status as such members, director or officer.

(8) To compel the directors and officers, or any of them, of a charitable corporation which has been dissolved under section 1011 (Dissolution for failure to file certificate of type of Not-for-Profit Corporation Law under section 113) to account for the assets of the dissolved corporation.

(9) Upon application, ex parte, for an order to the supreme court at a special term held within the judicial district where the office of the corporation is located, and if the court so orders, to enforce any right given under this chapter to members, a director or an officer of a non-charitable corporation. For such purpose, the attorney-general shall have the same status as such members, director or officer.

(10) To enjoin, void or rescind any related party transaction, or seek additional damages or remedies pursuant to section 715 (Related party transactions) of this chapter.

(b) In an action or special proceeding brought by the attorney-general under any of the provisions of this chapter:

(1) If an action, it is triable by jury as a matter of right.

(2) The court may confer immunity in accordance with the provisions of section six hundred nineteen-c of the code of criminal procedure.

(3) A temporary restraining order to restrain the commission or continuance of the unlawful acts which form the basis of action or special proceeding may be granted upon proof, by affidavit, that the defendant or defendants have committed or are about to commit such acts. Application for such restraining or may be made ex parte or upon such notice as the court may direct.

(4) If the action or special proceeding is against a foreign corporation, the attorney-general may apply to the court at any stage thereof for the appointment of a temporary receiver of the assets in this state of such foreign corporation, whenever it has assets or property of any kind whatsoever, tangible or intangible, within this state.

(5) When final judgment in such action or special proceeding rendered against the defendant or defendants, the court may direct the costs to be collected by execution against any or all of the defendants or by order of attachment or other process against the person of any director or officer of a corporate defendant.

(6) In connection with any such proposed action or special proceeding, the attorney-general may take proof and issue subpoenas in accordance with the civil practice law and rules.

(c) In any such action or special proceeding against a foreign corporation which has not designated the secretary of state as agent for service of process under section 304 (Statutory designation of secretary of state as agent for service of process), any of the following acts in this state by such foreign corporation shall constitute the appointment by it of the secretary of state as its agent upon whom process against such foreign corporation may served.

(1) As used in this paragraph the term "resident" shall include individuals, domestic corporations of any type or kind and foreign corporations of any kind authorized to do business or carry on activities in the state.

(2) Any act done, or representation made as part of a course of the solicitation of orders, or the issuance, or the delivery of contracts for, or the sale of, property, or the performance of services to residents which involves or promotes a plan or scheme to defraud residents in violation of the laws or the public policy of the state.

(3) Any act done as part of a course of conduct of business or activities in the solicitation of orders from residents for property, goods or services, to be delivered or rendered within this state to, or on their behalf, where the orders or contracts are executed by such residents within this state and where such orders or contracts are accompanied or followed by an earnest money deposit or other down payment or any installment payment thereon or any other form of payment, which payment is either delivered in or transmitted from the state.

(4) Any act done as part of the conduct of a course of business or activities with residents which defrauds such residents or otherwise involves or promotes an attempt by such foreign corporation to circumvent the laws of this state.

(d) Paragraphs (b), (c), (d) and (e) of section 307 (Service of process of unauthorized foreign corporation) shall apply to process served under paragraph (c).

§ 114. Visitation of supreme court

Charitable corporations, whether formed under general or special laws, with their books and vouchers, shall be subject to the visitation and inspection of a justice of the supreme court, or of any person appointed by the court for that purpose. If it appears by the verified petition of a member or creditor of any such corporation, that it, or its directors, officers, members, key persons or agents, have misappropriated any of the funds or property of the corporation, or diverted them from the purpose of its incorporation, or that the corporation has acquired property in excess of the amount which it is authorized by law to hold, or has engaged in any business other than that stated in its certificate of incorporation, the court may order that notice of at least eight days, with a copy of the petition, be served on the corporation, the attorney general and the persons charged with misconduct, requiring them to show cause at a time and place specified, why they should not be required to make and file an inventory and account of the property, effects and liabilities of such corporation with a detailed statement of its transactions during the twelve months next preceding the granting of such order. On the hearing of such application, the court may make an order requiring such inventory, account and statement to be filed, and proceed to take and state an account of the property and liabilities of the corporation, or may appoint a referee for that purpose. When such account is taken and stated, after hearing all the parties to the application, the court may enter a final order determining the amount of property so held by the corporation, its annual income, whether any of the property or funds of the corporation have been misappropriated or diverted to any other purpose than that for which such corporation was incorporated, and whether such corporation has been engaged in any activity not covered by its certificate of incorporation. An appeal may be taken from the order by any party aggrieved to the appellate division of the supreme court, and to the court of appeals, as in a civil action. No corporation shall be required to make and file more than one inventory and account in any one year, nor to make a second account and inventory, while proceedings are pending for the statement of an account under this section.

§ 115. Power to solicit contributions for charitable purposes

(a) No corporation required to obtain approval or provide notice of formation pursuant to section 404 (Approvals, notices and consents) of this chapter may solicit contributions for any purpose requiring such approval or notice unless and until such corporation (1) obtains and submits any approval or notice required thereunder, and (2) is in compliance with the registration and reporting requirements of article seven-A of the executive law and section 8–1.4 of the estates, powers and trusts law.

(b) The attorney general may maintain an action or proceeding pursuant to the provisions of subparagraph one of paragraph (a) of section one hundred twelve of this article against any corporation that solicits contributions in violation of paragraph (a) of this section. Such an action may also be maintained in relation to a corporation hereinafter incorporated if the name, purposes, objects or the activities of such corporation may, in any manner, lead to the belief that the corporation possesses or may exercise any of such purposes.

§ 201. Purposes

(a) A corporation, as defined in paragraph (a) of § 102 (Definitions), may be formed under this chapter as a charitable corporation or a non-charitable corporation unless it may be formed under any other corporate law of this state, in which event it may not be formed under this chapter unless such other corporate law expressly so provides.

(b) A corporation formed under this chapter on or after July first, two thousand fourteen shall either be a charitable corporation or a non-charitable corporation. Any corporation formed for both charitable purposes and non-charitable purposes shall be deemed a charitable corporation for purposes of this chapter. A type A not-for-profit corporation formed prior to July first, two thousand fourteen shall be deemed a non-charitable corporation under this chapter. Any submission or filing by such corporation to any person or entity shall be deemed to have been submitted or filed by a non-charitable corporation, and any reference in any such filing or submission referring to the status of such corporation as a type A corporation shall be deemed to refer to a non-charitable corporation.

(c) A type B or C not-for-profit corporation formed prior to July first, two thousand fourteen shall be deemed a charitable corporation for all purposes under this chapter. Any submission or filing by such corporation to any person or entity shall be deemed to have been submitted or filed by a charitable corporation, and any reference in any such filing or submission referring to the status of such corporation as a type B or type C corporation shall be deemed to refer to a charitable corporation.

(d) A type D not-for-profit corporation formed prior to July first, two thousand fourteen for charitable purposes shall be deemed a charitable corporation. Any submission or filing by such corporation to any person or entity shall be deemed to have been submitted or filed by a charitable corporation, and any reference in any such filing or submission referring to the status of such corporation as a type D corporation shall be deemed to refer to a charitable corporation. Any other type D not-for-profit corporations formed prior to July first, two thousand fourteen shall be deemed a non-charitable corporation. Any submission or filing by such corporation to any person or entity shall be deemed to have been submitted or filed by a non-charitable corporation, and any reference in any such filing or submission referring to the status of such corporation as a type D corporation shall be deemed to refer to a non-charitable corporation.

§ 202. General and special powers

(a) Each corporation, subject to any limitations provided in this chapter or any other statute of this state or its certificate of incorporation, shall have power in furtherance of its corporate purposes:

(1) To have perpetual duration.

(2) To sue and be sued in all courts and to participate in actions and proceedings, whether judicial. administrative, arbitrative, or otherwise, in like cases as natural persons.

(3) To have a corporate seal, and to alter such seal at pleasure, and to use it by causing it or a facsimile to be affixed or impressed or reproduced in any other manner.

(4) To purchase, receive, take by grant, gift, devise, bequest or otherwise, lease, or otherwise acquire, own, hold, improve, employ, use and otherwise deal in and with, real or personal property, or any interest therein, wherever situated.

(5) To sell, convey, lease, exchange, transfer or otherwise dispose of, or mortgage or pledge, or create a security interest in, all or any of its property, or any interest therein, wherever situated.

(6) To purchase, take, receive, subscribe for, or otherwise acquire, own, hold, vote, employ, sell, lend, lease, exchange, transfer, or otherwise dispose of, mortgage, pledge, use and otherwise deal in and with, bonds and other obligations, shares, or other securities or interests issued by others, whether engaged in similar or different business, governmental, or other activities.

(7) To make capital contributions or subventions to other not-for-profit corporations.

(8) To accept subventions from other persons or any unit of government.

(9) To make contracts, give guarantees and incur liabilities, borrow money at such rates of interest as the corporation may determine, issue its notes, bonds and other obligations, and secure any of its obligations by mortgage or pledge of all or any of its property or any interest therein, wherever situated.

(10) To lend money, invest and reinvest its funds, and take and hold real and personal property as security for the payment of funds so loaned or invested.

(11) To conduct the activities of the corporation and have offices and exercise the powers granted by this chapter in any jurisdiction within or without the United States.

(12) To elect or appoint officers, employees and other agents of the corporation, define their duties, fix their reasonable compensation and the reasonable compensation of directors, and to indemnify corporate personnel. Such compensation shall be commensurate with services performed.

(13) To adopt, amend or repeal by-laws, including emergency by-laws made pursuant to subdivision seventeen of section twelve of the state defense emergency act, relating to the activities of the corporation, the conduct of its affairs, its rights or powers or the rights or powers of its members, directors or officers.

(14) To make donations, irrespective of corporate benefit, for the public welfare or for community fund, hospital, charitable, educational, scientific, civic or similar purposes, and in time of war or other national emergency in aid thereof.

(15) To be a member, associate or manager of other non-profit activities or to the extent permitted in any other jurisdiction to be an incorporator of other corporations, and to be a partner in a redevelopment company formed under the private housing finance law.

(16) To have and exercise all powers necessary to effect any or all of the purposes for which the corporation is formed.

(b) If any general or special law heretofore passed, or any certificate of incorporation, shall limit the amount of property a corporation may take or hold, or the yearly income from the corporate assets or any part thereof, such corporation may take and hold property of the value of fifty million dollars or less, or the yearly income derived from which shall be six million dollars or less, or may receive yearly income from such corporate assets of six million dollars or less, notwithstanding any such limitations. In computing the value of such property, no increase in value arising otherwise than from improvements made thereon shall be taken into account.

(c) When any corporation shall have sold or conveyed any part of its real property, the supreme court, notwithstanding a restriction in any general or special law, may authorize it to purchase and hold from time to time other real property, upon satisfactory proof that the value of the property so purchased does not exceed the value of the property so sold and conveyed within the three years next preceding the application.

(d) A corporation formed under general or special law to provide parks playgrounds or cemeteries, or buildings and grounds for camp or grove meetings, Sunday school assemblies, cemetery purposes, temperance, missionary, educational, scientific, musical and other meetings, subject to the ordinances and police regulations of the county, city, town, or village in which such parks, playgrounds, cemeteries, buildings and grounds are situated, may appoint from time to time one or more special police officers, with power to remove the same at pleasure. Such special police officers shall preserve order in and about such parks, playgrounds, cemeteries, buildings and grounds, and the approaches thereto, and to protect the same from injury, and shall enforce the established rules and regulations of the corporation. Every police officer so appointed shall within fifteen days after his appointment and before entering upon the duties of his office, take and subscribe the oath of office prescribed in the thirteenth article of the constitution of the state of New York, which oath shall be filed in the office of the county clerk of the county where such grounds are situated. A police officer appointed under this section when on duty shall wear conspicuously a metallic shield with the name of the corporation which appointed him inscribed thereon. The compensation of police officers appointed under this section shall be paid by the corporation by which they are appointed.

(e) Any wilful trespass in or upon any of the parks, playgrounds, buildings or grounds provided for the purposes mentioned in the preceding paragraph, or upon the approaches thereto, and any wilful injury to any of the said parks, playgrounds, buildings or grounds, or to any trees, shrubbery, fences, fixtures or other property thereon or pertaining thereto, and any wilful disturbance of the peace thereon by intentional breach of the rules and regulations of the corporation, is a misdemeanor.

(f) No corporation shall conduct activities in New York state under any name, other than that appearing in its certificate of incorporation, without compliance with the filing provisions of section one hundred thirty of the general business law governing the conduct of business under an assumed name.

(g) Every corporation receiving any kind of state funding shall ensure the provision on any form required to be completed at application or recertification for the purpose of obtaining financial assistance pursuant to this chapter, that the application form shall contain a check-off question asking whether the applicant or recipient or a member of his or her family served in the United States military, and an option to answer in the affirmative. Where the applicant or recipient answers in the affirmative to such question, the not-for-profit corporation shall ensure that contact information for the state department of veterans' services is provided to such applicant or recipient in addition to any other materials provided.

§ 204. Limitation on activities

Notwithstanding any other provision of this chapter or any other general law, a corporation of any kind to which this chapter applies shall conduct no activities for pecuniary profit or financial gain, whether or not in furtherance of its corporate purposes, except to the extent that such activity supports its other lawful activities then being conducted.

§ 205. Conveyance of real property to members for dwelling houses

A not-for-profit corporation, if its by-laws so provide, and pursuant to the provisions thereof, and without leave of the court, may convey to a member of the corporation a portion of its real property for the erection thereupon of a cottage or other dwelling-house with suitable out-buildings. When so conveyed the title to such portion, together with the buildings thereon, shall continue in such member and on his death pass to his heirs or devisees, but the land shall not be alienable except to the corporation or to a member thereof.

§ 402. Certificate of incorporation; contents

(a) A certificate, entitled "Certificate of Incorporation of .... (name of corporation), under section 402 of the Not-for-Profit Corporation Law," shall be signed by each incorporator with his name and address included in such certificate and delivered to the department of state. It shall set forth:

(1) The name of the corporation.

(2) That the corporation is a corporation as defined in subparagraph (5) of paragraph (a) of section 102 (Definitions).

(2–a) the purpose or purposes for which it is formed, it being sufficient to state that the purpose of the corporation is any purpose for which corporations may be organized under this chapter as a charitable or non-charitable corporation, and whether it is a charitable corporation or a non-charitable corporation under section 201 (Purposes). Any corporation may also set forth any activities that it intends to carry out in furtherance of such purpose or purposes; provided that this subparagraph shall not be interpreted to require that the certificate of incorporation set forth such activities or otherwise state how the corporation's purposes will be achieved.

(2–b) If it is not formed to engage in any activity or for any purpose requiring consent or approval of any state official, department, board, agency or other body, a statement that no such consent or approval is required. Such statement shall be deemed conclusive for purposes of filing by the department of state. If subsequent to submitting the certificate of incorporation for filing, the corporation plans to engage in any activity requiring consent or approval pursuant to section 404 (approvals, notices and consents) of this chapter, the corporation shall obtain such consent or approval and accordingly amend its certificate of incorporation pursuant to article eight of this chapter.

(3) The county within the state in which the office of the corporation is to be located. It may also set forth the post office address of an office without the state, at which, pursuant to section 621 (Books and records; right of inspection; prima facie evidence), the books and records of account of the corporation shall be kept.

(4) The names and addresses of the initial directors.

(5) The duration of the corporation if other than perpetual.

(6) A designation of the secretary of state as agent of the corporation upon whom process against it may be served and the post office address within or without this state to which the secretary of state shall mail a copy of any process against it served upon him or her. The corporation may include an email address to which the secretary of state shall email a notice of the fact that process against it has been electronically served upon him or her.

(7) If the corporation is to have a registered agent, his name and address within this state and a statement that the registered agent is to be the agent of the corporation upon whom process against it may be served.

(8) The statements, if any, with respect to special not-for-profit corporations required under article 14 (Special not-for-profit corporations).

(b) If the certificate is for the incorporation of an existing unincorporated association or group it shall have annexed thereto an affidavit of the subscribers of such certificate stating that they constitute a majority of the members of a committee duly authorized to incorporate such association or group.

(c) The certificate of incorporation may set forth any provision, not inconsistent with this chapter or any other statute of the state, which provision is:

(1) For the regulation of the internal affairs of the corporation, including types or classes of membership and the distribution of assets on dissolution or final liquidation, or;

(2) Required by any governmental body or officer or other person or body as a condition for giving the consent or approval required for the filing of such certificate of incorporation.

§ 404. Approvals, notices and consents

(a) Every certificate of incorporation which includes among its purposes the formation of a trade or business association shall have endorsed thereon or annexed thereto the consent of the attorney-general.

(b)(1) Every certificate of incorporation which includes among its purposes the care of destitute, delinquent, abandoned, neglected or dependent children; the establishment or operation of any adult care facility, or the establishment or operation of a residential program for victims of domestic violence as defined in subdivision four of section four hundred fifty-nine-a of the social services law, or the placing-out or boarding-out of children or a home or shelter for unmarried mothers, excepting the establishment or maintenance of a hospital or facility providing health-related services as those terms are defined in article twenty-eight of the public health law and a facility for which an operating certificate is required by articles sixteen, nineteen, twenty-two and thirty-one of the mental hygiene law; or the solicitation of contributions for any such purpose or purposes, shall have endorsed thereon or annexed thereto the approval of the commissioner of the office of children and family services or with respect to any adult care facility, the commissioner of health.

(2) A corporation whose statement of purposes specifically includes the establishment or operation of a child day care center, as that term is defined in section three hundred ninety of the social services law, shall provide a certified copy of the certificate of incorporation, each amendment thereto, and any certificate of merger, consolidation or dissolution involving such corporation to the office of children and family services within thirty days after the filing of such certificate, amendment, merger, consolidation or dissolution with the department of state. This requirement shall also apply to any foreign corporation filing an application for authority under section thirteen hundred four of this chapter, any amendments thereto, and any surrender of authority or termination of authority in this state of such corporation

(c) Every certificate of incorporation which includes among the purposes of the corporation, the establishment, maintenance and operation of a hospital service or a health service or a medical expense indemnity plan or a dental expense indemnity plan as permitted in article forty-three of the insurance law, shall have endorsed thereon or annexed thereto the approval of the superintendent of insurance and the commissioner of health.

(d) Every corporation whose certificate of incorporation includes among its purposes the operation of a school; a college, university or other entity providing post secondary education; a library; or a museum or historical society shall have endorsed thereon or annexed thereto the approval of the commissioner of education, or in the case of a college or a university, the written authorization of the Regents of the university of the State of New York. Any other corporation the certificate of incorporation of which includes a purpose for which a corporation might be chartered by the regents of the university of the State of New York shall provide a certified copy of the certificate of incorporation to the commissioner of education within thirty business days after the corporation receives confirmation from the department of state that the certificate has been accepted for filing.

(e) Every certificate of incorporation of a cemetery corporation, except those within the exclusionary provisions of section 1503 (Cemetery corporations) shall have endorsed thereon or annexed thereto the approval of the cemetery board.

(f) Every certificate of incorporation of a fire corporation shall have endorsed thereon or annexed thereto the approval, signed and acknowledged, of the authorities of each city, village, town or fire district in which the corporation proposes to act. Such authorities shall be: in a city, the mayor; in a village, a majority of the trustees; in a town, a majority of the members of the town board; in a fire district, a majority of the fire commissioners. The members of the town board of a town, or the trustees of a village, shall not consent to the formation of a fire corporation as hereinbefore provided, until such board shall have held a public hearing on the question of whether the fire company should be incorporated. The notice shall be published at least once in each week for two successive weeks in the official newspaper published in the county in which such fire corporation intends to locate, prior to the regular meeting of such board designated by the chairman of the board to consider the matter. Such notice shall contain the name of the proposed company, the names of the persons signing the certificate of incorporation, a brief description of the territory to be protected by the fire company and that all persons interested shall be heard. If no newspaper is published in the county the publication of the notice shall be in a newspaper in an adjoining county selected by the chairman of such board. All expenses in connection with such publication shall be borne by the parties making the application and paid before the hearing.

(g) Every certificate of incorporation of a corporation for prevention of cruelty to animals shall have endorsed thereon or annexed thereto the approval of the American Society for the Prevention of Cruelty to Animals, or, if such approval be withheld thirty days after application therefor, a certified copy of an order of a justice of the supreme court of the judicial district in which the office of the corporation is to be located, dispensing with such approval, granted upon eight days' notice to such society.

(h) Every certificate of incorporation of a Young Men's Christian Association shall have endorsed thereon or annexed thereto the approval of the chairman of the national board of Young Men's Christian Associations.

(i) Every certificate of incorporation which indicates that the proposed corporation is to solicit funds for or otherwise benefit the armed forces of the United States or of any foreign country, or their auxiliaries, or of this or any other state or any territory, shall have endorsed thereon or annexed thereto the approval of the adjutant general. The department of state, in conjunction with the division of military and naval affairs, shall establish and maintain on the department's website a public listing of all approved not-for-profit corporations soliciting funds for or otherwise benefiting the armed forces of the United States or of any foreign country, or their auxiliaries, or of this or any other state or territory.

(j) Every certificate of incorporation which includes among its purposes the organization of wage-earners for their mutual betterment, protection and advancement; the regulation of hours of labor, working conditions, or wages; or the performance, rendition or sale of services as labor consultant, labor-management advisor, negotiator, arbitrator, or specialist; and every certificate of incorporation in which the name of the proposed corporation includes "union", "labor", "council" or "industrial organization", or any abbreviation or derivative thereof in a context that indicates or implies that the corporation is formed for any of the above purposes, shall have endorsed thereon or annexed thereto the approval of the industrial board of appeals. The board shall make such inquiry into the purposes of the proposed corporation as it shall deem advisable and shall order a hearing if necessary to determine whether or not such purposes are in all respects consistent with public policy and the labor law. Notice of the time and place of hearing shall be given to the applicants and such other persons as the board may determine.

(k) Every certificate of incorporation for a corporation which has as its exclusive purpose the promotion of the interests of savings bank life insurance or the promotion of the interests of member banks may, if the approval of the superintendent of banks is endorsed thereon or annexed thereto, use as a part of the corporate name any of the words or phrases, or any abbreviation or derivative thereof, set forth in subparagraph (5) of paragraph (a) of section 301 (Corporate name; general).

(*l*) Every certificate of incorporation for a corporation which has as its exclusive purpose the creation of an association of licensed insurance agents, licensed insurance brokers, or licensed insurance underwriters and every application for authority of a foreign corporation which is an independent laboratory engaged in testing for public safety, or which has as its purpose the advancement of corporate, governmental, and institutional risk and insurance management, or which has as its exclusive purpose the creation of an association of insurers, each of which is duly licensed in this state or, if it does no business or is not licensed in this state, is duly licensed in another state or foreign jurisdiction may, if the approval of the superintendent of insurance is endorsed thereon or annexed thereto, use as a part of the corporate name any of the words or phrases, or any abbreviation or derivative thereof, set forth in subparagraph (5) of paragraph (a) of section 301 (Corporate name; general).

(m) Every certificate of incorporation in which the name of the proposed corporation includes the name of a political party shall have endorsed thereon or annexed thereto the consent of the chairman of the county committee of such political party of the county in which the office of the corporation is to be located, except in cases where the supreme court finds that the withholding of such consent of the county chairman is unreasonable.

(n) Every certificate of incorporation in which the name of the proposed corporation includes the words "American Legion," shall have endorsed thereon or annexed thereto the approval of the Department of New York, the American Legion, duly acknowledged by its commander or adjutant.

(*o*) Every certificate of incorporation which includes among its corporate purposes or powers the establishment or maintenance of any hospital, as defined in article twenty-eight of the public health law, or the solicitation of contributions for any such purpose, or purposes, shall have endorsed thereon or annexed thereto the approval of the public health council.

(p) Every certificate of incorporation of a medical corporation as defined in article forty-four of the public health law and organized pursuant thereto and pursuant to this chapter, shall have endorsed thereon or annexed thereto the consent of the commissioner of health and the approval of the public health and health planning council.

(q) Every certificate of incorporation which includes among its corporate purposes or powers the establishment, or operation of a facility for which an operating certificate from the commissioner of mental health or mental retardation and developmental disabilities is required by article thirty-one or sixteen of the mental hygiene law, or the solicitation of contributions for any such purpose, shall have endorsed thereon or annexed thereto the approval of the commissioner of mental health or mental retardation and developmental disabilities.

(r) Every certificate of incorporation of a health maintenance organization as defined in article forty-four of the public health law and organized pursuant thereto and pursuant to this chapter, shall have endorsed thereon or annexed thereto the consent of the commissioner of health.

* * *

(t) Every certificate of incorporation which includes among its purposes and powers the establishment or maintenance of a hospital or facility providing health related services, as those terms are defined in article twenty-eight of the public health law, or the solicitation of contributions for any such purpose or two or more of such purposes, shall have endorsed thereon the approval of the public health council.

(u) Every certificate of incorporation which includes among, substance dependent, alcohol abuse, alcoholism, or chemical abuse or dependence program, or the solicitation of contributions for any such purpose, shall have endorsed thereon or annexed thereto the consent of the commissioner of the office of alcoholism and substance abuse services to its filing by the department of state.

(v) Every certificate of incorporation which includes among the purposes of the corporation, the establishment or operation of a nonprofit property/casualty insurance company, pursuant to article sixty-seven of the insurance law, shall have endorsed thereon or annexed thereto the approval of the superintendent of financial services.

§ 406. Private foundation, as defined in the United States internal revenue code of 1954: provisions included in the certificate of incorporation

(a) The following provisions are hereby included in the certificate of incorporation of every domestic corporation, heretofore or hereafter formed, to which this chapter applies in whole or in part, and which is a "private foundation" as defined in section 509 of the United States internal revenue code of 1954 ("code"):

(1) The corporation shall distribute such amounts for each taxable year at such time and in such manner as not to subject the corporation to tax on undistributed income under section 4942 of the code.

(2) The corporation shall not engage in any act or* [of] self-dealing which is subject to tax under section 4941 of the code.

(3) The corporation shall not retain any excess business holdings which are subject to tax under section 4943 of the code.

(4) The corporation shall not make any investments in such manner as to subject the corporation to tax under section 4944 of the code.

(5) The corporation shall not make any taxable expenditures which are subject to tax under section 49 of the code. Except as provided in paragraph (b), this paragraph applies notwithstanding any other provision of the certificate of incorporation or any direction in an instrument referred to in section 513 (Administration of assets received for specific purposes).

(b) Paragraph (a) shall not apply to the extent that it conflicts with any mandatory direction in an instrument by which assets referred to in section 513 were transferred to the corporation prior to the effective date of this section unless such conflicting direction is removed as impracticable under article eight of the estates, powers and trusts law or in any other manner provided by law. The absence of a specific provision in the section 513 instrument for the current use of the principal of the fund, or the presence in such an instrument of a provision, as to the principal of a fund, limited to the principal's being held, invested and reinvested, is not such a conflicting mandatory direction.

(c) All references in this section to sections of the code shall be to such sections as amended from time to time, or to corresponding provisions of subsequent internal revenue laws.

(d) Nothing in this section shall impair the rights and powers of the courts or the attorney-general of this state.

* * *

---

* Appears in original, Eds.

§ 501. Stock and shares prohibited; membership certificates authorized

A corporation shall not have stock or shares or certificates for stock or for shares, but may issue non-transferable membership certificates or cards to evidence membership, whether or not connected with any financial contribution to the corporation, as provided in section 601 (Members). The fact that the corporation is a not-for-profit corporation, and that the membership certificate or card is non-transferable shall be noted conspicuously on the face or back of each such certificate or card.

§ 508. Income from corporate activities

A corporation whose lawful activities involve among other things the charging of fees or prices for its services or products shall have the right to receive such income and, in so doing, may make an incidental profit. All such incidental profits shall be applied to the maintenance, expansion or operation of the lawful activities of the corporation, and in no case shall be divided or distributed in any manner whatsoever among the members, directors, or officers of the corporation.

§ 509. Purchase, sale, mortgage and lease of real property

(a) No corporation shall purchase real property unless such purchase is authorized by the vote of a majority of directors of the board or of a majority of a committee authorized by the board, provided that if such property would, upon purchase thereof, constitute all, or substantially all, of the assets of the corporation, then the vote of two-thirds of the entire board shall be required, or, if there are twenty-one or more directors, the vote of a majority of the entire board shall be sufficient.

(b) No corporation shall sell, mortgage, lease, exchange or otherwise dispose of its real property unless authorized by the vote of a majority of directors of the board or of a majority of a committee authorized by the board; provided that if such property constitutes all, or substantially all, of the assets of the corporation, then the vote of two-thirds of the entire board shall be required, or, if there are twenty-one or more directors, the vote of a majority of the entire board shall be sufficient.

(c) If a corporation authorizes a committee to act pursuant to paragraphs (a) and (b) of this section, the committee shall promptly report any actions taken to the board, and in no event after the next regularly scheduled meeting of the board.

§ 513. Administration of assets received for specific purposes

(a) A corporation which is, or would be if formed under this chapter, a charitable corporation shall hold full ownership rights in any assets consisting of funds or other real or personal property of any kind, that may be given, granted, bequeathed or devised to or otherwise vested in such corporation in trust for, or with a direction to apply the same to, any purpose specified in its certificate of incorporation, and shall not be deemed a trustee of an express trust of such assets. Any other corporation subject to this chapter may similarly hold assets so received, unless otherwise provided by law or in the certificate of incorporation.

(b) Except as may be otherwise permitted under article eight of the estates, powers and trusts law or section 555 (Release or modification of restrictions on management, investment, or purpose), the governing board shall apply all assets thus received to the purposes specified in the gift instrument as defined in section 551 (Definitions) and to the payment of the reasonable and proper expenses of administration of such assets. The governing board shall cause accurate accounts to be kept of such assets separate and apart from the accounts of other assets of the corporation. Unless the terms of the particular gift instrument provide otherwise, the treasurer shall make an annual report to the members (if there be members) or to the governing board (if there be no members) concerning the assets held under this section and the use made of such assets and of the income thereof.

§ 514. Delegation of investment management

(a) Except as otherwise provided by the applicable gift instrument as defined in section 551 (Definitions), the governing board may delegate to its committees, officers or employees of the corporation or the fund the authority to act in place of the governing board in investment and reinvestment of institutional funds as defined in section 551 (Definitions). Each contract, if any, pursuant to which authority is so delegated shall provide that it may be terminated by the governing board at any time, without penalty, upon not more than sixty days' notice. Section 554 (Delegation of management and investment functions) shall govern external delegation.

(b) The governing board shall exercise the standard of care required by section 717 (Duty of directors and officers) in the selection of persons to whom authority is delegated or with whom contracts are made under paragraph (a) of this section and in the continuation or termination of such delegation or contracts. The governing board shall be relieved of all liability for the investment and reinvestment of institutional funds by, and for the other acts or omissions of, persons to whom authority is so delegated or with whom contracts are so made.

§ 515. Dividends prohibited; certain distributions of cash or property authorized

(a) A corporation shall not pay dividends or distribute any part of its income or profit to its members, directors, or officers.

(b) A corporation may pay compensation in a reasonable amount to members, directors, or officers for services rendered, and may make distributions of cash or property to members upon dissolution or final liquidation as permitted by this chapter. No person who may benefit from such compensation may be present at or otherwise participate in any board or committee deliberation or vote concerning such person's compensation: provided that nothing in this section shall prohibit the board or authorized committee from requesting that a person who may benefit from such compensation present information as background or answer questions at a committee or board meeting prior to the commencement of deliberations or voting relating thereto. Nothing in this section or in paragraph (h) of section seven hundred fifteen of this chapter shall be construed to prohibit a director from deliberating or voting concerning compensation for service on the board that is to be made available or provided to all directors of the corporation on the same or substantially similar terms.

§ 519. Annual report of directors

(a) The board shall present at the annual meeting of members a report, verified by the president and treasurer or by a majority of the directors, or certified by an independent public or certified public accountant or a firm of such accountants selected by the board, showing in appropriate detail the following:

(1) The assets and liabilities, including the trust funds, of the corporation as of the end of a twelve month fiscal period terminating not more than six months prior to said meeting.

(2) The principal changes in assets and liabilities, including trust funds, during said fiscal period.

(3) The revenue or receipts of the corporation, both unrestricted and restricted to particular purposes during said fiscal period.

(4) The expenses or disbursements of the corporation, for both general and restricted purposes, during said fiscal period.

(5) The number of members of the corporation as of the date of the report, together with a statement of increase or decrease in such number during said fiscal period, and a statement of the place where the names and places of residence of the current members may be found.

(b) The annual report of directors shall be filed with the records of the corporation and either a copy or an abstract thereof entered in the minutes of the proceedings of the annual meeting of members.

(c) The board of a corporation having no members shall direct the president and treasurer to present at the annual meeting of the board a report in accordance with paragraph (a), but omitting the requirement of subparagraph (5). This report shall be filed with the minutes of the annual meeting of the board.

§ 520. Reports of corporation

Each domestic corporation, and each foreign corporation authorized to conduct activities in this state, shall from time to time file such reports on its activities as may be required by the laws of this state. All registration and reporting requirements pursuant to EPTL 8–1.4, or related successor provisions, are, without limitation on the foregoing, expressly included as reports required by the laws of this state to be filed within the meaning of this section. Willful failure of a corporation to file a report as required by law shall constitute a breach of the directors' duty to the corporation and shall subject the corporation, at the suit of the attorney-general, to an action or special proceeding for dissolution under article 11 (Judicial dissolution) in the case of a domestic corporation, or under '1303 (Violations) in the case of a foreign corporation.

§ 521. Liability for failure to disclose required information

Failure of the corporation to comply in good faith with the notice of disclosure or reporting provisions of section 501 (Stock and shares prohibited; membership certificates authorized), or paragraph (c) of section 503 (Capital certificates), or paragraph (c) of section 505 (Subvention certificates), or paragraph (b) of section 513 (Administration of assets received for specific purposes), or section 518 (Reports to comptroller), or section 519 (Annual report of directors), or section 520 (Reports of corporation), shall make the corporation liable for any damage sustained by any person in consequence thereof.

§ 603. Meetings of members

(a) Meetings of members may held at such place, within or without this state, as may be fixed by or under the by-laws or, if not so fixed, as determined by the board of directors. For the duration of the state disaster emergency declared by executive order two hundred two that began on March seventh, two thousand twenty, the board of directors may, in its sole discretion, determine that meetings of members be held partially or solely by means of electronic communication, the electronic service and/or platform by which the meeting is held shall be the place of the meeting for purposes of this article if a meeting is held solely by means of electronic communication. Meetings conducted partially or solely by means of electronic communications in reliance upon this paragraph and any member's electronic participation in such meetings shall be subject to those guidelines and procedures as the board adopts, provided the board shall implement reasonable measures to: (1) verify that each person participating electronically is a member or a proxy of a member; (2) provide each member participating electronically with a reasonable opportunity to participate in the meeting, including an opportunity to propose, object to, and vote upon a specific action to be taken by the members, and to see, read or hear the proceedings of the meeting substantially concurrently with those proceedings; and (3) record and maintain a record of any votes or other actions taken by electronic communication at the meeting.

(b) A meeting of the members shall be held annually for the election of directors and the transaction of other business on a date fixed by or under the by-laws. Failure to hold the annual meeting on the date so fixed or to elect a sufficient number of directors to conduct the business of the corporation shall not work a forfeiture or give cause for dissolution of the corporation, except as provided in paragraph (a) of section 1102 (Judicial dissolution; petition by directors or members; petition in case of deadlock among directors or members).

(c) Special meetings of the members may be called by the board and by such person or persons as may be authorized by the certificate of incorporation or the by-laws. In any case, such meetings may be convened by the members entitled to cast ten per cent of the total number of votes entitled to be cast at such meeting, who may, in writing, demand the call of a special meeting specifying the date and month thereof, which shall not be less than two nor more than three months from the date of such written demand. The secretary of the corporation upon receiving the written demand shall promptly give notice of such meeting, or if he fails to do so within five business days thereafter, any member signing such demand may give such notice. The meeting shall be held at the place fixed in the by-laws or, if not so fixed, at the office of the corporation.

(d) A corporation may provide in its certificate of incorporation or by-laws adopted by the members for the election of representatives or delegates, who, when assembled within or without the state as directed by the certificate of incorporation or the by-laws, shall have and may exercise all of the powers, rights and privileges of members at an annual meeting. When so exercising the powers, rights and privileges of members, such representatives or delegates shall be subject in all respects to the provisions of this chapter governing members.

§ 621. Books and records; right of inspection; prima facie evidence

(a) Except as otherwise provided herein, every corporation shall keep, at the office of the corporation, correct and complete books and records of account and minutes of the proceedings of its members, board and executive committee, if any, and shall keep at such office or at the office of its transfer agent or registrar in this state, a list or a record containing the names and addresses of all members, the class or classes of membership or capital certificates and the number of capital certificates held by each and the dates when they respectively became the holders of record thereof. A corporation may keep its books and records of account in an office of the corporation without the state as specified in its certificate of incorporation. Any of the foregoing books, minutes and records may be in written form or in any other form capable of being converted into written form within a reasonable time.

(b) Any person who shall have been a member of record of a corporation for at least six months immediately preceding his demand, or any person holding, or thereunto authorized in writing by the holders of, at least five percent of any class of the outstanding capital certificates, upon at least five days written demand shall have the right to examine in person or by agent or attorney, during usual business hours, its minutes of the proceedings of its members and list or record of members and to make extracts therefrom.

(c) An inspection authorized by paragraph (b) may be denied to such member or other person upon his refusal to furnish to the corporation, its transfer agent or registrar an affidavit that such inspection is not desired and will not be used for a purpose which is in the interest of a business or object other than the business of the corporation and that he has not within five years given, sold or offered for sale any list or record of members of any domestic or foreign corporation or aided or abetted, or attempted or offered to aid or abet, any person in procuring any such list or record of members for any such purpose.

(d) Upon refusal by the corporation or by an officer or agent of the corporation to permit an inspection of the minutes of the proceedings of its members or of the list or record of members, as herein provided, the person making the demand for inspection may apply to the supreme court in the judicial district where the office of the corporation is located, upon such notice as the court may direct, for an order directing the corporation, its officer or agent to show cause why an order should not be granted permitting such inspection by the applicant. Upon the return day of the order to show cause, the court shall hear the parties summarily, by affidavit or otherwise, and if it appears that the applicant is qualified and entitled to such inspection, the court shall grant an order compelling such inspection and awarding such further relief as to the court may seem just and proper.

(e) Upon the written request of any person who shall have been a member of record for at least six months immediately preceding his request, or of any person holding, or thereunto authorized in writing by the holders of, at least five percent of any class of the outstanding capital certificates, the corporation shall provide to such member an annual balance sheet and profit and loss statement or a financial statement performing a similar function for the preceding fiscal year, and, if any interim balance sheet or profit and loss or similar financial statement has been distributed to its members or otherwise made available to the public, the most recent such interim balance sheet or profit and loss or similar financial statement. The corporation shall be allowed a reasonable time to prepare such annual balance sheet and profit and loss or similar financial statement.

(e-1) In addition to those documents described in paragraph (e) of this section, members of a homeowners association incorporated pursuant to the provisions of this chapter shall also be entitled to review, upon request to the homeowners association's governing board, invoices, ledgers, bank accounts, reconciliations, contracts, and any documents related to the expenditure of homeowners association dues.

(f) Nothing herein contained shall impair the power of courts to compel the production for examination of the books and records of a corporation.

(g) The books and records specified in paragraph (a) shall be prima facie evidence of the facts therein stated in favor of the plaintiff in any action or special proceeding against such corporation or any of its officers, directors or members.

(h) Nothing in this chapter shall require an employee organization certified or recognized for any collective negotiating unit of an employer pursuant to article fourteen of the civil service law to disclose the home address of any member or former member of such organization.

§ 712–a. Audit oversight

(a) The board, or a designated audit committee of the board comprised solely of independent directors, of any corporation required to file an independent certified public accountant's audit report with the attorney general pursuant to subdivision one of section one hundred seventy-two-b of the executive law shall oversee the accounting and financial reporting processes of the corporation and the audit of the corporation's financial statements. The board or designated audit committee shall annually retain or renew the retention of an independent auditor to conduct the audit and, upon completion thereof, review the results of the audit and any related management letter with the independent auditor.

(b) The board, or a designated audit committee of the board comprised solely of independent directors, of any corporation required to file an independent certified public accountant's audit report with the attorney general pursuant to subdivision one of section one hundred seventy-two-b of the executive law and that in the prior fiscal year had or in the current fiscal year reasonably expects to have annual revenue in excess of one million dollars shall, in addition to those duties set forth in paragraph (a) of this section:

(1) review with the independent auditor the scope and planning of the audit prior to the audit's commencement;

(2) upon completion of the audit, review and discuss with the independent auditor: (A) any material risks and weaknesses in internal controls identified by the auditor; (B) any restrictions on the scope of the auditor's activities or access to requested information; (C) any significant disagreements between the auditor and management; and (D) the adequacy of the corporation's accounting and financial reporting processes;

(3) annually consider the performance and independence of the independent auditor; and

(4) if the duties required by this section are performed by an audit committee, report on the committee's activities to the board.

(c) [Repealed.]

(d) If a corporation controls a group of corporations, the board or designated audit committee of the board of the controlling corporation may perform the duties required by this section for one or more of the controlled corporations and, if independent directors, directors from one or more of such controlled corporations may serve on any designated audit committee of the board of such controlling corporation, and perform the duties required by this section for each corporation and any controlled corporations.

(e) Only independent directors may participate in any board or committee deliberations or voting relating to matters set forth in this section, provided that nothing in this paragraph shall prohibit the board or designated audit committee from requesting that a person with an interest in the matter present information as background or answer questions at a committee or board meeting prior to the commencement of deliberations or voting relating thereto.

(f) Any corporation that is a state authority or a local authority as defined in section two of the public authorities law and that has complied substantially with sections twenty-eight hundred two and twenty-eight hundred twenty-four of such law shall be deemed in compliance with this section.

§ 715. Related party transactions

(a) No corporation shall enter into any related party transaction unless the transaction is determined by the board, or an authorized committee thereof, to be fair, reasonable and in the corporation's best interest at the time of such determination. Any director, officer or key person who has an interest in a related party transaction shall disclose in good faith to the board, or an authorized committee thereof, the material facts concerning such interest.

(b) With respect to any related party transaction involving a charitable corporation and in which a related party has a substantial financial interest, the board of such corporation, or an authorized committee thereof, shall:

(1) Prior to entering into the transaction, consider alternative transactions to the extent available;

(2) Approve the transaction by not less than a majority vote of the directors or committee members present at the meeting; and

(3) Contemporaneously document in writing the basis for the board or authorized committee's approval, including its consideration of any alternative transactions.

(c) The certificate of incorporation, by-laws or any policy adopted by the board may contain additional restrictions on related party transactions and additional procedures necessary for the review and approval of such transactions, or provide that any transaction in violation of such restrictions shall be void or voidable.

(d) Unless otherwise provided in the certificate of incorporation or the by-laws, the board shall have authority to fix the compensation of directors for services in any capacity.

(e) The fixing of compensation of officers, if not done in or pursuant to the by-laws, shall require the affirmative vote of a majority of the entire board unless a higher proportion is set by the certificate of incorporation or by-laws.

(f) The attorney general may bring an action to enjoin, void or rescind any related party transaction or proposed related party transaction that violates any provision of this chapter or was otherwise not reasonable or in the best interests of the corporation at the time the transaction was approved, or to seek restitution, and the removal of directors or officers, or seek to require any person or entity to:

(1) Account for any profits made from such transaction, and pay them to the corporation;

(2) Pay the corporation the value of the use of any of its property or other assets used in such transaction;

(3) Return or replace any property or other assets lost to the corporation as a result of such transaction, together with any income or appreciation lost to the corporation by reason of such transaction, or account for any proceeds of sale of such property, and pay the proceeds to the corporation together with interest at the legal rate; and

(4) Pay, in the case of willful and intentional conduct, an amount up to double the amount of any benefit improperly obtained.

(g) The powers of the attorney general provided in this section are in addition to all other powers the attorney general may have under this chapter or any other law.

(h) No related party may participate in deliberations or voting relating to a related party transaction in which he or she has an interest; provided that nothing in this section shall prohibit the board or authorized committee from requesting that a related party present information as background or answer concerning a related party transaction at a board or committee meeting prior to the commencement of deliberations or voting relating thereto.

(i) In an action by any person or entity other than the attorney general, it shall be a defense to a claim of violation of any provisions of this section that a transaction was fair, reasonable and in the corporation's best interest at the time the corporation approved the transaction.

(j) In an action by the attorney general with respect to a related party transaction not approved in accordance with paragraphs (a) or (b) of this section at the time it was entered into, whichever is applicable, it shall be a defense to a claim of violation of any provisions of this section that (1) the transaction was fair, reasonable and in the corporation's best interest at the time the corporation approved the transaction and (2) prior to receipt of any request for information by the attorney general regarding the transaction, the board has: (A) ratified the transaction by finding in good faith that it was fair, reasonable and in the corporation's best interest at the time the corporation approved the transaction; and, with respect to any related party transaction involving a charitable corporation and in which a related party has a substantial financial interest, considered alternative transactions to the extent available, approving the transaction by not less than a majority vote of the directors or committee members present at the meeting; (B) documented in writing the nature of the violation and the basis for the board's or committee's ratification of the transaction; and (C) put into place procedures to ensure that the corporation complies with paragraphs (a) and (b) of this section as to related party transactions in the future.

§ 715–a. Conflict of interest policy

(a) Except as provided in paragraph (d) of this section, the board shall adopt, and oversee the implementation of, and compliance with, a conflict of interest policy to ensure that its directors, officers and key employees act in the corporation's best interest and comply with applicable legal requirements, including but not limited to the requirements set forth in section seven hundred fifteen of this article.

(b) The conflict of interest policy shall include, at a minimum, the following provisions:

(1) a definition of the circumstances that constitute a conflict of interest;

(2) procedures for disclosing a conflict of interest, or possible conflict of interest to the board or to a committee of the board, and procedures for the board or committee to determine whether a conflict exists;

(3) a requirement that the person with the conflict of interest not be present at or participate in board or committee deliberation or vote on the matter giving rise to such conflict, provided that nothing in this section shall prohibit the board or a committee from requesting that the person with the conflict of interest present information as background or answer questions at a committee or board meeting prior to the commencement of deliberations or voting relating thereto;

(4) a prohibition against any attempt by the person with the conflict to influence improperly the deliberation or voting on the matter giving rise to such conflict;

(5) a requirement that the existence and resolution of the conflict be documented in the corporation's records, including in the minutes of any meeting at which the conflict was discussed or voted upon; and

(6) procedures for disclosing, addressing, and documenting related party transactions in accordance with section seven hundred fifteen of this article.

(c) The conflict of interest policy shall require that prior to the initial election of any director, and annually thereafter, such director shall complete, sign and submit to the secretary of the corporation or a designated compliance officer a written statement identifying, to the best of the director's knowledge, any entity of which such director is an officer, director, trustee, member, owner (either as a sole proprietor or a partner), or employee and with which the corporation has a relationship, and any transaction in which the corporation is a participant and in which the director might have a conflicting interest. The policy shall require that each director annually resubmit such written statement. The secretary of the corporation or a designated compliance officer shall provide a copy of all completed statements to the chair of the audit committee or, if there is no audit committee, to the chair of the board.

(d) A corporation that has adopted and possesses a conflict of interest policy pursuant to federal, state or local laws that is substantially consistent with the provisions of paragraph (b) of this section shall be deemed in compliance with provisions of this section. In addition, any corporation that is a state authority or a local authority as defined in section two of the public authorities law, and that has complied substantially with section twenty-eight hundred twenty-four and subdivision three of section twenty-eight hundred twenty-five of such law, shall be deemed in compliance with this section.

(e) Nothing in this section shall be interpreted to require a corporation to adopt any specific conflict of interest policy not otherwise required by this section or any other law or rule, or to supersede or limit any requirement or duty governing conflicts of interest required by any other law or rule.

§ 715–b. Whistleblower policy

(a) Except as provided in paragraph (c) of this section, every corporation that has twenty or more employees and in the prior fiscal year had annual revenue in excess of one million dollars shall adopt a whistleblower policy to protect from retaliation persons who report suspected improper conduct. Such policy shall provide that no director, officer, employee or volunteer of a corporation who in good faith reports any action or suspected action taken by or within the corporation that is illegal, fraudulent or in violation of any adopted policy of the corporation shall suffer intimidation, harassment, discrimination or other retaliation or, in the case of employees, adverse employment consequence.

(b) The whistleblower policy shall include the following provisions:

(1) Procedures for the reporting of violations or suspected violations of laws or corporate policies, including procedures for preserving the confidentiality of reported information;

(2) A requirement that an employee, officer or director of the corporation be designated to administer the whistleblower policy and to report to the board or an authorized committee thereof, except that directors who are employees may not participate in any board or committee deliberations or voting relating to administration of the whistleblower policy;

(3) A requirement that the person who is the subject of a whistleblower complaint not be present at or participate in board or committee deliberations or vote on the matter relating to such complaint, provided that nothing in this subparagraph shall prohibit the board or committee from requesting that the person who is subject to the complaint present information as background or answer questions at a committee or board meeting prior to the commencement of deliberations or voting relating thereto; and

(4) A requirement that a copy of the policy be distributed to all directors, officers, employees and to volunteers who provide substantial services to the corporation. For purposes of this subdivision, posting the policy on the corporation's website or at the corporation's offices in a conspicuous location accessible to employees and volunteers are among the methods a corporation may use to satisfy the distribution requirement.

(c) A corporation that has adopted and possesses a whistleblower policy pursuant to federal, state or local laws that is substantially consistent with the provisions of paragraph (b) of this section shall be deemed in compliance with provisions of this section. In addition, any corporation that is a state authority or local authority as defined in section two of the public authorities law, and that has complied substantially with section twenty-eight hundred twenty-four of such law and is subject to the provisions of section twenty-eight hundred fifty-seven of such law, shall be deemed in compliance with the provisions of this section.

(d) Nothing in this section shall be interpreted to relieve any corporation from any additional requirements in relation to internal compliance, retaliation, or document retention required by any other law or rule.

§ 716. Loans to directors and officers

No loans, other than through the purchase of bonds, debentures, or similar obligations of the type customarily sold in public offerings, or through ordinary deposit of funds in a bank, shall be made by a corporation to its directors, officers or key persons, or to any other corporation, firm, association or other entity in which one or more of its directors, officers or key persons, are directors or officers or hold a substantial financial interest, except a loan by one charitable corporation to another charitable corporation to another charitable corporation. A loan made in violation of this section shall be a violation of the duty to the corporation of the directors or officers authorizing it or participating in it, but the obligation of the borrower with respect to the loan shall not be affected thereby.

§ 717. Duty of directors and officers

(a) Directors, officers and key persons shall discharge the duties of their respective positions in good faith and with the care an ordinarily prudent person in a like position would exercise under similar circumstances. The factors set forth in subparagraph one of paragraph (e) of section 552 (Standard of conduct in managing and investing an institutional fund), if relevant, must be considered by a governing board delegating investment management of institutional funds pursuant to section 514 (Delegation of investment management). For purposes of this paragraph, the term institutional fund is defined in section 551 (Definitions).

(b) In discharging their duties, directors, officers and key persons, when acting in good faith, may rely on information, opinions, reports or statements including financial statements and other financial data, in each case prepared or presented by:

(1) one or more officers or employees of the corporation, whom the director believes to be reliable and competent in the matters presented,

(2) counsel, public accountants or other persons as to matters which the directors, officers or key persons believe to be within such person's professional or expert competence or

(3) a committee of the board upon which they do not serve, duly designated in accordance with a provision of the certificate of incorporation or the bylaws, as to matters within its designated authority, which committee the directors, officers or key persons believe to merit confidence, so long as in so relying they shall be acting in good faith and with that degree of care specified in paragraph (a) of this section. Persons shall not be considered to be acting in good faith if they have knowledge concerning the matter in question that would cause such reliance to be unwarranted. Persons who so perform their duties shall have no liability by reason of being or having been directors, officers or key persons of the corporation.

§ 719. Liability of directors in certain cases

(a) Directors of a corporation who vote for or concur in any of the following corporate actions shall be jointly and severally liable to the corporation for the benefit of its creditors or members or the ultimate beneficiaries of its activities, to the extent of any injury suffered by such persons, respectively, as a result of such action, or, if there be no creditors or members or ultimate beneficiaries so injured, to the corporation, to the extent of any injury suffered by the corporation as a result of such action:

(1) The distribution of the corporation's cash or property to members, directors or officers, other than a distribution permitted under section 515 (Dividends prohibited; certain distributions of cash or property authorized).

(2) The redemption of capital certificates, subvention certificates or bonds, to the extent such redemption is contrary to the provisions of section 502 (Member's capital contributions), section 504 (Subventions), or section 506 (Bonds and security interests).

(3) The payment of a fixed or contingent periodic sum to the holders of subvention certificates or of interest to the holders or beneficiaries of bonds to the extent such payment is contrary to the provisions of section 504 or section 506.

(4) The distribution of assets after dissolution of the corporation in violation of section 1005 (Procedure after dissolution) or without paying or adequately providing for all known liabilities of the corporation, excluding any claims not filed by creditors within the time limit set in a notice given to creditors under articles 10 (non-judicial dissolution) or 11 (Judicial dissolution).

(5) The making of any loan contrary to section 716 (Loans to directors and officers).

(b) A director who is present at a meeting of the board, or any committee thereof, at which action specified in paragraph (a) is taken shall be presumed to have concurred in the action unless his dissent thereto shall be entered in the minutes of the meeting, or unless he shall submit his written dissent to the person acting as the secretary of the meeting before the adjournment thereof, or shall deliver or send by registered mail such dissent to the secretary of the corporation promptly after the adjournment of the meeting. Such right to dissent shall not apply to a director who voted in favor of such action. A director who is absent from a meeting of the board, or any committee thereof, at which such action is taken shall be presumed to have concurred in the action unless he shall deliver or send by registered mail his dissent thereto to the secretary of the corporation or shall cause such dissent to be filed with the minutes of the proceedings of the board or committee within a reasonable time after learning of such action.

(c) Any director against whom a claim is successfully asserted under this section shall be entitled to contribution from the other directors who voted for or concurred in the action upon which the claim is asserted.

(d) Directors against whom a claim is successfully asserted under this section shall be entitled, to the extent of the amounts paid by them to the corporation as a result of such claims:

(1) Upon reimbursement to the corporation of any amount of an improper distribution of the corporation's cash or property, to be subrogated to the rights of the corporation

against members, directors or officers who received such distribution with knowledge of facts indicating that it was not authorized by this chapter, in proportion to the amounts received by them respectively.

(2) Upon reimbursement to the corporation of an amount representing an improper redemption of a capital certificate, subvention or bond, to have the corporation rescind such improper redemption and recover the amount paid, for their benefit but at their expense, from any member or holder who received such payment with knowledge of facts indicating that such redemption by the corporation was not authorized by this chapter.

(3) Upon reimbursement to the corporation of an amount representing all or part of an improper payment of a fixed or contingent periodic sum to the holder of a subvention certificate, or of interest to the holder or beneficiary of a bond, to have the corporation recover the amount so paid, for their benefit but at their expense, from any holder or beneficiary who received such payment with knowledge of facts indicating that such payment by the corporation was not authorized by this chapter.

(4) Upon payment to the corporation of the claim of the attorney general or of any creditor by reason of a violation of subparagraph (a)(4), to be subrogated to the rights of the corporation against any person who received an improper distribution of assets.

(5) Upon reimbursement to the corporation of the amount of any loan made contrary to section 716 (Loans to directors and officers), to be subrogated to the rights of the corporation against a director or officer who received the improper loan.

(e) A director or officer shall not be liable under this section if, in the circumstances, he discharged his duty to the corporation under section 717 (Duty of directors and officers).

(f) This section shall not affect any liability otherwise imposed by law upon any director or officer.

§ 720. Actions against directors, officers and key employees

(a) An action may be brought against one or more directors, officers, or key persons of a corporation to procure a judgment for the following relief:

(1) To compel the defendant to account for his official conduct in the following cases:

(A) The neglect of, or failure to perform, or other violation of his duties in the management and disposition of corporate assets committed to his charge.

(B) The acquisition by himself, transfer to others, loss or waste of corporate assets due to any neglect of, or failure to perform, or other violation of his duties.

(2) To set aside an unlawful conveyance, assignment or transfer of corporate assets, where the transferee knew of its unlawfulness.

(3) To enjoin a proposed unlawful conveyance, assignment or transfer of corporate assets, where there are reasonable grounds for belief that it will be made.

(b) An action may be brought for the relief provided in this section and in paragraph (a) of section 719 (Liabilities of directors in certain cases) by the attorney general, by the corporation, or, in the right of the corporation, by any of the following:

(1) A director or officer of the corporation.

(2) A receiver, trustee in bankruptcy, or judgment creditor thereof.

(3) Under section 623 (Members' derivative action brought in the right of the corporation to procure a judgment in its favor), by one or more of the members thereof.

(4) If the certificate of incorporation or the by-laws so provide, by any holder of a subvention certificate or any other contributor to the corporation of cash or property of the value of $1,000 or more.

(c) In a corporation having no members, an action may be brought by a director against third parties to obtain a judgment in favor of the corporation. The complaint shall set forth with particularity the efforts of the plaintiff to secure the initiation of such action by the board or the reason for not making such efforts. The court in its discretion shall determine whether it is in the interest of the corporation that the action be maintained, and if the action is successful in whole or in part, what reimbursement if any should be made out of the corporate treasury to the plaintiff for his reasonable expenses including attorney's fees, incurred in the prosecution of the action.

§ 720–a. Liability of directors, officers and trustees

Except as provided in sections seven hundred nineteen and seven hundred twenty of this chapter, and except any action or proceeding brought by the attorney general or, in the case of a charitable trust, an action or proceeding against a trustee brought by a beneficiary of such trust, no person serving without compensation as a director, officer or trustee of a corporation, association, organization or trust described in section 501(c)(3) of the United States internal revenue code shall be liable to any person other than such corporation, association, organization or trust based solely on his or her conduct in the execution of such office unless the conduct of such director, officer or trustee with respect to the person asserting liability constituted gross negligence or was intended to cause the resulting harm to the person asserting such liability. For purposes of this section, such a director, officer or trustee shall not be considered compensated solely by reason of payment of his or her actual expenses incurred in attending meetings or otherwise in the execution of such office.

MODEL NONPROFIT CORPORATION ACT (1964)

SECTION 4. PURPOSES

Corporations may be organized under this Act for any lawful purpose or purposes, including, without being limited to, any one or more of the following purposes: charitable; benevolent; eleemosynary; educational; civic; patriotic; political; religious; social; fraternal; literary; cultural; athletic; scientific; agricultural; horticultural; animal husbandry; and professional, commercial, industrial or trade association; but labor unions, cooperative organizations, and organizations subject to any of the provisions of the insurance laws of this State may not be organized under this Act.

Division 2. *Purposes.* (Alternative Section)

SECTION 4. PURPOSES

Corporations may be organized under this Act for any lawful purpose or purposes except [list, if any].

REVISED MODEL NONPROFIT CORPORATION ACT

Chapter 6

MEMBERS AND MEMBERSHIPS

* * *

Subchapter C. Resignation and Termination

Section 6.21. Termination, Expulsion and Suspension

(a) No member of a public benefit or mutual benefit corporation may be expelled or suspended, and no membership or memberships in such corporations may be terminated or suspended except pursuant to a procedure that is fair and reasonable and is carried out in good faith.

(b) A procedure is fair and reasonable when either:

(1) The articles or bylaws set forth a procedure that provides:

(i) not less than fifteen days prior written notice of the expulsion, suspension or termination and the reasons therefore; and

(ii) an opportunity for the member to be heard, orally or in writing, not less than five days before the effective date of the expulsion, suspension or termination by a person or persons authorized to decide that the proposed expulsion, termination or suspension not take place; or

(2) It is fair and reasonable taking into consideration all of the relevant facts and circumstances.

(c) Any written notice given by mail must be given by first-class or certified mail sent to the last address of the member shown on the corporation's records.

(d) Any proceeding challenging an expulsion, suspension or termination, including a proceeding in which defective notice is alleged, must be commenced within one year after the effective date of the expulsion, suspension or termination.

(e) A member who has been expelled or suspended may be liable to the corporation for dues, assessments or fees as a result of obligations incurred or commitments made prior to expulsion or suspension.

RESTATEMENT OF THE LAW CHARITABLE NONPROFIT ORGANIZATIONS

Section **Page**

Chapter 6
Standing of Private Parties

Chapter 1
Definition and Choice of Form

§ 1.01. Definition of a Charity

(a) A charity is a legal entity with exclusively charitable purposes, established for the benefit of indefinite beneficiaries, and prohibited from providing impermissible private benefit.

(b) Charitable purposes include:

(1) the relief of poverty;

(2) the advancement of knowledge or education;

(3) the advancement of religion;

(4) the promotion of health;

(5) governmental or municipal purposes; and

(6) other purposes that are beneficial to the community.

(c) A purpose is not charitable if it is unlawful, its performance requires the commission of criminal or tortious activity, or it is otherwise contrary to fundamental public policy.

§ 1.02. Choice of Legal Form

A charity may be organized as a nonprofit corporation, trust, unincorporated association, or other legal form recognized by law.

§ 1.03. Charities with Members

(a) A charity that is:

(1) a corporation need not have members, but may have one or more members;

(2) an unincorporated association must have at least two members;

(3) a limited liability company must have at least one member.

(b) In a charity with members, one or more classes of members must have the rights to:

(1) vote in elections for the governing body,

(2) vote on proposals to make material amendments to the organizational documents, and

(3) examine the charity's records in accordance with § 2.07.

(c) The rights of members may reside in a single class of membership or be divided among classes of members. However, members must have the right to vote on any amendments to the organizational documents that would change any rights held by members in their membership class.

(d) A charity's members may be natural persons, organizations, or both.

(e) A membership interest in a charity is not transferable, except that a membership interest held by a charity may be transferred to another charity.

Chapter 2
Governance and Management of Assets

§ 2.01. Fiduciary Defined and Scope of Duties

(a) A fiduciary of a charity is a person who has substantial powers with respect to a charity.

(b) Fiduciaries include members of the board, officers, and other persons holding similar powers with respect to a charity.

(c) Fiduciaries owe duties commensurate with their powers with respect to a charity.

§ 2.02. Duty of Loyalty

A fiduciary of a charity has a duty to:

(a) act in good faith and in a manner the fiduciary reasonably believes to be in the best interests of the charity in light of its purposes;

(b) address reasonably situations that involve the potential for self-dealing in which the interests of a fiduciary or related person may conflict with the interests of the charity; and

(c) seek court application of the doctrine of cy pres or the doctrine of deviation when such relief is appropriate.

§ 2.03. Duty of Care and the Business Judgment Rule

(a) A fiduciary of a charity has a duty to act in good faith with the care a person of ordinary prudence in a like position would exercise under similar circumstances.

(b) A fiduciary of a charity who makes a decision in good faith should not be subject to further review for breach of the duty of care under subsection (a) for that decision if, at the time the decision is made, the fiduciary:

(1) has no interest, direct or indirect, in the subject of the decision and is otherwise able to exercise independent judgment;

(2) is reasonably informed with respect to the subject of the decision using material information reasonably available under the circumstances; and

(3) reasonably believes that the decision is in the best interests of the charity in light of its purposes.

§ 2.04. Management, Investment, and Expenditure of a Charity's Assets

(a) The management, investment, and expenditure of a charity's assets are governed by the fiduciary duties set forth in §§ 2.02 and 2.03.

(b) A charity must manage its assets that are held for investment as a prudent investor would in light of the purposes of the charity, in accordance with any valid terms governing the assets in question, and considering any other relevant circumstances.

(c) A charity may appropriate for expenditure or accumulate:

(1) funds in an endowment

(A) to the extent the charity determines it to be prudent given the uses, benefits, purposes, and duration for which the endowment was established,

(B) in light of the purposes of the charity, and

(C) in accordance with any additional, valid terms governing the funds in question; and

(2) funds not in an endowment

(A) in light of the purposes of the charity, and

(B) in accordance with any additional, valid terms governing the funds in question.

§ 2.05. Definition and Duty of the Board

A board is the body that holds ultimate responsibility for the affairs of a charity. It has a duty to adopt policies to advance the purposes of the charity it governs and oversee implementation of those policies.

§ 2.06. Delegation to Board Committees

The board may delegate to committees the authority to perform board functions, subject to the board's duty to govern as set forth in § 2.05 and except for those matters specifically reserved to the board by law or by the charity's organizational documents.

§ 2.07. Fiduciaries' Rights to Information

(a) A fiduciary is entitled to inspect and copy, for proper purposes and under reasonable circumstances, all books, records, reports, and information prepared by or for the charity.

(b) A proper purpose is one that reasonably relates to the fulfillment of the fiduciary's duties to the charity.

(c) A request for information related to board duties by a member of the board, as defined in § 2.05, is presumed to be for a proper purpose.

§ 2.08. Modification of Fiduciary Duties and Exculpation of Fiduciaries

The organizational documents of a charity may contain terms modifying the duties of and exculpating its fiduciaries, but may not modify fiduciary duties or exculpate a fiduciary for breach of these duties in a manner that:

(a) permits intentional, knowing, reckless, grossly negligent, or illegal misconduct;

(b) permits any actions in bad faith or with disregard for the purposes of the charity; or

(c) nullifies the duties of care or loyalty.

§ 2.09. Immunity, Indemnity, and Insurance for Indemnification

(a) An individual who volunteers for a charity, including a member of the board or an officer of a charity, generally is immune from liability to a third party for a negligent act or omission that occurs within the scope of the individual's responsibilities as a volunteer for the charity.

(b) Subject to subsection (c), a charity may or, when required by a charity's organizational documents, applicable law, or a valid court order, must indemnify a person who is or was a member of the board, an officer, an agent, or an employee of the charity:

(1) for amounts the person is required to pay as a judgment or settlement and reasonable expenses that person incurred:

(A) in connection with the defense of an action to which that person is a party because of that person's service to the charity, or

(B) as a plaintiff in a derivative action, as defined in § 6.02, that has been resolved in that person's favor; and

(2) in accordance with terms in the charity's organizational documents;

(3) in compliance with a valid court order; or

(4) in compliance with applicable law.

(c) A charity may not indemnify any person for:

(1) any financial benefit that the person received, directly or indirectly, and that the person has been adjudged not to have been entitled to receive, or

(2) an act or omission that:

(A) involved reckless, knowing, or intentional misconduct;

(B) in the case of any criminal proceeding, the person had reason to believe was unlawful;

(C) was performed in bad faith or with knowing disregard for the purposes of the charity; or

(D) involved a conflict of interest that was not approved by the charity in accordance with § 2.02(b) and, therefore, breached the duty of loyalty.

(d) Regardless of whether a charity has the obligation or power to indemnify a person under subsection (b), a charity may purchase and maintain insurance on behalf of such person for reasonable costs and attorney's fees incurred in a legal proceeding related to that person's service to the charity, except that such coverage may not indemnify the person if that person was found, in an adjudication, to have:

(1) acted with deliberate dishonesty in a manner material to the cause of action in question, or

(2) intentionally engaged in self-dealing that was not approved by the charity in accordance with § 2.02(b).

(e) A charity may pay for or reimburse the reasonable expenses incurred by a person who is a party to a proceeding in advance of final disposition of the proceeding if:

(1) the person furnishes the charity with a written affirmation of the person's good-faith belief that the person has not engaged in conduct that would preclude indemnification under this Section;

(2) the person furnishes the charity with a written undertaking to repay the advance if it is ultimately determined that the person engaged in conduct that would preclude indemnification under this Section; and

(3) the board making the decision to advance funds is not aware of any facts reasonably available to it, at the time the decision to advance funds is made, that would preclude indemnification under this Section.

(f) A charity may not indemnify, insure, or provide an advance to a person under this Section if the decision to do so would breach the decisionmakers' fiduciary duties to the charity.

Chapter 3
Changes to Purposes and Organization

§ 3.02. The Doctrine of Cy Pres

If it is or becomes unlawful, impossible, impracticable, or wasteful for a charity to carry out its purposes, the court should direct application of the assets or an appropriate portion thereof to charitable purposes that reasonably approximate the designated purposes.

§ 3.03. The Doctrine of Deviation

(a) A court may modify an administrative term governing one or more charitable assets or direct or permit a deviation from such a term if deviation will further the purposes governing an asset because:

(1) compliance with the term has become unlawful, impossible, impracticable, or wasteful;

(2) the term impairs the prudent management or investment of an asset; or

(3) circumstances exist that had not been anticipated by the donor.

(b) If it is unclear whether a particular term governing the use of a charitable asset applies to either the administration of the asset or the purposes to which it is devoted, the court should apply the doctrine of deviation rather than the doctrine of cy pres set forth in § 3.02.

§ 3.04. Change of Structure: Fundamental Transactions

(a) A charity may merge, consolidate, or engage in other change of legal form that involves all or substantially all of that charity's assets and results in those assets being held by one or more charities:

(1) pursuant to any applicable terms in its organizational documents;

(2) in accordance with any applicable laws governing the transaction; and

(3) with prior notice to the state attorney general.

(b) A charity may convert or transfer all or substantially all of its assets from charitable to noncharitable status:

(1) pursuant to any applicable terms in its organizational documents;

(2) in accordance with any applicable laws governing the conversion or transaction, or in a state with no laws governing the conversion or transaction, with court approval; and

(3) with prior notice to the state attorney general.

(c) A charity must receive fair market value for a sale, conversion of status, or other transfer of all or substantially all its assets to an entity that is not a charity. A charity may not pay more than fair market value for the purchase, conversion of status, or other transfer of assets from an entity that is not a charity.

Chapter 4
Restrictions on Assets; Pledges; Solicitation

4.03. Release or Modification of a Specific Restriction on a Charitable Asset

A specific restriction on a charitable asset may be released or modified only:

(a) by following the terms governing the asset, including any terms identifying procedures for releasing or modifying a specific restriction, subject to an applicable statute;

(b) by following the procedures required by an applicable statute; or

(c) as authorized in a judicial proceeding to which the state attorney general is a necessary party and in which the court applies the doctrine of cy pres to modify the purposes to which the asset must be devoted, as provided in § 3.02, or the doctrine of deviation to modify an administrative term governing the asset, as provided in § 3.03.

§ 4.05. Solicitation of Charitable Assets

If required by applicable law of a state or subdivision thereof, both a charity, for itself and on behalf of its board members, officers, employees, and volunteers, and any person who is compensated for soliciting donations on behalf of or providing fundraising advice to the charity must:

(a) register with the state attorney general or other designated authority before soliciting donations in the state;

(b) file periodic financial reports on the solicitation of donations with the state attorney general or other designated authority; and

(c) comply with any other requirements related to solicitation in the state or subdivision thereof.

Chapter 5
Government Regulation of Charities

§ 5.01. Role of the State Attorney General

The state attorney general:

(a) has the authority to protect charitable assets and interests within the jurisdiction of the state and to seek judicial relief to protect the public's interest in those assets and interests;

(b) must be notified of all judicial actions that implicate the protection of charitable assets and interests described in subsection (a) and has the right to intervene in such actions; and

(c) has all the powers necessary to carry out the authority and rights described in subsections (a) and (b), including the powers to investigate claims, obtain documents, call witnesses, and issue subpoenas, as provided under state law.

Chapter 6
Standing of Private Parties

§ 6.01. Standing of a Private Party to Bring or Intervene in an Action Directly Against a Charity

(a) A court should recognize standing of a current or former member of the board, as defined in § 2.05, or current or former member of a charity, as defined in § 1.03, to bring or intervene in an action directly against the charity to establish that person's status with respect to the charity and to protect or exercise any right accorded to that person as provided by the charity's organizational documents or applicable law.

(b) A court should recognize standing of a private party to bring or intervene in an action directly against a charity to enforce that party's interest in the charity's property as provided by the documents governing the property in question or applicable law.

(c) The state attorney general must be provided notice of an action directly against a charity in accordance with § 5.01.

§ 6.02. Standing of a Private Party to Bring an Action on Behalf of a Charity: The Derivative Action

(a) A derivative action on behalf of a charity is one in which a private party seeks a judgment in favor of the charity and against one or more of its current or former fiduciaries or other parties who have allegedly harmed the charity.

(b) For a court to recognize the standing of a private party to bring a derivative action on behalf of a charity, that private party must demonstrate to the court that:

(1) it fairly and adequately represents the interests of the charity in light of the charity's purposes,

(2) it is or consists of:

(A) a current member of the board of the charity, as defined in § 2.05,

(B) a former member of the board of the charity who is no longer a member for reasons related to that member's attempt to address the alleged harm to the charity,

(C) current members of the charity, as defined in § 1.03, who satisfy the statutory criteria requiring them to represent a specified number of members, percentage of the membership, or percentage of the voting power of the membership, or

(D) a private party with a special interest, as defined in § 6.05;

(3) it made a written, formal demand upon the board of the charity to pursue suitable corrective measures or to prosecute the action itself and has provided the charity sufficient time to respond, unless the party is excused from making the demand; and

(4) the action is likely to be in the best interests of the charity in light of the charity's purposes.

(c) As a condition of maintaining an action under this Section, the state attorney general must be provided notice of any such action, as provided in § 5.01(b).

§ 6.03. Standing of a Private Party to Enforce the Purposes to Which Charitable Assets are Devoted and Administrative Terms Governing Charitable Assets

(a) For a court to recognize the standing of a private party to bring or intervene in an action to enforce the purposes to which charitable assets are devoted or the administrative terms that govern them, the private party must demonstrate to the court that:

(1) the private party:

(A) has standing according to the documents governing the assets,

(B) has standing under applicable law, or

(C) is a party with a special interest as defined in § 6.05; and

(2) the action is likely to be in the best interests of the charity in light of its purposes or, in the case of particular assets held by the charity, the action will advance the purposes to which those assets must be devoted.

(b) As a condition of maintaining an action under this Section, a private party must provide notice of the action to:

(1) any person with a right of reverter,

(2) any charity that is identified in the documents governing the assets in question as a beneficiary or alternative beneficiary, and

(3) the state attorney general, as provided in § 5.01.

§ 6.05. Standing of a Private Party with a Special Interest for Purposes of Standing

A private party has a special interest for purposes of bringing a derivative action on behalf of a charity under § 6.02, bringing or intervening in an action to enforce the purposes to which charitable assets are devoted and or the administrative terms that govern charitable assets under § 6.03, or bringing or intervening in a cy pres or deviation action under § 6.04 only upon demonstrating all of the following conditions:

(a) the state attorney general is not exercising the office's authority to protect the public's interest in the charitable assets at issue, as provided in § 5.01;

(b) the charitable assets at issue will not be protected without the grant of standing to the private party;

(c) the alleged misconduct is egregious or the circumstances are serious and exigent;

(d) the relief sought is appropriate to enforce the purposes of the charity or the purposes to which particular charitable assets are devoted; and

(e) the private party has a substantial connection to:

(1) the matter at issue and the charity, for an action under § 6.02, or

(2) the charitable assets at issue, for an action under §§ 6.03 or 6.04.

THE CLAYTON ACT
(15 U.S.C.)

§ 1. [15 U.S.C. § 12]. Words defined; short title

(a) "Antitrust laws," as used herein, includes the Act entitled "An Act to protect trade and commerce against unlawful restraints and monopolies," approved July second, eighteen hundred and ninety; section seventy-three to seventy-six, inclusive, of an Act entitled "An Act to reduce taxation, to provide revenue for the Government, and for other purposes," of August twenty-seventh, eighteen hundred and ninety-four; an Act entitled "An Act to amend sections seventy-three and seventy-six of the Act of August twenty-seventh, eighteen hundred and ninety-four, entitled 'An Act to reduce taxation, to provide revenue for the Government, and for other purposes,' " approved February twelfth, nineteen hundred and thirteen; and also this Act.

"Commerce," as used herein, means trade or commerce among the several States and with foreign nations, or between the District of Columbia or any Territory of the United States and any State, Territory, or foreign nation, or between any insular possessions or other places under the jurisdiction of the United States or the District of Columbia or any foreign nation, or within the District of Columbia or any Territory or any insular possession or other place under the jurisdiction of the United States; *Provided,* That nothing in this Act contained shall apply to the Philippine Islands.

The word "person" or "persons" wherever used in this Act shall be deemed to include corporations and associations existing under or authorized by the laws of either the United States, the laws of any of the Territories, the laws of any State, or the laws of any foreign country.

(b) This Act may be cited as the "Clayton Act."

§ 7. [15 U.S.C. § 18]. Acquisition by one corporation of stock of another

No person engaged in commerce or in any activity affecting commerce shall acquire, directly or indirectly, the whole or any part of the stock or other share capital and no person subject to the jurisdiction of the Federal Trade Commission shall acquire the whole or any part of the assets of another person engaged also in commerce or in any activity affecting commerce, where in any line of commerce or in any activity affecting commerce in any section of the country, the effect of such acquisition may be substantially to lessen competition, or to tend to create a monopoly.

No person shall acquire, directly or indirectly, the whole or any part of the stock or other share capital and no person subject to the jurisdiction of the Federal Trade Commission shall acquire the whole or any part of the assets of one or more persons engaged in commerce or in any activity affecting commerce, where in any line of commerce or in any activity affecting commerce in any section of the country, the effect of such acquisition, of such stocks or assets, or of the use of such stock by the voting or granting of proxies or otherwise, may be substantially to lessen competition, or to tend to create a monopoly.

This section shall not apply to persons purchasing such stock solely for investment and not using the same by voting or otherwise to bring about, or in attempting to bring about, the substantial lessening of competition. Nor shall anything contained in this section prevent a corporation engaged in commerce or in any activity affecting commerce from causing the formation of subsidiary corporations for the actual carrying on of their immediate lawful business, or the natural and legitimate branches or extensions thereof, or from owning and holding all or a part of the stock of such subsidiary corporations, when the effect of such formation is not to substantially lessen competition.

Nor shall anything herein contained be construed to prohibit any common carrier subject to the laws to regulate commerce from aiding in the construction of branches or short lines so located as to become feeders to the main line of the company so aiding in such construction or from acquiring or owning all or any part of the stock of such branch lines, nor to prevent any such common carrier from acquiring and owning all or any part of the stock of a branch or short line constructed by an independent company where there is no substantial competition between the company owning the branch line so constructed and the company owning the main line acquiring the property or an interest therein, nor to prevent such common carrier from extending any of its lines through the medium of the acquisition of stock or otherwise of any other common carrier where there is no substantial competition between the company extending its lines and the company whose stock, property, or an interest therein is so acquired.

Nothing contained in this section shall be held to affect or impair any right heretofore legally acquired: *Provided*, That nothing in this section shall be held or construed to authorize or make lawful anything heretofore prohibited or made illegal by the antitrust laws, nor to exempt any person from the penal provisions thereof or the civil remedies therein provided.

Nothing contained in this section shall apply to transactions duly consummated pursuant to authority given by the Secretary of Transportation, Federal Power Commission, Surface Transportation Board, the Securities and Exchange Commission in the exercise of its jurisdiction under section 79j of this title, the United States Maritime Commission, or the Secretary of Agriculture under any statutory provision vesting such power in such Commission, Board, or Secretary.

§ 11. [15 U.S.C. § 21]. Enforcement provisions

(a) Commission, Board, or Secretary authorized to enforce compliance

Authority to enforce compliance with sections 13, 14, 18, and 19 of this title by the persons respectively subject thereto is vested in the Surface Transportation Board where applicable to common carriers subject to jurisdiction under subtitle IV of Title 49; in the Federal Communications Commission where applicable to common carriers engaged in wire or radio communication or radio transmission of energy; in the Secretary of Transportation where applicable to air carriers and foreign air carriers subject to part A of subtitle VII of Title 49; in the Board of Governors of the Federal Reserve System where applicable to banks, banking associations, and trust companies; and in the Federal Trade Commission where applicable to all other character of commerce to be exercised as follows:

(b) Issuance of complaints for violations; hearing; intervention; filing of testimony; report; cease and desist orders; reopening and alteration of reports or orders

Whenever the Commission, Board, or Secretary vested with jurisdiction thereof shall have reason to believe that any person is violating or has violated any of the provisions of sections 13, 14, 18, and 19 of this title, it shall issue and serve upon such person and the Attorney General a complaint stating its charges in that respect, and containing a notice of a hearing upon a day and at a place therein fixed at least thirty days after the service of said complaint. The person so complained of shall have the right to appear at the place and time so fixed and show cause why an order should not be entered by the Commission, Board, or Secretary requiring such person to cease and desist from the violation of the law so charged in said complaint. The Attorney General shall have the right to intervene and appear in said proceeding and any person may make application, and upon good cause shown may be allowed by the Commission, Board, or Secretary, to intervene and appear in said proceeding by counsel or in person. The testimony in any such proceeding shall be reduced to writing and filed in the office of the Commission, Board, or Secretary. If upon such hearing the Commission, Board, or Secretary, as the case may be, shall be of the opinion that any of the provisions of said sections have been or are being violated, it shall make a report in writing, in which it shall state its findings as to the facts, and shall issue and cause to be served on such person an order requiring such person to cease and desist from such violations, and divest itself of the stock, or other share capital, or assets, held or rid itself of the directors chosen contrary to the provisions of sections 18 and 19 of this title, if any there be, in the manner and within the time fixed by said order. Until the expiration of the time allowed for filing a petition for review, if no such petition has been duly filed within such time, or, if a petition for review has been filed within such time then until the record in the proceeding has been filed in a court of appeals of the United States, as hereinafter provided, the Commission, Board, or Secretary may at any time, upon such notice and in such manner as it shall deem proper, modify or set aside, in whole or in part, any report or any order made or issued by it under this section. After the expiration of the time allowed for filing a petition for review, if no such petition has been duly filed within such time, the Commission, Board, or Secretary may at any time, after notice and opportunity for hearing, reopen and alter, modify, or set aside, in whole or in part, any report or order made or issued by it under this section, whenever in the opinion of the Commission, Board, or Secretary conditions of fact or of law have so changed as to require such action or if the public interest shall so require: *Provided, however,* That the said person may, within sixty days after service upon him or it of said report or order entered after such a reopening, obtain a review thereof in the appropriate court of appeals of the United States, in the manner provided in subsection (c) of this section.

(c) Review of orders; jurisdiction; filing of petition and record of proceeding; conclusiveness of findings; additional evidence; modification of findings; finality of judgment and decree

Any person required by such order of the commission, board, or Secretary to cease and desist from any such violation may obtain a review of such order in the court of appeals of the United States for any circuit within which such violation occurred or within which such person resides or carries on business, by filing in the court, within sixty days after the date of the service of such order, a written petition praying that the order of the commission, board, or Secretary be set aside. A copy of such petition shall be forthwith transmitted by the clerk of the court to the commission, board, or Secretary, and thereupon the commission, board, or Secretary shall file in the court the record in the proceeding, as provided in section 2112 of Title 28. Upon such filing of the petition the court shall have jurisdiction of the proceeding and of the question determined therein concurrently with the commission, board, or Secretary until the filing of the record, and shall have power to make and enter a decree affirming, modifying, or setting aside the order of the commission, board, or Secretary, and enforcing the same to the extent that such order is affirmed, and to issue such writs as are ancillary to its jurisdiction or are necessary in its judgment to prevent injury to the public or to competitors pendente lite. The findings of the commission, board, or Secretary as to the facts, if supported by substantial evidence, shall be conclusive. To the extent that the order of the commission, board, or Secretary is affirmed, the court shall issue its own order commanding obedience to the terms of such order of the commission, board, or Secretary. If either party shall apply to the court for leave to adduce additional evidence, and shall show to the satisfaction of the court that such additional evidence is material and that there were reasonable grounds for the failure to adduce such evidence in the proceeding before the commission, board, or Secretary, the court may order such additional evidence to be taken before the commission, board, or Secretary, and to be adduced upon the hearing in such manner and upon such terms and conditions as to the court may seem proper. The commission, board, or Secretary may modify its findings as to the facts, or make new findings, by reason of the additional evidence so taken, and shall file such modified or new findings, which if supported by substantial evidence, shall be conclusive, and its recommendation, if any, for the modification or setting aside of its original order, with the return of such additional evidence. The judgment and decree of the court shall be final, except that the same shall be subject to review by the Supreme Court upon certiorari, as provided in section 1254 of Title 28.

(d) Exclusive jurisdiction of Court of Appeals

Upon the filing of the record with its jurisdiction of the court of appeals to affirm, enforce, modify, or set aside orders of the commission, board, or Secretary shall be exclusive.

(e) Liability under antitrust laws

No order of the commission, board, or Secretary or judgment of the court to enforce the same shall in anywise relieve or absolve any person from any liability under the antitrust laws.

(f) Service of complaints, orders and other processes

Complaints, orders, and other processes of the commission, board, or Secretary under this section may be served by anyone duly authorized by the commission, board, or Secretary, either (1) by delivering a copy thereof to the person to be served, or to a member of the partnership to be served, or to the president, secretary, or other executive officer or a director of the corporation to be served; or (2) by leaving a copy thereof at the residence or the principal office or place of business of such person; or (3) by mailing by registered or certified mail a copy thereof addressed to such person at his or its residence or principal office or place of business. The verified return by the person so serving said complaint, order, or other process setting forth the manner of said service shall be proof of the same, and the return post office receipt for said complaint, order, or other process mailed by registered or certified mail as aforesaid shall be proof of the service of the same.

(g) Finality of orders generally

Any order issued under subsection (b) of this section shall become final—

(1) upon the expiration of the time allowed for filing a petition for review, if no such petition has been duly filed within such time; but the commission, board, or Secretary may thereafter modify or set aside its order to the extent provided in the last sentence of subsection (b) of this section; or

(2) upon the expiration of the time allowed for filing a petition for certiorari, if the order of the commission, board, or Secretary has been affirmed, or the petition for review has been dismissed by the court of appeals, and no petition for certiorari has been duly filed; or

(3) upon the denial of a petition for certiorari, if the order of the commission, board, or Secretary has been affirmed or the petition for review has been dismissed by the court of appeals; or

(4) upon the expiration of thirty days from the date of issuance of the mandate of the Supreme Court if such Court directs that the order of the commission, board, or Secretary be affirmed or the petition for review be dismissed.

(h) Finality of orders modified by Supreme Court

If the Supreme Court directs that the order of the commission, board, or Secretary be modified or set aside, the order of the commission, board, or Secretary rendered in accordance with the mandate of the Supreme Court shall become final upon the expiration of thirty days from the time it was rendered, unless within such thirty days either party has instituted proceedings to have such order corrected to accord with the mandate, in which event the order of the commission, board, or Secretary shall become final when so corrected.

(i) Finality of orders modified by Court of Appeals

If the order of the commission, board, or Secretary is modified or set aside by the court of appeals, and if (1) the time allowed for filing a petition for certiorari has expired and no such petition has been duly filed, or (2) the petition for certiorari has been denied, or (3) the decision of the court has been affirmed by the Supreme Court, then the order of the commission, board, or Secretary rendered in accordance with the mandate of the court of appeals shall become final on the expiration of thirty days from the time such order of the commission, board, or Secretary was rendered, unless within such thirty days either party has instituted proceedings to have such order corrected so that it will accord with the mandate, in which event the order of the commission, board, or Secretary shall become final when so corrected.

(j) Finality of orders issued on rehearing ordered by Court of Appeals or Supreme Court

If the Supreme Court orders a rehearing; or if the case is remanded by the court of appeals to the commission, board, or Secretary for a rehearing, and if (1) the time allowed for filing a petition for certiorari has expired, and no such petition has been duly filed, or (2) the petition for certiorari has been denied, or (3) the decision of the court has been affirmed by the Supreme Court, then the order of the commission, board, or Secretary rendered upon such rehearing shall become final in the same manner as though no prior order of the commission, board, or Secretary had been rendered.

(k) "Mandate" defined

As used in this section the term "mandate", in case a mandate has been recalled prior to the expiration of thirty days from the date of issuance thereof, means the final mandate.

(*l*) Penalties

Any person who violates any order issued by the commission, board, or Secretary under subsection (b) of this section after such order has become final, and while such order is in effect, shall forfeit and pay to the United States a civil penalty of not more than $5,000 for each violation, which shall accrue to the United States and may be recovered in a civil action brought by the United States. Each separate violation of any such order shall be a separate offense, except that in the case of a violation through continuing failure or neglect to obey a final order of the commission, board, or Secretary each day of continuance of such failure or neglect shall be deemed a separate offense.

THE FEDERAL TRADE COMMISSION ACT

(15 U.S.C.)

§ 4. [15 U.S.C. § 44]. Definitions

The words defined in this section shall have the following meaning when found in sections 41 to 46 and 47 to 58 of this title, to wit:

"Commerce" means commerce among the several States or with foreign nations, or in any Territory of the United States or in the District of Columbia, or between any such Territory and another, or between any such Territory and any State or foreign nation, or between the District of Columbia and any State or Territory or foreign nation.

"Corporation" shall be deemed to include any company, trust, so-called Massachusetts trust, or association, incorporated or unincorporated, which is organized to carry on business for its own profit or that of its members, and has shares of capital or capital stock or certificates of interest, and any company, trust, so-called Massachusetts trust, or association, incorporated or unincorporated, without shares of capital or capital stock or certificates of interest, except partnerships, which is organized to carry on business for its own profit or that of its members.

"Documentary evidence" includes all documents, papers, correspondence, books of account, and financial and corporate records.

"Acts to regulate commerce" means subtitle IV of Title 49 and the Communications Act of 1934 [47 U.S.C.A. § 151 et seq.] and all Acts amendatory thereof and supplementary thereto.

"Antitrust Acts" means the Act entitled "An Act to protect trade and commerce against unlawful restraints and monopolies," approved July 2, 1890; also sections 73 to 77, of an Act entitled "An Act to reduce taxation, to provide revenue for the Government, and for other purposes", approved August 27, 1894; also the Act entitled "An Act to amend sections 73 and 76 of the Act of August 27, 1894, entitled 'An Act to reduce taxation, to provide revenue for the Government, and for other purposes' ", approved February 12, 1913; and also the Act entitled "An Act to supplement existing laws against unlawful restraints and monopolies, and for other purposes", approved October 15, 1914.

"Banks" means the types of banks and other financial institutions referred to in section 57a(f)(2) of this title.

"Foreign law enforcement agency" means—

(1) any agency or judicial authority of a foreign government, including a foreign state, a political subdivision of a foreign state, or a multinational organization constituted by and

comprised of foreign states, that is vested with law enforcement or investigative authority in civil, criminal, or administrative matters; and

(2) any multinational organization, to the extent that it is acting on behalf of an entity described in paragraph (1).

§ 5. [15 U.S.C. § 45]. Unfair methods of competition unlawful; prevention by Commission

(a) Declaration of unlawfulness; power to prohibit unfair practices; inapplicability to foreign trade

(1) Unfair methods of competition in or affecting commerce, and unfair or deceptive acts or practices in or affecting commerce, are declared unlawful.

(2) The Commission is empowered and directed to prevent persons, partnerships, or corporations, except banks, savings and loan institutions described in section 57a(f)(3) of this title, Federal credit unions described in section 57a(f)(4) of this title, common carriers subject to the Acts to regulate commerce, air carriers and foreign air carriers subject to the Federal Aviation Act of 1958, and persons, partnerships, or corporations insofar as they are subject to the Packers and Stockyards Act, 1921, as amended [7 U.S.C.A. § 181 et seq.], except as provided in section 406(b) of said Act [7 U.S.C.A. § 227(a)], from using unfair methods of competition in or affecting commerce and unfair or deceptive acts or practices in or affecting commerce.

(3) This subsection shall not apply to unfair methods of competition involving commerce with foreign nations (other than import commerce) unless—

(A) such methods of competition have a direct, substantial, and reasonably foreseeable effect—

(i) on commerce which is not commerce with foreign nations, or on import commerce with foreign nations; or

(ii) on export commerce with foreign nations, of a person engaged in such commerce in the United States; and

(B) such effect gives rise to a claim under the provisions of this subsection, other than this paragraph.

If this subsection applies to such methods of competition only because of the operation of subparagraph (A)(ii), this subsection shall apply to such conduct only for injury to export business in the United States.

(4)(A) For purposes of subsection (a), the term "unfair or deceptive acts or practices" includes such acts or practices involving foreign commerce that—

(i) cause or are likely to cause reasonably foreseeable injury within the United States; or

(ii) involve material conduct occurring within the United States.

(B) All remedies available to the Commission with respect to unfair and deceptive acts or practices shall be available for acts and practices described in this paragraph, including restitution to domestic or foreign victims.

(b) Proceeding by Commission; modifying and setting aside orders

Whenever the Commission shall have reason to believe that any such person, partnership, or corporation has been or is using any unfair method of competition or unfair or deceptive act or practice in or affecting commerce, and if it shall appear to the Commission that a proceeding by it in respect thereof would be to the interest of the public, it shall issue and serve upon such person, partnership, or corporation a complaint stating its charges in that respect and containing a notice of a hearing upon a day and at a place therein fixed at least thirty days after the service of said complaint. The person, partnership, or corporation so complained of shall have the right to appear at the place and time so fixed and show cause why an order should not be entered by the Commission requiring such person, partnership, or corporation to cease and desist from the violation of the law so charged in said complaint. Any person, partnership, or corporation may make application, and upon good cause shown may be allowed by the Commission to intervene and appear in said proceeding by counsel or in person. The testimony in any such proceeding shall be reduced to writing and filed in the office of the Commission. If upon such hearing the Commission shall be of the opinion that the method of competition or the act or practice in question is prohibited by this subchapter, it shall make a report in writing in which it shall state its findings as to the facts and shall issue and cause to be served on such person, partnership, or corporation an order requiring such person, partnership, or corporation to cease and desist from using such method of competition or such act or practice. Until the expiration of the time allowed for filing a petition for review, if no such petition has been duly filed within such time, or, if a petition for review has been filed within such time then until the record in the proceeding has been filed in a court of appeals of the United States, as hereinafter provided, the Commission may at any time, upon such notice and in such manner as it shall deem proper, modify or set aside, in whole or in part, any report or any order made or issued by it under this section. After the expiration of the time allowed for filing a petition for review, if no such petition has been duly filed within such time, the Commission may at any time, after notice and opportunity for hearing, reopen and alter, modify, or set aside, in whole or in part, any report or order made or issued by it under this section, whenever in the opinion of the Commission conditions of fact or of law have so changed as to require such action or if the public interest shall so require, except that (1) the said person, partnership, or corporation may, within sixty days after service upon him or it of said report or order entered after such a reopening, obtain a review thereof in the appropriate court of appeals of the United States, in the manner provided in subsection (c) of this section; and (2) in the case of an order, the Commission shall reopen any such order to consider whether such order (including any affirmative relief provision contained in such order) should be altered, modified, or set aside, in whole or in part, if the person, partnership, or corporation involved files a request with the Commission which makes a satisfactory showing that changed conditions of law or fact require such order to be altered, modified, or set aside, in whole or in part. The Commission shall determine whether to alter, modify, or set aside any order of the Commission in response to a request made by a person, partnership, or corporation under paragraph (2) not later than 120 days after the date of the filing of such request.

(c) Review of order; rehearing

Any person, partnership, or corporation required by an order of the Commission to cease and desist from using any method of competition or act or practice may obtain a review of such order in the court of appeals of the United States, within any circuit where the method of competition or the act or practice in question was used or where such person, partnership, or corporation resides or carries on business, by filing in the court, within sixty days from the date of the service of such order, a written petition praying that the order of the Commission be set aside. A copy of such petition shall be forthwith transmitted by the clerk of the court to the Commission, and thereupon the Commission shall file in the court the record in the proceeding, as provided in section 2112 of Title 28. Upon such filing of the petition the court shall have jurisdiction of the proceeding and of the question determined therein concurrently with the Commission until the filing of the record and shall have power to make and enter a decree affirming, modifying, or setting aside the order of the Commission, and enforcing the same to the extent that such order is affirmed and to issue such writs as are ancillary to its jurisdiction or are necessary in its judgment to prevent injury to the public or to competitors pendente lite. The findings of the Commission as to the facts, if supported by evidence, shall be conclusive. To the extent that the order of the Commission is affirmed, the court shall thereupon issue its own order commanding obedience to the terms of such order of the Commission. If either party shall apply to the court for leave to adduce additional evidence, and shall show to the satisfaction of the court that such additional evidence is material and that there were reasonable grounds for the failure to adduce such evidence in the proceeding before the Commission, the court may order such additional evidence to be taken before the Commission and to be adduced upon the hearing in such manner and upon such terms and conditions as to the court may seem proper. The Commission may modify its findings as to the facts, or make new findings, by reason of the additional evidence so taken, and it shall file such modified or new findings, which, if supported by evidence, shall be conclusive, and its recommendation, if any, for the modification or setting aside of its original order, with the return of such additional evidence. The judgment and decree of the court shall be final, except that the same shall be subject to review by the Supreme Court upon certiorari, as provided in section 347 of Title 28.

(d) Jurisdiction of court

Upon the filing of the record with it the jurisdiction of the court of appeals of the United States to affirm, enforce, modify, or set aside orders of the Commission shall be exclusive.

(e) Exemption from liability

No order of the Commission or judgment of court to enforce the same shall in anywise relieve or absolve any person, partnership, or corporation from any liability under the Antitrust Acts.

(f) Service of complaints, orders and other processes; return

Complaints, orders, and other processes of the Commission under this section may be served by anyone duly authorized by the Commission, either (a) by delivering a copy thereof to the person to be served, or to a member of the partnership to be served, or the president, secretary, or other executive officer or a director of the corporation to be served; or (b) by leaving a copy thereof at the residence or the principal office or place of business of such person, partnership, or corporation; or (c) by mailing a copy thereof by registered mail or by certified mail addressed to such person, partnership, or corporation at his or its residence or principal office or place of business. The verified return by the person so serving said complaint, order, or other process setting forth the manner of said service shall be proof of the same, and the return post office receipt for said complaint, order, or other process mailed by registered mail or by certified mail as aforesaid shall be proof of the service of the same.

(g) Finality of order

An order of the Commission to cease and desist shall become final—

(1) Upon the expiration of the time allowed for filing a petition for review, if no such petition has been duly filed within such time; but the Commission may thereafter modify or set aside its order to the extent provided in the last sentence of subsection (b) of this section.

(2) Except as to any order provision subject to paragraph (4), upon the sixtieth day after such order is served, if a petition for review has been duly filed; except that any such order may be stayed, in whole or in part and subject to such conditions as may be appropriate, by—

(A) the Commission;

(B) an appropriate court of appeals of the United States, if (i) a petition for review of such order is pending in such court, and (ii) an application for such a stay was previously submitted to the Commission and the Commission, within the 30-day period beginning on the date the application was received by the Commission, either denied the application or did not grant or deny the application; or

(C) the Supreme Court, if an applicable petition for certiorari is pending.

(3) For purposes of subsection (m)(1)(B) of this section and of section 57b(a)(2) of this title, if a petition for review of the order of the Commission has been filed—

(A) upon the expiration of the time allowed for filing a petition for certiorari, if the order of the Commission has been affirmed or the petition for review has been dismissed by the court of appeals and no petition for certiorari has been duly filed;

(B) upon the denial of a petition for certiorari, if the order of the Commission has been affirmed or the petition for review has been dismissed by the court of appeals; or

(C) upon the expiration of 30 days from the date of issuance of a mandate of the Supreme Court directing that the order of the Commission be affirmed or the petition for review be dismissed.

(4) In the case of an order provision requiring a person, partnership, or corporation to divest itself of stock, other share capital, or assets, if a petition for review of such order of the Commission has been filed—

(A) upon the expiration of the time allowed for filing a petition for certiorari, if the order of the Commission has been affirmed or the petition for review has been dismissed by the court of appeals and no petition for certiorari has been duly filed;

(B) upon the denial of a petition for certiorari, if the order of the Commission has been affirmed or the petition for review has been dismissed by the court of appeals; or

(C) upon the expiration of 30 days from the date of issuance of a mandate of the Supreme Court directing that the order of the Commission be affirmed or the petition for review be dismissed.

(h) Modification or setting aside of order by Supreme Court

If the Supreme Court directs that the order of the Commission be modified or set aside, the order of the Commission rendered in accordance with the mandate of the Supreme Court shall become final upon the expiration of thirty days from the time it was rendered, unless within such thirty days either party has instituted proceedings to have such order corrected to accord with the mandate, in which event the order of the Commission shall become final when so corrected.

(i) Modification or setting aside of order by Court of Appeals

If the order of the Commission is modified or set aside by the court of appeals, and if (1) the time allowed for filing a petition for certiorari has expired and no such petition has been duly filed, or (2) the petition for certiorari has been denied, or (3) the decision of the court has been affirmed by the Supreme Court, then the order of the Commission rendered in accordance with the mandate of the court of appeals shall become final on the expiration of thirty days from the time such order of the Commission was rendered, unless within such thirty days either party has instituted proceedings to have such order corrected so that it will accord with the mandate, in which event the order of the Commission shall become final when so corrected.

(j) Rehearing upon order or remand

If the Supreme Court orders a rehearing; or if the case is remanded by the court of appeals to the Commission for a rehearing, and if (1) the time allowed for filing a petition for certiorari has expired, and no such petition has been duly filed, or (2) the petition for certiorari has been denied, or (3) the decision of the court has been affirmed by the Supreme Court, then the order of the Commission rendered upon such rehearing shall become final in the same manner as though no prior order of the Commission had been rendered.

(k) "Mandate" definded

As used in this section the term "mandate", in case a mandate has been recalled prior to the expiration of thirty days from the date of issuance thereof, means the final mandate.

(*l*) Penalty for violation of order; injunctions and other appropriate equitable relief

Any person, partnership, or corporation who violates an order of the Commission after it has become final, and while such order is in effect, shall forfeit and pay to the United States a civil penalty of not more than $10,000 for each violation, which shall accrue to the United States and may be recovered in a civil action brought by the Attorney General of the United States. Each separate violation of such an order shall be a separate offense, except that in the case of a violation through continuing failure to obey or neglect to obey a final order of the Commission, each day of continuance of such failure or neglect shall be deemed a separate offense. In such actions, the United States district courts are empowered to grant mandatory injunctions and such other and further equitable relief as they deem appropriate in the enforcement of such final orders of the Commission.

(m) Civil actions for recovery of penalties for knowing violations of rules and cease and desist orders respecting unfair or deceptive acts or practices; jurisdiction; maximum amount of penalties; continuing violations; de novo determinations; compromise or settlement procedure

(1)(A) The Commission may commence a civil action to recover a civil penalty in a district court of the United States against any person, partnership, or corporation which violates any rule under this chapter respecting unfair or deceptive acts or practices (other than an interpretive rule or a rule violation of which the Commission has provided is not an unfair or deceptive act or practice in violation of subsection (a)(1) of this section) with actual knowledge or knowledge fairly implied on the basis of objective circumstances that such act is unfair or deceptive and is prohibited by such rule. In such action, such person, partnership, or corporation shall be liable for a civil penalty of not more than $10,000 for each violation.

(B) If the Commission determines in a proceeding under subsection (b) of this section that any act or practice is unfair or deceptive, and issues a final cease and desist order, other than a consent order, with respect to such act or practice, then the Commission may commence a civil action to obtain a civil penalty in a district court of the United States against any person, partnership, or corporation which engages in such act or practice—

(1) after such cease and desist order becomes final (whether or not such person, partnership, or corporation was subject to such cease and desist order), and

(2) with actual knowledge that such act or practice is unfair or deceptive and is unlawful under subsection (a)(1) of this section.

In such action, such person, partnership, or corporation shall be liable for a civil penalty of not more than $10,000 for each violation.

(C) In the case of a violation through continuing failure to comply with a rule or with subsection (a)(1) of this section, each day of continuance of such failure shall be treated as a separate violation, for purposes of subparagraphs (A) and (B). In determining the amount of such a civil penalty, the court shall take into account the degree of culpability, any history of prior such conduct, ability to pay, effect on ability to continue to do business, and such other matters as justice may require.

(2) If the cease and desist order establishing that the act or practice is unfair or deceptive was not issued against the defendant in a civil penalty action under paragraph (1)(B) the issues of fact in such action against such defendant shall be tried de novo. Upon request of any party to such an action against such defendant, the court shall also review the determination of law made by the Commission in the proceeding under subsection (b) of this section that the act or practice which was the subject of such proceeding constituted an unfair or deceptive act or practice in violation of subsection (a) of this section.

(3) The Commission may compromise or settle any action for a civil penalty if such compromise or settlement is accompanied by a public statement of its reasons and is approved by the court.

(n) Standard of proof; public policy considerations

The Commission shall have no authority under this section or section 57a of this title to declare unlawful an act or practice on the grounds that such act or practice is unfair unless the act or practice causes or is likely to cause substantial injury to consumers which is not reasonably avoidable by consumers themselves and not outweighed by countervailing benefits to consumers or to competition. In determining whether an act or practice is unfair, the Commission may consider established public policies as evidence to be considered with all other evidence. Such public policy considerations may not serve as a primary basis for such determination.

THE SHERMAN ACT
(15 U.S.C.)

§ 1. [15 U.S.C. § 1]. Trusts, etc., in restraint of trade illegal; penalty

Every contract, combination in the form of trust or otherwise, or conspiracy, in restraint of trade or commerce among the several States, or with foreign nations, is declared to be illegal. Every person who shall make any contract or engage in any combination or conspiracy hereby declared to be illegal shall be deemed guilty of a felony, and, on conviction thereof, shall be punished by fine not exceeding $10,000,000 if a corporation, or, if any other person, $350,000, or by imprisonment not exceeding three years, or by both said punishments, in the discretion of the court.

§ 2. [15 U.S.C. § 2]. Monopolizing trade a felony; penalty

Every person who shall monopolize, or attempt to monopolize, or combine or conspire with any other person or persons, to monopolize any part of the trade or commerce among the several States, or with foreign nations, shall be deemed guilty of a felony, and, on conviction thereof, shall be punished by fine not exceeding $10,000,000 if a corporation, or, if any other person, $350,000, or by imprisonment not exceeding three years, or by both said punishments, in the discretion of the court.

RESTATEMENT OF THE LAW SECOND, TRUSTS

§ 227. Investments Which a Trustee Can Properly Make

In making investments of trust funds the trustee is under a duty to the beneficiary

(a) in the absence of provisions in the terms of the trust or of a statute otherwise providing, to make such investments and only such investments as a prudent man would make of his own property having in view the preservation of the estate and the amount and regularity of the income to be derived;

(b) in the absence of provisions in the terms of the trust, to conform to the statutes, if any, governing investments by trustees;

(c) to conform to the terms of the trust, except as stated in § 165–168.

§ 228. Distribution of Risk of Loss

Except as otherwise provided by the terms of the Trust, the trustee is under a duty to the beneficiary to distribute the risk of loss by a reasonable diversification of investments, unless under the circumstances it is prudent not to do so.

RESTATEMENT OF THE LAW THIRD, TRUSTS

§ 28. Charitable Purposes

Charitable trust purposes include:

(a) the relief of poverty;

(b) the advancement of knowledge or education;

(c) the advancement of religion;

(d) the promotion of health;

(e) governmental or municipal purposes; and

(f) other purposes that are beneficial to the community.

§ 66. Power of Court to Modify: Unanticipated Circumstances

(1) The court may modify an administrative or distributive provision of a trust, or direct or permit the trustee to deviate from an administrative or distributive provision, if because of circumstances not anticipated by the settlor the modification or deviation will further the purposes of the trust.

(2) If a trustee knows or should know of circumstances that justify judicial action under Subsection (1) with respect to an administrative provision, and of the potential of those circumstances to cause substantial harm to the trust or its beneficiaries, the trustee has a duty to petition the court for appropriate modification of or deviation from the terms of the trust.

§ 67. Failure Of Designated Charitable Purpose: The Doctrine Of Cy Pres

Unless the terms of the trust provide otherwise, where property is placed in trust to be applied to a designated charitable purpose and it is or becomes unlawful, impossible, or impracticable to carry out that purpose, or to the extent it is or becomes wasteful to apply all of the property to the designated purpose, the charitable trust will not fail but the court will direct application of the property or appropriate portion thereof to a charitable purpose that reasonably approximates the designated purpose.

§ 77. Duty of Prudence

(1) The trustee has a duty to administer the trust as a prudent person would, in light of the purposes, terms, and other circumstances of the trust.

(2) The duty of prudence requires the exercise of reasonable care, skill, and caution.

(3) If the trustee possesses, or procured appointment by purporting to possess, special facilities or greater skill than that of a person of ordinary prudence, the trustee has a duty to use such facilities or skill.

§ 80. Duty With Respect to Delegation

(1) A trustee has a duty personally to perform the responsibilities of the trusteeship except as a prudent person might delegate those responsibilities to others.

(2) In deciding whether, to whom and in what manner to delegate fiduciary authority in the administration of a trust, and thereafter in supervising or monitoring agents, the trustee has a duty to exercise fiduciary discretion and to act as a prudent person of comparable skill would act in similar circumstances.

§ 85. Extent of Trustees' Powers

(1) In administering a trust, the trustee has, except as limited by statute or the terms of the trust,

(a) all of the powers over trust property that a legally competent, unmarried individual has with respect to individually owned property, as well as

(b) powers granted by statute or the terms of the trust and

(c) powers specifically applicable to trust administration that are recognized in other Sections of this Restatement.

(2) Except as otherwise provided by the terms of the trust, the powers of a trustee under Subsection (1) pass to and are exercisable by substitute or successor trustees.

§ 86. Fiduciary Duties and the Exercise of Trustee Powers

A trustee, in deciding whether and how to exercise the powers of the trusteeship, is subject to and must act in accordance with the fiduciary duties stated in Chapter 15 and elsewhere in this Restatement.

§ 90. General Standard of Prudent Investment

The trustee has a duty to the beneficiaries to invest and manage the funds of the trust as a prudent investor would, in light of the purposes, terms, distribution requirements, and other circumstances of the trust.

(a) This standard requires the exercise of reasonable care, skill, and caution, and is to be applied to investments not in isolation but in the context of the trust portfolio and as a part of an overall investment strategy, which should incorporate risk and return objectives reasonably suitable to the trust.

(b) In making and implementing investment decisions, the trustee has a duty to diversify the investments of the trust unless, under the circumstances, it is prudent not to do so.

(c) In addition, the trustee must:

(1) conform to fundamental fiduciary duties of loyalty (§ 78) and impartiality (§ 79);

(2) act with prudence in deciding whether and how to delegate authority and in the selection and supervision of agents (§ 80); and

(3) incur only costs that are reasonable in amount and appropriate to the investment responsibilities of the trusteeship (§ 88).

(d) The trustee's duties under this Section are subject to the rule of § 91, dealing primarily with contrary investment provisions of a trust or statute.

§ 91. Investment Provisions of Statute or Trust

In investing the funds of the trust, the trustee

(a) has a duty to conform to any applicable statutory provisions governing investment by trustees; and

(b) has the powers expressly or impliedly granted by the terms of the trust and, except as provided in §§ 66 and 76, has a duty to conform to the terms of the trust directing or restricting investments by the trustee.

§ 100. Liability of Trustee for Breach of Trust

A trustee who commits a breach of trust is chargeable with

(a) the amount required to restore the values of the trust estate and trust distributions to what they would have been if the portion of the trust affected by the breach had been properly administered; or

(b) the amount of any benefit to the trustee personally as a result of the breach.

§ 101. Offsetting Profit Against Loss

The amount of a trustee's liability for breach of trust may not be reduced by a profit resulting from other misconduct unless the acts of misconduct causing the loss and the profit constitute a single breach.

UNIFORM PRUDENT MANAGEMENT OF INSTITUTIONAL FUNDS ACT

SECTION 1. SHORT TITLE. This [act] may be cited as the Uniform Prudent Management of Institutional Funds Act.

SECTION 2. DEFINITIONS. In this [act]:

(1) "Charitable purpose" means the relief of poverty, the advancement of education or religion, the promotion of health, the promotion of a governmental purpose, or any other purpose the achievement of which is beneficial to the community.

(2) "Endowment fund" means an institutional fund or part thereof that, under the terms of a gift instrument, is not wholly expendable by the institution on a current basis. The term does not include assets that an institution designates as an endowment fund for its own use.

(3) "Gift instrument" means a record or records, including an institutional solicitation, under which property is granted to, transferred to, or held by an institution as an institutional fund.

(4) "Institution" means:

(A) a person, other than an individual, organized and operated exclusively for charitable purposes;

(B) a government or governmental subdivision, agency, or instrumentality, to the extent that it holds funds exclusively for a charitable purpose; or

(C) a trust that had both charitable and noncharitable interests, after all noncharitable interests have terminated.

(5) "Institutional fund" means a fund held by an institution exclusively for charitable purposes. The term does not include:

(A) program-related assets;

(B) a fund held for an institution by a trustee that is not an institution; or

(C) a fund in which a beneficiary that is not an institution has an interest,

other than an interest that could arise upon violation or failure of the purposes of the fund.

(6) "Person" means an individual, corporation, business trust, estate, trust, partnership, limited liability company, association, joint venture, public corporation, government or governmental subdivision, agency, or instrumentality, or any other legal or commercial entity.

(7) "Program-related asset" means an asset held by an institution primarily to accomplish a charitable purpose of the institution and not primarily for investment.

(8) "Record" means information that is inscribed on a tangible medium or that is stored in an electronic or other medium and is retrievable in perceivable form.

SECTION 3. STANDARD OF CONDUCT IN MANAGING AND INVESTING INSTITUTIONAL FUND.

(a) Subject to the intent of a donor expressed in a gift instrument, an institution, in managing and investing an institutional fund, shall consider the charitable purposes of the institution and the purposes of the institutional fund.

(b) In addition to complying with the duty of loyalty imposed by law other than this [act], each person responsible for managing and investing an institutional fund shall manage and invest the fund in good faith and with the care an ordinarily prudent person in a like position would exercise under similar circumstances.

(c) In managing and investing an institutional fund, an institution:

(1) may incur only costs that are appropriate and reasonable in relation to the assets, the purposes of the institution, and the skills available to the institution; and

(2) shall make a reasonable effort to verify facts relevant to the management and investment of the fund.

(d) An institution may pool two or more institutional funds for purposes of management and investment.

(e) Except as otherwise provided by a gift instrument, the following rules apply:

(1) In managing and investing an institutional fund, the following factors, if relevant, must be considered:

(A) general economic conditions;

(B) the possible effect of inflation or deflation;

(C) the expected tax consequences, if any, of investment decisions or strategies;

(D) the role that each investment or course of action plays within the overall investment portfolio of the fund;

(E) the expected total return from income and the appreciation of investments;

(F) other resources of the institution;

(G) the needs of the institution and the fund to make distributions and to preserve capital; and

(H) an asset's special relationship or special value, if any, to the charitable purposes of the institution.

(2) Management and investment decisions about an individual asset must be made not in isolation but rather in the context of the institutional fund's portfolio of investments as a whole and as a part of an overall investment strategy having risk and return objectives reasonably suited to the fund and to the institution.

(3) Except as otherwise provided by law other than this [act], an institution may invest in any kind of property or type of investment consistent with this section.

(4) An institution shall diversify the investments of an institutional fund unless the institution reasonably determines that, because of special circumstances, the purposes of the fund are better served without diversification.

(5) Within a reasonable time after receiving property, an institution shall make and carry out decisions concerning the retention or disposition of the property or to rebalance a portfolio, in order to bring the institutional fund into compliance with the purposes, terms, and distribution requirements of the institution as necessary to meet other circumstances of the institution and the requirements of this [act].

(6) A person that has special skills or expertise, or is selected in reliance upon the person's representation that the person has special skills or expertise, has a duty to use those skills or that expertise in managing and investing institutional funds.

SECTION 4. APPROPRIATION FOR EXPENDITURE OR ACCUMULATION OF ENDOWMENT FUND; RULES OF CONSTRUCTION.

(a) Subject to the intent of a donor expressed in the gift instrument [and to subsection (d)], an institution may appropriate for expenditure or accumulate so much of an endowment fund as the institution determines is prudent for the uses, benefits, purposes, and duration for which the endowment fund is established. Unless stated otherwise in the gift instrument, the assets in an endowment fund are donor-restricted assets until appropriated for expenditure by the institution. In making a determination to appropriate or accumulate, the institution shall act in good faith, with the care that an ordinarily prudent person in a like position would exercise under similar circumstances, and shall consider, if relevant, the following factors:

(1) the duration and preservation of the endowment fund;

(2) the purposes of the institution and the endowment fund;

(3) general economic conditions;

(4) the possible effect of inflation or deflation;

(5) the expected total return from income and the appreciation of investments;

(6) other resources of the institution; and

(7) the investment policy of the institution.

(b) To limit the authority to appropriate for expenditure or accumulate under subsection (a), a gift instrument must specifically state the limitation.

(c) Terms in a gift instrument designating a gift as an endowment, or a direction or authorization in the gift instrument to use only "income", "interest", "dividends", or "rents, issues, or profits", or "to preserve the principal intact", or words of similar import:

(1) create an endowment fund of permanent duration unless other language in the gift instrument limits the duration or purpose of the fund; and

(2) do not otherwise limit the authority to appropriate for expenditure or accumulate under subsection (a).

[(d) The appropriation for expenditure in any year of an amount greater than seven percent of the fair market value of an endowment fund, calculated on the basis of market values determined at least quarterly and averaged over a period of not less than three years immediately preceding the year in which the appropriation for expenditure is made, creates a rebuttable presumption of imprudence. For an endowment fund in existence for fewer than three years, the fair market value of the endowment fund must be calculated for the period the endowment fund has been in existence. This subsection does not:

(1) apply to an appropriation for expenditure permitted under law other than this [act] or by the gift instrument; or

(2) create a presumption of prudence for an appropriation for expenditure of an amount less than or equal to seven percent of the fair market value of the endowment fund.]

[SECTION 5. DELEGATION OF MANAGEMENT AND INVESTMENT FUNCTIONS.

(a) Subject to any specific limitation set forth in a gift instrument or in law other than this [act], an institution may delegate to an external agent the management and investment of an institutional fund to the extent that an institution could prudently delegate under the circumstances. An institution shall act in good faith, with the care that an ordinarily prudent person in a like position would exercise under similar circumstances, in:

(1) selecting an agent;

(2) establishing the scope and terms of the delegation, consistent with the purposes of the institution and the institutional fund; and

(3) periodically reviewing the agent's actions in order to monitor the agent's performance and compliance with the scope and terms of the delegation.

(b) In performing a delegated function, an agent owes a duty to the institution to exercise reasonable care to comply with the scope and terms of the delegation.

(c) An institution that complies with subsection (a) is not liable for the decisions or actions of an agent to which the function was delegated.

(d) By accepting delegation of a management or investment function from an institution that is subject to the laws of this state, an agent submits to the jurisdiction of the courts of this state in all proceedings arising from or related to the delegation or the performance of the delegated function.

(e) An institution may delegate management and investment functions to its committees, officers, or employees as authorized by law of this state other than this [act].]

SECTION 6. RELEASE OR MODIFICATION OF RESTRICTIONS ON MANAGEMENT, INVESTMENT, OR PURPOSE.

(a) If the donor consents in a record, an institution may release or modify, in whole or in part, a restriction contained in a gift instrument on the management, investment, or purpose of an institutional fund. A release or modification may not allow a fund to be used for a purpose other than a charitable purpose of the institution.

(b) The court, upon application of an institution, may modify a restriction contained in a gift instrument regarding the management or investment of an institutional fund if the restriction has become impracticable or wasteful, if it impairs the management or investment of the fund, or if, because of circumstances not anticipated by the donor, a modification of a restriction will further the purposes of the fund. The institution shall notify the [Attorney General] of the application, and the [Attorney General] must be given an opportunity to be heard. To the extent practicable, any modification must be made in accordance with the donor's probable intention.

(c) If a particular charitable purpose or a restriction contained in a gift instrument on the use of an institutional fund becomes unlawful, impracticable, impossible to achieve, or wasteful, the court, upon application of an institution, may modify the purpose of the fund or the restriction on the use of the fund in a manner consistent with the charitable purposes expressed in the gift instrument. The institution shall notify the [Attorney General] of the application, and the [Attorney General] must be given an opportunity to be heard.

(d) If an institution determines that a restriction contained in a gift instrument on the management, investment, or purpose of an institutional fund is unlawful, impracticable, impossible to achieve, or wasteful, the institution, [60 days] after notification to the [Attorney General], may release or modify the restriction, in whole or part, if:

(1) the institutional fund subject to the restriction has a total value of less than [$25,000];

(2) more than [20] years have elapsed since the fund was established; and

(3) the institution uses the property in a manner consistent with the charitable purposes expressed in the gift instrument.

SECTION 7. REVIEWING COMPLIANCE. Compliance with this [act] is determined in light of the facts and circumstances existing at the time a decision is made or action is taken, and not by hindsight.

SECTION 8. APPLICATION TO EXISTING INSTITUTIONAL FUNDS. This [act] applies to institutional funds existing on or established after [the effective date of this act]. As applied to institutional funds existing on [the effective date of this act] this [act] governs only decisions made or actions taken on or after that date.

SECTION 9. RELATION TO ELECTRONIC SIGNATURES IN GLOBAL AND NATIONAL COMMERCE ACT. This [act] modifies, limits, and supersedes the Electronic Signatures in Global and National Commerce Act, 15 U.S.C. Section 7001 et seq., but does not modify, limit, or supersede Section 101 of that act, 15 U.S.C. Section 7001(a), or authorize electronic delivery of any of the notices described in Section 103 of that act, 15 U.S.C. Section 7003(b).

SECTION 10. UNIFORMITY OF APPLICATION AND CONSTRUCTION. In applying and construing this uniform act, consideration must be given to the need to promote uniformity of the law with respect to its subject matter among states that enact it.

SECTION 11. EFFECTIVE DATE. This [act] takes effect . . . .

SECTION 12. REPEAL. The following acts and parts of acts are repealed: * * * (a) [The Uniform Management of Institutional Funds Act]

UNIFORM PRUDENT INVESTOR ACT

Section 1. Prudent Investor Rule

(a) Except as provided in subsection (b), a trustee who invests and manages trust assets owes a duty to the beneficiaries of the trust to comply with the prudent investor rule, as set forth in Sections 2 through 9.

(b) The prudent investor rule is a default rule that may be expanded, restricted, eliminated, or otherwise altered by provisions of the trust. The trustee is not liable to a beneficiary to the extent that the trustee acted in reasonable reliance on provisions of the trust.

Section 2. Standard of Care; Portfolio Strategy; Risk and Return Objectives

(a) A trustee shall invest and manage trust assets as a prudent investor would, by considering the purposes, terms, distribution requirements, and other circumstances of the trust. In satisfying this standard, the trustee must exercise reasonable care, skill, and caution.

(b) A trustee's investment and management decisions respecting individual assets must be evaluated not in isolation, but in the context of the trust portfolio as a whole and as a part of an overall investment strategy having risk and return objectives reasonably suited to the trust.

(c) Among the circumstances that the trustee shall consider in investing and managing trust assets are such of the following as are relevant to the trust and its beneficiaries:

(1) general economic conditions;

(2) the possible effect of inflation or deflation;

(3) the expected tax consequences of investment decisions or strategies;

(4) the role that each investment or course of action plays within the overall trust portfolio, which may include financial assets, interests in closely held enterprises, tangible and intangible personalty, and real estate;

(5) the expected total return from income and the appreciation of capital;

(6) other resources of the beneficiaries;

(7) needs for liquidity, for regularity of income, and for preservation or appreciation of capital; and

(8) an asset's special relationship or special value, if any, to the purposes of the trust or to one or more of the beneficiaries.

(d) The trustee shall take reasonable steps to verify facts relevant to the investment and management of trust assets.

(e) Subject to the standards of this [Act], a trustee may invest in any kind of property or type of investment.

(f) A trustee who has special skills or expertise, or is named trustee in reliance upon the trustee's representation that the trustee has special skills or expertise, has a duty to use those special skills or expertise.

Section 3. Diversification

A trustee shall diversify the investments of the trust unless the trustee reasonably determines that, because of special circumstances, the purposes of the trust are better served without diversifying.

Section 4. Inception Assets

Within a reasonable time after accepting a trusteeship, the trustee shall review the trust assets and shall make and implement decisions concerning the retention and disposition of assets received at the inception of the trust, in order to bring the trust portfolio into compliance with the provisions of the trust instrument or with the requirements of this [Act].

Section 5. Loyalty

A trustee shall invest and manage the trust assets solely in the interest of the beneficiaries.

Section 6. Impartiality

If a trust has two or more beneficiaries, the trustee shall act impartially in investing and managing the trust assets, taking into account the differing interests of the beneficiaries.

Section 7. Investment Costs

In investing and managing trust assets, a trustee may only incur costs that are appropriate and reasonable in relation to the assets, the purposes of the trust, and the skills of the trustee.

Section 8. Reviewing Compliance

The prudent investor rule expresses a standard of conduct, not outcome. Compliance with the prudent investor rule is determined in light of the facts and circumstances existing at the time of the trustee's decision or action.

Section 9. Delegation of Investment and Management Functions

(a) A trustee may delegate investment and management functions that a prudent trustee of comparable skills could properly delegate under the circumstances. The trustee shall exercise reasonable care, skill, and caution in

(1) selecting an agent;

(2) establishing the scope and terms of the delegation consistent with the purposes and terms of the trust; and

(3) periodically reviewing the agent's actions in order to monitor the agent's performance and compliance with the scope and terms of the delegation.

(b) In performing a delegated function, the agent has a duty to the trust to exercise reasonable care to comply with the terms of the delegation.

(c) The trustee who complies with the requirements of subsection (a) is not liable to the beneficiaries or to the trust for the decisions or actions of the agent to whom the function was delegated.

(d) By accepting the delegation of a trust function from the trustee of a trust that is subject to the law of [this State], an agent submits to the jurisdiction of the courts of [this State].

Section 10. Language Invoking Standard of [Act]

The following terms or comparable language in a trust instrument, unless otherwise limited or modified by that instrument, must be construed as authorizing any investment or strategy permitted under this [Act]: "investments permissible by law for investment of trust funds," "legal investments," "authorized investments," "using the judgment and care under the circumstances then prevailing that persons of prudence, discretion, and intelligence exercise in the management of their own affairs, not in regard to speculation but in regard to the permanent disposition of their funds, considering the probable income as well as the probable safety of their capital," "prudent man rule," "prudent trustee rule," "prudent person rule," and "prudent investor rule."

Section 11. Effective Date

This [Act] applies to trusts existing on and created after its effective date. As applied to trusts existing on its effective date, this [Act] governs only actions or omissions occurring after that date.

Section 12. Short Title

This [Act] may be cited as the "[Name of Enacting State] Uniform Prudent Investor Act."

Section 13. Severability

If any provision of this [Act] or its application to any person or circumstance is held invalid, the invalidity does not affect other provisions or applications of this [Act] which can be given effect without the invalid provision or application, and to this end the provisions of this [Act] are severable.

REVISED UNIFORM UNINCORPORATED NONPROFIT ASSOCIATION ACT

SECTION 1. SHORT TITLE. This act may be cited as the Uniform Unincorporated Nonprofit Association Act.

SECTION 2. DEFINITIONS. In this [act]:

* * *

(3) "Manager" means a person that is responsible, alone or in concert with others, for the management of an unincorporated nonprofit association.

(4) "Member" means a person that, under the governing principles, may participate in the selection of persons authorized to manage the affairs of the unincorporated nonprofit association or in the development of the policies and activities of the association.

* * *

(11) "Unincorporated nonprofit association" means an unincorporated organization consisting of [two] or more members joined under an agreement that is oral, in a record, or implied from conduct, for one or more common, nonprofit purposes. The term does not include:

(A) a trust;

(B) a marriage, domestic partnership, common law domestic relationship, civil union, or other domestic living arrangement;

(C) an organization formed under any other statute that governs the organization and operation of unincorporated associations;

(D) a joint tenancy, tenancy in common, or tenancy by the entireties even if the co-owners share use of the property for a nonprofit purpose; or

(E) a relationship under an agreement in a record that expressly provides that the relationship between the parties does not create an unincorporated nonprofit association.

SECTION 3. RELATION TO OTHER LAW.

(a) A statute governing a specific type of unincorporated nonprofit association prevails over an inconsistent provision in this [act], to the extent of the inconsistency.

(b) This [act] supplements the law of this state that applies to nonprofit associations operating in this state. If a conflict exists, that law applies.

(c) Unless displaced by a particular provision of this [act], the principles of law and equity supplement this [act].

* * *

SECTION 5. ENTITY; PERPETUAL EXISTENCE; POWERS.

(a) An unincorporated nonprofit association is a legal entity distinct from its members and managers.

(b) An unincorporated nonprofit association has perpetual duration unless the governing principles specify otherwise.

(c) An unincorporated nonprofit association has the same powers as an individual to do all things necessary or convenient to carry on its purposes.

(d) An unincorporated nonprofit association may engage in profit-making activities but profits from any activities must be used or set aside for the association's nonprofit purposes.

SECTION 6. OWNERSHIP AND TRANSFER OF PROPERTY.

(a) An unincorporated nonprofit association may acquire, hold, encumber, or transfer in its name an interest in real or personal property.

(b) An unincorporated nonprofit association may be a beneficiary of a trust or contract, a legatee or a devisee.

SECTION 7. STATEMENT OF AUTHORITY AS TO REAL PROPERTY.

(a) In this section, "statement of authority" means a statement authorizing a person to transfer an interest in real property held in the name of an unincorporated nonprofit association.

(b) An interest in real property held in the name of an unincorporated nonprofit association may be transferred by a person authorized to do so in a statement of authority [filed] [recorded] by the association in the office in the [county] in which a transfer of the property would be [filed] [recorded].

* * *

(g) Unless canceled earlier, a [filed] [recorded] statement of authority and its most recent amendment expire [five] years after the date of the most recent [filing] [recording].

(h) If the record title to real property is in the name of an unincorporated nonprofit association and the statement of authority is [filed] [recorded] in the office of the [county] in which a transfer of the property would be [filed] [recorded], the authority of the person named in the statement to transfer is conclusive in favor of a person that gives value without notice that the person lacks authority.

SECTION 8. LIABILITY.

(a) A debt, obligation, or other liability of an unincorporated nonprofit association is solely the debt, obligation, or other liability of the association. A member or manager is not personally liable, directly or indirectly, by way of contribution or otherwise for a debt, obligation, or other liability of the association solely by reason of being or acting as a member or manager. This subsection applies regardless of the dissolution of the organization.

(b) A person's status as a member or manager does not prevent or restrict law other than this [act] from imposing liability on the person or the association because of the person's conduct.

(c) The failure of an unincorporated association to observe formalities relating to the exercise of its powers or management of its activities and affairs is not a ground for imposing liability on a member or manager of the association for a debt, obligation, or other liability of the association.

SECTION 9. ASSERTION AND DEFENSE OF CLAIMS.

(a) An unincorporated nonprofit association may sue or be sued in its own name.

(b) A member or manager may assert a claim the member or manager has against the unincorporated nonprofit association. An association may assert a claim it has against a member or manager.

SECTION 10. EFFECT OF JUDGMENT OR ORDER. A judgment or order against an unincorporated nonprofit association is not by itself a judgment or order against a member or manager.

[**SECTION 11. SERVICE OF PROCESS.** In an action or proceeding against an unincorporated nonprofit association, process may be served on an agent authorized by appointment to receive service of process, on a manager of the association, or in any other manner authorized by the law of this state.]

* * *

SECTION 14. MEMBER NOT AGENT. A member is not an agent of the association solely by reason of being a member.

SECTION 15. APPROVAL BY MEMBERS.

(a) Except as otherwise provided in the governing principles, an unincorporated nonprofit association must have the approval of its members to:

(1) admit, suspend, dismiss, or expel a member;

(2) select or dismiss a manager;

(3) adopt, amend, or repeal the governing principles;

(4) sell, lease, exchange, or otherwise dispose of all, or substantially all, of the association's property, with or without the association's goodwill, outside the ordinary course of its activities;

(5) dissolve under section 7(a) or merge under section 31;

(6) undertake any other act outside the ordinary course of the association's activities; or

(7) determine the policy and purposes of the association.

(b) An unincorporated nonprofit association must have the approval of the members to do any other act or exercise a right that the governing principles require to be approved by members.

SECTION 16. MEMBER MEETINGS; PROCEDURAL REQUIREMENTS.

(a) Unless the governing principles provide otherwise:

(1) approval of a matter by members requires an affirmative majority of the votes cast at a meeting of members; and

(2) each member is entitled to one vote on each matter that is submitted for approval by members.

(b) The governing principles may provide for the:

(1) calling, location, and timing of member meetings;

(2) notice and quorum requirements for member meetings;

(3) conduct of member meetings;

(4) taking of action by the members by consent without a meeting or casting ballots; and

(5) participation by members in a member meeting by telephone or other means of electronic communication.

(c) If the governing principles do not provide for a matter described in subsection (b), customary usages and principles of parliamentary law and procedure apply.

SECTION 17. DUTIES OF MEMBER.

(a) A member does not have a fiduciary duty to an unincorporated nonprofit association or to another member solely by being a member.

(b) A member shall discharge the duties to the unincorporated nonprofit association and the other members and exercise any rights under this [act] consistent with the governing principles and the obligation of good faith and fair dealing.

SECTION 18. ADMISSION, SUSPENSION, DISMISSAL, OR EXPULSION OF MEMBERS.

(a) A person becomes a member and may be suspended, dismissed, or expelled in accordance with the association's governing principles. If there are no applicable governing principles, a person may become a member or be suspended, dismissed, or expelled from an association only by a vote of its members. A person may not be admitted as a member without the person's consent.

(b) Unless the governing principles provide otherwise, the suspension, dismissal, or expulsion of a member does not relieve the member from any unpaid capital contribution, dues, assessments, fees, or other obligation incurred or commitment made by the member before the suspension, dismissal, or expulsion.

SECTION 19. MEMBER'S RESIGNATION.

(a) A member may resign as a member in accordance with the governing principles. In the absence of applicable governing principles, a member may resign at any time.

(b) Unless the governing principles provide otherwise, resignation of a member does not relieve the member from any unpaid capital contribution, dues, assessments, fees, or other obligation incurred or commitment made by the member before resignation.

SECTION 20. MEMBERSHIP INTEREST NOT TRANSFERABLE. Except as otherwise provided in the governing principles, a member's interest or any right under the governing principles is not transferable.

SECTION 21. SELECTION OF MANAGERS; MANAGEMENT RIGHTS OF MANAGERS. Except as otherwise provided in this [act] or the governing principles:

(1) only the members may select a manager or managers;

(2) a manager may be a member or a nonmember;

(3) if a manager is not selected, all members are managers;

(4) each manager has equal rights in the management and conduct of the association's activities;

(5) all matters relating to the association's activities are decided by its managers except for matters reserved for approval by members in section 16; and

(6) a difference among managers is decided by a majority of the managers.

SECTION 22. DUTIES OF MANAGERS.

(a) A manager owes to the unincorporated nonprofit association and to its members the fiduciary duties of loyalty and care.

(b) A manager shall manage the unincorporated nonprofit association in good faith, in a manner the manager reasonably believes to be in the best interests of the association, and with such care, including reasonable inquiry, as a prudent person would reasonably exercise in a similar position and under similar circumstances. A manager may rely in good faith upon any opinion, report, statement, or other information provided by another person that the manager reasonably believes is a competent and reliable source for the information.

(c) After full disclosure of all material facts, a specific act or transaction that would otherwise violate the duty of loyalty by a manager may be authorized or ratified by a majority of the members that are not interested directly or indirectly in the act or transaction.

(d) A manager that makes a business judgment in good faith satisfies the duties specified in subsection (a) if the manager:

(1) is not interested, directly or indirectly, in the subject of the business judgment and is otherwise able to exercise independent judgment;

(2) is informed with respect to the subject of the business judgment to the extent the manager reasonably believes to be appropriate under the circumstances; and

(3) believes that the business judgment is in the best interests of the unincorporated nonprofit association and in accordance with its purposes.

(e) The governing principles in a record may limit or eliminate the liability of a manager to the unincorporated nonprofit association or its members for damages for any action taken, or for failure to take any action, as a manager, except liability for:

(1) the amount of financial benefit improperly received by a manager;

(2) an intentional infliction of harm on the association or one or more of its members;

(3) an intentional violation of criminal law;

(4) breach of the duty of loyalty; or

(5) improper distributions.

* * *

SECTION 24. RIGHT OF MEMBER OR MANAGER TO INFORMATION.

(a) On reasonable notice, a member or manager of an unincorporated nonprofit association may inspect and copy during the unincorporated nonprofit association's regular operating hours, at a reasonable location specified by the association, any record maintained by the association regarding its activities, financial condition, and other circumstances, to the extent the information is material to the member's or manager's rights and duties under the governing principles.

(b) An unincorporated nonprofit association may impose reasonable restrictions on access to and use of information to be furnished under this section, including designating the information confidential and imposing obligations of nondisclosure and safeguarding on the recipient.

(c) An unincorporated nonprofit association may charge a person that makes a demand under this section reasonable copying costs, limited to the costs of labor and materials.

(d) A former member or manager is entitled to information to which the member or manager was entitled while a member or manager if the information pertains to the period during which the person was a member or manager, the former member or manager seeks the information in good faith, and the former member or manager satisfies subsections (a) through (c).

SECTION 25. DISTRIBUTIONS PROHIBITED; COMPENSATION AND OTHER PERMITTED PAYMENTS.

(a) Except as otherwise provided in subsection (b), an unincorporated nonprofit association may not pay dividends or make distributions to a member or manager.

(b) An unincorporated nonprofit association may:

(1) pay reasonable compensation or reimburse reasonable expenses to a member or manager for services rendered;

(2) confer benefits on a member or manager in conformity with its nonprofit purposes;

(3) repurchase a membership and repay a capital contribution made by a member to the extent authorized by its governing principles; or

(4) make distributions of property to members upon winding up and termination to the extent permitted by section 29.

* * *

SECTION 27. DISSOLUTION.

(a) An unincorporated nonprofit association may be dissolved as follows:

(1) if the governing principles provide a time or method for dissolution, at that time or by that method;

(2) if the governing principles do not provide a time or method for dissolution, upon approval by the members;

(3) if no member can be located and the association's operations have been discontinued for at least three years, by the managers or, if the association has no current manager, by its last manager;

(4) by court order; or

(5) under law other than this act.

(b) After dissolution, an unincorporated nonprofit association continues in existence until its activities have been wound up and it is terminated pursuant to section 29.

SECTION 28. WINDING UP AND TERMINATION. Winding up and termination of an unincorporated nonprofit association must proceed in accordance with the following rules:

(1) All known debts and liabilities must be paid or adequately provided for.

(2) Any property subject to a condition requiring return to the person designated by the donor must be transferred to that person.

(3) Any property subject to a trust must be distributed in accordance with the trust agreement.

(4) Any remaining property must be distributed as follows:

(A) as required by law other than this [act] that requires assets of an association to be distributed to another person with similar nonprofit purposes;

(B) in accordance with the association's governing principles or in the absence of applicable governing principles, to the members of the association per capita or as the members direct; or

(C) if neither subparagraph (A) nor (B) applies, under [cite the unclaimed property law in this state.]

* * *

EMPLOYEE RETIREMENT INCOME SECURITY ACT OF 1974 ("ERISA")

§ 404. (codified in 29 U.S.C.A. § 1104(a)(1).)

§ 1104. Fiduciary duties.

(a) Prudent man standard of care.

(1) Subject To sections 403(c) and (d), 4042, and 4044, a fiduciary shall discharge his duties with respect to a plan solely in the interest of the participants and beneficiaries and—

(A) for the exclusive purpose of:

(i) providing benefits to participants and their beneficiaries; and

(ii) defraying reasonable expenses of administering the plan;

(B) with the care, skill, prudence, and diligence under the circumstances then prevailing that a prudent man acting in a like capacity and familiar with such matters would use in the conduct of an enterprise of a like character and with like aims;

(C) by diversifying the investments of the plan so as to minimize the risk of large losses, unless under the circumstances it is clearly prudent not to do so; and

(D) in accordance with the documents and instruments governing the plan insofar as such documents and instruments are consistent with the provisions of this title.

(2) in the case of an eligible individual account plan (as defined in section 407(d)(3)), the diversification requirement of paragraph (1)(C) and the prudence requirement (only to the extent that it requires diversification) of paragraph (1)(B) is not violated by acquisition or holding of qualifying employer real property or qualifying employer securities (as defined in section 1107(d)(4) and (5) of this title).

(b) Indicia of ownership of assets outside jurisdiction of district courts. Except as authorized by the secretary by regulation, no fiduciary may maintain the indicia of ownership of any assets of a plan outside the jurisdiction of the district courts of the United States.

(c) Control over assets by participant or beneficiary.

(1) in the case of a pension plan which provides for individual accounts and permits a participant or beneficiary to exercise control over assets in his account, If a participant or beneficiary exercises control over the assets in his account (as determined under regulations of the Secretary)—

(A) such participant or beneficiary shall not be deemed to be a fiduciary by reason of such exercise, and

(B) no person who is otherwise a fiduciary shall be liable under this part for any loss, or by reason of any breach, which results from such participant's or beneficiary's exercise of control.

U.S. Department of Labor Reg. 29 C.F.R. § 2550.404a–1. Investment Duties.

(a) In general. Section 404(a)(1)(B) of the Employee Retirement Income Security Act of 1974 (the Act) provides, in part, that a fiduciary shall discharge his duties with respect to a plan with the care, skill, prudence, and diligence under the circumstances then prevailing that a prudent man acting in a like capacity and familiar with such matters would use in the conduct of an enterprise of a like character and with like aims.

(b) Investment Duties.

(1) With regard to an investment or investment course of action taken by a fiduciary of an employee benefit plan pursuant to his investment duties, the requirements of section 404(a)(1)(B) of the Act set forth in subsection (a) of this section are satisfied if the fiduciary:

(i) Has given appropriate consideration to those facts and circumstances that, given the scope of such fiduciary's investment duties, the fiduciary knows or should know are relevant to the particular investment or investment course of action involved, including the role the investment or investment course of action plays in that portion of the plan's investment portfolio with respect to which the fiduciary has investment duties; and

(ii) Has acted accordingly.

(2) For purposes of paragraph (b)(1) of this section, "appropriate consideration" shall include, but is not necessarily limited to,

(i) A determination by the fiduciary that the particular investment or investment course of action is reasonably designed, as part of the portfolio (or, where applicable, that portion of the plan portfolio with respect to which the fiduciary has investment duties), to further the purposes of the plan, taking into consideration the risk of loss and the opportunity for gain (or other return) associated with the investment or investment course of action, and

(ii) Consideration of the following factors as they relate to such portion of the portfolio:

(A) The composition of the portfolio with regard to diversification;

(B) The liquidity and current return of the portfolio relative to the anticipated cash flow requirements of the plan; and

(C) The projected return of the portfolio relative to the funding objectives of the plan.

(3) An investment manager appointed, pursuant to the provisions of section 402(c)(3) of the Act, to manage all or part of the assets of a plan, may, for purposes of compliance with the provisions of paragraphs (b)(1) and (2) of this section, rely on, and act upon the basis of, information pertaining to the plan provided by or at the direction of the appointing fiduciary, if—

(i) Such information is provided for the stated purpose of assisting the manager in the performance of his investment duties, and

(ii) The manager does not know and has no reason to know that the information is incorrect.

(c) Definitions. For purposes of this section:

(1) The term "investment duties" means any duties imposed upon, or assumed or undertaken by, a person in connection with the investment of plan assets which make or will make such person a fiduciary of an employee benefit plan or which are performed by such person as a fiduciary of an employee benefit plan as defined in section 3(21)(A)(i) or (ii) of the Act.

(2) The term "investment course of action" means any series or program of investments or actions related to a fiduciary's performance of his investment duties.

(3) The term "plan" means an employee benefit plan to which Title I of the Act applies.

THE VOLUNTEER PROTECTION ACT OF 1997 (42 U.S.C. 14501–14505)

UNITED STATES CODE ANNOTATED
TITLE 42. THE PUBLIC HEALTH AND WELFARE
CHAPTER 139—VOLUNTEER PROTECTION

§ 14501. Findings and purpose

(a) Findings

The Congress finds and declares that—

(1) the willingness of volunteers to offer their services is deterred by the potential for liability actions against them;

(2) as a result, many nonprofit public and private organizations and governmental entities, including voluntary associations, social service agencies, educational institutions, and other civic programs, have been adversely affected by the withdrawal of volunteers from boards of directors and service in other capacities;

(3) the contribution of these programs to their communities is thereby diminished, resulting in fewer and higher cost programs than would be obtainable if volunteers were participating;

(4) because Federal funds are expended on useful and cost-effective social service programs, many of which are national in scope, depend heavily on volunteer participation, and represent some of the most successful public-private partnerships, protection of volunteerism through clarification and limitation of the personal liability risks assumed by the volunteer in connection with such participation is an appropriate subject for Federal legislation;

(5) services and goods provided by volunteers and nonprofit organizations would often otherwise be provided by private entities that operate in interstate commerce;

(6) due to high liability costs and unwarranted litigation costs, volunteers and nonprofit organizations face higher costs in purchasing insurance, through interstate insurance markets, to cover their activities; and

(7) clarifying and limiting the liability risk assumed by volunteers is an appropriate subject for Federal legislation because—

(A) of the national scope of the problems created by the legitimate fears of volunteers about frivolous, arbitrary, or capricious lawsuits;

(B) the citizens of the United States depend on, and the Federal Government expends funds on, and provides tax exemptions and other consideration to, numerous social programs that depend on the services of volunteers;

(C) it is in the interest of the Federal Government to encourage the continued operation of volunteer service organizations and contributions of volunteers because the Federal Government lacks the capacity to carry out all of the services provided by such organizations and volunteers; and

(D)(i) liability reform for volunteers, will promote the free flow of goods and services, lessen burdens on interstate commerce and uphold constitutionally protected due process rights; and

(ii) therefore, liability reform is an appropriate use of the powers contained in article 1, section 8, clause 3 of the United States Constitution, and the fourteenth amendment to the United States Constitution.

(b) Purpose

The purpose of this chapter is to promote the interests of social service program beneficiaries and taxpayers and to sustain the availability of programs, nonprofit organizations, and governmental entities that depend on volunteer contributions by reforming the laws to provide certain protections from liability abuses related to volunteers serving nonprofit organizations and governmental entities.

§ 14502. Preemption and election of State nonapplicability

(a) Preemption

This chapter preempts the laws of any State to the extent that such laws are inconsistent with this chapter, except that this chapter shall not preempt any State law that provides additional protection from liability relating to volunteers or to any category of volunteers in the performance of services for a nonprofit organization or governmental entity.

(b) Election of State regarding nonapplicability

This chapter shall not apply to any civil action in a State court against a volunteer in which all parties are citizens of the State if such State enacts a statute in accordance with State requirements for enacting legislation—

(1) citing the authority of this subsection;

(2) declaring the election of such State that this chapter shall not apply, as of a date certain, to such civil action in the State; and

(3) containing no other provisions.

§ 14503. Limitation on liability for volunteers

(a) Liability protection for volunteers

Except as provided in subsections (b) and (d) of this section, no volunteer of a nonprofit organization or governmental entity shall be liable for harm caused by an act or omission of the volunteer on behalf of the organization or entity if—

(1) the volunteer was acting within the scope of the volunteer's responsibilities in the nonprofit organization or governmental entity at the time of the act or omission;

(2) if appropriate or required, the volunteer was properly licensed, certified, or authorized by the appropriate authorities for the activities or practice in the State in which the harm occurred, where the activities were or practice was undertaken within the scope of the volunteer's responsibilities in the nonprofit organization or governmental entity;

(3) the harm was not caused by willful or criminal misconduct, gross negligence, reckless misconduct, or a conscious, flagrant indifference to the rights or safety of the individual harmed by the volunteer; and

(4) the harm was not caused by the volunteer operating a motor vehicle, vessel, aircraft, or other vehicle for which the State requires the operator or the owner of the vehicle, craft, or vessel to—

(A) possess an operator's license; or

(B) maintain insurance.

(b) Concerning responsibility of volunteers to organizations and entities

Nothing in this section shall be construed to affect any civil action brought by any nonprofit organization or any governmental entity against any volunteer of such organization or entity.

(c) No effect on liability of organization or entity

Nothing in this section shall be construed to affect the liability of any nonprofit organization or governmental entity with respect to harm caused to any person.

(d) Exceptions to volunteer liability protection

If the laws of a State limit volunteer liability subject to one or more of the following conditions, such conditions shall not be construed as inconsistent with this section:

(1) A State law that requires a nonprofit organization or governmental entity to adhere to risk management procedures, including mandatory training of volunteers.

(2) A State law that makes the organization or entity liable for the acts or omissions of its volunteers to the same extent as an employer is liable for the acts or omissions of its employees.

(3) A State law that makes a limitation of liability inapplicable if the civil action was brought by an officer of a State or local government pursuant to State or local law.

(4) A State law that makes a limitation of liability applicable only if the nonprofit organization or governmental entity provides a financially secure source of recovery for individuals who suffer harm as a result of actions taken by a volunteer on behalf of the organization or entity. A financially secure source of recovery may be an insurance policy within specified limits, comparable coverage from a risk pooling mechanism, equivalent assets, or alternative arrangements that satisfy the State that the organization or entity will be able to pay for losses up to a specified amount. Separate standards for different types of liability exposure may be specified.

(e) Limitation on punitive damages based on the actions of volunteers

(1) General rule

Punitive damages may not be awarded against a volunteer in an action brought for harm based on the action of a volunteer acting within the scope of the volunteer's responsibilities to a nonprofit organization or governmental entity unless the claimant establishes by clear and convincing evidence that the harm was proximately caused by an action of such volunteer which constitutes willful or criminal misconduct, or a conscious, flagrant indifference to the rights or safety of the individual harmed.

(2) Construction

Paragraph (1) does not create a cause of action for punitive damages and does not preempt or supersede any Federal or State law to the extent that such law would further limit the award of punitive damages.

(f) Exceptions to limitations on liability

(1) In general

The limitations on the liability of a volunteer under this chapter shall not apply to any misconduct that—

(A) constitutes a crime of violence (as that term is defined in section 16 of Title 18) or act of international terrorism (as that term is defined in section 2331 of Title 18) for which the defendant has been convicted in any court;

(B) constitutes a hate crime (as that term is used in the Hate Crime Statistics Act (28 U.S.C. 534 note));

(C) involves a sexual offense, as defined by applicable State law, for which the defendant has been convicted in any court;

(D) involves misconduct for which the defendant has been found to have violated a Federal or State civil rights law; or

(E) where the defendant was under the influence (as determined pursuant to applicable State law) of intoxicating alcohol or any drug at the time of the misconduct.

(2) Rule of construction

Nothing in this subsection shall be construed to effect subsection (a)(3) or (e) of this section.

§ 14504. Liability for noneconomic loss

(a) General rule

In any civil action against a volunteer, based on an action of a volunteer acting within the scope of the volunteer's responsibilities to a nonprofit organization or governmental entity, the liability of the volunteer for noneconomic loss shall be determined in accordance with subsection (b) of this section.

(b) Amount of liability

(1) In general

Each defendant who is a volunteer, shall be liable only for the amount of noneconomic loss allocated to that defendant in direct proportion to the percentage of responsibility of that defendant (determined in accordance with paragraph (2)) for the harm to the claimant with respect to which that defendant is liable. The court shall render a separate judgment against each defendant in an amount determined pursuant to the preceding sentence.

(2) Percentage of responsibility

For purposes of determining the amount of noneconomic loss allocated to a defendant who is a volunteer under this section, the trier of fact shall determine the percentage of responsibility of that defendant for the claimant's harm.

§ 14505. Definitions

For purposes of this chapter:

(1) Economic loss

The term "economic loss" means any pecuniary loss resulting from harm (including the loss of earnings or other benefits related to employment, medical expense loss, replacement services loss, loss due to death, burial costs, and loss of business or employment opportunities) to the extent recovery for such loss is allowed under applicable State law.

(2) Harm

The term "harm" includes physical, nonphysical, economic, and noneconomic losses.

(3) Noneconomic losses

The term "noneconomic losses" means losses for physical and emotional pain, suffering, inconvenience, physical impairment, mental anguish, disfigurement, loss of enjoyment of life, loss of society and companionship, loss of consortium (other than loss of domestic service), hedonic damages, injury to reputation and all other nonpecuniary losses of any kind or nature.

(4) Nonprofit organization

The term "nonprofit organization" means—

(A) any organization which is described in section 501(c)(3) of Title 26 and exempt from tax under section 501(a) of Title 26 and which does not practice any action which constitutes a hate crime referred to in subsection (b)(1) of the first section of the Hate Crime Statistics Act (28 U.S.C. 534 note); or

(B) any not-for-profit organization which is organized and conducted for public benefit and operated primarily for charitable, civic, educational, religious, welfare, or health purposes and which does not practice any action which constitutes a hate crime referred to in subsection (b)(1) of the first section of the Hate Crime Statistics Act (28 U.S.C. 534 note).

(5) State

The term "State" means each of the several States, the District of Columbia, the Commonwealth of Puerto Rico, the Virgin Islands, Guam, American Samoa, the Northern Mariana Islands, any other territory or possession of the United States, or any political subdivision of any such State, territory, or possession.

(6) Volunteer

The term "volunteer" means an individual performing services for a nonprofit organization or a governmental entity who does not receive—

(A) compensation (other than reasonable reimbursement or allowance for expenses actually incurred); or

(B) any other thing of value in lieu of compensation, in excess of $500 per year, and such term includes a volunteer serving as a director, officer, trustee, or direct service volunteer.

MODEL PROTECTION OF CHARITABLE ASSETS ACT (SELECTED PROVISIONS)

Section 3. Authority of [Attorney General] to Protect Charitable Assets.

(a) The [Attorney General] shall represent the public interest in the protection of charitable assets and may:

(1) enforce the application of a charitable asset in accordance with:

(A) the law and terms governing the use, management, investment, distribution, and expenditure of the charitable asset; and

(B) the charitable purpose of the person holding the asset;

(2) act to prevent or remedy:

(A) the misapplication, diversion, or waste of a charitable asset; or

(B) a breach of fiduciary or other legal duty in the governance, management, or administration of a charitable asset; and

(3) commence or intervene in an action to:

(A) prevent, remedy, or obtain damages for the misapplication, diversion, or waste of a charitable asset or for a breach of fiduciary or other legal duty in the governance, management, or administration of a charitable asset;

(B) enforce this [act]; or

(C) determine that an asset is a charitable asset.

(b) If the [Attorney General] has reason to believe an investigation is necessary to determine whether action may be advisable under this [act], the [Attorney General] may conduct an investigation, including exercising administrative subpoena power under [section of the law of the state providing for administrative subpoena power].

(c) This [act] does not limit the powers and duties of the [Attorney General] under law of this state other than this [act].

(d) The [Attorney General] shall promulgate regulations to implement [this act] [Section 4(a) and (e), 5(a), 6, 7(b) and 8.

Section 4. Registration.

(a) The [Attorney General] shall establish and maintain a public registry of persons registered under this section.

* * *

Section 5. Annual Report.

(a) Unless the [Attorney General] grants a waiver under Section 8, a person required to register under Section 4 which holds charitable assets with a value in excess of $[50,000] at the end of the person's most recent annual accounting period or receives charitable assets with a total value that exceeds $[50,000] during the period shall file with the [Attorney General], on or before the later of four months and 15 days after the end of the period or the date authorized for filing an informational return with the Internal Revenue Service, including all extensions, an annual report providing [and verifying][and certifying the accuracy of] the following information:

(1) the name and address of the person;

(2) the name and address of the statutory agent of the person or the individual on whom service of process may be made;

(3) the name and contact information of a responsible individual of the person during the period;

(4) a description of the person's most significant charitable activities, not exceeding three, during the period;

(5) whether during the period the person:

(A) engaged in an event described in Section 6(a) or (b);

(B) entered into a contract, loan, lease, or other financial transaction with an officer, director, trustee, or other fiduciary of the person, or a family member of an officer, director, trustee, or other fiduciary of the person, either directly or with an entity in which the officer, director, trustee, other fiduciary or family member had a material financial interest;

(C) became aware of an embezzlement, theft, or diversion of a charitable asset of the person;

(D) became aware of use of a charitable asset of the person to pay any penalty, fine, or judgment;

(E) became aware of the payment by an officer, director, trustee, or other fiduciary of the person of a penalty, fine, or judgment with respect to the person;

(F) became aware of the use of restricted funds of the person for a purpose other than the charitable purpose specified in the restriction; or

(G) received notice of revocation, modification, or denial of its federal or state charitable [income] tax exemption.

(6) an explanation of an affirmative answer reported under paragraph (5)[.][;][; and]

[(7) the person's total revenue relating to its charitable assets for the period; [and]

(8) the value of the person's charitable assets as of the last day of the period[.][;][; and]

[(9)] a change to any information provided under Section 4 [.][; and]

(10) the name under which the person has registered under [the state's solicitation statute] and the registration number, if any.]

(b) If a person required to file an annual report under subsection (a) is required to file a federal information return with the IRS, the person shall attach to the annual report a copy of the publicly available part of the most recently filed return.

Section 6. Notice to [Attorney General] of Reportable Event.

(a) A person required to register under Section 4 shall give notice in a record to the [Attorney General] not later than [20] days before the occurrence of any of the following proposed events:

(1) dissolution of the person;

(2) termination of the person;

(3) disposition by the person of all or substantially all of the charitable assets of the person;

(4) removal of the person from the jurisdiction of this state;

(5) removal of significant charitable assets of the person from this state; or

(6) any amendment of the record that describes the charitable purpose of the person and the use and administration of charitable assets held by the person.

(b) A person required to register under Section 4 shall give notice in a record to the [Attorney General] not later than [90] days before the proposed consummation of a merger, conversion, or domestication of the person.

(c) A transfer of a charitable asset in connection with an event described in subsection (a) or (b) which occurs earlier than [20] days after delivery of the notice required by subsection (a) or [90] days after delivery of the notice required by subsection (b) is a violation of this [act] unless before the transfer the person receives from the [Attorney General] in a record consent to the proposed event or notice that the [Attorney General] will take no action regarding the event.

(d) If a decedent's estate opened by a court in this state involves, or may involve, the distribution of property to a person holding charitable assets, unless the distribution is a nonresiduary devise with a value of less than $[50,000] to a named person holding charitable assets, the [personal representative] shall deliver to the [Attorney General] not later than [90] days after the date the [personal representative] is appointed:

(1) a copy of the will;

(2) a copy of the [application] [petition] for probate; and

(3) a copy of the inventory or, if none is filed with the court, a statement of the value of the estate.

(e) If a revocable trust becomes irrevocable because of the settlor's death, has its principal place of administration in this state after the settlor's death, and provides for a distribution of property to a person holding charitable assets, unless the distribution is a nonresiduary devise with a value of less than $[50,000] to a named person holding charitable assets, the trustee shall deliver to the [Attorney General] not later than [90] days after the date of the settlor's death:

(1) a description of the charitable interests; and

(2) a statement of the value of the trust assets.

(f) A person required to register under Section 4 shall give notice in a record to the [Attorney General] not later than [20] days after receipt of a notice of revocation, modification, or denial of its federal or state [income] tax exemption.

Section 7. Notice to Attorney General of Action or Proceeding.

(a) This section applies to an action or proceeding in a federal or state court in this state:

(1) by, against or on behalf of a person holding a charitable asset in which the relief sought relates to a gift of a charitable asset;

(2) concerning the use of a charitable asset or a breach of duty or other obligation owed to a person holding a charitable asset;

(3) by, against, or on behalf of a person holding a charitable asset in which the relief sought includes:

(A) instruction, injunction, or declaratory relief relating to the management, use, or distribution of a charitable asset;

(B) construction of a record under which a charitable asset is held;

(C) modification, interpretation, or termination of the terms of a record under which a charitable asset is held;

(D) removal, appointment, or replacement of a trustee of a charitable trust; or

(E) a challenge to the administration of or a distribution from a decedent's estate or a trust in which matters affecting a charitable asset may be decided; and

(4) for bankruptcy under federal law, receivership under [state receivership statute] or a similar receivership statute of another state, or relief in any other insolvency proceeding.

(b) If an action or proceeding to which this section applies is commenced by or brought against a person in this state, the party seeking relief shall give notice in a record to the [Attorney General]. The notice must include a copy of the initial pleading. An order, decree, or judgment rendered in an action in which notice is required by this section is not binding on the [Attorney General] if the notice has not been given.

Section 8. Waiver of Filing.

(a) The [Attorney General] may waive a filing required under Section 4 if a person required to register only by Section 4(b)(3) or (4) is registered in another state under a law that is substantially similar to this [act] and files with the [Attorney General] a copy of the registration filed in the other state.

(b) The [Attorney General] may waive a filing required under Section 5 if a person required to register only by Section 4 files a report pursuant to [insert state solicitation statute or other statute].

INTERNAL REVENUE CODE OF 1986 (SELECTED PROVISIONS)

SUBTITLE A. INCOME TAXES

Chapter 1. Normal Taxes and Surtaxes

Subchapter B. Computation of Taxable Income

Subchapter F. Exempt Organizations

Subchapter J. Estates, Trusts, Beneficiaries, and Decedents

Subchapter C. Political Expenditures of Section 501(c)(3) Organizations

Subchapter D. Failure by Certain Charitable Organizations to Meet Certain Qualification Requirements

Subchapter E. Abatement of First and Second Tier Taxes in Certain Cases

Subchapter F. Tax Shelter Transactions

Subchapter G. Donor Advised Funds

Subchapter H. Excise Tax Based on Investment Income of Private Colleges and Universities

SUBTITLE F. PROCEDURE AND ADMINISTRATION

Chapter 61. Information and Returns

Subchapter A. Returns and Records

SUBTITLE A. INCOME TAXES

Chapter 1. Normal Taxes and Surtaxes

Subchapter B. Computation of Taxable Income

§ 25F. Qualified elementary and secondary education scholarships.

(a) Allowance of credit.—In the case of an individual who is a citizen or resident of the United States (within the meaning of section 7701(a)(9)), there shall be allowed as a credit against the tax imposed by this chapter for the taxable year an amount equal to the aggregate amount of qualified contributions made by the taxpayer during the taxable year.

(b) Limitations.—

(1) In general.—The credit allowed under subsection (a) to any taxpayer for any taxable year shall not exceed $1,700.

(2) Reduction based on State credit.—The amount allowed as a credit under subsection (a) for a taxable year shall be reduced by the amount allowed as a credit on any State tax return of the taxpayer for qualified contributions made by the taxpayer during the taxable year.

(c) Definitions.—For purposes of this section—

(1) Covered state.—The term "covered State" means one of the States, or the District of Columbia, that, for a calendar year, voluntarily elects to participate under this section and to identify scholarship granting organizations in the State, in accordance with subsection (g).

(2) Eligible student.—The term "eligible student" means an individual who—

(A) is a member of a household with an income which, for the calendar year prior to the date of the application for a scholarship, is not greater than 300 percent of the area median gross income (as such term is used in section 42), and

(B) is eligible to enroll in a public elementary or secondary school.

(3) Qualified contribution.—The term "qualified contribution" means a charitable contribution of cash to a scholarship granting organization that uses the contribution to fund scholarships for eligible students solely within the State in which the organization is listed pursuant to subsection (g).

(4) Qualified elementary or secondary education expense.—The term "qualified elementary or secondary education expense" means any expense of an eligible student which is described in section 530(b)(3)(A).

(5) Scholarship granting organization.—The term "scholarship granting organization" means any organization—

(A) which—

(i) is described in section 501(c)(3) and exempt from tax under section 501(a), and

(ii) is not a private foundation,

(B) which prevents the co-mingling of qualified contributions with other amounts by maintaining one or more separate accounts exclusively for qualified contributions,

(C) which satisfies the requirements of subsection (d), and

(D) which is included on the list submitted for the applicable covered State under subsection (g) for the applicable year.

(d) Requirements for scholarship granting organizations.—

(1) In general.—An organization meets the requirements of this subsection if—

(A) such organization provides scholarships to 10 or more students who do not all attend the same school,

(B) such organization spends not less than 90 percent of the income of the organization on scholarships for eligible students,

(C) such organization does not provide scholarships for any expenses other than qualified elementary or secondary education expenses,

(D) such organization provides a scholarship to eligible students with a priority for—

(i) students awarded a scholarship the previous school year, and

(ii) after application of clause (i), any eligible students who have a sibling who was awarded a scholarship from such organization,

(E) such organization does not earmark or set aside contributions for scholarships on behalf of any particular student, and

(F) such organization—

(i) verifies the annual household income and family size of eligible students who apply for scholarships to ensure such students meet the requirement of subsection (c)(2)(A), and

(ii) limits the awarding of scholarships to eligible students who are a member of a household for which the income does not exceed the amount established under subsection (c)(2)(A).

(2) Prohibition on self-dealing.—

(A) In general.—A scholarship granting organization may not award a scholarship to any disqualified person.

(B) Disqualified person.—For purposes of this paragraph, a disqualified person shall be determined pursuant to rules similar to the rules of section 4946.

(e) Denial of double benefit.—Any qualified contribution for which a credit is allowed under this section shall not be taken into account as a charitable contribution for purposes of section 170.

(f) Carryforward of unused credit.—

(1) In general.—If the credit allowable under subsection (a) for any taxable year exceeds the limitation imposed by section 26(a) for such taxable year reduced by the sum of the credits allowable under this subpart (other than this section, section 23, and section 25D), such excess shall be carried to the succeeding taxable year and added to the credit allowable under subsection (a) for such taxable year.

(2) Limitation.—No credit may be carried forward under this subsection to any taxable year following the fifth taxable year after the taxable year in which the credit arose. For purposes of the preceding sentence, credits shall be treated as used on a first-in first-out basis.

(g) State list of scholarship granting organizations.—

(1) List.—

(A) In general.—Not later than January 1 of each calendar year (or, with respect to the first calendar year for which this section applies, as early as practicable), a State that voluntarily elects to participate under this section shall provide to the Secretary a list of the scholarship granting organizations that meet the requirements described in subsection (c)(5) and are located in the State.

(B) Process.—The election under this paragraph shall be made by the Governor of the State or by such other individual, agency, or entity as is designated under State law to make such elections on behalf of the State with respect to Federal tax benefits.

(2) Certification.—Each list submitted under paragraph (1) shall include a certification that the individual, agency, or entity submitting such list on behalf of the State has the authority to perform this function.

(h) Regulations and guidance.—The Secretary shall issue such regulations or other guidance as the Secretary determines necessary to carry out the purposes of this section, including regulations or other guidance—

(1) providing for enforcement of the requirements under subsections (d) and (g), and

(2) with respect to recordkeeping or information reporting for purposes of administering the requirements of this section.

§ 63. Taxable income defined.

(a) In general.—Except as provided in subsection (b), for purposes of this subtitle, the term "taxable income" means gross income minus the deductions allowed by this chapter (other than the standard deduction).

(b) Individuals who do not itemize their deductions.—In the case of an individual who does not elect to itemize his deductions for the taxable year, for purposes of this subtitle, the term "taxable income" means adjusted gross income, minus—

(1) the standard deduction,

(2) the deduction for personal exemptions provided in section 151,

(3) any deduction provided in section 199A, and

(4) the deduction provided in section 170(p).

* * *

§ 68. Overall limitation on itemized deductions.

(a) In general.—In the case of an individual, the amount of the itemized deductions otherwise allowable for the taxable year (determined without regard to this section) shall be reduced by $\frac{2}{37}$ of the lesser of—

(1) such amount of itemized deductions, or

(2) so much of the taxable income of the taxpayer for the taxable year (determined without regard to this section and increased by such amount of itemized deductions) as exceeds the dollar amount at which the 37 percent rate bracket under section 1 begins with respect to the taxpayer.

(b) Coordination with other limitations.—This section shall be applied after the application of any other limitation on the allowance of any itemized deduction.

§ 115. Income of States, municipalities, etc.

Gross income does not include—

(1) income derived from any public utility or the exercise of any essential governmental function and accruing to a State or any political subdivision thereof, or the District of Columbia; or

(2) income accruing to the government of any possession of the United States, or any political subdivision thereof.

§ 145. Qualified 501(c)(3) bond.

(a) In general.—For purposes of this part, except as otherwise provided in this section, the term "qualified 501(c)(3) bond" means any private activity bond issued as part of an issue if—

(1) all property which is to be provided by the net proceeds of the issue is to be owned by a 501(c)(3) organization or a governmental unit, and

(2) such bond would not be a private activity bond if—

(A) 501(c)(3) organizations were treated as governmental units with respect to their activities which do not constitute unrelated trades or businesses, determined by applying section 513(a), and

(B) paragraphs (1) and (2) of section 141(b) were applied by substituting "5 percent" for "10 percent" each place it appears and by substituting "net proceeds" for "proceeds" each place it appears.

(b) $150,000,000 limitation on bonds other than hospital bonds.—

(1) In general.—A bond (other than a qualified hospital bond) shall not be treated as a qualified 501(c)(3) bond if the aggregate authorized face amount of the issue (of which such bond is a part) allocated to any 501(c)(3) organization which is a test-period beneficiary (when increased by the outstanding tax-exempt nonhospital bonds of such organization) exceeds $150,000,000.

(2) Outstanding tax-exempt nonhospital bonds.

(A) In general.—For purposes of applying paragraph (1) with respect to any issue, the outstanding tax-exempt nonhospital bonds of any organization which is a test-period beneficiary with respect to such issue is the aggregate amount of tax-exempt bonds referred to in subparagraph (B)—

(i) which are allocated to such organization, and

(ii) which are outstanding at the time of such later issue (not including as outstanding any bond which is to be redeemed (other than in an advance refunding) from the net proceeds of the later issue).

(B) Bonds taken into account.—For purposes of subparagraph (A), the bonds referred to in this subparagraph are—

(i) any qualified 501(c)(3) bond other than a qualified hospital bond, and

(ii) any bond to which section 141(a) does not apply if—

(I) such bond would have been an industrial development bond (as defined in section 103(b)(2), as in effect on the day before the date of the enactment of the Tax Reform Act of 1986) if 501(c)(3) organizations were not exempt persons, and

(II) such bond was not described in paragraph (4), (5), or (6) of such section 103(b)(as in effect on the date such bond was issued).

(C) Only nonhospital portion of bonds taken into account.

(i) In general.—A bond shall be taken into account under subparagraph (B) only to the extent that the proceeds of the issue of which such bond is a part are not used with respect to a hospital.

(ii) Special rule.—If 90 percent or more of the net proceeds of an issue are used with respect to a hospital, no bond which is part of such issue shall be taken into account under subparagraph (B)(ii).

(3) Aggregation rule.—For purposes of this subsection, 2 or more organizations under common management or control shall be treated as 1 organization.

(4) Allocation of face amount of issue; test-period beneficiary.—Rules similar to the rules of subparagraphs (C), (D), and (E) of section 144(a)(10) shall apply for purposes of this subsection.

(5) Termination of limitation.—This subsection shall not apply with respect to bonds issued after the date of the enactment of this paragraph as part of an issue 95 percent or more of the net proceeds of which are to be used to finance capital expenditures incurred after such date.

(c) Qualified hospital bond.—For purposes of this section, the term "qualified hospital bond" means any bond issued as part of an issue 95 percent or more of the net proceeds of which are to be used with respect to a hospital.

* * *

(e) Election out.—This section shall not apply to an issue if—

(1) the issuer elects not to have this section apply to such issue, and

(2) such issue is an issue of exempt facility bonds, or qualified redevelopment bonds, to which section 146 applies.

§ 162. Trade or business expenses.

* * *

(e) Denial of deduction for certain lobbying and political expenditures.—

(1) In general.—No deduction shall be allowed under subsection (a) for any amount paid or incurred in connection with—

(A) influencing legislation,

(B) participation in, or intervention in, any political campaign on behalf of (or in opposition to) any candidate for public office,

(C) Any attempt to influence the general public, or segments thereof, with respect to elections, legislative matters, or referendums, or

(D) any direct communication with a covered executive branch official in an attempt to influence the official actions or positions of such official.

(2) Application to dues of tax-exempt organizations.—No deduction shall be allowed under subsection (a) for the portion of dues or other similar amounts paid by the taxpayer to an organization which is exempt from tax under this subtitle which the organization notifies the taxpayer under section 6033(e)(1)(A)(ii) is allocable to expenditures to which paragraph (1) applies.

(3) Influencing legislation.—For purposes of this subsection—

(A) In general.—The term 'influencing legislation' means any attempt to influence any legislation through communication with any member or employee of a legislative body, or with any government official or employee who may participate in the formulation of legislation.

(B) Legislation.—The term 'legislation' has the meaning given such term by section 4911(e)(2).

(4) Other special rules.—

(A) Exception for certain taxpayers.—In the case of any taxpayer engaged in the trade or business of conducting activities described in paragraph (1), paragraph (1) shall not apply to expenditures of the taxpayer in conducting such activities directly on behalf of another person (but shall apply to payments by such other person to the taxpayer for conducting such activities).

(B) De minimis exception.—

(i) In general.—Paragraph (1) shall not apply to any in-house expenditures for any taxable year if such expenditures do not exceed $2,000. In determining whether a taxpayer exceeds the $2,000 limit under this clause, there shall not be taken into account overhead costs otherwise allocable to activities described in paragraphs (1)(A) and (D).

(ii) In-house expenditures.—For purposes of clause (i), the term "in-house expenditures" means expenditures described in paragraphs (1)(A) and (D) other than—

(I) payments by the taxpayer to a person engaged in the trade or business of conducting activities described in paragraph (1) for the conduct of such activities on behalf of the taxpayer, or

(II) dues or other similar amounts paid or incurred by the taxpayer which are allocable to activities described in paragraph (1).

(C) Expenses incurred in connection with lobbying and political activities.—Any amount paid or incurred for research for, or preparation, planning, or coordination of, any activity described in paragraph (1) shall be treated as paid or incurred in connection with such activity.

(5) Covered executive branch official.—For purposes of this subsection, the term "covered executive branch official" means—

(A) the President,

(B) the Vice President,

(C) any officer or employee of the White House Office of the Executive Office of the President, and the 2 most senior level officers of each of the other agencies in such Executive Office, and

(D)(i) any individual serving in a position in level I of the Executive Schedule under section 5312 of title 5, United States Code, (ii) any other individual designated by the President as having Cabinet level status, and (iii) any immediate deputy of an individual described in clause (i) or (ii).

(6) Cross reference.—For reporting requirements and alternative taxes related to this subsection, see section 6033(e).

§ 170. Charitable, etc., contributions and gifts.

(a) Allowance of deduction.—

(1) General rule.—There shall be allowed as a deduction any charitable contribution (as defined in subsection (c)) payment of which is made within the taxable year. A charitable contribution shall be allowable as a deduction only if verified under regulations prescribed by the Secretary.

(2) Corporations on an accrual basis.—In the case of a corporation reporting its taxable income on the accrual basis, if—

(A) the board of directors authorizes a charitable contribution during any taxable year, and

(B) payment of such contribution is made after the close of such taxable year and on or before the 15th day of the fourth month following the close of such taxable year,

then the taxpayer may elect to treat such contribution as paid during such taxable year. The election may be made only at the time of the filing of the return for such taxable year, and shall be signified in such manner as the Secretary shall by regulations prescribe.

(3) Future interests in tangible personal property.—For purposes of this section, payment of a charitable contribution which consists of a future interest in tangible personal property shall be treated as made only when all intervening interests in, and rights to the actual possession or enjoyment of, the property have expired or are held by persons other than the taxpayer or those standing in a relationship to the taxpayer described in section 267(b) or 707(b). For purposes of the preceding sentence, a fixture which is intended to be severed from the real property shall be treated as tangible personal property.

(b) Percentage limitations.—

(1) Individuals.—In the case of an individual, the deduction provided in subsection (a) shall be limited as provided in the succeeding subparagraphs.

(A) General rule.—Any charitable contribution to—

(i) a church or a convention or association of churches,

(ii) an educational organization which normally maintains a regular faculty and curriculum and normally has a regularly enrolled body of pupils or students in attendance at the place where its educational activities are regularly carried on,

(iii) an organization the principal purpose or functions of which are the providing of medical or hospital care or medical education or medical research, if the organization is a hospital, or if the organization is a medical research organization directly engaged in the continuous active conduct of medical research in conjunction with a hospital, and during the calendar year in which the contribution is made such organization is committed to spend such contributions for such research before January 1 of the fifth calendar year which begins after the date such contribution is made.

(iv) an organization which normally receives a substantial part of its support (exclusive of income received in the exercise or performance by such organization of its charitable, educational, or other purpose or function constituting the basis for its exemption under section 501(a)) from the United States or any State or political subdivision thereof or from direct or indirect contributions from the general public, and which is organized and operated exclusively to receive, hold, invest, and administer property and to make expenditures to or for the benefit of a college or university which is an organization referred to in clause (ii) of this subparagraph and which is an agency or instrumentality of a State or political subdivision thereof, or which is owned or operated by a State or political subdivision thereof or by an agency or instrumentality of one or more States or political subdivisions,

(v) a governmental unit referred to in subsection (c)(1),

(vi) an organization referred to in subsection (c)(2) which normally receives a substantial part of its support (exclusive of income received in the exercise or performance by such organization of its charitable, educational, or other purpose or function constituting the basis for its exemption under section 501(a)) from a governmental unit referred to in subsection (c)(1) or from direct or indirect contributions from the general public,

(vii) a private foundation described in subparagraph (F),

(viii) an organization described in section 509(a)(2) or (3), or

(ix) an agricultural research organization directly engaged in the continuous active conduct of agricultural research (as defined in section 1404 of the National Agricultural Research, Extension, and Teaching Policy Act of 1977) in conjunction with a land-grant college or university (as defined in such section) or a non-land grant college of agriculture (as defined in such section), and during the calendar year in which the contribution is made such organization is committed to spend such contribution for such research before January 1 of the fifth calendar year which begins after the date such contribution is made,

(x) an organization described in section 501(c)(19) that is a federally chartered corporation,

shall be allowed to the extent that the aggregate of such contributions does not exceed 50 percent of the taxpayer's contribution base for the taxable year.

(B) Other contributions.—Any charitable contribution other than a charitable contribution to which subparagraph (A) or (G) applies shall be allowed to the extent that the aggregate of such contributions does not exceed the lesser of—

(i) 30 percent of the taxpayer's contribution base for the taxable year, or

(ii) the excess of 50 percent of the taxpayer's contribution base for the taxable year over—

(I) the amount of charitable contributions allowable under subparagraph (A) (determined without regard to subparagraph (C)) and subparagraph (G), reduced by

(II) so much of the contributions taken into account under subparagraph (G) as does not exceed 10 percent of the taxpayer's contribution base.

If the aggregate of such contributions exceeds the limitation of the preceding sentence, such excess shall be treated (in a manner consistent with the rules of subsection (d)(1)) as a charitable contribution (to which subparagraph (A) or (G) does not apply) in each of the 5 succeeding taxable years in order of time.

(C) Special limitation with respect to contributions described in subparagraph (A) of certain capital gain property.—

(i) In the case of charitable contributions described in subparagraph (A) of capital gain property to which subsection (e)(1)(B) does not apply, the total amount of contributions of such property which may be taken into account under subsection (a) for any taxable year shall not exceed 30 percent of the taxpayer's contribution base for such year. For purposes of this subsection, contributions of capital gain property to which this subparagraph applies shall be taken into account after all other charitable contributions (other than charitable contributions to which subparagraph (D) applies).

(ii) If charitable contributions described in subparagraph (A) of capital gain property to which clause (i) applies exceeds 30 percent of the taxpayer's contribution base for any taxable year, such excess shall be treated, in a manner consistent with the rules of subsection (d)(1), as a charitable contribution of capital gain property to which clause (i) applies in each of the 5 succeeding taxable years in order of time.

(iii) At the election of the taxpayer (made at such time and in such manner as the Secretary prescribes by regulations), subsection (e)(1) shall apply to all contributions of capital gain property (to which subsection (e)(1)(B) does not otherwise apply) made by the taxpayer during the taxable year. If such an election is made, clauses (i) and (ii) shall not apply to contributions of capital gain property made during the taxable year, and, in applying subsection (d)(1) for such taxable year with respect to contributions of capital gain property made in any prior contribution year for which an election was not made under this clause, such contributions shall be reduced as if subsection (e)(1) had applied to such contributions in the year in which made.

(iv) For purposes of this paragraph, the term "capital gain property" means with respect to any contribution, any capital asset the sale of which at its fair market value at the time of the contribution would have resulted in gain which would have been long-term capital gain. For purposes of the preceding sentence, any property which is property used in the trade or business (as defined in section 1231(b)) shall be treated as a capital asset.

(D) Special limitation with respect to contributions of capital gain property to organizations not described in subparagraph (A).—

(i) In general.—In the case of charitable contributions (other than charitable contributions to which subparagraph (A) applies) of capital gain property, the total amount of such contributions of such property taken into account under subsection (a) for any taxable year shall not exceed the lesser of—

(I) 20 percent of the taxpayer's contribution base for the taxable year, or

(II) the excess of 30 percent of the taxpayer's contribution base for the taxable year over the amount of the contributions of capital gain property to which subparagraph (C) applies.

For purposes of this subsection, contributions of capital gain property to which this subparagraph applies shall be taken into account after all other charitable contributions.

(ii) Carryover.—If the aggregate amount of contributions described in clause (i) exceeds the limitation of clause (i), such excess shall be treated (in a manner consistent with the rules of subsection (d)(1)) as a charitable contribution of capital gain property to which clause (i) applies in each of the 5 succeeding taxable years in order of time.

(E) Contributions of qualified conservation contributions.—

(i) In general.—Any qualified conservation contribution (as defined in subsection (h)(1)) shall be allowed to the extent the aggregate of such contributions does not exceed the excess of 50 percent of the taxpayer's contribution base over the amount of all other charitable contributions allowable under this paragraph.

(ii) Carryover.—If the aggregate amount of contributions described in clause (i) exceeds the limitation of clause (i), such excess shall be treated (in a manner consistent with the rules of subsection (d)(1)) as a charitable contribution to which clause (i) applies in each of the 15 succeeding years in order of time.

(iii) Coordination with other subparagraphs.—For purposes of applying this subsection and subsection (d)(1), contributions described in clause (i) shall not be treated as described in subparagraph (A), (B), (C), or (D) and such subparagraphs shall apply without regard to such contributions.

(iv) Special rule for contribution of property used in agriculture or livestock production.—

(I) In general.—If the individual is a qualified farmer or rancher for the taxable year for which the contribution is made, clause (i) shall be applied by substituting "100 percent" for "50 percent".

(II) Exception.—Subclause (I) shall not apply to any contribution of property made after the date of the enactment of this subparagraph which is used in agriculture or livestock production (or available for such production) unless such contribution is subject to a restriction that such property remain available for such production. This subparagraph shall be applied separately with respect to property to which subclause (I) does not apply by reason of the preceding sentence prior to its application to property to which subclause (I) does apply.

(v) Definition.—For purposes of clause (iv), the term "qualified farmer or rancher" means a taxpayer whose gross income from the trade or business of farming (within the meaning of section 2032A(e)(5)) is greater than 50 percent of the taxpayer's gross income for the taxable year.

(F) Certain private foundations.—The private foundations referred to in subparagraph (A)(vii) and subsection (e)(1)(B) are—

(i) a private operating foundation (as defined in section 4942(j)(3)),

(ii) any other private foundation (as defined in section 509(a)) which, not later than the 15th day of the third month after the close of the foundation's taxable year in which contributions are received, makes qualifying distributions (as defined in section 4942(g), without regard to paragraph (3) thereof), which are treated, after the application of section 4942(g)(3), as distributions out of corpus (in accordance with section 4942(h)) in an amount equal to 100 percent of such contributions, and with respect to which the taxpayer obtains adequate records or other sufficient evidence from the foundation showing that the foundation made such qualifying distributions, and

(iii) a private foundation all of the contributions to which are pooled in a common fund and which would be described in section 509(a)(3) but for the right of any substantial contributor (hereafter in this clause called "donor") or his spouse to designate annually the recipients, from among organizations described in paragraph (1) of section 509(a), of the income attributable to the donor's contribution to the fund and to direct (by deed or by will) the payment, to an organization described in such paragraph (1), of the corpus in the common fund attributable to the donor's contribution; but this clause shall apply only if all of the income of the common fund is required to be (and is) distributed to one or more organizations described in such paragraph (1) not later than the 15th day of the third month after the close of the taxable year in which the income is realized by the fund and only if all of the corpus attributable to any donor's contribution to the fund is required to be (and is) distributed to one or more of such organizations not later than one year after his death or after the death of his surviving spouse if she has the right to designate the recipients of such corpus.

(G) Increased limitation for cash contributions.—

(i) In general.—For taxable years beginning after December 31, 2017, any contribution of cash to an organization described in subparagraph (A) shall be allowed as a deduction under subsection (a) to the extent that the aggregate of such contributions does not exceed the excess of—

(I) 60 percent of the taxpayer's contribution base for the taxable year, over

(II) the aggregate amount of contributions taken into account under subparagraph (A) for such taxable year.

(ii) Carryover.—If the aggregate amount of contributions described in clause (i) exceeds the applicable limitation under clause (i) for any taxable year described in such clause, such excess shall be treated (in a manner consistent with the rules of subsection (d)(1)) as a charitable contribution to which clause (i) applies in each of the 5 succeeding years in order of time.

(iii) Coordination with subparagraph (A).

(I) In general.—Contributions taken into account under this subparagraph shall not be taken into account under subparagraph (A).

(II) Limitation reduction.—For each taxable year described in clause (i), and each taxable year to which any contribution under this subparagraph is carried over under clause (ii), subparagraph (A) shall be applied by reducing (but not below zero) the contribution limitation allowed for the taxable year under such subparagraph by the aggregate contributions allowed under this subparagraph for such taxable year.

(H) Contribution base defined.—For purposes of this section, the term "contribution base" means adjusted gross income (computed without regard to any net operating loss carryback to the taxable year under section 172).

(I) 0.5-percent floor.—Any charitable contribution otherwise allowable (without regard to this subparagraph) as a deduction under this section shall be allowed only to the extent that the aggregate of such contributions exceeds 0.5 percent of the taxpayer's contribution base for the taxable year. The preceding sentence shall be applied—

(i) first, by taking into account charitable contributions to which subparagraph (D) applies to the extent thereof,

(ii) second, by taking into account charitable contributions to which subparagraph (C) applies to the extent thereof,

(iii) third, by taking into account charitable contributions to which subparagraph (B) applies to the extent thereof,

(iv) fourth, by taking into account charitable contributions to which subparagraph (E) applies to the extent thereof,

(v) fifth, by taking into account charitable contributions to which subparagraph (A) applies to the extent thereof, and

(vi) sixth, by taking into account charitable contributions to which subparagraph (G) applies to the extent thereof.

(2) Corporations.—In the case of a corporation—

(A) In general.—Any charitable contribution otherwise allowable (without regard to this subparagraph) as a deduction under this section for any taxable year, other than any contribution to which subparagraph (B) or (C) applies, shall be allowed only to the extent that the aggregate of such contributions—

(i) exceeds 1 percent of the taxpayer's taxable income for the taxable year, and

(ii) does not exceed 10 percent of the taxpayer's taxable income for the taxable year.

(B) Qualified conservation contributions by certain corporate farmers and ranchers.—

(i) In general.—Any qualified conservation contribution (as defined in subsection (h)(1))—

(I) which is made by a corporation which, for the taxable year during which the contribution is made, is a qualified farmer or rancher (as defined in paragraph (1)(E)(v)) and the stock of which is not readily tradable on an established securities market at any time during such year, and

(II) which, in the case of contributions made after the date of the enactment of this subparagraph, is a contribution of property which is used in agriculture or livestock production (or available for such production) and which is subject to a restriction that such property remain available for such production,

shall be allowed to the extent the aggregate of such contributions does not exceed the excess of the taxpayer's taxable income over the amount of charitable contributions allowable under subparagraph (A).

(ii) Carryover.—If the aggregate amount of contributions described in clause (i) exceeds the limitation of clause (i), such excess shall be treated (in a manner consistent with the rules of subsection (d)(2) other than subparagraph (C) thereof) as a charitable contribution to which clause (i) applies in each of the 15 succeeding taxable years in order of time.

* * *

(D) Taxable income.—For purposes of this paragraph, taxable income shall be computed without regard to—

(i) this section,

(ii) part VIII (except section 248),

(iii) any net operating loss carryback to the taxable year under section 172,

(iv) any capital loss carryback to the taxable year under section 1212(a)(1),

(v) section 199A(g).

(c) Charitable contribution defined.—For purposes of this section, the term "charitable contribution" means a contribution or gift to or for the use of—

(1) A State, a possession of the United States, or any political subdivision of any of the foregoing, or the United States or the District of Columbia, but only if the contribution or gift is made for exclusively public purposes.

(2) A corporation, trust, or community chest, fund, or foundation—

(A) created or organized in the United States or in any possession thereof, or under the law of the United States, any State, the District of Columbia, or any possession of the United States;

(B) organized and operated exclusively for religious, charitable, scientific, literary, or educational purposes, or to foster national or international amateur sports competition (but only if no part of its activities involve the provision of athletic facilities or equipment), or for the prevention of cruelty to children or animals;

(C) no part of the net earnings of which inures to the benefit of any private shareholder or individual; and

(D) which is not disqualified for tax exemption under section 501(c)(3) by reason of attempting to influence legislation, and which does not participate in, or intervene in (including the publishing or distributing of statements), any political campaign on behalf of (or in opposition to) any candidate for public office.

A contribution or gift by a corporation to a trust, chest, fund, or foundation shall be deductible by reason of this paragraph only if it is to be used within the United States or any of its possessions exclusively for purposes specified in subparagraph (B). Rules similar to the rules of section 501(j) shall apply for purposes of this paragraph.

(3) A post or organization of war veterans, or an auxiliary unit or society of, or trust or foundation for, any such post or organization—

(A) organized in the United States or any of its possessions, and

(B) no part of the net earnings of which inures to the benefit of any private shareholder or individual.

(4) In the case of a contribution or gift by an individual, a domestic fraternal society, order, or association, operating under the lodge system, but only if such contribution or gift is to be used exclusively for religious, charitable, scientific, literary, or educational purposes, or for the prevention of cruelty to children or animals.

(5) A cemetery company owned and operated exclusively for the benefit of its members, or any corporation chartered solely for burial purposes as a cemetery corporation and not permitted by its charter to engage in any business not necessarily incident to that purpose, if such company or corporation is not operated for profit and no part of the net earnings of such company or corporation inures to the benefit of any private shareholder or individual.

(6) An organization described in section 501(c)(19) that is a federally chartered corporation.

For purposes of this section, the term "charitable contribution" also means an amount treated under subsection (g) as paid for the use of an organization described in paragraph (2), (3), or (4).

(d) Carryovers of excess contributions.—

(1) Individuals.—

(A) In general.—In the case of an individual, if the amount of charitable contributions described in subsection (b)(1)(A) payment of which is made within a taxable year (hereinafter in this paragraph referred to as the "contribution year") exceeds 50 percent of the taxpayer's contribution base for such year, such excess shall be treated as a charitable contribution described in subsection (b)(1)(A) paid in each of the 5 succeeding taxable years in order of time, but, with respect to any such succeeding taxable year, only to the extent of the lesser of the two following amounts:

(i) the amount by which 50 percent of the taxpayer's contribution base for such succeeding taxable year exceeds the sum of the charitable contributions described in subsection (b)(1)(A) payment of which is made by the taxpayer within such succeeding taxable year (determined without regard to this subparagraph) and the charitable contributions described in subsection (b)(1)(A) payment of which was made in taxable years before the contribution year which are treated under this subparagraph as having been paid in such succeeding taxable year; or

(ii) in the case of the first succeeding taxable year, the amount of such excess, and in the case of the second, third, fourth, or fifth succeeding taxable year, the portion of such excess not treated under this subparagraph as a charitable contribution described in subsection(b)(1)(A) paid in any taxable year intervening between the contribution year and such succeeding taxable year.

(B) Special rule for net operating loss carryovers.—In applying subparagraph (A), the excess determined under subparagraph (A) for the contribution year shall be reduced to the extent that such excess reduces taxable income (as computed for purposes of the second sentence of section 172(b)(2)) and increases the net operating loss deduction for a taxable year succeeding the contribution year.

(C) Contributions disallowed by 0.5-percent floor carried forward only from years in which limitation is exceeded.—

(i) In general.—In the case of any taxable year from which an excess is carried forward (determined without regard to this subparagraph) under any carryover rule, the applicable carryover rule shall be applied by increasing the excess determined under such applicable carryover rule for the contribution year (before the application of subparagraph (B)) by the amount attributable to the charitable contributions to which such rule applies which is not allowed as a deduction for the contribution year by reason of subsection (b)(1)(I).

(ii) Carryover rule.—For purposes of this subparagraph, the term "carryover rule" means—

(I) subparagraph (A) of this paragraph,

(II) subparagraphs (C)(ii), (D)(ii), (E)(ii), and (G)(ii) of subsection (b)(1), and

(III) the second sentence of subsection (b)(1)(B).

(iii) Applicable carryover rule.—For purposes of this subparagraph, the term "applicable carryover rule" means any carryover rule applicable to charitable contributions which were (in whole or in part) not allowed as a deduction for the contribution year by reason of subsection (b)(1)(I).

(2) Corporations.—

(A) In general.—Any charitable contribution taken into account under subsection (b)(2)(A) for any taxable year which is not allowed as a deduction by reason of clause (ii) thereof shall be taken into account as a charitable contribution for the succeeding taxable year, except that, for purposes of determining under this subparagraph whether such contribution is allowed in such succeeding taxable year, contributions in such succeeding taxable year (determined without regard to this paragraph) shall be taken into account under subsection (b)(2)(A) before any contribution taken into account by reason of this paragraph.

(B) 5-year carryforward.—No charitable contribution may be carried forward under subparagraph (A) to any taxable year following the fifth taxable year after the taxable year in which the charitable contribution was first taken into account. For purposes of the preceding sentence, contributions shall be treated as allowed on a first-in first-out basis.

(C) Contributions disallowed by 1-percent floor carried forward only from years in which 10 percent limitation is exceeded.—In the case of any taxable year from which a charitable contribution is carried forward under subparagraph (A) (determined without regard this subparagraph), subparagraph (A) shall be applied by substituting "clause (i) or (ii)" for "clause (ii)".

(D) Special rule for net operating loss carryovers.—The amount of charitable contributions carried forward under subparagraph (A) shall be reduced to the extent that such carryforward would (but for this subparagraph) reduce taxable income (as computed for purposes of the second sentence of section 172(b)(2)) and increase a net operating loss carryover under section 172 to a succeeding taxable year.

(e) Certain contributions of ordinary income and capital gain property.—

(1) General rule.—The amount of any charitable contribution of property otherwise taken into account under this section shall be reduced by the sum of—

(A) the amount of gain which would not have been long-term capital gain (determined without regard to section 1221(b)(3)) if the property contributed had been sold by the taxpayer at its fair market value (determined at the time of such contribution), and

(B) in the case of a charitable contribution—

(i) of tangible personal property—

(I) if the use by the donee is unrelated to the purpose or function constituting the basis for its exemption under section 501 (or, in the case of a governmental unit, to any purpose or function described in subsection (c)), or

(II) which is applicable property (as defined in paragraph (7)(C)) which is sold, exchanged, or otherwise disposed of by the donee before the last day of the taxable year in which the contribution was made and with respect to which the donee has not made a certification in accordance with paragraph (7)(D),

(ii) to or for the use of a private foundation (as defined in section 509(a)), other than a private foundation described in subsection (b)(1)(E),

(iii) of any patent, copyright (other than a copyright described in section 1221(a)(3) or 1231(b)(1)(C)), trademark, trade name, trade secret, know-how, software (other than software described in section 197(e)(3)(A)(i)), or similar property, or applications or registrations of such property, or

(iv) of any taxidermy property which is contributed by the person who prepared, stuffed, or mounted the property or by any person who paid or incurred the cost of such preparation, stuffing, or mounting,

the amount of gain which would have been long-term capital gain if the property contributed had been sold by the taxpayer at its fair market value (determined at the time of such contribution). For purposes of applying this paragraph (other than in the case of gain to which section 617(d)(1), 1245(a), 1250(a), 1252(a) or 1254(a) applies), property which is property used in the trade or business (as defined in section 1231(b)) shall be treated as a capital asset. For purposes of applying this paragraph in the case of a charitable contribution of stock in an S corporation, rules similar to the rules of Section 751 shall apply in determining whether gain on such stock would have been long-term capital gain if such stock were sold by the taxpayer.

(2) Allocation of basis.—For purposes of paragraph (1), in the case of a charitable contribution of less than the taxpayer's entire interest in the property contributed, the taxpayer's adjusted basis in such property shall be allocated between the interest contributed and any interest not contributed in accordance with regulations prescribed by the Secretary.

(3) Special rule for certain contributions of inventory and other property.—

(A) Qualified contributions.—For purposes of this paragraph, a qualified contribution shall mean a charitable contribution of property described in paragraph (1) or (2) of section 1221(a), by a corporation (other than a corporation which is an S corporation) to an organization which is described in section 501(c)(3) and is exempt under section 501(a) (other than a private foundation, as defined in section 509(a), which is not an operating foundation, as defined in section 4942(j)(3)), but only if—

(i) the use of the property by the donee is related to the purpose or function constituting the basis for its exemption under section 501 and the property is to be used by the donee solely for the care of the ill, the needy, or infants;

(ii) the property is not transferred by the donee in exchange for money, other property, or services;

(iii) the taxpayer receives from the donee a written statement representing that its use and disposition of the property will be in accordance with the provisions of clauses (i) and (ii); and

(iv) in the case where the property is subject to regulation under the Federal Food, Drug, and Cosmetic Act, as amended, such property must fully satisfy the applicable requirements of such Act and regulations promulgated thereunder on the date of transfer and for one hundred and eighty days prior thereto.

(B) Amount of reduction.—The reduction under paragraph (1)(A) for any qualified contribution (as defined in subparagraph (A)) shall be no greater than the sum of—

(i) one-half of the amount computed under paragraph (1)(A) (computed without regard to this paragraph), and

(ii) the amount (if any) by which the charitable contribution deduction under this section for any qualified contribution (computed by taking into account the amount determined in clause (i), but without regard to this clause) exceeds twice the basis of such property.

(C) Special rule for contributions of food inventory.—

(i) General rule.—In the case of a charitable contribution of food from any trade or business of the taxpayer, this paragraph shall be applied—

(I) without regard to whether the contribution is made by a C corporation, and

(II) only to food that is apparently wholesome food.

(ii) Limitation.—The aggregate amount of such contributions for any taxable year which may be taken into account under this section shall not exceed—

(I) in the case of any taxpayer other than a C corporation, 15 percent of the taxpayer's aggregate net income for such taxable year from all trades or businesses from which such contributions were made for such year, computed without regard to this section, and

(II) in the case of a C corporation, 15 percent of taxable income (as defined in subsection (b)(2)(D)).

(iii) Rules related to limitation.—

(I) Carryover.—If such aggregate amount exceeds the limitation imposed under clause (ii), such excess shall be treated (in a manner consistent with the rules of subsection (d)) as a charitable contribution described in clause (i) in each of the 5 succeeding taxable years in order of time.

(II) Coordination with overall corporate limitation.—In the case of any charitable contribution which is allowable after the application of clause (ii)(II), subsection (b)(2)(A) shall not apply to such contribution, but the limitation imposed by such subsection shall be reduced (but not below zero) by the aggregate amount of such contributions. For purposes of subsection (b)(2)(B), such contributions shall be treated as allowable under subsection (b)(2)(A).

(iv) Determination of basis for certain taxpayers.—If a taxpayer—

(I) does not account for inventories under section 471, and

(II) is not required to capitalize indirect costs under section 263A,

the taxpayer may elect, solely for purposes of subparagraph (B), to treat the basis of any apparently wholesome food as being equal to 25 percent of the fair market value of such food.

(v) Determination of fair market value.—In the case of any such contribution of apparently wholesome food which cannot or will not be sold solely by reason of internal standards of the taxpayer, lack of market, or similar circumstances, or by reason of being produced by the taxpayer exclusively for the purposes of transferring the food to an organization described in subparagraph (A), the fair market value of such contribution shall be determined—

(I) without regard to such internal standards, such lack of market, such circumstances, or such exclusive purpose, and

(II) by taking into account the price at which the same or substantially the same food items (as to both type and quality) are sold by the taxpayer at the time of the contribution (or, if not so sold at such time, in the recent past).

(vi) Apparently wholesome food.—For purposes of this subparagraph, the term "apparently wholesome food" has the meaning given to such term by section 22(b)(2) of the Bill Emerson Good Samaritan Food Donation Act (42 U.S.C. 1791(b)(2)), as in effect on the date of the enactment of this subparagraph.

* * *

(E) This paragraph shall not apply to so much of the amount of the gain described in paragraph (1)(A) which would be long-term capital gain but for the application of sections 617, 1245, 1250, or 1252.

(4) Special rule for contributions of scientific property used for research.—

(A) Limit on reduction.—In the case of a qualified research contribution, the reduction under paragraph (1)(A) shall be no greater than the amount determined under paragraph (3)(B).

(B) Qualified research contributions.—For purposes of this paragraph, the term "qualified research contribution" means a charitable contribution by a corporation of tangible personal property described in paragraph (1) of section 1221(a), but only if—

(i) the contribution is to an organization described in subparagraph (A) or subparagraph (B) of section 41(e)(6),

(ii) the property is constructed or assembled by the taxpayer,

(iii) the contribution is made not later than 2 years after the date the construction or assembly of the property is substantially completed,

(iv) the original use of the property is by the donee,

(v) the property is scientific equipment or apparatus substantially all of the use of which by the donee is for research or experimentation (within the meaning of section 174), or for research training, in the United States in physical or biological sciences,

(vi) the property is not transferred by the donee in exchange for money, other property, or services, and

(vii) the taxpayer receives from the donee a written statement representing that its use and disposition of the property will be in accordance with the provisions of clauses (v) and (vi).

(C) Construction of property by taxpayer.—For purposes of this paragraph, property shall be treated as constructed by the taxpayer only if the cost of the parts used in the construction of such property (other than parts manufactured by the taxpayer or a related person) do not exceed 50 percent of the taxpayer's basis in such property.

(D) Corporation.—For purposes of this paragraph, the term "corporation" shall not include—

(i) an S corporation,

(ii) a personal holding company (as defined in section 542), and

(iii) a service organization (as defined in section 414(m)(3)).

(5) Special rule for contributions of stock for which market quotations are readily available.—

(A) In general.—Subparagraph (B)(ii) of paragraph (1) shall not apply to any contribution of qualified appreciated stock.

(B) Qualified appreciated stock.—Except as provided in subparagraph (C), for purposes of this paragraph, the term "qualified appreciated stock" means any stock of a corporation—

(i) for which (as of the date of the contribution) market quotations are readily available on an established securities market, and

(ii) which is capital gain property (as defined in subsection (b)(1)(C)(iv)).

(C) Donor may not contribute more than 10 percent of stock of corporation.—

(i) In general.—In the case of any donor, the term "qualified appreciated stock" shall not include any stock of a corporation contributed by the donor in a contribution to which paragraph (1)(B)(ii) applies (determined without regard to this paragraph) to the extent that the amount of the stock so contributed (when increased by the aggregate amount of all prior such contributions by the donor of stock in such corporation) exceeds 10 percent (in value) of all of the outstanding stock of such corporation.

(ii) Special rule.—For purposes of clause (i), an individual shall be treated as making all contributions made by any member of his family (as defined in section 267(c)(4)).

* * *

(7) Recapture of deduction on certain dispositions of exempt use property.—

(A) In general.—In the case of an applicable disposition of applicable property, there shall be included in the income of the donor of such property for the taxable year of such donor in which the applicable disposition occurs an amount equal to the excess (if any) of—

(i) the amount of the deduction allowed to the donor under this section with respect to such property, over

(ii) the donor's basis in such property at the time such property was contributed.

(B) Applicable disposition.—For purposes of this paragraph, the term "applicable disposition" means any sale, exchange, or other disposition by the donee of applicable property—

(i) after the last day of the taxable year of the donor in which such property was contributed, and

(ii) before the last day of the 3-year period beginning on the date of the contribution of such property,

unless the donee makes a certification in accordance with subparagraph (D).

(C) Applicable property.—For purposes of this paragraph, the term "applicable property" means charitable deduction property (as defined in section 6050L(a)(2)(A))—

(i) which is tangible personal property the use of which is identified by the donee as related to the purpose or function constituting the basis of the donee's exemption under section 501, and

(ii) for which a deduction in excess of the donor's basis is allowed.

(D) Certification.—A certification meets the requirements of this subparagraph if it is a written statement which is signed under penalty of perjury by an officer of the donee organization and—

(i) which—

(I) certifies that the use of the property by the donee was substantial and related to the purpose or function constituting the basis for the donee's exemption under section 501, and

(II) describes how the property was used and how such use furthered such purpose or function, or

(ii) which—

(I) states the intended use of the property by the donee at the time of the contribution, and

(II) certifies that such intended use has become impossible or infeasible to implement.

(f) Disallowance of deduction in certain cases and special rules.—

(1) In general.—No deduction shall be allowed under this section for a contribution to or for the use of an organization or trust described in section 508(d) or 4948(c)(4) subject to the conditions specified in such sections.

(2) Contributions of property placed in trust.—

(A) Remainder interest.—In the case of property transferred in trust, no deduction shall be allowed under this section for the value of a contribution of a remainder interest unless the trust is a charitable remainder annuity trustor a charitable remainder unitrust (described in section 664), or a pooled income fund (described in section 642(c)(5)).

(B) Income interests, etc.—No deduction shall be allowed under this section for the value of any interest in property (other than a remainder interest) transferred in trust unless the interest is in the form of a guaranteed annuity or the trust instrument specifies that the interest is a fixed percentage distributed yearly of the fair market value of the trust property (to be determined yearly) and the grantor is treated as the owner of such interest for purposes of applying section 671. If the donor ceases to be treated as the owner of such an interest for purposes of applying section 671, at the time the donor ceases to be so treated, the donor shall for purposes of this chapter be considered as having received an amount of income equal to the amount of any deduction he received under this section for the contribution reduced by the discounted value of all amounts of income earned by the trust and taxable to him before the time at which he ceases to be treated as the owner of the interest. Such amounts of income shall be discounted to the date of the contribution. The Secretary shall prescribe such regulations as may be necessary to carry out the purposes of this subparagraph.

(C) Denial of deduction in case of payments in certain trusts.—In any case in which a deduction is allowed under this section for the value of an interest in property described in subparagraph (B), transferred in trust, no deduction shall be allowed under this section to the grantor or any other person for the amount of any contribution made by the trust with respect to such interest.

(D) Exception.—This paragraph shall not apply in a case in which the value of all interests in property transferred in trust are deductible under subsection (a).

(3) Denial of deduction in case of certain contributions of partial interests in property.—

(A) In general.—In the case of a contribution (not made by a transfer in trust) of an interest in property which consists of less than the taxpayer's entire interest in such property, a deduction shall be allowed under this section only to the extent that the value of the interest contributed would be allowable as a deduction under this section if such interest had been transferred in trust. For purposes of this subparagraph, a contribution by a taxpayer of the right to use property shall be treated as a contribution of less than the taxpayer's entire interest in such property.

(B) Exceptions.—Subparagraph (A) shall not apply to—

(i) a contribution of a remainder interest in a personal residence or farm,

(ii) a contribution of an undivided portion of the taxpayer's entire interest in property, and

(iii) a qualified conservation contribution.

(4) Valuation of remainder interests in real property.—For purposes of this section, in determining the value of a remainder interest in real property, depreciation (computed on the straight line method) and depletion of such property shall be taken into account, and such value shall be discounted at a rate of 6 percent per annum, except that the Secretary may prescribe a different rate.

(5) Reduction for certain interest.—If, in connection with any charitable contribution, a liability is assumed by the recipient or by any other person, or if a charitable contribution is of property which is subject to a liability, then, to the extent necessary to avoid the duplication of amounts, the amount taken into account for purposes of this section as the amount of the charitable contribution—

(A) shall be reduced for interest (i) which has been paid (or is to be paid) by the taxpayer, (ii) which is attributable to the liability, and (iii) which is attributable to any period after the making of the contribution, and

(B) in the case of a bond, shall be further reduced for interest (i) which has been paid (or is to be paid) by the taxpayer on indebtedness incurred or continued to purchase or carry such bond, and (ii) which is attributable to any period before the making of the contribution.

The reduction pursuant to subparagraph (B) shall not exceed the interest (including interest equivalent) on the bond which is attributable to any period before the making of the contribution and which is not (under the taxpayer's method of accounting) includible in the gross income of the taxpayer for any taxable year. For purposes of this paragraph, the term "bond" means any bond, debenture, note, or certificate or other evidence of indebtedness.

(6) Deductions for out-of-pocket expenditures.—No deduction shall be allowed under this section for an out-of-pocket expenditure made by any person on behalf of an organization described in subsection (c) (other than an organization described in section 501(h)(5) (relating to churches, etc.)) if the expenditure is made for the purpose of influencing legislation (within the meaning of section 501(c)(3)).

(7) Reformations to comply with paragraph (2).—

(A) In general.—A deduction shall be allowed under subsection (a) in respect of any qualified reformation (within the meaning of section 2055(e)(3)(B)).

(B) Rules similar to section 2055(e)(3) to apply.—For purposes of this paragraph, rules similar to the rules of section 2055(e)(3) shall apply.

(8) Substantiation requirement for certain contributions.—

(A) General rule.—No deduction shall be allowed under subsection (a) for any contribution of $250 or more unless the taxpayer substantiates the contribution by a contemporaneous written acknowledgment of the contribution by the donee organization that meets the requirements of subparagraph (B).

(B) Content of acknowledgement.—An acknowledgement meets the requirements of this subparagraph if it includes the following information:

(i) The amount of cash and a description (but not value) of any property other than cash contributed.

(ii) Whether the donee organization provided any goods or services in consideration, in whole or in part, for any property described in clause (i).

(iii) A description and good faith estimate of the value of any goods or services referred to in clause (ii) or, if such goods or services consist solely of intangible religious benefits, a statement to that effect.

For purposes of this subparagraph, the term 'intangible religious benefit' means any intangible religious benefit which is provided by an organization organized exclusively for religious purposes and which generally is not sold in a commercial transaction outside the donative context.

(C) Contemporaneous.—For purposes of subparagraph (A), an acknowledgment shall be considered to be contemporaneous if the taxpayer obtains the acknowledgment on or before the earlier of—

(i) the date on which the taxpayer files a return for the taxable year in which the contribution was made, or

(ii) the due date (including extensions) for filing such return.

(D) Regulations.—The Secretary shall prescribe such regulations as may be necessary or appropriate to carry out the purposes of this paragraph, including regulations that may provide that some or all of the requirements of this paragraph do not apply in appropriate cases.

(9) Denial of deduction where contribution for lobbying activities.—No deduction shall be allowed under this section for a contribution to an organization which conducts activities to which section 162(e)(1) applies on matters of direct financial interest to the donor's trade or business, if a principal purpose of the contribution was to avoid Federal income tax by securing a deduction for such activities under this section which would be disallowed by reason of section 162(e) if the donor had conducted such activities directly. No deduction shall be allowed under section 162(a) for any amount for which a deduction is disallowed under the preceding sentence.

* * *

(11) Qualified appraisal and other documentation for certain contributions.—

(A) In general.—

(i) Denial of deduction.—In the case of an individual, partnership, or corporation, no deduction shall be allowed under subsection (a) for any contribution of property for which a deduction of more than $500 is claimed unless such person meets the requirements of subparagraphs (B), (C), and (D), as the case may be, with respect to such contribution.

(ii) Exceptions.—

(I) Readily valued property.—Subparagraphs (C) and (D) shall not apply to cash, property described in subsection (e)(1)(B)(iii) or section 1221(a)(1), publicly traded securities (as defined in section 6050L(a)(2)(B)), and any qualified vehicle described in paragraph (12)(A)(ii) for which an acknowledgement under paragraph (12)(B)(iii) is provided.

(II) Reasonable cause.—Clause (i) shall not apply if it is shown that the failure to meet such requirements is due to reasonable cause and not to willful neglect.

(B) Property description for contributions of more than $500—In the case of contributions of property for which a deduction of more than $500 is claimed, the requirements of this subparagraph are met if the individual, partnership or corporation includes with the return for the taxable year in which the contribution is made a description of such property and such other information as the Secretary may require. The requirements of this subparagraph shall not apply to a C corporation which is not a personal service corporation or a closely held C corporation.

(C) Qualified appraisal for contributions of more than $5,000—In the case of contributions of property for which a deduction of more than $5,000 is claimed, the requirements of this subparagraph are met if the individual, partnership, or corporation obtains a qualified appraisal of such property and attaches to the return for the taxable year in which such contribution is made such information regarding such property and such appraisal as the Secretary may require.

(D) Substantiation for contributions of more than $500,000.—In the case of contributions of property for which a deduction of more than $500,000 is claimed, the requirements of this subparagraph are met if the individual, partnership, or corporation attaches to the return for the taxable year a qualified appraisal of such property.

(E) Qualified appraisal and appraiser.—For purposes of this paragraph—

(i) Qualified appraisal.—The term "qualified appraisal" means, with respect to any property, an appraisal of such property which—

(I) is treated for purposes of this paragraph as a qualified appraisal under regulations or other guidance prescribed by the Secretary, and

(II) is conducted by a qualified appraiser in accordance with generally accepted appraisal standards and any regulations or other guidance prescribed under subclause (I).

(ii) Qualified appraiser.—Except as provided in clause (iii), the term "qualified appraiser" means an individual who—

(I) has earned an appraisal designation from a recognized professional appraiser organization or has otherwise met minimum education and experience requirements set forth in regulations prescribed by the Secretary,

(II) regularly performs appraisals for which the individual receives compensation, and

(III) meets such other requirements as may be prescribed by the Secretary in regulations or other guidance.

(iii) Specific appraisals.—An individual shall not be treated as a qualified appraiser with respect to any specific appraisal unless—

(I) the individual demonstrates verifiable education and experience in valuing the type of property subject to the appraisal, and

(II) the individual has not been prohibited from practicing before the Internal Revenue Service by the Secretary under section 330(c) of title 31, United States Code, at any time during the 3-year period ending on the date of the appraisal.

(F) Aggregation of similar items of property.—For purposes of determining thresholds under this paragraph, property and all similar items of property donated to 1 or more donees shall be treated as 1 property.

(G) Special rule for pass-thru entities.—In the case of a partnership or S corporation, this paragraph shall be applied at the entity level, except that the deduction shall be denied at the partner or shareholder level.

(H) Regulations.—The Secretary may prescribe such regulations as may be necessary or appropriate to carry out the purposes of this paragraph, including regulations that may provide that some or all of the requirements of this paragraph do not apply in appropriate cases.

(12) Contributions of used motor vehicles, boats, and airplanes.—

(A) In general.—In the case of a contribution of a qualified vehicle the claimed value of which exceeds $500—

(i) paragraph (8) shall not apply and no deduction shall be allowed under subsection (a) for such contribution unless the taxpayer substantiates the contribution by a contemporaneous written acknowledgement of the contribution by the donee organization that meets the requirements of subparagraph (B) and includes the acknowledgement with the taxpayer's return of tax which includes the deduction, and

(ii) if the organization sells the vehicle without any significant intervening use or material improvement of such vehicle by the organization, the amount of the deduction allowed under subsection (a) shall not exceed the gross proceeds received from such sale.

(B) Content of acknowledgement.—An acknowledgement meets the requirements of this subparagraph if it includes the following information:

(i) The name and taxpayer identification number of the donor.

(ii) The vehicle identification number or similar number.

(iii) In the case of a qualified vehicle to which subparagraph (A)(ii) applies—

(I) a certification that the vehicle was sold in an arm's length transaction between unrelated parties,

(II) the gross proceeds from the sale, and

(III) a statement that the deductible amount may not exceed the amount of such gross proceeds.

(iv) In the case of a qualified vehicle to which subparagraph (A)(ii) does not apply—

(I) a certification of the intended use or material improvement of the vehicle and the intended duration of such use, and

(II) a certification that the vehicle would not be transferred in exchange for money, other property, or services before completion of such use or improvement.

(v) Whether the donee organization provided any goods or services in consideration, in whole or in part, for the qualified vehicle.

(vi) A description and good faith estimate of the value of any goods or services referred to in clause (v) or, if such goods or services consist solely of intangible religious benefits (as defined in paragraph (8)(B)), a statement to that effect.

(C) Contemporaneous.—For purposes of subparagraph (A), an acknowledgement shall be considered to be contemporaneous if the donee organization provides it within 30 days of—

(i) the sale of the qualified vehicle, or

(ii) in the case of an acknowledgement including a certification described in subparagraph (B)(iv), the contribution of the qualified vehicle.

(D) Information to Secretary.—A donee organization required to provide an acknowledgement under this paragraph shall provide to the Secretary the information contained in the acknowledgement. Such information shall be provided at such time and in such manner as the Secretary may prescribe.

(E) Qualified vehicle.—For purposes of this paragraph, the term "qualified vehicle" means any—

(i) motor vehicle manufactured primarily for use on public streets, roads, and highways,

(ii) boat, or

(iii) airplane.

Such term shall not include any property which is described in section 1221(a)(1).

(F) Regulations or other guidance.—The Secretary shall prescribe such regulations or other guidance as may be necessary to carry out the purposes of this paragraph. The Secretary may prescribe regulations or other guidance which exempts sales by the donee organization which are in direct furtherance of such organization's charitable purpose from the requirements of subparagraphs (A)(ii) and (B)(iv)(II).

(13) Contributions of certain interests in buildings located in registered historic districts.—

(A) In general.—No deduction shall be allowed with respect to any contribution described in subparagraph (B) unless the taxpayer includes with the return for the taxable year of the contribution a $500 filing fee.

(B) Contribution described.—A contribution is described in this subparagraph if such contribution is a qualified conservation contribution (as defined in subsection (h)) which is a restriction with respect to the exterior of a building described in subsection (h)(4)(C)(ii) and for which a deduction is claimed in excess of $10,000.

(C) Dedication of fee.—Any fee collected under this paragraph shall be used for the enforcement of the provisions of subsection (h).

(14) Reduction for amounts attributable to rehabilitation credit.—In the case of any qualified conservation contribution (as defined in subsection (h)), the amount of the deduction allowed under this section shall be reduced by an amount which bears the same ratio to the fair market value of the contribution as—

(A) the sum of the credits allowed to the taxpayer under section 47 for the 5 preceding taxable years with respect to any building which is a part of such contribution, bears to

(B) the fair market value of the building on the date of the contribution.

(15) Special rule for taxidermy property.—

(A) Basis.—For purposes of this section and notwithstanding section 1012, in the case of a charitable contribution of taxidermy property which is made by the person who prepared, stuffed, or mounted the property or by any person who paid or incurred the cost of such preparation, stuffing, or mounting, only the cost of the preparing, stuffing, or mounting shall be included in the basis of such property.

(B) Taxidermy property.—For purposes of this section, the term "taxidermy property" means any work of art which—

(i) is the reproduction or preservation of an animal, in whole or in part,

(ii) is prepared, stuffed, or mounted for purposes of recreating one or more characteristics of such animal, and

(iii) contains a part of the body of the dead animal.

(16) Contributions of clothing and household items.—

(A) In general.—In the case of an individual, partnership, or corporation, no deduction shall be allowed under subsection (a) for any contribution of clothing or a household item unless such clothing or household item is in good used condition or better.

(B) Items of minimal value.—Notwithstanding subparagraph (A), the Secretary may by regulation deny a deduction under subsection (a) for any contribution of clothing or a household item which has minimal monetary value.

(C) Exception for certain property.—Subparagraphs (A) and (B) shall not apply to any contribution of a single item of clothing or a household item for which a deduction of more than $500 is claimed if the taxpayer includes with the taxpayer's return a qualified appraisal with respect to the property.

(D) Household items.—For purposes of this paragraph—

(i) In general.—The term "household items" includes furniture, furnishings, electronics, appliances, linens, and other similar items.

(ii) Excluded items.—Such term does not include—

(I) food,

(II) paintings, antiques, and other objects of art,

(III) jewelry and gems, and

(IV) collections.

(E) Special rule for pass-thru entities.—In the case of a partnership or S corporation, this paragraph shall be applied at the entity level, except that the deduction shall be denied at the partner or shareholder level.

(17) Recordkeeping.—No deduction shall be allowed under subsection (a) for any contribution of a cash, check, or other monetary gift unless the donor maintains as a record of such contribution a bank record or a written communication from the donee showing the name of the donee organization, the date of the contribution, and the amount of the contribution.

(18) Contributions to donor advised funds.—A deduction otherwise allowed under subsection (a) for any contribution to a donor advised fund (as defined in section 4966(d)(2)) shall only be allowed if—

(A) the sponsoring organization (as defined in section 4966(d)(1)) with respect to such donor advised fund is not—

(i) described in paragraph (3), (4), or (5) of subsection (c), or

(ii) a type III supporting organization (as defined in section 4943(f)(5)(A)) which is not a functionally integrated type III supporting organization (as defined in section 4943(f)(5)(B)), and

(B) the taxpayer obtains a contemporaneous written acknowledgment (determined under rules similar to the rules of paragraph (8)(C)) from the sponsoring organization (as so defined) of such donor advised fund that such organization has exclusive legal control over the assets contributed.

(19) Certain qualified conservation contributions.—

(A) In general.—In the case of a qualified conservation contribution to which this paragraph applies, no deduction shall be allowed under subsection (a) for such contribution unless the partnership making such contribution—

(i) includes on its return for the taxable year in which the contribution is made a statement that the partnership made such a contribution, and

(ii) provides such information about the contribution as the Secretary may require.

(B) Contributions to which this paragraph applies.—This paragraph shall apply to any qualified conservation contribution—

(i) the conservation purpose of which is the preservation of any building which is a certified historic structure (as defined in subsection (h)(4)(C)),

(ii) which is made by a partnership (whether directly or as a distributive share of a contribution of another partnership), and

(iii) the amount of which exceeds 2.5 times the sum of each partner's relevant basis (as defined in subsection (h)(7)) in the partnership making the contribution.

(C) Application to other pass-through entities.—Except as may be otherwise provided by the Secretary, the rules of this paragraph shall apply to S corporations and other pass-through entities in the same manner as such rules apply to partnerships.

(g) Amounts paid to maintain certain students as members of taxpayer's household.—

(1) In general.—Subject to the limitations provided by paragraph (2), amounts paid by the taxpayer to maintain an individual (other than a dependent, as defined in section 152 determined without regard to subsection (b)(1), (b)(2), and (d)(1)(B) thereof, or a relative of the taxpayer) as a member of his household during the period that such individual is—

(A) a member of the taxpayer's household under a written agreement between the taxpayer and an organization described in paragraph (2), (3), or (4) of subsection (c) to implement a program of the organization to provide educational opportunities for pupils or students in private homes, and

(B) a full-time pupil or student in the twelfth or any lower grade at an educational organization described in section 170(b)(1)(A)(ii) located in the United States,

shall be treated as amounts paid for the use of the organization.

(2) Limitations.—

(A) Amount.—Paragraph (1) shall apply to amounts paid within the taxable year only to the extent that such amounts do not exceed $50 multiplied by the number of full calendar months during the taxable year which fall within the period described in paragraph (1). For purposes of the preceding sentence, if 15 or more days of a calendar month fall within such period such month shall be considered as a full calendar month.

(B) Compensation or reimbursement.—Paragraph (1) shall not apply to any amount paid by the taxpayer within the taxable year if the taxpayer receives any money or other property as compensation or reimbursement for maintaining the individual in his household during the period described in paragraph (1).

(3) Relative defined.—For purposes of paragraph (1), the term "relative of the taxpayer" means an individual who, with respect to the taxpayer, bears any of the relationships described in subparagraphs (A) through (G) of section 152(d)(2).

(4) No other amount allowed as deduction.—No deduction shall be allowed under subsection (a) for any amount paid by a taxpayer to maintain an individual as a member of his household under a program described in paragraph (1)(A) except as provided in this subsection.

(h) Qualified conservation contribution.—

(1) In general.—For purposes of subsection (f)(3)(B)(iii), the term "qualified conservation contribution" means a contribution—

(A) of a qualified real property interest,

(B) to a qualified organization,

(C) exclusively for conservation purposes.

(2) Qualified real property interest.—For purposes of this subsection, the term "qualified real property interest" means any of the following interests in real property:

(A) the entire interest of the donor other than a qualified mineral interest,

(B) a remainder interest, and

(C) a restriction (granted in perpetuity) on the use which may be made of the real property.

(3) Qualified organization.—For purposes of paragraph (1), the term "qualified organization" means an organization which—

(A) is described in clause (v) or (vi) of subsection (b)(1)(A), or

(B) is described in section 501(c)(3) and—

(i) meets the requirements of section 509(a)(2), or

(ii) meets the requirements of section 509(a)(3) and is controlled by an organization described in subparagraph (A) or in clause (i) of this subparagraph.

(4) Conservation purpose defined.—

(A) In general.—For purposes of this subsection, the term "conservation purpose" means—

(i) the preservation of land areas for outdoor recreation by, or the education of, the general public,

(ii) the protection of a relatively natural habitat of fish, wildlife, or plants, or similar ecosystem,

(iii) the preservation of open space (including farmland and forest land) where such preservation is—

(I) for the scenic enjoyment of the general public, or

(II) pursuant to a clearly delineated Federal, State, or local governmental conservation policy,

and will yield a significant public benefit, or

(iv) the preservation of an historically important land area or a certified historic structure.

(B) Special rules with respect to buildings in registered historic districts.—In the case of any contribution of a qualified real property interest which is a restriction with respect to the exterior of a building described in subparagraph (C)(ii), such contribution shall not be considered to be exclusively for conservation purposes unless—

(i) such interest—

(I) includes a restriction which preserves the entire exterior of the building (including the front, sides, rear, and height of the building), and

(II) prohibits any change in the exterior of the building which is inconsistent with the historical character of such exterior,

(ii) the donor and donee enter into a written agreement certifying, under penalty of perjury, that the donee—

(I) is a qualified organization (as defined in paragraph (3)) with a purpose of environmental protection, land conservation, open space preservation, or historic preservation, and

(II) has the resources to manage and enforce the restriction and a commitment to do so, and

(iii) in the case of any contribution made in a taxable year beginning after the date of the enactment of this subparagraph, the taxpayer includes with the taxpayer's return for the taxable year of the contribution—

(I) a qualified appraisal (within the meaning of subsection (f)(11)(E)) of the qualified property interest,

(II) photographs of the entire exterior of the building, and

(III) a description of all restrictions on the development of the building.

(C) Certified historic structure.—For purposes of subparagraph (A)(iv), the term "certified historic structure" means—

(i) any building, structure, or land area which is listed in the National Register, or

(ii) any building which is located in a registered historic district (as defined in section 47(c)(3)(B)) and is certified by the Secretary of the Interior to the Secretary as being of historic significance to the district.

A building, structure, or land area satisfies the preceding sentence if it satisfies such sentence either at the time of the transfer or on the due date (including extensions) for filing the transferor's return under this chapter for the taxable year in which the transfer is made.

(5) Exclusively for conservation purposes.—For purposes of this subsection—

(A) Conservation purpose must be protected.—A contribution shall not be treated as exclusively for conservation purposes unless the conservation purpose is protected in perpetuity.

(B) No surface mining permitted.—

(i) In general.—Except as provided in clause (ii), in the case of a contribution of any interest where there is a retention of a qualified mineral interest, subparagraph (A) shall not be treated as met if at any time there may be extraction or removal of minerals by any surface mining method.

(ii) Special rule.—With respect to any contribution of property in which the ownership of the surface estate and mineral interests has been and remains separated, subparagraph (A) shall be treated as met if the probability of surface mining occurring on such property is so remote as to be negligible.

(6) Qualified mineral interest.—For purposes of this subsection, the term "qualified mineral interest" means—

(A) subsurface oil, gas, or other minerals, and

(B) the right to access to such minerals.

(7) Limitation on deduction for qualified conservation contributions made by pass-through entities.

(A) In general.—A contribution by a partnership (whether directly or as a distributive share of a contribution of another partnership) shall not be treated as a qualified conservation contribution for purposes of this section if the amount of such contribution exceeds 2.5 times the sum of each partner's relevant basis in such partnership.

(B) Relevant basis.—For purposes of this paragraph—

(i) In general.—The term "relevant basis" means, with respect to any partner, the portion of such partner's modified basis in the partnership which is allocable (under rules similar to the rules of section 755) to the portion of the real property with respect to which the contribution described in subparagraph (A) is made.

(ii) Modified basis.—The term "modified basis" means, with respect to any partner, such partner's adjusted basis in the partnership as determined—

(I) immediately before the contribution described in subparagraph (A),

(II) without regard to section 752, and

(III) by the partnership after taking into account the adjustments described in subclauses (I) and (II) and such other adjustments as the Secretary may provide.

(C) Exception for contributions outside 3-year holding period.—Subparagraph (A) shall not apply to any contribution which is made at least 3 years after the latest of—

(i) the last date on which the partnership that made such contribution acquired any portion of the real property with respect to which such contribution is made,

(ii) the last date on which any partner in the partnership that made such contribution acquired any interest in such partnership, and

(iii) if the interest in the partnership that made such contribution is held through 1 or more partnerships—

(I) the last date on which any such partnership acquired any interest in any other such partnership, and

(II) the last date on which any partner in any such partnership acquired any interest in such partnership.

(D) Exception for family partnerships.—

(i) In general—Subparagraph (A) shall not apply with respect to any contribution made by any partnership if substantially all of the partnership interests in such partnership are held, directly or indirectly, by an individual and members of the family of such individual.

(ii) Members of the family.—For purposes of this subparagraph, the term "members of the family" means, with respect to any individual—

(I) the spouse of such individual, and

(II) any individual who bears a relationship to such individual which is described in subparagraphs (A) through (G) of section 152(d)(2).

(E) Exception for contributions to preserve certified historic structures.—Subparagraph (A) shall not apply to any qualified conservation contribution the conservation purpose of which is the preservation of any building which is a certified historic structure (as defined in paragraph (4)(C)).

(F) Application to other pass-through entities.—Except as may be otherwise provided by the Secretary, the rules of this paragraph shall apply to S corporations and other pass-through entities in the same manner as such rules apply to partnerships.

(G) Regulations.—The Secretary shall prescribe such regulations or other guidance as may be necessary or appropriate to carry out the purposes of this paragraph, including regulations or other guidance—

(i) to require reporting, including reporting related to tiered partnerships and the modified basis of partners, and

(ii) to prevent the avoidance of the purposes of this paragraph.

(i) Standard mileage rate for use of passenger automobile.—For purposes of computing the deduction under this section for use of a passenger automobile the standard mileage rate shall be 14 cents per mile.

(j) Denial of deduction for certain travel expenses.—No deduction shall be allowed under this section for traveling expenses (including amounts expended for meals and lodging) while away from home, whether paid directly or by reimbursement, unless there is no significant element of personal pleasure, recreation, or vacation in such travel.

* * *

(*l*) Treatment of certain amounts paid to or for the benefit of institutions of higher education.—

(1) In general.—No deduction shall be allowed under this section for any amount described in paragraph (2).

(2) Amount described.—For purposes of paragraph (1), an amount is described in this paragraph if—

(A) the amount is paid by the taxpayer to or for the benefit of an educational organization—

(i) which is described in subsection (b)(1)(A)(ii), and

(ii) which is an institution of higher education (as defined in section 3304(f)), and

(B) the taxpayer receives (directly or indirectly) as a result of paying such amount the right to purchase tickets for seating at an athletic event in an athletic stadium of such institution.

If any portion of a payment is for the purchase of such tickets, such portion and the remaining portion (if any) of such payment shall be treated as separate amounts for purposes of this subsection.

(m) Certain donee income from intellectual property treated as an additional charitable contribution.—

(1) Treatment as additional contribution.—In the case of a taxpayer who makes a qualified intellectual property contribution, the deduction allowed under subsection (a) for each taxable year of the taxpayer ending on or after the date of such contribution shall be increased (subject to the limitations under subsection (b)) by the applicable percentage of qualified donee income with respect to such contribution which is properly allocable to such year under this subsection.

(2) Reduction in additional deductions to extent of initial deduction.—With respect to any qualified intellectual property contribution, the deduction allowed under subsection (a) shall be increased under paragraph (1) only to the extent that the aggregate amount of such increases with respect to such contribution exceed the amount allowed as a deduction under subsection (a) with respect to such contribution determined without regard to this subsection.

(3) Qualified donee income.—For purposes of this subsection, the term "qualified donee income" means any net income received by or accrued to the donee which is properly allocable to the qualified intellectual property.

(4) Allocation of qualified donee income to taxable years of donor.—For purposes of this subsection, qualified donee income shall be treated as properly allocable to a taxable year of the donor if such income is received by or accrued to the donee for the taxable year of the donee which ends within or with such taxable year of the donor.

(5) 10-year limitation.—Income shall not be treated as properly allocable to qualified intellectual property for purposes of this subsection if such income is received by or accrued to the donee after the 10-year period beginning on the date of the contribution of such property.

(6) Benefit limited to life of intellectual property.—Income shall not be treated as properly allocable to qualified intellectual property for purposes of this subsection if such income is received by or accrued to the donee after the expiration of the legal life of such property.

(7) Applicable percentage.—For purposes of this subsection, the term "applicable percentage" means the percentage determined under the following table which corresponds to a taxable year of the donor ending on or after the date of the qualified intellectual property contribution:

Taxable Year of Donor Ending on or After Date of Contribution:	Applicable Percentage:
1st	100
2nd	100
3rd	90
4th	80
5th	70
6th	60
7th	50
8th	40
9th	30
10th	20
11th	10
12th	10.

(8) Qualified intellectual property contribution.—For purposes of this subsection, the term "qualified intellectual property contribution" means any charitable contribution of qualified intellectual property—

(A) the amount of which taken into account under this section is reduced by reason of subsection (e)(1), and

(B) with respect to which the donor informs the donee at the time of such contribution that the donor intends to treat such contribution as a qualified intellectual property contribution for purposes of this subsection and section 6050L.

(9) Qualified intellectual property.—For purposes of this subsection, the term "qualified intellectual property" means property described in subsection (e)(1)(B)(iii) (other than property contributed to or for the use of an organization described in subsection (e)(1)(B)(ii)).

(10) Other special rules.—

(A) Application of limitations on charitable contributions.—Any increase under this subsection of the deduction provided under subsection (a) shall be treated for purposes of subsection (b) as a deduction which is attributable to a charitable contribution to the donee to which such increase relates.

(B) Net income determined by donee.—The net income taken into account under paragraph (3) shall not exceed the amount of such income reported under section 6050L(b)(1).

(C) Deduction limited to 12 taxable years.—Except as may be provided under subparagraph (D)(i), this subsection shall not apply with respect to any qualified intellectual property contribution for any taxable year of the donor after the 12th taxable year of the donor which ends on or after the date of such contribution.

(D) Regulations.—The Secretary may issue regulations or other guidance to carry out the purposes of this subsection, including regulations or guidance—

(i) modifying the application of this subsection in the case of a donor or donee with a short taxable year, and

(ii) providing for the determination of an amount to be treated as net income of the donee which is properly allocable to qualified intellectual property in the case of a donee who uses such property to further a purpose or function constituting the basis of the donee's exemption under section 501 (or, in the case of a governmental unit, any purpose described in section 170(c)) and does not possess a right to receive any payment from a third party with respect to such property.

(n) Expenses paid by certain whaling captains in support of native Alaskan subsistence whaling.—

(1) In general.—In the case of an individual who is recognized by the Alaska Eskimo Whaling Commission as a whaling captain charged with the responsibility of maintaining and carrying out sanctioned whaling activities and who engages in such activities during the taxable year, the amount described in paragraph (2) (to the extent such amount does not exceed $50,000 for the taxable year) shall be treated for purposes of this section as a charitable contribution.

(2) Amount described.—

(A) In general.—The amount described in this paragraph is the aggregate of the reasonable and necessary whaling expenses paid by the taxpayer during the taxable year in carrying out sanctioned whaling activities.

(B) Whaling expenses.—For purposes of subparagraph (A), the term "whaling expenses" includes expenses for—

(i) the acquisition and maintenance of whaling boats, weapons, and gear used in sanctioned whaling activities,

(ii) the supplying of food for the crew and other provisions for carrying out such activities, and

(iii) storage and distribution of the catch from such activities.

(3) Sanctioned whaling activities.—For purposes of this subsection, the term "sanctioned whaling activities" means subsistence bowhead whale hunting activities conducted pursuant to the management plan of the Alaska Eskimo Whaling Commission.

(4) Substantiation of expenses.—The Secretary shall issue guidance requiring that the taxpayer substantiate the whaling expenses for which a deduction is claimed under this subsection, including by maintaining appropriate written records with respect to the time, place, date, amount, and nature of the expense, as well as the taxpayer's eligibility for such deduction, and that (to the extent provided by the Secretary) such substantiation be provided as part of the taxpayer's return of tax.

(*o*) Special rules for fractional gifts.—

(1) Denial of deduction in certain cases.—

(A) In general.—No deduction shall be allowed for a contribution of an undivided portion of a taxpayer's entire interest in tangible personal property unless all interests in the property are held immediately before such contribution by—

(i) the taxpayer, or

(ii) the taxpayer and the donee.

(B) Exceptions.—The Secretary may, by regulation, provide for exceptions to subparagraph (A) in cases where all persons who hold an interest in the property make proportional contributions of an undivided portion of the entire interest held by such persons.

(2) Valuation of subsequent gifts.—In the case of any additional contribution, the fair market value of such contribution shall be determined by using the lesser of—

(A) the fair market value of the property at the time of the initial fractional contribution, or

(B) the fair market value of the property at the time of the additional contribution.

(3) Recapture of deduction in certain cases; addition to tax.—

(A) Recapture.—The Secretary shall provide for the recapture of the amount of any deduction allowed under this section (plus interest) with respect to any contribution of an undivided portion of a taxpayer's entire interest in tangible personal property—

(i) in any case in which the donor does not contribute all of the remaining interests in such property to the donee (or, if such donee is no longer in existence, to any person described in section 170(c)) on or before the earlier of—

(I) the date that is 10 years after the date of the initial fractional contribution, or

(II) the date of the death of the donor, and

(ii) in any case in which the donor has not, during the period beginning on the date of the initial fractional contribution and ending on the date described in clause (I)—

(I) had substantial physical possession of the property, and

(II) used the property in a use which is related to a purpose or function constituting the basis for the organizations' exemption under section 501.

(B) Addition to tax.—The tax imposed under this chapter for any taxable year for which there is a recapture under subparagraph (A) shall be increased by 10 percent of the amount so recaptured.

(4) Definitions.—For purposes of this subsection—

(A) Additional contribution.—The term "additional contribution" means any charitable contribution by the taxpayer of any interest in property with respect to which the taxpayer has previously made an initial fractional contribution.

(B) Initial fractional contribution.—The term "initial fractional contribution" means, with respect to any taxpayer, the first charitable contribution of an undivided portion of the taxpayer's entire interest in any tangible personal property.

(p) Special rule for taxpayers who do not elect to itemize deductions.—In the case of any taxable year, if the individual does not elect to itemize deductions for such taxable year, the deduction under this section shall be equal to the deduction, not in excess of $1,000 ($2,000 in the case of a joint return), which would be determined under this section if the only charitable contributions taken into account in determining such deduction were contributions made in cash during such taxable year (determined without regard to subsections (b)(1)(G)(ii), (b)(1)(I), and (d)(1)) to an organization described in section 170(b)(1)(A) and not—

(1) to an organization described in section 509(a)(3), or

(2) for the establishment of a new, or maintenance of an existing donor advised fund (as defined in section 4966(d)(2)).

(q) Other cross references.—

(1) For treatment of certain organizations providing child care, see section 501(k).

(2) For charitable contributions of estates and trusts, see section 642(c).

(3) For nondeductibility of contributions by common trust funds, see section 584.

(4) For charitable contributions of partners, see section 702.

(5) For charitable contributions of nonresident aliens, see section 873.

(6) For treatment of gifts for benefit of or use in connection with the Naval Academy as gifts to or for the use of the United States, see section 6973 of title 10, United States Code.

(7) For treatment of gifts accepted by the Secretary of State, the Director of the International Communication Agency, or the Director of the United States International Development Cooperation Agency, as gifts to or for the use of the United States, see section 25 of the State Department Basic Authorities Act of 1956.

(8) For treatment of gifts of money accepted by the Attorney General for credit to the "Commissary Funds Federal Prisons" as gifts to or for the use of the United States, see section 4043 of title 18, United States Code.

(9) For charitable contributions to or for the use of Indian tribal governments (or their subdivisions), see section 7871.

* * *

Subchapter F. Exempt Organizations

§ 501. Exemption from tax on corporations, certain trusts, etc.

(a) Exemption from taxation.—An organization described in subsection (c) or (d) or section 401(a) shall be exempt from taxation under this subtitle unless such exemption is denied under section 502 or 503.

(b) Tax on unrelated business income and certain other activities.—An organization exempt from taxation under subsection (a) shall be subject to tax to the extent provided in parts II, III, and VI of this subchapter, but (notwithstanding parts II, III, and VI of this subchapter) shall be considered an organization exempt from income taxes for the purpose of any law which refers to organizations exempt from income taxes.

(c) List of exempt organizations.—The following organizations are referred to in subsection (a):

(1) Any corporation organized under Act of Congress which is an instrumentality of the United States but only if such corporation—

(A) is exempt from Federal income taxes—

(i) under such Act as amended and supplemented before July 18, 1984, or

(ii) under this title without regard to any provision of law which is not contained in this title and which is not contained in a revenue Act, or

(B) is described in subsection (*l*).

(2) Corporations organized for the exclusive purpose of holding title to property, collecting income therefrom, and turning over the entire amount thereof, less expenses, to an organization which itself is exempt under this section. Rules similar to the rules of subparagraph (G) of paragraph (25) shall apply for purposes of this paragraph.

(3) Corporations, and any community chest, fund, or foundation, organized and operated exclusively for religious, charitable, scientific, testing for public safety, literary, or educational purposes, or to foster national or international amateur sports competition (but only if no part of its activities involve the provision of athletic facilities or equipment), or for the prevention of cruelty to children or animals, no part of the net earnings of which inures to the benefit of any private shareholder or individual, no substantial part of the activities of which is carrying on propaganda, or otherwise attempting, to influence legislation (except as otherwise provided in subsection (h)), and which does not participate in, or intervene in (including the publishing or distributing of statements), any political campaign on behalf of (or in opposition to) any candidate for public office.

(4)(A) Civic leagues or organizations not organized for profit but operated exclusively for the promotion of social welfare, or local associations of employees, the membership of which is limited to the employees of a designated person or persons in a particular municipality, and the net earnings of which are devoted exclusively to charitable, educational, or recreational purposes.

(B) Subparagraph (A) shall not apply to an entity unless no part of the net earnings of such entity inures to the benefit of any of any private shareholder or individual.

(5) Labor, agricultural, or horticultural organizations.

(6) Business leagues, chambers of commerce, real-estate boards, boards of trade, or professional football leagues (whether or not administering a pension fund for football players) not organized for profit and no part of the net earnings of which inures to the benefit of any private shareholder or individual.

(7) Clubs organized for pleasure, recreation, and other nonprofitable purposes, substantially all of the activities of which are for such purposes and no part of the net earnings of which inures to the benefit of any private shareholder.

(8) Fraternal beneficiary societies, orders, or associations—

(A) operating under the lodge system or for the exclusive benefit of the members of a fraternity itself operating under the lodge system, and

(B) providing for the payment of life, sick, accident, or other benefits to the members of such society, order, or association or their dependents.

(9) Voluntary employees' beneficiary associations providing for the payment of life, sick, accident, or other benefits to the members of such association or their dependents or designated beneficiaries, if no part of the net earnings of such association inures (other than through such payments) to the benefit of any private shareholder or individual.* * *

(10) Domestic fraternal societies, orders, or associations, operating under the lodge system—

(A) the net earnings of which are devoted exclusively to religious, charitable, scientific, literary, educational, and fraternal purposes, and

(B) which do not provide for the payment of life, sick, accident, or other benefits.

* * *

(13) Cemetery companies owned and operated exclusively for the benefit of their members or which are not operated for profit; and any corporation chartered solely for the purpose of the disposal of bodies by burial or cremation which is not permitted by its charter to engage in any business not necessarily incident to that purpose and no part of the net earnings of which inures to the benefit of any private shareholder or individual.

(14)(A) Credit unions without capital stock organized and operated for mutual purposes and without profit.

* * *

(19) A post or organization of past or present members of the Armed Forces of the United States, or an auxiliary unit or society of, or a trust or foundation for, any such post or organization—

(A) organized in the United States or any of its possessions,

(B) at least 75 percent of the members of which are past or present members of the Armed Forces of the United States and substantially all of the other members of which are individuals who are cadets or are spouses, widows, widowers, ancestors, or lineal descendants of past or present members of the Armed Forces of the United States or of cadets, and

(C) no part of the net earnings of which inures to the benefit of any private shareholder or individual.

* * *

(23) Any association organized before 1880 more than 75 percent of the members of which are present or past members of the Armed Forces and a principal purpose of which is to provide insurance and other benefits to veterans or their dependents.

* * *

(25)(A) Any corporation or trust which—

(i) has no more than 35 shareholders or beneficiaries,

(ii) has only 1 class of stock or beneficial interest, and

(iii) is organized for the exclusive purposes of—

(I) acquiring real property and holding title to, and collecting income from, such property, and

(II) remitting the entire amount of income from such property (less expenses) to 1 or more organizations described in subparagraph (C) which are shareholders of such corporation or beneficiaries of such trust.

For purposes of clause (iii), the term "real property" shall not include any interest as a tenant in common (or similar interest) and shall not include any indirect interest.

(B) A corporation or trust shall be described in subparagraph (A) without regard to whether the corporation or trust is organized by 1 or more organizations described in subparagraph (C).

(C) An organization is described in this subparagraph if such organization is—

(i) a qualified pension, profit sharing, or stock bonus plan that meets the requirements of section 401(a),

(ii) a governmental plan (within the meaning of section 414(d)),

(iii) the United States, any State or political subdivision thereof, or any agency or instrumentality of any of the foregoing, or

(iv) any organization described in paragraph (3).

(D) A corporation or trust shall in no event be treated as described in subparagraph (A) unless such corporation or trust permits its shareholders or beneficiaries—

(i) to dismiss the corporation's or trust's investment adviser, following reasonable notice, upon a vote of the shareholders or beneficiaries holding a majority of interest in the corporation or trust, and

(ii) to terminate their interest in the corporation or trust by either, or both, of the following alternatives, as determined by the corporation or trust:

(I) by selling or exchanging their stock in the corporation or interest in the trust (subject to any Federal or State securities law) to any organization described in subparagraph (C) so long as the sale or exchange does not increase the number of shareholders or beneficiaries in such corporation or trust above 35, or

(II) by having their stock or interest redeemed by the corporation or trust after the shareholder or beneficiary has provided 90 days notice to such corporation or trust.

(E)(i) For purposes of this title—

(I) a corporation which is a qualified subsidiary shall not be treated as a separate corporation, and

(II) all assets, liabilities, and items of income, deduction, and credit of a qualified subsidiary shall be treated as assets, liabilities, and such items (as the case may be) of the corporation or trust described in subparagraph (A).

(ii) For purposes of this subparagraph, the term "qualified subsidiary" means any corporation if, at all times during the period such corporation was in existence, 100 percent of the stock of such corporation is held by the corporation or trust described in subparagraph (A).

(iii) For purposes of this subtitle, if any corporation which was a qualified subsidiary ceases to meet the requirements of clause (ii), such corporation shall be treated as a new corporation acquiring all of its assets (and assuming all of its liabilities) immediately before such cessation from the corporation or trust described in subparagraph (A) in exchange for its stock.

(F) For purposes of subparagraph (A), the term "real property" includes any personal property which is leased under, or in connection with, a lease of real property, but only if the rent attributable to such personal property (determined under the rules of section 856(d)(1)) for the taxable year does not exceed 15 percent of the total rent for the taxable year attributable to both the real and personal property leased under, or in connection with, such lease.

(G)(i) An organization shall not be treated as failing to be described in this paragraph merely by reason of the receipt of any otherwise disqualifying income which is incidentally derived from the holding of real property.

(ii) Clause (i) shall not apply if the amount of gross income described in such clause exceeds 10 percent of the organization's gross income for the taxable year unless the organization establishes to the satisfaction of the Secretary that the receipt of gross income described in clause (i) in excess of such limitation was inadvertent and reasonable steps are being taken to correct the circumstances giving rise to such income.

* * *

(d) Religious and apostolic organizations.—The following organizations are referred to in subsection (a): Religious or apostolic associations or corporations, if such associations or corporations have a common treasury or community treasury, even if such associations or corporations engage in business for the common benefit of the members, but only if the members thereof include (at the time of filing their returns) in their gross income their entire pro rata shares, whether distributed or not, of the taxable income of the association or corporation for such year. Any amount so included in the gross income of a member shall be treated as a dividend received.

(e) Cooperative hospital service organizations.—For purposes of this title, an organization shall be treated as an organization organized and operated exclusively for charitable purposes, if—

(1) such organization is organized and operated solely—

(A) to perform, on a centralized basis, one or more of the following services which, if performed on its own behalf by a hospital which is an organization described in subsection (c)(3) and exempt from taxation under subsection (a), would constitute activities in exercising or performing the purpose or function constituting the basis for its exemption: data processing, purchasing (including the purchasing of insurance on a group basis), warehousing, billing and collection (including the purchase of patron accounts receivable on a recourse basis), food, clinical, industrial engineering,laboratory, printing, communications, record center, and personnel (including selection, testing, training, and education of personnel) services; and

(B) to perform such services solely for two or more hospitals each of which is—

(i) an organization described in subsection (c)(3) which is exempt from taxation under subsection (a),

(ii) a constituent part of an organization described in subsection (c)(3) which is exempt from taxation under subsection (a) and which, if organized and operated as a separate entity, would constitute an organization described in subsection (c)(3), or

(iii) owned and operated by the United States, a State, the District of Columbia, or a possession of the United States, or a political subdivision or an agency or instrumentality of any of the foregoing;

(2) such organization is organized and operated on a cooperative basis and allocates or pays, within 8-1/2 months after the close of its taxable year, all net earnings to patrons on the basis of services performed for them; and

(3) if such organization has capital stock, all of such stock outstanding is owned by its patrons.

For purposes of this title, any organization which, by reason of the preceding sentence, is an organization described in subsection (c)(3) and exempt from taxation under subsection (a), shall be treated as a hospital and as an organization referred to in section 170(b)(1)(A)(iii).

(f) Cooperative service organizations of operating educational organizations.—For purposes of this title, if an organization is—

(1) organized and operated solely to hold, commingle, and collectively invest and reinvest (including arranging for and supervising the performance by independent contractors of investment services related thereto) in stocks and securities, the moneys contributed thereto by each of the members of such organization, and to collect income therefrom and turn over the entire amount thereof, less expenses, to such members,

(2) organized and controlled by one or more such members, and

(3) comprised solely of members that are organizations described in clause (ii) or (iv) of section 170(b)(1)(A)—

(A) which are exempt from taxation under subsection (a), or

(B) the income of which is excluded from taxation under section 115(a),

then such organization shall be treated as an organization organized and operated exclusively for charitable purposes.

(g) Definition of agricultural.—For purposes of subsection (c)(5), the term "agricultural" includes the art or science of cultivating land, harvesting crops or aquatic resources, or raising livestock.

(h) Expenditures by public charities to influence legislation.—

(1) General rule.—In the case of an organization to which this subsection applies, exemption from taxation under subsection (a) shall be denied because a substantial part of the activities of such organization consists of carrying on propaganda, or otherwise attempting, to influence legislation, but only if such organization normally—

(A) makes lobbying expenditures in excess of the lobbying ceiling amount for such organization for each taxable year, or

(B) makes grass roots expenditures in excess of the grass roots ceiling amount for such organization for each taxable year.

(2) Definitions.—For purposes of this subsection—

(A) Lobbying expenditures.—The term "lobbying expenditures" means expenditures for the purpose of influencing legislation (as defined in section 4911(d)).

(B) Lobbying ceiling amount.—The lobbying ceiling amount for any organization for any taxable year is 150 percent of the lobbying nontaxable amount for such organization for such taxable year, determined under section 4911.

(C) Grass roots expenditures.—The term "grass roots expenditures" means expenditures for the purpose of influencing legislation (as defined in section 4911(d) without regard to paragraph (1)(B) thereof).

(D) Grass roots ceiling amount.—The grass roots ceiling amount for any organization for any taxable year is 150 percent of the grass roots nontaxable amount for such organization for such taxable year, determined under section 4911.

(3) Organizations to which this subsection applies.—This subsection shall apply to any organization which has elected (in such manner and at such time as the Secretary may prescribe) to have the provisions of this subsection apply to such organization and which, for the taxable year which includes the date the election is made, is described in subsection (c)(3) and—

(A) is described in paragraph (4), and

(B) is not a disqualified organization under paragraph (5).

(4) Organizations permitted to elect to have this subsection apply.—An organization is described in this paragraph if it is described in—

(A) section 170(b)(1)(A)(ii) (relating to educational institutions),

(B) section 170(b)(1)(A)(iii) (relating to hospitals and medical research organizations),

(C) section 170(b)(1)(A)(iv) (relating to organizations supporting government schools),

(D) section 170(b)(1)(A)(vi) (relating to organizations publicly supported by charitable contributions),

(E) section 170(b)(1)(A)(ix) (relating to agricultural research organizations),

(F) section 509(a)(2) (relating to organizations publicly supported by admissions, sales, etc.), or

(G) section 509(a)(3) (relating to organizations supporting certain types of public charities) except that for purposes of this subparagraph, section 509(a)(3) shall be applied without regard to the last sentence of section 509(a).

(5) Disqualified organizations.—For purposes of paragraph (3) an organization is a disqualified organization if it is—

(A) described in section 170(b)(1)(A)(i) (relating to churches),

(B) an integrated auxiliary of a church or of a convention or association of churches, or

(C) a member of an affiliated group of organizations (within the meaning of section 4911(f)(2)) if one or more members of such group is described in subparagraph (A) or (B).

(6) Years for which election is effective.—An election by an organization under this subsection shall be effective for all taxable years of such organization which—

(A) end after the date the election is made, and

(B) begin before the date the election is revoked by such organization (under regulations prescribed by the Secretary).

(7) No effect on certain organizations.—With respect to any organization for a taxable year for which—

(A) such organization is a disqualified organization (within the meaning of paragraph (5)), or

(B) an election under this subsection is not in effect for such organization,

nothing in this subsection or in section 4911 shall be construed to affect the interpretation of the phrase, "no substantial part of the activities of which is carrying on propaganda, or otherwise attempting, to influence legislation," under subsection (c)(3).

(8) Affiliated organizations.—For rules regarding affiliated organizations, see section 4911(f).

(i) Prohibition of discrimination by certain social clubs.—Notwithstanding subsection (a), an organization which is described in subsection (c)(7) shall not be exempt from taxation under subsection (a) for any taxable year if, at any time during such taxable year, the charter, bylaws, or other governing instrument, of such organization or any written policy statement of such organization contains a provision which provides for discrimination against any person on the basis of race, color, or religion. The preceding sentence to the extent it relates to discrimination on the basis of religion shall not apply to—

(1) an auxiliary of a fraternal beneficiary society if such society—

(A) is described in subsection (c)(8) and exempt from tax under subsection (a), and

(B) limits its membership to the members of a particular religion, or

(2) a club which in good faith limits its membership to the members of a particular religion in order to further the teachings or principles of that religion, and not to exclude individuals of a particular race or color.

(j) Special rules for certain amateur sports organizations.—

(1) In general.—In the case of a qualified amateur sports organization—

(A) the requirement of subsection (c)(3) that no part of its activities involve the provision of athletic facilities or equipment shall not apply, and

(B) such organization shall not fail to meet the requirements of subsection (c)(3) merely because its membership is local or regional in nature.

(2) Qualified amateur sports organization defined.—For purposes of this subsection, the term "qualified amateur sports organization" means any organization organized and operated exclusively to foster national or international amateur sports competition if such organization is also organized and operated primarily to conduct national or international competition in sports or to support and develop amateur athletes for national or international competition in sports.

(k) Treatment of certain organizations providing child care.—For purposes of subsection (c)(3) of this section and sections 170(c)(2), 2055(a)(2), and 2522(a)(2), the term "educational purposes" includes the providing of care of children away from their homes if—

(1) substantially all of the care provided by the organization is for purposes of enabling individuals to be gainfully employed, and

(2) the services provided by the organization are available to the general public.

***(l)* Government corporations exempt under subsection (c)(1).**—For purposes of subsection (c)(1), the following organizations are described in this subsection:

(1) The Central Liquidity Facility established under title III of the Federal Credit Union Act (12 U.S.C. 1795 et seq.).

(2) The Resolution Trust Corporation established under section 21A of the Federal Home Loan Bank Act.

(3) The Resolution Funding Corporation established under section 21—of the Federal Home Loan Bank Act.

(m) Certain organizations providing commercial-type insurance not exempt from tax.—

(1) Denial of tax exemption where providing commercial-type insurance is substantial part of activities.—An organization described in paragraph (3) or (4) of subsection (c) shall be exempt from tax under subsection (a) only if no substantial part of its activities consists of providing commercial-type insurance.

(2) Other organizations taxed as insurance companies on insurance business.—In the case of an organization described in paragraph (3) or (4) of subsection (c) which is exempt from tax under subsection (a) after the application of paragraph (1) of this subsection—

(A) the activity of providing commercial-type insurance shall be treated as an unrelated trade or business (as defined in section 513), and

(B) in lieu of the tax imposed by section 511 with respect to such activity, such organization shall be treated as an insurance company for purposes of applying subchapter L with respect to such activity.

(3) Commercial-type insurance.—For purposes of this subsection, the term "commercial-type insurance" shall not include—

(A) insurance provided at substantially below cost to a class of charitable recipients,

(B) incidental health insurance provided by a health maintenance organization of a kind customarily provided by such organizations,

(C) property or casualty insurance provided (directly or through an organization described in section 414(e)(3)(B)(ii)) by a church or convention or association of churches for such church or convention or association of churches,

(D) providing retirement or welfare benefits (or both) by a church or a convention or association of churches (directly or through an organization described in section 414(e)(3)(A) or 414(e)(3)(B)(ii)) for the employees (including employees described in section 414(e)(3)(B)) of such church or convention or association of churches or the beneficiaries of such employees, and

(E) charitable gift annuities.

(4) Insurance includes annuities.—For purposes of this subsection, the issuance of annuity contracts shall be treated as providing insurance.

(5) Charitable gift annuity.—For purposes of paragraph (3)(E), the term "charitable gift annuity" means an annuity if—

(A) a portion of the amount paid in connection with the issuance of the annuity is allowable as a deduction under section 170 or 2055, and

(B) the annuity is described in section 514(c)(5) (determined as if any amount paid in cash in connection with such issuance were property).

* * *

(*o*) Treatment of hospitals participating in provider-sponsored organizations.—An organization shall not fail to be treated as organized and operated exclusively for a charitable purpose for purposes of subsection (c)(3) solely because a hospital which is owned and operated by such organization participates in a provider-sponsored organization (as defined in section 1855(d) of the Social Security Act), whether or not the provider-sponsored organization is exempt from tax. For purposes of subsection (c)(3), any person with a material financial interest in such a provider-sponsored organization shall be treated as a private shareholder or individual with respect to the hospital.

(p) Suspension of tax-exempt status of terrorist organizations.—

(1) In general.—The exemption from tax under subsection (a) with respect to any organization described in paragraph (2), and the eligibility of any organization described in paragraph (2) to apply for recognition of exemption under subsection (a), shall be suspended during the period described in paragraph (3).

(2) Terrorist organizations.—An organization is described in this paragraph if such organization is designated or otherwise individually identified—

(A) under section 212(a)(3)(B)(vi)(II) or 219 of the Immigration and Nationality Act as a terrorist organization or foreign terrorist organization,

(B) in or pursuant to an Executive order which is related to terrorism and issued under the authority of the International Emergency Economic Powers Act or section 5 of the United Nations Participation Act of 1945 for the purpose of imposing on such organization an economic or other sanction, or

(C) in or pursuant to an Executive order issued under the authority of any Federal law if—

(i) the organization is designated or otherwise individually identified in or pursuant to such Executive order as supporting or engaging in terrorist activity (as defined in section 212(a)(3)(B) of the Immigration and Nationality Act) or supporting terrorism (as defined in section 140(d)(2) of the Foreign Relations Authorization Act, Fiscal Years 1988 and 1989); and

(ii) such Executive order refers to this subsection.

(3) Period of suspension.—With respect to any organization described in paragraph (2), the period of suspension—

(A) begins on the later of—

(i) the date of the first publication of a designation or identification described in paragraph (2) with respect to such organization, or

(ii) the date of the enactment of this subsection, and

(B) ends on the first date that all designations and identifications described in paragraph (2) with respect to such organization are rescinded pursuant to the law or Executive order under which such designation or identification was made.

(4) Denial of deduction.—No deduction shall be allowed under any provision of this title, including sections 170, 545(b)(2), 556(b)(2), 642(c), 2055, 2106(a)(2), and 2522, with respect to any contribution to an organization described in paragraph (2) during the period described in paragraph (3).

(5) Denial of administrative or judicial challenge of suspension or denial of deduction.—Notwithstanding section 7428 or any other provision of law, no organization or other person may challenge a suspension under paragraph (1), a designation or identification described in paragraph (2), the period of suspension described in paragraph (3), or a denial of a deduction under paragraph (4) in any administrative or judicial proceeding relating to the Federal tax liability of such organization or other person.

(6) Erroneous designation.—

(A) In general.—If—

(i) the tax exemption of any organization described in paragraph (2) is suspended under paragraph (1),

(ii) each designation and identification described in paragraph (2) which has been made with respect to such organization is determined to be erroneous pursuant to the law or Executive order under which such designation or identification was made, and

(iii) the erroneous designations and identifications result in an overpayment of income tax for any taxable year by such organization, credit or refund (with interest) with respect to such overpayment shall be made.

(B) Waiver of limitations.—If the credit or refund of any overpayment of tax described in subparagraph (A)(iii) is prevented at any time by the operation of any law or rule of law (including res judicata), such credit or refund may nevertheless be allowed or made if the claim therefor is filed before the close of the 1-year period beginning on the date of the last determination described in subparagraph (A)(ii).

(7) Notice of suspensions.—If the tax exemption of any organization is suspended under this subsection, the Internal Revenue Service shall update the listings of tax-exempt organizations and shall publish appropriate notice to taxpayers of such suspension and of the fact that contributions to such organization are not deductible during the period of such suspension.

(q) Special Rules for Credit Counseling Organizations—

(1) In general.—An organization with respect to which the provision of credit counseling services is a substantial purpose shall not be exempt from tax under subsection (a) unless such organization is described in paragraph (3) or (4) of subsection (c) and such organization is organized and operated in accordance with the following requirements:

(A) The organization—

(i) provides credit counseling services tailored to the specific needs and circumstances of consumers,

(ii) makes no loans to debtors (other than loans with no fees or interest) and does not negotiate the making of loans on behalf of debtors,

(iii) provides services for the purpose of improving a consumer's credit record, credit history, or credit rating only to the extent that such services are incidental to providing credit counseling services, and

(iv) does not charge any separately stated fee for services for the purpose of improving any consumer's credit record, credit history, or credit rating.

(B) The organization does not refuse to provide credit counseling services to a consumer due to the inability of the consumer to pay, the ineligibility of the consumer for debt management plan enrollment, or the unwillingness of the consumer to enroll in a debt management plan.

(C) The organization establishes and implements a fee policy which—

(i) requires that any fees charged to a consumer for services are reasonable,

(ii) allows for the waiver of fees if the consumer is unable to pay, and

(iii) except to the extent allowed by State law, prohibits charging any fee based in whole or in part on a percentage of the consumer's debt, the consumer's payments to be made pursuant to a debt management plan, or the projected or actual savings to the consumer resulting from enrolling in a debt management plan.

(D) At all times the organization has a board of directors or other governing body—

(i) which is controlled by persons who represent the broad interests of the public, such as public officials acting in their capacities as such, persons having special knowledge or expertise in credit or financial education, and community leaders,

(ii) not more than 20 percent of the voting power of which is vested in persons who are employed by the organization or who will benefit financially, directly or indirectly, from the organization's activities (other than through the receipt of reasonable directors" fees or the repayment of consumer debt to creditors other than the credit counseling organization or its affiliates), and

(iii) not more than 49 percent of the voting power of which is vested in persons who are employed by the organization or who will benefit financially, directly or indirectly, from the organization's activities (other than through the receipt of reasonable directors" fees).

(E) The organization does not own more than 35 percent of—

(i) the total combined voting power of any corporation (other than a corporation which is an organization described in subsection (c)(3) and exempt from tax under subsection (a)) which is in the trade or business of lending money, repairing credit, or providing debt management plan services, payment processing, or similar services,

(ii) the profits interest of any partnership (other than a partnership which is an organization described in subsection (c)(3) and exempt from tax under subsection (a)) which is in the trade or business of lending money, repairing credit, or providing debt management plan services, payment processing, or similar services, and

(iii) the beneficial interest of any trust or estate (other than a trust which is an organization described in subsection (c)(3) and exempt from tax under subsection (a)) which is in the trade or business of lending money, repairing credit, or providing debt management plan services, payment processing, or similar services.

(F) The organization receives no amount for providing referrals to others for debt management plan services, and pays no amount to others for obtaining referrals of consumers.

(2) Additional requirements for organizations described in subsection (c)(3)—

(A) In general.—In addition to the requirements under paragraph (1), an organization with respect to which the provision of credit counseling services is a substantial purpose and which is described in paragraph (3) of subsection (c) shall not be exempt from tax under subsection (a) unless such organization is organized and operated in accordance with the following requirements:

(i) The organization does not solicit contributions from consumers during the initial counseling process or while the consumer is receiving services from the organization.

(ii) The aggregate revenues of the organization which are from payments of creditors of consumers of the organization and which are attributable to debt management plan services do not exceed the applicable percentage of the total revenues of the organization.

(B) Applicable percentage—

(i) In general.—For purposes of subparagraph (A)(ii), the applicable percentage is 50 percent.

(ii) Transition rule.—Notwithstanding clause (i), in the case of an organization with respect to which the provision of credit counseling services is a substantial purpose and which is described in paragraph (3) of subsection (c) and exempt from tax under subsection (a) on the date of the enactment of this subsection, the applicable percentage is—

(I) 80 percent for the first taxable year of such organization beginning after the date which is 1 year after the date of the enactment of this subsection, and

(II) 70 percent for the second such taxable year beginning after such date, and

(III) 60 percent for the third such taxable year beginning after such date.

(3) Additional requirement for organizations described in subsection (c)(4).—In addition to the requirements under paragraph (1), an organization with respect to which the provision of credit counseling services is a substantial purpose and which is described in paragraph (4) of subsection (c)) shall not be exempt from tax under subsection (a) unless such organization notifies the Secretary, in such manner as the Secretary may by regulations prescribe, that it is applying for recognition as a credit counseling organization.

(4) Credit counseling services; debt management plan services.—For purposes of this subsection—

(A) Credit counseling services.—The term "credit counseling services" means—

(i) the providing of educational information to the general public on budgeting, personal finance, financial literacy, saving and spending practices, and the sound use of consumer credit,

(ii) the assisting of individuals and families with financial problems by providing them with counseling, or

(iii) a combination of the activities described in clauses (i) and (ii).

(B) Debt management plan services.—The term "debt management plan services" means services related to the repayment, consolidation, or restructuring of a consumer's debt, and includes the negotiation with creditors of lower interest rates, the waiver or reduction of fees, and the marketing and processing of debt management plans.

(r) Additional requirements for certain hospitals.—

(1) In general.—A hospital organization to which this subsection applies shall not be treated as described in subsection (c)(3) unless the organization—

(A) meets the community health needs assessment requirements described in paragraph (3),

(B) meets the financial assistance policy requirements described in paragraph (4),

(C) meets the requirements on charges described in paragraph (5), and

(D) meets the billing and collection requirement described in paragraph (6).

(2) Hospital organizations to which subsection applies.—

(A) In general.—This subsection shall apply to—

(ii) an organization which operates a facility which is required by a State to be licensed, registered, or similarly recognized as a hospital, and

(ii) any other organization which the Secretary determines has the provision of hospital care as its principal function or purpose constituting the basis for its exemption under subsection (c)(3) (determined without regard to this subsection).

(B) Organizations with more than 1 hospital facility.—If a hospital organization operates more than 1 hospital facility—

(i) the organization shall meet the requirements of this subsection separately with respect to each such facility, and

(ii) the organization shall not be treated as described in subsection (c)(3) with respect to any such facility for which such requirements are not separately met.

(3) Community health needs assessments.—

(A) In general.—An organization meets the requirements of this paragraph with respect to any taxable year only if the organization—

(i) has conducted a community health needs assessment which meets the requirements of subparagraph (B) in such taxable year or in either of the 2 taxable years immediately preceding such taxable year, and

(ii) has adopted an implementation strategy to meet the community health needs identified through such assessment.

(B) Community health needs assessment.—A community health needs assessment meets the requirements of this paragraph if such community needs health assessment—

(i) takes into account input from persons who represent the broad interests of the community served by the hospital facility, including those with special knowledge of or expertise in public health, and

(ii) is made widely available to the public.

(4) Financial assistance policy.—An organization meets the requirements of this paragraph if the organization establishes the following policies:

(A) Financial assistance policy.—A written financial assistance policy which includes—

(i) eligibility criteria for financial assistance, and whether such assistance includes free or discounted care,

(ii) the basis for calculating amounts charged to patients,

(iii) the method for applying for financial assistance,

(iv) in the case of an organization which does not have a separate billing and collections policy, the actions the organization may take in the event of non-payment, including collections action and reporting to credit agencies, and

(v) measures to widely publicize the policy within the community to be served by the organization.

(B) Policy relating to emergency medical care.—A written policy requiring the organization to provide, without discrimination, care for emergency medical conditions (within the meaning of section 1867 of the Social Security Act (42 U.S.C. 1395dd)) to individuals regardless of their eligibility under the financial assistance policy described in subparagraph (A).

(5) Limitation on charges.—An organization meets the requirements of this paragraph if the organization—

(A) limits amounts charged for emergency or other medically necessary care provided to individuals eligible for assistance under the financial assistance policy described in paragraph (4)(A) to not more than the lowest amounts charged to individuals who have insurance covering such care, and

(B) prohibits the use of gross charges.

(6) Billing and collection requirements.—An organization meets the requirements of this paragraph only if the organization does not engage in extraordinary collection actions before the organization has made reasonable efforts to determine whether the individual is eligible for assistance under the financial assistance policy described in paragraph (4)(A).

(7) Regulatory authority.—The Secretary shall issue such regulations and guidance as may be necessary to carry out the provisions of this subsection, including guidance relating to what constitutes reasonable efforts to determine the eligibility of a patient under a financial assistance policy for purposes of paragraph (6).

(s) Cross reference.—For nonexemption of Communist-controlled organizations, see section 11(b) of the Internal Security Act of 1950 (64 Stat. 997; 50 U.S.C. 790(b)).

§ 502. Feeder organizations.

(a) General rule.—An organization operated for the primary purpose of carrying on a trade or business for profit shall not be exempt from taxation under section 501 on the ground that all of its profits are payable to one or more organizations exempt from taxation under section 501.

(b) Special rule.—For purposes of this section, the term "trade or business" shall not include—

(1) the deriving of rents which would be excluded under section 512(b)(3), if section 512 applied to the organization,

(2) any trade or business in which substantially all the work in carrying on such trade or business is performed for the organization without compensation, or

(3) any trade or business which is the selling of merchandise, substantially all of which has been received by the organization as gifts or contributions.

§ 504. Status after organization ceases to qualify for exemption under section 501(c)(3) because of substantial lobbying or because of political activities.

(a) General rule.—An organization which—

(1) was exempt (or was determined by the Secretary to be exempt) from taxation under section 501(a) by reason of being an organization described in section 501(c)(3), and

(2) is not an organization described in section 501(c)(3)—

(A) by reason of carrying on propaganda, or otherwise attempting, to influence legislation, or

(B) by reason of participating in, or intervening in, any political campaign on behalf of (or in opposition to) any candidate for public office, shall not at any time thereafter be treated as an organization described in section 501(c)(4).

(b) Regulations to prevent avoidance.—The Secretary shall prescribe such regulations as may be necessary or appropriate to prevent the avoidance of subsection (a), including regulations relating to a direct or indirect transfer of all or part of the assets of an organization to an organization controlled (directly or indirectly) by the same person or persons who control the transferor organization.

(c) Churches, etc.—Subsection (a) shall not apply to any organization which is a disqualified organization within the meaning of section 501(h)(5) (relating to churches, etc.) for the taxable year immediately preceding the first taxable year for which such organization is described in paragraph (2) of subsection (a).

* * *

§ 506. Organizations required to notify Secretary of intent to operate under 501(c)(4).

(a) In general.—An organization described in section 501(c)(4) shall, not later than 60 days after the organization is established, notify the Secretary (in such manner as the Secretary shall by regulation prescribe) that it is operating as such.

(b) Contents of notice.—The notice required under subsection (a) shall include the following information:

(1) The name, address, and taxpayer identification number of the organization.

(2) The date on which, and the State under the laws of which, the organization was organized.

(3) A statement of the purpose of the organization.

(c) Acknowledgment of receipt.—Not later than 60 days after receipt of such a notice, the Secretary shall send to the organization an acknowledgment of such receipt.

(d) Extension for reasonable cause.—The Secretary may, for reasonable cause, extend the 60-day period described in subsection (a).

(e) User fee.—The Secretary shall impose a reasonable user fee for submission of the notice under subsection (a).

(f) Request for determination.—Upon request by an organization to be treated as an organization described in section 501(c)(4), the Secretary may issue a determination with respect to such treatment. Such request shall be treated for purposes of section 6104 an application for exemption from taxation under section 501(a).

§ 507. Termination of private foundation status.

(a) General rule.—Except as provided in subsection (b), the status of any organization as a private foundation shall be terminated only if—

(1) such organization notifies the Secretary (at such time and in such manner as the Secretary may by regulations prescribe) of its intent to accomplish such termination, or

(2)(A) with respect to such organization, there have been either willful repeated acts (or failures to act), or a willful and flagrant act (or failure to act), giving rise to liability for tax under chapter 42, and

(B) the Secretary notifies such organization that, by reason of subparagraph (A), such organization is liable for the tax imposed by subsection (c),

and either such organization pays the tax imposed by subsection (c) (or any portion not abated under subsection (g)) or the entire amount of such tax is abated under subsection (g).

(b) Special rules.—

(1) Transfer to, or operation as, public charity.—The status as a private foundation of any organization, with respect to which there have not been either willful repeated acts (or failures to act) or a willful and flagrant act (or failure to act) giving rise to liability for tax under chapter 42, shall be terminated if—

(A) such organization distributes all of its net assets to one or more organizations described in section 170(b)(1)(A) (other than in clauses (vii) and (viii)) each of which has been in existence and so described for a continuous period of at least 60 calendar months immediately preceding such distribution, or

(B)(i) such organization meets the requirements of paragraph (1), (2), or (3) of section 509(a) by the end of the 12-month period beginning with its first taxable year which begins after December 31, 1969, or for a continuous period of 60 calendar months beginning with the first day of any taxable year which begins after December 31, 1969,

(ii) such organization notifies the Secretary (in such manner as the Secretary may by regulations prescribe) before the commencement of such 12-month or 60-month period (or before the 90th day after the day on which regulations first prescribed under this subsection become final) that it is terminating its private foundation status, and

(iii) such organization establishes to the satisfaction of the Secretary (in such manner as the Secretary may by regulations prescribe) immediately after the expiration of such 12-month or 60-month period that such organization has complied with clause (i).

If an organization gives notice under subparagraph (B)(ii) of the commencement of a 60-month period and such organization fails to meet the requirements of paragraph (1), (2), or (3) of section 509(a) for the entire 60-month period, this part and chapter 42 shall not apply to such organization for any taxable year within such 60-month period for which it does meet such requirements.

(2) Transferee foundations.—For purposes of this part, in the case of a transfer of assets of any private foundation to another private foundation pursuant to any liquidation, merger, redemption, recapitalization, or other adjustment, organization, or reorganization, the transferee foundation shall not be treated as a newly created organization.

(c) Imposition of tax.—There is hereby imposed on each organization which is referred to in subsection (a) a tax equal to the lower of—

(1) the amount which the private foundation substantiates by adequate records or other corroborating evidence as the aggregate tax benefit resulting from the section 501(c)(3) status of such foundation, or

(2) the value of the net assets of such foundation.

(d) Aggregate tax benefit.—

(1) In general.—For purposes of subsection (c), the aggregate tax benefit resulting from the section 501(c)(3) status of any private foundation is the sum of—

(A) the aggregate increases in tax under chapters 1, 11, and 12 (or the corresponding provisions of prior law) which would have been imposed with respect to all substantial contributors to the foundation if deductions for all contributions made by such contributors to the foundation after February 28, 1913, had been disallowed, and

(B) the aggregate increases in tax under chapter 1 (or the corresponding provisions of prior law) which would have been imposed with respect to the income of the private foundation for taxable years beginning after December 31, 1912, if (i) it had not been exempt from tax under section 501(a) (or the corresponding provisions of prior law), and (ii) in the case of a trust, deductions under section 642(c) (or the corresponding provisions of prior law) had been limited to 20 percent of the taxable income of the trust (computed without the benefit of section 642(c) but with the benefit of section 170(b)(1)(A)), and

(C) interest on the increases in tax determined under subparagraphs (A) and (B) from the first date on which each such increase would have been due and payable to the date on which the organization ceases to be a private foundation.

(2) Substantial contributor.—

(A) Definition.—For purposes of paragraph (1), the term "substantial contributor" means any person who contributed or bequeathed an aggregate amount of more than

$5,000 to the private foundation, if such amount is more than 2 percent of the total contributions and bequests received by the foundation before the close of the taxable year of the foundation in which the contribution or bequest is received by the foundation from such person. In the case of a trust, the term "substantial contributor" also means the creator of the trust.

(B) Special rules.—For purposes of subparagraph (A)—

(i) each contribution or bequest shall be valued at fair market value on the date it was received,

(ii) in the case of a foundation which is in existence on October 9, 1969, all contributions and bequests received on or before such date shall be treated (except for purposes of clause (i)) as if received on such date,

(iii) an individual shall be treated as making all contributions and bequests made by his spouse, and

(iv) any person who is a substantial contributor on any date shall remain a substantial contributor for all subsequent periods.

(C) Person ceases to be substantial contributor in certain cases.—

(i) In general.—A person shall cease to be treated as a substantial contributor with respect to any private foundation as of the close of any taxable year of such foundation if—

(I) during the 10-year period ending at the close of such taxable year such person (and all related persons) have not made any contribution to such private foundation,

(II) at no time during such 10-year period was such person (or any related person) a foundation manager of such private foundation, and

(III) the aggregate contributions made by such person (and related persons) are determined by the Secretary to be insignificant when compared to the aggregate amount of contributions to such foundation by one other person.

For purposes of subclause (III), appreciation on contributions while held by the foundation shall be taken into account.

(ii) Related person.—For purposes of clause (i), the term "related person" means, with respect to any person, any other person who would be a disqualified person (within the meaning of section 4946) by reason of his relationship to such person. In the case of a contributor which is a corporation, the term also includes any officer or director of such corporation.

(3) Regulations.—For purposes of this section, the determination as to whether and to what extent there would have been any increase in tax shall be made in accordance with regulations prescribed by the Secretary.

(e) Value of assets.—For purposes of subsection (c), the value of the net assets shall be determined at whichever time such value is higher: (1) the first day on which action is taken by the organization which culminates in its ceasing to be a private foundation, or (2) the date on which it ceases to be a private foundation.

(f) Liability in case of transfers of assets from private foundation.—For purposes of determining liability for the tax imposed by subsection (c) in the case of assets transferred by the private foundation, such tax shall be deemed to have been imposed on the first day on which action is taken by the organization which culminates in its ceasing to be a private foundation.

(g) Abatement of taxes.—The Secretary may abate the unpaid portion of the assessment of any tax imposed by subsection (c), or any liability in respect thereof, if—

(1) the private foundation distributes all of its net assets to one or more organizations described in section 170(b)(1)(A) (other than in clauses (vii) and (viii)) each of which has been in existence and so described for a continuous period of at least 60 calendar months, or

(2) following the notification prescribed in section 6104(c) to the appropriate State officer, such State officer within one year notifies the Secretary, in such manner as the Secretary may by regulations prescribe, that corrective action has been initiated pursuant to State law to insure that the assets of such private foundation are preserved for such charitable or other purposes specified in section 501(c)(3) as may be ordered or approved by a court of competent jurisdiction, and upon completion of the corrective action, the Secretary receives certification from the appropriate State officer that such action has resulted in such preservation of assets.

§ 508. Special rules with respect to section 501(c)(3) organizations.

(a) New organizations must notify Secretary that they are applying for recognition of section 501(c)(3) status.—Except as provided in subsection (c), an organization organized after October 9, 1969, shall not be treated as an organization described in section 501(c)(3)—

(1) unless it has given notice to the Secretary in such manner as the Secretary may by regulations prescribe, that it is applying for recognition of such status, or

(2) for any period before the giving of such notice, if such notice is given after the time prescribed by the Secretary by regulations for giving notice under this subsection.

(b) Presumption that organizations are private foundations.—Except as provided in subsection (c), any organization (including an organization in existence on October 9,

1969) which is described in section 501(c)(3) and which does not notify the Secretary, at such time and in such manner as the Secretary may by regulations prescribe, that it is not a private foundation shall be presumed to be a private foundation.

(c) Exceptions.—

(1) Mandatory exceptions.—Subsections (a) and (b) shall not apply to—

(A) churches, their integrated auxiliaries, and conventions or associations of churches, or

(B) any organization which is not a private foundation (as defined in section 509(a)) and the gross receipts of which in each taxable year are normally not more than $5,000.

(2) Exceptions by regulations.—The Secretary may by regulations exempt (to the extent and subject to such conditions as may be prescribed in such regulations) from the provisions of subsection (a) or (b) or both—

(A) educational organizations described in section 170(b)(1)(A)(ii), and

(B) any other class of organizations with respect to which the Secretary determines that full compliance with the provisions of subsections (a) and (b) is not necessary to the efficient administration of the provisions of this title relating to private foundations.

(d) Disallowance of certain charitable, etc., deductions.—

(1) Gift or bequest to organizations subject to section 507(c) tax.—No gift or bequest made to an organization upon which the tax provided by section 507(c) has been imposed shall be allowed as a deduction under section 170, 545(b)(2), 642(c), 2055, 2106(a)(2), or 2522, if such gift or bequest is made—

(A) by any person after notification is made under section 507(a), or

(B) by a substantial contributor (as defined in section 507(d)(2)) in his taxable year which includes the first day on which action is taken by such organization which culminates in the imposition of tax under section 507(c) and any subsequent taxable year.

(2) Gift or bequest to taxable private foundation, section 4947 trust, etc.—No gift or bequest made to an organization shall be allowed as a deduction under section 170, 545(b)(2), 642(c), 2055, 2106(a)(2), or 2522, if such gift or bequest is made—

(A) to a private foundation or a trust described in section 4947 in a taxable year for which it fails to meet the requirements of subsection (e) (determined without regard to subsection (e)(2)), or

(B) to any organization in a period for which it is not treated as an organization described in section 501(c)(3) by reason of subsection (a).

(3) Exception.—Paragraph (1) shall not apply if the entire amount of the unpaid portion of the tax imposed by section 507(c) is abated by the Secretary under section 507(g).

(e) Governing instruments.—

(1) General rule.—A private foundation shall not be exempt from taxation under section 501(a) unless its governing instrument includes provisions the effects of which are—

(A) to require its income for each taxable year to be distributed at such time and in such manner as not to subject the foundation to tax under section 4942, and

(B) to prohibit the foundation from engaging in any act of self-dealing (as defined in section 4941(d)), from retaining any excess business holdings (as defined in section 4943(c)), from making any investments in such manner as to subject the foundation to tax under section 4944, and from making any taxable expenditures (as defined in section 4945(d)).

* * *

(f) Additional provisions relating to supporting organizations. A sponsoring organization (as defined in section 4966(d)(1)) shall give notice to the Secretary (in such manner as the Secretary may provide) whether such organization maintains or intends to maintain donor advised funds (as defined in section 4966(d)(2)) and the manner in which such organization plans to operate such funds.

§ 509. Private foundation defined.

(a) General rule.—For purposes of this title, the term "private foundation" means a domestic or foreign organization described in section 501(c)(3) other than—

(1) an organization described in section 170(b)(1)(A) (other than in clauses (vii) and (viii));

(2) an organization which—

(A) normally receives more than one-third of its support in each taxable year from any combination of—

(i) gifts, grants, contributions, or membership fees, and

(ii) gross receipts from admissions, sales of merchandise, performance of services, or furnishing of facilities, in an activity which is not an unrelated trade or business (within the meaning of section 513), not including such receipts from any person, or from any bureau or similar agency of a governmental unit (as described in section 170(c)(1)), in any taxable year to the extent such receipts exceed the greater of $5,000 or 1 percent of the organization's support in such taxable year, from persons other than disqualified persons (as defined in section 4946) with respect to the organization, from governmental units described in section 170(c)(1), or from organizations described in section 170(b)(1)(A) (other than in clauses (vii) and (viii)), and

(B) normally receives not more than one-third of its support in each taxable year from the sum of—

(i) gross investment income (as defined in subsection (e)) and

(ii) the excess (if any) of the amount of the unrelated business taxable income (as defined in section 512) over the amount of the tax imposed by section 511;

(3) an organization which—

(A) is organized, and at all times thereafter is operated, exclusively for the benefit of, to perform the functions of, or to carry out the purposes of one or more specified organizations described in paragraph (1) or (2),

(B) is—

(i) operated, supervised, or controlled by one or more organizations described in paragraph (1) or (2),

(ii) supervised or controlled in connection with one or more such organizations, or

(iii) operated in connection with one or more such organizations, and

(C) is not controlled directly or indirectly by one or more disqualified persons (as defined in section 4946) other than foundation managers and other than one or more organizations described in paragraph (1) or (2);

(4) an organization which is organized and operated exclusively for testing for public safety.

For purposes of paragraph (3), an organization described in paragraph (2) shall be deemed to include an organization described in section 501(c)(4), (5), or (6) which would be described in paragraph (2) if it were an organization described in section 501(c)(3).

(b) Continuation of private foundation status.—For purposes of this title, if an organization is a private foundation (within the meaning of subsection (a)) on October 9, 1969, or becomes a private foundation on any subsequent date, such organization shall be treated as a private foundation for all periods after October 9, 1969, or after such subsequent date, unless its status as such is terminated under section 507.

(c) Status of organization after termination of private foundation status.—For purposes of this part, an organization the status of which as a private foundation is terminated under section 507 shall (except as provided in section 507(b)(2)) be treated as an organization created on the day after the date of such termination.

(d) Definition of support.—For purposes of this part and chapter 42, the term "support" includes (but is not limited to)—

(1) gifts, grants, contributions, or membership fees,

(2) gross receipts from admissions, sales of merchandise, performance of services, or furnishing of facilities in any activity which is not an unrelated trade or business (within the meaning of section 513),

(3) net income from unrelated business activities, whether or not such activities are carried on regularly as a trade or business,

(4) gross investment income (as defined in subsection (e)),

(5) tax revenues levied for the benefit of an organization and either paid to or expended on behalf of such organization, and

(6) the value of services or facilities (exclusive of services or facilities generally furnished to the public without charge) furnished by a governmental unit referred to in section 170(c)(1) to an organization without charge.

Such term does not include any gain from the sale or other disposition of property which would be considered as gain from the sale or exchange of a capital asset, or the value of exemption from any Federal, State, or local tax or any similar benefit.

(e) Definition of gross investment income.—For purposes of subsection (d), the term "gross investment income" means the gross amount of income from interest, dividends, payments with respect to securities loans (as defined in section 512(a)(5)),rents, and royalties, but not including any such income to the extent included in computing the tax imposed by section 511. Such term shall also include income from sources similar to those in the preceding sentence.

(f) Requirements for supporting organizations.—

(1) Type III supporting organizations.—For purposes of subsection (a)(3)(B)(iii), an organization shall not be considered to be operated in connection with any organization described in paragraph (1) or (2) of subsection (a) unless such organization meets the following requirements:

(A) Responsiveness. For each taxable year beginning after the date of the enactment of this subsection, the organization provides to each supported organization such information as the Secretary may require to ensure that such organization is responsive to the needs or demands of the supported organization.

(B) Foreign supported organizations.—

(i) In general.—The organization is not operated in connection with any supported organization that is not organized in the United States.

(ii) Transition rule for existing organizations.—If the organization is operated in connection with an organization that is not organized in the United States on the date of the enactment of this subsection, clause (i) shall not apply until the first day of the third taxable year of the organization beginning after the date of the enactment of this subsection.

(2) Organizations controlled by donors—

(A) In general.—For purposes of subsection (a)(3)(B), an organization shall not be considered to be—

(i) operated, supervised, or controlled by any organization described in paragraph (1) or (2) of subsection (a), or

(ii) operated in connection with any organization described in paragraph (1) or (2) of subsection (a), if such organization accepts any gift or contribution from any person described in subparagraph (B).

(B) Person described.—A person is described in this subparagraph if, with respect to a supported organization of an organization described in subparagraph (A), such person is—

(i) a person (other than an organization described in paragraph (1), (2), or (4) of section 509(a)) who directly or indirectly controls, either alone or together with persons described in clauses (ii) and (iii), the governing body of such supported organization,

(ii) a member of the family (determined under section 4958(f)(4)) of an individual described in clause (i), or

(iii) a 35-percent controlled entity (as defined in section 4958(f)(3) by substituting "persons described in clause (i) or (ii) of section 509(f)(2)(B)" for "persons described in subparagraph (A) or (B) of paragraph (1)" in subparagraph (A)(i) thereof).

(3) Supported organization.—For purposes of this subsection, the term "supported organization" means, with respect to an organization described in subsection (a)(3), an organization described in paragraph (1) or (2) of subsection (a)—

(A) for whose benefit the organization described in subsection (a)(3) is organized and operated, or

(B) with respect to which the organization performs the functions of, or carries out the purposes of.

§ 511. Imposition of tax on unrelated business income of charitable, etc., organizations.

(a) Charitable, etc., organizations taxable at corporation rates.—

(1) Imposition of tax.—There is hereby imposed for each taxable year on the unrelated business taxable income (as defined in section 512) of every organization described in paragraph (2) a tax computed as provided in section 11. In making such computation for purposes of this section, the term "taxable income" as used in section 11 shall be read as "unrelated business taxable income".

(2) Organizations subject to tax.—

(A) Organizations described in sections 401(a) and 501(c).—The tax imposed by paragraph (1) shall apply in the case of any organization (other than a trust described in subsection (b) or an organization described in section 501(c)(1)) which is exempt, except as provided in this part or part II (relating to private foundations), from taxation under this subtitle by reason of section 501(a).

(B) State colleges and universities.—The tax imposed by paragraph (1) shall apply in the case of any college or university which is an agency or instrumentality of any government or any political subdivision thereof, or which is owned or operated by a government or any political subdivision thereof, or by any agency or instrumentality of one or more governments or political subdivisions. Such tax shall also apply in the case of any corporation wholly owned by one or more such colleges or universities.

(b) Tax on charitable, etc., trusts.—

(1) Imposition of tax.—There is hereby imposed for each taxable year on the unrelated business taxable income of every trust described in paragraph (2) a tax computed as provided in section 1(e). In making such computation for purposes of this section, the term "taxable income" as used in section 1 shall be read as "unrelated business taxable income" as defined in section 512.

(2) Charitable, etc., trusts subject to tax.—The tax imposed by paragraph (1) shall apply in the case of any trust which is exempt, except as provided in this part or part II (relating to private foundations), from taxation under this subtitle by reason of section 501(a) and which, if it were not for such exemption, would be subject to subchapter J (sec. 641 and following, relating to estates, trusts, beneficiaries, and decedents).

(c) Special rule for section 501(c)(2) corporations.—If a corporation described in section 501(c)(2)—

(1) pays any amount of its net income for a taxable year to an organization exempt from taxation under section 501(a) (or which would pay such an amount but for the fact that the expenses of collecting its income exceed its income), and

(2) such corporation and such organization file a consolidated return for the taxable year,

such corporation shall be treated, for purposes of the tax imposed by subsection (a), as being organized and operated for the same purposes as such organization, in addition to the purposes described in section 501(c)(2).

§ 512. Unrelated business taxable income.

(a) Definition.—For purposes of this title—

(1) General rule.—Except as otherwise provided in this subsection, the term "unrelated business taxable income" means the gross income derived by any organization from any unrelated trade or business (as defined in section 513) regularly carried on by it, less the deductions allowed by this chapter which are directly connected with the carrying on of such trade or business, both computed with the modifications provided in subsection (b).

(2) Special rule for foreign organizations.—In the case of an organization described in section 511 which is a foreign organization, the unrelated business taxable income shall be—

(A) its unrelated business taxable income which is derived from sources within the United States and which is not effectively connected with the conduct of a trade or business within the United States, plus

(B) its unrelated business taxable income which is effectively connected with the conduct of a trade or business within the United States.

(3) Special rules applicable to organizations described in paragraph (7), (9), (17), or (20) of section 501(c).—

(A) General rule.—In the case of an organization described in paragraph (7), (9), (17), or (20) of section 501(c), the term "unrelated business taxable income" means the gross income (excluding any exempt function income), less the deductions allowed by this chapter which are directly connected with the production of the gross income (excluding exempt function income), both computed with the modifications provided in paragraphs (6), (10), (11), and (12) of subsection (b). For purposes of the preceding sentence, the deductions provided by sections 243, 244, and 245 (relating to dividends received by corporations) shall be treated as not directly connected with the production of gross income.

(B) Exempt function income.—For purposes of subparagraph (A), the term "exempt function income" means the gross income from dues, fees, charges, or similar amounts paid by members of the organization as consideration for providing such members or their dependents or guests goods, facilities, or services in furtherance of the purposes constituting the basis for the exemption of the organization to which such income is paid. Such term also means all income (other than an amount equal to the gross income derived from any unrelated trade or business regularly carried on by such organization computed as if the organization were subject to paragraph (1)), which is set aside—

(i) for a purpose specified in section 170(c)(4), or

(ii) in the case of an organization described in paragraph (9), (17), or (20) of section 501(c), to provide for the payment of life, sick, accident, or other benefits,

including reasonable costs of administration directly connected with a purpose described in clause (i) or (ii). If during the taxable year, an amount which is attributable to income so set aside is used for a purpose other than that described in clause (i) or (ii), such amount shall be included, under subparagraph (A), in unrelated business taxable income for the taxable year.

(C) Applicability to certain corporations described in section 501(c)(2).— In the case of a corporation described in section 501(c)(2), the income of which is payable to an organization described in paragraph (7), (9), (17), or (20) of section 501(c), subparagraph (A) shall apply as if such corporation were the organization to which the income is payable. For purposes of the preceding sentence, such corporation shall be treated as having exempt function income for a taxable year only if it files a consolidated return with such organization for such year.

(D) Nonrecognition of gain.—If property used directly in the performance of the exempt function of an organization described in paragraph (7), (9), (17), or (20) of section 501(c) is sold by such organization, and within a period beginning 1 year before the date of such sale, and ending 3 years after such date, other property is purchased and used by such organization directly in the performance of its exempt function, gain (if any) from such sale shall be recognized only to the extent that such organization's sales price of the old property exceeds the organization's cost of purchasing the other property. For purposes of this subparagraph, the destruction in whole or in part, theft, seizure, requisition, or condemnation of property, shall be treated as the sale of such property, and rules similar to the rules provided by subsections (b), (c), (e), and (j) of section 1034 (as in effect on the day before the date of the enactment of the Taxpayer Relief Act of 1997) shall apply.

(E) Limitation on amount of set aside in the case of organizations described in paragraph (9), (17), or (20) of section 501(c).—

(i) In general.—In the case of any organization described in paragraph (9), (17), or (20) of section 501(c), a set-aside for any purpose specified in clause (ii) of subparagraph (B) may be taken into account under subparagraph (B) only to the extent that such set-aside does not result in an amount of assets set aside for such purpose in excess of the account limit determined under section 419A (without regard to subsection (f)(6) thereof) for the taxable year (not taking into account any reserve described in section 419A(c)(2)(A) for post-retirement medical benefits).

(ii) Treatment of existing reserves for post-retirement medical or life insurance benefits.—

(I) Clause (i) shall not apply to any income attributable to an existing reserve for post-retirement medical or life insurance benefits.

(II) For purposes of subclause (I), the term "reserve for post-retirement medical or life insurance benefits" means the greater of the amount of assets set aside for purposes of post-retirement medical or life insurance benefits to be provided to covered employees as of the close of the last plan year ending before the date of the enactment of the Tax Reform Act of 1984 or on July 18, 1984.

(III) All payments during plan years ending on or after the date of the enactment of the Tax Reform Act of 1984 of post-retirement medical benefits or life insurance benefits shall be charged against the reserve referred to in subclause (II). Except to the extent provided in regulations prescribed by the Secretary, all plans of an employer shall be treated as 1 plan for purposes of the preceding sentence.

(iii) Treatment of tax exempt organizations.—This subparagraph shall not apply to any organization if substantially all of the contributions to such organization are made by employers who were exempt from tax under this chapter throughout the 5-taxable year period ending with the taxable year in which the contributions are made.

(4) Special rule applicable to organizations described in section 501(c)(19).— In the case of an organization described in section 501(c)(19), the term "unrelated business taxable income" does not include any amount attributable to payments for life, sick, accident, or health insurance with respect to members of such organizations or their dependents which is set aside for the purpose of providing for the payment of insurance benefits or for a purpose specified in section 170(c)(4). If an amount set aside under the preceding sentence is used during the taxable year for a purpose other than a purpose described in the preceding sentence, such amount shall be included, under paragraph (1), in unrelated business taxable income for the taxable year.

(5) Definition of payments with respect to securities loans.—

(A) The term "payments with respect to securities loans" includes all amounts received in respect of a security (as defined in section 1236(c)) transferred by the owner to another person in a transaction to which section 1058 applies (whether or not title to the security remains in the name of the lender) including—

(i) amounts in respect of dividends, interest, or other distributions,

(ii) fees computed by reference to the period beginning with the transfer of securities by the owner and ending with the transfer of identical securities back to the transferor by the transferee and the fair market value of the security during such period,

(iii) income from collateral security for such loan, and

(iv) income from the investment of collateral security.

(B) Subparagraph (A) shall apply only with respect to securities transferred pursuant to an agreement between the transferor and the transferee which provides for—

(i) reasonable procedures to implement the obligation of the transferee to furnish to the transferor, for each business day during such period, collateral with a fair market value not less than the fair market value of the security at the close of business on the preceding business day,

(ii) termination of the loan by the transferor upon notice of not more than 5 business days, and

(iii) return to the transferor of securities identical to the transferred securities upon termination of the loan.

(6) Special Rule for Organization with More than 1 Unrelated Trade or Business.—In the case of any organization with more than 1 unrelated trade or business—

(A) unrelated business taxable income, including for purposes of determining any net operating loss deduction, shall be computed separately with respect to each such trade or business and without regard to subsection (b)(12),

(B) the unrelated business taxable income of such organization shall be the sum of the unrelated business taxable income so computed with respect to each such trade or business, less a specific deduction under subsection (b)(12), and

(C) for purposes of subparagraph (B), unrelated business taxable income with respect to any such trade or business shall not be less than zero.

(b) Modifications.—The modifications referred to in subsection (a) are the following:

(1) There shall be excluded all dividends, interest, payments with respect to securities loans (as defined in subsection (a)(5)), amounts received or accrued as consideration for entering into agreements to make loans, and annuities, and all deductions directly connected with such income.

(2) There shall be excluded all royalties (including overriding royalties) whether measured by production or by gross or taxable income from the property, and all deductions directly connected with such income.

(3) In the case of rents—

(A) Except as provided in subparagraph (B), there shall be excluded—

(i) all rents from real property (including property described in section 1245(a)(3)(C)), and

(ii) all rents from personal property (including for purposes of this paragraph as personal property any property described in section 1245(a)(3)(B)) leased with such real property, if the rents attributable to such personal property are an incidental amount of the total rents received or accrued under the lease, determined at the time the personal property is placed in service.

(B) Subparagraph (A) shall not apply—

(i) if more than 50 percent of the total rent received or accrued under the lease is attributable to personal property described in subparagraph (A)(ii), or

(ii) if the determination of the amount of such rent depends in whole or in part on the income or profits derived by any person from the property leased (other than an amount based on a fixed percentage or percentages of receipts or sales).

(C) There shall be excluded all deductions directly connected with rents excluded under subparagraph (A).

(4) Notwithstanding paragraph (1), (2), (3), or (5), in the case of debt-financed property (as defined in section 514) there shall be included, as an item of gross income derived from an unrelated trade or business, the amount ascertained under section 514(a)(1), and there shall be allowed, as a deduction, the amount ascertained under section 514(a)(2).

(5) There shall be excluded all gains or losses from the sale, exchange, or other disposition of property other than—

(A) stock in trade or other property of a kind which would properly be includible in inventory if on hand at the close of the taxable year, or

(B) property held primarily for sale to customers in the ordinary course of the trade or business.

There shall also be excluded all gains or losses recognized, in connection with the organization's investment activities, from the lapse or termination of options to buy or sell securities (as defined in section 1236(c)) or real property and all gains or losses from the forfeiture of good-faith deposits (that are consistent with established business practice) for the purchase, sale, or lease of real property in connection with the organization's investment activities. This paragraph shall not apply with respect to the cutting of timber which is considered, on the application of section 631, as a sale or exchange of such timber.

(6) The net operating loss deduction provided in section 172 shall be allowed, except that—

(A) the net operating loss for any taxable year, the amount of the net operating loss carryback or carryover to any taxable year, and the net operating loss deduction for any taxable year shall be determined under section 172 without taking into account any amount of income or deduction which is excluded under this part in computing the unrelated business taxable income; and

(B) the terms "preceding taxable year" and "preceding taxable years" as used in section 172 shall not include any taxable year for which the organization was not subject to the provisions of this part.

(7) There shall be excluded all income derived from research for (A) the United States, or any of its agencies or instrumentalities, or (B) any State or political subdivision thereof; and there shall be excluded all deductions directly connected with such income.

(8) In the case of a college, university, or hospital, there shall be excluded all income derived from research performed for any person, and all deductions directly connected with such income.

(9) In the case of an organization operated primarily for purposes of carrying on fundamental research the results of which are freely available to the general public, there shall be excluded all income derived from research performed for any person, and all deductions directly connected with such income.

(10) In the case of any organization described in section 511(a), the deduction allowed by section 170 (relating to charitable etc. contributions and gifts) shall be allowed (whether or not directly connected with the carrying on of the trade or business), but shall not exceed 10 percent of the unrelated business taxable income computed without the benefit of this paragraph.

(11) In the case of any trust described in section 511(b), the deduction allowed by section 170 (relating to charitable etc. contributions and gifts) shall be allowed (whether or not directly connected with the carrying on of the trade or business), and for such purpose a distribution made by the trust to a beneficiary described in section 170 shall be considered as a gift or contribution. The deduction allowed by this paragraph shall be allowed with the limitations prescribed in section 170(b)(1)(A) and (B) determined with reference to the unrelated business taxable income computed without the benefit of this paragraph (in lieu of with reference to adjusted gross income).

(12) Except for purposes of computing the net operating loss under section 172 and paragraph (6), there shall be allowed a specific deduction of $1,000. In the case of a diocese, province of a religious order, or a convention or association of churches, there shall also be allowed, with respect to each parish, individual church, district, or other local unit, a specific deduction equal to the lower of—

(A) $1,000, or

(B) the gross income derived from any unrelated trade or business regularly carried on by such local unit.

(13) Special rules for certain amounts received from controlled entities—

(A) In general—If an organization (in this paragraph referred to as the "controlling organization") receives or accrues (directly or indirectly) a specified payment from another entity which it controls (in this paragraph referred to as the "controlled entity"), notwithstanding paragraphs (1), (2), and (3), the controlling organization shall include such payment as an item of gross income derived from an unrelated trade or business to the extent such payment reduces the net unrelated income of the controlled entity (or increases any net unrelated loss of the controlled entity). There shall be allowed all deductions of the controlling organization directly connected with amounts treated as derived from an unrelated trade or business under the preceding sentence.

(B) Net unrelated income or loss—For purposes of this paragraph—

(i) Net unrelated income—The term "net unrelated income" means—

(I) in the case of a controlled entity which is not exempt from tax under section 501(a), the portion of such entity's taxable income which would be unrelated business taxable income if such entity were exempt from tax under section and had the same exempt purposes as the controlling organization, or

(II) in the case of a controlled entity which is exempt from tax under section 501(a), the amount of the unrelated business taxable income of the controlled entity.

(ii) Net unrelated loss—The term "net unrelated loss" means the net operating loss adjusted under rules similar to the rules of clause (i).

(C) Specified payment—For purposes of this paragraph, the term "specified payment" means any interest, annuity, royalty, or rent.

(D) Definition of control—For purposes of this paragraph—

(i) Control—The term "control" means—

(I) in the case of a corporation, ownership (by vote or value) of more than 50 percent of the stock in such corporation,

(II) in the case of a partnership, ownership of more than 50 percent of the profits interests or capital interests in such partnership, or

(III) in any other case, ownership of more than 50 percent of the beneficial interests in the entity.

(ii) Constructive ownership—Section 318 (relating to constructive ownership of stock) shall apply for purposes of determining ownership of stock in a corporation. Similar principles shall apply for purposes of determining ownership of interests in any other entity.

(E) Paragraph to apply only to certain excess payments.—

(i) In general.—Subparagraph (A) shall apply only to the portion of a qualifying specified payment received or accrued by the controlling organization that exceeds the amount which would have been paid or accrued if such payment met the requirements prescribed under section 482.

(ii) Addition to tax for valuation misstatements.—The tax imposed by this chapter on the controlling organization shall be increased by an amount equal to 20 percent of the larger of—

(I) such excess determined without regard to any amendment or supplement to a return of tax, or

(II) such excess determined with regard to all such amendments and supplements.

(iii) Qualifying specified payment.—The term "qualifying specified payment" means a specified payment which is made pursuant to—

(I) a binding written contract in effect on the date of the enactment of this subparagraph, or

(II) a contract which is a renewal, under substantially similar terms, of a contract described in subclause (I).

(F) Related persons—The Secretary shall prescribe such rules as may be necessary or appropriate to prevent avoidance of the purposes of this paragraph through the use of related persons.

* * *

(15) Except as provided in paragraph (4), in the case of a trade or business—

(A) which consists of providing services under license issued by a Federal regulatory agency,

(B) which is carried on by a religious order or by an educational organization described in section 170(b)(1)(A)(ii) maintained by such religious order, and which was so carried on before May 27, 1959, and

(C) less than 10 percent of the net income of which for each taxable year is used for activities which are not related to the purpose constituting the basis for the religious order's exemption,

there shall be excluded all gross income derived from such trade or business and all deductions directly connected with the carrying on of such trade or business, so long as it is established to the satisfaction of the Secretary that the rates or other charges for such services are competitive with rates or other charges charged for similar services by persons not exempt from taxation.

* * *

(c) Special rules for partnerships.—

(1) In general.—If a trade or business regularly carried on by a partnership of which an organization is a member is an unrelated trade or business with respect to such organization, such organization in computing its unrelated business taxable income shall, subject to the exceptions, additions, and limitations contained in subsection (b), include its share (whether or not distributed) of the gross income of the partnership from such unrelated trade or business and its share of the partnership deductions directly connected with such gross income.

(2) Special rule where partnership year is different from organization's year.—If the taxable year of the organization is different from that of the partnership, the amounts to be included or deducted in computing the unrelated business taxable income under paragraph (1) shall be based upon the income and deductions of the partnership for any taxable year of the partnership ending within or with the taxable year of the organization.

(d) Treatment of dues of agricultural or horticultural organizations.—

(1) In general.—If—

(A) an agricultural or horticultural organization described in section requires annual dues to be paid in order to be a member of such organization, and

(B) the amount of such required annual dues does not exceed $100,

in no event shall any portion of such dues be treated as derived by such organization from an unrelated trade or business by reason of any benefits or privileges to which members of such organization are entitled.

(2) Indexation $100 amount.—In the case of any taxable year beginning in a calendar year after 1995, the $100 amount in paragraph (1) shall be increased by an amount equal to—

(A) $100, multiplied by

(B) the cost-of-living adjustment determined under section for the calendar year in which the taxable year begins by, substituting "calendar year 1994" for "calendar year 2016" in subparagraph (B) thereof.

(3) Dues.—For purposes of this subsection, the term "dues" means any payment (whether or not designated as dues) which is required to be made in order to be recognized by the organization as a member of the organization.

(e) Special rules applicable to S corporations.

(1) In general.—If an organization described in section 1361(c)(2)(A)(vi) or 1361(c)(6) holds stock in an S corporation—

(A) such interest shall be treated as an interest in an unrelated trade or business, and

(B) notwithstanding any other provision of this part—

(i) all items of income, loss, or deduction taken into account under section 1366(a), and

(ii) any gain or loss on the disposition of the stock in the S corporation,

shall be taken into account in computing the unrelated business taxable income of such organization.

(2) Basis reduction.—Except as provided in regulations, for purposes of paragraph (1), the basis of any stock acquired by purchase (as defined in section 1361(e)(1)(C)) shall be reduced by the amount of any dividends received by the organization with respect to the stock.

(3) Exception for ESOPs.—This subsection shall not apply to employer securities (within the meaning of section 409(*l*) held by an employee stock ownership plan described in section 4975(e)(7).

§ 513. Unrelated trade or business.

(a) General rule.—The term "unrelated trade or business" means, in the case of any organization subject to the tax imposed by section 511, any trade or business the conduct of which is not substantially related (aside from the need of such organization for income or funds or the use it makes of the profits derived) to the exercise or performance by such organization of its charitable, educational, or other purpose or function constituting the basis for its exemption under section 501 (or, in the case of an organization described in section 511(a)(2)(B), to the exercise or performance of any purpose or function described in section 501(c)(3)), except that such term does not include any trade or business—

(1) in which substantially all the work in carrying on such trade or business is performed for the organization without compensation; or

(2) which is carried on, in the case of an organization described in section 501(c)(3) or in the case of a college or university described in section 511(a)(2)(B), by the organization primarily for the convenience of its members, students, patients, officers, or employees, or, in the case of a local association of employees described in section 501(c)(4) organized before May 27, 1969, which is the selling by the organization of items of work-related clothes and equipment and items normally sold through vending machines, through food dispensing facilities, or by snack bars, for the convenience of its members at their usual places of employment; or

(3) which is the selling of merchandise, substantially all of which has been received by the organization as gifts or contributions.

(b) Special rule for trusts.—The term "unrelated trade or business" means, in the case of—

(1) a trust computing its unrelated business taxable income under section 512 for purposes of section 681; or

(2) a trust described in section 401(a), or section 501(c)(17), which is exempt from tax under section 501(a);

any trade or business regularly carried on by such trust or by a partnership of which it is a member.

(c) Advertising, etc., activities.—For purposes of this section, the term "trade or business" includes any activity which is carried on for the production of income from the sale of goods or the performance of services. For purposes of the preceding sentence, an activity does not lose identity as a trade or business merely because it is carried on within a larger aggregate of similar activities or within a larger complex of other endeavors which may, or may not, be related to the exempt purposes of the organization. Where an activity carried on for profit constitutes an unrelated trade or business, no part of such trade or business shall be excluded from such classification merely because it does not result in profit.

(d) Certain activities of trade shows, State fairs, etc.—

(1) General rule.—The term "unrelated trade or business" does not include qualified public entertainment activities of an organization described in paragraph (2)(C), or qualified convention and trade show activities of an organization described in paragraph (3)(C).

(2) Qualified public entertainment activities.—For purposes of this subsection—

(A) Public entertainment activity.—The term "public entertainment activity" means any entertainment or recreational activity of a kind traditionally conducted at fairs or expositions promoting agricultural and educational purposes, including, but not limited to, any activity one of the purposes of which is to attract the public to fairs or expositions or to promote the breeding of animals or the development of products or equipment.

(B) Qualified public entertainment activity.—The term "qualified public entertainment activity" means a public entertainment activity which is conducted by a qualifying organization described in subparagraph (C) in—

(i) conjunction with an international, national, State, regional, or local fair or exposition,

(ii) accordance with the provisions of State law which permit the activity to be operated or conducted solely by such an organization, or by an agency, instrumentality, or political subdivision of such State, or

(iii) accordance with the provisions of State law which permit such an organization to be granted a license to conduct not more than 20 days of such activity on payment to the State of a lower percentage of the revenue from such licensed activity than the State requires from organizations not described in section 501(c)(3), (4), or (5).

(C) Qualifying organization.—For purposes of this paragraph, the term "qualifying organization" means an organization which is described in section 501(c)(3), (4), or (5) which regularly conducts, as one of its substantial exempt purposes, an agricultural and educational fair or exposition.

(3) Qualified convention and trade show activities.—

(A) Convention and trade show activities.—The term "convention and trade show activity" means any activity of a kind traditionally conducted at conventions, annual meetings, or trade shows, including, but not limited to, any activity one of the purposes of which is to attract persons in an industry generally (without regard to membership in the sponsoring organization) as well as members of the public to the show for the purpose of displaying industry products or to stimulate interest in, and demand for, industry products or services, or to educate persons engaged in the industry in the development of new products and services or new rules and regulations affecting the industry.

(B) Qualified convention and trade show activity.—The term "qualified convention and trade show activity" means a convention and trade show activity carried out by a qualifying organization described in subparagraph (C) in conjunction with an international, national, State, regional, or local convention, annual meeting, or show conducted by an organization described in subparagraph (C) if one of the purposes of such organization in sponsoring the activity is the promotion and stimulation of interest in, and demand for, the products and services of that industry in general or to educate persons in attendance regarding new developments or products and services related to the exempt activities of the organization, and the show is designed to achieve such purpose through the character of the exhibits and the extent of the industry products displayed.

(C) Qualifying organization.—For purposes of this paragraph, the term "qualifying organization" means an organization described in section 501(c)(3), (4), (5), or (6) which regularly conducts as one of its substantial exempt purposes a show which stimulates interest in, and demand for, the products of a particular industry or segment of such industry or which educates persons in attendance regarding new developments or products and services related to the exempt activities of the organization.

(4) Such activities not to affect exempt status.—An organization described in section 501(c)(3), (4), or (5) shall not be considered as not entitled to the exemption allowed under section 501(a) solely because of qualified public entertainment activities conducted by it.

(e) Certain hospital services.—In the case of a hospital described in section 170(b)(1)(A)(iii), the term "unrelated trade or business" does not include the furnishing of one or more of the services described in section 501(e)(1)(A) to one or more hospitals described in section 170(b)(1)(A)(iii) if—

(1) such services are furnished solely to such hospitals which have facilities to serve not more than 100 inpatients;

(2) such services, if performed on its own behalf by the recipient hospital, would constitute activities in exercising or performing the purpose or function constituting the basis for its exemption; and

(3) such services are provided at a fee or cost which does not exceed the actual cost of providing such services, such cost including straight line depreciation and a reasonable amount for return on capital goods used to provide such services.

(f) Certain bingo games.—

(1) In general.—The term "unrelated trade or business" does not include any trade or business which consists of conducting bingo games.

(2) Bingo game defined.—For purposes of paragraph (1), the term "bingo game" means any game of bingo—

(A) of a type in which usually—

(i) the wagers are placed,

(ii) the winners are determined, and

(iii) the distribution of prizes or other property is made,

in the presence of all persons placing wagers in such game,

(B) the conducting of which is not an activity ordinarily carried out on a commercial basis, and

(C) the conducting of which does not violate any State or local law.

(g) Certain pole rentals.—In the case of a mutual or cooperative telephone or electric company, the term "unrelated trade or business" does not include engaging in qualified pole rentals (as defined in section 501(c)(12)(D)).

(h) Certain distributions of low cost articles without obligation to purchase and exchanges and rentals of member lists.—

(1) In general.—In the case of an organization which is described in section 501 and contributions to which are deductible under paragraph (2) or (3) of section 170(c), the term "unrelated trade or business" does not include—

(A) activities relating to the distribution of low cost articles if the distribution of such articles is incidental to the solicitation of charitable contributions, or

(B) any trade or business which consists of—

(i) exchanging with another such organization names and addresses of donors to (or members of) such organization, or

(ii) renting such names and addresses to another such organization.

(2) Low cost article defined.—For purposes of this subsection—

(A) In general.—The term "low cost article" means any article which has a cost not in excess of $5 to the organization which distributes such item (or on whose behalf such item is distributed).

(B) Aggregation rule.—If more than 1 item is distributed by or on behalf of an organization to a single distributee in any calendar year, the aggregate of the items so distributed in such calendar year to such distributee shall be treated as 1 article for purposes of subparagraph (A).

(C) Indexation of $5 amount.—In the case of any taxable year beginning in a calendar year after 1987, the $5 amount in subparagraph (A) shall be increased by an amount equal to—

(i) $5, multiplied by

(ii) the cost-of-living adjustment determined under section 1(f)(3) for the calendar year in which the taxable year begins by substituting "calendar year 1987" for "calendar year 2016" in subparagraph (B) thereof.

(3) Distribution which is incidental to the solicitation of charitable contributions described.—For purposes of this subsection, any distribution of low cost articles by an organization shall be treated as a distribution incidental to the solicitation of charitable contributions only if—

(A) such distribution is not made at the request of the distributee,

(B) such distribution is made without the express consent of the distributee, and

(C) the articles so distributed are accompanied by—

(i) a request for a charitable contribution (as defined in section 170(c)) by the distributee to such organization, and

(ii) a statement that the distributee may retain the low cost article regardless of whether such distributee makes a charitable contribution to such organization.

(i) Treatment of certain sponsorship payments.—

(1) In general.—The term "unrelated trade or business" does not include the activity of soliciting and receiving qualified sponsorship payments.

(2) Qualified sponsorship payments.—For purposes of this subsection—

(A) In general.—The term "qualified sponsorship payment" means any payment made by any person engaged in a trade or business with respect to which there is no arrangement or expectation that such person will receive any substantial return benefit other than the use or acknowledgement of the name or logo (or product lines) of such person's trade or business in connection with the activities of the organization that receives such payment. Such a use or acknowledgement does not include advertising such person's products or services (including messages containing qualitative or comparative language, price information, or other indications of savings or value, an endorsement, or an inducement to purchase, sell, or use such products or services).

(B) Limitations.—

(i) Contingent payments.—The term "qualified sponsorship payment" does not include any payment if the amount of such payment is contingent upon the level of attendance at one or more events, broadcast ratings, or other factors indicating the degree of public exposure to one or more events.

(ii) Safe harbor does not apply to periodicals and qualified convention and trade show activities.—The term "qualified sponsorship payment" does not include—

(I) any payment which entitles the payor to the use or acknowledgement of the name or logo (or product lines) of the payor's trade or business in regularly scheduled and printed material published by or on behalf of the payee organization that is not related to and primarily distributed in connection with a specific event conducted by the payee organization, or

(II) any payment made in connection with any qualified convention or trade show activity (as defined in subsection (d)(3)(B)).

(3) Allocation of portions of single payment.—For purposes of this subsection, to the extent that a portion of a payment would (if made as a separate payment) be a qualified sponsorship payment, such portion of such payment and the other portion of such payment shall be treated as separate payments.

* * *

§ 514. Unrelated debt-financed income.

(a) Unrelated debt-financed income and deductions.—In computing under section 512 the unrelated business taxable income for any taxable year—

(1) Percentage of income taken into account.—There shall be included with respect to each debt-financed property as an item of gross income derived from an unrelated trade or business an amount which is the same percentage (but not in excess of 100 percent) of the total gross income derived during the taxable year from or on account of such property as (A) the average acquisition indebtedness (as defined in subsection (c)(7)) for the taxable year with respect to the property is of (B) the average amount (determined under regulations prescribed by the Secretary) of the adjusted basis of such property during the period it is held by the organization during such taxable year.

(2) Percentage of deductions taken into account.—There shall be allowed as a deduction with respect to each debt-financed property an amount determined by applying (except as provided in the last sentence of this paragraph) the percentage derived under paragraph (1) to the sum determined under paragraph (3). The percentage derived under this paragraph shall not be applied with respect to the deduction of any capital loss resulting from the carryback or carryover of net capital losses under section 1212.

(3) Deductions allowable.—The sum referred to in paragraph (2) is the sum of the deductions under this chapter which are directly connected with the debt-financed property or the income therefrom, except that if the debt-financed property is of a character which is subject to the allowance for depreciation provided in section 167, the allowance shall be computed only by use of the straight-line method.

(b) Definition of debt-financed property.—

(1) In general.—For purposes of this section, the term "debt-financed property" means any property which is held to produce income and with respect to which there is an acquisition indebtedness (as defined in subsection (c)) at any time during the taxable year (or, if the property was disposed of during the taxable year, with respect to which there was an acquisition indebtedness at anytime during the 12-month period ending with the date of such disposition), except that such term does not include—

(A)(i) any property substantially all the use of which is substantially related (aside from the need of the organization for income or funds) to the exercise or performance by such organization of its charitable, educational, or other purpose or function constituting the basis for its exemption under section 501 (or, in the case of an organization described in section 511(a)(2)(B), to the exercise or performance of any purpose or function designated in section 501(c)(3)), or (ii) any property to which clause (i) does not apply, to the extent that its use is so substantially related;

(B) except in the case of income excluded under section 512(b)(5), any property to the extent that the income from such property is taken into account in computing the gross income of any unrelated trade or business;

(C) any property to the extent that the income from such property is excluded by reason of the provisions of paragraph (7), (8), or (9) of section 512(b) in computing the gross income of any unrelated trade or business;

(D) any property to the extent that it is used in any trade or business described in paragraph (1), (2), or (3) of section 513(a); or

(E) any property the gain or loss from the sale or exchange, or other disposition of which would be excluded by reason of the provisions of section 512(b)(19) in computing the gross income of any unrelated trade or business.

For purposes of subparagraph (A), substantially all the use of a property shall be considered to be substantially related to the exercise or performance by an organization of its charitable, educational, or other purpose or function constituting the basis for its exemption under section 501 if such property is real property subject to a lease to a medical clinic entered into primarily for purposes which are substantially related (aside from the need of such organization for income or funds or the use it makes of the rents derived) to the exercise or performance by such organization of its charitable, educational, or other purpose or function constituting the basis for its exemption under section 501.

(2) Special rule for related uses.—For purposes of applying paragraphs (1)(A), (C), and (D), the use of any property by an exempt organization which is related to an organization shall be treated as use by such organization.

(3) Special rules when land is acquired for exempt use within 10 years.—

(A) Neighborhood land.—If an organization acquires real property for the principal purpose of using the land (commencing within 10 years of the time of acquisition) in the manner described in paragraph (1)(A) and at the time of acquisition the property is in the neighborhood of other property owned by the organization which is used in such manner, the real property acquired for such future use shall not be treated as debt-financed property so long as the organization does not abandon its intent to so use the land within the 10-year period. The preceding sentence shall not apply for any period after the expiration of the 10-year period, and shall apply after the first 5 years of the 10-year period only if the organization establishes to the satisfaction of the Secretary that it is reasonably certain that the land will be used in the described manner before the expiration of the 10-year period.

(B) Other cases.—If the first sentence of subparagraph (A) is inapplicable only because—

(i) the acquired land is not in the neighborhood referred to in subparagraph (A), or

(ii) the organization (for the period after the first 5 years of the 10-year period) is unable to establish to the satisfaction of the Secretary that it is reasonably certain that the land will be used in the manner described in paragraph (1)(A) before the expiration of the 10-year period,

but the land is converted to such use by the organization within the 10-year period, the real property (subject to the provisions of subparagraph (D)) shall not be treated as debt-financed property for any period before such conversion. For purposes of this subparagraph, land shall not be treated as used in the manner described in paragraph (1)(A) by reason of the use made of any structure which was on the land when acquired by the organization.

(C) Limitations.—Subparagraphs (A) and (B)—

(i) shall apply with respect to any structure on the land when acquired by the organization, or to the land occupied by the structure, only if (and so long as) the intended future use of the land in the manner described in paragraph (1)(A) requires that the structure be demolished or removed in order to use the land in such manner;

(ii) shall not apply to structures erected on the land after the acquisition of the land; and

(iii) shall not apply to property subject to a lease which is a business lease (as defined in this section immediately before the enactment of the Tax Reform Act of 1976).

(D) Refund of taxes when subparagraph (B) applies.—If an organization for any taxable year has not used land in the manner to satisfy the actual use condition of subparagraph (B) before the time prescribed by law(including extensions thereof) for filing the return for such taxable year, the tax for such year shall be computed without regard to the application of subparagraph (B), but if and when such use condition is satisfied, the provisions of subparagraph (B) shall then be applied to such taxable year. If the actual use condition of subparagraph (B) is satisfied for any taxable year after such time for filing the return, and if credit or refund of any overpayment for the taxable year resulting from the satisfaction of such use condition is prevented at the close of the taxable year in which the use condition is satisfied, by the operation of any law or rule of law (other than chapter 74, relating to closing agreements and compromises), credit or refund of such overpayment may nevertheless be allowed or made if claim therefor is filed before the expiration of 1 year after the close of the taxable year in which the use condition is satisfied.

(E) Special rule for churches.—In applying this paragraph to a church or convention or association of churches, in lieu of the 10-year period referred to in subparagraphs (A) and (B) a 15-year period shall be applied, and subparagraphs (A) and (B)(ii) shall apply whether or not the acquired land meets the neighborhood test.

(c) Acquisition indebtedness.—

(1) General rule.—For purposes of this section, the term "acquisition indebtedness" means, with respect to any debt-financed property, the unpaid amount of—

(A) the indebtedness incurred by the organization in acquiring or improving such property;

(B) the indebtedness incurred before the acquisition or improvement of such property if such indebtedness would not have been incurred but for such acquisition or improvement; and

(C) the indebtedness incurred after the acquisition or improvement of such property if such indebtedness would not have been incurred but for such acquisition or improvement and the incurrence of such indebtedness was reasonably foreseeable at the time of such acquisition or improvement.

(2) Property acquired subject to mortgage, etc.—For purposes of this subsection—

(A) General rule.—Where property (no matter how acquired) is acquired subject to a mortgage or other similar lien, the amount of the indebtedness secured by such mortgage or lien shall be considered as an indebtedness of the organization incurred in acquiring such property even though the organization did not assume or agree to pay such indebtedness.

(B) Exceptions.—Where property subject to a mortgage is acquired by an organization by bequest or devise, the indebtedness secured by the mortgage shall not be treated as acquisition indebtedness during a period of 10 years following the date of the acquisition. If an organization acquires property by gift subject to a mortgage which was placed on the property more than 5 years before the gift, which property was held by the donor more than 5 years before the gift, the indebtedness secured by such mortgage shall not be treated as acquisition indebtedness during a period of 10 years following the date of such gift. This subparagraph shall not apply if the organization, in order to acquire the equity in the property by bequest, devise, or gift, assumes and agrees to pay the indebtedness secured by the mortgage, or if the organization makes any payment for the equity in the property owned by the decedent or the donor.

(C) Liens for taxes or assessments.—Where State law provides that—

(i) a lien for taxes, or

(ii) a lien for assessments,

made by a State or a political subdivision thereof attaches to property prior to the time when such taxes or assessments become due and payable, then such lien shall be treated as similar to a mortgage (within the meaning of subparagraph (A)) but only after such taxes or assessments become due and payable and the organization has had an opportunity to pay such taxes or assessments in accordance with State law.

(3) Extension of obligations.—For purposes of this section, an extension, renewal, or refinancing of an obligation evidencing a pre-existing indebtedness shall not be treated as the creation of a new indebtedness.

(4) Indebtedness incurred in performing exempt purpose.—For purposes of this section, the term "acquisition indebtedness" does not include indebtedness the incurrence of which is inherent in the performance or exercise of the purpose or function constituting the basis of the organization's exemption, such as the indebtedness incurred by a credit union described in section 501(c)(14) in accepting deposits from its members.

(5) Annuities.—For purposes of this section, the term "acquisition indebtedness" does not include an obligation to pay an annuity which—

(A) is the sole consideration (other than a mortgage to which paragraph (2)(B) applies) issued in exchange for property if, at the time of the exchange, the value of the annuity is less than 90 percent of the value of the property received in the exchange,

(B) is payable over the life of one individual in being at the time the annuity is issued, or over the lives of two individuals in being at such time, and

(C) is payable under a contract which—

(i) does not guarantee a minimum amount of payments or specify a maximum amount of payments, and

(ii) does not provide for any adjustment of the amount of the annuity payments by reference to the income received from the transferred property or any other property.

(6) Certain Federal financing.—

(A) In general.—For purposes of this section, the term "acquisition indebtedness" does not include—

(i) an obligation, to the extent that it is insured by the Federal Housing Administration, to finance the purchase, rehabilitation, or construction of housing for low and moderate income persons, or

(ii) indebtedness incurred by a small business investment company licensed after the date of the enactment of the American Jobs Creation Act of 2004 under the Small Business Investment Act of 1958 if such indebtedness is evidenced by a debenture—

(I) issued by such company under section 303(a) of such Act, and

(II) held or guaranteed by the Small Business Administration.

(B) Limitation.—Subparagraph (A)(ii) shall not apply with respect to any small business investment company during any period that—

(i) any organization which is exempt from tax under this title (other than a governmental unit) owns more than 25 percent of the capital or profits interest in such company, or

(ii) organizations which are exempt from tax under this title (including governmental units other than any agency or instrumentality of the United States) own, in the aggregate, 50 percent or more of the capital or profits interest in such company.

(7) Average acquisition indebtedness.—For purposes of this section, the term "average acquisition indebtedness" for any taxable year with respect to a debt-financed property means the average amount, determined under regulations prescribed by the Secretary of the acquisition indebtedness during the period the property is held by the organization during the taxable year, except that for the purpose of computing the percentage of any gain or loss to be taken into account on a sale or other disposition of debt-financed property, such term means the highest amount of the acquisition indebtedness with respect to such property during the 12-month period ending with the date of the sale or other disposition.

(8) Securities subject to loans.—For purposes of this section—

(A) payments with respect to securities loans (as defined in section 512(a)(5)) shall be deemed to be derived from the securities loaned and not from collateral security or the investment of collateral security from such loans,

(B) any deductions which are directly connected with collateral security for such loan, or with the investment of collateral security, shall be deemed to be deductions which are directly connected with the securities loaned, and

(C) an obligation to return collateral security shall not be treated as acquisition indebtedness (as defined in paragraph (1)).

(9) Real property acquired by a qualified organization.—

(A) In general.—Except as provided in subparagraph (B), the term "acquisition indebtedness" does not, for purposes of this section, include indebtedness incurred by a qualified organization in acquiring or improving any real property. For purposes of this paragraph, an interest in a mortgage shall in no event be treated as real property.

(B) Exceptions.—The provisions of subparagraph (A) shall not apply in any case in which—

(i) the price for the acquisition or improvement is not a fixed amount determined as of the date of the acquisition or the completion of the improvement;

(ii) the amount of any indebtedness or any other amount payable with respect to such indebtedness, or the time for making any payment of any such amount, is dependent, in whole or in part, upon any revenue, income, or profits derived from such real property;

(iii) the real property is at any time after the acquisition leased by the qualified organization to the person selling such property to such organization or to any person who bears a relationship described in section 267(b) or 707(b) to such person;

(iv) the real property is acquired by a qualified trust from, or is at any time after the acquisition leased by such trust to, any person who—

(I) bears a relationship which is described in subparagraph (C), (E), or (G) of section 4975(e)(2) to any plan with respect to which such trust was formed, or

(II) bears a relationship which is described in subparagraph (F) or (H) of section 4975(e)(2) to any person described in subclause (I);

(v) any person described in clause (iii) or (iv) provides the qualified organization with financing in connection with the acquisition or improvement; or

(vi) the real property is held by a partnership unless the partnership meets the requirements of clauses (i) through (v) and unless—

(I) all of the partners of the partnership are qualified organizations,

(II) each allocation to a partner of the partnership which is a qualified organization is a qualified allocation (within the meaning of section 168(h)(6)), or

(III) such partnership meets the requirements of subparagraph (E).

For purposes of subclause (I) of clause (vi), an organization shall not be treated as a qualified organization if any income of such organization is unrelated business taxable income.

(C) Qualified organization.—For purposes of this paragraph, the term "qualified organization" means—

(i) an organization described in section 170(b)(1)(A)(ii) and its affiliated support organizations described in section 509(a)(3);

(ii) any trust which constitutes a qualified trust under section 401;

(iii) an organization described in section 501(c)(25); or

(iv) a retirement income account described in section 403(b)(9).

(D) Other pass-thru entities; tiered entities.—Rules similar to the rules of subparagraph (B)(vi) shall also apply in the case of any pass-thru entity other than a partnership and in the case of tiered partnerships and other entities.

(E) Certain allocations permitted.—

(i) In general.—A partnership meets the requirements of this subparagraph if—

(I) the allocation of items to any partner which is a qualified organization cannot result in such partner having a share of the overall partnership income for any taxable year greater than such partner's share of the overall partnership loss for the taxable year for which such partner's loss share will be the smallest, and

(II) each allocation with respect to the partnership has substantial economic effect within the meaning of section 704(b)(2).

For purposes of this clause, items allocated under section 704(c) shall not be taken into account.

(ii) Special rules.—

(I) Chargebacks.—Except as provided in regulations, a partnership may without violating the requirements of this subparagraph provide for chargebacks with respect to disproportionate losses previously allocated to qualified organizations and disproportionate income previously allocated to other partners. Any chargeback referred to in the preceding sentence shall not be at a ratio in excess of the ratio under which the loss or income (as the case may be) was allocated.

(II) Preferred rates of return, etc.—To the extent provided in regulations, a partnership may without violating the requirements of this subparagraph provide for reasonable preferred returns or reasonable guaranteed payments.

(iii) Regulations.—The Secretary shall prescribe such regulations as may be necessary to carry out the purposes of this subparagraph, including regulations which may provide for exclusion or segregation of items.

(F) Special rules for organizations described in section 501(c)(25).—

(i) In general.—In computing under section 512 the unrelated business taxable income of a disqualified holder of an interest in an organization described in section 501(c)(25), there shall be taken into account—

(I) as gross income derived from an unrelated trade or business, such holder's pro rata share of the items of income described in clause (ii)(I) of such organization, and

(II) as deductions allowable in computing unrelated business taxable income, such holder's pro rata share of the items of deduction described in clause (ii)(II) of such organization.

Such amounts shall be taken into account for the taxable year of the holder in which (or with which) the taxable year of such organization ends.

(ii) Description of amounts.—For purposes of clause (i)—

(I) gross income is described in this clause to the extent such income would (but for this paragraph) be treated under subsection (a) as derived from an unrelated trade or business, and

(II) any deduction is described in this clause to the extent it would (but for this paragraph) be allowable under subsection (a)(2) in computing unrelated business taxable income.

(iii) Disqualified holder.—For purposes of this subparagraph, the term "disqualified holder" means any shareholder (or beneficiary) which is not described in clause (i) or (ii) of subparagraph (C).

(G) Special rules for purposes of the exceptions.—Except as otherwise provided by regulations—

(i) Small leases disregarded.—For purposes of clauses (iii) and (iv) of subparagraph (B), a lease to a person described in such clause (iii) or (iv) shall be disregarded if no more than 25 percent of the leasable floor space in a building (or complex of buildings) is covered by the lease and if the lease is on commercially reasonable terms.

(ii) Commercially reasonable financing.—Clause (v) of subparagraph (B) shall not apply if the financing is on commercially reasonable terms.

(H) Qualifying sales by financial institutions.—

(i) In general.—In the case of a qualifying sale by a financial institution, except as provided in regulations, clauses (i) and (ii) of subparagraph (B) shall not apply with respect to financing provided by such institution for such sale.

(ii) Qualifying sale.—For purposes of this clause, there is a qualifying sale by a financial institution if—

(I) a qualified organization acquires property described in clause (iii) from a financial institution and any gain recognized by the financial institution with respect to the property is ordinary income,

(II) the stated principal amount of the financing provided by the financial institution does not exceed the amount of the outstanding indebtedness (including accrued but unpaid interest) of the financial institution with respect to the property described in clause (iii) immediately before the acquisition referred to in clause (iii) or (v), whichever is applicable, and

(III) the present value (determined as of the time of the sale and by using the applicable Federal rate determined under section 1274(d)) of the maximum amount payable pursuant to the financing that is determined by reference to the revenue, income, or profits derived from the property cannot exceed 30 percent of the total purchase price of the property (including the contingent payments).

(iii) Property to which subparagraph applies.—Property is described in this clause if such property is foreclosure property, or is real property which—

(I) was acquired by the qualified organization from a financial institution which is in conservatorship or receivership, or from the conservator or receiver of such an institution, and

(II) was held by the financial institution at the time it entered into conservatorship or receivership.

(iv) Financial institution.—For purposes of this subparagraph, the term "financial institution" means—

(I) any financial institution described in section 581 or 591(a),

(II) any other corporation which is a direct or indirect subsidiary of an institution referred to in subclause (I) but only if, by virtue of being affiliated with such institution, such other corporation is subject to supervision and examination by a Federal or State agency which regulates institutions referred to in subclause (I), and

(III) any person acting as a conservator or receiver of an entity referred to in subclause (I) or (II) (or any government agency or corporation succeeding to the rights or interest of such person).

(v) Foreclosure property.—For purposes of this subparagraph, the term `foreclosure property' means any real property acquired by the financial institution as the result of having bid on such property at foreclosure, or by operation of an agreement or process of law, after there was a default (or a default was imminent) on indebtedness which such property secured.

(d) Basis of debt-financed property acquired in corporate liquidation.—For purposes of this subtitle, if the property was acquired in a complete or partial liquidation of a corporation in exchange for its stock, the basis of the property shall be the same as it would be in the hands of the transferor corporation, increased by the amount of gain recognized to the transferor corporation upon such distribution and by the amount of any gain to the organization which was included, on account of such distribution, in unrelated business taxable income under subsection (a).

(e) Allocation rules.—Where debt-financed property is held for purposes described in subsection (b)(1)(A), (B), (C), or (D) as well as for other purposes, proper allocation shall be made with respect to basis, indebtedness, and income and deductions. The allocations required by this section shall be made in accordance with regulations prescribed by the Secretary to the extent proper to carry out the purposes of this section.

(f) Personal property leased with real property.—For purposes of this section, the term "real property" includes personal property of the lessor leased by it to a lessee of its real estate if the lease of such personal property is made under, or in connection with, the lease of such real estate.

(g) Regulations.—The Secretary shall prescribe such regulations as may be necessary or appropriate to carry out the purposes of this section, including regulations to prevent the circumvention of any provision of this section through the use of segregated asset accounts.

§ 515. Taxes of foreign countries and possessions of the United States.

The amount of taxes imposed by foreign countries and possessions of the United States shall be allowed as a credit against the tax of an organization subject to the tax imposed by section 511 to the extent provided in section 901; and in the case of the tax imposed by section 511, the term "taxable income" as used in section 901 shall be read as "unrelated business taxable income".

* * *

§ 521. Exemption of certain farmers' cooperatives from tax.

(a) Exemption from tax.—A farmers' cooperative organization described in subsection (b)(1) shall be exempt from taxation under this subtitle except as otherwise provided in part I of subchapter T (sec. 1381 and following). Notwithstanding part I of subchapter T (sec. 1381 and following), such an organization shall be considered an organization exempt from income taxes for purposes of any law which refers to organizations exempt from income taxes.

(b) Applicable rules.—

(1) Exempt farmers' cooperatives.—The farmers' cooperatives exempt from taxation to the extent provided in subsection (a) are farmers', fruit growers', or like associations organized and operated on a cooperative basis (A) for the purpose of marketing the products of members or other producers, and turning back to them the proceeds of sales, less the necessary marketing expenses, on the basis of either the quantity or the value of the products furnished by them, or (B) for the purpose of purchasing supplies and equipment for the use of members or other persons, and turning over such supplies and equipment to them at actual cost, plus necessary expenses.

(2) Organizations having capital stock.—Exemption shall not be denied any such association because it has capital stock, if the dividend rate of such stock is fixed at not to exceed the legal rate of interest in the State of incorporation or 8 percent per annum, whichever is greater, on the value of the consideration for which the stock was issued, and if substantially all such stock (other than nonvoting preferred stock, the owners of which are not entitled or permitted to participate, directly or indirectly, in the profits of the association, upon dissolution or otherwise, beyond the fixed dividends) is owned by producers who market their products or purchase their supplies and equipment through the association.

(3) Organizations maintaining reserve.—Exemption shall not be denied any such association because there is accumulated and maintained by it a reserve required by State law or a reasonable reserve for any necessary purpose.

(4) Transactions with nonmembers.—Exemption shall not be denied any such association which markets the products of nonmembers in an amount the value of which does not exceed the value of the products marketed for members, or which purchases supplies and equipment for nonmembers in an amount the value of which does not exceed the value of the supplies and equipment purchased for members, provided the value of the purchases made for persons who are neither members nor producers does not exceed 15 percent of the value of all its purchases.

(5) Business for the United States.—Business done for the United States or any of its agencies shall be disregarded in determining the right to exemption under this section.

(6) Netting of losses.—Exemption shall not be denied any such association because such association computes its net earnings for purposes of determining any amount available for distribution to patrons in the manner described in paragraph (1) of section 1388(j).

(7) Cross reference.—For treatment of value-added processing involving animals, see section 1388(k).

§ 527. Political organizations.

(a) General rule.—A political organization shall be subject to taxation under this subtitle only to the extent provided in this section. A political organization shall be considered an organization exempt from income taxes for the purpose of any law which refers to organizations exempt from income taxes.

(b) Tax imposed.—A tax is hereby imposed for each taxable year on the political organization taxable income of every political organization. Such tax shall be computed by multiplying the political organization taxable income by the highest rate of tax specified in section 11(b).

(c) Political organization taxable income defined.—

(1) Taxable income defined.—For purposes of this section, the political organization taxable income of any organization for any taxable year is an amount equal to the excess (if any) of—

(A) the gross income for the taxable year (excluding any exempt function income), over

(B) the deductions allowed by this chapter which are directly connected with the production of the gross income (excluding exempt function income), computed with the modifications provided in paragraph (2).

(2) Modifications.—For purposes of this subsection—

(A) there shall be allowed a specific deduction of $100,

(B) no net operating loss deduction shall be allowed under section 172, and

(C) no deduction shall be allowed under part VIII of subchapter—(relating to special deductions for corporations).

(3) Exempt function income.—For purposes of this subsection, the term "exempt function income" means any amount received as—

(A) a contribution of money or other property,

(B) membership dues, a membership fee or assessment from a member of the political organization,

(C) proceeds from a political fundraising or entertainment event, or proceeds from the sale of political campaign materials, which are not received in the ordinary course of any trade or business, or

(D) proceeds from the conducting of any bingo game (as defined in section 513(f)(2)),

to the extent such amount is segregated for use only for the exempt function of the political organization.

(d) Certain uses not treated as income to candidate.—For purposes of this title, if any political organization—

(1) contributes any amount to or for the use of any political organization which is treated as exempt from tax under subsection (a) of this section,

(2) contributes any amount to or for the use of any organization described in paragraph (1) or (2) of section 509(a) which is exempt from tax under section 501(a), or

(3) deposits any amount in the general fund of the Treasury or in the general fund of any State or local government,

such amount shall be treated as an amount not diverted for the personal use of the candidate or any other person. No deduction shall be allowed under this title for the contribution or deposit of any amount described in the preceding sentence.

(e) Other definitions.—For purposes of this section—

(1) Political organization.—The term "political organization" means a party, committee, association, fund, or other organization (whether or not incorporated) organized and operated primarily for the purpose of directly or indirectly accepting contributions or making expenditures, or both, for an exempt function.

(2) Exempt function.—The term "exempt function" means the function of influencing or attempting to influence the selection, nomination, election, or appointment of any individual to any Federal, State, or local public office or office in a political organization, or the election of Presidential or Vice-Presidential electors, whether or not such individual or electors are selected, nominated, elected, or appointed. Such term includes the making of expenditures relating to an office described in the preceding sentence which, if incurred by the individual, would be allowable as a deduction under section 162(a).

(3) Contributions.—The term "contributions" has the meaning given to such term by section 271(b)(2).

(4) Expenditures.—The term "expenditures" has the meaning given to such term by section 271(b)(3).

(5) Qualified state or local political organization.—

(A) In general.—The term "qualified State or local political organization" means a political organization—

(i) all the exempt functions of which are solely for the purposes of influencing or attempting to influence the selection, nomination, election, or appointment of any individual to any State or local public office or office in a State or local political organization,

(ii) which is subject to State law that requires the organization to report (and it so reports)—

(I) information regarding each separate expenditure from and contribution to such organization, and

(II) information regarding the person who makes such contribution or receives such expenditure,

which would otherwise be required to be reported under this section, and

(iii) with respect to which the reports referred to in clause (ii) are (I) made public by the agency with which such reports are filed, and (II) made publicly available for inspection by the organization in the manner described in section 6104(d).

(B) Certain State law differences disregarded.—An organization shall not be treated as failing to meet the requirements of subparagraph (A)(ii) solely by reason of 1 or more of the following:

(i) The minimum amount of any expenditure or contribution required to be reported under State law is not more than $300 greater than the minimum amount required to be reported under subsection (j).

(ii) The State law does not require the organization to identify 1 or more of the following:

(I) The employer of any person who makes contributions to the organization.

(II) The occupation of any person who makes contributions to the organization.

(III) The employer of any person who receives expenditures from the organization.

(IV) The occupation of any person who receives expenditures from the organization.

(V) The purpose of any expenditure of the organization.

(VI) The date any contribution was made to the organization.

(VII) The date of any expenditure of the organization.

(C) De minimis errors.—An organization shall not fail to be treated as a qualified State or local political organization solely because such organization makes de minimis errors in complying with the State reporting requirements and the public inspection requirements described in subparagraph (A) as long as the organization corrects such errors within a reasonable period after the organization becomes aware of such errors.

(D) Participation of Federal candidate or office holder.—The term "qualified State or local political organization" shall not include any organization otherwise described in subparagraph (A) if a candidate for nomination or election to Federal elective public office or an individual who holds such office—

(i) controls or materially participates in the direction of the organization,

(ii) solicits contributions to the organization (unless the Secretary determines that such solicitations resulted in de minimis contributions and were made without the prior knowledge and consent, whether explicit or implicit, of the organization or its officers, directors, agents, or employees), or

(iii) directs, in whole or in part, disbursements by the organization.

(f) Exempt organization, which is not political organization, must include certain amounts in gross income.—

(1) In general.—If an organization described in section 501(c) which is exempt from tax under section 501(a) expends any amount during the taxable year directly (or through another organization) for an exempt function (within the meaning of subsection (e)(2)), then, notwithstanding any other provision of law, there shall be included in the gross income of such organization for the taxable year, and shall be subject to tax under subsection (b) as if it constituted political organization taxable income, an amount equal to the lesser of—

(A) the net investment income of such organization for the taxable year, or

(B) the aggregate amount so expended during the taxable year for such an exempt function.

(2) Net investment income.—For purposes of this subsection, the term "net investment income" means the excess of—

(A) the gross amount of income from interest, dividends, rents, and royalties, plus the excess (if any) of gains from the sale or exchange of assets over the losses from the sale or exchange of assets, over

(B) the deductions allowed by this chapter which are directly connected with the production of the income referred to in subparagraph (A).

For purposes of the preceding sentence, there shall not be taken into account items taken into account for purposes of the tax imposed by section 511 (relating to tax on unrelated business income).

(3) Certain separate segregated funds.—For purposes of this subsection and subsection (e)(1), a separate segregated fund (within the meaning of section 610 of title 18) or of any similar State statute, or within the meaning of any State statute which permits the segregation of dues moneys for exempt functions (within the meaning of subsection (e)(2)) which is maintained by an organization described in section 501(c) which is exempt from tax under section 501(a) shall be treated as a separate organization.

(g) Treatment of newsletter funds.—

(1) In general.—For purposes of this section, a fund established and maintained by an individual who holds, has been elected to, or is a candidate (within the meaning of paragraph (3)) for nomination or election to, any Federal, State, or local elective public office, for use by such individual exclusively for the preparation and circulation of such individual's newsletter shall, except as provided in paragraph (2), be treated as if such fund constituted a political organization.

(2) Additional modifications.—In the case of any fund described in paragraph (1)—

(A) the exempt function shall be only the preparation and circulation of the newsletter, and

(B) the specific deduction provided by subsection (c)(2)(A) shall not be allowed.

(3) Candidate.—For purposes of paragraph (1), the term "candidate" means, with respect to any Federal, State, or local elective public office, an individual who—

(A) publicly announces that he is a candidate for nomination or election to such office, and

(B) meets the qualifications prescribed by law to hold such office.

(h) Special rule for principal campaign committees.—

(1) In general.—In the case of a political organization, which is a principal campaign committee, paragraph (1) of subsection (b) shall be applied by substituting "the appropriate rates" for "the highest rate".

(2) Principal campaign committee defined.—

(A) In general.—For purposes of this subsection, the term "principal campaign committee" means the political committee designated by a candidate for Congress as his principal campaign committee for purposes of—

(i) section 302(e) of the Federal Election Campaign Act of 1971 (52 U.S.C. 30102(e)), and

(ii) this subsection.

(B) Designation.—A candidate may have only 1 designation in effect under subparagraph (A)(ii) at any time and such designation—

(i) shall be made at such time and in such manner as the Secretary may prescribed by regulations, and

(ii) once made, may be revoked only with the consent of the Secretary.

Nothing in this subsection shall be construed to require any designation where there is only one political committee with respect to a candidate.

(i) Organizations must notify Secretary that they are section 527 organizations.—

(1) In general.—Except as provided in paragraph (5), an organization shall not be treated as an organization described in this section—

(A) unless it has given notice to the Secretary electronically that it is to be so treated, or

(B) if the notice is given after the time required under paragraph (2), the organization shall not be so treated for any period before such notice is given or, in the case of any material change in the information required under paragraph (3), for the period beginning on the date on which the material change occurs and ending on the date on which such notice is given.

(2) Time to give notice.—The notice required under paragraph (1) shall be transmitted not later than 24 hours after the date on which the organization is established or, in the case of any material change in the information required under paragraph (3), not later than 30 days after such material change.

(3) Contents of notice.—The notice required under paragraph (1) shall include information regarding—

(A) the name and address of the organization (including any business address, if different) and its electronic mailing address,

(B) the purpose of the organization,

(C) the names and addresses of its officers, highly compensated employees, contact person, custodian of records, and members of its Board of Directors,

(D) the name and address of, and relationship to, any related entities (within the meaning of section 168(h)(4)),

(E) whether the organization intends to claim an exemption from the requirements of subsection (j) or section 6033, and

(F) such other information as the Secretary may require to carry out the internal revenue laws.

(4) Effect of failure.—In the case of an organization failing to meet the requirements of paragraph (1) for any period, the taxable income of such organization shall be computed by taking into account any exempt function income (and any deductions directly connected with the production of such income) or, in the case of a failure relating to a material change, by taking into account such income and deductions only during the period beginning on the date on which the material change occurs and ending on the date on which notice is given under this subsection. For purposes of the preceding sentence, the term "exempt function income" means any amount described in a subparagraph of subsection (c)(3), whether or not segregated for use for an exempt function.

(5) Exceptions.—This subsection shall not apply to any organization—

(A) to which this section applies solely by reason of subsection (f)(1),

(B) which reasonably anticipates that it will not have gross receipts of $25,000 or more for any taxable year, or

(C) which is a political committee of a State or local candidate or which is a State or local committee of a political party.

(6) Coordination with other requirements.—This subsection shall not apply to any person required (without regard to this subsection) to report under the Federal Election Campaign Act of 1971 (52 U.S.C. 30101 et seq.) as a political committee.

(j) Required disclosure of expenditures and contributions.—

(1) Penalty for failure.—In the case of—

(A) a failure to make the required disclosures under paragraph (2) at the time and in the manner prescribed therefor, or

(B) a failure to include any of the information required to be shown by such disclosures or to show the correct information,

there shall be paid by the organization an amount equal to the rate of tax specified in subsection (b)(1) multiplied by the amount to which the failure relates. For purposes of subtitle F, the amount imposed by this paragraph shall be assessed and collected in the same manner as penalties imposed by section 6652(c).

(2) Required disclosure.—A political organization which accepts a contribution, or makes an expenditure, for an exempt function during any calendar year shall file with the Secretary either—

(A)(i) in the case of a calendar year in which a regularly scheduled election is held—

(I) quarterly reports, beginning with the first quarter of the calendar year in which a contribution is accepted or expenditure is made, which shall be filed not later than the fifteenth day after the last day of each calendar quarter, except that the report for the quarter ending on December 31 of such calendar year shall be filed not later than January 31 of the following calendar year,

(II) a pre-election report, which shall be filed not later than the twelfth day before (or posted by registered or certified mail not later than the fifteenth day before) any election with respect to which the organization makes a contribution or expenditure, and which shall be complete as of the twentieth day before the election, and

(III) a post-general election report, which shall be filed not later than the thirtieth day after the general election and which shall be complete as of the twentieth day after such general election, and

(ii) in the case of any other calendar year, a report covering the period beginning January 1 and ending June 30, which shall be filed no later than July 31 and a report covering the period beginning July 1 and ending December 31, which shall be filed no later than January 31 of the following calendar year, or

(B) monthly reports for the calendar year, beginning with the first month of the calendar year in which a contribution is accepted or expenditure is made, which shall be filed not later than the twentieth day after the last day of the month and shall be complete as if the last day of the month, except that, in lieu of filing the reports otherwise due in November and December of any year in which a regularly scheduled general election is held, a pre-general election report shall be filed in accordance with subparagraph (A)(i)(II), a post-general election report shall be filed in accordance with subparagraph (A)(i)(III), and a year end report shall be filed not later than January 31 of the following calendar year.

(3) Contents of report.—A report required under paragraph (2) shall contain the following information:

(A) The amount, date, and purpose of each expenditure made to a person if the aggregate amount of expenditures to such person during the calendar year equals or exceeds $500 and the name and address of the person (in the case of an individual, including the occupation and name of employer of such individual).

(B) The name and address (in the case of an individual, including the occupation and name of employer of such individual) of all contributors which contributed an aggregate amount of $200 or more to the organization during the calendar year and the amount and date of the contribution.

Any expenditure or contribution disclosed in a previous reporting period is not required to be included in the current reporting period.

(4) Contracts to spend or contribute.—For purposes of this subsection, a person shall be treated as having made an expenditure or contribution if the person has contracted or is otherwise obligated to make the expenditure or contribution.

(5) Coordination with other requirements.—This subsection shall not apply—

(A) to any person required (without regard to this subsection) to report under the Federal Election Campaign Act of 1971 (52 U.S.C. 30101 et seq.) as a political committee,

(B) to any State or local committee of a political party or political committee of a State or local candidate,

(C) to any organization which is a qualified State or local political organization,

(D) to any organization which reasonably anticipates that it will not have gross receipts of $25,000 or more for any taxable year,

(E) to any organization to which this section applies solely by reason of subsection (f)(1), or

(F) with respect to any expenditure which is an independent expenditure (as defined in section 301 of such Act).

(6) Election.—For purposes of this subsection, the term "election" means—

(A) a general, special, primary, or runoff election for a Federal office,

(B) a convention or caucus of a political party which has authority to nominate a candidate for Federal office,

(C) a primary election held for the selection of delegates to a national nominating convention of a political party, or

(D) a primary election held for the expression of a preference for the nomination of individuals for election to the office of President.

(7) Electronic filing.—Any report required under paragraph (2) with respect to any calendar year shall be filed in electronic form if the organization has, or has reason to expect to have, contributions exceeding $50,000 or expenditures exceeding $50,000 in such calendar year.

(k) Public availability of notices and reports.—

(1) In general.—The Secretary shall make any notice described in subsection (i)(1) or report described in subsection (j)(7) available for public inspection on the Internet not later than 48 hours after such notice or report has been filed (in addition to such public availability as may be made under section 6104(d)(7)).

(2) Access.—The Secretary shall make the entire database of notices and reports which are made available to the public under paragraph (1) searchable by the following items (to the extent the items are required to be included in the notices and reports):

(A) Names, States, zip codes, custodians of records, directors, and general purposes of the organizations.

(B) Entities related to the organizations.

(C) Contributors to the organizations.

(D) Employers of such contributors.

(E) Recipients of expenditures by the organizations.

(F) Ranges of contributions and expenditures.

(G) Time periods of the notices and reports.

Such database shall be downloadable.

(*l*) Authority to waive.—The Secretary may waive all or any portion of the—

(1) tax assessed on an organization by reason of the failure of the organization to comply with the requirements of subsection (i), or

(2) amount imposed under subsection (j) for a failure to comply with the requirements thereof on a showing that such failure was due to reasonable cause and not due to willful neglect.

§ 528. Certain homeowners associations.

(a) General rule.—A homeowners association (as defined in subsection (c)) shall be subject to taxation under this subtitle only to the extent provided in this section. A homeowners association shall be considered an organization exempt from income taxes for the purpose of any law which refers to organizations exempt from income taxes.

(b) Tax imposed.—A tax is hereby imposed for each taxable year on the homeowners association taxable income of every homeowners association. Such tax shall be equal to 30 percent of the homeowners association taxable income (32 percent of such income in the case of a timeshare association).

(c) Homeowners association defined.—For purposes of this section—

(1) Homeowners association.—The term "homeowners association" means an organization which is a condominium management association or a residential real estate management association or a timeshare association if—

(A) such organization is organized and operated to provide for the acquisition, construction, management, maintenance, and care of association property,

(B) 60 percent or more of the gross income of such organization for the taxable year consists solely of amounts received as membership dues, fees, or assessments from—

(i) owners of residential units in the case of a condominium management association, or

(ii) owners of residences or residential lots in the case of a residential real estate management association, or

(iii) owners of timeshare rights to use, or timeshare ownership interests in, association property in the case of timeshare association,

(C) 90 percent or more of the expenditures of the organization for the taxable year are expenditures for the acquisition, construction, management, maintenance, and care of association property,

(D) no part of the net earnings of such organization inures (other than by acquiring, constructing, or providing management, maintenance, and care of association property, and other than by a rebate of excess membership dues, fees, or assessments) to the benefit of any private shareholder or individual, and

(E) such organization elects (at such time and in such manner as the Secretary by regulations prescribes) to have this section apply for the taxable year.

(2) Condominium management association.—The term "condominium management association" means any organization meeting the requirement of subparagraph (A) of paragraph (1) with respect to a condominium project substantially all of the units of which are used by individuals for residences.

(3) Residential real estate management association.—The term "residential real estate management association" means any organization meeting the requirements of subparagraph (A) of paragraph (1) with respect to a subdivision, development, or similar area substantially all the lots or buildings of which may only be used by individuals for residences.

(4) Timeshare association.—The term "timeshare association" means any organization (other than a condominium management association) meeting the requirement of subparagraph (A) of paragraph (1) with respect to a subdivision, development, or similar area substantially all of the lots or buildings of which may only be used by individuals for residences.

(5) Association property.—The term "association property" means—

(A) property held by the organization,

(B) property commonly held by the members of the organization,

(C) property within the organization privately held by the members of the organization, and

(D) property owned by a governmental unit and used for the benefit of residents of such unit.

(d) Homeowners association taxable income defined.—

(1) Taxable income defined.—For purposes of this section, the homeowners association taxable income of any organization for any taxable year is an amount equal to the excess (if any) of—

(A) the gross income for the taxable year (excluding any exempt function income), over

(B) the deductions allowed by this chapter which are directly connected with the production of the gross income (excluding exempt function income), computed with the modifications provided in paragraph (2).

(2) Modifications.—For purposes of this subsection—

(A) there shall be allowed a specific deduction of $100,

(B) no net operating loss deduction shall be allowed under section 172, and

(C) no deduction shall be allowed under part VIII of subchapter—(relating to special deductions for corporations).

(3) Exempt function income.—For purposes of this subsection, the term "exempt function income" means any amount received as membership dues, fees, or assessments from—

(A) owners of condominium housing units in the case of a condominium management association, or

(B) owners of real property in the case of a residential real estate management association, or

(C) owners of timeshare rights to use, or timeshare ownership interests in, real property in the case of a timeshare association.

Subchapter J. Estates, Trusts, Beneficiaries, and Decedents

§ 642. Special rules for credits and deductions.

* * *

(c) Deduction for amounts paid or permanently set aside for a charitable purpose.—

(1) General rule.—In the case of an estate or trust (other then a trust meeting the specifications of subpart B), there shall be allowed as a deduction in computing its taxable income (in lieu of the deduction allowed by section 170(a), relating to deduction for charitable, etc., contributions and gifts) any amount of the gross income, without limitation, which pursuant to the terms of the governing instrument is, during the taxable year, paid for a purpose specified in section 170(c) (determined without regard to section 170(c)(2)(A)). If a charitable contribution is paid after the close of such taxable year and on or before the last day of the year following the close of such taxable year, then the trustee or administrator may elect to treat such contribution as paid during such taxable year. The election shall be made at such time and in such manner as the Secretary prescribes by regulations.

(2) Amounts permanently set aside.—In the case of an estate, and in the case of a trust (other than a trust meeting the specifications of subpart B) required by the terms of its governing instrument to set aside amounts which was—

(A) created on or before October 9, 1969, if—

(i) an irrevocable remainder interest is transferred to or for the use of an organization described in section 170(c), or

(ii) the grantor is at all times after October 9, 1969, under a mental disability to change the terms of the trust; or

(B) established by a will executed on or before October 9, 1969, if—

(i) the testator dies before October 9, 1972, without having republished the will after October 9, 1969, by codicil or otherwise,

(ii) the testator at no time after October 9, 1969, had the right to change the portions of the will which pertain to the trust, or

(iii) the will is not republished by codicil or otherwise before October 9, 1972, and the testator is on such date and at all times thereafter under a mental disability to republish the will by codicil or otherwise, there shall also be allowed as a deduction in computing its taxable income any amount of the gross income, without limitation, which pursuant to the terms of the governing instrument is, during the taxable year, permanently set aside for a purpose specified in section 170(c), or is to be used exclusively for religious, charitable, scientific, literary, or educational purposes, or for the prevention of cruelty to children or animals, or for the establishment, acquisition, maintenance, or operation of a public cemetery not operated for profit. In the case of a trust, the preceding sentence shall apply only to gross income earned with respect to amounts transferred to the trust before October 9, 1969, or transferred under a will to which subparagraph (B) applies.

(3) Pooled income funds.—In the case of a pooled income fund (as defined in paragraph (5)), there shall also be allowed as a deduction in computing its taxable income any amount of the gross income attributable to gain from the sale of a capital asset held for more than 6 months, without limitation, which pursuant to the terms of the governing instrument is, during the taxable year, permanently set aside for a purpose specified in section 170(c).

(4) Adjustments.—To the extent that the amount otherwise allowable as a deduction under this subsection consists of gain described in section 1202(a), proper adjustment shall be made for any exclusion allowable to the estate or trust under section 1202. In the case of a trust, the deduction allowed by this subsection shall be subject to section 681 (relating to unrelated business income).

(5) Definition of pooled income fund.—For purposes of paragraph (3), a pooled income fund is a trust—

(A) to which each donor transfers property, contributing an irrevocable remainder interest in such property to or for the use of an organization described in section 170(b)(1)(A) (other than in clauses (vii) or (viii)), and retaining an income interest for the life of one or more beneficiaries (living at the time of such transfer),

(B) in which the property transferred by each donor is commingled with property transferred by other donors who have made or make similar transfers,

(C) which cannot have investments in securities which are exempt from the taxes imposed by this subtitle,

(D) which includes only amounts received from transfers which meet the requirements of this paragraph,

(E) which is maintained by the organization to which the remainder interest is contributed and of which no donor or beneficiary of an income interest is a trustee, and

(F) from which each beneficiary of an income interest receives income, for each year for which he is entitled to receive the income interest referred to in subparagraph (A), determined by the rate of return earned by the trust for such year.

For purposes of determining the amount of any charitable contribution allowable by reason of a transfer of property to a pooled fund, the value of the income interest shall be determined on the basis of the highest rate of return earned by the fund for any of the 3 taxable years immediately preceding the taxable year of the fund in which the transfer is made. In the case of funds in existence less than 3 taxable years preceding the taxable year of the fund in which a transfer is made the rate of return shall be deemed to be 6 percent per annum, except that the Secretary may prescribe a different rate of return.

(6) Taxable private foundations.—In the case of a private foundation which is not exempt from taxation under section 501(a) for the taxable year, the provisions of this subsection shall not apply and the provisions of section 170 shall apply.

§ 664. Charitable remainder trusts.

(a) General rule.—Notwithstanding any other provision of this subchapter, the provisions of this section shall, in accordance with regulations prescribed by the Secretary, apply in the case of a charitable remainder annuity trust and a charitable remainder unitrust.

(b) Character of distributions.—Amounts distributed by a charitable remainder annuity trust or by a charitable remainder unitrust shall be considered as having the following characteristics in the hands of a beneficiary to whom is paid the annuity described in subsection (d)(1)(A) or the payment described in subsection (d)(2)(A):

(1) First, as amounts of income (other than gains, and amounts treated as gains, from the sale or other disposition of capital assets) includible in gross income to the extent of such income of the trust for the year and such undistributed income of the trust for prior years;

(2) Second, as a capital gain to the extent of the capital gain of the trust for the year and the undistributed capital gain of the trust for prior years;

(3) Third, as other income to the extent of such income of the trust for the year and such undistributed income of the trust for prior years; and

(4) Fourth, as a distribution of trust corpus.

For purposes of this section, the trust shall determine the amount of its undistributed capital gain on a cumulative net basis.

(c) Taxation of trusts.—

(1) Income tax.—A charitable remainder annuity trust and a charitable remainder unitrust shall, for any taxable year, not be subject to any tax imposed by this subtitle.

(2) Excise tax.—

(A) In general.—In the case of a charitable remainder annuity trust or a charitable remainder unitrust which has unrelated business taxable income (within the meaning of section 512, determined as if part III of subchapter F applied to such trust) for a taxable year, there is hereby imposed on such trust or unitrust an excise tax equal to the amount of such unrelated business taxable income.

(B) Certain rules to apply.—The tax imposed by subparagraph (A) shall be treated as imposed by chapter 42 for purposes of this title other than subchapter E of chapter 42.

(C) Tax court proceedings.—For purposes of this paragraph, the references in section 6212(c)(1) to section 4940 shall be deemed to include references to this paragraph.

(d) Definitions.—

(1) Charitable remainder annuity trust.—For purposes of this section, a charitable remainder annuity trust is a trust—

(A) from which a sum certain (which is not less than 5 percent nor more than 50 percent of the initial net fair market value of all property placed in trust) is to be paid, not less often than annually, to one or more persons (at least one of which is not an organization described in section 170(c) and, in the case of individuals, only to an individual who is living at the time of the creation of the trust) for a term of years (not in excess of 20 years) or for the life or lives of such individual or individuals,

(B) from which no amount other than the payments described in subparagraph (A) may be paid to or for the use of any person other than an organization described in section 170(c), and

(C) following the termination of the payments described in subparagraph (A), the remainder interest in the trust is to be transferred to, or for the use of, an organization described in section 170(c) or is to be retained by the trust for such a use or, to the extent the remainder interest is in qualified employer securities (as defined in subsection (g)(4)), all or part of such securities are to be transferred to an employee stock ownership plan (as defined in section 4975(e)(7)) in a qualified gratuitous transfer (as defined by subsection (g)), and

(D) the value (determined under section 7520) of such remainder interest is at least 10 percent of the initial fair market value of all property placed in the trust.

(2) Charitable remainder unitrust.—For purposes of this section, a charitable remainder unitrust is a trust—

(A) from which a fixed percentage (which is not less than 5 percent no more than 50 percent) of the net fair market value of its assets, valued annually, is to be paid, not less often than annually, to one or more persons (at least one of which is not an organization described in section 170(c) and, in the case of individuals, only to an individual who is living at the time of the creation of the trust) for a term of years (not in excess of 20 years) or for the life or lives of such individual or individuals,

(B) from which no amount other than the payments described in subparagraph (A) may be paid to or for the use of any person other than an organization described in section 170(c), and

(C) following the termination of the payments described in subparagraph (A), the remainder interest in the trust is to be transferred to, or for the use of, an organization described in section 170(c) or is to be retained by the trust for such a use.

(D) with respect to each contribution of property to the trust, the value (determined under 7520) of such remainder interest in such property is at least 10 percent of the net fair market value of such property as of the date such property is contributed to the trust.

(3) Exception.—Notwithstanding the provisions of paragraphs (2)(A) and (B), the trust instrument may provide that the trustee shall pay the income beneficiary for any year—

(A) the amount of the trust income, if such amount is less than the amount required to be distributed under paragraph (2)(A), and

(B) any amount of the trust income which is in excess of the amount required to be distributed under paragraph (2)(A), to the extent that (by reason of subparagraph (A)) the aggregate of the amounts paid in prior years was less than the aggregate of such required amounts.

(4) Severance of certain additional contributions.—If—

(A) any contribution is made to a trust which before the contribution is a charitable remainder unitrust, and

(B) such contribution would (but for this paragraph) result in such trust ceasing to be a charitable unitrust by reason of paragraph (2)(D),

such contribution shall be treated as a transfer to a separate trust under regulations prescribed by the Secretary.

(e) Valuation for purposes of charitable contribution.—For purposes of determining the amount of any charitable contribution, the remainder interest of a charitable remainder annuity trust or charitable remainder unitrust shall be computed on the basis that an amount equal to 5 percent of the net fair market value of its assets (or a greater amount, if required under the terms of the trust instrument) is to be distributed each year.

(f) Certain contingencies permitted.—

(1) General rule.—If a trust would, but for a qualified contingency, meet the requirements of paragraph (1)(A) or (2)(A) of subsection (d), such trust shall be treated as meeting such requirements.

(2) Value determined without regard to qualified contingency.—For purposes of determining the amount of any charitable contribution (or the actuarial value of any interest), a qualified contingency shall not be taken into account.

(3) Qualified contingency.—For purposes of this subsection, the term "qualified contingency" means any provision of a trust which provides that, upon the happening of a contingency, the payments described in paragraph (1)(A) or (2)(A) of subsection (d) (as the case may be) will terminate not later than such payments would otherwise terminate under the trust.

* * *

Subchapter O. Gain or Loss on Disposition of Property

§ 1011. Adjusted basis for determining gain or loss.

* * *

(b) Bargain sale to a charitable organization.—If a deduction is allowable under section 170 (relating to charitable contributions) by reason of a sale, then the adjusted basis for determining the gain from such sale shall be that portion of the adjusted basis which bears the same ratio to the adjusted basis as the amount realized bears to the fair market value of the property.

Subchapter S. Tax Treatment of S Corporations and Their Shareholders

§ 1361. S corporation defined.

* * *

(c) Special rules for applying subsection (b).—

* * *

(6) Certain exempt organizations permitted as shareholders.—For purposes of subsection (b)(1)(B), an organization which is—

(A) described in section 401(a) or 501(c)(3), and

(B) exempt from taxation under section 501(a),

may be a shareholder in an S corporation.

SUBTITLE B. ESTATE AND GIFT TAXES

Chapter 11. Estate Tax

Subchapter A. Estates of Citizens or Residents

§ 2055. Transfers for public, charitable, and religious uses.

(a) In general.—For purposes of the tax imposed by section 2001, the value of the taxable estate shall be determined by deducting from the value of the gross estate the amount of all bequests, legacies, devises, or transfers—

(1) to or for the use of the United States, any State, any political subdivision thereof, or the District of Columbia, for exclusively public purposes;

(2) to or for the use of any corporation organized and operated exclusively for religious, charitable, scientific, literary, or educational purposes, including the encouragement of art, or to foster national or international amateur sports competition (but only if no part of its activities involve the provision of athletic facilities or equipment), and the prevention of cruelty to children or animals, no part of the net earnings of which inures to the benefit of any private stockholder or individual, which is not disqualified for tax exemption under section 501(c)(3) by reason of attempting to influence legislation, and which does not participate in, or intervene in (including the publishing or distributing of statements), any political campaign on behalf of (or in opposition to) any candidate for public office;

(3) to a trustee or trustees, or a fraternal society, order, or association operating under the lodge system, but only if such contributions or gifts are to be used by such trustee or trustees, or by such fraternal society, order, or association, exclusively for religious, charitable, scientific, literary, or educational purposes, or for the prevention of cruelty to children or animals, such trust, fraternal society, order, or association would not be disqualified for tax exemption under section 501(c)(3) by reason of attempting to influence legislation, and such trustee or trustees, or such fraternal society, order, or association, does not participate in, or intervene in (including the publishing or distributing of statements), any political campaign on behalf of (or in opposition to) any candidate for public office;

(4) to or for the use of any veteran's organization incorporated by Act of Congress, or of its departments or local chapters or posts, no part of the net earnings of which inures to the benefit of any private shareholder or individual; or

(5) to an employee stock ownership plan if such transfer qualifies as a qualified gratuitous transfer of qualified employer securities within the meaning of section 664(g).

For purposes of this subsection, the complete termination before the date prescribed for the filing of the estate tax return of a power to consume, invade, or appropriate property for the benefit of an individual before such power has been exercised by reason of the death of such individual or for any other reason shall be considered and deemed to be a qualified disclaimer with the same full force and effect as though he had filed such qualified disclaimer. Rules similar to the rules of section 501(j) shall apply for purposes of paragraph (2).

(b) Powers of appointment.—Property includible in the decedent's gross estate under section 2041 (relating to powers of appointment) received by a donee described in this section shall, for purposes of this section, be considered a bequest of such decedent.

(c) Death taxes payable out of bequests.—If the tax imposed by section 2001, or any estate, succession, legacy, or inheritance taxes, are, either by the terms of the will, by the law of the jurisdiction under which the estate is administered, or by the law of the jurisdiction imposing the particular tax, payable in whole or in part out of the bequests, legacies, or devises otherwise deductible under this section, then the amount deductible under this section shall be the amount of such bequests, legacies, or devises reduced by the amount of such taxes.

(d) Limitation on deduction.—The amount of the deduction under this section for any transfer shall not exceed the value of the transferred property required to be included in the gross estate.

(e) Disallowance of deductions in certain cases.—

(1) No deduction shall be allowed under this section for a transfer to or for the use of an organization or trust described in section 508(d) or 4948(c)(4) subject to the conditions specified in such sections.

(2) Where an interest in property (other than an interest described in section 170(f)(3)(B)) passes or has passed from the decedent to a person, or for a use, described in subsection (a), and an interest (other than an interest which is extinguished upon the decedent's death) in the same property passes or has passed (for less than an adequate and full consideration in money or money's worth) from the decedent to a person, or for a use, not described in subsection (a), no deduction shall be allowed under this section for the interest which passes or has passed to the person, or for the use, described in subsection (a) unless—

(A) in the case of a remainder interest, such interest is in a trust which is a charitable remainder annuity trust or a charitable remainder unitrust (described in section 664) or a pooled income fund (described in section 642(c)(5)), or

(B) in the case of any other interest, such interest is in the form of a guaranteed annuity or is a fixed percentage distributed yearly of the fair market value of the property (to be determined yearly).

(3) Reformations to comply with paragraph (2).—

(A) In general.—A deduction shall be allowed under subsection (a) in respect of any qualified reformation.

(B) Qualified reformation.—For purposes of this paragraph, the term "qualified reformation" means a change of a governing instrument by reformation, amendment, construction, or otherwise which changes a reformable interest into a qualified interest but only if—

(i) any difference between—

(I) the actuarial value (determined as of the date of the decedent's death) of the qualified interest, and

(II) the actuarial value (as so determined) of the reformable interest,

does not exceed 5 percent of the actuarial value (as so determined) of the reformable interest,

(ii) in the case of—

(I) a charitable remainder interest, the nonremainder interest (before and after the qualified reformation) terminated at the same time, or

(II) any other interest, the reformable interest and the qualified interest are for the same period, and

(iii) such change is effective as of the date of the decedent's death.

A nonremainder interest (before reformation) for a term of years in excess of 20 years shall be treated as satisfying subclause (I) of clause (ii) if such interest (after reformation) is for a term of 20 years.

(C) Reformable interest.—For purposes of this paragraph—

(i) In general.—The term "reformable interest" means any interest for which a deduction would be allowable under subsection (a) at the time of the decedent's death but for paragraph (2).

(ii) Beneficiary's interest must be fixed.—The term "reformable interest" does not include any interest unless, before the remainder vests in possession, all payments to persons other than an organization described in subsection (a) are expressed either in specified dollar amounts or a fixed percentage of the fair market value of the property. For purposes of determining whether all such payments are expressed as a fixed percentage of the fair market value of the property, section 664(d)(3) shall be taken into account.

(iii) Special rule where timely commencement of reformation.—Clause (ii) shall not apply to any interest if a judicial proceeding is commenced to change such interest into a qualified interest not later than the 90th day after—

(I) if an estate tax return is required to be filed, the last date (including extensions) for filing such return, or

(II) if no estate tax return is required to be filed, the last date (including extensions) for filing the income tax return for the 1st taxable year for which such a return is required to be filed by the trust.

(iv) Special rule for will executed before January 1, 1979, etc.—In the case of any interest passing under a will executed before January 1, 1979, or under a trust created before such date, clause (ii) shall not apply.

(D) Qualified interest.—For purposes of this paragraph, the term "qualified interest" means an interest for which a deduction is allowable under subsection (a).

(E) Limitation.—The deduction referred to in subparagraph (A) shall not exceed the amount of the deduction which would have been allowable for the reformable interest but for paragraph (2).

(F) Special rule where income beneficiary dies.—If (by reason of the death of any individual, or by termination or distribution of a trust in accordance with the terms of the trust instrument) by the due date for filing the estate tax return (including any extension thereof) a reformable interest is in a wholly charitable trust or passes directly to a person or for a use described in subsection (a), a deduction shall be allowed for such reformable interest as if it had met the requirements of paragraph (2) on the date of the decedent's death. For purposes of the preceding sentence, the term "wholly charitable trust" means a charitable trust which, upon the allowance of a deduction, would be described in section 4947(a)(1).

(G) Statute of limitations.—The period for assessing any deficiency of any tax attributable to the application of this paragraph shall not expire before the date 1 year after the date on which the Secretary is notified that such reformation (or other proceeding pursuant to subparagraph (J)) has occurred.

(H) Regulations.—The Secretary shall prescribe such regulations as may be necessary to carry out the purposes of this paragraph, including regulations providing such adjustments in the application of the provisions of section 508 (relating to special rules relating to section 501(c)(3) organizations), subchapter J (relating to estates, trusts, beneficiaries, and decedents), and chapter 42 (relating to private foundations) as may be necessary by reason of the qualified reformation.

(I) Reformations permitted in case of remainder interests in residence or farm, pooled income funds, etc.—The Secretary shall prescribe regulations (consistent with the provisions of this paragraph) permitting reformations in the case of any failure—

(i) to meet the requirements of section 170(f)(3)(B) (relating to remainder interests in personal residence or farm, etc.), or

(ii) to meet the requirements of section 642(c)(5).

(J) Void or reformed trust in cases of insufficient remainder interests.—In the case of a trust that would qualify (or could be reformed to qualify pursuant to subparagraph (B)) but for failure to satisfy the requirement of paragraph (1)(D) or (2)(D) of section 664(d), such trust may be—

(i) declared null and void ab initio, or

(ii) changed by reformation, amendment, or otherwise to meet such requirement by reducing the payout rate or the duration (or both) or any noncharitable beneficiary's interest to the extent necessary to satisfy such requirement,

pursuant to a proceeding that is commenced within the period required in subparagraph (C)(iii). In a case described in clause (i), no deduction shall be allowed under this title for any transfer to the trust and any transactions entered into by the trust prior to being declared void shall be treated as entered into by the transferor.

(4) Works of art and their copyrights treated as separate properties in certain cases.—

(A) In general.—In the case of a qualified contribution of a work of art, the work of art and the copyright on such work of art shall be treated as separate properties for purposes of paragraph (2).

(B) Work of art defined.—For purposes of this paragraph, the term "work of art" means any tangible personal property with respect to which there is a copyright under Federal law.

(C) Qualified contribution defined.—For purposes of this paragraph, the term "qualified contribution" means any transfer of property to a qualified organization if the use of the property by the organization is related to the purpose or function constituting the basis for its exemption under section 501.

(D) Qualified organization defined.—For purposes of this paragraph, the term "qualified organization" means any organization described in section 501(c)(3) other than a private foundation (as defined in section 509). For purposes of the preceding sentence, a private operating foundation (as defined in section 4942(j)(3)) shall not be treated as a private foundation.

(5) Contributions to donor advised funds.—A deduction otherwise allowed under subsection (a) for any contribution to a donor advised fund (as defined in section 4966(d)(2)) shall only be allowed if—

(A) the sponsoring organization (as defined in section 4966(d)(1)) with respect to such donor advised fund is not—

(i) described in paragraph (3) or (4) of subsection (a), or

(ii) a type III supporting organization (as defined in section 4943(f)(5)(A)) which is not a functionally integrated type III supporting organization (as defined in section 4943(f)(5)(B)), and

(B) the taxpayer obtains a contemporaneous written acknowledgment (determined under rules similar to the rules of section 170(f)(8)(C)) from the sponsoring organization (as so defined) of such donor advised fund that such organization has exclusive legal control over the assets contributed.

(f) Special rule for irrevocable transfers of easements in real property.—A deduction shall be allowed under subsection (a) in respect of any transfer of a qualified real property interest (as defined in section 170(h)(2)(C)) which meets the requirements of section 170(h) (without regard to paragraph (4)(A) thereof).

* * *

Chapter 12. Gift Tax

Subchapter C. Deductions

§ 2522. Charitable and similar gifts.

(a) Citizens or residents.—In computing taxable gifts for the calendar year, there shall be allowed as a deduction in the case of a citizen or resident the amount of all gifts made during such year to or for the use of—

(1) the United States, any State, or any political subdivision thereof, or the District of Columbia, for exclusively public purposes;

(2) a corporation, or trust, or community chest, fund, or foundation, organized and operated exclusively for religious, charitable, scientific, literary, or educational purposes, or to foster national or international amateur sports competition (but only if no part of its activities involve the provision of athletic facilities or equipment), including the encouragement of art and the prevention of cruelty to children or animals, no part of the net earnings of which inures to the benefit of any private stockholder or individual, which is not disqualified for tax exemption under section 501(c)(3) by reason of attempting to influence legislation, and which does not participate in, or intervene in (including the publishing or distributing of statements), any political campaign on behalf of (or in opposition to) any candidate for public office;

(3) a fraternal society, order, or association operating under the lodge system, but only if such gifts are to be used exclusively for religious, charitable, scientific, literary, or educational purposes, including the encouragement of art and the prevention of cruelty to children or animals;

(4) posts or organizations of war veterans, or auxiliary units or societies of any such posts, organizations, units, or societies are organized in the United States or any of its possessions, and if no part of their net earnings inures to the benefit of any private shareholder or individual.

* * *

(c) Disallowance of deductions in certain cases.—* * *

(2) Where a donor transfers an interest in property (other than an interest described in section 170(f)(3)(B)) passes or has passed from the decedent to a person, or for a use, described in subsection (a) or (b) and an interest in the same property is retained by the donor, or is transferred or has been transferred (for less than an adequate and full consideration in money or money's worth) from the donor to a person, or for a use, not described in subsection (a) or (b), no deduction shall be allowed under this section for the interest which is, or has been transferred, to the person, or for the use, described in subsection (a) or (b), unless—

(A) in the case of a remainder interest, such interest is in a trust which is a charitable remainder annuity trust or a charitable remainder unitrust (described in section 664) or a pooled income fund (described in section 642(c)(5)), or

(B) in the case of any other interest, such interest is in the form of a guaranteed annuity or is a fixed percentage distributed yearly of the fair market value of the property (to be determined yearly).

* * *

(5) Contributions to donor advised funds.—A deduction otherwise allowed under subsection (a) for any contribution to a donor advised fund (as defined in section 4966(d)(2)) shall only be allowed if—

(A) the sponsoring organization (as defined in section 4966(d)(1)) with respect to such donor advised fund is not—

(i) described in paragraph (3) or (4) of subsection (a), or

(ii) a type III supporting organization (as defined in section 4943(f)(5)(A)) which is not a functionally integrated type III supporting organization (as defined in section 4943(f)(5)(B)), and

(B) the taxpayer obtains a contemporaneous written acknowledgment (determined under rules similar to the rules of section 170(f)(8)(C)) from the sponsoring organization (as so defined) of such donor advised fund that such organization has exclusive legal control over the assets contributed.

* * *

(e) Special rules for fractional gifts.—

(1) Denial of deduction in certain cases.—

(A) In general.—No deduction shall be allowed for a contribution of an undivided portion of a taxpayer's entire interest in tangible personal property unless all interests in the property are held immediately before such contribution by—

(i) the taxpayer, or

(ii) the taxpayer and the donee.

(B) Exceptions.—The Secretary may, by regulation, provide for exceptions to subparagraph (A) in cases where all persons who hold an interest in the property make proportional contributions of an undivided portion of the entire interest held by such persons.

(2) Recapture of deduction in certain cases; addition to tax.—

(A) In general.—The Secretary shall provide for the recapture of an amount equal to any deduction allowed under this section (plus interest) with respect to any contribution of an undivided portion of a taxpayer's entire interest in tangible personal property—

(i) in any case in which the donor does not contribute all of the remaining interests in such property to the donee (or, if such donee is no longer in existence, to any person described in section 170(c)) on or before the earlier of—

(I) the date that is 10 years after the date of the initial fractional contribution, or

(II) the date of the death of the donor, and

(ii) in any case in which the donee has not, during the period beginning on the date of the initial fractional contribution and ending on the date described in clause (I)—

(I) had substantial physical possession of the property, and

(II) used the property in a use which is related to a purpose or function constituting the basis for the organizations' exemption under section 501.

(B) Addition to tax.—The tax imposed under this chapter for any taxable year for which there is a recapture under subparagraph (A) shall be increased by 10 percent of the amount so recaptured.

(C) Initial fractional contribution.—For purposes of this paragraph, the term "initial fractional contribution" means, with respect to any donor, the first gift of an undivided portion of the donor's entire interest in any tangible personal property for which a deduction is allowed under subsection (a) or (b).

* * *

SUBTITLE D. MISCELLANEOUS EXCISE TAXES

Chapter 41. Public Charities

§ 4911. Tax on excess expenditures to influence legislation.

(a) Tax imposed.—

(1) In general.—There is hereby imposed on the excess lobbying expenditures of any organization to which this section applies a tax equal to 25 percent of the amount of the excess lobbying expenditures for the taxable year.

(2) Organizations to which this section applies.—This section applies to any organization with respect to which an election under section 501(h) (relating to lobbying expenditures by public charities) is in effect for the taxable year.

(b) Excess lobbying expenditures.—For purposes of this section, the term "excess lobbying expenditures" means, for a taxable year, the greater of—

(1) the amount by which the lobbying expenditures made by the organization during the taxable year exceed the lobbying nontaxable amount for such organization for such taxable year, or

(2) the amount by which the grass roots expenditures made by the organization during the taxable year exceed the grass roots nontaxable amount for such organization for such taxable year.

(c) Definitions.—For purposes of this section—

(1) Lobbying expenditures.—The term "lobbying expenditures" means expenditures for the purpose of influencing legislation (as defined in subsection (d)).

(2) Lobbying nontaxable amount.—The lobbying nontaxable amount for any organization for any taxable year is the lesser of (A) $1,000,000 or (B) the amount determined under the following table:

If the exempt purpose expenditures are—	The lobbying nontaxable amount is—
Not over $500,000	20 percent of the exempt purpose expenditures.
Over $500,000 but not over $1,000,000	$100,000, plus 15 percent of the excess of the exempt purpose expenditures over $500,000.
Over $1,000,000 but not over $1,500,000	$175,000 plus 10 percent of the excess of the exempt purpose expenditures over $1,000,000.
Over $1,500,000	$225,000 plus 5 percent of the excess of the exempt purpose expenditures over $1,500,000.

(3) Grass roots expenditures.—The term "grass roots expenditures" means expenditures for the purpose of influencing legislation (as defined in subsection (d) without regard to paragraph (1)(B) thereof).

(4) Grass roots nontaxable amount.—The grass roots nontaxable amount for any organization for any taxable year is 25 percent of the lobbying nontaxable amount (determined under paragraph (2)) for such organization for such taxable year.

(d) Influencing legislation.—

(1) General rule.—Except as otherwise provided in paragraph (2), for purposes of this section, the term "influencing legislation" means—

(A) any attempt to influence any legislation through an attempt to affect the opinions of the general public or any segment thereof, and

(B) any attempt to influence any legislation through communication with any member or employee of a legislative body, or with any government official or employee who may participate in the formulation of the legislation.

(2) Exceptions.—For purposes of this section, the term "influencing legislation," with respect to an organization, does not include—

(A) making available the results of nonpartisan analysis, study, or research;

(B) providing of technical advice or assistance (where such advice would otherwise constitute the influencing of legislation) to a governmental body or to a committee or other subdivision thereof in response to a written request by such body or subdivision, as the case may be;

(C) appearances before, or communications to, any legislative body with respect to a possible decision of such body which might affect the existence of the organization, its powers and duties, tax-exempt status, or the deduction of contributions to the organization;

(D) communications between the organization and its bona fide members with respect to legislation or proposed legislation of direct interest to the organization and such members, other than communications described in paragraph (3); and

(E) any communication with a governmental official or employee, other than—

(i) a communication with a member or employee of a legislative body (where such communication would otherwise constitute the influencing of legislation), or

(ii) a communication the principal purpose of which is to influence legislation.

(3) Communications with members.—

(A) A communication between an organization and any bona fide member of such organization to directly encourage such member to communicate as provided in paragraph (1)(B) shall be treated as a communication described in paragraph (1)(B).

(B) A communication between an organization and any bona fide member of such organization to directly encourage such member to urge persons other than members to communicate as provided in either subparagraph (A) or subparagraph (B) of paragraph (1) shall be treated as a communication described in paragraph (1)(A).

(e) Other definitions and special rules.—For purposes of this section—

(1) Exempt purpose expenditures.—

(A) In general.—The term "exempt purpose expenditures" means, with respect to any organization for any taxable year, the total of the amounts paid or incurred by such organization to accomplish purposes described in section 170(c)(2)(B) (relating to religious, charitable, educational, etc., purposes).

(B) Certain amounts included.—The term "exempt purpose expenditures" includes—

(i) administrative expenses paid or incurred for purposes described in section 170(c)(2)(B), and

(ii) amounts paid or incurred for the purpose of influencing legislation (whether or not for purposes described in section 170(c)(2)(B)).

(C) Certain amounts excluded.—The term "exempt purpose expenditures" does not include amounts paid or incurred to or for—

(i) a separate fundraising unit of such organization, or

(ii) one or more other organizations, if such amounts are paid or incurred primarily for fundraising.

(2) Legislation.—The term "legislation" includes action with respect to Acts, bills, resolutions, or similar items by the Congress, any State legislature, any local council, or similar governing body, or by the public in a referendum, initiative, constitutional amendment, or similar procedure.

(3) Action.—The term "action" is limited to the introduction, amendment, enactment, defeat, or repeal of Acts, bills, resolutions, or similar items.

(4) Depreciation, etc., treated as expenditures.—In computing expenditures paid or incurred for the purpose of influencing legislation (within the meaning of subsection (b)(1) or (b)(2)) or exempt purpose expenditures (as defined in paragraph (1)), amounts properly chargeable to capital account shall not be taken into account. There shall be taken into account a reasonable allowance for exhaustion, wear and tear, obsolescence, or amortization. Such allowance shall be computed only on the basis of the straight-line method of depreciation. For purposes of this section, a determination of whether an amount is properly chargeable to capital account shall be made on the basis of the principles that apply under subtitle A to amounts which are paid or incurred in a trade or business.

(f) Affiliated organizations.—

(1) In general.—Except as otherwise provided in paragraph (4), if for a taxable year two or more organizations described in section 501(c)(3) are members of an affiliated group of organizations as defined in paragraph (2), and an election under section 501(h) is effective for at least one such organization for such year, then—

(A) the determination as to whether excess lobbying expenditures have been made and the determination as to whether the expenditure limits of section 501(h)(1) have been exceeded shall be made as though such affiliated group is one organization,

(B) if such group has excess lobbying expenditures, each such organization as to which an election under section 501(h) is effective for such year shall be treated as an organization which has excess lobbying expenditures in an amount which equals such organization's proportionate share of such group's excess lobbying expenditures,

(C) if the expenditure limits of section 501(h)(1) are exceeded, each such organization as to which an election under section 501(h) is effective for such year shall be treated as an organization which is not described in section 501(c)(3) by reason of the application of 501(h), and

(D) subparagraphs (C) and (D) of subsection (d)(2), paragraph (3) or subsection (d), and clause (i) of subsection (e)(1)(C) shall be applied as if such affiliated group were one organization.

(2) Definition of affiliation.—For purposes of paragraph (1), two organizations are members of an affiliated group of organizations but only if—

(A) the governing instrument of one such organization requires it to be bound by decisions of the other organization on legislative issues, or

(B) the governing board of one such organization includes persons who—

(i) are specifically designated representatives of another such organization or are members of the governing board, officers, or paid executive staff members of such other organization, and

(ii) by aggregating their votes, have sufficient voting power to cause or prevent action on legislative issues by the first such organization.

(3) Different taxable years.—If members of an affiliated group of organizations have different taxable years, their expenditures shall be computed for purposes of this section in a manner to be prescribed by regulations promulgated by the Secretary.

(4) Limited control.—If two or more organizations are members of an affiliated group of organizations (as defined in paragraph (2) without regard to subparagraph (B) thereof), no two members of such affiliated group are affiliated (as defined in paragraph (2) without regard to subparagraph (A) thereof), and the governing instrument of no such organization requires it to be bound by decisions of any of the other such organizations on legislative issues other than as to action with respect to Acts, bills, resolutions, or similar items by the Congress, then—

(A) in the case of any organization whose decisions bind one or more members of such affiliated group, directly or indirectly, the determination as to whether such organization has paid or incurred excess lobbying expenditures and the determination as to whether such organization has exceeded the expenditure limits of section 501(h)(1) shall be made as though such organization has paid or incurred those amounts paid or incurred by such members of such affiliated group to influence legislation with respect to Acts, bills, resolutions, or similar items by the Congress, and

(B) in the case of any organization to which subparagraph (A) does not apply, but which is a member of such affiliated group, the determination as to whether such organization has paid or incurred excess lobbying expenditures and the determination as to whether such organization has exceeded the expenditure limits of section 501(h) (1) shall be made as though such organization is not a member of such affiliated group.

§ 4912. Tax on disqualifying lobbying expenditures of certain organizations.

(a) Tax on organization.—If an organization to which this section applies is not described in section 501(c)(3) for any taxable year by reason of making lobbying expenditures, there is hereby imposed a tax on the lobbying expenditures of such organization for such taxable year equal to 5 percent of the amount of such expenditures. The tax imposed by this subsection shall be paid by the organization.

(b) On management.—If tax is imposed under subsection (a) on the lobbying expenditures of any organization, there is hereby imposed on the agreement of any organization manager to the making of any such expenditures, knowing that such expenditures are likely to result in the organization not being described in section 501(c)(3), a tax equal to 5 percent of the amount of such expenditures, unless such agreement is not willful and is due to reasonable cause. The tax imposed by this subsection shall be paid by any manager who agreed to the making of the expenditures.

(c) Organizations to which section applies.—

(1) In general.—Except as provided in paragraph (2), this section shall apply to any organization which was exempt (or was determined by the Secretary to be exempt) from taxation under section 501(a) by reason of being an organization described in section 501(c)(3).

(2) Exceptions.—This section shall not apply to any organization—

(A) to which an election under section 501(h) applies,

(B) which is a disqualified organization (within the meaning of section 501(h)(5)), or

(C) which is a private foundation.

(d) Definitions.—

(1) Lobbying expenditures.—The term "lobbying expenditure" means any amount paid or incurred by the organization in carrying on propaganda, or otherwise attempting to influence legislation.

(2) Organization manager.—The term "organization manager" has the meaning given to such term by section 4955(f)(2).

(3) Joint and several liability.—If more than 1 person is liable under subsection (b), all such persons shall be jointly and severally liable under such subsection.

* * *

Chapter 42. Private Foundations and Certain Other Tax-Exempt Organizations

Subchapter A. Private Foundations

§ 4940. Excise tax based on investment income.

(a) Tax-exempt foundations.—There is hereby imposed on each private foundation which is exempt from taxation under section 501(a) for the taxable year, with respect to the carrying on its activities, a tax equal to 1.39 percent of the net investment income of such foundation for the taxable year.

(b) Taxable foundations.—There is hereby imposed on each private foundation which is not exempt from taxation under section 501(a) for the taxable year, with respect to the carrying on of its activities, a tax equal to—

(1) the amount (if any) by which the sum of (A) the tax imposed under subsection (a) (computed as if such subsection applied to such private foundation for the taxable year), plus (B) the amount of the tax which would have been imposed under section 511 for the taxable year if such private foundation had been exempt from taxation under section 501(a), exceeds

(2) the tax imposed under subtitle A on such private foundation for the taxable year.

(c) Net investment income defined.—

(1) In general.—For purposes of subsection (a), the net investment income is the amount by which (A) the sum of the gross investment income and the capital gain net income exceeds (B) the deductions allowed by paragraph (3). Except to the extent inconsistent with the provisions of this section, net investment income shall be determined under the principles of subtitle A.

(2) Gross investment income.—For purposes of paragraph (1), the term "gross investment income" means the gross amount of income from interest, dividends, rents, payments with respect to securities loans (as defined in section 512(a)(5)), and royalties, but not including any such income to the extent included in computing the tax imposed by section 511. Such term shall also include income from sources similar to those in the preceding sentence.

(3) Deductions.—

(A) In general.—For purposes of paragraph (1), there shall be allowed as a deduction all the ordinary and necessary expenses paid or incurred for the production or collection of gross investment income or for the management, conservation, or maintenance of property held for the production of such income, determined with the modifications set forth in subparagraph (B).

(B) Modifications.—For purposes of subparagraph (A)—

(i) The deduction provided by section 167 shall be allowed, but only on the basis of the straight line method of depreciation.

(ii) The deduction for depletion provided by section 611 shall be allowed, but such deduction shall be determined without regard to section 613 (relating to percentage depletion).

(4) Capital gains and losses.—For purposes of paragraph (1) in determining capital gain net income—

(A) There shall not be taken into account any gain or loss from the sale or other disposition of property to the extent that such gain or loss is taken into account for purposes of computing the tax imposed by section 511.

(B) The basis for determining gain in the case of property held by the private foundation on December 31, 1969, and continuously thereafter to the date of its disposition shall be deemed to be not less than the fair market value of such property on December 31, 1969.

(C) Losses from sales or other dispositions of property shall be allowed only to the extent of gains from such sales or other dispositions, and there shall be no capital loss carryovers or carrybacks.

(D) Except to the extent provided by regulation, under rules similar to the rules of section 1031 (including the exception under subsection (a)(2) thereof), no gain or loss shall be taken into account with respect to any portion of property used for a period of not less than 1 year for a purpose or function constituting the basis of the private foundation's exemption if the entire property is exchanged immediately following such period solely for property of like kind which is to be used primarily for a purpose or function constituting the basis for such foundation's exemption.

(5) Tax-exempt income.—For purposes of this section, net investment income shall be determined by applying section 103 (relating to State and local bonds) and section 265 (relating to expenses and interest relating to tax-exempt income).

(d) Exemption for certain operating foundations.—

(1) In general.—No tax shall be imposed by this section on any private foundation which is an exempt operating foundation for the taxable year.

(2) Exempt operating foundation.—For purposes of this subsection, the term "exempt operating foundation" means, with respect to any taxable year, any private foundation if—

(A) such foundation is an operating foundation (as defined in section 4942(j)(3)),

(B) such foundation has been publicly supported for at least 10 taxable years,

(C) at all times during the taxable year, the governing body of such foundation—

(i) consists of individuals at least 75 percent of whom are not disqualified individuals, and

(ii) is broadly representative of the general public, and

(D) at no time during the taxable year does such foundation have an officer who is a disqualified individual.

(3) Definitions.—For purposes of this subsection—

(A) Publicly supported.—A private foundation is publicly supported for a taxable year if it meets the requirements of section 170(b)(1)(A)(vi) or 509(a)(2) for such taxable year.

(B) Disqualified individual.—The term "disqualified individual" means, with respect to any private foundation, an individual who is—

(i) a substantial contributor to the foundation,

(ii) an owner of more than 20 percent of—

(I) the total combined voting power of a corporation,

(II) the profits interest of a partnership, or

(III) the beneficial interest of a trust or unincorporated enterprise,

which is a substantial contributor to the foundation, or

(iii) a member of the family of any individual described in clause (i) or (ii).

(C) Substantial contributor.—The term "substantial contributor" means a person who is described in section 507(d)(2).

(D) Family.—The term "family" has the meaning given to such term by section 4946(d).

(E) Constructive ownership.—The rules of paragraphs (3) and (4) of section 4946(a) shall apply for purposes of subparagraph (B)(ii).

§ 4941. Taxes on self-dealing.

(a) Initial taxes.—

(1) On self-dealer.—There is hereby imposed a tax on each act of self-dealing between a disqualified person and a private foundation. The rate of tax shall be equal to

10 percent of the amount involved with respect to the act of self-dealing for each year (or part thereof) in the taxable period. The tax imposed by this paragraph shall be paid by any disqualified person (other than a foundation manager acting only as such) who participates in the act of self-dealing. In the case of a government official (as defined in section 4946(c)), a tax shall be imposed by this paragraph only if such disqualified person participates in the act of self-dealing knowing that it is such an act.

(2) On foundation manager.—In any case in which a tax is imposed by paragraph (1), there is hereby imposed on the participation of any foundation manager in an act of self-dealing between a disqualified person and a private foundation, knowing that it is such an act, a tax equal to 5 percent of the amount involved with respect to the act of self-dealing for each year (or part thereof) in the taxable period, unless such participation is not willful and is due to reasonable cause. The tax imposed by this paragraph shall be paid by any foundation manager who participated in the act of self-dealing.

(b) Additional taxes.—

(1) On self-dealer.—In any case in which an initial tax is imposed by subsection (a)(1) on an act of self-dealing by a disqualified person with a private foundation and the act is not corrected within the taxable period, there is hereby imposed a tax equal to 200 percent of the amount involved. The tax imposed by this paragraph shall be paid by any disqualified person (other than a foundation manager acting only as such) who participated in the act of self-dealing.

(2) On foundation manager.—In any case in which an additional tax is imposed by paragraph (1), if a foundation manager refused to agree to part or all of the correction, there is hereby imposed a tax equal to 50 percent of the amount involved. The tax imposed by this paragraph shall be paid by any foundation manager who refused to agree to part or all of the correction.

(c) Special rules.—For purposes of subsections (a) and (b)—

(1) Joint and several liability.—If more than one person is liable under any paragraph of subsection (a) or (b) with respect to any one act of self-dealing, all such persons shall be jointly and severally liable under such paragraph with respect to such act.

(2) $20,000 limit for management.—With respect to any one act of self-dealing, the maximum amount of the tax imposed by subsection (a)(2) shall not exceed $20,000, and the maximum amount of the tax imposed by subsection (b)(2) shall not exceed $20,000.

(d) Self-dealing.—

(1) In general.—For purposes of this section, the term "self-dealing" means any direct or indirect—

(A) sale or exchange, or leasing, of property between a private foundation and a disqualified person;

(B) lending of money or other extension of credit between a private foundation and a disqualified person;

(C) furnishing of goods, services, or facilities between a private foundation and a disqualified person;

(D) payment of compensation (or payment or reimbursement of expenses) by a private foundation to a disqualified person;

(E) transfer to, or use by or for the benefit of, a disqualified person of the income or assets of a private foundation; and

(F) agreement by a private foundation to make any payment of money or other property to a government official (as defined in section 4946(c)), other than an agreement to employ such individual for any period after the termination of his government service if such individual is terminating his government service within a 90-day period.

(2) Special rules.—For purposes of paragraph (1)—

(A) the transfer of real or personal property by a disqualified person to a private foundation shall be treated as a sale or exchange if the property is subject to a mortgage or similar lien which the foundation assumes or if it is subject to a mortgage or similar lien which a disqualified person placed on the property within the 10-year period ending on the date of the transfer;

(B) the lending of money by a disqualified person to a private foundation shall not be an act of self-dealing if the loan is without interest or other charge (determined without regard to section 7872) and if the proceeds of the loan are used exclusively for purposes specified in section 501(c)(3);

(C) the furnishing of goods, services, or facilities by a disqualified person to a private foundation shall not be an act of self-dealing if the furnishing is without charge and if the goods, services, or facilities so furnished are used exclusively for purposes specified in section 501(c)(3);

(D) the furnishing of goods, services, or facilities by a private foundation to a disqualified person shall not be an act of self-dealing if such furnishing is made on a basis no more favorable than that on which such goods, services, or facilities are made available to the general public;

(E) except in the case of a government official (as defined in section 4946(c)), the payment of compensation (and the payment or reimbursement of expenses) by a private foundation to a disqualified person for personal services which are reasonable and necessary to carrying out the exempt purpose of the private foundation shall not be an act of self-dealing if the compensation (or payment or reimbursement) is not excessive;

(F) any transaction between a private foundation and a corporation which is a disqualified person (as defined in section 4946(a)), pursuant to any liquidation, merger, redemption, recapitalization, or other corporate adjustment, organization, or reorganization, shall not be an act of self-dealing if all of the securities of the same class as that held by the foundation are subject to the same terms and such terms provide for receipt by the foundation of no less than fair market value;

(G) in the case of a government official (as defined in section 4946(c)), paragraph (1) shall in addition not apply to—

(i) prizes and awards which are subject to the provisions of section 74(b) (without regard to paragraph (3) thereof), if the recipients of such prizes and awards are selected from the general public,

(ii) scholarships and fellowship grants which would be subject to the provisions of section 117(a) (as in effect on the day before the date of the enactment of the Tax Reform Act of 1986) and are to be used for study at an educational organization described in section 170(b)(1)(A)(ii),

(iii) any annuity or other payment (forming part of a stock-bonus, pension, or profit-sharing plan) by a trust which is a qualified trust under section 401,

(iv) any annuity or other payment under a plan which meets the requirements of section 404(a)(2),

(v) any contribution or gift (other than a contribution or gift of money) to, or services or facilities made available to, any such individual, if the aggregate value of such contributions, gifts, services, and facilities to, or made available to, such individual during any calendar year does not exceed $25,

(vi) any payment made under chapter 41 of title 5, United States Code, or

(vii) any payment or reimbursement of traveling expenses for travel solely from one point in the United States to another point in the United States, but only if such payment or reimbursement does not exceed the actual cost of the transportation involved plus an amount for all other traveling expenses not in excess of 125 percent of the maximum amount payable under section 5702 of title 5, United States Code, for like travel by employees of the United States;

* * *

(e) Other definitions.—For purposes of this section—

(1) Taxable period.—The term "taxable period" means, with respect to any act of self-dealing, the period beginning with the date on which the act of self-dealing occurs and ending on the earliest of—

(A) the date of mailing a notice of deficiency with respect to the tax imposed by subsection (a)(1) under section 6212,

(B) the date on which the tax imposed by subsection (a)(1) is assessed, or

(C) the date on which correction of the act of self-dealing is completed.

(2) Amount involved.—The term "amount involved" means, with respect to any act of self-dealing, the greater of the amount of money and the fair market value of the other property given or the amount of money and the fair market value of the other property received; except that, in the case of services described in subsection (d)(2)(E), the amount involved shall be only the excess compensation. For purposes of the preceding sentence, the fair market value—

(A) in the case of the taxes imposed by subsection (a), shall be determined as of the date on which the act of self-dealing occurs; and

(B) in the case of the taxes imposed by subsection (b), shall be the highest fair market value during the taxable period.

(3) Correction.—The terms "correction" and "correct" mean, with respect to any act of self-dealing, undoing the transaction to the extent possible, but in any case placing the private foundation in a financial position not worse than that in which it would be if the disqualified person were dealing under the highest fiduciary standards.

§ 4942. Taxes on failure to distribute income.

(a) Initial tax.—There is hereby imposed on the undistributed income of a private foundation for any taxable year, which has not been distributed before the first day of the second (or any succeeding) taxable year following such taxable year (if such first day falls within the taxable period), a tax equal to 30 percent of the amount of such income remaining undistributed at the beginning of such second (or succeeding) taxable year. The tax imposed by this subsection shall not apply to the undistributed income of a private foundation—

(1) for any taxable year for which it is an operating foundation (as defined in subsection (j)(3)), or

(2) to the extent that the foundation failed to distribute any amount solely because of an incorrect valuation of assets under subsection (e), if—

(A) the failure to value the assets properly was not willful and was due to reasonable cause,

(B) such amount is distributed as qualifying distributions (within the meaning of subsection (g)) by the foundation during the allowable distribution period (as defined in subsection (j)(2)),

(C) the foundation notifies the Secretary that such amount has been distributed (within the meaning of subparagraph (B)) to correct such failure, and

(D) such distribution is treated under subsection (h)(2) as made out of the undistributed income for the taxable year for which a tax would (except for this paragraph) have been imposed under this subsection.

(b) Additional tax.—In any case in which an initial tax is imposed under subsection (a) on the undistributed income of a private foundation for any taxable year, if any portion of such income remains undistributed at the close of the taxable period, there is hereby imposed a tax equal to 100 percent of the amount remaining undistributed at such time.

(c) Undistributed income.—For purposes of this section, the term "undistributed income" means, with respect to any private foundation for any taxable year as of any time, the amount by which—

(1) the distributable amount for such taxable year, exceeds

(2) the qualifying distributions made before such time out of such distributable amount.

(d) Distributable amount.—For purposes of this section, the term "distributable amount" means, with respect to any foundation for any taxable year, an amount equal to—

(1) the sum of the minimum investment return plus the amounts described in subsection (f)(2)(C), reduced by

(2) the sum of the taxes imposed on such private foundation for the taxable year under subtitle A and section 4940.

(e) Minimum investment return.—

(1) In general.—For purposes of subsection (d), the minimum investment return for any private foundation for any taxable year is 5 percent of the excess of—

(A) the aggregate fair market value of all assets of the foundation other than those which are used (or held for use) directly in carrying out the foundation's exempt purpose, over

(B) the acquisition indebtedness with respect to such assets (determined under section 514(c)(1) without regard to the taxable year in which the indebtedness was incurred).

(2) Valuation.—

(A) In general.—For purposes of paragraph (1)(A), the fair market value of securities for which market quotations are readily available shall be determined on a monthly basis. For all other assets, the fair market value shall be determined at such times and in such manner as the Secretary shall by regulations prescribe.

(B) Reductions in value for blockage or similar factors.—In determining the value of any securities under this paragraph, the fair market value of such securities (determined without regard to any reduction in value) shall not be reduced unless, and only to the extent that, the private foundation establishes that as a result of—

(i) the size of the block of such securities,

(ii) the fact that the securities held are securities in a closely held corporation, or

(iii) the fact that the sale of such securities would result in a forced or distress sale,

the securities could not be liquidated within a reasonable period of time except at a price less than such fair market value. Any reduction in value allowable under this subparagraph shall not exceed 10 percent of such fair market value.

(f) Adjusted net income.—

(1) Defined.—For purposes of subsection (j), the term "adjusted net income" means the excess (if any) of—

(A) the gross income for the taxable year (determined with the income modifications provided by paragraph (2)), over

(B) the sum of the deductions (determined with the deduction modifications provided by paragraph (3)) which would be allowed to a corporation subject to the tax imposed by section 11 for the taxable year.

(2) Income modifications.—The income modifications referred to in paragraph (1)(A) are as follows:

(A) section 103 (relating to State and local bonds) shall not apply,

(B) capital gains and losses from the sale or other disposition of property shall be taken into account only in an amount equal to any net short-term capital gain for the taxable year;

(C) there shall be taken into account—

(i) amounts received or accrued as repayments of amounts which were taken into account as a qualifying distribution within the meaning of subsection (g)(1)(A) for any taxable year;

(ii) notwithstanding subparagraph (B), amounts received or accrued from the sale or other disposition of property to the extent that the acquisition of such property was taken into account as a qualifying distribution (within the meaning of subsection (g)(1)(B)) for any taxable year; and

(iii) any amount set aside under subsection (g)(2) to the extent it is determined that such amount is not necessary for the purposes for which it was set aside; and

(D) section 483 (relating to imputed interest) shall not apply in the case of a binding contract made in a taxable year beginning before January 1, 1970.

(3) Deduction modifications.—The deduction modifications referred to in paragraph (1)(B) are as follows:

(A) no deduction shall be allowed other than all the ordinary and necessary expenses paid or incurred for the production or collection of gross income or for the management, conservation, or maintenance of property held for the production of such income and the allowances for depreciation and depletion determined under section 4940(c)(3)(B), and

(B) section 265 (relating to expenses and interest relating to tax-exempt interest) shall not apply.

(4) Transitional rule.—For purposes of paragraph (2)(B), the basis (for purposes of determining gain) of property held by a private foundation on December 31, 1969, and continuously thereafter to the date of its disposition, shall be deemed to be not less than the fair market value of such property on December 31, 1969.

(g) Qualifying distributions defined.—

(1) In general.—For purposes of this section, the term "qualifying distribution" means—

(A) any amount (including that portion of reasonable and necessary administrative expenses) paid to accomplish one or more purposes described in section 170(c)(2)(B), other than any contribution to (i) an organization controlled (directly or indirectly) by the foundation or one or more disqualified persons (as defined in section 4946) with respect to the foundation, except as provided in paragraph (3), or (ii) a private foundation which is not an operating foundation (as defined in subsection (j)(3)), except as provided in paragraph (3), or

(B) any amount paid to acquire an asset used (or held for use) directly in carrying out one or more purposes described in section 170(c)(2)(B).

(2) Certain set-asides.—

(A) In general.—Subject to such terms and conditions as may be prescribed by the Secretary, an amount set aside for a specific project which comes within one or more purposes described in section 170(c)(2)(B) may be treated as a qualifying distribution if it meets the requirements of subparagraph (B).

(B) Requirements.—An amount set aside for a specific project shall meet the requirements of this subparagraph if at the time of the set-aside the foundation establishes to the satisfaction of the Secretary that the amount will be paid for the specific project within 5 years, and either—

(i) at the time of the set-aside the private foundation establishes to the satisfaction of the Secretary that the project is one which can better be accomplished by such set-aside than by immediate payment of funds, or

(ii)(I) the project will not be completed before the end of the taxable year of the foundation in which the set-aside is made,

(II) the private foundation in each taxable year beginning after December 31, 1975 (or after the end of the fourth taxable year following the year of its creation, whichever is later), distributes amounts, in cash or its equivalent, equal to not less than the distributable amount determined under subsection (d) (without regard to subsection (i)) for purposes described in section 170(c)(2)(B) (including but not limited to payments with respect to set-asides which were treated as qualifying distributions in one or more prior years), and

(III) the private foundation has distributed (including but not limited to payments with respect to set-asides which were treated as qualifying distributions in one or more prior years) during the four taxable years immediately preceding its first taxable year beginning after December 31, 1975, or the fifth taxable year following the year of its creation, whichever is later, an aggregate amount, in cash or its equivalent, of not less than the sum of the following: 80 percent of the first preceding taxable year's distributable amount; 60 percent of the second preceding taxable year's distributable amount; 40 percent of the third preceding taxable year's distributable amount; and 20 percent of the fourth preceding taxable year's distributable amount.

(C) Certain failures to distribute.—If, for any taxable year to which clause (ii)(II) of subparagraph (B) applies, the private foundation fails to distribute in cash or its equivalent amounts not less than those required by such clause and—

(i) the failure to distribute such amounts was not willful and was due to reasonable cause, and

(ii) the foundation distributes an amount in cash or its equivalent which is not less than the difference between the amounts required to be distributed under clause (ii)(II) of subparagraph (B) and the amounts actually distributed in cash or its equivalent during that taxable year within the correction period (as defined in section 4963(e)),

such distribution in cash or its equivalent shall be treated for the purposes of this subparagraph as made during such year.

(D) Reduction in distribution amount.—If, during the taxable years in the adjustment period for which the organization is a private foundation, the foundation distributes amounts in cash or its equivalent which exceed the amount required to be distributed under clause (ii)(II) of subparagraph (B) (including but not limited to payments with respect to set-asides which were treated as qualifying distributions in prior years), then for purposes of this subsection the distribution required under clause (ii)(II) of subparagraph (B) for the taxable year shall be reduced by an amount equal to such excess.

(E) Adjustment period.—For purposes of subparagraph (D), with respect to any taxable year of a private foundation, the taxable years in the adjustment period are the taxable years (not exceeding 5) beginning after December 31, 1975, and immediately preceding the taxable year.

In the case of a set-aside which satisfies the requirements of clause (i) of subparagraph (B), for good cause shown, the period for paying the amount set aside may be extended by the Secretary.

(3) Certain contributions to section 501(c)(3) organizations.—For purposes of this section, the term "qualifying distribution" includes a contribution to a section 501(c)(3) organization described in paragraph (1)(A)(i) or (ii) if—

(A) not later than the close of the first taxable year after its taxable year in which such contribution is received, such organization makes a distribution equal to the amount of such contribution and such distribution is a qualifying distribution (within the meaning of paragraph (1) or (2), without regard to this paragraph) which is treated under subsection (h) as a distribution out of corpus (or would be so treated if such section 501(c)(3) organization were a private foundation which is not an operating foundation), and

(B) the private foundation making the contribution obtains adequate records or other sufficient evidence from such organization showing that the qualifying distribution described in subparagraph (A) has been made by such organization.

(4) Limitation on distributions by nonoperating private foundations to supporting organizations—

(A) In general.—For purposes of this section, the term "qualifying distribution" shall not include any amount paid by a private foundation which is not an operating foundation to—

(i) any type III supporting organization (as defined in section 4943(f)(5)(A)) which is not a functionally integrated type III supporting organization (as defined in section 4943(f)(5)(B)), and

(ii) any organization which is described in subparagraph (B) or (C) if—

(I) a disqualified person of the private foundation directly or indirectly controls such organization or a supported organization (as defined in section 509(f)(3)) of such organization, or

(II) the Secretary determines by regulations that a distribution to such organization otherwise is inappropriate.

(B) Type I and type II supporting organizations.—An organization is described in this subparagraph if the organization meets the requirements of subparagraphs (A) and (C) of section 509(a)(3) and is—

(i) operated, supervised, or controlled by one or more organizations described in paragraph (1) or (2) of section 509(a), or

(ii) supervised or controlled in connection with one or more such organizations.

(C) Functionally integrated type III supporting organizations.—An organization is described in this subparagraph if the organization is a functionally integrated type III supporting organization (as defined under section 4943(f)(5)(B)).

(h) Treatment of qualifying distributions.—

(1) In general.—Except as provided in paragraph (2), any qualifying distribution made during a taxable year shall be treated as made—

(A) first out of the undistributed income of the immediately preceding taxable year (if the private foundation was subject to the tax imposed by this section for such preceding taxable year) to the extent thereof,

(B) second out of the undistributed income for the taxable year to the extent thereof, and

(C) then out of corpus.

For purposes of this paragraph, distributions shall be taken into account in the order of time in which made.

(2) Correction of deficient distributions for prior taxable years, etc.—In the case of any qualifying distribution which (under paragraph (1)) is not treated as made out of the undistributed income of the immediately preceding taxable year, the foundation may elect to treat any portion of such distribution as made out of the undistributed income of a designated prior taxable year or out of corpus. The election shall be made by the foundation at such time and in such manner as the Secretary shall by regulations prescribe.

(i) Adjustment of distributable amount where distributions during prior years have exceeded income.—

(1) In general.—If, for the taxable years in the adjustment period for which an organization is a private foundation—

(A) the aggregate qualifying distributions treated (under subsection (h)) as made out of the undistributed income for such taxable year or as made out of corpus (except to the extent subsection (g)(3) with respect to the recipient private foundation or section 170(b)(1)(F)(ii) applies) during such taxable years, exceed

(B) the distributable amounts for such taxable years (determined without regard to this subsection),

then, for purposes of this section (other than subsection (h)), the distributable amount for the taxable year shall be reduced by an amount equal to such excess.

(2) Taxable years in adjustment period.—For purposes of paragraph (1), with respect to any taxable year of a private foundation the taxable years in the adjustment period are the taxable years (not exceeding 5) immediately preceding the taxable year.

(j) Other definitions.—For purposes of this section—

(1) Taxable period.—The term "taxable period" means, with respect to the undistributed income for any taxable year, the period beginning with the first day of the taxable year and ending on the earlier of—

(A) the date of mailing of a notice of deficiency with respect to the tax imposed by subsection (a) under section 6212, or

(B) the date on which the tax imposed by subsection (a) is assessed.

(2) Allowable distribution period.—The term "allowable distribution period" means, with respect to any private foundation, the period beginning with the first day of the first taxable year following the taxable year in which the incorrect valuation (described in subsection (a)(2)) occurred and ending 90 days after the date of mailing of a notice of deficiency (with respect to the tax imposed by subsection (a)) under section 6212 extended by—

(A) any period in which a deficiency cannot be assessed under section 6213(a), and

(B) any other period which the Secretary determines is reasonable and necessary to permit a distribution of undistributed income under this section.

(3) Operating foundation.—For purposes of this section, the term "operating foundation" means any organization—

(A) which makes qualifying distributions (within the meaning of paragraph (1) or (2) of subsection (g)) directly for the active conduct of the activities constituting the purpose or function for which it is organized and operated equal to substantially all of the lesser of—

(i) its adjusted net income (as defined in subsection (f)), or

(ii) its minimum investment return; and

(B)(i) substantially more than half of the assets of which are devoted directly to such activities or to functionally related businesses (as defined in paragraph (4)), or to both, or are stock of a corporation which is controlled by the foundation and substantially all of the assets of which are so devoted.

(ii) which normally makes qualifying distributions (within the meaning of paragraph (1) or (2) of subsection (g)) directly for the active conduct of the activities constituting the purpose or function for which it is organized and operated in an amount not less than two-thirds of its minimum investment return (as defined in subsection (e)), or

(iii) substantially all of the support (other than gross investment income as defined in section 509(e)) of which is normally received from the general public and from 5 or more exempt organizations which are not described in section 4946(a)(1)(H) with respect to each other or the recipient foundation; not more than 25 percent of the support (other than gross investment income) of which is normally received from any one such exempt organization; and not more than half of the support of which is normally received from gross investment income.

Notwithstanding the provisions of subparagraph (A), if the qualifying distributions (within the meaning of paragraph (1) or (2) of subsection (g)) of an organization for the taxable year exceed the minimum investment return for the taxable year, clause (ii) of subparagraph (A) shall not apply unless substantially all of such qualifying distributions are made directly for the active conduct of the activities constituting the purpose or function for which it is organized and operated.

(4) Functionally related business.—The term "functionally related business" means—

(A) a trade or business which is not an unrelated trade or business (as defined in section 513), or

(B) an activity which is carried on within a larger aggregate of similar activities or within a larger complex of other endeavors which is related (aside from the need of the organization for income or funds or the use it makes of the profits derived) to the exempt purposes of the organization.

(5) Certain elderly care facilities.—For purposes of this section (but no other provisions of this title), the term "operating foundation" includes any organization which, on May 26, 1969, and at all times thereafter before the close of the taxable year, operated and maintained as its principal functional purpose facilities for the long-term care, comfort, maintenance, or education of permanently and totally disabled persons, elderly persons, needy widows, or children but only if such organization meets the requirements of paragraph (3)(B)(ii).

§ 4943. Taxes on excess business holdings.

(a) Initial tax.—

(1) Imposition.—There is hereby imposed on the excess business holdings of any private foundation in a business enterprise during any taxable year which ends during the taxable period a tax equal to 10 percent of the value of such holdings.

(2) Special rules.—The tax imposed by paragraph (1)—

(A) shall be imposed on the last day of the taxable year, but

(B) with respect to the private foundation's holdings in any business enterprise, shall be determined as of that day during the taxable year when the foundation's excess holdings in such enterprise were the greatest.

(b) Additional tax.—In any case in which an initial tax is imposed under subsection (a) with respect to the holdings of a private foundation in any business enterprise, if, at the close of the taxable period with respect to such holdings, the foundation still has excess business holdings in such enterprise, there is hereby imposed a tax equal to 200 percent of such excess business holdings.

(c) Excess business holdings.—For purposes of this section—

(1) In general.—The term "excess business holdings" means, with respect to the holdings of any private foundation in any business enterprise, the amount of stock or other interest in the enterprise which the foundation would have to dispose of to a person other than a disqualified person in order for the remaining holdings of the foundation in such enterprise to be permitted holdings.

(2) Permitted holdings in a corporation.—

(A) In general.—The permitted holdings of any private foundation in an incorporated business enterprise are—

(i) 20 percent of the voting stock, reduced by

(ii) the percentage of the voting stock owned by all disqualified persons.

In any case in which all disqualified persons together do not own more than 20 percent of the voting stock of an incorporated business enterprise, nonvoting stock held by the private foundation shall also be treated as permitted holdings.

(B) 35 percent rule where third person has effective control of enterprise.—If—

(i) the private foundation and all disqualified persons together do not own more than 35 percent of the voting stock of an incorporated business enterprise, and

(ii) it is established to the satisfaction of the Secretary that effective control of the corporation is in one or more persons who are not disqualified persons with respect to the foundation,

then subparagraph (A) shall be applied by substituting 35 percent for 20 percent.

(C) 2 percent de minimis rule.—A private foundation shall not be treated as having excess business holdings in any corporation in which it (together with all other private foundations which are described in section 4946(a)(1)(H)) owns not more than 2 percent of the voting stock and not more than 2 percent in value of all outstanding shares of all classes of stock.

(3) Permitted holdings in partnerships, etc.—The permitted holdings of a private foundation in any business enterprise which is not incorporated shall be determined under regulations prescribed by the Secretary. Such regulations shall be consistent in principle with paragraphs (2) and (4), except that—

(A) in the case of a partnership or joint venture, "profits interest" shall be substituted for "voting stock", and "capital interest" shall be substituted for "nonvoting stock",

(B) in the case of a proprietorship, there shall be no permitted holdings, and

(C) in any other case, "beneficial interest" shall be substituted for "voting stock".

(4) Present holdings.—

(A)(i) In applying this section with respect to the holdings of any private foundation in a business enterprise, if such foundation and all disqualified persons together have holdings in such enterprise in excess of 20 percent of the voting stock on May 26, 1969, the percentage of such holdings shall be substituted for "20 percent," and for "35 percent" (if the percentage of such holdings is greater than 35 percent), wherever it appears in paragraph (2), but in no event shall the percentage so substituted be more than 50 percent.

* * *

(5) Holdings acquired by trust or will.—Paragraph (4) (other than subparagraph (B)(i)) shall apply to any interest in a business enterprise which a private foundation acquires under the terms of a trust which was irrevocable on May 26, 1969, or under the terms of a will executed on or before such date, which are in effect on such date and at all times thereafter, as if such interest were held on May 26, 1969, except that the 15-year and 10-year periods prescribed in clauses (ii) and (iii) of paragraph (4)(B) shall commence with respect to such interest on the date of distribution under the trust or will in lieu of May 26, 1969.

(6) 5-year period to dispose of gifts, bequests, etc.—Except as provided in paragraph (5), if, after May 26, 1969, there is a change in the holdings in a business enterprise (other than by purchase by the private foundation or by a disqualified person) which causes the private foundation to have—

(A) excess business holdings in such enterprise, the interest of the foundation in such enterprise (immediately after such change) shall (while held by the foundation) be treated as held by a disqualified person (rather than by the foundation) during the 5-year period beginning on the date of such change in holdings; or

(B) an increase in excess business holdings in such enterprise (determined without regard to subparagraph (A)), subparagraph (A) shall apply, except that the excess holdings immediately preceding the increase therein shall not be treated, solely because of such increase, as held by a disqualified person (rather than by the foundation).

In any case where an acquisition by a disqualified person would result in a substitution under clause (i) or (ii) of subparagraph (D) of paragraph (4), the preceding sentence shall be applied with respect to such acquisition as if it did not contain the phrase "or by a disqualified person" in the material preceding subparagraph (A).

(7) 5-year extension of period to dispose of certain large gifts and bequests.—The Secretary may extend for an additional 5-year period the period under paragraph (6) for disposing of excess business holdings in the case of an unusually large gift or bequest of diverse business holdings or holdings with complex corporate structures if—

(A) the foundation establishes that—

(i) diligent efforts to dispose of such holdings have been made within the initial 5-year period, and

(ii) disposition within the initial 5-year period has not been possible (except at a price substantially below fair market value) by reason of such size and complexity or diversity of such holdings,

(B) before the close of the initial 5-year period—

(i) the private foundation submits to the Secretary a plan for disposing of all of the excess business holdings involved in the extension, and

(ii) the private foundation submits the plan described in clause (i) to the Attorney General (or other appropriate State official) having administrative or supervisory authority or responsibility with respect to the foundation's disposition of the excess business holdings involved and submits to the Secretary any response received by the private foundation from the Attorney General (or other appropriate State official) to such plan during such 5-year period, and

(C) the Secretary determines that such plan can reasonably be expected to be carried out before the close of the extension period.

(d) Definitions; special rules.—For purposes of this section—

(1) Business holdings.—In computing the holdings of a private foundation, or a disqualified person (as defined in section 4946) with respect thereto, in any business enterprise, any stock or other interest owned, directly or indirectly, by or for a corporation, partnership, estate, or trust shall be considered as being owned proportionately by or for its shareholders, partners, or beneficiaries. The preceding sentence shall not apply with respect to an income or remainder interest of a private foundation in a trust described in section 4947(a)(2), but only if, in the case of property transferred in trust after May 26, 1969, such foundation holds only an income interest or only a remainder interest in such trust.

(2) Taxable period.—The term "taxable period" means, with respect to any excess business holdings of a private foundation in a business enterprise, the period beginning on the first day on which there are excess holdings and ending on the earlier of—

(A) the date of mailing of a notice of deficiency with respect to the tax imposed by subsection (a) under section 6212 in respect of such holdings, or

(B) the date on which the tax imposed by subsection (a) in respect of such holdings is assessed.

(3) Business enterprise.—The term "business enterprise" does not include—

(A) a functionally related business (as defined in section 4942(j)(4)), or

(B) a trade or business at least 95 percent of the gross income of which is derived from passive sources.

For purposes of subparagraph (B), gross income from passive sources includes the items excluded by section 512(b)(1), (2), (3), and (5), and income from the sale of goods (including charges or costs passed on at cost to purchasers of such goods or income received in settlement of a dispute concerning or in lieu of the exercise of the right to sell such goods) if the seller does not manufacture, produce, physically receive or deliver, negotiate sales of, or maintain inventories in such goods.

(4) Disqualified person.—The term "disqualified person" (as defined in section 4946(a)) does not include a plan described in section 4975(e)(7) with respect to the holdings of a private foundation described in paragraphs (4) and (5) of subsection (c).

(e) Application of tax to donor advised funds—

(1) In general.—For purposes of this section, a donor advised fund (as defined in section 4966(d)(2)) shall be treated as a private foundation.

(2) Disqualified person.—In applying this section to any donor advised fund (as so defined), the term "disqualified person" means, with respect to the donor advised fund, any person who is—

(A) described in section 4966(d)(2)(A)(iii),

(B) a member of the family of an individual described in subparagraph (A), or

(C) a 35-percent controlled entity (as defined in section 4958(f)(3) by substituting "persons described in subparagraph (A) or (B) of section 4943(e)(2)" for "persons described in subparagraph (A) or (B) of paragraph (1)" in subparagraph (A)(i) thereof).

(3) Present holdings.—For purposes of this subsection, rules similar to the rules of paragraphs (4), (5), and (6) of subsection (c) shall apply to donor advised funds (as so defined), except that—

(A) "the date of the enactment of this subsection" shall be substituted for "May 26, 1969" each place it appears in paragraphs (4), (5), and (6), and

(B) "January 1, 2007" shall be substituted for "January 1, 1971" in paragraph (4)(E).

(f) Application of tax to supporting organizations.—

(1) In general.—For purposes of this section, an organization which is described in paragraph (3) shall be treated as a private foundation.

(2) Exception.—The Secretary may exempt the excess business holdings of any organization from the application of this subsection if the Secretary determines that such holdings are consistent with the purpose or function constituting the basis for its exemption under section 501.

(3) Organizations described.—An organization is described in this paragraph if such organization is—

(A) a type III supporting organization (other than a functionally integrated type III supporting organization), or

(B) an organization which meets the requirements of subparagraphs (A) and (C) of section 509(a)(3) and which is supervised or controlled in connection with one or more organizations described in paragraph (1) or (2) of section 509(a), but only if such organization accepts any gift or contribution from any person described in section 509(f)(2)(B).

(4) Disqualified person—

(A) In general.—In applying this section to any organization described in paragraph (3), the term "disqualified person" means, with respect to the organization—

(i) any person who was, at any time during the 5-year period ending on the date described in subsection (a)(2)(A), in a position to exercise substantial influence over the affairs of the organization,

(ii) any member of the family (determined under section 4958(f)(4)) of an individual described in clause (i),

(iii) any 35-percent controlled entity (as defined in section 4958(f)(3) by substituting "persons described in clause (i) or (ii) of section 4943(f)(4)(A)" for "persons described in subparagraph (A) or (B) of paragraph (1)" in subparagraph (A)(i) thereof),

(iv) any person described in section 4958(c)(3)(B), and

(v) any organization—

(I) which is effectively controlled (directly or indirectly) by the same person or persons who control the organization in question, or

(II) substantially all of the contributions to which were made (directly or indirectly) by the same person or persons described in subparagraph (B) or a member of the family (within the meaning of section 4946(d)) of such a person.

(B) Persons described.—A person is described in this subparagraph if such person is—

(i) a substantial contributor to the organization (as defined in section 4958(c)(3)(C)),

(ii) an officer, director, or trustee of the organization (or an individual having powers or responsibilities similar to those of the officers, directors, or trustees of the organization), or

(iii) an owner of more than 20 percent of—

(I) the total combined voting power of a corporation,

(II) the profits interest of a partnership, or

(III) the beneficial interest of a trust or unincorporated enterprise,

which is a substantial contributor (as so defined) to the organization.

(5) Type III supporting organization; functionally integrated type III supporting organization.—For purposes of this subsection—

(A) Type III supporting organization.—The term "type III supporting organization" means an organization which meets the requirements of subparagraphs (A) and (C) of section 509(a)(3) and which is operated in connection with one or more organizations described in paragraph (1) or (2) of section 509(a).

(B) Functionally integrated type III supporting organization.—The term "functionally integrated type III supporting organization" means a type III supporting organization which is not required under regulations established by the Secretary to make payments to supported organizations (as defined under section 509(f)(3)) due to the activities of the organization related to performing the functions of, or carrying out the purposes of, such supported organizations.

(6) Special rule for certain holdings of type III supporting organizations.—For purposes of this subsection, the term "excess business holdings" shall not include any holdings of a type III supporting organization in any business enterprise if, as of November 18, 2005, the holdings were held (and at all times thereafter, are held) for the benefit of the community pursuant to the direction of a State attorney general or a State official with jurisdiction over such organization.

(7) Present holdings.—For purposes of this subsection, rules similar to the rules of paragraphs (4), (5), and (6) of subsection (c) shall apply to organizations described in section 509(a)(3), except that—

(A) "the date of the enactment of this subsection" shall be substituted for "May 26, 1969" each place it appears in paragraphs (4), (5), and (6), and

(B) "January 1, 2007" shall be substituted for "January 1, 1971" in paragraph (4)(E).

(g) Exception for certain holdings limited to independently-operated philanthropic business.—

(1) In general.—Subsection (a) shall not apply with respect to the holdings of a private foundation in any business enterprise which meets the requirements of paragraphs (2), (3), and (4) for the taxable year.

(2) Ownership.—The requirements of this paragraph are met if—

(A) 100 percent of the voting stock in the business enterprise is held by the private foundation at all times during the taxable year, and

(B) all the private foundation's ownership interests in the business enterprise were acquired by means other than by purchase.

(3) All profits to charity.—

(A) In General.—The requirements of this paragraph are met if the business enterprise, not later than 120 days after the close of the taxable year, distributes an amount equal to its net operating income for such taxable year to the private foundation.

(B) Net operating income.—For purposes of this paragraph, the net operating income of any business enterprise for any taxable year is an amount equal to the gross income of the business enterprise for the taxable year, reduced by the sum of—

(i) the deductions allowed by chapter 1 for the taxable year which are directly connected with the production of such income,

(ii) the tax imposed by chapter 1 on the business enterprise for the taxable year, and

(iii) an amount for a reasonable reserve for working capital and other business needs of the business enterprise.

(4) Independent operation.—The requirements of this paragraph are met if, at all times during the taxable year—

(A) no substantial contributor (as defined in section 4958(c)(3)(C)) to the private foundation or family member (as determined under section 4958(f)(4)) of such a contributor is a director, officer, trustee, manager, employee, or contractor of the business enterprise (or an individual having powers or responsibilities similar to any of the foregoing),

(B) at least a majority of the board of directors of the private foundation are persons who are not—

(i) directors or officers of the business enterprise, or

(ii) family members (as so determined) of a substantial contributor (as so defined) to the private foundation, and

(C) there is no loan outstanding from the business enterprise to a substantial contributor (as so defined) to the private foundation or to any family member of such a contributor (as so determined).

(5) Certain deemed private foundations excluded.—This subsection shall not apply to—

(A) any fund or organization treated as a private foundation for purposes of this section by reason of subsection (e) or (f),

(B) any trust described in section 4947(a)(1) (relating to charitable trusts), and

(C) any trust described in section 4947(a)(2) (relating to split-interest trusts).

§ 4944. Taxes on investments which jeopardize charitable purpose.

(a) Initial taxes.—

(1) On the private foundation.—If a private foundation invests any amount in such a manner as to jeopardize the carrying out of any of its exempt purposes, there is hereby imposed on the making of such investment a tax equal to 10 percent of the amount so invested for each year (or part thereof) in the taxable period. The tax imposed by this paragraph shall be paid by the private foundation.

(2) On the management.—In any case in which a tax is imposed by paragraph (1), there is hereby imposed on the participation of any foundation manager in the making of the investment, knowing that it is jeopardizing the carrying out of any of the foundation's exempt purposes, a tax equal to 10 percent of the amount so invested for each year (or part thereof) in the taxable period, unless such participation is not willful and is due to reasonable cause. The tax imposed by this paragraph shall be paid by any foundation manager who participated in the making of the investment.

(b) Additional taxes.—

(1) On the foundation.—In any case in which an initial tax is imposed by subsection (a)(1) on the making of an investment and such investment is not removed from jeopardy within the taxable period, there is hereby imposed a tax equal to 25 percent of the amount of the investment. The tax imposed by this paragraph shall be paid by the private foundation.

(2) On the management.—In any case in which an additional tax is imposed by paragraph (1), if a foundation manager refused to agree to part or all of the removal from jeopardy, there is hereby imposed a tax equal to 5 percent of the amount of the investment. The tax imposed by this paragraph shall be paid by any foundation manager who refused to agree to part or all of the removal from jeopardy.

(c) Exception for program-related investments.—For purposes of this section, investments, the primary purpose of which is to accomplish one or more of the purposes described in section 170(c)(2)(B), and no significant purpose of which is the production of income or the appreciation of property, shall not be considered as investments which jeopardize the carrying out of exempt purposes.

(d) Special rules.—For purposes of subsections (a) and (b)—

(1) Joint and several liability.—If more than one person is liable under subsection (a)(2) or (b)(2) with respect to any one investment, all such persons shall be jointly and severally liable under such paragraph with respect to such investment.

(2) Limit for management.—With respect to any one investment, the maximum amount of the tax imposed by subsection (a)(2) shall not exceed $10,000, and the maximum amount of the tax imposed by subsection (b)(2) shall not exceed $20,000.

(e) Definitions.—For purposes of this section—

(1) Taxable period.—The term "taxable period" means, with respect to any investment which jeopardizes the carrying out of exempt purposes, the period beginning with the date on which the amount is so invested and ending on the earliest of—

(A) the date of mailing of a notice of deficiency with respect to the tax imposed by subsection (a)(1) under section 6212,

(B) the date on which the tax imposed by subsection (a)(1) is assessed, or

(C) the date on which the amount so invested is removed from jeopardy.

(2) Removal from jeopardy.—An investment which jeopardizes the carrying out of exempt purposes shall be considered to be removed from jeopardy when such investment is sold or otherwise disposed of, and the proceeds of such sale or other disposition are not investments which jeopardize the carrying out of exempt purposes.

§ 4945. Taxes on taxable expenditures.

(a) Initial taxes.—

(1) On the foundation.—There is hereby imposed on each taxable expenditure (as defined in subsection (d)) a tax equal to 20 percent of the amount thereof. The tax imposed by this paragraph shall be paid by the private foundation.

(2) On the management.—There is hereby imposed on the agreement of any foundation manager to the making of an expenditure, knowing that it is a taxable expenditure, a tax equal to 5 percent of the amount thereof, unless such agreement is not willful and is due to reasonable cause. The tax imposed by this paragraph shall be paid by any foundation manager who agreed to the making of the expenditure.

(b) Additional taxes.—

(1) On the foundation.—In any case in which an initial tax is imposed by subsection (a)(1) on a taxable expenditure and such expenditure is not corrected within the taxable period, there is hereby imposed a tax equal to 100 percent of the amount of the expenditure. The tax imposed by this paragraph shall be paid by the private foundation.

(2) On the management.—In any case in which an additional tax is imposed by paragraph (1), if a foundation manager refused to agree to part or all of the correction, there is hereby imposed a tax equal to 50 percent of the amount of the taxable expenditure. The tax imposed by this paragraph shall be paid by any foundation manager who refused to agree to part or all of the correction.

(c) Special rules.—For purposes of subsections (a) and (b)—

(1) Joint and several liability.—If more than one person is liable under subsection (a)(2) or (b)(2) with respect to the making of a taxable expenditure, all such persons shall be jointly and severally liable under such paragraph with respect to such expenditure.

(2) Limit for management.—With respect to any one taxable expenditure, the maximum amount of the tax imposed by subsection (a)(2) shall not exceed $10,000, and the maximum amount of the tax imposed by subsection (b)(2) shall not exceed $20,000.

(d) Taxable expenditure.—For purposes of this section, the term "taxable expenditure" means any amount paid or incurred by a private foundation—

(1) to carry on propaganda, or otherwise to attempt, to influence legislation, within the meaning of subsection (e),

(2) except as provided in subsection (f), to influence the outcome of any specific public election, or to carry on, directly or indirectly, any voter registration drive,

(3) as a grant to an individual for travel, study, or other similar purposes by such individual, unless such grant satisfies the requirements of subsection (g),

(4) as a grant to an organization unless—

(A) such organization—

(i) is described in paragraph (1) or (2) of section 509(a),

(ii) is an organization described in section 509(a)(3) (other than an organization described in clause (i) or (ii) of section 4942(g)(4)(A)), or

(iii) is an exempt operating foundation (as defined in section 4940(d)(2)), or

(B) the private foundation exercises expenditure responsibility with respect to such grant in accordance with subsection (h), or

(5) for any purpose other than one specified in section 170(c)(2)(B).

(e) Activities within subsection (d)(1)—For purposes of subsection (d)(1), the term "taxable expenditure" means any amount paid or incurred by a private foundation for—

(1) any attempt to influence any legislation through an attempt to affect the opinion of the general public or any segment thereof, and

(2) any attempt to influence legislation through communication with any member or employee of a legislative body, or with any other government official or employee who may participate in the formulation of the legislation (except technical advice or assistance provided to a governmental body or to a committee or other subdivision thereof in response to a written request by such body or subdivision, as the case may be),

other than through making available the results of nonpartisan analysis, study, or research. Paragraph (2) of this subsection shall not apply to any amount paid or incurred in connection with an appearance before, or communication to, any legislative body with respect to a possible decision of such body which might affect the existence of the private foundation, its powers and duties, its tax-exempt status, or the deduction of contributions to such foundation.

(f) Nonpartisan activities carried on by certain organizations.—Subsection (d)(2) shall not apply to any amount paid or incurred by any organization—

(1) which is described in section 501(c)(3) and exempt from taxation under section 501(a),

(2) the activities of which are nonpartisan, are not confined to one specific election period, and are carried on in 5 or more States,

(3) substantially all of the income of which is expended directly for the active conduct of the activities constituting the purpose or function for which it is organized and operated,

(4) substantially all of the support (other than gross investment income as defined in section 509(e)) of which is received from exempt organizations, the general public, governmental units described in section 170(c)(1), or any combination of the foregoing; not more than 25 percent of such support is received from any one exempt organization (for this purpose treating private foundations which are described in section 4946(a)(1)(H) with respect to each other as one exempt organization); and not more than half of the support of which is received from gross investment income, and

(5) contributions to which for voter registration drives are not subject to conditions that they may be used only in specified States, possessions of the United States, or political subdivisions or other areas of any of the foregoing, or the District of Columbia, or that they may be used in only one specific election period.

In determining whether the organization meets the requirements of paragraph (4) for any taxable year of such organization, there shall be taken into account the support received by such organization during such taxable year and during the immediately preceding 4 taxable years of such organization. Subsection (d)(4) shall not apply to any grant to an organization which meets the requirements of this subsection.

(g) Individual grants.—Subsection (d)(3) shall not apply to an individual grant awarded on an objective and nondiscriminatory basis pursuant to a procedure approved in advance by the Secretary, if it is demonstrated to the satisfaction of the Secretary that—

(1) the grant constitutes a scholarship or fellowship grant which would be subject to the provisions of section 117(a) (as in effect on the day before the date of the enactment of the Tax Reform Act of 1986) and is to be used for study at an educational organization described in section 170(b)(1)(A)(ii),

(2) the grant constitutes a prize or award which is subject to the provisions of section 74(b)(without regard to paragraph (3) thereof), if the recipient of such prize or award is selected from the general public, or

(3) the purpose of the grant is to achieve a specific objective, produce a report or other similar product, or improve or enhance a literary, artistic, musical, scientific, teaching, or other similar capacity, skill, or talent of the grantee.

(h) Expenditure responsibility.—The expenditure responsibility referred to in subsection (d)(4) means that the private foundation is responsible to exert all reasonable efforts and to establish adequate procedures—

(1) to see that the grant is spent solely for the purpose for which made,

(2) to obtain full and complete reports from the grantee on how the funds are spent, and

(3) to make full and detailed reports with respect to such expenditures to the Secretary.

(i) Other definitions.—For purposes of this section—

(1) Correction.—The terms "correction" and "correct" means, with respect to any taxable expenditure, (A) recovering part or all of the expenditure to the extent recovery is possible, and where full recovery is not possible such additional corrective action as is prescribed by the Secretary by regulations, or (B) in the case of a failure to comply with subsection (h)(2) or (h)(3), obtaining or making the report in question.

(2) Taxable period.—The term "taxable period" means, with respect to any taxable expenditure, the period beginning with the date on which the taxable expenditure occurs and ending on the earlier of—

(A) the date of mailing a notice of deficiency with respect to the tax imposed by subsection (a)(1) under section 6212, or

(B) the date on which the tax imposed by subsection (a)(1) is assessed.

§ 4946. Definitions and special rules.

(a) Disqualified person.—

(1) In general.—For purposes of this subchapter, the term "disqualified person" means, with respect to a private foundation, a person who is—

(A) a substantial contributor to the foundation,

(B) a foundation manager (within the meaning of subsection (b)(1)),

(C) an owner of more than 20 percent of—

(i) the total combined voting power of a corporation,

(ii) the profits interest of a partnership, or

(iii) the beneficial interest of a trust or unincorporated enterprise,

which is a substantial contributor to the foundation,

(D) a member of the family (as defined in subsection (d)) of any individual described in subparagraph (A), (B), or (C),

(E) a corporation of which persons described in subparagraph (A), (B), (C), or (D) own more than 35 percent of the total combined voting power,

(F) a partnership in which persons described in subparagraph (A), (B), (C), or (D) own more than 35 percent of the profits interest,

(G) a trust or estate in which persons described in subparagraph (A), (B), (C), or (D) hold more than 35 percent of the beneficial interest,

(H) only for purposes of section 4943, a private foundation—

(i) which is effectively controlled (directly or indirectly) by the same person or persons who control the private foundation in question, or

(ii) substantially all of the contributions to which were made (directly or indirectly) by the same person or persons described in subparagraph (A), (B), or (C), or members of their families (within the meaning of subsection (d)), who made (directly or indirectly) substantially all of the contributions to the private foundation in question, and

(I) only for purposes of section 4941, a government official (as defined in subsection (c)).

(2) Substantial contributors.—For purposes of paragraph (1), the term "substantial contributor" means a person who is described in section 507(d)(2).

(3) Stockholdings.—For purposes of paragraphs (1)(C)(i) and (1)(E), there shall be taken into account indirect stockholdings which would be taken into account under section 267(c), except that, for purposes of this paragraph, section 267(c)(4) shall be treated as providing that the members of the family of an individual are the members within the meaning of subsection (d).

(4) Partnerships; trusts.—For purposes of paragraphs (1)(C)(ii) and (iii), (1)(F), and (1)(G), the ownership of profits or beneficial interests shall be determined in accordance with the rules for constructive ownership of stock provided in section 267(c) (other than paragraph (3) thereof), except that section 267(c)(4) shall be treated as providing that the members of the family of an individual are the members within the meaning of subsection (d).

(b) Foundation manager.—For purposes of this subchapter, the term "foundation manager" means, with respect to any private foundation—

(1) an officer, director, or trustee of a foundation (or an individual having powers or responsibilities similar to those of officers, directors, or trustees of the foundation), and

(2) with respect to any act (or failure to act), the employees of the foundation having authority or responsibility with respect to such act (or failure to act).

(c) Government official.—For purposes of subsection (a)(1)(I) and section 4941, the term "government official" means, with respect to an act of self-dealing described in section 4941, an individual who, at the time of such act, holds any of the following offices or positions (other than as a "special Government employee", as defined in section 202(a) of title 18, United States Code):

(1) an elective public office in the executive or legislative branch of the Government of the United States,

(2) an office in the executive or judicial branch of the Government of the United States, appointment to which was made by the President,

(3) a position in the executive, legislative, or judicial branch of the Government of the United States—

(A) which is listed in schedule C of rule VI of the Civil Service Rules, or

(B) the compensation for which is equal to or greater than the lowest rate of basic pay for the Senior Executive Service under section 5382 of title 5, United States Code.

(4) a position under the House of Representatives or the Senate of the United States held by an individual receiving gross compensation at an annual rate of $15,000 or more,

(5) an elective or appointive public office in the executive, legislative, or judicial branch of the government of a State, possession of the United States, or political subdivision or other area of any of the foregoing, or of the District of Columbia, held by an individual receiving gross compensation at an annual rate of $20,000 or more, or

(6) a position as personal or executive assistant or secretary to any of the foregoing, or

(7) a member of the Internal Revenue Service Oversight Board.

(d) Members of family.—For purposes of subsection (a)(1), the family of any individual shall include only his spouse, ancestors, children, grandchildren, great grandchildren, and the spouses of children, grandchildren, and great grandchildren.

§ 4947. Application of taxes to certain nonexempt trusts.

(a) Application of tax.—

(1) Charitable trusts.—For purposes of part II of subchapter F of chapter 1 (other than section 508(a), (b), and (c)) and for purposes of this chapter, a trust which is not exempt from taxation under section 501(a), all of the unexpired interests in which are devoted to one or more of the purposes described in section 170(c)(2)(B), and for which a deduction was allowed under section 170, 545(b)(2), 642(c), 2055, 2106(a)(2), or 2522 (or the corresponding provisions of prior law), shall be treated as an organization described in section 501(c)(3). For purposes of section 509(a)(3)(A), such a trust shall be treated as if organized on the day on which it first becomes subject to this paragraph.

(2) Split-interest trusts.—In the case of a trust which is not exempt from tax under section 501(a), not all of the unexpired interests in which are devoted to one or more of the purposes described in section 170(c)(2)(B), and which has amounts in trust for which a deduction was allowed under section 170, 545(b)(2), 642(c), 2055, 2106(a)(2), or 2522, section 507 (relating to termination of private foundation status), section 508(e) (relating to governing instruments) to the extent applicable to a trust described in this paragraph, section 4941 (relating to taxes on self-dealing), section 4943 (relating to taxes on excess business holdings) except as provided in subsection (b)(3), section 4944 (relating to investments which jeopardize charitable purpose) except as provided in subsection (b)(3), and section 4945 (relating to taxes on taxable expenditures) shall apply as if such trust were a private foundation. This paragraph shall not apply with respect to—

(A) any amounts payable under the terms of such trust to income beneficiaries, unless a deduction was allowed under section 170(f)(2)(B), 2055(e)(2)(B), or 2522(c)(2)(B),

(B) any amounts in trust other than amounts for which a deduction was allowed under section 170, 545(b)(2), 642(c), 2055, 2106(a)(2), or 2522, if such other amounts are segregated from amounts for which no deduction was allowable, or

(C) any amounts transferred in trust before May 27, 1969.

(3) Segregated amounts.—For purposes of paragraph (2)(B), a trust with respect to which amounts are segregated shall separately account for the various income, deduction, and other items properly attributable to each of such segregated amounts.

(b) Special rules.—

(1) Regulations.—The Secretary shall prescribe such regulations as may be necessary to carry out the purposes of this section.

(2) Limit to segregated amounts.—If any amounts in the trust are segregated within the meaning of subsection (a)(2)(B) of this section, the value of the net assets for purposes of subsections (c)(2) and (g) of section 507 shall be limited to such segregated amounts.

(3) Sections 4943 and 4944.—Sections 4943 and 4944 shall not apply to a trust which is described in subsection (a)(2) if—

(A) all the income interest (and none of the remainder interest) of such trust is devoted solely to one or more of the purposes described in section 170(c)(2)(B), and all amounts in such trust for which a deduction was allowed under section 170, 545(b)(2), 642(c), 2055, 2106(a)(2), or 2522 have an aggregate value not more than 60 percent of the aggregate fair market value of all amounts in such trusts, or

(B) a deduction was allowed under section 170, 545(b)(2), 642(c), 2055, 2106(a)(2), or 2522 for amounts payable under the terms of such trust to every remainder beneficiary but not to any income beneficiary.

(4) Section 507.—The provisions of section 507(a) shall not apply to a trust which is described in subsection (a)(2) by reason of a distribution of qualified employer securities (as defined in section 664(g)(4)) to an employee stock ownership plan (as defined in section 4975(e)(7)) in a qualified gratuitous transfer (as defined by section 664(g)).

§ 4948. Application of taxes and denial of exemption with respect to certain foreign organizations.

(a) Tax on income of certain foreign organizations.—In lieu of the tax imposed by section 4940, there is hereby imposed for each taxable year on the gross investment income (within the meaning of section 4940(c)(2)) derived from sources within the United States (within the meaning of section 861) by every foreign organization which is a private foundation for the taxable year a tax equal to 4 percent of such income.

(b) Certain sections inapplicable.—Section 507 (relating to termination of private foundation status), section 508 (relating to special rules with respect to section 501(c)(3) organizations), and this chapter (other than this section) shall not apply to any foreign organization which has received substantially all of its support (other than gross investment income) from sources outside the United States.

(c) Denial of exemption to foreign organizations engaged in prohibited transactions.—

(1) General rule.—A foreign organization described in subsection (b) shall not be exempt from taxation under section 501(a) if it has engaged in a prohibited transaction after December 31, 1969.

(2) Prohibited transactions.—For purposes of this subsection, the term "prohibited transaction" means any act or failure to act (other than with respect to section 4942(e)) which would subject a foreign organization described in subsection (b), or a disqualified person (as defined in section 4946) with respect thereto, to liability for a penalty under section 6684 or a tax under section 507 if such foreign organization were a domestic organization.

(3) Taxable years affected.—

(A) Except as provided in subparagraph (B), a foreign organization described in subsection (b) shall be denied exemption from taxation under section 501(a) by reason of paragraph (1) for all taxable years beginning with the taxable year during which it is notified by the Secretary that it has engaged in a prohibited transaction. The Secretary shall publish such notice in the Federal Register on the day on which he so notifies such foreign organization.

(B) Under regulations prescribed by the Secretary any foreign organization described in subsection (b) which is denied exemption from taxation under section 501(a) by reason of paragraph (1) may, with respect to the second taxable year following the taxable year in which notice is given under subparagraph (A) (or any taxable year thereafter), file claim for exemption from taxation under section 501(a). If the Secretary is satisfied that such organization will not knowingly again engage in a prohibited transaction, such organization shall not, with respect to taxable years beginning with the taxable year with respect to which such claim is filed, be denied exemption from taxation under section 501(a) by reason of any prohibited transaction which was engaged in before the date on which such notice was given under subparagraph (A).

(4) Disallowance of certain charitable deductions.—No gift or bequest shall be allowed as a deduction under section 170, 545(b)(2), 642(c), 2055, 2106(a)(2), or 2522, if made—

(A) to a foreign organization described in subsection (b) after the date on which the Secretary publishes notice under paragraph (3)(A) that he has notified such organization that it has engaged in a prohibited transaction, and

(B) in a taxable year of such organization for which it is not exempt from taxation under section 501(a) by reason of paragraph (1).

Subchapter C. Political Expenditures of Section 501(c)(3) Organizations

§ 4955. Taxes on political expenditures of section 501(c)(3) organizations.

(a) Initial taxes.—

(1) On the organization.—There is hereby imposed on each political expenditure by a section 501(c)(3) organization a tax equal to 10 percent of the amount thereof. The tax imposed by this paragraph shall be paid by the organization.

(2) On the management.—There is hereby imposed on the agreement of any organization manager to the making of any expenditure, knowing that it is a political expenditure, a tax equal to 2-1/2 percent of the amount thereof, unless such agreement is not willful and is due to reasonable cause. The tax imposed by this paragraph shall be paid by any organization manager who agreed to the making of the expenditure.

(b) Additional taxes.—

(1) On the organization.—In any case in which an initial tax is imposed by subsection (a)(1) on a political expenditure and such expenditure is not corrected within the taxable period, there is hereby imposed a tax equal to 100 percent of the amount of the expenditure. The tax imposed by this paragraph shall be paid by the organization.

(2) On the management.—In any case in which an additional tax is imposed by paragraph (1), if an organization manager refused to agree to part or all of the correction, there is hereby imposed a tax equal to 50 percent of the amount of the political expenditure. The tax imposed by this paragraph shall be paid by any organization manager who refused to agree to part or all of the correction.

(c) Special rules.—For purposes of subsections (a) and (b)—

(1) Joint and several liability.—If more than 1 person is liable under subsection (a)(2) or (b)(2) with respect to the making of a political expenditure, all such persons shall be jointly and severally liable under such subsection with respect to such expenditure.

(2) Limit for management.—With respect to any 1 political expenditure, the maximum amount of the tax imposed by subsection (a)(2) shall not exceed $5,000, and the maximum amount of the tax imposed by subsection (b)(2) shall not exceed $10,000.

(d) Political expenditure.—For purposes of this section—

(1) In general.—The term "political expenditure" means any amount paid or incurred by a section 501(c)(3) organization in any participation in, or intervention in (including the publication or distribution of statements), any political campaign on behalf of (or in opposition to) any candidate for public office.

(2) Certain other expenditures included.—In the case of an organization which is formed primarily for purposes of promoting the candidacy (or prospective candidacy) of an individual for public office (or which is effectively controlled by a candidate or prospective candidate and which is availed of primarily for such purposes), the term "political expenditure" includes any of the following amounts paid or incurred by the organization:

(A) Amounts paid or incurred to such individual for speeches or other services.

(B) Travel expenses of such individual.

(C) Expenses of conducting polls, surveys, or other studies, or preparing papers or other materials, for use by such individual.

(D) Expenses of advertising, publicity, and fundraising for such individual.

(E) Any other expense which has the primary effect of promoting public recognition, or otherwise primarily accruing to the benefit, of such individual.

(e) Coordination with sections 4945 and 4958.—If tax is imposed under this section with respect to any political expenditure, such expenditure shall not be treated as a taxable expenditure for purposes of section 4945 or an excess benefit for purposes of section 4958.

(f) Other definitions.—For purposes of this section—

(1) Section 501(c)(3) organization.—The term "section 501(c)(3) organization" means any organization which (without regard to any political expenditure) would be described in section 501(c)(3) and exempt from taxation under section 501(a).

(2) Organization manager.—The term "organization manager" means—

(A) any officer, director, or trustee of the organization (or individual having powers or responsibilities similar to those of officers, directors, or trustees of the organization), and

(B) with respect to any expenditure, any employee of the organization having authority or responsibility with respect to such expenditure.

(3) Correction.—The terms "correction" and "correct" mean, with respect to any political expenditure, recovering part or all of the expenditure to the extent recovery is possible, establishment of safeguards to prevent future political expenditures, and where full recovery is not possible, such additional corrective action as is prescribed by the Secretary by regulations.

(4) Taxable period.—The term "taxable period" means, with respect to any political expenditure, the period beginning with the date on which the political expenditure occurs and ending on the earlier of—

(A) the date of mailing a notice of deficiency under section 6212 with respect to the tax imposed by subsection (a)(1), or

(B) the date on which tax imposed by subsection (a)(1) is assessed.

Subchapter D. Failure by Certain Charitable Organizations to Meet Certain Qualification Requirements

§ 4958. Taxes on excess benefit transactions.

(a) Initial taxes—

(1) On the disqualified person.—There is hereby imposed on each excess benefit transaction a tax equal to 25 percent of the excess benefit. The tax imposed by this paragraph shall be paid by any disqualified person referred to in subsection (f)(1) with respect to such transaction.

(2) On the management.—In any case in which a tax is imposed by paragraph (1), there is hereby imposed on the participation of any organization manager in the excess benefit transaction, knowing that it is such a transaction, a tax equal to 10 percent of the excess benefit, unless such participation is not willful and is due to reasonable cause. The tax imposed by this paragraph shall be paid by any organization manager who participated in the excess benefit transaction.

(b) Additional tax on the disqualified person.—In any case in which an initial tax is imposed by subsection (a)(1) on an excess benefit transaction and the excess benefit involved in such transaction is not corrected within the taxable period, there is hereby imposed a tax equal to 200 percent of the excess benefit involved. The tax imposed by this subsection shall be paid by any disqualified person referred to in subsection (f)(1) with respect to such transaction.

(c) Excess benefit transaction; excess benefit.—For purposes of this section—

(1) Excess benefit transaction.—

(A) In general.—The term "excess benefit transaction" means any transaction in which an economic benefit is provided by an applicable tax-exempt organization directly or indirectly to or for the use of any disqualified person if the value of the economic benefit provided exceeds the value of the consideration (including the performance of services) received for providing such benefit. For purposes of the preceding sentence, an economic benefit shall not be treated as consideration for the performance of services unless such organization clearly indicated its intent to so treat such benefit.

(B) Excess benefit.—The term "excess benefit" means the excess referred to in subparagraph (A).

(2) Special rules for donor advised funds.—In the case of any donor advised fund (as defined in section 4966(d)(2))—

(A) the term "excess benefit transaction" includes any grant, loan, compensation, or other similar payment from such fund to a person described in subsection (f)(7) with respect to such fund, and

(B) the term "excess benefit" includes, with respect to any transaction described in subparagraph (A), the amount of any such grant, loan, compensation, or other similar payment.

(3) Special rules for supporting organizations—

(A) In general.—In the case of any organization described in section 509(a)(3)—

(i) the term "excess benefit transaction" includes—

(I) any grant, loan, compensation, or other similar payment provided by such organization to a person described in subparagraph (B), and

(II) any loan provided by such organization to a disqualified person (other than an organization described in subparagraph (C)(ii)), and

(ii) the term "excess benefit" includes, with respect to any transaction described in clause (i), the amount of any such grant, loan, compensation, or other similar payment.

(B) Person described.—A person is described in this subparagraph if such person is—

(i) a substantial contributor to such organization,

(ii) a member of the family (determined under section 4958(f)(4)) of an individual described in clause (i), or

(iii) a 35-percent controlled entity (as defined in section 4958(f)(3) by substituting "persons described in clause (i) or (ii) of section 4958(c)(3)(B)" for "persons described in subparagraph (A) or (B) of paragraph (1)" in subparagraph (A)(i) thereof).

(C) Substantial contributor.—For purposes of this paragraph—

(i) In general.—The term "substantial contributor" means any person who contributed or bequeathed an aggregate amount of more than $5,000 to the organization, if such amount is more than 2 percent of the total contributions and bequests received by the organization before the close of the taxable year of the organization in which the contribution or bequest is received by the organization from such person. In the case of a trust, such term also means the creator of the trust. Rules similar to the rules of subparagraphs (B) and (C) of section 507(d)(2) shall apply for purposes of this subparagraph.

(ii) Exception.—Such term shall not include—

(I) any organization described in paragraph (1), (2), or (4) of section 509(a), and

(II) any organization which is treated as described in such paragraph (2) by reason of the last sentence of section 509(a) and which is a supported organization (as defined in section 509(f)(3)) of the organization to which subparagraph (A) applies.

(4) Authority to include certain other private inurement.—To the extent provided in regulations prescribed by the Secretary, the term "excess benefit transaction" includes any transaction in which the amount of any economic benefit provided to or for the use of a disqualified person is determined in whole or in part by the revenues of 1 or more activities of the organization but only if such transaction results in inurement not permitted under paragraph (3) or (4) of section 501(c), as the case may be. In the case of any such transaction, the excess benefit shall be the amount of the inurement not so permitted.

(d) Special rules.—For purposes of this section—

(1) Joint and several liability.—If more than 1 person is liable for any tax imposed by subsection (a) or subsection (b), all such persons shall be jointly and severally liable for such tax.

(2) Limit for management.—With respect to any 1 excess benefit transaction, the maximum amount of the tax imposed by subsection (a)(2) shall not exceed $20,000.

(e) Applicable tax-exempt organization.—For purposes of this subchapter, the term "applicable tax-exempt organization" means—

(1) any organization which (without regard to any excess benefit) would be described in paragraph (3), (4), or (29) of section 501(c) and exempt from tax under section 501(a), and

(2) any organization which was described in paragraph (1) at any time during the 5-year period ending on the date of the transaction.

Such term shall not include a private foundation (as defined in section 509(a)).

(f) Other definitions.—For purposes of this section—

(1) Disqualified person.—The term "disqualified person" means, with respect to any transaction—

(A) any person who was, at any time during the 5-year period ending on the date of such transaction, in a position to exercise substantial influence over the affairs of the organization.

(B) a member of the family of an individual described in subparagraph (A),

(C) a 35-percent controlled entity,

(D) any person who is described in subparagraph (A), (B), or (C) with respect to an organization described in section 509(a)(3) and organized and operated exclusively for the benefit of, to perform the functions of, or to carry out the purposes of the applicable tax-exempt organization.

(E) which involves a donor advised fund (as defined in section 4966(d)(2)), any person who is described in paragraph (7) with respect to such donor advised fund (as so defined), and

(F) which involves a sponsoring organization (as defined in section 4966(d)(1)), any person who is described in paragraph (8) with respect to such sponsoring organization (as so defined).

(2) Organization manager.—The term "organization manager" means, with respect to any applicable tax-exempt organization, any officer, director, or trustee of such organization (or any individual having powers or responsibilities similar to those of officers, directors, or trustees of the organization).

(3) 35-percent controlled entity.—

(A) In general.—The term "35-percent controlled entity" means—

(i) a corporation in which persons described in subparagraph (A) or (B) of paragraph (1) own more than 35 percent of the total combined voting power,

(ii) a partnership in which such persons own more than 35 percent of the profits interest, and

(iii) a trust or estate in which such persons own more than 35 percent of the beneficial interest.

(B) Constructive ownership rules.—Rules similar to the rules of paragraphs (3) and (4) of section 4946(a) shall apply for purposes of this paragraph.

(4) Family members.—The members of an individual's family shall be determined under section 4946(d); except that such members also shall include the brothers and sisters (whether by the whole or half blood) of the individual and their spouses.

(5) Taxable period.—The term "taxable period" means, with respect to any excess benefit transaction, the period beginning with the date on which the transaction occurs and ending on the earliest of—

(A) the date of mailing a notice of deficiency under section 6212 with respect to the tax imposed by subsection (a)(1), or

(B) the date on which the tax imposed by subsection (a)(1) is assessed.

(6) Correction.—The terms "correction" and "correct" mean, with respect to any excess benefit transaction, undoing the excess benefit to the extent possible, and taking any additional measures necessary to place the organization in a financial position not worse than that in which it would be if the disqualified person were dealing under the highest fiduciary standards.

(7) Donors and donor advisors.—For purposes of paragraph (1)(E), a person is described in this paragraph if such person—

(A) is described in section 4966(d)(2)(A)(iii),

(B) is a member of the family of an individual described in subparagraph (A), or

(C) is a 35-percent controlled entity (as defined in paragraph (3) by substituting "persons described in subparagraph (A) or (B) of paragraph (7)" for "persons described in subparagraph (A) or (B) of paragraph (1)" in subparagraph (A)(i) thereof).

(8) Investment advisors.—For purposes of paragraph (1)(F)—

(A) In general.—A person is described in this paragraph if such person—

(i) is an investment advisor,

(ii) is a member of the family of an individual described in clause (i), or

(iii) is a 35-percent controlled entity (as defined in paragraph (3) by substituting "persons described in clause (i) or (ii) of paragraph (8)(A)" for "persons described in subparagraph (A) or (B) of paragraph (1)" in subparagraph (A)(i) thereof).

(B) Investment advisor defined.—For purposes of subparagraph (A), the term "investment advisor" means, with respect to any sponsoring organization (as defined in section 4966(d)(1)), any person (other than an employee of such organization) compensated by such organization for managing the investment of, or providing investment advice with respect to, assets maintained in donor advised funds (as defined in section 4966(d)(2)) owned by such organization.

§ 4959. Taxes on failures by hospital organizations.

If a hospital organization to which section 501(r) applies fails to meet the requirement of section 501(r)(3) for any taxable year, there is imposed on the organization a tax equal to $50,000.

§ 4960. Tax on excess tax-exempt organization executive compensation.

(a) Tax imposed.—There is hereby imposed a tax equal to the product of the rate of tax under section 11 and the sum of—

(1) so much of the remuneration paid (other than any excess parachute payment) by an applicable tax-exempt organization for the taxable year with respect to employment of any covered employee in excess of $1,000,000, plus

(2) any excess parachute payment paid by such an organization to any covered employee.

For purposes of the preceding sentence, remuneration shall be treated as paid when there is no substantial risk of forfeiture (within the meaning of section 475(f)(3)(B)) of the rights to such remuneration.

(b) Liability for tax.—The employer shall be liable for the tax imposed under subsection (a).

(c) Definitions and special rules.—For purposes of this section—

(1) Applicable tax-exempt organization.—The term 'applicable tax-exempt organization' means any organization which for the taxable year—

(A) is exempt from taxation under section 501(a),

(B) is a farmers' cooperative organization described in section 521(b)(1),

(C) has income excluded from taxation under section 115(1), or

(D) is a political organization described in section 527(e)(1).

(2) Covered employee.—For purposes of this section, the term "covered employee" means any employee of an applicable tax-exempt organization (or any predecessor of such an organization) and any former employee of such an organization (or predecessor) who was such an empoloyee during any taxable year beginning after December 31, 2016.

(3) Remuneration.—For purposes of this section:

(A) In general.—The term 'remuneration' means wages (as defined in section 3401(a)), except that such term shall not include any designated Roth contribution (as defined in section 402A(e)) and shall include amounts required to be included in gross income under section 457(f).

(B) Exception for remuneration for medical services.—The term 'remuneration' shall not include the portion of any remuneration paid to a licensed medical professional (including a veterinarian) which is for the performance of medical or veterinary services by such professional.

(4) Remuneration from related organizations.—

(A) In general.—Remuneration of a covered employee by an applicable tax-exempt organization shall include any remuneration paid with respect to employment of such employee by any related person or governmental entity.

(B) Related organizations.—A person or governmental entity shall be treated as related to an applicable tax-exempt organization if such person or governmental entity—

(i) controls, or is controlled by, the organization,

(ii) is controlled by one or more persons which control the organization,

(iii) is a supported organization (as defined in section 509(f)(3)) during the taxable year with respect to the organization,

(iv) is a supporting organization described in section 509(a)(3) during the taxable year with respect to the organization, or

(v) in the case of an organization which is a voluntary employees' beneficiary association described in section 501(c)(9), establishes, maintains or makes contributions to such voluntary employees' beneficiary association.

(C) Liability for tax.—In any case in which remuneration from more than one employer is taken into account under this paragraph in determining the tax imposed by subsection (a), each such employer shall be liable for such tax in an amount which bears the same ratio to the total tax determined under subsection (a) with respect to such remuneration as—

(i) the amount of remuneration paid by such employer with respect to such employee, bears to

(ii) the amount of remuneration paid by all such employers to such employee.

(5) Excess parachute payment.—For purposes of determining the tax imposed by subsection (a)(2)—

(A) In general.—The term 'excess parachute payment' means an amount equal to the excess of any parachute payment over the portion of the base amount allocated to such payment.

(B) Parachute payment.—The term 'parachute payment' means any payment in the nature of compensation to (or for the benefit of) a covered employee if—

(i) such payment is contingent on such employee's separation from employment with the employer, and

(ii) the aggregate present value of the payments in the nature of compensation to (or for the benefit of) such individual which are contingent on such separation equals or exceeds an amount equal to 3 times the base amount.

(C) Exception.—Such term does not include any payment—

(i) described in section 280G(b)(6) (relating to exemption for payments under qualified plans),

(ii) made under or to an annuity contract described in section 403(b) or a plan described in section 457(b),

(iii) to a licensed medical professional (including a veterinarian) to the extent that such payment is for the performance of medical or veterinary services by such professional, or

(iv) to an individual who is not a highly compensated employee as defined in section 414(q).

(D) Base amount.—Rules similar to the rules of 280G(b)(3) shall apply for purposes of determining the base amount.

(E) Property transfers; present value.—Rules similar to the rules of paragraphs (3) and (4) of section 280G(d) shall apply.

(6) Coordination with deduction limitation.—Remuneration the deduction for which is not allowed by reason of section 162(m) shall not be taken into account for purposes of this section.

(d) Regulations.—The Secretary shall prescribe such regulations as may be necessary to prevent avoidance of the tax under this section, including regulations to prevent avoidance of such tax through the performance of services other than as an employee or by providing compensation through a pass-through or other entity to avoid such tax.

Subchapter E. Abatement of First and Second Tier Taxes in Certain Cases

§ 4961. Abatement of second tier taxes when there is correction.

(a) General rule.—If any taxable event is corrected during the correction period for such event, then any second tier tax imposed with respect to such event (including interest, additions to the tax, and additional amounts) shall not be assessed, and if assessed the assessment shall be abated, and if collected shall be credited or refunded as an overpayment.

(b) Supplemental proceeding.—If the determination by a court that the taxpayer is liable for a second tier tax has become final, such court shall have jurisdiction to conduct any necessary supplemental proceeding to determine whether the taxable event was corrected during the correction period. Such a supplemental proceeding may be begun only during the period which ends on the 90th day after the last day of the correction period. Where such a supplemental proceeding has begun, the reference in the second sentence of section 6213(a) to a final decision of the Tax Court shall be treated as including a final decision in such supplemental proceeding.

(c) Suspension of period of collection for second tier tax.—

(1) Proceeding in District Court or United States Court of Federal Claims.—If, not later than 90 days after the day on which the second tier tax is assessed, the first tier tax is paid in full and a claim for refund of the amount so paid is filed, no levy or proceeding in court for the collection of the second tier tax shall be made, begun, or prosecuted until a final resolution of a proceeding begun as provided in paragraph (2) (and of any supplemental proceeding with respect thereto under subsection (b)). Notwithstanding section 7421(a), the collection by levy or proceeding may be enjoined during the time such prohibition is in force by a proceeding in the proper court.

(2) Suit must be brought to determine liability.—If, within 90 days after the day on which his claim for refund is denied, the person against whom the second tier tax was assessed fails to begin a proceeding described in section 7422 for the determination of his liability for such tax, paragraph (1) shall cease to apply with respect to such tax, effective on the day following the close of the 90-day period referred to in this paragraph.

(3) Suspension of running of period of limitations on collection.—The running of the period of limitations provided in section 6502 on the collection by levy or by a proceeding in court with respect to any second tier tax described in paragraph (1) shall be suspended for the period during which the Secretary is prohibited from collecting by levy or a proceeding in court.

(4) Jeopardy collection.—If the Secretary makes a finding that the collection of the second tier tax is in jeopardy, nothing in this subsection shall prevent the immediate collection of such tax.

§ 4962. Abatement of first tier taxes in certain cases.

(a) General rule.—If it is established to the satisfaction of the Secretary that—

(1) a taxable event was due to reasonable cause and not to willful neglect, and

(2) such event was corrected within the correction period for such event, then any qualified first tier tax imposed with respect to such event (including interest) shall not be assessed and, if assessed, the assessment shall be abated and, if collected, shall be credited or refunded as an overpayment.

(b) Qualified first tier tax.—For purposes of this section, the term "qualified first tier tax" means any first tier tax imposed by subchapter A, C, D, or G of this chapter, except that such term shall not include the tax imposed by section 4941(a) (relating to initial tax on self-dealing).

(c) Special rule for tax on political expenditures of section 501(c)(3) organizations.—In the case of the tax imposed by section 4955(a), subsection (a)(1) shall be applied by substituting "not willful and flagrant" for "due to reasonable cause and not to willful neglect.

§ 4963. Definitions.

(a) First tier tax.—For purposes of this subchapter, the term "first tier tax" means any tax imposed by subsection (a) of section 4941, 4942, 4943, 4944, 4945, 4951, 4952, 4955, 4958, 4966, 4967, 4971, or 4975.

(b) Second tier tax.—For purposes of this subchapter, the term "second tier tax" means any tax imposed by subsection (b) of section 4941, 4942, 4943, 4944, 4945, 4951, 4952, 4955, 4958, 4971, or 4975.

(c) Taxable event.—For purposes of this subchapter, the term "taxable event" means any act (or failure to act) giving rise to liability for tax under section 4941, 4942, 4943, 4944, 4945, 4951, 4952, 4955, 4958, 4966, 4967, 4971, or 4975.

(d) Correct.—For purposes of this subchapter—

(1) In general.—Except as provided in paragraph (2), the term "correct" has the same meaning as when used in the section which imposes the second tier tax.

(2) Special rules.—The term "correct" means—

(A) in the case of the second tier tax imposed by section 4942(b), reducing the amount of the undistributed income to zero,

(B) in the case of the second tier tax imposed by section 4943(b), reducing the amount of the excess business holdings to zero, and

(C) in the case of the second tier tax imposed by section 4944, removing the investment from jeopardy.

(e) Correction period.—For purposes of this subchapter—

(1) In general.—The term "correction period" means, with respect to any taxable event, the period beginning on the date on which such event occurs and ending 90 days after the date of mailing under section 6212 of a notice of deficiency with respect to the second tier tax imposed on such taxable event, extended by—

(A) any period in which a deficiency cannot be assessed under section 6213(a) (determined without regard to the last sentence of section 4961(b)), and

(B) any other period which the Secretary determines is reasonable and necessary to bring about correction of the taxable event.

(2) Special rules for when taxable event occurs.—For purposes of paragraph (1), the taxable event shall be treated as occurring—

(A) in the case of section 4942, on the first day of the taxable year for which there was a failure to distribute income,

(B) in the case of section 4943, on the first day on which there are excess business holdings,

(C) in the case of section 4971, on the last day of the plan year in which there is an accumulated funding deficiency, and

(D) in any other case, the date on which such event occurred.

* * *

Subchapter F. Tax Shelter Transactions

§ 4965. Excise tax on certain tax-exempt entities entering into prohibited tax shelter transactions.

(a) Being a party to and approval of prohibited transactions.—

(1) Tax-exempt entity.—

(A) In General.—If a transaction is a prohibited tax shelter transaction at the time any tax-exempt entity described in paragraph (1), (2), or (3) of subsection (c) becomes a party to the transaction, such entity shall pay a tax for the taxable year in which the entity becomes such a party and any subsequent taxable year in the amount determined under subsection (b)(1).

(B) Post-Transaction determination.—If any tax-exempt entity described in paragraph (1), (2), or (3) of subsection (c) is a party to a subsequently listed transaction at any time during a taxable year, such entity shall pay a tax for such taxable year in the amount determined under subsection (b)(1).

(2) Entity manager.—If any entity manager of a tax-exempt entity approves such entity as (or otherwise causes such entity to be) a party to a prohibited tax shelter transaction at any time during the taxable year and knows or has reason to know that the transaction is a prohibited tax shelter transaction, such manager shall pay a tax for such taxable year in the amount determined under subsection (b)(2).

(b) Amount of tax.—

(1) Entity.—In the case of a tax-exempt entity—

(A) In general.—Except as provided in subparagraph (B), the amount of the tax imposed under subsection (a)(1) with respect to any transaction for a taxable year shall be an amount equal to the product of the highest rate of tax under section 11, and the greater of—

(i) the entity's net income (after taking into account any tax imposed by this subtitle (other than by this section) with respect to such transaction) for such taxable year which—

(I) in the case of a prohibited tax shelter transaction (other than a subsequently listed transaction), is attributable to such transaction, or

(II) in the case of a subsequently listed transaction, is attributable to such transaction and which is properly allocable to the period beginning on the later of the date such transaction is identified by guidance as a listed transaction by the Secretary or the first day of the taxable year, or

(ii) 75 percent of the proceeds received by the entity for the taxable year which—

(I) in the case of a prohibited tax shelter transaction (other than a subsequently listed transaction), are attributable to such transaction, or

(II) in the case of a subsequently listed transaction, are attributable to such transaction and which are properly allocable to the period beginning on the later of the date such transaction is identified by guidance as a listed transaction by the Secretary or the first day of the taxable year.

(B) Increase in tax for certain knowing transactions.—In the case of a tax-exempt entity which knew, or had reason to know, a transaction was a prohibited tax shelter transaction at the time the entity became a party to the transaction, the amount of the tax imposed under subsection (a)(1)(A) with respect to any transaction for a taxable year shall be the greater of—

(i) 100 percent of the entity's net income (after taking into account any tax imposed by this subtitle (other than by this section) with respect to the prohibited tax shelter transaction) for such taxable year which is attributable to the prohibited tax shelter transaction, or

(ii) 75 percent of the proceeds received by the entity for the taxable year which are attributable to the prohibited tax shelter transaction.

This subparagraph shall not apply to any prohibited tax shelter transaction to which a tax exempt entity became a party on or before the date of the enactment of this section.

(2) Entity manager.—In the case of each entity manager, the amount of the tax imposed under subsection (a)(2) shall be $ 20,000 for each approval (or other act causing participation) described in subsection (a)(2).

(c) Tax-exempt entity.—For purposes of this section, the term 'tax-exempt entity' means an entity which is—

(1) described in section 501(c) or 501(d),

(2) described in section 170(c) (other than the United States),

(3) an Indian tribal government (within the meaning of section 7701(a)(40)),

(4) described in paragraph (1), (2), or (3) of section 4979(e),

(5) a program described in section 529,

(6) an eligible deferred compensation plan described in section 457(b) which is maintained by an employer described in section 457(e)(1)(A), or

(7) an arrangement described in section 4973(a).

(d) Entity manager.—For purposes of this section, the term 'entity manager' means—

(1) in the case of an entity described in paragraph (1), (2), or (3) of subsection (c)—

(A) the person with authority or responsibility similar to that exercised by an officer, director, or trustee of an organization, and

(B) with respect to any act, the person having authority or responsibility with respect to such act, and

(2) in the case of an entity described in paragraph (4), (5), (6), or (7) of subsection (c), the person who approves or otherwise causes the entity to be a party to the prohibited tax shelter transaction.

(e) Prohibited tax shelter transaction; subsequently listed transaction.—For purposes of this section—

(1) Prohibited tax shelter transaction.—

(A) In general.—The term "prohibited tax shelter transaction" means—

(i) any listed transaction, and

(ii) any prohibited reportable transaction.

(B) Listed transaction.—The term "listed transaction" has the meaning given such term by section 6707A(c)(2).

(C) Prohibited reportable transaction.—The term "prohibited reportable transaction" means any confidential transaction or any transaction with contractual protection (as defined under regulations prescribed by the Secretary) which is a reportable transaction (as defined in section 6707A(c)(1)).

(2) Subsequently listed transaction.—The term "subsequently listed transaction" means any transaction to which a tax-exempt entity is a party and which is determined by the Secretary to be a listed transaction at any time after the entity has become a party to the transaction. Such term shall not include a transaction which is a prohibited reportable transaction at the time the entity became a party to the transaction.

(f) Regulatory authority.—The Secretary is authorized to promulgate regulations which provide guidance regarding the determination of the allocation of net income or proceeds of a tax-exempt entity attributable to a transaction to various periods, including before and after the listing of the transaction or the date which is 90 days after the date of the enactment of this section.

(g) Coordination with other taxes and penalties.—The tax imposed by this section is in addition to any other tax, addition to tax, or penalty imposed under this title.

Subchapter G. Donor Advised Funds

§ 4966. Taxes on taxable distributions.

(a) Imposition of taxes.—

(1) On the sponsoring organization.—There is hereby imposed on each taxable distribution a tax equal to 20 percent of the amount thereof. The tax imposed by this paragraph shall be paid by the sponsoring organization with respect to the donor advised fund.

(2) On the fund management.—There is hereby imposed on the agreement of any fund manager to the making of a distribution, knowing that it is a taxable distribution, a tax equal to 5 percent of the amount thereof. The tax imposed by this paragraph shall be paid by any fund manager who agreed to the making of the distribution.

(b) Special rules.—For purposes of subsection (a)—

(1) Joint and several liability.—If more than one person is liable under subsection (a)(2) with respect to the making of a taxable distribution, all such persons shall be jointly and severally liable under such paragraph with respect to such distribution.

(2) Limit for management.—With respect to any one taxable distribution, the maximum amount of the tax imposed by subsection (a)(2) shall not exceed $10,000.

(c) Taxable distribution.—For purposes of this section—

(1) In general.—The term "taxable distribution" means any distribution from a donor advised fund—

(A) to any natural person, or

(B) to any other person if—

(i) such distribution is for any purpose other than one specified in section 170(c)(2)(B), or

(ii) the sponsoring organization does not exercise expenditure responsibility with respect to such distribution in accordance with section 4945(h).

(2) Exceptions.—Such term shall not include any distribution from a donor advised fund—

(A) to any organization described in section 170(b)(1)(A) (other than a disqualified supporting organization),

(B) to the sponsoring organization of such donor advised fund, or

(C) to any other donor advised fund.

(d) Definitions.—For purposes of this subchapter—

(1) Sponsoring organization.—The term "sponsoring organization" means any organization which—

(A) is described in section 170(c) (other than in paragraph (1) thereof, and without regard to paragraph (2)(A) thereof),

(B) is not a private foundation (as defined in section 509(a)), and

(C) maintains 1 or more donor advised funds.

(2) Donor advised fund.—

(A) In general.—Except as provided in subparagraph (B) or (C), the term "donor advised fund" means a fund or account—

(i) which is separately identified by reference to contributions of a donor or donors,

(ii) which is owned and controlled by a sponsoring organization, and

(iii) with respect to which a donor (or any person appointed or designated by such donor) has, or reasonably expects to have, advisory privileges with respect to the distribution or investment of amounts held in such fund or account by reason of the donor's status as a donor.

(B) Exceptions.—The term "donor advised fund" shall not include any fund or account—

(i) which makes distributions only to a single identified organization or governmental entity, or

(ii) with respect to which a person described in subparagraph (A)(iii) advises as to which individuals receive grants for travel, study, or other similar purposes, if—

(I) such person's advisory privileges are performed exclusively by such person in the person's capacity as a member of a committee all of the members of which are appointed by the sponsoring organization,

(II) no combination of persons described in subparagraph (A)(iii) (or persons related to such persons) control, directly or indirectly, such committee, and

(III) all grants from such fund or account are awarded on an objective and nondiscriminatory basis pursuant to a procedure approved in advance by the board of directors of the sponsoring organization, and such procedure is designed to ensure that all such grants meet the requirements of paragraph (1), (2), or (3) of section 4945(g).

(C) Secretarial authority.—The Secretary may exempt a fund or account not described in subparagraph (B) from treatment as a donor advised fund—

(i) if such fund or account is advised by a committee not directly or indirectly controlled by the donor or any person appointed or designated by the donor for the purpose of advising with respect to distributions from such fund (and any related parties), or

(ii) if such fund benefits a single identified charitable purpose.

(3) Fund manager.—The term "fund manager" means, with respect to any sponsoring organization—

(A) an officer, director, or trustee of such sponsoring organization (or an individual having powers or responsibilities similar to those of officers, directors, or trustees of the sponsoring organization), and

(B) with respect to any act (or failure to act), the employees of the sponsoring organization having authority or responsibility with respect to such act (or failure to act).

(4) Disqualified supporting organization.—

(A) In general.—The term "disqualified supporting organization" means, with respect to any distribution—

(i) any type III supporting organization (as defined in section 4943(f)(5)(A)) which is not a functionally integrated type III supporting organization (as defined in section 4943(f)(5)(B)), and

(ii) any organization which is described in subparagraph (B) or (C) if—

(I) the donor or any person designated by the donor for the purpose of advising with respect to distributions from a donor advised fund (and any related parties) directly or indirectly controls a supported organization (as defined in section 509(f)(3)) of such organization, or

(II) the Secretary determines by regulations that a distribution to such organization otherwise is inappropriate.

(B) Type I and type II supporting organizations.—An organization is described in this subparagraph if the organization meets the requirements of subparagraphs (A) and (C) of section 509(a)(3) and is—

(i) operated, supervised, or controlled by one or more organizations described in paragraph (1) or (2) of section 509(a), or

(ii) supervised or controlled in connection with one or more such organizations.

(C) Functionally integrated type III supporting organizations.—An organization is described in this subparagraph if the organization is a functionally integrated type III supporting organization (as defined under section 4943(f)(5)(B)).

§ 4967. Taxes on prohibited benefits.

(a) Imposition of taxes.—

(1) On the donor, donor advisor, or related person.—There is hereby imposed on the advice of any person described in subsection (d) to have a sponsoring organization make a distribution from a donor advised fund which results in such person or any other person described in subsection (d) receiving, directly or indirectly, a more than incidental benefit as a result of such distribution, a tax equal to 125 percent of such benefit. The tax imposed by this paragraph shall be paid by any person described in subsection (d) who advises as to the distribution or who receives such a benefit as a result of the distribution.

(2) On the fund management.—There is hereby imposed on the agreement of any fund manager to the making of a distribution, knowing that such distribution would confer a benefit described in paragraph (1), a tax equal to 10 percent of the amount of such benefit. The tax imposed by this paragraph shall be paid by any fund manager who agreed to the making of the distribution.

(b) Exception.—No tax shall be imposed under this section with respect to any distribution if a tax has been imposed with respect to such distribution under section 4958.

(c) Special rules.—For purposes of subsection (a)—

(1) Joint and several liability.—If more than one person is liable under paragraph (1) or (2) of subsection (a) with respect to a distribution described in subsection (a), all such persons shall be jointly and severally liable under such paragraph with respect to such distribution.

(2) Limit for management.—With respect to any one distribution described in subsection (a), the maximum amount of the tax imposed by subsection (a)(2) shall not exceed $10,000.

(d) Person described.—A person is described in this subsection if such person is described in section 4958(f)(7) with respect to a donor advised fund.

Subchapter H. Excise Tax Based on Investment Income of Private Colleges and Universities

§ 4968. Excise tax based on investment income of private colleges and universities.

(a) Tax imposed.—There is hereby imposed on each applicable educational institution for the taxable year a tax equal to the applicable percentage of the net investment income of such institution for the taxable year.

(b) Applicable percentage.—For purposes of this section, the term "applicable percentage" means—

(1) 1.4 percent in the case of an institution with a student adjusted endowment of at least $500,000, and not in excess of $750,000,

(2) 4 percent in the case of an institution with a student adjusted endowment in excess of $750,000, and not in excess of $2,000,000, and

(3) 8 percent in the case of an institution with a student adjusted endowment in excess of $2,000,000.

(c) Applicable educational institution.—For purposes of this subchapter, the term "applicable educational institution" means an eligible educational institution (as defined in section 25A(f)(2))—

(1) which had at least 3,000 tuition-paying students during the preceding taxable year,

(2) more than 50 percent of the tuition-paying students of which are located in the United States,

(3) the student adjusted endowment of which is at least $500,000, and

(4) which is not described in the first sentence of section 511(a)(2)(B) (relating to State colleges and universities).

(d) Student adjusted endowment.—For purposes of this section, the term "student adjusted endowment" means, with respect to any institution for any taxable year—

(1) the aggregate fair market value of the assets of such institution (determined as of the end of the preceding taxable year), other than those assets which are used directly in carrying out the institution's exempt purpose, divided by

(2) the number of students of such institution.

(e) Determination of number of students.—For purposes of subsections (c) and (d), the number of students of an institution (including for purposes of determining the number of students at a particular location) shall be based on the daily average number of full-time students attending such institution (with part-time students taken into account on a full-time student equivalent basis).

(f) Net investment income.—For purposes of this section—

(1) In general.—Net investment income shall be determined under rules similar to the rules of section 4940(c).

(2) Override of certain regulatory exceptions.—

(A) Student loan interest.—Net investment income shall be determined by taking into account any interest income from a student loan made by the applicable educational institution (or any related organization) as gross investment income.

(B) Federally-subsidized royalty income.—

(i) In general.—Net investment income shall be determined by taking into account any Federally-subsidized royalty income as gross investment income.

(ii) Federally-subsidized royalty income.—For purposes of this subparagraph—

(I) In general.—The term "Federally-subsidized royalty income" means any otherwise-regulatory-exempt royalty income if any Federal funds were used in the research, development, or creation of the patent, copyright, or other intellectual or intangible property from which such royalty income is derived.

(II) Otherwise-regulatory-exempt royalty income.—For purposes of this subparagraph, the term "otherwise-regulatory-exempt royalty income" means royalty income which (but for this subparagraph) would not be taken into account as gross investment income by reason of being derived from patents, copyrights, or other intellectual or intangible property which resulted from the work of students or faculty members in their capacities as such with the applicable educational institution.

(III) Federal funds.—The term "Federal funds" includes any grant made by, and any payment made under any contract with, any Federal agency to the applicable educational institution, any related organization, or any student or faculty member referred to in subclause (II).

(g) Assets and net investment income of related organizations.—

(1) In general.—For purposes of subsections (d) and (f), assets and net investment income of any related organization with respect to an educational institution shall be treated as assets and net investment income, respectively, of the educational institution, except that—

(A) no such amount shall be taken into account with respect to more than 1 educational institution, and

(B) unless such organization is controlled by such institution or is described in section 509(a)(3) with respect to such institution for the taxable year, assets and net investment income which are not intended or available for the use or benefit of the educational institution shall not be taken into account.

(2) Related organization.—For purposes of this subsection, the term "related organization" means, with respect to an educational institution, any organization which—

(A) controls, or is controlled by, such institution,

(B) is controlled by 1 or more persons which also control such institution, or

(C) is a supported organization (as defined in section 509(f)(3)), or an organization described in section 509(a)(3), during the taxable year with respect to such institution.

(h) Regulations.—The Secretary shall prescribe such regulations or other guidance as may be necessary to prevent avoidance of the tax under this section, including regulations or other guidance to prevent avoidance of such tax through the restructuring of endowment funds or other arrangements designed to reduce or eliminate the value of net investment income or assets subject to the tax imposed by this section.

SUBTITLE F. PROCEDURE AND ADMINISTRATION

Chapter 61. Information and Returns

Subchapter A. Returns and Records

* * *

§ 6033. Returns by exempt organizations.

(a) Organizations required to file.—

(1) In general.—Except as provided in paragraph (2), every organization exempt from taxation under section 501(a) shall file an annual return, stating specifically the items of gross income, receipts, and disbursements, and such other information for the purpose of carrying out the internal revenue laws as the Secretary may by forms or regulations prescribe, and shall keep such records, render under oath such statements, make such other returns, and comply with such rules and regulations as the Secretary may from time to time prescribe; except that, in the discretion of the Secretary, any organization described in section 401(a) may be relieved from stating in its return any information which is reported in returns filed by the employer which established such organization.

(2) Being a party to certain reportable transactions.—Every tax-exempt entity described in section 4965(c) shall file (in such form and manner and at such time as determined by the Secretary) a disclosure of—

(A) such entity's being a party to any prohibited tax shelter transaction (as defined in section 4965(e)), and

(B) the identity of any other party to such transaction which is known by such tax-exempt entity.

(3) Exceptions from filing.—

(A) Mandatory exceptions.—Paragraph (1) shall not apply to—

(i) churches, their integrated auxiliaries, and conventions or associations of churches,

(ii) any organization (other than a private foundation, as defined in section 509(a)) described in subparagraph (C), the gross receipts of which in each taxable year are normally not more than $5,000, or

(iii) the exclusively religious activities of any religious order.

(B) Discretionary exceptions.—The Secretary may relieve any organization required under paragraph (1) to file an information return from filing such a return where he determines that such filing is not necessary to the efficient administration of the internal revenue laws.

(C) Certain organizations.—The organizations referred to in subparagraph (A)(ii) are—

(i) a religious organization described in section 501(c)(3);

(ii) an educational organization described in section 170(b)(1)(A)(ii);

(iii) a charitable organization, or an organization for the prevention of cruelty to children or animals, described in section 501(c)(3), if such organization is supported, in whole or in part, by funds contributed by the United States or any State or political subdivision thereof, or is primarily supported by contributions of the general public;

(iv) an organization described in section 501(c)(3), if such organization is operated, supervised, or controlled by or in connection with a religious organization described in clause (i);

(v) an organization described in section 501(c)(8); and

(vi) an organization described in section 501(c)(1), if such organization is a corporation wholly owned by the United States or any agency or instrumentality thereof, or a wholly-owned subsidiary of such a corporation.

(b) Certain organizations described in section 501(c)(3).—Every organization described in section 501(c)(3) which is subject to the requirements of subsection (a) shall furnish annually information, at such time and in such manner as the Secretary may by forms or regulations prescribe, setting forth—

(1) its gross income for the year,

(2) its expenses attributable to such income and incurred within the year,

(3) its disbursements within the year for the purposes for which it is exempt,

(4) a balance sheet showing its assets, liabilities, and net worth as of the beginning of such year,

(5) the total of the contributions and gifts received by it during the year, and the names and addresses of all substantial contributors,

(6) the names and addresses of its foundation managers (within the meaning of section 4946(b)(1)) and highly compensated employees,

(7) the compensation and other payments made during the year to each individual described in paragraph (6),

(8) in the case of an organization with respect to which an election under section 501(h) is effective for the taxable year, the following amounts for such organization for such taxable year:

(A) the lobbying expenditures (as defined in section 4911(c)(1)),

(B) the lobbying nontaxable amount (as defined in section 4911(c)(2)),

(C) the grass roots expenditures (as defined in section 4911(c)(3)), and

(D) the grass roots nontaxable amount (as defined in section 4911(c)(4)),

(9) such other information with respect to direct or indirect transfers to, and other direct or indirect transactions and relationships with, other organizations described in section 501(c) (other than paragraph (3) thereof) or section 527 as the Secretary may require to prevent—

(A) diversion of funds from the organization's exempt purpose, or

(B) misallocation of revenues or expenses,

(10) the respective amounts (if any) of the taxes imposed on the organization, or any organization manager of the organization, during the taxable year under any of the following provisions (and the respective amounts (if any) of reimbursements paid by the organization during the taxable year with respect to taxes imposed on any such organization manager under any of such provisions):

(A) section 4911 (relating to tax on excess expenditures to influence legislation),

(B) section 4912 (relating to tax on disqualifying lobbying expenditures of certain organizations), and

(C) section 4955 (relating to taxes on political expenditures of section 501(c)(3) organizations), except to the extent that, by reason of section 4962, the taxes imposed under such section are not required to be paid or are credited or refunded,

(11) the respective amounts (if any) of—

(A) the taxes imposed with respect to the organization on any organization manager, or any disqualified person, during the taxable year under section 4958 (relating to taxes on private excess benefit from certain charitable organizations), and

(B) reimbursements paid by the organization during the taxable year with respect to taxes imposed under such section,

except to the extent that, by reason of section 4962, the taxes imposed under such section are not required to be paid or are credited or refunded,

(12) such information as the Secretary may require with respect to any excess benefit transaction (as defined in section 4958),

(13) such information with respect to disqualified persons as the Secretary may prescribe, and

(14) such other information for purposes of carrying out the internal revenue laws as the Secretary may require.

For purposes of paragraph (8), if section 4911(f) applies to the organization for the taxable year, such organization shall furnish the amounts with respect to the affiliated group as well as with respect to such organization.

(c) Additional provisions relating to private foundations.—In the case of an organization which is a private foundation (within the meaning of section 509(a))—

(1) the Secretary shall by regulations provide that the private foundation shall include in its annual return under this section such information (not required to be furnished by subsection (b) or the forms or regulations prescribed thereunder) as would have been required to be furnished under section 6056 (relating to annual reports by private foundations) as such section 6056 was in effect on January 1, 1979,

(2) the foundation managers shall furnish copies of the annual return under this section to such State officials, at such times, and under such conditions, as the Secretary may by regulations prescribe.

Nothing in paragraph (1) shall require the inclusion of the name and address of any recipient (other than a disqualified person within the meaning of section 4946) of 1 or more charitable gifts or grants made by the foundation to such recipient as an indigent or needy person if the aggregate of such gifts or grants made by the foundation to such recipient during the year does not exceed $1,000.

(d) Section to apply to nonexempt charitable trusts and nonexempt private foundations.—The following organizations shall comply with the requirements of this section in the same manner as organizations described in section 501(c)(3) which are exempt from tax under section 501(a):

(1) Nonexempt charitable trusts.—A trust described in section 4947(a)(1) (relating to nonexempt charitable trusts).

(2) Nonexempt private foundations.—A private foundation which is not exempt from tax under section 501(a).

(e) Special rules relating to lobbying activities.—

(1) Reporting requirements.—

(A) In general.—If this subsection applies to an organization for any taxable year, such organization—

(i) shall include on any return required to be filed under subsection (a) for such year information setting forth the total expenditures of the organization to which section 162(e)(1) applies and the total amount of the dues or other similar amounts paid to the organization to which such expenditures are allocable, and

(ii) except as provided in paragraphs (2)(A)(i) and (3), shall, at the time of assessment or payment of such dues or other similar amounts, provide notice to each person making such payment which contains a reasonable estimate of the portion of such dues or other similar amounts to which such expenditures are so allocable.

(B) Organizations to which subsection applies.—

(i) In general.—This subsection shall apply to any organization which is exempt from taxation under this subtitle other than an organization described in section 501(c)(3).

(ii) Special rule for in-house expenditures.—This subsection shall not apply to the in-house expenditures (within the meaning of section 162(e)(4)(B)(ii)) of an organization for a taxable year if such expenditures do not exceed $2,000. In determining whether a taxpayer exceeds the $2,000 limit under this clause, there shall not be taken into account overhead costs otherwise allocable to activities described in subparagraphs (A) and (D) of section 162(e)(1).

(iii) Coordination with section 527(f).—This subsection shall not apply to any amount on which tax is imposed by reason of section 527(f).

(C) Allocation.—For purposes of this paragraph—

(i) In general.—Expenditures to which section 162(e)(1) applies shall be treated as paid out of dues or other similar amounts to the extent thereof.

(ii) Carryover of lobbying expenditures in excess of dues.—If expenditures to which section 162(e)(1) applies exceed the dues or other similar amounts for any taxable year, such excess shall be treated as expenditures to which section 162(e)(1) applies which are paid or incurred by the organization during the following taxable year.

(2) Tax imposed where organization does not notify.—

(A) In general.—If an organization—

(i) elects not to provide the notices described in paragraph (1)(A) for any taxable year, or

(ii) fails to include in such notices the amount allocable to expenditures to which section 162(e)(1) applies (determined on the basis of actual amounts rather than the reasonable estimates under paragraph (1)(A)(ii)),

then there is hereby imposed on such organization for such taxable year a tax in an amount equal to the product of the highest rate of tax imposed by section 11 for the taxable year and the aggregate amount not included in such notices by reason of such election or failure.

(B) Waiver where future adjustments made.—The Secretary may waive the tax imposed by subparagraph (A)(ii) for any taxable year if the organization agrees to adjust its estimates under paragraph (1)(A)(ii) for the following taxable year to correct any failures.

(C) Tax treated as income tax—For purposes of this title, the tax imposed by subparagraph (A) shall be treated in the same manner as a tax imposed by chapter 1 (relating to income taxes).

(3) Exception where dues generally nondeductible.—Paragraph (1)(A) shall not apply to an organization which establishes to the satisfaction of the Secretary that substantially all of the dues or other similar amounts paid by persons to such organization are not deductible without regard to section 162(e).

(f) Certain organizations described in section 501(c)(4).—Every organization described in section 501(c)(4) which is subject to the requirements of subsection (a) shall include on the return required under subsection (a)—

(1) the information referred to in paragraphs (11), (12), and (13) of subsection (b) with respect to such organization, and

(2) in the case of the first such return filed by such an organization after submitting a notice to the Secretary under section 506(a), such information as the Secretary shall by regulation require in support of the organization's treatment as an organization described in section 501(c)(4).

(g) Returns required by political organizations.—

(1) In general.—This section shall apply to a political organization (as defined by section 527(e)(1)) which has gross receipts of $25,000 or more for the taxable year. In the case of a political organization which is a qualified State or local political organization (as defined in section 527(e)(5)), the preceding sentence shall be applied by substituting "$100,000" for "$25,000".

(2) Annual returns.—Political organizations described in paragraph (1) shall file an annual return—

(A) containing the information required, and complying with the other requirements, under subsection (a)(1) for organizations exempt from taxation under section 501(a), with such modifications as the Secretary considers appropriate to require only information which is necessary for the purposes of carrying out section 527, and

(B) containing such other information as the Secretary deems necessary to carry out the provisions of this subsection.

(3) Mandatory exceptions from filing.—Paragraph (2) shall not apply to an organization—

(A) which is a State or local committee of a political party, or political committee of a State or local candidate,

(B) which is a caucus or association of State or local officials,

(C) which is an authorized committee (as defined in section 301(6) of the Federal Election Campaign Act of 1971) of a candidate for Federal office,

(D) which is a national committee (as defined in section 301(14) of the Federal Election Campaign Act of 1971) of a political party,

(E) which is a United States House of Representatives or United States Senate campaign committee of a political party committee,

(F) which is required to report under the Federal Election Campaign Act of 1971 as a political committee (as defined in section 301(4) of such Act), or

(G) to which section 527 applies for the taxable year solely by reason of subsection (f)(1) of such section.

(4) Discretionary exception.—The Secretary may relieve any organization required under paragraph (2) to file an information return from filing such a return if the Secretary determines that such filing is not necessary to the efficient administration of the internal revenue laws.

(h) Controlling organizations.—Each controlling organization (within the meaning of section 512(b)(13)) which is subject to the requirements of subsection (a) shall include on the return required under subsection (a)—

(1) any interest, annuities, royalties, or rents received from each controlled entity (within the meaning of section 512(b)(13)),

(2) any loans made to each such controlled entity, and

(3) any transfers of funds between such controlling organization and each such controlled entity.

(i) Additional notification requirements.—Any organization the gross receipts of which in any taxable year result in such organization being referred to in subsection (a)(3)(A)(ii) or (a)(3)(B)—

(1) shall furnish annually, in electronic form, and at such time and in such manner as the Secretary may by regulations prescribe, information setting forth—

(A) the legal name of the organization,

(B) any name under which such organization operates or does business,

(C) the organization's mailing address and Internet web site address (if any),

(D) the organization's taxpayer identification number,

(E) the name and address of a principal officer, and

(F) evidence of the continuing basis for the organization's exemption from the filing requirements under subsection (a)(1), and

(2) upon the termination of the existence of the organization, shall furnish notice of such termination.

(j) Loss of exempt status for failure to file return or notice.—

(1) In general.—If an organization described in subsection (a)(1) or (i) fails to file an annual return or notice required under either subsection for 3 consecutive years, such organization's status as an organization exempt from tax under section 501(a) shall be considered revoked on and after the date set by the Secretary for the filing of the third annual return or notice. The Secretary shall publish and maintain a list of any organization the status of which is so revoked.

(2) Application necessary for reinstatement.—Any organization the tax-exempt status of which is revoked under paragraph (1) must apply in order to obtain reinstatement of such status regardless of whether such organization was originally required to make such an application.

(3) Retroactive reinstatement if reasonable cause shown for failure.—If, upon application for reinstatement of status as an organization exempt from tax under section 501(a), an organization described in paragraph (1) can show to the satisfaction of the Secretary evidence of reasonable cause for the failure described in such paragraph, the organization's exempt status may, in the discretion of the Secretary, be reinstated effective from the date of the revocation under such paragraph.

(k) Additional provisions relating to sponsoring organizations.—Every organization described in section 4966(d)(1) shall, on the return required under subsection (a) for the taxable year—

(1) list the total number of donor advised funds (as defined in section 4966(d)(2)) it owns at the end of such taxable year,

(2) indicate the aggregate value of assets held in such funds at the end of such taxable year, and

(3) indicate the aggregate contributions to and grants made from such funds during such taxable year.

(*l*) Additional provisions relating to supporting organizations.—Every organization described in section 509(a)(3) shall, on the return required under subsection (a)—

(1) list the supported organizations (as defined in section 509(f)(3)) with respect to which such organization provides support,

(2) indicate whether the organization meets the requirements of clause (i), (ii), or (iii) of section 509(a)(3)(B), and

(3) certify that the organization meets the requirements of section 509(a)(3)(C).

* * *

(*o*) Requirement to report certain information with respect to excise tax based on investment income of private colleges and universities.—Each applicable educational institution described in section 4968(c) which is subject to the requirements of subsection (a) shall include on teh return required under subsection (a)—

(1) the number of tuition-paying students taken into account under section 4968(c), and

(2) the number of students of such institution (determined under the rules of section 4968(e)).

(p) Cross references.—For provisions relating to statements, etc., regarding exempt status of organizations, see section 6001.

For reporting requirements as to certain liquidations, dissolutions, terminations, and contractions, see section 6043(b). For provisions relating to penalties for failure to file a return required by this section, see section 6652(c).

For provisions relating to information required in connection with certain plans of deferred compensation, see section 6058.

§ 6034. Returns by certain trusts.

(a) Split-interest trusts.—Every trust described in section 4947(a)(2) shall furnish such information with respect to the taxable year as the Secretary may by forms or regulations require.

(b) Trusts claiming certain charitable deductions.—

(1) In general.—Every trust not required to file a return under subsection (a) but claiming a deduction under section 642(c) for the taxable year shall furnish such information with respect to such taxable year as the Secretary may by forms or regulations prescribe, including—

(A) the amount of the deduction taken under section 642(c) within such year,

(B) the amount paid out within such year which represents amounts for which deductions under section 642(c) have been taken in prior years,

(C) the amount for which such deductions have been taken in prior years but which has not been paid out at the beginning of such year,

(D) the amount paid out of principal in the current and prior years for the purposes described in section 642(c),

(E) the total income of the trust within such year and the expenses attributable thereto, and

(F) a balance sheet showing the assets, liabilities, and net worth of the trust as of the beginning of such year.

(2) Exceptions.—Paragraph (1) shall not apply to a trust for any taxable year if—

(A) all the net income for such year, determined under the applicable principles of the law of trusts, is required to be distributed currently to the beneficiaries, or

(B) the trust is described in section 4947(a)(1).

§ 6050L. Returns relating to certain donated property.

(a) Dispositions of donated property—

(1) In general.—If the donee of any charitable deduction property sells, exchanges, or otherwise disposes of such property within 3 years after its receipt, the donee shall make a return (in accordance with forms and regulations prescribed by the Secretary) showing—

(A) the name, address, and TIN of the donor,

(B) a description of the property,

(C) the date of the contribution,

(D) the amount received on the disposition,

(E) the date of such disposition,

(F) a description of the donee's use of the property, and

(G) a statement indicating whether the use of the property was related to the purpose or function constituting the basis for the donee's exemption under section 501.

In any case in which the donee indicates that the use of applicable property (as defined in section 170(e)(7)(C)) was related to the purpose or function constituting the basis for the exemption of the donee under section 501 under subparagraph (G), the donee shall include with the return the certification described in section 170(e)(7)(D) if such certification is made under section 170(e)(7).

(2) Definitions.—For purposes of this subsection:

(A) Charitable deduction property.—The term "charitable deduction property" means any property (other than publicly traded securities) contributed in a contribution for which a deduction was claimed under section 170 if the claimed value of such property (plus the claimed value of all similar items of property donated by the donor to 1 or more donees) exceeds $5,000.

(B) Publicly traded securities.—The term "publicly traded securities" means securities for which (as of the date of the contribution) market quotations are readily available on an established securities market.

(b) Qualified intellectual property contributions.—

(1) In general.—Each donee with respect to a qualified intellectual property contribution shall make a return (at such time and in such form and manner as the Secretary may by regulations prescribe) with respect to each specified taxable year of the donee showing—

(A) the name, address, and TIN of the donor,

(B) a description of the qualified intellectual property contributed,

(C) the date of the contribution, and

(D) the amount of net income of the donee for the taxable year which is properly allocable to the qualified intellectual property (determined without regard to paragraph (10)(B) of section 170(m) and with the modifications described in paragraphs (5) and (6) of such section).

(2) Definitions.—For purposes of this subsection:

(A) In general.—Terms used in this subsection which are also used in section 170(m) have the respective meanings given such terms in such section.

(B) Specified taxable year.—The term "specified taxable year" means, with respect to any qualified intellectual property contribution, any taxable year of the donee any portion of which is part of the 10-year period beginning on the date of such contribution.

(c) Statement to be furnished to donors.—Every person making a return under subsection (a) or (b) shall furnish a copy of such return to the donor at such time and in such manner as the Secretary may by regulations prescribe.

Subchapter B. Miscellaneous Provisions

§ 6104. Publicity of information required from certain exempt organizations and certain trusts.

(a) Inspection of applications for tax exemption or notice of status.—

(1) Public inspection.—

(A) Organizations described in section 501 or 527.—If an organization described in section 501(c) or (d) is exempt from taxation under section 501(a) for any taxable year or a political organization is exempt from taxation under section 527 for any taxable year, the application filed by the organization with respect to which the Secretary made his determination that such organization was entitled to exemption under section 501(a) or notice of status filed by the organization under section 527(i), together with any papers submitted in support of such application or notice, and any letter or other document issued by the Internal Revenue Service with respect to such application or notice shall be open to public inspection at the national office of the Internal Revenue Service. In the case of any application or notice filed after the date of the enactment of this subparagraph, a copy of such application or notice and such letter or document shall be open to public inspection at the appropriate field office of the Internal Revenue Service (determined under regulations prescribed by the Secretary). Any inspection under this subparagraph may be made at such times, and in such manner, as the Secretary shall by regulations prescribe. After the application of any organization for exemption from taxation under section 501(a) has been opened to public inspection under this subparagraph, the Secretary shall, on the request of any person with respect to such organization, furnish a statement indicating the subsection and paragraph of section 501 which it has been determined describes such organization.

(B) Pension, etc., plans.—The following shall be open to public inspection at such times and in such places as the Secretary may prescribe:

(i) any application filed with respect to the qualification of a pension, profit-sharing, or stock bonus plan under section 401(a) or 403(a), an individual retirement account described in section 408(a), or an individual retirement annuity described in section 408(b),

(ii) any application filed with respect to the exemption from tax under section 501(a) of an organization forming part of a plan or account referred to in clause (i),

(iii) any papers submitted in support of an application referred to in clause (i) or (ii), and

(iv) any letter or other document issued by the Internal Revenue Service and dealing with the qualification referred to in clause (i) or the exemption from tax referred to in clause (ii).

Except in the case of a plan participant, this subparagraph shall not apply to any plan referred to in clause (i) having not more than 25 participants.

(C) Certain names and compensation not to be opened to public inspection.—In the case of any application, document, or other papers, referred to in subparagraph (B), information from which the compensation (including deferred compensation) of any individual may be ascertained shall not be open to public inspection under subparagraph (B).

(D) Withholding of certain other information.—Upon request of the organization submitting any supporting papers described in subparagraph (A) or (B), the Secretary shall withhold from public inspection any information contained therein which he determines relates to any trade secret, patent, process, style of work, or apparatus, of the organization, if he determines that public disclosure of such information would adversely affect the organization. The Secretary shall withhold from public inspection any information contained in supporting papers described in subparagraph (A) or (B) the public disclosure of which he determines would adversely affect the national defense.

(2) Inspection by committees of Congress.—Section 6103(f) shall apply with respect to—

(A) the application for exemption of any organization described in section 501(c) or (d) which is exempt from taxation under section 501(a) for any taxable year or notice of status of any political organization which is exempt from taxation under section 527 for any taxable year, and any application referred to in subparagraph (B) of subsection (a)(1) of this section, and

(B) any other papers which are in the possession of the Secretary and which relate to such application,

as if such papers constituted returns.

(3) Information available on Internet and in person.—

(A) In general.—The Secretary shall make publicly available, on the Internet and at the offices of the Internal Revenue Service—

(i) a list of all political organizations which file a notice with the Secretary under section 527(i), and

(ii) the name, address, electronic mailing address, custodian of records, and contact person for such organization.

(B) Time to make information available.—The Secretary shall make available the information required under subparagraph (A) not later than 5 business days after the Secretary receives a notice from a political organization under section 527(i).

(b) Inspection of annual returns.—The information required to be furnished by sections 6033, 6034, and 6058, together with the names and addresses of such organizations and trusts, shall be made available to the public at such times and in such places as the Secretary may prescribe. Nothing in this subsection shall authorize the Secretary to disclose the name or address of any contributor to any organization or trust (other than a private foundation, as defined in section 509(a) or a political organization exempt from taxation under section 527) which is required to furnish such information. In the case of an organization described in section 501(d), this subsection shall not apply to copies referred to in section 6031(b) with respect to such organization. In the case of a trust which is required to file a return under section 6034(a), this subsection shall not apply to information regarding beneficiaries which are not organizations described in section 170(c). Any annual return which is filed under section 6011 by an organization described in section 501(c)(3) and which relates to any tax imposed by section 511 (relating to imposition of tax on unrelated business income of charitable, etc., organizations) shall be treated for purposes of this subsection in the same manner as if furnished under section 6033.

(c) Publication to State officials.—

(1) General rule for charitable organizations.—In the case of any organization which is described in section 501(c)(3) and exempt from taxation under section 501(a), or has applied under section 508(a) for recognition as an organization described in section 501(c)(3), the Secretary at such times and in such manner as he may by regulations prescribe shall—

(A) notify the appropriate State officer of a refusal to recognize such organization as an organization described in section 501(c)(3), or of the operation of such organization in a manner which does not meet, or no longer meets, the requirements of its exemption,

(B) notify the appropriate State officer of the mailing of a notice of deficiency of tax imposed under section 507 or chapter 41 or 42, and

(C) at the request of such appropriate State officer, make available for inspection and copying such returns, filed statements, records, reports, and other information, relating to a determination under subparagraph (A) or (B) as are relevant to any determination under State law.

(2) Disclosure of proposed actions related to charitable organizations.—

(A) Specific notifications.—In the case of an organization to which paragraph (1) applies, the Secretary may disclose to the appropriate State officer—

(i) a notice of proposed refusal to recognize such organization as an organization described in section 501(c)(3) or a notice of proposed revocation of such organization's recognition as an organization exempt from taxation,

(ii) the issuance of a letter of proposed deficiency of tax imposed under section 507 or chapter 41 or 42, and

(iii) the names, addresses, and taxpayer identification numbers of organizations which have applied for recognition as organizations described in section 501(c)(3).

(B) Additional disclosures.—Returns and return information of organizations with respect to which information is disclosed under subparagraph (A) may be made available for inspection by or disclosed to an appropriate State officer.

(C) Procedures for disclosure.—Information may be inspected or disclosed under subparagraph (A) or (B) only—

(i) upon written request by an appropriate State officer, and

(ii) for the purpose of, and only to the extent necessary in, the administration of State laws regulating such organizations.

Such information may only be inspected by or disclosed to a person other than the appropriate State officer if such person is an officer or employee of the State and is designated by the appropriate State officer to receive the returns or return information under this paragraph on behalf of the appropriate State officer.

(D) Disclosures other than by request.—The Secretary may make available for inspection or disclose returns and return information of an organization to which paragraph (1) applies to an appropriate State officer of any State if the Secretary determines that such returns or return information may constitute evidence of noncompliance under the laws within the jurisdiction of the appropriate State officer.

(3) Disclosure with respect to certain other exempt organizations.—Upon written request by an appropriate State officer, the Secretary may make available for inspection or disclosure returns and return information of any organization described in section 501(c) (other than organizations described in paragraph (1) or (3) thereof) for the purpose of, and only to the extent necessary in, the administration of State laws regulating the solicitation or administration of the charitable funds or charitable assets of such organizations. Such information may only be inspected by or disclosed to a person other than the appropriate State officer if such person is an officer or employee of the State and is designated by the appropriate State officer to receive the returns or return information under this paragraph on behalf of the appropriate State officer.

(4) Use in civil judicial and administrative proceedings.—Returns and return information disclosed pursuant to this subsection may be disclosed in civil administrative and civil judicial proceedings pertaining to the enforcement of State laws regulating such organizations in a manner prescribed by the Secretary similar to that for tax administration proceedings under section 6103(h)(4).

(5) No disclosure if impairment.—Returns and return information shall not be disclosed under this subsection, or in any proceeding described in paragraph (4), to the extent that the Secretary determines that such disclosure would seriously impair Federal tax administration.

(6) Definitions.—For purposes of this subsection—

(A) Return and return information.—The terms "return" and "return information" have the respective meanings given to such terms by section 6103(b).

(B) Appropriate State officer.—The term "appropriate State officer" means—

(i) the State attorney general,

(ii) the State tax officer,

(iii) in the case of an organization to which paragraph (1) applies, any other State official charged with overseeing organizations of the type described in section 501(c)(3), and

(iv) in the case of an organization to which paragraph (3) applies, the head of an agency designated by the State attorney general as having primary responsibility for overseeing the solicitation of funds for charitable purposes.

(d) Public inspection of certain annual returns, reports, applications for exemption, and notices of status.—

(1) In general.—In the case of an organization described in subsection (c) or (d) of section 501 and exempt from taxation under section 501(a) or an organization exempt from taxation under section 527(a)—

(A) a copy of—

(i) the annual return filed under section 6033 (relating to returns by exempt organizations) by such organization,

(ii) any annual return which is filed under section 6011 by an organization described in section 501(c)(3) and which relates to any tax imposed by section 511 (relating to imposition of tax on unrelated business income of charitable, etc., organizations),

(iii) if the organization filed an application for recognition of exemption under section 501 or notice of status under section 527(i), the exempt status application materials or any notice materials of such organization, and

(iv) the reports filed under section 527(j) (relating to required disclosure of expenditures and contributions) by such organization,

shall be made available by such organization for inspection during regular business hours by any individual at the principal office of such organization and, if such organization regularly maintains 1 or more regional or district offices having 3 or more employees, at each such regional or district office, and

(B) upon request of an individual made at such principal office or such a regional or district office, a copy of such annual return, reports, and exempt status application materials or such notice materials shall be provided to such individual without charge other than a reasonable fee for any reproduction and mailing costs.

The request described in subparagraph (B) must be made in person or in writing. If such request is made in person, such copy shall be provided immediately and, if made in writing, shall be provided within 30 days.

(2) 3-year limitation on inspection of returns.—Paragraph (1) shall apply to an annual return filed under section 6011 or 6033 only during the 3-year period beginning on the last day prescribed for filing such return (determined with regard to any extension of time for filing).

(3) Exceptions from disclosure requirement.—

(A) Nondisclosure of contributors, etc.—In the case of an organization which is not a private foundation (within the meaning of section 509(a)) or a political organization exempt from taxation under section 527, paragraph (1) shall not require the disclosure of the name or address of any contributor to the organization. In the case of an organization described in section 501(d), paragraph (1) shall not require the disclosure of the copies referred to in section 6031(b) with respect to such organization.

(B) Nondisclosure of certain other information.—Paragraph (1) shall not require the disclosure of any information if the Secretary withheld such information from public inspection under subsection (a)(1)(D).

(4) Limitation on providing copies.—Paragraph (1)(B) shall not apply to any request if, in accordance with regulations promulgated by the Secretary, the organization has made the requested documents widely available, or the Secretary determines, upon application by an organization, that such request is part of a harassment campaign and that compliance with such request is not in the public interest.

(5) Exempt status application materials.—For purposes of paragraph (1), the term "exempt status application materials" means the application for recognition of exemption under section 501 and any papers submitted in support of such application and any letter or other document issued by the Internal Revenue Service with respect to such application.

(6) Notice materials.—For purposes of paragraph (1), the term "notice materials" means the notice of status filed under section 527(i) and any papers submitted in support of such notice and any letter or other document issued by the Internal Revenue Service with respect to such notice.

(7) Disclosure of reports by Internal Revenue Service.—Any report filed by an organization under section 527(j) (relating to required disclosure of expenditures and contributions) shall be made available to the public at such times and in such places as the Secretary may prescribe.

(8) Application to nonexempt charitable trusts and nonexempt private foundations.—The organizations referred to in paragraphs (1) and (2) of section 6033(d) shall comply with the requirements of this subsection relating to annual returns filed under section 6033 in the same manner as the organizations referred to in paragraph (1).

§ 6113. Disclosure of nondeductibility of contributions.

(a) General rule.—Each fundraising solicitation by (or on behalf of) an organization to which this section applies shall contain an express statement (in a conspicuous and easily recognizable format) that contributions or gifts to such organization are not deductible as charitable contributions for Federal income tax purposes.

(b) Organizations to which section applies.—

(1) In general.—Except as otherwise provided in this subsection, this section shall apply to any organization which is not described in section 170(c) and which—

(A) is described in subsection (c) (other than paragraph (1) thereof) or (d) of section 501 and exempt from taxation under section 501(a),

(B) is a political organization (as defined in section 527(e)), or

(C) was an organization described in subparagraph (A) or (B) at any time during the 5-year period ending on the date of the fundraising solicitation or is a successor to an organization so described at any time during such 5-year period.

(2) Exception for small organizations.—

(A) Annual gross receipts do not exceed $100,000.—This section shall not apply to any organization the gross receipts of which in each taxable year are normally not more than $100,000.

(B) Multiple organization rule.—The Secretary may treat any group of 2 or more organizations as 1 organization for purposes of subparagraph (A) where necessary or appropriate to prevent the avoidance of this section through the use of multiple organizations.

(3) Special rule for certain fraternal organizations.—For purposes of paragraph (1), an organization described in section 170(c)(4) shall be treated as described in section 170(c) only with respect to solicitations for contributions or gifts which are to be used exclusively for purposes referred to in section 170(c)(4).

(c) Fundraising solicitation.—For purposes of this section—

(1) In general.—Except as provided in paragraph (2), the term "fundraising solicitation" means any solicitation of contributions or gifts which is made—

(A) in written or printed form,

(B) by television or radio, or

(C) by telephone.

(2) Exception for certain letters or calls.—The term "fundraising solicitation" shall not include any letter or telephone call if such letter or call is not part of a coordinated fundraising campaign soliciting more than 10 persons during the calendar year.

§ 6115. Disclosure related to quid pro quo contributions.

(a) Disclosure requirement.—If an organization described in section 170(c) (other than paragraph (1) thereof) receives a quid pro quo contribution in excess of $75, the organization shall, in connection with the solicitation or receipt of the contribution, provide a written statement which—

(1) informs the donor that the amount of the contribution that is deductible for Federal income tax purposes is limited to the excess of the amount of any money and the value of any property other than money contributed by the donor over the value of the goods or services provided by the organization, and

(2) provides the donor with a good faith estimate of the value of such goods or services.

(b) Quid pro quo contribution.—For purposes of this section, the term 'quid pro quo contribution' means a payment made partly as a contribution and partly in consideration for goods or services provided to the payor by the donee organization. A quid pro quo contribution does not include any payment made to an organization, organized exclusively for religious purposes, in return for which the taxpayer receives solely an intangible religious benefit that generally is not sold in a commercial transaction outside the donative context.

Chapter 68. Additions to the Tax, Additional Amounts, and Assessable Penalties

Subchapter A. Additions to the Tax and Additional Amounts

§ 6662. Imposition of accuracy-related penalty.

* * *

(e) Substantial valuation misstatement under Chapter 1.—

(1) In general.—For purposes of this section, there is a substantial valuation misstatement under chapter 1 if—

(A) the value of any property (or the adjusted basis of any property) claimed on any return of tax imposed by chapter 1 is 150 percent or more of the amount determined to be the correct amount of such valuation or adjusted basis (as the case may be), or

(B)(i) the price for any property or services (or for the use of property) claimed on any such return in connection with any transaction between persons described in section 482 is 200 percent or more (or 50 percent or less) of the amount determined under section 482 to be the correct amount of such price, or

(ii) the net section 482 transfer price adjustment for the taxable year exceeds the lesser of $5,000,000 or 10 percent of the taxpayer's gross receipts.

(2) Limitation.—No penalty shall be imposed by reason of subsection (b)(3) unless the portion of the underpayment for the taxable year attributable to substantial valuation misstatements under chapter 1 exceeds $5,000 ($10,000 in the case of a corporation other than an S corporation or a personal holding company (as defined in section 542).

* * *

(*l*) Increase in penalty in case of overstatement of qualified charitable contributions.—In the case of any portion of an underpayment which is attributable to one or more overstatements of the deduction provided in section 170(p), subsection (a) shall be applied with respect to such portion by substituting "50 percent" for "20 percent."

§ 6664. Definitions and special rules.

* * *

(c) Reasonable cause exception for underpayments.—

(1) In general.—No penalty shall be imposed under section 6662 and 6663 with respect to any portion of an underpayment if it is shown that there was a reasonable cause for such portion and that the taxpayer acted in good faith with respect to such portion.

(2) Special rule for certain valuation overstatements.—In the case of any underpayment attributable to a substantial or gross valuation overstatement under chapter 1 with respect to charitable deduction property, paragraph (1) shall not apply unless—

(A) the claimed value of the property was based on a qualified appraisal made by a qualified appraiser, and

(B) in addition to obtaining such appraisal, the taxpayer made a good faith investigation of the value of the contributed property.

(3) Definitions.—For purposes of this subsection—

(A) Charitable deduction property.—The term "charitable deduction property" means any property contributed by the taxpayer in a contribution for which a deduction was claimed under section 170. For purposes of paragraph (2), such term shall not include any securities for which (as of the date of the contribution) market quotations are readily available on an established securities market.

(B) Qualified appraiser.—The term "qualified appraiser" has the meaning given such term by section 170(f)(11)(E)(i).

(C) Qualified appraisal.—The term "qualified appraisal" has the meaning given such term by section 170(f)(11)(E)(ii).

Subchapter B. Assessable Penalties

§ 6685. Assessable penalty with respect to public inspection requirements for certain tax-exempt organizations.

In addition to the penalty imposed by section 7207 (relating to fraudulent returns, statements, or other documents), any person who is required to comply with the requirements of subsection (d) or (e) of section 6104 and who fails to so comply with respect to any return or application, if such failure is willful, shall pay a penalty of $5,000 with respect to each such return or application.

§ 6710. Failure to disclose that contributions are nondeductible.

(a) Imposition of penalty.—If there is a failure to meet the requirement of section 6113 with respect to a fundraising solicitation by (or on behalf of) an organization to which section 6113 applies, such organization shall pay a penalty of $1,000 for each day on which such a failure occurred. The maximum penalty imposed under this subsection on failures by any organization during any calendar year shall not exceed $10,000.

(b) Reasonable cause exception.—No penalty shall be imposed under this section with respect to any failure if it is shown that such failure is due to reasonable cause.

(c) $10,000 limitation not to apply where intentional disregard.—If any failure to which subsection (a) applies is due to intentional disregard of the requirement of section 6113—

(1) the penalty under subsection (a) for the day on which such failure occurred shall be the greater of—

(A) $1,000, or

(B) 50 percent of the aggregate cost of the solicitations which occurred on such day and with respect to which there was such a failure,

(2) the $10,000 limitation of subsection (a) shall not apply to any penalty under subsection (a) for the day on which such failure occurred, and

(3) such penalty shall not be taken into account in applying such limitation to other penalties under subsection (a).

(d) Day on which failure occurs.—For purposes of this section, any failure to meet the requirement of section 6113 with respect to a solicitation—

(1) by television or radio, shall be treated as occurring when the solicitation was telecast or broadcast,

(2) by mail, shall be treated as occurring when the solicitation was mailed,

(3) not by mail but in written or printed form, shall be treated as occurring when the solicitation was distributed, or

(4) by telephone, shall be treated as occurring when the solicitation was made.

§ 6711. Failure by tax-exempt organization to disclose that certain information or service available from Federal Government.

(a) Imposition of penalty—

If—

(1) a tax-exempt organization offers to sell (or solicits money for) specific information or a routine service for any individual which could be readily obtained by such individual free of charge (or for a nominal charge) from an agency of the Federal Government,

(2) the tax-exempt organization, when making such offer or solicitation, fails to make an express statement in a conspicuous and easily recognizable format) that the information or service can be so obtained, and

(3) such failure is due to intentional disregard of the requirements of this subsection, such organization shall pay a penalty determined under subsection (b) for such day on which such a failure occurred.

(b) Amount of penalty.—The penalty under subsection (a) for any day on which a failure referred to in such subsection occurred shall be the greater of—

(1) $1,000, or

(2) 50 percent of the aggregate cost of the offers and solicitations referred to in subsection (a)(1) which occurred on such day and with respect to which there was such a failure.

(c) Definitions.—For purposes of this section—

(1) Tax-exempt organization. The term "tax-exempt organization" means any organization which—

(A) is described in subsection (c) or (d) of section 501 and exempt from taxation under section 501(a), or

(B) is a political organization (as defined in section 527(e)).

(2) Day on which failure occurs.—The day on which any failure referred to in subsection (a) occurs shall be determined under rules similar to the rules of section 6710(d).

§ 6714. Failure to meet disclosure requirements applicable to quid pro quo contributions.

(a) Imposition of penalty.—If an organization fails to meet the disclosure requirement of section 6115 with respect to a quid pro quo contribution, such organization shall pay a penalty of $10 for each contribution in respect of which the organization fails to make the required disclosure, except that the total penalty imposed by this subsection with respect to a particular fundraising event or mailing shall not exceed $5,000.

(b) Reasonable cause exception.—No penalty shall be imposed under this section with respect to any failure if it is shown that such failure is due to reasonable cause.

* * *

Chapter 70. Judicial Receiverships, Etc.

Subchapter A. Jeopardy

§ 6852. Termination assessments in case of flagrant political expenditures of section 501(c)(3) organizations.

(a) Authority to make.—

(1) In general.—If the Secretary finds that—

(A) a section 501(c)(3) organization has made political expenditures, and

(B) such expenditures constitute a flagrant violation of the prohibition against making political expenditures,

the Secretary shall immediately make a determination of any income tax payable by such organization for the current or immediately preceding taxable year, or both, and shall immediately make a determination of any tax payable under section 4955 by such organization or any manager thereof with respect to political expenditures during the current or preceding taxable year, or both. Notwithstanding any other provision of law, any such tax shall become immediately due and payable. The Secretary shall immediately assess the amount of tax so determined (together with all interest, additional amounts, and additions to the tax provided by law) for the current year or the preceding taxable year, or both, and shall cause notice of such determination and assessment to be given to the organization or any manager thereof, as the case may be, together with a demand for immediate payment of such tax.

(2) Computation of tax.—In the case of a current taxable year, the Secretary shall determine the taxes for the period beginning on the 1st day of such current taxable year and ending on the date of the determination under paragraph (1) as though such period were a taxable year of the organization, and shall take into account any prior determination made under this subsection with respect to such current taxable year.

(3) Treatment of amounts collected.—Any amounts collected as a result of any assessments under this subsection shall, to the extent thereof, be treated as a payment of income tax for such taxable year, or tax under section 4955 with respect to the expenditure, as the case may be.

(4) Section inapplicable to assessments after due date.—This section shall not authorize any assessment of tax for the preceding taxable year which is made after the due date of the organization's return for such taxable year (determined with regard to any extensions).

(b) Definitions and special rules.—

(1) Definitions.—For purposes of this section, the terms "section 501(c)(3) organization", "political expenditure", and "organization manager" have the respective meanings given to such terms by section 4955.

(2) Certain rules made applicable.—The provisions of sections 6851(b), 6861(f), and 6861(g) shall apply with respect to any assessment made under subsection (a), except that determinations under section 6861(g) shall be made on the basis of whether the requirements of subsection (a)(1)(B) of this section are met in lieu of whether jeopardy exists.

Chapter 76. Judicial Proceedings

Subchapter A. Civil Actions by the United States

§ 7409. Action to enjoin flagrant political expenditures of section 501(c)(3) organizations.

(a) Authority to seek injunction.—

(1) In general. If the requirements of paragraph (2) are met, a civil action in the name of the United States may be commenced at the request of the Secretary to enjoin any section 501(c)(3) organization from further making political expenditures and for such other relief as may be appropriate to ensure that the assets of such organization are preserved for charitable or other purposes specified in section 501(c)(3). Any action under this section shall be brought in the district court of the United States for the district in which such organization has its principal place of business or for any district in which it has made political expenditures. The court may exercise its jurisdiction over such action (as provided in section 7402(a)) separate and apart from any other action brought by the United States against such organization.

(2) Requirements. An action may be brought under subsection (a) only if—

(A) the Internal Revenue Service has notified the organization of its intention to seek an injunction under this section if the making of political expenditures does not immediately cease, and

(B) the Commissioner of Internal Revenue has personally determined that—

(i) such organization has flagrantly participated in, or intervened in (including the publication or distribution of statements), any political campaign on behalf of (or in opposition to) any candidate for public office, and

(ii) injunctive relief is appropriate to prevent future political expenditures.

(b) Adjudication and decree.—In any action under subsection (a), if the court finds on the basis of clear and convincing evidence that—

(1) such organization has flagrantly participated in, or intervened in (including the publication or distribution of statements), any political campaign on behalf of (or in opposition to) any candidate for public office, and

(2) injunctive relief is appropriate to prevent future political expenditures,the court may enjoin such organization from making political expenditures and may grant such other relief as may be appropriate to ensure that the assets of such organization are preserved for charitable or other purposes specified in section 501(c)(3).

(c) Definitions.—For purposes of this section, the terms "section 501(c)(3) organization" and "political expenditures" have the respective meanings given to such terms by section 4955.

Subchapter B. Proceedings by Taxpayers and Third Parties

§ 7428. Declaratory judgments relating to status and classification of organizations under section 501(c)(3), etc.

(a) Creation of remedy.—In a case of actual controversy involving—

(1) a determination by the Secretary—

(A) with respect to the initial qualification or continuing qualification of an organization as an organization described in section 501(c)(3) which is exempt from tax under section 501(a) or as an organization described in section 170(c)(2),

(B) with respect to the initial classification or continuing classification of an organization as a private foundation (as defined in section 509(a)), or

(C) with respect to the initial classification or continuing classification of an organization as a private operating foundation (as defined in section 4942(j)(3)),

(D) with respect to the initial classification or continuing classification of a cooperative an an organization described in section 521(b) which is exempt from tax under section 521(a), or

(E) with respect to the initial classification or continuing qualification of an organization as an organization described in section 501(c) (other than paragraph (3)) or 501(d) and exempt from tax under section 501(a), or

(2) a failure by the Secretary to make a determination with respect to an issue referred to in paragraph (1),

upon the filing of an appropriate pleading, the United States Tax Court, the United States Claims Court, or the district court of the United States for the District of Columbia may make a declaration with respect to such initial qualification or continuing qualification or with respect to such initial classification or continuing classification. Any such declaration shall have the force and effect of a decision of the Tax Court or a final judgment or decree of the district court or the Claims Court, as the case may be, and shall be reviewable as such. For purposes of this section, a determination with respect to a continuing qualification or continuing classification includes any revocation of or other change in a qualification or classification.

(b) Limitations.—

(1) Petitioner.—A pleading may be filed under this section only by the organization the qualification or classification of which is at issue.

(2) Exhaustion of administrative remedies.—A declaratory judgment or decree under this section shall not be issued in any proceeding unless the Tax Court, the Claims Court, or the district court of the United States for the District of Columbia determines that the organization involved has exhausted administrative remedies available to it within the Internal Revenue Service. An organization requesting the determination of an issue referred to in subsection (a)(1) shall be deemed to have exhausted its administrative remedies with respect to a failure by the Secretary to make a determination with respect to such issue at the expiration of 270 days after the date on which the request for such determination was made if the organization has taken, in a timely manner, all reasonable steps to secure such determination.

(3) Time for bringing action.—If the Secretary sends by certified or registered mail notice of his determination with respect to an issue referred to in subsection (a)(1) to the organization referred to in paragraph (1), no proceeding may be initiated under this section by such organization unless the pleading is filed before the 91st day after the date of such mailing.

(4) Nonapplication for certain revocations—No action may be brought under this section with respect to any revocation of status described in section 6033(j)(1).

(c) Validation of certain contributions made during pendency of proceedings.—

(1) In general.—If—

(A) the issue referred to in subsection (a)(1) involves the revocation of a determination that the organization is described in section 170(c)(2),

(B) a proceeding under this section is initiated within the time provided by subsection (b)(3), and

(C) either—

(i) a decision of the Tax Court has become final (within the meaning of section 7481), or

(ii) a judgment of the district court of the United States for the District of Columbia has been entered, or

(iii) a judgment of the Claims Court, has been entered,

and such decision or judgment, as the case may be, determines that the organization was not described in section 170(c)(2), then, notwithstanding such decision or judgment, such organization shall be treated as having been described in section 170(c)(2) for purposes of section 170 for the period beginning on the date on which the notice of the revocation was published and ending on the date on which the court first determined in such proceeding that the organization was not described in section 170(c)(2).

(2) Limitation.—Paragraph (1) shall apply only—

(A) with respect to individuals, and only to the extent that the aggregate of the contributions made by any individual to or for the use of the organization during the period specified in paragraph (1) does not exceed $1,000 (for this purpose treating a husband and wife as one contributor), and

(B) with respect to organizations described in section 170(c)(2) which are exempt from tax under section 501(a) (for this purpose excluding any such organization with respect to which there is pending a proceeding to revoke the determination under section 170(c)(2)).

(3) Exception.—This subsection shall not apply to any individual who was responsible, in whole or in part, for the activities (or failures to act) on the part of the organization which were the basis for the revocation.

(d) Subpoena power for district court for District of Columbia.—In any action brought under this section in the district court of the United States for the District of Columbia, a subpoena requiring the attendance of a witness at a trial or hearing may be served at any place in the United States.

Subchapter C. The Tax Court.

§ 7454. Burden of proof in fraud, foundation manager, and transferee cases.

(a) Fraud. In any proceeding involving the issue whether the petitioner has been guilty of fraud with intent to evade tax, the burden of proof in respect of such issue shall be upon the Secretary.

(b) Foundation managers. In any proceeding involving the issue whether a foundation manager (as defined in section 4946(b) has "knowingly" participated in an act of self-dealing (within the meaning of section 4941, participated in an investment which jeopardizes the carrying out of exempt purposes (within the meaning of section 4944, or agreed to the making of a taxable expenditure (within the meaning of section 4945, or whether the trustee of a trust described in section 501(c)(21) has "knowingly" participated in an act of self-dealing (within the meaning of section 4951 or agreed to the making of a taxable expenditure (within the meaning of section 4952, or whether an organization manager (as defined in section 4955(f)(2)) has "knowingly" agreed to the making of a political expenditure (within the meaning of section 4955, or whether an organization manager (as defined in section 4912(d)(2) has "knowingly" agreed to the making of disqualifying lobbying expenditures within the meaning of section 4912(b), or whether an organization manager (as defined in section 4958(f)(2) has "knowingly" participated in an excess benefit transaction (as defined in section 4958(c), the burden of proof in respect of such issue shall be upon the Secretary.

* * *

Chapter 77. Miscellaneous Provisions

§ 7520. Valuation tables.

(a) General rule.—For purposes of this title, the value of any annuity, any interest for life or a term of years, or any remainder or reversionary interest shall be determined—

(1) under tables prescribed by the Secretary, and

(2) by using an interest rate (rounded to the nearest 2/10ths of 1 percent) equal to 120 percent of the Federal midterm rate in effect under section 1274(d)(1) for the month in which the valuation date falls.

If an income, estate, or gift tax charitable contribution is allowable for any part of the property transferred, the taxpayer may elect to use such Federal midterm rate for either of the 2 months preceding the month in which the valuation date falls for purposes of paragraph (2). In the case of transfers of more than 1 interest in the same property with respect to which the taxpayer may use the same rate under paragraph (2), the taxpayer shall use the same rate with respect to each such interest.

(b) Section not to apply for certain purposes.—This section shall not apply for purposes of part I of subchapter D of chapter 1 or any other provision specified in regulations.

* * *

Chapter 78. Discovery of Liability and Enforcement of Title

Subchapter A. Examination and Inspection

§ 7611. Restrictions on church tax inquiries and examinations.

(a) Restrictions on inquiries.—

(1) In general.—The Secretary may begin a church tax inquiry only if—

(A) the reasonable belief requirements of paragraph (2), and

(B) the notice requirements of paragraph (3), have been met.

(2) Reasonable belief requirements.—The requirements of this paragraph are met with respect to any church tax inquiry if an appropriate high-level Treasury official reasonably believes (on the basis of facts and circumstances recorded in writing) that the church—

(A) may not be exempt, by reason of its status as a church, from tax under section 501(a), or

(B) may be carrying on an unrelated trade or business (within the meaning of section 513) or otherwise engaged in activities subject to taxation under this title.

(3) Inquiry notice requirements.—

(A) In general.—The requirements of this paragraph are met with respect to any church tax inquiry if, before beginning such inquiry, the Secretary provides written notice to the church of the beginning of such inquiry.

(B) Contents of inquiry notice.—The notice required by this paragraph shall include—

(i) an explanation of—

(I) the concerns which gave rise to such inquiry, and

(II) the general subject matter of such inquiry, and

(ii) a general explanation of the applicable—

(I) administrative and constitutional provisions with respect to such inquiry (including the right to a conference with the Secretary before any examination of church records), and

(II) provisions of this title which authorize such inquiry or which may be otherwise involved in such inquiry.

(b) Restrictions on examinations.—

(1) In general.—The Secretary may begin a church tax examination only if the requirements of paragraph (2) have been met and such examination may be made only—

(A) in the case of church records, to the extent necessary to determine the liability for, and the amount of, any tax imposed by this title, and

(B) in the case of religious activities, to the extent necessary to determine whether an organization claiming to be a church is a church for any period.

(2) Notice of examination; opportunity for conference.—The requirements of this paragraph are met with respect to any church tax examination if—

(A) at least 15 days before the beginning of such examination, the Secretary provides the notice described in paragraph (3) to both the church and the appropriate regional counsel of the Internal Revenue Service, and

(B) the church has a reasonable time to participate in a conference described in paragraph (3)(A)(iii), but only if the church requests such a conference before the beginning of the examination.

(3) Contents of examination notice, et cetera.—

(A) In general.—The notice described in this paragraph is a written notice which includes—

(i) a copy of the church tax inquiry notice provided to the church under subsection (a),

(ii) a description of the church records and activities which the Secretary seeks to examine,

(iii) an offer to have a conference between the church and the Secretary in order to discuss, and attempt to resolve, concerns relating to such examination, and

(iv) a copy of all documents which were collected or prepared by the Internal Revenue Service for use in such examination and the disclosure of which is required by the Freedom of Information Act (5 U.S.C. 552).

(B) Earliest day examination notice may be provided.—The examination notice described in subparagraph (A) shall not be provided to the church before the 15th day after the date on which the church tax inquiry notice was provided to the church under subsection (a).

(C) Opinion of regional counsel with respect to examination.—Any regional counsel of the Internal Revenue Service who receives an examination notice under paragraph (1) may, within 15 days after such notice is provided, submit to the regional commissioner for the region an advisory objection to the examination.

(4) Examination of records and activities not specified in notice.—Within the course of a church tax examination which (at the time the examination begins) meets the requirements of paragraphs (1) and (2), the Secretary may examine any church records or religious activities which were not specified in the examination notice to the extent such examination meets the requirement of subparagraph (A) or (B) of paragraph (1) (whichever applies).

(c) Limitation on period of inquiries and examinations.—

(1) Inquiries and examinations must be completed within 2 years.—

(A) In general.—The Secretary shall complete any church tax status inquiry or examination (and make a final determination with respect thereto) not later than the date which is 2 years after the examination notice date.

(B) Inquiries not followed by examinations.—In the case of a church tax inquiry with respect to which there is no examination notice under subsection (b), the Secretary shall complete such inquiry (and make a final determination with respect thereto) not later than the date which is 90 days after the inquiry notice date.

(2) Suspension of 2-year period.—The running of the 2-year period described in paragraph (1)(A) and the 90-day period in paragraph (1)(B) shall be suspended—

(A) for any period during which—

(i) a judicial proceeding brought by the church against the Secretary with respect to the church tax inquiry or examination is pending or being appealed,

(ii) a judicial proceeding brought by the Secretary against the church (or any official thereof) to compel compliance with any reasonable request of the Secretary in a church tax examination for examination of church records or religious activities is pending or being appealed, or

(iii) the Secretary is unable to take actions with respect to the church tax inquiry or examination by reason of an order issued in any judicial proceeding brought under section 7609,

(B) for any period in excess of 20 days (but not in excess of 6 months) in which the church or its agents fail to comply with any reasonable request of the Secretary for church records or other information, or

(C) for any period mutually agreed upon by the Secretary and the church.

(d) Limitations on revocation of tax-exempt status, etc.—

(1) In general.—The Secretary may—

(A) determine that an organization is not a church which—

(i) is exempt from taxation by reason of section 501(a), or

(ii) is described in section 170(c), or

(B)(i) send a notice of deficiency of any tax involved in a church tax examination, or

(ii) in the case of any tax with respect to which subchapter B of chapter 63 (relating to deficiency procedures) does not apply, assess any underpayment of such tax involved in a church tax examination,

only if the appropriate regional counsel of the Internal Revenue Service determines in writing that there has been substantial compliance with the requirements of this section and approves in writing of such revocation, notice of deficiency, or assessment.

(2) Limitations on period of assessment.—

(A) Revocation of tax-exempt status.—

(i) 3-year statute of limitations generally.—In the case of any church tax examination with respect to the revocation of tax-exempt status under section 501(a), any tax imposed by chapter 1 (other than section 511) may be assessed, or a proceeding in court for collection of such tax may be begun without assessment, only for the 3 most recent taxable years ending before the examination notice date.

(ii) 6-year statute of limitations where tax-exempt status revoked.—If an organization is not a church exempt from tax under section 501(a) for any of the 3 taxable years described in clause (i), clause (i) shall be applied by substituting "6 most recent taxable years" for "3 most recent taxable years".

(B) Unrelated business tax.—In the case of any church tax examination with respect to the tax imposed by section 511 (relating to unrelated business income), such tax may be assessed, or a proceeding in court for the collection of such tax may be begun without assessment, only with respect to the 6 most recent taxable years ending before the examination notice date.

(C) Exception where shorter statute of limitations otherwise applicable.—Subparagraphs (A) and (B) shall not be construed to increase the period otherwise applicable under subchapter A of chapter 66 (relating to limitations on assessment and collection).

(e) Information not collected in substantial compliance with procedures to stay summons proceeding.—

(1) In general.—If there has not been substantial compliance with—

(A) the notice requirements of subsection (a) or (b),

(B) the conference requirement described in subsection (b)(3)(A)(iii), or

(C) the approval requirement of subsection (d)(1) (if applicable),

with respect to any church tax inquiry or examination, any proceeding to compel compliance with any summons with respect to such inquiry or examination shall be stayed until the court finds that all practicable steps to correct the noncompliance have been taken. The period applicable under paragraph (1) or subsection (c) shall not be suspended during the period of any stay under the preceding sentence.

(2) Remedy to be exclusive.—No suit may be maintained, and no defense may be raised in any proceeding (other than as provided in paragraph (1)), by reason of any noncompliance by the Secretary with the requirements of this section.

(f) Limitations on additional inquiries and examinations.—

(1) In general.—If any church tax inquiry or examination with respect to any church is completed and does not result in—

(A) a revocation, notice of deficiency, or assessment described in subsection (d)(1), or

(B) a request by the Secretary for any significant change in the operational practices of the church (including the adequacy of accounting practices),

no other church tax inquiry or examination may begin with respect to such church during the applicable 5-year period unless such inquiry or examination is approved in writing by the Assistant Commissioner for Employee Plans and Exempt Organizations of the Internal Revenue Service or does not involve the same or similar issues involved in the preceding inquiry or examination. For purposes of the preceding sentence, an inquiry or examination shall be treated as completed not later than the expiration of the applicable period under paragraph (1) of subsection (c).

(2) Applicable 5-year period.—For purposes of paragraph (1), the term "applicable 5-year period" means the 5-year period beginning on the date the notice taken into account for purposes of subsection (c)(1) was provided. For purposes of the preceding sentence, the rules of subsection (c)(2) shall apply.

(g) Treatment of final report of revenue agent.—Any final report of an agent of the Internal Revenue Service shall be treated as a determination of the Secretary under paragraph (1) of section 7428(a), and any church receiving such a report shall be treated for purposes of sections 7428 and 7430 as having exhausted the administrative remedies available to it.

(h) Definitions.—For purposes of this section—

(1) Church.—The term "church" includes—

(A) any organization claiming to be a church, and

(B) any convention or association of churches.

(2) Church tax inquiry.—The term "church tax inquiry" means any inquiry to a church (other than an examination) to serve as a basis for determining whether a church—

(A) is exempt from tax under section 501(a) by reason of its status as a church, or

(B) is carrying on an unrelated trade or business (within the meaning of section 513) or otherwise engaged in activities which may be subject to taxation under this title.

(3) Church tax examination.—The term "church tax examination" means any examination for purposes of making a determination described in paragraph (2) of—

(A) church records at the request of the Internal Revenue Service, or

(B) the religious activities of any church.

(4) Church records.—

(A) In general.—The term "church records" means all corporate and financial records regularly kept by a church, including corporate minute books and lists of members and contributors.

(B) Exception.—Such term shall not include records acquired—

(i) pursuant to a summons to which section 7609 applies, or

(ii) from any governmental agency.

(5) Inquiry notice date.—The term "inquiry notice date" means the date the notice with respect to a church tax inquiry is provided under subsection (a).

(6) Examination notice date.—The term "examination notice date" means the date the notice with respect to a church tax examination is provided under subsection (b) to the church.

(7) Appropriate high-level Treasury official.—The term "appropriate high-level Treasury official" means the Secretary of the Treasury or any delegate of the Secretary whose rank is no lower than that of a principal Internal Revenue officer for an internal revenue region.

(i) Section not to apply to criminal investigations, etc.—This section shall not apply to—

(1) any criminal investigation,

(2) any inquiry or examination relating to the tax liability of any person other than a church,

(3) any assessment under section 6851 (relating to termination assessments of income tax), section 6852 (relating to termination assessments in case of flagrant political expenditures of section 501(c)(3) organizations), or section 6861 (relating to jeopardy assessments of income taxes, etc.),

(4) any willful attempt to defeat or evade any tax imposed by this title, or

(5) any knowing failure to file a return of tax imposed by this title.

TREASURY REGULATIONS

INCOME TAX REGULATIONS

EXCISE TAX REGULATIONS

PROCEDURAL REGULATIONS

INCOME TAX REGULATIONS

BUSINESS DEDUCTIONS

§ 1.162–28. Allocation of costs to lobbying activities.

(a) Introduction—(1) In general. Section 162(e)(1) denies a deduction for certain amounts paid or incurred in connection with activities described in section 162(e)(1)(A) and (D) (lobbying activities). To determine the nondeductible amount, a taxpayer must allocate costs to lobbying activities. This section describes costs that must be allocated to lobbying activities and prescribes rules permitting a taxpayer to use a reasonable method to allocate those costs. This section does not apply to taxpayers subject to section 162(e)(5)(A). In addition, this section does not apply for purposes of section 4911 and 4945 and the regulations thereunder.

(2) Recordkeeping. For recordkeeping requirements, see section 6001 and the regulations thereunder.

(b) Reasonable method of allocating costs.—(1) In General. A taxpayer may use a reasonable method to allocate the costs described in paragraph (c) of this section to lobbying activities. A method is not reasonable unless it is applied consistently and is consistent with the special rules in paragraph (g) of this section. Except as provided in paragraph (b)(2) of this section, reasonable methods of allocating costs to lobbying activities include (but are not limited to)—

(i) The ratio method described in paragraph (d) of this section;

(ii) The gross-up method described in paragraph (e) of this section; and

(iii) A method that applies the principles of section 263A and the regulations thereunder (see paragraph (f) of this section).

(2) Taxpayers not permitted to use certain methods. A taxpayer (other than one subject to section 6033(e)) that does not pay or incur reasonable labor costs for persons engaged in lobbying activities may not use the gross-up method. For example, a partnership or sole proprietorship in which the lobbying activities are performed by the owners who do not receive a salary or guaranteed payment for services does not pay or incur reasonable labor costs for persons engaged in those activities and may not use the gross-up method.

(c) Costs allocable to lobbying activities.—(1) In general. Costs properly allocable to lobbying activities include labor costs and general and administrative costs.

(2) Labor costs. For each taxable year, labor costs allocable to lobbying activities include costs attributable to full-time, part-time, and contract employees. Labor costs include all elements of compensation, such as basic compensation, overtime pay, vacation pay, holiday pay, sick leave pay, payroll taxes, pension costs, employee benefits, and payments to a supplemental unemployment benefit plan.

(3) General and administrative costs. For each taxable year, general and administrative costs include depreciation, rent, utilities, insurance, maintenance costs, security costs, and other administrative department costs (for example, payroll, personnel, and accounting).

(d) Ratio method.—(1) In general. Under the ratio method described in this paragraph (d), a taxpayer allocates to lobbying activities the sum of its third-party costs (as defined in paragraph (d)(5) of this section) allocable to lobbying activities and the costs determined by using the following formula:

(Lobbying labor hours/Total labor hours) x Total costs of operations.

(2) Lobbying labor hours. Lobbying labor hours are the hours that a taxpayer's personnel spend on lobbying activities during the taxable year. A taxpayer may use any reasonable method to determine the number of labor hours spent on lobbying activities and may use the de minimis rule of paragraph (g)(1) of this section. A taxpayer may treat as zero the lobbying labor hours of personnel engaged in secretarial, clerical, support, and other administrative activities (as opposed to activities involving significant judgment with respect to lobbying activities). Thus, for example, the hours spent on lobbying activities by para-professionals and analysts may not be treated as zero.

(3) Total labor hours. Total labor hours means the total number of hours of labor that a taxpayer's personnel spend on a taxpayer's trade or business during the taxable year. A taxpayer may make reasonable assumptions concerning total hours worked by its personnel during the year. For example, it may be reasonable, based on all the facts and circumstances, to assume that all full-time personnel spend 1,800 hours per year on a taxpayer's trade or business. If, under paragraph (d)(2) of this section, a taxpayer treats as zero the lobbying labor hours of personnel engaged in secretarial, clerical, support, and other administrative activities, the taxpayer must also treat as zero the total labor hours of all personnel engaged in those activities.

(4) Total costs of operations. A taxpayer's total costs of operations means the total costs of the taxpayer's trade or business for a taxable year, excluding third-party costs (as defined in paragraph (d)(5) of this section).

(5) Third-party costs. Third-party costs are amounts paid or incurred for lobbying activities conducted by third parties (such as amounts paid to taxpayers subject to section 162(e)(5)(A) or dues or other similar amounts that are not deductible under section 162(e)(3)) and amounts paid or incurred for travel (including meals and lodging while away from home) and entertainment relating to lobbying activities.

(e) Gross-up method—(1) In general. Under the gross-up method described in this paragraph (e)(1), the taxpayer allocates to lobbying activities the sum of its third-party costs (as defined in paragraph (d)(5) of this section) allocable to lobbying activities and 175 percent of its basic lobbying labor costs (as defined in paragraph (e)(3) of this section) of all personnel.

(2) Alternative gross-up method. Under the alternative gross-up method described in this paragraph (e)(2), the taxpayer allocates to lobbying activities the sum of its third-party costs (as defined in paragraph (d)(5) of this section) allocable to lobbying activities and 225 percent of its basic lobbying labor costs (as defined in paragraph (e)(3)), excluding the costs of personnel who engage in secretarial, clerical, support, and other administrative activities (as opposed to activities involving significant judgment with respect to lobbying activities).

(3) Basic lobbying labor costs. For purposes of this paragraph (e), basic lobbying labor costs are the basic costs of lobbying labor hours (as defined in paragraph (d)(2) of this section) determined for the appropriate personnel. For purposes of this paragraph (e), basic costs of lobbying labor hours are wages or other similar costs of labor, including, for example, guaranteed payments for services. Basic costs do not include pension, profit-sharing, employee benefits, and supplemental unemployment benefit plan costs, or other similar costs.

* * *

(g) Special rules. The following rules apply to any reasonable method of allocating costs to lobbying activities.

(1) De minimis rule for labor hours. Subject to the exception provided in paragraph (g)(2) of this section, a taxpayer may treat time spent by an individual on lobbying activities as zero if less than five percent of the person's time is spent on lobbying activities. Reasonable methods must be used to determine if less than five percent of a person's time is spent on lobbying activities.

(2) Direct contact lobbying labor hours. Notwithstanding paragraph (g)(1) of this section, a taxpayer must treat all hours spent by a person on direct contact lobbying (as well as the hours that person spends in connection with direct contact lobbying, including time spent traveling that is allocable to the direct contact lobbying) as labor hours allocable to lobbying activities. An activity is direct contact lobbying if it is a meeting, telephone conversation, letter, or other similar means of communication with a legislator (other than a local legislator) or covered executive branch official (as defined in section 162(e)(6)) and otherwise qualifies as a lobbying activity. A person who engages in research, preparation, and other background activities related to direct contact lobbying but who does not make direct contact with a legislator or covered executive branch official is not engaged in direct contact lobbying.

(3) Taxpayer defined. For purposes of this section, a taxpayer includes a tax-exempt organization subject to section 6033(e).

* * *

§ 1.162–29. Influencing legislation.

(a) Scope. This section provides rules for determining whether an activity is influencing legislation for purposes of section 162(e)(1)(A). This section does not apply for purposes of sections 4911 and 4945 and the regulations thereunder.

(b) Definitions. For purposes of this section—

(1) Influencing legislation. Influencing legislation means—

(i) Any attempt to influence any legislation through a lobbying communication; and

(ii) All activities, such as research, preparation, planning, and coordination, including deciding whether to make a lobbying communication, engaged in for a purpose of making or supporting a lobbying communication, even if not yet made. See paragraph (c) of this section for rules for determining the purposes for engaging in an activity.

(2) Attempt to influence legislation. An attempt to influence any legislation through a lobbying communication is making the lobbying communication.

(3) Lobbying communications. A lobbying communication is any communication (other than any communication compelled by subpoena, or otherwise compelled by Federal or State law) with any member or employee of a legislative body or any other government official or employee who may participate in the formulation of the legislation that—

(i) Refers to specific legislation and reflects a view on that legislation; or

(ii) Clarifies, amplifies, modifies, or provides support for views reflected in a prior lobbying communication.

(4) Legislation. Legislation includes any action with respect to Acts, bills, resolutions, or other similar items by a legislative body. Legislation includes a proposed treaty required to be submitted by the President to the Senate for its advice and consent from the time the President's representative begins to negotiate its position with the prospective parties to the proposed treaty.

(5) Specific legislation. Specific legislation includes a specific legislative proposal that has not been introduced in a legislative body.

(6) Legislative bodies. Legislative bodies are Congress, state legislatures, and other similar governing bodies, excluding local councils (and similar governing bodies), and executive, judicial, or administrative bodies. For this purpose, administrative bodies include school boards, housing authorities, sewer and water districts, zoning boards, and other similar Federal, State, or local special purpose bodies, whether elective or appointive.

(7) Examples. The provisions of this paragraph (b) are illustrated by the following examples.

Example 1. Taxpayer P's employee, A, is assigned to approach members of Congress to gain their support for a pending bill. A drafts and P prints a position letter on the bill. P distributes the letter to members of Congress. Additionally, A personally contacts several members of Congress or their staffs to seek support for P's position on the bill. The letter and the personal contacts are lobbying communications. Therefore, P is influencing legislation.

Example 2. Taxpayer R is invited to provide testimony at a congressional oversight hearing concerning the implementation of The Financial Institutions Reform, Recovery, and Enforcement Act of 1989. Specifically, the hearing concerns a proposed regulation increasing the threshold value of commercial and residential real estate transactions for which an appraisal by a state licensed or certified appraiser is required. In its testimony, R states that it is in favor of the proposed regulation. Because R does not refer to any specific legislation or reflect a view on any such legislation, R has not made a lobbying communication. Therefore, R is not influencing legislation.

Example 3. State X enacts a statute that requires the licensing of all day-care providers. Agency B in State X is charged with writing rules to implement the statute. After the enactment of the statute, Taxpayer S sends a letter to Agency B providing detailed proposed rules that S recommends Agency B adopt to implement the statute on licensing of day-care providers. Because the letter to Agency B neither refers to nor reflects a view on any specific legislation, it is not a lobbying communication. Therefore, S is not influencing legislation.

Example 4. Taxpayer T proposes to a State Park Authority that it purchase a particular tract of land for a new park. Even if T's proposal would necessarily require the State Park Authority eventually to seek appropriations to acquire the land and develop the new park, T has not made a lobbying communication because there has been no reference to, nor any view reflected on, any specific legislation. Therefore, T's proposal is not influencing legislation.

Example 5. (i) Taxpayer U prepares a paper that asserts that lack of new capital is hurting State X's economy. The paper indicates that State X residents either should invest more in local businesses or increase their savings so that funds will be available to others interested in making investments. U forwards a summary of the unpublished paper to legislators in State X with a cover letter that states in part:

> You must take action to improve the availability of new capital in the state.

(ii) Because neither the summary nor the cover letter refers to any specific legislative proposal and no other facts or circumstances indicate that they refer to an existing legislative proposal, forwarding the summary to legislators in State X is not a lobbying communication. Therefore, U is not influencing legislation.

(iii) Q, a member of the legislature of State X, calls U to request a copy of the unpublished paper from which the summary was prepared. U forwards the paper with a cover letter that simply refers to the enclosed materials. Because U's letter to Q and the unpublished paper do not refer to any specific legislation or reflect a view on any such legislation, the letter is not a lobbying communication. Therefore, U is not influencing legislation.

Example 6. (i) Taxpayer V prepares a paper that asserts that lack of new capital is hurting the national economy. The paper indicates that lowering the capital gains rate would increase the availability of capital and increase tax receipts from the capital gains tax. V forwards the paper to its representatives in Congress with a cover letter that says, in part:

> I urge you to support a reduction in the capital gains tax rate.

(ii) V's communication is a lobbying communication because it refers to and reflects a view on a specific legislative proposal (i.e., lowering the capital gains rate). Therefore, V is influencing legislation.

Example 7. Taxpayer W, based in State A, notes in a letter to a legislator of State A that State X has passed a bill that accomplishes a stated purpose and then says that State A should pass such a bill. No such bill has been introduced into the State A legislature. The communication is a lobbying communication because it refers to and reflects a view on a specific legislative proposal. Therefore, W is influencing legislation.

Example 8. (i) Taxpayer Y represents citrus fruit growers. Y writes a letter to a United States senator discussing how pesticide O has benefited citrus fruit growers and disputing problems linked to its use. The letter discusses a bill pending in Congress and states in part:

> This bill would prohibit the use of pesticide O. If citrus growers are unable to use this pesticide, their crop yields will be severely reduced, leading to higher prices for consumers and lower profits, even bankruptcy, for growers.

(ii) Y's views on the bill are reflected in this statement. Thus, the communication is a lobbying communication, and Y is influencing legislation.

Example 9. (i) B, the president of Taxpayer Z, an insurance company, meets with Q, who chairs the X state legislature's committee with jurisdiction over laws regulating insurance companies, to discuss the possibility of legislation to address current problems with surplus-line companies. B recommends that legislation be introduced that would create minimum capital and surplus requirements for surplus-line companies and create clearer guidelines concerning the risks that surplus-line companies can insure. B's discussion with Q is a lobbying communication because B refers to and reflects a view on a specific legislative proposal. Therefore, Z is influencing legislation.

(ii) Q is not convinced that the market for surplus-line companies is substantial enough to warrant such legislation and requests that B provide information on the amount and types of risks covered by surplus-line companies. After the meeting, B has employees of Z prepare estimates of the percentage of property and casualty insurance risks handled by surplus-line companies. B sends the estimates with a cover letter that simply refers to the enclosed materials. Although B's follow-up letter to Q does not refer to specific legislation or reflect a view on such legislation, B's letter supports the views reflected in the earlier communication. Therefore, the letter is a lobbying communication and Z is influencing legislation.

(c) Purpose for engaging in an activity—

(1) In general. The purposes for engaging in an activity are determined based on all the facts and circumstances. Facts and circumstances include, but are not limited to—

(i) Whether the activity and the lobbying communication are proximate in time;

(ii) Whether the activity and the lobbying communication relate to similar subject matter;

(iii) Whether the activity is performed at the request of, under the direction of, or on behalf of a person making the lobbying communication;

(iv) Whether the results of the activity are also used for a nonlobbying purpose; and

(v) Whether, at the time the taxpayer engages in the activity, there is specific legislation to which the activity relates.

(2) Multiple purposes. If a taxpayer engages in an activity both for the purpose of making or supporting a lobbying communication and for some nonlobbying purpose, the taxpayer must treat the activity as engaged in partially for a lobbying purpose and partially for a nonlobbying purpose. This division of the activity must result in a reasonable allocation of costs to influencing legislation. See section 1.162–28 (allocation rules for certain expenditures to which section 162(e)(1) applies). A taxpayer's treatment of these multiple-purpose activities will, in general, not result in a reasonable allocation if it allocates to influencing legislation—

(i) Only the incremental amount of costs that would not have been incurred but for the lobbying purpose; or

(ii) An amount based solely on the number of purposes for engaging in that activity without regard to the relative importance of those purposes.

(3) Activities treated as having no purpose to influence legislation. A taxpayer that engages in any of the following activities is treated as having done so without a purpose of making or supporting a lobbying communication—

(i) Before evidencing a purpose to influence any specific legislation referred to in paragraph (c)(3)(i)(A) or (B) of this section (or similar legislation)—

(A) Determining the existence or procedural status of specific legislation, or the time, place, and subject of any hearing to be held by a legislative body with respect to specific legislation; or

(B) Preparing routine, brief summaries of the provisions of specific legislation;

(ii) Performing an activity for purposes of complying with the requirements of any law (for example, satisfying state or federal securities law filing requirements);

(iii) Reading any publications available to the general public or viewing or listening to other mass media communications; and

(iv) Merely attending a widely attended speech.

(4) Examples. The provisions of this paragraph (c) are illustrated by the following examples.

Example 1. (i) *Facts.* In 1997, Agency F issues proposed regulations relating to the business of Taxpayer W. There is no specific legislation during 1997 that is similar to the regulatory proposal. W undertakes a study of the impact of the proposed regulations on its business. W incorporates the results of that study in comments sent to Agency F in 1997. In 1998, legislation is introduced in Congress that is similar to the regulatory proposal. Also in 1998, W writes a letter to Senator P stating that it opposes the proposed legislation. W encloses with the letter a copy of the comments it sent to Agency F.

(ii) *Analysis.* W's letter to Senator P refers to and reflects a view on specific legislation and therefore is a lobbying communication. Although W's study of the impact of the proposed regulations is proximate in time and similar in subject matter to its lobbying communication, W performed the study and incorporated the results in comments sent to Agency F when no legislation with a similar subject matter was pending (a nonlobbying use). On these facts, W engaged in the study solely for a nonlobbying purpose.

Example 2. (i) *Facts.* The governor of State Q proposes a budget that includes a proposed sales tax on electricity. Using its records of electricity consumption, Taxpayer Y estimates the additional costs that the budget proposal would impose upon its business. In the same year, Y writes to members of the state legislature and explains that it opposes the proposed sales tax. In its letter, Y includes its estimate of the costs that the sales tax would impose on its business. Y does not demonstrate any other use of its estimates.

(ii) *Analysis.* The letter is a lobbying communication (because it refers to and reflects a view on specific legislation, the governor's proposed budget). Y's estimate of additional costs under the proposal supports the lobbying communication, is proximate in time and similar in subject matter to a specific legislative proposal then in existence, and is not used for a nonlobbying purpose. Based on these facts, Y estimated its additional costs under the budget proposal solely to support the lobbying communication.

Example 3. (i) *Facts.* A senator in the State Q legislature announces her intention to introduce legislation to require health insurers to cover a particular medical procedure in all policies sold in the state. Taxpayer Y has different policies for two groups of employees, one of which covers the procedure and one of which does not. After the bill is introduced, Y's legislative affairs staff asks Y's human resources staff to estimate the additional cost to cover the procedure for both groups of employees. Y's human resources staff prepares a study estimating Y's increased costs and forwards it to the legislative affairs staff. Y's legislative staff then writes to members of the state legislature and explains that it opposes the proposed change in insurance coverage based on the study. Y's legislative affairs staff thereafter forwards the study, prepared for its use in opposing the statutory proposal, to its labor relations staff for use in negotiations with employees scheduled to begin later in the year.

(ii) *Analysis.* The letter to legislators is a lobbying communication (because it refers to and reflects a view on specific legislation). The activity of estimating Y's additional costs under the proposed legislation relate to the same subject as the lobbying communication, occurs close in time to the lobbying communication, is conducted at the request of a person making a lobbying communication, and relates to specific legislation then in existence. Although Y used the study in its labor negotiations, mere use for that purpose does not establish that Y estimated its additional costs under the proposed legislation in part for a nonlobbying purpose. Thus, based on all the facts and circumstances, Y estimated the additional costs it would incur under the proposal solely to make or support the lobbying communication.

Example 4. (i) *Facts.* After several years of developmental work under various contracts, in 1996, Taxpayer A contracts with the Department of Defense (DOD) to produce a prototype of a new generation military aircraft. A is aware that DOD will be able to fund the contract only if Congress appropriates an amount for that purpose in the upcoming appropriations process. In 1997, A conducts simulation tests of the aircraft and revises the specifications of the aircraft's expected performance capabilities, as required under the contract. A submits the results of the tests and the revised specifications to DOD. In 1998, Congress considers legislation to appropriate funds for the contract. In that connection, A summarizes the results of the simulation tests and of the aircraft's expected performance capabilities, and submits the summary to interested members of Congress with a cover letter that encourages them to support appropriations of funds for the contract.

(ii) *Analysis.* The letter is a lobbying communication (because it refers to specific legislation (i.e., appropriations) and requests passage). The described activities in 1996, 1997, and 1998 relate to the same subject as the lobbying communication. The summary was prepared specifically for, and close in time to, that communication. Based on these facts, the summary was prepared solely for a lobbying purpose. In contrast, A conducted the tests and revised the specifications to comply with its production contract with DOD. A conducted the tests and revised the specifications solely for a nonlobbying purpose.

Example 5. (i) *Facts.* C, president of Taxpayer W, travels to the state capital to attend a two-day conference on new manufacturing processes. C plans to spend a third day in the capital meeting with state legislators to explain why W opposes a pending bill unrelated to the subject of the conference. At the meetings with the legislators, C makes lobbying communications by referring to and reflecting a view on the pending bill.

(ii) *Analysis.* C's traveling expenses (transportation and meals and lodging) are partially for the purpose of making or supporting the lobbying communications and partially for a nonlobbying purpose. As a result, under paragraph (c)(2) of this section, W must reasonably allocate C's traveling expenses between these two purposes. Allocating to influencing legislation only C's incremental transportation expenses (i.e., the taxi fare to meet with the state legislators) does not result in a reasonable allocation of traveling expenses.

Example 6. (i) *Facts.* On February 1, 1997, a bill is introduced in Congress that would affect Company E. Employees in E's legislative affairs department, as is customary, prepare a brief summary of the bill and periodically confirm the procedural status of the bill through conversations with employees and members of Congress. On March 31, 1997, the head of E's legislative affairs department meets with E's President to request that B, a chemist, temporarily help the legislative affairs department analyze the bill. The President agrees, and suggests that B also be assigned to draft a position letter in opposition to the bill. Employees of the legislative affairs department continue to confirm periodically the procedural status of the bill. On October 31, 1997, B's position letter in opposition to the bill is delivered to members of Congress.

(ii) *Analysis.* B's letter is a lobbying communication because it refers to and reflects a view on specific legislation. Under paragraph (c)(3)(i) of this section, the assignment of B to assist the legislative affairs department in analyzing the bill and in drafting a position letter in opposition to the bill evidences a purpose to influence legislation. Neither the activity of periodically confirming the procedural status of the bill nor the activity of preparing the routine, brief summary of the bill before March 31 constitutes influencing legislation. In contrast, periodically confirming the procedural status of the bill on or after March 31 relates to the same subject as, and is close in time to, the lobbying communication and is used for no nonlobbying purpose. Consequently, after March 31, E determined the procedural status of the bill for the purpose of supporting the lobbying communication by B.

(d) Lobbying communication made by another. If a taxpayer engages in activities for a purpose of supporting a lobbying communication to be made by another person (or by a group of persons), the taxpayer's activities are treated under paragraph (b) of this section as influencing legislation. For example, if a taxpayer or an employee of the taxpayer (as a volunteer or otherwise) engages in an activity to assist a trade association in preparing its lobbying communication, the taxpayer's activities are influencing legislation even if the lobbying communication is made by the trade association and not the taxpayer. If, however, the taxpayer's employee, acting outside the employee's scope of employment, volunteers to engage in those activities, then the taxpayer is not influencing legislation.

(e) No lobbying communication. Paragraph (e) of this section applies if a taxpayer engages in an activity for a purpose of making or supporting a lobbying communication, but no lobbying communication that the activity supports has yet been made.

(1) Before the filing date. Under this paragraph (e)(1), if on the filing date of the return for any taxable year the taxpayer no longer expects, under any reasonably foreseeable circumstances, that a lobbying communication will be made that is supported by the activity, then the taxpayer will be treated as if it did not engage in the activity for a purpose of making or supporting a lobbying communication. Thus, the taxpayer need not treat any amount allocated to that activity for that year under section 1.162–28 as an amount to which section 162(e)(1)(A) applies. The filing date for purposes of paragraph (e) of this section is the earlier of the time the taxpayer files its timely return for the year or the due date of the timely return.

(2) After the filing date—(i) In general. If, at any time after the filing date, the taxpayer no longer expects, under any reasonably foreseeable circumstances, that a lobbying communication will be made that is supported by the activity, then any amount previously allocated under section 1.162–28 to the activity and disallowed under section 162(e)(1)(A) is treated as an amount that is not subject to section 162(e)(1)(A) and that is paid or incurred only at the time the taxpayer no longer expects that a lobbying communication will be made.

(ii) Special rule for certain tax-exempt organizations. For a tax-exempt organization subject to section 6033(e), the amounts described in paragraph (e)(2)(i) of this section are treated as reducing (but not below zero) its expenditures to which section 162(e)(1) applies beginning with that year and continuing for subsequent years to the extent not treated in prior years as reducing those expenditures.

(f) Anti-avoidance rule. If a taxpayer, alone or with others, structures its activities with a principal purpose of achieving results that are unreasonable in light of the purposes of section 162(e)(1)(A) and section 6033(e), the Commissioner can recast the taxpayer's activities for federal tax purposes as appropriate to achieve tax results that are consistent with the intent of section 162(e)(1)(A), section 6033(e) (if applicable), and this section, and the pertinent facts and circumstances.

(g) Taxpayer defined. For purposes of this section, a taxpayer includes a tax-exempt organization subject to section 6033(e).

* * *

CHARITABLE CONTRIBUTIONS

§ 1.170A-1. Charitable, etc., contributions and gifts; allowance of deduction.

(a) Allowance of deduction. Any charitable contribution, as defined in section 170(c), actually paid during the taxable year is allowable as a deduction in computing taxable income irrespective of the method of accounting employed or of the date on which the contribution is pledged. However, charitable contributions by corporations may under certain circumstances be deductible even though not paid during the taxable year as provided in section 170(a)(2) and § 1.170A–11. For rules relating to recordkeeping and return requirements in support of deductions for charitable contributions (whether by an itemizing or nonitemizing taxpayer) see §§ 1.170A–13 (generally applicable to contributions on or before July 30, 2018), 1.170A–14, 1.170A–15, 1.170A–16, 1.170A–17, and 1.170A–18. The deduction is subject to the limitations of section 170(b) and § 1.170A–8 or § 1.170A–11. Subject to the provisions of section 170(d) and ss 1.170A–10 and 1.170A–11, certain excess charitable contributions made by individuals and corporations shall be treated as paid in certain succeeding taxable years. * * * For a special rule relating to the computation of the amount of the deduction with respect to a charitable contribution of certain ordinary income or capital gain property, see section 170(e) and § 1.170A–4 and § 1.170A–4A. For rules for postponing the time for deduction of a charitable contribution of a future interest in tangible personal property, see section 170(a)(3) and § 1.170A–5. For rules with respect to transfers in trust and of partial interests in property, see section 170(e), section 170(f)(2) and (3), § 1.170A–4, § 1.170A–6, and § 1.170A–7. For definition of the term "section 170(b)(1)(A) organization," see § 1.170A–9. For valuation of a remainder interest in real property, see section 170(f)(4) and the regulations thereunder. The deduction for charitable contributions is subject to verification by the district director.

(b) Time of making contribution. Ordinarily, a contribution is made at the time delivery is effected. The unconditional delivery or mailing of a check which subsequently clears in due course will constitute an effective contribution on the date of delivery or mailing. If a taxpayer unconditionally delivers or mails a properly endorsed stock certificate to a charitable donee or the donee's agent, the gift is completed on the date of delivery or, if such certificate is received in the ordinary course of the mails, on the date of mailing. If the donor delivers the stock certificate to his bank or broker as the donor's agent, or to the issuing corporation or its agent, for transfer into the name of the donee, the gift is completed on the date the stock is transferred on the books of the corporation. For rules relating to the date of payment of a contribution consisting of a future interest in tangible personal property, see section 170(a)(3) and § 1.170A–5.

(c) Value of a contribution in property. (1) If a charitable contribution is made in property other than money, the amount of the contribution is the fair market value of the property at the time of the contribution reduced as provided in section 170(e)(1) and paragraph (a) of § 1.170A–4, or section 170(e)(3) and paragraph (c) of § 1.170A–4A.

(2) The fair market value is the price at which the property would change hands between a willing buyer and a willing seller, neither being under any compulsion to buy or sell and both having reasonable knowledge of relevant facts. If the contribution is made in property of a type which the taxpayer sells in the course of his business, the fair market value is the price which the taxpayer would have received if he had sold the contributed property in the usual market in which he customarily sells, at the time and place of the contribution and, in the case of a contribution of goods in quantity, in the quantity contributed. The usual market of a manufacturer or other producer consists of the wholesalersor other distributors to or through whom he customarily sells, but if he sells only at retail the usual market consists of his retail customers.

(3) If a donor makes a charitable contribution of property, such as stock in trade, at a time when he could not reasonably have been expected to realize its usual selling price, the value of the gift is not the usual selling price but is the amount for which the quantity of property contributed would have been sold by the donor at the time of the contribution.

(4) Any costs and expenses pertaining to the contributed property which were incurred in taxable years preceding the year of contribution and are properly reflected in the opening inventory for the year of contribution must be removed from inventory and are not a part of the cost of goods sold for purposes of determining gross income for the year of contribution. Any costs and expenses pertaining to the contributed property which are incurred in the year of contribution and would, under the method of accounting used, be properly reflected in the cost of goods sold for such year are to be treated as part of the costs of goods sold for such year. If costs and expenses incurred in producing or acquiring the contributed property are, under the method of accounting used, properly deducted under section 162 or other section of the Code, such costs and expenses will be allowed as deductions for the taxable year in which they are paid or incurred whether or not such year is the year of the contribution. Any such costs and expenses which are treated as part of the cost of goods sold for the year of contribution, and any such costs and expenses which are properly deducted under section 162 or other section of the Code, are not to be treated under any section of the Code as resulting in any basis for the contributed property. Thus, for example, the contributed property has no basis for purposes of determining under section 170(e)(1)(A) and paragraph (a) of § 1.170A-4 the amount of gain which would have been recognized if such property had been sold by the donor at its fair market value at the time of its contribution. The amount of any charitable contribution for the taxable year is not to be reduced by the amount of any costs or expenses pertaining to the contributed property which was properly deducted under section 162 or other section of the Code for any taxable year preceding the year of the contribution. This subparagraph applies only to property which was held by the taxpayer for sale in the course of a trade or business. * * *

(5) Transfers of property to an organization described in section 170(c) which bear a direct relationship to the taxpayer's trade or business and which are made with a reasonable expectation of financial return commensurate with the amount of the transfer may constitute allowable deductions as trade or business expenses rather than as charitable contributions. See section 162 and the regulations thereunder. For payments of transfers to an entity described in section 170(a) by a taxpayer carrying on a trade or business, see § 1.162-15(a).

* * *

(e) Transfers subject to a condition or power. If as of the date of a gift a transfer for charitable purposes is dependent upon the performance of some act or the happening of a precedent event in order that it might become effective, no deduction is allowable unless the possibility that the charitable transfer will not become effective is so remote as to be negligible. If an interest in property passes to, or is vested in, charity on the date of the gift and the interest would be defeated by the subsequent performance of some act or the happening of some event, the possibility of occurrence of which appears on the date of the gift to be so remote as to be negligible, the deduction is allowable. For example, A transfers land to a city government for as long as the land is used by the city for a public park. If on the date of the gift the city does plan to use the land for a park and the possibility that the city will not use the land for a public park is so remote as to be negligible, A is entitled to a deduction under section 170 for his charitable contribution.

* * *

(g) Contributions of services. No deduction is allowable under section 170 for a contribution of services. However, unreimbursed expenditures made incident to the rendition of services to an organization contributions to which are deductible may constitute a deductible contribution. For example, the cost of a uniform without general utility which is required to be worn in performing donated services is deductible. Similarly, out-of-pocket transportation expenses necessarily incurred in performing donated services are deductible. Reasonable expenditures for meals and lodging necessarily incurred while away from home in the course of performing donated services also are deductible. For the purposes of this paragraph, the phrase "while away from home" has the same meaning as that phrase is used for purposes of section 162 and the regulations thereunder.

(h) Payment in exchange for consideration—

(1) Burden on taxpayer to show that all or part of payment is a charitable contribution or gift. No part of a payment that a taxpayer makes to or for the use of an organization described in section 170(c) that is in consideration for (as defined in section 1.170A–13(f)(6)) goods or services (as defined in paragraph (h)(4)(ii) of this section) is a contribution or gift within the meaning of section 170(c) unless the taxpayer—

(i) Intends to make a payment in an amount that exceeds the fair market value of the goods or services; and

(ii) Makes a payment in an amount that exceeds the fair market value of the goods or services.

(2) Limitation on amount deductible—(i) In general. The charitable contribution deduction under section 170(a) for a payment a taxpayer makes partly in consideration for goods or services may not exceed the excess of—

(A) The amount of any cash paid and the fair market value of any property (other than cash) transferred by the taxpayer to an organization described in section 170(c); over

(B) The fair market value of the goods or services the organization provides in return.

(ii) Special rules. For special limits on the deduction for charitable contributions of ordinary income and capital gain property, see section 170(e) and sections 1.170A–4 and 1.170A–4A.

(3) Payments resulting in state or local tax benefits—(i) State or local tax credits. Except as provided in paragraph (h)(3)(vi) of this section, if a taxpayer makes a payment or transfers property to or for the use of an entity described in section 170(c), the amount of the taxpayer's charitable contribution deduction under section 170(a) is reduced by the amount of any state or local tax credit that the taxpayer receives or expects to receive in consideration for the taxpayer's payment or transfer.

(ii) State or local tax deductions—(A) In general. If a taxpayer makes a payment or transfers property to or for the use of an entity described in section 170(c), and the taxpayer receives or expects to receive state or local tax deductions that do not exceed the amount of the taxpayer's payment or the fair market value of the property transferred by the taxpayer to the entity, the taxpayer is not required to reduce its charitable contribution deduction under section 170(a) on account of the state or local tax deductions.

(B) Excess state or local tax deductions. If the taxpayer receives or expects to receive a state or local tax deduction that exceeds the amount of the taxpayer's payment or the fair market value of the property transferred, the taxpayer's charitable contribution deduction under section 170(a) is reduced.

(iii) In consideration for. For purposes of paragraph (h) of this section, the term in consideration for has the meaning set forth in paragraph (h)(4)(i) of this section.

(iv) Amount of reduction. For purposes of paragraph (h)(3)(i) of this section, the amount of any state or local tax credit is the maximum credit allowable that corresponds to the amount of the taxpayer's payment or transfer to the entity described in section 170(c).

(v) State or local tax. For purposes of paragraph (h)(3) of this section, the term state or local tax means a tax imposed by a State, a possession of the United States, or by a political subdivision of any of the foregoing, or by the District of Columbia.

(vi) Exception. Paragraph (h)(3)(i) of this section shall not apply to any payment or transfer of property if the total amount of the state and local tax credits received or expected to be received by the taxpayer is 15 percent or less of the taxpayer's payment, or

15 percent or less of the fair market value of the property transferred by the taxpayer.

(vii) Examples. The following examples illustrate the provisions of this paragraph (h)(3). The examples in paragraph (h)(6) of this section are not illustrative for purposes of this paragraph (h)(3).

(A) **Example 1.** A, an individual, makes a payment of $1,000 to X, an entity described in section 170(c). In exchange for the payment, A receives or expects to receive a state tax credit of 70 percent of the amount of A's payment to X. Under paragraph (h)(3)(i) of this section, A's charitable contribution deduction is reduced by $700 (0.70 x $1,000). This reduction occurs regardless of whether A is able to claim the state tax credit in that year. Thus, A's charitable contribution deduction for the $1,000 payment to X may not exceed $300.

(B) **Example 2.** B, an individual, transfers a painting to Y, an entity described in section 170(c). At the time of the transfer, the painting has a fair market value of $100,000. In exchange for the painting, B receives or expects to receive a state tax credit equal to 10 percent of the fair market value of the painting. Under paragraph (h)(3)(vi) of this section, B is not required to apply the general rule of paragraph (h)(3)(i) of this section because the amount of the tax credit received or expected to be received by B does not exceed 15 percent of the fair market value of the property transferred to Y. Accordingly, the amount of B's charitable contribution deduction for the transfer of the painting is not reduced under paragraph (h)(3)(i) of this section.

(C) **Example 3.** C, an individual, makes a payment of $1,000 to Z, an entity described in section 170(c). In exchange for the payment, under state M law, C is entitled to receive a state tax deduction equal to the amount paid by C to Z. Under paragraph (h)(3)(ii)(A) of this section, C's charitable contribution deduction under section 170(a) is not required to be reduced on account of C's state tax deduction for C's payment to Z.

(viii) Safe harbor for payments by C corporations and specified passthrough entities. For payments by a C corporation or by a specified passthrough entity to an entity described in section 170(c), where the C corporation or specified passthrough entity receives or expects to receive a State or local tax credit that reduces the charitable contribution deduction for such payments under paragraph (h)(3) of this section, see § 1.162–15(a)(3) (providing safe harbors under section 162(a) to the extent of that reduction).

(ix) Safe harbor for individuals. Under certain circumstances, an individual who itemizes deductions and makes a payment to an entity described in section 170(c) in consideration for a State or local tax credit may treat the portion of such payment for which a charitable contribution deduction is disallowed under paragraph (h)(3) of this section as a payment of State or local taxes under section 164. See § 1.164–3(j), providing a safe harbor for certain payments by individuals in exchange for State or local tax credits.

(x) Effective/applicability date. This paragraph (h)(3) applies to amounts paid or property transferred by a taxpayer after August 27, 2018.

(4) Definitions. For purposes of this paragraph (h), the following definitions apply:

(i) In consideration for. A taxpayer receives goods or services in consideration for a taxpayer's payment or transfer to an entity described in section 170(c) if, at the time the taxpayer makes the payment to such entity, the taxpayer receives or expects to receive goods or services from that entity or any other party in return.

(ii) Goods or services. Goods or services means cash, property, services, benefits, and privileges.

(iii) Applicability date. The definitions provided in this paragraph (h)(4) are applicable to amounts paid or property transferred on or after December 17, 2019.

(5) Certain goods or services disregarded. For purposes of section 170(a) and paragraphs (h)(1) and (h)(2) of this section, goods or services described in section 1.170A–13(f)(8)(i) or section 1.170A13(f)(9)(i) are disregarded.

(6) Donee estimates of the value of goods or services may be treated as fair market value—(i) In general. For purposes of section 170(a), a taxpayer may rely on either a contemporaneous written acknowledgment provided under section 170(f)(8) and section 1.170A–13(f) or a written disclosure statement provided under section 6115 for the fair market value of any goods or services provided to the taxpayer by the donee organization.

(ii) Exception. A taxpayer may not treat an estimate of the value of goods or services as their fair market value if the taxpayer knows, or has reason to know, that such treatment is unreasonable. For example, if a taxpayer knows, or has reason to know, that there is an error in an estimate provided by an organization described in section 170(c) pertaining to goods or services that have a readily ascertainable value, it is unreasonable for the taxpayer to treat the estimate as the fair market value of the goods or services. Similarly, if a taxpayer is a dealer in the type of goods or services provided in consideration for the taxpayer's payment and knows, or has reason to know, that the estimate is in error, it is unreasonable for the taxpayer to treat the estimate as the fair market value of the goods or services.

(7) Examples. The following examples illustrate the rules of this paragraph (h).

Example 1. Certain goods or services disregarded. Taxpayer makes a $50 payment to Charity B, an organization described in section 170(c), in exchange for a family membership. The family membership entitles Taxpayer and members of Taxpayer's family to certain benefits. These benefits include free admission to weekly poetry readings, discounts on merchandise sold by B in its gift shop or by mail order, and invitations to special events for members only, such as lectures or informal receptions. When B first offers its membership package for the year, B reasonably projects that each special event for members will have a cost to B, excluding any allocable overhead, of $5 or less per person attending the event. Because the family membership benefits are disregarded pursuant to section 1.170A–13(f)(8)(i), Taxpayer may treat the $50 payment as a contribution or gift within the meaning of section 170(c), regardless of Taxpayer's intent and whether or not the payment exceeds the fair market value of the goods or services. Furthermore, any charitable contribution deduction available to Taxpayer may be calculated without regard to the membership benefits.

Example 2. Treatment of good faith estimate at auction as fair market value. Taxpayer attends an auction held by Charity C, an organization described in section 170(c). Prior to the auction, C publishes a catalog that meets the requirements for a written disclosure statement under section 6115(a) (including C's good faith estimate of the value of items that will be available for bidding). A representative of C gives a copy of the catalog to each individual (including Taxpayer) who attends the auction. Taxpayer notes that in the catalog C's estimate of the value of a vase is $100. Taxpayer has no reason to doubt the accuracy of this estimate. Taxpayer successfully bids and pays $500 for the vase. Because Taxpayer knew, prior to making her payment, that the estimate in the catalog was less than the amount of her payment, Taxpayer satisfies the requirement of paragraph (h)(1)(i) of this section. Because Taxpayer makes a payment in an amount that exceeds that estimate, Taxpayer satisfies the requirements of paragraph (h)(1)(ii) of this section. Taxpayer may treat C's estimate of the value of the vase as its fair market value in determining the amount of her charitable contribution deduction.

Example 3. Good Faith estimate not in error. Taxpayer makes a $200 payment to Charity D, an organization described in section 170(c). In return for Taxpayer's payment, D gives Taxpayer a book that Taxpayer could buy at retail prices typically ranging from $18 to $25. D provides Taxpayer with a good faith estimate, in a written disclosure statement under section 6115(a), of $20 for the value of the book. Because the estimate is within the range of typical retail prices for the book, the estimate contained in the written disclosure statement is not in error. Although Taxpayer knows that the book is sold for as much as $25, Taxpayer may treat the estimate of $20 as the fair market value of the book in determining the amount of his charitable contribution deduction.

* * *

§ 1.170A-4. Reduction in amount of charitable contributions of certain appreciated property.

(a) Amount of reduction. Section 170(e)(1) requires that the amount of the charitable contribution which would be taken into account under section 170(a) without regard to section 170(e) shall be reduced before applying the percentage limitations under section 170(b):

(1) In the case of a contribution by an individual or by a corporation of ordinary income property, as defined in paragraph (b)(1) of this section, by the amount of gain (hereinafter in this section referred to as ordinary income) which would have been recognized as gain which is not long-term capital gain if the property had been sold by the donor at its fair market value at the time of its contribution to the charitable organization,

* * *

Section 170(e)(1) and this paragraph do not apply to reduce the amount of the charitable contribution where, by reason of the transfer of the contributed property, ordinary income or capital gain is recognized by the donor in the same taxable year in which the contribution is made. Thus, where income or gain is recognized under section 453(d) upon the transfer of an installment obligation to a charitable organization, or under section 454(b) upon the transfer of an obligation issued at a discount to such an organization, or upon the assignment of income to such an organization, section 170(e)(1) and this paragraph do not apply if recognition of the income or gain occurs in the same taxable year in which the contribution is made. Section 170(e)(1) and this paragraph apply to a charitable contribution of an interest in ordinary income property or section 170(e) capital gain property which is described in paragraph (b) of § 1.170A-6, or paragraph (b) of § 1.170A-7. For purposes of applying section 170(e)(1) and this paragraph it is immaterial whether the charitable contribution is made "to" the charitable organization or whether it is made "for the use of" the charitable organization. See § 1.170A-8(a)(2).

(b) Definitions and other rules. For purposes of this section:

(1) Ordinary income property. The term "ordinary income property" means property any portion of the gain on which would not have been long term capital gain if the property had been sold by the donor at its fair market value at the time of its contribution to the charitable organization. Such term includes, for example, property held by the donor primarily for sale to customers in the ordinary course of his trade or business, a work of art created by the donor, a manuscript prepared by the donor, letters and memorandums prepared by or for the donor, a capital asset held by the donor for not more than 1 year (6 months for taxable years beginning before 1977; 9 months for taxable years beginning in 1977), and stock described in section 306(a), 341(a), or 1248(a) to the extent that, after applying such section, gain on its disposition would not have been long-term capital gain. The term does not include an income interest in respect of which a deduction is allowed under section 170(f)(2)(B) and paragraph (c) of § 1.170A–6.

(2) Section 170(e) capital gain property. The term "section 170(e) capital gain property" means property any portion of the gain on which would have been treated as long-term capital gain if the property had been sold by the donor at its fair market value at the time of its contribution to the charitable organization and which:

(i) Is contributed to or for the use of a private foundation, as defined in section 509(a) and the regulations thereunder, other than a private foundation described in section 170(b)(1)(E),

(ii) Constitutes tangible personal property contributed to or for the use of a charitable organization, other than a private foundation to which subdivision (i) of this subparagraph applies, which is put to an unrelated use by the charitable organization within the meaning of subparagraph (3) of this paragraph, or

(iii) Constitutes property not described in subdivision (i) or (ii) of this subparagraph which is 30-percent capital gain property to which an election under paragraph (d)(2) of § 1.170A–8 applies.

For purposes of this subparagraph a fixture which is intended to be severed from real property shall be treated as tangible personal property.

(3) Unrelated use—(i) In general. The term "unrelated use" means a use which is unrelated to the purpose or function constituting the basis of the charitable organization's exemption under section 501 or, in the case of a contribution of property to a governmental unit, the use of such property by such unit for other than exclusively public purposes. For example, if a painting contributed to an educational institution is used by that organization for educational purposes by being placed in its library for display and study by art students, the use is not an unrelated use; but if the painting is sold and the proceeds used by the organization for educational purposes, the use of the property is an unrelated use. If furnishings contributed to a charitable organization are used by it in its offices and buildings in the course of carrying out its functions, the use of the property is not an unrelated use. If a set or collection of items of tangible personal property is contributed to a charitable organization or governmental unit, the use of the set or collection is not an unrelated use if the donee sells or otherwise disposes of only an insubstantial portion of the set or collection. The use by a trust of tangible personal property contributed to it for the benefit of a charitable organization is an unrelated use if the use by the trust is one which would have been unrelated if made by the charitable organization.

(ii) Proof of use. For purposes of applying subparagraph (2)(ii) of this paragraph, a taxpayer who makes a charitable contribution of tangible personal property to or for the use of a charitable organization or governmental unit may treat such property as not being put to an unrelated use by the donee if:

(a) He establishes that the property is not in fact put to an unrelated use by the donee, or

(b) At the time of the contribution or at the time the contribution is treated as made, it is reasonable to anticipate that the property will not be put to an unrelated use by the donee. In the case of a contribution of tangible personal property to or for the use of a museum, if the object donated is of a general type normally retained by such museum or other museums for museum purposes, it will be reasonable for the donor to anticipate, unless he has actual knowledge to the contrary, that the object will not be put to an unrelated use by the donee, whether or not the object is later sold or exchanged by the donee.

(4) Property used in trade or business. For purposes of applying subparagraphs (1) and (2) of this paragraph, property which is used in the trade or business, as defined in section 1231(b), shall be treated as a capital asset, except that any gain in respect of such property which would have been recognized if the property had been sold by the donor at its fair market value at the time of its contribution to the charitable organization shall be treated as ordinary income to the extent that such gain would have constituted ordinary income by reason of the application of section 617(d)(1), 1245(a), 1250(a), 1251(c), 1252(a), or 1254(a).

* * *

(c) Allocation of basis and gain—(1) In general. Except as provided in subparagraph (2) of this paragraph:

(i) If a taxpayer makes a charitable contribution of less than his entire interest in appreciated property, whether or not the transfer is made in trust, as, for example, in the case of a transfer of appreciated property to a pooled income fund described in section 642(c)(5) and § 1.642(c)–5, and is allowed a deduction under section 170 for a portion of the fair market value of such property, then for purposes of applying the reduction rules of section 170(e)(1) and this section to the contributed portion of the property the taxpayer's adjusted basis in such property at the time of the contribution shall be allocated under section 170(e)(2) between the contributed portion of the property and the noncontributed portion.

(ii) The adjusted basis of the contributed portion of the property shall be that portion of the adjusted basis of the entire property which bears the same ratio to the total adjusted basis as the fair market value of the contributed portion of the property bears to the fair market value of the entire property.

(iii) The ordinary income and the long-term capital gain which shall be taken into account in applying section 170(e)(1) and paragraph (a) of this section to the contributed portion of the property shall be the amount of gain which would have been recognized as ordinary income and long-term capital gain if such contributed portion had been sold by the donor at its fair market value at the time of its contribution to the charitable organization.

(2) Bargain sale. (i) Section 1011(b) and § 1.1011–2 apply to bargain sales of property to charitable organizations. For purposes of applying the reduction rules of section 170(e)(1) and this section to the contributed portion of the property in the case of a bargain sale, there shall be allocated under section 1011(b) to the contributed portion of the property that portion of the adjusted basis of the entire property that bears the same ratio to the total adjusted basis as the fair market value of the contributed portion of the property bears to the fair market value of the entire property. For purposes of applying section 170(e)(1) and paragraph (a) of this section to the contributed portion of the property in such a case, there shall be allocated to the contributed portion the amount of gain that is not recognized on the bargain sale but that would have been recognized if such contributed portion had been sold by the donor at its fair market value at the time of its contribution to the charitable organization.

(ii) The term "bargain sale", as used in this subparagraph, means a transfer of property which is in part a sale or exchange of the property and in part a charitable contribution, as defined in section 170(c), of the property.

(3) Ratio of ordinary income and capital gain. For purposes of applying subparagraphs (1)(iii) and (2)(i) of this paragraph, the amount of ordinary income (or long-term capital gain) which would have been recognized if the contributed portion of the property had been sold by the donor at its fair market value at the time of its contribution shall be that amount which bears the same ratio to the ordinary income (or long-term capital gain) which would have been recognized if the entire property had been sold by the donor at its fair market value at the time of its contribution as (i) the fair market value of the contributed portion at such time bears to (ii) the fair market value of the entire property at such time. In the case of a bargain sale, the fair market value of the contributed portion for purposes of subdivision (i) is the amount determined by subtracting from the fair market value of the entire property the amount realized on the sale.

(4) Donee's basis of property acquired. The adjusted basis of the contributed portion of the property, as determined under subparagraph (1) or (2) of this paragraph, shall be used by the donee in applying to the contributed portion such provisions as section 514(a)(1), relating to adjusted basis of debt-financed property; section 1015(a), relating to basis of property acquired by gift; section 4940(c)(4), relating to capital gains and losses in determination of net investment income; and section 4942(f)(2)(B), relating to net short-term capital gain in determination of tax on failure to distribute income. The fair market value of the contributed portion of the property at the time of the contribution shall not be used by the donee as the basis of such contributed portion.

* * *

§ 1.170A–5. Future interests in tangible personal property.

(a) In general. (1) A contribution consisting of a transfer of a future interest in tangible personal property shall be treated as made only when all intervening interests in, and rights to the actual possession or enjoyment of, the property:

(i) Have expired, or

(ii) Are held by persons other than the taxpayer or those standing in a relationship to the taxpayer described in section 267(b) and the regulations thereunder, relating to losses, expenses, and interest with respect to transactions between related taxpayers.

(2) Section 170(a)(3) and this section have no application in respect of a transfer of an undivided present interest in property. For example, a contribution of an undivided one-quarter interest in a painting with respect to which the donee is entitled to possession during 3 months of each year shall be treated as made upon the receipt by the donee of a formally executed and acknowledged deed of gift. However, the period of initial possession by the donee may not be deferred in time for more than 1 year.

(3) Section 170(a)(3) and this section have no application in respect of a transfer of a future interest in intangible personal property or in real property. However, a fixture which is intended to be severed from real property shall be treated as tangible personal property. For example, a contribution of a future interest in a chandelier which is attached to a building is considered a contribution which consists of a future interest in tangible personal property if the transferor intends that it be detached from the building at or prior to the time when the charitable organization's right to possession or enjoyment of the chandelier is to commence.

(4) For purposes of section 170(a)(3) and this section, the term "future interest" has generally the same meaning as it has when used in section 2503 and § 25.2503–3 of this chapter (Gift Tax Regulations); it includes reversions, remainders, and other interests or estates, whether vested or contingent, and whether or not supported by a particular interest or estate, which are limited to commence in use, possession, or enjoyment at some future date or time. The term "future interest" includes situations in which a donor purports to give tangible personal property to a charitable organization, but has an understanding, arrangement, agreement, etc., whether written or oral, with the charitable organization which has the effect of reserving to, or retaining in, such donor a right to the use, possession, or enjoyment of the property.

(5) In the case of a charitable contribution of a future interest to which section 170(a)(3) and this section apply the other provisions of section 170 and the regulations thereunder are inapplicable to the contribution until such time as the contribution is treated as made under section 170(a)(3).

(b) Illustrations. The application of this section may be illustrated by the following examples:

Example (1). On December 31, 1970, A, an individual who reports his income on the calendar year basis, conveys by deed of gift to a museum title to a painting, but reserves to himself the right to the use, possession, and enjoyment of the painting during his lifetime. It is assumed that there was no intention to avoid the application of section 170(f)(3)(A) by the conveyance. At the time of the gift the value of the painting is $90,000. Since the contribution consists of a future interest in tangible personal property in which the donor has retained an intervening interest, no contribution is considered to have been made in 1970.

Example (2). Assume the same facts as in example (1) except that on December 31, 1971, A relinquishes all of his right to the use, possession, and enjoyment of the painting and delivers the painting to the museum. Assuming that the value of the painting has increased to $95,000, A is treated as having made a charitable contribution of $95,000 in 1971 for which a deduction is allowable without regard to section 170(f)(3)(A).

Example (3). Assume the same facts as in example (1) except A dies without relinquishing his right to the use, possession, and enjoyment of the painting. Since A did not relinquish his right to the use, possession, and enjoyment of the property during his life, A is treated as not having made a charitable contribution of the painting for income tax purposes.

Example (4). Assume the same facts as in example (1) except A, on December 31, 1971, transfers his interest in the painting to his son, B, who reports his income on the calendar year basis. Since the relationship between A and B is one described in section 267(b), no contribution of the remainder interest in the painting is considered to have been made in 1971.

Example (5). Assume the same facts as in example (4). Also assume that on December 31, 1972, B conveys to the museum the interest measured by A's life. B has made a charitable contribution of the present interest in the painting conveyed to the museum. In addition, since all intervening interests in, and rights to the actual possession or enjoyment of the property, have expired, a charitable contribution of the remainder interest is treated as having been made by A in 1972 for which a deduction is allowable without regard to section 170(f)(3)(A). Such remainder interest is valued according to § 20.2031–7A(c) of this chapter (estate tax regulations), determined by subtracting the value of B's interest measured by A's life expectancy in 1972, and B receives a deduction in 1972 for the life interest measured by A's life expectancy and valued according to Table A(1) in such section.

Example (6). On December 31, 1970, C, an individual who reports his income on the calendar year basis, transfers a valuable painting to a pooled income fund described in section 642(c)(5), which is maintained by a university. C retains for himself for life an income interest in the painting, the remainder interest in the painting being contributed to the university. Since the contribution consists of a future interest in tangible personal property in which the donor has retained an intervening interest, no charitable contribution is considered to have been made in 1970.

Example (7). On January 15, 1972, D, an individual who reports his income on the calendar year basis, transfers a capital asset held for more than 6 months consisting of a valuable painting to a pooled income fund described in section 642(c)(5), which is maintained by a university, and creates an income interest in such painting for E for life. E is an individual not standing in a relationship to D described in section 267(b). The remainder interest in the property is contributed by D to the university. The trustee of the pooled income fund puts the painting to an unrelated use within the meaning of paragraph (b)(3) of § 1.170A–4. Accordingly, D is allowed a deduction under section 170 in 1972 for the present value of the remainder interest in the painting, after reducing such amount under section 170(e)(1)(B)(i) and paragraph (a)(2) of § 1.170A–4. This reduction in the amount of the contribution is required since under paragraph (b)(3) of that section the use by the pooled income fund of the painting is a use which would have been an unrelated use if it had been made by the university.

* * *

§ 1.170A–6. Charitable contributions in trust.

(a) In general. (1) No deduction is allowed under section 170 for the fair market value of a charitable contribution of any interest in property which is less than the donor's entire interest in the property and which is transferred in trust unless the transfer meets the requirements of paragraph (b) or (c) of this section. If the donor's entire interest in the property is transferred in trust and is contributed to a charitable organization described in section 170(c), a deduction is allowed under section 170. Thus, if on July 1, 1972, property is transferred in trust with the requirement that the income of the trust be paid for a term of 20 years to a church and thereafter the remainder be paid to an educational organization described in section 170(b)(1)(A), a deduction is allowed for the value of such property. See section 170(f)(2) and (3)(B), and paragraph (b)(1) of § 1.170A–7.

(2) A deduction is allowed without regard to this section for a contribution of a partial interest in property if such interest is the taxpayer's entire interest in the property, such as an income interest or a remainder interest. If, however, the property in which such partial interest exists was divided in order to create such interest and thus avoid section 170(f)(2), the deduction will not be allowed. Thus, for example, assume that a taxpayer desires to contribute to a charitable organization the reversionary interest in certain stocks and bonds which he owns. If the taxpayer transfers such property in trust with the requirement that the income of the trust be paid to his son for life and that the reversionary interest be paid to himself and immediately after creating the trust contributes the reversionary interest to a charitable organization, no deduction will be allowed under section 170 for the contribution of the taxpayer's entire interest consisting of the reversionary interest in the trust.

(b) Charitable contribution of a remainder interest in trust—(1) In general. No deduction is allowed under section 170 for the fair market value of a charitable contribution of a remainder interest in property which is less than the donor's entire interest in the property and which the donor transfers in trust unless the trust is:

(i) A pooled income fund described in section 642(c)(5) and § 1.642(c)-5,

(ii) A charitable remainder annuity trust described in section 664(d)(1) and § 1.664-2, or

(iii) A charitable remainder unitrust described in section 664(d)(2) and § 1.664-3.

(2) Value of a remainder interest. The fair market value of a remainder interest in a pooled income fund shall be computed under § 1.642(c)-6. The fair market value of a remainder interest in a charitable remainder annuity trust shall be computed under § 1.664-2. The fair market value of a remainder interest in a charitable remainder unitrust shall be computed under § 1.664-4. However, in some cases a reduction in the amount of a charitable contribution of the remainder interest may be required. See section 170(e) and § 1.170A-4.

(c) Charitable contribution of an income interest in trust—(1) In general. No deduction is allowed under section 170 for the fair market value of a charitable contribution of an income interest in property which is less than the donor's entire interest in the property and which the donor transfers in trust unless the income interest is either a guaranteed annuity interest or a unitrust interest, as defined in paragraph (c)(2) of this section, and the grantor is treated as the owner of such interest for purposes of applying section 671, relating to grantors and others treated as substantial owners. See section 4947(a)(2) for the application to such income interests in trust of the provisions relating to private foundations and section 508(e) for rules relating to provisions required in the governing instruments.

(2) Definitions. For purposes of this paragraph:

(i) Guaranteed annuity interest. (A) An income interest is a "guaranteed annuity interest", only if it is an irrevocable right pursuant to the governing instrument of the trust to receive a guaranteed annuity. A guaranteed annuity is an arrangement under which a determinable amount is paid periodically, but not less often than annually, for a specified term or for the life or lives of an individual or individuals, each of whom must be living at the date of transfer and can be ascertained at such date. For example, the annuity may be paid for the life of A plus a term of years. An amount is determinable if the exact amount which must be paid under the conditions specified in the governing instrument of the trust can be ascertained as of the date of transfer. For example, the amount to be paid may be a stated sum for a term, or for the life of an individual, at the expiration of which it may be changed by a specified amount, but it may not be redetermined by reference to a fluctuating index such as the cost of living index. In further illustration, the amount to be paid may be expressed in terms of a fraction or percentage of the cost of living index on the date of transfer.

(B) An income interest is a guaranteed annuity interest only if it is a guaranteed annuity interest in every respect. For example, if the income interest is the right to receive from a trust each year a payment equal to the lesser of a sum certain or a fixed percentage of the net fair market value of the trust assets, determined annually, such interest is not a guaranteed annuity interest.

(C) Where a charitable interest is in the form of a guaranteed annuity interest, the governing instrument of the trust may provide that income of the trust which is in excess of the amount required to pay the guaranteed annuity interest shall be paid to or for the use of a charitable organization. Nevertheless, the amount of the deduction under section 170(f)(2)(B) shall be limited to the fair market value of the guaranteed annuity interest as determined under paragraph (c)(3) of this section. For a rule relating to treatment by the grantor of any contribution made by the trust in excess of the amount required to pay the guaranteed annuity interest, see paragraph (d)(2)(ii) of this section.

(D) If the present value on the date of transfer of all the income interests for a charitable purpose exceeds 60 percent of the aggregate fair market value of all amounts in the trust (after the payment of liabilities), the income interest will not be considered a guaranteed annuity interest unless the governing instrument of the trust prohibits both the acquisition and the retention of assets which would give rise to a tax under section 4944 if the trustee had acquired such assets. The requirement in this subdivision (D) for a prohibition in the governing instrument against the retention of assets which would give rise to a tax under section 4944 if the trustee had acquired the assets shall not apply to a transfer in trust made on or before May 21, 1972.

(E) An income interest consisting of an annuity transferred in trust after May 21, 1972, will not be considered a guaranteed annuity interest if any amount other than an amount in payment of a guaranteed annuity interest may be paid by the trust for a private purpose before the expiration of all the income interests for a charitable purpose, unless such amount for a private purpose is paid from a group of assets which, pursuant to the governing instrument of the trust, are devoted exclusively to private purposes and to which section 4947(a)(2) is inapplicable by reason of section 4947(a)(2)(B). The exception in the immediately preceding sentence with respect to any guaranteed annuity for a private purpose shall apply only if the obligation to pay the annuity for a charitable purpose begins as of the date of creation of the trust and the obligation to pay the guaranteed annuity for a private purpose does not precede in point of time the obligation to pay the annuity for a charitable purpose and only if the governing instrument of the trust does not provide for any preference or priority in respect of any payment of the guaranteed annuity for a private purpose as opposed to any payment of any annuity for a charitable purpose. For purposes of this subdivision (E), an amount is not paid for a private purpose if it is paid for an adequate and full consideration in money or money's worth. See § 53.4947–1(c) of this chapter (Foundation Excise Tax Regulations) for rules relating to the inapplicability of § 4947(a)(2) to segregated amounts in a split-interest trust.

Example. In 1975, E transfers $75,000 in trust with the requirement that an annuity of $5,000 a year, payable annually at the end of each year, be paid to B, an individual, for a period of 5 years and thereafter an annuity of $5,000 a year, payable annually at the end of each year, be paid to M Charity for a period of 5 years. The remainder is to be paid to C, an individual. No deduction is allowed under subparagraph (1) of this paragraph with respect to the charitable annuity because it is not a "guaranteed annuity interest" within the meaning of this subdivision.

(F) For rules relating to certain governing instrument requirements and to the imposition of certain excise taxes where the guaranteed annuity interest is in trust and for rules governing payment of private income interests by a split-interest trust, see section 4947(a)(2) and (b)(3)(A), and the regulations thereunder.

(ii) Unitrust interest. (A) An income interest is a "unitrust interest" only if it is an irrevocable right pursuant to the governing instrument of the trust to receive payment, not less often than annually of a fixed percentage of the net fair market value of the trust assets, determined annually. In computing the net fair market value of the trust assets, all assets and liabilities shall be taken into account without regard to whether particular items are taken into account in determining the income of the trust. The net fair market value of the trust assets may be determined on any one date during the year or by taking the average of valuations made on more than one date during the year, provided that the same valuation date or dates and valuation methods are used each year. Where the governing instrument of the trust does not specify the valuation date or dates, the trustee shall select such date or dates and shall indicate his selection on the first return on Form 1041 which the trust is required to file. Payments under a unitrust interest may be paid for a specified term or for the life or lives of an individual or individuals, each of whom must be living at the date of transfer and can be ascertained at such date. For example, the unitrust interest may be paid for the life of A plus a term of years.

(B) An income interest is a unitrust interest only if it is a unitrust interest in every respect. For example, if the income interest is the right to receive from a trust each year a payment equal to the lesser of a sum certain or a fixed percentage of the net fair market value of the trust assets, determined annually, such interest is not a unitrust interest.

(C) Where a charitable interest is in the form of a unitrust interest, the governing instrument of the trust may provide that income of the trust which is in excess of the amount required to pay the unitrust interest shall be paid to or for the use of a charitable organization. Nevertheless, the amount of the deduction under section 170(f)(2)(B) shall be limited to the fair market value of the unitrust interest as determined under paragraph (c)(3) of this section. For a rule relating to treatment by the grantor of any contribution made by the trust in excess of the amount required to pay the unitrust interest, see paragraph (d)(2)(ii) of this section.

(D) An income interest in the form of a unitrust interest will not be considered a unitrust interest if any amount other than an amount in payment of a unitrust interest may be paid by the trust for a private purpose before the expiration of all the income interests for a charitable purpose, unless such amount for a private purpose is paid from a group of assets which, pursuant to the governing instrument of the trust, are devoted exclusively to private purposes and to which section 4947(a)(2) is inapplicable by reason of section 4947(a)(2)(B). The exception in the immediately preceding sentence with respect to any unitrust interest for a private purpose shall apply only if the obligation to pay the unitrust interest for a charitable purpose begins as of the date of creation of the trust and the obligation to pay the unitrust interest for a private purpose does not precede in point of time the obligation to pay the unitrust interest for a charitable purpose and only if the governing instrument of the trust does not provide for any preference or priority in respect of any payment of the unitrust interest for a private purpose as opposed to any payments of any unitrust interest for a charitable purpose. For purposes of this subdivision (D), an amount is not paid for a private purpose if it is paid for an adequate and full consideration in money or money's worth. See § 53.4947–1(c) of this chapter (Foundation Excise Tax Regulations) for rules relating to the inapplicability of section 4947(a)(2) to segregated amounts in a split-interest trust.

(E) For rules relating to certain governing instrument requirements and to the imposition of certain excise taxes where the unitrust interest is in trust and for rules governing payment of private income interests by a split-interest trust, see section 4947(a)(2) and (b)(3)(A), and the regulations thereunder.

* * *

(d) Denial of deduction for certain contributions by a trust. (1) If by reason of section 170(f)(2)(B) and paragraph (c) of this section a charitable contributions deduction is allowed under section 170 for the fair market value of an income interest transferred in trust, neither the grantor of the income interest, the trust, nor any other person shall be allowed a deduction under section 170 or any other section for the amount of any charitable contribution made by the trust with respect to, or in fulfillment of, such income interest.

(2) Section 170(f)(2)(C) and subparagraph (1) of this paragraph shall not be construed, however, to:

(i) Disallow a deduction to the trust, pursuant to section 642(c)(1) and the regulations thereunder, for amounts paid by the trust after the grantor ceases to be treated as the owner of the income interest for purposes of applying section 671 and which are not taken into account in determining the amount of recapture under paragraph (c)(4) of this section, or

(ii) Disallow a deduction to the grantor under section 671 and § 1.671–2(c) for a charitable contribution made by the trust in excess of the contribution required to be made by the trust under the terms of the trust instrument with respect to, or in fulfillment of, the income interest.

(3) Although a deduction for the fair market value of an income interest in property which is less than the donor's entire interest in the property and which the donor transfers in trust is disallowed under section 170 because such interest is not a guaranteed annuity interest, or a unitrust interest, as defined in paragraph (c)(2) of this section, the donor may be entitled to a deduction under section 671 and § 1.671–2(c) for any charitable contributions made by the trust if he is treated as the owner of such interest for purposes of applying section 671.

* * *

§ 1.170A–7. Contributions not in trust of partial interests in property.

(a) In general. (1) In the case of a charitable contribution, not made by a transfer in trust, of any interest in property which consists of less than the donor's entire interest in such property, no deduction is allowed under section 170 for the value of such interest unless the interest is an interest described in paragraph (b) of this section. See section 170(f)(3)(A). For purposes of this section, a contribution of the right to use property which the donor owns, for example, a rent-free lease, shall be treated as a contribution of less than the taxpayer's entire interest in such property.

(2)(i) A deduction is allowed without regard to this section for a contribution of a partial interest in property if such interest is the taxpayer's entire interest in the property, such as an income interest or a remainder interest. Thus, if securities are given to A for life, with the remainder over to B, and B makes a charitable contribution of his remainder interest to an organization described in section 170(c), a deduction is allowed under section 170 for the present value of B's remainder interest in the securities. If, however, the property in which such partial interest exists was divided in order to create such interest and thus avoid section 170(f)(3)(A), the deduction will not be allowed. Thus, for example, assume that a taxpayer desires to contribute to a charitable organization an income interest in property held by him, which is not of a type described in paragraph (b)(2) of this section. If the taxpayer transfers the remainder interest in such property to his son and immediately thereafter contributes the income interest to a charitable organization, no deduction shall be allowed under section 170 for the contribution of the taxpayer's entire interest consisting of the retained income interest. In further illustration, assume that a taxpayer desires to contribute to a charitable organization the reversionary interest in certain stocks and bonds held by him, which is not of a type described in paragraph (b)(2) of this section. If the taxpayer grants a life estate in such property to his son and immediately thereafter contributes the reversionary interest to a charitable organization, no deduction will be allowed under section 170 for the contribution of the taxpayer's entire interest consisting of the reversionary interest.

(ii) A deduction is allowed without regard to this section for a contribution of a partial interest in property if such contribution constitutes part of a charitable contribution not in trust in which all interests of the taxpayer in the property are given to a charitable organization described in section 170(c). Thus, if on March 1, 1971, an income interest in property is given not in trust to a church and the remainder interest in the property is given not in trust to an educational organization described in section 170(b)(1)(A), a deduction is allowed for the value of such property.

(3) A deduction shall not be disallowed under section 170(f)(3)(A) and this section merely because the interest which passes to, or is vested in, the charity may be defeated by the performance of some act or the happening of some event, if on the date of the gift it appears that the possibility that such act or event will occur is so remote as to be negligible. See paragraph (e) of § 1.170A-1.

(b) Contributions of certain partial interests in property for which a deduction is allowed. A deduction is allowed under section 170 for a contribution not in trust of a partial interest which is less than the donor's entire interest in property and which qualifies under one of the following subparagraphs:

(1) Undivided portion of donor's entire interest. (i) A deduction is allowed under section 170 for the value of a charitable contribution not in trust of an undivided portion of a donor's entire interest in property. An undivided portion of a donor's entire interest in property must consist of a fraction or percentage of each and every substantial interest or right owned by the donor in such property and must extend over the entire term of the donor's interest in such property and in other property into which such property is converted. For example, assuming that in 1967 B has been given a life estate in an office building for the life of A and that B has no other interest in the office building, B will be allowed a deduction under section 170 for his contribution in 1972 to charity of a one-half interest in such life estate in a transfer which is not made in trust. Such contribution by B will be considered a contribution of an undivided portion of the donor's entire interest in property. In further illustration, assuming that in 1968 C has been given the remainder interest in a trust created under the will of his father and C has no other interest in the trust, C will be allowed a deduction under section 170 for his contribution in 1972 to charity of a 20-percent interest in such remainder interest in a transfer which is not made in trust. Such contribution by C will be considered a contribution of an undivided portion of the donor's entire interest in property. If a taxpayer owns 100 acres of land and makes a contribution of 50 acres to a charitable organization, the charitable contribution is allowed as a deduction under section 170. A deduction is allowed under section 170 for a contribution of property to a charitable organization whereby such organization is given the right, as a tenant in common with the donor, to possession, dominion, and control of the property for a portion of each year appropriate to its interest in such property. However, for purposes of this subparagraph a charitable contribution in perpetuity of an interest in property not in trust where the donor transfers some specific rights and retains other substantial rights will not be considered a contribution of an undivided portion of the donor's entire interest in property to which section 170(f)(3)(A) does not apply. Thus, for example, a deduction is not allowable for the value of an immediate and perpetual gift not in trust of an interest in original historic motion picture films to a charitable organization where the donor retains the exclusive right to make reproductions of such films and to exploit such reproductions commercially.

* * *

(2) Partial interests in property which would be deductible in trust. A deduction is allowed under section 170 for the value of a charitable contribution not in trust of a partial interest in property which is less than the donor's entire interest in the property and which would be deductible under section 170(f)(2) and § 1.170A–6 if such interest had been transferred in trust.

(3) Contribution of a remainder interest in a personal residence. A deduction is allowed under section 170 for the value of a charitable contribution not in trust of an irrevocable remainder interest in a personal residence which is not the donor's entire interest in such property. Thus, for example, if a taxpayer contributes not in trust to an organization described in section 170(c) a remainder interest in a personal residence and retains an estate in such property for life or for a term of years, a deduction is allowed under section 170 for the value of such remainder interest not transferred in trust. For purposes of section 170(f)(3)(B)(i) and this subparagraph, the term "personal residence" means any property used by the taxpayer as his personal residence even though it is not used as his principal residence. For example, the taxpayer's vacation home may be a personal residence for purposes of this subparagraph. The term "personal residence" also includes stock owned by a taxpayer as a tenant-stockholder in a cooperative housing corporation (as those terms are defined in section 216(b)(1) and (2)) if the dwelling which the taxpayer is entitled to occupy as such stockholder is used by him as his personal residence.

(4) Contribution of a remainder interest in a farm. A deduction is allowed under section 170 for the value of a charitable contribution not in trust of an irrevocable remainder interest in a farm which is not the donor's entire interest in such property. Thus, for example, if a taxpayer contributes not in trust to an organization described in section 170(c) a remainder interest in a farm and retains an estate in such farm for life or for a term of years, a deduction is allowed under section 170 for the value of such remainder interest not transferred in trust. For purposes of section 170(f)(3)(B)(i) and this subparagraph, the term "farm" means any land used by the taxpayer or his tenant for the production of crops, fruits, or other agricultural products or for the sustenance of livestock. The term "livestock" includes cattle, hogs, horses, mules, donkeys, sheep, goats, captive fur-bearing animals, chickens, turkeys, pigeons, and other poultry. A farm includes the improvements thereon.

(5) Qualified conservation contribution. A deduction is allowed under section 170 for the value of a qualified conservation contribution. For the definition of a qualified conservation contribution, see § 1.170A–14.

(c) Valuation of a partial interest in property. Except as provided in § 1.170A–14, the amount of the deduction under section 170 in the case of a charitable contribution of a partial interest in property to which paragraph (b) of this section applies is the fair market value of the partial interest at the time of the contribution. See § 1.170A–1(c). The fair market value of such partial interest must be determined in accordance with § 20.2031–7 of this chapter (Estate Tax Regulations), except that, in the case of a charitable contribution of a remainder interest in real property which is not transferred in trust, the fair market value of such interest must be determined in accordance with section 170(f)(4) and § 1.170A–12. In the case of a charitable contribution of a remainder interest in the form of a remainder interest in a pooled income fund, a charitable remainder annuity trust, or a charitable remainder unitrust, the fair market value of the remainder interest must be determined as provided in paragraph (b)(2) of § 1.170A–6. However, in some cases a reduction in the amount of a charitable contribution of the remainder interest may be required. See section 170(e) and paragraph (a) of § 1.170A–4.

(d) Illustrations. The application of this section may be illustrated by the following examples:

Example (1). A, an individual owning a 10-story office building, donates the rent-free use of the top floor of the building for the year 1971 to a charitable organization. Since A's contribution consists of a partial interest to which section 170(f)(3)(A) applies, he is not entitled to a charitable contributions deduction for the contribution of such partial interest.

Example (2). In 1971, B contributes to a charitable organization an undivided one-half interest in 100 acres of land, whereby as tenants in common they share in the economic benefits from the property. The present value of the contributed property is $50,000. Since B's contribution consists of an undivided portion of his entire interest in the property to which section 170(f)(3)(B) applies, he is allowed a deduction in 1971 for his charitable contribution of $50,000.

Example (3). In 1971, D loans $10,000 in cash to a charitable organization and does not require the organization to pay any interest for the use of the money. Since D's contribution consists of a partial interest to which section 170(f)(3)(A) applies, he is not entitled to a charitable contributions deduction for the contribution of such partial interest.

* * *

§ 1.170A–8. Limitations on charitable deductions by individuals.

(a) Percentage limitations—(1) In general. An individual's charitable contributions deduction is subject to 20-, 30-, and 50-percent limitations unless the individual qualifies for the unlimited charitable contributions deduction under section 170(b)(1)(C). For a discussion of these limitations and examples of their application, see paragraphs (b) through (f) of this section. If a husband and wife make a joint return, the deduction for contributions is the aggregate of the contributions made by the spouses, and the limitations in section 170(b) and this section are based on the aggregate contribution base of the spouses. A charitable contribution by an individual to or for the use of an organization described in section 170(c) may be deductible even though all, or some portion, of the funds of the organization may be used in foreign countries for charitable or educational purposes.

(2) "To" or "for the use of" defined. For purposes of section 170, a contribution of an income interest in property, whether or not such contributed interest is transferred in trust, for which a deduction is allowed under section 170(f)(2)(B) or (3)(A) shall be considered as made "for the use of" rather than "to" the charitable organization. A contribution of a remainder interest in property, whether or not such contributed interest is transferred in trust, for which a deduction is allowed under section 170(f)(2)(A) or (3)(A), shall be considered as made "to" the charitable organization except that, if such interest is transferred in trust and, pursuant to the terms of the trust instrument, the interest contributed is, upon termination of the predecessor estate, to be held in trust for the benefit of such organization, the contribution shall be considered as made "for the use of" such organization. Thus, for example, assume that A transfers property to a charitable remainder annuity trust described in section 664(d)(1) which is required to pay to B for life an annuity equal to 5 percent of the initial fair market value of the property transferred in trust. The trust instrument provides that after B's death the remainder interest in the trust is to be transferred to M Church or, in the event M Church is not an organization described in section 170(c) when the amount is to be irrevocably transferred to such church, to an organization which is described in section 170(c) at that time. The contribution by A of the remainder interest shall be considered as made "to" M Church. However, if in the trust instrument A had directed that after B's death the remainder interest is to be held in trust for the benefit of M Church, the contribution shall be considered as made "for the use of" M Church. This subparagraph does not apply to the contribution of a partial interest in property, or of an undivided portion of such partial interest, if such partial interest is the donor's entire interest in the property and such entire interest was not created to avoid section 170(f)(2) or (3)(A). See paragraph (a)(2) of § 1.170A–6 and paragraphs (a)(2)(i) and (b)(1) of § 1.170A–7.

* * *

(d) 30-percent limitation—(1) In general. An individual may deduct charitable contributions of 30-percent capital gain property, as defined in subparagraph (3) of this paragraph, made during a taxable year to or for the use of any charitable organization described in section 170(c) to the extent that such contributions in the aggregate do not exceed 30-percent of his contribution base, as defined in paragraph (e) of this section, subject, however, to the 50- and 20-percent limitations prescribed by paragraphs (b) and (c) of this section. For purposes of applying the 50-percent and 20-percent limitations described in paragraphs (b) and (c) of this section, charitable contributions of 30-percent capital gain property paid during the taxable year, and limited as provided by this subparagraph, shall be taken into account after all other charitable contributions paid during the taxable year. For provisions relating to the carryover of certain contributions of 30-percent capital gain property in excess of 30-percent of an individual's contribution base, see section 170(b)(1)(D)(ii) and paragraph (c) of § 1.170A–10.

(2) Election by an individual to have section 170(e)(1)(B) apply to contributions—(i) In general. (A) An individual may elect under section 170(b)(1)(D)(iii) for any taxable year to have the reduction rule of section 170(e)(1)(B) and paragraph (a) of § 1.170A–4 apply to all his charitable contributions of 30-percent capital gain property made during such taxable year or carried over to such taxable year from a taxable year beginning after December 31, 1969. If such election is made such contributions shall be treated as contributions of section 170(e) capital gain property in accordance with paragraph (b)(2)(iii) of § 1.170A–4. The election may be made with respect to contributions of 30-percent capital gain property carried over to the taxable year even though the individual has not made any contribution of 30-percent capital gain property in such year. If such an election is made, section 170(b)(1)(D)(i) and (ii) and subparagraph (1) of this paragraph shall not apply to such contributions made during such year. However, such contributions must be reduced as required under section 170(e)(1)(B) and paragraph (a) of § 1.170A–4.

(B) If there are carryovers to such taxable year of charitable contributions of 30-percent capital gain property made in preceding taxable years beginning after December 31, 1969, the amount of such contributions in each such preceding year shall be reduced as if section 170(e)(1)(B) had applied to them in the preceding year and shall be carried over to the taxable year and succeeding taxable years under section 170(d)(1) and paragraph (b) of § 1.170A–10 as contributions of property other than 30-percent capital gain property. For purposes of applying the immediately preceding sentence, the percentage limitations under section 170(b) for the preceding taxable year and for any taxable years intervening between such year and the year of the election shall not be redetermined and the amount of any deduction allowed for such years under section 170 in respect of the charitable contributions of 30-percent capital gain property in the preceding taxable year shall not be redetermined. However, the amount of the deduction so allowed under section 170 in the preceding taxable year must be subtracted from the reduced amount of the charitable contributions made in such year in order to determine the excess amount which is carried over from such year under section 170(d)(1). If the amount of the deduction so allowed in the preceding taxable year equals or exceeds the reduced amount of the charitable contributions, there shall be no carryover from such year to the year of the election.

(C) An election under this subparagraph may be made for each taxable year in which charitable contributions of 30-percent capital gain property are made or to which they are carried over under section 170(b)(1)(D)(ii). If there are also carryovers under section 170(d)(1) to the year of the election by reason of an election made under this subparagraph for a previous taxable year, such carryovers under section 170(d)(1) shall not be redetermined by reason of the subsequent election.

(ii) Husband and wife making joint return. If a husband and wife make a joint return of income for a contribution year and one of the spouses elects under this subparagraph in a later year when he files a separate return, or if a spouse dies after a contribution year for which a joint return is made, any excess contribution of 30-percent capital gain property which is carried over to the election year from the contribution year shall be allocated between the husband and wife as provided in paragraph (d)(4)(i) and (iii) of § 1.170A–10. If a husband and wife file separate returns in a contribution year, any election under this subparagraph in a later year when a joint return is filed shall be applicable to any excess contributions of 30-percent capital gain property of either taxpayer carried over from the contribution year to the election year. The immediately preceding sentence shall also apply where two single individuals are subsequently married and file a joint return. A remarried individual who filed a joint return with his former spouse for a contribution year and thereafter files a joint return with his present spouse shall treat the carryover to the election year as provided in paragraph (d)(4)(ii) of § 1.170A–10.

(iii) Manner of making election. The election under subdivision (i) of this subparagraph shall be made by attaching to the income tax return for the election year a statement indicating that the election under section 170(b)(1)(D)(iii) and this subparagraph is being made. If there is a carryover to the taxable year of any charitable contributions of 30-percent capital gain property from a previous taxable year or years, the statement shall show a recomputation, in accordance with this subparagraph and § 1.170A–4, of such carryover, setting forth sufficient information with respect to the previous taxable year or any intervening year to show the basis of the recomputation. The statement shall indicate the district director, or the director of the internal revenue service center, with whom the return for the previous taxable year or years was filed, the name or names in which such return or returns were filed, and whether each such return was a joint or separate return.

(3) 30-percent capital gain property defined. If there is a charitable contribution of a capital asset which, if it were sold by the donor at its fair market value at the time of its contribution, would result in the recognition of gain all, or any portion, of which would be long-term capital gain and if the amount of such contribution is not required to be reduced under section 170(e)(1)(B) and § 1.170A–4(a)(2), such capital asset shall be treated as "30-percent capital gain property" for purposes of section 170 and the regulations thereunder. For such purposes any property which is property used in the trade or business, as defined in section 1231(b), shall be treated as a capital asset. However, see paragraph (b)(4) of § 1.170A–4. For the treatment of such property as section 170(e) capital gain property, see paragraph (b)(2)(iii) of § 1.170A–4.

(e) Contribution base defined. For purposes of section 170 the term "contribution base" means adjusted gross income under section 62, computed without regard to any net operating loss carryback to the taxable year under section 172. See section 170(b)(1)(F).

* * *

§ 1.170A–9. Definition of section 170(b)(1)(A) organization.

(a) The term "section 170(b)(1)(A) organization" as used in the regulations under section 170 means any organization described in paragraphs (a) through (i) of this section, effective with respect to taxable years beginning after December 31, 1969, except as otherwise provided. Section 1.170–2(b) shall continue to be applicable with respect to taxable years beginning prior to January 1, 1970. The term "one or more organizations described in section 170(b)(1)(A) (other than in clauses (vii) and (viii))" as used in sections 507 and 509 of the Code and the regulations thereunder means one or more organizations described in paragraphs (a) through (e) of this section, except as modified by the regulations under part II of subchapter F of chapter I or under chapter 42.

(b) Church or a convention or association of churches. An organization is described in section 170(b)(1)(A)(i) if it is a church or a convention or association of churches.

(c) Educational organization and organizations for the benefit of certain State and municipal colleges and universities—(1) Educational organization. An educational organization is described in section 170(b)(1)(A)(ii) if its primary function is the presentation of formal instruction and it normally maintains a regular faculty and curriculum and normally has a regularly enrolled body of pupils or students in attendance at the place where its educational activities are regularly carried on. The term includes institutions such as primary, secondary, preparatory, or high schools, and colleges and universities. It includes Federal, State, and other public-supported schools which otherwise come within the definition. It does not include organizations engaged in both educational and noneducational activities unless the latter are merely incidental to the educational activities. A recognized university which incidentally operates a museum or sponsors concerts is an educational organization within the meaning of section 170(b)(1)(A)(ii). However, the operation of a school by a museum does not necessarily qualify the museum as an educational organization within the meaning of this subparagraph.

(2) Organizations for the benefit of certain State and municipal colleges and universities. (i) An organization is described in section 170(b)(1)(A)(iv) if it meets the support requirements of subdivision (ii) of this subparagraph and is organized and operated exclusively to receive, hold, invest, and administer property and to make expenditures to or for the benefit of a college or university which is an organization described in subdivision (iii) of this subparagraph. The phrase "expenditures to or for the benefit of a college or university" includes expenditures made for any one or more of the normal functions of colleges and universities such as the acquisition and maintenance of real property comprising part of the campus area; the erection of, or participation in the erection of, college or university buildings; the acquisition and maintenance of equipment and furnishings used for, or in conjunction with, normal functions of colleges and universities; or expenditures for scholarships, libraries and student loans.

(ii) To qualify under section 170(b)(1)(A)(iv), the organization receiving the contribution must normally receive a substantial part of its support from the United States or any State or political subdivision thereof or from direct or indirect contributions from the general public, or from a combination of two or more of such sources. For such purposes, the term "support" does not include income received in the exercise or performance by the organization of its charitable, educational, or other purpose or function constituting the basis for its exemption under section 501(a). An example of an indirect contribution from the public is the receipt by the organization of its share of the proceeds of an annual collection campaign of a community chest, community fund, or united fund. In determining the amount of support received by such organization with respect to a contribution of property which is subject to reduction under section 170(e), the fair market value of the property shall be taken into account.

(iii) The college or university (including a land grant college or university) to be benefited must be an educational organization referred to in section 170(b)(1)(A)(ii) and subparagraph (1) of this paragraph which is an agency or instrumentality of a State or political subdivision thereof, or which is owned or operated by a State or political subdivision thereof or by an agency or instrumentality of one or more States or political subdivisions.

(d) Hospitals and medical research organizations—(1) Hospitals. An organization (other than one described in subparagraph (2) of this paragraph) is described in section 170(b)(1)(a)(iii) if:

(i) It is a hospital, and

(ii) Its principal purpose or function is the providing of medical or hospital care or medical education or medical research.

(A) The term "hospital" includes (1) Federal hospitals and (2) State, county, and municipal hospitals which are instrumentalities of governmental units referred to in section 170(c)(1) and otherwise come within the definition. A rehabilitation institution, outpatient clinic, or community mental health or drug treatment center may qualify as a "hospital" within the meaning of subdivision (i) of this subparagraph if its principal purpose or function is the providing of hospital or medical care. For purposes of this subdivision, the term "medical care" shall include the treatment of any physical or mental disability or condition, whether on an inpatient or outpatient basis, provided the cost of such treatment is deductible under section 213 by the person treated. An organization, all the accommodations of which qualify as being part of a "skilled nursing facility" within the meaning of 42 U.S.C. 1395x(j), may qualify as a "hospital" within the meaning of subdivision (i) of this subparagraph if its principal purpose or function is the providing of hospital or medical care. For taxable years ending after June 28, 1968, the term "hospital" also includes cooperative hospital service organizations which meet the requirements of section 501(e) and § 1.501(e)–1.

(B) The term "hospital" does not, however, include convalescent homes or homes for children or the aged, nor does the term include institutions whose principal purpose or function is to train handicapped individuals to pursue some vocation. An organization whose principal purpose or function is the providing of medical education or medical research will not be considered a "hospital" within the meaning of subdivision (i) of this subparagraph, unless it is also actively engaged in providing medical or hospital care to patients on its premises or in its facilities, on an inpatient or outpatient basis, as an integral part of its medical education or medical research functions. See, however, subparagraph (2) of this paragraph with respect to certain medical research organizations.

* * *

(e) Governmental unit. A governmental unit is described in section 170(b)(1)(A)(v) if it is referred to in section 170(c)(1).

(f) Definition of section 170(b)(1)(A)(vi) organization—(1) In general. An organization is described in section 170(b)(1)(A)(vi) if it:

(i) Is referred to in section 170(c)(2) (other than an organization specifically described in paragraphs (b) through (e) of this section); and

(ii) Normally receives a substantial part of its support from a governmental unit referred to in section 170(c)(1) or from direct or indirect contributions from the general public ("publicly supported"). For purposes of this paragraph (f)(1)(ii), an organization is publicly supported if it meets the requirements of either paragraph (f)(2) of this section (33 1/3 percent support test) or paragraph (f)(3) of this section (facts and circumstances test). Paragraph (f)(4) of this section defines normally for purposes of the 33 1/3 percent support test, the facts and circumstances test and for new organizations in the first 5 years of the organization's existence as a section 501(c)(3) organization. Paragraph (f)(5) of this section provides for determinations of foundation classification and rules for reliance by donors and contributors. Paragraphs (f)(6), (7), and (8) of this section list the items that are included and excluded from the term support. Paragraph (f)(9) of this section provides examples of the application of this paragraph. Types of organizations that, subject to the provisions of this paragraph, generally qualify under section 170(b)(1)(A)(vi) as "publicly supported" are publicly or governmentally supported museums of history, art, or science, libraries, community centers to promote the arts, organizations providing facilities for the support of an opera, symphony orchestra, ballet, or repertory drama or for some other direct service to the general public.

(2) Determination whether an organization is "publicly supported"; 33 1/3 percent support test. An organization is publicly supported if the total amount of support (see paragraphs (f)(6), (7), and (8) of this section) that the organization normally (see paragraph (f)(4)(i) of this section) receives from governmental units referred to in section 170(c)(1), from contributions made directly or indirectly by the general public, or from a combination of these sources, equals at least 33 1/3 percent of the total support normally received by the organization. See paragraph (f)(9) Example 1 of this section.

(3) Determination whether an organization is "publicly supported"; facts and circumstances test. Even if an organization fails to meet the 33 1/3 percent support test, it is publicly supported if it normally receives a substantial part of its support from governmental units, from contributions made directly or indirectly by the general public, or from a combination of these sources, and meets the other requirements of this paragraph (f)(3). In order to satisfy the facts and circumstances test, an organization must meet the requirements of paragraphs (f)(3)(i) and (f)(3)(ii) of this section. In addition, the organization must be in the nature of an organization that is publicly supported, taking into account all relevant facts and circumstances, including the factors listed in paragraphs (f)(3)(iii)(A) through (f)(3)(iii)(E) of this section.

(i) Ten percent support limitation. The percentage of support (see paragraphs (f)(6), (f)(7) and (f)(8) of this section) normally (see paragraph (f)(4) of this section) received by an organization from governmental units, from contributions made directly or indirectly by the general public, or from a combination of these sources, must be substantial. For purposes of this paragraph (f)(3), an organization will not be treated as normally receiving a substantial amount of governmental or public support unless the total amount of governmental and public support normally received equals at least 10 percent of the total support normally received by such organization.

(ii) Attraction of public support. An organization must be so organized and operated as to attract new and additional public or governmental support on a continuous basis. An organization will be considered to meet this requirement if it maintains a continuous and bona fide program for solicitation of funds from the general public, community, or membership group involved, or if it carries on activities designed to attract support from governmental units or other organizations described in section 170(b)(1)(A)(i) through (vi). In determining whether an organization maintains a continuous and bona fide program for solicitation of funds from the general public or community, consideration will be given to whether the scope of its fundraising activities is reasonable in light of its charitable activities. Consideration will also be given to the fact that an organization may, in its early years of existence, limit the scope of its solicitation to persons deemed most likely to provide seed money in an amount sufficient to enable it to commence its charitable activities and expand its solicitation program.

(iii) In addition to the requirements set forth in paragraphs (f)(3)(i) and (f)(3)(ii) of this section that must be satisfied, all pertinent facts and circumstances, including the following factors, will be taken into consideration in determining whether an organization is "publicly supported" within the meaning of paragraph (f)(1) of this section. However, an organization is not generally required to satisfy all of the factors in paragraphs (f)(3)(iii)(A) through (f)(3)(iii)(E) of this section. The factors relevant to each case and the weight accorded to any one of them may differ depending upon the nature and purpose of the organization and the length of time it has been in existence.

(A) *Percentage of financial support.* The percentage of support received by an organization from public or governmental sources will be taken into consideration in determining whether an organization is "publicly supported." The higher the percentage of support above the 10 percent requirement of paragraph (f)(3)(i) of this section from public or governmental sources, the lesser will be the burden of establishing the publicly supported nature of the organization through other factors described in this paragraph (f)(3), while the lower the percentage, the greater will be the burden. If the percentage of the organization's support from public or governmental sources is low because it receives a high percentage of its total support from investment income on its endowment funds, such fact will be treated as evidence of compliance with this subdivision if such endowment funds were originally contributed by a governmental unit or by the general public. However, if such endowment funds were originally contributed by a few individuals or members of their families, such fact will increase the burden on the organization of establishing compliance with the other factors described in paragraph (f)(3)(iii) of this section.

(B) *Sources of support.* The fact that an organization meets the requirement of paragraph (f)(3)(i) of this section through support from governmental units or directly or indirectly from a representative number of persons, rather than receiving almost all of its support from the members of a single family, will be taken into consideration in determining whether an organization is "publicly supported." In determining what is a "representative number of persons," consideration will be given to the type of organization involved, the length of time it has been in existence, and whether it limits its activities to a particular community or region or to a special field which can be expected to appeal to a limited number of persons.

(C) *Representative governing body.* The fact that an organization has a governing body which represents the broad interests of the public, rather than the personal or private interests of a limited number of donors (or persons standing in a relationship to such donors which is described in section 4946(a)(1)(C) through (G)), will be taken into account in determining whether an organization is "publicly supported." An organization will be treated as meeting this requirement if it has a governing body (whether designated in the organization's governing instrument or bylaws as a Board of Directors, Board of Trustees, etc.) which is comprised of public officials acting in their capacities as such; of individuals selected by public officials acting in their capacities as such; of persons having special knowledge or expertise in the particular field or discipline in which the organization is operating; of community leaders, such as elected or appointed officials, clergymen, educators, civic leaders, or other such persons representing a broad cross-section of the views and interests of the community; or, in the case of a membership organization, of individuals elected pursuant to the organization's governing instrument or bylaws by a broadly based membership.

(D) *Availability of public facilities or services; public participation in programs or policies.* (1) The fact that an organization is of the type which generally provides facilities or services directly for the benefit of the general public on a continuing basis (such as a museum or library which holds open its building or facilities to the public, a symphony orchestra which gives public performances, a conservation organization which provides educational services to the public through the distribution of educational materials, or an old age home which provides domiciliary or nursing services for members of the general public) will be considered evidence that such organization is "publicly supported."

(2) The fact that an organization is an educational or research institution which regularly publishes scholarly studies that are widely used by colleges and universities or by members of the general public will also be considered evidence that such organization is "publicly supported."

(3) The following factors will also be considered evidence that an organization is "publicly supported":

(i) The participation in, or sponsorship of, the programs of the organization by members of the public having special knowledge or expertise, public officials, or civic or community leaders.

(ii) The maintenance of a definitive program by an organization to accomplish its charitable work in the community, such as combating community deterioration in an economically depressed area that has suffered a major loss of population and jobs.

(iii) The receipt of a significant part of its funds from a public charity or governmental agency to which it is in some way held accountable as a condition of the grant, contract, or contribution.

(E) *Additional factors pertinent to membership organizations.* The following are additional factors to be considered in determining whether a membership organization is "publicly supported":

(1) Whether the solicitation for dues-paying members is designed to enroll a substantial number of persons in the community or area, or in a particular profession or field of special interest (taking into account the size of the area and the nature of the organization's activities).

(2) Whether membership dues for individual (rather than institutional) members have been fixed at rates designed to make membership available to a broad cross section of the interested public, rather than to restrict membership to a limited number of persons.

(3) Whether the activities of the organization will be likely to appeal to persons having some broad common interest or purpose, such as educational activities in the case of alumni associations, musical activities in the case of symphony societies, or civic affairs in the case of parent-teacher associations. See Examples 2 through 5 contained in paragraph (f)(9) of this section for illustrations of this paragraph (f)(3).

(4) Definition of normally; general rule—(i) Normally; 33 1/3 percent support test. An organization "normally" receives the requisite amount of public support and meets the 33 1/3 percent support test for a taxable year and the taxable year immediately succeeding that year, if, for the taxable year being tested and the four taxable years immediately preceding that taxable year, the organization meets the 33 1/3 percent support test on an aggregate basis.

(ii) Normally; facts and circumstances test. An organization "normally" receives the requisite amount of public support and meets the facts and circumstances test of paragraph (f)(3) for a taxable year and the taxable year immediately succeeding that year, if, for the taxable year being tested and the four taxable years immediately preceding that taxable year, the organization meets the facts and circumstances test on an aggregate basis. In the case of paragraphs (f)(3)(iii)(A) and (f)(3)(iii)(B) of this section, facts pertinent to years preceding the five-year period may also be taken into consideration. The combination of factors set forth in paragraphs (f)(3)(iii)(A) through (f)(3)(iii)(E) of this section that an organization normally must meet does not have to be the same for each five-year period so long as there exists a sufficient combination of factors to show compliance with the facts and circumstances test.

(iii) Special rule. The fact that an organization has normally met the requirements of the 33 1/3 percent support test for a current taxable year, but is unable normally to meet such requirements for a succeeding taxable year, will not in itself prevent such organization from meeting the facts and circumstances test for such succeeding taxable year.

(iv) Example. The application of paragraphs (f)(4)(i), (f)(4)(ii), and (f)(4)(iii) of this section may be illustrated by the following example:

Example. (i) X is recognized as an organization described in section 501(c)(3). On the basis of support received during taxable years 2008, 2009, 2010, 2011, and 2012, in the aggregate, X receives at least 33 1/3 percent of its support from governmental units referred to in section 170(c)(1), from contributions made directly or indirectly by the general public, or from a combination of these sources. Consequently, X meets the 33 1/3 percent support test for taxable year 2012 (the current taxable year). X also meets the 33 1/3 support test for 2013, as the immediately succeeding taxable year.

(ii) In taxable years 2009, 2010, 2011, 2012, and 2013, in the aggregate, X does not receive at least 33 1/3 percent of its support from governmental units referred to in section 170(c)(1), from contributions made directly or indirectly by the general public, or from a combination of these sources. However, X still meets the 33 1/3 percent support test for taxable year 2013 based on the aggregate support received for taxable years 2008 through 2012.

(iii) In taxable years 2010, 2011, 2012, 2013, and 2014, in the aggregate, X does not receive at least 33 1/3 percent of its support from governmental units referred to in section 170(c)(1), from contributions made directly or indirectly by the general public, or from a combination of these sources. X does not meet the 33 1/3 percent support test for taxable year 2014.

(iv) X meets the facts and circumstances test for taxable year 2013 and for taxable year 2014 (the immediately succeeding taxable year) based on the aggregate support X receives, X's fundraising program, and consideration of other factors, including those listed in paragraphs (f)(3)(iii)(A) through (f)(3)(iii)(E) of this section, during taxable years 2009, 2010, 2011, 2012, and 2013. Therefore, even though X does not meet the 33 1/3 percent support test for taxable year 2014, X is still an organization described in section 170(b)(1)(A)(vi) for that year.

(v) Normally; first five years of an organization's existence. (A) An organization "normally" receives the requisite amount of public support and meets the 33 1/3 percent public support test or the facts and circumstances test during its first five taxable years as a section 501(c)(3) organization if the organization can reasonably be expected to meet the requirements of the 33 1/3 percent support test or the facts and circumstances test during that period. With respect to such organization's sixth taxable year, the general definition of normally set forth in paragraphs (f)(4)(i), (f)(4)(ii), and (f)(4)(iii) of this section apply. Alternatively, the organization shall be treated as "normally" meeting the 33 1/3 percent support test or the facts and circumstances test for its sixth taxable year (but not its seventh taxable year) if it meets the 33 1/3 percent support test or the facts and circumstances test under the definition of normally set forth in paragraphs (f)(4)(i), (f)(4)(ii), and (f)(4)(iii) of this section for its fifth taxable year (based on support received in its first through fifth taxable years).

(B) Basic consideration. In determining whether an organization can reasonably be expected (within the meaning of paragraph (f)(4)(v)(A) of this section) to meet the requirements of the 33 1/3 percent support test or the facts and circumstances test during its first five taxable years, the basic consideration is whether its organizational structure, current or proposed programs or activities, and actual or intended method of operation are such as can reasonably be expected to attract the type of broadly based support from the general public, public charities, and governmental units that is necessary to meet such tests. The factors that are relevant to this determination, and the weight accorded to each of them, may differ from case to case, depending on the nature and functions of the organization. The information to be considered for this purpose shall consist of all pertinent facts and circumstances, including the factors set forth in paragraph (f)(3) of this section.

(vi) Example. The application of paragraph (f)(4)(v) of this section may be illustrated by the following example:

Example. (i) Organization Y was formed in January 2008, and uses a taxable year ending December 31. After September 9, 2008, and before December 31, 2008, Organization Y filed Form 1023 requesting recognition of exemption as an organization described in section 501(c)(3) and in sections 170(b)(1)(A)(vi) and 509(a)(1). In its application, Organization Y established that it can reasonably be expected to operate as a publicly supported organization under paragraph (f)(2) or (f)(3) and paragraph (f)(4)(v) of this section. Subsequently, Organization Y received a ruling or determination letter that it is an organization described in section 501(c)(3) and sections 170(b)(1)(A)(vi) and 509(a)(1) effective as of the date of its formation.

(ii) Organization Y is described in sections 170(b)(1)(A)(vi) and 509(a)(1) for its first five taxable years (the taxable years ending December 31, 2008, through December 31, 2012).

(iii) Organization Y can qualify as a publicly supported organization for the taxable year ending December 31, 2013, if Organization Y can meet the requirements of either paragraph (f)(2) or paragraph (f)(3) of this section or § 1.509(a)–3(a) and § 1.509(a)–(3)(b) for the taxable years ending December 31, 2009, through December 31, 2013, or for the taxable years ending December 31, 2008, through December 31, 2012.

(vii) Organizations reclassified as private foundations. (A) New publicly supported organizations. If a new publicly supported organization described under section 170(b)(1)(A)(vi) cannot meet the requirements of the 33 1/3 percent test of paragraph (f)(2) or the facts and circumstances test of paragraph (f)(3) for its sixth taxable year under the general definition of normally set forth in paragraphs (f)(4)(i), (f)(4)(ii), and (f)(4)(iii) of this section or under the alternate rule set forth in paragraph (f)(4)(v) of this section (effectively failing to meet a public support test for both its fifth and sixth taxable years), it will be treated as a private foundation as of the first day of its sixth taxable year only for purposes of sections 507, 4940, and 6033. Such an organization must file a Form 990-PF, "Return of Private Foundation or Section 4947(a)(1) Nonexempt Charitable Trust Treated as a Private Foundation," and will be liable for the net investment tax imposed by section 4940 and, if applicable, the private foundation termination tax imposed by section 507(c), for its sixth taxable year. For succeeding taxable years, the organization will be treated as a private foundation for all purposes.

(B) Other publicly supported organizations. A publicly supported organization described in section 170(b)(1)(A)(vi) (other than a new publicly supported organization described in paragraph (f)(4)(vii)(A) of this section) that has failed to meet both the 33 1/3 percent support test and the facts and circumstances test for any two consecutive taxable years will be treated as a private foundation as of the first day of the second consecutive taxable year only for purposes of sections 507, 4940, and 6033. Such an organization must file a Form 990-PF, "Return of Private Foundation or Section 4947(a)(1) Nonexempt Charitable Trust Treated as a Private Foundation," and will be liable for the net investment tax imposed by section 4940 and, if applicable, the private foundation termination tax imposed by section 507(c), for the second consecutive failed taxable year. For succeeding taxable years, the organization will be treated as a private foundation for all purposes.

(5) Determinations of foundation classification and reliance. (i) A ruling or determination letter that an organization is described in section 170(b)(1)(A)(vi) may be issued to an organization. Such determination may be made in conjunction with the recognition of the organization's tax-exempt status or at such other time as the organization believes it is described in section 170(b)(1)(A)(vi). The ruling or determination letter that the organization is described in section 170(b)(1)(A)(vi) may be revoked if, upon examination, the organization has not met the requirements of paragraph (f) of this section. The ruling or determination letter that the organization is described in section 170(b)

(1)(A)(vi) also may be revoked if the organization's application for a ruling or determination contained one or more material misstatements or omissions of fact or if such application was part of a scheme or plan to avoid or evade any provision of the Internal Revenue Code. The revocation of the determination that an organization is described in section 170(b)(1)(A)(vi) does not preclude revocation of the determination that the organization is described in section 501(c)(3).

(ii) Status of grantors or contributors. For purposes of sections 170, 507, 545(b)(2), 642(c), 4942, 4945, 4966, 2055, 2106(a)(2), and 2522, grantors or contributors may rely upon a determination letter or ruling that an organization is described in section 170(b)(1)(A)(vi) until the IRS publishes notice of a change of status (for example, in the Internal Revenue Bulletin or Publication 78, "Cumulative List of Organizations described in Section 170(c) of the Internal Revenue Code of 1986," which can be searched at http://www.irs.gov.) For this purpose, grantors or contributors also may rely on an advance ruling that expires on or after June 9, 2008. However, a grantor or contributor may not rely on such an advance ruling or any determination letter or ruling if the grantor or contributor was responsible for, or aware of, the act or failure to act that resulted in the organization's loss of classification under section 170(b)(1)(A)(vi) or acquired knowledge that the IRS had given notice to such organization that it would be deleted from such classification.

(iii) Reliance by grantors or contributors. A grantor or contributor, other than one of the organization's founders, creators, or foundation managers (within the meaning of section 4946(b)), will not be considered to be responsible for, or aware of, the act or failure to act that resulted in the loss of the organization's "publicly supported" classification under section 170(b)(1)(A)(vi), if such grantor or contributor has made such grant or contribution in reliance upon a written statement by the grantee organization that such grant or contribution will not result in the loss of such organization's classification as a publicly supported organization as described in section 170(b)(1)(A)(vi). Such statement must be signed by a responsible officer of the grantee organization and must set forth sufficient information, including a summary of the pertinent financial data for the five taxable years immediately preceding the current taxable year, to assure a reasonably prudent person that his grant or contribution will not result in the loss of the grantee organization's classification as a publicly supported organization as described in section 170(b)(1)(A)(vi). If a reasonable doubt exists as to the effect of such grant or contribution, or if the grantor or contributor is one of the organization's founders, creators, or foundation managers, the procedure set forth in paragraph (f)(6)(iv) of this section for requesting a determination from the IRS may be followed by the grantee organization for the protection of the grantor or contributor.

(6) Definition of support; meaning of general public—(i) In general. In determining whether the 33 ⅓ percent support test or the 10 percent support limitation described in paragraph (f)(3)(i) of this section is met, contributions by an individual, trust, or corporation shall be taken into account as support from direct or indirect contributions from the general public only to the extent that the total amount of the contributions by any such individual, trust, or corporation during the period described in paragraph (f)(4)(i) or paragraph (f)(4)(ii) of this section does not exceed two percent of the organization's total support for such period, except as provided in paragraph (f)(6)(ii) of this section. Therefore, for example, any contribution by one individual will be included in full in the denominator of the fraction determining the 33 ⅓ percent support or the 10 percent support limitation, but will be includible in the numerator of such fraction only to the extent that such amount does not exceed two percent of the denominator. In applying the two percent limitation, all contributions made by a donor and by any person or persons standing in a relationship to the donor that is described in section 4946(a)(1)(C) through (a)(1)(G) and the related regulations shall be treated as made by one person. The two percent limitation shall not apply to support received from governmental units referred to in section 170(c)(1) or to contributions from organizations described in section 170(b)(1)(A)(vi), except as provided in paragraph (f)(6)(v) of this section. For purposes of paragraphs (f)(2), (f)(3)(i), and (f)(7)(iii)(A)(2) of this section, the term indirect contributions from the general public includes contributions received by the organization from organizations (such as section 170(b)(1)(A)(vi) organizations) that normally receive a substantial part of their support from direct contributions from the general public, except as provided in paragraph (f)(6)(v) of this section. See the examples in paragraph (f)(9) of this section for the application of this paragraph (f)(6)(i). For purposes of this paragraph (f), the term contributions includes qualified sponsorship payments (as defined in § 1.513–4) in the form of money or property (but not services).

(ii) Exclusion of unusual grants. (A) For purposes of applying the 2 percent limitation described in paragraph (f)(6)(i) of this section to determine whether the 33 1/3 percent support test or the 10 percent support limitation in paragraph (f)(3)(i) of this section is satisfied, one or more contributions may be excluded from both the numerator and the denominator of the applicable support fraction if such contributions meet the requirements of paragraph (f)(6)(iii) of this section. The exclusion provided by this paragraph (f)(6)(ii) is generally intended to apply to substantial contributions or bequests from disinterested parties, which contributions or bequests—

(1) Are attracted by reason of the publicly supported nature of the organization;

(2) Are unusual or unexpected with respect to the amount thereof; and

(3) Would, by reason of their size, adversely affect the status of the organization as normally being publicly supported for the applicable period described in paragraph (f)(4) of this section.

(B) In the case of a grant (as defined in § 1.509(a)–3(g)) that meets the requirements of this paragraph (f)(6)(ii), if the terms of the granting instrument (whether executed before or after 1969) require that the funds be paid to the recipient organization over a period of years, the amount received by the organization each year pursuant to the terms of such grant may be excluded for such year. However, no item of gross investment income may be excluded under this paragraph (f)(6). The provisions of this paragraph (f)(6) shall apply to exclude unusual grants made during any of the applicable periods described in paragraph (f)(4) or (f)(6) of this section. See paragraph (f)(6)(iv) of this section as to reliance by a grantee organization upon an unusual grant ruling under this paragraph (f)(6).

(iii) Determining factors. In determining whether a particular contribution may be excluded under paragraph (f)(6)(ii) of this section all pertinent facts and circumstances will be taken into consideration. No single factor will necessarily be determinative. For some of the factors similar to the factors to be considered, see § 1.509(a)–3T(c)(4).

(iv) Grantors and contributors. Prior to the making of any grant or contribution that will allegedly meet the requirements for exclusion under paragraph (f)(6)(ii) of this section, a potential grantee organization may request a determination whether such grant or contribution may be so excluded. Requests for such determination may be filed by the grantee organization. The issuance of such determination will be at the sole discretion of the Commissioner. The organization must submit all information necessary to make a determination on the factors referred to in paragraph (f)(6)(iii) of this section. If a favorable ruling is issued, such ruling may be relied upon by the grantor or contributor of the particular contribution in question for purposes of sections 170, 507, 545(b)(2), 642(c), 4942, 4945, 2055 2106(a)(2), and 2522 and by the grantee organization for purposes of paragraph (f)(6)(ii) of this section.

(v) Grants from public charities. Pursuant to paragraph (f)(6)(i) of this section, contributions received from a governmental unit or from a section 170(b)(1)(A)(vi) organization are not subject to the 2 percent limitation described in paragraph (f)(6)(i) of this section unless such contributions represent amounts which have been expressly or impliedly earmarked by a donor to such governmental unit or section 170(b)(1)(A)(vi) organization as being for, or for the benefit of, the particular organization claiming section 170(b)(1)(A)(vi) status. See § 1.509(a)–3(j)(3) for examples illustrating the rules of this paragraph (f)(6)(v).

(7) Definition of support; special rules and meaning of terms—(i) Definition of support. For purposes of this paragraph (f)(7), the term "support" shall be as defined in section 509(d) (without regard to section 509(d)(2)). The term "support" does not include—

(A) Any amounts received from the exercise or performance by an organization of its charitable, educational, or other purpose or function constituting the basis for its exemption under section 501(a). In general, such amounts include amounts received from any activity the conduct of which is substantially related to the furtherance of such purpose or function (other than through the production of income); or

(B) Contributions of services for which a deduction is not allowable.

(ii) For purposes of the 33 1/3 percent support test and the 10 percent support limitation in paragraph (f)(3)(i) of this section, all amounts received that are described in paragraphs (f)(7)(i)(A) or (B) of this section are to be excluded from both the numerator and the denominator of the fractions determining compliance with such tests, except as provided in paragraph (f)(7)(iii) of this section.

(iii) Organizations dependent primarily on gross receipts from related activities. (A) Notwithstanding the provisions of paragraph (f)(7)(i) of this section, an organization will not be treated as satisfying the 33 1/3 percent support test or the 10 percent support limitation in paragraph (f)(3)(i) of this section if it receives—

(1) Almost all of its support (as defined in section 509(d)) from gross receipts from related activities; and

(2) An insignificant amount of its support from governmental units (without regard to amounts referred to in paragraph (f)(7)(i)(A) of this section) and contributions made directly or indirectly by the general public.

(B) Example. The application of this paragraph (f)(7)(iii) may be illustrated by the following example:

Example. Z, an organization described in section 501(c)(3), is controlled by A, its president. Z received $500,000 during the period consisting of the current taxable year and the four immediately preceding taxable years under a contract with the Department of Transportation, pursuant to which Z has engaged in research to improve a particular vehicle used primarily by the Federal government.

During this same period, the only other support received by Z consisted of $5,000 in small contributions primarily from Z's employees and business associates. The $500,000 amount constitutes support under sections 509(d)(2) and 509(a)(2)(A). Under these circumstances, Z meets the conditions of paragraphs (f)(7)(iii)(A)(1) and (2) of this section and will not be treated as meeting the requirements of either the 33 1/3 percent support test or the facts and circumstances test. As to the rules applicable to organizations that fail to qualify under section 170(b)(1)(A)(vi) because of the provisions of this paragraph (f)(7)(ii), see section 509(a)(2) and the accompanying regulations. For the distinction between gross receipts (as referred to in section 509(d)(2)) and gross investment income (as referred to in section 509(d)(4)), see § 1.509(a)–3(m).

(iv) Membership fees. For purposes of this paragraph (f)(7), the term support shall include "membership fees" within the meaning of § 1.509(a)–3(h) (that is, if the basic purpose for making a payment is to provide support for the organization rather than to purchase admissions, merchandise, services, or the use of facilities).

(v) Unrelated business activities. The term net income from unrelated business activities in section 509(d)(3) includes (but is not limited to) an organization's unrelated business taxable income (UBTI) within the meaning of section 512. However, when calculating UBTI for purposes of determining support (within the meaning of this paragraph (f)(7)), section 512(a)(6) does not apply. Accordingly, in the case of an organization that derives gross income from the regular conduct of two or more unrelated business activities, support includes the aggregate of gross income from all such unrelated business activities less the aggregate of the deductions allowed with respect to all such unrelated business activities. Nonetheless, when determining support, such organization can use either its UBTI calculated under section 512(a)(6) or its UBTI calculated in the aggregate.

(8) Support from a governmental unit. (i) For purposes of the 33 1/3 percent support test and the 10 percent support limitation described in paragraph (f)(3)(i) of this section, the term support from a governmental unit includes any amounts received from a governmental unit, including donations or contributions and amounts received in connection with a contract entered into with a governmental unit for the performance of services or in connection with a government research grant. However, such amounts will not constitute support from a governmental unit for such purposes if they constitute amounts received from the exercise or performance of the organization's exempt functions as provided in paragraph (f)(7)(i)(A) of this section.

(ii) For purposes of paragraph (f)(8)(i) of this section, any amount paid by a governmental unit to an organization is not to be treated as received from the exercise or performance of its charitable, educational, or other purpose or function constituting the basis for its exemption under section 501(a) (within the meaning of paragraph (f)(7)(i)(A) of this section) if the purpose of the payment is primarily to enable the organization to provide a service to, or maintain a facility for, the direct benefit of the public (regardless of whether part of the expense of providing such service or facility is paid for by the public), rather than to serve the direct and immediate needs of the payor. For example—

(A) Amounts paid for the maintenance of library facilities which are open to the public;

(B) Amounts paid under government programs to nursing homes or homes for the aged in order to provide health care or domiciliary services to residents of such facilities; and

(C) Amounts paid to child placement or child guidance organizations under government programs for services rendered to children in the community, are considered payments the purpose of which is primarily to enable the recipient organization to provide a service or maintain a facility for the direct benefit of the public, rather than to serve the direct and immediate needs of the payor. Furthermore, any amount received from a governmental unit under circumstances such that the amount would be treated as a "grant" within the meaning of § 1.509(a)–3(g) will generally constitute "support from a governmental unit" described in this paragraph (f)(8), rather than an amount described in paragraph (f)(7)(i)(A) of this section.

(9) Examples. The application of paragraphs (f)(1) through (8) of this paragraph may be illustrated by the following examples:

Example 1. (i) M is recognized as an organization referred to in section 501(c)(3). For the years 2008 through 2012 (the applicable period with respect to the taxable year 2012 under paragraph (f)(4) of this paragraph), M received support (as defined in paragraphs (f)(6) through (8) of this section) of $600,000 from the following sources:

Investment Income	$ 300,000
City Y (a governmental unit described in section 170(c)(1)	40,000
United Fund (an organization described in section 170(b)(1)(A)(vi)	40,000
Contributions	220,000
Total Support	$ 600,000

(ii) With respect to the taxable year 2012, M's public support is computed as follows:

Support from a governmental unit described in section 170(c)(1)	40,000
Indirect contributions from the general public (United Fund)	40,000
Contributions by various donors no one having made contributions which total in excess of $12,000—2 percent of total support)	50,000
Six contributions (each in excess of $12,000—2 percent total support) 6 x $12,000	72,000
	$ 202,000

(iii) M's support from governmental units referred to in section 170(c)(1) and from direct and indirect contributions from the general public (as defined in paragraph (f)(6) of this section with respect to the taxable year 2012 normally exceeds 33 1/3 percent of M's total support for the applicable period (2008 through 2012). M meets the 33 1/3 percent-of-support test with respect to 2012 and is therefore publicly supported for the taxable years 2012 and 2013.

Example 2. N is recognized as an organization described in section 501(c)(3). It was created to maintain public gardens containing botanical specimens and displaying statuary and other art objects. The facilities, works of art, and a large endowment were all contributed by a single contributor. The members of the governing body of the organization are unrelated to its creator. The gardens are open to the public without charge and attract a substantial number of visitors each year. For the current taxable year and the four taxable years immediately preceding the current taxable year, 95 percent of the organization's total support was received from investment income from its original endowment. N also maintains a membership society that is supported by members of the general public who wish to contribute to the upkeep of the gardens by paying a small annual membership fee. Over the 5-year period in question, these fees from the general public constituted the remaining 5 percent of the organization's total support for such period. Under these circumstances, N does not meet the 33 1/3 percent support test for its current taxable year. Furthermore, because only 5 percent of its total support is, with respect to the current taxable year, normally received from the general public, N does not satisfy the 10 percent support limitation described in paragraph (f)(3)(i) of this section and therefore does not qualify as publicly supported under the facts and circumstances test. Because N has failed to satisfy the 10 percent support limitation under paragraph (f)(3)(i) of this section, none of the other requirements or factors set forth in paragraphs (f)(3)(iii)(A) through (E) of this section can be considered in determining whether N qualifies as a publicly supported organization. For its current taxable year, N therefore is not an organization described in section 170(b)(1)(A)(vi).

Example 3. (i) O, an art museum, is recognized as an organization described in section 501(c)(3). In 1930, O was founded in S City by the members of a single family to collect, preserve, interpret, and display to the public important works of art. O is governed by a Board of Trustees that originally consisted almost entirely of members of the founding family. However, since 1945, members of the founding family or persons standing in a relationship to the members of such family described in section 4946(a)(1)(C) through (G) have annually constituted less than one-fifth of the Board of Trustees. The remaining board members are citizens of S City from a variety of professions and occupations who represent the interests and views of the people of S City in the activities carried on by the organization rather than the personal or private interests of the founding family. O solicits contributions from the general public and for the current taxable year and each of the four taxable years immediately preceding the current taxable year, O has received total contributions (in small sums of less than $100, none of which exceeds 2 percent of O's total support for such period) in excess of $10,000. These contributions from the general public (as defined in paragraph (f)(6) of this section) represent 25 percent of the organization's total support for such 5-year period. For this same period, investment income from several large endowment funds has constituted 75 percent of O's total support. O expends substantially all of its annual income for its exempt purposes and thus depends upon the funds it annually solicits from the public as well as its investment income in order to carry out its activities on a normal and continuing basis and to acquire new works of art. O has, for the entire period of its existence, been open to the public and more than 300,000 people (from S City and elsewhere) have visited the museum in each of the current taxable year and the four most recent taxable years.

(ii) Under these circumstances, O does not meet the 33 1/3 percent support test for its current year because it has received only 25 percent of its total support for the applicable 5-year period from the general public. However, under the facts set forth above, O has met the 10 percent support limitation under paragraph (f)(3)(i) of this section, as well as the requirements of paragraph (f)(3)(ii) of this section. Under all of the facts set forth in this example, O is considered as meeting the requirements of the facts and circumstances test on the basis of satisfying paragraphs (f)(3)(i) and (ii) of this section and the factors set forth in paragraphs (f)(3)(iii)(A) through (D) of this section. O is therefore publicly supported for its current taxable year and the immediately succeeding taxable year.

Example 4. (i) In 1960, the P Philharmonic Orchestra was organized in T City through the combined efforts of a local music society and a local women's club to present to the public a wide variety of musical programs intended to foster music appreciation in the community. P is recognized as an organization described in section 501(c)(3). The orchestra is composed of professional musicians who are paid by the association. Twelve performances open to the public are scheduled each year. A small admission fee is charged for each of these performances. In addition, several performances are staged annually without charge. During the current taxable year and the four taxable years immediately preceding the current taxable year, P has received separate contributions of $200,000 each from A and B (not members of a single family) and support of $120,000 from the T Community Chest, a public federated fundraising organization operating in T City. P depends on these funds in order to carry out its activities and will continue to depend on contributions of this type to be made in the future. P has also begun a fundraising campaign in an attempt to expand its activities for the coming years. P is governed by a Board of Directors comprised of 5 individuals. A faculty member of a local college, the president of a local music society, the head of a local banking institution, a prominent doctor, and a member of the governing body of the local chamber of commerce currently serve on P's Board and represent the interests and views of the community in the activities carried on by P.

(ii) With respect to P's current taxable year, P's sources of support are computed on the basis of the current taxable year and the four taxable years immediately preceding the current taxable year, as follows:

Contributions	$ 520,000
Receipts from performances	100,000
Total support	620,000
Less:	
Receipts from performances (excluded under paragraph (f)7(i)(a) of this paragraph)	100,000
Total support for purposes of paragraphs (f)(2) and (f)(3)(i) of this paragraph	$ 520,000

(iii) For purposes of paragraphs (f)(2) and (f)(3)(i) of this paragraph, P's support is computed as follows:

T Community Chest (indirect support from the general public)	$ 120,000
Two contributions (each in excess of $10,400—2 percent of total support) 2 x $10,400	20,800
Total	$ 140,800

(iv) P's support from the direct and indirect contributions from the general public does not meet the 33 1/3 percent support test ($140,800/$520,000 = 27 percent of total support). However, because P receives 27 percent of its total support from the general public, it meets the 10 percent support limitation under paragraph (f)(3)(i) of this section. P also meets the requirements of paragraph (f)(3)(ii) of this section. As a result of satisfying these requirements and the factors set forth in paragraphs (f)(3)(iii)(A) through (D) of this section, P is considered to meet the facts and circumstances test and therefore qualifies as a publicly supported organization under paragraph (f)(1) of this section for its current taxable year and the immediately succeeding taxable year.

Example 5. (i) Q is recognized as an organization described in section 501(c)(3). It is a philanthropic organization founded in 1965 by C for the purpose of making annual contributions to worthy charities. C created Q as a charitable trust by the transfer of appreciated securities worth $500,000 to Q. Pursuant to the trust agreement, C and two other members of his family are the sole trustees of Q and are vested with the right to appoint successor trustees. In each of the current taxable year and the four taxable years immediately preceding the current taxable year, Q received $15,000 in investment income from its original endowment. Each year Q makes a solicitation for funds by operating a charity ball at C's residence. Guests are invited and requested to make contributions of $100 per couple. During the 5-year period at issue, $15,000 was received from the proceeds of these events. C and his family have also made contributions to Q of $25,000 over the 5-year period at issue. Q makes disbursements each year of substantially all of its net income to the public charities chosen by the trustees.

(ii) Q's sources of support for the current taxable year and the four taxable years immediately preceding the current taxable year as follows:

Investment Income	$ 60,000
Contributions	40,000
Total support	$ 100,000

(iii) For purposes of paragraphs (f)(2) and (f)(3)(i) of this section, Q's support is computed as follows:

Contributions from the general public	$ 15,000
One contribution (in excess of $2,000—2% of total support) 1 x $2,000	2,000
Total	$ 17,000

(iv) Q's support from the general public does not meet the 33 1/3 percent support test ($17,000/$100,000 = 17 percent of total support). Thus, Q's classification as a "publicly supported" organization depends on whether it meets the requirements of the facts and circumstances test. Even though it satisfies the 10 percent support limitation under paragraph (f)(3)(i) of this section, its method of solicitation makes it questionable whether Q satisfies the requirements of paragraph (f)(3)(ii) of this section. Because of its method of operating, Q also has a greater burden of establishing its publicly supported nature under paragraph (f)(3)(iii)(A) of this section. Based upon the foregoing and upon Q's failure to receive favorable consideration under the remaining factors set forth in paragraphs (f)(3)(iii)(B), (C) and (D) of this section, Q does not satisfy the facts and circumstances test.

(10) Community trusts; introduction. Community trusts have often been established to attract large contributions of a capital or endowment nature for the benefit of a particular community or area, and often such contributions have come initially from a small number of donors. While the community trust generally has a governing body comprised of representatives of the particular community or area, its contributions are often received and maintained in the form of separate trusts or funds, which are subject to varying degrees of control by the governing body. To qualify as a "publicly supported" organization, a community trust must meet the 33 1/3 percent-of-support test of paragraph (e)(2) of this section, or, if it cannot meet that test, be organized and operated so as to attract new and additional public or governmental support on a continuous basis sufficient to meet the facts and circumstances test of paragraph (e)(3) of this section. Such facts and circumstances test includes a requirement of attraction of public support in paragraph (e)(3)(ii) of this section which, as applied to community trusts will generally satisfied, if they seek gifts and bequests from a wide range of potential donors in the community or area served, through banks or trust companies, through attorneys or other professional persons, or in other appropriate ways which call attention to the community trust as a potential recipient of gifts and bequests made for the benefit of the community or area served. A community trust is not required to engage in periodic, community-wide, fund-raising campaigns directed toward attracting a large number of small contributions in a manner similar to campaigns conducted by a community chest or united fund. * * *

* * *

(13) Method of accounting. For purposes of section 170(b)(1)(A)(vi), an organization's support will be determined under the method of accounting on the basis of which the organization regularly computes its income in keeping its books under section 446. For example, if a grantor makes a grant to an organization payable over a term of years, such grant will be includible in the support fraction of the grantee organization under the method of accounting on the basis of which the grantee organization regularly computes its income in keeping its books under section 446.

§ 1.170A-13. Recordkeeping and return requirements for deductions for charitable contributions.

* * *

(f) Substantiation of charitable contributions of $250 or more—(1) In general. No deduction is allowed under section 170(a) for all or part of any contribution of $250 or more unless the taxpayer substantiates the contribution with a contemporaneous written acknowledgment from the donee organization. A taxpayer who makes more than one contribution of $250 or more to a donee organization in a taxable year may substantiate the contributions with one or more contemporaneous written acknowledgments. Section 170(f)(8) does not apply to a payment of $250 or more if the amount contributed (as determined under section

1.170A–1(h)) is less than $250. Separate contributions of less than $250 are not subject to the requirements of section 170(f)(8), regardless of whether the sum of the contributions made by a taxpayer to a donee organization during a taxable year equals $250 or more.

(2) Written acknowledgement. Except as otherwise provided in paragraphs (f)(8) through (f)(11) and (f)(13) of this section, a written acknowledgment from a donee organization must provide the following information—

(i) The amount of any cash the taxpayer paid and a description (but not necessarily the value) of any property other than cash the taxpayer transferred to the donee organization;

(ii) A statement of whether or not the donee organization provides any goods or services in consideration, in whole or in part, for any of the cash or other property transferred to the donee organization;

(iii) If the donee organization provides any goods or services other than intangible religious benefits (as described in section 170(f)(8)), a description and good faith estimate of the value of those goods or services; and

(iv) If the donee organization provides any intangible religious benefits, a statement to that effect.

(3) Contemporaneous. A written acknowledgment is contemporaneous if it is obtained by the taxpayer on or before the earlier of—

(i) The date the taxpayer files the original return for the taxable year in which the contribution was made; or

(ii) The due date (including extensions) for filing the taxpayer's original return for that year.

(4) Donee organization. For purposes of this paragraph (f), a donee organization is an organization described in section 170(c).

(5) Goods or services. Goods or services means cash, property, services, benefits, and privileges.

(6) In consideration for. A donee organization provides goods or services in consideration for a taxpayer's payment if, at the time the taxpayer makes the payment to the donee organization, the taxpayer receives or expects to receive goods or services in exchange for that payment. Goods or services a donee organization provides in consideration for a payment by a taxpayer include goods or services provided in a year other than the year in which the taxpayer makes the payment to the donee organization.

(7) Good faith estimate. For purposes of this section, good faith estimate means a donee organization's estimate of the fair market value of any goods or services, without regard to the manner in which the organization in fact made that estimate. See section 1.170A–1(h)(6) for rules regarding when a taxpayer may treat a donee organization's estimate of the value of goods or services as the fair market value.

(8) Certain goods or services disregarded.—(i) In general. For purposes of section 170(f)(8), the following goods or services are disregarded—

(A) Goods or services that have insubstantial value under the guidelines provided in Revenue Procedures 90–12, 1990–1 C.B. 471, 92–49, 1992–1 C.B. 987, and any successor documents. (See section 601.601(d)(2)(ii) of the Statement of Procedural Rules, 26 CFR part 601.); and

(B) Annual membership benefits offered to a taxpayer in exchange for a payment of $75 or less per year that consist of—

(1) Any rights or privileges, other than those described in section 170(*l*), that the taxpayer can exercise frequently during the membership period. Examples of such rights and privileges may include, but are not limited to, free or discounted admission to the organization's facilities or events, free or discounted parking, preferred access to goods or services, and discounts on the purchase of goods or services; and

(2) Admission to events during the membership period that are open only to members of a donee organization and for which the donee organization reasonably projects that the cost per person (excluding any allocable overhead) attending each such event is within the limits established for "low cost articles" under section 513(h)(2). The projected cost to the donee organization is determined at the time the organization first offers its membership package for the year (using section 3.07 of Revenue Procedure 90–12, or any successor documents, to determine the cost of any items or services that are donated).

(ii) Examples. The following examples illustrate the rules of this paragraph (f)(8).

Example 1. Membership benefits disregarded. Performing Arts Center E is an organization described in section 170(c). In return for a payment of $75, E offers a package of basic membership benefits that includes the right to purchase tickets to performances one week before they go on sale to the general public, free parking in E's garage during evening and weekend performances, and a 10% discount on merchandise sold in E's gift shop. In return for a payment of $150, E offers a package of preferred membership benefits that includes all of the benefits in the $75 package as well as a poster that is sold in E's gift shop for $20. The basic membership and the preferred membership are each valid for twelve months, and there are approximately 50 performances of various productions at E during a twelve-month period. E's gift shop is open for several hours each week and at performance times. F, a patron of the arts, is solicited by E to make a contribution. E offers F the preferred membership benefits in return for a payment of $150 or more. F makes a payment of $300 to E. F can satisfy the substantiation requirement of section 170(f)(8) by obtaining a contemporaneous written acknowledgment from E that includes a description of the poster and a good faith estimate of its fair market value ($20) and disregards the remaining membership benefits.

Example 2. Contemporaneous written acknowledgement need not mention rights or privileges that can be disregarded. The facts are the same as in Example 1, except that F made a payment of $300 and received only a basic membership. F can satisfy the section 170(f)(8) substantiation requirement with a contemporaneous written acknowledgment stating that no goods or services were provided.

Example 3. Rights or privileges that cannot be exercised frequently. Community Theater Group G is an organization described in section 170(c). Every summer, G performs four different plays. Each play is performed two times. In return for a membership fee of $60, G offers its members free admission to any of its performances. Non-members may purchase tickets on a performance by performance basis for $15 a ticket. H, an individual who is a sponsor of the theater, is solicited by G to make a contribution. G tells H that the membership benefit will be provided in return for any payment of $60 or more. H chooses to make a payment of $350 to G and receives in return the membership benefit. G's membership benefit of free admission is not described in paragraph (f)(8)(i)(B) of this section because it is not a privilege that can be exercised frequently (due to the limited number of performances offered by G). Therefore, to meet the requirements of section 170(f)(8), a contemporaneous written acknowledgment of H's $350 payment must include a description of the free admission benefit and a good faith estimate of its value.

Example 4. Multiple memberships. In December of each year, K, an individual, gives each of her six grandchildren a junior membership in

Dinosaur Museum, an organization described in section 170(c). Each junior membership costs $50, and K makes a single payment of $300 for all six memberships. A junior member is entitled to free admission to the museum and to weekly films, slide shows, and lectures about dinosaurs. In addition, each junior member receives a bi-monthly, non-commercial quality newsletter with information about dinosaurs and upcoming events. K's contemporaneous written acknowledgment from Dinosaur Museum may state that no goods or services were provided in exchange for K's payment.

(9) Goods or services provided to employees or partners of donors—(i) Certain goods or services disregarded. For purposes of section 170(f)(8), goods or services provided by a donee organization to employees of a donor, or to partners of a partnership that is a donor, in return for a payment to the organization may be disregarded to the extent that the goods or services provided to each employee or partner are the same as those described in paragraph (f)(8)(i) of this section.

(ii) No good faith estimate required for other goods or services. If a taxpayer makes a contribution of $250 or more to a donee organization and, in return, the donee organization offers the taxpayer's employees or partners goods or services other than those described in paragraph (f)(9)(i) of this section, the contemporaneous written acknowledgment of the taxpayer's contribution is not required to include a good faith estimate of the value of such goods or services but must include a description of those goods or services.

(iii) Example. The following example illustrates the rules of this paragraph (f)(9).

Example. Museum J is an organization described in section 170(c). For a payment of $40, J offers a package of basic membership benefits that includes free admission and a 10% discount on merchandise sold in J's gift shop. J's other membership categories are for supporters who contribute $100 or more. Corporation K makes a payment of $50,000 to J and, in return, J offers K's employees free admission for one year, a tee-shirt with J's logo that costs J $4.50, and a gift shop discount of 25% for one year. The free admission for K's employees is the same as the benefit made available to holders of the $40 membership and is otherwise described in paragraph (f)(8)(i)(B) of this section. The tee-shirt given to each of K's employees is described in paragraph (f)(8)(i)(A) of this section. Therefore, the contemporaneous written acknowledgment of K's payment is not required to include a description or good faith estimate of the value of the free admission or the tee-shirts. However, because the gift shop discount offered to K's employees is different than that offered to those who purchase the $40 membership, the discount is not described in paragraph (f)(8)(i) of this section. Therefore, the contemporaneous written acknowledgment of K's payment is required to include a description of the 25% discount offered to K's employees.

(10) Substantiation of out-of-pocket expenses. A taxpayer who incurs unreimbursed expenditures incident to the rendition of services, within the meaning of section 1.170A–1(g), is treated as having obtained a contemporaneous written acknowledgment of those expenditures if the taxpayer—

(i) Has adequate records under paragraph (a) of this section to substantiate the amount of the expenditures; and

(ii) Obtains by the date prescribed in paragraph (f)(3) of this section a statement prepared by the donee organization containing—

(A) A description of the services provided by the taxpayer;

(B) A statement of whether or not the donee organization provides any goods or services in consideration, in whole or in part, for the unreimbursed expenditures; and

(C) The information required by paragraphs (f)(2)(iii) and (iv) of this section.

(11) Contributions made by payroll deduction—(i) Form of substantiation. A contribution made by means of withholding from a taxpayer's wages and payment by the taxpayer's employer to a donee organization may be substantiated, for purposes of section 170(f)(8), by both—

(A) A pay stub, Form W-2, or other document furnished by the employer that sets forth the amount withheld by the employer for the purpose of payment to a donee organization; and

(B) A pledge card or other document prepared by or at the direction of the donee organization that includes a statement to the effect that the organization does not provide goods or services in whole or partial consideration for any contributions made to the organization by payroll deduction.

(ii) Application of $250 threshold. For the purpose of applying the $250 threshold provided in section 170(f)(8)(A) to contributions made by the means described in paragraph (f)(11)(i) of this section, the amount withheld from each payment of wages to a taxpayer is treated as a separate contribution.

(12) Distributing organizations as donees. An organization described in section 170(c), or an organization described in 5 CFR 950.105 (a Principal Combined Fund Organization for purposes of the Combined Federal Campaign) and acting in that capacity, that receives a payment made as a contribution is treated as a donee organization solely for purposes of section 170(f)(8), even if the organization (pursuant to the donor's instructions or otherwise) distributes the amount received to one or more organizations described in section 170(c). This paragraph (f)(12) does not apply, however, to a case in which the distributee organization provides goods or services as part of a transaction structured with a view to avoid taking the goods or services into account in determining the amount of the deduction to which the donor is entitled under section 170.

(13) Transfers to certain trusts. Section 170(f)(8) does not apply to a transfer of property to a trust described in section 170(f)(2)(B), a charitable remainder annuity trust (as defined in section 664(d)(1)), or a charitable remainder unitrust (as defined in section 664(d)(2) or (d)(3) or section 1.664(3)(a)(1)(i)(b)). Section 170(f)(8) does apply, however, to a transfer to a pooled income fund (as defined in section 642(c)(5)); for such a transfer, the contemporaneous written acknowledgment must state that the contribution was transferred to the donee organization's pooled income fund and indicate whether any goods or services (in addition to an income interest in the fund) were provided in exchange for the transfer. The contemporaneous written acknowledgment is not required to include a good faith estimate of the income interest.

(14) Substantiation of payments to a college or university for the right to purchase tickets to athletic events. For purposes of paragraph (f)(2)(iii) of this section, the right to purchase tickets for seating at an athletic event in exchange for a payment described in section 170(*l*) is treated as having a value equal to twenty percent of such payment. For example, when a taxpayer makes a payment of $312.50 for the right to purchase tickets for seating at an athletic event, the right to purchase tickets is treated as having a value of $62.50. The remaining $250 is treated as a charitable contribution, which the taxpayer must substantiate in accordance with the requirements of this section.

(15) Substantiation of charitable contributions made by a partnership or an S corporation. If a partnership or an S corporation makes a charitable contribution of $250 or more, the partnership or S corporation will be treated as the taxpayer for purposes of section 170(f)(8). Therefore, the partnership or S corporation must substantiate the contribution with a contemporaneous written acknowledgment from the donee organization before reporting the contribution on its income tax return for the year in which the contribution was made and must maintain the contemporaneous written acknowledgment in its records. A partner of a partnership or a shareholder of an S corporation is not required to obtain any additional substantiation for his or her share of the partnership's or S corporation's charitable contribution.

(16) Purchase of an annuity. If a taxpayer purchases an annuity from a charitable organization and claims a charitable contribution deduction of $250 or more for the excess of the amount paid over the value of the annuity, the contemporaneous written acknowledgment must state whether any goods or services in addition to the annuity were provided to the taxpayer. The contemporaneous written acknowledgment is not required to include a good faith estimate of the value of the annuity. See section 1.170A1(d)(2) for guidance in determining the value of the annuity.

(17) Substantiation of matched payments—(i) In general. For purposes of section 170, if a taxpayer's payment to a donee organization is matched, in whole or in part, by another payor, and the taxpayer receives goods or services in consideration for its payment and some or all of the matching payment, those goods or services will be treated as provided in consideration for the taxpayer's payment and not in consideration for the matching payment.

(ii) Example. The following example illustrates the rules of this paragraph (f)(17).

Example. Taxpayer makes a $400 payment to Charity L, a donee organization. Pursuant to a matching payment plan, Taxpayer's employer matches Taxpayer's $400 payment with an additional payment of $400. In consideration for the combined payments of $800, L gives Taxpayer an item that it estimates has a fair market value of $100. L does not give the employer any goods or services in consideration for its contribution. The contemporaneous written acknowledgment provided to the employer must include a statement that no goods or services were provided in consideration for the employer's $400 payment. The contemporaneous written acknowledgment provided to Taxpayer must include a statement of the amount of Taxpayer's payment, a description of the item received by Taxpayer, and a statement that L's good faith estimate of the value of the item received by Taxpayer is $100.

* * *

§ 1.170A–15. Substantiation requirements for charitable contribution of a cash, check, or other monetary gift.

(a) In general—(1) Bank record or written communication required. No deduction is allowed under sections 170(a) and 170(f)(17) for a charitable contribution in the form of a cash, check, or other monetary gift, as described in paragraph (b)(1) of this section, unless the donor substantiates the deduction with a bank record, as described in paragraph (b)(2) of this section, or a written communication, as described in paragraph (b)(3) of this section, from the donee showing the name of the donee, the date of the contribution, and the amount of the contribution.

(2) Additional substantiation required for contributions of $250 or more. No deduction is allowed under section 170(a) for any contribution of $250 or more unless the donor substantiates the contribution with a contemporaneous written acknowledgment, as described in section 170(f)(8) and § 1.170A–13(f), from the donee.

(3) Single document may be used. The requirements of paragraphs (a)(1) and (2) of this section may be met by a single document that contains all the information required by paragraphs (a)(1) and (2) of this section, if the document is obtained by the donor no later than the date prescribed by paragraph (c) of this section.

(b) Terms—(1) Monetary gift includes a transfer of a gift card redeemable for cash, and a payment made by credit card, electronic fund transfer (as described in section 5061(e)(2)), an online payment service, or payroll deduction.

(2) Bank record includes a statement from a financial institution, an electronic fund transfer receipt, a canceled check, a scanned image of both sides of a canceled check obtained from a bank website, or a credit card statement.

(3) Written communication includes email.

(c) Deadline for receipt of substantiation. The substantiation described in paragraph (a) of this section must be received by the donor on or before the earlier of—

(1) The date the donor files the original return for the taxable year in which the contribution was made; or

(2) The due date, including any extension, for filing the donor's original return for that year.

(d) Special rules—(1) Contributions made by payroll deduction. In the case of a charitable contribution made by payroll deduction, a donor is treated as meeting the requirements of section 170(f)(17) and paragraph (a) of this section if, no later than the date described in paragraph (c) of this section, the donor obtains—

(i) A pay stub, Form W-2, "Wage and Tax Statement," or other employer-furnished document that sets forth the amount withheld during the taxable year for payment to a donee; and

(ii) A pledge card or other document prepared by or at the direction of the donee that shows the name of the donee.

(2) Distributing organizations as donees. The following organizations are treated as donees for purposes of section 170(f)(17) and paragraph (a) of this section, even if the organization (pursuant to the donor's instructions or otherwise) distributes the amount received to one or more organizations described in section 170(c):

(i) An organization described in section 170(c).

(ii) An organization described in 5 CFR 950.105 (a Principal Combined Fund Organization (PCFO) for purposes of the Combined Federal Campaign (CFC)) and acting in that capacity. For purposes of the requirement for a written communication under section 170(f)(17), if the donee is a PCFO, the name of the local CFC campaign may be treated as the name of the donee organization.

(e) Substantiation of out-of-pocket expenses. Paragraph (a)(1) of this section does not apply to a donor who incurs unreimbursed expenses of less than $250 incident to the rendition of services, within the meaning of § 1.170A–1(g). For substantiation of unreimbursed out-of-pocket expenses of $250 or more, see § 1.170A–13(f)(10).

(f) Charitable contributions made by partnership or S corporation. If a partnership or an S corporation makes a charitable contribution, the partnership or S corporation is treated as the donor for purposes of section 170(f)(17) and paragraph (a) of this section.

(g) Transfers to certain trusts. The requirements of section 170(f)(17) and paragraphs (a)(1) and (3) of this section do not apply to a transfer of a cash, check, or other monetary gift to a trust described in section 170(f)(2)(B); a charitable remainder annuity trust, as described in section 664(d)(1) and the corresponding regulations; or a charitable remainder unitrust, as described in section 664(d)(2) or (d)(3) and the corresponding regulations. The requirements of section 170(f)(17) and paragraphs (a)(1) and (2) of this section do apply, however, to a transfer to a pooled income fund, as defined in section 642(c)(5).

(h) Effective/applicability date. This section applies to contributions made after July 30, 2018. Taxpayers may rely on the rules of this section for contributions made in taxable years beginning after August 17, 2006.

§ 1.170A–16. Substantiation and reporting requirements for noncash charitable contributions.

(a) Substantiation of charitable contributions of less than $250—(1) Individuals, partnerships, and certain corporations required to obtain receipt. Except as provided in paragraph (a)(2) of this section, no deduction is allowed under section 170(a) for a noncash charitable contribution of less than $250 by an individual, partnership, S corporation, or C corporation that is a personal service corporation or closely held corporation unless the donor maintains for each contribution a receipt from the donee showing the following information:

(i) The name and address of the donee;

(ii) The date of the contribution;

(iii) A description of the property in sufficient detail under the circumstances (taking into account the value of the property) for a person who is not generally familiar with the type of property to ascertain that the described property is the contributed property; and

(iv) In the case of securities, the name of the issuer, the type of security, and whether the securities are publicly traded securities within the meaning of § 1.170A–13(c)(7)(xi).

(2) Substitution of reliable written records—(i) In general. If it is impracticable to obtain a receipt (for example, where a donor deposits property at a donee's unattended drop site), the donor may satisfy the recordkeeping rules of this paragraph (a) by maintaining reliable written records, as described in paragraphs (a)(2)(ii) and (iii) of this section, for the contributed property.

(ii) Reliable written records. The reliability of written records is to be determined on the basis of all of the facts and circumstances of a particular case, including the proximity in time of the written record to the contribution.

(iii) Contents of reliable written records. Reliable written records must include—

(A) The information required by paragraph (a)(1) of this section;

(B) The fair market value of the property on the date the contribution was made;

(C) The method used in determining the fair market value; and

(D) In the case of a contribution of clothing or a household item as defined in § 1.170A–18(c), the condition of the item.

(3) Additional substantiation rules may apply. For additional substantiation rules, see paragraph (f) of this section.

(b) Substantiation of charitable contributions of $250 or more but not more

than $500. No deduction is allowed under section 170(a) for a noncash charitable contribution of $250 or more but not more than $500 unless the donor substantiates the contribution with a contemporaneous written acknowledgment, as described in section 170(f)(8) and § 1.170A–13(f).

(c) Substantiation of charitable contributions of more than $500 but not more than $5,000—(1) In general. No deduction is allowed under section 170(a) for a noncash charitable contribution of more than $500 but not more than $5,000 unless the donor substantiates the contribution with a contemporaneous written acknowledgment, as described in section 170(f)(8) and § 1.170A–13(f), and meets the applicable requirements of this section.

(2) Individuals, partnerships, and certain corporations also required to file Form 8283 (Section A). No deduction is allowed under section 170(a) for a noncash charitable contribution of more than $500 but not more than $5,000 by an individual, partnership, S corporation, or C corporation that is a personal service corporation or closely held corporation unless the donor completes Form 8283 (Section A), "Noncash Charitable Contributions," as provided in paragraph (c)(3) of this section, or a successor form, and files it with the return on which the deduction is claimed.

(3) Completion of Form 8283 (Section A). A completed Form 8283 (Section A) includes—

(i) The donor's name and taxpayer identification number (for example, a social security number or employer identification number);

(ii) The name and address of the donee;

(iii) The date of the contribution;

(iv) The following information about the contributed property:

(A) A description of the property in sufficient detail under the circumstances, taking into account the value of the property, for a person who is not generally familiar with the type of property to ascertain that the described property is the contributed property;

(B) In the case of real or tangible personal property, the condition of the property;

(C) In the case of securities, the name of the issuer, the type of security, and whether the securities are publicly traded securities within the meaning of § 1.170A–13(c)(7)(xi);

(D) The fair market value of the property on the date the contribution was made and the method used in determining the fair market value;

(E) The manner of acquisition (for example, by purchase, gift, bequest, inheritance, or exchange), and the approximate date of acquisition of the property by the donor (except that in the case of a contribution of publicly traded securities as defined in § 1.170A–13(c)(7)(xi), a representation that the donor held the securities for more than one year is sufficient) or, if the property was created, produced, or manufactured by or for the donor, the approximate date the property was substantially completed;

(F) The cost or other basis, adjusted as provided by section 1016, of the property (except that the cost or basis is not required for contributions of publicly traded securities (as defined in § 1.170A–13(c)(7)(xi)) that would have resulted in long-term capital gain if sold on the contribution date, unless the donor has elected to limit the deduction to basis under section 170(b)(1)(C)(iii));

(G) In the case of tangible personal property, whether the donee has certified it for a use related to the purpose or function constituting the donee's basis for exemption under section 501, or in the case of a governmental unit, an exclusively public purpose; and

(v) Any other information required by Form 8283 (Section A) or the instructions to Form 8283 (Section A).

(4) Additional requirement for certain vehicle contributions. In the case of a contribution of a qualified vehicle described in section 170(f)(12)(E) for which an acknowledgment by the donee organization is required under section 170(f)(12)(D), the donor must attach a copy of the acknowledgment to the Form 8283 (Section A) for the return on which the deduction is claimed.

(5) Additional substantiation rules may apply. For additional substantiation rules, see paragraph (f) of this section.

(d) Substantiation of charitable contributions of more than $5,000—(1) In general. Except as provided in paragraph (d)(2) of this section, no deduction is allowed under section 170(a) for a noncash charitable contribution of more than $5,000 unless the donor—

(i) Substantiates the contribution with a contemporaneous written acknowledgment, as described in section 170(f)(8) and § 1.170A–13(f);

(ii) Obtains a qualified appraisal, as defined in § 1.170A–17(a)(1), prepared by a qualified appraiser, as defined in § 1.170A–17(b)(1); and

(iii) Completes Form 8283 (Section B), as provided in paragraph (d)(3) of this section, or a successor form, and files it with the return on which the deduction is claimed.

(2) Exception for certain noncash contributions. A qualified appraisal is not required, and a completed Form 8283 (Section A) containing the information required in paragraph (c)(3) of this section meets the requirements of paragraph (d)(1)(iii) of this section for contributions of—

(i) Publicly traded securities as defined in § 1.170A–13(c)(7)(xi);

(ii) Property described in section 170(e)(1)(B)(iii) (certain intellectual property);

(iii) A qualified vehicle described in section 170(f)(12)(A)(ii) for which an acknowledgment under section 170(f)(12)(B)(iii) is provided; and

(iv) Property described in section 1221(a)(1) (inventory and property held by the donor primarily for sale to customers in the ordinary course of the donor's trade or business).

(3) Completed Form 8283 (Section B). A completed Form 8283 (Section B) includes—

(i) The donor's name and taxpayer identification number (for example, a social security number or employer identification number);

(ii) The donee's name, address, taxpayer identification number, signature, the date signed by the donee, and the date the donee received the property;

(iii) The appraiser's name, address, taxpayer identification number, appraiser declaration, as described in paragraph (d)(4) of this section, signature, and the date signed by the appraiser;

(iv) The following information about the contributed property:

(A) The fair market value on the valuation effective date, as defined in § 1.170A–17(a)(5)(i).

(B) A description in sufficient detail under the circumstances, taking into account the value of the property, for a person who is not generally familiar with the type of property to ascertain that the described property is the contributed property.

(C) In the case of real property or tangible personal property, the condition of the property;

(v) The manner of acquisition (for example, by purchase, gift, bequest, inheritance, or exchange), and the approximate date of acquisition of the property by the donor, or, if the property was created, produced, or manufactured by or for the donor, the approximate date the property was substantially completed;

(vi) The cost or other basis of the property, adjusted as provided by section 1016;

(vii) A statement explaining whether the charitable contribution was made by means of a bargain sale and, if so, the amount of any consideration received for the contribution; and

(viii) Any other information required by Form 8283 (Section B) or the instructions to Form 8283 (Section B).

(4) Appraiser declaration. The appraiser declaration referred to in paragraph (d)(3)(iii) of this section must include the following statement: "I understand that my appraisal will be used in connection with a return or claim for refund. I also understand that, if there is a substantial or gross valuation misstatement of the value of the property claimed on the return or claim for refund that is based on my appraisal, I may be subject to a penalty under section 6695A of the Internal Revenue Code, as well as other applicable penalties. I affirm that I have not been at any time in the three-year period ending on the date of the appraisal barred from presenting evidence or testimony before the Department of the Treasury or the Internal Revenue Service pursuant to 31 U.S.C. 330(c)."

(5) Donee signature—(i) Person authorized to sign. The person who signs Form 8283 (Section B) for the donee must be either an official authorized to sign the tax or information returns of the donee, or a person specifically authorized to sign Forms 8283 (Section B) by that official. In the case of a donee that is a governmental unit, the person who signs Form 8283 (Section B) for the donee must be an official of the governmental unit.

(ii) Effect of donee signature. The signature of the donee on Form 8283 (Section B) does not represent concurrence in the appraised value of the contributed property. Rather, it represents acknowledgment of receipt of the property described in Form 8283 (Section B) on the date specified in Form 8283 (Section B) and that the donee understands the information reporting requirements imposed by section 6050L and § 1.6050L–1.

(iii) Certain information not required on Form 8283 (Section B) before donee signs. Before Form 8283 (Section B) is signed by the donee, Form 8283 (Section B) must be completed (as described in paragraph (d)(3) of this section), except that it is not required to contain the following:

(A) The appraiser declaration or information about the qualified appraiser.

(B) The manner or date of acquisition.

(C) The cost or other basis of the property.

(D) The appraised fair market value of the contributed property.

(E) The amount claimed as a charitable contribution.

(6) Additional substantiation rules may apply. For additional substantiation rules, see paragraph (f) of this section.

(7) More than one appraiser. More than one appraiser may appraise the donated property. If more than one appraiser appraises the property, the donor does not have to use each appraiser's appraisal for purposes of substantiating the charitable contribution deduction under this paragraph (d). If the donor uses the appraisal of more than one appraiser, or if two or more appraisers contribute to a single appraisal, each appraiser shall comply with the requirements of this paragraph (d) and the requirements in § 1.170A–17, including signing the qualified appraisal and appraisal summary.

(e) Substantiation of noncash charitable contributions of more than $500,000—(1) In general. Except as provided in paragraph (e)(2) of this section, no deduction is allowed under section 170(a) for a noncash charitable contribution of more than $500,000 unless the donor—

(i) Substantiates the contribution with a contemporaneous written acknowledgment, as described in section 170(f)(8) and § 1.170A–13(f);

(ii) Obtains a qualified appraisal, as defined in § 1.170A–17(a)(1), prepared by a qualified appraiser, as defined in § 1.170A–17(b)(1);

(iii) Completes, as described in paragraph (d)(3) of this section, Form 8283 (Section B) and files it with the return on which the deduction is claimed; and

(iv) Attaches the qualified appraisal of the property to the return on which the deduction is claimed.

(2) Exception for certain noncash contributions. For contributions of property described in paragraph (d)(2) of this section, a qualified appraisal is not required, and a completed Form 8283 (Section A), containing the information required in paragraph (c)(3) of this section, meets the requirements of paragraph (e)(1)(iii) of this section.

(3) Additional substantiation rules may apply. For additional substantiation rules, see paragraph (f) of this section.

(f) Additional substantiation rules—(1) Form 8283 (Section B) furnished by donor to donee. A donor who presents a Form 8283 (Section B) to a donee for signature must furnish to the donee a copy of the Form 8283 (Section B).

(2) Number of Forms 8283 (Section A or Section B)—(i) In general. For each item of contributed property for which a Form 8283 (Section A or Section B) is required under paragraphs (c), (d), or (e) of this section, a donor must attach a separate Form 8283 (Section A or Section B) to the return on which the deduction for the item is claimed.

(ii) Exception for similar items. The donor may attach a single Form 8283 (Section A or Section B) for all similar items of property, as defined in § 1.170A–13(c)(7)(iii), contributed to the same donee during the donor's taxable year, if the donor includes on Form 8283 (Section A or Section B) the information required by paragraph (c)(3) or (d)(3) of this section for each item of property.

(3) Substantiation requirements for carryovers of noncash contribution deductions. The rules in paragraphs (c), (d), and (e) of this section (regarding substantiation that must be submitted with a return) also apply to the return for any carryover year under section 170(d).

(4) Partners and S corporation shareholders—(i) Form 8283 (Section A or Section B) must be provided to partners and S corporation shareholders. If the donor is a partnership or S corporation, the donor must provide a copy of the completed Form 8283 (Section A or Section B) to every partner or shareholder who receives an allocation of a charitable contribution deduction under section 170 for the property described in Form 8283 (Section A or Section B). Similarly, a recipient partner or shareholder that is a partnership or S corporation must provide a copy of the completed Form 8283 (Section A or Section B) to each of its partners or shareholders who receives an allocation of a charitable contribution deduction under section 170 for the property described in Form 8283 (Section A or Section B).

(ii) Partners and S corporation shareholders must attach Form 8283 (Section A or Section B) to return. A partner of a partnership or shareholder of an S corporation who receives an allocation of a charitable contribution deduction under section 170 for property to which paragraph (c), (d), or (e) of this section applies must attach a copy of the partnership's or S corporation's completed Form 8283 (Section A or Section B) to the return on which the deduction is claimed.

(5) Determination of deduction amount for purposes of substantiation rules—(i) In general. In determining whether the amount of a donor's deduction exceeds the amounts set forth in section 170(f)(11)(B) (noncash contributions exceeding $500), 170(f)(11)(C) (noncash contributions exceeding $5,000), or 170(f)(11)(D) (noncash contributions exceeding $500,000), the rules of paragraphs (f)(5)(ii) and (iii) of this section apply.

(ii) Similar items of property must be aggregated. Under section 170(f)(11)(F), the donor must aggregate the amount claimed as a deduction for all similar items of property, as defined in § 1.170A–13(c)(7)(iii), contributed during the taxable year. For rules regarding the number of qualified appraisals and Forms 8283 (Section A or Section B) required if similar items of property are contributed, see § 1.170A–13(c)(3)(iv)(A) and (4)(iv)(B).

(iii) For contributions of certain inventory and scientific property, excess of amount claimed over cost of goods sold taken into account—(A) In general. In determining the amount of a donor's contribution of property to which section 170(e)(3) (relating to contributions of inventory and other property) or (e)(4) (relating to contributions of scientific property used for research) applies, the donor must take into account only the excess of the amount claimed as a deduction over the amount that would have been treated as the cost of goods sold if the donor had sold the contributed property to the donee.

(B) Example. The following example illustrates the rule of this paragraph (f)(5)(iii):

Example. X Corporation makes a contribution of inventory described in section 1221(a)(2). The contribution, described in section 170(e)(3), is for the care of the needy. The cost of the property to X Corporation is $5,000 and the fair market value of the property at the time of the contribution is $11,000. Pursuant to section 170(e)(3)(B), X Corporation claims a charitable contribution deduction of $8,000 ($5,000 + ½ x ($11,000 - 5,000) = $8,000). The amount taken into account for purposes of determining the $5,000 threshold of paragraph (d) of this section is $3,000 ($8,000-$5,000).

(g) Effective/applicability date. This section applies to contributions made after July 30, 2018. Taxpayers may rely on the rules of this section for contributions made after June 3, 2004, or appraisals prepared for returns or submissions filed after August 17, 2006.

§ 1.170A–17. Qualified appraisal and qualified appraiser.

(a) Qualified appraisal—(1) Definition. For purposes of section 170(f)(11) and § 1.170A–16(d)(1)(ii) and (e)(1)(ii), the term qualified appraisal means an appraisal document that is prepared by a qualified appraiser (as defined in paragraph (b)(1) of this section) in accordance with generally accepted appraisal standards (as defined in paragraph (a)(2) of this section) and otherwise complies with the requirements of this paragraph (a).

(2) Generally accepted appraisal standards defined. For purposes of paragraph (a)(1) of this section, generally accepted appraisal standards means the substance and principles of the Uniform Standards of Professional Appraisal Practice, as developed by the Appraisal Standards Board of the Appraisal Foundation.

(3) Contents of qualified appraisal. A qualified appraisal must include—

(i) The following information about the contributed property:

(A) A description in sufficient detail under the circumstances, taking into account the value of the property, for a person who is not generally familiar with the type of property to ascertain that the appraised property is the contributed property.

(B) In the case of real property or tangible personal property, the condition of the property.

(C) The valuation effective date, as defined in paragraph (a)(5)(i) of this section.

(D) The fair market value, within the meaning of § 1.170A–1(c)(2), of the contributed property on the valuation effective date;

(ii) The terms of any agreement or understanding by or on behalf of the donor and donee that relates to the use, sale, or other disposition of the contributed property, including, for example, the terms of any agreement or understanding that—

(A) Restricts temporarily or permanently a donee's right to use or dispose of the contributed property;

(B) Reserves to, or confers upon, anyone, other than a donee or an organization participating with a donee in cooperative fundraising, any right to the income from the contributed property or to the possession of the property, including the right to vote contributed securities, to acquire the property by purchase or otherwise, or to designate the person having income, possession, or right to acquire; or

(C) Earmarks contributed property for a particular use;

(iii) The date, or expected date, of the contribution to the donee;

(iv) The following information about the appraiser:

(A) Name, address, and taxpayer identification number.

(B) Qualifications to value the type of property being valued, including the appraiser's education and experience.

(C) If the appraiser is acting in his or her capacity as a partner in a partnership, an employee of any person, whether an individual, corporation, or partnership, or an independent contractor engaged by a person other than the donor, the name, address, and taxpayer identification number of the partnership or the person who employs or engages the qualified appraiser;

(v) The signature of the appraiser and the date signed by the appraiser (appraisal report date);

(vi) The following declaration by the appraiser: "I understand that my appraisal will be used in connection with a return or claim for refund. I also understand that, if there is a substantial or gross valuation misstatement of the value of the property claimed on the return or claim for refund that is based on my appraisal, I may be subject to a penalty under section 6695A of the Internal Revenue Code, as well as other applicable penalties. I affirm that I have not been at any time in the three-year period ending on the date of the appraisal barred from presenting evidence or testimony before the Department of the Treasury or the Internal Revenue Service pursuant to 31 U.S.C. 330(c)";

(vii) A statement that the appraisal was prepared for income tax purposes;

(viii) The method of valuation used to determine the fair market value, such as the income approach, the market-data approach, or the replacement-cost-less-depreciation approach; and

(ix) The specific basis for the valuation, such as specific comparable sales transactions or statistical sampling, including a justification for using sampling and an explanation of the sampling procedure employed.

(4) Timely appraisal report. A qualified appraisal must be signed and dated by the qualified appraiser no earlier than 60 days before the date of the contribution and no later than—

(i) The due date, including extensions, of the return on which the deduction for the contribution is first claimed;

(ii) In the case of a donor that is a partnership or S corporation, the due date, including extensions, of the return on which the deduction for the contribution is first reported; or

(iii) In the case of a deduction first claimed on an amended return, the date on which the amended return is filed.

(5) Valuation effective date—(i) Definition. The valuation effective date is the date to which the value opinion applies.

(ii) Timely valuation effective date. For an appraisal report dated before the date of the contribution, as described in § 1.170A–1(b), the valuation effective date must be no earlier than 60 days before the date of the contribution and no later than the date of the contribution. For an appraisal report dated on or after the date of the contribution, the valuation effective date must be the date of the contribution.

(6) Exclusion for donor knowledge of falsity. An appraisal is not a qualified appraisal for a particular contribution, even if the requirements of this paragraph (a) are met, if the donor either failed to disclose or misrepresented facts, and a reasonable person would expect that this failure or misrepresentation would cause the appraiser to misstate the value of the contributed property.

(7) Number of appraisals required. A donor must obtain a separate qualified appraisal for each item of property for which an appraisal is required under section 170(f)(11)(C) and (D) and paragraph (d) or (e) of § 1.170A–16 and that is not included in a group of similar items of property, as defined in § 1.170A–13(c)(7)(iii). For rules regarding the number of appraisals required if similar items of property are contributed, see section 170(f)(11)(F) and § 1.170A–13(c)(3)(iv)(A).

(8) Time of receipt of qualified appraisal. The qualified appraisal must be received by the donor before the due date, including extensions, of the return on which a deduction is first claimed, or reported in the case of a donor that is a partnership or S corporation, under section 170 with respect to the donated property, or, in the case of a deduction first claimed, or reported, on an amended return, the date on which the return is filed.

(9) Prohibited appraisal fees. The fee for a qualified appraisal cannot be based to any extent on the appraised value of the property. For example, a fee for an appraisal will be treated as based on the appraised value of the property if any part of the fee depends on the amount of the appraised value that is allowed by the Internal Revenue Service after an examination.

(10) Retention of qualified appraisal. The donor must retain the qualified appraisal for so long as it may be relevant in the administration of any internal revenue law.

(11) Effect of appraisal disregarded pursuant to 31 U.S.C. 330(c). If an appraiser has been prohibited from practicing before the Internal Revenue Service by the Secretary under 31 U.S.C. 330(c) at any time during the three-year period ending on the date the appraisal is signed by the appraiser, any appraisal prepared by the appraiser will be disregarded as to value, but could constitute a qualified appraisal if the requirements of this section are otherwise satisfied, and the donor had no knowledge that the signature, date, or declaration was false when the appraisal and Form 8283 (Section B) were signed by the appraiser.

(12) Partial interest. If the contributed property is a partial interest, the appraisal must be of the partial interest.

(b) Qualified appraiser—(1) Definition. For purposes of section 170(f)(11) and § 1.170A–16(d)(1)(ii) and (e)(1)(ii), the term qualified appraiser means an individual with verifiable education and experience in valuing the type of property for which the appraisal is performed, as described in paragraphs (b)(2) through (4) of this section.

(2) Education and experience in valuing the type of property—(i) In general. An individual is treated as having education and experience in valuing the type of property within the meaning of paragraph (b)(1) of this section if, as of the date the individual signs the appraisal, the individual has—

(A) Successfully completed (for example, received a passing grade on a final examination) professional or college-level coursework, as described in paragraph (b)(2)(ii) of this section, in valuing the type of property, as described in paragraph (b)(3) of this section, and has two or more years of experience in valuing the type of property, as described in paragraph (b)(3) of this section; or

(B) Earned a recognized appraiser designation, as described in paragraph (b)(2)(iii) of this section, for the type of property, as described in paragraph (b)(3) of this section.

(ii) Coursework must be obtained from an educational organization, generally recognized professional trade or appraiser organization, or employer educational program. For purposes of paragraph (b)(2)(i)(A) of this section, the coursework must be obtained from—

(A) A professional or college-level educational organization described in section 170(b)(1)(A)(ii);

(B) A generally recognized professional trade or appraiser organization that regularly offers educational programs in valuing the type of property; or

(C) An employer as part of an employee apprenticeship or educational program substantially similar to the educational programs described in paragraphs (b)(2)(ii)(A) and (B) of this section.

(iii) Recognized appraiser designation defined. A recognized appraiser designation means a designation awarded by a generally recognized professional appraiser organization on the basis of demonstrated competency.

(3) Type of property defined—(i) In general. The type of property means the category of property customary in the appraisal field for an appraiser to value.

(ii) Examples. The following examples illustrate the rule of paragraphs (b)(2)(i) and (b)(3)(i) of this section:

Example (1). Coursework in valuing type of property. There are very few professional-level courses offered in widget appraising, and it is customary in the appraisal field for personal property appraisers to appraise widgets. Appraiser A has successfully completed professional-level coursework in valuing personal property generally but has completed no coursework in valuing widgets. The coursework completed by Appraiser A is for the type of property under paragraphs (b)(2)(i) and (b)(3)(i) of this section.

Example (2). Experience in valuing type of property. It is customary for professional antique appraisers to appraise antique widgets. Appraiser B has 2 years of experience in valuing antiques generally and is asked to appraise an antique widget. Appraiser B has obtained experience in valuing the type of property under paragraphs (b)(2)(i) and (b)(3)(i) of this section.

Example (3). No experience in valuing type of property. It is not customary for professional antique appraisers to appraise new widgets. Appraiser C has experience in appraising antiques generally but no experience in appraising new widgets. Appraiser C is asked to appraise a new widget. Appraiser C does not have experience in valuing the type of property under paragraphs (b)(2)(i) and (b)(3)(i) of this section.

(4) Verifiable. For purposes of paragraph (b)(1) of this section, education and experience in valuing the type of property are verifiable if the appraiser specifies in the appraisal the appraiser's education and experience in valuing the type of property, as described in paragraphs (b)(2) and (3) of this section, and the appraiser makes a declaration in the appraisal that, because of the appraiser's education and experience, the appraiser is qualified to make appraisals of the type of property being valued.

(5) Individuals who are not qualified appraisers. The following individuals are not qualified appraisers for the appraised property:

(i) An individual who receives a fee prohibited by paragraph (a)(9) of this section for the appraisal of the appraised property.

(ii) The donor of the property.

(iii) A party to the transaction in which the donor acquired the property (for example, the individual who sold, exchanged, or gave the property to the donor, or any individual who acted as an agent for the transferor or for the donor for the sale, exchange, or gift), unless the property is contributed within 2 months of the date of acquisition and its appraised value does not exceed its acquisition price.

(iv) The donee of the property.

(v) Any individual who is either—

(A) Related, within the meaning of section 267(b), to, or an employee of, an individual described in paragraph (b)(5)(ii), (iii), or (iv) of this section;

(B) Married to an individual described in paragraph (b)(5)(v)(A) of this section; or

(C) An independent contractor who is regularly used as an appraiser by any of the individuals described in paragraph (b)(5)(ii), (iii), or (iv) of this section, and who does not perform a majority of his or her appraisals for others during the taxable year.

(vi) An individual who is prohibited from practicing before the Internal Revenue Service by the Secretary under 31 U.S.C. 330(c) at any time during the three-year period ending on the date the appraisal is signed by the individual.

(c) Effective/applicability date. This section applies to contributions made on or after January 1, 2019. Taxpayers may rely on the rules of this section for appraisals prepared for returns or submissions filed after August 17, 2006.

§ 1.170A–18. Contributions of clothing and household items.

(a) In general. Except as provided in paragraph (b) of this section, no deduction is allowed under section 170(a) for a contribution of clothing or a household item (as described in paragraph (c) of this section) unless—

(1) The item is in good used condition or better at the time of the contribution; and

(2) The donor meets the substantiation requirements of § 1.170A–16.

(b) Certain contributions of clothing or household items with claimed value of more than $500. The rule described in paragraph (a)(1) of this section does not apply to a contribution of a single item of clothing or a household item for which a deduction of more than $500 is claimed, if the donor submits with the return on which the deduction is claimed a qualified appraisal, as defined in § 1.170A–17(a)(1), of the property prepared by a qualified appraiser, as defined in § 1.170A–17(b)(1), and a completed Form 8283 (Section B), "Noncash Charitable Contributions," as described in § 1.170A–16(d)(3).

(c) Definition of household items. For purposes of section 170(f)(16) and this section, the term household items includes furniture, furnishings, electronics, appliances, linens, and other similar items. Food, paintings, antiques, and other objects of art, jewelry, gems, and collections are not household items.

(d) Effective/applicability date. This section applies to contributions made after July 30, 2018. Taxpayers may rely on the rules of this section for contributions made after August 17, 2006.

QUALIFICATION FOR EXEMPTION

§ 1.501(a)–1. Exemption from taxation.

(a) In general; proof of exemption. (1) Section 501(a) provides an exemption from income taxes for organizations which are described in section 501(c) or (d) and section 401(a), unless such organization is a "feeder organization" (see section 502), or unless it engages in a transaction described in section 503. However, the exemption does not extend to "unrelated business taxable income" of such an organization (see Part III (Section 511 and following), subchapter F, chapter 1, of the Code.)

* * *

§ 1.501(c)(3)–1. Organizations organized and operated for religious, charitable, scientific, testing for public safety, literary, or educational purposes, or for the prevention of cruelty to children or animals.

(a) Organizational and operational tests.—(1) In order to be exempt as an organization described in section 501(c)(3), an organization must be both organized and operated exclusively for one or more of the purposes specified in such section. If an organization fails to meet either the organizational test or the operational test, it is not exempt.

(2) The term exempt purpose or purposes, as used in this section, means any purpose or purposes specified in section 501(c)(3), as defined and elaborated in paragraph (d) of this section.

(b) Organizational test—(1) In general. (i) An organization is organized exclusively for one or more exempt purposes only if its articles of organization (referred to in this section as its articles) as defined in subparagraph (2) of this paragraph:

(a) Limit the purposes of such organization to one or more exempt purposes; and

(b) Do not expressly empower the organization to engage, otherwise than as an insubstantial part of its activities, in activities which in themselves are not in furtherance of one or more exempt purposes.

(ii) In meeting the organizational test, the organization's purposes, as stated in its articles, may be as broad as, or more specific than, the purposes stated in section 501(c)(3). Therefore, an organization which, by the terms of its articles, is formed for literary and scientific purposes within the meaning of section 501(c)(3) of the Code shall, if it otherwise meets the requirements in this paragraph, be considered to have met the organizational test. Similarly, articles stating that the organization is created solely to receive contributions and pay them over to organizations which are described in section 501(c)(3) and exempt from taxation under section 501(a) are sufficient for purposes of the organizational test. Moreover, it is sufficient if the articles set for the purpose of the organization to be the operation of a school for adult education and describe in detail the manner of the operation of such school. In addition, if the articles state that the organization is formed for charitable purposes, such articles ordinarily shall be sufficient for purposes of the organizational test (see subparagraph (5) of this paragraph for rules relating to construction of terms).

(iii) An organization is not organized exclusively for one or more exempt purposes if its articles expressly empower it to carry on, otherwise than as an insubstantial part of its activities, activities which are not in furtherance of one or more exempt purposes, even though such organization is, by the terms of such articles, created for a purpose that is no broader than the purposes specified in section 501(c)(3). Thus, an organization that is empowered by its articles to engage in a manufacturing business, or to engage in the operation of a social club does not meet the organizational test regardless of the fact that its articles may state that such organization is created for charitable purposes within the meaning of section 501(c)(3) of the Code.

(iv) In no case shall an organization be considered to be organized exclusively for one or more exempt purposes, if, by the terms of its articles, the purposes for which such organization is created are broader than the purposes specified in section 501(c)(3). The fact that the actual operations of such an organization have been exclusively in furtherance of one or more exempt purposes shall not be sufficient to permit the organization to meet the organizational test. Similarly, such an organization will not meet the organizational test as a result of statements or other evidence that the members thereof intend to operate only in furtherance of one or more exempt purposes.

(v) Unless otherwise prescribed by applicable regulations or other guidance published in the Internal Revenue Bulleting, an organization must, in order to establish its exemption, submit a detailed statement of its proposed activities with and as a part of its application for exemption (see § 1.501(a)–1(b)).

(2) Articles of organization. For purposes of this section, the term articles of organization or articles includes the trust instrument, the corporate charter, the articles of association, or any other written instrument by which an organization is created.

(3) Authorization of legislative or political activities. An organization is not organized exclusively for one or more exempt purposes if its articles expressly empower it:

(i) To devote more than an insubstantial part of its activities to attempting to influence legislation by propaganda or otherwise; or

(ii) Directly or indirectly to participate in, or intervene in (including the publishing or distributing of statements), any political campaign on behalf of or in opposition to any candidate for public office; or

(iii) To have objectives and to engage in activities which characterize it as an action organization as defined in paragraph (c)(3) of this section.

The terms used in subdivisions (i), (ii), and (iii) of this subparagraph shall have the meanings provided in paragraph (c)(3) of this section. An organization's articles will not violate the provisions of paragraph (b)(3)(i) of this section even though the organization's articles expressly empower it to make the election provided for in section 501(h) with respect to influencing legislation and, only if it so elects, to make lobbying or grass roots expenditures that do not normally exceed the ceiling amounts prescribed by section 501(h)(2)(B) and (D).

(4) Distribution of assets on dissolution. An organization is not organized exclusively for one or more exempt purposes unless its assets are dedicated to an exempt purpose. An organization's assets will be considered dedicated to an exempt purpose, for example, if, upon dissolution, such assets would, by reason of a provision in the organization's articles or by operation of law, be distributed for one or more exempt purposes, or to the Federal Government, or to a State or local government, for a public purpose, or would be distributed by a court to another organization to be used in such manner as in the judgment of the court will best accomplish the general purposes for which the dissolved organization was organized. However, an organization does not meet the organizational test if its articles or the law of the State in which it was created provide that its assets would, upon dissolution, be distributed to its members or shareholders.

(5) Construction of terms. The law of the State in which an organization is created shall be controlling in construing the terms of its articles. However, any organization which contends that such terms have under State law a different meaning from their generally accepted meaning must establish such special meaning by clear and convincing reference to relevant court decisions, opinions of the State attorney-general, or other evidence of applicable State law.

(6) Applicability of the organizational test. A determination by the Commissioner that an organization is described in section 501(c)(3) and exempt under section 501(a) will not be granted after July 26, 1959, regardless of when the application is filed, unless such organization meets the organizational test prescribed by this paragraph (b). If, before July 27, 1959, an organization has been determined by the Commissioner or district director to be exempt as an organization described in section 501(c)(3) or in a corresponding provision of prior law and such determination has not been revoked before such date, the fact that such organization does not meet the organizational test prescribed by this paragraph (b) shall not be a basis for revoking such determination. Accordingly, an organization which has been determined to be exempt before July 27, 1959, and which does not seek a new determination of exemption is not required to amend its articles of organization to conform to the rules of this paragraph (b), but any organization which seeks a determination of exemption after July 26, 1959, must have articles of organization which meet the rules of this paragraph (b). For the rules relating to whether an organization determined to be exempt before July 27, 1959, is organized exclusively for one or more exempt purposes, see 26 CFR (1939) 39.101(6)–1 (Regulations 118) as made applicable to the Code by Treasury Decision 6091, approved August 16, 1954 (19 FR 5167; 1954–2 CB, 47).

(c) Operational test—(1) Primary activities. An organization will be regarded as operated exclusively for one or more exempt purposes only if it engages primarily in activities which accomplish one or more of such exempt purposes specified in section 501(c)(3). An organization will not be so regarded if more than an insubstantial part of its activities is not in furtherance of an exempt purpose.

(2) Distribution of earnings. An organization is not operated exclusively for one or more exempt purposes if its net earnings inure in whole or in part to the benefit of private shareholders or individuals. For the definition of the words private shareholder or individual, see paragraph (c) of § 1.501(a)–1.

(3) Action organizations. (i) An organization is not operated exclusively for one or more exempt purposes if it is an action organization as defined in subdivisions (ii), (iii), or (iv) of this subparagraph.

(ii) An organization is an action organization if a substantial part of its activities is attempting to influence legislation by propaganda or otherwise. For this purpose, an organization will be regarded as attempting to influence legislation if the organization:

(a) Contacts, or urges the public to contact, members of a legislative body for the purpose of proposing, supporting, or opposing legislation; or

(b) Advocates the adoption or rejection of legislation.

The term legislation, as used in this subdivision, includes action by the Congress, by any State legislature, by any local council or similar governing body, or by the public in a referendum, initiative, constitutional amendment, or similar procedure. An organization will not fail to meet the operational test merely because it advocates, as an insubstantial part of its activities, the adoption or rejection of legislation. An organization for which the expenditure test election of section 501(h) is in effect for a taxable year will not be considered an action organization by reason of this paragraph (c)(3)(ii) for that year if it is not denied exemption from taxation under section 501(a) by reason of section 501(h).

(iii) An organization is an action organization if it participates or intervenes, directly or indirectly, in any political campaign on behalf of or in opposition to any candidate for public office.

The term candidate for public office means an individual who offers himself, or is proposed by others, as a contestant for an elective public office, whether such office be national, State, or local. Activities which constitute participation or intervention in a political campaign on behalf of or in opposition to a candidate include, but are not limited to, the publication or distribution of written or printed statements or the making of oral statements on behalf of or in opposition to such a candidate.

(iv) An organization is an action organization if it has the following two characteristics: (a) Its main or primary objective or objectives (as distinguished from its incidental or secondary objectives) may be attained only by legislation or a defeat of proposed legislation; and (b) it advocates, or campaigns for, the attainment of such main or primary objective or objectives as distinguished from engaging in nonpartisan analysis, study, or research and making the results thereof available to the public. In determining whether an organization has such characteristics, all the surrounding facts and circumstances, including the articles and all activities of the organization, are to be considered.

(v) An action organization, described in subdivisions (ii) or (iv) of this subparagraph, though it cannot qualify under section 501(c)(3), may nevertheless qualify as a social welfare organization under section 501(c)(4) if it meets the requirements set out in paragraph (a) of § 1.501(c)(4)–1.

(d) Exempt purposes—(1) In general. **(i)** An organization may be exempt as an organization described in section 501(c)(3) if it is organized and operated exclusively for one or more of the following purposes:

(a) Religious,

(b) Charitable,

(c) Scientific,

(d) Testing for public safety,

(e) Literary,

(f) Educational, or

(g) Prevention of cruelty to children or animals.

(ii) An organization is not organized or operated exclusively for one or more of the purposes specified in subdivision (i) of this subparagraph unless it serves a public rather than a private interest. Thus, to meet the requirement of this subdivision, it is necessary for an organization to establish that it is not organized or operated for the benefit of private interests such as designated individuals, the creator or his family, shareholders of the organization, or persons controlled, directly or indirectly, by such private interests.

(iii) Examples. The following examples illustrate the requirement of paragraph (d)(1)(ii) of this section that an organization serve a public rather than a private interest:

Example 1. (i) O is an educational organization the purpose of which is to study history and immigration. O's educational activities include sponsoring lectures and publishing a journal. The focus of O's historical studies is the genealogy of one family, tracing the descent of its present members. O actively solicits for membership only individuals who are members of that one family. O's research is directed toward publishing a history of that family that will document the pedigrees of family members. A major objective of O's research is to identify and locate living descendants of that family to enable those descendants to become acquainted with each other.

(ii) O's educational activities primarily serve the private interests of members of a single family rather than a public interest. Therefore, O is operated for the benefit of private interests in violation of the restriction on private benefit in paragraph (d)(1)(ii) of this section. Based on these facts and circumstances, O is not operated exclusively for exempt purposes and, therefore, is not described in section 501(c)(3).

Example 2. (i) O is an art museum. O's principal activity is exhibiting art created by a group of unknown but promising local artists. O's activity, including organized tours of its art collection, promotes the arts. O is governed by a board of trustees unrelated to the artists whose work O exhibits. All of the art exhibited is offered for sale at prices set by the artist. Each artist whose work is exhibited has a consignment arrangement with O. Under this arrangement, when art is sold, the museum retains 10 percent of the selling price to cover the costs of operating the museum and gives the artist 90 percent.

(ii) The artists in this situation directly benefit from the exhibition and sale of their art. As a result, the principal activity of O serves the private interests of these artists. Because O gives 90 percent of the proceeds from its sole activity to the individual artists, the direct benefits to the artists are substantial and O's provision of these benefits to the artists is more than incidental to its other purposes and activities. This arrangement causes O to be operated for the benefit of private interests in violation of the restriction on private benefit in paragraph (d)(1)(ii) of this section. Based on these facts and circumstances, O is not operated exclusively for exempt purposes and, therefore, is not described in section 501(c)(3).

Example 3. (i) O is an educational organization the purpose of which is to train individuals in a program developed by P, O's president. The program is of interest to academics and professionals, representatives of whom serve on an advisory panel to O. All of the rights to the program are owned by Company K, a for-profit corporation owned by P. Prior to the existence of O, the teaching of the program was conducted by Company K. O licenses, from Company K, the right to conduct seminars and lectures on the program and to use the name of the program as part of O's name, in exchange for specified royalty payments. Under the license agreement, Company K provides O with the services of trainers and with course materials on the program. O may develop and copyright new course materials on the program but all such materials must be assigned to Company K without consideration if and when the license agreement is terminated. Company K sets the tuition for the seminars and lectures on the program conducted by O. O has agreed not to become involved in any activity resembling the program or its implementation for 2 years after the termination of O's license agreement.

(ii) O's sole activity is conducting seminars and lectures on the program. This arrangement causes O to be operated for the benefit of P and Company K in violation of the restriction on private benefit in paragraph (d)(1)(ii) of this section, regardless of whether the royalty payments from O to Company K for the right to teach the program are reasonable. Based on these facts and circumstances, O is not operated exclusively for exempt purposes and, therefore, is not described in section 501(c)(3).

(iv) Since each of the purposes specified in subdivision (i) of this subparagraph is an exempt purpose in itself, an organization may be exempt if it is organized and operated exclusively for any one or more of such purposes. If, in fact, an organization is organized and operated exclusively for an exempt purpose or purposes, exemption will be granted to such an organization regardless of the purpose or purposes specified in its application for exemption. For example, if an organization claims exemption on the ground that it is educational, exemption will not be denied if, in fact, it is charitable.

(2) Charitable defined. The term charitable is used in section 501(c)(3) in its generally accepted legal sense and is, therefore, not to be construed as limited by the separate enumeration in section 501(c)(3) of other tax-exempt purposes which may fall within the broad outlines of charity as developed by judicial decisions. Such term includes: Relief of the poor and distressed or of the underprivileged; advancement of religion; advancement of education or science; erection or maintenance of public buildings, monuments, or works; lessening of the burdens of Government; and promotion of social welfare by organizations designed to accomplish any of the above purposes, or (i) to lessen neighborhood tensions; (ii) to eliminate prejudice and discrimination; (iii) to defend human and civil rights secured by law; or (iv) to combat community deterioration and juvenile delinquency. The fact that an organization which is organized and operated for the relief of indigent persons may receive voluntary contributions from the persons intended to be relieved will not necessarily prevent such organization from being exempt as an organization organized and operated exclusively for charitable purposes. The fact that an organization, in carrying out its primary purpose, advocates social or civic changes or presents opinion on controversial issues with the intention of molding public opinion or creating public sentiment to an acceptance of its views does not preclude such organization from qualifying under section 501(c)(3) so long as it is not an action organization of any one of the types described in paragraph (c)(3) of this section.

(3) Educational defined—(i) In general. The term educational, as used in section 501(c)(3), relates to:

(a) The instruction or training of the individual for the purpose of improving or developing his capabilities; or

(b) The instruction of the public on subjects useful to the individual and beneficial to the community.

An organization may be educational even though it advocates a particular position or viewpoint so long as it presents a sufficiently full and fair exposition of the pertinent facts as to permit an individual or the public to form an independent opinion or conclusion. On the other hand, an organization is not educational if its principal function is the mere presentation of unsupported opinion.

(ii) Examples of educational organizations. The following are examples of organizations which, if they otherwise meet the requirements of this section, are educational:

Example 1. An organization, such as a primary or secondary school, a college, or a professional or trade school, which has a regularly scheduled curriculum, a regular faculty, and a regularly enrolled body of students in attendance at a place where the educational activities are regularly carried on.

Example 2. An organization whose activities consist of presenting public discussion groups, forums, panels, lectures, or other similar programs. Such programs may be on radio or television.

Example 3. An organization which presents a course of instruction by means of correspondence or through the utilization of television or radio.

Example 4. Museums, zoos, planetariums, symphony orchestras, and other similar organizations.

(4) Testing for public safety defined. The term testing for public safety, as used in section 501(c)(3), includes the testing of consumer products, such as electrical products, to determine whether they are safe for use by the general public.

(5) Scientific defined.

(i) Since an organization may meet the requirements of section 501(c)(3) only if it serves a public rather than a private interest, a scientific organization must be organized and operated in the public interest (see subparagraph (1)(ii) of this paragraph). Therefore, the term scientific, as used in section 501(c)(3), includes the carrying on of scientific research in the public interest. Research when taken alone is a word with various meanings; it is not synonymous with scientific; and the nature of particular research depends upon the purpose which it serves. For research to be scientific, within the meaning of section 501(c)(3), it must be carried on in furtherance of a scientific purpose. The determination as to whether research is scientific does not depend on whether such research is classified as fundamental or basic as contrasted with applied or practical. On the other hand, for purposes of the exclusion from unrelated business taxable income provided by section 512(b)(9), it is necessary to determine whether the organization is operated primarily for purposes of carrying on fundamental, as contrasted with applied, research.

(ii) Scientific research does not include activities of a type ordinarily carried on as an incident to commercial or industrial operations, as, for example, the ordinary testing or inspection of materials or products or the designing or construction of equipment, buildings, etc.

(iii) Scientific research will be regarded as carried on in the public interest:

(a) If the results of such research (including any patents, copyrights, processes, or formulae resulting from such research) are made available to the public on a nondiscriminatory basis;

(b) If such research is performed for the United States, or any of its agencies or instrumentalities, or for a State or political subdivision thereof; or

(c) If such research is directed toward benefiting the public. The following are examples of scientific research which will be considered as directed toward benefiting the public, and, therefore, which will be regarded as carried on in the public interest: (1) Scientific research carried on for the purpose of aiding in the scientific education of college or university students; (2) scientific research carried on for the purpose of obtaining scientific information, which is published in a treatise, thesis, trade publication, or in any other form that is available to the interested public; (3) scientific research carried on for the purpose of discovering a cure for a disease; or (4) scientific research carried on for the purpose of aiding a community or geographical area by attracting new industry to the community or area or by encouraging the development of, or retention of, an industry in the community or area. Scientific research described in this subdivision will be regarded as carried on in the public interest even though such research is performed pursuant to a contract or agreement under which the sponsor or sponsors of the research have the right to obtain ownership or control of any patents, copyrights, processes, or formulae resulting from such research.

(iv) An organization will not be regarded as organized and operated for the purpose of carrying on scientific research in the public interest and, consequently, will not qualify under section 501(c)(3) as a scientific organization, if:

(a) Such organization will perform research only for persons which are (directly or indirectly) its creators and which are not described in section 501(c)(3), or

(b) Such organization retains (directly or indirectly) the ownership or control of more than an insubstantial portion of the patents, copyrights, processes, or formulae resulting from its research and does not make such patents, copyrights, processes, or formulae available to the public. For purposes of this subdivision, a patent, copyright, process, or formula shall be considered as made available to the public if such patent, copyright, process, or formula is made available to the public on a nondiscriminatory basis. In addition, although one person is granted the exclusive right to the use of a patent, copyright, process, or formula, such patent, copyright, process, or formula shall be considered as made available to the public if the granting of such exclusive right is the only practicable manner in which the patent, copyright, process, or formula can be utilized to benefit the public. In such a case, however, the research from which the patent, copyright, process, or formula resulted will be regarded as carried on in the public interest (within the meaning of subdivision (iii) of this subparagraph) only if it is carried on for a person described in subdivision (iii)(b) of this subparagraph or if it is scientific research described in subdivision (iii)(c) of this subparagraph.

(v) The fact that any organization (including a college, university, or hospital) carries on research which is not in furtherance of an exempt purpose described in section 501(c)(3) will not preclude such organization from meeting the requirements of section

501(c)(3) so long as the organization meets the organizational test and is not operated for the primary purpose of carrying on such research (see paragraph (e) of this section, relating to organizations carrying on a trade or business). See paragraph (a)(5) of § 1.513–2, with respect to research which constitutes an unrelated trade or business, and section 512(b)(7), (8), and (9), with respect to income derived from research which is excludable from the tax on unrelated business income.

(vi) The regulations in this subparagraph are applicable with respect to taxable years beginning after December 31, 1960.

(e) Organizations carrying on trade or business—(1) In general. An organization may meet the requirements of section 501(c)(3) although it operates a trade or business as a substantial part of its activities, if the operation of such trade or business is in furtherance of the organization's exempt purpose or purposes and if the organization is not organized or operated for the primary purpose of carrying on an unrelated trade or business, as defined in section 513. In determining the existence or nonexistence of such primary purpose, all the circumstances must be considered, including the size and extent of the trade or business and the size and extent of the activities which are in furtherance of one or more exempt purposes. An organization which is organized and operated for the primary purpose of carrying on an unrelated trade or business is not exempt under section 501(c)(3) even though it has certain religious purposes, its property is held in common, and its profits do not inure to the benefit of individual members of the organization. See, however, section 501(d) and § 1.501(d)–1, relating to religious and apostolic organizations.

(2) Taxation of unrelated business income. For provisions relating to the taxation of unrelated business income of certain organizations described in section 501(c)(3), see sections 511 to 515, inclusive, and the regulations thereunder.

(f) Interaction with section 4958—(1) Application process. An organization that applies for recognition of exemption under section 501(a) as an organization described in section 501(c)(3) must establish its eligibility under this section. The Commissioner may deny an application for exemption for failure to establish any of section 501(c)(3)'s requirements for exemption. Section 4958 does not apply to transactions with an organization that has failed to establish that it satisfies all of the requirements for exemption under section 501(c)(3). See § 53.4958–2.

(2) Substantive requirements for exemption still apply to applicable tax-exempt organizations described in section 501(c)(3)—(i) In general. Regardless of whether a particular transaction is subject to excise taxes under section 4958, the substantive requirements for tax exemption under section 501(c)(3) still apply to an applicable tax-exempt organization (as defined in section 4958(e) and § 53.4958–2) described in section 501(c)(3) whose disqualified persons or organization managers are subject to excise taxes under section 4958. Accordingly, an organization will no longer meet the requirements for tax-exempt status under section 501(c)(3) if the organization fails to satisfy the requirements of paragraph (b), (c) or (d) of this section. See § 53.4958–8(a).

(ii) Determination of whether revocation of tax-exempt status is appropriate when section 4958 excise taxes also apply. In determining whether to continue to recognize the tax-exempt status of an applicable tax-exempt organization (as defined in section 4958(e) and § 53.4958–2) described in section 501(c)(3) that engages in one or more excess benefit transactions (as defined in section 4958(c) and § 53.4958–4) that violate the prohibition on inurement under section 501(c)(3), the Commissioner will consider all relevant facts and circumstances, including, but not limited to, the following—

(A) The size and scope of the organization's regular and ongoing activities that further exempt purposes before and after the excess benefit transaction or transactions occurred;

(B) The size and scope of the excess benefit transaction or transactions (collectively, if more than one) in relation to the size and scope of the organization's regular and ongoing activities that further exempt purposes;

(C) Whether the organization has been involved in multiple excess benefit transactions with one or more persons;

(D) Whether the organization has implemented safeguards that are reasonably calculated to prevent excess benefit transactions; and

(E) Whether the excess benefit transaction has been corrected (within the meaning of section 4958(f)(6) and § 53.4958–7), or the organization has made good faith efforts to seek correction from the disqualified person(s) who benefited from the excess benefit transaction.

(iii) All factors will be considered in combination with each other. Depending on the particular situation, the Commissioner may assign greater or lesser weight to some factors than to others. The factors listed in paragraphs (f)(2)(ii)(D) and (E) of this section will weigh more heavily in favor of continuing to recognize exemption where the organization discovers the excess benefit transaction or transactions and takes action before the Commissioner discovers the excess benefit transaction or transactions. Further, with respect to the factor listed in paragraph (f)(2)(ii)(E) of this section, correction after the excess benefit transaction or transactions are discovered by the Commissioner, by itself, is never a sufficient basis for continuing to recognize exemption.

(iv) Examples. The following examples illustrate the principles of paragraph (f)(2)(ii) of this section. For purposes of each example, assume that O is an applicable tax-exempt organization (as defined in section 4958(e) and § 53.4958–2) described in section 501(c)(3). The examples read as follows:

Example 1. (i) O was created as a museum for the purpose of exhibiting art to the general public. In Years 1 and 2, O engages in fundraising and in selecting, leasing, and preparing an appropriate facility for a museum. In Year 3, a new board of trustees is elected. All of the new trustees are local art dealers. Beginning in Year 3 and continuing to the present, O uses a substantial portion of its revenues to purchase art solely from its trustees at prices that exceed fair market value. O exhibits and offers for sale all of the art it purchases. O's Form 1023, "Application for Recognition of Exemption," did not disclose the possibility that O would purchase art from its trustees.

(ii) O's purchases of art from its trustees at more than fair market value constitute excess benefit transactions between an applicable tax-exempt organization and disqualified persons under section 4958. Therefore, these transactions are subject to the applicable excise taxes provided in that section. In addition, O's purchases of art from its trustees at more than fair market value violate the proscription against inurement under section 501(c)(3) and paragraph (c)(2) of this section.

(iii) The application of the factors in paragraph (f)(2)(ii) of this section to these facts is as follows. Beginning in Year 3, O does not engage primarily in regular and ongoing activities that further exempt purposes because a substantial portion of O's activities consists of purchasing art from its trustees and dealing in such art in a manner similar to a commercial art gallery. The size and scope of the excess benefit transactions collectively are significant in relation to the size and scope of any of O's ongoing activities that further exempt purposes. O has been involved in multiple excess benefit transactions, namely, purchases of art from its trustees at more than fair market value. O has not implemented safeguards that are reasonably calculated to prevent such improper purchases in the future. The excess benefit transactions have not been corrected, nor has O made good faith efforts to seek correction from the disqualified persons who benefited from the excess benefit transactions (the trustees). The trustees continue to control O's Board. Based on the application of the factors to these facts, O is no longer described in section 501(c)(3) effective in Year 3.

Example 2. (i) The facts are the same as in Example 1, except that in Year 4, O's entire board of trustees resigns, and O no longer offers all exhibited art for sale. The former board is replaced with members of the community who are not in the business of buying or selling art and who have skills and experience running charitable and educational programs and institutions. O promptly discontinues the practice of purchasing art from current or former trustees, adopts a written conflicts of interest policy, adopts written art valuation guidelines, hires legal counsel to recover the excess amounts O had paid its former trustees, and implements a new program of activities to further the public's appreciation of the arts.

(ii) O's purchases of art from its former trustees at more than fair market value constitute excess benefit transactions between an applicable tax-exempt organization and disqualified persons under section 4958. Therefore, these transactions are subject to the applicable excise taxes provided in that section. In addition, O's purchases of art from its trustees at more than fair market value violate the proscription against inurement under section501(c)(3) and paragraph (c)(2) of this section.

(iii) The application of the factors in paragraph (f)(2)(ii) of this section to these facts is as follows. In Year 3, O does not engage primarily in regular and ongoing activities that further exempt purposes. However, in Year 4, O elects a new board of trustees comprised of individuals who have skills and experience running charitable and educational programs and implements a new program of activities to further the public's appreciation of the arts. As a result of these actions, beginning in Year 4, O engages in regular and ongoing activities that further exempt purposes. The size and scope of the excess benefit transactions that occurred in Year 3, taken collectively, are significant in relation to the size and scope of O's regular and ongoing exempt function activities that were conducted in Year 3. Beginning in Year 4, however, as O's exempt function activities grow, the size and scope of the excess benefit transactions that occurred in Year 3 become less and less significant as compared to the size and scope of O's regular and ongoing exempt function activities. O was involved in multiple excess benefit transactions in Year 3. However, by discontinuing its practice of purchasing art from its current and former trustees, by replacing its former board with independent members of the community, and by adopting a conflicts of interest policy and art valuation guidelines, O has implemented safeguards that are reasonably calculated to prevent future violations. In addition, O has made a good faith effort to seek correction from the disqualified persons who benefited from the excess benefit transactions (its former trustees). Based on the application of the factors to these facts, O continues to meet the requirements for tax exemption under section 501(c)(3).

Example 3. (i) O conducts educational programs for the benefit of the general public. Since its formation, O has employed its founder, C, as its Chief Executive Officer. Beginning in Year 5 of O's operations and continuing to the present, C caused O to divert significant portions of O's funds to pay C's personal expenses. The diversions by C significantly reduced the funds available to conduct O's ongoing educational programs. The board of trustees never authorized C to cause O to pay C's personal expenses from O's funds. Certain members of the board were aware that O was paying C's personal expenses. However, the board did not terminate C's employment and did not take any action to seek repayment from C or to prevent C from continuing to divert O's funds to pay C's personal expenses. C claimed that O's payments of

C's personal expenses represented loans from O to C. However, no contemporaneous loan documentation exists, and C never made any payments of principal or interest.

(ii) The diversions of O's funds to pay C's personal expenses constitute excess benefit transactions between an applicable tax-exempt organization and a disqualified person under section 4958. Therefore, these transactions are subject to the applicable excise taxes provided in that section. In addition, these transactions violate the proscription against inurement under section 501(c)(3) and paragraph (c)(2) of this section.

(iii) The application of the factors in paragraph (f)(2)(ii) of this section to these facts is as follows. O has engaged in regular and ongoing activities that further exempt purposes both before and after the excess benefit transactions occurred. However, the size and scope of the excess benefit transactions engaged in by O beginning in Year 5, collectively, are significant in relation to the size and scope of O's activities that further exempt purposes. Moreover, O has been involved in multiple excess benefit transactions. O has not implemented any safeguards that are reasonably calculated to prevent future diversions. The excess benefit transactions have not been corrected, nor has O made good faith efforts to seek correction from C, the disqualified person who benefited from the excess benefit transactions. Based on the application of the factors to these facts, O is no longer described in section 501(c)(3) effective in Year 5.

Example 4. (i) O conducts activities that further exempt purposes. O uses several buildings in the conduct of its exempt activities. In Year 1, O sold one of the buildings to Company K for an amount that was substantially below fair market value. The sale was a significant event in relation to O's other activities. C, O's Chief Executive Officer, owns all of the voting stock of Company K. When O's board of trustees approved the transaction with Company K, the board did not perform due diligence that could have made it aware that the price paid by Company K to acquire the building was below fair market value. Subsequently, but before the IRS commences an examination of O, O's board of trustees determines that Company K paid less than the fair market value for the building. Thus, O concludes that an excess benefit transaction occurred. After the board makes this determination, it promptly removes C as Chief Executive Officer, terminates C's employment with O, and hires legal counsel to recover the excess benefit from Company K. In addition, O promptly adopts a conflicts of interest policy and new contract review procedures designed to prevent future recurrences of this problem.

(ii) The sale of the building by O to Company K at less than fair market value constitutes an excess benefit transaction between an applicable tax-exempt organization and a disqualified person under section 4958 in Year 1. Therefore, this transaction is subject to the applicable excise taxes provided in that section. In addition, this transaction violates the proscription against inurement under section 501(c)(3) and paragraph (c)(2) of this section.

(iii) The application of the factors in paragraph (f)(2)(ii) of this section to these facts is as follows. O has engaged in regular and ongoing activities that further exempt purposes both before and after the excess benefit transaction occurred. Although the size and scope of the excess benefit transaction were significant in relation to the size and scope of O's activities that further exempt purposes, the transaction with Company K was a one-time occurrence. By adopting a conflicts of interest policy and new contract review procedures and by terminating C, O has implemented safeguards that are reasonably calculated to prevent future violations. Moreover, O took corrective actions before the IRS commenced an examination of O. In addition, O has made a good faith effort to seek correction from Company K, the disqualified person who benefited from the excess benefit transaction. Based on the application of the factors to these facts, O continues to be described in section 501(c)(3).

Example 5. (i) O is a large organization with substantial assets and revenues. O conducts activities that further its exempt purposes. O employs C as its Chief Financial Officer. During Year 1, O pays $2,500 of C's personal expenses. O does not make these payments pursuant to an accountable plan, as described in § 53.4958–4(a)(4)(ii). In addition, O does not report any of these payments on C's Form W-2, "Wage and Tax Statement," or on a Form 1099-MISC, "Miscellaneous Income," for C for Year 1, and O does not report these payments as compensation on its Form 990, "Return of Organization Exempt From Income Tax," for Year 1. Moreover, none of these payments can be disregarded as nontaxable fringe benefits under § 53.4958–4(c)(2) and none consisted of fixed payments under an initial contract under § 53.4958–4(a)(3). C does not report the $2,500 of payments as income on his individual Federal income tax return for Year 1. O does not repeat this reporting omission in subsequent years and, instead, reports all payments of C's personal expenses not made under an accountable plan as income to C.

(ii) O's payment in Year 1 of $2,500 of C's personal expenses constitutes an excess benefit transaction between an applicable tax-exempt organization and a disqualified person under section 4958. Therefore, this transaction is subject to the applicable excise taxes provided in that section. In addition, this transaction violates the proscription against inurement in section 501(c)(3) and paragraph (c)(2) of this section.

(iii) The application of the factors in paragraph (f)(2)(ii) of this section to these facts is as follows. O engages in regular and ongoing activities that further exempt purposes. The payment of $2,500 of C's personal expenses represented only a de minimis portion of O's assets and revenues; thus, the size and scope of the excess benefit transaction were not significant in relation to the size and scope of O's activities that further exempt purposes. The reporting omission that resulted in the excess benefit transaction in Year 1 occurred only once and is not repeated in subsequent years. Based on the application of the factors to these facts, O continues to be described in section 501(c)(3).

Example 6. (i) O is a large organization with substantial assets and revenues. O furthers its exempt purposes by providing social services to the population of a specific geographic area. O has a sizeable workforce of employees and volunteers to conduct its work. In Year 1, O's board of directors adopted written procedures for setting executive compensation at O. O's executive compensation procedures were modeled on the procedures for establishing a rebuttable presumption of reasonableness under § 53.4958–6. In accordance with these procedures, the board appointed a compensation committee to gather data on compensation levels paid by similarly situated organizations for functionally comparable positions. The members of the compensation committee were disinterested within the meaning of § 53.4958–6(c)(1)(iii). Based on its research, the compensation committee recommended a range of reasonable compensation for several of O's existing top executives (the Top Executives). On the basis of the committee's recommendations, the board approved new compensation packages for the Top Executives and timely documented the basis for its decision in board minutes. The board members were all disinterested within the meaning of § 53.4958–6(c)(1)(iii). The Top Executives were not involved in setting their own compensation. In Year 1, even though payroll expenses represented a significant portion of O's total operating expenses, the total compensation paid to O's Top Executives represented only an insubstantial portion of O's total payroll expenses. During a subsequent examination, the IRS found that the compensation committee relied exclusively on compensation data from organizations that perform similar social services to O. The IRS concluded, however, that the organizations were not similarly situated because they served substantially larger geographic regions with more diverse populations and were larger than O in terms of annual revenues, total operating budget, number of employees, and number of beneficiaries served. Accordingly, the IRS concluded that the compensation committee did not rely on "appropriate data as to comparability" within the meaning of § 53.4958–6(c)(2) and, thus, failed to establish the rebuttable presumption of reasonableness under § 53.4958–6. Taking O's size and the nature of the geographic area and population it serves into account, the IRS concluded that the Top Executives' compensation packages for Year 1 were excessive. As a result of the examination, O's board added new members to the compensation committee who have expertise in compensation matters and also amended its written procedures to require the compensation committee to evaluate a number of specific factors, including size, geographic area, and population covered by the organization, in assessing the comparability of compensation data. O's board renegotiated the Top Executives' contracts in accordance with the recommendations of the newly constituted compensation committee on a going forward basis. To avoid potential liability for damages under state contract law, O did not seek to void the Top Executives' employment contracts retroactively to Year 1 and did not seek correction of the excess benefit amounts from the Top Executives. O did not terminate any of the Top Executives.

(ii) O's payments of excessive compensation to the Top Executives in Year 1 constituted excess benefit transactions between an applicable tax-exempt organization and disqualified persons under section 4958. Therefore, these payments are subject to the applicable excise taxes provided under that section, including second-tier taxes if there is no correction by the disqualified persons. In addition, these payments violate the proscription against inurement under section 501(c)(3) and paragraph (c)(2) of this section.

(iii) The application of the factors in paragraph (f)(2)(ii) of this section to these facts is as follows. O has engaged in regular and ongoing activities that further exempt purposes both before and after the excess benefit transactions occurred. The size and scope of the excess benefit transactions, in the aggregate, were not significant in relation to the size and scope of O's activities that further exempt purposes. O engaged in multiple excess benefit transactions. Nevertheless, prior to entering into these excess benefit transactions, O had implemented written procedures for setting the compensation of its top management that were reasonably calculated to prevent the occurrence of excess benefit transactions. O followed these written procedures in setting the compensation of the Top Executives for Year 1. Despite the board's failure to rely on appropriate comparability data, the fact that O implemented and followed these written procedures in setting the compensation of the Top Executives for Year 1 is a factor favoring continued exemption. The fact that O amended its written procedures to ensure the use of appropriate comparability data and renegotiated the Top Executives' compensation packages on a going-forward basis are also factors favoring continued exemption, even though O did not void the Top Executives' existing contracts and did not seek correction from the Top Executives. Based on the application of the factors to these facts, O continues to be described in section 501(c)(3).

(3) Applicability. The rules in paragraph (f) of this section will apply with respect to excess benefit transactions occurring after March 28, 2008.

* * *

§ 1.501(c)(4)–1. Civic organizations and local associations of employees.

(a) Civic organizations—(1) In general. A civic league or organization may be exempt as an organization described in section 501(c)(4) if—

(i) It is not organized or operated for profit; and

(ii) It is operated exclusively for the promotion of social welfare.

(2) Promotion of social welfare—(i) In general. An organization is operated exclusively for the promotion of social welfare if it is primarily engaged in promoting in some way the common good and general welfare of the people of the community. An organization embraced within this section is one which is operated primarily for the purpose of bringing about civic betterments and social improvements. A social welfare organization will qualify for exemption as a charitable organization if it falls within the definition of charitable set forth in paragraph (d)(2) of § 1.501(c)(3)–1 and is not an action organization as set forth in paragraph (c)(3) of § 1.501(c)(3)–1.

(ii) Political or social activities. The promotion of social welfare does not include direct or indirect participation or intervention in political campaigns on behalf of or in opposition to any candidate for public office. Nor is an organization operated primarily for the promotion of social welfare if its primary activity is operating a social club for the benefit, pleasure, or recreation of its members, or is carrying on a business with the general public in a manner similar to organizations which are operated for profit. See, however, section 501(c)(6) and § 1.501(c)(6)–1, relating to business leagues and similar organizations. A social welfare organization that is not, at any time after October 4, 1976, exempt from taxation as an organization described in section 501(c)(3) may qualify under section 501(c)(4) even though it is an action organization described in § 1.501(c)(3)–1(c)(3)(ii) or (iv), if it otherwise qualifies under this section. For rules relating to an organization that is, after October 4, 1976, exempt from taxation as an organization described in section 501(c)(3), see section 504 and § 1.504–1.

(b) Local associations of employees. Local associations of employees described in section 501(c)(4) are expressly entitled to exemption under section 501(a). As conditions to exemption, it is required (1) that the membership of such an association be limited to the employees of a designated person or persons in a particular municipality, and (2) that the net earnings of the association be devoted exclusively to charitable, educational, or recreational purposes. The word local is defined in paragraph (b) of § 1.501(c)(12)–1. See paragraph (d)(2) and (3) of § 1.501(c)(3)–1 with reference to the meaning of charitable and educational as used in this section.

§ 1.501(c)(5)–1. Labor, agricultural, and horticultural organizations.

(a) The organizations contemplated by section 501(c)(5) as entitled to exemption from income taxation are those which:

(1) Have no net earnings inuring to the benefit of any member, and

(2) Have as their objects the betterment of the conditions of those engaged in such pursuits, the improvement of the grade of their products, and the development of a higher degree of efficiency in their respective occupations.

(b)(1) General rule. An organization is not a organization described in section 501(c)(5) if the principal activity of the organization is to receive, hold, invest, disburse or otherwise manage funds associated with savings or investment plans or programs, including pension or other retirement savings plans or programs.

(2) Exception. Paragraph (b)(1) of this section shall not apply to an organization which—

(i) Is established and maintained by another labor organization described in section 501(c)(5), (determined without regard to this paragraph (b)(2));

(ii) Is not directly or indirectly established or maintained in whole or in part by one or more—

(A) Employers;

(B) Governments or agencies or instrumentalities thereof; or

(C) Government controlled entities;

(iii) Is funded by membership dues from members of the labor organization described in this paragraph (b)(2) and earnings thereon;

(iv) Has not at any time after September 2, 1974 (the date of enactment of the Employee Retirement Income Security Act of 1974, Pub. L. 93–406, 88 Stat. 829) provided for, permitted or accepted employer contributions.

(3) Example. The principles of this paragraph (b) are illustrated by the following example:

Example. Trust A is organized in accordance with a collective bargaining agreement between labor union K and multiple employers. Trust A forms part of a plan that is established and maintained pursuant to the agreement and which covers employees of the signatory employers who are members of K. Representatives of both the employers and K serve as trustees. A receives contributions from the employers who are subject to the agreement. Retirement benefits paid to K's members as specified in the agreement are funded exclusively by the employers' contributions and accumulated earnings. A also provides information to union members about their retirement benefits and assists them with administrative tasks associated with the benefits. Most of A's activities are devoted to these functions. From time to time, A also participates in the renegotiation of the collective bargaining agreement. A's principal activity is to receive, hold, invest, disburse, or otherwise manage funds associated with a retirement savings plan. In addition, A does not satisfy all the requirements of the exception described in paragraph (b)(2) of this section. (For example, A accepts contributions from employers). Therefore, A is not a labor organization described in section 501(c)(5).

(c) Organizations described in section 501(c)(5) and otherwise exempt from tax under section 501(a) are taxable upon their unrelated business taxable income. See part II (section 511 and following), subchapter F, chapter 1 of the Code, and the regulations thereunder.

§ 1.501(c)(6)–1. Business leagues, chambers of commerce, real estate boards, and boards of trade.

A business league is an association of persons having some common business interest, the purpose of which is to promote such common interest and not to engage in a regular business of a kind ordinarily carried on for profit. It is an organization of the same general class as a chamber of commerce or board of trade. Thus, its activities should be directed to the improvement of business conditions of one or more lines of business as distinguished from the performance of particular services for individual persons. An organization whose purpose is to engage in a regular business of a kind ordinarily carried on for profit, even though the business is conducted on a cooperative basis or produces only sufficient income to be self-sustaining, is not a business league. An association engaged in furnishing information to prospective investors, to enable them to make sound investments, is not a business league, since its activities do not further any common business interest, even though all of its income is devoted to the purpose stated. A stock or commodity exchange is not a business league, a chamber of commerce, or a board of trade within the meaning of section 501(c)(6) and is not exempt from tax. Organizations otherwise exempt from tax under this section are taxable upon their unrelated business taxable income. See part II (section 511 and following), subchapter F, chapter 1 of the Code, and the regulations thereunder.

§ 1.501(c)(7)–1. Social clubs.

(a) The exemption provided by section 501(a) for organizations described in section 501(c)(7) applies only to clubs which are organized and operated exclusively for pleasure, recreation, and other nonprofitable purposes, but does not apply to any club if any part of its net earnings inures to the benefit of any private shareholder. In general, this exemption extends to social and recreation clubs which are supported solely by membership fees, dues, and assessments. However, a club otherwise entitled to exemption will not be disqualified because it raises revenue from members through the use of club facilities or in connection with club activities.

(b) A club which engages in business, such as making its social and recreational facilities available to the general public or by selling real estate, timber, or other products, is not organized and operated exclusively for pleasure, recreation, and other nonprofitable purposes, and is not exempt under section 501(a). Solicitation by advertisement or otherwise for public patronage of its facilities is prima facie evidence that the club is engaging in business and is not being operated exclusively for pleasure, recreation, or social purposes. However, an incidental sale of property will not deprive a club of its exemption.

§ 1.501(h)–1. Application of the expenditure test to expenditures to influence legislation; introduction.

(a) Scope. (1) There are certain requirements an organization must meet in order to be a charity described in section 501(c)(3). Among other things, section 501(c)(3) states that "no substantial part of the activities of [a charity may consist of] carrying on propaganda, or otherwise attempting to influence legislation, (except as otherwise provided in subsection (h))." This requirement is called the substantial part test.

(2) Under section 501(h), many public charities may elect the expenditure test as a substitute for the substantial part test. The expenditure test is described in section 501(h) and this § 1.501(h). A public charity is any charity that is not a private foundation under section 509(a). (Unlike a public charity, a private foundation may not make any lobbying expenditures: If a private foundation does make a lobbying expenditure, it is subject to an excise tax under section 4945). Section 1.501(h)–2 lists which public charities are eligible to make the expenditure test election. Section 1.501(h)–2 also provides information about how a public charity makes and revokes the election to be covered by the expenditure test.

(3) A public charity that makes the election may make lobbying expenditures within specified dollar limits. If an electing public charity's lobbying expenditures are within the dollar limits determined under section 4911(c), the electing public charity will not owe tax under section 4911 nor will it lose its tax exempt status as a charity by virtue of section 501(h). If, however, that electing public charity's lobbying expenditures exceed its section 4911 lobbying limit, the organization is subject to an excise tax on the excess lobbying expenditures. Further, under section 501(h), if an electing public charity's lobbying expenditures normally are more than 150 percent of its section 4911 lobbying limit, the organization will cease to be a charity described in section 501(c)(3).

(4) A public charity that elects the expenditure test may nevertheless lose its tax exempt status if it is an action organization under § 1.501(c)(3)–1(c)(3)(iii) or (iv). A public charity that does not elect the expenditure test remains subject to the substantial part test. The substantial part test is applied without regard to the provisions of section 501(h) and 4911 and the related regulations.

(b) Effective date. The provisions of § 1.501(h)–1 through § 1.501(h)–3, are effective for taxable years beginning after August 31, 1990. An election made before August 31, 1990, under the provisions of § 301.9100–

12T(c)(4) or the instructions to Form 5768, will be effective under these regulations without again filing Form 5768.

§ 1.501(h)-2. Electing the expenditure test.

(a) In general. The election to be governed by section 501(h) may be made by an eligible organization (as described in paragraph (b) of this section) for any taxable year of the organization beginning after December 31, 1976, other than the first taxable year for which a voluntary revocation of the election is effective (see paragraph (d) of this section). The election is made by filing a completed Form 5768, Election/Revocation of Election by an Eligible Section 501(c)(3) Organization to Make Expenditures to Influence Legislation, with the appropriate Internal Revenue Service Center listed on that form. Under section 501(h)(6), the election is effective with the beginning of the taxable year in which the form is filed. For example, if an eligible organization whose taxable year is the calendar year files Form 5768 on December 31, 1979, the organization is governed by section 501(h) for its taxable year beginning January 1, 1979. Once made, the expenditure test election is effective (without again filing Form 5768) for each succeeding taxable year for which the organization is an eligible organization and which begins before a notice of revocation is filed under paragraph (d) of this section.

(b) Organizations eligible to elect the expenditure test—(1) In general. For purposes of section 501(h) and the regulations thereunder, an organization is an eligible organization for a taxable year if, for that taxable year, it is—

(i) Described in section 501(c)(3) (determined, in any year for which an election is in effect, without regard to the substantial part test of section 501(c)(3)),

(ii) Described in section 501(h)(4) and paragraph (b)(2) of this section, and

(iii) Not a disqualified organization described in section 501(h)(5) and paragraph (b)(3) of this section.

(2) Certain organizations listed. An organization is described in section 501(h)(4) and this paragraph (b)(2) if it is an organization described in—

(i) Section 170(b)(1)(A)(ii) (relating to educational institutions),

(ii) Section 170(b)(1)(A)(iii) (relating to hospitals and medical research organizations),

(iii) Section 170(b)(1)(A)(iv) (relating to organizations supporting government schools),

(iv) Section 170(b)(1)(A)(vi) (relating to organizations publicly supported by charitable contributions),

(v) Section 509(a)(2) (relating to organizations publicly supported by admissions, sales, etc.), or

(vi) Section 509(a)(3) (relating to organizations supporting public charities), except that for purposes of this paragraph (b)(2), section 509(a)(3) shall be applied without regard to the last sentence of section 509(a).

(3) Disqualified organizations. An organization is a disqualified organization described in section 501(h)(5) and this paragraph (b)(3) if the organization is—

(i) Described in section 170(b)(1)(A)(i) (relating to churches),

(ii) An integrated auxiliary of a church or of a convention or association of churches see (§ 1.6033-2(g)(5)), or

(iii) Described in section 501(c)(3) and affiliated (within the meaning of I.R.C. § 56.4911–7) with one or more organizations described in paragraph (b)(3)(i) or (ii) of this section.

(4) Other organizations ineligible to elect. Under section 501(h)(4), certain organizations, although not disqualified organizations, are not eligible to elect the expenditure test. For example, organizations described in section 509(a)(4) are not listed in section 501(h)(4) and therefore are not eligible to elect. Similarly, private foundations (within the meaning of section 509(a)) are not eligible to elect. For the treatment of expenditures by a private foundation for the purpose of carrying on propaganda, or otherwise attempting, to influence legislation, see § 53.4945–2.

(c) New organizations. A newly created organization may submit Form 5768 to elect the expenditure test under section 501(h) before it is determined to be an eligible organization and may submit Form 5768 at the time it submits its application for recognition of exemption (Form 1023). If the newly created organization is determined to be an eligible organization, the election will be effective under the provisions of paragraph (a) of this section, that is, with the beginning of the taxable year in which the Form 5768 is filed by the eligible organization. However, if a newly created organization is determined by the Service not to be an eligible organization, the organization's election will not be effective and the substantial part test will apply from the effective date of its section 501(c)(3) classification.

(d) Voluntary revocation of expenditure test election—(1) Revocation effective. An organization may voluntarily revoke an expenditure test election by filing a notice of voluntary revocation with the appropriate Internal Revenue Service Center listed on Form 5768. Under section 501(h)(6)(B), a voluntary revocation is effective with the beginning of the first taxable year after the taxable year in which the notice is filed. If an organization voluntarily revokes its election, the substantial part test of section 501(c)(3) will apply with respect to the organization's activities in attempting to influence legislation beginning with the taxable year for which the voluntary revocation is effective.

(2) Re-election of expenditure test. If an organization's expenditure test election is voluntarily revoked, the organization may again make the expenditure test election, effective no earlier than for the taxable year following the first taxable year for which the revocation is effective.

(3) Example. X, an organization whose taxable year is the calendar year, plans to voluntarily revoke its expenditure test election effective beginning with its taxable year 1985. X must file its notice of voluntary revocation on Form 5768 after December 31, 1983, and before January 1, 1985. If X files a notice of voluntary revocation on December 31, 1984, the revocation is effective beginning with its taxable year 1985. The organization may again elect the expenditure test by filing Form 5768. Under paragraph (d)(2) of this section, the election may not be made for taxable year 1985. Under paragraph (a) of this section, a new expenditure test election will be effective for taxable years beginning with taxable year 1986, if the Form 5768 is filed after December 31, 1985, and before January 1, 1987.

(e) Involuntary revocation of expenditure test election. If, while an election by an eligible organization is in effect, the organization ceases to be an eligible organization, its election is automatically revoked. The revocation is effective with the beginning of the first full taxable year for which it is determined that the organization is not an eligible organization. If an organization's expenditure test election is involuntarily revoked under this paragraph (e) but the organization continues to be described in section 501(c)(3), the substantial part test of section 501(c)(3) will apply with respect to the organization's activities in attempting to influence legislation beginning with the first taxable year for which the involuntary revocation is effective.

* * *

§ 1.501(h)–3. Lobbying or grass roots expenditures normally in excess of ceiling amount.

(a) Scope. This section provides rules under section 501(h) for determining whether an organization that has elected the expenditure test and that is not a member of an affiliated group of organizations (as defined in § 56.4911–7(e)) either normally makes lobbying expenditures in excess of its lobbying ceiling amount or normally makes grass roots expenditures in excess of its grass roots ceiling amount. Under section 501(h) and this section, an organization that has elected the expenditure test and that normally makes expenditures in excess of the corresponding ceiling amount will cease to be exempt from tax under section 501(a) as an organization described in section 501(c)(3). For similar rules relating to members of an affiliated group of organizations, see § 56.4911–9.

(b) Loss of exemption—(1) In general. Under section 501(h)(1), an organization that has elected the expenditure test shall be denied exemption from taxation under section 501(a) as an organization described in section 501(c)(3) for the taxable year following a determination year if—

(i) The sum of the organization's lobbying expenditures for the base years exceeds 150 percent of the sum of its lobbying nontaxable amounts for the base years, or **(ii)** The sum of the organization's grass roots expenditures for its base years exceeds 150 percent of the sum of its grass roots nontaxable amounts for the base years.

The organization thereafter shall not be exempt from tax under section 501(a) as an organization described in section 501(c)(3) unless, pursuant to paragraph (d) of this section, the organization reapplies for recognition of exemption and is recognized as exempt.

(2) Special exception for organization's first election. For the first, second, or third consecutive determination year for which an organization's first expenditure test election is in effect, no determination is required under paragraph (b)(1) of this section, and the organization will not be denied exemption from tax by reason of section 501(h) and this section if, taking into account as base years only those years for which the expenditure test election is in effect—

(i) The sum of the organization's lobbying expenditures for such base years does not exceed 150 percent of the sum of its lobbying nontaxable amounts for the same base years, and

(ii) The sum of the organization's grass roots expenditure for those base years does not exceed 150 percent of the sum of its grass roots nontaxable amounts for such base years. If an organization does not satisfy the requirements of this paragraph (b)(2), paragraph (b)(1) of this section will apply.

(c) Definitions. For purposes of this section—**(1)** The term lobbying expenditures means lobbying expenditures as defined in section 4911(c)(1) or section 4911(f)(4)(A) and § 56.4911–2(a).

(2) The term lobbying nontaxable amount is defined in § 56.4911–1(c)(1).

(3) An organization's lobbying ceiling amount is 150 percent of the organization's lobbying nontaxable amount for a taxable year.

(4) The term grass roots expenditures means expenditures for grass roots lobbying communications as defined in section 4911(c)(3) or section 4911(f)(4)(A) and §§ 56.4911–2 and 56.4911–3.

(5) The term grass roots nontaxable amount is defined in § 56.4911–1(c)(2).

(6) An organization's grass roots ceiling amount is 150 percent of the organization's grass roots nontaxable amount for a taxable year.

(7) In general, the term base years means the determination year and the three taxable years immediately preceding the determination year. The base years, however, do not include any taxable year preceding the taxable year for which the organization is first treated as described in section 501(c)(3).

(8) A taxable year is a determination year if it is a year for which the expenditure test election is in effect, other than the taxable year for which the organization is first treated as described in section 501(c)(3).

(d) Reapplication for recognition of exemption—(1) Time of application. An organization that is denied exemption from taxation under section 501(a) by reason of section 501(h) and this section may apply on Form 1023 for recognition of exemption as an organization described in section 501(c)(3) for any taxable year following the first taxable year for which exemption is so denied. See paragraphs (d)(2) and (d)(3) of this section for material to be included with an application described in the preceding sentence.

(2) Section 501(h) calculation. An application described in paragraph (d)(1) of this section must demonstrate that the organization would not be denied exemption from taxation under section 501(a) by reason of section 501(h) if the expenditure test election has been in effect for all of its last taxable year ending before the application is made by providing the calculations, described either in paragraphs (b)(1)(i) and (ii) of this section or in § 56.4911–9(b), that would have applied to the organization for that year.

(3) Operations not disqualifying. An application described in paragraph (d)(1) of this section must include information that demonstrates to the satisfaction of the Commissioner that the organization will not knowingly operate in a manner that would disqualify the organization for tax exemption under section 501(c)(3) by reason of attempting to influence legislation.

(4) Reelection of expenditure test. If an organization is denied exemption from tax for a taxable year by reason of section 501(h) and this section, and thereafter is again recognized as an organization described in section 501(c)(3) pursuant to this paragraph (d), it may again elect the expenditure test under section 501(h) in accordance with § 1.501(h)–2(a).

(e) Examples. The provisions of this section are illustrated by the following examples, which also illustrate the operation of the tax imposed by section 4911.

Example 1. (1) The following table contains information used in this example concerning organization X.

			Lobbying	
Year	Exempt purpose expenditures (EPE)	Calculation	Nontaxable amount (LNTA)	Lobbying expenditures (LE)
1979	$400,000	(20% of $400,000=)	$80,000	$100,000
1980	300,000	(20% of $300,000=)	60,000	100,000
1981	600,000	(20% of $500,000 + 15% of $100,000=)	115,000	120,000
1982	500,000	(20% of $500,000=)	100,000	100,000
Totals	$1,800,000		$355,000	$420,000

(2) Organization X, whose taxable year is the calendar year, was organized in 1971. X first made the expenditure test election under section 501(h) effective for taxable years beginning with 1979 and has not revoked the election. None of X's lobbying expenditures for its taxable years 1979 through 1982 are grass roots expenditures. Under section 4911(a) and § 56.4911–1(a), X must determine for each year for which the expenditure test election is effective whether it is liable for the 25 percent excise tax imposed by section 4911(a) on excess lobbying expenditures. X is liable for this tax for each of its taxable years 1979, 1980, and 1981, because in each year its lobbying expenditures exceeded its lobbying nontaxable amount for the year. For 1979, the tax imposed by section 4911(a) is $5,000 / 25% x ($100,000-$80,000)'$5,000. For 1980, the tax is $10,000. For 1981, the tax is $1,250.

(3) The taxable years 1979 through 1981 are all determination years under paragraph (c)(8) of this section. On its annual return for determination year 1979, the first year of its first election, X can demonstrate, under paragraph (b)(2) of this section, that its lobbying expenditures during 1979 ($100,000) do not exceed 150 percent of its lobbying nontaxable amount for 1979 ($120,000). For determination year 1980, under paragraph (b)(2), X can demonstrate that the sum of its lobbying expenditures for 1979 and 1980 ($200,000) does not exceed 150 percent of the sum of its lobbying nontaxable amounts for 1979 and 1980 ($210,000). For 1981, under paragraph (b)(2), X can demonstrate that the sum of its lobbying expenditures for 1979, 1980, and 1981 ($320,000) does not exceed 150 percent of the sum of its lobbying nontaxable amounts for 1979, 1980, and 1981 ($382,500). For each of the determination years 1979, 1980, and 1981, the first three years of its first election, X satisfies the requirements of paragraph (b)(2). Accordingly, no determination under paragraph (b)(1) of this section is required for those years, and X is not denied tax exemption by reason of section 501(h).

(4) Under paragraph (b)(1) of this section, X must determine for its determination year 1982 whether it has normally made lobbying expenditures in excess of the lobbying ceiling amount. This determination takes into account expenditures in base years 1979 through 1982. The sum of X's lobbying expenditures for the base years ($420,000) does not exceed 150 percent of the sum of the lobbying nontaxable amounts for the base years (150% x $355,000=$532,500). Accordingly, X is not denied tax exemption by reason of section 501(h).

Example 2. (1) The following table contains information used in this example concerning W.

Year	Exempt purpose expenditures (EPE) (dollars)	Calculation
1979	700,000	(20% of $500,000 + 15% of $200,000=).
1980	800,000	(20% of $500,000 + 15% of $300,000=).
1981	800,000	(20% of $500,000 + 15% of $300,000=).
1982	900,000	(20% of $500,000 + 15% of $400,000=).
Total	$ 3,200,000	

Year	Lobbying nontaxable amount (LNTA) (dollars)	Lobbying expenditures (LE) (dollars)	Grass Roots nontaxable amount (25 percent of LNTA (dollars)	Grass root expenditure (dollars)
1979	130,000	120,000	32,500	30,000
1980	145,000	100,000	36,250	60,000
1981	145,000	100,000	36,250	65,000
1982	160,000	150,000	40,000	65,000
Total	$ 580,000	$ 470,000	$ 145,000	$ 220,000

(2) Organization W, whose taxable year is the calendar year, made the expenditure test election under section 501(h) effective for taxable years beginning with 1979 and has not revoked the election. W has been treated as an organization described in section 501(c)(3) for each of its taxable years beginning within its taxable year 1974.

(3) Under section 4911(a) and section 56.4911–1(a), W must determine for each year for which the expenditure test election is effective whether it is liable for the 25 percent excise tax imposed by section 4911(a) on excess lobbying expenditures. In 1980, 1981, and 1982, W has excess lobbying expenditures because its grass roots expenditures in each of those years exceeded its grass roots nontaxable amount for the year. Therefore, W is liable for the excise tax under section 4911(a) for those years. The tax imposed by section 4911(a) for 1980 is $5,937.50 / {25% x ($60,000-$36,250)= $5,937.50}. For 1981, the tax is $7,187.50. For 1982, the tax is $6,250.

(4) On its annual return for its determination years 1979, 1980, and 1981, the first three years of its first election, W demonstrates that it satisfies the requirements of paragraph (b)(2) of this section. Accordingly, no determination under paragraph (b)(1) of this section is required for those years, and W is not denied tax exemption by reason of section 501(h).

(5) On its annual return for its determination year 1982, W must determine under paragraph (b)(1) whether it has normally made lobbying expenditures or grass roots expenditures in excess of the corresponding ceiling amount.

This determination takes into account expenditures in base years 1979 through 1982. The sum of W's lobbying expenditures for the base years ($470,000) does not exceed 150% of the sum of W's lobbying nontaxable amounts for those years (150% x $580,000=$870,000). However, the sum of W's grass roots expenditures for the base years ($220,000) does exceed 150% of the sum of W's grass roots nontaxable amounts for those years (150% x $145,000=$217,500). Under section 501(h), W is denied tax exemption under section 501(a) as an organization described in section 501(c)(3) for its taxable year 1983. For its taxable year 1984 and any taxable year thereafter, W is exempt from tax as an organization described in section 501(c)(3) only if W applies for recognition of its exempt status under paragraph (d) of this section and is recognized as exempt from tax.

Example 3. (1) The following table contains information used in this example concerning organization Y.

Taxable Year	Exempt purpose expenditures (EPE) (dollars)	Calculation
1977	$700,000	(20% of $500,000 + 15% of $200,000=
1978	$800,000	(20% of $500,000 + 15% of $300,000=
Subtotal	$1,500,000	
1979	$ 900,000	(20% of $500,000 + 15% of $400,000=
Totals:	$ 2,400,000	

Taxable Year	Lobbying nontaxable amount (LNTA) (dollars)	Lobbying expenditures (LE)(dollars)	Grass roots nontaxable amount (25 percent of (LNTA)(dollars)	Grass roots expenditures (dollars)
1977	130,000	182,000	32,500	30,000
1978	145,000	224,750	36,250	35,000
Subtotal	$ 275,000	$ 406,750	$ 68,750	$ 65,000
1979	160,000	264,000	40,000	50,000
Totals:	$ 435,000	$ 670,750	$ 108,750	$ 115,000

(2) Organization Y, whose taxable year is the calendar year, was first treated as an organization described in section 501(c)(3) on February 1, 1977. Y made the expenditure test election under section 501(h) effective for taxable years beginning with 1977 and has not revoked the election.

(3) For 1977, Y has excess lobbying expenditures of $52,000 because its lobbying expenditures ($182,000) exceed its lobbying nontaxable amount ($130,000) for the taxable year. Accordingly, Y is liable for the 25 percent excise tax imposed by section 4911(a). The amount of the tax is $13,000 [25% x ($182,000-$130,000)=$13,000].

(4) For 1978, Y again has excess lobbying expenditures and is again liable for the 25 percent excise tax imposed by section 4911(a). The amount of the tax is $19,937.50 [25% x ($224,750 - $145,000) = $ 19,937.50.]

(5) For 1979, Y's lobbying expenditures ($264,000) exceed its lobbying nontaxable amount ($160,000) by $104,000, and its grass roots expenditures ($50,000) exceed its grass roots nontaxable amount ($40,000) by $10,000. Under § 56.4911–1(b), Y's excess lobbying expenditures are the greater of $104,000 or $10,000. The amount of the tax, therefore, is $26,000 [25% x $104,000=$26,000].

(6) Under paragraph (c)(8) of this section, 1977 is not a determination year because it is the first year for which the organization is treated as described in section 501(c)(3). For 1977, Y need not determine whether it has normally made lobbying expenditures or grass roots expenditures in excess of the corresponding ceiling amount for purposes of determining whether it is denied exemption under section 501(h) for its taxable year 1978.

(7) For determination year 1978, Y must determine whether it has normally made lobbying or grass roots expenditures in excess of the corresponding ceiling amount, taking into account expenditures for the base years 1977 and 1978. For Y, the determination under paragraph (b)(2) of this section considers the same base years as the determination under paragraph (b)(1) of this section and is, therefore, redundant. Accordingly, Y proceeds to determine, under (b)(1), whether it is denied exemption. Y's grass roots expenditures for 1977 and 1978 ($65,000) did not exceed 150 percent of the sum of its grass roots nontaxable amounts for those years ($103,125). Y's lobbying expenditures for 1977 and 1978 ($406,750) did not exceed 150% of its lobbying nontaxable amount for those years (150% x $275,000=$412,500). Therefore, Y is not denied tax exemption under section 501(h) for its taxable year 1979.

(8) For determination year 1979, the sum of Y's grass roots expenditures in base years 1977, 1978, and 1979 does not exceed 150 percent of its grass roots nontaxable amount (calculation omitted). However, the sum of Y's lobbying expenditures for the base years ($670,750) does exceed 150% of the sum of the lobbying nontaxable amounts for those years (150% x $435,000=$652,500). Since Y was not described in section 501(c)(3) prior to 1977, only the years 1977, 1978, and 1979 may be considered in determining whether Y has normally made lobbying expenditures in excess of its lobbying ceiling. Therefore, Y determines that it has normally made lobbying expenditures in excess of its lobbying ceiling. Under section 501(h), Y is denied tax exemption under section 501(a) as an organization described in section 501(c)(3) for its taxable year 1980. For its taxable year 1981, and any taxable year thereafter, Y is exempt from tax as an organization described in section 501(c)(3) only if Y applies for recognition of its exempt status under paragraph (d) of this section and is recognized as exempt from tax.

Example 4. Organization M made the expenditure test election under section 501(h) effective for taxable years beginning with 1977 and has not revoked the election. M has $500,000 of exempt purpose expenditures during each of the years 1981 through 1984. In addition, during each of those years, M spends $75,000 for direct lobbying and $25,000 for grass roots lobbying. Since the amount expended for M's lobbying (both total lobbying and grass roots lobbying) is within the respective nontaxable expenditure limitations, M is not liable for the 25 percent excise tax imposed under section 4911(a) upon excess lobbying expenditures, nor is M denied tax-exempt status by reason of section 501(h).

Example 5. Assume the same facts as in Example 4, except that, on behalf of M, numerous unpaid volunteers conduct substantial lobbying activities with no reimbursement. Since the substantial lobbying activities of the unpaid volunteers are not counted towards the expenditure limitations and the amount expended for M's lobbying is within the respective nontaxable expenditure limitations, M is not liable for the 25 percent excise tax under section 4911, nor is M denied tax-exempt status by reason of section 501(h).

§ 1.502–1. Feeder organizations.

(a) In the case of an organization operated for the primary purpose of carrying on a trade or business for profit, exemption is not allowed under section 501 on the ground that all the profits of such organization are payable to one or more organizations exempt from taxation under section 501. In determining the primary purpose of an organization, all the circumstances must be considered, including the size and extent of the trade or business and the size and extent of those activities of such organization which are specified in the applicable paragraph of section 501.

(b) If a subsidiary organization of a tax-exempt organization would itself be exempt on the ground that its activities are an integral part of the exempt activities of the parent organization, its exemption will not be lost because, as a matter of accounting between the two organizations, the subsidiary derives a profit from its dealings with its parent organization, for example, a subsidiary organization which is operated for the sole purpose of furnishing electric power used by its parent organization, a tax-exempt educational organization, in carrying on its educational activities. However, the subsidiary organization is not exempt from tax if it is operated for the primary purpose of carrying on a trade or business which would be an unrelated trade or business (that is, unrelated to exempt activities) if regularly carried on by the parent organization. For example, if a subsidiary organization is operated primarily for the purpose of furnishing electric power to consumers other than its parent organization (and the parent's tax-exempt subsidiary organizations), it is not exempt since such business would be an unrelated trade or business if regularly carried on by the parent organization. Similarly, if the organization is owned by several unrelated exempt organizations, and is operated for the purpose of furnishing electric power to each of them, it is not exempt since such business would be an unrelated trade or business if regularly carried on by any one of the tax-exempt organizations. For purposes of this paragraph, organizations are related only if they consist of:

(1) A parent organization and one or more of its subsidiary organizations; or

(2) Subsidiary organizations having a common parent organization.

An exempt organization is not related to another exempt organization merely because they both engage in the same type of exempt activities.

(c) In certain cases an organization which carries on a trade or business for profit but is not operated for the primary purpose of carrying on such trade or business is subject to the tax imposed under section 511 on its unrelated business taxable income.

§ 1.504–1. Attempts to influence legislation; certain organizations formerly described in section 501(c)(3) denied exemption.

Section 504(a) and this section apply to an organization that is exempt from taxation at any time after October 4, 1976, as an organization described in section 501(c)(3), and that ceases to be described in that section because it—

(a) Is an action organization within the meaning of section 1.501(c)(3)–1(c)(3)(ii) or (iv), on account of activities occurring after October 4, 1976, or

(b) Is denied exemption under the provisions of section 501(h) (see section 1.501(h)–3 or section 56.4911–9).

This section does not apply, however, to an organization that was described in section 501(h)(5) and section 1.501(h)–2(b)(3) (relating generally to churches) for its taxable year immediately preceding the first taxable year for which it is no longer an organization described in section 501(c)(3). An organization to which section 504(a) and this section apply shall not be treated as described in section 501(c)(4) at any time after the organization ceases to be described in section 501(c)(3). Further, an organization denied treatment as an organization described in section 501(c)(4) under this section may not be treated as an organization described in section 501(c) other than as an organization described in section 501(c)(3). For rules relating to recognition of exemption after exemption is denied under section 501(h), section 1.501(h)–3(d).

§ 1.504–2. Certain transfers made to avoid section 504(a).

(a) Scope. Under section 504(b), a transfer described in paragraph (b) or (c) of this section to an organization exempt from tax under section 501(a) may result in loss of exemption by the transferee unless the Commissioner determines, under paragraph (e) of this section, that the original transfer did not effect an avoidance of section 504(a). For purposes of this section, the term transfer includes any use by, or for the benefit of, the recipient of the transfer, but does not include any transfer made for adequate and full consideration.

(b) Transferor and transferee commonly controlled—(1) Loss of exemption. A transfer is described in this paragraph (b) if it is described in paragraphs (b)(2) through (b)(6). The transferee of a transfer described in this paragraph will cease to be exempt from tax under section 501(a), unless the provisions of paragraph (e) of this section apply.

(2) Transferor organization. A transfer is described in this paragraph (b)(2) only if it is from an organization that—

(i) Is or was described in section 501(c)(3), but not in section 501(h)(5), and

(ii) Is determined to be an "action" organization (as defined in section 1.501(c)(3)–1(c)(3)(ii) or (iv)), or is denied exemption from tax by reason of section 501(h) and either section 1.501(h)–3 or section 56.4911–9.

(3) Transferor and transferee commonly controlled. A transfer is described in this paragraph (b)(3) only if, at the time of the transfer or at any time during the transferee's ten taxable years following the year in which the transfer was made, the transferee is controlled (directly or indirectly), as defined in paragraph (f) of this section, by the same person or persons who control the transferor.

(4) Time of transfer. A transfer is described in this paragraph (b)(4) only if the transfer is made—

(i) After the date that is 24 months before the earliest of the effective date of the determination under section 501(h) that the transferor is not exempt, the effective date of the Commissioner's determination that the transferor is an "action" organization (as defined in section 1.501(c)(3)(ii) or (iv)), or the date on which the Commissioner proposes to treat it as no longer described in section 501(c)(3), and

(ii) Before the transferor again is recognized as an organization described in section 501(c)(3).

(5) Transferee. A transfer is described in this paragraph (b)(5) only if the transferee is exempt from tax under section 501(a) but the transferee is neither—

(i) An organization described in section 501(c)(3), nor

(ii) An organization described in section 401(a) to which the transferor contributes as an employer.

(6) Amount of transfer. A transfer is described in this paragraph (b)(6) only if the amount of the transfer exceeds the lesser of 30 percent of the net fair market value of the transferor's assets or 50 percent of the net fair market value of the transferee's assets, computed immediately before the transfer. For purposes of this paragraph (b)(6)—

(i) The amount of a transfer by a transferor is the sum of the amounts transferred to any number of transferees in any number of transfers, all of which are described in paragraphs (b)(2) through (b)(5) of this section, and the time of the transfer is the time of the first transfer so taken into account; and

(ii) The amount of a transfer to a transferee is the sum of the amounts transferred by a transferor to the transferee in any number of transfers, all of which are described in paragraphs (b)(2) through (b)(5) of this section, and the time of the transfer is the time of the first transfer so taken into account.

(c) Other transfers—(1) Transfers included. A transfer is described in this paragraph (c) if it would be described in paragraph (b) of this section except that either—

(i) The amount of the transfer is less than the amount determined in paragraph (b)(6) of this section, or

(ii) The transferor and transferee are not commonly controlled as described in paragraph (b)(3) of this section, or

(iii) The transferee is an organization described in sections 501(c)(3) and 501(h)(4).

(2) Loss of exemption. The transferee of a transfer described in this paragraph (c) will cease to be exempt under section 501(a) if the Commissioner determines on all the facts and circumstances that the transfer effected an avoidance of section 504(a). In determining whether a transfer effected an avoidance of section 504(a), the Commissioner may consider whether the transferee engages, or has engaged, in attempts to influence legislation and may also consider any factors enumerated in paragraph (e) of this section.

(d) Date of loss of exempt status. A transferee of a transfer described in paragraph (b), (c)(1)(ii), or (c)(1)(iii) of this section will cease to be exempt from tax under section 501(a) on the date that all requirements of paragraph (b), (c)(1)(ii), or (c)(1)(iii) (other than the determination by the Commissioner) are satisfied. A transferee of a transfer described in paragraph (c)(1)(i) of this section will cease to be exempt from tax under section 501(a) on the date of the last transfer preceding notification of the transferee that the Commissioner proposes to treat the transferee as other than an exempt organization.

(e) Transfers not in avoidance of section 504(a). Notwithstanding paragraph (b) of this section, if, based on all the facts and circumstances, the Commissioner determines that a transfer described in paragraph (b) did not effect an avoidance of section 504(a), the transferee will not be denied exemption from tax by reason of section 504(b) and this section. In making the determination called for in the preceding sentence, the Commissioner may consider all relevant factors including:

(1) Whether enforceable and effective conditions on the transfer preclude use of any of the transferred assets for any purpose that, if it were a substantial part of an organization's activities, would be inconsistent with exemption as an organization described in section 501(c)(3);

(2) In the absence of conditions described in paragraph (e)(1) of this section, whether the transferred assets are used exclusively for purposes that are consistent with the transferor's exemption as an organization described in section 501(c)(3);

(3) Whether the assets transferred would be described in section 53.4942(a)–(2)(c)(3) before, as well as after, the transfer if both the transferor and transferee were private foundations;

(4) Whether and to what extent the transfer would satisfy the provisions of section 1.507–2(a)(7) and (8) if the transferor were a private foundation;

(5) Whether all of the transferred assets have been expended during a period when the transferee was not controlled (directly or indirectly) by the same person or persons who controlled the transferor; and

(6) Whether the entire amount of the transferred assets were in turn transferred, before the close of the transferee's taxable year following the taxable year in which the transferred assets were received, to one or more organizations described in section 507(b)(1)(A) none of which are controlled (directly or indirectly) by the same persons who control either the original transferor or transferee.

(f) Control. For purposes of section 504 and the regulations thereunder—

(1) The transferor will be presumed to control any organization with which it is affiliated within the meaning of section 56.4911–7(a), or would be if both organizations were described in section 501(c)(3), and

(2) The transferee will be treated as controlled (directly of indirectly) by the same person or persons who control the transferor if the transferee would be treated as controlled under section 53.4942(a)–3(a)(3), for which purpose the transferor shall be treated as a private foundation.

§ 1.506–1. Organizations required to notify Commissioner of intent to operate under section 501(c)(4).

(a) Notification requirement—(1) In general. Except as provided in paragraph (b) of this section, an organization (whether domestic or foreign) described in section 501(c)(4) must, no later than 60 days after the date the organization is organized, notify the Commissioner that it is operating as an organization described in section 501(c)(4) by submitting a completed Form 8976, "Notice of Intent to Operate Under Section 501(c)(4)," or its successor (the notification). The notification must be submitted in accordance with the form and its instructions. The notification must include the information specified in paragraph (a)(2) of this section and be accompanied by payment of the user fee described in paragraph (a)(3) of this section. Additional guidance on the procedure for submitting the notification may be provided in published guidance in the Internal Revenue Bulletin (see § 601.601(d)(2) of this chapter) or in other guidance, such as forms or instructions, issued with respect to the notification.

(2) Contents of the notification. The notification must include the following information:

(i) The name, address, and taxpayer identification number of the organization.

(ii) The date on which, and the state or other jurisdiction under the laws of which, the organization was organized (that is, formed as a legal entity). For an organization formed outside the United States, the jurisdiction is the foreign country under the laws of which it is organized.

(iii) A statement of the purpose of the organization.

(iv) Such additional information as may be specified in published guidance in the Internal Revenue Bulletin (see § 601.601(d)(2) of this chapter) or in other guidance, such as forms or instructions, issued with respect to the notification.

(3) User fee. The notification must be accompanied by payment of the user fee set forth by published guidance in the Internal Revenue Bulletin (see § 601.601(d)(2) of this chapter) or in other guidance, such as forms or instructions, issued with respect to the notification.

(4) Extension for reasonable cause. The Commissioner may, for reasonable cause, extend the 60-day period for submitting the notification.

(b) Special rules for organizations that were organized on or before July 8, 2016—(1) Notification requirement does not apply to organizations that filed with the IRS on or before December 18, 2015. The requirement to submit the notification does not apply to any organization described in section 501(c)(4) that, on or before December 18, 2015, either—

(i) Applied for a written determination of recognition as an organization described in section 501(c)(4) in accordance with § 1.501(a)–1 and all applicable guidance published in the Internal Revenue Bulletin (see § 501.601(d)(2) of this chapter), forms, and instructions; or

(ii) Filed at least one annual information return or annual electronic notification required under section 6033(a)(1) or (i).

(2) Transition relief available for organizations that filed with the IRS on or before July 8, 2016. An organization described in section 501(c)(4) is not required to submit the notification if, on or before July 8, 2016, the organization either—

(i) Applied for a written determination of recognition as an organization described in section 501(c)(4) in accordance with § 1.501(a)–1 and all applicable guidance published in the Internal Revenue Bulletin (see § 601.601(d)(2) of this chapter), forms, and instructions; or

(ii) Filed at least one annual information return or annual electronic notification required under section 6033(a)(1) or (i).

(3) Extended due date. An organization that was organized on or before July 8, 2016, and is not described in paragraph (b)(1) or (2) of this section, satisfies the requirement to submit the notification if the notification was submitted on or before September 6, 2016.

(c) Failure to submit the notification. For information on the penalties for failure to submit the notification, the applicable reasonable cause exception, and applicable special rules, see section 6652(c)(4) through(6).

(d) Acknowledgment of receipt. Within 60 days after receipt of the notification, the Commissioner will send the organization an acknowledgment of such receipt. This acknowledgment is not a determination by the Commissioner that the organization qualifies for exemption under section 501(a) as an organization described in section 501(c)(4). See paragraph (e) of this section.

(e) Separate procedure by which an organization may request an IRS determination that it qualifies for section 501(c)(4) tax-exempt status. Submission of the notification does not constitute a request by an organization for a determination by the Commissioner that the organization qualifies for exemption under section 501(a) as an organization described in section 501(c)(4). An organization seeking IRS recognition of its tax-exempt status must separately request such a determination in accordance with § 1.501(a)–1 and all applicable guidance published in the Internal Revenue Bulletin (see § 601.601(d)(2) of this chapter), forms, and instructions.

(f) Applicability date. This section applies on and after July 8, 2016.

PRIVATE FOUNDATIONS

§ 1.507–1. General rule.

(a) In general.—Except as provided in § 1.507–2, the status of any organization as a private foundation shall be terminated only if—

(1) Such organization notifies the district director of its intent to accomplish such termination, or

(2)(i) With respect to such organization, there have been either willful repeated acts (or failures to act), or a willful and flagrant act (or failure to act) giving rise to liability for tax under chapter 42, and

(ii) the Commissioner notifies such organization that, by reason of subdivision (I) of this subparagraph, such organization is liable for the tax imposed by section 507(c),

and either such organization pays the tax imposed by section 507(c) (or any portion not abated under section 507(g)) or the entire amount of such tax is abated under section 507(g).

(b) Termination under section 507(a)(1). (1) In order to terminate its private foundation status under paragraph (a)(1) of this section, an organization must submit a statement to the district director of its intent to terminate its private foundation status under section 507(a)(1). Such statement must set forth in detail the computation and amount of tax imposed under section 507(c). Unless the organization requests abatement of such tax pursuant to section 507(g), full payment of such tax must be made at the time the statement is filed under section 507(a)(1). An organization may request the abatement of all of the tax imposed under section 507(c), or may pay any part thereof and request abatement of the unpaid portion of the amount of tax assessed. If the organization requests abatement of the tax imposed under section 507(c) and such request is denied, the organization must pay such tax in full upon notification by the Internal Revenue Service that such tax will not be abated. For purposes of subtitle F of the Code, the statement described in this subparagraph, once filed, shall be treated as a return.

(2) Termination of private foundation status under section 507(a)(1) does not relieve a private foundation, or any disqualified person with respect thereto, of liability for tax under chapter 42 with respect to acts or failures to act prior to termination or for any additional taxes imposed for failure to correct such acts or failures to act. See subparagraph (8) of this paragraph as to the possible imposition of transferee liability in cases not involving termination of private foundation status.

(3) In the case of an organization which has terminated its private foundation status under section 507(a) and continues in operation thereafter, if such organization wishes to be treated as described in section 501(c)(3), then pursuant to section 509(c) and § 1.509(c)–1 such organization must apply for recognition of exemption as an organization described in section 501(c)(3) in accordance with the provisions of section 508(a).

(4) See § 53.4947–1(c)(7) of this chapter as to the application of section 507(a) to certain split-interest trusts.

(5) For purposes of section 508(d)(1), the Internal Revenue Service shall make notice to the public (such as by publication in the

Internal Revenue Bulletin) of any notice received from a private foundation pursuant to section 507(a)(1) or of any notice given to a private foundation pursuant to section 507(a)(2).

(6) If a private foundation transfers all or part of its assets to one or more other private foundations (or one or more private foundations and one or more section 509(a)(1), (2), (3), or (4) organizations) pursuant to a transfer described in section 507(b)(2) and § 1.507–3(c), such transferor foundation will not have terminated its private foundation status under section 507(a)(1). See § 1.507–3, however, for the special rules applicable to private foundations participating in section 507(b)(2) transfers.

(7) Neither a transfer of all of the assets of a private foundation nor a significant disposition of assets (as defined in § 1.507–3(c)(2)) by a private foundation (whether or not any portion of such significant disposition of assets is made to another private foundation) shall be deemed to result in a termination of the transferor private foundation under section 507(a) unless the transferor private foundation elects to terminate pursuant to section 507(a)(1) or section 507(a)(2) is applicable. Thus, if a private foundation transfers all of its assets to one or more persons, but less than all of its net assets to one or more organizations described in section 509(a)(1) which have been in existence and so described for a continuous period of 60 calendar months, for purposes of this paragraph such transferor foundation will not be deemed by reason of such transfer to have terminated its private foundation status under section 507(a) or (b) unless section 507(a)(2) is applicable. Such foundation will continue to be treated as a private foundation for all purposes. For example, if a private foundation transfers all of its net assets to a section 509(a)(2) organization in 1971 and receives a bequest in 1973, the bequest will be regarded as having been made to a private foundation and the foundation will be subject to the provisions of chapter 42 with respect to such funds. If a private foundation makes a transfer of all of its net assets to a section 509(a)(2) or (3) organization, for example, it must retain sufficient income or assets to pay the tax imposed under section 4940 for that portion of its taxable year prior to such transfer. For additional rules applicable to a transfer by a private foundation of all of its net assets to a section 509(a)(1) organization which has not been in existence and so described for a continuous period of 60 calendar months, see § 1.507–3(e).

(8) If a private foundation makes a transfer described in subparagraph (7) of this paragraph and prior to, or in connection with, such transfer, liability for any tax under chapter 42 is incurred by the transferor foundation, transferee liability may be applied against the transferee organization for payment of such taxes. For purposes of this subparagraph, liability for any tax imposed under chapter 42 for failure to correct any act or failure to act shall be deemed incurred on the date on which the act or failure to act giving rise to the initial tax liability occurred.

(9) A private foundation which transfers all of its net assets is required to file the annual information return required by section 6033, and the foundation managers are required to file the annual report of a private foundation required by section 6056, for the taxable year in which such transfer occurs. However, neither such foundation nor its foundation managers will be required to file such returns for any taxable year following the taxable year in which the last of any such transfers occurred, if at no time during the subsequent taxable years in question the foundation has either legal or equitable title to any assets or engages in any activity.

(c) Involuntary termination under section 507(a)(2). (1) For purposes of section 507(a)(2)(A), the term "willful repeated acts (or failures to act)" means at least two acts or failures to act both of which are voluntary, conscious, and intentional.

(2) For purposes of section 507(a)(2)(A), a "willful and flagrant act (or failure to act)" is one which is voluntarily, consciously, and knowingly committed in violation of any provision of chapter 42 (other than section 4940 or 4948(a)) and which appears to a reasonable man to be a gross violation of any such provision.

(3) An act (or failure to act) may be treated as an act (or failure to act) by the private foundation for purposes of section 507(a)(2) even though tax is imposed upon one or more foundation managers rather than upon the foundation itself.

(4) For purposes of section 507(a)(2), the failure to correct the act or acts (or failure or failures to act) which gave rise to liability for tax under any section of chapter 42 by the close of the correction period for such section may be a willful and flagrant act (or failure to act).

(5) No motive to avoid the restrictions of the law or the incurrence of any tax is necessary to make an act (or failure to act) willful. However, a foundation's act (or failure to act) is not willful if the foundation (or a foundation manager, if applicable) does not know that it is an act of self-dealing, a taxable expenditure, or other act (or failure to act) to which chapter 42 applies. Rules similar to the regulations under chapter 42 (see, for example, § 53.4945–1(a)(2)(iii) of this chapter) shall apply in determining whether a foundation or a foundation manager "knows" that an act (or failure to act) is an act of self-dealing a taxable expenditure or other such act (or failure to act).

§ 1.507–6. Substantial contributor defined.

(a) Definition—(1) In general. Except as provided in subparagraph (2) of this paragraph, the term "substantial contributor" means, with respect to a private foundation, any person (within the meaning of section 7701(a)(1)), whether or not exempt from taxation under section 501(a), who contributed or bequeathed an aggregate amount of more than $5,000 to the private foundation, if such amount is more than 2 percent of the total contributions and bequests received by the private foundation before the close of the taxable year of the private foundation in which a contribution or bequest is received by the foundation from such person. In the case of a trust, the term "substantial contributor" also means the creator of the trust. Such term does not include a governmental unit described in section 170(c)(1).

(2) Special rules. For purposes of sections 170(b)(1)(E)(iii), 507(d)(1), 508(d), 509(a)(1) and (3), and chapter 42, the term "substantial contributor" shall not include an organization which is described in section 509(a)(1), (2), or (3) or any other organization which is wholly owned by such section 509(a)(1), (2), or (3) organization. Furthermore, taking section 4941 (relating to taxes on self-dealing) in context, it would unduly restrict the activities of private foundations if the term "substantial contributor" were to include any section 501(c)(3) organizations. It was not intended, for example, that a large grant for charitable purposes from one private foundation to another would forever preclude the latter from making any grants to, or otherwise dealing with, the former. Accordingly, for purposes of section 4941 only, the term "substantial contributor" shall not only include any organization which is described in section 501(c)(3) (other than an organization described in section 509(a)(4)).

(b) Determination of substantial contributor—(1) In general. In determining under paragraph (a) of this section whether the aggregate of contributions and bequests from a person exceeds 2 percent of the total contributions and bequests received by a private foundation, both the total of such amounts received by the private foundation, and the aggregate of such amounts contributed and bequeathed by such person, shall be determined as of the last day of each taxable year commencing with the first taxable year ending after October 9, 1969. Generally, under section 507(d)(2) and this section, except for purposes of valuation under section 507(d)(2)(B)(i), all contributions and bequests made before October 9, 1969, are deemed to have been made on October 9, 1969. For purposes of section 509(a)(2) and the support test described in § 1.509(a)–3(c), contributions and bequests before October 9, 1969, will be taken into account in the year when actually made. For example, in the case of a contribution or bequest of $6,000 in 1967, such contribution or bequest shall be treated as made by a substantial contributor in 1967 for purposes of section 509(a)(2) and § 1.509(a)–3(c) if such person met the $5,000—2 percent test as of December 31, 1967, and December 31, 1969 (in the case of a calendar year accounting period). Although the determination of the percentage of total contributions and bequests represented by a given donor's contributions and bequests is not made until the end of the foundation's taxable year, a donor is a substantial contributor as of the first date when the foundation received from him an amount sufficient to make him a substantial contributor. Except as otherwise provided in this subparagraph, such amount is treated for all purposes as made by a substantial contributor. Thus, the total contributions and bequests received by the private foundation from all persons, and the aggregate contributions and bequests made by a particular person, are to be determined as of December 31, 1969 (in the case of a calendar year organization which was in existence on that date), and the amounts included in each respective total would be all contributions and bequests received by the organization on or before that date, and all contributions and bequests made by the person on or before that date. Thereafter, a similar determination is to be made with respect to such private foundation as of the end of each of its succeeding taxable years. Status as a substantial contributor, however, will date from the time when the donor first met the $5,000 and 2 percent test. Once a person is a substantial contributor with respect to a private foundation, he remains a substantial contributor even though he might not be so classified if a determination were first made at some later date. For instance, even though the aggregate contributions and bequests of a person become less than 2 percent of the total received by a private foundation (for example, because of subsequent contributions and bequests by other persons), such person remains a substantial contributor with respect to the foundation.

(2) Examples. The provisions of paragraph (a) of this section and this paragraph (b) may be illustrated by the following examples:

Example 1. On January 1, 1968, A, an individual, gave $4,500 to M, a private foundation on a calendar year basis. On June 1, 1969, A gave M the further sum of $1,500. Throughout its existence, through December 31, 1969, M has received $250,000 in contributions and bequests from all sources. As of June 1, 1969, A is a substantial contributor to M for purposes of section 509(a)(2).

Example 2. On September 9, 1966, B, an individual, gave $3,500 to N, a private foundation on a calendar year basis. On March 15, 1970, B gave N the further sum of $3,500. Throughout its existence, through December 31, 1970, N has received $200,000 in contributions and bequests from all sources. B is a substantial contributor to N as of March 15, 1970, since that is the first date on which his contributions met the 2 percent-$5,000 test.

Example 3. On July 21, 1964, X, a corporation, gave $2,000 to O, a private foundation on a calendar year basis. As of December 31, 1969, O had received $150,000 from all sources. On September 17, 1970, X gave O the further sum of $3,100. Through September 17, 1970, O had received $245,000 from all sources as total contributions and bequests. Between September 17, 1970, and December 31, 1970, however, O received $50,000 in contributions and bequests from others. X is not a substantial contributor to O, since X's contributions to O were not more than 2 percent of the total contributions and bequests received by O by December 31, 1970, the end of O's taxable year, even though X's contributions met that test at one point during the year.

Example 4. On September 16, 1970, C, an individual, gave $10,000 to P, a private foundation on a calendar year basis. Throughout its existence, and through December 31, 1970, the close of its taxable year, P had received a total of $100,000 in contributions and bequests. On January 3, 1971, P received a bequest of $1 million. C is a substantial contributor to P since he was a substantial contributor as of September 16, 1970, and therefore remains one even though he no longer meets the 2-percent test on a later date after the end of the taxable year of the foundation in which he first became a substantial contributor.

(c) Special rules—(1) Contributions defined. The term "contribution" shall, for purposes of section 507(d)(2), have the same meaning as such term has under section 170(c) and also include bequests, legacies, devises, and transfers within the meaning of section 2055 or 2106(a)(2). Thus, for purposes of section 507(d)(2), any payment of money or transfer of property without adequate consideration shall be considered a "contribution". Where payment is made or property transferred as consideration for admissions, sales of merchandise, performance of services, or furnishing of facilities to the donor, the qualification of all or any part of such payment or transfer as a contribution under section 170(c) shall determine whether and to what extent such payment or transfer constitutes a "contribution" under section 507(d)(2).

(2) Valuation of contributions and bequests. Each contribution or bequest to a private foundation shall be valued at fair market value when actually received by the private foundation.

(3) Contributions and bequests by a spouse. An individual shall be considered, for purposes of this section, to have made all contributions and bequests made by his spouse during the period of their marriage. Thus, for example, where W contributed $500,000 to P, a private foundation, in 1941 and that amount exceeded 2 percent of the total contributions received by P as of the end of P's first taxable year ending after October 9, 1969, H (W's spouse at the time of the 1941 gift) is considered to have made such contribution (even if W died prior to October 9, 1969, or their marriage was otherwise terminated prior to such date). Similarly, any bequest or devise shall be treated as having been made by the decedent's surviving spouse.

§ 1.508-1. Notices.

(a) New organizations must notify the Commissioner that they are applying for recognition of section 501(c)(3) status—(1) In general. Except as provided in subparagraph (3) of this paragraph, an organization that is organized after October 9, 1969, will not be treated as described in section 501(c)(3):

(i) Unless such organization has given the Commissioner notice in the manner prescribed in subparagraph (2) of this paragraph; or

(ii) For any period before the giving of such notice, unless such notice is given in the manner and within the time prescribed in subparagraph (2) of this paragraph.

No organization shall be exempt from taxation under section 501(a) by reason of being described in section 501(c)(3) whenever such organization is not treated as described in section 501(c)(3) by reason of section 508(a) and this paragraph. See section 508(d)(2)(B) and § 1.508–2(b) regarding the deductibility of charitable contributions to an organization during the period such organization is not exempt under section 501(a) as an organization described in section 501(c)(3) by reason of failing to file a notice under section 508(a) and this subparagraph. See also § 1.508–2(b)(1)(viii) regarding the deductibility of charitable contributions to trusts described in section 4947(a)(1).

(2) Filing of notice. (i) For purposes of subparagraph (1) of this paragraph, except as provided in subparagraph (3) of this paragraph, an organization seeking exemption under section 501(c)(3) must file the notice described in section 508(a) within 15 months from the end of the month in which the organization was organized, or before March 22, 1973, whichever comes later. Such notice is filed by submitting a properly completed and executed Form 1023, exemption application. Notice should be filed with the district director. A request for extension of time for the filing of such notice should be submitted to such district director. Such request may be granted if it demonstrates that additional time is required.

(ii) Although the information required by Form 1023 must be submitted to satisfy the notice required by this section, the failure to supply, within the required time, all of the information required to complete such form is not alone sufficient to deny exemption from the date of organization to the date such complete information is submitted by the organization. If the information which is submitted within the required time is incomplete, and the organization supplies the necessary additional information at the request of the Commissioner within the additional time period allowed by him, the original notice will be considered timely.

(iii) For purposes of subdivision (i) of this subparagraph and paragraph (b)(2)(i) of this section, an organization shall be considered "organized" on the date it becomes an organization described in section 501(c)(3) (determined without regard to section 508(a)).

(iv) Since a trust described in section 4947(a)(2) is not an organization described in section 501(c)(3), it is not required to file a notice described in section 508(a).

(v) For the treatment of community trusts, and the trusts or funds comprising them, under section 508, see the special rules under § 1.170A–9(e).

(vi) A foreign organization shall, for purposes of section 508, be treated in the same manner as a domestic organization, except that section 508 shall not apply to a foreign organization which is described in section 4948(b).

(3) Exceptions from notice. (i) Subparagraphs (1) and (2) of this paragraph are inapplicable to the following organizations:

(a) Churches, interchurch organizations of local units of a church, conventions or associations of churches, or integrated auxiliaries of a church, such as a men's or women's organization, religious school, mission society, or youth group;

(b) Any organization which is not a private foundation (as defined in section 509(a)) and the gross receipts of which in each taxable year are normally not more than $5,000 (as described in subdivision (ii) of this subparagraph);

(c) Subordinate organizations (other than private foundations) covered by a group exemption letter;

(d) Solely for purposes of sections 507, 508(d)(1), 508(d)(2)(A) and 508(d)(3), 508(e), 509 and chapter 42, a trust described in section 4947(a)(1). (However, a trust described in section 501(c)(3) which was organized after October 9, 1969, shall be exempt under section 501(a) by reason of being described in section 501(c)(3) only if it files such notice); and

(e) Any other class of organization that the Commissioner from time to time excludes from the requirement of filing notice under section 508(a).

(ii) For purposes of subdivision (i)(b) of this subparagraph and paragraph (b)(7)(ii) of this section, the gross receipts (as defined in subdivision (iii) of this subparagraph) of an organization are normally not more than $5,000 if:

(a) During the first taxable year of the organization the organization has received gross receipts of $7,500 or less;

(b) During its first 2 taxable years the aggregate gross receipts received by the organization are $12,000 or less; and

(c) In the case of an organization which has been in existence for at least 3 taxable years, the aggregate gross receipts received by the organization during the immediately preceding 2 taxable years, plus the current year are $15,000 or less.

If an organization fails to meet the requirements of (a), (b), or (c) of this subdivision, then with respect to the organization, such organization shall be required to file the notices described in section 508(a) and (b) within 90 days after the end of the period described in (a), (b), or (c) of this subdivision or before March 22, 1973, whichever is later, in lieu of the period prescribed in subparagraph (2)(i) of this paragraph. Thus, for example, if an organization meets the $7,500 requirement of (a) of this subdivision for its first taxable year, but fails to meet the $12,000 requirement of (b) of this subdivision for the period ending with its second taxable year, then such organization shall meet the notification requirements of section 508(a)(1) and 508(b) and subparagraph (2)(i) of this paragraph if it files such notification within 90 days after the close of its second taxable year. If an organization which has been in existence at least 3 taxable years meets the requirements of (a), (b), and (c) with respect to all prior taxable years, but fails to meet the requirements of (c) of this subdivision with respect to the current taxable year, then even if the organization fails to make such notification within 90 days after the close of the current taxable year, section 508(a)(1) and 508(b) shall not apply with respect to its prior years. In such a case, the organization shall not be treated as described in section 501(c)(3) for a period beginning with such current taxable year and ending when such notice is given under section 508(a)(2).

(iii) For a definition of "gross receipts" for purposes of subdivision (i)(b) of this subparagraph and paragraph (b)(7)(ii) of this section, see § 1.6033–2(g)(4).

(4) Voluntary filings by new organizations excepted from filing notice. Any organization excepted from the requirement of filing notice under section 508(a) will be exempt from taxation under section 501(c)(3) if it meets the requirements of that section, whether or not it files such notice. However, in order to establish its exemption with the Internal Revenue Service and receive a ruling or determination letter recognizing its exempt status, an organization excepted from the notice requirement by reason of subparagraph (3) of this paragraph should file proof of its exemption in the manner prescribed in § 1.501(a)–1.

(b) Presumption that old and new organizations are private foundations—(1) In general. Except as provided in subparagraph (7) of this paragraph, any organization (including an organization in existence on October 9, 1969) which is described in section 501(c)(3), and which does not notify the Commissioner within the time and in the manner prescribed in subparagraph (2) that it is not a private foundation, will be presumed to be a private foundation.

(2) Filing of notice. (i) Except as provided in subparagraph (7) of this paragraph, an organization must file the notice described in section 508(b) and subparagraph (1) of this paragraph within 15 months from the end of the month in which such organization was organized, or before March 22, 1973, whichever comes later. See paragraph (a)(2)(iii) of this section, for rules pertaining to when an organization is "organized".

* * *

(3) Effect of notice upon the filing organization. (i) The notice filed under this paragraph may not be relied upon by the organization so filing unless and until the Internal Revenue Service notifies the organization that it is an organization described in paragraph (1), (2), (3), or (4), of section 509(a). For purposes of the preceding sentence, an organization that has filed notice under section 508(b), and has previously received a ruling that it is an organization described in section 170(b)(1)(A) (other than clauses (vii) and (viii) thereof), will be considered to have been notified by the Internal Revenue Service that it is an organization described in paragraph (1) of section 509(a) if (a) the facts and circumstances forming the basis for the issuance of such ruling have not substantially changed, and (b) the ruling issued under that section has not been revoked expressly or by a subsequent change of the law or regulations under which the ruling was issued.

(ii) If an organization has filed a notice under section 508(b) stating that it is not a private foundation and designating only one paragraph of section 509(a) under which it claims recognition of its classification (such as an organization described in section 509(a)(2)), and if it has received a ruling or determination letter which recognizes that it is not a private foundation but which fails to designate the paragraph under section 509(a) in which it is described, then such organization will be treated as described under the paragraph designated by it, until such ruling or determination letter is modified or revoked. The rule in the preceding sentence shall not apply to an organization which indicated that it does not know its status under section 509(a) or which claimed recognition of its status under more than one paragraph of section 509(a).

(4) Effect of notice upon grantors or contributors to the filing organization. In the case of grants, contributions, or distributions made prior to:

(i) In the case of community trusts, 6 months after the date on which corrective and clarifying regulations designated as § 1.170A–9(e)(10) become final;

(ii) In the case of medical research organizations, 6 months after the date on which corrective and clarifying regulations designated as § 1.170A–9(b)(2), become final, and

(iii) In all other cases, January 1, 1976, any organization which has properly filed the notice described in section 508(b) prior to March 22, 1973 will not be treated as a private foundation for purposes of making any determination under the internal revenue laws with respect to a grantor, contributor or distributor (as for example, a private foundation distributing all of its net assets pursuant to a section 507(b)(1)(A) termination) thereto, unless the organization is controlled directly or indirectly by such grantor, contributor or distributor, if by the 30th day after the day on which such notice is filed, the organization has not been notified by the Commissioner that the notice filed by such organization has failed to establish that such organization is not a private foundation. See subparagraph (6) of this paragraph for the effect of an adverse notice by the Internal Revenue Service. For purposes of this subparagraph, an organization which has properly filed notice described in section 508(b) prior to March 22, 1973, and which has claimed recognition of its status under only one paragraph of section 509(a) in such notice, will be treated only for purposes of grantors, contributors or distributors as having the classification claimed in the notice if the provisions of this subparagraph are otherwise satisfied.

(5) Statement that old and new organizations are operating foundations. (i) Any organization (including an organization in existence on October 9, 1969) which is described in section 501(c)(3) may submit a statement, in the form and manner provided for notice in subparagraph (2) of this paragraph, that it is an operating foundation (as defined in section 4942(j)(3)) and include in such statement:

(a) Necessary supporting information as required by the regulations under section 4942(j)(3) to confirm such determination (including a statement identifying the clause of section 4942(j)(3)(B) that is applicable); and

(b) A written declaration by the principal officer, manager, or authorized trustee that there is a reasonable basis in law and in fact that the organization so filing is an operating foundation, and that to the best of the knowledge and belief of such officer, manager or trustee, the information submitted is complete and correct.

(ii) The statement filed under this subparagraph may not be relied upon by the organization so filing unless and until the Internal Revenue Service notifies the organization that it is an operating foundation described in section 4942(j)(3).

* * *

(6) Effect of notice by Internal Revenue Service concerning organization's notice or statement. Subparagraph (4) and subdivision (iii) of subparagraph (5) of this paragraph shall have no effect:

(i) With respect to a grantor, contributor, or distributor to any organization for any period after the date on which the Internal Revenue Service makes notice to the public (such as by publication in the Internal Revenue Bulletin) that a grantor, contributor, or distributor to such organization can no longer rely upon the notice or statement submitted by such organization; and

(ii) Upon any grant, contribution, or distribution made to an organization on or after the date on which a grantor, contributor, or distributor acquired knowledge that the Internal Revenue Service has given notice to such organization that its notice or statement has failed to establish that such organization either is not a private foundation, or is an operating foundation, as the case may be.

(7) Exceptions from notice. Subparagraphs (1) and (2) of this paragraph are inapplicable to the following organizations:

(i) Churches, interchurch organizations of local units of a church, conventions or associations of churches, or integrated auxiliaries of a church, such as a men's or women's organization, religious school, mission society, or youth group;

(ii) Any organization which is not a private foundation (as defined in section 509(a)) and the gross receipts of which in each taxable year are normally not more than $5,000 (as determined under paragraph (a)(3)(ii) of this section);

(iii) Subordinate organizations (other than private foundations) covered by a group exemption letter but only if the parent or supervisory organization submits a notice covering the subordinates;

(iv) Trusts described in section 4947(a)(1); and

(v) Any other class of organization that the Commissioner from time to time excludes from the notification requirements of section 508(b).

(8) Voluntary filings by organizations excepted from filing notice. Any organization excepted from the requirement of filing notice under section 508(b) by reason of subdivisions (i), (ii), and (v) of subparagraph (7) of this paragraph may receive the benefits of subparagraph (4) of this paragraph by filing such notice.

§ 1.508–2. Disallowance of certain charitable, etc., deductions.

(a) Gift or bequest to organizations subject to section 507(c) tax—(1) General rule. No gift or bequest made to an organization upon which the tax provided by section 507(c) has been imposed shall be allowed as a deduction under section 170, 545(b)(2), 556(b)(2), 642(c), 2055, 2106(a)(2), or 2522, if such gift or bequest is made:

(i) By any person after notification has been made by the organization under section 507(a)(1) or after notification has been made by the Commissioner under section 507(a)(2)(B), or

(ii) By a substantial contributor (as defined in section 507(d)(2)) in his taxable year which includes the first day on which action is taken by such organization which culminates in the imposition of tax under section 507(c) and any subsequent taxable year.

For purposes of subdivision (ii) of this subparagraph, the first day on which action is taken by an organization which culminates in the imposition of tax under section 507(c) shall be determined under the rules set forth in § 1.507–7(b)(1) and (2).

(2) Exception. Subparagraph (1) of this paragraph shall not apply if the entire amount of the unpaid portion of the tax imposed by section 507(c) is abated by the Commissioner under section 507(g).

(b) Gift or bequest to taxable private foundation, section 4947 trust, etc.—(1) General rule. (i) Except as provided in subparagraph (2) of this paragraph, no gift or bequest made to an organization shall be allowed as a deduction under section 170, 545(b)(2), 556(b)(2), 642(c), 2055, 2106(a)(2), or 2522, if such gift or bequest is made:

(a) To a private foundation or a trust described in section 4947(a)(2) in a taxable year for which it fails to meet the requirements of section 508(e) (determined without regard to section 508(e)(2)(B) and (C)), or

(b) To any organization in a period for which it is not treated as an organization described in section 501(c)(3) by reason of section 508(a).

(ii) For purposes of subdivision (i)(a) of this subparagraph the term "taxable year" refers to the taxable year of the donee or beneficiary organization. In the event abequest is made to a private foundation or trust described in section 4947(a)(2) which is not in existence at the date of the testator's death (but which is created under the terms of the testator's will), the term "taxable year" shall mean the first taxable year of the private foundation or trust.

(iii) For purposes of subdivision (i)(a) of this subparagraph, an organization does not fail to meet the requirements of section 508(e) for a taxable year, unless it fails to meet such requirements for the entire year. Therefore, even if a donee organization fails to meet the requirements of section 508(e) on the date it receives a grant from a donor, the donor's grant will not be disallowed by operation of section 508(d)(2)(A) and subdivision (i)(a) of this subparagraph, if the organization meets the requirements of section 508(e) (determined without regard to section 508(e)(2)(B) or (C)) by the end of its taxable year.

(iv) No deduction will be disallowed under section 508(d)(2)(A) with respect to a deduction under section 170, 545(b)(2), 556(b)(2), 642(c), 2055, 2106(a)(2), or 2522 if during the taxable year in question, the private foundation or trust described in section 4947(a)(2) has instituted a judicial proceeding which is necessary to reform its governing instrument or other instrument in order to meet the requirements of section 508(e)(1). This subdivision shall not apply unless within a reasonable time such judicial proceedings succeed in so reforming such instrument.

(v) No deduction will be disallowed under section 508(d)(2)(A) and subdivision (i)(a) of this subparagraph for any taxable year beginning before January 1, 1972, with respect to a private foundation or trust described in section 4947 organized before January 1, 1970. See also § 1.508–3(g) regarding transitional rules for extending compliance with section 508(e)(1).

(vi)(a) In the case of a contribution or bequest to a trust described in section 4947(a)(2) other than to a trust to which subdivision (vii) of this subparagraph applies, no deduction shall be disallowed by reason of section 508(d)(2)(A) on the grounds that such trust's governing instrument contains no provisions with respect to section 4942. Similarly, if for a taxable year such trust is also a trust described in section 4947(b)(3), no deduction for such year shall be so disallowed on the grounds that the governing instrument contains no provision with respect to section 4943 or 4944.

(b) This subdivision may be illustrated by the following example:

Example. H executes a will on January 1, 1977, establishing a charitable remainder trust (as described in section 664) with income payable to W, his wife, for life, remainder to X university, an organization described in section 170(b)(1)(A)(ii). The will provides that the trust is prohibited from engaging in activities which would subject itself, its foundation manager or a disqualified person to taxes under section 4941 or 4945 of the Code. The will is silent as to sections 4942, 4943, and 4944. H dies February 12, 1978. Section 508(d)(2)(A) will not operate to disallow any deduction to H's estate under section 2055 with respect to such trust.

(vii)(a) In the case of a trust described in section 4947(a)(2) which by its terms will become a trust described in section 4947(a)(1) and the governing instrument of which is executed after March 22, 1973, the governing instrument shall not meet the requirements of section 508(e)(1) if it does not contain provisions to the effect that the trust must comply with the provisions of section 4942, or sections 4942, 4943, and 4944 (as the case may be) to the extent such section or sections shall become applicable to such trust.

(b) This subdivision may be illustrated by the following example:

Example. H executes a will on January 1, 1977, establishing a charitable remainder trust (as described in section 664) with income payable to W, his wife, for life, remainder in trust in perpetuity for the benefit of an organization described in section 170(c). By its terms the trust will become a trust described in section 4947(a)(1), and will become a private foundation. The will provides that the trust is prohibited from engaging in activities which would subject itself, its foundation manager or a disqualified person to taxes under sections 4941 or 4945 of the Code. The will is silent as to sections 4942, 4943, and 4944. H dies February 12, 1978. Unless the trust's governing instrument is amended prior to the end of the trust's first taxable year, or judicial proceedings have been instituted under subdivision (iv) of this subparagraph, section 508(d)(2)(A) will operate to disallow any deduction to H's estate under section 2055 with respect to such trust.

(viii) Since a charitable trust described in section 4947(a)(1) is not required to file a notice under section 508(a), section 508(d)(2)(B) and subdivision (i)(b) of this subparagraph are not applicable to such a trust.

* * *

§ 1.509(a)–1. Definition of private foundation.

In general. Section 509(a) defines the term private foundation to mean any domestic or foreign organization described in section 501(c)(3) other than an organization described in section 509(a)(1), (2), (3), or (4). Organizations which fall into the categories excluded from the definition of private foundation are generally those which either have broad public support or actively function in a supporting relationship to such organizations. Organizations which test for public safety are also excluded.

§ 1.509(a)–2. Exclusion for certain organizations described in section 170(b)(1)(A).

(a) General rule. Organizations described in section 170(b)(1)(A) (other than in clauses (vii) and (viii)) are excluded from the definition of private foundation by section 509(a)(1). For the requirements to be met by organizations described in section 170(b)(1)(A)(i) through (vi), see § 1.170A–9(a) through (e) and paragraph (b) of this section. For purposes of this section, the parenthetical language other than in clauses (vii) and (viii) used in section 509(a)(1) means other than an organization which is described only in clause (vii) or (viii). For purposes of this section, an organization may qualify as a section 509(a)(1) organization regardless of the fact that it does not satisfy section 170(c)(2) because:

(1) Its funds are not used within the United States or its possessions, or

(2) It was created or organized other than in, or under the law of, the United States, any State or territory, the District of Columbia, or any possession of the United States.

(b) Medical research organizations. In order to qualify under section 509(a)(1) as a medical research organization described in section 170(b)(1)(A)(iii), an organization must meet the requirements of section 170(b)(1)(A)(iii) and § 1.170A–9(c)(2), except that, solely for purposes of classification as a section 509(a)(1) organization, such organization need not be committed to spend every contribution for medical research before January 1 of the fifth calendar year which begins after the date such contribution is made.

§ 1.509(a)–3. Broadly, publicly supported organizations.

(a) In general—(1) General rule. Section 509(a)(2) excludes certain types of broadly, publicly supported organizations from private foundation status. An organization will be excluded under section 509(a)(2) if it meets the one-third support test under section 509(a)(2)(A) and the not-more-than-one-third support test under section 509(a)(2)(B).

(2) One-third support test. An organization will meet the one-third support test if it normally (within the meaning of paragraph (c) or (d) of this section) receives more than one-third of its support in each taxable year from any combination of—

(i) Gifts, grants, contributions, or membership fees; and

(ii) Gross receipts from admissions, sales of merchandise, performance of services, or furnishing of facilities, in an activity that is not an unrelated trade or business (within the meaning of section 513), subject to certain limitations described in paragraph (b) of this section, from permitted sources. For purposes of this section, governmental units, organizations described in section 509(a)(1) and persons other than disqualified persons with respect to the organization shall be referred to as permitted sources. For purposes of this section, the amount of support received from the sources described in paragraph (a)(2)(i) of this section and this paragraph (a)(2)(ii) (subject to the limitations referred to in this paragraph (a)(2)) will be referred to as the numerator of the one-third support fraction, and the total amount of support received (as defined in section 509(d)) will be referred to as the denominator of the one-third support fraction. For purposes of section 509(a)(2), § 1.509(a)–3(f) distinguishes gifts and contributions from gross receipts; § 1.509(a)–3(g) distinguishes grants from gross receipts; § 1.509(a)–3(h) defines membership fees; § 1.509(a)–3(i) defines "any bureau or similar agency of a governmental unit"; § 1.509(a)–3(j) describes the treatment of certain indirect forms of support; paragraph (k) of this section describes the method of accounting for support; § 1.509(a)–3(*l*) describes the treatment of gross receipts from section 513(a)(1), (2), or (3) activities; and § 1.509(a)–3(m) distinguishes gross receipts from gross investment income.

(3) Not-more-than-one-third support test—(i) In general. An organization will meet the not-more-than-one-third support test under section 509(a)(2)(B) if it normally (within the meaning of paragraph (c) or (d) of this section) receives not more than one-third of its support in each taxable year from the sum of its gross investment income (as defined in section 509(e)) and the excess (if any) of the amount of its unrelated business taxable income (as defined in section 512, without regard to section 512(a)(6), or with regard to section 512(a)(6), if the organization so chooses) derived from trades or businesses that were acquired by the organization after June 30, 1975, over the amount of tax imposed on such income by section 511. For purposes of this section the amount of support received from items described in section 509(a)(2)(B) will be referred to as the numerator of the not-more-than-one-third support fraction, and the total amount of support (as defined in section 509(d)) will be referred to as the denominator of the not-more-than-one-third support fraction. For purposes of section 509(a)(2), paragraph (m) of this section distinguishes gross receipts from gross investment income. For purposes of section 509(e), gross investment income includes the items of investment income described in § 1.512(b)–1(a).

* * *

(4) Unrelated business activities. The denominator of the one-third support fraction and the denominator of the not-more-than-one-third support fraction both include net income from unrelated business activities, whether or not such activities are carried on regularly as a trade or business. The term *net income from unrelated business activities* includes (but is not limited to) an organization's unrelated business taxable income (UBTI) within the meaning of section 512. However, when calculating UBTI for purposes of determining the denominator of both support fractions, section 512(a)(6) does not apply. Accordingly, in the case of an organization that derives gross income from the regular conduct of two or more unrelated business activities, support includes the aggregate of gross income from all such unrelated business activities less the aggregate of the deductions allowed with respect to all such unrelated business activities. Nonetheless, when determining support, such organization can use either its UBTI calculated under section 512(a)(6) or its UBTI calculated in the aggregate.

* * *

(b) Limitation on gross receipts—(1) General rule. In computing the amount of support received from gross receipts under section 509(a)(2)(A)(ii) for purposes of the one-third support test of section 509(a)(2)(A), gross receipts from related activities received from any person, or from any bureau or similar agency of a governmental unit, are includible in any taxable year only to the extent that such receipts do not exceed the greater of $5,000 or 1 percent of the organization's support in such taxable year.

(2) Examples. The application of this paragraph may be illustrated by the examples set forth below. For purposes of these examples, the term general public is defined as persons other than disqualified persons and other than persons from whom the foundation receives gross receipts in excess of the greater of $5,000 or 1 percent of its support in any taxable year, and the term gross receipts is limited to receipts from activities which are not unrelated trade or business (within the meaning of section 513).

Example (1). For the taxable year 1970, X, an organization described in section 501(c)(3), received support of $10,000 from the following sources:

Bureau M (a governmental bureau from which X received gross receipts for services rendered	$ 25,000
Bureau N (a governmental bureau from which X received gross receipts for services rendered	25,000
General public (gross receipts for services rendered)	20,000
Gross investment income	15,000
Contributions from individual substantial contributors (defined as disqualified persons under section 4946(a)(2))	15,000
Total support	$ 100,000

Since the $25,000 received from each bureau amounts to more than the greater of $5,000 or 1 percent of X's support for 1970 (1% of $100,000=$1,000) under section 509(a)(2)(A)(ii), each amount is includible in the numerator of the one-third support fraction only to the extent of $5,000. Thus, for the taxable year 1970, X received support from sources which are taken into account in meeting the one-third support test of section 509(a)(2)(A) computed as follows:

Bureau M	$ 5,000
Bureau N	5,000
General public	20,000
Total	$ 30,000

Therefore, in making the computations required under paragraph (c), (d), or (e) of this section, only $30,000 is includible in the aggregate numerator and $100,000 is includible in the aggregate denominator of the support fraction.

Example (2). For the taxable year 1970, Y, an organization described in section 501(c)(3), received support of $600,000 from the following sources:

Bureau O (gross receipts-services rendered)	$ 10,000
Bureau P (gross receipts-services rendered)	10,000
General public (gross receipts-services rendered)	150,000
General public (contributions)	40,000
Gross investment income	150,000
Contributions from substantial contributors	240,000
Total support	$ 600,000

Since the $10,000 received from each bureau amounts to more than the greater of $5,000 or 1 percent of Y's support for 1970 (1% of $600,000=$6,000), each amount is includible in the numerator of the one-third support fraction only to the extent of $6,000. Thus,for the taxable year 1970, Y received support from sources required to meet the one-third support test of section 509(a)(2)(A) computed as follows:

Bureau O	$ 6,000
Bureau P	6,000
General public (gross receipts)	150,000
General public (contributions)	40,000
Total	$ 202,000

Therefore, in making the computations required under paragraph (c), (d), or (e) of this section, $202,000 is includible in the aggregate numerator and $600,000 is includible in the aggregate denominator of the support fraction.

(c) Normally—(1) In general—(i) Definition. The support tests set forth in section 509(a)(2) are to be computed on the basis of the nature of the organization's normal sources of support. An organization will be considered as normally receiving one third of its support from any combination of gifts, grants, contributions, membership fees, and gross receipts from permitted sources (subject to the limitations described in § 1.509(a)–3(b)) and not more than one third of its support from items described in section 509(a)(2)(B) for its current taxable year and the taxable year immediately succeeding its current year, if, for the current taxable year and the four taxable years immediately preceding the current taxable year, the aggregate amount of the support received during the applicable period from gifts, grants, contributions, membership fees, and gross receipts from permitted sources (subject to the limitations described in § 1.509(a)–3(b)) is more than one third, and the aggregate amount of the support received from items described in section 509(a)(2)(B) is not more than one third, of the total support of the organization for such 5-year period.

(ii) First five years of an organization's existence. See paragraph (d)(1) of this section for the definition of "normally" for organizations in the first five years of their existence.

* * *

(3) Exclusion of unusual grants. For purposes of applying the 5-year aggregation test for support set forth in paragraph (c)(1) of this section, one or more contributions may be excluded from the numerator of the one-third support fraction and from the denominator of both the one-third support and not-more-than-one-third support fractions only if such a contribution meets the requirements of this paragraph (c)(3). The exclusion provided by this paragraph (c)(3) is generally intended to apply to substantial contributions and bequests from disinterested parties, which contributions or bequests—

(i) Are attracted by reason of the publicly supported nature of the organization;

(ii) Are unusual or unexpected with respect to the amount thereof; and

(iii) Would by reason of their size, adversely affect the status of the organization as normally meeting the one-third support test for any of the applicable periods described in this paragraph (c) or paragraph (d) of this section. In the case of a grant (as defined in § 1.509(a)–3(g)) that meets the requirements of this paragraph (c)(3), if the terms of the granting instrument (whether executed before or after 1969) require that the funds be paid to the recipient organization over a period of years, the amount received by the organization each year pursuant to the terms of such grant may be excluded for such year. However, no item described in section 509(a)(2)(B) may be excluded under this paragraph (c)(3). The provisions of this paragraph (c)

(3) shall apply to exclude unusual grants made during any of the applicable periods described in this paragraph (c) or paragraph (d) of this section. See paragraph (c)(5)(ii) of this section as to reliance by a grantee organization upon an unusual grant ruling under this paragraph (c)(3).

(4) Determining factors. In determining whether a particular contribution may be excluded under paragraph (c)(3) of this section, all pertinent facts and circumstances will be taken into consideration. No single factor will necessarily be determinative. Among the factors to be considered are—

(i) Whether the contribution was made by any person (or persons standing in a relationship to such person which is described in section 4946(a)(1)(C) through (G)) who created the organization, previously contributed a substantial part of its support or endowment, or stood in a position of authority, such as a foundation manager (within the meaning of section 4946(b)), with respect to the organization. A contribution made by a person other than those persons described in this paragraph (c)(4)(i) will ordinarily be given more favorable consideration than a contribution made by a person described in this paragraph (c)(4)(i);

(ii) Whether the contribution was a bequest or an inter vivos transfer. A bequest will ordinarily be given more favorable consideration than an inter vivos transfer;

(iii) Whether the contribution was in the form of cash, readily marketable securities, or assets which further the exempt purposes of the organization, such as a gift of a painting to a museum;

(iv) Except in the case of a new organization, whether, prior to the receipt of the particular contribution, the organization has carried on an actual program of public solicitation and exempt activities and has been able to attract a significant amount of public support;

(v) Whether the organization may reasonably be expected to attract a significant amount of public support subsequent to the particular contribution. In this connection, continued reliance on unusual grants to fund an organization's current operating expenses (as opposed to providing new endowment funds) may be evidence that the organization cannot reasonably be expected to attract future support from the general public;

(vi) Whether, prior to the year in which the particular contribution was received, the organization met the one-third support test described in paragraph (c)(1) of this section without the benefit of any exclusions of unusual grants pursuant to paragraph (c)(3) of this section;

(vii) Whether neither the contributor nor any person standing in a relationship to such contributor which is described in section 4946(a)(1)(C) through (G) continues directly or indirectly to exercise control over the organization;

(viii) Whether the organization has a representative governing body as described in § 1.509(a)–3(d)(3)(i); and

(ix) Whether material restrictions or conditions (within the meaning of § 1.507–2T(a)(7)) have been imposed by the transferor upon the transferee in connection with such transfer.

(5) Grantors and contributors. Prior to the making of any grant or contribution expected to meet the requirements for exclusion under paragraph (c)(3) of this section, a potential grantee organization may request a ruling whether such grant or contribution may be so excluded. Requests for such ruling may be filed by the grantee organization. The issuance of such determination will be at the sole discretion of the Commissioner. The organization must submit all information necessary to make a determination of the applicability of paragraph (c)(3) of this section, including all information relating to the factors described in paragraph (c)(4) of this section. If a favorable ruling is issued, such ruling may be relied upon by the grantor or contributor of the particular contribution in question for purposes of sections 170, 507, 545(b)(2), 642(c), 4942 4945, 2055, 2106(a)(2), and 2522 and by the grantee organization for purposes of paragraph (c)(3) of this section.

(6) Examples. The application of the principles set forth in this paragraph are illustrated by the examples as follows. For purposes of these examples, the term general public is defined as persons other than disqualified persons and other than persons from whom the foundation received gross receipts in excess of the greater of $5,000 or 1 percent of its support in any taxable year, the term gross investment income is as defined in section 509(e), and the term gross receipts is limited to receipts from activities which are not unrelated trades or businesses (within the meaning of section 513).

Example 1. (i) For the years 2008 through 2012, X, an organization exempt under section 501(c)(3) that makes scholarship grants to needy students of a particular city, received support from the following sources:

2008:

Gross receipts (general public)	$35,000
Contributions (substantial contributors)	36,000
Gross investment income	29,000
Total support	$ 100,000

2009:

Gross receipts (general public)	34,000
Contributions (substantial contributors)	35,000
Gross investment income	31,000
Total support	$ 100,000

2010:

Gross receipts (general public)	35,000
Contributions (substantial contributors)	30,000
Gross investment income	35,000
Total support	$ 100,000

2011:

Gross receipts (general public)	33,000
Contributions (substantial contributors)	32,000
Gross investment income	35,000
Total support	$ 100,000

2012:

Gross receipts (general public)	31,000
Contributions (substantial contributors)	39,000
Gross investment income	30,000
Total support	$ 100,000

(ii) In applying section 509(a)(2) to the taxable year 2012, on the basis of paragraph (c)(1)(i) of this section, the total amount of support from gross receipts from the general public ($168,000) for the period 2008 through 2012, was more than one third, and the total amount of support from gross investment income ($160,000) was less than one third, of X's total support for the same period ($500,000). For the taxable years 2012 and 2013, X is therefore considered normally to receive more than one third of its support from the public sources described in section 509(a)(2)(A) and less than one third of its support from items described in section 509(a)(2)(B). The fact that X received less than one third of its support from section 509(a)(2)(A) sources in 2012 and more than one third of its support from items described in section 509(a)(2)(B) in 2011 does not affect its status because it met the normally test over a 5-year period.

Example 2. Assume the same facts as in Example 1 except that in 2012, X also received an unexpected bequest of $50,000 from A, an elderly widow who was interested in encouraging the work of X, but had no other relationship to it. Solely by reason of the bequest, A became a disqualified person. X used the bequest to create 5 new scholarships. Its operations otherwise remained the same. Under these circumstances X could not meet the 5-year support test because the total amount received from gross receipts from the general public ($168,000) would not be more than one-third of its total support for the 5-year period ($550,000). Because A is a disqualified person, her bequest cannot be included in the numerator of the one-third support test under section 509(a)(2)(A). However, based on the factors set forth in paragraph (c)(4) of this section, A's bequest may be excluded as an unusual grant under paragraph (c)(3) of this section. Therefore, X will be considered to have met the support test for the taxable years 2012 and 2013.

Example 3. Y, an organization described in section 501(c)(3), was created by A, the holder of all the common stock in M corporation, B, A's wife, and C, A's business associate. The purpose of Y was to sponsor and equip athletic teams for underprivileged children in the community. Each of the three creators makes small cash contributions to Y. A, B, and C have been active participants in the affairs of Y since its creation. Y regularly raises small amounts of contributions through fundraising drives and selling admission to some of the sponsored sporting events. The operations of Y are carried out on a small scale, usually being restricted to the sponsorship of two to four baseball teams of underprivileged children. In 2009, M recapitalizes and creates a first and second class of 6 percent nonvoting preferred stock, most of which is held by A and B. In 2010, A contributes 49 percent of his common stock in M to Y. A's contribution of M's common stock was substantial and constitutes 90 percent of Y's total support for 2010. A combination of the facts and circumstances described in paragraph (c)(4) of this section preclude A's contribution of M's common stock in 2010 from being excluded as an unusual grant under paragraph (c)(3) of this section for purposes of determining whether Y meets the one-third support test under section 509(a)(2).

Example 4. (i) M is organized in 2009 to promote the appreciation of ballet in a particular region of the United States. Its principal activities consist of erecting a theater for the performance of ballet and the organization and operation of a ballet company. M receives a determination letter that it is an organization described in section 501(c)(3) and that it is a public charity described in section 509(a)(2). The governing body of M consists of 9 prominent unrelated citizens residing in the region who have either an expertise in ballet or a strong interest in encouraging appreciation of the art form.

(ii) In 2010, Z, a private foundation, proposes to makes a grant of $500,000 in cash to M to provide sufficient capital for M to commence its activities. Although A, the creator of Z, is one of the nine members of M's governing body, was one of M's original founders, and continues to lend his prestige to M's activities and fund raising efforts, A does not, directly or indirectly, exercise any control over M. M also receives a significant amount of support from a number of smaller contributions and pledges from other members of the general public. M charges admission to the ballet performances to the general public.

(iii) Although the support received in 2010 will not impact M's status as a public charity for its first 5 taxable years, it will be relevant to the determination of whether M meets the one-third support test under section 509(a)(2) for the 2014 taxable year, using the computation period 2010 through 2014. Within the appropriate timeframe, M may submit a request for a private letter ruling that the $500,000 contribution from Z qualifies as an unusual grant.

(iv) Under the above circumstances, even though A was a founder and member of the governing body of M, M may exclude Z's contribution of $500,000 in 2010 as an unusual grant under paragraph (c)(3) of this section for purposes of determining whether M meets the one-third support test under section 509(a)(2) for 2014.

Example 5. (i) Assume the same facts as Example 4. In 2013, B, a widow, passes away and bequeaths $4 million to M. During 2009 through

2013, B made small contributions to M, none exceeding $10,000 in any year. During 2009 through 2013, M received approximately $550,000 from receipts for admissions and contributions from the general public. At the time of B's death, no person standing in a relationship to B described in section 4946(a)(1)(C) through (G) was a member of M's governing body. B's bequest was in the form of cash and readily marketable securities. The only condition placed upon the bequest was that it be used by M to advance the art of ballet.

(ii) Although the support received in 2013 will not impact M's status as a public charity for its first five taxable years, it will be relevant to the determination of whether M meets the one-third support test under section 509(a)(2) for future years. Within the appropriate timeframe, M may submit a request for a private letter ruling that the $4 million bequest from B qualifies as an unusual grant.

(iii) Under the above circumstances, M may exclude B's bequest of $4 million in 2013 as an unusual grant under paragraph (c)(3) of this section for purposes of determining whether M meets the one-third support test under section 509(a)(2) for 2014 and subsequent years.

Example 6. (i) N is a research organization that was created by A in 2009 for the purpose of carrying on economic studies primarily through persons receiving grants from N and engaging in the sale of economic publications. N received a determination letter that it is described in section 501(c)(3) and that it is a public charity described in 509(a)(2). N's five-member governing body consists of A, A's sons, B and C, and two unrelated economists. In 2009, A made a contribution to N of $100,000 to help establish the organization. During 2009 through 2013, A made annual contributions to N averaging $20,000 a year. During the same period, N received annual contributions from members of the general public averaging $15,000 per year and receipts from the sale of its publications averaging $50,000 per year. In 2013, B made an inter vivos contribution to N of $600,000 in cash and readily marketable securities.

(ii) Although the support received in 2013 will not impact N's status as a public charity for its first 5 taxable years, it will be relevant to the determination of whether N meets the one-third support test under section 509(a)(2) for future years. In determining whether B's contribution of $600,000 in 2013 may be excluded as an unusual grant, the support N received in 2009 through 2013 is relevant in considering the factor described in paragraph (c)(4)(vi) of this section, notwithstanding that N received a determination letter that it is described in section 509(a)(2).

(iii) Based on the application of the factors in paragraphs (c)(4)(i) through (ix) of this section to N's circumstances, in particular the facts that B is a disqualified person described in section 4946(a)(1)(D) and N does not have a representative governing body as described in paragraphs (c)(4)(viii) and (d)(3)(i) of this section, N cannot exclude B's contribution of $600,000 in 2013 as an unusual grant under paragraph (c)(3) of this section for purposes of determining whether N meets the one-third support test under section 509(a)(2) for 2014 and future years.

Example 7. (i) O is an educational organization created in 2009. O received a determination letter that it is described in section 501(c)(3) and that it is a public charity described in section 509(a)(2). The governing body of O has 9 members, consisting of A, a prominent civic leader and 8 other unrelated civic leaders and educators in the community, all of whom participated in the creation of O. During 2009 through 2013, the principal source of income for O has been receipts from the sale of its educational periodicals. These sales have amounted to $200,000 for this period. Small contributions amounting to $50,000 have also been received during the same period from members of the governing body, including A, as well as other members of the general public.

(ii) In 2013, A contributed $750,000 of the nonvoting stock of S, a closely held corporation, to O. A retained a substantial portion of the voting stock of S. By a majority vote, the governing body of O decided to retain the S stock for a period of at least 5 years.

(iii) Although the support received in 2013 will not impact O's status as a public charity for its first 5 taxable years, it will be relevant to the determination of whether O meets the one-third support test under section 509(a)(2) for future years. In determining whether A's contribution of the S stock in 2013 may be excluded as an unusual grant, the support O received in 2009 through 2013 is relevant in considering the factor described in paragraph (c)(4)(vi) of this section, notwithstanding that O received a determination letter that it is described in section 509(a)(2).

(iv) Based on the application of the factors in paragraphs (c)(4)(i) through (ix) of this section to O's circumstances, in particular the facts that A is a foundation manager within the meaning of section 4946(b) and A's contribution is in the form of closely held stock, O cannot exclude A's contribution of the S stock in 2013 as an unusual grant under paragraph (c)(3) of this section for purposes of determining whether O meets the one-third support test under section 509(a)(2) for 2014 and future years.

(d) Definition of normally; first five years of an organization's existence—(1) In general. An organization will "normally" meet the one-third support test and the not-more-than-one-third support test during its first five taxable years as a section 501(c)(3) organization if the organization can reasonably be expected to meet the requirements of the one-third support test and the not-more-than-one-third support test during that period. With respect to an organization's sixth taxable year, the general definition of normally in paragraph (c)(1) of this section applies. Alternatively, the organization shall be treated as normally meeting the one-third support test and the not-more-than-one-third support test for its sixth taxable year (but not its seventh taxable year) if it meets the one-third support test and the not-more-than-one-third support test under the definition of normally set forth in paragraph (c)(1)(i) of this section for its fifth taxable year (based on support received in its first through fifth taxable years). If a new publicly supported organization described under section 509(a)(2) cannot meet the requirements of the one-third support test or the not-more-than-one-third support test for its sixth taxable year using either the general definition of normally in paragraph (c)(1) of this section or the alternate rule above (effectively failing to meet a public support test for both its fifth and sixth years), it will be reclassified as a private foundation as of the first day of its sixth taxable year only for purposes of sections 507, 4940, and 6033. Such an organization must file a Form 990-PF, "Return of Private Foundation or Section 4947(a)(1) Nonexempt Charitable Trust Treated as a Private Foundation," and is liable for the net investment tax imposed by section 4940 and, if applicable, the private foundation termination tax imposed by section 507(c), for its sixth taxable year. Beginning the first day of its seventh taxable year, the organization will be treated as a private foundation for all purposes.

(2) Basic consideration. In determining whether an organization can reasonably be expected (within the meaning of paragraph (c)(1)(i) of this section) to meet the one-third support test under section 509(a)(2)(A) and the not-more-than-one-third support test under section 509(a)(2)(B) described in paragraph (a) of this section during its first five taxable years, the basic consideration is whether its organizational structure, current or proposed programs or activities, and actual or intended method of operation are such as to attract the type of broadly based support from the general public, public charities, and governmental units that is necessary to meet such tests. The factors that are relevant to this determination, and the weight accorded to each of them, may differ from case to case, depending on the nature and functions of the organization. An organization cannot reasonably be expected to meet the one-third support test and the not-more-than-one-third support test where the facts indicate that an organization is likely during its first five taxable years to receive less than one-third of its support from permitted sources (subject to the limitations of paragraph (b) of this section) or to receive more than one-third of its support from items described in section 509(a)(2)(B).

(3) Factors taken into account. All pertinent facts and circumstances shall be taken into account under paragraph (d)(2) of this section in determining whether the organizational structure, programs or activities, and method of operation of an organization are such as to enable it to meet the tests under section 509(a)(2) during its first five taxable years. Some of the pertinent factors are:

(i) Whether the organization has or will have a representative governing body which is comprised of public officials, or individuals chosen by public officials acting in their capacity as such; of persons having special knowledge in the particular field or discipline in which the organization is operating; of community leaders, such as elected officials, clergymen, and educators; or, in the case of a membership organization, of individuals elected pursuant to the organization's governing instrument or bylaws by a broadly based membership. This characteristic does not exist if the membership of the organization's governing body is such as to indicate that it represents the personal or private interests of disqualified persons, rather than the interests of the community or the general public.

(ii) Whether a substantial portion of the organization's initial funding is to be provided by the general public, by public charities, or by government grants, rather than by a limited number of grantors or contributors who are disqualified persons with respect to the organization. The fact that the organization plans to limit its activities to a particular community or region or to a special field which can be expected to appeal to a limited number of persons will be taken into consideration in determining whether those persons providing the initial support for the organization are representative of the general public. On the other hand, the subsequent sources of funding which the organization can reasonably expect to receive after it has become established and fully operational will also be taken into account.

(iii) Whether a substantial proportion of the organization's initial funds are placed, or will remain, in an endowment, and whether the investment of such funds is unlikely to result in more than one third of its total support being received from items described in section 509(a)(2)(B).

(iv) In the case of an organization that carries on fundraising activities, whether the organization has developed a concrete plan for solicitation of funds from the general public on a community or area-wide basis; whether any steps have been taken to implement such plan; whether any firm commitments of financial or other support have been made to the organization by civic, religious, charitable, or similar groups within the community; and whether the organization has made any commitments to, or established any working relationships with, those organizations or classes of persons intended as the future recipients of its funds.

(v) In the case of an organization that carries on community services, such as combating community deterioration in an economically depressed area that has suffered a major loss of population and jobs, whether the organization has a concrete program to carry out its work in the community; whether any steps have been taken to implement that program; whether it will receive any part of its funds from a public charity or governmental agency to which it is in some way held accountable as a condition of the grant or contribution; and whether it has enlisted the sponsorship or support of other civic or community leaders involved in community service programs similar to those of the organization.

(vi) In the case of an organization that carries on educational or other exempt activities for, or on behalf of, members, whether the solicitation for dues-paying members is designed to enroll a substantial number of persons in the community, area, profession, or field of special interest (depending on the size of the area and the nature of the organization's activities); whether membership dues for individual (rather than institutional) members have been fixed at rates designed to make membership available to a broad cross-section of the public rather than to restrict membership to a limited number of persons; and whether the activities of the organization will be likely to appeal to persons having some broad common interest or purpose, such as educational activities in the case of alumni associations, musical activities in the case of symphony societies, or civic affairs in the case of parent-teacher associations.

(vii) In the case of an organization that provides goods, services, or facilities, whether the organization is or will be required to make its services, facilities, performances, or products available (regardless of whether a fee is charged) to the general public, public charities, or governmental units, rather than to a limited number of persons or organizations; whether the organization will avoid executing contracts to perform services for a limited number of firms or governmental agencies or bureaus; and whether the service to be provided is one which can be expected to meet a special or general need among a substantial portion of the general public.

(4) Example. The application of this paragraph (d) may be illustrated by the following example:

Example. (i) Organization X was formed in January 2008 and uses a taxable year ending December 31. After September 9, 2008, and before December 31, 2008, Organization X filed Form 1023 requesting recognition of exemption as an organization described in section 501(c)(3) and in section 509(a)(2). In its application, Organization X established that it can reasonably be expected to operate as a publicly supported organization under paragraph (d) of this section. Subsequently, Organization X received a ruling or determination letter that it is an organization described in sections 501(c)(3) and 509(a)(2) effective as of the date of its formation.

(ii) Organization X is described in section 509(a)(2) for its first five taxable years (for the taxable years ending December 31, 2008, through December 31, 2012).

(iii) Organization X can qualify as a publicly supported organization beginning with the taxable year ending December 31, 2013, if Organization X can meet the requirements of either § 1.170A–9(f)(2) or § 1.170A–9(f)(3) or paragraphs (a) and (b) of this section for the taxable years ending December 31, 2009, through December 31, 2013, or for the taxable years ending December 31, 2008, through December 31, 2012.

(e) Determinations on foundation classification and reliance. (1) A ruling or determination letter that an organization is described in section 509(a)(2) may be issued to an organization. Such determination may be made in conjunction with the recognition of the organization's tax-exempt status or at such other time as the organization believes it is described in section 509(a)(2). The ruling or determination letter that the organization is described in section 509(a)(2) may be revoked if, upon examination, the organization has not met the requirements of this section. The ruling or determination letter that the organization is described in section 509(a)(2) also may be revoked if the organization's application for a ruling or determination contained one or more material misstatements of fact or such application was part of a scheme or plan to avoid or evade any provision of the Internal Revenue Code. The revocation of the determination that an organization is described in section 509(a)(2) does not preclude revocation of the determination that the organization is described in section 501(c)(3).

(2) Status of grantors or contributors. For purposes of sections 170, 507, 545(b)(2), 642(c), 4942, 4945, 2055, 2106(a)(2), and 2522, grantors and contributors may rely upon a determination letter or ruling that an organization is described in section 509(a)(2) until the Internal Revenue Service publishes notice of a change of status (for example, in the Internal Revenue Bulletin or Publication 78, "Cumulative List of Organizations described in Section 170(c) of the Internal Revenue Code of 1986," which can be searched at www.irs.gov). For this purpose, grantors or contributors may also rely on an advance ruling that expires on or after June 9, 2008. However, a grantor or contributor may not rely on such an advance ruling or any determination letter or ruling if the grantor or contributor was responsible for, or aware of, the act or failure to act that resulted in the organization's loss of classification under section 509(a)(2) or acquired knowledge that the Internal Revenue Service had given notice to such organization that it would be deleted from such classification.

(3) Examples. The provisions of this paragraph (e) may be illustrated by the following examples:

Example 1. Y, a calendar year organization described in section 501(c)(3), is created in February 2008 for the purpose of displaying African art. On its exemption application Y shows, under penalties of perjury, that it can reasonably, in accordance with the requirements of paragraph (d) of this section, expect to receive support from the public in 2008 through 2012 that will satisfy the one-third support and not-more-than-one-third support tests described in section 509(a)(2) for its first 5 taxable years, 2008 through 2012. Y may therefore receive a determination that it meets the requirements of paragraph (a) of this section. Pursuant to such determination, Y will be a public charity for its first five taxable years (2008, 2009, 2010, 2011, and 2012), regardless of the public support Y in fact receives during this period.

Example 2. Z, a calendar year organization described in section 501(c)(3), is created in July 2008. On its exemption application Z shows, under penalties of perjury, that it can reasonably, in accordance with the requirements of paragraph (d) of this section, expect to receive support from the public in 2008 through 2012 that will satisfy the one-third support and not-more-than-one-third support tests described in section 509(a)(2) for its first 5 taxable years, 2008 through 2012. Z receives a determination that it is described in section 509(a)(2). However, the support actually received from the public over Z's first 5 taxable years (2008 through 2012) does not satisfy the one-third support and not-more-than-one-third support tests described in section 509(a)(2), nor does the support Z receives from 2009 through and including its sixth taxable year, 2013, meet the one-third support and not-more-than-one-third support tests described in section 509(a)(2). Z is described in section 509(a)(2) during its first five years for all purposes. But, because Z has not met the requirements of paragraph (a) of this section either for 2008 through 2012 or 2009 through 2013, Z is not described in section 509(a)(2) for its taxable year 2013. If Z is not described in section 509(a)(1), (3), or (4), then Z is a private foundation as of 2013, and Z will be treated as a private foundation for all purposes (except as provided in paragraph (e)(2) of this section with respect to grantors and contributors).

(f) Gifts and contributions distinguished from gross receipts—(1) In general. In determining whether an organization normally receives more than one-third of its support from permitted sources, all gifts and contributions (within the meaning of section 509(a)(2)(A)(i)) received from permitted sources, are includible in the numerator of the support fraction in each taxable year. However, gross receipts (within the meaning of section 509(a)(2)(A)(ii)) from admissions, sales of merchandise, performance of services, or furnishing of facilities, in an activity which is not an unrelated trade or business, are includible in the numerator of the support fraction in any taxable year only to the extent that such gross receipts do not exceed the limitation with respect to the greater of $5,000 or 1 percent of support which is describing paragraph (b) of this section. The terms gifts and contributions shall, for purposes of section 509(a)(2), have the same meaning as such terms have under section 170(c) and also include bequests, legacies, devises, and transfers within the meaning of section 2055 or 2106(a)(2). Thus, for purposes of section 509(a)(2)(A), any payment of money or transfer of property without adequate consideration shall be considered a gift or contribution. Where payment is made or property transferred as consideration for admissions, sales of merchandise, performance of services, or furnishing of facilities to the donor, the status of the payment or transfer under section 170(c) shall determine whether and to what extent such payment or transfer constitutes a gift or contribution under section 509(a)(2)(A)(i) as distinguished from gross receipts from related activities under section 509(a)(2)(A)(ii). For purposes of section 509(a)(2), the term contributions includes qualified sponsorship payments (as defined in § 1.513–4) in the form of money or property (but not services).

(2) Valuation of property. For purposes of section 509(a)(2), the amount includible in computing support with respect to gifts, grants or contributions of property or use of such property shall be the fair market or rental value of such property at the date of such gift or contribution.

(3) Examples. The provisions of this paragraph (f) may be illustrated by the following examples:

Example (1). P is a local agricultural club described in section 501(c)(3). In order to encourage interest and proficiency by young people in farming and raising livestock, it makes awards at its annual fair for outstanding specimens of produce and livestock. Most of these awards are cash or other property donated by local businessmen. When the awards are made, the donors are given recognition for their donations by being identified as the donor of the award. The recognition given to donors is merely incidental to the making of the award to worthy youngsters. For these reasons, the donations will constitute contributions for purposes of section 509(a)(2)(A)(i). The amount includible in computing support with respect to such contributions is equal to the cash contributed or the fair market value of other property on the dates contributed.

Example (2). Q, a performing arts center, enters into a contract with a large company to be the exclusive sponsor of the center's theatrical events. The company makes a payment of cash and products in the amount of $100,000 to Q, and in return, Q agrees to make a broadcast announcement thanking the company before each show and to provide $2,000 of advertising in the show's program (2% of $100,000 is $2,000). The announcement constitutes use or acknowledgment pursuant to section 513(i)(2). Because the value of the advertising does not exceed 2% of the total payment, the entire $100,000 is a qualified sponsorship payment under section 513(i), and $100,000 is treated as a contribution for purposes of section 509(a)(2)(A)(i).

Example (3). R, a charity, enters into a contract with a law firm to be the exclusive sponsor of the charity's outreach program. Instead of making a cash payment, the law firm agrees to perform $100,000 of legal services for the charity. In return, R agrees to acknowledge the law firm in all its informational materials. The total fair market value of the legal services, or $100,000, is a qualified sponsorship payment under section 513(i), but no amount is treated as a contribution under section 509(a)(2)(A)(i) because the contribution is of services.

(g) Grants distinguished from gross receipts—(1) In general. In determining whether an organization normally receives more than one-third of its support from public sources, all grants (within the meaning of section 509(a)(2)(A)(i)) received from permitted sources are includible in full in the numerator of the support fraction in each taxable year. However, gross receipts (within the meaning of section 509(a)(2)(A)(ii)) from admissions, sales of merchandise, performance of services, or furnishing of facilities, in an activity which is not an unrelated trade or business, are includible in the numerator of the support fraction in any taxable year only to the extent that such gross receipts do not exceed the limitation with respect to the greater of $5,000 or 1 percent of support which is described in paragraph (b) of this section. A grant is normally made to encourage the grantee organization to carry on certain programs or activities in furtherance of its exempt purposes. It may contain certain terms and conditions imposed by the grantor to insure that the grantee's programs or activities are conducted in a manner compatible with the grantor's own programs and policies and beneficial to the public. The grantee may also perform a service or produce a work product which incidentally benefits the grantor. Because of the imposition of terms and conditions, the frequent similarity of public purposes of grantor and grantee, and the possibility of benefit resulting to the grantor, amounts received as grants for the carrying on of exempt activities are sometimes difficult to distinguish from amounts received as gross receipts from the carrying on of exempt activities. The fact that the agreement, pursuant to which payment is made, is designated a contract or a grant is not controlling for purposes of classifying the payment under section 509(a)(2).

(2) Distinguishing factors. For purposes of section 509(a)(2)(A)(ii), in distinguishing the term gross receipts from the term grants, the term gross receipts means amounts received from an activity which is not an unrelated trade or business, if a specific service, facility, or product is provided to serve the direct and immediate needs of the payor, rather than primarily to confer a direct benefit upon the general public. In general, payments made primarily to enable the payor to realize or receive some economic or physical benefit as a result of the service, facility, or product obtained will be treated as gross receipts with respect to the payee. The fact that a profitmaking organization would, primarily for its own economic or physical betterment, contract with a nonprofit organization for the rendition of a comparable service, facility or product from such organization constitutes evidence that any payments received by the nonprofit payee organization (whether from a governmental unit, a nonprofit or a profitmaking organization) for such services, facilities or products are primarily for the economic or physical benefit of the payor and would therefore be considered gross receipts, rather than grants with respect to the payee organization. For example, if a nonprofit hospital described in section 170(b)(1)(A)(iii) engages an exempt research and development organization to develop a more economical system of preparing food for its own patients and personnel, and it can be established that a hospital operated for profit might engage the services of such an organization to perform a similar benefit for its economic betterment, such fact would constitute evidence that the payments received by the research and development organization constitute gross receipts, rather than grants. Research leading to the development of tangible products for the use or benefit of the payor will generally be treated as a service provided to serve the direct and immediate needs of the payor, while basic research or studies carried on in the physical or social sciences will generally be treated as primarily to confer a direct benefit upon the general public.

(3) Examples. The application of this paragraph may be illustrated by the following examples:

Example (1). M, a nonprofit research organization described in section 501(c)(3), engages in some contract research. It receives funds from the government to develop a specific electronic device needed to perfect articles of space equipment. The initiative for the project came solely from the government. Furthermore, the government could have contracted with profitmaking research organizations which carry on similar activities. The funds received from the government for this project are gross receipts and do not constitute grants within the meaning of section 509(a)(2)(A)(i). M provided a specific product at the government's request and thus was serving the direct and immediate needs of the payor within the meaning of subparagraph (2) of this paragraph.

Example (2). N is a nonprofit educational organization described in section 501(c)(3). Its principal activity is to operate institutes to train employees of various industries in the principles of management and administration. The government pays N to set up a special institute for certain government employees and to train them over a 2-year period. Management training is also provided by profitmaking organizations. The funds received are included as gross receipts. The particular services rendered were to serve the direct and immediate needs of the government in the training of its employees within the meaning of subparagraph (2) of this paragraph.

Example (3). The Office of Economic Opportunity makes a community action program grant to O, an organization described in section 509(a)(1). O serves as a delegate agency of OEO for purposes of financing a local community action program. As part of this program, O signs an agreement with X, an educational and charitable organization described in section 501(c)(3), to carry out a housing program for the benefit of poor families. Pursuant to this agreement, O pays X out of the funds provided by OEO to build or rehabilitate low income housing and to provide advisory services to other nonprofit organizations in order for them to meet similar housing objectives, all on a nonprofit basis. Payments made from O to X constitute grants for purposes of section 509(a)(2)(A) because such program is carried on primarily for the direct benefit of the community.

Example (4). P is an educational institute described in section 501(c)(3). It carries on studies and seminars to assist institutions of higher learning. It receives funds from the government to research and develop a program of black studies for institutions of higher learning. The performance of such a service confers a direct benefit upon the public. Because such program is carried on primarily for the direct benefit of the public, the funds are considered a grant.

Example (5). Q is an organization described in section 501(c)(3) which carries on medical research. Its efforts have primarily been directed toward cancer research. Q sought funds from the government for a particular project being contemplated in connection with its work. In order to encourage its activities, the government gives Q the sum of $25,000. The research project sponsored by government funds is primarily to provide direct benefit to the general public, rather than to serve the direct and immediate needs of the government. The funds are therefore considered a grant.

Example (6). R is a public service organization described in section 501(c)(3) and composed of State and local officials involved in public works activities. The Bureau of Solid Waste, Management of the Department of Health, Education, and Welfare paid R to study the feasibility of a particular system for disposal of solid waste. Upon completion of the study, R was required to prepare a final report setting forth its findings and conclusions. Although R is providing the Bureau of Solid Waste Management with a final report, such report is the result of basic research and study in the physical sciences and is primarily to provide direct benefit to the general public by serving to further the general functions of government, rather than a direct and immediate governmental needs. The funds paid to R are therefore a grant within the meaning of section 509(a)(2).

Example (7). R is the public service organization referred to in example (6). W, a municipality described in section 170(c)(1), decides to construct a sewage disposal plant. W pays R to study a number of possible locations for such plant and to make recommendations to W, based upon a number of factors, as to the best location. W instructed R that in making its recommendation, primary consideration should be given to minimizing the costs of the project to W. Since the study commissioned by W was primarily directed toward producing an economic benefit to W in the form of minimizing the costs of its project, the services rendered are treated as serving W's direct and immediate needs and are includible as gross receipts by R.

Example (8). S in an organization described in section 501(c)(3). It was organized and is operated to further African development and strengthen understanding between the United States and Africa. To further these purposes, S receives funds from the Agency for International Development and the Department of State under which S is required to carry out the following programs: Selection, transportation, orientation, counseling, and language training of African students admitted to American institutions of higher learning; payment of tuition, other fees, and maintenance of such students; and operation of schools and vocational training programs in underdeveloped countries for residents of those countries. Since the programs carried on by S are primarily to provide direct benefit to the general public, all of the funds received by S from the Federal agencies are considered grants within the meaning of section 509(a)(2).

(h) Definition of membership fees—(1) General rule. For purposes of section 509(a)(2), the fact that a membership organization provides services, admissions, facilities, or merchandise to its members as part of its overall activities will not, in itself, result in the classification of fees received from members as gross receipts rather than membership fees. If an organization uses membership fees as a means of selling admissions, merchandise, services, or the use of facilities to members of the general public who have no common goal or interest (other than the desire to purchase such admissions, merchandise, services, or use of facilities), then the income received from such fees shall not constitute membership fees under section 509(a)(2)(A)(i), but shall, if from a related activity, constitute gross receipts under section 509(a)(2)(A)(ii). On the other hand, to the extent the basic purpose for making the payment is to provide support for the organization rather than to purchase admissions, merchandise, services, or the use of facilities, the income received from such payment shall constitute membership fees.

(2) Examples. The provisions of this paragraph may be illustrated by the following examples:

Example (1). M is a symphony society described in section 501(c)(3). Its primary purpose is to support the local symphony orchestra. The organization has three classes of membership. Contributing members pay annual dues of $10, sustaining members pay $25, and honorary members pay $100. The dues are placed in a maintenance fund which is used to provide financial assistance in underwriting the orchestra's annual deficit. Members have the privilege of purchasing subscriptions to the concerts before they go on sale to the general public, but must pay the same price as any other member of the public. They also are entitled to attend a number of rehearsals each season without charge. Under these circumstances, M's receipts from the members constitute membership fees for purposes of section 509(a)(2)(A)(i).

Example (2). N is a theater association described in section 501(c)(3). Its purpose is to support a repertory company in the community in order to make live theatrical performances available to the public. The organization sponsors six plays each year. Members of the organization are entitled to a season subscription to the plays. The fee paid as dues approximates the retail price of the six plays, less a 10-percent discount. Tickets to each performance are also sold directly to the general public. The organization also holds a series of lectures on the theater which members may attend. Under these circumstances, the fees paid by members as dues will be considered gross receipts from a related activity. Although the fees are designated as membership fees, they are actually admissions to a series of plays.

(i) Bureau defined—(1) In general. The term any bureau or similar agency of a governmental unit (within the meaning of section 509(a)(2)(A)(ii)), refers to a specialized operating unit of the executive, judicial, or legislative branch of government where business is conducted under certain rules and regulations. Since the term bureau refers to a unit functioning at the operating, as distinct from the policymaking, level of government, it is normally descriptive of a subdivision of a department of government. The term bureau, for purposes of section 509(a)(2)(A)(ii), would therefore not usually include those levels of government which are basically policymaking or administrative, such as the office of the Secretary or Assistant Secretary of a department, but would consist of the highest operational level under such policymaking or administrative levels. Each subdivision of a larger unit within the Federal Government, which is headed by a Presidential appointee holding a position at or above Level V of the Executive Schedule under 5 U.S.C. 5316, will normally be considered an administrative or policymaking, rather than an operating, unit. Amounts received from a unit functioning at the policymaking or administrative level of government will be treated as received from one bureau or similar agency of such unit. Units of a governmental agency above the operating level shall be aggregated and considered a separate bureau for this purpose. Thus, an organization receiving gross receipts from both a policymaking or administrative unit and an operational unit of a department will be treated as receiving gross receipts from two bureaus within the meaning of section 509(a)(2)(A)(ii). For purposes of this subparagraph, the Departments of Air Force, Army, and Navy are separate departments and each is considered as having its own policymaking, administrative, and operating units.

(2) Examples. The provisions of this paragraph may be illustrated by the following examples:

Example (1). The Bureau of Health Insurance is considered a bureau within the meaning of section 509(a)(2)(A)(ii). It is a part of the Department of Health, Education, and Welfare, whose Secretary performs a policymaking function, and is under the Social Security Administration, which is basically an administrative unit. The Bureau of Health Insurance is in the first operating level within the Social Security Administration. Similarly, the National Cancer Institute would be considered a bureau, as it is an operating part of the National Institutes of Health within the Department of Health, Education, and Welfare.

Example (2). The Bureau for Africa and the Bureau for Latin America are considered bureaus within the meaning of section 509(a)(2)(A)(ii). Both are separate operating units under the administrator of the Agency for International development, a policymaking official. If an organization received gross receipts from both of these bureaus, the amount of gross receipts received from each would be subject to the greater of $5,000 or 1 percent limitation under section 509(a)(2)(A)(ii).

Example (3). The Bureau of International Affairs of the Civil Aeronautics Board is considered a bureau within the meaning of section 509(a)(2)

(A)(ii). It is an operating unit under the administrative office of the Executive Director. The subdivisions of the Bureau of International Affairs are Geographic Areas and Project Development Staff. If an organization received gross receipts from these subdivisions, the total gross receipts from these subdivisions would be considered gross receipts from the same bureau, the Bureau of International Affairs, and would be subject to the greater of $5,000 or 1 percent limitation under section 509(a)(2)(A)(ii).

Example (4). The Department of Mental Health, a State agency which is an operational part of State X's Department of Public Health, is considered a bureau. The Department of Public Health is basically an administrative agency and the Department of Mental Health is at the first operational level within it.

Example (5). The Aeronautical Systems Division of the Air Force Systems Command, and other units on the same level, are considered separate bureaus with the meaning of section 509(a)(2)(A)(ii). They are part of the Department of the Air Force which is a separate department for this purpose, as are the Army and Navy. The Secretary and the Under Secretary of the Air Force perform the policymaking function, the Chief of Staff and the Air Force Systems Command are basically administrative, having a comprehensive complement of staff functions to provide administration for the various divisions. The Aeronautical Systems Division and other units on the same level are thus the first operating level, as evidenced by the fact that they are the units that let contracts and perform the various operating functions.

Example (6). The Division of Space Nuclear Systems, the Division of Biology and Medicine, and other units on the same level within the Atomic Energy Commission are each separate bureaus within the meaning of section 509(a)(2)(A)(ii). The Commissioners (which make up the Commission) are the policymakers. The general manager and the various assistant general managers perform the administrative function. The various divisions perform the operating function as evidenced by the fact that each has separate programs to pursue and contracts specifically for these various programs.

(j) Grants from public charities—(1) General rule. For purposes of the one-third support test in section 509(a)(2)(A), grants (as defined in paragraph (g) of this section) received from an organization described in section 509(a)(1) (hereinafter referred to in this subparagraph as a public charity) are generally includible in full in computing the numerator of the recipient's support fraction of the taxable year in question. It is sometimes necessary to determine whether the recipient of a grant from a public charity has received such support from the public charity as a grant, or whether the recipient has in fact received such support as an indirect contribution from a donor to the public charity. If the amount received is considered a grant from the public charity, it is fully includible in the numerator of the support fraction under section 509(a)(2)(A). However, if the amount received is considered to be an indirect contribution from one of the public charity's donors which has passed through the public chairty to the recipient organization, such amount will retain its character as a contribution from such donor and, if, for example, the donor is a substantial contributor (as defined in section 507(d)(2)) with respect to the ultimate recipient, such amount shall be excluded from the numerator of the support fraction under section 509(a)(2). If a public charity makes both an indirect contribution from its donor and an additional grant to the ultimate recipient, the indirect contribution shall be treated as made first.

(2) Indirect contributions. For purposes of subparagraph (1) of this paragraph, an indirect contribution is one which is expressly or impliedly ear-marked by the donor as being for, or for the benefit of, a particular recipient (rather than for a particular purpose).

(3) Examples. The provisions of this paragraph may be illustrated by the following examples:

Example (1). M, a national foundation for the encouragement of the musical arts, is an organization described in section 170(b)(1)(A)(vi). A gives M a donation of $5,000 without imposing any restrictions or conditions upon the gift. M subsequently makes a $5,000 grant to X, an organization devoted to giving public performances of chamber music. Since the grant to X is treated as being received from M, it is fully includible in the numerator of X's support fraction for the taxable year of receipt.

Example (2). Assume M is the same organization described in example (1). B gives M a donation of $10,000, but requires that M spend the money for the purpose of supporting organizations devoted to the advancement of contemporary American music. M has complete discretion as to the organizations of the type described to which it will make a grant. M decides to make grants of $5,000 each to Y and Z, both being organizations described in section 501(c)(3) and devoted to furthering contemporary American music. Since the grants to Y and Z are treated as being received from M, Y and Z may each include one of the $5,000 grants in the numerator of its support fraction for purposes of section 509(a)(2)(A). Although the donation to M was conditioned upon the use of the funds for a particular purpose, M was free to select the ultimate recipient.

Example (3). N is a national foundation for the encouragement of art and is an organization described in section 170(b)(1)(A)(vi). Grants to N are permitted to be earmarked for particular purposes. O, which is an art workshop devoted to training young artists and claiming status under section 509(a)(2), persuades C, a private foundation, to make a grant of $25,000 to N. C is a disqualified person with respect to O. C made the grant to N with the understanding that N would be bound to make a grant to O in the sum of $25,000, in addition to a matching grant of N's funds to O in the sum of $25,000. Only the $25,000 received directly from N is considered a grant from N. The other $25,000 is deemed an indirect contribution from C to O and is to be excluded from the numerator of O's support fraction.

(k) Method of accounting. For purposes of section 509(a)(2), an organization's support will be determined under the method of accounting on the basis of which the organization regularly computes its income in keeping its books under section 446. For example, if a grantor makes a grant to an organization payable over a term of years, such grant will be includible in the support fraction of the grantee organization under the method of accounting on the basis of which it regularly computes its income in keeping its books under section 446.

(*l*) Gross receipts from section 513(a)(1), (2), or (3) activities. For purposes of section 509(a)(2)(A)(ii), gross receipts from activities described in section 513(a)(1), (2), or (3) will be considered gross receipts from activities which are not unrelated trade or business.

(m) Gross receipts distinguished from gross investment income. (1) For purposes of section 509(a)(2), where the charitable purpose of an organization described in section 501(c)(3) is accomplished through the furnishing of facilities for a rental fee or loans to a particular class of persons, such as aged, sick, or needy persons, the support received from such persons will be considered gross receipts (within the meaning of section 509(d)(2)) from an activity which is not an unrelated trade or business, rather than gross investment income. However, if such organization also furnishes facilities or loans to persons who are not members of such class and such furnishing does not contribute importantly to the accomplishment of such organization's exempt purposes (aside from the need of such organization for income or funds or the use it makes of the profits derived), the support received from such furnishing will be considered rents or interest and therefore will be treated as gross investment income within the meaning of section 509(d)(4), unless such income is included in computing the tax imposed by section 511.

(2) The provisions of this paragraph may be illustrated by the following example:

Example. X, an organization described in section 501(c)(3), is organized and operated to provide living facilities for needy widows of deceased servicemen. X charges such widows a small rental fee for the use of such facilities. Since X is accomplishing its exempt purpose through the rental of such facilities, the support received from the widows is considered gross receipts within the meaning of section 509(d)(2). However, if X rents part of its facilities to persons having no relationship to X's exempt purpose, the support received from such rental will be considered gross investment income within the meaning of section 509(d)(4), unless such income is included in computing the tax imposed by section 511.

* * *

§ 1.509(a)–4. Supporting organizations.

(a) In general. (1) Section 509(a)(3) excludes from the definition of private foundation those organizations which meet the requirements of subparagraphs (A), (B), and (C) thereof.

(2) Section 509(a)(3)(A) provides that a section 509(a)(3) organization must be organized, and at all times thereafter operated, exclusively for the benefit of, to perform the functions of, or to carry out the purposes of one or more specified organizations described in section 509(a)(1) or (2). Section 509(a)(3)(A) describes the nature of the support or benefit which a section 509(a)(3) organization must provide to one or more section 509(a)(1) or (2) organizations. For purposes of section 509(a)(3)(A), paragraph (b) of this section generally describes the organizational and operational tests; paragraph (c) of this section describes permissible purposes under the organizational test; paragraph (d) of this section describes the requirement of supporting or benefiting one or more specified publicly supported organizations; and paragraph (e) of this section describes permissible beneficiaries and activities under the operational test.

(3) Section 509(a)(3)(B) provides that a section 509(a)(3) organization must be operated, supervised, or controlled by or in connection with one or more organizations described in section 509(a)(1) or (2). Section 509(a)(3)(B) and paragraph (f) of this section describe the nature of the relationship which must exist between the section 509(a)(3) and section 509(a)(1) or (2) organizations. For purposes of section 509(a)(3)(B), paragraph (g) of this section defines operated, supervised, or controlled by; paragraph (h) of this section defines supervised or controlled in connection with; and paragraph (i) of this section defines operated in connection with.

(4) Section 509(a)(3)(C) provides that a section 509(a)(3) organization must not be controlled directly or indirectly by disqualified persons (other than foundation managers or organizations described in section 509(a)(1) or (2)). Section 509(a)(3)(C) and paragraph (j) of this section prescribe a limitation on the control over the section 509(a)(3) organization.

(5) For purposes of this section, the term supporting organization means either an organization described in section 509(a)(3) or an organization seeking section 509(a)(3) status, depending upon its context. For purposes of this section, the term publicly supported organization means an organization described in section 509(a)(1) or (2).

(6) For purposes of paragraph (i) of this section, the term "supported organization" means a specified publicly supported organization described in paragraphs (d)(2)(iv) or (d)(4) of this section.

(b) Organizational and operational tests. (1) Under subparagraph (A) of section 509(a)(3), in order to qualify as a supporting organization, an organization must be both organized and operated exclusively for the benefit of, to perform the functions of, or to carry out the purposes of (hereinafter referred to in this section as being organized and operated to support or benefit) one or more specified publicly supported organizations. If an organization fails to meet either the organizational or the operational test, it cannot qualify as a supporting organization. * * *

(c) Organizational test—(1) In general. An organization is organized exclusively for one or more of the purposes specified in section 509(a)(3)(A) only if its articles of organization (as defined in § 1.501(c)(3)–1(b)(2)):

(i) Limit the purposes of such organization to one or more of the purposes set forth in section 509(a)(3)(A);

(ii) Do not expressly empower the organization to engage in activities which are not in furtherance of the purposes referred to in subdivision (i) of this subparagraph;

(iii) State the specified publicly supported organizations on whose behalf such organization is to be operated (within the meaning of paragraph (d) of this section); and

(iv) Do not expressly empower the organization to operate to support or benefit any organization other than the specified publicly supported organizations referred to in subdivision (iii) of this subparagraph.

(2) Purposes. In meeting the organizational test, the organization's purposes, as stated in its articles, may be as broad as, or more specific than, the purposes set forth in section 509(a)(3)(A). Therefore, an organization which, by the terms of its articles, is formed for the benefit of one or more specified publicly supported organizations shall, if it otherwise meets the other requirements of this paragraph, be considered to have met the organizational test. Similarly, articles which state that an organization is formed to perform the publishing functions of a specified university are sufficient to comply with the organizational test. An organization which is operated, supervised, or controlled by (within the meaning of paragraph (g) of this section) or supervised or controlled in connection with (within the meaning of paragraph (h) of this section) one or more sections 509(a)(1) or (2) organizations to carry out the purposes of such organizations, will be considered as meeting the requirements of this paragraph if the purposes set forth in its articles are similar to, but no broader than, the purposes set forth in the articles of its controlling section 509(a)(1) or (2) organizations. If, however, the organization by which it is operated, supervised, or controlled is a publicly supported section 501(c)(4), (5), or (6) organization (deemed to be a section 509(a)(2) organization for purposes of section 509(a)(3) under the provisions of section 509(a)), the supporting organization will be considered as meeting the requirements of this paragraph if its articles require it to carry on charitable, etc., activities within the meaning of section 170(c)(2).

(3) Limitations. An organization is not organized exclusively for the purposes set forth in section 509(a)(3)(A) if its articles expressly permit it to operate to support or benefit any organization other than those specified publicly supported organizations referred to in subparagraph (1)(iii) of this paragraph. Thus, for example, an organization will not meet the organizational test under section 509(a)(3)(A) if its articles expressly empower it to pay over any part of its income to, or perform any service for, any organization other than those publicly supported organizations specified in its articles (within the meaning of paragraph (d) of this section). The fact that the actual operations of such organization have been exclusively for the benefit of the specified publicly supported organizations shall not be sufficient to permit it to meet the organizational test.

(d) Specified organizations—(1) In general. In order to meet the requirements of section 509(a)(3)(A), an organization must be organized and operated exclusively to support or benefit one or more specified publicly supported organizations. The manner in which the publicly supported organizations must be specified in the articles for purposes of section 509(a)(3)(A) will depend upon whether the supporting organization is operated, supervised, or controlled by or supervised or controlled in connection with (within the meaning of paragraphs (g) and (h) of this section) such organizations or whether it is operated in connection with (within the meaning of paragraph (i) of this section) such organizations.

(2) Nondesignated publicly supported organizations; requirements. (i) Except as provided in paragraph (d)(2)(iv) of this section, in order to meet the requirements of paragraph (d)(1) of this section, the articles of the supporting organization must designate each of the specified organizations by name unless:

(A) The supporting organization is operated, supervised, or controlled by (within the meaning of paragraph (g) of this section), or is supervised or controlled in connection with (within the meaning of paragraph (h) of this section) one or more publicly supported organizations; and

(B) The articles of organization of the supporting organization require that it be operated to support or benefit one or more beneficiary organizations which are designated by class or purpose and which include:

(1) The publicly supported organizations referred to in paragraph (d)(2)(i)(A) of this section (without designating such organizations by name); or

(2) Publicly supported organizations which are closely related in purpose or function to those publicly supported organizations referred to in paragraph (d)(2)(i)(A) of this section or this paragraph (d)(2)(i)(B)(2) (without designating such organization by name).

(ii) If a supporting organization is described in paragraph (d)(2)(i)(A) of this section, it will not be considered as failing to meet the requirements of paragraph (d)(1) of this section that the publicly supported organizations be specified merely because its articles of organization permit the conditions described in paragraphs (d)(3)(i) through (iii) and (d)(4)(i)(A) and (B) of this section.

(iii) This paragraph (d)(2) may be illustrated by the following examples:

(A) **Example 1.** X is an organization described in section 501(c)(3) which operates for the benefit of institutions of higher learning in the State of Y. X is controlled by these institutions (within the meaning of paragraph (g) of this section) and such institutions are all section 509(a)(1) organizations. X's articles will meet the organizational test if they require X to operate for the benefit of institutions of higher learning or educational organizations in the State of Y (without naming each institution). X's articles would also meet the organizational test if they provided for the giving of scholarships to enable students to attend institutions of higher learning but only in the State of Y.

(B) **Example 2.** M is an organization described in section 501(c)(3) which was organized and operated by representatives of N church to run a home for the aged. M is controlled (within the meaning of paragraph (g) of this section) by N church, a section 509(a)(1) organization. The care of the sick and the aged are longstanding temporal functions and purposes of organized religion. By operating a home for the aged, M is operating to support or benefit N church in carrying out one of its temporal purposes. Thus M's articles will meet the organizational test if they require M to care for the aged since M is operating to support one of N church's purposes (without designating N church by name).

(iv) A supporting organization will meet the requirements of paragraph (d)(1) of this section even though its articles do not designate each of the specified organizations by name if:

(A) There has been an historic and continuing relationship between the supporting organization and the section 509(a)(1) or (2) organizations; and

(B) By reason of such relationship, there has developed a substantial identity of interests between such organizations.

(3) Nondesignated publicly supported organizations; scope of rule. If the requirements of paragraph (d)(2)(i)(A) of this section are met, a supporting organization will not be considered as failing the test of being organized for the benefit of specified organizations solely because its articles:

(i) Permit the substitution of one publicly supported organization within a designated class for another publicly supported organization either in the same or a different class designated in the articles;

(ii) Permit the supporting organization to operate for the benefit of new or additional publicly supported organizations of the same or a different class designated in the articles; or

(iii) Permit the supporting organization to vary the amount of its support among different publicly supported organizations within the class or classes of organizations designated by the articles.

For example, X is an organization which operates for the benefit of private colleges in the State of Y. If X is controlled by these colleges (within the meaning of paragraph (g) of this section) and such colleges are all section 509(a)(1) organizations, X's articles will meet the organization test even if they permit X to operate for the benefit of any new colleges created in State Y in addition to the existing colleges or in lieu of one which has ceased to operate, or if they permit X to vary its support by paying more to one college than to another in a particular year.

(4) Designated publicly supported organizations. (i) If an organization is organized and operated to support one or more publicly supported organizations and it is operated in connection with such organization or organizations, then, except as provided in paragraph (d)(2)(iv) of this section, its articles of organization must, for purposes of satisfying the organizational test under section 509(a)(3)(A), designate the specified organizations by name. Under the circumstances described in this paragraph (d)(4), a supporting organization which has one or more specified organizations designated by name in its articles, will not be considered as failing the test of being organized for the benefit of specified organizations solely because its articles:

(A) Permit a publicly supported organization which is designated by class or purpose, rather than by name, to be substituted for the publicly supported organization or organizations designated by name in the articles, but only if such substitution is conditioned upon the occurrence of an event which is beyond the control of the supporting organization, such as loss of exemption, substantial failure or abandonment of operations, or dissolution of the publicly supported organization or organizations designated in the articles;

(B) Permit the supporting organization to operate for the benefit of a beneficiary organization which is not a publicly supported organization, but only if such supporting organization is currently operating for the benefit of a publicly supported organization and the possibility of its operating for the benefit of other than a publicly supported organization is a remote contingency; or

(C) Permit the supporting organization to vary the amount of its support between different designated organizations, so long as it meets the requirements of the integral part test set forth in paragraph (i)(1)(iii) of this section with respect to at least one beneficiary organization.

(ii) If the beneficiary organization referred to in paragraph (d)(4)(i)(B) of this section is not a publicly supported organization, the supporting organization will not then meet the operational test of paragraph (e)(1) of this section. Therefore, if a supporting organization substituted in accordance with such paragraph (d)(4)(i)(B) a beneficiary other than a publicly supported organization and operated in support of such beneficiary organization, the supporting organization would not be described in section 509(a)(3).

(iii) This paragraph (d)(4) may be illustrated by the following example:

(A) **Example.** X is a charitable trust described in section 4947(a)(1) organized in 1968. Under the terms of its trust instrument, X's trustees are required to pay over all of X's annual income to M University Medical School for urological research. If M University Medical School is unable or unwilling to devote these funds to urological research, the trustees are required to pay all of such income to N University Medical School. However if N University Medical School is also unable or unwilling to devote these funds to urological research, X's trustees are directed to choose a similar organization willing to apply X's funds for urological research. From 1968 to 1973, X pays all of its net income to M University Medical School pursuant to the terms of the trust. M and N are publicly supported organizations. Although the contingent remainderman may not be a publicly supported organization, the possibility that X may operate for the benefit of other than a publicly supported organization is, in 1973, a remote possibility, and X will be considered as operating for the benefit of a specified publicly supported organization under subdivision (i)(b) of this subparagraph. However, if, at some future date, X actually substituted a nonpublicly supported organization as beneficiary, X would fail the requirements of the operational test set forth in paragraph (e)(1) of this section.

(B) [Reserved]

(e) Operational test—(1) Permissible beneficiaries. A supporting organization will be regarded as operated exclusively to support one or more specified publicly supported organizations (hereinafter referred to as the operational test) only if it engages solely in activities which support or benefit the specified publicly supported organizations. Such activities may include making payments to or for the use of, or providing services or facilities for, individual members of the charitable class benefited by the specified publicly supported organization. A supporting organization may also, for example, make a payment indirectly through another unrelated organization to a member of a charitable class benefited by the specified publicly supported organization, but only if such a payment constitutes a grant to an individual rather than a grant to an organization. In determining whether a grant is indirectly to an individual rather than to an organization the same standard shall be applied as in § 53.4945–4(a)(4) of this chapter. Similarly, an organization will be regarded as operated exclusively to support or benefit one or more specified publicly supported organizations even if it supports or benefits an organization, other than a private foundation, which is described in section 501(c)(3) and is operated, supervised, or controlled directly by or in connection with such publicly supported organizations, or which is described in section 511(a)(2)(B). However, an organization will not be regarded as operated exclusively if any part of its activities is in furtherance of a purpose other than supporting or benefiting one or more specified publicly supported organizations.

(2) Permissible activities. A supporting organization is not required to pay over its income to the publicly supported organizations in order to meet the operational test. It may satisfy the test by using its income to carry on an independent activity or program which supports or benefits the specified publicly supported organizations. All such support must, however, be limited to permissible beneficiaries in accordance with subparagraph (1) of this paragraph. The supporting organization may also engage in fund raising activities, such as solicitations, fund raising dinners, and unrelated trade or business to raise funds for the publicly supported organizations, or for the permissible beneficiaries.

(3) Examples. The provisions of this paragraph (e) may be illustrated by the following examples:

(i) Example (1). M is a separately incorporated alumni association of X University and is an organization described in section 501(c)(3). X University is designated in M's articles as the sole beneficiary of its support. M uses all of its dues and income to support its own program of educational activities for alumni, faculty, and students of X University and to encourage alumni to maintain a close relationship with the university and to make contributions to it. M does not distribute any of its income directly to X for the latter's general purposes. M pays no part of its funds to, or for the benefit of, any organization other than X. Under these circumstances, M is considered as operated exclusively to perform the functions and carry out the purpose of X. Although it does not pay over any of its funds to X, it carries on a program which both supports and benefits X.

(ii) Example (2). N is a separately incorporated religious and educational organization described in section 501(c)(3). It was formed and is operated by Y Church to provide religious training for the members of the church. While it does not maintain a regular faculty, N conducts a Sunday school, weekly adult education lectures on religious subjects, and other similar activities for the benefit of the church members. All of its funds are disbursed in furtherance of such activities and no part of its funds is paid to, or for the benefit of, any organization other than Y Church. N is considered as operated exclusively to perform the educational functions of Y Church and to carry out its religious purposes by providing various forms of religious instruction.

(iii) Example (3). P is an organization described in section 501(c)(3). Its primary activity is providing financial assistance to S, a publicly supported organization which aids underdeveloped nations in Central America. P's articles of organization designate S as the principal recipient of P's assistance. However, P also makes a small annual general purpose grant to T, a private foundation engaged in work similar to that carried on by S. T performs a particular function that assists in the overall aid program carried on by S. Even though P is operating primarily for the benefit of S, a specified publicly supported organization, it is not considered as operated exclusively for the purposes set forth in section 509(a)(3)(A). The grant to T, a private foundation, prevents it from complying with the operational test under section 509(a)(3)(A).

(iv) Example (4). Assume the same facts as example (3), except that T is a section 501(c)(3) organization other than a private foundation and is operated in connection with S. Under these circumstances, P will be considered as operated exclusively to support S within the meaning of section 509(a)(3)(A).

(v) Example (5). Assume the same facts as example (3) except that instead of the annual general purpose grant made to T, each grant made by P to T is specifically earmarked for the training of social workers and teachers, designated by name, from Central America. Under these circumstances, P's grants to T would be treated as grants to the individual social workers and teachers under section 4945(d)(3) and § 53.4945–4(a)(4), rather than as grants to T under section 4945(d)(4). These social workers and teachers are part of the charitable class benefitted by S. P would thus be considered as operating exclusively to support S within the meaning of section 509(a)(3)(A).

(f) Nature of relationship required between organizations—(1) In general. Section 509(a)(3)(B) describes the nature of the relationship required between a section 501(c)(3) organization and one or more publicly supported organizations in order for such section 501(c)(3) organization to qualify under the provisions of section 509(a)(3). To meet the requirements of section 509(a)(3), an organization must be operated, supervised, or controlled by or in connection with one or more publicly supported organizations. If an organization does not stand in one of such relationships (as provided in this paragraph) to one or more publicly supported organizations, it is not an organization described in section 509(a)(3).

(2) Types of relationships. Section 509(a)(3)(B) sets forth three different types of relationships, one of which must be met in order to meet the requirements of subparagraph (1) of this paragraph. Thus, a supporting organization may be:

(i) Operated, supervised, or controlled by,

(ii) Supervised or controlled in connection with, or

(iii) Operated in connection with, one or more publicly supported organizations.

(3) Requirements of relationships. Although more than one type of relationship may exist in any one case, any relationship described in section 509(a)(3)(B) must insure that:

(i) The supporting organization will be responsive to the needs of demands of one or more publicly supported organizations; and

(ii) The supporting organization will constitute an integral part of, or maintain a significant involvement in, the operations of one or more publicly supported organizations.

(4) General description of relationships. In the case of supporting organizations which are operated, supervised, or controlled by one or more publicly supported organizations, the distinguishing feature of this type of relationship is the presence of a substantial degree of direction by the publicly supported organizations over the conduct of the supporting organization, as described in paragraph (g) of this section. In the case of supporting organizations which are supervised or controlled in connection with one or more publicly supported organizations, the distinguishing feature is the presence of common supervision or control among the governing bodies of all organizations involved, such as the presence of common directors, as described in paragraph (h) of this section. In the case of a supporting organization which is operated in connection with one or more publicly supported organizations, the distinguishing feature is that the supporting organization is responsive to, and significantly involved in the operations of, the publicly supported organization, as described in paragraph (i) of this section.

(5) Contributions from controlling donors—(i) In general. For any taxable year, a supporting organization shall not be considered to be operated, supervised, or controlled by, or operated in connection with, one or more publicly supported organizations, if the supporting organization accepts any gift or contribution from any person who is—

(A) A person (other than an organization described in section 509(a)(1), (2), or (4)) who directly or indirectly controls, either alone or together with persons described in paragraphs (f)(5)(i)(B) or (f)(5)(i)(C) of this section, the governing body of a specified publicly supported organization supported by such supporting organization;

(B) A member of the family (determined under section 4958(f)(4)) of an individual described in paragraph (f)(5)(i)(A) of this section; or

(C) A 35-percent controlled entity (as defined in section 4958(f)(3) by substituting "clause (i) or (ii) of section 509(f)(2)(B)" for "subparagraph (A) or (B) of paragraph (1)" in paragraph (f)(3)(A)(i) thereof).

(ii) Meaning of control. For purposes of paragraph (f)(5)(i) of this section, the governing body of a supported organization will be considered controlled by a person described in paragraph (f)(5)(i)(A) of this section if that person, alone or by aggregating the person's votes or positions of authority with persons described in paragraph (f)(5)(i)(B) or (C) of this section, may require the governing body of the supported organization to perform any act that significantly affects its operations or may prevent the governing body of the supported organization from performing any such act. The governing body of a supported organization will be considered to be controlled directly or indirectly by one or more persons described in paragraph (f)(5)(i)(A), (B), or (C) of this section if the voting power of such persons is 50 percent or more of the total voting power of such governing body or if one or more of such persons have the right to exercise veto power over the actions of the governing body of the supported organization. Thus, if the governing body of a supported organization is composed of five members, none of whom has a veto power over the actions of the supported organization, and no more than two members are at any time described in paragraph (f)(5)(i)(A), (B), or (C) of this section, such supported organization will not be considered to be controlled directly or indirectly by such persons by reason of this fact alone. However, all pertinent facts and circumstances will be taken into consideration in determining whether one or more persons do in fact directly or indirectly control the governing body of a supported organization.

(g) Meaning of operated, supervised, or controlled by. (1)(i) Each of the items operated by, supervised by, and controlled by, as used in section 509(a)(3)(B), presupposes a substantial degree of direction over the policies, programs, and activities of a supporting organization by one or more publicly supported organizations. The relationship required under any one of these terms is comparable to that of a parent and subsidiary, where the subsidiary is under the direction of, and accountable or responsible to, the parent organization. This relationship is established by the fact that a majority of the officers, directors, or trustees of the supporting organization are appointed or elected by the governing body, members of the governing body, officers acting in their official capacity, or the membership of one or more publicly supported organizations.

(ii) A supporting organization may be operated, supervised, or controlled by one or more publicly supported organizations within the meaning of section 509(a)(3)(B) even though its governing body is not comprised of representatives of the specified publicly supported organizations for whose benefit it is operated within the meaning of section 509(a)(3)(A). A supporting organization may be operated, supervised, or controlled by one or more publicly supported organizations (within the meaning of section 509(a)(3)(B)) and be operated for the benefit of one or more different publicly supported organizations (within the meaning of section 509(a)(3)(A)) only if it can be demonstrated that the purposes of the former organizations are carried out by benefitting the latter organizations.

(2) The provisions of this paragraph (g) may be illustrated by the following examples:

(i) **Example (1).** X is a university press which is organized and operated as a nonstock educational corporation to perform the publishing and printing for M University, a publicly supported organization. Control of X is vested in a Board of Governors appointed by the Board of Trustees of M University upon the recommendation of the president of the university. X is considered to be operated, supervised, or controlled by M University within the meaning of section 509(a)(3)(B).

(ii) **Example (2).** Y Council was organized under the joint sponsorship of seven independent publicly supported organizations, each of which is dedicated to the advancement of knowledge in a particular field of social science. The sponsoring organizations organized Y Council as a means of pooling their ideas and resources for the attainment of common objectives, including the conducting of scholarly studies and formal discussions in various fields of social science. Under Y Council's by-laws, each of the seven sponsoring organizations elects three members to Y's board of trustees for 3-year terms. Y's board also includes the president of Y Council and eight other individuals elected at large by the board. Pursuant to policies established or approved by the board, Y Council engages in research, planning, and evaluation in the social sciences and sponsors or arranges conferences, seminars, and similar programs for scholars and social scientists. It carries out these activities through its own full-time professional staff, through a part-time committee of scholars, and through grant recipients. Under the above circumstances, Y Council is subject to a substantial degree of direction by the sponsoring publicly supported organizations. It is therefore considered to be operated, supervised, or controlled by such sponsoring organizations within the meaning of section 509(a)(3)(B).

(iii) **Example (3).** Z is a charitable trust created by A in 1972. It has three trustees, all of whom are appointed by M University, a publicly supported organization. The trust was organized and is operated to pay over all of its net income for medical research to N, O, and P, each of which is specified in the trust, is a hospital described in section 509(a)(1), and is located in the same city as M. Members of M's biology department are permitted to use the research facilities of N, O, and P. Under paragraph (1)(ii) of this section, Z is considered to be operated, supervised, or controlled by M within the meaning of section 509(a)(3)(B), even though it is operated for the benefit of N, O, and P within the meaning of section 509(a)(3)(A).

(h) Meaning of supervised or controlled in connection with. (1) In order for a supporting organization to be supervised or controlled in connection with one or more publicly supported organizations, there must be common supervision or control by the persons supervising or controlling both the supporting organization and the publicly supported organizations to insure that the supporting organization will be responsive to the needs and requirements of the publicly supported organizations. Therefore, in order to meet such requirement, the control or management of the supporting organization must be vested in the same persons that control or manage the publicly supported organizations.

(2) A supporting organization will not be considered to be supervised or controlled in connection with one or more publicly supported organizations if such organization merely makes payments (mandatory or discretionary) to one or more named publicly supported organizations, even if the obligation to make payments to the named beneficiaries is enforceable under State law by such beneficiaries and the supporting organization's governing instrument contains provisions whose effect is described in section 508(e)(1)(A) and (B). Such arrangements do not provide a sufficient connection between the payor organization and the needs and requirements of the publicly supported organizations to constitute supervision or control in connection with such organizations.

(3) The provisions of this paragraph (h) may be illustrated by the following examples:

(i) **Example 1.** A, a philanthropist, founded X school for orphan boys (a publicly supported organization). At the same time A founded X school, he also established Y trust into which he transferred all of the operating assets of the school, together with a substantial endowment for it. Under the provisions of the trust instrument, the same persons who control and manage the school also control and manage the trust. The sole function of Y trust is to hold legal title to X school's operating and endowment assets, to invest the endowment assets and to apply the income from the endowment to the benefit of the school in accordance with direction from the school's governing body. Under these circumstances, Y trust is organized and operated for the benefit of X school and is supervised or controlled in connection with such organization within the meaning of section 509(a)(3). The fact that the same persons control both X and Y insures Y's responsiveness to X's needs.

(ii) **Example 2.** In 1972, B, a philanthropist, created P, a charitable trust for the benefit of Z, a symphony orchestra described in section 509(a)(2). B transferred 100 shares of common stock to P. Under the terms of the trust instrument, the trustees (none of whom is under the control of B) were required to pay over all of the income produced by the trust assets to Z. The governing instrument of P contains certain provisions whose effect is described in section 508(e)(1)(A) and (B). Under applicable State law, Z can enforce the provisions of the trust instrument and compel payment to Z in a court of equity. There is no relationship between the trustees of P and the governing body of Z. Under these circumstances P is not supervised or controlled in connection with a publicly supported organization. Because of the lack of any common supervision or control by the trustees of P and the governing body of Z, P is not supervised or controlled in connection with Z within the meaning of section 509(a)(3)(B).

(iii) **Example 3.** T is a charitable trust described in section 501(c)(3) and created under the will of D. Prior to his death, D was a leader and very active in C church, a publicly supported organization. D created T to perpetuate his interest in, and assistance to, C. The sole purpose of T was to provide financial support for C and its related institutions. All of the original named trustees of T are members of C, are leaders in C, and hold important offices in one or more of C's related institutions. Successor trustees of T are by the terms of the charitable trust instrument to be chosen by the remaining trustees and are also to be members of C. All of the original trustees have represented that any successor trustee will be a leader in C and will hold an important office in one or more of C's related institutions. By reason of the foregoing relationship T and its trustees are responsive to the needs and requirements of C and its related institutions. Under these circumstances, T trust is organized and operated for the benefit of C and is supervised or controlled in connection with C and its related institutions within the meaning of section 509(a)(3)(B).

(i) Meaning of operated in connection with—(1) General rule. For each taxable year, a supporting organization is operated in connection with one or more supported organizations (that is, is a "Type III supporting organization") only if it is not disqualified by reason of paragraph (f)(5) (relating to acceptance of contributions from controlling donors) or paragraph (i)(10) (relating to foreign supported organizations) of this section, and it satisfies—

(i) The notification requirement, which is set forth in paragraph (i)(2) of this section;

(ii) The responsiveness test, which is set forth in paragraph (i)(3) of this section; and

(iii) The integral part test, which is satisfied by maintaining significant involvement in the operations of one or more supported organizations and providing support on which the supported organization(s) are dependent; in order to satisfy this test, the supporting organization must meet the requirements either for—

(A) Functionally integrated Type III supporting organizations set forth in paragraph (i)(4) of this section; or

(B) Non-functionally integrated Type III supporting organizations set forth in paragraph (i)(5) of this section.

(2) Notification requirement—(i) Annual notification. For each taxable year (Reporting Year), a Type III supporting organization must provide the following documents to each of its supported organizations:

(A) A written notice addressed to a principal officer of the supported organization describing the type and amount of all of the support (including all of the distributions described in paragraph (i)(6) of this section, if applicable) the supporting organization provided to the supported organization during the supporting organization's taxable year immediately preceding the Reporting Year (and during any other taxable year of the supporting organization ending after December 28, 2012, for which such support information has not previously been provided), including a brief narrative description of the support provided and sufficient financial detail for the recipient to identify the types and amounts of support being reported;

(B) A copy of the supporting organization's Form 990, "Return of Organization Exempt from Income Tax," or other annual information return required to be filed under section 6033 (although the supporting organization may redact from the return the name and address of any contributor to the organization) that was most recently filed as of the date the notification is provided (and any such return for any other taxable year of the supporting organization ending after December 28, 2012, that has not previously been provided to the supported organization); and

(C) A copy of the supporting organization's governing documents as in effect on the date the notification is provided, including its articles of organization and bylaws (if any) and any amendments to such documents, unless such documents have been previously provided and not subsequently amended.

(ii) Electronic media. The notification documents required by this paragraph (i)(2) may be provided by electronic media.

(iii) Due date. The notification documents required by this paragraph (i)(2) must be delivered or electronically transmitted by the last day of the fifth calendar month of the Reporting Year.

(iv) Principal officer. For purposes of paragraph (i)(2)(i)(A) of this section, a principal officer includes, but is not limited to, a person who, regardless of title, has ultimate responsibility for—

(A) Implementing the decisions of the governing body of a supported organization;

(B) Supervising the management, administration, or operation of the supported organization; or

(C) Managing the finances of the supported organization.

(3) Responsiveness test—(i) General rule. A supporting organization meets the responsiveness test if it is responsive to the needs or demands of each of its supported organizations. Except as provided in paragraph (i)(3)(v) of this section, in order to meet this test, a supporting organization must satisfy the requirements of paragraphs (i)(3)(ii) and (i)(3)(iii) of this section with respect to each of its supported organizations.

(ii) Relationship of officers, directors, or trustees. A supporting organization satisfies the requirements of this paragraph (i)(3)(ii) with respect to a supported organization only if—

(A) One or more officers, directors, or trustees of the supporting organization are elected or appointed by the officers, directors, trustees, or membership of the supported organization;

(B) One or more members of the governing body of the supported organization are also officers, directors, or trustees of, or hold other important offices in, the supporting organization; or

(C) The officers, directors, or trustees of the supporting organization maintain a close and continuous working relationship with the officers, directors, or trustees of the supported organization.

(iii) Significant voice. A supporting organization satisfies the requirements of this paragraph (i)(3)(iii) only if, by reason of paragraphs (i)(3)(ii)(A), (i)(3)(ii)(B), or (i)(3)(ii)(C) of this section, the officers, directors, or trustees of the supported organization have a significant voice in the investment policies of the supporting organization, the timing of grants, the manner of making grants, and the selection of grant recipients by such supporting organization, and in otherwise directing the use of the income or assets of the supporting organization.

(iv) Examples. The provisions of this paragraph (i)(3) may be illustrated by the following examples:

(A) **Example 1.** X, an organization described in section 501(c)(3), is a trust created under the last will and testament of Decedent. The trustee of X (Trustee) is a bank. Under the trust instrument, X supports M, a private university described in section 509(a)(1). The trust instrument provides that Trustee has discretion regarding the timing and amount of distributions consistent with the Trustee's fiduciary duties. Representatives of Trustee and an officer of M have quarterly face-to-face or telephonic meetings during which they discuss M's projected needs and ways in which M would like X to use its income and invest its assets. Additionally, Trustee communicates regularly with that officer of M regarding X's investments and plans for distributions from X. Trustee provides the officer of M with quarterly investment statements, the information required under paragraph (i)(2) of this section, and an annual accounting statement. Based on these facts, X meets the responsiveness test of this paragraph (i)(3) with respect to M.

(B) **Example 2.** Y is an organization described in section 501(c)(3) and is a trust under State law. The trustee of Y (Trustee) is a bank. Y supports charities P, Q, and R, each an organization described in section 509(a)(1). Y makes annual cash payments to P, Q, and R. Once a year, Trustee sends to P, Q, and R the cash payment, the information required under paragraph (i)(2) of this section, and an accounting statement. Trustee has no other communication with P, Q, or R. Y does not meet the responsiveness test of this paragraph (i)(3).

(C) **Example 3.** Z is described in section 501(c)(3). Z's organizational documents provide that it supports ten different organizations, each of which is described in section 509(a)(1). One of the directors of S (one of the supported organizations) is a voting member of Z's board of directors and participates in Z's regular board meetings. Officers of Z hold regularly scheduled face-to-face or telephonic meetings during the year, to which officers of all the supported organizations are invited. Z's meetings with the supported organizations may be held jointly or separately. Prior to the meetings, Z makes available to the supported organizations (including by email) up-to-date information about its activities, including its assets and liabilities, receipts and distributions, and investment policies and returns. In the meetings, officers of each of the supported organizations have an opportunity to ask questions and discuss with officers of Z the projected needs of their organizations, as well as Z's investment and grant making policies and practices. In addition to holding these meetings with the supported organizations, Z provides the contact information of one of its officers to each of the supported organizations and encourages them to contact that officer if they have questions, or if they wish to schedule additional meetings to discuss the projected needs of their organization and how Z should distribute its income and invest its assets. Z provides the information required under paragraph (i)(2) of this section and a copy of its annual audited financial statements to the principal officers of the supported organizations. Z meets the relationship requirement of paragraph (i)(3)(ii)(B) or (C) of this section with respect to each of its supported organizations. Based on these facts, Z also satisfies the significant voice requirement of paragraph (i)(3)(iii) of this section, and therefore meets the responsiveness test of this paragraph (i)(3) with respect to each of its ten supported organizations.

* * *

(4) Integral part test—functionally integrated Type III supporting organization—(i) General rule. A supporting organization meets the integral part test and will be considered functionally integrated within the meaning of section 4943(f)(5)(B), if it—

(A) Engages in activities substantially all of which directly further the exempt purposes of one or more supported organizations and otherwise meets the requirements described in paragraph (i)(4)(ii) of this section;

(B) Is the parent of each of its supported organizations, as described in paragraph (i)(4)(iii) of this section; or

(C) Supports a governmental supported organization and otherwise meets the requirements of paragraph (i)(4)(iv) of this section.

(ii) Substantially all activities directly further exempt purposes—(A) In general. A supporting organization meets the requirements of this paragraph (i)(4)(ii) if it engages in activities substantially all of which—

(1) Directly further the exempt purposes of one or more supported organizations by performing the functions of, or carrying out the purposes of, such supported organization(s); and

(2) But for the involvement of the supporting organization, would normally be engaged in by such supported organization(s).

(B) Meaning of substantially all. For purposes of paragraph (i)(4)(ii)(A) of this section, in determining whether substantially all of a supporting organization's activities directly further the exempt purposes of one or more supported organization(s), all pertinent facts and circumstances will be taken into consideration.

(C) Meaning of directly further. Activities "directly further" the exempt purposes of one or more supported organizations for purposes of this paragraph (i)(4) only if they are conducted by the supporting organization itself, rather than by a supported organization. Holding title to and managing exempt-use assets described in paragraph (i)(8)(ii) of this section are activities that directly further the exempt purposes of the supported organization within the meaning of this paragraph (i)(4). Conversely, except as provided in paragraph (i)(4)(ii)(D) of this section, fundraising, making grants (whether to the supported organization or to third parties), and investing and managing non-exempt-use assets are not activities that directly further the exempt purposes of the supported organization within the meaning of this paragraph (i)(4).

(D) Payments to individual beneficiaries. The making or awarding of grants, scholarships, or other payments to individual beneficiaries who are members of the charitable class benefited by a supported organization will be treated as an activity that directly furthers the exempt purposes of that supported organization for purposes of this paragraph (i)(4) only if—

(1) The individual beneficiaries are selected on an objective and nondiscriminatory basis (as described in § 53.4945–4(b));

(2) The officers, directors, or trustees of the supported organization have a significant voice in the timing of the payments, the manner of making them, and the selection of recipients; and

(3) The making or awarding of such payments is part of an active program of the supporting organization that directly furthers the exempt purposes of the supported organization and in which the supporting organization maintains significant involvement, as defined in § 53.4942(b)–1(b)(2)(ii) (except that "supporting organization" shall be substituted for "foundation").

(iii) Parent of supported organization(s)—(A) In general. For purposes of paragraph (i)(4)(i)(B) of this section, in order for a supporting organization to qualify as the parent of each of its supported organizations—

(1) The supporting organization and its supported organizations must be part of an integrated system (such as, for example, a hospital system);

(2) The supporting organization must direct the overall policies, programs, and activities of the supported organizations (such as, for example, coordinating the activities of the supported organizations and engaging in overall planning, policy development, budgeting, and resource allocation); and

(3) The supporting organization's governing body, members of the governing body, or officers (acting in their official capacities) must appoint or elect, directly or indirectly, a majority of the officers, directors, or trustees of each supported organization and have the power to remove and replace such directors, officers, or trustees, or otherwise have an ongoing power to appoint or elect such directors, officers or trustees with reasonable frequency.

(B) Subsidiary organizations. A supporting organization may meet the requirements of paragraph (i)(4)(iii)(A)(3) of this section with respect to a second-tier (or lower) subsidiary provided that the supporting organization, by control of its first-tier subsidiary, has the power to appoint or elect (as described in paragraph (i)(4)(iii)(A)(3) of this section) a majority of the officers, directors, or trustees of the lower-tier subsidiary. For example, if the board of directors of supporting organization A elects a majority of the directors of supported organization B, and the board of directors of B, in turn elect, by a simple majority vote, a majority of the directors of supported organization C, the directors of supporting organization A will be treated as electing a majority of the directors of both supported organization B and supported organization C.

(iv) Supporting a governmental supported organization—(A) In general. A supporting organization satisfies the requirements of this paragraph (i)(4)(iv) if—

(1) The supporting organization only supports one or more governmental supported organizations;

(2) In any case in which the supporting organization supports more than one governmental supported organization, all of the governmental supported organizations either—

(i) Operate within the same city, county, or metropolitan area; or

(ii) Work in close coordination or collaboration with one another to conduct a service, program, or activity that the supporting organization supports; and

(3) A substantial part of the supporting organization's total activities are activities that directly further, as defined by paragraph (i)(4)(ii)(C) of this section, the exempt purposes of at least one governmental supported organization.

(B) Governmental supported organization defined. For purposes of paragraph (i)(4)(iv)(A) of this section, the term governmental supported organization means a supported organization that is:

(1) A governmental unit described in section 170(c)(1), including all of its agencies, departments, and divisions (all of which will be treated as one governmental supported organization for purposes of this paragraph (i)(4)(iv)); or

(2) An organization described in section 170(c)(2) and (b)(1)(A) (other than in clauses (vii) and (viii)) that is an instrumentality of one or more governmental units described in section 170(c)(1).

(C) Close coordination or collaboration. To satisfy the close coordination or collaboration requirement of paragraph (i)(4)(iv)(A)(2) of this section, the supporting organization must maintain on file a letter from each of the governmental supported organizations (or a joint letter from all of them) describing their coordination or collaboration efforts with respect to the particular service, program, or activity.

(D) Substantial part. For purposes of paragraph (i)(4)(iv)(A)(3) of this section, in determining whether a substantial part of a supporting organization's activities directly further the exempt purposes of one or more governmental supported organization(s), all pertinent facts and circumstances will be taken into consideration.

(E) Exception for organizations supporting a governmental supported organization on or before February 19, 2016. A Type III supporting organization in existence on or before February 19, 2016, will be treated as meeting the requirements of this paragraph (i)(4)(iv) if it met and continues to meet the following requirements:

(1) It supports one or more governmental supported organizations described in paragraph (i)(4)(iv)(B) of this section and does not support more than one supported organization that is not a governmental supported organization;

(2) Each of the supported organizations is designated by the supporting organization as provided in paragraph (d)(4) of this section on or before February 19, 2016; and

(3) A substantial part (as defined in paragraph (i)(4)(iv)(D) of this section) of the supporting organization's total activities are activities that directly further (as defined by paragraph (i)(4)(ii)(C) of this section) the exempt purposes of its governmental supported organization(s).

* * *

(v) Examples. The provisions of this paragraph (i)(4) may be illustrated by the following examples:

(A) **Example 1.** N, an organization described in section 501(c)(3), is the parent organization of a healthcare system consisting of two hospitals (Q and R) and an outpatient clinic (S), each of which is described in section 509(a)(1), and a taxable subsidiary (T). N is the sole member of each of Q, R, and S. Under the charter and bylaws of each of Q, R, and S, N appoints all members of the board of directors of each corporation. N engages in the overall coordination and supervision of the health-care system's exempt subsidiary corporations Q, R, and S in approval of their budgets, strategic planning, marketing, resource allocation, securing tax-exempt bond financing, and community education. N also manages and invests assets that serve as endowments of Q, R, and S. Based on these facts, N qualifies as a functionally integrated Type III supporting organization under paragraph (i)(4)(i)(B) of this section.

(B) **Example 2.** V, an organization described in section 501(c)(3), is organized and operated as a supporting organization to L, a church described in section 509(a)(1). V meets the responsiveness test described in paragraph (i)(3) of this section with respect to L. L transferred to V title to the buildings in which L conducts religious services, Bible study, and community enrichment programs. Substantially all of V's activities consist of holding and maintaining these buildings, which L continues to use, free of charge, to further its exempt purposes. But for the activities of V, L would hold and maintain the buildings. Based on these facts, V satisfies the requirements of paragraph (i)(4)(ii) of this section.

(C) **Example 3.** O is a local nonprofit food pantry described in section 501(c)(3). O collects donated food from local growers, grocery stores, and individuals and distributes this food free of charge to poor and needy people in O's community. O is organized and operated as a supporting organization to eight churches of a particular denomination located in O's community, each of which is described in section 509(a)(1). Control of O is vested in a five-member Board of Directors, which includes an official from one of the churches as well as four lay members of the churches' congregations. The officers of O maintain a close and continuing working relationship with each of the eight churches and as a result of such relationship, each of the eight churches has a significant voice in directing the use of the income and assets of O. As a result, O is responsive to its supported organizations. All of O's activities directly further the exempt purposes of the eight supported organizations to which it is responsive. Additionally, but for the activities of O, the churches would normally operate food pantries themselves. Based on these facts, O satisfies the requirements of paragraph (i)(4)(ii) of this section.

(D) **Example 4.** M, an organization described in section 501(c)(3), was created by B, an individual, to provide scholarships for students of U, a private secondary school and an organization described in section 509(a)(1). U establishes the scholarship criteria, publicizes the scholarship program, solicits and reviews applications, and selects the scholarship recipients. M invests its assets and disburses the funds for scholarships to the recipients selected by U. M does not provide the scholarships as part of an active program in which it maintains significant involvement, as defined in § 53.4942(b)–1(b)(2)(ii). Based on these facts, M does not satisfy the requirements of paragraph (i)(4)(ii) of this section.

(E) **Example 5.** J, an organization described in section 501(c)(3), is organized as a supporting organization to community foundation G, an organization described in section 509(a)(1). J meets the responsiveness test described in paragraph (i)(3) of this section with respect to G. In addition to maintaining field-of-interest funds, sponsoring donor advised funds, and conducting general grant-making activities, G also engages in activities to beautify and maintain local parks. Substantially all of J's activities consist of maintaining all of the local parks in the area of community foundation G by performing activities such as establishing and maintaining trails, planting trees, and removing trash. But for the activities of J, G would normally engage in these efforts to beautify and maintain the local parks. Based on these facts, J satisfies the requirements of paragraph (i)(4)(ii) of this section.

(F) **Example 6.** X, an organization described in section 501(c)(3), is organized and operated as a supporting organization to two organizations, City and Park. X meets the responsiveness test described in paragraph (i)(3) of this section with respect to both City and Park. City and Park are both governmental units described in section 170(c)(1). Park maintains a state park located within the same county as City. X does not support any other organizations. X supports Park by operating an information center for visitors to Park. The information center provides educational material and informational sessions to visitors to Park. X's activities related to operating the Park information center constitute a substantial part of X's activities. X also makes grants directly to City to fund City's other programs. X's grant making activities constitute a substantial part of X's activities. X meets the requirements of paragraph (i)(4)(iv)(A)(1) of this section because X only supports City and Park, both of which are governmental supported organizations described in paragraph (i)(4)(iv)(B) of this section. X meets the requirements of paragraph (i)(4)(iv)(A)(2) of this section because City and Park operate within the same county in accordance with paragraph (i)(4)(iv)(A)(2)(i) of this section. Finally, X meets the requirements of paragraph (i)(4)(iv)(A)(3) of this section because a substantial part of X's activities directly further (within the meaning of paragraph (i)(4)(ii)(C) of this section) Park's exempt purposes, even though X's grants to City are also a substantial part of X's activities. Based on these facts, X qualifies as functionally integrated under paragraph (i)(4)(iv) of this section.

(5) Integral part test—non-functionally integrated Type III supporting organization—(i) General rule. A supporting organization meets the integral part test and will be considered non-functionally integrated if it satisfies either—

(A) The distribution requirement of paragraph (i)(5)(ii) of this section and the attentiveness requirement of paragraph (i)(5)(iii) of this section; or

(B) The pre-November 20, 1970 trust requirements of paragraph (i)(9) of this section.

(ii) Distribution requirement—(A) Annual distribution. With respect to each taxable year, a supporting organization must make distributions described in paragraph (i)(6) of this section in a total amount equaling or exceeding the supporting organization's distributable amount for the taxable year, as defined in paragraph (i)(5)(ii)(B) of this section, on or before the last day of the taxable year.

(B) Distributable amount. Except as provided in paragraphs (i)(5)(ii)(D) and (E) of this section, the distributable amount for a taxable year is an amount equal to the greater of 85 percent of the supporting organization's adjusted net income (as determined by applying the principles of section 4942(f) and § 53.4942(a)–2(d) of this chapter) for the taxable year immediately preceding the taxable year of the required distribution (immediately preceding taxable year) or its minimum asset amount (as defined in paragraph (i)(5)(ii)(C) of this section) for the immediately preceding taxable year.

(C) Minimum asset amount. For purposes of this paragraph (i)(5), a supporting organization's minimum asset amount for the immediately preceding taxable year is 3.5 percent of the excess of the aggregate fair market value of all of the supporting organization's non-exempt-use assets (determined under paragraph (i)(8) of this section) in that immediately preceding taxable year over the acquisition indebtedness with respect to such non-exempt-use assets (determined under section 514(c)(1) without regard to the taxable year in which the indebtedness was incurred), increased by—

(1) Amounts received or accrued during the immediately preceding taxable year as repayments of amounts which were taken into account by the organization to meet the distribution requirement imposed in this paragraph (i)(5)(ii) for any taxable year;

(2) Amounts received or accrued during the immediately preceding taxable year from the sale or other disposition of property to the extent that the acquisition of such property was taken into account by the organization to meet the distribution requirement imposed in this paragraph (i)(5)(ii) for any taxable year; and

(3) Any amount set aside under paragraph (i)(6)(v) of this section to the extent it is determined during the immediately preceding taxable year that such amount is not necessary for the purposes for which it was set aside and such amount was taken into account by the organization to meet the distribution requirement imposed in this paragraph (i)(5)(ii) for any taxable year.

(D) First taxable year. The distributable amount for the first taxable year an organization is treated as a non-functionally integrated Type III supporting organization is zero. Notwithstanding the foregoing, for purposes of determining whether an excess amount is created under paragraph (i)(7)(ii) of this section, the distributable amount for the first taxable year an organization is treated as a non-functionally integrated Type III supporting organization is the distributable amount that would apply under paragraph (i)(5)(ii)(B) of this section in the absence of this paragraph (i)(5)(ii)(D).

(E) Emergency temporary reduction. The Secretary may provide by publication in the Internal Revenue Bulletin (see § 601.601(d)(2)(ii)(b) of this chapter) for a temporary reduction in the distributable amount in the case of a disaster or emergency.

(F) Reasonable cause exception. A non-functionally integrated Type III supporting organization that fails to meet the distribution requirement of this paragraph (i)(5)(ii) will not be classified as a private foundation for the taxable year in which it fails to meet the distribution requirement if the organization establishes to the satisfaction of the Secretary that—

(1) The failure was due solely to unforeseen events or circumstances that are beyond the organization's control, a clerical error, or an incorrect valuation of assets;

(2) The failure was due to reasonable cause and not to willful neglect; and

(3) The distribution requirement is met within 180 days after the organization is first able to distribute its distributable amount notwithstanding the unforeseen events or circumstances, or 180 days after the date the incorrect valuation or clerical error was or should have been discovered; however, no amounts paid to meet a distribution requirement for a prior taxable year under this paragraph (i)(5)(ii)(F)(3) may be counted toward the distribution requirement for the taxable year in which such amounts are paid.

(iii) Attentiveness requirement—(A) General rule. With respect to each taxable year, a non-functionally integrated Type III supporting organization must distribute one-third or more of its distributable amount to one or more supported organizations that are attentive to the operations of the supporting organization (within the meaning of paragraph (i)(5)(iii)(B) of this section).

(B) Attentiveness. A supported organization is attentive to the operations of the supporting organization during a taxable year if, in the taxable year, at least one of the following requirements is satisfied:

(1) The supporting organization distributes to the supported organization amounts equaling or exceeding 10 percent of the supported organization's total support (or, in the case of a particular department or school of a university, hospital, or church, the total support of the department or school) received

during the supported organization's last taxable year ending before the beginning of the supporting organization's taxable year.

(2) The amount of support received from the supporting organization is necessary to avoid the interruption of the carrying on of a particular function or activity of the supported organization. The support is necessary if the supporting organization or the supported organization earmarks the support for a particular program or activity of the supported organization, even if such program or activity is not the supported organization's primary program or activity, as long as such program or activity is a substantial one.

(3) Based on the consideration of all pertinent factors, including the number of supported organizations, the length and nature of the relationship between the supported organization and supporting organization, and the purpose to which the funds are put, the amount of support received from the supporting organization is a sufficient part of a supported organization's total support (or, in the case of a particular department or school of a university, hospital, or church, the total support of the department or school) to ensure attentiveness. Normally the attentiveness of a supported organization is influenced by the amounts received from the supporting organization. Thus, the more substantial the amount involved in terms of a percentage of the supported organization's total support, the greater the likelihood that the required degree of attentiveness will be present. However, in determining whether the amount received from the supporting organization is sufficient to ensure the attentiveness of the supported organization to the operations of the supporting organization (including attentiveness to the nature and yield of the supporting organization's investments), evidence of actual attentiveness by the supported organization is of almost equal importance. A supported organization is not considered to be attentive solely because it has enforceable rights against the supporting organization under state law.

(C) Distribution to donor advised fund disregarded. Notwithstanding paragraph (i)(5)(iii)(B) of this section, in determining whether a supported organization will be considered attentive to the operations of a supporting organization, any amount received from the supporting organization that is held by the supported organization in a donor advised fund described in section 4966(d)(2) will be disregarded.

(D) Examples. This paragraph (i)(5)(iii) is illustrated by the following examples:

(1) **Example 1.** K, an organization described in section 501(c)(3), annually pays an aggregate amount equaling or exceeding its distributable amount described in § 1.509(a)–4T(i)(5)(ii)(B) to L, a museum described in section 509(a)(2). K meets the responsiveness test described in paragraph (i)(3) of this section with respect to L. In recent years, L has earmarked the income received from K to underwrite the cost of carrying on a chamber music series consisting of 12 performances a year that are performed for the general public free of charge at its premises. The chamber music series is not L's primary activity but it is a substantial activity. L could not continue the performances without K's support. Based on these facts, K meets the requirements of paragraph (i)(5)(iii)(B)(2) of this section.

(2) **Example 2.** M, an organization described in section 501(c)(3), annually pays an aggregate amount equaling or exceeding its distributable amount described in § 1.509(a)–4T(i)(5)(ii)(B) to the Law School of N University, an organization described in section 509(a)(1). M meets the responsiveness test described in paragraph (i)(3) of this section with respect to N. M has earmarked the income paid over to N's Law School to endow a chair in International Law. Without M's continued support, N could not continue to maintain this chair. The chair is not N's primary activity but it is a substantial activity. Based on these facts, M

meets the requirements of paragraph (i)(5)(iii)(B)(2) of this section.

(3) **Example 3.** R is a charitable trust created under the will of B, who died in 1969. R's purpose is to hold assets as an endowment for S (a hospital), T (a university), and U (a national medical research organization), all organizations described in section 509(a)(1) and specifically named in the trust instrument, and to distribute all of the income each year in equal shares among the three named beneficiaries. Each year, R pays to S, T, and U an aggregate amount equaling or exceeding its distributable amount described in § 1.509(a)–4T(i)(5)(ii)(B). Such payments equal less than one percent of the total support that each supported organization received in its most recently completed taxable year. Based on these facts, R does not meet the requirements of paragraph (i)(5)(iii)(B)(1) of this section. However, because B died prior to November 20, 1970, R could meet the requirements of paragraph (i)(5)(i)(B) of this section upon meeting all of the requirements of paragraph (i)(9) of this section.

(4) **Example 4.** O is an organization described in section 501(c)(3). O is organized to support five private universities, V, W, X, Y, and Z, each of which is described in section 509(a)(1). O meets the responsiveness test described in paragraph (i)(3) of this section with respect to each of its supported organizations. Each year, O distributes an aggregate amount that equals its distributable amount described in paragraph (i)(5)(ii)(B) of this section and distributes an equal amount to each of the five universities. O distributes annually to each of V and W an amount that equals more than 10 percent of each university's total annual support received in its most recently completed taxable year. Based on these facts, O meets the requirements of paragraph (i)(5)(iii) of this section because it distributes two-fifths (more than the required one-third) of its distributable amount to supported organizations that are attentive to O.

(6) Distributions that count toward distribution requirement. For purposes of this paragraph (i)(6), the amount of a distribution made to a supported organization is the amount of cash distributed or the fair-market value of the property distributed as of the date the distribution is made. The amount of a distribution will be determined solely on the cash receipts and disbursements method of accounting described in section 446(c)(1). Distributions by the supporting organization that count toward the distribution requirement imposed in paragraph (i)(5)(ii) of this section are limited to—

(i) Any amount paid to a supported organization to accomplish the supported organization's exempt purposes;

(ii) Any amount paid by the supporting organization to perform an activity that satisfies the requirements of paragraph (i)(4)(ii) of this section, but only to the extent such amount exceeds any income derived by the supporting organization from the activity;

(iii) Any reasonable and necessary—

(A) Administrative expenses paid to accomplish the exempt purposes of the supported organization, which do not include expenses incurred in the production of investment income or expenses incurred in the conduct of fundraising activities (except solicitation expenses described in paragraph (i)(6)(iii)(B) of this section); and

(B) Expenses incurred to solicit contributions that are received directly by a supported organization (rather than by the supporting organization), but only to the extent the amount of the reasonable and necessary expenses the supporting organization incurs for each solicitation does not exceed the amount of contributions that are actually received by the supported organization directly from donors as a result of each such solicitation, as substantiated in a written report by the supported organization to the supporting organization that is postmarked or electronically transmitted by the due date of the supporting organization's Form 990 (or successor form) for the year of the solicitation(s) (without regard to extensions);

(iv) Any amount paid to acquire an exempt-use asset described in paragraph (i)(8)(ii) of this section; and

(v) Any amount set aside for a specific project that accomplishes the exempt purposes of a supported organization to which the supporting organization is responsive, with such set aside counting toward the distribution requirement for the taxable year in which the amount is set aside but not in the year in which it is actually paid, if at the time of the set-aside, the supporting organization—

(A) Obtains a written statement from each supported organization whose exempt purposes the specific project accomplishes, signed under penalty of perjury by one of the supported organization's principal officers, as defined in paragraph (i)(2)(iv) of this section, stating that the supported organization approves the project as one that accomplishes one or more of the supported organization's exempt purposes and also approves the supporting organization's determination that the project is one that can be better accomplished by such a set-aside than by the immediate payment of funds;

(B) Establishes to the satisfaction of the Commissioner, by meeting the approval and information requirements described in § 53.4942(a)–3(b)(7)(i) of this chapter and by providing the written statement described in paragraph (i)(6)(v)(A) of this section, that the amount set aside will be paid for the specific project within 60 months after it is set aside and that the project is one that can better be accomplished by the set-aside than by the immediate payment of funds; and

(C) Evidences the set-aside by the entry of a dollar amount on the books and records of the supporting organization as a pledge or obligation to be paid at a future date or dates within 60 months of the set aside.

(7) Carryover of excess amounts—(i) In general. If with respect to any taxable year, an excess amount, as defined in paragraph (i)(7)(ii) of this section, is created, such excess amount may be used to reduce the distributable amount in any of the five taxable years immediately following the taxable year in which the excess amount is created. An excess amount created in a taxable year can only be carried over for five taxable years.

(ii) Excess amount. An excess amount is created for any taxable year beginning after December 28, 2012, if the total distributions made in that taxable year that count toward the distribution requirement exceed the supporting organization's distributable amount for the taxable year, as determined under § 1.509(a)–4T(i)(5)(ii)(B). With respect to any taxable year to which an excess amount is carried over, in determining whether an excess amount is created in that taxable year, the distributable amount is first reduced by any excess amounts carried over (with the oldest excess amounts applied first) and then by any distributions made in that taxable year.

(8) Valuation of non-exempt-use assets. For purposes of determining its distributable amount for a taxable year, a supporting organization determines its minimum asset amount, as defined in paragraph (i)(5)(ii)(C) of this section, by determining the aggregate fair market value of all of its non-exempt-use assets in the immediately preceding taxable year. For these purposes, the determination of the aggregate fair market value of all non-exempt-use assets shall be made using the valuation methods described in § 53.4942(a)–2(c) of this chapter. The aggregate fair market value of the supporting organization's non-exempt-use assets shall not be reduced by any amount that is set aside under paragraph (i)(6)(v) of this section. For these purposes, the non-exempt use assets of the supporting organization are all assets of the supporting organization other than—

(i) Assets described in § 53.4942(a)–2(c)(2)(i) through (iv) of this chapter (with the term "supporting organization" being substituted for "foundation" or "private foundation" and the date "August 17, 2006" being substituted for "December 31, 1969"); and

(ii) Exempt-use assets, which are assets that are used (or held for use) directly in carrying out the exempt purposes of the supporting organization's supported organization(s) (determined by applying the principles described in § 53.4942(a)–2(c)(3) of this chapter) by either—

(A) The supporting organization; or

(B) One or more supported organizations, but only if the supporting organization makes the asset available to the supported organization(s) at no cost (or nominal rent) to the supported organization(s).

* * *

(10) Foreign supported organizations. A supporting organization is not operated in connection with one or more supported organizations if it supports any supported organization organized outside of the United States.

* * *

(j) Control by disqualified persons—(1) In general. Under the provisions of section 509(a)(3)(C) a supporting organization may not be controlled directly or indirectly by one or more disqualified persons (as defined in section 4946) other than foundation managers and other than one or more publicly supported organizations. If a person who is a disqualified person with respect to a supporting organization, such as a substantial contributor to the supporting organization, is appointed or designated as a foundation manager of the supporting organization by a publicly supported beneficiary organization to serve as the representative of such publicly supported organization, then for purposes of this paragraph such person will be regarded as a disqualified person, rather than as a representative of the publicly supported organization. An organization will be considered controlled, for purposes of section 509(a)(3)(C), if the disqualified persons, by aggregating their votes or positions of authority, may require such organization to perform any act which significantly affects its operation or may prevent such organization from performing such act. This includes, but is not limited to, the right of any substantial contributor or his spouse to designate annually the recipients, from among the publicly supported organizations of the income attributable to his contribution to the supporting organization. Except as provided in subparagraph (2) of this paragraph, a supporting organization will be considered to be controlled directly or indirectly by one or more disqualified persons if the voting power of such persons is 50 percent or more of the total voting power of the organization's governing body or if one or more of such persons have the right to exercise veto power over the actions of the organization. Thus, if the governing body of a foundation is composed of five trustees, none of whom has a veto power over the actions of the foundation, and no more than two trustees are at any time disqualified persons, such foundation will not be considered to be controlled directly or indirectly by one or more disqualified persons by reason of this fact alone. However, all pertinent facts and circumstances including the nature, diversity, and income yield of an organization's holdings, the length of time particular stocks, securities, or other assets are retained, and its manner of exercising its voting rights with respect to stocks in which members of its governing body also have some interest, will be taken into consideration in determining whether a disqualified person does in fact indirectly control an organization.

(2) Proof of independent control. Notwithstanding subparagraph (1) of this paragraph, an organization shall be permitted to establish to the satisfaction of the Commissioner that disqualified persons do not directly or indirectly control it. For example, in the case of a religious organization operated in connection with a church, the fact that the majority of the organization's governing body is composed of lay persons who are substantial contributors to the organization will not disqualify the organization under section 509(a)(3)(C) if a representative of the church, such as a bishop or other official, has control over the policies and decisions of the organization.

(k) Organizations operated in conjunction with certain section 501(c)(4), (5), or (6) organizations. (1) For purposes of section 509(a)(3), an organization which is operated in conjunction with an organization described in section 501(c)(4), (5), or (6) (such as a social welfare organization, labor or agricultural organization, business league, or real estate board) shall, if it otherwise meets the requirements of section 509(a)(3), be considered an organization described in section 509(a)(3) if such section 501(c)(4), (5), or (6) organization would be described in section 509(a)(2) if it were an organization described in section 501(c)(3). The section 501(c)(4), (5), or (6) organization, which the supporting organization is operating in conjunction with, must therefore meet the one-third tests of a publicly supported organization set forth in section 509(a)(2).

(2) This paragraph (k) may be illustrated by the following example:

(i) Example. X medical association, described in section 501(c)(6), is supported by membership dues and funds resulting from the performance of its exempt activities. This support, which is entirely from permitted sources, constitutes more than one-third of X's support. X does not normally receive more than one-third of its support from items described in section 509(a)(2)(B). X organized and operated an endowment fund for the sole purpose of furthering medical education. The fund is an organization described in section 501(c)(3). Since more than one-third of X's support is derived from membership dues and from funds resulting from the performance of exempt purposes (all of which are from permitted sources) and not more than one-third of its support is from items described in section 509(a)(2)(B), it would be a publicly supported organization described in section 509(a)(2) if it were described in section 501(c)(3) rather than section 501(c)(6). Accordingly, if the fund otherwise meets the requirements of section 509(a)(3) with respect to X, it will be considered an organization described in section 509(a)(3).

(ii) [Reserved]

§ 1.509(a)–5. Special rules of attribution.

(a) Retained character of gross investment income. (1) For purposes of determining whether an organization meets the not-more-than-one-third support test set forth in section 509(a)(2)(B), amounts received by such organization from:

(i) An organization which seeks to be described in section 509(a)(3) by reason of its support of such organization; or

(ii) A charitable trust, corporation, fund, or association described in section 501(c)(3) (including a charitable trust described in section 4947(a)(1)) or a split interest trust described in section 4947(a)(2), which is required by its governing instrument or otherwise to distribute, or which normally does distribute, at least 25 percent of its adjusted net income (within the meaning of section 4942(f)) to such organization, and such distribution normally comprises at least 5 percent of such distributee organization's adjusted net income,

will retain their character as gross investment income (rather than gifts or contributions) to the extent that such amounts are characterized as gross investment income in the possession of the distributing organization described in subdivision (i) or (ii) of this subparagraph or, if the distributing organization is a split interest trust described in section 4947(a)(2), to the extent that such amounts would be characterized as gross investment income attributable to transfers in trust after May 26, 1969, if such trust were a private foundation. For purposes of this section, all income which is characterized as gross investment income in the possession of the distributing organization shall be deemed to be distributed first by such organization and shall retain its character as such in the possession of the recipient of amounts described in this paragraph. If an organization described in subdivision (i) or (ii) of this subparagraph makes distributions to more than one organization, the amount of gross investment income deemed distributed shall be prorated among the distributees.

(2) For purposes of subparagraph (1) of this paragraph, amounts paid by an organization to provide goods, services, or facilities for the direct benefit of an organization seeking section 509(a)(2) status (rather than for the direct benefit of the general public) shall be treated in the same manner as amounts received by the latter organization. Such amounts will be treated as gross investment income to the extent that such amounts are characterized as gross investment income in the possession of the organization spending such amounts. For example, X is an organization described in subparagraph (1)(i) of this paragraph. It uses part of its funds to provide Y, an organization seeking section 509(a)(2) status, with certain services which Y would otherwise be required to purchase on its own. To the extent that the funds used by X to provide such services for Y are characterized as gross investment income in the possession of X, such funds will be treated as gross investment income received by Y.

(3) An organization seeking section 509(a)(2) status shall file a separate statement with its return required by section 6033, setting forth all amounts received from organizations described in paragraph (a)(1) (i) or (ii) of this section.

(b) Relationships created for avoidance purposes. (1) If a relationship between an organization seeking section 509(a) (3) status and an organization seeking section 509(a)(2) status:

(i) Is established or availed of after October 9, 1969, and

(ii) One of the purposes of establishing or utilizing such relationship is to avoid classification as a private foundation with respect to either organization, the character and amount of support received by the section 509(a)(3) organization will be attributed to the section 509(a)(2) organization for purposes of determining whether the latter meets the one-third support test and the not-more-than-one-third support test under section 509(a)(2). If a relationship described in this subparagraph is established or utilized by an organization seeking section 509(a)(3) status and two or more organizations seeking section 509(a)(2) status, the amount of support received by the former organization will be prorated among the latter organizations and the character of each class of support (as defined in section 509(d)) will be attributed pro rata to each such organization. The provisions of this paragraph and of paragraph (a) of this section are not mutually exclusive.

(2) In determining whether a relationship between one or more organizations seeking section 509(a)(2) status (hereinafter referred to as "beneficiary organizations") and an organization seeking section 509(a)(3) status (hereinafter referred to as the "supporting organization") has been established or availed of to avoid classification as a private foundation (within the meaning of subparagraph (1) of this paragraph), all pertinent facts and circumstances, including the following, shall be taken into account as evidence that a relationship was not established or availed of to avoid classification as a private foundation:

(i) The supporting organization is operated to support or benefit several specified beneficiary organizations.

(ii) The beneficiary organization has a substantial number of dues-paying members (in relation to the public it serves and the nature of its activities) and such members have an effective voice in the management of both the supporting and beneficiary organizations.

(iii) The beneficiary organization is composed of several membership organizations, each of which has a substantial number of members (in relation to the public it serves and the nature of its activities), and such membership organizations have an effective voice in the management of the supporting and beneficiary organizations.

(iv) The beneficiary organization receives a substantial amount of support from the general public, public charities, or governmental grants.

(v) The supporting organization uses its funds to carry on a meaningful program of activities to support or benefit the beneficiary organization and such use would, if such supporting organization were a private foundation, be sufficient to avoid the imposition of any tax upon such organization under section 4942.

(vi) The supporting organization is not able to exercise substantial control or influence over the beneficiary organization by reason of the former's receiving support or holding assets which are disproportionately large in comparison with the support received or the assets held by the latter.

(vii) Different persons manage the operations of the beneficiary and supporting organizations and each organization performs a different function.

(3) The provisions of this paragraph may be illustrated by the following examples:

Example 1. M, an organization described in section 509(a)(2), is a council composed of 10 learned societies. Each member society has a large membership of scholars interested in a particular academic area. In 1970 M established N, an organization seeking section 509(a)(3) status, for the purpose of carrying on research and study projects of interest to the member societies. The principal source of funds for N's activities is from foundation and government grants and contracts. The principal source of funds for M's activities after the creation of N is membership dues. M continued to maintain a wide variety of activities for its members, such as publishing periodicals and carrying on seminars and conferences. N is subject to complete control by the governing body of M. Under these circumstances, the relationship between these organizations is not one which is described in subparagraph (1) of this paragraph.

Example 2. Q is a local medical research organization described in section 509(a)(2). Its fixed assets are negligible and it carries on research activities on a limited scale. It also makes a limited number of grants to scientists and doctors who are engaged in medical research of interest to Q. It receives support through small government grants and a few research contracts from private foundations. R is an organization described in section 501(c)(3). As of January 1, 1970, R was classified as a private foundation under section 509. It has a substantial endowment which it uses to make grants to various charitable and scientific organizations described in section 501(c)(3). During 1970, R agrees to subsidize the research activities of Q. R amends its governing instrument to provide specifically that all of R's support will be used for research activities which are approved and supervised by Q. R also amends its bylaws to permit a minority of Q's board of directors to be members of R's governing body. R then gives timely notification under section 507(b)(1)(B)(ii) that R is terminating its private foundation status by meeting the requirements of section 509(a)(3) by the end of the 12-month period described in section 507(b)(1)(B)(i). For purposes of determining whether R has met the requirements of section 509(a)(3) by the end of the 12-month period, as well as determining Q's status under section 509(a)(2), the character and amount of support received by R will be attributed to Q.

(c) Effect on organizations claiming section 509(a)(3) status. If an organization claiming section 509(a)(2) status fails to meet either the one-third support test or the not-more-than-one-third support test under section 509(a)(2) by reason of the application of the provisions of paragraph (a) or (b) of this section, and such organization is one of the specified organizations (within the meaning of section 509(a)(3)(A)) for whose support or benefit an organization claiming section 509(a)(3) status is operated, the organization claiming section 509(a)(3) status will not be considered to be operated exclusively to support or benefit one or more section 509(a)(1) or (2) organizations.

§ 1.509(a)–6. Classification under section 509(a).

If an organization is described in section 509(a)(1) and also in another paragraph of section 509(a), it will be treated as described in section 509(a)(1). For purposes of this section, the parenthetical language "other than in clauses (vii) and (viii)" used in section 509(a)(1) shall be construed to mean "other than an organization which is described only in clause (vii) or (viii)". For example, X is an organization which is described in section 170(b)(1)(A)(vi), but could also meet the description of section 170(b)(1)(A)(viii) as an organization described in section 509(a)(2). For purposes of the one-third support test in section 509(a)(2)(A), contributions from X to other organizations will be treated as support from an organization described in section 170(b)(1)(A)(vi) rather than from an organization described in section 170(b)(1)(A)(viii).

§ 1.509(a)–7. Reliance by grantors and contributors to section 509(a)(1), (2), and (3) organizations.

(a) General rule. Once an organization has received a final ruling or determination letter classifying it as an organization described in section 509(a)(1), (2), or (3), the treatment of grants and contributions and the status of grantors and contributors to such organization under sections 170, 507, 545(b)(2), 556(b)(2), 642(c), 4942, 4945, 2055, 2106(a)(2), and 2522 will not be affected by reason of a subsequent revocation by the service of the organization's classification as described in section 509(a)(1), (2), or (3) until the date on which notice of change of status is made to the public (such as by publication in the Internal Revenue Bulletin) or another applicable date, if any, specified in such public notice. In appropriate cases, however, the treatment of grants and contributions and the status of grantors and contributors to an organization described in section 509(a)(1), (2), or (3) may be affected pending verification of the continued classification of such organization under section 509(a)(1), (2), or (3). Notice to this affect will be made in a public announcement by the service. In such cases the effect of grants and contributions made after the date of the announcement will depend upon the statutory qualification of the organization as an organization described in section 509(a)(1), (2), or (3).

(b) Exceptions. (1) Paragraph (a) of this section shall not apply if the grantor or contributor:

(i) Had knowledge of the revocation of the ruling or determination letter classifying the organization as an organization described in section 509(a)(1), (2), or (3), or

(ii) Was in part responsible for, or was aware of, the act, the failure to act, or the substantial and material change on the part of the organization which gave rise to the revocation of the ruling or determination letter classifying the organization as an organization described in section 509(a)(1), (2), or (3).

(2) Paragraph (a) of this section shall not apply where a different rule is otherwise expressly provided in the regulations under sections 170(b)(1)(A), 507(b)(1)(B), or 509.

§ 1.509(d)–1. Definition of support.

For purposes of section 509(a)(2), the term "support" does not include amounts received in repayment of the principal of a loan or other indebtedness. See, however, section 509(e) as to amounts received as interest on a loan or other indebtedness.

§ 1.509(e)–1. Definition of gross investment income.

For the distinction between gross receipts and gross investment income, see § 1.509(a)–3(m).

UNRELATED BUSINESS INCOME TAX

§ 1.511–1. Imposition and rates of tax.

Section 511(a) imposes a tax upon the unrelated business taxable income of certain organizations otherwise exempt from Federal income tax. Under section 511(a)(1), organizations described in section 511(a)(2)(A) and in paragraph (a) of § 1.511–2 and organizations described in section 511(a)(2)(B) are subject to normal tax and surtax at the corporate rates provided by section 11. Under section 511(b)(1), trusts described in section 511(b)(2) are subject to tax at the individual rates prescribed in section 1(d) of the Code as amended by the Tax Reform Act of 1969 (section 1 for taxable years ending before Jan. 1, 1971). The deduction for personal exemption provided in section 642(b) in the case of a trust taxable under subchapter J, chapter 1 of the Code, is not allowed in computing unrelated business taxable income.

§ 1.511–2. Organizations subject to tax.

(a) Organizations other than trusts and title holding companies.

(1)(i) The taxes imposed by section 511(a)(1) apply in the case of any organization (other than a trust described in section 511(b)(2) or an organization described in section 501(c)(1)) which is exempt from taxation under section 501(a) (except as provided in sections 507 through 515). For special rules concerning corporations described in section 501(c)(2), see paragraph (c) of this section.

(ii) In the case of an organization described in section 501(c)(4), (7), (8), (9), (10), (11), (12), (13), (14)(A), (15), (16), or (18), the taxes imposed by section 511(a)(1) apply only for taxable years beginning after December 31, 1969. In the case of an organization described in section 501(c)(14)(B) or (C), the taxes imposed by section 511(a)(1) apply only for taxable years beginning after February 2, 1966.

(2) The taxes imposed by section 511(a) apply in the case of any college or university which is an agency or instrumentality of any government or any political subdivision thereof, or which is owned or operated by a government or any political subdivision thereof or by any agency or instrumentality of any one or more governments or political subdivisions. Such taxes also apply in the case of any corporation wholly owned by one or more such colleges or universities. As here used, the word government includes any foreign government (to the extent not contrary to any treaty obligation of the United States) and all domestic governments (the United States and any of its Territories or possessions, any State, and the District of Columbia). Elementary and secondary schools operated by such governments are not subject to the tax on unrelated business income.

(3)(i) For taxable years beginning before January 1, 1970, churches and associations or conventions of churches are exempt from the taxes imposed by section 511. The exemption is applicable only to an organization which itself is a church or an association or convention of churches. Subject to the provisions of subdivision (ii) of this subparagraph, religious organizations, including religious orders, if not themselves churches or associations or conventions of churches, and all other organizations which are organized or operated under church auspices, are subject to the tax imposed by section 511, whether or not they engage in religious, educational, or charitable activities approved by a church.

(ii) The term church includes a religious order or a religious organization if such order or organization (a) is an integral part of a church, and (b) is engaged in carrying out the functions of a church, whether as a civil law corporation or otherwise. In determining whether a religious order or organization is an integral part of a church, consideration will be given to the degree to which it is connected with, and controlled by, such church. A religious order or organization shall be considered to be engaged in carrying out the functions of a church if its duties include the ministration of sacerdotal functions and the conduct of religious worship. If a religious order or organization is not an integral part of a church, or if such an order or organization is not authorized to carry out the functions of a church (ministration of sacerdotal functions and conduct of religious worship) then it is subject to the tax imposed by section 511 whether or not it engages in religious, educational, or charitable activities approved by a church. What constitutes the conduct of religious worship or the ministration of sacerdotal functions depends on the tenets and practices of a particular religious body constituting a church. If a religious order or organization can fully meet the requirements stated in this subdivision, exemption from the tax imposed by section 511 will apply to all its activities, including those which it conducts through a separate corporation (other than a corporation described in section 501(c)(2)) or other separate entity which it wholly owns and which is not operated for the primary purpose of carrying on a trade or business for profit. Such exemption from tax will also apply to activities conducted through a separate corporation (other than a corporation described in section 501(c)(2)) or other separate entity which is wholly owned by more than one religious order or organization, if all such orders or organizations fully meet the requirements stated in this subdivision and if such corporation or other entity is not operated for the primary purpose of carrying on a trade or business for profit.

(iii) For taxable years beginning after December 31, 1969, churches and conventions or associations of churches are subject to the taxes imposed by section 511, unless otherwise entitled to the benefit of the transitional rules of section 512(b)(14) and § 1.512(b)–1(i).

(b) Trusts—(1) In general. The taxes imposed by section 511(b) apply in the case of any trust which is exempt from taxation under section 501(a) (except as provided in sections 507 through 515), and which, if it were not for such exemption, would be subject to the provisions of subchapter J, Chapter 1, of the Code. An organization which is considered as trustee of a stock bonus, pension, or profit-sharing plan described in section 401(a), a supplemental unemployment benefit trust described in section 501(c)(17), or a pension plan described in section 501(c)(18) (regardless of the form of such organization) is subject to the taxes imposed by section 511(b)(1) on its unrelated business income. However, if such an organization conducts a business which is a separate taxable entity on the basis of all the facts and circumstances, for example, an association taxable as a corporation, the business will be taxable as a feeder organization described in section 502.

(2) Effective dates. In the case of a trust described in section 501(c)(3), the taxes imposed by section 511(b) apply for taxable years beginning after December 31, 1953. In the case of a trust described in 401(a), the taxes imposed by section 511(b) apply for taxable years beginning after June 30, 1954. In the case of a trust described in section 501(c)(17), the taxes imposed by section 511(b) apply for taxable years beginning after December 31, 1959. In the case of any other trust described in subparagraph (1) of this paragraph, the taxes imposed by section 511(b) apply for taxable years beginning after December 31, 1969.

(c) Title Holding Companies—(1) In general. If a corporation described in section 501(c)(2) pays any amount of its net income for a taxable year to an organization exempt from taxation under section 501(a) (or would pay such an amount but for the fact that the expenses of collecting its income exceed its income), and if such corporation and such organization file a consolidated income tax return for such taxable year, then such corporation shall be treated, for purposes of the tax imposed by section 511(a), as being organized and operated for the same purposes as such organization, as well as for its title-holding purpose. Therefore, if an item of income of the section 501(c)(2) corporation is derived from a source which is related to the exempt function of the exempt organization to which such income is payable and with which such corporation files a consolidated return, such item is, together with all deductions directly connected therewith, excluded from the determination of unrelated business taxable income under section 512 and shall not be subject to the tax imposed by section 511(a). If, however, such item of income is derived from a source which is not so related, then such item, less all deductions directly connected therewith, is, subject to the modifications provided in section 512(b), unrelated business taxable income subject to the tax imposed by section 511(a).

(2) The provisions of subparagraph (1) of this paragraph may be illustrated by the following example:

Example. The income of X, a section 501(c)(2) corporation, is required to be distributed to exempt organization A. During the taxable year X realizes net income of $900,000 from source M and $100,000 from source N. Source M is related to A's exempt function, while source N is not so related. X and A file a consolidated return for such taxable year. X has net unrelated business income of $100,000, subject to the modifications in section 512(b).

(3) Cross reference. For rules relating generally to the filing of consolidated returns by certain organizations exempt from taxation under section 501(a), see section 1504(e) of the Code and § 1.1502–100.

(4) Effective dates. Subparagraphs (1) through (3) of this paragraph apply with respect to taxable years beginning after December 31, 1969. For taxable years beginning before January 1, 1970, a corporation described in section 501(c)(2) and otherwise exempt from taxation under section 501(a) is taxable upon its unrelated business taxable income only if such income is payable either:

(i) To a church or convention or association of churches, or

(ii) To any organization subject, for taxable years beginning before January 1, 1970, to the tax imposed by section 511(a)(1).

(d) The fact that any class of organizations exempt from taxation under section 501(a) is subject to the unrelated business income tax under section 511 and this section does not in any way enlarge the permissible scope of business activities of such class for purposes of the continued qualification of such class under section 501(a).

* * *

§ 1.512(a)–1. Definition.

(a) In general. Except as otherwise provided in § 1.512(a)–3, § 1.512(a)–4, or paragraph (f) of this section, section 512(a)(1) defines unrelated business taxable income as the gross income derived from any unrelated trade or business regularly carried on, less those deductions allowed by chapter 1 of the Internal Revenue Code (Code) which are directly connected with the carrying on of such trade or business, subject to certain modifications referred to in § 1.512(b)–1. To be deductible in computing unrelated business taxable income, therefore, expenses, depreciation, and similar items not only must qualify as deductions allowed by chapter 1 of the Code, but also must be directly connected with the carrying on of unrelated trade or business. Except as provided in paragraph (d)(2) of this section, to be directly connected with the conduct of unrelated business for purposes of section 512, an item of deduction must have proximate and primary relationship to the carrying on of that business. In the case of an organization with more than one unrelated trade or business, unrelated business taxable income is calculated separately with respect to each such trade or business. See § 1.512(a)–6. For the treatment of amounts of income or loss of common trust funds, see § 1.584–2(c)(3).

(b) Expenses attributable solely to unrelated business activities. Expenses, depreciation, and similar items attributable solely to the conduct of unrelated business activities are proximately and primarily related to that business activity, and therefore qualify for deduction to the extent that they meet the requirements of section 162, section 167, or other relevant provisions of the Code. Expenses, depreciation, and similar items attributable solely to the conduct of unrelated business activities are proximately and primarily related to that business activity, and therefore qualify for deduction to the extent that they meet the requirements of section 162, section 167, or other relevant provisions of the Code. Thus, for example, salaries of personnel employed full-time in carrying on unrelated business activities are directly connected with the conduct of that activity and are deductible in computing unrelated business taxable income if they otherwise qualify for deduction under the requirements of section 162. Similarly, depreciation of a building used entirely in the conduct of unrelated business activities would be an allowable deduction to the extent otherwise permitted by section 167.

(c) Dual use of facilities or personnel. Where facilities are used both to carry on exempt activities and to conduct unrelated trade or business activities, expenses, depreciation and similar items attributable to such facilities (as, for example, items of overhead), shall be allocated between the two uses on a reasonable basis. Similarly, where personnel are used both to carry on exempt activities and to conduct unrelated trade or business activities, expenses and similar items attributable to such personnel (as, for example, items of salary) shall be allocated between the two uses on a reasonable basis. The portion of any such item so allocated to the unrelated trade or business activity is proximately and primarily related to that business activity, and shall be allowable as a deduction in computing unrelated business taxable income in the manner and to the extent permitted by section 162, section 167, or other relevant provisions of the Code. Thus, for example, assume that X, an exempt organization subject to the provisions of section 511, pays its president a salary of $20,000 a year. X derives gross income from the conduct of unrelated trade or business activities. The president devotes approximately 10 percent of his time during the year to the unrelated business activity. For purposes of computing X's unrelated business taxable income, a deduction of $2,000 (10 percent of $20,000), would be allowable for the salary paid to its president. However, allocation of expenses, depreciation, and similar items is not reasonable if the cost of providing a good or service in a related and an unrelated activity is substantially the same, but the price charged for that good or service in the unrelated activity is greater than the price charged in the related activity and no adjustment is made to equalize the price difference for purposes of allocating expenses, depreciation, and similar items based on revenue between related and unrelated activities. For example, if a social club described in section 501(c)(7) charges nonmembers a higher price than it charges members for the same good or service but does not adjust the price of the good or service provided to members for purposes of allocating expenses, depreciation, and similar items attributable to the provision of that good or service, the allocation method is not reasonable.

(d) Exploitation of exempt activities—(1) In general. In certain cases, gross income is derived from an unrelated trade or business activity which exploits an exempt activity. One example of such exploitation is the sale of advertising in a periodical of an exempt organization which contains editorial material related to the accomplishment of the organization's exempt purpose. Except as specified in subparagraph (2) of this paragraph and paragraph (f) of this section, in such cases, expenses, depreciation and similar items attributable to the conduct of the exempt activities are not deductible in computing unrelated business taxable income. Since such items are incident to an activity which is carried on in furtherance of the exempt purpose of the organization, they do not possess the necessary proximate and primary relationship to the unrelated trade or business activity and are therefore not directly connected with that business activity.

(2) Allowable deductions. Where an unrelated trade or business activity is of a kind carried on for profit by taxable organizations and where the exempt activity exploited by the business is a type of activity normally conducted by taxable organizations in pursuance of such business, expenses, depreciation, and similar items which are attributable to the exempt activity qualify as directly connected with the carrying on of the unrelated trade or business activity to the extent that:

(i) The aggregate of such items exceeds the income (if any) derived from or attributable to the exempt activity; and

(ii) The allocation of such excess to the unrelated trade or business activity does not result in a loss from such unrelated trade or business activity.

Under the rule of the preceding sentence, expenses, depreciation and similar items paid or incurred in the performance of an exempt activity must be allocated first to the exempt activity to the extent of the income derived from or attributable to the performance of that activity. Furthermore, such items are in no event allocable to the unrelated trade or business activity exploiting such exempt activity to the extent that their deduction would result in a loss carryover or carryback with respect to that trade or business activity. Similarly, they may not be taken into account in computing unrelated business taxable income attributable to any unrelated trade or business activity not exploiting the same exempt activity. See paragraph (f) of this section for the application of these rules to periodicals published by exempt organizations.

(e) Example. This section is illustrated by the following examples:

Example 1. W is an exempt business league with a large membership. Under an arrangement with an advertising agency W regularly mails brochures, pamphlets and other advertising materials to its members, charging the agency an agreed amount per enclosure. The distribution of the advertising materials does not contribute importantly to the accomplishment of the purpose for which W is granted exemption. Accordingly, the payments made to W by the advertising agency constitute gross income from an unrelated trade or business activity. In computing W's unrelated business taxable income, the expenses attributable solely to the conduct of the business, or allocable to such business under the rule of paragraph (c) of this section, are allowable as deductions in accordance with the provisions of section 162. Such deductions include the costs of handling and mailing, the salaries of personnel used full-time in the unrelated business activity and an allocable portion of the salaries of personnel used both to carry on exempt activities and to conduct the unrelated business activity. However, costs of developing W's membership and carrying on its exempt activities are not deductible. Those costs are necessary to the maintenance of the intangible asset exploited in the unrelated business activity—W's membership—but are incurred primarily in connection with W's fundamental purpose as an exempt organization. As a consequence, they do not have proximate and primary relationship to the conduct of the unrelated business activity and do not qualify as directly connected with it.

Example 2. (i) P, a manufacturer of photographic equipment, underwrites a photography exhibition organized by M, an art museum described in section 501(c)(3). In return for a payment of $100,000, M agrees that the exhibition catalog sold by M in connection with the exhibit will advertise P's product. The exhibition catalog will also include educational material, such as copies of photographs included in the exhibition, interviews with photographers, and an essay by the curator of M's department of photography. For purposes of this example, assume that none of the $100,000 is a qualified sponsorship payment within the meaning of section 513(i) and § 1.513–4, that M's advertising activity is regularly carried on, and that the entire amount of the payment is unrelated business taxable income to M. Expenses directly connected with generating the unrelated business taxable income (i.e., direct advertising costs) total $25,000. Expenses directly connected with the preparation and publication of the exhibition catalog (other than direct advertising costs) total $110,000. M receives $60,000 of gross revenue from sales of the exhibition catalog. Expenses directly connected with the conduct of the exhibition total $500,000.

(ii) The computation of unrelated business taxable income is as follows:

(A) Unrelated trade or business (sale of advertising):

Income	$ 100,000
Directly-connected expenses	(25,000)
Subtotal	$ 75,000

(B) Exempt function (publication of exhibition catalog):

Income (from catalog sales)	$ 60,000
Directly-connected expenses	(110,000)
Net exempt function income (loss)	($50,000)
Unrelated business taxable income	$ 25,000

(iii) Expenses related to publication of the exhibition catalog exceed revenues by $50,000. Because the unrelated business activity (the sale of advertising) exploits an exempt activity (the publication of the exhibition catalog), and because the publication of editorial material is an activity normally conducted by taxable entities that sell advertising, the net loss from the exempt publication activity is allowed as a deduction from unrelated business income under paragraph (d)(2) of this section. In contrast, the presentation of an exhibition is not an activity normally conducted by taxable entities engaged in advertising and publication activity for purposes of paragraph (d)(2) of this section. Consequently, the $500,000 cost of presenting the exhibition is not directly connected with the conduct of the unrelated advertising activity and does not have a proximate and primary relationship to that activity. Accordingly, M has unrelated business taxable income of $25,000.

(f) Determination of unrelated business taxable income derived from sale of advertising in exempt organization periodicals—(1) In general. Under section 513 (relating to the definition of unrelated trade or business) and § 1.513–1, amounts realized by an exempt organization from the sale of advertising in a periodical constitute gross income from an unrelated trade or business activity involving the exploitation of an exempt activity; namely, the circulation and readership of the periodical developed through the production and distribution of the readership content of the periodical. Paragraph (d) of this section provides for the allowance of deductions attributable to the production and distribution of the readership content of the periodical. Thus, subject to the limitations of paragraph (d)(2) of this section, where the circulation and readership of an exempt organization periodical are utilized in connection with the sale of advertising in the periodical, expenses, depreciation, and similar items of deductions attributable to the production and distribution of the editorial or readership content of the periodical shall qualify as items of deductions directly connected with the unrelated advertising activity. Subparagraphs (2) through (6) of this paragraph provide rules for determining the amount of unrelated business taxable income attributable to the sale of advertising in exempt organization periodicals. Subparagraph (7) of this paragraph provides rules for determining when the unrelated business taxable income of two or more exempt organization periodicals may be determined on a consolidated basis.

(2) Computation of unrelated business taxable income attributable to sale of advertising—(i) Excess advertising costs. If the direct advertising costs of an exempt organization periodical (determined under subparagraph (6)(ii) of this paragraph) exceed gross advertising income (determined under subparagraph (3)(ii) of this paragraph), such excess shall be allowable as a deduction in determining unrelated business taxable income from any unrelated trade or business activity carried on by the organization.

(ii) Excess advertising income. If the gross advertising income of an exempt organization periodical exceeds direct advertising costs, paragraph (d)(2) of this section provides that items of deduction attributable to the production and distribution of the readership content of an exempt organization periodical shall qualify as items of deduction directly connected with unrelated advertising activity in computing the amount of unrelated business taxable income derived from the advertising activity to the extent that such items exceed the income derived from or attributable to such production and distribution, but only to the extent that such items do not result in a loss from such advertising activity. Furthermore, such items of deduction shall not qualify as directly connected with such advertising activity to the extent that their deduction would result in a loss carryback or carryover with respect to such advertising activity. Similarly, such items of deduction shall not be taken into account in computing unrelated business taxable income attributable to any unrelated trade or business activity other than such advertising activity. Thus:

(a) If the circulation income of the periodical (determined under subparagraph (3)(iii) of this paragraph) equals or exceeds the readership costs of such periodical (determined under subparagraph (6)(iii) of this paragraph), the unrelated business taxable income attributable to the periodical is the excess of the gross advertising income of the periodical over direct advertising costs; but

(b) If the readership costs of an exempt organization periodical exceed the circulation income of the periodical, the unrelated business taxable income is the excess, if any, of the total income attributable to the periodical (determined under subparagraph (3) of this paragraph) over the total periodical costs (as defined in subparagraph (6)(i) of this paragraph).

See subparagraph (7) of this paragraph for rules relating to the consolidation of two or more periodicals.

(iii) Examples. The application of this paragraph may be illustrated by the following examples. For purposes of these examples it is assumed that the production and distribution of the readership content of the periodical is related to the organization's exempt purpose.

Example 1. X, an exempt trade association, publishes a single periodical which carries advertising. During 1971, X realizes a total of $40,000 from the sale of advertising in the periodical (gross advertising income) and $60,000 from the sales of the periodical to members and nonmembers (circulation income). The total periodical costs are $90,000 of which $50,000 is directly connected with the sale and publication of advertising (direct advertising costs) and $40,000 is attributable to the production and distribution of the readership content (readership costs). Since the direct advertising costs of the periodical ($50,000) exceed gross advertising income ($40,000), pursuant to subdivision (i) of this subparagraph, the unrelated business taxable income attributable to advertising is determined solely on the basis of the income and deductions directly connected with the production and sale of the advertising:

Gross advertising revenue	$40,000
Direct advertising costs	(50,000)
Loss attributable to advertising	(10,000)

X has realized a loss of $10,000 from its advertising activity. This loss is an allowable deduction in computing X's unrelated business taxable income derived from any other unrelated trade or business activity.

Example 2. Assume the facts as stated in example (1), except that the circulation income of X periodical is $100,000 instead of $60,000, and that of the total periodical costs, $25,000 are direct advertising costs, and $65,000 are readership costs. Since the circulation income ($100,000) exceeds the total readership costs ($65,000), pursuant to subdivision (ii)(a) of this subparagraph the unrelated business taxable income attributable to the advertising activity is $15,000, the excess of gross advertising income ($40,000) over direct advertising costs ($25,000).

Example 3. Assume the facts as stated in example (1), except that of the total periodical costs, $20,000 are direct advertising costs and $70,000 are readership costs. Since the readership costs of the periodical ($70,000), exceed the circulation income ($60,000), pursuant to subdivision (ii)(b) of this subparagraph the unrelated business taxable income attributable to advertising is the excess of the total income attributable to the periodical over the total periodical costs. Thus, X has unrelated business taxable income attributable to the advertising activity of $10,000 ($100,000 total income attributable to the periodical less $90,000 total periodical costs).

Example 4. Assume the facts as stated in example (1), except that the total periodical costs are $120,000 of which $30,000 are direct advertising costs and $90,000 are readership costs. Since the readership costs of the periodical ($90,000), exceed the circulation income ($60,000), pursuant to subdivision (ii)(b) of this subparagraph the unrelated business taxable income attributable to advertising is the excess, if any, of the total income attributable to the periodical over the total periodical costs. Since the total income of the periodical ($100,000) does not exceed the total periodical costs ($120,000), X has not derived any unrelated business taxable income from the advertising activity. Further, only $70,000 of the $90,000 of readership costs may be deducted in computing unrelated business taxable income since as provided in subdivision (ii) of this subparagraph, such costs may be deducted, to the extent they exceed circulation income, only to the extent they do not result in a loss from the advertising activity. Thus, there is no loss from such activity, and no amount may be deducted on this account in computing X's unrelated trade or business income derived from any other unrelated trade or business activity.

(3) Income attributable to exempt organization periodicals—(i) In general. For purposes of this paragraph the total income attributable to an exempt organization periodical is the sum of its gross advertising income and its circulation income.

(ii) Gross advertising income. The term gross advertising income means all amounts derived from the unrelated advertising activities of an exempt organization periodical (or for purposes of this paragraph in the case of a taxable organization, all amounts derived from the advertising activities of the taxable organization).

(iii) Circulation income. The term circulation income means the income attributable to the production, distribution or circulation of a periodical (other than gross advertising income) including all amounts realized from or attributable to the sale or distribution of the readership content of the periodical, such as amounts realized from charges made for reprinting or republishing articles and special items in the periodical and amounts realized from sales of back issues. Where the right to receive an exempt organization periodical is associated with membership or similar status in such organization for which dues, fees or other charges are received (hereinafter referred to as membership receipts), circulation income includes the portion of such membership receipts allocable to the periodical (hereinafter referred to as allocable membership receipts). Allocable membership receipts is the amount which would have been charged and paid if:

(a) The periodical was that of a taxable organization.

(b) The periodical was published for profit, and

(c) The member was an unrelated party dealing with the taxable organization at arm's length.

See subparagraph (4) of this paragraph for a discussion of the factors to be considered in determining allocable membership receipts of an exempt organization periodical under the standard described in the preceding sentence.

(4) Allocable membership receipts. The allocable membership receipts of an exempt organization periodical shall be determined in accordance with the following rules:

(i) Subscription price charged to nonmembers. If 20 percent or more of the total circulation of a periodical consist of sales to nonmembers, the subscription price charged to such nonmembers shall determine the price of the periodical for purposes of allocating membership receipts to the periodical.

(ii) Subscription price to nonmembers. If paragraph (f)(4)(i) of this section does not apply and if the membership dues from 20 percent or more of the members of an exempt organization are less than those received from the other members because the former members do not receive the periodical, the amount of the reduction in membership dues for a member not receiving the periodical shall determine the price of the periodical for purposes of allocating membership receipts to the periodical.

(iii) Pro rata allocation of membership receipts. Since it may generally be assumed that membership receipts and gross advertising income are equally available for all the exempt activities (including the periodical) of the organization, the share of membership receipts allocated to the periodical, where paragraphs (f)(4)(i) and (ii) of this section do not apply, shall be an amount equal to the organization's membership receipts multiplied by a fraction the numerator of which is the total periodical costs and the denominator of which is such costs plus the cost of other exempt activities of the organization. For example, assume that an exempt organization has total periodical costs of $30,000 and other exempt costs of $70,000. Further assume that the membership receipts of the organization are $60,000 and that paragraphs (f)(4)(i) and (ii) of this section do not apply. Under these circumstances $18,000 ($60,000 times $30,000/$100,000) is allocated to the periodical's circulation income.

(5) Examples. The rules set forth in paragraph (f)(4) of this section may be illustrated by the following examples. For purposes of these examples it is assumed that the exempt organization periodical contains advertising, and that the production and distribution of the readership content of the periodical is related to the organization's exempt purpose.

Example 1. U is an exempt scientific organization with 10,000 members who pay annual dues of $15 per year. One of U's activities is the publication of a monthly periodical which is distributed to all of its members. U also distributes 5,000 additional copies of its periodical to nonmember subscribers at a cost of $10 per year. Pursuant to paragraph (f)(4)(i) of this section, since the nonmember circulation of U's periodical represents 33 1/3 percent of its total circulation the subscription price charged to nonmembers will be used to determine the portion of U's membership receipts allocable to the periodical. Thus, U's allocable membership receipts will be $100,000 ($10 times 10,000 members), and U's total circulation income for the periodical will be $150,000 ($100,000 from members plus $50,000 from sales to nonmembers).

Example 2. Assume the facts as stated in example (1), except that U sells only 500 copies of its periodical to nonmembers, at a price of $10 per year. Assume further that U's members may elect not to receive the periodical, in which case their annual dues are reduced from $15 per year to $6 per year, and that only 3,000 members elect to receive the periodical and pay the full dues of $15 per year. U's stated subscription price to members of $9 consistently results in an excess of total income (including gross advertising income) attributable to the periodical over total costs of the periodical. Since the 500 copies of the periodical distributed to nonmembers represents only 14 percent of the 3,500 copies distributed, pursuant to paragraph (f)(4)(i) of this section, the $10 subscription price charged to nonmembers will not be used in determining the portion of membership receipts allocable to the periodical. On the other hand, since 70 percent of the members elect not to receive the periodical and pay $9 less per year in dues, pursuant to paragraph (f)(4)(ii) of this section, such $9 price will be used in determining the subscription price charged to members. Thus, the allocable membership receipts will be $9 per member, or $27,000 ($9 times 3,000 copies) and U's total circulation income will be $32,000 ($27,000 plus $5,000).

Example 3. (a) W, an exempt trade association, has 800 members who pay annual dues of $50 per year. W publishes a monthly journal the editorial content and advertising of which are directed to the business interests of its own members. The journal is distributed to all of W's members and no receipts are derived from nonmembers.

(b) W has total receipts of $100,000 of which $40,000 ($50 x 800) are membership receipts and $60,000 are gross advertising income. W's total costs for the journal and other exempt activities is $100,000. W has total periodical costs of $76,000 of which $41,000 are direct advertising costs and $35,000 are readership costs.

(c) Paragraph (f)(4)(i) of this section will not apply since no copies are available to nonmembers. Therefore, the allocation of membership receipts shall be made in accordance with paragraph (f)(4)(iii) of this section. Based upon pro rata allocation of membership receipts (40,000) by a fraction the numerator of which is total periodical costs ($76,000) and the denominator of which is the total costs of the journal and the other exempt activities ($100,000), $30,400 ($76,000/$100,000 times $40,000) of membership receipts is circulation income.

(6) Deductions attributable to exempt organization periodicals—(i) In general. For purposes of this paragraph the term total periodical costs means the total deductions attributable to the periodical. For purposes of this paragraph the total periodical costs of an exempt organization periodical are the sum of the direct advertising costs of the periodical (determined under subdivision (ii) of this subparagraph) and the readership costs of the periodical (determined under subdivision (iii) of this subparagraph). Items of deduction properly attributable to exempt activities other than the publication of an exempt organization periodical may not be allocated to such periodical. Where items are attributable both to an exempt organization periodical and to other activities of an exempt organization, the allocation of such items must be made on a reasonable basis which fairly reflects the portion of such item properly attributable to each such activity. The method of allocation will vary with the nature of the item, but once adopted, a reasonable method of allocation with respect to an item must be used consistently. Thus, for example, salaries may generally be allocated among various activities on the basis of the time devoted to each activity; occupancy costs such as rent, heat and electricity may be allocated on the basis of the portion of space devoted to each activity; and depreciation may be allocated on the basis of space occupied and the portion of the particular asset utilized in each activity. Allocations based on dollar receipts from various exempt activities will generally not be reasonable since such receipts are usually not an accurate reflection of the costs associated with activities carried on by exempt organizations.

(ii) Direct advertising costs. (a) The direct advertising costs of an exempt organization periodical include all expenses, depreciation, and similar items of deduction which are directly connected with the sale and publication of advertising as determined in accordance with paragraphs (a), (b), and (c) of this section. These items are allowable as deductions in the computation of unrelated business income of the organization for the taxable year to the extent they meet the requirements of section 162, section 167, or other relevant provisions of the Code. The items allowable as deductions under this subdivision do not include any items of deduction attributable to the production or distribution of the readership content of the periodical.

(b) The items allowable as deductions under this subdivision would include agency commissions and other direct selling costs, such as transportation and travel expenses, office salaries, promotion and research expenses, and direct office overhead directly connected with the sale of advertising lineage in the periodical. Also included would be other items of deduction commonly classified as advertising costs under standard account classification, such as art work and copy preparation, telephone, telegraph, postage, and similar costs directly connected with advertising.

(c) In addition to the items of deduction normally included in standard account classifications relating to advertising costs, it is also necessary to ascertain the portion of mechanical and distribution costs attributable to advertising lineage. For this purpose, the general account classifications of items includible in mechanical and distribution costs ordinarily employed in business-paper and consumer publication accounting provide a guide for the computation. Thus, the mechanical and distribution costs in such cases would include the portion of the costs and other expenses of composition, presswork, binding, mailing (including paper and wrappers used for mailing), and the bulk postage attributable to the advertising lineage of the publication. The portion of mechanical and distribution costs attributable to advertising lineage of the periodical will be determined on the basis of the ratio of advertising lineage to total lineage of the periodical, and the application of that ratio to the total mechanical and distribution costs of the periodical, where records are not kept in such a manner as to reflect more accurately the allocation of mechanical and distributions costs to advertising lineage of the periodical, and where there is no factor in the character of the periodical to indicate that such an allocation would be unreasonable.

(iii) Readership costs. The readership costs of an exempt organization periodical include expenses, depreciation or similar items which are directly connected with the production and distribution of the readership content of the periodical and which would otherwise be allowable as deductions in determining unrelated business taxable income under section 512 and the regulations thereunder if such production and distribution constituted an unrelated trade or business activity. Thus, readership costs include all the items of deduction attributable to an exempt organization periodical which are not allocated to direct advertising costs under subdivision (ii) of this subparagraph, including the portion of such items attributable to the readership content of the periodical, as opposed to the advertising content, and the portion of mechanical and distribution costs which is not attributable to advertising lineage in the periodical.

(7) Consolidation—(i) In general. Where an exempt organization subject to unrelated business income tax under section 511 publishes two or more periodicals for the production of income, it may treat the gross income from all (but not less than all) of such periodicals and the items of deduction directly connected with such periodicals (including readership costs of such periodicals), on a consolidated basis as if such periodicals were one periodical in determining the amount of unrelated business taxable income derived from the sale of advertising in such periodical. Such treatment must, however, be followed consistently and once adopted shall be binding unless the consent of the Commissioner is obtained as provided in sections 446(e) and § 1.446–1(e).

(ii) Production of income. For purposes of this subparagraph, an exempt organization periodical is published for the production of income if:

(a) The organization generally receives gross advertising income from the periodical equal to at least 25 percent of the readership costs of such periodical, and

(b) The publication of such periodical is an activity engaged in for profit.

For purposes of the preceding sentence, the determination whether the publication of a periodical is an activity engaged in for profit is to be made by reference to objective standards taking into account all the facts and circumstances involved in each case. The facts and circumstances must indicate that the organization carries on the activity with the objective that the publication of the periodical will result in economic profit (without regard to tax consequences), although not necessarily in a particular year. Thus, an exempt organization periodical may be treated as having been published with such an objective even though in a particular year its total periodical costs exceed its total income. Similarly, if an exempt organization begins publishing a new periodical, the fact that the total periodical costs exceed the total income for the startup years because of a lack of advertising sales does not mean that the periodical was published without an objective of economic profit. The organization may establish that the activity was carried on with such an objective. This might be established by showing, for example, that there is a reasonable expectation that the total income, by reason of an increase in advertising sales, will exceed costs within a reasonable time. See § 1.183–2 for additional factors bearing on this determination.

(iii) Example. This subparagraph may be illustrated by the following example:

Example. Y, an exempt trade association, publishes three periodicals which it distributes to its members: a weekly newsletter, a monthly magazine, and quarterly journal. Both the monthly magazine and the quarterly journal contain advertising which accounts for gross advertising income equal to more than 25 percent of their respective readership costs. Similarly, the total income attributable to each such periodical has exceeded the total deductions attributable to each such periodical for substantially all the years they have been published. The newsletter carries no advertising and its annual subscription price is not intended to cover the cost of publication. The newsletter is a service of Y distributed to all of its members in an effort to keep them informed of changes occurring in the business world and is not engaged in for profit. Under these circumstances, Y may consolidate the income and deductions from the monthly and quarterly journals in computing its unrelated business taxable income, but may not consolidate the income and deductions attributable to the publication of the newsletter with the income and deductions of its other periodicals since the newsletter is not published for the production of income.

* * *

§ 1.512(a)–6. Special rule for organizations with more than one unrelated trade or business.

(a) More than one unrelated trade or business—(1) In general. An organization with more than one unrelated trade or business must compute unrelated business taxable income (UBTI) separately with respect to each such trade or business, without regard to the specific deduction in section 512(b)(12), including for purposes of determining any net operating loss (NOL) deduction. An organization with more than one unrelated trade or business computes its total UBTI under paragraph (g) of this section.

(2) Separate trades or businesses. An organization determines whether it regularly carries on unrelated trades or businesses by applying sections 511 through 514. For purposes of section 512(a)(6)(A) and paragraph (a)(1) of this section, an organization identifies its separate unrelated trades or businesses using the methods described in paragraphs (b) through (e) of this section.

(3) Reporting changes in identification. An organization that changes the identification of a separate unrelated trade or business under paragraph (a)(2) of this section must report the change in the taxable year of that change in accordance with forms and instructions. For this purpose, a change in identification of a separate unrelated trade or business includes the changed identification of the separate unrelated trade or business with respect to a partnership interest that was incorrectly designated as a qualifying partnership interest (QPI). In the case of an incorrect designation of a QPI, paragraph (c)(2)(iii) of this section (regarding designation of qualifying partnership interests) does not apply. In all cases, to report the change in identification, an organization must provide the following information with respect to each separate change in identification—

(i) The identification of the separate unrelated trade or business in the previous taxable year;

(ii) The identification of the separate unrelated trade or business in the current taxable year; and

(iii) The reason for the change.

(b) North American Industry Classification System—(1) In general. Except as provided in paragraphs (c) through (e) of this section, an organization identifies each of its separate unrelated trades or businesses using the first two digits of the North American Industry Classification System code (NAICS 2-digit code) that most accurately describes the unrelated trade or business based on the more specific NAICS code, such as at the 6-digit level, that describes the activity it conducts and subject to the requirements of paragraph (b)(2) and (3) of this section. The descriptions in the current NAICS manual (available at www.census.gov) of trades or businesses using more than two digits of the NAICS codes are relevant in this determination. In the case of the sale of goods, both online and in stores, the separate unrelated trade or business is identified by the goods sold in stores if the same goods generally are sold both online and in stores.

(2) Codes must identify the unrelated trade or business. The NAICS 2-digit code must identify the unrelated trade or business in which the organization engages (directly or indirectly) and not activities the conduct of which are substantially related to the exercise or performance by such organization of its charitable, educational, or other purpose or function constituting the basis for its exemption under section 501 (or, in the case of an organization described in section 511(a)(2)(B), to the exercise or performance of any purpose or function described in section 501(c)(3)). For example, a college or university described in section 501(c)(3) cannot use the NAICS 2-digit code for educational services to identify all its separate unrelated trades or businesses, and a qualified retirement plan described in section 401(a) cannot use the NAICS 2-digit code for finance and insurance to identify all of its unrelated trades or businesses.

(3) Codes only reported once. An organization will report each NAICS 2-digit code only once. For example, a hospital organization that operates several hospital facilities in a geographic area (or multiple geographic areas), all of which include pharmacies that sell goods to the general public, would include all the pharmacies under the NAICS 2-digit code for retail trade, regardless of whether the hospital organization keeps separate books and records for each pharmacy.

(c) Activities in the nature of investments—(1) In general. An organization's activities in the nature of investments (investment activities) are treated collectively as a separate unrelated trade or business for purposes of section 512(a)(6) and paragraph (a) of this section. Except as provided in paragraphs (c)(7) and (c)(8) of this section, an organization's investment activities are limited to its—

(i) Qualifying partnership interests (described in paragraph (c)(2) of this section);

(ii) Qualifying S corporation interests (described in paragraph (e)(2)(i) of this section); and

(iii) Debt-financed property or properties (within the meaning of section 514).

(2) Qualifying partnership interests—(i) Directly-held partnership interests. An interest in a partnership is a qualifying partnership interest (QPI) if the exempt organization holds a direct interest in the partnership (directly-held partnership interest) that meets the requirements of either the de minimis test (described in paragraph (c)(3) of this section) or the participation test (described in paragraph (c)(4) of this section).

(ii) Indirectly-held partnership interests—(A) Look through rule. If an organization holds a direct interest in a partnership but that directly-held partnership interest is not a QPI because it does not meet the requirements of the de minimis test (described in paragraph (c)(3) of this section) or the participation test (described in paragraph (c)(4) of this section), any partnership in which the organization holds an indirect interest through the directly-held partnership interest (indirectly-held partnership interest) may be a QPI if the indirectly-held partnership interest meets the requirements of paragraph (c)(2)(ii)(B) or (c)(2)(ii)(C) of this section.

(B) Indirectly-held partnership interests that meet the requirements of the de minimis test. An indirectly-held partnership interest meets the requirements of this paragraph (c)(2)(ii)(B) if the indirectly-held partnership interest meets the requirements of the de minimis test described in paragraph (c)(3) of this section with regard to the organization. For example, if an organization directly holds 50 percent of the capital interests of a partnership and the directly-held partnership holds 4 percent of the capital and profits interest of lower-tier partnership A, the organization may aggregate its interest in lower-tier partnership A with its other QPIs because the organization indirectly holds 2 percent of the capital and profits interests of lower-tier partnership A (4 percent x 50 percent).

(C) Indirectly-held partnership interests that meet the requirements of the participation test. An indirectly-held partnership interest meets the requirements of this paragraph (c)(2)(ii)(C) if the indirectly-held partnership interest meets the requirements of the participation test (described in paragraph (c)(4) of this section) with respect to the partnership that directly owns the interest in the indirectly-held partnership. For purposes of applying the participation test to a partnership, the term organization in paragraph (c)(4) of this section refers to the partnership that directly holds the indirectly-held partnership interest being tested for QPI status. Additionally, the list of officers, directors, trustees, or employees of an organization found in paragraphs (c)(4)(iii)(B) and (C) includes a general partner that directly owns an interest in the lower-tier partnership.

(D) Example—(I) Organization D is described in section 501(c) and is exempt from Federal income tax under section 501(a). Organization D owns 50 percent of the capital interest in Partnership A. Partnership A owns 30 percent of the capital interest in Partnership B, but Partnership A does not significantly participate in Partnership B within the meaning of paragraph (c)(4)(iii) of this section. Further, Partnership B owns 15 percent of the capital interest in Partnership C, in which Partnership B does not significantly participate within the meaning of paragraph (c)(4)(iii) of this section. No other organizations related (within the meaning of paragraph (c)(4)(ii) of this section) to either Organization D or the partnerships owns an interest in any of the lower-tier partnerships.

(II) Neither the interest in Partnership A nor B is a QPI. Organization D's interest in Partnership A does not meet the requirements of either the de minimis test or the participation test because it owns 50 percent of the interest in the partnership. Organization D's indirect interest in Partnership B

(50 percent of 30 percent, or 15 percent) does not meet the de minimis test. Additionally, because Partnership A owns greater than 20 percent interest in Partnership B, Partnership A's interest in Partnership B does not meet the participation test. However, Organization D's interest in Partnership C is a QPI because Partnership C meets the participation test. That is, Partnership B holds a 15 percent interest in Partnership C and does not significantly participate in Partnership C.

(iii) Designation. An organization that has a partnership interest meeting the requirements of paragraph (c)(2)(i) or (ii) of this section in a taxable year may designate that partnership interest as a QPI by including its share of partnership gross income (and directly connected deductions) with the gross income (and directly connected deductions) from its other investment activities (see paragraph (c)(1) of this section) in accordance with forms and instructions. Any partnership interest that is designated as a QPI remains a QPI unless and until it no longer meets the requirements of paragraph (c)(2)(i) or (ii) of this section. For example, if an organization designates a directly-held partnership interest that meets the requirements of the de minimis rule as a QPI in one taxable year, the organization cannot, in the next taxable year, use NAICS 2-digit codes to describe the partnership trades or businesses that are unrelated trades or businesses with respect to the organization unless the directly-held partnership interest fails to meet the requirements of both the de minimis test and the participation test (after application of the grace period described in paragraph (c)(6) of this section, if appropriate).

(3) De minimis test. A partnership interest is a QPI that meets the requirements of the de minimis test if the organization holds directly (within the meaning of paragraph (c)(2)(i) of this section) or indirectly (within the meaning of paragraph (c)(2)(ii) of this section) no more than 2 percent of the profits interest and no more than 2 percent of the capital interest during the organization's taxable year with which or in which the partnership's taxable year ends.

(4) Participation test—(i) In general. A partnership interest is a QPI that meets the requirements of the participation test if the organization holds directly (within the meaning of paragraph (c)(2)(i) of this section) or indirectly (within the meaning of paragraph (c)(2)(ii) of this section) no more than 20 percent of the capital interest during the organization's taxable year with which or in which the partnership's taxable year ends and the organization does not significantly participate in the partnership within the meaning of paragraph (c)(4)(iii) of this section.

(ii) Combining related interests. When determining an organization's percentage interest in a partnership for purposes of paragraph (c)(4)(i) of this section, the interests of a supporting organization (as defined in section 509(a)(3) and § 1.509(a)–4), other than a Type III supporting organization (as defined in § 1.509(a)–4(i)) that is not a parent of its supported organization, or of a controlled entity (as defined in section 512(b)(13)(D) and § 1.512(b)–1(*l*)) in the same partnership will be taken into account. For example, if an organization owns 10 percent of the capital interests in a partnership, and its Type I supporting organization owns an additional 15 percent capital interest in that partnership, the organization would not meet the requirements of the participation test because its aggregate percentage interest exceeds 20 percent (10 percent + 15 percent = 25 percent).

(iii) Significant Participation. An organization significantly participates in a partnership if—

(A) The organization, by itself, may require the partnership to perform, or may prevent the partnership from performing (other than through a unanimous voting requirement or through minority consent rights), any act that significantly affects the operations of the partnership;

(B) Any of the organization's officers, directors, trustees, or employees have rights to participate in the management of the partnership at any time;

(C) Any of the organization's officers, directors, trustees, or employees have rights to conduct the partnership's business at any time; or

(D) The organization, by itself, has the power to appoint or remove any of the partnership's officers or employees or a majority of directors.

(5) Determining percentage interest—(i) Profits interest. For purposes of the de minimis test described in paragraph (c)(3) of this section, an organization's profits interest in a partnership is determined in the same manner as its distributive share of partnership taxable income. See section 704(b) (relating to the determination of the distributive share by the income or loss ratio) and §§ 1.704–1 through 1.704–4.

(ii) Capital interest. For purposes of the de minimis test (described in paragraph (c)(3) of this section) and the participation test (described in paragraph (c)(4)(i) of this section), in the absence of a provision in the partnership agreement, an organization's capital interest in a partnership is determined on the basis of its interest in the assets of the partnership which would be distributable to such organization upon its withdrawal from the partnership, or upon liquidation of the partnership, whichever is the greater.

(iii) Average percentage interest. For purposes of the de minimis test (described in paragraph (c)(3) of this section) and the participation test (described in paragraph (c)(4)(i) of this section), an organization determines its percentage interest by taking the average of the organization's percentage interest at the beginning and the end of the partnership's taxable year, or, in the case of a partnership interest held for less than a year, the percentage interest held at the beginning and end of the period of ownership within the partnership's taxable year. For example, if an organization acquires an interest in a partnership that files on a calendar year basis in May and the partnership reports on Schedule K-1 (Form 1065) that the partner held a 3 percent profits interest at the date of acquisition but held a 1 percent profits interest at the end of the calendar year, the organization will be considered to have held 2 percent of the profits interest in that partnership for that year ((3 percent + 1 percent)/2).

(iv) Reliance on Schedule K-1 (Form 1065). When determining the organization's average percentage interest (described in paragraph (c)(5)(iii) of this section) in a partnership for purposes of the de minimis test (described in paragraph (c)(3) of this section) and the participation test (described in paragraph (c)(4) of this section), an organization may rely on the Schedule K-1 (Form 1065) (or its successor) it receives from the partnership if the form lists the organization's percentage profits interest or its percentage capital interest, or both, at the beginning and end of the year. However, the organization may not rely on the form to the extent that any information about the organization's percentage interest is not specifically provided. For example, if the Schedule K-1 (Form 1065) an organization receives from a partnership lists the organization's profits interest as "variable" but lists its percentage capital interest at the beginning and end of the year, the organization may rely on the form only with respect to its percentage capital interest.

(6) Changes in percentage interest. A partnership interest that fails to meet the requirements of the de minimis test (described in paragraph (c)(3) of this section) or the participation test (described in paragraph (c)(4) of this section) because of an increase in percentage interest in the organization's current taxable year may be treated for the taxable year of the change as meeting the requirements of the test it met in the prior taxable year if—

(i) The partnership interest met the requirements of the de minimis test or participation test, respectively, in the organization's prior taxable year without application of this paragraph (c)(6);

(ii) The increase in percentage interest is solely due to the actions of one or more partners other than the organization; and

(iii) In the case of a partnership interest that met the requirements of the participation test in the prior taxable year, the interest of the partner or partners that caused the increase in paragraph (c)(6)(ii) of this section was not combined for the prior taxable year and is not combined for the taxable year of the change with the organization's partnership interest for purposes of paragraph (c)(4)(ii) of this section.

(7) UBTI from the investment activities of organizations subject to section 512(a)(3). For purposes of paragraph (c)(1) of this section, UBTI from the investment activities of an organization subject to section 512(a)(3) includes any amount that—

(i) Would be excluded from the calculation of UBTI under section 512(b)(1), (2), (3), or (5) if the organization were subject to section 512(a)(1);

(ii) Is attributable to income set aside (and not in excess of the set aside limit described in section 512(a)(3)(E)), but not used, for a purpose described in section 512(a)(3)(B)(i) or (ii); or

(iii) Is in excess of the set aside limit described in section 512(a)(3)(E).

(8) Limitations—(i) Social clubs. Paragraphs (c)(2) (regarding QPIs) and (c)(9) (transition rule for certain partnership interests) of this section do not apply to social clubs described in section 501(c)(7).

(ii) General partnership interests. Any partnership in which an organization, or an organization whose interest is combined with that organization's interest for purposes of paragraph (c)(4)(ii) of this section, is a general partner under applicable state law is not a QPI within the meaning of paragraph (c)(2) of this section, regardless of the organization's percentage interest. Such partnership interest cannot be a QPI for any organization or for any of the organizations whose interest is combined with that organization's interest for purposes of paragraph (c)(4)(ii) of this section.

(iii) Application of other sections. This paragraph (c) does not otherwise impact application of section 512(c) and the fragmentation rule under section 513(c).

(9) Transition rule for certain partnership interests—(i) In general. If a directly-held partnership interest acquired prior to August 21, 2018, is not a QPI, an organization may treat such partnership interest as a separate unrelated trade or business for purposes of section 512(a)(6) regardless of the number of unrelated trades or businesses directly or indirectly conducted by the partnership. For example, if an organization has a 35 percent capital interest in a partnership acquired prior to August 21, 2018, it can treat the partnership as a single trade or business even if the partnership's investments generated UBTI from lower-tier partnerships that were engaged in multiple trades or businesses. A partnership interest acquired prior to August 21, 2018, will continue to meet the requirement of this rule even if the organization's percentage interest in such partnership changes before the end of the transition period (see paragraph (c)(9)(iii) of this section).

(ii) Exclusivity. An organization may apply either the transition rule in paragraph (c)(9)(i) of this section or the look-through rule in paragraph (c)(2)(ii) of this section, but not both, to a partnership interest described in paragraph (c)(9)(i) of this section that also qualifies for application of the look-through rule described in paragraph (c)(2)(ii).

(iii) Transition period. An organization may rely on this transition rule until the first day of the organization's first taxable year beginning after December 2, 2020.

(d) Income from certain controlled entities—(1) Specified payments from controlled entities. If an organization (controlling organization) controls another entity (within the meaning of section 512(b)(13)(D)) (controlled entity), all specified payments (as defined in section 512(b)(13)(C)) received by a controlling organization from that controlled entity are treated as gross income from a separate unrelated trade or business for purposes of paragraph (a) of this section. If a controlling organization receives specified payments from two different controlled entities, the payments from each controlled entity are treated as a separate unrelated trade or business. For example, a controlling organization that receives rental payments from two controlled entities has two separate unrelated trades or businesses, one for each controlled entity. The specified payments from a controlled entity are treated as gross income from one trade or business regardless of whether the controlled entity engages in more than one unrelated trade or business or whether the controlling organization receives more than one type of specified payment from that controlled entity.

(2) Certain amounts derived from controlled foreign corporations. All amounts included in UBTI under section 512(b)(17) are treated as income derived from a separate unrelated trade or business for purposes of paragraph (a) of this section.

(e) S corporation interests—(1) In general. Except as provided in paragraph (e)(2) of this section, if an organization owns stock in an S corporation (S corporation interest), such S corporation interest is treated as an interest in a separate unrelated trade or business for purposes of paragraph (a) of this section. Thus, if an organization owns two S corporation interests, neither of which is described in paragraph (e)(2) of this section, the exempt organization reports two separate unrelated trades or businesses, one for each S corporation interest. The UBTI from an S corporation interest is the amount described in section 512(e)(1)(B).

(2) Exception for a qualifying S corporation interest. Notwithstanding paragraph (e)(1) of this section, an organization may aggregate its UBTI from an S corporation interest with its UBTI from other investment activities (described in paragraph (c)(1) of this section) if the organization's ownership interest in the S corporation meets the criteria for a QPI as described in paragraph (c)(2)(i) of this section (substituting "S corporation" for "partnership" and "shareholder" or "shareholders" for "partner" or "partners," as applicable, throughout paragraphs (c)(2)(i), (c)(3), (c)(4), (c)(5)(iii), (c)(5)(iv), and (c)(6) of this section; "no more than 2 percent of stock ownership" for "no more than 2 percent of the profits interest and no more than 2 percent of the capital interest" in paragraph (c)(3) of this section; "no more than 20 percent of stock ownership" in place of "no more than

20 percent of the capital interest" in paragraph (c)(4)(i) of this section; and "Schedule K-1 (Form 1120-S)" for "Schedule K-1 (Form 1065)" for purposes of paragraph (c)(5)(iv) of this section). Paragraphs (c)(5)(i) and (c)(5)(ii) do not apply for purposes of determining an organization's ownership interest in an S corporation; rather, the average percentage stock ownership determined under paragraph (c)(5)(iii) of this section applies for purposes of this paragraph (e)(2). For purposes of paragraph (c)(5)(iv) of this section, an organization can rely on the Schedule K-1 (Form 1120-S) (or its successor) it receives from the S corporation only if the form lists information sufficient to determine the organization's percentage of stock ownership for the year. A Schedule K-1 (Form 1120-S) that reports "zero" as the organization's number of shares of stock in either the beginning or end of the S corporation's taxable year does not list information sufficient to determine the organization's percentage of stock ownership for the year. The grace period described in paragraph (c)(6) of this section applies to changes in an exempt organization's percentage of stock ownership in an S corporation.

(f) Allocation of deductions. An organization must allocate deductions between separate unrelated trades or businesses using the method described in § 1.512(a)–1(c).

(g) Total UBTI—(1) In general. The total UBTI of an organization with more than one unrelated trade or business is the sum of the UBTI computed with respect to each separate unrelated trade or business (as identified under paragraph (a)(2) of this section and subject to the limitation described in paragraph (g)(2) of this section), less a charitable contribution deduction, an NOL deduction for losses arising in taxable years beginning before January 1, 2018 (pre-2018 NOLs), and a specific deduction under section 512(b)(12), as applicable.

(2) UBTI not less than zero. For purposes of paragraph (g)(1) of this section, the UBTI with respect to any separate unrelated trade or business identified under paragraph (a)(2) of this section cannot be less than zero.

(h) Net operating losses—(1) In general. For taxable years beginning after December 31, 2017, an exempt organization with more than one unrelated trade or business determines the NOL deduction allowed by sections 172(a) and 512(b)(6) separately with respect to each of its unrelated trades or businesses. Accordingly, if an exempt organization has more than one unrelated trade or business, § 1.512(b)–1(e) applies separately with respect to each such unrelated trade or business.

(2) Coordination of pre-2018 and post-2017 NOLs. An organization with pre-2018 NOLs, and with losses arising in a taxable year beginning after December 31, 2017 (post-2017 NOLs), deducts its pre-2018 NOLs from total UBTI before deducting any post-2017 NOLs with regard to a separate unrelated trade or business against the UBTI from such trade or business. Pre-2018 NOLs are taken against the total UBTI as determined under paragraph (g) of this section in a manner that allows for maximum utilization of post-2017 NOLs in a taxable year. For example, an organization could choose to allocate all of its pre-2018 NOLs to one of its separate unrelated trade or business or it could allocate its pre-2018 NOLs ratably among its separate unrelated trades or businesses, whichever results in the greatest utilization of the post-2017 NOLs in that taxable year.

(3) Treatment of NOLs upon the termination, sale, exchange, or other disposition of a separate unrelated trade or business. After offsetting any gain resulting from the termination, sale, exchange, or disposition of a separate unrelated trade or business, any NOL remaining is suspended. However, the suspended NOLs may be used if that previous separate unrelated trade or business is later resumed or if a new unrelated trade or business that is accurately identified using the same NAICS 2-digit code as the previous separate unrelated trade or business is commenced or acquired in a future taxable year.

(4) Treatment of NOLs when the identification of a separate unrelated trade or business changes—(i) In general. For purposes of section 512(a)(6) and this section, a separate unrelated trade or business for which the appropriate identification (within the meaning of paragraph (a) of this section) changes is treated as if the originally identified separate unrelated trade or business is terminated and a new separate unrelated trade or business is commenced. None of the NOLs from the previously identified separate unrelated trade or business will be carried over to the newly identified separate unrelated trade or business. For example, if the nature of a separate unrelated trade or business changes such that it is more accurately described by another NAICS 2-digit code, the separate unrelated trade or business is treated as a new separate unrelated trade or business with no NOLs. The change in identification may apply to all or a part of the originally identified separate unrelated trade or business. If the change in identification applies to the originally identified separate trade or business in its entirety, any NOLs attributable to that separate unrelated trade or business are suspended in accordance with paragraph (h)(3) of this section. If the change in identification applies to the originally identified separate unrelated trade or business in part, the originally identified separate unrelated trade or business that is not changing retains the full NOLs attributable to the originally identified separate unrelated trade or business, without allocation to the portion that became a newly identified separate unrelated trade or business. This paragraph (h)(4) also applies to each QPI that becomes a non-QPI. In this case, any NOLs attributable to the QPI that became a non-QPI are retained with the organization's investment activities described in paragraph (c) of this section.

(ii) Exception for non-material changes. In the case of a separate unrelated trade or business that is accidentally identified using the wrong NAICS 2-digit code or if an organization has determined that a separate unrelated trade or business that has not materially changed is more accurately identified by another NAICS 2-digit code, any NOL attributable to the originally identified separate unrelated trade or business becomes an NOL of the newly identified separate unrelated trade or business.

(iii) Effective date of change in identification. A change in identification described in this paragraph (h)(4) is effective on the first day of the taxable year in which the change in identification is made. Accordingly, the newly identified separate unrelated trade or business is treated as commencing on this date.

(iv) Examples—(A) *In general.* The following examples illustrate the rules described in this paragraph (h)(4).

(B) Example 1. *Erroneous code*—(I) Organization G is described in section 501(c) and is exempt from Federal income tax under section 501(a). In addition to its investment activities, Organization G has two separate unrelated trades or businesses—Q and R—that are identified with different NAICS 2-digit codes. Both Q and R have NOLs carried over from post-2017 taxable years.

(II) In Year 2 (a post-2017 taxable year), Organization G realizes that it accidentally used the wrong NAICS 2-digit code to identify R. The NOLs attributable to R under the old NAICS 2-digit code become the NOLs of

R under the new NAICS 2-digit code as of the first day of Year 2.

(C) Example 2. Material change—(I) Same facts as Example 1, except assume that, in addition to its investment activities, Organization G has three separate unrelated trades or businesses—Q, R, and S—that are identified with different NAICS 2-digit codes. Q, R, and S all have NOLs carried over from post-2017 taxable years.

(II) Organization G changes the NAICS 2-digit code identifying R to the same NAICS 2-digit code identifying S because the nature of the unrelated trade or business materially changed. Any post-2017 NOLs attributable to R are suspended (see paragraph (h)(4)(i) of this section). Organization G now has two separate unrelated trades or businesses—Q and S—as of the first day of Year 2.

(D) Example 3. Partial material change—(I) Same facts as Example 1, except assume that Organization G determines that a part of R has materially changed such that R should be identified as two separate unrelated trades or businesses—R1 and R2. R1 retains the NAICS 2-digit code originally identifying R, and R2 is identified with a new NAICS 2-digit code that is not the same NAICS 2-digit code identifying Q. R2 is treated as a new separate unrelated trade or business with no NOLs as of the first day of Year 2. Any post-2017 NOLs attributable to R remain with R1.

(E) Example 4. QPI to non-QPI—(I) Same facts as Example 1, but assume that Organization G has a partnership interest in T that was, for prior taxable years, a QPI included with Organization G's investment activities. In Year 3 (a post-2017 taxable year), Organization G acquires more than 20 percent of the capital interests in T. The grace period described in paragraph (c)(6) of this section does not apply because the increase in percentage interest was not due to the actions of other partners.

(II) T conducts two trade or business activities that are unrelated trade or business activities with respect to Organization G—T1 and T2. Both T1 and T2 will be treated as new separate unrelated trades or business as of the first day of Year 2. Organization G identifies T1 with the same NAICS 2-digit code used to identify Q and T2 with a NAICS 2-digit code that is different than the NAICS 2-digit codes used to identify Q and R. In addition to its investment activities, Organization G has three separate unrelated trades or businesses—Q, R, and T2. Any post-2017 NOLs attributable to the QPI remain with Organization G's other investment activities separate unrelated trade or business.

§ 1.512(b)-1. Modifications.

Whether a particular item of income falls within any of the modifications provided in section 512(b) shall be determined by all the facts and circumstances of each case. For example, if a payment termed rent by the parties is in fact a return of profits by a person operating the property for the benefit of the tax-exempt organization or is a share of the profits retained by such organization as a partner or joint venturer, such payment is not within the modification for rents. The modifications provided in section 512(b) are as follows:

(a) Certain investment income. (1) In general. Dividends (including an inclusion of subpart F income under section 951(a)(1)(A) or an inclusion of global intangible low-taxed income (GILTI) under section 951A(a), both of which are treated in the same manner as a dividend for purposes of section 512(b)(1)), interest, payments with respect to securities loans (as defined in section 512(a)(5)), annuities, income from notional principal contracts (as defined in § 1.837-7 or regulations issued under section 446), other substantially similar income from ordinary and routine investments to the extent determined by the Commissioner, and all deductions directly connected with any of the foregoing items of income must be excluded in computing unrelated business taxable income.

(2) Limitations.—The exclusions under paragraph (a)(1) of this section do not apply to income derived from and deductions in connection with debt-financed property (as defined in section 514(b)). Moreover, the exclusions under paragraph (a)(1) of this section do not apply to gains or losses from the sale, exchange, or other disposition of any property, or to gains or losses from the lapse or termination of options to buy or sell securities. For rules regarding the treatment of these gains and losses, see section 512(b)(5) and section 1.512(b)-l(d). Furthermore, the exclusions under paragraph (a)(1) of this section do not apply to interest and annuities derived from and deductions in connection with controlled organizations. For rules regarding the treatment of such amounts, see section 512(b)(13) and section 1.512(b)–1(*l*). Finally, the exclusions under paragraph (a)(1) of this section of income from notional principal contracts and income that the Commissioner determines to be substantially similar income from ordinary and routine investments do not apply to income earned by brokers or dealers (including organizations that make a market in derivative financial products, as described in Treasury Regulations 26 CFR 1.954–2T(a)(4)(iii)(B)).

* * *

(b) Royalties. Royalties, including overriding royalties, and all deductions directly connected with such income shall be excluded in computing unrelated business taxable income. However, for taxable years beginning after December 31, 1969, certain royalties from and certain deductions in connection with either, debt-financed property (as defined in section 514(b)) or controlled organizations (as defined in paragraph (*l*) of this section) shall be included in computing unrelated business taxable income. Mineral royalties shall be excluded whether measured by production or by gross or taxable income from the mineral property. However, where an organization owns a working interest in a mineral property, and is not relieved of its share of the development costs by the terms of any agreement with an operator, income received from such an interest shall not be excluded. To the extent not treated as a loan under section 636, payments in discharge of mineral production payments shall be treated in the same manner as royalty payments for the purpose of computing unrelated business taxable income. To the extent treated as a loan under section 636, the amount of any payment in discharge of a production payment which is the equivalent of interest shall be treated as interest for purposes of section 512(b)(1) and paragraph (a) of this section.

(c) Rents—* * *

(2) Taxable years beginning after December 31, 1969.—(i) In general. For taxable years beginning after December 31, 1969, except as provided in subdivision (iii) of this subparagraph, rents from property described in subdivision (ii) of this subparagraph, and the deductions directly connected therewith, shall be excluded in computing unrelated business taxable income. However, notwithstanding subdivision (ii) of this subparagraph, certain rents from and certain deductions in connection with either debt-financed property (as defined in section 514(b)) or property rented to controlled organizations (as defined in paragraph (*l*) of this section) shall be included in computing unrelated business taxable income.

(ii) Excluded rents. The rents which are excluded from unrelated business income under section 512(b)(3)(A) and this paragraph are:

(a) Real property. All rents from real property; and

(b) Personal property. All rents from personal property leased with real property if the rents attributable to such personal property are an incidental amount of the total rents received or accrued under the lease, determined at the time personal property are an incidental amount service by the lessee.

For purposes of the preceding sentence, rents attributable to personal property generally are not an incidental amount of the total rents if such rents exceed 10 percent of the total rents from all the property leased. For example, if the rents attributable to the personal property leased are determined to be $3,000 per year, and the total rents from all property leased are $10,000 per year, then such $3,000 amount is not to be excluded from the computation of unrelated business taxable income by operation of section 512(b)(3)(A)(ii) and this paragraph, since such amount is not an incidental portion of the total rents.

(iii) Exception. Subdivision (ii) of this subparagraph shall not apply, if either:

(a) Excess personal property rents. More than 50 percent of the total rents are attributable to personal property, determined at the time such personal property is first placed in service by the lessee; or

(b) Net profits. The determination of the amount of such rents depends in whole or in part on the income or profits derived by any person from the property leased, other than an amount based on a fixed percentage or percentages of the gross receipts or sales. For purposes of the preceding sentence, the rules contained in paragraph (b)(3) and (6) (other than paragraph (b)(6)(ii)) of § 1.856–4 shall apply.

(iv) Illustration. This subparagraph may be illustrated by the following example:

Example. A, an exempt organization, owns a printing factory which consists of a building housing two printing presses and other equipment necessary for printing. On January 1, 1971, A rents the building and the printing equipment to B for $10,000 a year. The lease states that $9,000 of such rent is for the building and $1,000 for the printing equipment. However, it is determined that notwithstanding the terms of the lease $4,000, or 40 percent ($4,000/$10,000), of the rent is actually attributable to the printing equipment. During 1971, A has $3,000 of deductions, all of which are properly allocable to the land and building. Under these circumstances, A shall not take into account in computing its unrelated business taxable income the $6,000 of rent attributable to the building and the $3,000 of deductions directly connected with such rent. However, the $4,000 of rent attributable to the printing equipment is not excluded from the computation of A's unrelated business taxable income by operation of section 512(b)(3)(A)(ii) or this paragraph since such rent represents more than an incidental portion of the total rents.

(3) Definitions and special rules. For purposes of subparagraph (2) of this paragraph:

(i) Real property defined. The term real property means all real property, including any property described in sections 1245(a)(3)(C) and 1250(c) and the regulations thereunder.

(ii) Personal property defined. The term personal property means all personal property, including any property described in section 1245(a)(3)(B) and the regulations thereunder.

(iii) Multiple leases. If separate leases are entered into with respect to real and personal property, and such properties have an integrated use (e.g., one or more leases for real property and another lease or leases for personal property to be used upon such real property), all such leases shall be considered as one lease.

(iv) Placed in service. Property is placed in service by the lessee when it is first subject to his use in accordance with the terms of the lease. For example, property subject to a lease entered into on November 1, 1971, for a term commencing on January 1, 1972, shall be considered as placed in service on January 1, 1972, regardless of when the property is first actually used by the lessee.

(v) Changes in rent charged or personal property rented. If:

(a) By reason of the placing of additional or substitute personal property in service, there is an increase of 100 percent or more in the rent attributable to all the personal property leased, or

(b) There is a modification of the lease by which there is a change in the rent charged (whether or not there is a change in the amount of personal property rented), the rent attributable to personal property shall be recomputed to determine whether the exclusion under subparagraph (2)(ii)(b) of this paragraph or the exception under subparagraph (2)(iii)(a) of this paragraph applies. Any change in the treatment of rents, attributable to a recomputation under this subdivision, shall be effective only with respect to rents for the period beginning with the event which occasioned the recomputation.

(4) Examples. Subparagraphs (2) and (3) of this paragraph may be illustrated by the following examples:

Example 1. On January 1, 1971, A, an exempt organization, executes two leases with B. One is for the rental of a computer, with a stated annual rent of $750. The other is for the rental of office space in which to use the computer, at a stated annual rent of $7,250. The total annual rent under both leases for 1971 is $8,000. At the time the computer is first placed in service, however, taking both leases into consideration, it is determined that notwithstanding the terms of the leases $3,000, or 37.5 percent ($3,000/$8,000), of the rent is actually attributable to the computer. Therefore, for 1971, only the $5,000 ($8,000-$3,000) attributable to the rental of the office space is excluded from the computation of A's unrelated business taxable income by operation of section 512(b)(3).

Example 2. Assume the facts as stated in example (1). Assume further that the leases to which the computer and office space are subject in example (1) provide that the rent may be increased or decreased, depending upon the prevailing rental value for similar computers and office space. On January 1, 1972, the total annual rent is increased in the computer lease to $2,000, and in the office space lease to $9,000. For 1972, it is determined that notwithstanding the terms of the leases $6,000, or 54.5 percent ($6,000/$11,000), of the total rent is actually attributable to the computer as of that time. Even though the rent attributable to personal property now exceeds 50 percent of the total rent, the rent attributable to real property will continue to be excluded, since there was no modification of the terms of the leases and since the increase in the rent was not attributable to the placing of new personal property in service. See subparagraph (3)(v) of this paragraph. Thus, for 1972 the $5,000 of rent attributable to the office space continues to be excluded from the computation of A's unrelated business taxable income by operation of section 512(b)(3).

Example 3. Assume the facts as stated in example (1), except that on January 1, 1973, B rents a second computer from A, which is placed in service on that date. The total rent is increased to $2,000 for the computer lease and to $10,000 for the office space lease. It is determined at the time the second computer is first placed in service that notwithstanding the terms of the leases $7,000 of the rent is actually attributable to the computers. Since the rent attributable to personal property has increased by more than 100 percent

($4,000/$3,000=133 percent), a redetermination must be made pursuant to subparagraph (3)(v)(a) of this paragraph. As a result, 58.3 percent ($7,000/$12,000) of the total rent is determined to be attributable to personal property. Accordingly, since more than 50 percent of the total rent A receives is attributable to the personal property leased, none of the rents are excluded from the computation of A's unrelated business taxable income by operation of section 512(b)(3).

Example 4. Assume the facts as stated in example (3), except that on June 30, 1975, the lease between B and A is modified. The total rent for the computer lease is reduced to $1,500 and the total rent for the office space lease is reduced to $7,500. Pursuant to subdivision (3)(v)(b) of this paragraph, a redetermination is made as of June 30, 1975. As of the modification date, it is determined that notwithstanding the terms of the leases, the rent actually attributable to the computers is $4,000, or 44.4 percent ($4,000/$9,000), of the total rent. Since less than 50 percent of the total rent is now attributable to personal property, the rent attributable to real property ($5,000), for periods after June 30, 1975, is excluded from the computation of A's unrelated business taxable income by operation of section 512(b)(3). However, the rent attributable to personal property ($4,000) is not excluded from unrelated business taxable income for such periods by operation of section 512(b)(3), since it represents more than an incidental portion of the total rent.

(5) Rendering of services. For purposes of this paragraph, payments for the use or occupancy of rooms and other space where services are also rendered to the occupant, such as for the use or occupancy of rooms or other quarters in hotels, boarding houses, or apartment houses furnishing hotel services, or in tourist camps or tourist homes, motor courts, or motels, or for the use of occupancy of space in parking lots, warehouses, or storage garages, does not constitute rent from real property. Generally, services are considered rendered to the occupant if they are primarily for his convenience and are other than those usually or customarily rendered in connection with the rental of rooms or other space for occupancy only. The supplying of maid service, for example, constitutes such service; whereas the furnishing of heat and light, the cleaning of public entrances, exists, stairways, and lobbies, the collection of trash, etc., are not considered as services rendered to the occupant. Payments for the use or occupancy of entire private residences or living quarters in duplex or multiple housing units, of offices in any office building, etc., are generally treated as rent from real property.

(d)(1) Gains and losses from the sale, etc. of property. There shall also be excluded from the computation of unrelated business taxable income gains or losses from the sale, exchange, or other disposition of property other than (i) stock in trade or other property of a kind which would properly be included in the inventory of the organization if on hand at the close of the taxable year, or (ii) property held primarily for sale to customers in the ordinary course of the trade or business. This exclusion does not apply with respect to the cutting of timber which is considered, upon the application of section 631(a), as a sale or exchange of such timber. In addition, for taxable years beginning after December 31, 1969, this exclusion does not apply to the gain derived from the sale or other disposition of debt-financed property (as defined in section 514(b)). Otherwise, the exclusion under section 512(b)(5) applies with respect to gains and losses from involuntary conversions, casualties, etc.

(2) There shall be excluded from the computation of unrelated business taxable income any gain from the lapse or termination after December 31, 1975, of options to buy or sell securities (as that term is defined in section 1236(c)). An option is considered terminated when the organization's obligation under the option ceases by any means other than by reason of the exercise or lapse of such option. If the exclusion is otherwise available it will apply whether or not the organization owns the securities upon which the option is written, that is, whether or not the option is covered. However, income from the lapse or termination of an option is excludable only if the option is written in connection with the organization's investment activities. Thus, for example, if the securities upon which the options are written are held by the organization as inventory or for sale to customers in the ordinary course of a trade or business, the income from the lapse or termination will not be excludable under the provisions of this paragraph. Similarly, if an organization is engaged in the trade or business of writing options (whether or not such options are covered) the exclusion will not be available.

(e) Net operating losses. (1) The net operating loss deduction provided in section 172 shall be allowed in computing unrelated business taxable income. However, the net operating loss carryback or carryover (from a taxable year for which the taxpayer is subject to the provisions of section 511) shall be determined under section 172 without taking into account any amount of income or deduction which is not included under section 511 in computing unrelated business taxable income. For example, a loss attributable to an unrelated trade or business shall not be diminished by reason of the receipt of dividend income.

(2) For the purpose of computing the net operating loss deduction provided by section 172, any prior taxable year for which an organization was not subject to the provisions of section 511, or a corresponding provision of prior law, shall not be taken into account. Thus, if the organization was not subject to the provisions of section 511 or Supplement U of the Internal Revenue Code of 1939 for a preceding taxable year, the net operating loss is not a carryback to such preceding taxable year, and the net operating loss carryover to succeeding taxable years is not reduced by the taxable income for such preceding taxable year.

(3) A net operating loss carryback or carryover shall be allowed only from a taxable year for which the taxpayer is subject to the provisions of section 511, or a corresponding provision of prior law.

(4) In determining the span of years for which a net operating loss may be carried for purposes of section 172, taxable years in which an organization was not subject to the provisions of section 511 or a corresponding provision of prior law shall be taken into account. Thus, for example, if an organization is subject to the provisions of section 511 for the taxable year 1955 and has a net operating loss for that year, the last taxable year to which any part thereof may be carried over is the year 1960 regardless of whether the organization is subject to the provisions of section 511 in any of the intervening taxable years.

(5) See § 1.512(a)–6(h) regarding the computation of the net operating loss deduction when an organization has more than one unrelated trade or business.

(f) Research. (1) Income derived from research for the United States or any of its agencies or instrumentalities or a State or political subdivision thereof, and all deductions directly connected with such income, shall be excluded in computing unrelated business taxable income.

(2) In the case of a college, university, or hospital, all income derived from research performed for any person and all deductions directly connected with such income, shall be excluded in computing unrelated business taxable income.

(3) In the case of an organization operated primarily for the purpose of carrying on fundamental research (as distinguished from applied research) the results of which are freely available to the general public, all income derived from research performed for any person and all deductions directly connected with such income shall be excluded in computing unrelated business taxable income.

(4) For the purpose of §§ 1.512(a)–1, 1.512(a)–2, and this section, the term research does not include activities of a type ordinarily carried on as an incident to commercial or industrial operations, for example, the ordinary testing or inspection of materials or products or the designing or construction of equipment, buildings, etc. The term fundamental research does not include research carried on for the primary purpose of commercial or industrial application.

(g) Charitable, etc., contributions. **(1)** In computing the unrelated business taxable income of an organization described in section 511(a)(2) the deduction from gross income allowed by section 170 (relating to charitable contributions and gifts) shall be allowed, whether or not the contribution is directly connected with the carrying on of the trade or business. Section 512(b)(10) provides that this deduction shall not exceed 5 percent of the organization's unrelated business taxable income computed without regard to that deduction. The provisions of section 170(b)(2) are not applicable to contributions by the organizations described in section 511(a)(2).

(2) In computing the unrelated business taxable income of a trust described in section 511(b)(2), the deduction allowed by section 170 (relating to charitable contributions and gifts) shall be allowed whether or not the contribution is directly connected with the carrying on of the trade or business. The deduction is limited as provided in section 170(b)(1)(A) and (B), except that the amounts so allowed are determined on the basis of unrelated business taxable income computed without regard to this deduction (rather than on the basis of adjusted gross income). For purposes of this deduction, a distribution by a trust described in section 511(b)(2) made pursuant to the trust instrument to a beneficiary described in section 170 shall be treated in the same manner as gifts or contributions.

(3) The contribution, whether made by a trust or other exempt organization, must be paid to another organization to be allowable. For example, a university described in section 501(c)(3) which is exempt from tax and which operates an unrelated business, shall be allowed a deduction, not in excess of 5 percent of its unrelated business taxable income, for gifts or contributions to another university described in section 501(c)(3) for educational work but shall not be allowed any deduction for amounts expended in administering its own educational program.

(4) The term unrelated business taxable income as used in section 512(b)(10) and (11) refers to unrelated business taxable income after application of section 512(a)(6).

* * *

(h) Specific deduction—(1) In general. In computing unrelated business taxable income a specific deduction from gross income of $1,000 is allowed. However, for taxable years beginning after December 31, 1969, such specific deduction is not allowed in computing the net operating loss under section 172 and paragraph (6) of section 512(b).

(2) Special rule for a diocese, province of a religious order, or a convention or association of churches. (i) In the case of a diocese, province of a religious order, or a convention or association of churches, there shall be allowed with respect to each parish, individual church, district, or other local unit a specific deduction equal to the lower of $1,000 or the gross income derived from an unrelated trade or business regularly conducted by such local unit. However, a diocese, province of a religious order, or a convention or association of churches shall not be entitled to a specific deduction for a local unit which, for a taxable year, files a separate return. In the case of a local unit which, for a taxable year, files a separate return, such local unit may claim a specific deduction equal to the lower of $1,000 or the gross income derived from any unrelated trade or business which it regularly conducts.

(ii) The provisions of this subparagraph may be illustrated by the following example:

Example. X is an association of churches on the calendar year basis. X is divided into local units A, B, C, and D. During 1973, A, B, C, and D derive gross income of, respectively, $1,200, $800, $1,500, and $700 from unrelated businesses which they regularly conduct. Furthermore, for such taxable year, D files a separate return. X may claim a specific deduction of $1,000 with respect to A, $800 with respect to B, and $1,000 with respect to C. X may not claim a specific deduction with respect to D. D, however, may claim a specific deduction of $700 on its return.

* * *

(k) Income and deductions from debt-financed property. For taxable years beginning after December 31, 1969, in the case of debt-financed property (as defined in section 514(b)), there shall be included in the unrelated business taxable income of an exempt organization, as an item of gross income derived from an unrelated trade or business, the amount of unrelated debt-financed income determined under section 514(a)(1) and § 1.514(a)–1(a), and there shall be allowed, as a deduction with respect to such income, the amount determined under section 514(a)(2) and § 1.514(a)–1(b).

(*l*) Interest, annuities, royalties, and rents from controlled organizations.—

(1) In general. For taxable years beginning after December 31, 1969, if an exempt organization (hereinafter referred to as the controlling organization) has control (as defined in subparagraph (4) of this paragraph) of another organization (hereinafter referred to as the controlled organization), the controlling organization shall include as an item of gross income in computing its unrelated business taxable income, the amount of interest, annuities, royalties, and rents derived from the controlled organization determined under subparagraph (2) or (3) of this paragraph. The preceding sentence shall apply whether or not the activity conducted by the controlling organization to derive such amounts represents a trade or business or is regularly carried on. Thus, amounts received by a controlling organization from the rental of its real property to a controlled organization may be included in the unrelated business taxable income of the controlling organization, even though the rental of such property is not an activity regularly carried on by the controlling organization.

(2) Exempt controlled organization.—(i) In general. If the controlled organization is exempt from taxation under section 501(a), the amount referred to in subparagraph (1) of this paragraph is an amount which bears the same ratio to the interest, annuities, royalties, and rents received by the controlling organization from the controlled organization as the unrelated business taxable income of the controlled organization bears to whichever of the following amounts is the greater:

(*a*) The taxable income of the controlled organization, computed as though the controlled organization were not exempt from taxation under section 501(a), or

(*b*) The unrelated business taxable income of the controlled organization, both determined without regard to any amounts paid directly or indirectly to the controlling organization. The controlling organization shall be allowed all deductions directly connected with amounts included in gross income under the preceding sentence.

(ii) Examples. This subparagraph may be illustrated by the following examples:

Example 1. A, an exempt scientific organization described in section 501(c)(3), owns all the stock of B, another exempt scientific organization described in section 501(c)(3). During 1971, A rents space for a laboratory to B for $15,000 a year. A's total deductions for 1971 with respect to the leased property are $3,000: $1,000 for maintenance and $2,000 for depreciation. If B were not an exempt organization, its total taxable income would be $300,000, disregarding rent paid to A. B's unrelated business taxable income, disregarding rent paid to A, is $100,000. Under these circumstances, $4,000 of the rent paid by B will be included by A as net rental income in determining its unrelated business taxable income, computed as follows:

B's unrelated business taxable income (disregarding rent paid to A)	$100,000
B's taxable income (computed as though B were not exempt and disregarding rent paid to A)	300,000
Ratio ($100,000/$300,000)	1/3
Total rent	15,000
Total deductions	3,000
Rental income treated as gross income from an unrelated trade or business (1/3 of $15,000)	5,000
Less deductions directly connected with such income (1/3 of $3,000)	1,000
Net rental income included by A in computing its unrelated business taxable income	$ 4,000

Example 2. Assume the facts as stated in example (1), except that B's taxable income is $90,000 (computed as though B were not an exempt organization, and disregarding rents paid to A). B's unrelated business taxable income ($100,000) is therefore greater than its taxable income ($90,000). Thus, the ratio used to determine the portion of rent received by A which is to be taken into account is one since both the numerator and denominator of such ratio is B's unrelated business taxable income. Consequently, all the rent received by A from B ($15,000), and all the deductions directly connected therewith ($3,000), are included by A in computing its unrelated business taxable income.

(3) Nonexempt controlled organization—(i) In general. If the controlled organization is not exempt from taxation under section 501(a), the amount referred to in subparagraph (1) of this paragraph is an amount which bears the same ratio to the interest, annuities, royalties, and rents received by the controlling organization from the controlled organization as the excess taxable income (as defined in subdivision (ii) of this subparagraph) of the controlled organization bears to whichever of the following amounts is the greater:

(a) The taxable income of the controlled organization, or

(b) The excess taxable income of the controlled organization,

both determined without regard to any amount paid directly or indirectly to the controlling organization. The controlling organization shall be allowed all deductions which are directly connected with amounts included in gross income under the preceding sentence.

(ii) Excess taxable income. For purposes of this paragraph, the term excess taxable income means the excess of the controlled organization's taxable income over the amount of such taxable income which, if derived directly by the controlling organization, would not be unrelated business taxable income.

(iii) Examples. This subparagraph may be illustrated by the following examples:

Example 1. A, an exempt university described in section 501(c)(3), owns all the stock of M, a nonexempt organization. During 1971, M leases a factory and a dormitory from A for a total annual rent of $100,000. During the taxable year, M has $500,000 of taxable income, disregarding the rent paid to A: $150,000 from a dormitory for students of A university, and $350,000 from the operation of a factory which is a business unrelated to A's exempt purpose. A's deductions for 1971 with respect to the leased property are $4,000 for the dormitory and $16,000 for the factory. Under these circumstances, $56,000 of the rent paid by M will be included by A as net rental income in determining its unrelated business taxable income, computed as follows:

M's taxable income (disregarding rent paid to A)	$ 500,000
Less taxable income from dormitory	150,000
Excess taxable income	$350,000
Ratio ($350,000/$500,000)	7/10
Total rent paid to A	$100,000
Total deductions ($4,000 + $16,000)	20,000
Rental income treated as gross income from an unrelated trade or business (7/10 of $100,000)	70,000
Less deductions directly connected with such income (7/10 of $20,000)	14,000
Net rental income included by A in computing its unrelated business taxable income	$ 56,000

Example 2. Assume the facts as stated in example (1), except that M's taxable income (disregarding rent paid to A) is $300,000, consisting of $350,000 from the operation of the factory and a $50,000 loss from the operation of the dormitory. Thus, M's excess taxable income is also $300,000, since none of M's taxable income would be excluded from the computation of A's unrelated business taxable income if received directly by A. The ratio of M's excess taxable income to its taxable income is therefore one ($300,000/$300,000). Thus, all the rent received by A from M ($100,000), and all the deductions directly connected therewith ($20,000), are included in the computation of A's unrelated business taxable income.

(4) Control. (i) In general. For purposes of this paragraph—

(a) Stock corporation. In the case of an organization which is a stock corporation, the term control means ownership by an exempt organization of stock possessing at least 80 percent of the total combined voting power of all classes of stock entitled to vote and at least 80 percent of the total number of shares of all other classes of stock of such corporation.

(b) Nonstock organization. In the case of a nonstock organization, the term control means that at least 80 percent of the directors or trustees of such organization are either representatives of or directly or indirectly controlled by an exempt organization. A trustee or director is a representative of an exempt organization if he is a trustee, director, agent, or employee of such exempt organization. A trustee or director is controlled by an exempt organization if such organization has the power to remove such trustee or director and designate a new trustee or director.

(ii) Gain or loss of control. If control of an organization (as defined in subdivision (i) of this subparagraph) is acquired or relinquished during the taxable year, only the interest, annuities, royalties, and rents paid or accrued to the controlling organization in accordance with its method of accounting for that portion of the taxable year it has control shall be subject to the tax on unrelated business income.

(5) Amounts taxable under other provisions of the Code—(i) In general. Except as provided in subdivision (ii) of this subparagraph, section 512(b)(13) and this paragraph do not apply to amounts which are included in the computation of unrelated business taxable income by operation of any other provision of the Code. However, amounts which are not included in unrelated business taxable income by operation of section 512(a)(1), or which are excluded by operation of section 512(b)(1), (2), or (3), may be included in unrelated business taxable income by operation of section 512(b)(13) and this paragraph.

(ii) Debt-financed property. Rents deprived from the lease of debt-financed property by a controlling organization to a controlled organization are subject to the rules contained in section 512(b)(13) and this paragraph. Thus, if a controlling organization leases debt-financed property to a controlled organization, the amount of rents includible in the controlling organization's unrelated business taxable income shall first be determined under section 512(b)(13) and this paragraph, and only the portion of such rents not taken into account by operation of section 512(b)(13) are taken into account by operation of section 514. See example (3) of § 1.514(b)–1(b)(3).

§ 1.513–1. Definition of unrelated trade or business.

(a) In general. As used in section 512 the term unrelated business taxable income means the gross income derived by an organization from any unrelated trade or business regularly carried on by it, less the deductions and subject to the modifications provided in section 512. Section 513 specifies with certain exceptions that the phrase unrelated trade or business means, in the case of an organization subject to the tax imposed by section 511, any trade or business the conduct of which is not substantially related (aside from the need of such organization for income or funds or the use it makes of the profits derived) to the exercise or performance by such organization of its charitable, educational, or other purpose or function constituting the basis for its exemption under section 501 (or, in the case of an organization described in section 511(a)(2)(B), to the exercise or performance of any purpose or function described in section 501(c)(3)). For certain exceptions from this definition, see paragraph (e) of this section. For a special definition of unrelated trade or business applicable to certain trusts, see paragraph (f) of this section. Therefore, unless one of the specific exceptions of section 512 or 513 is applicable, gross income of an exempt organization subject to the tax imposed by section 511 is includible in the computation of unrelated business taxable income if: (1) It is income from trade or business; (2) such trade or business is regularly carried on by the organization; and (3) the conduct of such trade or business is not substantially related (other than through the production of funds) to the organization's performance of its exempt functions.

(b) Trade or business. The primary objective of adoption of the unrelated business income tax was to eliminate a source of unfair competition by placing the unrelated business activities of certain exempt organizations upon the same tax basis as the nonexempt business endeavors with which they compete. On the other hand, where an activity does not possess the characteristics of a trade or business within the meaning of section 162, such as when an organization sends out low-cost articles incidental to the solicitation of charitable contributions, the unrelated business income tax does not apply since the organization is not in competition with taxable organizations. However, in general, any activity of a section 511 organization which is carried on for the production of income and which otherwise possesses the characteristics required to constitute trade or business within the meaning of section 162—and which, in addition, is not substantially related to the performance of exempt functions—presents sufficient likelihood of unfair competition to be within the policy of the tax. Accordingly, for purposes of section 513 the term trade or business has the same meaning it has in section 162, and generally includes any activity carried on for the production of income from the sale of goods or performance of services. Thus, the term trade or business in section 513 is not limited to integrated aggregates of assets, activities and good will which comprise businesses for the purposes of certain other provisions of the Internal Revenue Code. Activities of producing or distributing goods or performing services from which a particular amount of gross income is derived do not lose identity as trade or business merely because they are carried on within a larger aggregate of similar activities or within a larger complex of other endeavors which may, or may not, be related to the exempt purposes of the organization. Thus, for example, the regular sale of pharmaceutical supplies to the general public by a hospital pharmacy does not lose identity as trade or business merely because the pharmacy also furnishes supplies to the hospital and patients of the hospital in accordance with its exempt purposes or in compliance with the terms of section 513(a)(2). Similarly, activities of soliciting, selling, and publishing commercial advertising do not lose identity as a trade or business even though the advertising is published in an exempt organization periodical which contains editorial matter related to the exempt purposes of the organization. However, where an activity carried on for the production of income constitutes an unrelated trade or business, no part of such trade or business shall be excluded from such classification merely because it does not result in profit.

(c) Regularly carried on—(1) General principles. In determining whether trade or business from which a particular amount of gross income derives is regularly carried on, within the meaning of section 512, regard must be had to the frequency and continuity with which the activities productive of the income are conducted and the manner in which they are pursued. This requirement must be applied in light of the purpose of the unrelated business income tax to place exempt organization business activities upon the same tax basis as the nonexempt business endeavors with which they compete. Hence, for example, specific business activities of an exempt organization will ordinarily be deemed to be regularly carried on if they manifest a frequency and continuity, and are pursued in a manner, generally similar to comparable commercial activities of nonexempt organizations.

(2) Application of principles in certain cases—(i) Normal time span of activities. Where income producing activities are of a kind normally conducted by nonexempt commercial organizations on a year-round basis, the conduct of such activities by an exempt organization over a period of only a few weeks does not constitute the regular carrying on of trade or business. For example, the operation of a sandwich stand by a hospital auxiliary for only 2 weeks at a state fair would not be the regular conduct of trade or business. However, the conduct of year-round business activities for one day each week would constitute the regular carrying on of trade or business. Thus, the operation of a commercial parking lot on Saturday of each week would be the regular conduct of trade or business. Where income producing activities are of a kind normally undertaken by nonexempt commercial organizations only on a seasonal basis, the conduct of such activities by an exempt organization during a significant portion of the season ordinarily constitutes the regular conduct of trade or business. For example, the operation of a track for horse racing for several weeks of a year would be considered the regular conduct of trade or business because it is usual to carry on such trade or business only during a particular season.

(ii) Intermittent activities; in general. In determining whether or not intermittently conducted activities are regularly carried on, the manner of conduct of the activities must be compared with the manner in which commercial activities are normally pursued by nonexempt organizations. In general, exempt organization business activities which are engaged in only discontinuously or periodically will not be considered regularly carried on if they are conducted without the competitive and promotional efforts typical of commercial endeavors. For example, the publication of advertising in programs for sports events or music or drama performances will not ordinarily be deemed to be the regular carrying on of business. Similarly, where an organization sells certain types of goods or services to a particular class of persons in pursuance of its exempt functions or primarily for the convenience of such persons within the meaning of section 513(a)(2) (as, for example, the sale of books by a college bookstore to students or the sale of pharmaceutical supplies by a hospital pharmacy to patients of the hospital), casual sales in the course of such activity which do not qualify as related to the exempt function involved or as described in section 513(a)(2) will not be treated as regular. On the other hand, where the nonqualifying sales are not merely casual, but are systematically and consistently promoted and carried on by the organization, they meet the section 512 requirement of regularity.

(iii) Intermittent activities; special rule in certain cases of infrequent conduct. Certain intermittent income producing activities occur so infrequently that neither their recurrence nor the manner of their conduct will cause them to be regarded as trade or business regularly carried on. For example, income producing or fund raising activities lasting only a short period of time will not ordinarily be treated as regularly carried on if they recur only occasionally or sporadically. Furthermore, such activities will not be regarded as regularly carried on merely because they are conducted on an annually recurrent basis. Accordingly, income derived from the conduct of an annual dance or similar fund raising event for charity would not be income from trade or business regularly carried on.

(d) Substantially related—(1) In general. Gross income derives from unrelated trade or business, within the meaning of section 513(a), if the conduct of the trade or business which produces the income is not substantially related (other than through the production of funds) to the purposes for which exemption is granted. The presence of this requirement necessitates an examination of the relationship between the business activities which generate the particular income in question—the activities, that is, of producing or distributing the goods or performing the services involved—and the accomplishment of the organization's exempt purposes.

(2) Type of relationship required. Trade or business is related to exempt purposes, in the relevant sense, only where the conduct of the business activities has causal relationship to the achievement of exempt purposes (other than through the production of income); and it is substantially related, for purposes of section 513, only if the causal relationship is a substantial one. Thus, for the conduct of trade or business from which a particular amount of gross income is derived to be substantially related to purposes for which exemption is granted, the production or distribution of the goods or the performance of the services from which the gross income is derived must contribute importantly to the accomplishment of those purposes. Where the production or distribution of the goods or the performance of the services does not contribute importantly to the accomplishment of the exempt purposes of an organization, the income from the sale of the goods or the performance of the services does not derive from the conduct of related trade or business. Whether activities productive of gross income contribute importantly to the accomplishment of any purpose for which an organization is granted exemption depends in each case upon the facts and circumstances involved.

(3) Size and extent of activities. In determining whether activities contribute importantly to the accomplishment of an exempt purpose, the size and extent of the activities involved must be considered in relation to the nature and extent of the exempt function which they purport to serve. Thus, where income is realized by an exempt organization from activities which are in part related to the performance of its exempt functions, but which are conducted on a larger scale than is reasonably necessary for performance of such functions, the gross income attributable to that portion of the activities in excess of the needs of exempt functions constitutes gross income from the conduct of unrelated trade or business. Such income is not derived from the production or distribution of goods or the performance of services which contribute importantly to the accomplishment of any exempt purpose of the organization.

(4) Application of principles—(i) Income from performance of exempt functions.

(A) In general. Gross income derived from charges for the performance of exempt functions does not constitute gross income from the conduct of unrelated trade or business.

(B) Examples. The following examples illustrate the application of this paragraph (d)(4)(i):

Example 1. M, an organization described in section 501(c)(3), operates a school for training children in the performing arts, such as acting, singing, and dancing. It presents performances by its students and derives gross income from admission charges for the performances. The students' participation in performances before audiences is an essential part of their training. Since the income realized from the performances derives from activities which contribute importantly to the accomplishment of M's exempt purposes, it does not constitute gross income from unrelated trade or business. (For specific exclusion applicable in certain cases of contributed services, see section 513(a)(1) and paragraph (e)(1) of this section.)

Example 2. N is a trade union qualified for exemption under section 501(c)(5). To improve the trade skills of its members, N conducts refresher training courses and supplies handbooks and technical manuals. N receives payments from its members for these services and materials. However, the development and improvement of the skills of its members is one of the purposes for which exemption is granted N; and the activities described contribute importantly to that purpose. Therefore, the income derived from these activities does not constitute gross income from unrelated trade or business.

Example 3. O is an industry trade association qualified for exemption under section 501(c)(6). It presents a trade show in which members of its industry join in an exhibition of industry products. O derives income from charges made to exhibitors for exhibit space and admission fees charged patrons or viewers of the show. The show is not a sales facility for individual exhibitors; its purpose is the promotion and stimulation of interest in, and demand for, the industry's products in general, and it is conducted in a manner reasonably calculated to achieve that purpose. The stimulation of demand for the industry's products in general is one of the purposes for which exemption is granted O. Consequently, the activities productive of O's gross income from the show—that is, the promotion, organization and conduct of the exhibition—contribute importantly to the achievement of an exempt purpose, and the income does not constitute gross income from unrelated trade or business. See also section 513(d) and regulations thereunder regarding sales activity.

* * *

(ii) Disposition of product of exempt functions. Ordinarily, gross income from the sale of products which result from the performance of exempt functions does not constitute gross income from the conduct of unrelated trade or business if the product is sold in substantially the same state it is in on completion of the exempt functions. Thus, in the case of an organization described in section 501(c)(3) and engaged in a program of rehabilitation of handicapped persons, income from sale of articles made by such persons as a part of their rehabilitation training would not be gross income from conduct of unrelated trade or business. The income in such case would be from sale of products, the production of which contributed importantly to the accomplishment of purposes for which exemption is granted the organization—namely, rehabilitation of the handicapped. On the other hand, if a product resulting from an exempt function is utilized or exploited in further business endeavor beyond that reasonably appropriate or necessary for disposition in the state it is in upon completion of exempt functions, the gross income derived therefrom would be from conduct of unrelated trade or business. Thus, in the case of an experimental dairy herd maintained for scientific purposes by a research organization described in section 501(c)(3), income from sale of milk and cream produced in the ordinary course of operation of the project would not be gross income from conduct of unrelated trade or business. On the other hand, if the organization were to utilize the milk and cream in the further manufacture of food items such as ice cream, pastries, etc., the gross income from the sale of such products would be from the conduct of unrelated trade or business unless the manufacturing activities themselves contribute importantly to the accomplishment of an exempt purpose of the organization.

(iii) Dual use of assets or facilities. In certain cases, an asset or facility necessary to the conduct of exempt functions may also be employed in a commercial endeavor. In such cases, the mere fact of the use of the asset or facility in exempt functions does not, by itself, make the income from the commercial endeavor gross income from related trade or business. The test, instead, is whether the activities productive of the income in question contribute importantly to the accomplishment of exempt purposes. Assume, for example, that a museum exempt under section 501(c)(3) has a theater auditorium which is specially designed and equipped for showing of educational films in connection with its program of public education in the arts and sciences. The theater is a principal feature of the museum and is in continuous operation during the hours the museum is open to the public. If the organization were to operate the theater as an ordinary motion picture theater for public entertainment during the evening hours when the museum was closed, gross income from such operation would be gross income from conduct of unrelated trade or business.

(iv) Exploitation of exempt functions. In certain cases, activities carried on by an organization in the performance of exempt functions may generate good will or other intangibles which are capable of being exploited in commercial endeavors. Where an organization exploits such an intangible in commercial activities, the mere fact that the resultant income depends in part upon an exempt function of the organization does not make it gross income from related trade or business. In such cases, unless the commercial activities themselves contribute importantly to the accomplishment of an exempt purpose, the income which they produce is gross income from the conduct of unrelated trade or business. The application of this subdivision is illustrated in the following examples:

Example 1. U, an exempt scientific organization, enjoys an excellent reputation in the field of biological research. It exploits this reputation regularly by selling endorsements of various items of laboratory equipment to manufacturers. The endorsing of laboratory equipment does not contribute importantly to the accomplishment of any purpose for which exemption is granted U. Accordingly, the income derived from the sale of endorsements is gross income from unrelated trade or business.

Example 2. V, an exempt university, has a regular faculty and a regularly enrolled student body. During the school year, V sponsors the appearance of professional theater companies and symphony orchestras which present drama and musical performances for the students and faculty members. Members of the general public are also admitted. V advertises these performances and supervises advance ticket sales at various places, including such university facilities as the cafeteria and the university bookstore. V derives gross income from the conduct of the performances. However, while the presentation of the performances makes use of an intangible generated by V's exempt educational functions—the presence of the student body and faculty—the presentation of such drama and music events contributes importantly to the overall educational and cultural function of the university. Therefore, the income which V receives does not constitute gross income from the conduct of unrelated trade or business.

Example 3. W is an exempt business league with a large membership. Under an arrangement with an advertising agency, W regularly mails brochures, pamphlets and other commercial advertising materials to its members, for which service W charges the agency an agreed amount per enclosure. The distribution of the advertising materials does not contribute importantly to the accomplishment of any purpose for which W is granted exemption. Accordingly, the payments made to W by the advertising agency constitute gross income from unrelated trade or business.

Example 4. X, an exempt organization for the advancement of public interest in classical music, owns a radio station and operates it in a manner which contributes importantly to the accomplishment of the purposes for which the organization is granted exemption. However, in the course of the operation of the station the organization derives gross income from the regular sale of advertising time and services to commercial advertisers in the manner of an ordinary commercial station. Neither the sale of such time nor the performance of such services contributes importantly to the accomplishment of any purpose for which the organization is granted exemption. Notwithstanding the fact that the production of the advertising income depends upon the existence of the listening audience resulting from performance of exempt functions, such income is gross income from unrelated trade or business.

Example 5. Y, an exempt university, provides facilities, instruction and faculty supervision for a campus newspaper operated by its students. In addition to news items and editorial commentary, the newspaper publishes paid advertising. The solicitation, sale, and publication of the advertising are conducted by students, under the supervision and instruction of the university. Although the services rendered to advertisers are of a commercial character, the advertising business contributes importantly to the university's educational program through the training of the students involved. Hence, none of the income derived from publication of the newspaper constitutes gross income from unrelated trade or business. The same result would follow even though the newspaper is published by a separately incorporated section 501(c)(3) organization, qualified under the university rules for recognition of student activities, and even though such organization utilizes its own facilities and is independent of faculty supervision, but carries out its educational purposes by means of student instruction of other students in the editorial and advertising activities and student participation in those activities.

Example 6. Z is an association exempt under section 501(c)(6), formed to advance the interests of a particular profession and drawing its membership from the members of that profession. Z publishes a monthly journal containing articles and other editorial material which contribute importantly to the accomplishment of purposes for which exemption is granted the organization. Income from the sale of subscriptions to members and others in accordance with the organization's exempt purposes, therefore, does not constitute gross income from unrelated trade or business. In connection with the publication of the journal, Z also derives income from the regular sale of space and services for general consumer advertising, including advertising of such products as soft drinks, automobiles, articles of apparel, and home appliances. Neither the publication of such advertisements nor the performance of services for such commercial advertisers contributes importantly to the accomplishment of any purpose for which exemption is granted. Therefore, notwithstanding the fact that the production of income from advertising utilizes the circulation developed and maintained in performance of exempt functions, such income is gross income from unrelated trade or business.

Example 7. The facts are as described in the preceding example, except that the advertising in Z's journal promotes only products which are within the general area of professional interest of its members. Following a practice common among taxable magazines which publish advertising, Z requires its advertising to comply with certain general standards of taste, fairness, and accuracy; but within those limits the form, content, and manner of presentation of the advertising messages are governed by the basic objective of the advertisers to promote the sale of the advertised products. While the advertisements contain certain information, the informational function of the advertising is incidental to the controlling aim of stimulating demand for the advertised products and differs in no essential respect from the informational function of any commercial advertising. Like taxable publishers of advertising, Z accepts advertising only from those who are willing to pay its prescribed rates. Although continuing education of its members in matters pertaining to their profession is one of the purposes for which Z is granted exemption, the publication of advertising designed and selected in the manner of ordinary commercial advertising is not an educational activity of the kind contemplated by the exemption statute; it differs fundamentally from such an activity both in its governing objective and in its method. Accordingly, Z's publication of advertising does not contribute importantly to the accomplishment of its exempt purposes; and the income which it derives from advertising constitutes gross income from unrelated trade or business.

(e) Exceptions. Section 513(a) specifically states that the term unrelated trade or business does not include:

(1) Any trade or business in which substantially all the work in carrying on such trade or business is performed for the organization without compensation; or

(2) Any trade or business carried on by an organization described in section 501(c)(3) or by a governmental college or university described in section 511(a)(2)(B), primarily for the convenience of its members, students, patients, officers, or employees; or, any trade or business carried on by a local association of employees described in section 501(c)(4) organized before May 27, 1969, which consists of the selling by the organization of items of work-related clothes and equipment and items normally sold through vending machines, through food dispensing facilities, or by snack bars, for the convenience of its members at their usual places of employment; or

(3) Any trade or business which consists of selling merchandise, substantially all of which has been received by the organization as gifts or contributions.

An example of the operation of the first of the exceptions mentioned above would be an exempt orphanage operating a retail store and selling to the general public, where substantially all the work in carrying on such business is performed for the organization by volunteers without compensation. An example of the first part of the second exception, relating to an organization described in section 501(c)(3) or a governmental college or university described in section 511(a)(2)(B), would be a laundry operated by a college for the purpose of laundering dormitory linens and the clothing of students. The latter part of the second exception, dealing with certain sales by local employee associations, will not apply to sales of these items at locations other than the usual place of employment of the employees; therefore sales at such other locations will continue to be treated as unrelated trade or business. The third exception applies to so-called thrift shops operated by a tax-exempt organization where those desiring to benefit such organization contribute old clothes, books, furniture, et cetera, to be sold to the general public with the proceeds going to the exempt organization.

(f) Special definition of "unrelated trade or business" for trusts. In the case of a trust computing its unrelated business taxable income under section 512 for purposes of section 681, or a trust described in section 401(a) or section 501(c)(17), which is exempt from tax under section 501(a), section 513(b) provides that the term *unrelated trade or business* means any trade or business regularly carried on by such trust or by a partnership of which it is a member. This definition also applies to an individual retirement account described in section 408 that, under section 408(e), is subject to the tax imposed by section 511.

* * *

§ 1.513-4. Certain sponsorship not unrelated trade or business.

(a) In general. Under section 513(i), the receipt of qualified sponsorship payments by an exempt organization which is subject to the tax imposed by section 511 does not constitute receipt of income from an unrelated trade or business.

(b) Exception. The provisions of this section do not apply with respect to payments made in connection with qualified convention and trade show activities. For rules governing qualified convention and trade show activity, see § 1.513-3. The provisions of this section also do not apply to income derived from the sale of advertising or acknowledgments in exempt organization periodicals. For this purpose, the term periodical means regularly scheduled and printed material published by or on behalf of the exempt organization that is not related to and primarily distributed in connection with a specific event conducted by the exempt organization. For this purpose, printed material includes material that is published electronically. For rules governing the sale of advertising in exempt organization periodicals, see § 1.512(a)-1(f).

(c) Qualified sponsorship payment—(1) Definition. The term qualified sponsorship payment means any payment by any person engaged in a trade or business with respect to which there is no arrangement or expectation that the person will receive any substantial return benefit. In determining whether a payment is a qualified sponsorship payment, it is irrelevant whether the sponsored activity is related or unrelated to the recipient organization's exempt purpose. It is also irrelevant whether the sponsored activity is temporary or permanent. For purposes of this section, payment means the payment of money, transfer of property, or performance of services.

(2) Substantial return benefit—(i) In general. For purposes of this section, a substantial return benefit means any benefit other than a use or acknowledgment described in paragraph (c)(2)(iv) of this section, or disregarded benefits described in paragraph (c)(2)(ii) of this section.

(ii) Certain benefits disregarded. For purposes of paragraph (c)(2)(i) of this section, benefits are disregarded if the aggregate fair market value of all the benefits provided to the payor or persons designated by the payor in connection with the payment during the organization's taxable year is not more than 2% of the amount of the payment. If the aggregate fair market value of the benefits exceeds 2% of the amount of the payment, then (except as provided in paragraph (c)(2)(iv) of this section) the entire fair market value of such benefits, not merely the excess amount, is a substantial return benefit. Fair market value is determined as provided in paragraph (d)(1) of this section.

(iii) Benefits defined. For purposes of this section, benefits provided to the payor or persons designated by the payor may include:

(A) Advertising as defined in paragraph (c)(2)(v) of this section.

(B) Exclusive provider arrangements as defined in paragraph (c)(2)(vi)(B) of this section.

(C) Goods, facilities, services or other privileges.

(D) Exclusive or nonexclusive rights to use an intangible asset (e.g., trademark, patent, logo, or designation) of the exempt organization.

(iv) Use or acknowledgment. For purposes of this section, a substantial return benefit does not include the use or acknowledgment of the name or logo (or product lines) of the payor's trade or business in connection with the activities of the exempt organization. Use or acknowledgment does not include advertising as described in paragraph (c)(2)(v) of this section, but may include the following: exclusive sponsorship arrangements; logos and slogans that do not contain qualitative or comparative descriptions of the payor's products, services, facilities or company; a list of the payor's locations, telephone numbers, or Internet address; value-neutral descriptions, including displays or visual depictions, of the payor's product-line or services; and the payor's brand or trade names and product or service listings. Logos or slogans that are an established part of a payor's identity are not considered to contain qualitative or comparative descriptions. Mere display or distribution, whether for free or remuneration, of a payor's product by the payor or the exempt organization to the general public at the sponsored activity is not considered an inducement to purchase, sell or use the payor's product for purposes of this section and, thus, will not affect the determination of whether a payment is a qualified sponsorship payment.

(v) Advertising. For purposes of this section, the term advertising means any message or other programming material which is broadcast or otherwise transmitted, published, displayed or distributed, and which promotes or markets any trade or business, or any service, facility or product. Advertising includes messages containing qualitative or comparative language, price information or other indications of savings or value, an endorsement, or an inducement to purchase, sell, or use any company, service, facility or product. A single message that contains both advertising and an acknowledgment is advertising. This section does not apply to activities conducted by a payor on its own. For example, if a payor purchases broadcast time from a television station to advertise its product during commercial breaks in a sponsored program, the exempt organization's activities are not thereby converted to advertising.

(vi) Exclusivity arrangements—(A) Exclusive sponsor. An arrangement that acknowledges the payor as the exclusive sponsor of an exempt organization's activity, or the exclusive sponsor representing a particular trade, business or industry, generally does not, by itself, result in a substantial return benefit. For example, if in exchange for a payment, an organization announces that its event is sponsored exclusively by the payor (and does not provide any advertising or other substantial return benefit to the payor), the payor has not received a substantial return benefit.

(B) Exclusive provider. An arrangement that limits the sale, distribution, availability, or use of competing products, services, or facilities in connection with an exempt organization's activity generally results in a substantial return benefit. For example, if in exchange for a payment, the exempt organization agrees to allow only the payor's products to be sold in connection with an activity, the payor has received a substantial return benefit.

(d) Allocation of payment—(1) In general. If there is an arrangement or expectation that the payor will receive a substantial return benefit with respect to any payment, then only the portion, if any, of the payment that exceeds the fair market value of the substantial return benefit is a qualified sponsorship payment. However, if the exempt organization does not establish that the payment exceeds the fair market value of any substantial return benefit, then no portion of the payment constitutes a qualified sponsorship payment.

(i) Treatment of payments other than qualified sponsorship payments. The unrelated business income tax (UBIT) treatment of any payment (or portion thereof) that is not a qualified sponsorship payment is determined by application of sections 512, 513 and 514. For example, payments related to an exempt organization's providing facilities, services, or other privileges to the payor or persons designated by the payor, advertising, exclusive provider arrangements described in paragraph (c)(2)(vi)(B) of this section, a license to use intangible assets of the exempt organization, or other substantial return benefits, are evaluated separately in determining whether the exempt organization realizes unrelated business taxable income.

(ii) Fair market value. The fair market value of any substantial return benefit provided as part of a sponsorship arrangement is the price at which the benefit would be provided between a willing recipient and a willing provider of the benefit, neither being under any compulsion to enter into the arrangement and both having reasonable knowledge of relevant facts, and without regard to any other aspect of the sponsorship arrangement.

(iii) Valuation date. In general, the fair market value of the substantial return benefit is determined when the benefit is provided. However, if the parties enter into a binding, written sponsorship contract, the fair market value of any substantial return benefit provided pursuant to that contract is determined on the date the parties enter into the sponsorship contract. If the parties make a material change to a sponsorship contract, it is treated as a new sponsorship contract as of the date the material change is effective. A material change includes an extension or renewal of the contract, or a more than incidental change to any amount payable (or other consideration) pursuant to the contract.

(iv) Examples. The following examples illustrate the provisions of this section:

Example 1. On June 30, 2001, a national corporation and Z, a charitable organization, enter into a five-year binding, written contract effective for years 2002 through 2007. The contract provides that the corporation will make an annual payment of $5,000 to Z, and in return the corporation will receive no benefit other than advertising. On June 30, 2001, the fair market value of the advertising to be provided to the corporation in each year of the agreement is $75, which is less than the disregarded benefit amount provided for in paragraph (c)(2)(ii) of this section (2% of $5,000 is $100). In 2002, pursuant to the sponsorship contract, the corporation makes a payment to Z of $5,000, and receives the specified benefit (advertising). As of January 1, 2002, the fair market value of the advertising to be provided by Z each year has increased to $110. However, for purposes of this section, the fair market value of the advertising benefit is determined on June 30, 2001, the date the parties entered into the sponsorship contract. Therefore, the entire $5,000 payment received in 2002 is a qualified sponsorship payment.

Example 2. The facts are the same as Example 1, except that the contract provides for an initial payment by the corporation to Z of $5,000 in 2002, followed by annual payments of $1,000 during each of years 2003–2007. In 2003, pursuant to the sponsorship contract, the corporation makes a payment to Z of $1,000, and receives the specified advertising benefit. In 2003, the fair market value of the benefit provided ($75, as determined on June 30, 2001) exceeds 2% of the total payment received (2% of $1,000 is $20). Therefore, only $925 of the $1,000 payment received in 2003 is a qualified sponsorship payment.

(2) Anti-abuse provision. To the extent necessary to prevent avoidance of the rule stated in paragraphs (d)(1) and (c)(2) of this section, where the exempt organization fails to make a reasonable and good faith valuation of any substantial return benefit, the Commissioner (or the Commissioner's delegate) may determine the portion of a payment allocable to such substantial return benefit and may treat two or more related payments as a single payment.

(e) Special rules—(1) Written agreements. The existence of a written sponsorship agreement does not, in itself, cause a payment to fail to be a qualified sponsorship payment. The terms of the agreement, not its existence or degree of detail, are relevant to the determination of whether a payment is a qualified sponsorship payment. Similarly, the terms of the agreement and not the title or responsibilities of the individuals negotiating the agreement determine whether a payment (or any portion thereof) made pursuant to the agreement is a qualified sponsorship payment.

(2) Contingent payments. The term qualified sponsorship payment does not include any payment the amount of which is contingent, by contract or otherwise, upon the level of attendance at one or more events, broadcast ratings, or other factors indicating the degree of public exposure to the sponsored activity. The fact that a payment is contingent upon sponsored events or activities actually being conducted does not, by itself, cause the payment to fail to be a qualified sponsorship payment.

(3) Determining public support. Qualified sponsorship payments in the form of money or property (but not services) are treated as contributions received by the exempt organization for purposes of determining public support to the organization under section 170(b)(1)(A)(vi) or 509(a)(2). See §§ 1.509(a)–3(f)(1) and 1.170A–9(e)(6)(i). The fact that a payment is a qualified sponsorship payment that is treated as a contribution to the payee organization does not determine whether the payment is deductible by the payor under section 162 or 170.

(f) Examples. The provisions of this section are illustrated by the following examples. The tax treatment of any payment (or portion of a payment) that does not constitute a qualified sponsorship payment is governed by general UBIT principles. In these examples, the recipients of the payments at issue are section 501(c) organizations. The expectations or arrangements of the parties are those specifically indicated in the example. The examples are as follows:

Example 1. M, a local charity, organizes a marathon and walkathon at which it serves to participants drinks and other refreshments provided free of charge by a national corporation. The corporation also gives M prizes to be awarded to winners of the event. M recognizes the assistance of the corporation by listing the corporation's name in promotional fliers, in newspaper advertisements of the event and on T-shirts worn by participants. M changes the name of its event to include the name of the corporation. M's activities constitute acknowledgment of the sponsorship. The drinks, refreshments and prizes provided by the corporation are a qualified sponsorship payment, which is not income from an unrelated trade or business.

Example 2. N, an art museum, organizes an exhibition and receives a large payment from a corporation to help fund the exhibition. N recognizes the corporation's support by using the corporate name and established logo in materials publicizing the exhibition, which include banners, posters, brochures and public service announcements. N also hosts a dinner for the corporation's executives. The fair market value of the dinner exceeds 2% of the total payment. N's use of the corporate name and logo in connection with the exhibition constitutes acknowledgment of the sponsorship. However, because the fair market value of the dinner exceeds 2% of the total payment, the dinner is a substantial return benefit. Only that portion of the payment, if any, that N can demonstrate exceeds the fair market value of the dinner is a qualified sponsorship payment.

Example 3. O coordinates sports tournaments for local charities. An auto manufacturer agrees to underwrite the expenses of the tournaments. O recognizes the auto manufacturer by including the manufacturer's name and established logo in the title of each tournament as well as on signs, scoreboards and other printed material. The auto manufacturer receives complimentary admission passes and pro-am playing spots for each tournament that have a combined fair market value in excess of 2% of the total payment. Additionally, O displays the latest models of the manufacturer's premier luxury cars at each tournament. O's use of the manufacturer's name and logo and display of cars in the tournament area constitute acknowledgment of the sponsorship. However, the admission passes and pro-am playing spots are a substantial return benefit. Only that portion of the payment, if any, that O can demonstrate exceeds the fair market value of the admission passes and pro-am playing spots is a qualified sponsorship payment.

Example 4. P conducts an annual college football bowl game. P sells to commercial broadcasters the right to broadcast the bowl game on television and radio. A major corporation agrees to be the exclusive sponsor of the bowl game. The detailed contract between P and the corporation provides that in exchange for a $1,000,000 payment, the name of the bowl game will include the name of the corporation. In addition, the contract provides that the corporation's name and established logo will appear on player's helmets and uniforms, on the scoreboard and stadium signs, on the playing field, on cups used to serve drinks at the game, and on all related printed material distributed in connection with the game. P also agrees to give the corporation a block of game passes for its employees and to provide advertising in the bowl game program book. The fair market value of the passes is $6,000, and the fair market value of the program advertising is $10,000. The agreement is contingent upon the game being broadcast on television and radio, but the amount of the payment is not contingent upon the number of people attending the game or the television ratings. The contract provides that television cameras will focus on the corporation's name and logo on the field at certain intervals during the game. P's use of the corporation's name and logo in connection with the bowl game constitutes acknowledgment of the sponsorship. The exclusive sponsorship arrangement is not a substantial return benefit. Because the fair market value of the game passes and program advertising ($16,000) does not exceed 2% of the total payment (2% of $1,000,000 is $20,000), these benefits are disregarded and the entire payment is a qualified sponsorship payment, which is not income from an unrelated trade or business.

Example 5. Q organizes an amateur sports team. A major pizza chain gives uniforms to players on Q's team, and also pays some of the team's operational expenses. The uniforms bear the name and established logo of the pizza chain. During the final tournament series, Q distributes free of charge souvenir flags bearing Q's name to employees of the pizza chain who come out to support the team. The flags are valued at less than 2% of the combined fair market value of the uniforms and operational expenses paid. Q's use of the name and logo of the pizza chain in connection with the tournament constitutes acknowledgment of the sponsorship. Because the fair market value of the flags does not exceed 2% of the total payment, the entire amount of the funding and supplied uniforms are a qualified sponsorship payment, which is not income from an unrelated trade or business.

Example 6. R is a liberal arts college. A soft drink manufacturer enters into a binding, written contract with R that provides for a large payment to be made to the college's English department in exchange for R agreeing to name a writing competition after the soft drink manufacturer. The contract also provides that R will allow the soft drink manufacturer to be the exclusive provider of all soft drink sales on campus. The fair market value of the exclusive provider component of the contract exceeds 2% of the total payment. R's use of the manufacturer's name in the writing competition constitutes acknowledgment of the sponsorship. However, the exclusive provider arrangement is a substantial return benefit. Only that portion of the payment, if any, that R can demonstrate exceeds the fair market value of the exclusive provider arrangement is a qualified sponsorship payment.

Example 7. S is a noncommercial broadcast station that airs a program funded by a local music store. In exchange for the funding, S broadcasts the following message: "This program has been brought to you by the Music Shop, located at 123 Main Street. For your music needs, give them a call today at 555–1234. This station is proud to have the Music Shop as a sponsor." Because this single broadcast message contains both advertising and an acknowledgment, the entire message is advertising. The fair market value of the advertising exceeds 2% of the total payment. Thus, the advertising is a substantial return benefit. Unless S establishes that the amount of the payment exceeds the fair market value of the advertising, none of the payment is a qualified sponsorship payment.

Example 8. T, a symphony orchestra, performs a series of concerts. A program guide that contains notes on guest conductors and other information concerning the evening's program is distributed by T at each concert. The Music Shop makes a $1,000 payment to T in support of the concert series. As a supporter of the event, the Music Shop receives complimentary concert tickets with a fair market value of $85, and is recognized in the program guide and on a poster in the lobby of the concert hall. The lobby poster states that, "The T concert is sponsored by the Music Shop, located at 123 Main Street, telephone number 555-1234." The program guide contains the same information and also states, "Visit the Music Shop today for the finest selection of music CDs and cassette tapes." The fair market value of the advertisement in the program guide is $15. T's use of the Music Shop's name, address and telephone number in the lobby poster constitutes acknowledgment of the sponsorship. However, the combined fair market value of the advertisement in the program guide and complimentary tickets is $100 ($15 + $85), which exceeds 2% of the total payment (2% of $1,000 is $20). The fair market value of the advertising and complimentary tickets, therefore, constitutes a substantial return benefit and only that portion of the payment, or $900, that exceeds the fair market value of the substantial return benefit is a qualified sponsorship payment.

Example 9. U, a national charity dedicated to promoting health, organizes a campaign to inform the public about potential cures to fight a serious disease. As part of the campaign, U sends representatives to community health fairs around the country to answer questions about the disease and inform the public about recent developments in the search for a cure. A pharmaceutical company makes a payment to U to fund U's booth at a health fair. U places a sign in the booth displaying the pharmaceutical company's name and slogan, "Better Research, Better Health," which is an established part of the company's identity. In addition, U grants the pharmaceutical company a license to use U's logo in marketing its products to health care providers around the country. The fair market value of the license exceeds 2% of the total payment received from the company. U's display of the pharmaceutical company's name and slogan constitutes acknowledgment of the sponsorship. However, the license granted to the pharmaceutical company to use U's logo is a substantial return benefit. Only that portion of the payment, if any, that U can demonstrate exceeds the fair market value of the license granted to the pharmaceutical company is a qualified sponsorship payment.

Example 10. V, a trade association, publishes a monthly scientific magazine for its members containing information about current issues and developments in the field. A textbook publisher makes a large payment to V to have its name displayed on the inside cover of the magazine each month. Because the monthly magazine is a periodical within the meaning of paragraph (b) of this section, the section 513(i) safe harbor does not apply. See § 1.512(a)–1(f).

Example 11. W, a symphony orchestra, maintains a Web site containing pertinent information and its performance schedule. The Music Shop makes a payment to W to fund a concert series, and W posts a list of its sponsors on its Web site, including the Music Shop's name and Internet address. W's Web site does not promote the Music Shop or advertise its merchandise. The Music Shop's Internet address appears as a hyperlink from W's Web site to the Music Shop's Web site. W's posting of the Music Shop's name and Internet address on its Web site constitutes acknowledgment of the sponsorship. The entire payment is a qualified sponsorship payment, which is not income from an unrelated trade or business.

Example 12. X, a health-based charity, sponsors a year-long initiative to educate the public about a particular medical condition. A large pharmaceutical company manufactures a drug that is used in treating the medical condition, and provides funding for the initiative that helps X produce educational materials for distribution and post information on X's Web site. X's Web site contains a hyperlink to the pharmaceutical company's Web site. On the pharmaceutical company's Web site, the statement appears, "X endorses the use of our drug, and suggests that you ask your doctor for a prescription if you have this medical condition." X reviewed the endorsement before it was posted on the pharmaceutical company's Web site and gave permission for the endorsement to appear. The endorsement is advertising. The fair market value of the advertising exceeds 2% of the total payment received from the pharmaceutical company. Therefore, only the portion of the payment, if any, that X can demonstrate exceeds the fair market value of the advertising on the pharmaceutical company's Web site is a qualified sponsorship payment.

§ 1.513–7. Travel and tour activities of tax exempt organizations.

(a) Travel tour activities that constitute a trade or business, as defined in section 1.513–1(b), and that are not substantially related to the purposes for which exemption has been granted to the organization constitute an unrelated trade or business with respect to that organization. Whether travel tour activities conducted by an organization are substantially related to the organization's exempt purpose is determined by looking at all relevant facts and circumstances, including, but not limited to, how a travel tour is developed, promoted and operated. Section 513(c) and section 1.513–1(b) also apply to travel tour activity. Application of the rules of section 513(c) and section 1.513–1(b) may result in different treatment for individual tours within an organization's travel tour program.

(b) Examples. The provisions of this section are illustrated by the following examples. In all of these examples, the travel tours are priced to produce a profit for the exempt organization. The examples are as follows:

Example 1. O, a university alumni association, is exempt from federal income tax under section 501(a) as an educational organization described in section 501(c)(3). As part of its activities, O operates a travel tour program. The program is open to all current members of O and their guests. O works with travel agencies to schedule approximately 10 tours annually to various destinations around the world. Members of O pay $x to the organizing travel agency to participate in a tour. The travel agency pays O a per person fee for each participant. Although the literature advertising the tours encourages O's members to continue their lifelong learning by joining the tours, and a faculty member of O's related university frequently joins the tour as a guest of the alumni association, none of the tours includes any scheduled instruction or curriculum related to the destinations being visited. The travel tours made available to O's members do not contribute importantly to the accomplishment of O's educational purpose. Rather, O's program is designed to generate revenues for O by regularly offering its members travel services. Accordingly, O's tour program is an unrelated trade or business within the meaning of section 513(a).

Example 2. N is an organization formed for the purpose of educating individuals about the geography and culture of the United States. It is exempt from federal income tax under section 501(a) as an educational and cultural organization described in section 501(c)(3). N engages in a number of activities to accomplish its purposes, including offering courses and publishing periodicals and books. As one of its activities, N conducts study tours to national parks and other locations within the United States. The study tours are conducted by teachers and other personnel certified by the Board of Education of the State of P. The tours are directed toward students enrolled in degree programs at educational institutions in P, as reflected in the promotional materials, but are open to all who agree to participate in the required study program. Each tour's study program consists of instruction on subjects related to the location being visited on the tour. During the tour, five or six hours per day are devoted to organized study, preparation of reports, lectures, instruction and recitation by the students. Each tour group brings along a library of material related to the subject being studied on the tour. Examinations are given at the end of each tour and the P State Board of Education awards academic credit for tour participation. Because the tours offered by N include a substantial amount of required study, lectures, report preparation, examinations and qualify for academic credit, the tours are substantially related to N's educational purpose. Accordingly, N's tour program is not an unrelated trade or business within the meaning of section 513(a).

Example 3. R is a section 501(c)(4) social welfare organization devoted to advocacy on a particular issue. On a regular basis throughout the year, R organizes travel tours for its members to Washington, DC. While in Washington, the members follow a schedule according to which they spend substantially all of their time during normal business hours over several days attending meetings with legislators and government officials and receiving briefings on policy developments related to the issue that is R's focus. Members do have some time on their own in the evenings to engage in recreational or social activities of their own choosing. Bringing members to Washington to participate in advocacy on behalf of the organization and learn about developments relating to the organization's principal focus is substantially related to R's social welfare purpose. Therefore, R's operation of the travel tours does not constitute an unrelated trade or business within the meaning of section 513(a).

Example 4. S is a membership organization formed to foster cultural unity and to educate X Americans about X, their country of origin. It is exempt from federal income tax under section 501(a) and is described in section 501(c)(3) as an educational and cultural organization. Membership in S is open to all Americans interested in the X heritage. As part of its activities, S sponsors a program of travel tours to X. The tours are divided into two categories. Category A tours are trips to X that are designed to immerse participants in the X history, culture and language. Substantially all of the daily itinerary includes scheduled instruction on the X language, history and cultural heritage, and visits to destinations selected because of their historical or cultural significance or because of instructional resources they offer. Category B tours are also trips to X, but rather than offering scheduled instruction, participants are given the option of taking guided tours of various X locations included in their itinerary. Other than the optional guided tours, Category B tours offer no instruction or curriculum. Destinations of principally recreational interest, rather than historical or cultural interest, are regularly included on Category B tour itineraries. Based on the facts and circumstances, sponsoring Category A tours is an activity substantially related to S's exempt purposes, and does not constitute an unrelated trade or business within the meaning of section 513(a). However, sponsoring Category B tours does not contribute importantly to S's accomplishment of its exempt purposes and, thus, constitutes an unrelated trade or business within the meaning of section 513(a).

Example 5. T is a scientific organization engaged in environmental research. T is exempt from federal income tax under section 501(a) as an organization described in section 501(c)(3). T is engaged in a long-term study of how agricultural pesticide and fertilizer use affects the populations of various bird species. T collects data at several bases located in an important agricultural region of country U. The minutes of a meeting of T's Board of Directors state that, after study, the Board has determined that non-scientists can reliably perform needed data collection in the field, under supervision of T's biologists. The Board minutes reflect that the Board approved offering one-week trips to T's bases in U, where participants will assist T's biologists in collecting data for the study. Tour participants collect data during the same hours as T's biologists. Normally, data collection occurs during the early morning and evening hours, although the work schedule varies by season. Each base has rustic accommodations and few amenities, but country U is renowned for its beautiful scenery and abundant wildlife. T promotes the trips in its newsletter and on its Internet site and through various conservation organizations. The promotional materials describe the work schedule and emphasize the valuable contribution made by trip participants to T's research activities. Based on the facts and circumstances, sponsoring trips to T's bases in country U is an activity substantially related to T's exempt purpose, and, thus, does not constitute an unrelated trade or business within the meaning of section 513(a).

Example 6. V is an educational organization devoted to the study of ancient history and cultures and is exempt from federal income tax under section 501(a) as an organization described in section 501(c)(3). In connection with its educational activities, V conducts archaeological expeditions around the world, including in the Y region of country Z. In cooperation with the National Museum of Z, V recently presented an exhibit on ancient civilizations of the Y region of Z, including artifacts from the collection of the Z National Museum. V instituted a program of travel tours to V's archaeological sites located in the Y region. The tours were initially proposed by V staff members as a means of educating the public about ongoing field research conducted by V. V engaged a travel agency to handle logistics such as accommodations and transportation arrangements. In preparation for the tours, V developed educational materials relating to each archaeological site to be visited on the tour, describing in detail the layout of the site, the methods used by V's researchers in exploring the site, the discoveries made at the site, and their historical significance. V also arranged special guided tours of its exhibit on the Y region for individuals registered for the travel tours. Two archaeologists from V (both of whom had participated in prior archaeological expeditions in the Y region) accompanied the tours. These experts led guided tours of each site and explained the significance of the sites to tour participants. At several of the sites, tour participants also met with a working team of archaeologists from V and the National Museum of Z, who shared their experiences. V prepared promotional materials describing the educational nature of the tours, including the daily trips to V's archaeological sites and the educational background of the tour leaders, and providing a recommended reading list. The promotional materials do not refer to any particular recreational or sightseeing activities. Based on the facts and circumstances, sponsoring trips to the Y region is an activity substantially related to V's exempt purposes. The scheduled activities, which include tours of archaeological sites led by experts, are part of a coordinated educational program designed to educate tour participants about the ancient history of the Y region of Z and V's ongoing field research. Therefore, V's tour program does not constitute an unrelated trade or business within the meaning of section 513(a).

Example 7. W is an educational organization devoted to the study of the performing arts and is exempt from federal income tax under section 501(a) as an organization described in section 501(c)(3). In connection with its educational activities, W presents public performances of musical and theatrical works. Individuals become members of W by making an annual contribution to W of $q. Each year, W offers members an opportunity to travel as a group to one or more major cities in the United States or abroad. In each city, tour participants are provided tickets to attend a public performance of a play, concert or dance program each evening. W also arranges a sightseeing tour of each city and provides evening receptions for tour participants. W views its tour program as an important means to develop and strengthen bonds between W and its members, and to increase their financial and volunteer support of W. W engaged a travel agency to handle logistics such as accommodations and transportation arrangements. No educational materials are prepared by W or provided to tour participants in connection with the tours. Apart from attendance at the evening cultural events, the tours offer no scheduled instruction, organized study or group discussion. Although several members of W's administrative staff accompany each tour group, their role is to facilitate member interaction. The staff members have no special expertise in the performing arts and play no educational role in the tours. W prepared promotional materials describing the sightseeing opportunities on the tours and emphasizing the opportunity for members to socialize informally and interact with one another and with W staff members, while pursuing shared interests. Although W's tour program may foster goodwill among W members, it does not contribute importantly to W's educational purposes. W's tour program is primarily social and recreational in nature. The scheduled activities, which include sightseeing and attendance at various cultural events, are not part of a coordinated educational program. Therefore, W's tour program is an unrelated trade or business within the meaning of section 513(a).

§ 1.514(a)-1. Unrelated debt-financed income and deductions.

(a) Income includible in gross income. (1) Percentage of income taken into account—(i) In general. For taxable years beginning after December 31, 1969, there shall be included with respect to each debt-financed property (as defined in section 514 and § 1.514(b)-1) as an item of gross income derived from an unrelated trade or business the amount of unrelated debt-financed income (as defined in subdivision (ii) of this subparagraph). See paragraph (a)(5) of § 1.514(c)-1 for special rules regarding indebtedness incurred before June 28, 1966, applicable for taxable years beginning before January 1, 1972, and for special rules applicable to churches or conventions or associations of churches.

(ii) Unrelated debt-financed income. The unrelated debt-financed income with respect to each debt-financed property is an amount which is the same percentage (but not in excess of 100 percent) of the total gross income derived during the taxable year from or on account of such property as:

(a) The average acquisition indebtedness (as defined in subparagraph (3) of this paragraph) with respect to the property is of

(b) The average adjusted basis of such property (as defined in subparagraph (2) of this paragraph).

(iii) Debt/basis percentage. The percentage determined under subdivision (ii) of this subparagraph is hereinafter referred to as the debt/basis percentage.

(iv) Example. Subdivisions (i), (ii), and (iii) of this subparagraph are illustrated by the following example. For purposes of this example it is assumed that the property is debt-financed property.

Example. X, an exempt trade association, owns an office building which in 1971 produces $10,000 of gross rental income. The average adjusted basis of the building for 1971 is $100,000, and the average acquisition indebtedness with respect to the building for 1971 is $50,000. Accordingly, the debt/basis percentage for 1971 is 50 percent (the ratio of $50,000 to $100,000). Therefore, the unrelated debt-financed income with respect to the building for 1971 is $5,000 (50 percent of $10,000).

(v) Gain from sale or other disposition. If debt-financed property is sold or otherwise disposed of, there shall be included in computing unrelated business taxable income an amount with respect to such gain (or loss) which is the same percentage (but not in excess of 100 percent) of the total gain (or loss) derived from such sale or other disposition as:

(a) The highest acquisition indebtedness with respect to such property during the 12-month period, preceding the date of disposition, is of

(b) The average adjusted basis of such property.

The tax on the amount of gain (or loss) included in unrelated business taxable income pursuant to the preceding sentence shall be determined in accordance with the rules set forth in Subchapter P, Chapter 1 of the Code (relating to capital gains and losses). See also section 511(d) and the regulations thereunder (relating to the minimum tax for tax preferences).

(2) Average adjusted basis—(i) In general. The average adjusted basis of debt-financed property is the average amount of the adjusted basis of such property during that portion of the taxable year it is held by the organization. This amount is the average of:

(a) The adjusted basis of such property as of the first day during the taxable year that the organization holds the property, and

(b) The adjusted basis of such property as of the last day during the taxable year that the organization holds the property.

See section 1011 and the regulations thereunder for determination of the adjusted basis of property.

(ii) Adjustments for prior taxable years. For purposes of subdivision (i) of this subparagraph, the determination of the average adjusted basis of debt-financed property is not affected by the fact that the organization was exempt from taxation for prior taxable years. Proper adjustment must be made under section 1011 for the entire period since the acquisition of the property. For example, adjustment must be made for depreciation for all prior taxable years whether or not the organization was exempt from taxation for any such years. Similarly, the fact that only a portion of the depreciation allowance may be taken into account in computing the percentage of deductions allowable under section 514(a)(2) does not affect the amount of the adjustment for depreciation which is used in determining average adjusted basis.

(iii) Cross reference. For the determination of the basis of debt-financed property acquired in a complete or partial liquidation of a corporation in exchange for its stock, see § 1.514(d)–1.

(iv) Example. This subparagraph may be illustrated by the following example. For purposes of this example it is assumed that the property is debt-financed property.

Example. On July 10, 1970, X, an exempt educational organization, purchased an office building for $510,000, using $300,000 of borrowed funds. During 1970 the only adjustment to basis is $20,000 for depreciation. As of December 31, 1970, the adjusted basis of the building is $490,000 and the indebtedness is still $300,000. X files its return on a calendar year basis. Under these circumstances, the debt/basis percentage for 1970 is 60 percent, calculated in the following manner:

	Basis
As of July 10, 1970 (acquisition date)	$ 510,000
As of December 31, 1970	490,000
Total	$ 1,000,000

Average adjusted basis:

$1,000,000 / 2 = $500,000

Debt/basis percentage:

Average acquisition indebtedness ($300,000)

Average adjusted basis ($500,000) = 60 percent

For an illustration of the determination of the debt/basis percentage as changes in the acquisition indebtedness occur, see example (1) of subparagraph (3)(iii) of this paragraph.

(3) Average acquisition indebtedness—(i) In general. The average acquisition indebtedness with respect to debt-financed property is the average amount of the outstanding principal indebtedness during that portion of the taxable year the property is held by the organization.

(ii) Computation. The average acquisition indebtedness is computed by determining the amount of the outstanding principal indebtedness on the first day in each calendar month during the taxable year that the organization holds the property, adding these amounts together, and then dividing this sum by the total number of months during the taxable year that the organization held such property. A fractional part of a month shall be treated as a full month in computing average acquisition indebtedness.

* * *

(4) Indeterminate price—(i) In general. If an exempt organization acquires (or improves) property for an indeterminate price, the initial acquisition indebtedness and the unadjusted basis shall be determined in accordance with subdivisions (ii) and (iii) of this paragraph, unless the organization has obtained the consent of the Commissioner to use another method to compute such amounts.

(ii) Unadjusted basis. For purposes of this subparagraph, the unadjusted basis of property (or of an improvement) is the fair market value of the property (or improvement) on the date of acquisition (or the date of completion of the improvement). The average adjusted basis of such property shall be determined in accordance with paragraph (a)(2) of this section.

(iii) Initial acquisition indebtedness. For purposes of this subparagraph, the initial acquisition indebtedness is the fair market value of the property (or improvement) on the date of acquisition (or the date of completion of the improvement) less any down payment or other initial payment applied to the principal indebtedness. The average acquisition indebtedness with respect to such property shall be computed in accordance with paragraph (a)(3) of this section.

(iv) Example. The application of this subparagraph may be illustrated by the following example. For purposes of this example it is assumed that the property is debt-financed property.

Example. On January 1, 1971, X, an exempt trade association, acquires an office building for a down payment of $310,000 and an agreement to pay 10 percent of the income generated by the building for 10 years. Neither the sales price nor the amount which X is obligated to pay in the future is certain. The fair market value of the building on the date of acquisition is $600,000. The depreciation allowance for 1971 is $40,000. Unless X obtains the consent of the Commissioner to use another method, the unadjusted basis of the property is $600,000 (the fair market value of the property on the date of acquisition), and the initial acquisition indebtedness is $290,000 (fair market value of $600,000 less initial payment of $310,000). Under these circumstances, the average adjusted basis of the property for 1971 is $580,000, calculated as follows:

[Initial fair market value + (initial fair market value less depreciation)] / 2 =

[$600,000 + ($600,000-$40,000)]/ 2 = $580,000.

If no payment other than the initial payment is made in 1971, the average acquisition indebtedness for 1971 is $290,000. Thus, the debt/basis percentage for 1971 is 50 percent, calculated as follows:

Average acquisition indebtedness / average adjusted basis=$290,000 / $580,000=50 percent

(b) Deductions—(1) Percentage of deductions taken into account. Except as provided in subparagraphs (4) and (5) of this paragraph, there shall be allowed as a deduction with respect to each debt-financed property an amount determined by applying the debt/basis percentage to the sum of the deductions allowable under subparagraph (2) of this paragraph.

(2) Deductions allowable. The deductions allowable are those items allowed as deductions by chapter 1 of the Code which are directly connected with the debt-financed property or the income therefrom (including the dividends received deductions allowed by sections 243, 244, and 245), except that:

(i) The allowable deductions are subject to the modifications provided by section 512(b) on computation of the unrelated business taxable income, and

(ii) If the debt-financed property is of a character which is subject to the allowance for depreciation provided in section 167, such allowance shall be computed only by use of the straight-line method of depreciation.

(3) Directly connected with. To be directly connected with debt-financed property or the income therefrom, an item of deduction must have proximate and primary relationship to such property or the income therefrom. Expenses, depreciation, and similar items attributable solely to such property are proximately and primarily related to such property or the income therefrom, and therefore qualify for deduction, to the extent they meet the requirements of subparagraph (2) of this paragraph. Thus, for example, if the straight-line depreciation allowance for an office building is $10,000 a year, an organization would be allowed a deduction for depreciation of $10,000 if the entire building were debt-financed property. However, if only one-half of the building were treated as debt-financed property, then the depreciation allowed as a deduction would be $5,000. (See example (2) of § 1.514(b)–1(b)(1)(iii).)

(4) Capital losses—(i) In general. If the sale or exchange of debt-financed property results in a capital loss, the amount of such loss taken into account in the taxable year in which the loss arises shall be computed in accordance with paragraph (a)(1)(v) of this section. If, however, any portion of such capital loss not taken into account in such year may be carried back or carried over to another taxable year, the debt/basis percentage is not applied to determine what portion of such capital loss may be taken as a deduction in the year to which such capital loss is carried.

(ii) Example. This subparagraph is illustrated by the following example. For purposes of this example it is assumed that the property is debt-financed property.

Example. X, an exempt educational organization, owns securities which are capital assets and which it has held for more than 6 months. In 1972 X sells the securities at a loss of $20,000. The debt/basis percentage with respect to computing the gain (or loss) derived from the sale of the securities is 40 percent. Thus, X has sustained a capital loss of $8,000 (40 percent of $20,000) with respect to the sale of the securities. For 1972 and the preceding three taxable years X has no other capital transactions. Under these circumstances, the $8,000 of capital loss may be carried over to the succeeding 5 taxable years without further application of the debt/basis percentage.

(5) Net operating loss—(i) In general. If, after applying the debt/basis percentage to the income derived from debt-financed property and the deductions directly connected with such income, such deductions exceed such income, the organization has sustained a net operating loss for the taxable year. This amount may be carried back or carried over to other taxable years in accordance with section 512(b)(6). However, the debt/basis percentage shall not be applied in such other years to determine the amounts that may be taken as a deduction in those years.

(ii) Example. This subparagraph may be illustrated by the following example. For purposes of this example it is assumed that the property is debt-financed property.

Example. During 1974, Y, an exempt organization, receives $20,000 of rent from a building which it owns. Y has no other unrelated business taxable income for 1974. For 1974 the deductions directly connected with this building are property taxes of $5,000, interest of $5,000 on the acquisition indebtedness, and salary of $15,000 to the manager of the building. The debt/basis percentage for 1974 with respect to the building is 50 percent. Under these circumstances, Y shall take into account in computing its unrelated business taxable income for 1974, $10,000 of income (50 percent of $20,000) and $12,500 (50 percent of $25,000) of the deductions directly connected with such income. Thus, for 1974 Y has sustained a net operating loss of $2,500 ($10,000 of income less $12,500 of deductions) which may be carried back or carried over to other taxable years without further application of the debt/basis percentage.

§ 1.514(b)–1. Definition of debt-financed property.

(a) In general. For purposes of section 514 and the regulations thereunder, the term debt-financed property means any property which is held to produce income (e.g., rental real estate, tangible personal property, and corporate stock), and with respect to which there is an acquisition indebtedness (determined without regard to whether the property is debt-financed property) at any time during the taxable year. The term income is not limited to recurring income but applies as well to gains from the disposition of property. Consequently, when any property held to produce income by an organization which is not used in a manner described in section 514(b)(1)(A), (B), (C), or (D) is disposed of at a gain during the taxable year, and there was an acquisition indebtedness outstanding with respect to such property at any time during the 12-month period preceding the date of disposition (even though such period covers more than 1 taxable year), such property is debt-financed property. For example, assume that on June 1, 1972, an organization is given mortgaged, unimproved property which it does not use in a manner described in section 514(b)(1)(A), (B), (C), or (D) and that the organization assumes payment of the mortgage on such property. On July 15, 1972, the organization sells such property for a gain. Such property is debt-financed property and such gain is taxable as unrelated debt-financed income. See section 514(c) and

§ 1.514(c)–1 for rules relating to when there is acquisition indebtedness with respect to property. See paragraph (a) of § 1.514(a)–1 for rules determining the amount of income or gain from debt-financed property which is treated as unrelated debt-financed income.

(b) Exceptions—(1) Property related to certain exempt purposes. (i) To the extent that the use of any property is substantially related (aside from the need of the organization for income or funds or the use it makes of the profits derived) to the exercise or performance by an organization of its charitable, educational, or other purpose or function constituting its basis for exemption under section 501 (or, in the case of an organization described in section 511(a)(2)(B), to the exercise or performance of any purpose or function designated in section 501(c)(3)) such property shall not be treated as debt-financed property. See § 1.513–1 for principles applicable in determining whether there is a substantial relationship to the exempt purpose of the organization.

(ii) If substantially all of any property is used in a manner described in subdivision (i) of this subparagraph, such property shall not be treated as debt-financed property. In general the preceding sentence shall apply if 85 percent or more of the use of such property is devoted to the organization's exempt purpose. The extent to which property is used for a particular purpose shall be determined on the basis of all the facts and circumstances. These may include (where appropriate):

(a) A comparison of the portion of time such property is used for exempt purposes with the total time such property is used,

(b) A comparison of the portion of such property that is used for exempt purposes with the portion of such property that is used for all purposes, or

(c) Both the comparisons described in (a) and (b) of this subdivision.

(iii) This subparagraph may be illustrated by the following examples. For purposes of these examples it is assumed that the indebtedness is acquisition indebtedness.

Example 1. W, an exempt organization, owns a computer with respect to which there is an outstanding principal indebtedness and which is used by W in the performance of its exempt purpose. W sells time for the use of the computer to M corporation on occasions when the computer is not in full-time use by W. W uses the computer in furtherance of its exempt purpose more than 85 percent of the time it is in use and M uses the computer less than 15 percent of the total operating time the computer is in use. In this situation, substantially all the use of the computer is related to the performance of W's exempt purpose. Therefore, no portion of the computer is treated as debt-financed property.

Example 2. X, an exempt college, owns a four story office building which has been purchased with borrowed funds. In 1971, the lower two stories of the building are used to house computers which are used by X for administrative purposes. The top two stories are rented to the public for purposes not described in section 514(b)(1)(A), (B), (C), or (D). The gross income derived by X from the building is $6,000, all of which is attributable to the rents paid by tenants. There are $2,000 of expenses, allocable equally to each use of the building. The average adjusted basis of the building for 1971 is $100,000, and the outstanding principal indebtedness throughout 1971 is $60,000. Thus, the average acquisition indebtedness for 1971 is $60,000. In accordance with subdivision (i) of this subparagraph, only the upper half of the building is debt-financed property. Consequently, only the rental income and the deductions directly connected with such income are to be taken into account in computing unrelated business taxable income. The portion of such amounts to be taken into account is determined by multiplying the $6,000 of rental income and $1,000 of deductions directly connected with such rental income by the debt/basis percentage. The debt/basis percentage is the ratio which the allocable part of the average acquisition indebtedness is of the allocable part of the average adjusted basis of the property, that is, the ratio which $30,000 (one-half of $60,000) bears to $50,000 (one-half of $100,000). Thus, the debt/basis percentage for 1971 is 60 percent (the ratio of $30,000 to $50,000). Under these circumstances, X shall include net rental income of $3,000 in its unrelated business taxable income for 1971, computed as follows:

Total rental income	$ 6,000
Deductions directly connected with rental income	1,000
Debt/basis percentage ($30,000/$50,000)	60%
Rental income treated as gross income from an unrelated trade or business (60 percent of $6,000)	3,600
Less the allowable portion of deductions directly connected with such income (60 percent of $1,000)	600
Net rental income included by X in computing its unrelated business taxable income pursuant to section 514	$ 3,000

Example 3. Assume the facts as stated in example (2) except that on December 31, 1971, X sells the building and realizes a long-term capital gain of $10,000. This is X's only capital transaction for 1971. An allocable portion of this gain is subject to tax. This amount is determined by multiplying the gain related to the nonexempt use, $5,000 (one-half of $10,000), by the ratio which the indebtedness for the 12-month period preceding the date of sale, $30,000 (one-half of $60,000), is of the allocable part of the average adjusted basis, $50,000 (one-half of $100,000). Thus, the debt/basis percentage with respect to computing the gain (or loss) derived from the sale of the building is 60 percent (the ratio of $30,000 to $50,000). Consequently, $3,000 (60 percent of $5,000) is a net section 1201 gain (capital gain net income for taxable years beginning after December 31, 1976). The portion of such gain which is taxable shall be determined in accordance with rules contained in subchapter P, chapter 1 of the Code (relating to capital gains and losses). See also section 511(d) and the regulations thereunder (relating to the minimum tax for tax preferences).

(2) Property used in an unrelated trade or business—(i) In general. To the extent that the gross income from any property is treated as income from the conduct of an unrelated trade or business, such property shall not be treated as debt-financed property. However, any gain on the disposition of such property which is not included in the income of an unrelated trade or business by reason of section 512(b)(5) is includible as gross income derived from or on account of debt-financed property under paragraph (a)(1) of § 1.514(a)–1.

(ii) Amounts specifically taxable under other provisions of the Code. Section 514 does not apply to amounts which are otherwise included in the computation of unrelated business taxable income, such as rents from personal property includible pursuant to section 512(b)(13) or rents and interest from controlled organizations includible pursuant to section 512(b)(3). See paragraph (l)(5) of § 1.512(b)–1 for the rules determining the manner in which amounts are taken into account where such amounts may be included in the computation of unrelated business taxable income by operation of more than one provision of the Code.

(3) Examples. Subparagraphs (1) and (2) of this paragraph may be illustrated by the following examples. For purposes of these examples it is assumed that the indebtedness is acquisition indebtedness.

Example 1. X, an exempt scientific organization, owns a 10-story office building. During 1972, four stories are occupied by X's administrative offices, and the remaining six stories are rented to the public for purposes not described in section 514(b)(1)(A), (B), (C), or (D). On December 31, 1972, the building is sold and X realizes a long-term capital gain of $100,000. This is X's only capital transaction for 1972. The debt/basis percentage with respect to computing the gain (or loss) derived from the sale of the building is 30 percent. Since 40 percent of the building was used for X's exempt purpose, only 60 percent of the building is debt-financed property. Thus, only $60,000 of the gain (60 percent of $100,000) is subject to this section. Consequently, the amount of gain treated as unrelated debt-financed income is $18,000 ($60,000 multiplied by the debt/basis percentage of 30 percent).The portion of such $18,000 which is taxable shall be determined in accordance with the rules contained in subchapter P, chapter 1 of the Code. See also section 511(d) and the regulations thereunder (relating to the minimum tax for tax preferences).

Example 2. Y, an exempt organization, owns two properties, a restaurant and an office building. In 1972, all the space in the office building, except for the portion utilized by Y to house the administrative offices of the restaurant, is rented to the public for purposes not described in section 514(b)(1)(A), (B), (C), or (D). The average adjusted basis of the office building for 1972 is $2 million. The outstanding principal indebtedness throughout 1972 is $1 million. Thus, the highest acquisition indebtedness in the calendar year of 1972 is $1 million. It is determined that 30 percent of the space in the office building is used for the administrative functions engaged in by the employees of the organization with respect to the restaurant. Since the income attributable to the restaurant is attributable to the conduct of an unrelated trade or business, only 70 percent of the building is treated as debt-financed property for purposes of determining the portion of the rental income which is unrelated debt-financed income. On December 31, 1972, the office building is sold and Y realizes a long-term capital gain of $250,000. This is Y's only capital transaction for 1972. In accordance with subparagraph (2)(i) of this paragraph, all the gain derived from this sale is taken into account in computing the amount of such gain subject to tax. The portion of such gain which is taxable is determined by multiplying the $250,000 gain by the debt/basis percentage. The debt/basis percentage is the ratio which the highest acquisition indebtedness for the 12-month period preceding the date of sale, $1 million, is of the average adjusted basis, $2 million. Thus, the debt/basis percentage with respect to computing the gain (or loss) derived from the sale of the building is 50 percent (the ratio of $1 million to $2 million). Consequently, $125,000 (50 percent of $250,000) is a net section 1201 gain (net capital gain for taxable years beginning after December 31, 1976). The amount of such gain which is taxable shall be determined in accordance with the rules contained in subchapter P, chapter 1 of the Code. See also section 511(d) and the regulations thereunder.

Example 3. (a) Z, an exempt university, owns all the stock of M, a nonexempt corporation. During 1971 M leases from Z University a factory unrelated to Z's exempt purpose and a dormitory for the students of Z, for a total annual rent of $100,000: $80,000 for the factory and $20,000 for the dormitory. During 1971, M has $500,000 of taxable income, disregarding the rent paid to Z: $150,000 from the dormitory and $350,000 from the factory. The factory is subject to a mortgage of $150,000. Its average adjusted basis for 1971 is determined to be $300,000. Z's deductions for 1971 with respect to the leased property are $4,000 for the dormitory and $16,000 for the factory. In accordance with subdivision (ii) of this subparagraph, section 514 applies only to that portion of the rent which is excluded from the computation of unrelated business taxable income by operation of section 512(b)(3) and not included in such computation pursuant to section 512(b)(13). Since all the rent received by Z is derived from real property, section 512(b)(3) would exclude all such rent from computation of Z's unrelated business taxable income. However, 70 percent of the rent paid to Z with respect to the factory and 70 percent of the deductions directly connected with such rent shall be taken into account by Z in determining its unrelated business taxable income pursuant to section 512(b)(15), computed as follows:

M's taxable income (disregarding rent paid to Z)	$500,000
Less taxable income from dormitory	150,000
Excess taxable income	$350,000

Ratio ($350,000/$500,000)	7/10
Total rent paid to Z	100,000
Total deductions ($4,000 + $16,000)	20,000
Rental income treated under section 512(b)(15) as gross income from an unrelated trade or business (7/10 of $100,000)	70,000
Less deductions directly connected with such income (7/10 of $20,000)	14,000
Net rental income included by Z in computing its unrelated business taxable income pursuant to section 512(b)(15)	$56,000

(b) Since only that portion of the rent derived from the factory and the deductions directly connected with such rent not taken into account pursuant to section 512(b)(15) may be included in computing unrelated business taxable income by operation of section 514, only $10,000 ($80,000 minus $70,000) of rent and $2,000 ($16,000 minus $14,000) of deductions are so taken into account. The portion of such amounts to be taken into account is determined by multiplying the $10,000 of income and $2,000 of deductions by the debt/basis percentage. The debt/basis percentage is the ratio which the average acquisition indebtedness ($150,000) is of the average adjusted basis of the property ($300,000). Thus, the debt/basis percentage for 1971 is 50 percent (the ratio of $150,000 to $300,000). Under these circumstances, Z shall include net rental income of $4,000 in its unrelated business taxable income for 1971, computed as follows:

Total rents	$ 10,000
Deductions directly connected with such rents	2,000
Debt/basis percentage ($150,000/$300,000)	50%
Rental income treated as gross income from an unrelated trade or business (50 percent of $10,000)	5,000
Less the allowable portion of deductions directly connected with such income (50 percent of $2,000)	1,000
Net rental income included by Z in computing its unrelated business taxable income pursuant to section 514	$ 4,000

(4) Property related to research activities. To the extent that the gross income from any property is derived from research activities excluded from the tax on unrelated business income by paragraph (7), (8), or (9) of section 512(b), such property shall not be treated as debt-financed property.

(5) Property used in thrift shops, etc. To the extent that property is used in any trade or business which is excepted from the definition of unrelated trade or business by paragraph (1), (2), or (3) of section 513(a), such property shall not be treated as debt-financed property.

(6) Use by a related organization. For purposes of subparagraph (1), (4), or (5) of this paragraph, use of property by a related exempt organization (as defined in paragraph (c)(2)(ii) of this section) for a purpose described in such subparagraphs shall be taken into account in order to determine the extent to which such property is used for a purpose described in such subparagraphs.

* * *

(d) Property acquired for prospective exempt use—(1) Neighborhood land—(i) In general. If an organization acquires real property for the principal purpose of using the land in the exercise or performance of its exempt purpose, commencing within 10 years of the time of acquisition, such property will not be treated as debt-financed property, so long as (a) such property is in the neighborhood of other property owned by the organization which is used in the performance of its exempt purpose, and (b) the organization does not abandon its intent to use the land in such a manner within the 10-year period. The rule expressed in this subdivision is hereinafter referred to as the neighborhood land rule.

(ii) Neighborhood defined. Property shall be considered in the neighborhood of property owned and used by the organization in the performance of its exempt purpose if the acquired property is contiguous with the exempt purpose property or would be contiguous with such property except for the interposition of a road, street, railroad, stream, or similar property. If the acquired property is not contiguous with exempt function property, it may still be in the neighborhood of such property, but only if it is within 1 mile of such property and the facts and circumstances of the particular situation make the acquisition of contiguous property unreasonable. Some of the criteria to consider in determining this question include the availability of land and the intended future use of the land. For example, a university attempts to purchase land contiguous to its present campus but cannot do so because the owners either refuse to sell or ask unreasonable prices. The nearest land of sufficient size and utility is a block away from the campus. The university purchases such land. Under these circumstances, the contiguity requirement is unreasonable and the land purchased would be considered neighborhood land.

(iii) Exception. The neighborhood land rule shall not apply to any property after the expiration of 10 years from the date of acquisition. Further, the neighborhood land rule shall apply after the first 5 years of the 10-year period only if the organization establishes to the satisfaction of the Commissioner that future use of the acquired land in furtherance of the organization's exempt purpose before the expiration of the 10-year period is reasonably certain. In order to satisfy the Commissioner, the organization does not necessarily have to show binding contracts. However, it must at least have a definite plan detailing a specific improvement and a completion date, and some affirmative action toward the fulfillment of such a plan. This information shall be forwarded to the Commissioner of Internal Revenue, Washington, D.C. 20224, for a ruling at least 90 days before the end of the fifth year after acquisition of the land.

(2) Actual use. If the neighborhood land rule is inapplicable because:

(i) The acquired land is not in the neighborhood of other property used by the organization in performance of its exempt purpose, or

(ii) The organization (for the period after the first 5 years of the 10-year period) is unable to establish to the satisfaction of the Commissioner that the use of the acquired land for its exempt purposes within the 10-year period is reasonably certain, but the land is actually used by the organization in furtherance of its exempt purpose within the 10-year period, such property (subject to the provisions of subparagraph (4) of this paragraph) shall not be treated as debt-financed property for any period prior to such conversion.

(3) Limitations—(i) Demolition or removal required. (a) Subparagraphs (1) and (2) of this paragraph shall apply with respect to any structure on the land when acquired by the organization, or to the land occupied by the structure, only so long as the intended future use of the land in furtherance of the organization's exempt purpose requires that the structure be demolished or removed in order to use the land in such a manner. Thus, during the first 5 years after acquisition (and for subsequent years if there is a favorable ruling in accordance with subparagraph (1)(iii) of this paragraph) improved property is not debt-financed so long as the organization does not abandon its intent to demolish the existing structures and use the land in furtherance of its exempt purpose. Furthermore, if there is an actual demolition of such structures, the use made of the land need not be the one originally intended. Therefore, the actual use requirement of this subdivision may be satisfied by using the land in any manner which furthers the exempt purpose of the organization.

(b) Subdivision (i)(a) of this subparagraph may be illustrated by the following examples. For purposes of the following examples it is assumed that but for the application of the neighborhood land rule such property would be debt-financed property.

Example 1. An exempt university acquires a contiguous tract of land on which there is an apartment building. The university intends to demolish the apartment building and build classrooms and does not abandon this intent during the first 4 years after acquisition. In the fifth year after acquisition it abandons the intent to demolish and sells the apartment building. Under these circumstances, such property is not debt-financed property for the first 4 years after acquisition even though there was no eventual demolition or use made of such land in furtherance of the university's exempt purpose. However, such property is debt-financed property as of the time in the fifth year that the intent to demolish the building is abandoned and any gain on the sale of property is subject to section 514.

Example 2. Assume the facts as stated in Example 1 except that the university did not abandon its intent to demolish the existing building and construct a classroom building until the eighth year after acquisition when it sells the property. Assume further that the university did not receive a favorable ruling in accordance with subparagraph (1)(iii) of this paragraph. Under these circumstances, the building is debt-financed property for the sixth, seventh, and eighth years. It is not, however, treated as debt-financed property for the first 5 years after acquisition.

Example 3. Assume the facts as stated in Example 2 except that the university received a favorable ruling in accordance with subparagraph (1)(iii) of this paragraph. Under these circumstances, the building is not debt-financed property for the first 7 years after acquisition. It only becomes debt-financed property as of the time in the eighth year when the university abandoned its intent to demolish the existing structure.

Example 4. (1) Assume that a university acquires a contiguous tract of land containing an office building for the principal purpose of demolishing the office building and building a modern dormitory. Five years later the dormitory has not been constructed, and the university has failed to satisfy the Commissioner that the office building will be demolished and the land will be used in furtherance of its exempt purpose (and consequently has failed to obtain a favorable ruling under subparagraph (1)(iii) of this paragraph). In the ninth taxable year after acquisition the university converts the office building into an administration building. Under these circumstances, during the sixth, seventh, and eighth years after acquisition, the office building is treated as debt-financed property because the office building was not demolished or removed. Therefore, the income derived from such property during these years shall be subject to the tax on unrelated business income.

(2) Assume that instead of converting the office building to an administration building, the university demolishes the office building in the ninth taxable year after acquisition and then constructs a new administration building. Under these circumstances, the land would not be considered debt-financed property for any period following the acquisition, and the university would be entitled to a refund of taxes paid on the income derived from such property for the sixth through eighth taxable years after the acquisition in accordance with subparagraph (4) of this paragraph.

(ii) Subsequent construction. Subparagraphs (1) and (2) of this paragraph do not apply to structures erected on the land after the acquisition of the land.

(iii) Property subject to business lease. Subparagraphs (1) and (2) of this paragraph do not apply to property subject to a lease which is a business lease (as defined in § 1.514(f)–1) whether the organization acquired the property subject to the lease or whether it executed the lease subsequent to acquisition. If only a portion of the real property is subject to a lease, paragraph (c) of § 1.514(f)–1 applies in determining whether such lease is a business lease.

(4) Refund of taxes. (i) If an organization has not satisfied the actual use condition of subparagraph (2) of this paragraph or paragraph (e)(3) of this section before the date prescribed by law (including extensions) for filing the return for the taxable year, the tax for such year shall be computed without regard to the application of such actual use condition. However, if:

(a) A credit or refund of any overpayment of taxes is allowable for a prior taxable year as a result of the satisfaction of such actual use condition, and

(b) Such credit or refund is prevented by the operation of any law or rule of law (other than chapter 74, relating to closing agreements and compromises),

such credit or refund may nevertheless be allowed or made, if a claim is filed within 1 year after the close of the taxable year in which such actual use condition is satisfied. For a special rule with respect to the payment of interest at the rate of 4 percent per annum, see section 514(b)(3)(D), prior to its amendment by section 7(b) of the Act of January 3, 1975 (Pub. L. 93–625, 88 Stat. 2115).

(ii) This subparagraph may be illustrated by the following example. For purposes of this example it is assumed that but for the neighborhood land rule such property would be debt-financed property.

Example. Y, a calendar year exempt organization, acquires real property in January 1970, which is contiguous with other property used by Y in furtherance of its exempt purpose. However, Y does not satisfy the Commissioner by January 1975, that the existing structure will be demolished and the land will be used in furtherance of its exempt purpose. In accordance with this subparagraph, from 1975 until the property is converted to an exempt use, the income derived from such property shall be subject to the tax on unrelated business income. During July 1979, Y demolishes the existing structure on the land and begins using the land in furtherance of its exempt purpose. At this time Y may file claims for refund for the open years 1976 through 1978. Further, in accordance with this subparagraph, Y may also file a claim for refund for 1975, even though a claim for such taxable year may be barred by the statute of limitations, provided such claim is filed before the close of 1980.

(e) Churches—(1) In general. If a church or association or convention of churches acquires real property, for the principal purpose of using the land in the exercise or performance of its exempt purpose, commencing within 15 years of the time of acquisition, such property shall not be treated as debt-financed property so long as the organization does not abandon its intent to use the land in such a manner within the 15-year period.

(2) Exception. This paragraph shall not apply to any property after the expiration of the 15-year period. Further, this paragraph shall apply after the first 5 years of the 15-year period only if the church or association or convention of churches establishes to the satisfaction of the Commissioner that use of the acquired land in furtherance of the organization's exempt purpose before the expiration of the 15-year period is reasonably certain. For purposes of the preceding sentence, the rules contained in paragraph (d)(1)(iii) of this section with respect to satisfying the Commissioner that the exempt organization intends to use the land within the prescribed time in furtherance of its exempt purpose shall apply.

(3) Actual use. If the church or association or convention of churches for the period after the first 5 years of the 15-year period is unable to establish to the satisfaction of the Commissioner that the use of the acquired land for its exempt purpose within the 15-year period is reasonably certain, but such land is in fact converted to an exempt use within the 15-year period, the land (subject to the provisions of paragraph (d)(4) of this section) shall not be treated as debt-financed property for any period prior to such conversion.

(4) Limitations. The limitations stated in paragraph (d)(3)(i) and (ii) of this section shall similarly apply to the rules contained in this paragraph.

§ 1.514(c)–1. Acquisition indebtedness.

(a) In general—(1) Definition of acquisition indebtedness. For purposes of section 514 and the regulations thereunder, the term "acquisition indebtedness" means, with respect to any debt-financed property, the outstanding amount of—

(i) The principal indebtedness incurred by the organization in acquiring or improving such property.

(ii) The principal indebtedness incurred before the acquisition or improvement of such property if such indebtedness would not have been incurred but for such acquisition or improvement; and

(iii) The principal indebtedness incurred after the acquisition or improvement of such property if such indebtedness would not have been incurred but for such acquisition or improvement and the incurrence of such indebtedness was reasonably foreseeable at the time of such acquisition or improvement.

Whether the incurrence of an indebtedness is reasonably foreseeable depends upon the facts and circumstances of each situation. The fact that an organization did not actually foresee the need for the incurrence of an indebtedness prior to the acquisition or improvement does not necessarily mean that the subsequent incurrence of indebtedness was not reasonably foreseeable.

(2) Examples. The application of subparagraph (1) of this paragraph may be illustrated by the following examples:

Example 1. X, an exempt organization, pledges some of its investment securities with a bank for a loan and uses the proceeds of such loan to purchase an office building which it leases to the public for purposes other than those described in section 514(b)(1)(A), (B), (C), or (D). The outstanding principal indebtedness with respect to the loan constitutes acquisition indebtedness incurred prior to the acquisition which would not have been incurred but for such acquisition.

Example 2. Y, an exempt scientific organization, mortgages its laboratory to replace working capital used in remodeling an office building which Y rents to an insurance company for purposes not described in section 514(b)(1)(A), (B), (C), or (D). The indebtedness is "acquisition indebtedness" since such indebtedness, though incurred subsequent to the improvement of the office building, would not have been incurred but for such improvement, and the indebtedness was reasonably foreseeable when, to make such improvement, Y reduced its working capital below the amount necessary to continue current operations.

Example 3. (a) U, an exempt private preparatory school, as its sole educational facility owns a classroom building which no longer meets the needs of U's students. In 1971, U sells this building for $3 million to Y, a corporation which it does not control. U receives $1 million as a down payment from Y and takes back a purchase money mortgage of $2 million which bears interest at 10 percent per annum. At the time U became the mortgagee of the $2 million purchase money mortgage, U realized that it would have to construct a new classroom building and knew that it would have to incur an indebtedness in the construction of the new classroom building. In 1972, U builds a new classroom building for a cost of $4 million. In connection with the construction of this building, U borrows $2.5 million from X Bank pursuant to a deed of trust bearing interest at 6 percent per annum. Under these circumstances, $2 million of the $2.5 million borrowed to finance construction of the new classroom building would not have been borrowed but for the retention of the $2 million purchase money mortgage. Since such indebtedness was reasonably foreseeable, $2 million of the $2.5 million borrowed to finance the construction of the new classroom building is acquisition indebtedness with respect to the purchase money mortgage and the purchase money mortgage is debt-financed property.

(b) In 1972, U receives $200,000 in interest from Y (10 percent of $2 million) and makes a $150,000 interest payment to X (6 percent of $2.5 million). In addition, assume that for 1972 the debt/basis percentage is 100 percent ($2 million/$2 million). Accordingly, all the interest and all the deductions directly connected with such interest income are to be taken into account in computing unrelated business taxable income. Thus, $200,000 of interest income and $120,000 ($150,000 x $2 million/$2.5 million) of deductions directly connected with such interest income are taken into account. Under these circumstances, U shall include net interest income of $80,000 ($200,000 of income less $120,000 of deductions directly connected with such income) in its unrelated business taxable income for 1972.

Example 4. In 1972 X, an exempt organization, forms a partnership with A and B. The partnership agreement provides that all three partners shall share equally in the profits of the partnership, shall each invest $3 million, and that X shall be a limited partner. X invests $1 million of its own funds in the partnership and $2 million of borrowed funds. The partnership purchases as its sole asset an office building which is leased to the general public for purposes other than those described in section 514(b)(1)(A), (B), (C), or (D). The office building cost the partnership $24 million of which $15 million is borrowed from Y bank. This loan is secured by a mortgage on the entire office building. By agreement with Y bank, X is held not to be personally liable for payment of such mortgage. By reason of section 702(b) the character of any item realized by the partnership and included in the partner's distributive share shall be determined as if the partner realized such item directly from the source from which it was realized by the partnership and in the same manner. Therefore, a portion of X's income from the building is debt-financed income. Under these circumstances, since both the $2 million indebtedness incurred by X in acquiring its partnership interest and $5 million, the allocable portion of the partnership's indebtedness incurred with respect to acquiring the office building which is attributable to X in computing the debt/basis percentage (one-third of $15 million), were incurred in acquiring income-producing property, X has acquisition indebtedness of $7 million ($2 million plus $5 million). Similarly, the allocable portion of the partnership's adjusted basis in the office building which is attributable to X in computing the debt/basis percentage is $8 million (one-third of $24 million). Assuming no payment with respect to either indebtedness and no adjustments to basis in 1972, X's average acquisition indebtedness is $7 million and X's average adjusted basis is $8 million for such year. Therefore, X's debt/basis percentage with respect to its share of the partnership income for 1972 is 87.5 percent ($7 million/$8 million).

(3) Changes in use of property. Since property used in a manner described in section 514(b)(1)(A), (B), (C), or (D) is not considered debt-financed property, indebtedness with respect to such property is not acquisition indebtedness. However, if an organization converts such property to a use which is not described in section 514(b)(1)(A), (B), (C), or (D) and such property is otherwise treated as debt-financed property, the outstanding principal indebtedness with respect to such property will thereafter be treated as "acquisition indebtedness". For example, assume that in 1971 a university borrows funds to acquire an apartment building as housing for married students. In 1974 the university rents the apartment building to the public for purposes not described in section 514(b)(1)(A), (B), (C), or (D). The outstanding principal indebtedness is "acquisition indebtedness" as of the time in 1974 when the building is first rented to the public.

(4) Continued indebtedness. If—

(i) An organization sells or exchanges property, subject to an indebtedness (incurred in a manner described in subparagraph (1) of this paragraph),

(ii) Acquires another property without retiring the indebtedness, and

(iii) The newly acquired property is otherwise treated as debt-financed property,

the outstanding principal indebtedness with respect to the acquired property is "acquisition indebtedness", even though the original property was not debt-financed property. For example, to house its administrative offices, an exempt organization purchases a building with $600,000 of its own funds and $400,000 of borrowed funds secured by a pledge of its securities. It later sells the building for $1,000,000 without redeeming the pledge. It uses these proceeds to purchase an apartment building which it rents to the public for purposes not described in section 514(b)(1)(A), (B), (C), or (D). The indebtedness of $400,000 is "acquisition indebtedness" with respect to the apartment building even though the office building was not debt-financed property.

* * *

(b) Property acquired subject to lien—(1) Mortgages. Except as provided in subparagraphs (3) and (4) of this paragraph, whenever property is acquired subject to a mortgage, the amount of the outstanding principal indebtedness secured by such mortgage is treated as "acquisition indebtedness" with respect to such property even though the organization did not assume or agree to pay such indebtedness. The preceding sentence applies whether property is acquired by purchase, gift, devise, bequest, or any other means. Thus, for example, assume that an exempt organization pays $50,000 for real property valued at $150,000 and subject to a $100,000 mortgage. The $100,000 of outstanding principal indebtedness is "acquisition indebtedness" just as though the organization had borrowed $100,000 to buy the property.

(2) Other liens. For purposes of this paragraph, liens similar to mortgages shall be treated as mortgages. A lien is similar to a mortgage if title to property is encumbered by the lien for the benefit of a creditor. However, in the case where State law provides that a tax lien attaches to property prior to the time when such lien becomes due and payable, such lien shall not be treated as similar to a mortgage until after it has become due and payable and the organization has had an opportunity to pay such lien in accordance with State law. Liens similar to mortgages include (but are not limited to):

(i) Deeds of trust,

(ii) Conditional sales contracts,

(iii) Chattel mortgages,

(iv) Security interests under the Uniform Commercial Code,

(v) Pledges,

(vi) Agreements to hold title in escrow, and

(vii) Tax liens (other than those described in the third sentence of this subparagraph).

(3) Certain encumbered property acquired by gift, bequest or devise—(i)

Bequest or devise. Where property subject to a mortgage is acquired by an organization by bequest or devise, the outstanding principal indebtedness secured by such mortgage is not to be treated as "acquisition indebtedness" during the 10-year period following the date of acquisition. For purposes of the preceding sentence, the date of acquisition is the date the organization receives the property.

(ii) Gifts. If an organization acquires property by gift subject to a mortgage, the outstanding principal indebtedness secured by such mortgage shall not be treated as "acquisition indebtedness" during the 10-year period following the date of such gift, so long as—

(a) The mortgage was placed on the property more than 5 years before the date of the gift, and

(b) The property was held by the donor for more than 5 years before the date of the gift.

For purposes of the preceding sentence, the date of the gift is the date the organization receives the property.

(iii) Limitation. Subdivisions (i) and (ii) of this subparagraph shall not apply if—

(a) The organization assumes and agrees to pay all or any part of the indebtedness secured by the mortgage, or

(b) The organization makes any payment for the equity owned by the decedent or the donor in the property (other than a payment pursuant to an annuity excluded from the definition of "acquisition indebtedness" by paragraph (e) of this section).

Whether an organization has assumed and agreed to pay all or any part of an indebtedness in order to acquire the property shall be determined by the facts and circumstances of each situation.

(iv) Examples. The application of this subparagraph may be illustrated by the following examples:

Example 1. A dies on January 1, 1971. His will devises an office building subject to a mortgage to U, an exempt organization described in section 501(c)(3). U does not at any time assume the mortgage. For the period 1971 through 1980, the outstanding principal indebtedness secured by the mortgage is not acquisition indebtedness. However, after December 31, 1980, the outstanding principal indebtedness secured by the mortgage is acquisition indebtedness if the building is otherwise treated as debt-financed property.

Example 2. Assume the facts as stated in example (1) except that on January 1, 1975, U assumes the mortgage. After January 1, 1975, the outstanding principal indebtedness secured by the mortgage is acquisition indebtedness if the building is otherwise treated as debt-financed property.

* * *

(c) Extension of obligations—(1) In general. An extension, renewal, or refinancing of an obligation evidencing a preexisting indebtedness is considered as a continuation of the old indebtedness to the extent the outstanding principal amount thereof is not increased. Where the principal amount of the modified obligation exceeds the outstanding principal amount of the preexisting indebtedness, the excess shall be treated as a separate indebtedness for purposes of section 514 and the regulations thereunder. For example, if the interest rate on an obligation incurred prior to June 28, 1966, by an exempt university is modified subsequent to such date, the modified obligation shall be deemed to have been incurred prior to June 28, 1966. Thus, such an indebtedness will not be treated as acquisition indebtedness for taxable years beginning before January 1, 1972, unless the original indebtedness was business lease indebtedness (as defined in § 1.514(g)–1).

(2) Extension or renewal. In general, any modification or substitution of the terms of an obligation by the organization shall be an extension or renewal of the original obligation, rather than the creation of a new indebtedness to the extent that the outstanding principal amount of the indebtedness is not increased. The following are examples of acts which result in the extension or renewal of an obligation:

(i) Substitution of liens to secure the obligation;

(ii) Substitution of obligees, whether or not with the consent of the organization;

(iii) Renewal, extension or acceleration of the payment terms of the obligation; and

(iv) Addition, deletion, or substitution of sureties or other primary or secondary obligors.

(3) Allocation. In cases where the outstanding principal amount of the modified obligation exceeds the outstanding principal amount of the unmodified obligation and only a portion of such refinanced indebtedness is to be treated as acquisition indebtedness, payments on the amount of the refinanced indebtedness shall be apportioned prorata between the amount of the preexisting indebtedness and the excess amount. For example, assume that an organization has an outstanding principal indebtedness of $500,000 which is treated as acquisition indebtedness. It borrows another $100,000, which is not acquisition indebtedness, from the same lending institution and gives the lender a $600,000 note for its total obligation. In this situation, a payment of $60,000 on the amount of the total obligation would reduce the acquisition indebtedness by $50,000 and the excess indebtedness by $10,000.

(d) Indebtedness incurred in performing exempt purpose. "Acquisition indebtedness" does not include the incurrence of an indebtedness inherent in the performance or exercise of the purpose or function constituting the basis of the organization's exemption. Thus, "acquisition indebtedness" does not include the indebtedness incurred by an exempt credit union in accepting deposits from its members or the obligation incurred by an exempt organization in accepting payments from its members to provide such members with insurance, retirement or other similar benefits.

* * *

(g) Certain obligations of charitable remainder trusts. For purposes of section 664(c) and § 1.664–1(c), a charitable remainder trust (as defined in § 1.664–1(a)(1)(iii)(a)) does not incur "acquisition indebtedness" when the sole consideration it is required to pay in exchange for unencumbered property is an "annuity amount" or a "unitrust amount" (as defined in § 1.664–1(a)(1)(iii)(b) and (c)).

* * *

§ 1.514(e)–1. Allocation rules.

Where only a portion of property is debt-financed property, proper allocation of the basis, indebtedness, income, and deductions with respect to such property must be made to determine the amount of income or gain derived from such property which is to be treated as unrelated debt-financed income. See examples (2) and (3) of paragraph (b)(1)(iii) of § 1.514–1 and examples (1), (2), and (3) of paragraph (b)(3) of § 1.514(b)–1 for illustrations of proper allocation.

POLITICAL ORGANIZATIONS

§ 1.527-6. Inclusion of certain amounts in the gross income of an exempt organization which is not a political organization.

(a) Exempt organizations—General rule. If an organization described in section 501(c) which is exempt from tax under section 501(a) expends any amount for an exempt function, it may be subject to tax. There is included in the gross income of such organization for the taxable year an amount equal to the lesser of:

(1) The net investment income of such organization for the taxable year, or

(2) The aggregate amount expended during the taxable year for an exempt function.

The amount included will be treated as political organization taxable income.

(b) Exempt function expenditures—(1) Directly related expenses. (i) Except as provided in this section, the term exempt function will generally have the same meaning it has in § 1.527–2(c). Thus, expenditures which are directly related to the selection process as defined in § 1.527–2(c)(1) are expenditures for an exempt function. Expenditures for indirect expenses as defined in § 1.527–2(c)(2), when made by a section 501(c) organization are for an exempt function only to the extent provided in paragraph (b)(2) of this section. Expenditures of a section 501(c) organization which are otherwise allowable under the Federal Election Campaign Act or similar State statute are for an exempt function only to the extent provided in paragraph (b)(3) of this section.

(ii) An expenditure may be made for an exempt function directly or through another organization. A section 501(c) organization will not be absolutely liable under section 527(f)(1) for amounts transferred to an individual or organization. A section 501(c) organization is, however, required to take reasonable steps to ensure that the transferee does not use such amounts for an exempt function.

(2) Indirect expenses. [Reserved]

(3) Expenditures allowed by Federal Election Campaign Act. [Reserved]

(4) Appointments or confirmations. Where an organization described in paragraph (a) of this section appears before any legislative body in response to a written request by such body for the purpose of influencing the appointment or confirmation of an individual to a public office, any expenditure directly related to such appearance is not treated as an expenditure for an exempt function.

(5) Nonpartisan activity. Expenditures for nonpartisan activities by an organization to which paragraph (a) of this section applies are not expenditures for an exempt function. Nonpartisan activities include voter registration and get-out-the-vote campaigns. To be nonpartisan voter registration and get-out-the-vote campaigns must not be specifically identified by the organization with any candidate or political party.

(c) Character of items included in gross income—(1) General rule. The items of income included in the gross income of an organization under paragraph (a) of this section retain their character as ordinary income or capital gain.

(2) Special rule in determining character of item. If the amount included in gross income is determined under paragraph (a)(2)(ii) of this section, the character of the items of income is determined by multiplying the total amount included in gross income under such paragraph by a fraction, the numerator of which is the portion of the organization's net investment income that is gain from the sale or exchange of a capital asset, and the denominator of which is the organization's net investment income. For example, if $5,000 is included in the gross income of an organization under paragraph (a)(2) of this section, and the organization had $100,000 of net investment income of which $10,000 is long term capital gain, then $500 would be treated as long term capital gain:

Capital gain net investment income	x	Amount expended on an exempt function	=	Portion of income subject to tax under section 1201

$$\frac{\$10{,}000}{\$100{,}000} \times \$5{,}000 = \$500$$

(d) Modifications. The modifications described in section 527(c)(2) apply in computing the tax under paragraph (a)(2) of this section. Thus, no net operating loss is allowed under section 172 nor is any deduction allowed under part VIII of subchapter B. However, there is allowed a specific deduction of $100.

(e) Transfer not treated as exempt function expenditures. Provided the provisions of this paragraph (e) are met, a transfer of political contributions or dues collected by a section 501(c) organization to a separate segregated fund as defined in paragraph (f) of this section is not treated as an expenditure for an exempt function (within the meaning of § 1.527–2(c)). Such transfers must be made promptly after the receipt of such amounts by the section 501(c) organization, and must be made directly to the separate segregated fund. A transfer is considered promptly and directly made if:

(1) The procedures followed by the section 501(c) organization satisfy the requirements of applicable Federal or State campaign law and regulations;

(2) The section 501(c) organization maintains adequate records to demonstrate that amounts transferred in fact consist of political contributions or dues, rather than investment income; and

(3) The political contributions or dues transferred were not used to earn investment income for the section 501(c) organization.

(f) Separate segregated fund. An organization or fund described in section 527(f)(3) is a separate segregated fund. To avoid the application of paragraph (a) of this section, an organization described in section 501(c) that is exempt from taxation under section 501(a) may, if it is consistent with its exempt status, establish and maintain such a separate segregated fund to receive contributions and make expenditures in a political campaign. If such a fund meets the requirements of § 1.527–2(a) (relating to the definition of a political organization), it shall be treated as a political organization subject to the provisions of section 527. A segregated fund established under the Federal Election Campaign Act will continue to be treated as a segregated fund when it engages in exempt function activities as defined in § 1.527–2(c), relating to State campaigns.

(g) Effect of expenditures on exempt status. Section 527(f) and this section do not sanction the intervention in any political campaign by an organization described in section 501(c) if such activity is inconsistent with its exempt status under section 501(c). For example, an organization described in section 501(c)(3) is precluded from engaging in any political campaign activities. The fact that section 527 imposes a tax on the exempt function (as defined in § 1.527–2(c)) expenditures of section 501(c) organizations and permits such organizations to establish separate segregated funds to engage in campaign activities does not sanction the participation in these activities by section 501(c)(3) organizations.

CHARITABLE REMAINDER TRUSTS

§ 1.664-1. Charitable remainder trusts.

(a) In general—(1) Introduction—(i) General description of a charitable remainder trust. Generally, a charitable remainder trust is a trust which provides for a specified distribution, at least annually, to one or more beneficiaries, at least one of which is not a charity, for life or for a term of years, with an irrevocable remainder interest to be held for the benefit of, or paid over to, charity. The specified distribution to be paid at least annually must be a sum certain which is not less than 5 percent of the initial net fair market value of all property placed in trust (in the case of a charitable remainder annuity trust) or a fixed percentage which is not less than 5 percent of the net fair market value of the trust assets, valued annually (in the case of a charitable remainder unitrust). A trust created after July 31, 1969, which is a charitable remainder trust is exempt from all of the taxes imposed by Subtitle A of the Code for any taxable year of the trust except a taxable year in which it has unrelated business taxable income.

(ii) Scope. This section provides definitions, general rules governing the creation and administration of a charitable remainder trust, and rules governing the taxation of the trust and its beneficiaries. For the application of certain foundation rules to charitable remainder trusts, see paragraph (b) of this section. If the trust has unrelated business taxable income, see paragraph (c) of this section. For the treatment of distributions to recipients, see paragraph (d) of this section. For the treatment of distributions to charity, see paragraph (e) of this section. For the time limitations for amendment of governing instruments, see paragraph (f) of this section. For transitional rules under which particular requirements are inapplicable to certain trusts, see paragraph (g) of this section. Section 1.664-2 provides rules relating solely to a charitable remainder annuity trust. Section 1.664-3 provides rules relating solely to a charitable remainder unitrust. Section 1.664-4 provides rules governing the calculation of the fair market value of the remainder interest in a charitable remainder unitrust. For rules relating to the filing of returns for a charitable remainder trust, see paragraph (a)(6) of § 1.6012-3 and section 6034 and the regulations thereunder.

(iii) Definitions. As used in this section and §§ 1.664-2, 1.664-3, and 1.664-4:

(a) Charitable remainder trust. The term charitable remainder trust means a trust with respect to which a deduction is allowable under section 170, 2055, 2106, or 2522 and which meets the description of a charitable remainder annuity trust (as described in § 1.664-2) or a charitable remainder unitrust (as described in § 1.664-3).

(b) Annuity amount. The term annuity amount means the amount described in paragraph (a)(1) of § 1.664-2 which is payable, at least annually, to the beneficiary of a charitable remainder annuity trust.

(c) Unitrust amount. The term unitrust amount means the amount described in paragraph (a)(1) of § 1.664-3 which is payable, at least annually, to the beneficiary of a charitable remainder unitrust.

(d) Recipient. The term recipient means the beneficiary who receives the possession or beneficial enjoyment of the annuity amount or unitrust amount.

(e) Governing instrument. The term governing instrument has the same meaning as in section 508(e) and the regulations thereunder.

(2) Requirement that the trust must be either a charitable remainder annuity trust or a charitable remainder unitrust. A trust is a charitable remainder trust only if it is either a charitable remainder annuity trust in every respect or a charitable remainder unitrust in every respect. For example, a trust which provides for the payment each year to a noncharitable beneficiary of the greater of a sum certain or a fixed percentage of the annual value of the trust assets is not a charitable remainder trust inasmuch as the trust is neither a charitable remainder annuity trust (for the reason that the payment for the year may be a fixed percentage of the annual value of the trust assets which is not a "sum certain") nor a charitable remainder unitrust (for the reason that the payment for the year may be a sum certain which is not a "fixed percentage" of the annual value of the trust assets).

(3) Restrictions on investments. A trust is not a charitable remainder trust if the provisions of the trust include a provision which restricts the trustee from investing the trust assets in a manner which could result in the annual realization of a reasonable amount of income or gain from the sale or disposition of trust assets. In the case of transactions with, or for the benefit of, a disqualified person, see section 4941(d) and the regulations thereunder for rules relating to the definition of self-dealing.

(4) Requirement that trust must meet definition of and function exclusively as a charitable remainder trust from its creation. In order for a trust to be a charitable remainder trust, it must meet the definition of and function exclusively as a charitable remainder trust from the creation of the trust. Solely for the purposes of section 664 and the regulations thereunder, the trust will be deemed to be created at the earliest time that neither the grantor nor any other person is treated as the owner of the entire trust under subpart E, part 1, subchapter J, chapter 1, subtitle A of the Code (relating to grantors and others treated as substantial owners), but in no event prior to the time property is first transferred to the trust. For purposes of the preceding sentence, neither the grantor nor his spouse shall be treated as the owner of the trust under such subpart E merely because the grantor or his spouse is named as a recipient. See examples 1 through 3 of subparagraph (6) of this paragraph for illustrations of the foregoing rule.

(5) Rules applicable to testamentary transfers—(i) Deferral of annuity or unitrust amount. Notwithstanding subparagraph (4) of this paragraph and §§ 1.664–2 and 1.664–3, for purposes of sections 2055 and 2106 a charitable remainder trust shall be deemed created at the date of death of the decedent (even though the trust is not funded until the end of a reasonable period of administration or settlement) if the obligation to pay the annuity or unitrust amount with respect to the property passing in trust at the death of the decedent begins as of the date of death of the decedent, even though the requirement to pay such amount is deferred in accordance with the rules provided in this subparagraph. If permitted by applicable local law or authorized by the provisions of the governing instrument, the requirement to pay such amount may be deferred until the end of the taxable year of the trust in which occurs the complete funding of the trust. Within a reasonable period after such time, the trust must pay (in the case of an underpayment) or must receive from the recipient (in the case of an overpayment) the difference between:

(a) Any annuity or unitrust amounts actually paid, plus interest on such amounts computed at the rate of interest specified in paragraph (a)(5)(iv) of this section, compounded annually, and

(b) The annuity or unitrust amounts payable, plus interest on such amounts computed at the rate of interest specified in paragraph (a)(5)(iv) of this section, compounded annually.

The amounts payable shall be retroactively determined by using the taxable year, valuation method, and valuation dates which are ultimately adopted by the charitable remainder trust. See subdivision (ii) of this subparagraph for rules relating to retroactive determination of the amount payable under a charitable remainder unitrust. See paragraph (d)(4) of this section for rules relating to the year of inclusion in the case of an underpayment to a recipient and the allowance of a deduction in the case of an overpayment to a recipient.

(ii) For purposes of retroactively determining the amount under subdivision (i)(b) of this subparagraph, the governing instrument of a charitable remainder unitrust may provide that the amount described in subdivision (i)(b) of this subparagraph with respect to property passing in trust at the death of the decedent for the period which begins on the date of death of the decedent and ends on the earlier of the date of death of the last recipient or the end of the taxable year of the trust in which occurs the complete funding of the trust shall be computed by multiplying:

(a) The sum of (1) the value, on the earlier of the date of death of the last recipient or the last day in such taxable year, of the property held in trust which is attributable to property passing to the trust at the death of the decedent, (2) any distributions in respect of unitrust amounts made by the trust or estate before such date, and (3) interest on such distributions computed at the rate of interest specified in paragraph (a)(5)(iv) of this section, compounded annually, from the date of distribution to such date by:

(b)(1) In the case of transfers made after November 30, 1983, for which the valuation date is before May 1, 1989, a factor equal to 1.000000 less the factor under the appropriate adjusted payout rate in Table D in § 1.664–4(e)(6) opposite the number of years in column 1 between the date of death of the decedent and the date of the earlier of the death of the last recipient or the last day of such taxable year.

(2) In the case of transfers for which the valuation date is after April 30, 1989, a factor equal to 1.000000 less the factor under the appropriate adjusted payout rate in Table D in § 1.664–4(e)(6) opposite the number of years in column 1 between the date of death of the decedent and the date of the earlier of the death of the last recipient or the last day of such taxable year. The appropriate adjusted payout rate is determined by using the appropriate Table F contained in § 1.664–4(e)(6) for the section 7520 rate for the month of the valuation date.

(3) If the number of years between the date of death and the date of the earlier of the death of the last recipient or the last day of such taxable year is between periods for which factors are provided, a linear interpolation must be made.

(iii) Treatment of distributions. The treatment of a distribution to a charitable remainder trust, or to a recipient in respect of an annuity or unitrust amount, paid, credited, or required to be distributed by an estate, or by a trust which is not a charitable remainder trust, shall be governed by the rules of subchapter J, chapter 1, subtitle A of the Code other than section 664. In the case of a charitable remainder trust which is partially or fully funded during the period of administration of an estate or settlement of a trust (which is not a charitable remainder trust), the treatment of any amount paid, credited, or required to be distributed by the charitable remainder trust shall be governed by the rules of section 664.

(iv) Rate of interest. The following rates of interest shall apply for purposes of paragraphs (a)(5)(i) through (ii) of this section:

(a) The section 7520 rate for the month in which the valuation date with respect to the transfer is (or one of the prior two months if elected under § 1.7520–2(b)) after April 30, 1989;

* * *

(7) Valuation of unmarketable assets—(i) In general. If unmarketable assets are transferred to or held by a trust, the trust will not be a trust with respect to which a deduction is available under section 170, 2055, 2106, or 2522, or will be treated as failing to function exclusively as a charitable remainder trust unless, whenever the trust is required to value such assets, the valuation is—

(a) Performed exclusively by an independent trustee; or

(b) Determined by a current qualified appraisal, from a qualified appraiser, as those terms are defined in—

(1) Section 1.170A–13(c)(3) and 1.170A–13(c)(5), respectively, for appraisals prepared for returns or submissions filed on or before August 17, 2006;

(2) Section 3 of Notice 2006–96, 2006–2 CB 902, for appraisals prepared for returns or submissions filed after August 17, 2006, if the donations are made before January 1, 2019; or

(3) Section 1.170A–17(a) and 1.170A–17(b), respectively, for appraisals prepared for returns or submissions for donations made on or after January 1, 2019.

(ii) Unmarketable assets. Unmarketable assets are assets that are not cash, cash equivalents, or other assets that can be readily sold or exchanged for cash or cash equivalents. For example, unmarketable assets include real property, closely-held stock, and an unregistered security for which there is no available exemption permitting public sale.

(iii) Independent trustee. An independent trustee is a person who is not the grantor of the trust, a noncharitable beneficiary, or a related or subordinate party to the grantor, the grantor's spouse, or a noncharitable beneficiary (within the meaning of section 672(c) and the applicable regulations).

(b) Application of certain foundation rules to charitable remainder trusts. See section 4947(a)(2) and section 4947(b)(3)(B) and the regulations thereunder for the application to charitable remainder trusts of certain provisions relating to private foundations. See section 508(e) for rules relating to required provisions in governing instruments prohibiting certain activities specified in section 4947(a)(2).

(c) Taxation of nonexempt charitable remainder trusts. If the charitable remainder trust has any unrelated business taxable income (within the meaning of section 512 and the regulations thereunder, determined as if part III, subchapter F, chapter 1, subtitle A of the Code applied to such trust) for any taxable year, the trust is subject to all of the taxes imposed by subtitle A of the Code for such taxable year. For taxable years beginning after December 31, 1969, unrelated business taxable income includes debt-financed income. The taxes imposed by subtitle A of the Code upon a nonexempt charitable remainder trust shall be computed under the rules prescribed by subparts A and C, part 1, subchapter J, chapter 1, subtitle A of the Code for trusts which may accumulate income or which distribute corpus. The provisions of subpart E, part 1 of such subchapter J are not applicable with respect to a nonexempt charitable remainder trust. The application of the above rules may be illustrated by the following example:

Example. In 1975, a charitable remainder trust which has a calendar year as its taxable year has $1,000 of ordinary income, including $100 of unrelated business taxable income, and no deductions other than under sections 642(b) and 661(a). The trust is required to pay out $700 for 1975 to a noncharitable recipient. Because the trust has some unrelated business taxable income in 1975, it is not exempt for such year. Consequently, the trust is taxable on all of its income as a complex trust. Under section 661(a) of the Code, the trust is allowed a deduction of $700. Under section 642(b) of the Code, the trust is allowed a deduction of $100. Consequently, the taxable income of the trust for 1975 is $200 ($1,000-$700-$100).

(d) Treatment of annual distributions to recipients—(1) Character of distributions—(i) Assignment of income to categories and classes at the trust level. (a) A trust's income, including income includible in gross income and other income, is assigned to one of three categories in the year in which it is required to be taken into account by the trust. These categories are—

(1) Gross income, other than gains and amounts treated as gains from the sale or other disposition of capital assets (referred to as the ordinary income category);

(2) Gains and amounts treated as gains from the sale or other disposition of capital assets (referred to as the capital gains category); and

(3) Other income (including income excluded under part III, subchapter B, chapter 1, subtitle A of the Internal Revenue Code).

(b) Items within the ordinary income and capital gains categories are assigned to different classes based on the Federal income tax rate applicable to each type of income in that category in the year the items are required to be taken into account by the trust. For example, for a trust with a taxable year ending December 31, 2004, the ordinary income category may include a class of qualified dividend income as defined in section 1(h)(11) and a class of all other ordinary income, and the capital gains category may include separate classes for short-term and long-term capital gains and losses, such as a short-term capital gain class, a 28-percent long-term capital gain class (gains and losses from collectibles and section 1202 gains), an unrecaptured section 1250 long-term capital gain class (long-term gains not treated as ordinary income that would be treated as ordinary income if section 1250(b)(1) included all depreciation), a qualified 5-year long-term capital gain class as defined in section 1(h)(9) prior to amendment by the Jobs and Growth Tax Relief Reconciliation Act of 2003 (JGTRRA), Public Law 108–27 (117 Stat. 752), and an all other long-term capital gain class. After items are assigned to a class, the tax rates may change so that items in two or more classes would be taxed at the same rate if distributed to the recipient during a particular year. If the changes to the tax rates are permanent, the undistributed items in those classes are combined into one class. If, however, the changes to the tax rates are only temporary (for example, the new rate for one class will sunset in a future year), the classes are kept separate.

(ii) Order of distributions. (a) The categories and classes of income (determined under paragraph (d)(1)(i) of this section) are used to determine the character of an annuity or unitrust distribution from the trust in the hands of the recipient irrespective of whether the trust is exempt from taxation under section 664(c) for the year of the distribution. The determination of the character of amounts distributed or deemed distributed at any time during the taxable year of the trust shall be made as of the end of that taxable year. The tax rate or rates to be used in computing the recipient's tax on the distribution shall be the tax rates that are applicable, in the year in which the distribution is required to be made, to the classes of income deemed to make up that distribution, and not the tax rates that are applicable to those classes of income in the year the income is received by the trust. The character of the distribution in the hands of the annuity or unitrust recipient is determined by treating the distribution as being made from each category in the following order:

(1) First, from ordinary income to the extent of the sum of the trust's ordinary income for the taxable year and its undistributed ordinary income for prior years.

(2) Second, from capital gain to the extent of the trust's capital gains determined under paragraph (d)(1)(iv) of this section.

(3) Third, from other income to the extent of the sum of the trust's other income for the taxable year and its undistributed other income for prior years.

(4) Finally, from trust corpus (with corpus defined for this purpose as the net fair market value of the trust assets less the total undistributed income (but not loss) in paragraphs (d)(1)(i)(a)(1) through (3) of this section).

(b) If the trust has different classes of income in the ordinary income category, the distribution from that category is treated as being made from each class, in turn, until exhaustion of the class, beginning with the class subject to the highest Federal income tax rate and ending with the class subject to the lowest Federal income tax rate. If the trust has different classes of net gain in the capital gains category, the distribution from that category is treated as being made first from the short-term capital gain class and then from each class of long-term capital gain, in turn, until exhaustion of the class, beginning with the class subject to the highest Federal income tax rate and ending with the class subject to the lowest rate. If two or more classes within the same category are subject to the same current tax rate, but at least one of those classes will be subject to a different tax rate in a future year (for example, if the current rate sunsets), the order of that class in relation to other classes in the category with the same current tax rate is determined based on the future rate or rates applicable to those classes. Within each category, if there is more than one type of income in a class, amounts treated as distributed from that class are to be treated as consisting of the same proportion of each type of income as the total of the current and undistributed income of that type bears to the total of the current and undistributed income of all types of income included in that class. For example, if rental income and interest income are subject to the same current and future Federal income tax rate and, therefore, are in the same class, a distribution from that class will be treated as consisting of a proportional amount of rental income and interest income.

(iii) Treatment of losses at the trust level—(a) Ordinary income category. A net ordinary loss for the current year is first used to reduce undistributed ordinary income for prior years that is assigned to the same class as the loss. Any excess loss is then used to reduce the current and undistributed ordinary income from other classes, in turn, beginning with the class subject to the highest Federal income tax rate and ending with the class subject to the lowest Federal income tax rate. If any of the loss exists after all the current and undistributed ordinary income from all classes has been offset, the excess is carried forward indefinitely to reduce ordinary income for future years and retains its class assignment. For purposes of this section, the amount of current income and prior years' undistributed income shall be computed without regard to the deduction for net operating losses provided by section 172 or 642(d).

(b) Other income category. A net loss in the other income category for the current year is used to reduce undistributed income in this category for prior years and any excess is carried forward indefinitely to reduce other income for future years.

(iv) Netting of capital gains and losses at the trust level. Capital gains of the trust are determined on a cumulative net basis under the rules of this paragraph (d)(1) without regard to the provisions of section 1212. For each taxable year, current and undistributed gains and losses within each class are netted to determine the net gain or loss for that class, and the classes of capital gains and losses are then netted against each other in the following order. First, a net loss from a class of long-term capital gain and loss (beginning with the class subject to the highest Federal income tax rate and ending with the class subject to the lowest rate) is used to offset net gain from each other class of long-term capital gain and loss, in turn, until exhaustion of the class, beginning with the class subject to the highest Federal income tax rate and ending with the class subject to the lowest rate. Second, either—

(a) A net loss from all the classes of long-term capital gain and loss (beginning with the class subject to the highest Federal income tax rate and ending with the class subject to the lowest rate) is used to offset any net gain from the class of short-term capital gain and loss; or

(b) A net loss from the class of short-term capital gain and loss is used to offset any net gain from each class of long-term capital gain and loss, in turn, until exhaustion of the class, beginning with the class subject to the highest Federal income tax rate and ending with the class subject to the lowest Federal income tax rate.

(v) Carry forward of net capital gain or loss by the trust. If, at the end of a taxable year, a trust has, after the application of paragraph (d)(1)(iv) of this section, any net loss or any net gain that is not treated as distributed under paragraph (d)(1)(ii)(a)(2) of this section, the net gain or loss is carried over to succeeding taxable years and retains its character in succeeding taxable years as gain or loss from its particular class.

(vi) Special transitional rules. To be eligible to be included in the class of qualified dividend income, dividends must meet the definition of section 1(h)(11) and must be received by the trust after December 31, 2002. Long-term capital gain or loss properly taken into account by the trust before January 1, 1997, is included in the class of all other long-term capital gains and losses. Long-term capital gain or loss properly taken into account by the trust on or after January 1, 1997, and before May 7, 1997, if not treated as distributed in 1997, is included in the class of all other long-term capital gains and losses. Long-term capital gain or loss (other than 28-percent gain (gains and losses from collectibles and section 1202 gains), unrecaptured section 1250 gain (long-term gains not treated as ordinary income that would be treated as ordinary income if section 1250(b)(1) included all depreciation), and qualified 5-year gain as defined in section 1(h)(9) prior to amendment by JGTRRA), properly taken into account by the trust before January 1, 2003, and distributed during 2003 is treated as if it were properly taken into account by the trust after May 5, 2003. Long-term capital gain or loss (other than 28-percent gain, unrecaptured section 1250 gain, and qualified 5-year gain), properly taken into account by the trust on or after January 1, 2003, and before May 6, 2003, if not treated as distributed during 2003, is included in the class of all other long-term capital gain. Qualified 5-year gain properly taken into account by the trust after December 31, 2000, and before May 6, 2003, if not treated as distributed by the trust in 2003 or a prior year, must be maintained in a separate class within the capital gains category until distributed. Qualified 5-year gain properly taken into account by the trust before January 1, 2003, and deemed distributed during 2003 is subject to the same current tax rate as deemed distributions from the class of all other long-term capital gain realized by the trust after May 5, 2003. Qualified 5-year gain properly taken into account by the trust on or after January 1, 2003, and before May 6, 2003, if treated as distributed by the trust in 2003, is subject to the tax rate in effect prior to the amendment of section 1(h)(9) by JGTRRA.

(vii) Application of section 643(a)(7). For application of the anti-abuse rule of section 643(a)(7) to distributions from charitable remainder trusts, see § 1.643(a)–8.

(viii) Examples. The following examples illustrate the rules in this paragraph (d)(1):

Example 1. (i) X, a charitable remainder annuity trust described in section 664(d)(1), is created on January 1, 2003. The annual annuity amount is $100. X's income for the 2003 tax year is as follows:

Interest income	$80
Qualified dividend income	50
Capital gains and losses	0
Tax-exempt income	0

(ii) In 2003, the year this income is received by the trust, qualified dividend income is subject to a different rate of Federal income tax than interest income and is, therefore, a separate class of income in the ordinary income category. The annuity amount is deemed to be distributed from the classes within the ordinary income category, beginning with the class subject to the highest Federal income tax rate and ending with the class subject to the lowest rate. Because during 2003 qualified dividend income is taxed at a lower rate than interest income, the interest income is deemed distributed prior to the qualified dividend income. Therefore, in the hands of the recipient, the 2003 annuity amount has the following characteristics:

Interest income	$80
Qualified dividend income	20

(iii) The remaining $30 of qualified dividend income that is not treated as distributed to the recipient in 2003 is carried forward to 2004 as undistributed qualified dividend income.

Example 2. (i) The facts are the same as in Example 1, and at the end of 2004, X has the following classes of income:

Interest income class	$ 5
Qualified dividend income class ($10 from 2004 and $30 carried forward from 2003)	40
Net short-term capital gain class	15
Net long-term capital loss in 28-percent class	(325)
Net long-term capital gain in unrecaptured section 1250 gain class	175
Net long-term capital gain in all other long-term capital gain class	350

(ii) In 2004, gain in the unrecaptured section 1250 gain class is subject to a 25-percent Federal income tax rate, and gain in the all other long-term capital gain class is subject to a lower rate. The net long-term capital loss in the 28-percent gain class is used to offset the net capital gains in the other classes of long-term capital gain and loss, beginning with the class subject to the highest Federal income tax rate and ending with the class subject to the lowest rate. The $325 net loss in the 28-percent gain class reduces the $175 net gain in the unrecaptured section 1250 gain class to $0. The remaining $150 loss from the 28-percent gain class reduces the $350 gain in the all other long-term capital gain class to $200. As in Example 1, qualified dividend income is taxed at a lower rate than interest income during 2004. The annuity amount is deemed to be distributed from all the classes in the ordinary income category and then from the classes in the capital gains category, beginning with the class subject to the highest Federal income tax rate and ending with the class subject to the lowest rate. In the hands of the recipient, the 2004 annuity amount has the following characteristics:

Interest income	$ 5
Qualified dividend income	40
Net short-term capital gain	15
Net long-term capital gain in all other LTCG class	40

(iii) The remaining $160 gain in the all other long-term capital gain class that is not treated as distributed to the recipient in 2004 is carried forward to 2005 as gain in that same class.

Example 3. (i) The facts are the same as in Examples 1 and 2, and at the end of 2005, X has the following classes of income:

Interest income class	$ 5
Qualified dividend income	20
Net loss in short-term capital gain class	(50)
Net long-term capital gain in 28-percent gain class	10
Net long-term capital gain in unrecaptured section 1250 gain class	135
Net long-term capital gain in all other long-term capital gain class (carried forward from 2004)	160

(ii) There are no long-term capital losses to net against the long-term capital gains. Thus, the net short-term capital loss is used to offset the net capital gains in the classes of long-term capital gain and loss, in turn, until exhaustion of the class, beginning with the class subject to the highest Federal income tax rate and ending with the class subject to the lowest rate. The $50 net short-term loss reduces the $10 net gain in the 28-percent gain class to $0. The remaining $40 net loss reduces the $135 net gain in the unrecaptured section 1250 gain class to $95. As in Examples 1 and 2, during 2005, qualified dividend income is taxed at a lower rate than interest income; gain in the unrecaptured section 1250 gain class is taxed at 25 percent; and gain in the all other long-term capital gain class is taxed at a rate lower than 25 percent. The annuity amount is deemed to be distributed from all the classes in the ordinary income category and then from the classes in the capital gains category, beginning with the class subject to the highest Federal income tax rate and ending with the class subject to the lowest rate. Therefore, in the hands of the recipient, the 2005 annuity amount has the following characteristics:

Interest income	$ 5
Qualified dividend income	20
Unrecaptured section 1250 gain	75

(iii) The remaining $20 gain in the unrecaptured section 1250 gain class and the $160 gain in the all other long-term capital gain class that are not treated as distributed to the recipient in 2005 are carried forward to 2006 as gains in their respective classes.

Example 4. (i) The facts are the same as in Examples 1, 2 and 3, and at the end of 2006, X has the following classes of income:

Interest income class	$ 95
Qualified dividend income class	10
Net loss in short-term capital gain class	(20)
Net long-term capital loss in 28-percent gain class	(350)
Net long-term capital gain in unrecaptured section 1250 gain class (carried forward from 2005)	20
Net long-term capital gain in all other long-term capital gain class (carried forward from 2005)	160

(ii) A net long-term capital loss in one class is used to offset the net capital gains in the other classes of long-term capital gain and loss, in turn, until exhaustion of the class, beginning with the class subject to the highest Federal income tax rate and ending with the class subject to the lowest rate. The $350 net loss in the 28 percent gain class reduces the $20 net gain in the unrecaptured section 1250 gain class to $0. The remaining $330 net loss reduces the $160 net gain in the all other long-term capital gain class to $0. As in Examples

1, 2 and 3, during 2006, qualified dividend income is taxed at a lower rate than interest income. The annuity amount is deemed to be distributed from all the classes in the ordinary income category and then from the classes in the capital gains category, beginning with the class subject to the highest Federal income tax rate and ending with the class subject to the lowest rate. In the hands of the recipient, the 2006 annuity amount has the following characteristics:

Interest income	$ 95
Qualified dividend income	5

(iii) The remaining $5 of qualified dividend income that is not treated as distributed to the recipient in 2006 is carried forward to 2007 as qualified dividend income. The $20 net loss in the short-term capital gain class and the $170 net loss in the 28-percent gain class are carried forward to 2007 as net losses in their respective classes.

Example 5. (i) X, a charitable remainder annuity trust described in section 664(d)(1), is created on January 1, 2002. The annual annuity amount is $100. Except for qualified 5-year gain of $200 realized before May 6, 2003, but not distributed, X has no other gains or losses carried over from former years. X's income for the 2007 tax year is as follows:

Interest income class	$ 10
Net gain in short-term capital gain class	5
Net long-term capital gain in 28% gain class	5
Net long-term capital gain in unrecaptured section 1250 gain class	10
Net long-term capital gain in all other long-term capital gain class	10

(ii) The annuity amount is deemed to be distributed from all the classes in the ordinary income category and then from the classes in the capital gains category, beginning with the class subject to the highest Federal income tax rate and ending with the class subject to the lowest rate. In 2007, gains distributed to a recipient from both the qualified 5-year gain class and the all other long-term capital gains class are taxed at a 15/5 percent tax rate. Since after December 31, 2008, gains distributed from the qualified 5-year gain class will be taxed at a lower rate than gains distributed from the other classes of long-term capital gain and loss, distributions from the qualified 5-year gain class are made after distributions from the other classes of long-term capital gain and loss. In the hands of the recipient, the 2007 annuity amount has the following characteristics:

Interest income	$ 10
Short-term capital gain	5
28-percent gain	5
Unrecaptured section 1250 gain	10
All other long-term capital gain	10
Qualified 5-year gain (taxed as all other long-term capital gain)	60

(iii) The remaining $140 of qualified 5-year gain that is not treated as distributed to the recipient in 2007 is carried forward to 2008 as qualified 5-year gain.

(ix) Effective dates. The rules in this paragraph (d)(1) that require long-term capital gains to be distributed in the following order: first, 28-percent gain (gains and losses from collectibles and section 1202 gains); second, unrecaptured section 1250 gain (long-term gains not treated as ordinary income that would be treated as ordinary income if section 1250(b)(1) included all depreciation); and then, all other long-term capital gains are applicable for taxable years ending on or after December 31, 1998. The rules in this paragraph (d)(1) that provide for the netting of capital gains and losses are applicable for taxable years ending on or after December 31, 1998. The rule in the second sentence of paragraph (d)(1)(vi) of this section is applicable for taxable years ending on or after December 31, 1998. The rule in the third sentence of paragraph (d)(1)(vi) of this section is applicable for distributions made in taxable years ending on or after December 31, 1998. All other provisions of this paragraph (d)(1) are applicable for taxable years ending after November 20, 2003.

(2) Allocation of deductions. Items of deduction of the trust for a taxable year of the trust which are deductible in determining taxable income (other than the deductions permitted by sections 642(b), 642(c), 661, and 1202) which are directly attributable to one or more classes of items within a category of income (determined under paragraph (d)(1)(i)(a) of this section) or to corpus shall be allocated to such classes of items or to corpus. All other allowable deductions for such taxable year which are not directly attributable to one or more classes of items within a category of income or to corpus (other than the deductions permitted by sections 642(b), 642(c), 661, and 1202) shall be allocated among the classes of items within the category (excluding classes of items with net losses) on the basis of the gross income of such classes for such taxable year reduced by the deductions allocated thereto under the first sentence of this subparagraph, but in no event shall the amount of expenses allocated to any class of items exceed such income of such class for the taxable year. Items of deduction which are not allocable under the above two sentences (other than the deductions permitted by sections 642(b), 642(c), 661, and 1202) may be allocated in any manner. All taxes imposed by subtitle A of the Code for which the trust is liable because it has unrelated business taxable income and all taxes imposed by chapter 42 of the Code shall be allocated to corpus. Any expense which is not deductible in determining taxable income and which is not allocable to any class of items described in paragraph (d)(1)(i)(a)(3) of this section shall be allocated to corpus. The deductions allowable to a trust under sections 642(b), 642(c), 661, and 1202 are not allowed in determining the amount or character of any class of items within a category of income described in paragraph (d)(1)(i)(a) of this section or to corpus.

(3) Allocation of income among recipients. If there are two or more recipients, each will be treated as receiving his pro rata portion of the categories of income and corpus. The application of this rule may be illustrated by the following example:

Example. X transfers $40,000 to a charitable remainder annuity trust which is to pay $3,000 per year to X and $2,000 per year to Y for a term of 5 years. During the first taxable year the trust has $3,000 of ordinary income, $500 of capital gain, and $500 of tax-exempt income after allocation of all expenses. X is treated as receiving ordinary income of $1,800 ($3,000/$5,000x$3,000), capital gain of $300 ($3,000/$5,000x$500), tax exempt income of $300 ($3,000/$5,000x$500), and corpus of $600 ($3,000/$5,000x[$5,000-$4,000]). Y is treated as receiving ordinary income of $1,200 ($2,000/$5,000x$3,000), capital gain of $200 ($2,000/$5,000x$500), tax exempt income of $200 ($2,000/$5,000x $500), and corpus of $400 ($2,000/$5,000x[$5,000-$4,000]).

(4) Year of inclusion—(i) General rule. To the extent required by this paragraph, the annuity or unitrust amount is includible in the recipient's gross income for the taxable year in which the annuity or unitrust amount is required to be distributed even though the annuity or unitrust amount is not distributed until after the close of the taxable year of the trust. If a recipient has a different taxable year (as defined in section 441 or 442) from the taxable year of the trust, the amount he is required to include in gross income to the extent required by this paragraph shall be included in his taxable year in which or with which ends the taxable year of the trust in which such amount is required to be distributed.

* * *

(e) Other distributions—(1) Character of distributions. An amount distributed by the trust to an organization described in section 170(c) other than the annuity or unitrust amount shall be considered as a distribution of corpus and of those categories of income specified in paragraph (d)(1)(i)(a) of this section in an order inverse to that prescribed in such paragraph. The character of such amount shall be determined as of the end of the taxable year of the trust in which the distribution is made after the character of the annuity or unitrust amount has been determined.

(2) Distributions in kind. In the case of a distribution of an amount to which subparagraph (1) of this paragraph applies, no gain or loss is realized by the trust by reason of a distribution in kind unless such distribution is in satisfaction of a right to receive a distribution of a specific dollar amount or in specific property other than that distributed.

(f) Effective date—(1) General rule. The provisions of this section are effective with respect to transfers in trust made after July 31, 1969. Any trust created (within the meaning of applicable local law) prior to August 1, 1969, is not a charitable remainder trust even if it otherwise satisfies the definition of a charitable remainder trust. The provisions of paragraph § 1.664–1(a)(7)(i)(b) apply as provided in that paragraph.

* * *

(4) Valuation of unmarketable assets. The rules contained in paragraph (a)(7) of this section are applicable for trusts created on or after December 10, 1998. A trust in existence as of December 10, 1998, whose governing instrument requires that an independent trustee value the trust's unmarketable assets may be amended or reformed to permit a valuation method that satisfies the requirements of paragraph (a)(7) of this section for taxable years beginning on or after December 10, 1998.

* * *

§ 1.664–2. Charitable remainder annuity trust.

(a) Description. A charitable remainder annuity trust is a trust which complies with the applicable provisions of § 1.664–1 and meets all of the following requirements:

(1) Required payment of annuity amount—(i) Payment of sum certain at least annually. The governing instrument provides that the trust will pay a sum certain not less often than annually to a person or persons described in paragraph (a)(3) of this section for each taxable year of the period specified in paragraph (a)(5) of this section.

(a) General rule applicable to all trusts. A trust will not be deemed to have engaged in an act of self-dealing (within the meaning of section 4941), to have unrelated debt-financed income (within the meaning of section 514), to have received an additional contribution (within the meaning of paragraph (b) of this section), or to have failed to function exclusively as a charitable remainder trust (within the meaning of § 1.664–1(a)(4)) merely because the annuity amount is paid after the close of the taxable year if such payment is made within a reasonable time after the close of such taxable year and the entire annuity amount in the hands of the recipient is characterized only as income from the categories described in section 664(b)(1), (2), or (3), except to the extent it is characterized as corpus described in section 664(b)(4) because—

(1) The trust pays the annuity amount by distributing property (other than cash) that it owned at the close of the taxable year to pay the annuity amount, and the trustee elects to treat any income generated by the distribution as occurring on the last day of the taxable year in which the annuity amount is due;

(2) The trust pays the annuity amount by distributing cash that was contributed to the trust (with respect to which a deduction was allowable under section 170, 2055, 2106, or 2522); or

(3) The trust pays the annuity amount by distributing cash received as a return of basis in any asset that was contributed to the trust (with respect to which a deduction was allowable under section 170, 2055, 2106, or 2522), and that is sold by the trust during the year for which the annuity amount is due.

(b) Special rule for trusts created before December 10, 1998. In addition to the circumstances described in paragraph (a)(1)(i)(a) of this section, a trust created before December 10, 1998, will not be deemed to have engaged in an act of self-dealing (within the meaning of section 4941), to have unrelated debt-financed income (within the meaning of section 514), to have received an additional contribution (within the meaning of paragraph (b) of this section), or to have failed to function exclusively as a charitable remainder trust (within the meaning of § 1.664–1(a)(4)) merely because the annuity amount is paid after the close of the taxable year if such payment is made within a reasonable time after the close of such taxable year and the sum certain to be paid each year as the annuity amount is 15 percent or less of the initial net fair market value of the property irrevocably passing in trust as determined for federal tax purposes.

(c) Reasonable time. For this paragraph (a)(1)(i), a reasonable time will not ordinarily extend beyond the date by which the trustee is required to file Form 5227, "Split-Interest Trust Information Return," (including extensions) for the taxable year.

(d) Example. The following example illustrates the rules in paragraph (a)(1)(i)(a) of this section:

Example. X is a charitable remainder annuity trust described in section 664(d)(1) that was created after December 10, 1998. The prorated annuity amount payable from X for Year 1 is $100. The trustee does not pay the annuity amount to the recipient by the close of Year 1. At the end of Year 1, X has only $95 in the ordinary income category under section 664(b)(1) and no income in the capital gain or tax-exempt income categories under section 664(b)(2) or (3), respectively. By April 15 of Year 2, in addition to $95 in cash, the trustee distributes to the recipient of the annuity a capital asset with a $5 fair market value and a $2 adjusted basis to pay the $100 annuity amount due for Year 1. The trust owned the asset at the end of Year 1. Under § 1.664–1(d)(5), the distribution is treated as a sale by X, resulting in X recognizing a $3 capital gain. The trustee elects to treat the capital gain as occurring on the last day of Year 1. Under § 1.664–1(d)(1), the character of the annuity amount for Year 1 in the recipient's hands is $95 of ordinary income, $3 of capital gain income, and $2 of trust corpus. For Year 1, X satisfied paragraph (a)(1)(i)(a) of this section.

(e) Effective date. This paragraph (a)(1)(i) is applicable for taxable years ending after April 18, 1997. However, paragraphs (a)(1)(i)(a)(2) and (3) of this section apply only to distributions made on or after January 5, 2001.

(ii) Definition of sum certain. A sum certain is a stated dollar amount which is the same either as to each recipient or as to the total amount payable for each year of such period. For example, a provision for an amount which is the same every year to A until his death and concurrently an amount which is the same every year to B until his death, with the amount to each recipient to terminate at his death, would satisfy the above rule. Similarly, provisions for an amount to A and B for their joint lives and then to the survivor would satisfy the above rule. In the case of a distribution to an organization described in section 170(c) at the death of a recipient or the expiration of a term of years, the governing instrument may provide for a reduction of the stated amount payable after such a distribution: Provided, That:

(a) The reduced amount payable is the same either as to each recipient or as to the total amount payable for each year of the balance of such period, and

(b) The requirements of subparagraph (2)(ii) of this paragraph are met.

(iii) Sum certain stated as a fraction or percentage. The stated dollar amount may be expressed as a fraction or a percentage of the initial net fair market value of the property irrevocably passing in trust as finally determined for Federal tax purposes. If the stated dollar amount is so expressed and such market value is incorrectly determined by the fiduciary, the requirement of this subparagraph will be satisfied if the governing instrument provides that in such event the trust shall pay to the recipient (in the case of an undervaluation) or be repaid by the recipient (in the case of an overvaluation) an amount equal to the difference between the amount which the trust should have paid the recipient if the correct value were used and the amount which the trust actually paid the recipient. Such payments or repayments must be made within a reasonable period after the final determination of such value. Any payment due to a recipient by reason of such incorrect valuation shall be considered to be a payment required to be distributed at the time of such final determination for purposes of paragraph (d)(4)(ii) of § 1.664–1. See paragraph (d)(4) of § 1.664–1 for rules relating to the year of inclusion of such payments and the allowance of a deduction for such repayments. See paragraph (b) of this section for rules relating to future contributions. For rules relating to required adjustments for underpayments or overpayments of the amount described in this paragraph in respect of payments made during a reasonable period of administration, see paragraph (a)(5) of § 1.664–1. The application of the rule permitting the stated dollar amount to be expressed as a fraction or a percentage of the initial net fair market value of the property irrevocably passing in trust as finally determined for Federal tax purposes may be illustrated by the following example:

Example. The will of X provides for the transfer of one-half of his residuary estate to a charitable remainder annuity trust which is required to pay to W for life an annuity equal to 5 percent of the initial net fair market value of the interest passing in trust as finally determined for Federal tax purposes. The annuity is to be paid on December 31 of each year computed from the date of X's death. The will also provides that if such initial net fair market value is incorrectly determined, the trust shall pay to W, in the case of an undervaluation, or be repaid by W, in the case of an overvaluation, an amount equal to the difference between the amount which the trust should have paid if the correct value were used and the amount which the trust actually paid. X dies on March 1, 1971. The executor files an estate tax return showing the value of the residuary estate as $250,000 before reduction for taxes and expenses of $50,000. The executor paid to W $4,192 ([$250,000-$50,000] x 1/2 x 5 percent x 306/365) on December 31, 1971. On January 1, 1972, the executor transfers one-half of the residue of the estate to the trust. The trust adopts the calendar year as its taxable year. The value of the residuary estate is finally determined for Federal tax purposes to be $240,000 ($290,000-$50,000). Accordingly, the amount which the executor should have paid to W is $5,030 ([$290,000-$50,000] x 1/2 x 5 percent x 306/365). Consequently, an additional amount of $838 ($5,030-$4,192) must be paid to W within a reasonable period after the final determination of value for Federal tax purposes.

(iv) Computation of annuity amount in certain circumstances—(a) Short taxable years. The governing instrument provides that, in the case of a taxable year which is for a period of less than 12 months other than the taxable year in which occurs the end of the period specified in subparagraph (5) of this paragraph, the annuity amount determined under subdivision (i) of this subparagraph shall be the amount otherwise determined under that subdivision multiplied by a fraction the numerator of which is the number of days in the taxable year of the trust and the denominator of which is 365 (366 if February 29 is a day included in the numerator).

(b) Last taxable year of period. The governing instrument provides that, in the case of the taxable year in which occurs the end of the period specified in subparagraph (5) of this paragraph, the annuity amount which must be distributed under subdivision (i) of this subparagraph shall be the amount otherwise determined under that subdivision multiplied by a fraction the numerator of which is the number of days in the period beginning on the first day of such taxable year and ending on the last day of the period specified in subparagraph (5) of this paragraph and the denominator of which is 365 (366 if February 29 is a day included in the numerator). See subparagraph (5) of this paragraph for a special rule allowing termination of payment of the annuity amount with the regular payment next preceding the termination of the period specified therein.

(2) Minimum annuity amount—(i) General rule. The total amount payable under subparagraph (1) of this paragraph is not less than 5 percent of the initial net fair market value of the property placed in trust as finally determined for Federal tax purposes.

(ii) Reduction of annuity amount in certain cases. A trust will not fail to meet the requirements of this subparagraph by reason of the fact that it provides for a reduction of the stated amount payable upon the death of a recipient or the expiration of a term of years provided that:

(a) A distribution is made to an organization described in section 170(c) at the death of such recipient or the expiration of such term of years, and

(b) The total amounts payable each year under subparagraph (1) of this paragraph after such distribution are not less than a stated dollar amount which bears the same ratio to 5 percent of the initial net fair market value of the trust assets as the net fair market value of the trust assets immediately after such distribution bears to the net fair market value of the trust assets immediately before such distribution.

(iii) Rule applicable to inter vivos trust which does not provide for payment of minimum annuity amount. In the case where the grantor of an inter vivos trust underestimates in good faith the initial net fair market value of the property placed in trust as finally determined for Federal tax purposes and specifies a fixed dollar amount for the annuity which is less than 5 percent of the initial net fair market value of the property placed in trust as finally determined for Federal tax purposes, the trust will be deemed to have met the 5 percent requirement if the grantor or his representative consents, by appropriate agreement with the District Director, to accept an amount equal to 20 times the annuity as the fair market value of the property placed in trust for purposes of determining the appropriate charitable contributions deduction.

(3) Permissible recipients—(i) General rule. The amount described in subparagraph (1) of this paragraph is payable to or for the use of a named person or persons, at least one of which is not an organization described in section 170(c). If the amount described in subparagraph (1) of this paragraph is to be paid to an individual or individuals, all such individuals must be living at the time of the creation of the trust. A named person or persons may include members of a named class provided that, in the case of a class which includes any individual, all such individuals must be alive and ascertainable at the time of the creation of the trust unless the period for which the annuity amount is to be paid to such class consists solely of a term of years. For example, in the case of a testamentary trust, the testator's will may provide that an amount shall be paid to his children living at his death.

(ii) Power to alter amount paid to recipients. A trust is not a charitable remainder annuity trust if any person has the power to alter the amount to be paid to any named person other than an organization described in section 170(c) if such power would cause any person to be treated as the owner of the trust, or any portion thereof, if Subpart E, Part 1, Subchapter J, Chapter 1, Subtitle A of the Code were applicable to such trust. See paragraph (a)(4) of this section for a rule permitting the retention by a grantor of a testamentary power to revoke or terminate the interest of any recipient other than an organization described in section 170(c). For example, the governing instrument may not grant the trustee the power to allocate the annuity among members of a class unless such power falls within one of the exceptions to section 674(a).

(4) Other payments. No amount other than the amount described in subparagraph (1) of this paragraph may be paid to or for the use of any person other than an organization described in section 170(c). An amount is not paid to or for the use of any person other than an organization described in section 170(c) if the amount is transferred for full and adequate consideration. The trust may not be subject to a power to invade, alter, amend, or revoke for the beneficial use of a person other than an organization described in section 170(c). Notwithstanding the preceding sentence, the grantor may retain the power exercisable only by will to revoke or terminate the interest of any recipient other than an organization described in section 170(c). The governing instrument may provide that any amount other than the amount described in subparagraph (1) of this paragraph shall be paid (or may be paid in the discretion of the trustee) to an organization described in section 170(c) provided that in the case of distributions in kind, the adjusted basis of the property distributed is fairly representative of the adjusted basis of the property available for payment on the date of payment. For example, the governing instrument may provide that a portion of the trust assets may be distributed currently, or upon the death of one or more recipients, to an organization described in section 170(c).

(5) Period of payment of annuity amount—(i) General rules. The period for which an amount described in subparagraph (1) of this paragraph is payable begins with the first year of the charitable remainder trust and continues either for the life or lives of a named individual or individuals or for a term of years not to exceed 20 years. Only an individual or an organization described in section 170(c) may receive an amount for the life of an individual. If an individual receives an amount for life, it must be solely for his life. Payment of the amount described in subparagraph (1) of this paragraph may terminate with the regular payment next preceding the termination of the period described in this subparagraph. The fact that the recipient may not receive such last payment shall not be taken into account for purposes of determining the present value of the remainder interest. In the case of an amount payable for a term of years, the length of the term of years shall be ascertainable with certainty at the time of the creation of the trust, except that the term may be terminated by the death of the recipient or by the grantor's exercise by will of a retained power to revoke or terminate the interest of any recipient other than an organization described in section 170(c). In any event, the period may not extend beyond either the life or lives of a named individual or individuals or a term of years not to exceed 20 years. For example, the governing instrument may not provide for the payment of an annuity amount to A for his life and then to B for a term of years because it is possible for the period to last longer than either the lives of recipients in being at the creation of the trust or a term of years not to exceed 20 years. On the other hand, the governing instrument may provide for the payment of an annuity amount to A for his life and then to B for his life or a term of years (not to exceed 20 years), whichever is shorter (but not longer), if both A and B are in being at the creation of the trust because it is not possible for the period to last longer than the lives of recipients in being at the creation of the trust.

(ii) Relationship to 5 percent requirement. The 5 percent requirement provided in subparagraph (2) of this paragraph must be met until the termination of all of the payments described in subparagraph (1) of this paragraph. For example, the following provisions would satisfy the above rules:

(a) An amount equal to at least 5 percent of the initial net fair market value of the property placed in trust to A and B for their joint lives and then to the survivor for his life;

(b) An amount equal to at least 5 percent of the initial net fair market value of the property placed in trust to A for life or for a term of years not longer than 20 years, whichever is longer (or shorter);

(c) An amount equal to at least 5 percent of the initial net fair market value of the property placed in trust to A for a term of years not longer than 20 years and then to B for life (provided B was living at the date of creation of the trust);

(d) An amount to A for his life and concurrently an amount to B for his life (the amount to each recipient to terminate at his death) if the amount given to each individual is not less than 5 percent of the initial net fair market value of the property placed in trust; or

(e) An amount to A for his life and concurrently an equal amount to B for his life, and at the death of the first to die, the trust to distribute one-half of the then value of its assets to an organization described in section 170(c), if the total of the amounts given to A and B is not less than 5 percent of the initial net fair market value of the property placed in trust.

(6) Permissible remaindermen—(i) General rule. At the end of the period specified in subparagraph (5) of this paragraph the entire corpus of the trust is required to be irrevocably transferred, in whole or in part, to or for the use of one or more organizations described in section 170(c) or retained, in whole or in part, for such use.

(ii) Treatment of trust. If all of the trust corpus is to be retained for such use, the taxable year of the trust shall terminate at the end of the period specified in subparagraph (5) of this paragraph and the trust shall cease to be treated as a charitable remainder trust for all purposes. If all or any portion of the trust corpus is to be transferred to or for the use of such organization or organizations, the trustee shall have a reasonable time after the period specified in subparagraph (5) of this paragraph to complete the settlement of the trust. During such time, the trust shall continue to be treated as a charitable remainder trust for all purposes, such as sections 664, 4947(a)(2), and 4947(b)(3)(B). Upon the expiration of such period, the taxable year of the trust shall terminate and the trust shall cease to be treated as a charitable remainder trust for all purposes. If the trust continues in existence, it will be subject to the provisions of section 4947(a)(1) unless the trust is exempt from taxation under section 501(a). For purposes of determining whether the trust is exempt under section 501(a) as an organization described in section 501(c)(3), the trust shall be deemed to have been created at the time it ceases to be treated as a charitable remainder trust.

(iii) Concurrent or successive remaindermen. Where interests in the corpus of the trust are given to more than one organization described in section 170(c) such interests may be enjoyed by them either concurrently or successively.

(iv) Alternative remaindermen. The governing instrument shall provide that if an organization to or for the use of which the trust corpus is to be transferred or for the use of which the trust corpus is to be retained is not an organization described in section 170(c) at the time any amount is to be irrevocably transferred to or for the use of such organization, such amount shall be transferred to or for the use of one or more alternative organizations which are described in section 170(c) at such time or retained for such use. Such alternative organization or organizations may be selected in any manner provided by the terms of the governing instrument.

(b) Additional contributions. A trust is not a charitable remainder annuity trust unless its governing instrument provides that no additional contributions may be made to the charitable remainder annuity trust after the initial contribution. For purposes of this section, all property passing to a charitable remainder annuity trust by reason of death of the grantor shall be considered one contribution.

(c) Calculation of the fair market value of the remainder interest of a charitable remainder annuity trust. For purposes of sections 170, 2055, 2106, and 2522, the fair market value of the remainder interest of a charitable remainder annuity trust (as described in this section) is the net fair market value (as of the appropriate valuation date) of the property placed in trust less the present value of the annuity. For purposes of this section, valuation date means, in general, the date on which the property is transferred to the trust by the donor regardless of when the trust is created. In the case of transfers to a charitable remainder annuity trust for which the valuation date is after April 30, 1989, if an election is made under section 7520 and § 1.7520–2(b) to compute the present value of the charitable interest by use of the interest rate component for either of the 2 months preceding the month in which the transfer is made, the month so elected is the valuation date for purposes of determining the interest rate and mortality tables. For purposes of section 2055 or 2106, the valuation date is the date of death unless the alternate valuation date is elected in accordance with section 2032, in which event, and within the limitations set forth in section 2032 and the regulations thereunder, the valuation date is the alternate valuation date. If the decedent's estate elects the alternate valuation date under section 2032 and also elects, under section 7520 and § 1.7520–2(b), to use the interest rate component for one of the 2 months preceding the alternate valuation date, the month so elected is the valuation date for purposes of determining the interest rate and mortality tables. The present value of an annuity is computed under § 20.2031–7(d) of this chapter (Estate Tax Regulations) for transfers for which the valuation date is after April 30, 1999, or under § 20.2031–7A(a) through (e) of this chapter, whichever is applicable, for transfers for which the valuation date is before May 1, 1999. See, however, § 1.7520–3(b) (relating to exceptions to the use of prescribed tables under certain circumstances).

(d) Deduction for transfers to a charitable remainder annuity trust. For rules relating to a deduction for transfers to a charitable remainder annuity trust, see section 170, 2055, 2106, or 2522 and the regulations thereunder. Any claim for deduction on any return for the value of a remainder interest in a charitable remainder annuity trust must be supported by a full statement attached to the return showing the computation of the present value of such interest. The deduction allowed by section 170 is limited to the fair market value of the remainder interest of a charitable remainder annuity trust regardless of whether an organization described in section 170(c) also receives a portion of the annuity. For a special rule relating to the reduction of the amount of a charitable contribution deduction with respect to a contribution of certain ordinary income property or capital gain property, see section 170(e)(1)(A) or 170(e)(1)(B)(i) and the regulations thereunder. For rules for postponing the time for deduction of a charitable contribution of a future interest in tangible personal property, see section 170(a)(3) and the regulations thereunder.

§ 1.664–3. Charitable remainder unitrust.

(a) Description. A charitable remainder unitrust is a trust which complies with the applicable provisions of § 1.664–1 and meets all of the following requirements:

(1) Required payment of unitrust amount—(i) Payment of fixed percentage at least annually—(a) General rule. The governing instrument provides that the trust will pay not less often than annually a fixed percentage of the net fair market value of the trust assets determined annually to a person or persons described in paragraph (a)(3) of this section for each taxable year of the period specified in paragraph (a)(5) of this section. This paragraph (a)(1)(i)(a) is applicable for taxable years ending after April 18, 1997.

(b) Income exception. Instead of the amount described in (a) of this subdivision (i), the governing instrument may provide that the trust shall pay for any year either the amount described in (1) or the total of the amounts described in (1) and (2) of this subdivision (b).

(1) The amount of trust income for a taxable year to the extent that such amount is not more than the amount required to be distributed under paragraph (a)(1)(i)(a) of this section.

(2) An amount of trust income for a taxable year that is in excess of the amount required to be distributed under paragraph (a)(1)(i)(a) of this section for such year to the extent that (by reason of paragraph (a)(1)(i)(b)(1) of this section) the aggregate of the amounts paid in prior years was less than the aggregate of such required amounts.

(3) For purposes of this paragraph (a)(1)(i)(b), trust income generally means income as defined under section 643(b) and the applicable regulations. However, trust income may not be determined by reference to a fixed percentage of the annual fair market value of the trust property, notwithstanding any contrary provision in applicable state law. Proceeds from the sale or exchange of any assets contributed to the trust by the donor must be allocated to principal and not to trust income at least to the extent of the fair market value of those assets on the date of their contribution to the trust. Proceeds from the sale or exchange of any assets purchased by the trust must be allocated to principal and not to trust income at least to the extent of the trust's purchase price of those assets. Except as provided in the two preceding sentences, proceeds from the sale or exchange of any assets contributed to the trust by the donor or purchased by the trust may be allocated to income, pursuant to the terms of the governing instrument, if not prohibited by applicable local law. A discretionary pow-

er to make this allocation may be granted to the trustee under the terms of the governing instrument but only to the extent that the state statute permits the trustee to make adjustments between income and principal to treat beneficiaries impartially.

(4) The rules in paragraph (a)(1)(i)(b)(1) and (2) of this section are applicable for taxable years ending after April 18, 1997. The rule in the first sentence of paragraph (a)(1)(i)(b)(3) is applicable for taxable years ending after April 18, 1997. The rules in the second, fourth, and fifth sentences of paragraph (a)(1)(i)(b)(3) are applicable for taxable years ending after January 2, 2004. The rule in the third sentence of paragraph (a)(1)(i)(b)(3) is applicable for sales or exchanges that occur after April 18, 1997. The rule in the sixth sentence of paragraph (a)(1)(i)(b)(3) is applicable for trusts created after January 2, 2004.

(c) Combination of methods. Instead of the amount described in paragraph (a)(1)(i)(a) or (b) of this section, the governing instrument may provide that the trust will pay not less often than annually the amount described in paragraph (a)(1)(i)(b) of this section for an initial period and then pay the amount described in paragraph (a)(1)(i)(a) of this section (calculated using the same fixed percentage) for the remaining years of the trust only if the governing instrument provides that—

(1) The change from the method prescribed in paragraph (a)(1)(i)(b) of this section to the method prescribed in paragraph (a)(1)(i)(a) of this section is triggered on a specific date or by a single event whose occurrence is not discretionary with, or within the control of, the trustees or any other persons;

(2) The change from the method prescribed in paragraph (a)(1)(i)(b) of this section to the method prescribed in paragraph (a)(1)(i)(a) of this section occurs at the beginning of the taxable year that immediately follows the taxable year during which the date or event specified under paragraph (a)(1)(i)(c)(1) of this section occurs; and

(3) Following the trust's conversion to the method described in paragraph (a)(1)(i)(a) of this section, the trust will pay at least annually to the permissible recipients the amount described only in paragraph (a)(1)(i)(a) of this section and not any amount described in paragraph (a)(1)(i)(b) of this section.

(d) Triggering event. For purposes of paragraph (a)(1)(i)(c)(1) of this section, a triggering event based on the sale of unmarketable assets as defined in § 1.664–1(a)(7)(ii), or the marriage, divorce, death, or birth of a child with respect to any individual will not be considered discretionary with, or within the control of, the trustees or any other persons.

(e) Examples. The following examples illustrate the rules in paragraph (a)(1)(i)(c) of this section. For each example, assume that the governing instrument of charitable remainder unitrust Y provides that Y will initially pay not less often than annually the amount described in paragraph (a)(1)(i)(b) of this section and then pay the amount described in paragraph (a)(1)(i)(a) of this section (calculated using the same fixed percentage) for the remaining years of the trust and that the requirements of paragraphs (a)(1)(i)(c)(2) and (3) of this section are satisfied. The examples are as follows:

Example 1. Y is funded with the donor's former personal residence. The governing instrument of Y provides for the change in method for computing the annual unitrust amount as of the first day of the year following the year in which the trust sells the residence. Y provides for a combination of methods that satisfies paragraph (a)(1)(i)(c) of this section.

Example 2. Y is funded with cash and an unregistered security for which there is no available exemption permitting public sale under the Securities and Exchange Commission rules. The governing instrument of Y provides that the change in method for computing the annual unitrust amount is triggered on the earlier of the date when the stock is sold or at the time the restrictions on its public sale lapse or are otherwise lifted. Y provides for a combination of methods that satisfies paragraph (a)(1)(i)(c) of this section.

Example 3. Y is funded with cash and with a security that may be publicly traded under the Securities and Exchange Commission rules. The governing instrument of Y provides that the change in method for computing the annual unitrust amount is triggered when the stock is sold. Y does not provide for a combination of methods that satisfies the requirements of paragraph (a)(1)(i)(c) of this section because the sale of the publicly-traded stock is within the discretion of the trustee.

Example 4. S establishes Y for her granddaughter, G, when G is 10 years old. The governing instrument of Y provides for the change in method for computing the annual unitrust amount as of the first day of the year following the year in which G turns 18 years old. Y provides for a combination of methods that satisfies paragraph (a)(1)(i)(c) of this section.

Example 5. The governing instrument of Y provides for the change in method for computing the annual unitrust amount as of the first day of the year following the year in which the donor is married. Y provides for a combination of methods that satisfies paragraph (a)(1)(i)(c) of this section.

Example 6. The governing instrument of Y provides that if the donor divorces, the change in method for computing the annual unitrust amount will occur as of the first day of the year following the year of the divorce. Y provides for a combination of methods that satisfies paragraph (a)(1)(i)(c) of this section.

Example 7. The governing instrument of Y provides for the change in method for computing the annual unitrust amount as of the first day of the year following the year in which the noncharitable beneficiary's first child is born. Y provides for a combination of methods that satisfies paragraph (a)(1)(i)(c) of this section.

Example 8. The governing instrument of Y provides for the change in method for computing the annual unitrust amount as of the first day of the year following the year in which the noncharitable beneficiary's father dies. Y provides for a combination of methods that satisfies paragraph (a)(1)(i)(c) of this section.

Example 9. The governing instrument of Y provides for the change in method for computing the annual unitrust amount as of the first day of the year following the year in which the noncharitable beneficiary's financial advisor determines that the beneficiary should begin receiving payments under the second prescribed payment method. Because the change in methods for paying the unitrust amount is triggered by an event that is within a person's control, Y does not provide for a combination of methods that satisfies paragraph (a)(1)(i)(c) of this section.

Example 10. The governing instrument of Y provides for the change in method for computing the annual unitrust amount as of the first day of the year following the year in which the noncharitable beneficiary submits a request to the trustee that the trust convert to the second prescribed payment method. Because the change in methods for paying the unitrust amount is triggered by an event that is within a person's control, Y does not provide for a combination of methods that satisfies paragraph (a)(1)(i)(c) of this section.

(f) Effective date—(1) General rule. Paragraphs (a)(1)(i)(c), (d), and (e) of this section are applicable for charitable remainder trusts created on or after December 10, 1998.

* * *

(g) Payment under general rule for fixed percentage trusts. When the unitrust amount is computed under paragraph (a)(1)(i)(a) of this section, a trust will not be deemed to have engaged in an act of self-dealing (within the meaning of section 4941), to have unrelated debt-financed income (within the meaning of section 514), to have received an additional contribution (within the meaning of paragraph (b) of this section), or to have failed to function exclusively as a charitable remainder trust (within the meaning of § 1.664–1(a)(4)) merely because the unitrust amount is paid after the close of the taxable year if such payment is made within a reasonable time after the close of such taxable year and the entire unitrust amount in the hands of the recipient is characterized only as income from the categories described in section 664(b)(1), (2), or (3), except to the extent it is characterized as corpus described in section 664(b)(4) because—

(1) The trust pays the unitrust amount by distributing property (other than cash) that it owned at the close of the taxable year, and the trustee elects to treat any income generated by the distribution as occurring on the last day of the taxable year in which the unitrust amount is due;

(2) The trust pays the unitrust amount by distributing cash that was contributed to the trust (with respect to which a deduction was allowable under section 170, 2055, 2106, or 2522); or

(3) The trust pays the unitrust amount by distributing cash received as a return of basis in any asset that was contributed to the trust (with respect to which a deduction was allowable under section 170, 2055, 2106, or 2522), and that is sold by the trust during the year for which the unitrust amount is due.

* * *

(j) Payment under income exception. When the unitrust amount is computed under paragraph (a)(1)(i)(b) of this section, a trust will not be deemed to have engaged in an act of self-dealing (within the meaning of section 4941), to have unrelated debt-financed income (within the meaning of section 514), to have received an additional contribution (within the meaning of paragraph (b) of this section), or to have failed to function exclusively as a charitable remainder trust (within the meaning of § 1.664–1(a)(4)) merely because payment of the unitrust amount is made after the close of the taxable year if such payment is made within a reasonable time after the close of such taxable year.

(k) Reasonable time. For paragraphs (a)(1)(i)(g), (h), and (j) of this section, a reasonable time will not ordinarily extend beyond the date by which the trustee is required to file Form 5227, "Split-Interest Trust Information Return," (including extensions) for the taxable year.

(*l*) Effective date. Paragraphs (a)(1)(i)(g), (h), (i), (j), and (k) of this section are applicable for taxable years ending after April 18, 1997. Paragraphs (a)(1)(i)(g)(2) and (3) apply only to distributions made on or after January 5, 2001.

(ii) Definition of fixed percentage. The fixed percentage may be expressed either as a fraction or as a percentage and must be payable each year in the period specified in subparagraph (5) of this paragraph. A percentage is fixed if the percentage is the same either as to each recipient or as to the total percentage payable each year of such period. For example, provision for a fixed percentage which is the same every year to A until his death and concurrently a fixed percentage which is the same every year to B until his death, the fixed percentage to each recipient to terminate at his death, would satisfy the rule. Similarly, provision for a fixed percentage to A and B for their joint lives and then to the survivor would satisfy the rule. In the case of a distribution to an organization described in section 170(c) at the death of a recipient or the expiration of a term of years, the governing instrument may provide for a reduction of the fixed percentage payable after such distribution Provided That:

(a) The reduced fixed percentage is the same either as to each recipient or as to the total amount payable for each year of the balance of such period, and

(b) The requirements of subparagraph (2)(ii) of this paragraph are met.

(iii) Rules applicable to incorrect valuations. The governing instrument provides that in the case where the net fair market value of the trust assets is incorrectly determined by the fiduciary, the trust shall pay to the recipient (in the case of an undervaluation) or be repaid by the recipient (in the case of an overvaluation) an amount equal to the difference between the amount which the trust should have paid the recipient if the correct value were used and the amount which the trust actually paid the recipient. Such payments or repayments must be made within a reasonable period after the final determination of such value. Any payment due to a recipient by reason of such incorrect valuation shall be considered to be a payment required to be distributed at the time of such final determination for purposes of paragraph (d)(4)(ii) of § 1.664-1. See paragraph (d)(4) of § 1.664-1 for rules relating to the year of inclusion of such payments and the allowance of a deduction for such repayments. See paragraph (b) of this section for rules relating to additional contributions.

(iv) Rules applicable to valuation. In computing the net fair market value of the trust assets there shall be taken into account all assets and liabilities without regard to whether particular items are taken into account in determining the income of the trust. The net fair market value of the trust assets may be determined on any one date during the taxable year of the trust, or by taking the average of valuations made on more than one date during the taxable year of the trust, so long as the same valuation date or dates and valuation methods are used each year. If the governing instrument does not specify the valuation date or dates, the trustee must select such date or dates and indicate the selection on the first return on Form 5227, "Split-Interest Trust Information Return," that the trust must file. The amount described in subdivision (i)(a) of this subparagraph which must be paid each year must be based upon the valuation for such year.

(v) Computation of unitrust amount in certain circumstances—(a) Short taxable years. The governing instrument provides that, in the case of a taxable year which is for a period of less than 12 months other than the taxable year in which occurs the end of the period specified in subparagraph (5) of this paragraph:

(1) The amount determined under subdivision (i)(a) of this subparagraph shall be the amount otherwise determined under that subdivision multiplied by a fraction the numerator of which is the number of days in the taxable year of the trust and the denominator of which is 365 (366 if February 29 is a day included in the numerator),

(2) The amount determined under subdivision (i)(b) of this subparagraph shall be computed by using the amount determined under subdivision (a)(1) of this subdivision (v), and

(3) If no valuation date occurs before the end of the taxable year of the trust, the trust assets shall be valued as of the last day of the taxable year of the trust.

(b) Last taxable year of period. (1) The governing instrument provides that, in the case of the taxable year in which occurs the end of the period specified in subparagraph (5) of this paragraph:

(i) The unitrust amount which must be distributed under subdivision (i)(a) of this subparagraph shall be the amount otherwise determined under that subdivision multiplied by a fraction the numerator of which is the number of days in the period beginning on the first day of such taxable year and ending on the last day of the period specified in subparagraph (5) of this paragraph and the denominator of which is 365 (366 if February 29 is a day included in the numerator),

(ii) The amount determined under subdivision (i)(b) of this subparagraph shall be computed by using the amount determined under (b)(1)(i) of this subdivision (v), and

(iii) If no valuation date occurs before the end of such period, the trust assets shall be valued as of the last day of such period.

(2) See subparagraph (5) of this paragraph for a special rule allowing termination of payment of the unitrust amount with the regular payment next preceding the termination of the period specified therein.

(2) Minimum unitrust amount—(i) General rule. The fixed percentage described in subparagraph (1)(i) of this paragraph with respect to all beneficiaries taken together is not less than 5 percent.

(ii) Reduction of unitrust amount in certain cases. A trust will not fail to meet the requirements of this subparagraph by reason of the fact that it provides for a reduction of the fixed percentage payable upon the death of a recipient or the expiration of a term of years Provided That:

(a) A distribution is made to an organization described in section 170(c) at the death of such recipient or the expiration of such term of years, and

(b) The total of the percentage payable under subparagraph (1) of this paragraph after such distribution is not less than 5 percent.

(3) Permissible recipients—(i) General rule. The amount described in subparagraph (1) of this paragraph is payable to or for the use of a named person or persons, at least one of which is not an organization described in section 170(c). If the amount described in subparagraph (1) of this paragraph is to be paid to an individual or individuals, all such individuals must be living at the time of creation of the trust. A named person or persons may include members of a named class except in the case of a class which includes any individual, all such individuals must be alive and ascertainable at the time of the creation of the trust unless the period for which the unitrust amount is to be paid to such class consists solely of a term of years. For example, in the case of a testamentary trust, the testator's will may provide that the required amount shall be paid to his children living at his death.

(ii) Power to alter amount paid to recipients. A trust is not a charitable remainder unitrust if any person has the power to alter the amount to be paid to any named person other than an organization described in section 170(c) if such power would cause any person to be treated as the owner of the trust, or any portion thereof, if subpart E, part 1, subchapter J, chapter 1, subtitle A of the Code were applicable to such trust. See paragraph (a)(4) of this section for a rule permitting the retention by a grantor of a testamentary power to revoke or terminate the interest of any recipient other than an organization described in section 170(c). For example, the governing instrument may not grant the trustee the power to allocate the fixed percentage among members of a class unless such power falls within one of the exceptions to section 674(a).

(4) Other payments. No amount other than the amount described in subparagraph (1) of this paragraph may be paid to or for the use of any person other than an organization described in section 170(c). An amount is not paid to or for the use of any person other than an organization described in section 170(c) if the amount is transferred for full and adequate consideration. The trust may not be subject to a power to invade, alter, amend, or revoke for the beneficial use of a person other than an organization described in section 170(c). Notwithstanding the preceding sentence, the grantor may retain the power exercisable only by will to revoke or terminate the interest of any recipient other than an organization described in section 170(c). The governing instrument may provide that any amount other than the amount described in subparagraph (1) of this paragraph shall be paid (or may be paid in the discretion of the trustee) to an organization described in section 170(c) provided that, in the case of distributions in kind, the adjusted basis of the property distributed is fairly representative of the adjusted basis of the property available for payment on the date of payment. For example, the governing instrument may provide that a portion of the trust assets may be distributed currently, or upon the death of one or more recipients, to an organization described in section 170(c).

(5) Period of payment of unitrust amount—(i) General rules. The period for which an amount described in subparagraph (1) of this paragraph is payable begins with the first year of the charitable remainder trust and continues either for the life or lives of a named individual or individuals or for a term of years not to exceed 20 years. Only an individual or an organization described in section 170(c) may receive an amount for the life of an individual. If an individual receives an amount for life, it must be solely for his life. Payment of the amount described in subparagraph (1) of this paragraph may terminate with the regular payment next preceding the termination of the period described in this subparagraph. The fact that the recipient may not receive such last payment shall not be taken into account for purposes of determining the present value of the remainder interest. In the case of an amount payable for a term of years, the length of the term of years shall be ascertainable with certainty at the time of the creation of the trust, except that the term may be terminated by the death of the recipient or by the grantor's exercise by will of a retained power to revoke or terminate the interest of any recipient other than an organization described in section 170(c). In any event, the period may not extend beyond either the life or lives of a named individual or individuals or a term of years not to exceed 20 years. For example, the governing instrument may not provide for the payment of a unitrust amount to A for his life and then to B for a term of years because it is possible for the period to last longer than either the lives of recipients in being at the creation of the trust or a term of years not to exceed 20 years. On the other hand, the governing instrument may provide for the payment of a unitrust amount to A for his life and then to B for his life or a term of years (not to exceed 20 years), whichever is shorter (but not longer), if both A and B are in being at the creation of the trust because it is not possible for the period to last longer than the lives of recipients in being at the creation of the trust.

(ii) Relationship to 5 percent requirement. The 5 percent requirement provided in subparagraph (2) of this paragraph must be met until the termination of all of the payments described in subparagraph (1) of this paragraph. For example, the following provisions would satisfy the above rules:

(a) A fixed percentage of at least 5 percent to A and B for their joint lives and then to the survivor for his life;

(b) A fixed percentage of at least 5 percent to A for life or for a term of years not longer than 20 years, whichever is longer (or shorter);

(c) A fixed percentage of at least 5 percent to A for life or for a term of years not longer than 20 years and then to B for life (provided B was living at the creation of the trust);

(d) A fixed percentage to A for his life and concurrently a fixed percentage to B for his life (the percentage to each recipient to terminate at his death) if the percentage given to each individual is not less than 5 percent;

(e) A fixed percentage to A for his life and concurrently an equal percentage to B for his life, and at the death of the first to die, the trust to distribute one-half of the then value of its assets to an organization described in section 170(c) if the total of the percentages is not less than 5 percent for the entire period described in this subparagraph.

(6) Permissible remaindermen—(i) General rule. At the end of the period specified in subparagraph (5) of this paragraph, the entire corpus of the trust is required to be irrevocably transferred, in whole or in part, to or for the use of one or more organizations described in section 170(c) or retained, in whole or in part, for such use.

(ii) Treatment of trust. If all of the trust corpus is to be retained for such use, the taxable year of the trust shall terminate at the end of the period specified in subparagraph (5) of this paragraph and the trust shall cease to be treated as a charitable remainder trust for all purposes. If all or any portion of the trust corpus is to be transferred to or for the use of such organization or organizations, the trustee shall have a reasonable time after the period specified in subparagraph (5) of this paragraph to complete the settlement of the trust. During such time, the trust shall continue to be treated as a charitable remainder trust for all purposes, such as section 664, 4947(a)(2), and 4947(b)(3)(B). Upon the expiration of such period, the taxable year of the trust shall terminate and the trust shall cease to be treated as a charitable remainder trust for all purposes. If the trust continues in existence, it will be subject to the provisions of section 4947(a)(1) unless the trust is exempt from taxation under section 501(a). For purposes of determining whether the trust is exempt under section 501(a) as an organization described in section 501(c)(3), the trust shall be deemed to have been created at the time it ceases to be treated as a charitable remainder trust.

(iii) Concurrent or successive remaindermen. Where interests in the corpus of the trust are given to more than one organization described in section 170(c) such interests may be enjoyed by them either concurrently or successively.

(iv) Alternative remaindermen. The governing instrument shall provide that if an organization to or for the use of which the trust corpus is to be transferred or for the use of which the trust corpus is to be retained is not an organization described in section 170(c) at the time any amount is to be irrevocably transferred to or for the use of such organization, such amount shall be transferred to or for the use of or retained for the use of one or more alternative organizations which are described in section 170(c) at such time. Such alternative organization or organizations may be selected in any manner provided by the terms of the governing instrument.

(b) Additional contributions. A trust is not a charitable remainder annuity trust unless its governing instrument either prohibits additional contributions to the trust after the initial contribution or provides that for the taxable year of the trust in which the additional contribution is made:

(1) Where no valuation date occurs after the time of the contribution and during the taxable year in which the contribution is made, the additional property shall be valued as of the time of contribution; and

(2) The amount described in paragraph (a)(1)(i)(a) of this section shall be computed by multiplying the fixed percentage by the sum of (i) the net fair market value of the trust assets (excluding the value of the additional property and any earned income from and any appreciation on such property after its contribution), and (ii) that proportion of the value of the additional property (that was excluded under subdivision (i) of this paragraph), which the number of days in the period which begins with the date of contribution and ends with the earlier of the last day of such taxable year or the last day of the period described in paragraph (a)(5) of this section bears to the number of days in the period which begins with the first day of such taxable year and ends with the earlier of the last day of such taxable year or the last day of the period described in paragraph (a)(5) of this section.

For purposes of this section, all property passing to a charitable remainder unitrust by reason of death of the grantor shall be considered one contribution. The application of the preceding rules may be illustrated by the following examples:

Example 1. On March 2, 1971, X makes an additional contribution of property to a charitable remainder unitrust. The taxable year of the trust is the calendar year and the regular valuation date is January 1 of each year. For purposes of computing the required payout with respect to the additional contribution for the year of contribution, the additional contribution is valued on March 2, 1971, the time of contribution. The property had a value on that date of $5,000. Income from such property in the amount of $250 was received on December 31, 1971. The required payout with respect to the additional contribution for the year of contribution is $208 (5 percent x $5,000 x 305/365). The income earned after the date of the contribution and after the regular valuation date does not enter into the computation.

Example 2. On July 1, 1971, X makes an additional contribution of $10,000 to a charitable remainder unitrust. The taxable year of the trust is the calendar year and the regular valuation date is December 31 of each year. The fixed percentage is 5 percent. Between July 1, 1971, and December 31, 1971, the additional property appreciates in value to $12,500 and earns $500 of income. Because the regular valuation date for the year of contribution occurs after the date of the additional contribution, the additional contribution including income earned by it is valued on the regular valuation date. Thus, the required payout with respect to the additional contribution is $325.87 (5 percent x [$12,500 + $500] x 183/365).

(c) Calculation of the fair market value of the remainder interest of a charitable remainder unitrust. See § 1.664–4 for rules relating to the calculation of the fair market value of the remainder interest of a charitable remainder unitrust.

(d) Deduction for transfers to a charitable remainder unitrust. For rules relating to a deduction for transfers to a charitable remainder unitrust, see section 170, 2055, 2106, or 2522 and the regulations thereunder. The deduction allowed by section 170 for transfers to charity is limited to the fair market value of the remainder interest of a charitable remainder unitrusts regardless of whether an organization described in section 170(c) also receives a portion of the amount described in § 1.664–3(a)(1). For a special rule relating to the reduction of the amount of a charitable contribution deduction with respect to a contribution of certain ordinary income property or capital gain property, see section 170(e)(1)(A) or (B)(i) and the regulations thereunder. For rules for postponing the time for deduction of a charitable contribution of a future interest in tangible personal property, see section 170(a)(3) and the regulations thereunder.

EXCISE TAX REGULATIONS

PUBLIC CHARITIES LOBBYING ELECTION

§ 56.4911–1. Tax on excess lobbying expenditures.

(a) In general. Section 4911(a) imposes an excise tax of 25 percent on the excess lobbying expenditures (as defined in paragraph (b) of this section) for a taxable year of an organization for which the expenditure test election under section 501(h) is in effect (an "electing public charity"). An electing public charity's annual limit on expenditures for influencing legislation (i.e., the amount of lobbying expenditures on which no tax is due) is the lobbying nontaxable amount or, on expenditures for influencing legislation through grass roots lobbying, the grass roots nontaxable amount (see paragraph (c) of this section). For rules concerning the application of the excise tax imposed by section 4911(a) to the members of an affiliated group of organizations (as defined in § 56.4911–7(e)), see § 56.4911–8.

(b) Excess lobbying expenditures. For any taxable year for which the expenditure test election under section 501(h) is in effect, the amount of an electing public charity's excess lobbying expenditures is the greater of—

(1) The amount by which the organization's lobbying expenditures (within the meaning of § 56.4911–2(a)) exceed the organization's lobbying nontaxable amount, or

(2) The amount by which the organization's grass roots expenditures (within the meaning of §§ 56.4911–2(a)) exceed the organization's grass roots nontaxable amount.

(c) Nontaxable amounts—(1) Lobbying nontaxable amount. Under section 4911(c)(2), the lobbying nontaxable amount for any taxable year for which the expenditure test election is in effect is the lesser of:

(i) $1,000,000, or

(ii) To the extent of the electing public charity's exempt purpose expenditures (within the meaning of § 56.4911–4) for that year, the sum of 20 percent of the first $500,000 of such expenditures, plus 15 percent of the second $500,000 of such expenditures, plus 10 percent of the third $500,000 of such expenditures, plus 5 percent of the remainder of such expenditures. (2) Grass roots nontaxable amount. Under section 4911(c)(4), an electing public charity's grass roots nontaxable amount for any taxable year is 25 percent of its lobbying nontaxable amount for that year.

(d) Examples. The provisions of this section are illustrated by the examples in § 1.501(h)–3.

§ 56.4911–2. Lobbying expenditures, direct lobbying communications, and grassroots lobbying communications.

(a) Lobbying expenditures—(1) In general. An electing public charity's lobbying expenditures for a year are the sum of its expenditures during that year for direct lobbying communications ("direct lobbying expenditures") plus its expenditures during that year for grass roots lobbying communications ("grass roots expenditures").

(2) Overview of § 56.4911–2 and the definitions of "direct lobbying communication" and "grass roots lobbying communication". Paragraph (b)(1) of this section defines the term "direct lobbying communication." Paragraph (b)(2) of this section provides the general definition of the term "grass roots lobbying communication." (But also see paragraph (b)(5) of this section (special rebuttable presumption regarding certain paid mass media communications) and § 56.4911–5 (special, more lenient, definitions for certain communications from an electing public charity to its bona fide members)). Paragraph (b)(3) of this section lists and cross-references various exceptions to the definitions set forth in paragraphs (b)(1) and (2) (the text of the exceptions, along with relevant definitions and examples, is generally set forth in paragraph (c)). Paragraph (b)(4) of this section contains numerous examples illustrating the application of paragraphs (b)(1), (2) and (3). As mentioned above, paragraph (b)(5) of this section sets forth the special rebuttable presumption regarding a limited number of paid mass media communications about highly publicized legislation. Paragraph (d) of this section contains definitions of (and examples illustrating) various terms used in this section.

(b) Influencing legislation: direct and grass roots lobbying communications defined—(1) Direct lobbying communication—

(i) Definition. A direct lobbying communication is any attempt to influence any legislation through communication with:

(A) Any member or employee of a legislative body; or

(B) Any government official or employee (other than a member or employee of a legislative body) who may participate in the formulation of the legislation, but only if the principal purpose of the communication is to influence legislation.

(ii) Required elements. A communication with a legislator or government official will be treated as a direct lobbying communication under this § 46.4911–2(b)(1) if, but only if, the communication:

(A) Refers to specific legislation (see paragraph (d)(1) of this section for a definition of the term "specific legislation"); and

(B) Reflects a view on such legislation.

(iii) Special rule for referenda, ballot initiatives or similar procedures. Solely for purposes of this section 4911, where a communication refers to and reflects a view on a measure that is the subject of a referendum, ballot initiative or similar procedure, the general public in the State or locality where the vote will take place constitutes the legislative body, and individual members of the general public area, for purposes of this paragraph (b)(1), legislators. Accordingly, if such a communication is made to one or more members of the general public in that state or locality, the communication is a direct lobbying communication (unless it is nonpartisan analysis, study or research (see paragraph (c)(1) of this section).

(2) Grass roots lobbying communication—

(i) Definition. A grass roots lobbying communication is any attempt to influence any legislation through an attempt to affect the opinions of the general public or any segment thereof.

(ii) Required elements. A communication will be treated as a grass roots lobbying communication under this § 56.4911–2(b)(2)(ii) if, but only if, the communication:

(A) Refers to specific legislation (see paragraph (d)(1) of this section for a definition of the term "specific legislation");

(B) Reflects a view on such legislation; and

(C) Encourages the recipient of the communication to take action with respect to such legislation (see paragraph (b)(2)(iii) of this section for the definition of encouraging the recipient to take action.

For special, more lenient rules regarding an organization's communications directed only or primarily to bona fide members of the organization, see § 56.4911–5. For special rules regarding certain paid mass media advertisements about highly publicized legislation, see paragraph (b)(5) of this section. For special rules regarding lobbying on referenda, ballot initiatives and similar procedures, see paragraph (b)(1)(iii) of this section).

(iii) Definition of encouraging recipient to take action. For purposes of this section, encouraging a recipient to take action with respect to legislation means that the communication:

(A) States that the recipient should contact a legislator or an employee of a legislative body, or should contact any other government official or employee who may participate in the formulation of legislation (but only if the principal purpose of urging contact with the government official or employee is to influence legislation);

(B) States the address, telephone number, or similar information of a legislator or an employee of a legislative body;

(C) Provides a petition, tear-off postcard or similar material for the recipient to communicate with a legislator or an employee of a legislative body, or with any other government official or employee who may participate in the formulation of legislation (but only if the principal purpose of so facilitating contact with the government official or employee is to influence legislation); or

(D) Specifically identifies one or more legislators who will vote on the legislation as: opposing the communication's view with respect to the legislation; being undecided with respect to the legislation; being the recipient's representative in the legislature; or being a member of the legislative committee or subcommittee that will consider the legislation. Encouraging the recipient to take action under this paragraph (b)(2)(iii)(D) does not include naming the main sponsor(s) of the legislation for purposes of identifying the legislation.

(iv) Definition of directly encouraging recipient to take action. Communications described in one or more of paragraphs (b)(2)(iii)(A) through (C) of this section not only "encourage," but also "directly encourage" the recipient to take action with respect to legislation. Communications described in paragraph (b)(2)(iii)(D) of this section, however, do not directly encourage the recipient to take action with respect to legislation. Thus, a communication would encourage the recipient to take action with respect to legislation, but not directly encourage such action, if the communication does no more than identify one or more legislators who will vote on the legislation as: opposing the communication's view with respect to the legislation; being undecided with respect to the legislation; being the recipient's representative in the legislature; or being a member of the legislative committee or subcommittee that will consider the legislation. Communications that encourage the recipient to take action with respect to legislation but that do not directly encourage the recipient to take action with respect to legislation may be within the exception for nonpartisan analysis, study or research (see paragraph (c)(1) of this section) and thus not be grass roots lobbying communications.

(v) Subsequent lobbying use of nonlobbying communications or research materials—(A) Limited effect of application. Even though certain communications or research materials are initially not grass roots lobbying communications under the general definition set forth in paragraph (b)(2)(ii) of this section, subsequent use of the communications or research materials for grass roots lobbying may cause them to be treated as grass roots lobbying communications. This paragraph (b)(2)(v) does not cause any communications or research materials to be considered direct lobbying communications.

(B) Limited scope of application. Under this paragraph (b)(2)(v), only "advocacy communications or research materials" are potentially treated as grass roots lobbying communications. Communications or research materials that are not "advocacy communications or research materials" are not treated as grass roots lobbying communications under this paragraph (b)(2)(v). "Advocacy communications or research materials" are any communications or materials that both refer to and reflect a view on specific legislation but that do not, in their initial format, contain a direct encouragement for recipients to take action with respect to legislation.

(C) Subsequent use in lobbying. Where advocacy communications or research materials are subsequently accompanied by a direct encouragement for recipients to take action with respect to legislation, the advocacy communications or research materials themselves are treated as grass roots lobbying communications unless the organization's primary purpose in undertaking or preparing the advocacy communications or research materials was not for use in lobbying. In such a case, all expenses of preparing and distributing the advocacy communications or research materials will be treated as grass roots expenditures.

(D) Time limit on application of subsequent use rule. The characterization of expenditures as grass roots lobbying expenditures under paragraph (b)(2)(v)(C) shall apply only to expenditures paid less than six months before the first use of the advocacy communications or research materials with a direct encouragement to action.

(E) Safe harbor in determining "primary purpose". The primary purpose of the organization in undertaking or preparing advocacy communications or research materials will not be considered to be for use in lobbying if, prior to or contemporaneously with the use of the advocacy communications or research materials with the direct encouragement to action, the organization makes a substantial nonlobbying distribution of the advocacy communications or research materials (without the direct encouragement to action). Whether a distribution is substantial will be determined by reference to all of the facts and circumstances, including the normal distribution pattern of similar nonpartisan analyses, studies or research by that and similar organizations.

(F) Special rule for partisan analysis, study or research. In the case of advocacy communications or research materials that are not nonpartisan analysis, study or research, the nonlobbying distribution thereof will not be considered "substantial" unless that distribution is at least as extensive as the lobbying distribution thereof.

(G) Factors considered in determining primary purpose. Where the nonlobbying distribution of advocacy communications or research materials is not substantial, all of the facts and circumstances must be weighed to determine whether the organization's primary purpose in preparing the advocacy communications or research materials was for use in lobbying. While not the only factor, the extent of the organization's nonlobbying distribution of the advocacy communications or research materials is particularly relevant, especially when compared to the extent of their distribution with the direct encouragement to action. Another particularly relevant factor is whether the lobbying use of the advocacy communications or research materials is by the organization that prepared the document, a related organization, or an unrelated organization.

Where the subsequent lobbying distribution is made by an unrelated organization, clear and convincing evidence (which must include evidence demonstrating cooperation or collusion between the two organizations will be required to establish that the primary purpose for preparing the communication for use in lobbying.

(H) Examples. The provisions of this paragraph (b)(2)(v) are illustrated by the following examples:

Example (1). Assume a nonlobbying "report" (that is not nonpartisan analysis, study or research) is prepared by an organization, but distributed to only 50 people. The report, in that format, refers to and reflects a view on specific legislation but does not contain a direct encouragement for the recipients to take action with respect to legislation. Two months later, the organization sends the report to 10,000 people along with a letter urging recipients to write their Senators about the legislation discussed in the report. Because the report's nonlobbying distribution is not as extensive as its lobbying distribution, the report's nonlobbying distribution is not substantial for purposes of this paragraph (b)(2)(v). Accordingly, the organization's primary purpose in preparing the report must be determined by weighing all of the facts and circumstances. In light of the relatively minimal nonlobbying distribution and the fact that the lobbying distribution is by the preparing organization rather than by an unrelated organization, and in the absence of evidence to the contrary, both the report and the letter are grass roots lobbying communications. Assume that all costs of preparing the report were paid within the six months preceding the mailing of the letter. Accordingly, all of the organization's expenditures for preparing and mailing the two documents are grass roots lobbying expenditures.

Example (2). Assume the same facts as in Example (1), except that the costs of the report are paid over the two month period of January and February. Between January 1 and 31, the organization pays $1,000 for the report. In February, the organization pays $500 for the report. Further assume that the report is first used with a direct encouragement to action on August 1. Six months prior to August 1 is February 1. Accordingly, no costs paid for the report before February 1 are treated as grass roots lobbying expenditures under the subsequent use rule. Under these facts, the subsequent use rule treats only the $500 paid for the report in February as grass roots lobbying expenditures.

(3) Exceptions to the definition of influencing legislation. In many cases, a communication is not a direct or grass roots lobbying communication under paragraph (b)(1) or (b)(2) of this section if it falls within one of the exceptions listed in paragraph (c) of this section. See paragraph (c)(1), Nonpartisan analysis, study or research; paragraph (c)(2), Examinations and discussions of broad social, economic and similar problems; paragraph (c)(3), Requests for technical advice; and paragraph (c)(4), Communications pertaining to self-defense by the organization. In addition, see § 56.4911–5, which provides special rules regarding the treatment of certain lobbying communications directed in whole or in part to members of an electing public charity.

(4) Examples. This paragraph (b)(4) provides examples to illustrate the rules set forth in the section regarding direct and grass roots lobbying. The expenditure test election under section 501(h) is assumed to be in effect for all organizations discussed in the examples in this paragraph (b)(4). In addition, it is assumed that the special rules of § 56.4911–5, regarding certain of a public charity's communications with its members, do not apply to any of the examples in this paragraph (b)(4).

(i) Direct lobbying. The provisions of this section regarding direct lobbying communications are illustrated by the following examples:

Example (1). Organization P's employee, X, is assigned to approach members of Congress to gain their support for a pending bill. X drafts and P prints a position letter on the bill. P distributes the letter to members of Congress. Additionally, X personally contacts several members of Congress or their staffs to seek support for P's position on the bill. The letter and the personal contacts are direct lobbying communications.

Example (2). Organization M's president writes a letter to the Congresswoman representing the district in which M is headquartered, requesting that the Congresswoman write an administrative agency regarding proposed regulations recently published by that agency. M's president also requests that the Congresswoman's letter to the agency state the Congresswoman's support of M's application for a particular type of permit granted by the agency. The letter written by M's president is not a direct lobbying communication.

Example (3). Organization Z prepares a paper on a particular state's environmental problems. The paper does not reflect a view on any specific pending legislation or on any specific legislative proposal that Z either supports or opposes. Z's representatives give the paper to a state legislator. Z's paper is not a direct lobbying communication.

Example (4). State X enacts a statute that requires the licensing of all day care providers. Agency B in State X is charged with preparing rules to implement the bill enacted by State X. One week after enactment of the bill, organization C sends a letter to Agency B providing detailed proposed rules that organization C suggests to Agency B as the appropriate standards to follow in implementing the statute on licensing of day care providers. Organization C's letter to Agency B is not a lobbying communication.

Example (5). Organization B researches, prepares and prints a code of standards of minimum safety requirements in an area of common electrical wiring. Organization B sells the code of standards booklet to the public and it is widely used by professional in the installation of electrical wiring. A number of states have codified all, or part, of the code of standards as mandatory safety standards. On occasion, B lobbies state legislators for passage of the code of standards for safety reasons. Because the primary purpose of preparing the code of standards was the promotion of public safety and the standards were specifically used in a profession for that purpose, separate from any legislative requirement, the research, preparation, printing and public distribution of the code of standards is not an expenditure for a direct (or grass roots) lobbying communication. Costs, such as transportation, photocopying, and other similar expenses, incurred in lobbying state legislators for passage of the code of standards into law are expenditures for direct lobbying communications.

Example (6). On the organization's own initiative, representatives of Organization F present written testimony to a Congressional committee. The news media report on the testimony of Organization F, detailing F's opposition to a pending bill. The testimony is a direct lobbying communication but is not a grass roots lobbying communication.

Example (7). Organization R's monthly newsletter contains an editorial column that refers to and reflects a view on specific pending bills. R sends the newsletter to 10,000 nonmember subscribers. Senator Doe is among the subscribers. The editorial column in the newsletter copy sent to Senator Doe is not a direct lobbying communication because the newsletter is sent to Senator Doe in her capacity as a subscriber rather than her capacity as a legislator. (Note, though, that the editorial column may be a grass roots lobbying communication if it encourages recipients to take action with respect to the pending bills it refers to and on which it reflects a view).

Example (8). Assume the same facts as in Example (7), except that one of Senator Doe's staff members sees Senator Doe's copy of the editorial and writes to R requesting additional information. R responds with a letter that refers to and reflects a view on specific legislation. R's letter is a direct lobbying communication unless it is within one of the exceptions set forth in paragraph (c) of this section (such as the exception for nonpartisan analysis, study or research). (R's letter is not within the scope of the exception for responses to written requests from a legislative body or committee for technical advice (see paragraph (c)(3) of this section) because the letter is not in response to a written request from a legislative body or committee).

(ii) Grass roots lobbying. The provisions of this section regarding grass roots lobbying communications are illustrated in paragraph (b)(4)(ii)(A) of this section by examples of communications that are not grass roots lobbying communications and in paragraph (b)(4)(ii)(B) by examples of communications that are grass roots lobbying communications. The provisions of this section are further illustrated in paragraph (b)(4)(ii)(C), with particular regard to the exception for nonpartisan analysis, study, or research:

(A) Communications that are not grass roots lobbying communications.

Example (1). Organization L places in its newsletter an article that asserts that lack of new capital is hurting State W's economy. The article recommends that State W residents either invest more in local businesses or increase their savings so that funds will be available to others interested in making investments. The article is an attempt to influence opinions with respect to a general problem that might receive legislative attention and is distributed in a manner so as to reach and influence many individuals. However, the article does not refer to specific legislation that is pending in a legislative body, nor does the article refer to a specific legislative proposal the organization either supports or opposes. The article is not a grass roots lobbying communication.

Example (2). Assume the same facts as Example (1), except that the article refers to a bill pending in State W's legislature that is intended to provide tax incentives for private savings. The article praises the pending bill and recommends that it be enacted. However, the article does not encourage readers to take action with respect to the legislation. The article is not a grass roots lobbying communication.

Example (3). Organization B sends a letter to all persons on its mailing list. The letter includes an update on numerous environmental issues with a discussion of general concerns regarding pollution, proposed federal regulations affecting the area, and several pending legislative proposals. The letter endorses two pending bills and opposes another pending bill, but does not name any legislator involved (other than the sponsor of one bill, for purposes of identifying the bill), nor does it otherwise encourage the reader to take action with respect to the legislation. The letter is not a grass roots lobbying communication.

Example (4). A pamphlet distributed by organization Z discusses the dangers of drugs and encourages the public to send their legislators a coupon, printed with the statement "I support a drug-free America." The term "drug-free America" is not widely identified with any of the many specific pending legislative proposals regarding drug issues. The pamphlet does not refer to any of the numerous pending legislative proposals, nor does the organization support or oppose a specific legislative proposal. The pamphlet is not a grass roots lobbying communication.

Example (5). A pamphlet distributed by organization B encourages readers to join an organization and "get involved in the fight against drugs." The text states, in the course of a discussion of several current drug issues, that organization B supports a specific bill before Congress that would establish an expanded drug control program. The pamphlet does not encourage readers to communicate with legislators about the bill (such as by including the names of undecided or opposed legislators). The pamphlet is not a grass roots lobbying communication.

Example (6). Organization E, an environmental organization, routinely summarizes in each edition of its newsletter the new environment-related bills that have been introduced in Congress since the last edition of the newsletter. The newsletter identifies each bill by a bill number and the name of the legislation's sponsor. The newsletter also reports on the status of previously introduced environment-related bills. The summaries and status reports do not encourage recipients of the newsletter to take action with respect to legislation, as described in paragraphs (b)(2)(iii)(A) through (D) of this section. Although the summaries and status reports refer to specific legislation and often reflect a view on such legislation, they do not encourage the newsletter recipients to take action with respect to such legislation. The summaries and status reports are not grass roots lobbying communications.

Example (7). Organization B prints in its newsletter a report on pending legislation that B supports, the Family Equity bill. The report refers to and reflects a view on the Family Equity bill, but does not directly encourage recipients to take action. Nor does the report specifically identify any legislator as opposing the communication's view on the legislation, as being undecided, or as being a member of the legislative committee or subcommittee that will consider the legislation. However, the report does state the following: Rep. Doe (D-Ky.) and Rep. Roe (R-Ma.), both ardent supporters of the Family Equity bill, spoke at B's annual convention last week. Both encouraged B's efforts to get the Family Equity bill enacted and stated that they thought the bill could be enacted even over a presidential veto. B's legislative affairs liaison questioned others, who seemed to agree with that assessment. For example, Sen. Roe (I-Ca.) said that he thinks the bill will pass with such a large majority, "the President won't even consider vetoing it." Assume the newsletter, and thus the report, is sent to individuals throughout the U.S., including some recipients in Kentucky, Massachusetts and California. Because the report is distributed nationally, the mere fact that the report identifies several legislators by party and state as part of its discussion does not mean the report specifically identifies the named legislators as the Kentucky, Massachusetts and California recipients' representatives in the legislature for purposes of paragraph (b)(2)(iii) of this section. The report is not a grass roots lobbying communication.

(B) Communications that are grass roots lobbying communications.

Example (1). A pamphlet distributed by organization Y states that the "President's plan for a drug-free America," which will establish a drug control program, should be passed. The pamphlet encourages readers to "write or call your senators and representatives and tell them to vote for the President's plan." No legislative proposal formally bears the name "President's plan for a drug-free America," but that and similar terms have been widely used in connection with specific legislation pending in Congress that was initially proposed by the President. Thus, the pamphlet refers to specific legislation, reflects a view on the legislation, and encourages readers to take action with respect to the legislation. The pamphlet is a grass roots lobbying communication.

Example (2). Assume the same facts as in Example (1), except that the pamphlet does not encourage the public to write or call representatives, but does list the members of the committee that will consider the bill. The pamphlet is a grass roots lobbying communication.

Example (3). Assume the same facts as in Example (1), except that the pamphlet encourages readers to "write the President to urge him to make the bill a top legislative priority" rather than encouraging readers to communicate with members of Congress. The pamphlet is a grass roots lobbying communication.

Example (4). Organization B, a nonmembership organization, includes in one of three sections of its newsletter an endorsement of two pending bills and opposition to another pending bill and also identifies several legislators as undecided on the three bills. The section of the newsletter devoted to the three pending bills is a grass roots lobbying communication.

Example (5). Organization D, a nonmembership organization, sends a letter to all persons on its mailing list. The letter includes an extensive discussion concluding that a significant increase in spending for the Air Force is essential in order to provide an adequate defense of the nation. Prior to a concluding fundraising request, the letter encourages readers to write their Congressional representatives urging increased appropriations to build the B–1 bomber. The letter is a grass roots lobbying communication.

Example (6). The President nominates X for a position in the President's cabinet. Organization Y disagrees with the views of X and does not believe X has the necessary administrative capabilities to effectively run a cabinet-level department. Accordingly, Y sends a general mailing requesting recipients to write to four Senators on the Senate Committee that will consider the nomination. The mailing is a grass roots lobbying communication.

Example (7). Organization F mails letters requesting that each recipient contribute money to or join F. In addition, the letters express F's opposition to a pending bill that is to be voted upon by the U.S. House of Representatives. Although the letters are form letters sent as a mass mailing, each letter is individualized to report to the recipient the name of the recipient's congressional representative. The letters are grass roots lobbying communications.

Example (8). Organization C sends a mailing that opposes a specific legislative proposal and includes a postcard addressed to the President for the recipient to sign stating opposition to the proposal. The letter requests that the recipient send to C a contribution as well as the postcard opposing the proposal. C states in the letter that it will deliver all the postcards to the White House. The letter is a grass roots lobbying communication.

(C) Additional examples.

Example (1). The newsletter of an organization concerned with drug issues is circulated primarily to individuals who are not members of the organization. A story in the newsletter reports on the prospects for passage of a specifically identified bill, stating that the organization supports the bill. The newsletter story identifies certain legislators as undecided, but does not state that readers should contact the undecided legislators. The story does not provide a full and fair exposition sufficient to qualify as nonpartisan analysis, study or research. The newsletter story is a grass roots lobbying communication.

Example (2). Assume the same facts as in Example (1), except that the newsletter story provides a full and fair exposition sufficient to qualify as nonpartisan analysis, study or research. The newsletter story is not a grass roots lobbying communication because it is within the exception for nonpartisan analysis, study or research (since it does not directly encourage recipients to take action).

Example (3). Assume the same facts as in Example (2), except that the newsletter story explicitly asks readers to contact the undecided legislators. Because the newsletter story directly encourages readers to take action with respect to the legislation, the newsletter story is not within the exception for nonpartisan analysis, study or research. Accordingly, the newsletter story is a grass roots lobbying communication.

Example (4). Assume the same facts as in Example (1), except that the story does not identify any undecided legislators. The story is not a grass roots lobbying communication.

Example (5). X organization places an advertisement that specifically identifies and opposes a bill that X asserts would harm the farm economy. The advertisement is not a mass media communication described in paragraph (b)(5)(ii) of this section and does not directly encourage readers to take action with respect to the bill. However, the advertisement does state that Senator Y favors the legislation. Because the advertisement refers to and reflects a view on specific legislation, and also encourages the readers to take action with respect to the legislation by specifically identifying a legislator who opposes X's views on the legislation, the advertisement is a grass roots lobbying communication.

Example (6). Assume the same facts as in Example (5), except that instead of identifying Senator Y as favoring the legislation, the advertisement identifies the "junior Senator from State Z" as favoring the legislation. The advertisement is a grass roots lobbying communication.

Example (7). Assume the same facts as in Example (5), except that instead of identifying Senator Y as favoring the legislation, the advertisement states: "Even though this bill will have a devastating effect upon the farm economy, most of the Senators from the Farm Belt states are inexplicably in favor of the bill." The advertisement does not specifically identify one or more legislators as opposing the advertisement's view on the bill in question. Accordingly, the advertisement is not a grass roots lobbying communication because it does not encourage readers to take action with respect to the legislation.

Example (8). Organization V trains volunteers to go door-to-door to seek signatures for petitions to be sent to legislators in favor of a specific bill. The volunteers are wholly unreimbursed for their time and expenses. The volunteers' costs (to the extent any are incurred) are not lobbying or exempt purpose expenditures made by V (but the volunteers may not deduct their out-of-pocket expenditures (see section 170(f)(6)). When V asks the volunteers to contact others and urge them to sign the petitions, V encourages those volunteers to take action in favor of the specific bill. Accordingly, V's costs of soliciting the volunteers' help and its costs of training the volunteers are grass roots expenditures. In addition, the costs of preparing, copying, distributing, etc. the petitions (and any other materials on the same specific subject used in the door-to-door signature gathering effort), are grass roots expenditures.

(5) Special rule for certain mass media advertisements—

(i) In general. A mass media advertisement that is not a grass roots lobbying communication under the three-part grass roots lobbying definition contained in paragraph (b)(2) of this section may be a grass roots lobbying communication by virtue of paragraph (b)(5)(ii) of this section. The special rule in paragraph (b)(5)(ii) generally applies only to a limited type of paid advertisements that appear in the mass media.

(ii) Presumption regarding certain paid mass media advertisements about highly publicized legislation. If within two weeks before a vote by a legislative body, or a committee (but not a subcommittee) thereof, on a highly publicized piece of legislation, an organization's paid advertisement appears in the mass media, the paid advertisement will be presumed to be a grass roots lobbying communication, but only if the paid advertisement both reflects a view on the general subject of such legislation and either: refers to the highly publicized legislation; or encourages the public to communicate with legislators on the general subject of such legislation. An organization can rebut this presumption by demonstrating that the paid advertisement is a type of communication regularly made by the organization in the mass media without regard to the timing of legislation (that is, a customary course of business exception) or that the timing of the paid advertisement was unrelated to the upcoming legislative action. Notwithstanding the fact that an organization successfully rebuts the presumption, a mass media communication described in this paragraph (b)(5)(ii) is a grass roots lobbying communication if the communication would be a grass roots lobbying communication under the rules contained in paragraph (b)(2) of this section.

(iii) Definitions—(A) Mass media. For purposes of this paragraph (b)(5), the term "mass media" means television, radio, billboards and general circulation newspapers and magazines. General circulation newspapers and magazines do not include newspapers or magazines published by an organization for which the expenditure test election under section 501(h) is in effect, except where both: The total circulation of the newspaper or magazine is greater than 100,000; and fewer than one-half of the recipients are members of the organization (as defined in § 56.4911–5(f)).

(B) Paid advertisement. For purposes of this paragraph (b)(5), where an electing public charity is itself a mass media publisher or broadcaster, all portions of that organization's mass media publications or broadcasts are treated as paid advertisements in the mass media, except those specific portions that are advertisements paid for by another person. The term "mass media" is defined in paragraph (b)(5)(iii)(A).

(C) Highly publicized. For purposes of this paragraph (b)(5), "highly publicized" means frequent coverage on television and radio, and in general circulation newspapers, during the two weeks preceding the vote by the legislative body or committee. In the case of state or local legislation, "highly publicized" means frequent coverage in the mass media that serve the State or local jurisdiction in question. Even where legislation receives frequent coverage, it is "highly publicized" only if the pendency of the legislation or the legislation's general terms, purpose, or effect are known to a significant segment of the general public (as opposed to the particular interest groups directly affected) in the area in which the paid mass media advertisement appears.

(iv) Examples. The special rule of this paragraph (b)(5) is illustrated by the following examples. The expenditure test election under section 501(h) is assumed to be in effect for all organizations discussed in the examples in this paragraph (b)(5)(iv):

Example (1). Organization X places a television advertisement advocating one of the President's major foreign policy initiatives, as outlined by the President in a series of speeches and as drafted into proposed legislation. The initiative is popularly known as "the President's World Peace Plan," and is voted upon by the Senate four days after X's advertisement. The advertisement concludes: "SUPPORT THE PRESIDENT'S WORLD PEACE PLAN!" The President's plan and position are highly publicized during the two weeks before the Senate vote, as evidenced by: coverage of the plan on several nightly television network news programs; more than one article about the plan on the front page of a majority of the country's ten largest daily general circulation newspapers; and an editorial about the plan in four of the country's ten largest daily general circulation newspapers. Although the advertisement does not encourage readers to contact legislators or other government officials, the advertisement does refer to specific legislation and reflect a view on the general subject of the legislation. The communication is presumed to be a grass roots lobbying communication.

Example (2). Assume the same facts as in Example (1), except that the advertisement appears three weeks before the Senate's vote on the plan. Because the advertisement appears more than two weeks before the legislative vote, the advertisement is not within the scope of the special rule for mass media communications on highly publicized legislation. Accordingly, the advertisement is a grass roots lobbying communication only if it is described in the general definition contained in paragraph (b)(2) of this section. Because the advertisement does not encourage recipients to take action with respect to the legislation in question, the advertisement is not a grass roots lobbying communication.

Example (3). Organization Y places a newspaper advertisement advocating increased government funding for certain public works projects the President has proposed and that are being considered by a legislative committee. The advertisement explains the President's proposals and concludes: "SUPPORT FUNDING FOR THESE VITAL PROJECTS!" The advertisement does not encourage readers to contact legislators or other government officials nor does it name any undecided legislators, but it does name the legislation being considered by the committee. The President's proposed funding of public works, however, is not highly publicized during the two weeks before the vote: there has been little coverage of the issue on nightly television network news programs, only one front-page article on the issue in the country's ten largest daily general circulation newspapers, and only one editorial about the issue in the country's ten largest daily general circulation newspapers. Two days after the advertisement appears, the committee votes to approve funding of the projects. Although the advertisement appears less than two weeks before the legislative vote, the advertisement is not within the scope of the special rule for mass media communications on highly publicized legislation because the issue of funding for public works projects is not highly publicized. Thus, the advertisement is a grass roots lobbying communication only if it is described in the general definition contained in paragraph (b)(2) of this section. Because the advertisement does not encourage recipients to take action with respect to the legislation in question, the advertisement is not a grass roots lobbying communication.

Example (4). Organization P places numerous advertisements in the mass media about a bill being considered by the State Assembly. The bill is highly publicized, as evidenced by numerous front-page articles, editorials and letters to the editor published in the state's general circulation daily newspapers, as well as frequent coverage of the bill by the television and radio stations serving the state. The advertisements run over a three week period and, in addition to showing pictures of a family being robbed at gunpoint, say: "The State Assembly is considering a bill to make gun ownership illegal. This outrageous legislation would violate your constitutional rights and the rights of other law-abiding citizens. If this legislation is passed, you and your family will be criminals if you want to exercise your right to protect yourselves." The advertisements refer to and reflect a view on a specific bill but do not encourage recipients to take action. Sixteen days after the last advertisement runs, a State Assembly committee votes to defeat the legislation. None of the advertisements is a grass roots lobbying communication.

Example (5). Assume the same facts as in Example (4), except that it is publicly announced prior to the advertising campaign that the committee vote is scheduled for five days after the last advertisement runs. Because of public pressure resulting from the advertising campaign, the bill is withdrawn and no vote is ever taken. None of the advertisements is a grass roots lobbying communication.

(c) Exceptions to the definitions of direct lobbying communication and grass roots lobbying communication—(1) Nonpartisan analysis, study, or research exception—

(i) In general. Engaging in nonpartisan analysis, study, or research and making available to the general public or a segment or members thereof or to governmental bodies, officials, or employees the results of such work constitute neither a direct lobbying communication under § 56.4911–2(b)(1) nor a grass roots lobbying communication under § 56.4911–2(b)(2).

(ii) Nonpartisan analysis, study, or research. For purposes of this section, "nonpartisan analysis, study, or research" means an independent and objective exposition of a particular subject matter, including any activity that is "educational" within the meaning of § 1.501(c)(3)–1(d)(3). Thus, "nonpartisan analysis, study, or research" may advocate a particular position or viewpoint so long as there is a sufficiently full and fair exposition of the pertinent facts to enable the public or an individual to form an independent opinion or conclusion. The mere presentation of unsupported opinion, however, does not qualify as "nonpartisan analysis, study, or research".

(iii) Presentation as part of a series. Normally, whether a publication or broadcast qualifies as "nonpartisan analysis, study, or research" will be determined on a presentation-by-presentation basis. However, if a publication or broadcast is one of a series prepared or supported by an electing organization and the series as a whole meets the standards of paragraph (c)(1)(ii) of this section, then any individual publication or broadcast within the series is not a direct or grass roots lobbying communication even though such individual broadcast or publication does not, by itself, meet the standards of paragraph (c)(1)(ii) of this section. Whether a broadcast or publication is considered part of a series will ordinarily depend upon all the facts and circumstances of each particular situation. However, with respect to broadcast activities, all broadcasts within any period of six consecutive months will ordinarily be eligible to be considered as part of a series. If an electing organization times or channels a part of a series which is described in this paragraph (c)(1)(iii) in a manner designed to influence the general public or the action of a legislative body with respect to a specific legislative proposal, the expenses of preparing and distributing such part of the analysis, study, or research will be expenditures for a direct or grass roots lobbying communications, as the case may be.

(iv) Making available results of nonpartisan analysis, study, or research. An organization may choose any suitable means, including oral or written presentations, to distribute the results of its nonpartisan analysis, study, or research, with or without charge. Such means include distribution of reprints of speeches, articles and reports; presentation of information through conferences, meetings and discussions; and dissemination to the news media, including radio, television and newspapers, and to other public forums. For purposes of this paragraph (c)(1)(iv), such communications may not be limited to, or be directed toward, persons who are interested solely in one side of a particular issue.

(v) Subsequent lobbying use of certain analysis, study or research. Even though certain analysis, study or research is initially within the exception for nonpartisan analysis, study or research, subsequent use of that analysis, study or research for grass roots lobbying may cause that analysis, study or research to be treated as a grass roots lobbying communication that is not within the exception for nonpartisan analysis, study or research. This paragraph (c)(1)(v) does not cause any analysis, study or research to be considered a direct lobbying communication. For rules regarding when analysis, study or research is treated as a grass roots lobbying communication that is not within the scope of the exception for nonpartisan analysis, study or research, see paragraph (b)(2)(v) of this section.

(vi) Directly encouraging action by recipients of a communication. A communication that reflects a view on specific legislation is not within the nonpartisan analysis, study, or research exception of this paragraph (c)(1) if the communication directly encourages the recipient to take action with respect to such legislation. For purposes of this section, a communication directly encourages the recipient to take action with respect to legislation if the communication is described in one or more of paragraphs (b)(2)(iii)(A) through (C) of this section. As described in paragraph (b)(2)(iv) of this section, a communication would encourage the recipient to take action with respect to legislation, but not directly encourage such action, if the communication does no more than specifically identify one or more legislators who will vote on the legislation as: opposing the communication's view with respect to the legislation; being undecided with respect to the legislation; being the recipient's representative in the legislature; or being a member of the legislative committee or subcommittee that will consider the legislation.

(vii) Examples. The provisions of this paragraph (c)(1) may be illustrated by the following examples:

Example (1). Organization M establishes a research project to collect information for the purpose of showing the dangers of the use of pesticides in raising crops. The information collected includes data with respect to proposed legislation, pending before several State legislatures, which would ban the use of pesticides. The project takes favorable positions on such legislation without producing a sufficiently full and fair exposition of the pertinent facts to enable the public or an individual to form an independent opinion or conclusion on the pros and cons of the use of pesticides. This project is not within the exception for nonpartisan analysis, study, or research because it is designed to present information merely on one side of the legislative controversy.

Example (2). Organization N establishes a research project to collect information concerning the dangers of the use of pesticides in raising crops for the ostensible purpose of examining and reporting information as to the pros and cons of the use of pesticides in raising crops. The information is collected and distributed in the form of a published report which analyzes the effects and costs of the use and nonuse of various pesticides under various conditions on humans, animals and crops. The report also presents the advantages, disadvantages, and economic cost of allowing the continued use of pesticides unabated, of controlling the use of pesticides, and of developing alternatives to pesticides. Even if the report sets forth conclusions that the disadvantages as a result of using pesticides are greater than the advantages of using pesticides and that prompt legislative regulation of the use of pesticides is needed, the project is within the exception for nonpartisan analysis, study, or research since it is designed to present information on both sides of the legislative controversy and presents a sufficiently full and fair exposition of the pertinent facts to enable the public or an individual to form an independent opinion or conclusion.

Example (3). Organization O establishes a research project to collect information on the presence or absence of disease in humans from eating food grown with pesticides and the presence or absence of disease in humans from eating food not grown with pesticides. As part of the research project, O hires a consultant who prepares a "fact sheet" which calls for the curtailment of the use of pesticides and which addresses itself to the merits of several specific legislative proposals to curtail the use of pesticides in raising crops which are currently pending before State Legislatures. The "fact sheet" presents reports of experimental evidence tending to support its conclusions but omits any reference to reports of experimental evidence tending to dispute its conclusions. O distributes ten thousand copies to citizens' groups. Expenditures by O in connection with this work of the consultant are not within the exception for nonpartisan analysis, study, or research.

Example (4). P publishes a bi-monthly newsletter to collect and report all published materials, ongoing research, and new developments with regard to the use of pesticides in raising crops. The newsletter also includes notices of proposed pesticide legislation with impartial summaries of the provisions and debates on such legislation. The newsletter does not encourage recipients to take action with respect to such legislation, but is designed to present information on both sides of the legislative controversy and does present such information fully and fairly. It is within the exception for nonpartisan analysis, study, or research.

Example (5). X is satisfied that A, a member of the faculty of Y University, is exceptionally well qualified to undertake a project involving a comprehensive study of the effects of pesticides on crop yields. Consequently, X makes a grant to A to underwrite the cost of the study and of the preparation of a book on the effect of pesticides on crop yields. X does not take any position on the issues or control the content of A's output. A produces a book which concludes that the use of pesticides often has a favorable effect on crop yields, and on that basis argues against pending bills which would ban the use of pesticides. A's book contains a sufficiently full and fair exposition of the pertinent facts, including known or potential disadvantages of the use of pesticides, to enable the public or an individual to form an independent opinion or conclusion as to whether pesticides should be banned as provided in the pending bills. The book does not directly encourage readers to take action with respect to the pending bills. Consequently, the book is within the exception for nonpartisan analysis, study, or research.

Example (6). Assume the same facts as Example (2), except that, instead of issuing a report, X presents within a period of 6 consecutive months a two-program television series relating to the pesticide issue. The first program contains information, arguments, and conclusions favoring legislation to restrict the use of pesticides. The second program contains information, arguments, and conclusions opposing legislation to restrict the use of pesticides. The programs are broadcast within 6 months of each other during commensurate periods of prime time. X's programs are within the exception for nonpartisan analysis, study, or research. Although neither program individually could be regarded as nonpartisan, the series of two programs constitutes a balanced presentation.

Example (7). Assume the same facts as in Example (6), except that X arranged for televising the program favoring legislation to restrict the use of pesticides at 8:00 on a Thursday evening and for televising the program opposing such legislation at 7:00 on a Sunday morning. X's presentation is not within the exception for nonpartisan analysis, study, or research, since X disseminated its information in a manner prejudicial to one side of the legislative controversy.

Example (8). Organization Z researches, writes, prints and distributes a study on the use and effects of pesticide X. A bill is pending in the U.S. Senate to ban the use of pesticide X. Z's study leads to the conclusion that pesticide X is extremely harmful and that the bill pending in the U.S. Senate is an appropriate and much needed remedy to solve the problems caused by pesticide X. The study contains a sufficiently full and fair exposition of the pertinent facts, including known or potential advantages of the use of pesticide X, to enable the public or an individual to form an independent opinion or conclusion as to whether pesticides should be banned as provided in the pending bills. In its analysis of the pending bill, the study names certain undecided Senators on the Senate committee considering the bill. Although the study meets the three part test for determining whether a communication is a grass roots lobbying communication, the study is within the exception for nonpartisan analysis, study or research, because it does not directly encourage recipients of the communication to urge a legislator to oppose the bill.

Example (9). Assume the same facts as in Example (8), except that, after stating support for the pending bill, the study concludes: "You should write to the undecided committee members to support this crucial bill." The study is not within the exception for nonpartisan analysis, study or research because it directly encourages the recipients to urge a legislator to support a specific piece of legislation.

Example (10). Organization X plans to conduct a lobbying campaign with respect to illegal drug use in the United States. It incurs $5,000 in expenses to conduct research and prepare an extensive report primarily for use in the lobbying campaign. Although the detailed report discusses specific pending legislation and reaches the conclusion that the legislation would reduce illegal drug use, the report contains a sufficiently full and fair exposition of the pertinent facts to enable the public or an individual to form an independent conclusion regarding the effect of the legislation. The report does not encourage readers to contact legislators regarding the legislation. Accordingly, the report does not, in and of itself, constitute a lobbying communication. Copies of the report are available to the public at X's office, but X does not actively distribute the report or otherwise seek to make the contents of the report available to the general public. Whether or not X's distribution is sufficient to meet the requirement in § 56.4911–2(c)(1)(iv) that a nonpartisan communication be made available, X's distribution is not substantial (for purposes of § 56.4911–2(b)(2)(v)(E)) in light of all of the facts and circumstances, including the normal distribution pattern of similar nonpartisan reports. X then mails copies of the report, along with a letter, to 10,000 individuals on X's mailing list. In the letter, X requests that individuals contact legislators urging passage of the legislation discussed in the report. Because X's research and report were primarily undertaken by X for lobbying purposes and X did not make a substantial distribution of the report (without an accompanying lobbying message) prior to or contemporaneously with the use of the report in lobbying, the report is a grass roots lobbying communication that is not within the exception for nonpartisan analysis, study or research.

Example (11). Assume the same facts as in Example (10), except that before using the report in the lobbying campaign, X sends the research and report (without an accompanying lobbying message) to universities and newspapers. At the same time, X also advertises the availability of the report in its newsletter. This distribution is similar in scope to the normal distribution pattern of similar nonpartisan reports. In light of all of the facts and circumstances, X's distribution of the report is substantial. Because of X's substantial distribution of the report, X's primary purpose will be considered to be other than for use in lobbying and the report will not be considered a grass roots lobbying communication. Accordingly, only the expenditures for copying and mailing the report to the 10,000 individuals on X's mailing list, as well as for preparing and mailing the letter, are expenditures for grass roots lobbying communications.

Example (12). Organization M pays for a bumper sticker that reads: "STOP ABORTION: Vote NO on Prop. X!" M also pays for a 30-second television advertisement and a billboard that similarly advocate opposition to Prop. X. In light of the limited scope of the communications, none of the communications is within the exception for nonpartisan analysis, study or research. First, none of the communications rises to the level of analysis, study or research. Second, none of the communications is nonpartisan because none contains a sufficiently full and fair exposition of the pertinent facts to enable the public or an individual to form an independent opinion or conclusion. Thus, each communication is a direct lobbying communcation.

(2) Examinations and discussions of broad social, economic, and similar problems. Examinations and discussions of broad social, economic, and similar problems are neither direct lobbying communications under § 56.4911–2(b)(1) nor grass roots lobbying communications under § 56.4911–2(b)(2) even if the problems are of the type with which government would be expected to deal ultimately. Thus, under §§ 56.4911–2(b)(1) and (2), lobbying communications do not include public discussion, or communications with members of legislative bodies or governmental employees, the general subject of which is also the subject of legislation before a legislative body, so long as such discussion does not address itself to the merits of a specific legislative proposal and so long as such discussion does not directly encourage recipients to take action with respect to legislation. For example, this paragraph (c)(2) excludes from grass roots lobbying under § 56.4911–2(b)(2) an organization's discussions of problems such as environmental pollution or population growth that are being considered by Congress and various State legislatures, but only where the discussions are not directly addressed to specific legislation being considered, and only where the discussions do not directly encourage recipients of the communication to contact a legislator, an employee of a legislative body, or a government official or employee who may participate in the formulation of legislation.

(3) Requests for technical advice. A communication is not a direct lobbying communication under § 56.4911–2(b)(1) if the communication is the providing of technical advice or assistance to a governmental body, a governmental committee, or a subdivision of either in response to a written request by the body, committee, or subdivision, as set forth in § 53.4945–2(d)(2).

(4) Communications pertaining to "self-defense" by the organization. A communication is not a direct lobbying communication under § 56.4911–2(b)(1) if either:

(i) The communication is an appearance before, or communication with, any legislative body with respect to a possible action by the body that might affect the existence of the electing public charity, its powers and duties, its tax-exempt status, or the deductibility of contributions to the organization, as set forth in § 53.4945–2(d)(3);

(ii) The communication is by a member of an affiliated group of organizations (within the meaning of § 56.4911–7(e)), and is an appearance before, or communication with, a legislative body with respect to a possible action by the body that might affect the existence of any other member of the group, its powers and duties, its tax-exempt status, or the deductibility of contributions to it;

(iii) The communication is by an electing public charity more than 75 percent of the members of which are other organizations that are described in section 501(c)(3), and is an appearance before, or communication with, any legislative body with respect to a possible action by the body which might affect the existence of one or more of the section 501(c)(3) member organizations, their powers, duties, or tax-exempt status, or the deductibility (under section 170) of contributions to one or more of the section 501(c)(3) member organizations, but only if the principal purpose of the appearance or communication is to defend the section 501(c)(3) member organizations (rather than the non-section 501(c)(3) member organizations; or

(iv) The communication is by an electing public charity that is a member of a limited affiliated group or organizations under § 56.4911–10, and is an appearance before, or communication with, the Congress of the United States with respect to a possible action by the Congress that might affect the existence of any member of the limited affiliated group, its powers and duties, tax-exempt status, or the deductibility of contributions to it.

(v) Under the self-defense exception of paragraphs (c)(4)(i) through (iv) of this section, a charity may communicate with an entire legislative body, with committees or subcommittees of a legislative body, with individual legislators, with legislative staff members, or with representatives of the executive branch who are involved with the legislative process, so long as such communication is limited to the prescribed subjects. Similarly, under the self-defense exception, a charity may make expenditures in order to initiate legislation if such legislation concerns only matters which might affect the existence of the charity, its powers and duties, its tax-exempt status, or the deductibility of contributions to such charity. For examples illustrating the application and scope of the self-defense exception of this paragraph (c)(4), see § 53.4945–2(d)(3)(ii).

(d) Definitions. For purposes of section 4911 and the regulations thereunder—

(1) Legislation—

(i) In general. "Legislation" includes action by the Congress, any state legislature, any local council, or similar legislative body, or by the public in a referendum, ballot initiative, constitutional amendment, or similar procedure. "Legislation" includes a proposed treaty required to be submitted by the President to the Senate for its advice and consent from the time the President's representative begins to negotiate its position with the prospective parties to the proposed treaty.

(ii) Definition of specific legislation. For purposes of paragraphs (b)(1) and (b)(2) of this section, "specific legislation" includes both legislation that has already been introduced in a legislative body and a specific legislative proposal that the organization either supports or opposes. In the case of a referendum, ballot initiative, constitutional amendment, or other measure that is placed on the ballot by petitions signed by a required number or percentage of voters, an item becomes "specific legislation" when the petition is first circulated among voters for signature.

(iii) Examples. The terms "legislation" and "specific legislation" are illustrated using the following examples:

Example (1). A nonmembership organization includes in its newsletter an article about problems with the use of pesticide X that states in part: "Legislation that is pending in Congress would prohibit the use of this very dangerous pesticide. Fortunately, the legislation will probably be passed. Write your congressional representatives about this important issue." This is a grass roots lobbying communication that refers to and reflects a view on specific legislation and that encourages recipients to take action with respect to that legislation.

Example (2). An organization based in State A notes in its newsletter that State Z has passed a bill to accomplish a stated purpose and then says that State A should pass such a bill. The organization urges readers to write their legislators in favor of such a bill. No such bill has been introduced into the State A legislature. The organization has referred to and reflected a view on a specific legislative proposal and has also encouraged readers to take action thereon.

(2) Action. The term "action" in paragraph (d)(1)(i) of this section is limited to the introduction, amendment, enactment, defeat or repeal of Acts, bills, resolutions, or similar items.

(3) Legislative body. "Legislative body" does not include executive, judicial, or administrative bodies.

(4) Administrative bodies. "Administrative bodies" includes school boards, housing authorities, sewer and water districts, zoning boards, and other similar Federal, State, or local special purpose bodies, whether elective or attempt to influence any legislation" does not include attempts to persuade an executive body or department to form, support the formation of, or to acquire property to be used for the formation or expansion of, a public park or equivalent preserves (such as public recreation areas, game, or forest preserves, and soil demonstration areas) established or to be established by act of Congress, by executive action in accordance with an act of Congress, or by a State, municipality or other governmental unit described in section 170(c)(1), as compared with attempts to persuade a legislative body, a member thereof, or other governmental official or employee, to promote the appropriation of funds for such an acquisition or other legislative authorization of such an acquisition. Therefore, for example, an organization would not be influencing legislation for purposes of section 4911, if it proposed to a Park Authority that it purchase a particular tract of land for a new park, even though such an attempt would necessarily require the Park Authority eventually to seek appropriations to support a new park. However, in such a case, the organization would be influencing legislation, for purposes of section 4911, if it provided the Park Authority with a proposed budget to be submitted to a legislative body, unless such submission is described by one of the exceptions set forth in paragraph (c) of this section.

§ 56.4911–3. Expenditures for direct and/or grass roots lobbying communications.

(a) Definition of term "expenditures for"—(1) In general. This § 56.4911–3 contains allocation rules regarding what portion of a lobbying communication's costs is a direct lobbying expenditure, what portion is a grass roots expenditure and what portion is, in certain cases, a nonlobbying expenditure. Except as otherwise indicated in this paragraph (a), all costs of preparing a direct or grass roots lobbying communication are included as expenditures for direct or grass roots lobbying. Expenditures for a direct or grass roots lobbying communication ("lobbying expenditures") include amounts paid or incurred as current or deferred compensation for an employee's services attributable to the direct or grass roots lobbying communication, and the allocable portion of administrative, overhead, and other general expenditures attributable to the direct or grass roots lobbying communication. For example, except as otherwise provided in this paragraph (a), all expenditures for researching, drafting, reviewing, copying, publishing and mailing a direct or grass roots lobbying communication, as well as an allocable share of overhead expenses, are included as expenditures for direct or grass roots lobbying.

(2) Allocation of mixed purpose expenditures—(i) Nonmembership communications. Except as provided in paragraph (a)(2)(ii) of this section, lobbying expenditures for a communication that also has a bona fide nonlobbying purpose must include all costs attributable to those parts of the communication that are on the same specific subject as the lobbying message. All costs attributable to those parts of the communication that are not on the same specific subject as the lobbying message are not included as lobbying expenditures for allocation purposes. Whether or not a portion of a communication is on the same specific subject as the lobbying message will depend on the surrounding facts and circumstances. In general, a portion of a communication will be on the same specific subject as the lobbying message if that portion discusses an activity or specific issue that would be directly affected by the specific legislation that is the subject of the lobbying message. Moreover, discussion of the background or consequences of the specific legislation, or discussion of the background or consequences of an activity or specific issue affected by the specific legislation, is also considered to be on the same specific subject as the lobbying communication.

(ii) Membership communications. In the case of lobbying expenditures for a communication that also has a bona fide nonlobbying purpose and that is sent only or primarily to members, an electing public charity must make a reasonable allocation between the amount expended for the lobbying purpose and the amount expended for the nonlobbying purpose. An electing public charity that includes as a lobbying expenditure only the amount expended for the specific sentence or sentences that encourage the recipient to take action with respect to legislation has not made a reasonable allocation. For purposes of this paragraph, a communication is sent only or primarily to members if more than half of the recipients of the communication are members of the electing public charity making the communication within the meaning of § 56.4911–5. See § 56.4911–5 for separate rules on communications sent only or primarily to members. Nothing in this paragraph (a) shall change any allocation required by § 56.4911–5.

(3) Allocation of mixed lobbying. If a communication (to which § 56.4911–5 does not apply) is both a direct lobbying communication and a grass roots lobbying communication, the communication will be treated as a grass roots lobbying communication except to the extent that the electing public charity demonstrates that the communication was made primarily for direct lobbying purposes, in which case a reasonable allocation shall be made between the direct and the grass roots lobbying purposes served by the communication.

(b) Examples. The provisions of paragraph (a) of this section are illustrated by the following examples. Except where otherwise explicitly stated, the expenditure test election under section 501(h) is assumed to be in effect for all organizations discussed in the examples in this paragraph (b). See § 56.4911–5 for special rules applying to the member communications described in some of the following examples.

Example (1). Organization R makes the services of E, one of its paid executives, available to S, an organization described in section 501(c)(4) of the Code. E works for several weeks to assist S in developing materials that urge voters to contact their congressional representatives to indicate their support for specific legislation. In performing this work, E uses office space and clerical assistance provided by R. R pays full salary and benefits to E during this period and receives no reimbursement from S for these payments or for the other facilities and assistance provided. All expenditures of R, including allocable office and overhead expenses, that are attributable to this assignment are grass roots expenditures because E was engaged in an attempt to influence legislation.

Example (2). An organization distributes primarily to nonmembers a pamphlet with two articles on unrelated subjects. The total cost of preparing, printing and mailing the pamphlet is $11,000, $1,000 for preparation and $10,000 for printing and mailing. The cost of preparing one article, a nonlobbying communication, is $600. The article is printed on three of the four pages in the pamphlet. The cost of preparing the second article, a grassroots lobbying communication that addresses only one specific subject, is $400. This article is printed on one page of the four page pamphlet. In this situation, $400 of preparation costs and $2,500 (25% of $10,000) of printing and mailing costs are expenditures for a grass roots lobbying communication.

Example (3). Assume the same facts as in Example (2), except that the pamphlet is distributed only to members. In addition, assume the second article states that the recipient members should contact their congressional representatives. The organization allocates $400 of preparation costs and $2,500 of printing and mailing costs as expenditures for direct lobbying (see § 56.4911–5(c)). The allocation is reasonable for purposes of § 56.4911–3(a)(2)(ii).

Example (4). Organization J places a full-page advertisement in a newspaper. The advertisement urges passage of pending legislation to build three additional nuclear powered submarines, and states that readers should write their Congressional representatives in favor of the legislation. The advertisement also provides a general description of J's purposes and activities, invites readers to become members of J and asks readers to contribute money to J. Except for the cost of the portion of the advertisement describing J's purposes and activities and the portion specifically seeking members and contributions, the entire cost of the advertisement is an expenditure for a grass roots lobbying communication, because the entire advertisement, except for the lines specifically describing J and specifically seeking members and contributions, is on the same specific subject as the grass roots lobbying message.

Example (5). Assume the same facts as in Example (4), except that J places in the newspaper two separate half-page advertisements instead of one full-page advertisement. One of the two advertisements discusses the need for three additional nuclear powered submarines and urges readers to write their Congressional representatives in favor of the pending legislation to build the three submarines. The other advertisement contains only the membership and fundraising appeals, along with a general description of J's purposes and activities. The half-page advertisement urging readers to write to Congress is a grass roots lobbying communication and all of J's expenditures for producing and placing that advertisement are expenditures for a grass roots lobbying communication. J's expenditures for the other half-page advertisement are not expenditures for a grass roots or direct lobbying communication.

Example (6). Assume the same facts as in Example (4), except that the communication by J is in a letter mailed only to members of J, rather than in newspaper advertisement, and the invitation to become a member of J is an invitation to join a new membership category. In addition, assume that the communication states that the member recipients should ask nonmembers to write their Congressional representatives. J allocates one-half of the cost of the mailing as an expenditure for a grass roots lobbying communication (see § 56.4911–5(d)). Because the communication had both bona fide nonlobbying (e.g., membership solicitation and fundraising) purposes as well as lobbying purposes, J's allocation of one-half of the cost of the communication to grass roots lobbying and one-half to nonlobbying is reasonable for purposes of § 56.4911–3(a)(2)(ii).

Example (7). A particular monthly issue of organization X's newsletter, which is distributed mainly to nonmembers of X, has three articles of equal length. The first article is a grass roots lobbying communication, the sole specific subject of which is pending legislation to help protect seals from being slaughtered in certain foreign countries. The second article discusses the rapid decline in the world's whale population, particularly because of the illegal hunting of whales by foreign countries. The third article deals with air pollution and the acid rain problem in North America. Because the first article is a grass roots lobbying communication, all of the costs allocable to that article (e.g., one-third of the newsletter's printing and mailing costs) are lobbying expenditures. The second article is not a lobbying communication and the pending legislation relating to seals addressed in the first article does not affect the illegal whale hunting activities. Because the second and third articles are not lobbying communications and are also not on the same specific subject as the first article, no portion of the costs attributable to those articles is a grass roots lobbying expenditure.

Example (8). Organization T, a nonmembership organization, prepares a three page document that is mailed to 3,000 persons on T's mailing list. The first two pages of the three page document, titled "The Need for Child Care," support the need for additional child care programs, and include statistics on the number of children living in homes where both parents work or in homes with a single parent. The two pages also make note of the inadequacy of the number of day care providers to meet the needs of these parents. The third page of the document, titled "H.R. 1," indicates T's support of H.R. 1, a bill pending in the U.S. House of Representatives. The document states that H.R. 1 will provide for $10,000,000 in additional subsidies to child care providers, primarily for those providers caring for lower income children. The third page of the document also notes that H.R. 1 includes new federal standards regulating the quality of child care providers. The document ends with T's request that recipients contact their congressional representative in support of H.R. 1. The entire three page document is on the same specific subject, and, therefore, all expenditures of preparing and distributing the three page document are grass roots lobbying expenditures.

Example (9). Assume the same facts as in Example (8), except that the document has a fourth page. The fourth page does not refer to the general need for child care or the specific need for additional child care providers. Instead, the fourth page advocates that a particular federal agency commence, under its existing statutory authority, licensing of day care providers in order to promote safe and effective child care. The cost of the fourth page is not a lobbying expenditure.

Example (10). Assume the same facts as in Example (8), except that T is a membership organization, 75 percent of the recipients of the three page document are members of T, and 25 percent of the recipients are nonmembers and are not subscribers within the meaning of § 56.4911–5(f)(5). Assume also that the document states that readers should write to Congress, but does not state that the readers should urge nonmembers to write to Congress. T treats the document as having a bona fide nonlobbying purpose, the purpose of educating its members about the need for child care. Accordingly, T allocates one-half of the cost of preparing and distributing the document as a lobbying expenditure (see § 56.4911–5(e)(2)(i)), of which 75 percent is a direct lobbying expenditure (see § 56.4911–5(e)(2)(iii)) and 25 percent is a grass roots lobbying expenditure (see § 56.4911–5(e)(2)(ii)). The remaining one-half is allocated as a nonlobbying expenditure. T's allocation is reasonable for purposes of § 56.4911–3(a)(2)(ii) and is correct for purposes of § 56.4911–5(e).

Example (11). Assume the same facts as in Example (10), except that T allocates one percent of the cost of preparing and distributing the document as a lobbying expenditure (for purposes of § 56.4911–5(e)(2)) and 99 percent as a nonlobbying expenditure. T's allocation is based upon the fact that out of 200 lines in the document, only two lines state that the recipient should contact legislators about the pending legislation. T's allocation is unreasonable for purposes of § 56.4911–3(a)(2)(ii).

Example (12). Organization F, a nonmembership organization, sends a one page letter to all persons on its mailing list. The only subject of the letter is the organization's opposition to a pending bill allowing private uses of certain national parks. The letter requests recipients to send letters opposing the bill to their congressional representatives. A second one page letter is sent in the same envelope. The second letter discusses the broad educational activities and publications of the organization in all areas of environmental protection and ends by requesting the recipient to make a financial contribution to organization F. Since the separate second letter is on a different subject from the lobbying letter, and the letters are of equal length, 50 percent of the mailing costs must be allocated as an expenditure for a grass roots lobbying communication.

Example (13). Assume the same facts as in Example (12), except that F is a membership organization and the letters in question are sent primarily (90 percent) to members. The other 10 percent of the recipients are nonmembers and are not subscribers within the meaning of § 56.4911–5(f)(5). Assume also that the first letter does not state that readers should urge nonmembers to write to legislators. F allocates one-half of the mailing costs as a lobbying expenditure, of which 90 percent is a direct lobbying expenditure and 10 percent is a grass roots lobbying expenditure (see § 56.4911–5(e)(2)). F's allocation is reasonable for purposes of § 56.4911–3(a)(2)(ii) and is correct for purposes of § 56.4911–5.

(c) Certain transfers treated as lobbying expenditures—(1) Transfer earmarked for grass roots purposes. A transfer is a grass roots expenditure to the extent that it is earmarked (as defined in § 56.4911–4(f)(4)) for grass roots lobbying purposes and is not described in § 56.4911–4(e).

(2) Transfer earmarked for direct and grass roots lobbying. A transfer that is earmarked for direct lobbying purposes or for direct lobbying and grass roots lobbying purposes is treated as a grass roots expenditure in full except to the extent the transferor demonstrates that all or part of the amounts transferred were expended for direct lobbying purposes, in which case that part of the amounts transferred is a direct lobbying expenditure by the transferor. This paragraph (c)(2) shall not apply to any expenditure described in § 56.4911–4(e).

(3) Certain transfers to noncharities that lobby—(i) Limited application of paragraph (c)(3)—(A) In general. This paragraph (c)(3) applies only to transfers for less than fair market value from an electing public charity to any noncharity that makes lobbying expenditures. A noncharity is any entity that is not described in section 501(c)(3). In order for this paragraph to apply, the electing public charity must transfer to a noncharity more in value than it receives in return. For example, this paragraph does not apply to an electing public charity's fair market value payment of rent to a landlord. However, this paragraph does apply where an electing public charity and a noncharity share office space and the electing public charity pays more than fair market value rent to the noncharity. Similarly, this paragraph applies where an electing public charity sells goods or services to a noncharity for less than fair market value. See paragraphs (c)(3)(i)(B), (C) and (D) of this section for exceptions where non-fair market value transfers are not covered by this paragraph (c)(3). See paragraph (c)(3)(i)(E) of this section to determine the amount of any non-fair market value transfer covered by this paragraph (c)(3). See paragraph (c)(3)(ii) of this section for the rules that apply to transfers governed by this paragraph (c)(3).

(B) Exception for controlled grants. Notwithstanding paragraph (c)(3)(i)(A) of this section, this paragraph (c)(3) does not apply where an electing public charity makes a grant to a noncharity that is a controlled grant (as defined in § 56.4911–4(f)(3)).

(C) Exception for transfers that artificially inflate exempt purpose expenditures. Notwithstanding paragraph (c)(3)(i)(A) of this section, this paragraph (c)(3) does not apply where an electing public charity makes a grant to a noncharity that is an expenditure described in § 56.4911–4(e) (relating to grants that artificially inflate exempt purpose expenditures).

(D) Exception for substantially related activity. Notwithstanding paragraph (c)(3)(i)(A) of this section, this paragraph (c)(3) does not apply where an electing public charity, in the course of an activity that is substantially related to the accomplishment of the electing public charity's exempt purposes, makes goods or services widely available for less than fair market value to individual members of the general public and those goods or services are actually purchased (or consumed for no charge) by a substantial number of wholly unrelated individual members of the general public for less than fair market value. For purposes of the preceding sentence, the term "individual member of the general public" does not include any person or entity directly or indirectly affiliated with the electing public charity in question. The following example illustrates this paragraph (c)(3)(i)(D):

Example. Organization P is an educational organization dedicated to preserving the environment. One of P's activities is educating the public about the benefits of installing cost-effective passive solar energy systems, thereby helping to preserve the environment. P charges for its extensive literature and advice, but the charges are less than the fair market value of the literature and advice. P makes its literature and advice widely available to individual members of the general public by advertising in various media and by pamphlets distributed in various areas. P annually provides its literature and advice for less than fair market value to 500 wholly unrelated families, businesses, and tax-exempt organizations. Several of the businesses and tax-exempt organizations make lobbying expenditures within the meaning of section 4911. P's provision of its goods and services to these entities is not covered by this paragraph (c)(3) (and thus does not give rise to a lobbying expenditure by P under paragraph (c)(3)(ii)).

(E) Determination of amount of transfer governed by paragraph (c)(3). Where an electing public charity receives nothing of value in return for its transfer, the amount of the transfer governed by this paragraph (c)(3) is the greater of the fair market value or the cost of the goods or services transferred to the noncharity. Where the noncharity transfers something of value to the electing public charity in return for the charity's transfer, but that payment is less than the fair market value of the charity's transfer to the noncharity, the amount of the transfer governed by this paragraph (c)(3) is the excess of: first, the greater of the fair market value or cost of the goods or services transferred to the noncharity over, second, the value of the amount transferred to the charity. For example, if an electing public charity transfers $10,000 of goods and services to a noncharity that makes lobbying expenditures in return for payment by the noncharity of $2,000, the amount of the transfer governed by this paragraph (c)(3) is $8,000.

(ii) Rules governing transfers to which paragraph (c)(3) applies. A transfer to which this paragraph (c)(3) applies is treated in whole or in part as a grass roots and/or direct lobbying expenditure by the transferor in accordance with paragraphs (c)(3)(ii)(A), (B) and (C) of this section. In applying those paragraphs, the expenditures of the transferee will be determined as if the regulations under section 4911 applied to the transferee. This paragraph (c)(3) discusses only when certain transfers are lobbying expenditures by the transferor. This paragraph does not address other issues that may arise when an electing public charity makes a noncontrolled grant to a noncharity. Nothing in this paragraph (c)(3) shall be used to interpret issues relating to noncontrolled grants by charities to noncharities, such as whether the noncontrolled grant is consistent with the continued tax-exempt status of the electing public charity.

(A) Transfers treated as grass roots expenditures. The transfer is treated as a grass roots expenditure to the extent of the lesser of two amounts: The amount of the transfer and the amount of the transferee's grass roots expenditures.

(B) Transfers treated as direct lobbying expenditures. If the transfer is greater than the transferee's grass roots expenditures, the excess is treated as a direct lobbying expenditure, but only to the extent of the transferee's direct lobbying expenditures. (If, however, the transfer is less than the transferee's grass roots expenditures, none of the transfer is a direct lobbying expenditure.)

(C) Transfers treated as nonlobbying. If the transfer is greater than the sum of the transferee's grass roots and direct lobbying expenditures, the excess of the transfer over those lobbying expenses is not a lobbying expenditure.

(iii) Example. The following example illustrates the application of this paragraph (c)(3):

Example. Organization C, an electing public charity, shares employee E with N, a noncharity that makes lobbying expenditures. N's grass roots expenditures are $5,000 and its direct lobbying expenditures are $25,000. Each organization pays one-half of the $100,000 in direct and overhead costs associated with E. E devotes one-quarter of his time to C and three-quarters of his time to N. In substance, this arrangement is a transfer (for less than fair market value) from C to N in the amount of $25,000 (one-quarter of the $100,000 of direct and overhead costs associated with E's work). Accordingly, C is treated as having made a $5,000 grass roots expenditure (the lesser of N's grass roots expenditures ($5,000) or the amount of the transfer ($25,000)). C is also treated as having made a $20,000 direct lobbying expenditure (the lesser of N's direct lobbying expenditures ($25,000) or the remaining amount of the transfer ($20,000)).

§ 56.4911–4. Exempt purpose expenditures.

(a) Application. This section provides rules under section 4911(e) for determining an electing public charity's "exempt purpose expenditures" for a taxable year for purposes of section 4911(c)(2) and § 56.4911–1(c)(2). Those two sections generally define an electing public charity's lobbying limit (lobbying nontaxable amount) as a sliding scale percentage of the organization's exempt purpose expenditures. In determining an electing public charity's exempt purpose expenditures, no expenditure shall be counted twice by an organization.

(b) Included expenditures. Amounts paid or incurred by an organization that are exempt purpose expenditures include—

(1) Amounts paid or incurred to accomplish a purpose enumerated in section 170(c)(2)(B), including (but not limited to) the amount of any transfer made by the organization (other than a transfer described in paragraph (e) of this section) to another organization to accomplish the transferor's exempt purposes, and including amounts expended by an organization out of transfers (other than a transfer described in paragraph (e) of this section) for which the organization is the transferee,

(2) Amounts paid or incurred as current or deferred compensation for an employee's services for a purpose enumerated in section 170(c)(2)(B),

(3) The allocable portion of administrative overhead, and other general expenditures attributable to the accomplishment of a purpose enumerated in section 170(c)(2)(B),

(4) Lobbying expenditures (as defined in § 56.4911–2(a)) whether or not for a purpose enumerated in section 170(c)(2)(B),

(5) Amounts paid or incurred for activities described in § 56.4911–2(c),

(6) Amounts paid or incurred for activities described in § 56.4811–5 that are not lobbying expenditures,

(7) A reasonable allowance for exhaustion, wear and tear, obsolescence or amortization, of assets to the extent used for one or more of the purposes described in paragraphs (b)(1) through (6) of this section, computed on a straight-line basis (for this purpose, an allowance for depreciation will be treated as reasonable if based on a useful life that would satisfy section 321(k)(3)(A) as in effect on January 1, 1985), and

(8) Fundraising expenditures (but see section 4911(e)(1)(C) and paragraphs (c)(3) and (4) of this section.)

(c) Excluded expenditures. Notwithstanding paragraph (b) of this section, exempt purpose expenditures do not include—

(1) Amounts paid or incurred that are neither expenditures to accomplish a purpose enumerated in section 170(c)(2)(B), lobbying expenditures (as defined in § 56.4911–2(a)), nor expenditures described in paragraph (b)(5), (6) or (8) of this section,

(2) The amounts of any transfer described in paragraph (e) of this section,

(3) Amounts paid to or incurred for a separate fundraising unit (as defined in paragraph (f)(2) of this section) of an organization or of an affiliated organization (see § 56.4911–7(a)),

(4) Amounts paid to or incurred for any person not an employee, or any organization not an affiliated organization, if paid or incurred primarily for fundraising, but only if such person or organization engages in fundraising, fundraising counselling or the provision of similar advice or services,

(5) Amounts paid or incurred that are properly chargeable to a capital account, determined in accordance with the principles that apply under section 263 or, as applicable, section 263A, with respect to an unrelated trade or business,

(6) Amounts paid or incurred for a tax that is not imposed in connection with the organization's efforts to accomplish a purpose described in section 170(c)(2)(B), such as taxes imposed under sections 511(a)(1) and 4911(a), and

(7) Amounts paid or incurred for the production of income. For purposes of this section, amounts are paid or incurred for the production of income if they are paid or incurred for a purpose or activity that is not substantially related (aside from the need of the organization for income or funds or the use it makes of the profits derived) to the exercise or performance by the organization of its charitable, educational or other purpose or function constituting the basis for its exemption under section 501. For example, the costs of managing an endowment are amounts that are paid or incurred for the production of income and are thus not exempt purpose expenditures. Fundraising expenditures are not, for purposes of this section, amounts that are paid or incurred for the production of income. Instead, the determination of whether fundraising costs are exempt purpose expenditures must be made with reference to section 4911(e)(1)(C) and paragraphs (b)(8), (c)(3) and (c)(4) of this section.

(d) Certain transfers treated as exempt purpose expenditures—(1) An organization's transfer will be treated as an exempt purpose expenditure under paragraph (b)(1) of this section if it is—

(i) Described in either paragraph (d)(2) or (d)(3) of this section, and

(ii) Not described in paragraph (e) of this section.

(2) A transfer is described in this paragraph (d)(2) if it is made to an organization described in section 501(c)(3) in furtherance of the transferor's exempt purposes and is not earmarked for any purpose other than a purpose described in section 170(c)(2)(B). Thus, a payment of dues by a local or state organization to, respectively, a state or national organization that is described in section 501(c)(3) is considered an exempt purpose expenditure of the transferor to the extent it is not otherwise earmarked.

(3) A transfer is described in this paragraph (d)(3) if it is a controlled grant (as defined in paragraph (f)(3) of this section), but only to the extent of the amounts that are paid or incurred by the transferee that would be exempt purpose expenditures if paid or incurred by the transferor.

(e) Transfers not exempt purpose expenditures—(1) An organization's transfer is described in this paragraph (e) if it is described in one of paragraphs (e)(2) through (e)(4).

(2) A transfer is described in this paragraph (e)(2) if it is made to a member of any affiliated group (as defined in § 56.4911–7(e)) of which the transferor is a member.

(3) A transfer is described in this paragraph (e)(3) if the Commissioner determines that the transfer artificially inflates the amount of the transferor's or transferee's exempt purpose expenditures. In general, the Commissioner will make that determination if a substantial purpose of a transfer is to inflate those exempt purpose expenditures. A transfer described in this paragraph will not be considered an exempt purpose expenditure of the transferor, but will be an exempt purpose expenditure of the transferee to the extent that the transferee expends the transfer in the active conduct of its charitable activities or attempts to influence legislation. Standards similar to those found in § 53.4942(b)–1(b) may be applied in determining whether the transferee has expended amounts in the "active conduct" of its charitable activities or attempts to influence legislation.

(4) A transfer is described in this paragraph (e)(4) if it is not a controlled grant and is made to an organization not described in section 501(c)(3) that does not attempt to influence legislation.

(f) Definitions—(1) For purposes of paragraph (c) of this section, "fundraising" includes—

(i) Soliciting dues or contributions from members of the organization, from persons whose dues are in arrears, or from the general public,

(ii) Soliciting grants from businesses or other organizations, including organizations described in section 501(c)(3), or

(iii) Soliciting grants from a governmental unit referred to in section 170(c)(1), or any agency or instrumentality thereof.

(2) For purposes of paragraph (c) of this section, a separate fundraising unit of any organization must consist of either two or more individuals a majority of whose time is spent on fundraising for the organization, or any separate accounting unit of the organization that is devoted to fundraising. For purposes of paragraph (c) of this section, amounts paid to or incurred for a separate fundraising unit include all amounts incurred for the creation, production, copying, and distribution of the fundraising portion of a separate fundraising unit's communication. (For example, an electing public charity that has a separate fundraising unit may not count the cost of postage for a separate fundraising unit's communication as an exempt purpose expenditure even though, under the electing public charity's accounting system, that cost is attributable to the mailroom rather than to the separate fundraising unit.)

(3) For purposes of this section, a "controlled grant" is a grant made by an eligible organization described in § 1.501(h)–2(b) to an organization not described in section 501(c)(3) that meets the following requirements: (i) The donor limits the grant to a specific project of the recipient that is in furtherance of the donor's (nonlobbying) exempt purposes; and (ii) The donor maintains records to establish that the grant is used in furtherance of the donor's (nonlobbying) exempt purposes.

(4) A transfer, including a grant or payment of dues, is "earmarked" for a specific purpose—

(i) To the extent that the transferor directs the transferee to add the amount transferred to a fund established to accomplish the purpose, or

(ii) To the extent of the amount transferred or, if less, the amount agreed upon to the expended to accomplish the purpose, if there exists an agreement, oral or written, whereby the transferor may cause the transferee to expend amounts to accomplish the purpose or whereby the transferee agrees to expend an amount to accomplish the purpose.

(g) Example. The provisions of this section are illustrated by the following example:

Example. Organization X is an exempt organization described in section 501(c)(3) that is organized for the purpose of rehabilitating alcoholics. X elected to be subject to the provisions of section 501(h) in 1981. For 1981, X had the following expenditures that are included in its exempt purpose expenditures to the extent indicated.

Description	Total	Includible
Cost of real estate purchased for use as half-way house for alcoholics, attributable to the following:		
Land	30,000	$ - 0 -
Building	200,000	- 0 -
Depreciation 40-year useful life	- 0 -	5,000
Expenses of operating half-way house	170,000	170,000

Administrative expenses of the organization allocated to the operation of its half-way house	95,000	95,000
Depreciation and allowances for equipment	10,000	10,000
Expenses related to attempts to influence legislation (lobbying expenditures)	40,000	40,000
Amounts paid to Z by the Organization for fundraising	35,000	- 0 -
Total	$580,000	$320,000

Note: For 1981, X's exempt purpose expenditures total $320,000. The $35,000 paid by X to Z for fundraising is not included in the exempt purpose expenditures total. All lobbying expenses are included in full. Only depreciation computed on a straight-line basis is included in exempt purpose expenditures.

§ 56.4911–5. Communications with members.

(a) In general. For purposes of section 4911, expenditures for certain communications between an organization and its members ("membership communications") are treated more leniently than are communications to nonmembers. This § 56.4911–5 contains rules about the more lenient treatment. In certain cases, this section provides that expenditures for a membership communication are not lobbying expenditures even though those expenditures would be lobbying expenditures if the communication were to nonmembers. In other cases, this section provides that expenditures for a membership communication are direct lobbying expenditures even though those expenditures would be grass roots expenditures if the communication were to nonmembers. Paragraphs (b), (c) and (d) of this section set forth the more lenient rules that apply for communications that are directed only to members. Paragraph (e) of this section sets forth the more lenient rules that apply for communications that are directed primarily, but not solely, to members. Paragraph (f) of this section sets forth certain definitions and special rules.

(b) Communications (directed only to members) that are not lobbying communications. Expenditures for a communication that refers to, and reflects a view on, specific legislation are not lobbying expenditures if the communication satisfies the following requirements:

(1) The communication is directed only to members of the organization;

(2) The specific legislation the communication refers to, and reflects a view on, is of direct interest to the organization and its members;

(3) The communication does not directly encourage the member to engage in direct lobbying (whether individually or through the organization); and

(4) The communication does not directly encourage the member to engage in grass roots lobbying (whether individually or through the organization).

(c) Communications (directed only to members) that are direct lobbying communications. Expenditures for a communication that refers to, and reflects a view on, specific legislation and that satisfies the requirements of paragraphs (b)(1), (b)(2), and (b)(4) of this section, but does not satisfy the requirements of paragraph (b)(3) of this section, are treated as expenditures for direct lobbying.

(d) Communications (directed only to members) that are grass roots lobbying communications. Expenditures for a communication that refers to, and reflects a view on, specific legislation and that satisfies the requirements of paragraphs (b)(1) and (b)(2) of this section, but does not satisfy the requirements of paragraph (b)(4) of this section, are treated as grass roots expenditures (whether or not the communication satisfies the requirements of paragraph (b)(3) of this section).

(e) Written communications directed to members and nonmembers—(1) In general. Expenditures for any written communication that is designed primarily for members of an organization (but not directed only to members) and that refers to, and reflects a view on, specific legislation of direct interest to the organization and its members, are treated as expenditures for direct or grass roots lobbying in accordance with paragraph (e)(2), (e)(3) or (e)(4) of this section. For purposes of this section, a communication is designed primarily for members of an organization if more than half of the recipients of the communication are members of the organization.

(2) Direct lobbying directly encouraged—(i) Lobbying expenditure amount. If a written communication described in paragraph (e)(1) of this section directly encourages readers to engage individually or through the organization in direct lobbying but does not directly encourage them to engage in grass roots lobbying, the cost of the communication is allocated between expenditures for direct lobbying and grass roots expenditures in accordance with paragraphs (e)(2)(ii) and (iii) of this section. The portion of the cost to be allocated includes all costs of preparing all the material with respect to which readers are urged to engage in direct lobbying plus the mechanical and distribution costs attributable to the lineage devoted to this material (see § 1.512(a)–1(f)(6)).

(ii) Grass roots amount. The amount allocable as a grass roots expenditure for a communication described in paragraph (e)(1) of this section is the amount calculated in paragraph (e)(2)(i) of this section multiplied by the sum of the nonmember subscribers percentage and all the other distribution percentage, both as defined in paragraph (f)(7) of this section. Solely for purposes of the allocation described in this paragraph (e)(2)(ii), the nonmember subscribers percentage is treated as zero unless it is greater than 15% of total distribution.

(iii) Direct lobbying amount. The amount allocable as an expenditure for direct lobbying for a communication described in paragraph (e)(1) of this section is the excess of the amount described in paragraph (e)(2)(i) of this section over the amount described in paragraph (e)(2)(ii) of this section.

(3) Grass roots expenditure if grass roots lobbying directly encouraged. If a written communication described in paragraph (e)(1) of this section directly encourages readers to engage individually or collectively (whether through the organization or otherwise) in grass roots lobbying (whether or not it also encourages readers to engage in direct lobbying), the grass roots expenditure includes all the costs of preparing all the material with respect to which readers are urged to engage in grass roots lobbying plus the mechanical and distribution costs attributable to the lineage devoted to this material (see § 1.512(a)–1(f)(6)).

(4) No direct encouragement of direct lobbying or of grass roots lobbying. If a written communication described in paragraph (e)(1) of this section does not directly encourage readers to engage in either direct lobbying or grass roots lobbying, expenditures for the communication are not lobbying expenditures.

(f) Definitions and special rules. For purposes of the regulations under section 4911—

(1) Member; general rule. A person is a member of an electing public charity if the person—

(i) Pays dues or makes a contribution of more than a nominal amount,

(ii) Makes a contribution of more than a nominal amount of time, or

(iii) Is one of a limited number of "honorary" or "life" members who have more than a nominal connection with the electing public charity and who have been chosen for a valid reason (such as length of service to the organization or involvement in activities forming the basis of the electing public charity's exemption) unrelated to the electing public charity's dissemination of information to its members.

(2) Member; special rule. A person not a member of an electing public charity within the meaning of paragraph (f)(1) of this section may be treated as a member if the electing public charity demonstrates to the satisfaction of the Internal Revenue Service that there is a good reason for its membership requirements not meeting the requirements of such paragraph (f)(1), and that its membership requirements do not operate to permit an abuse of the rules described in this section.

(3) Member; affiliated group of organizations. For purposes of this section, a person who is a member of an organization that is a member of an affiliated group of organizations (within the meaning of § 56.4911–7(e)) is treated as a member of each organization in the affiliated group.

(4) Member; limited affiliated group of organizations. For purposes of this section, a person who is a member of an organization that is a member of a limited affiliated group of organizations (within the meaning of § 56.4911–10(b)) is treated as a member of each organization in the limited affiliated group, but only to the extent that the communication relates to a national legislative issue (within the meaning of § 56.4911–10(g)).

(5) Subscriber. A person is a subscriber to a written communication if—

(i) The person is a member of the publishing organization and the membership dues expressly include the right to receive the written communication, or

(ii) The person has affirmatively expressed a desire to receive the written communication and has paid more than a nominal amount of the communication.

(6) Directly encourages—(i) Direct lobbying—(A) In general. For purposes of this section, a communication directly encourages a recipient to engage in direct lobbying, whether individually or through the organization, if the communication:

(1) States that the recipient should contact a legislator or an employee of a legislative body, or should contact any other government official or employee who may participate in the formulation of legislation (but only if the principal purpose of urging contact with the government official or employee is to influence legislation);

(2) States the address, telephone number, or similar information of a legislator or an employee of a legislative body; or

(3) Provides a petition, tear-off postcard or similar material for the recipient to communicate his or her views to a legislator or an employee of a legislative body, or to any other government official or employee who

may participate in the formulation of legislation (but only if the principal purpose of so facilitating contact with the government official or employee is to influence legislation).

(B) "Self-defense" exception for communications with members. Notwithstanding the provisions of paragraph (f)(6)(i)(A) of this section, for purposes of paragraphs (b)(3), (e)(2)(i), (e)(3) and (e)(4) of this section, a communication that directly encourages a member to engage in direct lobbying activities that are described in section 4911(d)(2)(C) and that would not be attempts to influence legislation if engaged in directly by the organization is treated as a communication that does not directly encourage a member to engage in direct lobbying.

(ii) Grass roots lobbying. For purposes of paragraphs (b)(4), (e)(3) and (e)(4) of this section, a communication directly encourages recipients to engage individually or collectively (whether through the organization or otherwise) in grass roots lobbying if the communication:

(A) States that the recipient should encourage any nonmember to contact a legislator or an employee of a legislative body, or to contact any other government official or employee who may participate in the formulation of legislation (but only if the principal purpose of urging contact with the government official or employee is to influence legislation);

(B) States that the recipient should provide to any nonmember the address, telephone number, or similar information of a legislator or an employee of a legislative body; or

(C) Provides (or requests that the recipient provide to nonmembers) a petition, tear-off postcard or similar material for the recipient (or nonmember) to use to ask any nonmember to communicate views to a legislator or an employee of a legislative body, or to any other government official or employee who may participate in the formulation of legislation, but only if the principal purpose of so facilitating contact with the government official or employee is to influence legislation. For purposes of this paragraph (f)(6)(ii)(C), a petition is provided for the recipient to use to ask any nonmember to communicate views if, for example, the petition has an entire page of preprinted signature blocks. Similarly, for purposes of this paragraph (f)(6)(ii)(C), where a communication is distributed to a single member and provides several tear-off postcards addressed to a legislator, the postcards are presumed to be provided for the member to use to ask a nonmember to communicate with the legislator.

(7) Percentages of total distribution. With respect to a communication described in paragraph (e)(1) of this section—

(i) "Member percentage" means the percentage of total distribution that represents distribution of a single copy to any member;

(ii) "Nonmember subscribers percentage" means the percentage of total distribution that represents distribution to nonmember subscribers (including libraries); and

(iii) "All other distribution percentage" means 100% reduced by the sum of the member percentage and the nonmember subscribers percentage.

(8) Reasonable allocation rule. In the case of lobbying expenditures for a communication that also has a bona fide nonlobbying purpose and that is sent only or primarily to members, an electing public charity must make a reasonable allocation between the amount expended for the lobbying purpose and the amount expended for the nonlobbying purpose. See § 56.4911–3(a)(2)(ii).

§ 56.4911–6. Records of lobbying and grass roots expenditures.

(a) Records of lobbying expenditures. An electing public charity must keep a record of its lobbying expenditures for the taxable year. Lobbying expenditures of which an organization must keep a record include the following:

(1) Expenditures for grass roots lobbying, as described in paragraph (b) of this section;

(2) Amounts directly paid or incurred for direct lobbying, including payments to another organization earmarked for direct lobbying, fees and expenses paid to individuals or organizations for direct lobbying, and printing, mailing, and other direct costs of reproducing and distributing materials used in direct lobbying;

(3) The portion of amounts paid or incurred as current or deferred compensation for an employee's services for direct lobbying;

(4) Amounts paid for out-of-pocket expenditures incurred on behalf of the organization and for direct lobbying, whether or not incurred by an employee;

(5) The allocable portion of administrative, overhead, and other general expenditures attributable to direct lobbying;

(6) Expenditures for publications or for communications with members to the extent the expenditures are treated as expenditures for direct lobbying under § 56.4911–5; and

(7) Expenditures for direct lobbying of a controlled organization (within the meaning of § 56.4911–10(c)) to the extent included by a controlling organization (within the meaning of § 56.4911–10(c)) in its lobbying expenditures.

(b) Records of grass roots expenditures. An electing public charity must keep a record of its grass roots expenditures for the taxable year. Grass roots expenditures of which an organization must keep a record include the following:

(1) Amounts directly paid or incurred for grass roots lobbying, including payments to other organizations earmarked for grass roots lobbying, fees and expenses paid to individuals or organizations for grass roots lobbying, and the printing, mailing, and other direct costs of reproducing and distributing materials used in grass roots lobbying;

(2) The portion of amounts paid or incurred as current or deferred compensation for an employee's services for grass roots lobbying;

(3) Amounts paid for out-of-pocket expenditures incurred on behalf of the organization and for grass roots lobbying, whether or not incurred by an employee;

(4) The allocable portion of administrative, overhead and other general expenditures attributable to grass roots lobbying;

(5) Expenditures for publication or communications that are treated as expenditures for grass roots lobbying under § 56.4911–5; and

(6) Expenditures for grass roots lobbying of a controlled organization (within the meaning of § 56.4911–10(c)) to the extent included by a controlling organization (within the meaning of § 56.4911–10(c)) in its grass roots expenditures.

§ 56.4911–7. Affiliated group of organizations.

(a) Affiliation between two organizations. Sections 4911(f)(1) through (3) contain a limited anti-abuse rule for groups of affiliated organizations. In general, the rule operates to prevent numerous organizations from being created for the purpose of avoiding the sliding-scale percentage limitation on an electing public charity's lobbying expenditures (as well as avoiding the $1,000,000 cap on a single electing public charity's lobbying expenditures). This is generally accomplished by treating the members of an affiliated group as a single organization for purposes of measuring both lobbying expenditures and permitted lobbying expenditures. The anti-abuse rule is implemented by this § 56.4911–7 and § 56.4911–8 and 56.4911–9. This § 56.4911–7 defines the term "affiliated group of organizations" and defines the taxable year of an affiliated group of organizations. Section 56.4911–8 provides rules concerning the exempt purpose expenditures, lobbying expenditures and grass roots expenditures of an affiliated group of organizations, as well as rules concerning the application of the excise tax imposed by section 4911(a) on excess lobbying expenditures by the group. Section 56.4911–9 provides rules concerning the application of the section 501(h) lobbying expenditure limits to members of an affiliated group of organizations. (For additional rules for members of a limited affiliated group of organizations (generally, organizations that are affiliated solely by reason of governing instrument provisions that extend control solely with respect to national legislation), see section 4911(f)(4) and § 56.4911–10).

(1) In general. For purposes of the regulations under section 4911, two organizations are affiliated, subject to the limitation described in paragraph (a)(2) of this section, if one organization is able to control action on legislative issues by the other by reason of interlocking governing boards (see paragraph (b) of this section) or by reason of provisions of the governing instruments of the controlled organization (see paragraph (c) of this section). The ability of the controlling organization to control action on legislative issues by the controlled organization is sufficient to establish that the organizations are affiliated; it is not necessary that the control be exercised.

(2) Organizations not described in section 501(c)(3). Two organizations, neither of which is described in section 501(c)(3), are affiliated only if there exists at least one organization described in section 501(c)(3) that is affiliated with both organizations.

(3) Action on legislative issues. For purposes of this section, the term "action on legislative issues" includes taking a position in the organization's name on legislation, authorizing any person to take a position in the organization's name on legislation, or authorizing any lobbying expenditures. The phrase does not include actions taken merely to correct unauthorized actions taken in the organization's name.

(b) Interlocking governing boards—(1) In general. Two organizations have interlocking governing boards if one organization (the controlling organization) has a sufficient number of representatives (within the meaning of paragraph (b)(5) of this section) on the governing board of the second organization (the controlled organization) so that by aggregating their votes, the representatives of the controlling organization can cause or prevent action on legislative issues by the controlled organization. If two organizations have interlocking governing boards, the organizations are affiliated without regard to how or whether the representatives of the controlling organization vote on any particular matter.

* * *

PRIVATE FOUNDATION EXCISE TAXES

§ 53.4940–1. Excise tax on net investment income.

(a) In general. For taxable years beginning after September 30, 1977, section 4940 imposes an excise tax of 2 percent [1.29 percent, effective for taxable years beginning after December 20, 2019. Eds.] of the net investment income (as defined in section 4940(c) and paragraph (c) of this section) of a tax-exempt private foundation (as defined in section 509). * * * The tax imposed by section 4940(b) and this section is to be paid annually at the time the organization is required to pay its income taxes imposed under subtitle A. Except as otherwise provided herein, no exclusions or deductions from gross investment income or credits against tax are allowable under this section.

* * *

(c) Net investment income defined—(1) In general. For purposes of section 4940(a), net investment income of a private foundation is the amount by which:

(i) The sum of the gross investment income (as defined in section 4940(c)(2) and paragraph (d) of this section) and the capital gain net income (net capital gain for taxable years beginning before January 1, 1977) (within the meaning of section 4940(c)(4) and paragraph (f) of this section) exceeds

(ii) The deductions allowed by section 4940(c)(3) and paragraph (e) of this section.

Except to the extent inconsistent with the provisions of this section, net investment income shall be determined under the principles of Subtitle A.

(2) Tax-exempt income. For purposes of computing net investment income under section 4940, the provisions of section 103 (relating to interest on certain governmental obligations) and section 265 (relating to expenses and interest relating to tax-exempt income) and the regulations thereunder shall apply.

(d) Gross investment income—(1) In general. For purposes of paragraph (c) of this section, "gross investment income" means the gross amounts of income from interest, dividends, rents, and royalties (including overriding royalties) received by a private foundation from all sources, but does not include such income to the extent included in computing the tax imposed by section 511. Under this definition, interest, dividends, rents, and royalties derived from assets devoted to charitable activities are includible in gross investment income. Therefore, for example, interest received on a student loan would be includible in the gross investment income of a private foundation making such loan. For purposes of paragraph (c) of this section, gross investment income also includes the items of investment income described in § 1.512(b)–1(a).

* * *

(e) Deductions—(1) In general. (i) For purposes of computing net investment income, there shall be allowed as a deduction from gross investment income all the ordinary and necessary expenses paid or incurred for the production or collection of gross investment income or for the management, conservation, or maintenance of property held for the production of such income, determined with the modifications set forth in subparagraph (2) of this paragraph. Such expenses include that portion of a private foundation's operating expenses which is paid or incurred for the production or collection of gross investment income. Taxes paid or incurred under this section are not paid or incurred for the production or collection of gross investment income. A private foundation's operating expenses include compensation of officers, other salaries and wages of employees, outside professional fees, interest, and rent and taxes upon property used in the foundation's operations. Where a private foundation's officers or employees engage in activities on behalf of the foundation for both investment purposes and for exempt purposes, compensation and salaries paid to such officers or employees must be allocated between the investment activities and the exempt activities. To the extent a private foundation's expenses are taken into account in computing the tax imposed by section 511, they shall not be deductible for purposes of computing the tax imposed by section 4940.

(ii) Where only a portion of property produces, or is held for the production of, income subject to the section 4940 excise tax, and the remainder of the property is used for exempt purposes, the deductions allowed by section 4940(c)(3) shall be apportioned between the exempt and non-exempt uses.

(iii) No amount is allowable as a deduction under this section to the extent it is paid or incurred for purposes other than those described in subdivision (i) of this subparagraph. Thus, for example, the deductions prescribed by the following sections are not allowable: (1) The charitable deduction prescribed under section 170 and 642(c); (2) the net operating loss deduction prescribed under section 172; and (3) the special deductions prescribed under Part VIII, Subchapter B, Chapter 1.

(2) Deduction modifications. The following modifications shall be made in determining deductions otherwise allowable under this paragraph:

(i) The depreciation deduction shall be allowed, but only on the basis of the straight line method provided in section 167(b)(1).

(ii) The depletion deduction shall be allowed, but such deduction shall be determined without regard to section 613, relating to percentage depletion.

(iii) The basis to be used for purposes of the deduction allowed for depreciation or depletion shall be the basis determined under the rules of Part II of Subchapter O of Chapter 1, subject to the provisions of section 4940(c)(3)(B), and without regard to section 4940(c)(4)(B), relating to the basis for determining gain, or section 362(c). Thus, a private foundation must reduce the cost or other substituted or transferred basis by an amount equal to the straight line depreciation or cost depletion, without regard to whether the foundation deducted such depreciation or depletion during the period prior to its first taxable year beginning after December 31, 1969. However, where a private foundation has previously taken depreciation or depletion deductions in excess of the amount which would have been taken had the straight line or cost method been employed, such excess depreciation or depletion also shall be taken into account to reduce basis. If the facts necessary to determine the basis of property in the hands of the donor or the last preceding owner by whom it was not acquired by gift are unknown to a donee private foundation, then the original basis to such foundation of such property shall be determined under the rules of § 1.1015–1(a)(3).

(iv) The deduction for expenses paid or incurred in any taxable year for the production of gross investment income earned as an incident to a charitable function shall be no greater than the income earned from such function which is includible as gross investment income for such year. For example, where rental income is incidentally realized in 1971 from historic buildings held open to the public, deductions for amounts paid or incurred in 1971 for the production of such income shall be limited to the amount of rental income includible as gross investment income for 1971.

(f) Capital gain and losses—(1) General rule. In determining capital gain net income (net capital gain for taxable years beginning before January 1, 1977) for purposes of the tax imposed by section 4940, there shall be taken into account only capital gains and losses from the sale or other disposition of property held by a private foundation for investment purposes (other than program-related investments, as defined in section 4944(c)), and property used for the production of income included in computing the tax imposed by section 511 except to the extent gain or loss from the sale or other disposition of such property is taken into account for purposes of such tax. For taxable years beginning after December 31, 1972, property shall be treated as held for investment purposes even though such property is disposed of by the foundation immediately upon its receipt, if it is property of a type which generally produces interest, dividends, rents, royalties, or capital gains through appreciation (for example, rental real estate, stock, bonds, mineral interests, mortgages, and securities). Under this subparagraph, gains and losses from the sale or other disposition of property used for the exempt purposes of the private foundation are excluded. For example, gain or loss on the sale of the buildings used for the exempt activities of a private foundation would not be subject to the section 4940 tax. Where the foundation uses property for its exempt purposes, but also incidentally derives income from such property which is subject to the tax imposed by section 4940(a), any gain or loss resulting from the sale or other disposition of such property is not subject to the tax imposed by section 4940(a). For example, if a tax-exempt private foundation maintains buildings of a historical nature and keeps them open for public inspection, but requires a number of its employees to live in these buildings and charges the employees rent, the rent would be subject to the tax imposed by section 4940(a), but any gain or loss resulting from the sale of such property would not be subject to such tax. However, where the foundation uses property for both exempt purposes and (other than incidentally) for investment purposes (for example, a building in which the foundation's charitable and investment activities are carried on), that portion of any gain or loss from the sale or other disposition of such property which is allocable to the investment use of such property must be taken into account in computing capital gain net income (net capital gain for taxable years beginning before January 1, 1977) for such taxable year. For purposes of this paragraph, a distribution of property for purposes described in section 170(c)(1) or (2)(B) which is a qualifying distribution under section 4942 shall not be treated as a sale or other disposition of property.

(2) Basis. (i) The basis for purposes of determining gain from the sale or other disposition of property shall be the greater of:

(A) Fair market value on December 31, 1969, plus or minus all adjustments after December 31, 1969, and before the date of disposition under the rules of Part II of Subchapter O of Chapter 1, provided that the property was held by the private foundation on December 31, 1969, and continuously thereafter to the date of disposition, or

(B) Basis as determined under the rules of Part II of Subchapter O of Chapter 1,

subject to the provisions of section 4940(c)(3)(B) (and without regard to section 362(c)).

(ii) For purposes of determining loss from the sale or other disposition of property, basis as determined in subdivision (i)(B) of this subparagraph shall apply.

(3) Losses. Where the sale or other disposition of property referred to in section

4940(c)(4)(A) results in a capital loss, such loss may be subtracted from capital gains from the sale or other disposition of other such property during the same taxable year, but only to the extent of such gains. Should losses from the sale or other disposition of such property exceed gains from the sale or other disposition of such property during the same taxable year, such excess may not be deducted from gross investment income under section 4940(c)(3) in any taxable year, nor may such excess be used to reduce gains in either prior or future taxable years, regardless of whether the foundation is a corporation or a trust.

(4) Examples. The provisions of this paragraph may be illustrated by the following examples:

Example (1). A private foundation holds certain depreciable real property on December 31, 1969, having a basis of $102,000. The fair market value of such property on that date was $100,000. For its taxable year 1970 the foundation was allowed depreciation for such property of $5,100 on the straight line method, the allowable amount computed on the $102,000 basis. The property was sold on January 1, 1971, for $100,000. Because fair market value on December 31, 1969, less straight line depreciation of $5,100 ($94,900) is less than basis as determined by Part II of Subchapter O of Chapter 1, $96,900 ($102,000 less $5,100), a gain of $3,100 is recognized (*i.e.*, sales price of $100,000 less the greater of the two possible bases).

Example (2). Assume the same facts in example 1, except that the sale price was $95,000. Because the sale price was $1,900 less than the basis for loss ($96,900 as determined by the application of subparagraph (2)(ii) of this paragraph), there is a capital loss of $1,900 which may be deducted against capital gains for 1971 (if any) in determining net capital gain (capital gain net income for taxable years beginning after December 31, 1976).

Example (3). A private foundation holds certain depreciable real property on December 31, 1969, having a basis of $102,000. The fair market value of such property on that date was $110,000. For its taxable year 1970 the foundation was allowed depreciation for such property of $5,100 on the straight line method, the allowable amount computed on the $102,000 basis. The property was sold on January 1, 1971, for $100,000. Fair market value on December 31, 1969, less straight line depreciation of $5,100 ($104,900) exceeds basis as determined by Part II of Subchapter O of Chapter 1, $96,900 ($102,000 less $5,100), and will be used for purposes of determining gain. Because basis for purposes of determining gain exceeds sale price, there is no gain. There is no loss because basis for purposes of determining loss ($96,900) is less than sale price.

§ 53.4941(a)-1. Imposition of initial taxes.

(a) Tax on self-dealer—(1) In general. Section 4941(a)(1) of the code imposes an excise tax on each act of self-dealing between a disqualified person (as defined in section 4946(a)) and a private foundation. Except as provided in subparagraph (2) of this paragraph, this tax shall be imposed on a disqualified person even though he had no knowledge at the time of the act that such act constituted self-dealing. Notwithstanding the preceding two sentences, however, a transaction between a disqualified person and a private foundation will not constitute an act of self-dealing if:

(i) The transaction is a purchase or sale of securities by a private foundation through a stockbroker where normal trading procedures on a stock exchange or recognized over-the-counter market are followed;

(ii) Neither the buyer nor the seller of the securities nor the agent of either knows the identity of the other party involved; and

(iii) The sale is made in the ordinary course of business, and does not involve a block of securities larger than the average daily trading volume of that stock over the previous 4 weeks.

However, the preceding sentence shall not apply to a transaction involving a dealer who is a disqualified person acting as a principal or to a transaction which is an act of self-dealing pursuant to section 4941(d)(1)(B) and § 53.4941(d)–2(c)(1). The tax imposed by section 4941(a)(1) is at the rate of 5 percent of the amount involved (as defined in section 4941(e)(2) and § 53.4941(e)–1(b)) with respect to the act of self-dealing for each year or partial year in the taxable period (as defined in section 4941(e)(1)) and shall be paid by any disqualified person (other than a foundation manager acting only in the capacity of a foundation manager) who participates in the act of self-dealing. However, if a foundation manager is also acting as a self-dealer, he may be liable for both the tax imposed by section 4941(a)(1) and the tax imposed by section 4941(a)(2).

(2) Government officials. In the case of a government official (as defined in sec. 4946(a)), the tax shall be imposed upon such government official who participates in an act of self-dealing, only if he knows that such act is an act of self-dealing. See paragraph (b)(3) of this section for a definition of knowing.

(3) Participation. For purposes of this paragraph, a disqualified person shall be treated as participating in an act of self-dealing in any case in which he engages or takes part in the transaction by himself or with others, or directs any person to do so.

(b) Tax on foundation manager—(1) In general. Section 4941(a)(2) of the code imposes an excise tax on the participation of any foundation manager in an act of self-dealing between a disqualified person and a private foundation. This tax is imposed only in cases in which the following circumstances are present:

(i) A tax is imposed by section 4941(a)(1),

(ii) Such participating foundation manager knows that the act is an act of self-dealing, and

(iii) The participation by the foundation manager is willful and is not due to reasonable cause.

The tax imposed by section 4941(a)(2) is at the rate of 2 1/2 percent of the amount involved with respect to the act of self-dealing for each year or partial year in the taxable period and shall be paid by any foundation manager described in subdivisions (ii) and (iii) of this subparagraph.

(2) Participation. The term "participation" shall include silence or inaction on the part of a foundation manager where he is under a duty to speak or act, as well as any affirmative action by such manager. However, a foundation manager will not be considered to have participated in an act of self-dealing where he has opposed such act in a manner consistent with the fulfillment of his responsibilities to the private foundation.

(3) Knowing. For purposes of section 4941, a person shall be considered to have participated in a transaction "knowing" that it is an act of self-dealing only if:

(i) He has actual knowledge of sufficient facts so that, based solely upon such facts, such transaction would be an act of self-dealing,

(ii) He is aware that such an act under these circumstances may violate the provisions of Federal tax law governing self-dealing, and

(iii) He negligently fails to make reasonable attempts to ascertain whether the transaction is an act of self-dealing, or he is in fact aware that it is such an act.

For purposes of this part and chapter 42, the term "knowing" does not mean "having reason to know". However, evidence tending to show that a person has reason to know of a particular fact or particular rule is relevant in determining whether he had actual knowledge of such fact or rule. Thus, for example, evidence tending to show that a person has reason to know of sufficient facts so that, based solely upon such facts, a transaction would be an act of self-dealing is relevant in determining whether he has actual knowledge of such facts.

(4) Willful. Participation by a foundation manager shall be deemed willful if it is voluntary, conscious, and intentional. No motive to avoid the restrictions of the law or the incurrence of any tax is necessary to make the participation willful. However, participation by a foundation manager is not willful if he does not know that the transaction in which he is participating is an act of self-dealing.

(5) Due to reasonable cause. A foundation manager's participation is due to reasonable cause if he has exercised his responsibility on behalf of the foundation with ordinary business care and prudence.

(6) Advice of counsel. If a person, after full disclosure of the factual situation to legal counsel (including house counsel), relies on the advice of such counsel expressed in a reasoned written legal opinion that an act is not an act of self-dealing under section 4941, although such act is subsequently held to be an act of self-dealing, the person's participation in such act will ordinarily not be considered "knowing" or "willful" and will ordinarily be considered "due to reasonable cause" within the meaning of section 4941(a)(2). For purposes of this subparagraph, a written legal opinion will be considered "reasoned" even if it reaches a conclusion which is subsequently determined to be incorrect so long as such opinion addresses itself to the facts and applicable law. However, a written legal opinion will not be considered "reasoned" if it does nothing more than recite the facts and express a conclusion. However, the absence of advice of counsel with respect to an act shall not, by itself, give rise to any inference that a person participated in such act knowingly, willfully, or without reasonable cause.

(c) Burden of proof. For provisions relating to the burden of proof in cases involving the issue whether a foundation manager or a government official has knowingly participated in an act of self-dealing, see section 7454(b).

§ 53.4941(b)–1. Imposition of additional taxes.

(a) Tax on self-dealer. Section 4941(b)(1) of the Code imposes an excise tax in any case in which an initial tax is imposed by section 4941(a)(1) on an act of self-dealing by a disqualified person with a private foundation and the act is not corrected within the taxable period (as defined in § 53.4941(e)–1(a)). The tax imposed by section 4941(b)(1) is at the rate of 200 percent of the amount involved and shall be paid by any disqualified person (other than a foundation manager action only in the capacity of a foundation manager) who participated in the act of self-dealing.

(b) Tax on foundation manager. Section 4941(b)(2) of the Code imposes an excise tax to be paid by a foundation manager in any case in which a tax is imposed by section 4941(b)(1) and the foundation manager refused to agree to part or all of the correction of the self-dealing act. The tax imposed by section 4941(b)(2) is at the rate of 50 percent of the amount involved and shall be paid by any foundation manager who refused to agree to part or all of the correction of the self-dealing act. For the limitations on liability of a foundation manager, see § 53.4941(c)–1(b).

§ 53.4941(c)–1. Special rules.

(a) Joint and several liability. (1) In any case where more than one person is liable for the tax imposed by any paragraph of section 4941(a) or (b), all such persons shall be jointly and severally liable for the taxes imposed under such paragraph with respect to such act of self-dealing.

(2) The provisions of this paragraph may be illustrated by the following example:

Example. A and B, who are managers of private foundation X, lend one of the foundation's paintings to G, a disqualified person, for display in G's office, in a transaction which gives rise to liability for tax under section 4941(a)(2) (relating to tax on foundation managers). An initial tax is imposed on both A and B with respect to the act of lending the foundation's painting to G. A and B are jointly and severally liable for the tax.

(b) Limits on liability for management. (1) The maximum aggregate amount of tax collectible under section 4941(a)(2) from all foundation managers with respect to any one act of self-dealing shall be $10,000, and the maximum aggregate amount of tax collectible under section 4941(b)(2) from all foundation managers with respect to any one act of self-dealing shall be $10,000.

(2) The provisions of this paragraph may be illustrated by the following example:

Example. A, a disqualified person with respect to private foundation Y, sells certain real estate having a fair market value of $500,000 to Y for $500,000 in cash. B, C, and D, all the managers of foundation Y, authorized the purchase on Y's behalf knowing that such purchase was an act of self-dealing. The actions of B, C, and D in approving the purchase were willful and not due to reasonable cause. Initial taxes are imposed upon the foundation managers under subsections (a)(2) and (c)(2) of section 4941. The tax to be paid by the foundation managers is $10,000 (the lesser of $10,000 or 2 1/2 percent of the amount involved). The managers are jointly and severally liable for this $10,000, and this sum may be collected by the Internal Revenue Service from any one of them.

§ 53.4941(d)–1. Definition of self-dealing.

(a) In general. For purposes of section 4941, the term "self-dealing" means any direct or indirect transaction described in § 53.4941(d)–2. For purposes of this section, it is immaterial whether the transaction results in a benefit or a detriment to the private foundation. The term "self-dealing" does not, however, include a transaction between a private foundation and a disqualified person where the disqualified person status arises only as a result of such transaction. For example, the bargain sale of property to a private foundation is not a direct act of self-dealing if the seller becomes a disqualified person only by reason of his becoming a substantial contributor as a result of the bargain element of the sale. For the effect of sections 4942, 4943, 4944, and 4945 upon an act of self-dealing which also results in the imposition of tax under one or more of such sections, see the regulations under those sections.

(b) Indirect self-dealing—(1) Certain business transactions. The term "indirect self-dealing" shall not include any transaction described in § 53.4941(d)–2 between a disqualified person and an organization controlled by a private foundation (within the meaning of paragraph (6)(5) of this section) if:

(i) The transaction results from a business relationship which was established before such transaction constituted an act of self-dealing (without regard to this paragraph),

(ii) The transaction was at least as favorable to the organization controlled by the foundation as an arm's-length transaction with an unrelated person, and

(iii) Either:

(a) The organization controlled by the foundation could have engaged in the transaction with someone other than a disqualified person only at a severe economic hardship to such organization, or

(b) Because of the unique nature of the product or services provided by the organization controlled by the foundation, the disqualified person could not have engaged in the transaction with anyone else, or could have done so only by incurring severe economic hardship. See example (2) of subparagraph (8) of this paragraph.

(2) Grants to intermediaries. The term "indirect self-dealing" shall not include a transaction engaged in with a government official by an intermediary organization which is a recipient of a grant from a private foundation and which is not controlled by such foundation (within the meaning of subparagraph (5) of this paragraph) if the private foundation does not earmark the use of the grant for any named government official and there does not exist an agreement, oral or written, whereby the grantor foundation may cause the selection of the government official by the intermediary organization. A grant by a private foundation is earmarked if such grant is made pursuant to an agreement, either oral or written, that the grant will be used by any named individual. Thus, a grant by a private foundation shall not constitute an indirect act of self-dealing even though such foundation had reason to believe that certain government officials would derive benefits from such grant so long as the intermediary organization exercises control, in fact, over the selection process and actually makes the selection completely independently of the private foundation. See example (3) of subparagraph (8) of this paragraph.

* * *

(4) Transactions with certain organizations. A transaction between a private foundation and an organization which is not controlled by the foundation (within the meaning of subparagraph (5) of this paragraph), and which is not described in section 4946(a)(1)(E), (F), or (G) because persons described in section 4946(a)(1)(A), (B), (C), or (D) own no more than 35 percent of the total combined voting power or profits or beneficial interest of such organization, shall not be treated as an indirect act of self-dealing between the foundation and such disqualified persons solely because of the ownership interest of such persons in such organization.

(5) Control. For purposes of this paragraph, an organization is controlled by a private foundation if the foundation or one or more of its foundation managers (acting only in such capacity) may, only by aggregating their votes or positions of authority, require the organization to engage in a transaction which if engaged in with the private foundation would constitute self-dealing. Similarly, for purposes of this paragraph, an organization is controlled by a private foundation in the case of such a transaction between the organization and a disqualified person, if such disqualified person, together with one or more persons who are disqualified persons by reason of such a person's relationship (within the meaning of section 4946(a)(1)(C) through (G)) to such disqualified person, may, only by aggregating their votes or positions of authority with that of the foundation, require the organization to engage in such a transaction. The "controlled" organization need not be a private foundation; for example, it may be any type of exempt or nonexempt organization including a school, hospital, operating foundation, or social welfare organization. For purposes of this paragraph, an organization will be considered to be controlled by a private foundation or by a private foundation and disqualified persons referred to in the second sentence of this subparagraph if such persons are able, in fact, to control the organization (even if their aggregate voting power is less than 50 percent of the total voting power of the organization's governing body) or if one or more of such persons has the right to exercise veto power over the actions of such organization relevant to any potential acts of self-dealing. A private foundation shall not be regarded as having control over an organization merely because it exercises expenditure responsibility (as defined in section 4945(d)(4) and (h)) with respect to contributions to such organization. See example (6) of subparagraph (8) of this paragraph.

(6) Certain transactions involving limited amounts. The term "indirect self-dealing" shall not include any transaction between a disqualified person and an organization controlled by a private foundation (within the meaning of subparagraph (5) of this paragraph) or between two disqualified persons where the foundation's assets may be affected by the transaction if:

(i) The transaction arises in the normal and customary course of a retail business engaged in with the general public,

(ii) In the case of a transaction between a disqualified person and an organization controlled by a private foundation, the transaction is at least as favorable to the organization controlled by the foundation as an arm's-length transaction with an unrelated person, and

(iii) The total of the amounts involved in such transactions with respect to any one such disqualified person in any one taxable year does not exceed $5,000.

See example (7) of subparagraph (8) of this paragraph.

(7) Applicability of statutory exceptions to indirect self-dealing. The term "indirect self-dealing" shall not include a transaction involving one or more disqualified persons to which a private foundation is not a party, in any case in which the private foundation, by reason of section 4941(d)(2), could itself engage in such a transaction. Thus, for example, even if a private foundation has control (within the meaning of subparagraph (5) of this paragraph) of a corporation, the corporation may pay to a disqualified person, except a government official, reasonable compensation for personal services.

(8) Examples. The provisions of this paragraph may be illustrated by the following examples:

Example (1). Private foundation P owns the controlling interest of the voting stock of corporation X, and as a result of such interest, elects a majority of the board of directors of X. Two of the foundation managers, A and B, who are also directors of corporation X, form corporation Y for the purpose of building and managing a country club. A and B receive a total of 40 percent of Y's stock, making Y a disqualified person with respect to P under section 4946(a)(1)(E). In order to finance the construction and operation of the country club, Y requested and received a loan in the amount of $4 million from X. The making of the loan by X to Y shall constitute an indirect act of self-dealing between P and Y.

Example (2). Private foundation W owns the controlling interest of the voting stock of corporation X, a manufacturer of certain electronic computers. Corporation Y, a disqualified person with respect to W, owns the patent for, and manufactures, one of the essential component parts used in the computers. X has been making regular purchases of the patented component from Y since 1965, subject to the same terms as all other purchasers of such component parts. X could not buy similar components from another source. Consequently, X would suffer severe economic hardship if it could not continue to purchase these components from Y, since it would then be forced to develop a computer which could be constructed with other components. Under these circumstances, the continued purchase by X from Y of these components shall not be an indirect act of self-dealing between W and Y.

Example (3). Private foundation Y made a grant to M University, an organization described in section 170(b)(1)(A)(ii), for the purpose of conducting a seminar to study methods for improving the administration of the judicial system. M is not controlled by Y within the meaning of subparagraph (5) of this paragraph. In conducting the seminar, M made payments to certain government officials. By the nature of the grant, Y had reason to believe that government officials would be compensated for participation in the seminar. M, however, had completely independent control over the selection of such participants. Thus, such grant by Y shall not constitute an indirect act of self-dealing with respect to the government officials.

Example (4). A, a substantial contributor to P, a private foundation, bequeathed one-half of his estate to his spouse and one-half of his estate to P. Included in A's estate is a one-third interest in AB, a partnership. The other two-thirds interest in AB is owned by B, a disqualified person with respect to P. The one-third interest in AB was subject to an option agreement when it was acquired by the estate. The executor of A's estate sells the one-third interest in AB to B pursuant to such option agreement at the price fixed in such option agreement in a sale which meets the requirements of subparagraph (3) of this paragraph. Under these circumstances, the sale does not constitute an indirect act of self-dealing between B and P.

Example (5). A bequeathed $100,000 to his wife and a piece of unimproved real estate of equivalent value to private foundation Z, of which A was the creator and a foundation manager. Under the laws of State Y, to which the estate is subject, title to the real estate vests in the foundation upon A's death. However, the executor has the power under State law to reallocate the property to another beneficiary. During a reasonable period for administration of the estate, the executor exercises this power and distributes the $100,000 cash to the foundation and the real estate to A's wife. The probate court having jurisdiction over the estate approves the executor's action. Under these circumstances, the executor's action does not constitute an indirect act of self-dealing between the foundation and A's wife.

Example (6). Private foundation P owns 20 percent of the voting stock of corporation W. A, a substantial contributor with respect to P, owns 16 percent of the voting stock of corporation W. B, A's son, owns 15 percent of the voting stock of corporation W. The terms of the voting stock are such that P, A, and B could vote their stock in a block to elect a majority of the board of directors of W. W is treated as controlled by P (within the meaning of subparagraph (5) of this paragraph) for purposes of this example A and B also own 50 percent of the stock of corporation Y, making Y a disqualified person with respect to P under section 4946(a)(1)(E). W makes a loan to Y of $1 million. The making of this loan by W to Y shall constitute an indirect act of self-dealing between P and Y.

Example (7). A, a disqualified person with respect to private foundation P, enters into a contract with corporation M, which is also a disqualified person with respect to P. P owns 20 percent of M's stock, and controls M within the meaning of subparagraph (5) of this paragraph. M is in the retail department store business. Purchases by A of goods sold by M in the normal and customary course of business at retail or higher prices are not indirect acts of self-dealing so long as the total of the amounts involved in all of such purchases by A in any one year does not exceed $5,000.

§ 53.4941(d)–2. Specific acts of self-dealing.

Except as provided in § 53.4941(d)–3 or § 53.4941(d)–4:

(a) Sale or exchange of property—(1) In general. The sale or exchange of property between a private foundation and a disqualified person shall constitute an act of self-dealing. For example, the sale of incidental supplies by a disqualified person to a private foundation shall be an act of self-dealing regardless of the amount paid to the disqualified person for the incidental supplies. Similarly, the sale of stock or other securities by a disqualified person to a private foundation in a "bargain sale" shall be an act of self-dealing regardless of the amount paid for such stock or other securities. An installment sale may be subject to the provisions of both section 4941(d)(1)(A) and section 4941(d)(1)(B).

(2) Mortgaged property. For purposes of subparagraph (1) of this paragraph, the transfer of real or personal property by a disqualified person to a private foundation shall be treated as a sale or exchange if the foundation assumes a mortgage or similar lien which was placed on the property prior to the transfer, or takes subject to a mortgage or similar lien which a disqualified person placed on the property within the 10-year period ending on the date of transfer. For purposes of this subparagraph, the term "similar lien" shall include, but is not limited to, deeds of trust and vendors' liens, but shall not include any other lien if such lien is insignificant in relation to the fair market value of the property transferred.

(b) Leases—(1) In general. Except as provided in subparagraphs (2) and (3)of this paragraph, the leasing of property between a disqualified person and a private foundation shall constitute an act of self-dealing.

(2) Certain leases without charge. The leasing of property by a disqualified person to a private foundation shall not be an act of self-dealing if the lease is without charge. For purposes of this subparagraph, a lease shall be considered to be without charge even though the private foundation pays for janitorial services, utilities, or other maintenance costs it incurs for the use of the property, so long as the payment is not made directly or indirectly to a disqualified person.

* * *

(c) Loans—(1) In general. Except as provided in subparagraphs (2), (3), and (4) of this paragraph, the lending of money or other extension of credit between a private foundation and a disqualified person shall constitute an act of self-dealing. Thus, for example, an act of self-dealing occurs where a third party purchases property and assumes a mortgage, the mortgagee of which is a private foundation, and subsequently the third party transfers the property to a disqualified person who either assumes liability under the mortgage or takes the property subject to the mortgage. Similarly, except in the case of the receipt and holding of a note pursuant to a transaction described in § 53.4941(d)–1(b)(3), an act of self-dealing occurs where a note, the obligor of which is a disqualified person, is transferred by a third party to a private foundation which becomes the creditor under the note.

(2) Loans without interest. Subparagraph (1) of this paragraph shall not apply to the lending of money or other extension of credit by a disqualified person to a private foundation if the loan or other extension of credit is without interest or other charge.

(3) Certain evidences of future gifts. The making of a promise, pledge, or similar arrangement to a private foundation by a disqualified person, whether evidenced by an oral or written agreement, a promissory note, or other instrument of indebtedness, to the extent motivated by charitable intent and unsupported by consideration, is not an extension of credit (within the meaning of this paragraph) before the date of maturity.

(4) General banking functions. Under section 4941(d)(2)(E) the performance by a bank or trust company which is a disqualified person of trust functions and certain general banking services for a private foundation is not an act of self-dealing, where the banking services are reasonable and necessary to carrying out the exempt purposes of the private foundation, if the compensation paid to the bank or trust company, taking into account the fair interest rate for the use of the funds by the bank or trust company, for such services is not excessive. The general banking services allowed by this subparagraph are:

(i) Checking accounts, as long as the bank does not charge interest on any overwithdrawals,

(ii) Savings accounts, as long as the foundation may withdraw its funds on no more than 30-days notice without subjecting itself to a loss of interest on its money for the time during which the money was on deposit, and

(iii) Safekeeping activities. See example (3) § 53.4941(d)–3(c)(2).

(d) Furnishing goods, services, or facilities—(1) In general. Except as provided in subparagraph (2) or (3) of this paragraph (or § 53.4941(d)–3(b)), the furnishing of goods, services, or facilities between a private foundation and a disqualified person shall constitute an act of self-dealing. This subparagraph shall apply, for example, to the furnishing of goods, services, or facilities such as office space, automobiles, auditoriums, secretarial help, meals, libraries, publications, laboratories, or parking lots. Thus, for example, if a foundation furnishes personal living quarters to a disqualified person (other than a foundation manager or employee) without charge, such furnishing shall be an act of self-dealing.

(2) Furnishing of goods, services, or facilities to foundation managers and employees. The furnishing of goods, services, or facilities such as those described in subparagraph (1) of this paragraph to a foundation manager in recognition of his services as a foundation manager, or to another employee (including an individual who would be an employee but for the fact that he receives no compensation for his services) in recognition of his services in such capacity, is not an act of self-dealing if the value of such furnishing (whether or not includible as compensation in his gross income) is reasonable and necessary to the performance of his tasks in carrying out the exempt purposes of the foundation and, taken in conjunction with any other payment of compensation or payment or reimbursement of expenses to him by the foundation, is not excessive. For example, if a foundation furnishes meals and lodging which are reasonable and necessary (but not excessive) to a foundation manager by reason of his being a foundation manager, then, without regard to whether such meals and lodging are excludable from gross income under section 119 as furnished for the convenience of the employer, such furnishing is not an act of self-dealing. For the effect of section 4945(d)(5) upon an expenditure for unreasonable administrative expenses, see § 53.4945–6(b)(2).

(3) Furnishing of goods, services, or facilities by a disqualified person without charge. The furnishing of goods, services, or facilities by a disqualified person to a private foundation shall not be an act of self-dealing if they are furnished without charge. Thus, for example, the furnishing of goods such as pencils, stationery, or other incidental supplies, or the furnishing of facilities such as a building, by a disqualified person to a foundation shall be allowed if such supplies or facilities are furnished without charge. Similarly, the furnishing of services (even though such services are not personal in nature) shall be permitted if such furnishing is without charge. For purposes of this subparagraph, a furnishing of goods shall be considered without charge even though the private foundation pays for transportation, insurance, or maintenance costs it incurs in obtaining or using the property, so long as the payment is not made directly or indirectly to the disqualified person.

(e) Payment of compensation. The payment of compensation (or payment or reimbursement of expenses) by a private foundation to a disqualified person shall constitute an act of self-dealing. See, however, § 53.4941(d)–3(c) for the exception for the payment of compensation by a foundation to a disqualified person for personal services which are reasonable and necessary to carry out the exempt purposes of the foundation.

(f) Transfer or use of the income or assets of a private foundation—(1) In general. The transfer to, or use by or for the benefit of, a disqualified person of the income or assets of a private foundation shall constitute an act of self-dealing. For purposes of the preceding sentence, the payment by a private foundation of any tax imposed on a disqualified person by Chapter 42 shall be treated as a transfer of the income or assets of a private foundation for the benefit of a disqualified person. Similarly, the payment by a private foundation of the premiums for an insurance policy providing liability insurance to a foundation manager for Chapter 42 taxes shall be an act of self-dealing under this paragraph unless such premiums are treated as part of the compensation paid to such manager. In addition, the purchase or sale of stock or other securities by a private foundation shall be an act of self-dealing if such purchase or sale is made in an attempt to manipulate the price of the stock or other securities to the advantage of a disqualified person. Similarly, the indemnification (of a lender) or guarantee (of repayment) by a private foundation with respect to a loan to a disqualified person shall be treated as a use for the benefit of a disqualified person of the income or assets of the foundation (within the meaning of this subparagraph). In addition, if a private foundation makes a grant or other payment which satisfies the legal obligation of a disqualified person, such grant or payment shall ordinarily constitute an act of self-dealing to which this subparagraph applies. However, if a private foundation makes a grant or payment which satisfies a pledge, enforceable under local law, to an organization described in section 501(c)(3), which pledge is made on or before April 16, 1973, such grant or payment shall not constitute an act of self-dealing to which this subparagraph applies so long as the disqualified person obtains no substantial benefit, other than the satisfaction of his obligation, from such grant or payment.

(2) Certain incidental benefits. The fact that a disqualified person receives an incidental or tenuous benefit from the use by a foundation of its income or assets will not, by itself, make such use an act of self-dealing. Thus, the public recognition a person may receive, arising from the charitable activities of a private foundation to which such person is a substantial contributor, does not in itself result in an act of self-dealing since generally the benefit is incidental and tenuous. For example, a grant by a private foundation to a section 509(a)(1), (2), or (3) organization will not be an act of self-dealing merely because such organization is located in the same area as a corporation which is a substantial contributor to the foundation, or merely because one of the section 509(a)(1), (2), or (3) organization's officers, directors, or trustees is also a manager of or a substantial contributor to the foundation. Similarly, a scholarship or a fellowship grant to a person other than a disqualified person, which is paid or incurred by a private foundation in accordance with a program which is consistent with:

(i) The requirements of the foundation's exempt status under section 501(c)(3),

(ii) The requirements for the allowance of deductions under section 170 for contributions made to the foundation, and

(iii) The requirements of section 4945(g)(1),

will not be an act of self-dealing under section 4941(d)(1) merely because a disqualified person indirectly receives an incidental benefit from such grant. Thus, a scholarship or a fellowship grant made by a private foundation in accordance with a program to award scholarships or fellowship grants to the children of employees of a substantial contributor shall not constitute an act of self-dealing if the requirements of the preceding sentence are satisfied. For an example of the kind of scholarship program with an employment nexus that meets the above requirements, see § 53.4945–4(b)(5) (example 1).

(3) Non-compensatory indemnification of foundation managers against liability for defense in civil proceedings. **(i)** Except as provided in section 53.4941(d)–3(c), section 4941(d)(1) shall not apply to the indemnification by a private foundation of a foundation manager, with respect to the manager's defense in any civil judicial or civil administrative proceeding arising out of the manager's performance of services (or failure to perform services) on behalf of the foundation, against all expenses (other than taxes, including taxes imposed by chapter 42, penalties, or expenses of correction) including attorneys' fees, judgments and settlement expenditures if—

(A) Such expenses are reasonably incurred by the manager in connection with such proceeding; and

(B) The manager has not acted willfully and without reasonable cause with respect to the act or failure to act which led to such proceeding or to liability for tax under chapter 42.

(ii) Similarly, except as provided in section 53.4941(d)–3(c), section 4941(d)(1) shall not apply to premiums for insurance to make or to reimburse a foundation for an indemnification payment allowed pursuant to this paragraph (f)(3). Neither shall an indemnification or payment of insurance allowed pursuant to this paragraph (f)(3) be treated as part of the compensation paid to such manager for purposes of determining whether the compensation is reasonable under chapter 42.

(4) Compensatory indemnification of foundation managers against liability for defense in civil proceedings. **(i)** The indemnification by a private foundation of a foundation manager for compensatory expenses shall be an act of self-dealing under this paragraph unless when such payment is added to other compensation paid to such manager the total compensation is reasonable under chapter 42. A compensatory expense for purposes of this paragraph (f) is—

(A) Any penalty, tax (including a tax imposed by chapter 42), or expense of correction that is owed by the foundation manager;

(B) Any expense not reasonably incurred by the manager in connection with a civil judicial or civil administrative proceeding arising out of the manager's performance of services on behalf of the foundation; or

(C) Any expense resulting from an act or failure to act with respect to which the manager has acted willfully and without reasonable cause.

(ii) Similarly, the payment by a private foundation of the premiums for an insurance policy providing liability insurance to a foundation manager for expenses described in this paragraph (f)(4) shall be an act of self-dealing under this paragraph (f) unless when such premiums are added to other compensation paid to such manager the total compensation is reasonable under chapter 42.

(5) Insurance Allocation. A private foundation shall not be engaged in an act of self-dealing if the foundation purchases a single insurance policy to provide its managers both the noncompensatory and the compensatory coverage discussed in this paragraph (f), provided that the total insurance premium is allocated and that each manager's portion of the premium attributable to the compensatory coverage is included in that manager's compensation for purposes of determining reasonable compensation under chapter 42.

(6) Indemnification. For purposes of this paragraph (f), the term indemnification shall include not only reimbursement by the foundation for expenses that the foundation manager has already incurred or anticipates incurring but also direct payment by the foundation of such expenses as the expenses arise.

(7) Taxable Income. The determination of whether any amount of indemnification or insurance premium discussed in this paragraph (f) is included in the manager's gross income for individual income tax purposes is made on the basis of the provisions of chapter 1 and without regard to the treatment of such amount for purposes of determining whether the manager's compensation is reasonable under chapter 42.

(8) De Minimis Items. Any property or service that is excluded from income under section 132(a)(4) may be disregarded for purposes of determining whether the recipient's compensation is reasonable under chapter 42.

(9) Examples. The provisions of this paragraph may be illustrated by the following examples:

Example (1). M, a private foundation, makes a grant of $50,000 to the governing body of N City for the purpose of alleviating the slum conditions which exist in a particular neighborhood of N. Corporation P, a substantial contributor to M, is located in the same area in which the grant is to be used. Although the general improvement of the area may constitute an incidental and tenuous benefit to P, such benefit by itself will not constitute an act of self-dealing.

Example (2). Private foundation X established a program to award scholarship grants to the children of employees of corporation M, a substantial contributor to X. After disclosure of the method of carrying out such program, X received a determination letter from the Internal Revenue Service stating that X is exempt from taxation under section 501(c)(3), that contributions to X are deductible under section 170, and that X's scholarship program qualifies under section 4945(g)(1). A scholarship grant to a person not a disqualified person with respect to X paid or incurred by X in accordance with such program shall not be an indirect act of self-dealing between X and M.

Example (3). Private foundation Y owns voting stock in corporation Z, the management of which includes certain disqualified persons with respect to Y. Prior to Z's annual stockholder meeting, the management solicits and receives the foundation's proxies. The transfer of such proxies in and of itself shall not be an act of self-dealing.

Example (4). A, a disqualified person with respect to private foundation S, contributes certain real estate to S for the purpose of building a neighborhood recreation center in a particular underprivileged area. As a condition of the gift, S agrees to name the recreation center after A. Since the benefit to A is only incidental and tenuous, the naming of the recreation center, by itself, will not be an act of self-dealing.

(g) Payment to a government official. Except as provided in section 4941(d)(2)(G) or § 53.4941(d)–3(e), the agreement by a private foundation to make any payment of money or other property to a government official, as defined in section 4946(c), shall constitute an act of self-dealing. For purposes of this paragraph, an individual who is otherwise described in section 4946(c) shall be treated as a government official while on leave of absence from the government without pay.

§ 53.4941(d)–3. Exceptions to self-dealing.

(a) General rule. In general, a transaction described in section 4941(d)(2)(B), (C), (D), (E), (F), (G), or (H) is not an act of self-dealing. Section 4941(d)(2)(B), (C), and (H) provide limited exceptions to certain specific transactions, as described in paragraphs (b)(2), (b)(3), (c)(2), and (d)(3) of § 53.4941(d)–2. Section 4941(d)(2)(D), (E), (F), and (G) and paragraphs (b) through (e) of this section described certain transactions which are not acts of self-dealing.

(b) Furnishing of goods, services, or facilities to a disqualified person—(1) In general. Under section 4941(d)(2)(D), the furnishing of goods, services, or facilities by a private foundation to a disqualified person shall not be an act of self-dealing if such goods, services, or facilities are made available to the general public on at least as favorable a basis as they are made available to the disqualified person. This subparagraph shall not apply, however, in the case of goods, services, or facilities furnished later than May 16, 1973, unless such goods, services, or facilities are functionally related, within the meaning of section 4942(j)(5), to the exercise or performance by a private foundation of its charitable, educational, or other purpose or function constituting the basis for its exemption under section 501(c)(3).

(2) General public. For purposes of this paragraph, the term "general public" shall include those persons who, because of the particular nature of the activities of the private foundation, would be reasonably expected to utilize such goods, services, or facilities. This paragraph shall not apply, however, unless there is a substantial number of persons other than disqualified persons who are actually utilizing such goods, services, or facilities. Thus, a private foundation which furnishes recreational or park facilities to the general public may furnish such facilities to a disqualified person provided they are furnished to him on a basis which is not more favorable than that on which they are furnished to the general public. Similarly, the sale of a book or magazine by a private foundation to disqualified persons shall not be an act of self-dealing if the publication of such book or magazine is functionally related to a charitable or educational activity of the foundation and the book or magazine is made available to the disqualified persons and the general public at the same price. In addition, if the terms of the sale require, for example, payment within 60 days from the date of delivery of the book or magazine, such terms are consistent with normal commercial practices, and payment is made within the 60-day period, the transaction shall not be treated as a loan or other extension of credit under § 53.4941(d)–2(c)(1).

(c) Payment of compensation for certain personal services—(1) In general. Under section 4941(d)(2)(E), except in the case of a Government official (as defined in section 4946(c)), the payment of compensation (and the payment or reimbursement of expenses, including reasonable advances for expenses anticipated in the immediate future) by a private foundation to a disqualified person for the performance of personal services which are reasonable and necessary to carry out the exempt purpose of the private foundation shall not be an act of self-dealing if such compensation (or payment or reimbursement) is not excessive. For purposes of this subparagraph the term "personal services" includes the services of a broker serving as agent for the private foundation, but not the services of a dealer who buys from the private foundation as principal and resells to third parties. For the determination whether compensation is excessive, see § 1.162–7 of this chapter (Income Tax Regulations). This paragraph applies without regard to whether the person who receives the compensation (or payment or reimbursement) is an individual. The portion of any payment which represents payment for property shall not be treated as payment of compensation (or payment or reimbursement of expenses) for the performance of personal services for purposes of this paragraph. For rules with respect to the performance of general banking services, see § 53.4941(d)–2(c)(4). Further, the making of a cash advance to a foundation manager or employee for expenses on behalf of the foundation is not an act of self-dealing, so long as the amount of the advance is reasonable in relation to the duties and expense requirements of the foundation manager. Except where reasonably allowable pursuant to subdivision (iii) of this subparagraph, such advances shall not ordinarily exceed $500. For example, if a foundation makes an advance to a foundation manager to cover anticipated out-of-pocket current expenses for a reasonable period (such as a month) and the manager accounts to the foundation under a periodic reimbursement program for actual expenses incurred, the foundation will not be regarded as having engaged in an act of self-dealing:

(i) When it makes the advance,

(ii) When it replenishes the funds upon receipt of supporting vouchers from the foundation manager, or

(iii) If it temporarily adds to the advance to cover extraordinary expenses anticipated to be incurred in fulfillment of a special assignment (such as long distance travel).

(2) Examples. The provisions of this paragraph may be illustrated by the following examples:

Example (1). M, a partnership, is a firm of 10 lawyers engaged in the practice of law. A and B, partners in M, serve as trustees to private foundation W and, therefore, are disqualified persons. In addition, A and B own more than 35 percent of the profits interest in M, thereby making M a disqualified person. M performs various legal services for W from time to time as such services are requested. The payment of compensation by W to M shall not constitute an act of self-dealing if the services performed are reasonable and necessary for the carrying out of W's exempt purposes and the amount paid by W for such services is not excessive.

Example (2). C, a manager of private foundation X, owns an investment counseling business. Acting in his capacity as an investment counselor, C manages X's investment portfolio for which he receives an amount which is determined to be not excessive. The payment of such compensation to C shall not constitute an act of self-dealing.

Example (3). M, a commercial bank, serves as a trustee for private foundation Y. In addition to M's duties as trustee, M maintains Y's checking and savings accounts and rents a safety deposit box to Y. The use of the funds by M and the payment of compensation by Y to M for such general banking services shall be treated as the payment of compensation for the performance of personal services which are reasonable and necessary to carry out the exempt purposes of Y if such compensation is not excessive.

Example (4). D, a substantial contributor to private foundation Z, owns a factory which manufactures microscopes. D contracts with Z to manufacture 100 microscopes for Z. Any payment to D under the contract shall constitute an act of self-dealing, since such payment does not constitute the payment of compensation for the performance of personal services.

(d) Certain transactions between a foundation and a corporation—(1) In general. Under section 4941(d)(2)(F), any transaction between a private foundation and a corporation which is a disqualified person will not be an act of self-dealing if such transaction is engaged in pursuant to a liquidation, merger, redemption, recapitalization, or other corporate adjustment, organization, or reorganization, so long as all the securities of the same class as that held (prior to such transaction) by the foundation are subject to the same terms and such terms provide for receipt by the foundation of no less than fair market value. For purposes of this paragraph, all of the securities are not "subject to the same terms unless, pursuant to such transaction," The corporation makes a bona fide offer on a uniform basis to the foundation and every other person who holds such securities. The fact that a private foundation receives property, such as debentures, while all other persons holding securities of the same class receive cash for their interests, will be evidence that such offer was not made on a uniform basis. This paragraph may apply even if no other person holds any securities of the class held by the foundation. In such event, however, the consideration received by holders of other classes of securities, or the interests retained by holders of such other classes, when considered in relation to the consideration received by the foundation, must indicate that the foundation received at least as favorable treatment in relation to its interests as the holders of any other class of securities. In addition, the foundation must receive no less than the fair market value of its interests.

(2) Examples. The provisions of this paragraph may be illustrated by the following examples:

Example (1). Private foundation X owns 50 percent of the class A preferred stock of corporation M, which is a disqualified person with respect to X. The terms of such securities provide that the stock may be called for redemption at any time by M at 105 percent of the face amount of the stock. M exercises this right and calls all the class A preferred stock by paying 105 percent of the face amount in cash. At the time of the redemption of the class A preferred stock, it is determined that the fair market value of the preferred stock is equal to its face amount. In such case, the redemption by M of the preferred stock of X is not an act of self-dealing.

Example (2). Private foundation Y, which is on a calendar year basis, acquires 60 percent of the class A preferred stock of corporation N by will on January 10, 1970. N, which is also on a calendar year basis, is a disqualified person with respect to Y. In 1971, N offers to redeem all of the class A preferred stock for a consideration equal to 100 percent of the face amount of such stock by the issuance of debentures. The offer expires January 2, 1972. Both Y and all other holders of the class A preferred stock accept the offer and enter into the transaction on January 2, 1972, at which time it is determined that the fair market value of the debentures is no less than the fair market value of the preferred stock. The transaction on January 2, 1972, shall not be treated as an act of self-dealing for 1972. However, because under § 53.4941(e)–1(e)(1)(i) an act of self dealing occurs on the first day of each taxable year or portion of a taxable year that an extension of credit from a foundation to a disqualified person goes uncorrected, if such debentures are held by Y after December 31, 1972, except as provided in § 53.4941(d)–4(c)(4), such extension of credit shall not be excepted from the definition of an act of self dealing by reason of the January 2, 1972, transaction. See § 53.4941(d)–4(c)(4) for rules indicating that under certain circumstances such debentures could be held by Y until December 31, 1979.

(e) Certain payments to government officials. Under section 4941(d)(2)(G), in the case of a government official, in addition to the exceptions provided in section 4941(d)(2)(B), (C), and (D), section 4941(d)(1) shall not apply to:

(1) A prize or award which is not includible in gross income under section 74(b), if the government official receiving such prize or award is selected from the general public;

(2) A scholarship or a fellowship grant which is excludable from gross income under section 117(a) and which is to be utilized for study at an educational institution described in section 151(e)(4);

(3) Any annuity or other payment (forming part of a stock-bonus, pension, or profit sharing plan) by a trust which constitutes a qualified trust under section 401;

(4) Any annuity or other payment under a plan which meets the requirements of section 404(a)(2);

(5) Any contribution or gift (other than a contribution or gift of money) to, or services or facilities made available to, any government official, if the aggregate value of such contributions, gifts, services, and facilities does not exceed $25 during any calendar year;

(6) Any payment made under 5 U.S.C. chapter 41 (relating to government employees' training programs);

(7) Any payment or reimbursement of traveling expenses (including amounts expended for meals and lodging, regardless of whether the government official is away from home within the meaning of section 162(a)(2), and including reasonable advances for such expenses anticipated in the immediate future) for travel solely from one point in the United States to another in connection with one or more purposes described in section 170(c)(1) or (2)(B), but only if such payment or reimbursement does not exceed the actual cost of the transportation involved plus an amount for all other traveling expenses not in excess of 125 percent of the maximum amount payable under 5 U.S.C. 5702(a) for like travel by employees of the United States;

(8) Any agreement to employ or make a grant to a government official for any period after the termination of his government service if such agreement is entered into within 90 days prior to such termination;

(9) If a government official attends or participates in a conference sponsored by a private foundation, the allocable portion of the cost of such conference and other nonmonetary benefits (for example, benefits of a professional, intellectual, or psychological nature, or benefits resulting from the publication or the distribution to participants of a record of the conference), as well as the payment or reimbursement of expenses (including reasonable advances for expenses anticipated in connection with such a conference in the near future), received by such government official as a result of such attendance or participation shall not be subject to section 4941(d)(1), so long as the conference is in furtherance of the exempt purposes of the foundation; or

(10) In the case of any government official who was on leave of absence without pay on December 31, 1969, pursuant to a commitment entered into on or before such date for the purpose of engaging in certain activities for which such individual was to be paid by one or more private foundations, any payment of compensation (or payment or reimbursement of expenses, including reasonable advances for expenses anticipated in the immediate future) by such private foundations to such individual for any continuous period after December 31, 1969, and prior to January 1, 1971, during which such individual remains on leave of absence to engage in such activities. A commitment is considered entered into on or before December 31, 1969, if on or before such date, the amount and nature of the payments to be made and the name of the individual receiving such payments were entered on the records of the payor, or were otherwise adequately evidenced, or the notice of the payment to be received was communicated to the payee orally or in writing.

§ 53.4941(e)–1. Definitions.

(a) Taxable period—(1) In general. For purposes of any act of self-dealing, the term "taxable period" means the period beginning with the date on which the act of self-dealing occurs and ending on the earliest of:

(i) The date of mailing of a notice of deficiency under section 6212 with respect to the tax imposed by section 4941(a)(1),

(ii) The date on which correction of the act of self-dealing is completed, or

(iii) The date on which the tax imposed by section 4941(a)(1) is assessed.

(2) Date of occurrence. An act of self-dealing occurs on the date on which all the terms and conditions of the transaction and the liabilities of the parties have been fixed. Thus, for example, if a private foundation gives a disqualified person a binding option on June 15, 1971, to purchase property owned by the foundation at any time before June 15, 1972, the act of self-dealing has occurred on June 15, 1971. Similarly, in the case of a conditional sales contract, the act of self-dealing shall be considered as occurring on the date the property is transferred subject only to the condition that the buyer make payment for receipt of such property.

(3) Special rule. Where a notice of deficiency referred to in subparagraph (1)(i) of this paragraph is not mailed because a waiver of the restrictions on assessment and collection of a deficiency has been accepted, or because the deficiency is paid, the date of filing of the waiver or the date of such payment, respectively, shall be treated as the end of the taxable period.

(4) Examples. The provisions of this paragraph may be illustrated by the following examples:

Example (1). On July 16, 1970, F, a manager of private foundation X acting on behalf of the foundation, knowing his act to be one of self-dealing, willfully and without reasonable cause engaged in an act of self-dealing by selling certain real estate to A, a disqualified person. On March 25, 1973, the Internal Revenue Service mailed a notice of deficiency to A with respect to the tax imposed on the sale under section 4941(a)(1). The taxable period with respect to the act of self-dealing for both A and F is July 16, 1970, through March 25, 1973.

Example (2). Assume the facts as stated in example (1), except that the act of self-dealing is corrected by A on March 17, 1971. The taxable period with respect to the act of self-dealing for both A and F is July 16, 1970, through March 17, 1971.

Example (3). Assume the facts as stated in example (1), except that on August 20, 1972, A files a waiver of the restrictions on assessment and collection of the tax imposed on the sale under section 4941(a)(1) which is accepted. The taxable period with respect to the act of self-dealing for both A and F is July 16, 1970, through August 20, 1972.

(b) Amount involved—(1) In general. Except as provided in subparagraph (2) of this paragraph, for purposes of any act of self-dealing, the term "amount involved" means the greater of the amount of money and the fair market value of the other property given or the amount of money and the fair market value of the other property received.

(2) Exceptions. (i) In the case of the payment of compensation for personal services to persons other than Government officials, the amount involved shall be only the excess compensation paid by the private foundation.

(ii) Where the use of money or other property is involved, the amount involved shall be the greater of the amount paid for such use or the fair market value of such use for the period for which the money or other property is used. Thus, for example, in the case of a lease of a building by a private foundation to a disqualified person, the amount involved is the greater of the amount of rent received by the private foundation from the disqualified person or the fair rental value of the building for the period such building is used by the disqualified person.

(iii) In cases in which a transaction would not have been an act of self-dealing had the private foundation received fair market value, the amount involved is the excess of the fair market value of the property transferred by the private foundation over the amount which the private foundation receives, but only if the parties have made a good faith effort to determine fair market value. For purposes of this subdivision a good faith effort to determine fair market value shall ordinarily have been made where:

(a) The person making the valuation is not a disqualified person with respect to the foundation and is both competent to make the valuation and not in a position, whether by stock ownership or otherwise, to derive an economic benefit from the value utilized, and

(b) The method utilized in making the valuation is a generally accepted method for valuing comparable property, stock, or securities for purposes of arm's-length business transactions where valuation is a significant factor.

See section 4941(d)(2)(F) and §§ 53.4941(d)–1(b)(3), 53.4941(d)–3(d)(1) and 53.4941(d)–4(b). Thus, for example, if a corporation which is a disqualified person with respect to a private foundation recapitalizes in a transaction which would be described in section 4941(d)(2)(F) but for the fact that the private foundation receives new stock worth only $95,000 in exchange for the stock which it previously held in the corporation and which has a fair market value of $100,000 at the time of the recapitalization, the amount involved would be $5,000 ($100,000-$95,000) if there had been a good faith attempt to value the stock. Similarly, if an estate enters into a transaction with a disqualified person with respect to a foundation and such transaction would be described in § 53.4941(d)–1(b)(3) but for the fact that the estate receives less than fair market value for the property exchanged, the amount involved is the excess of the fair market value of the property the estate transfers to the disqualified person over the money and the fair market value of the property received by the estate.

(3) Time for determining fair market value. The fair market value of the property or the use thereof, as the case may be, shall be determined as of the date on which the act of self-dealing occurred in the case of the initial taxes imposed by section 4941(a) and shall be the highest fair market value during the taxable period in the case of the additional taxes imposed by section 4941(b).

(4) Examples. The provisions of this paragraph may be illustrated by the following examples:

Example (1). A, a disqualified person with respect to private foundation M, uses an airplane owned by M on June 15 and June 16, 1970, for a 2-day trip to New York City on personal business and pays M $500 for the use of such airplane. The fair rental value for the use of the airplane for those 2 days is $3,000. For purposes of section 4941(a), the amount involved with respect to the act of self-dealing is $3,000.

Example (2). On April 10, 1970, B, a manager of private foundation P, borrows $100,000 from P at 6 percent interest per annum. Both principal and interest are to be paid 1 year from the date of the loan. The fair market value of the use of the money on April 10, 1970, is 10 percent per annum. Six months later, B and P terminate the loan, and B repays the $100,000 principal plus $3,000 ($100,000x6 percent for one-half year) interest. For purposes of section 4941(a), the amount involved with respect to the act of self-dealing is $5,000 ($100,000x10 percent for one-half year) for each year or partial year in the taxable period.

Example (3). C, a substantial contributor to private foundation S, leases office space in a building owned by S for $3,600 for 1 year beginning on January 1, 1971. The fair rental value of the building for a 1-year lease on January 1, 1971, is $5,600. On December 31, 1971, the lease is terminated. For purposes of section 4941(a), the amount involved with respect to the act of self-dealing is $5,600 for each year or partial year in the taxable period.

Example (4). D, a disqualified person with respect to private foundation T, purchases 100 shares of stock from T for $5,000 on June 15, 1982. The fair market value of the 100 shares of stock on that date is $4,800. D sells the 100 shares of stock on December 20, 1983, for $6,000. On December 27, 1983, a notice of deficiency with respect to the taxes imposed under subsections (a) and (b) of section 4941 is mailed to D and the taxable period ends. D fails to correct during the taxable period. Between June 15, 1982, and the end of the taxable period, the stock was quoted on the New York Stock Exchange at a high of $67 per share. The amount involved with respect to the tax imposed under subsection (a) is $5,000, and the amount involved with respect to the tax imposed under subsection (b) for failure to correct is $6,700 (100 shares at $67 per share), the highest fair market value during the taxable period.

Example (5). Corporation M, a disqualified person with respect to private foundation V, redeems all of its Class B common stock, some of which is held by V. The redemption of V's stock would be described in section 4941(d)(2)(F) but for the fact that V receives only $95,000 in exchange for stock which has a fair market value of $100,000 at the time of the transaction. The $95,000 value of V's stock, which is not publicly traded, was determined by investment bankers in accordance with accepted methods of valuation that would be utilized if the M stock held by V were to be offered for sale to the public. Therefore, the amount involved with respect to the transaction will ordinarily be limited to $5,000 ($100,000 - $95,000).

(c) Correction—(1) In general. Correction shall be accomplished by undoing the transaction which constituted the act of self-dealing to the extent possible, but in no case shall the resulting financial position of the private foundation be worse than that which it would be if the disqualified person were dealing under the highest fiduciary standards. For example, where a disqualified person sells property to a private foundation for cash, correction may be accomplished by recasting the transaction in the form of a gift by returning the cash to the foundation. Subparagraphs (2) through (6) of this paragraph illustrate the minimum standards of correction in the case of certain specific acts of self-dealing. Principles similar to the principles contained in such subparagraphs shall be applied with respect to other acts of self-dealing. Any correction pursuant to this paragraph and section 4941 shall not be an act of self-dealing.

(2) Sales by foundation. (i) In the case of a sale of property by a private foundation to a disqualified person for cash, undoing the transaction includes, but is not limited to, requiring recission of the sale where possible. However, in order to avoid placing the foundation in a position worse than that in which it would be if rescission were not required, the amount returned to the disqualified person pursuant to the rescission shall not exceed the lesser of the cash received by the private foundation or the fair market value of the property received by the disqualified person. For purposes of the preceding sentence, fair market value shall be the lesser of the fair market value at the time of the act of self-dealing or the fair market value at the time of rescission. In addition to rescission, the disqualified person is required to pay over to the private foundation any net profits he realized after the original sale with respect to the property he received from the sale. Thus, for example, the disqualified person must pay over to the foundation any income derived by him from the property he received from the original sale to the extent such income during the correction period exceeds the income derived by the foundation during the correction period from the cash which the disqualified person originally paid to the foundation.

(ii) If, prior to the end of the correction period, the disqualified person resells the property in an arm's-length transaction to a bona fide purchaser who is not the foundation or another disqualified person, no rescission is required. In such case, the disqualified person must pay over to the foundation the excess (if any) of the greater of the fair market value of such property on the date on which correction of the act of self-dealing occurs or the amount realized by the disqualified person from such arm's length resale over the amount which would have been returned to the disqualified person pursuant to subdivision (i) of this subparagraph if rescission had been required. In addition, the disqualified person is required to pay over to the foundation any net profits he realized, as described in subdivision (i) of this subparagraph.

(iii) Examples. The provisions of this subparagraph may be illustrated by the following examples:

Example (1). On July 1, 1970, private foundation M sold a painting to A, a disqualified person, for $5,000, in a transaction not within any of the exceptions to self-dealing. The fair market value of the painting on such date was $6,000. On March 25, 1971, the painting is still owned by A and has a fair market value of $7,200. A did not derive any income as a result of purchasing the painting. In order to correct the act of self-dealing under this subparagraph on March 25, 1971, the sale must be rescinded by the return of the painting to M. However, pursuant to such rescission, M must not pay A more than $5,000, the original consideration received by M.

Example (2). Assume the facts as stated in Example (1), except that A sold the painting on December 15, 1970, in an arm's-length transaction to C, a bona fide purchaser who is not a disqualified person, for $6,100. In addition, assume that the fair market value of the painting on March 25, 1971, is $7,600. In order to correct the act of self-dealing under this subparagraph on March 25, 1971, A must pay M $2,600 ($7,600, the fair market value at the time of correction, less $5,000, the amount which would have been returned to A if rescission had been required). Since the painting was sold to C in an arm's-length transaction prior to correction, no rescission is required.

(3) Sales to foundation. (i) In the case of a sale of property to a private foundation by a disqualified person for cash, undoing the transaction includes, but is not limited to, requiring rescission of the sale where possible. However, in order to avoid placing the foundation in a position worse than that in which it would be if rescission were not required, the amount received from the disqualified person pursuant to the rescission shall be the greatest of the cash paid to the disqualified person, the fair market value of the property at the time of the original sale, or the fair market value of the property at the time of rescission. In addition to rescission, the disqualified person is required to pay over to the private foundation any net profits he realized after the original sale with respect to the consideration he received from the sale. Thus, for example, the disqualified person must pay over to the foundation any income derived by him from the cash he received from the original sale to the extent such income during the correction period exceeds the income derived by the foundation during the correction period from the property which the disqualified person originally transferred to the foundation.

(ii) If, prior to the end of the correction period, the foundation resells the property in an arm's-length transaction to a bona fide purchaser who is not a disqualified person, no recission is required. In such case, the disqualified person must pay over to the foundation the excess (if any) of the amount which would have been received from the disqualified person pursuant to subdivision (i) of this subparagraph, if rescission had been required over the amount realized by the foundation upon resale of the property. In addition, the disqualified person is required to pay over to the foundation any net profits he realized, as described in subdivision (i) of this subparagraph.

(iii) Examples. The provisions of this subparagraph may be illustrated by the following examples:

Example (1). On February 10, 1972, D, a disqualified person with respect to private foundation P, sells 100 shares of X stock to P for $2,500 in a transaction which does not fall within any of the exceptions to selfdealing. The fair market value of the 100 shares of X stock on February 10, 1972, is $3,200. On June 1, 1973, the 100 shares of X stock have a fair market value of $2,900. From February 10, 1972, through June 1, 1973, P has received dividends of $90 from the stock, and D has received interest of $300 from the $2,500 which D received as consideration for the stock. In order to correct the act of self-dealing under this subparagraph on June 1, 1973, the sale must be rescinded by the return of the stock to D. However, pursuant to such rescission, D must pay P $3,200, the fair market value of the stock on the date of sale. In addition, D must pay P $210, the amount of income derived by D during the correction period from the $2,500 received from P ($300) minus the income derived by P during the correction period from the stock sold to P ($90).

Example (2). Assume the facts as stated in Example (1), except that on September 1, 1972, P sells the 100 shares of X stock to E, a bona fide purchaser who is not a disqualified person, in an arm's-length transaction for $2,750. Assume further that P has not received any dividends from the stock prior to the sale to E, but that P receives interest of $260 from the $2,750 received as consideration for the stock for the period from September 1, 1972, to June 1, 1973. In order to correct the act of self-dealing under this subparagraph on June 1, 1973, D must pay P $450 ($3,200, the amount which would have been received from D if rescission had been required, less $2,750, the amount realized by P from the sale to E). In addition, D must pay P $40, the amount of income derived by D during the correction period from the $2,500 received from P ($300) minus the income derived by P during the correction period from the stock sold to P ($260 from the $2,750 received as consideration for the stock). Since the stock was sold to E in an arm's-length transaction prior to correction, no rescission is required.

(4) Use of property by a disqualified person. (i) In the case of the use by a disqualified person of property owned by a private foundation, undoing the transaction includes, but is not limited to, terminating the use of such property. In addition to termination, the disqualified person must pay the foundation:

(a) The excess (if any) of the fair market value of the use of the property over the amount paid by the disqualified person for such use until such termination, and

(b) The excess (if any) of the amount which would have been paid by the disqualified person for the use of the property on or after the date of such termination, for the period such disqualified person would have used the property (without regard to any further extensions or renewals of such period) if such termination had not occurred, over the fair market value of such use for such period.

In applying (a) of this subdivision the fair market value of the use of property shall be the higher of the rate (that is, fair rental value per period in the case of use of property other than money or fair interest rate in the case of use of money) at the time of the act of self-dealing (within the meaning of paragraph (e)(1) of this section) or such rate at the time of correction of such act of self-dealing. In applying (b) of this subdivision the fair market value of the use of property shall be the rate at the time of correction.

(ii) The provisions of this subparagraph may be illustrated by the following examples:

Example (1). On January 1, 1972, private foundation S rented the third story of its office building to A, a disqualified person, for 1 year at an annual rent of $10,000, in a transaction not within any of the exceptions to self-dealing. Both S and A are on the calendar year basis. The fair rental value of such office space for a 1-year period on January 1, 1972, is $12,000. On June 30, 1972, the fair rental value of such office space for a 1-year period is $13,000. In order to correct the act of self-dealing under this subparagraph on June 30, 1972, A must terminate his use of the property. In addition, A must pay S $1,500, the excess of $6,500 (the fair rental value for 6 months as of June 30, 1972) over $5,000 (the amount paid to S from Jan. 1, 1972, to June 30, 1972).

Example (2). On January 1, 1972, private foundation R rented the fourth story of its office building to B, a disqualified person, for 1 year at an annual rent of $10,000, in a transaction not included in any of the exceptions to self-dealing. Both R and B are on the calendar year basis. On January 1, 1973, B continues to rent the office space as a periodic tenant paying his rent monthly at an annual rate of $10,000. The fair rental value of such office space for a 1-year period on January 1, 1972, is $12,000, and as of January 1, 1973, is $1,250 per month. As of December 31, 1973, the fair rental value of such office space is $14,000 for a 1-year period and $1,200 on a monthly basis. In order to correct his acts of self-dealing (within the meaning of paragraph (e)(1) of this section) under this subparagraph on December 31, 1973, B must terminate his use of the property. In addition, B must pay R $9,000, $4,000 for his use of the property for 1972 (the excess of $14,000, the fair rental value for 1 year as of Dec. 31, 1973, over $10,000, the amount B paid R for his use of the property for 1972) and $5,000 for his use of the property for 1973 (the excess of $15,000, the fair rental value for 12 months as of Jan. 1, 1973, over $10,000, the amount B paid R for his use of the property for 1973).

Example (3). B, a substantial contributor to private foundation T, leases office space in a building owned by T for $5,000 for 1 year beginning on November 10, 1972, in a transaction not included in any of the exceptions to self-dealing. The fair rental value of the building for a 1-year period on November 10, 1972, is $4,000. On May 10, 1973, the fair rental value of the building for the remaining period of the lease is $2,200. In order to correct the acts of self-dealing under this subparagraph on May 10, 1973, B and T must terminate the lease. In addition, B must pay T $300 (the excess of $2,500, the amount which would have been paid by B for the remaining period of the lease if it had not been terminated, over $2,200, the fair rental value at the time of correction for the remaining period of the lease).

(5) Use of property by a private foundation. (i) In the case of the use by a private foundation of property owned by a disqualified person, undoing the transaction includes, but is not limited to, terminating the use of such property. In addition to termination, the disqualified person must pay the foundation:

(a) The excess (if any) of the amount paid to the disqualified person for such use until such termination over the fair market value of the use of the property, and

(b) The excess (if any) of the fair market value of the use of the property, for the period the foundation would have used the property (without regard to any further extensions or renewals of such period) if such termination had not occurred, over the amount which would have been paid to the disqualified person on or after the date of such termination for such use for such period.

In applying (a) of this subdivision the fair market value of the use of property shall be the lesser of the rate (that is, fair rental value per period in the case of use of property other than money or fair interest rate in the case of use of money) at the time of the act of self-dealing (within the meaning of paragraph (e)(1) of this section) or such rate at the time of correction of such act of self-dealing. In applying (b) of this subdivision the fair market value of the use of property shall be the rate at the time of correction.

(ii) The provisions of this subparagraph may be illustrated by the following examples:

Example (1). On July 1, 1972, private foundation X leases office space in a building owned by C, a disqualified person, for 1 year at an annual rent of $6,000. Both X and C are on the calendar year basis. The fair rental value of such office space for a 1-year period as of July 1, 1972, is $4,200. As of January 1, 1973, the fair rental value of such office space for a 1-year period is $5,400, and as of June 30, 1973, the fair rental value of such office space for a 1-year period is $4,800. In order to correct his acts of self-dealing (within the meaning of paragraph (e)(1) of this section) under this subparagraph on June 30, 1973, C must terminate X's use of the property. In addition, C must pay X $1,500, $900 (the excess of $3,000, the amount paid to C from July 1, 1972, through December 31, 1972, over $2,100, the fair rental value for 6 months as of July 1, 1972) plus $600 (the excess of $3,000, the amount paid to C from January 1, 1973, through June 30, 1973, over $2,400, the fair rental value for 6 months as of June 30, 1973).

Example (2). On April 1, 1973, D, a disqualified person with respect to private foundation Y, loans $100,000 to Y at 6 percent interest per annum. Both principal and interest are to be paid on April 1, 1978. The fair market value of the use of the money on April 1, 1973, is 9 percent per annum. On April 1, 1974, D and Y terminate the loan. On such date, the fair market value of the use of $100,000 is 10 percent per annum. In order to correct the act of self-dealing on April 1, 1974, in addition to the termination of the loan from D to Y, D must pay Y $16,000, the excess of $40,000 ($100,000x10 percent, the fair market value of the use determined at the time of correction, from April 1, 1974, to April 1, 1978) over $24,000 (the amount of interest Y would have paid to D from April 1, 1974, to April 1, 1978, if the loan from D to Y had not been terminated).

(6) Payment of compensation to a disqualified person. In the case of the payment of compensation by a private foundation to a disqualified person for the performance of personal services which are reasonable and necessary to carry out the exempt purpose of such foundation, undoing the transaction requires that the disqualified person pay to the foundation any amount which is excessive. However, termination of the employment or independent contractor relationship is not required.

(7) Special rule for correction of valuation errors. (i) In the case of a transaction described in paragraph (b)(2)(iii) of this section, a "correction" of the act of self-dealing shall ordinarily be deemed to occur if the foundation is paid an amount of money equal to the amount involved (as defined in paragraph (b)(2)(iii) of this section) plus such additional amounts as are necessary to compensate it for the loss of the use of the money or other property during the period commencing on the date of the act of self-dealing and ending on the date the transaction is corrected pursuant to this subparagraph.

(ii) The provisions of this subparagraph may be illustrated by the following example:

Example. Assume the same facts as in example (5) of paragraph (b)(4) of this section. Such transaction shall be considered as corrected by a payment of $5,000 by M to V, together with an additional payment to V of an amount equal to the interest which V could have obtained on $5,000 for the period commencing on the date of the redemption and ending on the date the act is corrected.

(d) Cross reference. For rules relating to taxable events that are corrected within the correction period, defined in section 4963(e), see section 4961(a), and the regulations thereunder.

(e) Act of self-dealing—(1) Number of acts; use of money or property—(i) In general. If a transaction between a private foundation and a disqualified person is determined to be self-dealing (as defined in section 4941(d)), for purposes of section 4941 there is generally one act of self-dealing. For the date on which such act is treated as occurring, see paragraph (a)(2) of this section. If, however, such transaction relates to the leasing of property, the lending of money or other extension of credit, other use of money or property, or payment of compensation, the transaction will generally be treated (for purposes of section 4941 but not section 507 or section 6684) as giving rise to an act of self-dealing on the day the transaction occurs plus an act of self-dealing on the first day of each taxable year or portion of a taxable year which is within the taxable period and which begins after the taxable year in which the transaction occurs.

(ii) Examples. The provisions of this subparagraph may be illustrated by the following examples:

Example (1). On August 31, 1970, X, a private foundation, sells a building to A, a disqualified person with respect to X. A is on the calendar year basis. Under these circumstances, the transaction between A and X is one act of self-dealing which is treated for purposes of section 4941 as occurring on August 31, 1970.

Example (2). Assume the facts as stated in example (1), except that, instead of selling the building to A, X leases the building to A for a term of 4 years beginning July 31, 1970, at an annual rental of $12,000. The fair rental value of the building is also $12,000 per annum as of July 31, 1970, and throughout the next 4 years. This transaction is corrected on September 30, 1973, in accordance with paragraph (c)(4) of this section. Under these circumstances, the transaction between A and X constitutes four separate acts of self-dealing, which are treated for purposes of section 4941 as occurring on July 31, 1970, January 1, 1971, January 1, 1972, and January 1, 1973. Consequently, there are four taxable periods. The first taxable period is from July 31, 1970, to September 30, 1973; the second is from January 1, 1971, to September 30, 1973; the third is from January 1, 1972, to September 30, 1973; and the fourth is from January 1, 1973, to September 30, 1973. For purposes of the initial taxes in section 4941(a), the amount involved is $5,000 for the first taxable period, $12,000 for the second, $12,000 for the third, and $9,000 for the fourth. The initial taxes to be paid by A are thus $1,000 ($5,000 x 5% x 4 taxable years or partial taxable years in the taxable period) for the first act; $1,800 ($12,000 x 5% x 3) for the second act; $1,200 ($12,000 x 5% x 2) for the third act; and $450 ($9,000 x 5% x 1) for the fourth act.

Example (3). Assume the facts as stated in example (1) of § 53.4941(d)–4(c)(4)(ii). If the debentures are held by Y after December 31, 1979, the extension of credit will not be excepted from the definition of an act of self-dealing, because an act of self-dealing will be treated (for purposes of section 4941) as occurring on January 1, 1980.

(2) Number of acts; joint participation by disqualified persons—(i) In general. If joint participation in a transaction by two or more disqualified persons constitutes self-dealing (such as a joint sale of property to a private foundation or joint use of its money or property), such transaction shall generally be treated as a separate act of self-dealing with respect to each disqualified person for purposes of section 4941. For purposes of section 507 and, in the case of a foundation manager, section 6684, however, such transaction shall be treated as only one act of self-dealing. For purposes of this subparagraph, an individual and one or more members of his family (within the meaning of section 4946(d)) shall be treated as one person, regardless of whether a member of the family is a disqualified person not only by reason of section 4946(a)(1)(D) but also by reason of another subparagraph of section 4946(a)(1). However, the liability imposed on a disqualified person and one or more members of his family for joint participation in an act of self-dealing shall be joint and several in accordance with section 4941(c)(1) and § 53.4941(c)–1(a).

(ii) Examples. The provisions of this subparagraph may be illustrated by the following examples:

Example (1). Private foundation X permits A, a substantial contributor to X, and her spouse, H, to use an automobile owned by X and normally used in its foundation activities to travel from State Z to State Y for a vacation on December 1, 1971. The automobile is then returned to X until December 21, 1971, when X again permits them to use the automobile to return to their home in State Z. Under these circumstances, there is one act of self-dealing on December 1, 1971, and a second act of self-dealing on December 21, 1971.

Example (2). Assume the facts as stated in example (1), except that B joined A and H on their vacation and traveled with them both to and from State Y. B is a disqualified person with respect to X, but he is not related by blood or marriage to A or H. Assume also that X is not paid for the use of its automobile, but that the fair rental value during the taxable period is $300 (or $100 per person) for a one-way trip between State Y and State Z. Under these circumstances, there are four acts of self-dealing, two with respect to A and H and two with respect to B. The amount involved with respect to A and H is $200 for each act, and the amount involved with respect to B is $100 for each act.

(f) Fair market value. For purposes of §§ 53.4941(a)–1 through 53.4941(f)–1, fair market value shall be determined pursuant to the provisions of § 53.4942(a)–2(c)(4).

§ 53.4942(a)–1. Taxes for failure to distribute income.

(a) Imposition of tax—(1) Initial tax. Except as provided in paragraph (b) of this section, section 4942(a) imposes an excise tax of 15 percent on the undistributed income (as defined in paragraph (a) of § 53.4942(a)–2) of a private foundation for any taxable year which has not been distributed before the first day of the second (or any succeeding) taxable year following such taxable year (if such first day falls within the taxable period as defined in paragraph (c)(1) of this section). For purposes of section 4942 and this section, the term distributed means distributed as qualifying distributions under section 4942(g). See paragraph (d)(2) of § 53.4942(a)–3 with respect to correction of deficient distributions for prior taxable years.

(2) Additional tax. In any case in which an initial excise tax is imposed by section 4942(a) on the undistributed income of a private foundation for any taxable year, section 4942(b) imposes an additional excise tax on any portion of such income remaining undistributed at the close of the correction period (as defined in paragraph (c)(1) of this section). The tax imposed by section 4942(b) is equal to 100 percent of the amount remaining undistributed at the close of the taxable period.

(3) Payment of tax. Payment of the excise taxes imposed by section 4942(a) or (b) is in addition to, and not in lieu of, making the distribution of such undistributed income as required by section 4942. See section 507(a)(2) and the regulations thereunder.

(4) Examples. The provisions of this paragraph may be illustrated by the following examples:

Example (1). M, a private foundation which uses the calendar year as its taxable year, has at the end of 1981, $50,000 of undistributed income (as defined in paragraph (a) of § 53.4942(a)–2) for 1981. As of January 1, 1983, $40,000 is still undistributed. On August 15, 1983, a notice of deficiency with respect to the excise taxes imposed by section 4942(a) and (b) is mailed to M under section 6212(a) and the taxable period ends. Thus, under these facts, an initial excise tax of $6,000 (15 percent of $40,000) is imposed upon M. An additional excise tax of $40,000 (100 percent of $40,000) is imposed by section 4942(b). Under section 4961(a), however, if the undistributed income is reduced to zero during the correction period, this latter tax will not be assessed, and if assessed, it will be abated, and if collected, it will be credited or refunded as an overpayment.

Example (2). Assume the facts as stated in example (1), except that the notice of deficiency is mailed to M on September 7, 1984, and as of January 1, 1984, only $10,000 of the $50,000 of undistributed income with respect to 1981 is undistributed. Therefore, initial excise taxes of $6,000 (15 percent of $40,000, M's undistributed income from 1981, as of January 1, 1983) and $1,500 (15 percent of $10,000, M's undistributed income from 1981 as of January 1, 1984) are imposed by section 4942(a). If the $10,000 remains undistributed as of September 7, 1984, the end of the taxable period, an additional excise tax of $10,000 (100 percent of $10,000, M's undistributed income from 1981, as of September 7, 1984) is imposed by section 4942(b).

(b) Exceptions—(1) In general. The initial excise tax imposed by section 4942(a) shall not apply to the undistributed income of a private foundation:

(i) For any taxable year for which it is an operating foundation (as defined in section 4942(j)(3) and the regulations thereunder), or

(ii) To the extent that the foundation failed to distribute any amount solely because of incorrect valuation of assets under paragraph (c)(4) of § 53.4942(a)–2, if:

(a) The failure to value the assets properly was not willful and was due to reasonable cause,

(b) Such amount is distributed as qualifying distributions (within the meaning of paragraph (a) of § 53.4942(a)–3) by the foundation during the allowable distribution period (as defined in paragraph (c)(2) of this section),

(c) The foundation notifies the Commissioner that such amount has been distributed (within the meaning of subdivision (ii)(b) of this subparagraph) to correct such failure, and

(d) Such distribution is treated under paragraph (d)(2) of § 53.4942(a)–3 as made out of the undistributed income for the taxable year for which a tax would (except for this subdivision) have been imposed by section 4942(a).

(2) Improper valuation. For purposes of subparagraph (1)(ii) of this paragraph, failure to value an asset properly shall be regarded as "not willful" and "due to reasonable cause" whenever, under all the facts and circumstances, the foundation can show that it has made all reasonable efforts in good faith to value such an asset in accordance with the provisions of paragraph (c)(4) of § 53.4942(a)–2. If a foundation, after full disclosure of the factual situation, obtains a bona fide appraisal of the fair market value of an asset by a person qualified to make such an appraisal (whether or not such a person is a disqualified person with respect to the foundation), and such foundation relies upon such appraisal, then failure to value the asset properly shall ordinarily be regarded as "not willful" and "due to reasonable cause".

Notwithstanding the preceding sentence, the failure to obtain such a bona fide appraisal shall not, by itself, give rise to any inference that a foundation's failure to value an asset properly was willful or not due to reasonable cause.

(3) Example. The provisions of this paragraph may be illustrated by the following example:

Example. In 1976 M, a private foundation which was established in 1975 and which uses the calendar year as the taxable year, incorrectly values its assets under paragraph (c)(4) of § 53.4942(a)–2 in a manner which is not willful and is due to reasonable cause. As a result of the incorrect valuation of assets, $20,000 which should be distributed with respect to 1976 is not distributed, and as of January 1, 1978, such amount is still undistributed. On March 29, 1978, a notice of deficiency with respect to the excise taxes imposed by section 4942(a) and (b) is mailed to M under section 6212(a). On May 5, 1978 (within the allowable distribution period), M makes a qualifying distribution of $20,000 which is treated under paragraph (d)(2) of § 53.4942(a)–3 as made out of M's undistributed income for 1976. M notifies the Commissioner of its action. Under the stated facts, an initial excise tax of $3,000 (15 percent of $20,000) would (except for the exception contained in subparagraph (1)(ii) of this paragraph) have been imposed by section 4942(a), but since all of the requirements of such subparagraph are satisfied no tax is imposed by section 4942(a).

(c) Certain periods. For purposes of this section—

(1) Taxable period. (i) The term "taxable period" means, with respect to the undistributed income of a private foundation for any taxable year, the period beginning with the first day of the taxable year and ending on the earlier of:

(A) The date of mailing of a notice of deficiency under section 6212(a) with respect to the initial excise tax imposed under section 4942(a), or

(B) The date on which the initial excise tax imposed under section 4942(a) is assessed.

For example, assume M, a private foundation which uses the calendar year as the taxable year, has $15,000 of undistributed income for 1981. A notice of deficiency is mailed to M under section 6212(a) on June 1, 1983. With respect to the undistributed income of M for 1981, the taxable period began on January 1, 1981, and ended on June 1, 1983.

(ii) Where a notice of deficiency referred to in subdivision (i) of this subparagraph is not mailed because there is a waiver of the restrictions on assessment and collection of a deficiency, or because the deficiency is paid, the date of filing of the waiver or the date of such payment, respectively, shall be treated as the end of the taxable period.

(2) Allowable distribution period. (i) The term "allowable distribution period" means the period beginning with the first day of the first taxable year following the taxable year in which the incorrect valuation of foundation assets (described in paragraph (b)(1)(ii) of this section) occurred and ending 90 days after the date of mailing of a notice of deficiency under section 6212(a) with respect to the initial excise tax imposed by section 4942(a). This period shall be extended by any period in which a deficiency cannot be assessed under section 6213(a), and any other period which the Commissioner determines is reasonable and necessary to permit a distribution of undistributed income under section 4942.

(ii) Where a notice of deficiency referred to in subdivision (i) of this subparagraph is not mailed because there is a waiver of the restrictions on assessment and collection of a deficiency, or because the deficiency is paid, the date of filing of the waiver or the date of such payment, respectively, shall be treated as the end of the allowable distribution period.

(3) Cross reference. For rules relating to taxable events that are corrected within the correction period, defined in section 4963(e), see section 4961(a) and the regulations thereunder.

(4) Examples. The provisions of this paragraph may be illustrated by the following examples:

Example (1). In 1975 M, a private foundation which uses the calendar year as the taxable year, made an error in valuing its assets which was not willful and was due to reasonable cause. The error caused M not to distribute $25,000 that should have been distributed with respect to 1975. On March 1, 1978, a notice of deficiency with respect to the excise taxes imposed by section 4942(a) and (b) was mailed to M under section 6212(a). With respect to the undistributed income for 1975, the "taxable period" is the period from January 1, 1975, through March 1, 1978, and the "allowable distribution period" is the period from January 1, 1976, through May 30, 1978 (90 days after the mailing of the notice of deficiency).

Example (2). Assume the facts as stated in example (1), except that the Commissioner determines that it is reasonable and necessary to extend the period for distribution through June 15, 1978. Thus, the "allowable distribution period" is from January 1, 1976, through June 15, 1978.

(d) Effective date. Except as otherwise specifically provided, section 4942 and the regulations thereunder shall only apply with respect to taxable years beginning after December 31, 1969.

§ 53.4942(a)-2. Computation of undistributed income.

(a) Undistributed income. For purposes of section 4942, the term "undistributed income" means, with respect to any private foundation for any taxable year as of any time, the amount by which—

(1) The distributable amount (as defined in paragraph (b) of this section) for such taxable year, exceeds

(2) The qualifying distributions (as defined in § 53.4942(a)-3) made before such time out of such distributable amount.

(b) Distributable amount—(1) In general. For purposes of paragraph (a) of this section, the term "distributable amount" means—

(i) For taxable years beginning before January 1, 1982, an amount equal to the greater of the minimum investment return (as defined in paragraph (c) of this section) or the adjusted net income (as defined in paragraph (d) of this section); and

(ii) For taxable years beginning after December 31, 1981, an amount equal to the minimum investment return (as defined in paragraph (c) of this section), reduced by the sum of the taxes imposed on such private foundation for such taxable year under subtitle A of the Code and section 4940, and increased by the amounts received from trusts described in subparagraph (2) of this paragraph.

(2) Certain trust amounts—(i) In general. The distributable amount shall be increased by the income portion (as defined in subdivision (ii) of this subparagraph) of distributions from trusts described in section 4947(a)(2) with respect to amounts placed in trust after May 26, 1969. If such distributions are made with respect to amounts placed in trust both on or before and after

May 26, 1969, such distributions shall be allocated between such amounts to determine the extent to which such distributions shall be included in the foundation's distributable amount. For rules relating to the segregation of amounts placed in trust on or before May 26, 1969, from amounts placed in trust after such date and to the allocation of income derived from such amounts, see paragraph (c)(5) of § 53.4947–1.

(ii) Income portion of distributions to private foundations. For purposes of subdivision (i) of this subparagraph, the income portion of a distribution from a section 4947(a)(2) trust to a private foundation in a particular taxable year of such foundation shall be the greater of:

(a) The amount of such distribution which is treated as income (within the meaning of section 643(b)) of the trust, or

(b) The guaranteed annuity, or fixed percentage of the fair market value of the trust property (determined annually), which the private foundation is entitled to receive for such year, regardless of whether such amount is actually received in such year or in any prior or subsequent year.

(iii) Limitation. Notwithstanding subdivisions (i) and (ii) of this subparagraph, a private foundation shall not be required to distribute a greater amount for any taxable year than would have been required (without regard to this subparagraph) for such year had the corpus of the section 4947(a)(2) trust to which the distribution described in subdivision (ii) of this subparagraph is attributable been taken into account by such foundation as an asset described in paragraph (c)(1)(i) of this section.

(c) Minimum investment return—(1) In general. For purposes of paragraph (b) of this section, the "minimum investment return" for any private foundation for any taxable year is the amount determined by multiplying—

(i) The excess of the aggregate fair market value of all assets of the foundation, other than those described in subparagraph (2) or (3) of this paragraph, over the amount of the acquisition indebtedness with respect to such assets (determined under section 514(c)(1), but without regard to the taxable year in which the indebtedness was incurred), by

(ii) The applicable percentage (as defined in subparagraph (5) of this paragraph) for such year.

For purposes of subdivision (i) of this subparagraph, the aggregate fair market value of all assets of the foundation shall include the average of the fair market values on a monthly basis of securities for which market quotations are readily available (within the meaning of subparagraph (4)(i)(a) of this paragraph), the average of the foundation's cash balances on a monthly basis (less the cash balances excluded from the computation of the minimum investment return by operation of subparagraph (3)(iv) of this paragraph), and the fair market value of all other assets (except those assets described in subparagraph (2) or (3) of this paragraph) for the period of time during the taxable year for which such assets are held by the foundation. Any determination of the fair market value of an asset required pursuant to the provisions of this subparagraph shall be made in accordance with the rules of subparagraph (4) of this paragraph.

(2) Certain assets excluded. For purposes of this paragraph, the assets taken into account in determining minimum investment return shall not include the following:

(i) Any future interest (such as a vested or contingent remainder, whether legal or equitable) of a foundation in the income or corpus of any real or personal property, other than a future interest created by the private foundation after December 31, 1969, until all intervening interests in, and rights to the actual possession or enjoyment of, such property have expired, or, although not actually reduced to the foundation's possession, until such future interest has been constructively received by the foundation, as where it has been credited to the foundation's account, set apart for the foundation, or otherwise made available so that the foundation may acquire it at any time or could have acquired it if notice of intention to acquire had been given;

(ii) The assets of an estate until such time as such assets are distributed to the foundation or, due to a prolonged period of administration, such estate is considered terminated for Federal income tax purposes by operation of paragraph (a) of § 1.641(b)–3 of this chapter (Income Tax Regulations);

(iii) Any present interest of a foundation in any trust created and funded by another person (see, however, paragraph (b)(2) of this section with respect to amounts received from certain trusts described in section 4947(a)(2));

(iv) Any pledge to the foundation of money or property (whether or not the pledge may be legally enforced); and

(v) Any assets used (or held for use) directly in carrying out the foundation's exempt purpose.

(3) Assets used (or held for use) in carrying out the exempt purpose—(i) In general. For purposes of subparagraph (2)(v) of this paragraph, an asset is "used (or held for use) directly in carrying out the foundation's exempt purpose" only if the asset is actually used by the foundation in the carrying out of the charitable, educational, or other similar purpose which gives rise to the exempt status of the foundation, or if the foundation owns the asset and establishes to the satisfaction of the Commissioner that its immediate use for such exempt purpose is not practical (based on the facts and circumstances of the particular case) and that definite plans exist to commence such use within a reasonable period of time. Consequently, assets which are held for the production of income or for investment (for example, stocks, bonds, interest-bearing notes, endowment funds, or, generally, leased real estate) are not being used (or held for use) directly in carrying out the foundation's exempt purpose, even though the income from such assets is used to carry out such exempt purpose. Whether an asset is held for the production of income or for investment rather than used (or held for use) directly by the foundation to carry out its exempt purpose is a question of fact. For example, an office building used for the purpose of providing offices for employees engaged in the management of endowment funds of the foundation is not being used (or held for use) directly by the foundation to carry out its charitable, educational, or other similar exempt purpose. However, where property is used both for charitable, educational, or other similar exempt purposes and for other purposes, if such exempt use represents 95 percent or more of the total use, such property shall be considered to be used exclusively for a charitable, educational, or other similar exempt purpose. If such exempt use of such property represents less than 95 percent of the total use, reasonable allocation between such exempt and nonexempt use must be made for purposes of this paragraph. Property acquired by the foundation to be used in carrying out its charitable, educational, or other similar exempt purpose may be considered as used (or held for use) directly to carry out such exempt purpose even though the property, in whole or in part, is leased for a limited period of time during which arrangements are made for its conversion to the use for which it was acquired, provided such income-producing use of the property does not exceed a reasonable period of time. Generally, 1 year shall be deemed to be a reasonable period of time for purposes of the immediately preceding sentence. For treatment of the income derived from such income-producing use, see paragraph (d)(2)(viii) of this section. Where the income-producing use continues beyond a reasonable period of time, the property shall not be deemed to be used by the foundation to carry out its charitable, educational, or other similar exempt purpose, but, instead, as of the time the income-producing use becomes unreasonable, such property shall be treated as disposed of within the meaning of paragraph (d)(2)(iii)(b) of this section to the extent that the acquisition of the property was taken into account as a qualifying distribution (within the meaning of paragraph (a)(2) of § 53.4942(a)–3 for any taxable year. If, subsequently, the property is used by the foundation directly in carrying out its charitable, educational, or other similar exempt purpose, a qualifying distribution in the amount of its then fair market value, determined in accordance with the rules contained in subparagraph (4) of this paragraph, shall be deemed to have been made as of the time such exempt use begins.

(ii) Illustrations. Examples of assets which are "used (or held for use) directly in carrying out the foundation's exempt purpose" include, but are not limited to, the following:

(a) Administrative assets, such as office equipment and supplies which are used by employees or consultants of the foundation, to the extent such assets are devoted to and used directly in the administration of the foundation's charitable, educational or other similar exempt activities;

(b) Real estate or the portion of a building used by the foundation directly in its charitable, educational, or other similar exempt activities;

(c) Physical facilities used in such activities, such as paintings or other works of art owned by the foundation which are on public display, fixtures and equipment in classrooms, research facilities and related equipment which under the facts and circumstances serve a useful purpose in the conduct of such activities;

(d) Any interest in a functionally related business (as defined in subdivision (iii) of this subparagraph) or in a program-related investment (as defined in section 4944(c));

(e) The reasonable cash balances (as described in subdivision (iv) of this subparagraph) necessary to cover current administrative expenses and other normal and current disbursements directly connected with the foundation's charitable, educational, or other similar exempt activities; and

(f) Any property leased by a foundation in carrying out its charitable, educational, or other similar exempt purpose at no cost (or at a nominal rent) to the lessee or for a program-related purpose (within the meaning of section 4944(c)), such as the leasing of renovated apartments to low-income tenants at a low rental as part of the lessor foundation's program for rehabilitating a blighted portion of a community. For treatment of the income derived from such use, see paragraph (d)(2)(viii) of this section.

(iii) Functionally related business— (a) In general. The term "functionally related business" means—

(1) A trade or business which is not an unrelated trade or business (as defined in section 513), or

(2) An activity which is carried on within a larger aggregate of similar activities or within a larger complex of other endeavors which is related (aside from the need of the organization for income or funds or the use it makes of the profits derived) to the char-

itable, educational, or other similar exempt purpose of the organization.

(b) Examples. The provisions of this subdivision may be illustrated by the following examples:

Example (1). X, a private foundation, maintains a community of historic value which is open to the general public. For the convenience of the public, X, through a wholly owned, separately incorporated, taxable entity, maintains a restaurant and hotel in such community. Such facilities are within the larger aggregate of activities which makes available for public enjoyment the various buildings of historic interest and which is related to X's exempt purpose. Thus, the operation of the restaurant and hotel under such circumstances constitutes a functionally related business.

Example (2). Y, a private foundation, as part of its medical research program under section 501(c)(3), publishes a medical journal in carrying out its exempt purpose. Space in the journal is sold for commercial advertising. Notwithstanding the fact that the advertising activity may be subject to the tax imposed by section 511, such activity is within a larger complex of endeavors which makes available to the scientific community and the general public developments with respect to medical research and is therefore a functionally related business.

(iv) Cash held for charitable, etc. activities. For purposes of subdivision (ii)(e) of this subparagraph, the reasonable cash balances which a private foundation needs to have on hand to cover expenses and disbursements described in such subdivision will generally be deemed to be an amount, computed on an annual basis, equal to one and one-half percent of the fair market value of all assets described in subparagraph (1)(i) of this paragraph, without regard to subdivision (ii)(e) of this subparagraph. However, if the Commissioner is satisfied that under the facts and circumstances an amount in addition to such one and one-half percent is necessary for payment of such expenses and disbursements, then such additional amount may also be excluded from the amount of assets described in subparagraph (1)(i) of this paragraph. All remaining cash balances, including amounts necessary to pay any tax imposed by section 511 or any section of chapter 42 of the Code except section 4940, are to be included in the assets described in subparagraph (1)(i) of this paragraph.

(4) Valuation of assets—(i) Certain securities. (a) For purposes of subparagraph (1)(i) of this paragraph, a private foundation may use any reasonable method to determine the fair market value on a monthly basis of securities for which market quotations are readily available, as long as such method is consistently used. For purposes of this subparagraph, market quotations are readily available if a security is:

(1) Listed on the New York Stock Exchange, the American Stock Exchange, or any city or regional exchange in which quotations appear on a daily basis, including foreign securities listed on a recognized foreign national or regional exchange;

(2) Regularly traded in the national or regional over-the-counter market, for which published quotations are available; or

(3) Locally traded, for which quotations can readily be obtained from established brokerage firms.

(b) For purposes of this subdivision, commonly accepted methods of valuation must be used in making an appraisal. Valuations made in accordance with the principles stated in the regulations under section 2031 constitute acceptable methods of valuation. This paragraph (c)(4)(i)(b) applies only for taxable years beginning before January 1, 1976. See section 4942(e)(2)(B) and paragraph (c)(4)(i)(c) of this section for special valuation rules that apply for subsequent taxable years.

(c) For purposes of this subdivision (i) and with respect to taxable years beginning after December 31, 1975, if the private foundation can show that the value of securities determined on the basis of market quotations as provided by subdivision (i)(a) does not reflect the fair market value thereof because—

(1) The securities constitute a block of securities so large in relation to the volume of actual sales on the existing market that it could not be liquidated in a reasonable time without depressing the market.

(2) The securities are securities in a closely held corporation and sales are few or of a sporadic nature, and, or

(3) The sale of the securities would result in a forced or distress sale because the securities could not be offered to the public for sale without first being registered under the Securities Act of 1933 or because of other factors,

then the price at which the securities could be sold as such outside the usual market, as through an underwriter, may be a more accurate indication of value than market quotations. On the other hand, if the securities to be valued represents a controlling interest, either actual or effective, in a going business, the price at which other lots change hands may have little relation to the true value of the securities. No decrease in the fair market value of any given class of securities determined on the basis of market quotations as provided by subdivision (i)(a) shall be allowed except as authorized by this subdivision, and no such decrease shall in the aggregate exceed 10 percent of the fair market value of such class of securities so determined on the basis of market quotations and without regard to this subdivision.

(d) In the case of securities described in subdivision (i)(a) of this subparagraph, which are held in trust for, or on behalf of, a foundation by a bank or other financial institution which values such securities periodically by use of a computer, a foundation may determine the correct value of such securities by use of such computer pricing system, provided the Commissioner has accepted such computer pricing system as a valid method for valuing securities for Federal estate tax purposes.

(e) This subdivision may be illustrated by the following examples:

Example (1). U, a private foundation, owns 1,000 shares of the stock of M Corporation. M stock is regularly traded on the New York Stock Exchange. U consistently follows a practice of valuing its 1,000 shares of M stock on the last trading day of each month based upon the quoted closing price for M stock. U's method of valuing its M Corporation stock is permissible under the rules contained in subdivision (i)(a) of this subparagraph.

Example (2). Assume the facts as stated in example (1), except that U consistently follows a practice of valuing its 1,000 shares of M stock by taking the mean of the closing prices for M stock on the first and last trading days of each month and the trading day nearest the 15th day of each month. U's method of valuing its M stock is permissible under the rules contained in subdivision (i)(a) of this subparagraph.

Example (3). Assume the facts as stated in example (1), except that U consistently follows a practice of valuing its M stock by taking the mean of the highest and lowest quoted prices for the stock on the last trading day of each month. U's method of valuing its M stock is permissible under the rules contained in subdivision (1)(a) of this subparagraph.

Example (4). V, a private foundation, owns 1,000 shares of the stock of N Corporation. N stock is regularly traded in the national over-the-counter market and published quotations of the bid and asked prices for the stock are available. V consistently follows a practice of valuing its 1,000 shares of N stock on the first trading day of each month by taking the mean of the bid and asked prices on that day. V's method of valuing its N Corporation stock is permissible under the rules contained in subdivision (i)(a) of this subparagraph.

Example (5). W, a private foundation, owns 1,000 shares of the stock of O Corporation. O stock is locally traded and quotations can readily be obtained from established brokerage firms. W consistently follows a practice of valuing its O stock on the 15th day of each month by obtaining a bona fide quotation of bid and asked prices for the stock from an established brokerage firm and taking the mean of such prices on that day. If a quotation is unavailable on the regular valuation date, W values its O stock based upon a bona fide quotation on the first day thereafter on which such a quotation is available. W's method of valuing its O Corporation stock is permissible under the rules contained in subdivision (i)(a) of this subparagraph.

(ii) Cash. In order to determine the amount of a foundation's cash balances, the foundation shall value its cash on a monthly basis by averaging the amount of cash on hand as of the first day of each month and as of the last day of each month.

(iii) Common trust funds. If a private foundation owns a participating interest in a common trust fund (as defined in section 584) established and administered under a plan providing for the periodic valuation of participating interests during the fund's taxable year and the reporting of such valuations to participants, the value of the foundation's interest in the common trust fund based upon the average of the valuations reported to the foundation during its taxable year will ordinarily constitute an acceptable method of valuation.

(iv) Other Assets. (a) Except as otherwise provided in subdivision (iv)(b) of this subparagraph, the fair market value of assets other than those described in subdivisions (i) through (iii) of this subparagraph shall be determined annually. Thus, the fair market value of securities other than those described in subdivision (i) of this subparagraph shall be determined in accordance with this subdivision (a). If, however, a private foundation owns voting stock of an issuer of unlisted securities and has, or together with disqualified persons or another private foundation has, effective control of the issuer (within the meaning of § 53.4943–3(b)(3)(ii), then to the extent that the issuer's assets consist of shares of listed securities issues, such assets shall be valued monthly on the basis of market quotations or in accordance with section 4942(e)(2)(B), if applicable. Thus, for example, if a private foundation and a disqualified person together own all of the unlisted voting stock of a holding company which in turn holds a portfolio of securities of issues which are listed on the New York Stock Exchange, in determining the net worth of the holding company, the underlying portfolio securities are to be valued monthly by reference to market quotations for their issues unless a decrease in such value is authorized in accordance with section 4942(e)(2)(b). Such determination may be made by employees of the private foundation or by any other person, without regard to whether such person is a disqualified person with respect to the foundation. A valuation made pursuant to the provisions of this subdivision, if accepted by the Commissioner, shall be valid only for the taxable year for which it is made. A new valuation made in accordance with these provisions is required for the succeeding taxable year.

(b) If the requirements of this subdivision are met, the fair market value of any interest in real property, including any improvements thereon, may be determined on a 5-year basis. Such value must be determined by means of a certified, independent appraisal made in writing by a qualified person who is neither a disqualified person with respect to, nor an employee of, the private foundation. The appraisal is certified only if it contains a statement at the end thereof to the effect that, in the opinion of the appraiser, the values placed on the assets appraised were determined in accordance with valuation principles regularly employed in making appraisals of such property using all reasonable valuation methods. The foundation shall retain a copy of the independent appraisal for its records. If a valuation made pursuant to the provisions of this subdivision in fact falls within the range of reasonable values for the appraised property, such valuation may be used by the foundation for the taxable year for which the valuation is made and for each of the succeeding 4 taxable years. Any valuation made pursuant to the provisions of this subdivision may be replaced during the 5-year period by a subsequent 5-year valuation made in accordance with the rules set forth in this subdivision, or with an annual valuation made in accordance with subdivision (iv)(a) of this subparagraph, and the most recent such valuation of such assets shall be used in computing the foundation's minimum investment return. In the case of a foundation organized before May 27, 1969, a valuation made in accordance with this subdivision applicable to the foundation's first taxable year beginning after December 31, 1972, and the 4 succeeding taxable years must be made no later than the last day of such first taxable year. In the case of a foundation organized after May 26, 1969, a valuation made in accordance with this subdivision applicable to the foundation's first taxable year beginning after February 5, 1973 and the succeeding 4 taxable years must be made no later than the last day of such first taxable year. Any subsequent valuation made in accordance with this subdivision must be made no later than the last day of the first taxable year for which such new valuation is applicable. A valuation, if properly made in accordance with the rules set forth in this subdivision, will not be disturbed by the Commissioner during the 5-year period for which it applies even if the actual fair market value of such property changes during such period.

(c) For purposes of this subdivision, commonly accepted methods of valuation must be used in making an appraisal. Valuations made in accordance with the principles stated in the regulations under section 2031 constitute acceptable methods of valuation. The term "appraisal," as used in this subdivision, means a determination of fair market value and is not to be construed in a technical sense peculiar to particular property or interests therein, such as, for example, mineral interests in real property.

(v) Definition of "securities". For purposes of this subparagraph, the term "securities" includes, but is not limited to, common and preferred stocks, bonds, and mutual fund shares.

(vi) Valuation date. (a) In the case of an asset which is required to be valued on an annual basis as provided in subdivision (iv)(a) of this subparagraph, such asset may be valued as of any day in the private foundation's taxable year to which such valuation applies, provided the foundation follows a consistent practice of valuing such asset as of such date in all taxable years.

(b) A valuation described in subdivision (iv)(b) of this subparagraph may be made as of any day in the first taxable year of the private foundation to which such valuation is to be applied.

(vii) Assets held for less than a taxable year. For purposes of this paragraph, any asset described in subparagraph (1)(i) of this paragraph which is held by a foundation for only part of a taxable year shall be taken into account for purposes of determining the foundation's minimum investment return for such taxable year by multiplying the fair market value of such asset (as determined pursuant to this subparagraph) by a fraction, the numerator of which is the number of days in such taxable year that the foundation held such asset and the denominator of which is the number of days in such taxable year.

(5) Applicable percentage—(i) In general. For purposes of paragraph (c)(1)(ii) of this section, except as provided in paragraph (c)(5)(ii) or (iii) of this section, the applicable percentage is:

(a) Six percent for a taxable year beginning in 1970 or 1971;

(b) Five and a half percent for a taxable year beginning in 1972;

(c) Five and one-quarter percent for a taxable year beginning in 1973;

(d) Six percent for a taxable year beginning in 1974 or 1975; and

(e) Five percent for taxable years beginning after Dec. 31, 1975.

* * *

(iii) Short taxable periods. In any case in which a taxable year referred to in this subparagraph is a period less than 12 months, the applicable percentage to be applied to the amount determined under the provisions of subparagraph (1) of this paragraph shall be equal to the applicable percentage for the calendar year in which the short taxable period began multiplied by a fraction, the numerator of which is the number of days in such short taxable period and the denominator of which is 365.

(d) Adjusted net income—(1) Definition. For purposes of paragraph (b) of this section, the term "adjusted net income" means the excess (if any) of—

(i) The gross income for the taxable year (including gross income from any unrelated trade or business) determined with the income modifications provided by subparagraph (2) of this paragraph, over

(ii) The sum of the deductions (including deductions directly connected with the carrying on of any unrelated trade or business), determined with the deduction modifications provided by subparagraph (4) of this paragraph, which would be allowed to a corporation subject to the tax imposed by section 11 for the taxable year.

In computing the income includible under this paragraph as gross income and the deductions allowable under this paragraph from such income, the principles of subtitle A of the Code shall apply except to the extent such principles conflict with section 4942 and the regulations thereunder (without regard to this sentence). Except as otherwise provided in this paragraph, no exclusions or deductions from gross income or credits against tax are allowable under this paragraph. For purposes of subdivision (i) of this subparagraph, the term "gross income" does not include gifts, grants, or contributions received by the private foundation but does include income from a functionally related business (as defined in paragraph (c)(3)(iii) of this section).

(2) Income modifications. The income modifications referred to in subparagraph (1)(i) of this paragraph are as follows:

(i) Section 103 (relating to interest on certain governmental obligations) shall not apply. Hence, interest which would have been excluded from gross income by section 103 shall be included in gross income.

(ii) Capital gains and losses from the sale or other disposition of property shall be taken into account only in an amount equal to any net short-term capital gain (as defined in section 1222(5)) for the taxable year. Long-term capital gain or loss is not included in the computation of adjusted net income. Similarly, net section 1231 gains shall be excluded from the computation of adjusted net income. However, net section 1231 losses shall be included in the computation of adjusted net income, if such losses are otherwise described in subparagraph (1)(ii) of this paragraph. Any net short-term capital loss for a given taxable year shall not be taken into account in computing adjusted net income for such year or in computing net short-term capital gain for purposes of determining adjusted net income for prior or future taxable years regardless of whether the foundation is a corporation or a trust.

(iii) The following amounts shall be included in gross income for the taxable year—

(a) Amounts received or accrued as repayments of amounts which were taken into account as a qualifying distribution within the meaning of paragraph (a)(2)(i) of § 53.4942(a)–3 for any taxable year;

(b) Notwithstanding subdivision (ii) of this subparagraph, gross amounts received or accrued from the sale or other disposition of property to the extent that the acquisition of such property was taken into account as a qualifying distribution (within the meaning of paragraph (a)(2)(ii) of § 53.4942(a)–3) for any taxable year; and

(c) Any amount set aside under paragraph (b) of § 53.4942(a)–3 to the extent it is determined that such amount is not necessary for the purposes for which it was set aside.

(iv) Any distribution received by a private foundation from a disqualified person in redemption of stock held by such private foundation in a business enterprise shall be treated as not essentially equivalent to a dividend under section 302(b)(1) if all of the following conditions are satisfied:

(a) Such redemption is of stock which was owned by a private foundation on May 26, 1969 (or which is acquired by a private foundation under the terms of a trust which was irrevocable on May 26, 1969, or under the terms of a will executed on or before such date which are in effect on such date and at all times thereafter);

(b) Such foundation is required to dispose of such property in order not to be liable for tax under section 4943 (relating to taxes on excess business holdings) applied, in the case of a disposition before January 1, 1975, without taking section 4943(c)(4) into account; and

(c) Such foundation receives in return an amount which equals or exceeds the fair market value of such property at the time of such disposition or at the time a contract for such disposition was previously executed in a transaction which would not constitute a prohibited transaction (within the meaning of section 503(b) or the corresponding provisions of prior law).

(v) If, as of the date of distribution of property for purposes described in section 170(c)(1) or (2)(B), the fair market value of such property exceeds its adjusted basis, such excess shall not be deemed an amount includible in gross income.

(vi) The income received by a private foundation from an estate during the period of administration of such estate shall not be included in such foundation's gross income, unless, due to a prolonged period of administration, such estate is considered terminated for Federal income tax purposes by operation of paragraph (a) of § 1.641(b)–3 of this chapter (Income Tax Regulations).

(vii) Distributions received by a private foundation from a trust created and funded by another person shall not be included in the foundation's gross income. However, with respect to distributions from certain trusts described in section 4947(a)(2), see paragraph (b)(2) of this section.

(viii) Gross income shall include all amounts derived from, or in connection with, property held by the foundation, even though the fair market value of such property may not be included in such foundation's assets for purposes of determining minimum investment return by operation of paragraph (c)(3) of this section.

(ix) Gross income shall include amounts treated in a preceding taxable year as a "qualifying distribution" by operation of paragraph (c) of § 53.4942(a)–3 where such amounts are not redistributed by the close of the donee organization's succeeding taxable year in accordance with the rules prescribed in such paragraph (c). In such cases, such amounts shall be included in the donor foundation's gross income for such foundation's first taxable year beginning after the close of the donee organization's first taxable year following the donee organization's taxable year of receipt.

(x) For taxable years ending after October 4, 1976, section 4942(f)(2)(D) states that section 483 (relating to imputed interest on deferred payments) does not apply to payments made pursuant to a binding contract entered into in a taxable year beginning before January 1, 1970. Amounts that are not treated as imputed interest because of section 4942(f)(2)(D) and this subdivision will represent gain or loss from the sale of property. If the gain or loss is long term capital gain or loss, section 4942(f)(2)(B) excludes the gain or loss from the computation of the foundation's gross income. If, in a taxable year beginning after December 31, 1969, there is a substantial change in the terms of a contract entered into in a taxable year beginning before January 1, 1970, then any payment made pursuant to the changed contract is not considered a payment made pursuant to a contract entered into in a taxable year beginning before January 1, 1970. Whether or not a change in the terms of a contract (for example, a change relating to time of payment, sales price, or obligations under the contract) is a substantial change is determined by applying the rules under section 483 and § 1.483–1(b)(4). As used in this subdivision, a binding contract includes an irrevocable written option.

(3) Adjusted basis—(i) In general. For purposes of subparagraph (2)(ii) of this paragraph, the adjusted basis for purposes of determining gain from the sale or other disposition of property shall be determined in accordance with the rules set forth in subdivision (ii) of this subparagraph and the adjusted basis for purposes of determining loss from such disposition shall be determined in accordance with the rules set forth in subdivision (iii) of this subparagraph. Further, the provisions of this subparagraph do not apply for any purpose other than for purposes of subparagraph (2)(ii) of this paragraph. For example, the determination of gain pursuant to the provisions of section 341 is determined without regard to this subparagraph.

(ii) Gain from sale or other disposition. The adjusted basis for purposes of determining gain from the sale or other disposition of property shall be the greater of:

(a) The fair market value of such property on December 31, 1969, plus or minus all adjustments after December 31, 1969, and before the date of sale or other disposition under the rules of Part II, Subchapter O, Chapter 1 of the Code, provided that the property was held by the private foundation on December 31, 1969, and continuously thereafter to such date of sale or other disposition; or

(b) The adjusted basis as determined under the rules of Part II, Subchapter O, Chapter 1 of the Code, subject to the provisions of section 4940(c)(3)(B) and the regulations thereunder (and without regard to section 362(c)). With respect to assets acquired prior to December 31, 1969, which were subject to depreciation or depletion, for purposes of determining the adjustments to be made to basis between the date of acquisition and December 31, 1969, and amount equal to straight-line depreciation or cost depletion shall be taken into account. In addition, in determining such adjustments to basis, if any other adjustments would have been made during such period (such as a change in useful life based upon additional data or a change in facts), such adjustments shall also be taken into account.

(iii) Loss from sale or other disposition. For purposes of determining loss from the sale or other disposition of property, adjusted basis as determined in subdivision (ii) (b) of this subparagraph shall apply.

* * *

(4) Deduction modifications—(i) In general. For purposes of computing adjusted net income under subparagraph (1) of this paragraph, no deduction shall be allowed other than all the ordinary and necessary expenses paid or incurred for the production or collection of gross income or for the management, conservation, or maintenance of property held for the production of such income, except as provided in subdivision (ii) of this subparagraph. Such expenses include that portion of a private foundation's operating expenses which is paid or incurred for the production or collection of gross income. Operating expenses include compensation of officers, other salaries and wages of employees, interest, rent, and taxes. Where only a portion of the property produces (or is held for the production of) income subject to the provisions of section 4942, and the remainder of the property is used for charitable, educational, or other similar exempt purposes, the deductions allowed by this subparagraph shall be apportioned between the exempt and nonexempt uses. Similarly, where the deductions with respect to property used for a charitable, educational, or other similar exempt purpose exceed the income derived from such property, such excess shall not be allowed as a deduction, but may be treated as a qualifying distribution described in paragraph (a)(2)(ii) of § 53.4942(a)–3. Furthermore, this subdivision does not allow deductions which are not paid or incurred for the purposes herein prescribed. Thus, for example, the deductions prescribed by the following sections are not allowable: (a) The charitable contributions deduction prescribed under sections 170 and 642(c); (b) the net operating loss deduction prescribed under section 172; and (c) the special deductions prescribed under Part VIII, subchapter B, chapter 1 of the Code.

(ii) Special rules. For purposes of computing adjusted net income under subparagraph (1) of this paragraph: (a) The allowances for depreciation and depletion as determined under section 4940(c)(3)(B) and the regulations thereunder shall be taken into account, and (b) section 265 (relating to expenses and interest relating to tax-exempt interest) shall not apply.

* * *

§ 53.4942(a)–3. Qualifying distributions defined.

(a) In general—(1) Distributions generally. For purposes of section 4942 and the regulations thereunder, the amount of a qualifying distribution of property (as defined in subparagraph (2) of this paragraph) is the fair market value of such property as of the date such qualifying distribution is made. The amount of an organization's qualifying distributions will be determined solely on the cash receipts and disbursements method of accounting described in section 446(c)(1).

(2) Definition. The term "qualifying distribution" means—

(i) Any amount (including program-related investments, as defined in section 4944(c), and reasonable and necessary administrative expenses) paid to accomplish one or more purposes described in section 170(c)(1) or (2)(B), other than any contribution to—

(a) A private foundation which is not an operating foundation (as defined in section 4942(j)(3)), except as provided in paragraph (c) of this section, or

(b) An organization controlled (directly or indirectly) by the contributing private foundation or one or more disqualified persons with respect to such foundation, except as provided in paragraph (c) of this section; or

(c) An organization described in section 4942(g)(4)(A)(i) or (ii), if paid by a private foundation that is not an operating foundation.

(ii) Any amount paid to acquire an asset used (or held for use) directly in carrying out one or more purposes described in section 170(c)(1) or (2)(B). See paragraph (c)(3) of § 53.4942(a)–2 for the definition of "used (or held for use)"; or

(iii) Any amount set aside within the meaning of paragraph (b) of this section.

(3) Control. For purposes of subparagraph (2)(i)(b) of this paragraph, an organization is "controlled" by a foundation or one or more disqualified persons with respect to the foundation if any of such persons may, by aggregating their votes or positions of authority, require the donee organization to make an expenditure, or prevent the donee organization from making an expenditure, regardless of the method by which the control is exercised or exercisable. "Control" of a donee organization is determined without regard to any conditions imposed upon the donee as part of the distribution or any other restrictions accompanying the distribution as to the manner in which the distribution is to be used, unless such conditions or restrictions are described in paragraph (a)(8) of § 1.507–2 of this chapter (Income Tax Regulations). In general, it is the donee, not the distribution, which must be "controlled" by the distributing private foundation for the provisions of subparagraph (2)(i)(b) of this paragraph to apply. Thus, the furnishing of support to an organization and the consequent imposition of budgetary procedures upon that organization with respect to such support shall not in itself be treated as subjecting that organization to the distributing foundation's control within the meaning of this subparagraph. Such "budgetary procedures" include expenditure responsibility requirements under section 4945(d)(4). The "controlled" organization need not be a private foundation; it may be any type of exempt or nonexempt organization including a school, hospital, operating foundation, or social welfare organization.

(4) Borrowed funds—(i) In general. For purposes of this paragraph, if a private foundation borrows money in a particular taxable year to make expenditures for a specific charitable, educational, or other similar purpose, a qualifying distribution out of such borrowed funds will, except as otherwise provided in subdivision (ii) of this subparagraph, be deemed to have been made only at the time that such borrowed funds are actually distributed for such exempt purpose.

* * *

(5) Changes in use of an asset. If an asset not used (or held for use) directly in carrying out one or more purposes described in section 170(c)(1) or (2)(B) is subsequently converted to such a use, the foundation may treat such conversion as a qualifying distribution. The amount of such qualifying distribution shall be the fair market value of the converted asset as of the date of its conversion. For purposes of the preceding sentence, fair market value shall be determined by making a valuation of the converted asset as of the date of its conversion in accordance with the rules set forth in paragraph (c)(4) of § 53.4942(a)–2.

(6) Certain foreign organizations— (i) In general. A distribution for purposes described in section 170(c)(2)(B) to a foreign organization, which has not received a ruling or determination letter that it is an organization described in section 509(a)(1), (a)(2), or (a)(3) or in section 4942(j)(3), will be treated as a distribution made to an organization described in section 509(a)(1), (a)(2), or (a)(3) (other than an organization described in section 4942(g)(4)(A)(i) or (ii)) or in section 4942(j)(3) if the distributing foundation has made a good faith determination that the donee organization is an organization described in section 509(a)(1), (a)(2), or (a)(3) (other than an organization described in section 4942(g)(4)(A)(i) or (ii)) or in section 4942(j)(3). A determination ordinarily will be considered a good faith determination if the determination is based on current written advice received from a qualified tax practitioner concluding that the donee is an organization described in section 509(a)(1), (a)(2), or (a)(3) (other than an organization described in section 4942(g)(4)(A)(i) or (ii)) or in section 4942(j)(3), and if the foundation reasonably relied in good faith on the written advice in accordance with the requirements of § 1.6664–4(c)(1) of this chapter. The written advice must set forth sufficient facts concerning the operations and support of the donee organization for the Internal Revenue Service to determine that the donee organization would be likely to qualify as an organization described in section 509(a)(1), (a)(2), or (a)(3) (other than an organization described in section 4942(g)(4)(A)(i) or (ii)) or in section 4942(j)(3) as of the date of the written advice. For purposes of this section, except as provided in the next sentence, written advice will be considered current if, as of the date of distribution, the relevant law on which the advice is based has not changed since the date of the written advice and the factual information on which the advice is based is from the donee's current or prior taxable year (or annual accounting period if the donee does not have a taxable year for United States federal tax purposes). Written advice that a donee met the public support test under section 170(b)(1)(A)(vi) or section 509(a)(2) for a test period of five years will be treated as current for purposes of distributions to the donee during the two taxable years (or, as applicable, annual accounting periods) of the donee immediately following the end of the five-year test period.

(ii) Definitions. For purposes of this paragraph (a)(6)—

(a) The term "foreign organization" means any organization that is not described in section 170(c)(2)(A).

(b) The term "qualified tax practitioner" means an attorney, a certified public accountant, or an enrolled agent, within the meaning of 31 CFR 10.2 and 10.3, who is subject to the requirements in 31 CFR part 10.

(7) Payment of tax. The payment of any tax imposed under chapter 42 of the Code shall not be treated as a qualifying distribution.

(8) Examples. The provisions of this paragraph may be illustrated by the following examples:

Example (1). M, a private foundation which uses the calendar year as the taxable year, makes the following payments in 1970: (i) a payment of $44,000 to five employees for conducting a foundation program of educational grants for research and study; (ii) $20,000 for various items of overhead, 10 percent of which is attributable to the activities of the employees mentioned in payment (i) of this example and the other 90 percent of which is attributable to administrative expenses which were not paid to accomplish any section 170(c)(1) or (2)(B) purpose; and (iii) a $100,000 general purpose grant paid to an educational institution described in section 170(b)(1)(A)(ii) which is not controlled by M or any disqualified persons with respect to M. Payments (i) and (ii) of this example are qualifying distributions to the extent of $46,000 ($44,000 of salaries and 10 percent of the overhead, both of which are reasonable administrative expenses paid to accomplish section 170(c)(1) or (2)(B) purposes). Payment (iii) of this example is also a qualifying distribution, since it is a contribution for section 170(c)(2)(B) purposes to an organization which is not described in subparagraph (2)(i)(a) or (b) of this paragraph. The other 90 percent of payment (ii) of this example may constitute items of deduction under paragraph (d)(1)(ii) of § 53.4942(a)–2 if such items otherwise qualify under such paragraph.

Example (2). On February 21, 1972, N, a private foundation which uses the calendar year as the taxable year, pays $500,000 for real property on which it plans to build hospital facilities to be used for medical care and education. The real property produces no income and the hospital facilities will not be constructed until 1974 according to the set-aside plan submitted to and approved by the Commissioner pursuant to paragraph (b) of this section. The purchase of the land is a qualifying distribution under subparagraph (2)(ii) of this paragraph. If, however, the property used were to produce rental income for more than a reasonable period of time before construction of the hospital is begun, then as of the time such rental use becomes unreasonable (i) such purchase would no longer constitute a qualifying distribution under subparagraph (2)(ii) of this paragraph, and (ii) the amount of the qualifying distribution would be included in N's gross income. See paragraphs (c)(3)(i) and (d)(2)(iii)(b) of § 53.4942(a)–2.

Example (3). In 1971, X, a private foundation engaged in holding paintings and exhibiting them to the public, purchases an additional building to be used to exhibit the paintings. Such expenditure is a qualifying distribution under subparagraph (2)(ii) of this paragraph. In 1975, X sells the building. Under paragraph (d)(2)(iii)(b) of § 53.4942(a)–2, all of the proceeds of the sale (less direct costs of the sale) are included in X's adjusted net income for 1975.

Example (4). In January 1969, M, a private foundation which uses the calendar year as the taxable year, borrows $10 million to give to N, a private college, for the construction of a science center. M borrowed the money from X, a commercial bank. M is to repay X at the rate of $1.1 million per year ($1 million principal and $0.1 million interest) for 10 years, beginning in January, 1973. M distributed $5 million of the borrowed funds to N in February 1969 and the other $5 million in March 1970. M files a statement with the form it is required to file under section 6033 for 1973 which contains the information required by subparagraph (4)(ii)(b) of this paragraph. Pursuant to M's election, each repayment of loan principal constitutes a qualifying distribution in the year of repayment. Accordingly, the distribution of $5 million to N in March 1970 will not be treated as a qualifying distribution. Each payment of interest ($0.1 million annually) with respect to M's loan from X is treated as a deduction under paragraph (d)(1)(ii) of § 53.4942(a)–2 in the taxable year in which it is made.

Example (5). Private foundation Y engages in providing care for the aged. Y makes a distribution of cash to H, a hospital described in section 170(b)(1)(A)(iii) which is not controlled by Y or any disqualified person with respect to Y. The distribution is made subject to the conditions that H will invest the money as a separate fund which will bear a name commemorating the creator of Y and will use the income from such fund only for H's exempt hospital purposes which relate to care for the aged. Under these circumstances, the distribution from Y to H is a qualifying distribution pursuant to subparagraph (2)(i) of this paragraph.

(b) Certain set-asides—(1) In general. An amount set aside for a specific project that is for one or more of the purposes described in section 170(c)(1) or (2)(B) may be treated as a qualifying distribution in the year in which set aside (but not in the year in which actually paid), if the requirements of section 4942(g)(2) and this paragraph (b) are satisfied. The requirements of this paragraph (b) are satisfied if the private foundation establishes to the satisfaction of the Commissioner that the amount set aside will be paid for the specific project within 60 months after it is set aside, and

(i) The set-aside satisfies the suitability test described in subparagraph (2) of this paragraph, or

(ii) With respect to a set-aside made in a taxable year beginning after December 31, 1974, the private foundation satisfies the cash distribution test described in subparagraph (3) of this paragraph.

If the suitability test or cash distribution test is otherwise satisfied, the 60 month period for paying the amount set aside may, for good cause shown, be extended by the Commissioner.

(2) Suitability test. The suitability test is satisfied if the private foundation establishes to the satisfaction of the Commissioner that the specific project for which the amount is set aside is one that can be better accomplished by the set-aside than by the immediate payment of funds. Specific projects that can be better accomplished by the use of a set-aside include, but are not limited to, projects in which relatively long-term grants or expenditures must be made in order to assure the continuity of particular charitable projects or program-related investments (as defined in section 4944(c)) or where grants are made as part of a matching-grant program. Such projects include, for example, a plan to erect a building to house the direct charitable, educational, or other similar exempt activity of the private foundation (such as a museum building in which paintings are to be hung), even though the exact location and architectural plans have not been finalized; a plan to purchase an additional group of paintings offered for sale only as a unit that requires an expenditure of more than one year's income; or a plan to fund a specific research program that is of such magnitude as to require an accumulation of funds before beginning the research, even though not all of the details of the program have been finalized.

(3) Cash distribution test; in general. The cash distribution test is satisfied if—

(i) The specific project for which the amount is set aside will not be completed before the end of the taxable year in which the set-aside is made,

(ii) The private foundation actually distributes, in cash or its equivalent and for one or more of the purposes described in section 170(c)(1) or (2)(B), the "start-up period minimum amount" described in subparagraph (4) of this paragraph during the private foundation's start-up period, and

(iii) The private foundation actually distributes, in cash or its equivalent and for one or more of the purposes described in section 170(c)(1) or (2)(B), the "full-payment period minimum amount" described in subparagraph (5) of this paragraph in each taxable year of the private foundation's full-payment period.

For purposes of the cash distribution test, an amount set aside will be treated as distributed in the year in which actually paid and not in the year in which set aside.

* * *

(7) Approval and information requirements—(i) Suitability test. If an amount is set aside under the suitability test of section 4942(g)(2)(B)(i) and subparagraph (2) of this paragraph, the private foundation must apply for the Commissioner's approval of the set-aside before the end of the taxable year in which the amount is set aside. The Commissioner will either approve or disapprove the set-aside in writing. An otherwise proper set-aside will not be treated as a qualifying distribution under this paragraph (b) with respect to a taxable year if the Commissioner's approval is not sought before the end of the taxable year in which the amount is actually set aside. To obtain approval by the Commissioner for a set-aside under the suitability test, the private foundation must write to Commissioner of Internal Revenue, Attention: OP:E:EO:T, 1111 Constitution Avenue, NW., Washington, D.C. 20224, and include—

(a) A statement describing the nature and purposes of the specific project and the amount of the set-aside for which approval is requested;

(b) A statement describing the amounts and approximate dates of any planned additions to the set-aside after its initial establishment;

(c) A statement of the reasons why the project can be better accomplished by a set-aside than by the immediate payment of funds;

(d) A detailed description of the project, including estimated costs, sources of any future funds expected to be used for completion of the project, and the location or locations (general or specific) of any physical facilities to be acquired or constructed as part of the project; and

(e) A statement by an appropriate foundation manager (as defined in section 4946(b)) that the amounts to be set aside will actually be paid for the specific project within a specified period of time that ends not more than 60 months after the date of the first set-aside, or a statement showing good cause why the period for paying the amount set aside should be extended (including a showing that the proposed project could not be divided into two or more projects covering periods of no more than 60 months each) and setting forth the extension of time required.

(ii) Cash distribution test. If an amount is set aside under the cash distribution test of section 4942(g)(2)(B)(ii) and subparagraphs (3), (4), and (5) of this paragraph, then for taxable years ending after April 2, 1984, the private foundation must submit an attachment with the return required by section 6033 for the taxable year in which the amount is set aside and for certain subsequent taxable years. For the taxable year in which the amount is set aside the attachment must include—

(a) A statement describing the nature and purposes of the specific project for which amounts are to be set aside;

(b) A statement that the amounts set aside for the specific project will actually be paid for the specific project within a specified period of time that ends not more than 60 months after the date of the set-aside;

(c) A statement that the project will not be completed before the end of the taxable year of the private foundation in which the set-aside is made;

(d) A statement showing the distributable amounts determined under section 4942(d) for any past taxable years in the private foundation's start-up and full-payment periods; and

(e) A statement showing the aggregate amount of actual payments made in cash or its equivalent, for purposes described in section 170(c)(1) or (2)(B), during each taxable year in the private foundation's start-up and full-payment periods. This statement should include a detailed description of any payments that are to be treated, pursuant to the rules of subparagraphs (4)(iv) and (6)(ii) of this paragraph (b), as distributed during a taxable year prior to the taxable year in which such payments were actually made and, in addition, should explain the circumstances that justify the application of those rules.

For the five taxable years following the taxable year in which the amount is set aside (or, if longer, for each taxable year in the extended period for paying the amount set aside), the attachment must include the statements required by (d) and (e) of this subdivision (ii). The submission of the statement required by (b) of this subdivision (ii) will satisfy the requirement of section 4942(g)(2)(B) and subparagraph (1) of this paragraph (b) that the private foundation establish to the satisfaction of the Commissioner that the amount set aside will be paid for the specific project within 60 months after it is set aside.

(8) Evidence of set-aside. A set-aside that is approved by the Commissioner or which satisfies the cash distribution test shall be evidenced by the entry of a dollar amount on the books and records of a private foundation as a pledge or obligation to be paid at a future date or dates. Any amount which is set aside shall be taken into account for purposes of determining the private foundation's minimum investment return under § 53.4942(a)–2(c)(1), and any income attributable to such set-aside shall be taken into account in computing adjusted net income under § 53.4942(a)–2(d).

(9) Contingent set-aside. In the event a private foundation is involved in litigation and may not distribute assets or income because of a court order, the private foundation may (except as provided in § 53.4942(a)–2(e)(1)(i) or (ii)) seek and obtain a set-aside for a purpose described in § 53.4942(a)–3(a)(2). The amount to be set aside shall be equal to that portion of the private foundation's distributable amount which is attributable to the assets or income that are held pursuant to court order and which, but for the court order precluding the distribution of such assets or income, would have been distributed. In the event that the litigation encompasses more than one taxable year, the private foundation may seek additional contingent set-asides. Such amounts must actually be distributed by the last day of the taxable year following the taxable year in which the litigation is terminated. Amounts not distributed by the close of the appropriate taxable year shall be treated as described in § 53.4942(a)–2(d)(2)(iii)(c) for the succeeding taxable year.

(c) Certain contributions to section 501(c)(3) organizations—(1) In general. For purposes of this section, the term "qualifying distribution" includes (in the year in which it is paid) a contribution to an exempt organization described in section 501(c)(3) and described in paragraph (a)(2)(i)(a) or (b) of this section if—

(i) Not later than the close of the first taxable year after the donee organization's taxable year in which such contribution is received, such donee organization makes a distribution equal to the full amount of such contribution and such distribution is a qualifying distribution (within the meaning of paragraph (a) of this section, without regard to this paragraph) which is treated under paragraph (d) of this section as a distribution out of corpus (or would be so treated if such section 501(c)(3) organization were a private foundation which is not an operating foundation); and

(ii) The private foundation making the contribution obtains adequate records or other sufficient evidence from such donee organization (such as a statement by an appropriate officer, director, or trustee of such donee organization) showing (except as otherwise provided in this subparagraph) (a) that the qualifying distribution described in subdivision (i) of this subparagraph has been made by such organization, (b) the names and addresses of the recipients of such distribution and the amount received by each, and (c) that the distribution is treated as a distribution out of corpus under paragraph (d) of this section (or would be so treated if the donee organization were a private foundation which is not an operating foundation). Where a distribution is for an administrative expense which is part of a section 170(c)(1) or (2)(B) expenditure or is part of another section 170(c)(1) or (2)(B) expenditure that cannot reasonably be separately accounted for, the provisions of subdivision (ii) of this subparagraph may be satisfied by the submission by the donee organization of a statement setting forth the general purpose for which such expenditure was made and that the amount was distributed as a qualifying distribution described in subdivision (ii)(c) of this subparagraph.

(2) Distribution requirements. (i) In order for a donee organization to meet the distribution requirements of subparagraph (1)(i) of this paragraph, it must, not later than the close of the first taxable year after its taxable year in which any contributions are received, distribute (within the meaning of this subparagraph) an amount equal in value to the contributions received in such prior taxable year and have no remaining undistributed income for such prior taxable year. In the event that a donee organization redistributes less than an amount equal to the total contributions from donor organizations which are required to be redistributed by such donee organization by the close of the first taxable year following the taxable year in which such contributions were received, amounts treated as redistributions of such contributions shall be deemed to have been made pro rata out of all such contributions regardless of any earmarking or identification made by such donee organization with respect to the source of such distributions. See paragraph (d)(2)(ix) of § 53.4942(a)–2 for the treatment of amounts deemed not to have been so redistributed. For purposes of this paragraph, the term "contributions" means all contributions, whether of cash or property, and the fair market value of contributed property determined as of the date of the contribution must be used in determining whether an amount equal in value to the contributions received has been redistributed.

(ii) For purposes of this paragraph, the characterization of qualifying distributions made during the taxable year (i.e., whether out of the prior year's undistributed income, the current year's undistributed income, or corpus) is to be made as of the close of the taxable year in question, except to the extent that a different characterization is effected by means of the election provided for by paragraph (d)(2) of this section or by subdivision (iv) of this subparagraph. Once it is determined that a qualifying distribution is attributable to corpus, such distribution will first be charged to distributions which are required to be redistributed under this paragraph.

(iii) All amounts contributed to a specific exempt organization described in section 501(c)(3) and in paragraph (a)(2)(i)(a) or (b) of this section within any one taxable year of such organization shall be treated (with respect to the contributing private foundation) as one "contribution". If subparagraph (1)(i) or (ii) of this paragraph is not completely satisfied with respect to such contribution within the meaning of such subparagraph, only that portion of such contribution which was redistributed (within the meaning of subparagraph (1)(i) and (ii) of this paragraph) shall be treated as a qualifying distribution.

(iv) In order to satisfy distribution requirements under section 170(b)(1)(E)(ii) or this paragraph, a donee organization may elect to treat as a current distribution out of corpus any amount distributed in a prior taxable year which was treated as a distribution out of corpus under paragraph (d)(1)(iii) of this section provided that (a) such amount has not been availed of for any other purpose, such as a carryover under paragraph (e) of this section or a redistribution under this paragraph for a prior year, (b) such corpus distribution occurred within the preceding 5 years, and (c) such amount is not later availed of for any other purpose. Such election must be made by attaching a statement to the return the foundation is required to file under section 6033 with respect to the taxable year for which such election is to apply. Such statement must contain a declaration by an appropriate foundation manager (within the meaning of section 4946(b)(1)) that the foundation is making an election under this paragraph and it must specify that the distribution was treated under paragraph (d)(1)(iii) of this section as a distribution out of corpus in a designated prior taxable year (or years).

(3) Examples. The provisions of subparagraphs (1) and (2) of this paragraph may be illustrated by the following examples. It is assumed in these examples that all private foundations described use the calendar as the taxable year.

Example (1). In 1972 M, a private foundation, makes a contribution out of 1971 income to X, another private foundation which is not an operating foundation. The contribution is the only one received by X in 1972. In 1973 X makes a qualifying distribution to an art museum maintained by an operating foundation in an amount equal to the amount of the contribution received from M. X also distributes all of its undistributed income for 1972 and 1973 for other purposes described in section 170(c)(2)(B). Under the provisions of paragraph (d) of this section, such distribution to the museum is treated as a distribution out of corpus. Thus, M's contribution to X is a qualifying distribution out of M's 1971 income provided M obtains adequate records or other sufficient evidence from X showing the nature and amount of the distribution made by X, the identity of the recipient, and the fact that the distribution is treated as made out of corpus. If X's qualifying distributions during 1973 had been equal only to M's contribution to X and X's undistributed income for 1972, X could have made an election under paragraph (d)(2) of this section to treat the amount distributed in excess of its 1972 undistributed income as a distribution out of corpus and in that manner satisfied the requirements of this paragraph.

Example (2). Assume the facts stated in example (1), except that X is a private college described in section 170(b)(1)(A)(ii) which is controlled by disqualified persons with respect to M and that the records which X furnishes to M show that the distribution would have been treated as made out of corpus if X were a private nonoperating foundation. Under these circumstances, result is the same as in example (1).

Example (3). Assume the facts stated in example (1), except that X makes a distribution to the museum equal only to one-half of the contribution from M, that the remainder of such contribution is added to X's funds and used to pay charitable administrative expenses, and that the records obtained by M from X are not sufficient to show the amounts distributed or the identities of the recipients of the distributions. The contribution by M to X will be a qualifying distribution only to the extent that M can obtain (i) other sufficient evidence (such as statements from officers or employees of X or from the museum) showing the facts required by subparagraph (1)(ii)(a), (b), and (c) of this paragraph and (ii) a statement from X setting forth that the remainder of the contribution was used for charitable administrative expenses which constituted qualifying distributions described in paragraph (a)(2)(i) of this section.

Example (4). X and Y are private nonoperating foundations. A is an exempt organization which is not described in section 501(c)(3) but which supervises and conducts a program described in section 170(c)(2)(B). Y, but not X, controls A within the meaning of paragraph (a)(3) of this section. In 1972, X and Y each makes a grant to A of $100, specifically designated for use in the operation of A's section 170(c)(2)(B) program. X has made a qualifying distribution to A because the distribution is one described in paragraph (a)(2)(i) of this section. However, because A is controlled by Y, Y's grant of $100 to A does not constitute a qualifying distribution within the meaning of such paragraph (a)(2)(i). Furthermore, because A is not an exempt organization described in section 501(c)(3), Y's grant to A does not constitute a qualifying distribution by operation of the provisions of this paragraph.

Example (5). N, a private nonoperating foundation, had distributable amounts of $100 in 1970 and $125 in 1971. In 1970 N received total contributions of $540: $150 from Y, a public charity; $70 from Z, a private foundation; $140 from Q, a private foundation, subject to the requirement that N earmark the amount and distribute it before distributing Z's contribution; and, $180 from R, also a private foundation. However, R specifically instructed N that such contribution did not have to be redistributed because R already had made enough qualifying distributions to avoid all section 4942 taxes. N is not controlled by Y, Z, Q, or R, and N made no qualifying distributions in 1970. By the close of 1971, N had made qualifying distributions of $420, earmarking $140 as having been a distribution of Q's contribution, but had made no election under paragraph (d)(2) of this section to have any amount distributed which was in excess of N's 1970 undistributed income treated as distributed out of corpus. Therefore, the first $225 of qualifying distributions made in 1971 (the sum of $100 and $125, N's distributable amounts for 1970 and 1971, respectively) are treated as amounts described in paragraph (d)(1)(i) and (ii) of this section. Since Y's contribution is a contribution from a public charity and does not have to be "redistributed" and since R specifically instructed N that its contribution need not be "redistributed", the remaining $195 of qualifying distributions will be treated as distributed pro rata from Z's and Q's contributions, regardless of N's earmarking. Accordingly, of Z's original qualifying distribution of $70 only $65 ($195 multiplied by $70, Z's contribution, over $210, the total ($70 plus $140) of Z's and Q's contributions) will be treated as redistributed by N. Similarly, of Q's original qualifying distribution of $140 only $130 ($195 multiplied by $140 over $210) will be treated as redistributed by N. Thus, Z's gross income for 1972 will be increased by $5 ($70 less the $65 actually redistributed), and Q's gross income for 1972 will be increased by $10 ($140 less the $130 actually redistributed).

(4) Limitation. A contribution by a private foundation to a donee organization which the donee uses to make payments to another organization (the secondary donee) shall not be regarded as a contribution by the private foundation to the secondary donee if the distributing foundation does not earmark the use of the contribution for any named secondary donee and does not retain power to cause the selection of the secondary donee by the organization to which such foundation has made the contribution. For purposes of this subparagraph, a contribution described herein shall not be regarded as a contribution by the foundation to the secondary donee even though such foundation has reason to believe that certain organizations would derive benefits from such contribution so long as the original donee organization exercises control, in fact, over the selection process and actually makes the selection completely independently of such foundation.

* * *

(d) Treatment of qualifying distributions—(1) In general. Except as provided in subparagraph (2) of this paragraph, any qualifying distribution made during a taxable year shall be treated as made—

(i) First out of the undistributed income (as defined in paragraph (a) of § 53.4942(a)–2) of the immediately preceding taxable year (if the private foundation was subject to the initial excise tax imposed by section 4942(a) for such preceding taxable year) to the extent thereof;

(ii) Second out of the undistributed income for the taxable year to the extent thereof; and

(iii) Then out of corpus.

(2) Election. In the case of any qualifying distribution which (under subparagraph (1) of this paragraph) is not treated as made out of the undistributed income of the immediately preceding taxable year, the foundation may elect to treat any portion of such distribution as made out of the undistributed income of a designated prior taxable year or out of corpus. Such election must be made by filing a statement with the Commissioner during the taxable year in which such qualifying distribution is made or by attaching a statement to the return the foundation is required to file under section 6033 with respect to the taxable year in which such qualifying distribution was made. Such statement must contain a declaration by an appropriate foundation manager (within the meaning of section 4946(b)(1)) that the foundation is making an election under this subparagraph, and it must specify whether the distribution is made out of the undistributed income of a designated prior taxable year (or years) or is made out of corpus. In any case where the election described in this subparagraph is made during the taxable year in which the qualifying distribution is made, such election may be revoked in whole or in part by filing a statement with the Commissioner during such taxable year revoking such election in whole or in part or by attaching a statement to the return the foundation is required to file under section 6033 with respect to the taxable year in which the qualifying distribution was made revoking such election in whole or in part. Such statement must contain a declaration by an appropriate foundation manager (within the meaning of section 4946(b)(1)) that the foundation is revoking an election under this subparagraph in whole or in part, and it must specify the election or part thereof being revoked.

(3) Examples. The provisions of this paragraph may be illustrated by the following examples:

Example (1). M, a private foundation which was created in 1968 and which uses the calendar year as the taxable year, has distributable amounts and qualifying distributions for 1970 through 1976 as follows:

Year	1970	1971	1972	1973
Distributable amount	$100	$100	$100	$100
Qualifying distribution	0	100	250	100

Year	1974	1975	1976
Distributable amount	$100	$100	$100
Qualifying distribution	100	100	100

In 1971 the qualifying distribution of $100 is treated under subparagraph (1)(i) of this paragraph as made out of the $100 of undistributed income for 1970. The qualifying distribution of $250 in 1972 is treated as made: (i) $100 out of the undistributed income for 1971 under subparagraph (1)(i) of this paragraph; (ii) $100 out of the undistributed income for 1972 under subparagraph (1)(ii) of this paragraph; and (iii) $50 out of corpus in 1972 under subparagraph (1)(iii) of this paragraph. The qualifying distribution of $100 in each of the years 1973 through 1976 is treated as made out of the undistributed income for each of those respective years under subparagraph (1)(ii) of this paragraph. See paragraph (e) of this section for rules relating to the carryover of qualifying distributions out of corpus.

Example (2). M, a private foundation which uses the calendar year as the taxable year, has undistributed income of $300 for 1981, $200 for

1982, and $400 for 1983. On January 14, 1983, M makes its first qualifying distribution in 1983 when it sets aside (within the meaning of paragraph (b) of this section) $700 for construction of a hospital. On February 24, 1983 a notice of deficiency with respect to the excise taxes imposed by section 4942(a) and (b) in regard to M 's undistributed income for 1981 is mailed to M under section 6212(a). M notifies the Commissioner in writing on March 24, 1983, that it is making an election under subparagraph (2) of this paragraph to have its distribution of January 14th applied first against its undistributed income for 1982, next against its undistributed income for 1981, and last against its undistributed income for 1983. Thus, $200 of the $700 qualifying distribution is treated as made out of the undistributed income for 1982; $300, out of undistributed income for 1981; and $200 ($700 less the sum of $200 and $300), out of the undistributed income for 1983. Thus, an initial excise tax of $45 (15 percent of $300) is imposed under section 4942(a). Since M made the election described above, the $300 (treated as distributed out of undistributed income for 1981) corrects (within the meaning of section 4963(d)(2)) the taxable act because the undistributed income for 1981 is reduced to zero. Furthermore, correction is effected within the correction period (as defined in section 4963(e)(1) and § 53.4963–1(e)). Therefore, under the provisions of section 4961(a), the additional tax imposed by section 4942(b) will not be assessed.

(e) Carryover of excess qualifying distributions—(1) In general. If in any taxable year for which an organization is subject to the initial excise tax imposed by section 4942(a) there is created an excess of qualifying distributions (as determined under subparagraph (2) of this paragraph), such excess may be used to reduce distributable amounts in any taxable year of the adjustment period (as defined in subparagraph (3) of this paragraph). For purposes of section 4942, including paragraph (d) of this section, the distributable amount for a taxable year in the adjustment period shall be reduced to the extent of the lesser of (i) the excess of qualifying distributions made in prior taxable years to which such adjustment period applies or (ii) the remaining undistributed income at the close of such taxable year after applying any qualifying distributions made in such taxable year to the distributable amount for such taxable year (determined without regard to this paragraph). If during any taxable year of the adjustment period there is created another excess of qualifying distributions, such excess shall not be taken into account until any earlier excess of qualifying distributions has been completely applied against distributable amounts during its adjustment period.

(2) Excess qualifying distributions. An excess of qualifying distributions is created for any taxable year beginning after December 31, 1969, if—

(i) The total qualifying distributions treated (under paragraph (d) of this section) as made out of the undistributed income for such taxable year or as made out of corpus with respect to such taxable year (other than amounts distributed by an organization in satisfaction of section 170(b)(1)(E)(ii) or paragraph (c) of this section, or applied to a prior taxable year by operation of the elections contained in paragraphs (c)(2)(iv) and (d)(2) of this section), exceeds

(ii) The distributable amount for such taxable year (determined without regard to this paragraph).

(3) Adjustment period. For purposes of this paragraph, the taxable years in the adjustment period are the 5 taxable years immediately following the taxable year in which the excess of qualifying distributions is created. Thus, an excess (within the meaning of subparagraph (2) of this paragraph) for any 1 taxable year cannot be carried over beyond the succeeding 5 taxable years. However, if during any taxable year in the adjustment period an organization ceases to be subject to the initial excise tax imposed by section 4942(a), any portion of the excess of qualifying distributions, which prior to such taxable year has not been applied against distributable amounts, may not be carried over to such taxable year or subsequent taxable years in the adjustment period, even if during any of such taxable years the organization again becomes subject to the initial excise tax imposed by section 4942(a).

(4) Examples. The provisions of this paragraph may be illustrated by the following examples:

Example (1). (i) F, a private foundation which was created in 1967 and which uses the calendar year as the taxable year, has distributable amounts and qualifying distributions for 1970 through 1976 as follows:

Year	1970	1971	1972	1973
Distributable amount	$100	$100	$100	$100
Qualifying distribution	0	$250	$70	$140

Year	1974	1975	1976
Distributable amount	$100	$100	$100
Qualifying distribution	$60	$75	$105

(ii) The qualifying distributions made in 1971 will be treated under paragraph (d) of this section as $100 made out of the undistributed income for 1970, then as $100 made out of the undistributed income for 1971, and finally as $50 out of corpus in 1971. Since the total qualifying distributions for 1971 ($150) exceed the distributable amount for 1971 ($100), there exists a $50 excess of qualifying distributions which F may use to reduce its distributable amounts for the years 1972 through 1976 (the taxable years in the adjustment period with respect to the 1971 excess). Therefore, the $100 distributable amount for 1972 is reduced by $30 (the lesser of the 1971 excess ($50) and the remaining undistributed income at the close of 1972 ($30), after the qualifying distributions of $70 for 1972 were applied to the original distributable amount for 1972 of $100). Since the distributable amount for 1972 was reduced to $70, there is no remaining undistributed income for 1972. Accordingly, the qualifying distributions made in 1973 will be treated as $100 made out of the undistributed income for 1973 and as $40 out of corpus in 1973. Since this amount ($140) exceeds the distributable amount for 1973 ($100), there exists a $40 excess which F may use to reduce its distributable amounts for the years 1974 through 1978 (the taxable years in the adjustment period with respect to the 1973 excess). However, in accordance with subparagraph (1) of this paragraph such excess may not be used to reduce F's distributable amounts for the years 1974 through 1976 until the excess created in 1971 has been completely applied against distributable amounts during such years. The distributable amount for 1974 is reduced by $40 (the lesser of the unused portion of the 1971 excess ($20) plus the 1973 excess ($40) and the remaining undistributed income at the close of 1974 ($40), after the qualifying distributions of $60 for 1974 were applied to the original distributable amount for 1974 of $100). The distributable amount for 1975 is reduced by $20 (the lesser of the unused portion of the 1973 excess of qualifying distributions ($20) and the remaining undistributed income at the close of 1975 ($25), after the qualifying distributions of $75 for 1975 were applied to the original distributable amount for 1975 of $100). Consequently, qualifying distributions made in 1976 will be treated as made first out of the $5 of remaining undistributed income for 1975 and then as $100 made out of the undistributed income for 1976.

Example (2). Assume the facts as stated in example (1), except that in 1974 F receives a contribution of $300 from G, a private foundation which controls F (within the meaning of paragraph (a)(3) of this section), and F distributes such contribution in 1975 in satisfaction of paragraph (c) of this section. Under these circumstances, there would be no excess of qualifying distributions for 1975 with respect to such distribution, since such distribution is excluded from the computation of an excess of qualifying distributions by operation of subparagraph (2)(i) of this paragraph.

Example (3). Assume the facts as stated in example (1), except that in 1972 F is treated as an operating foundation (as such term is defined in section 4942(j)(3)). In accordance with subparagraph (3) of this paragraph since F is not subject to the initial excise tax imposed by section 4942(a) for 1972, the 1971 excess cannot be carried forward to 1972 or any subsequent year in the adjustment period with respect to the 1971 excess, even if F is subsequently treated as a private nonoperating foundation for any year during the period 1973 through 1976.

(f) Effective/applicability date and transition relief. Paragraphs (a)(2)(i) and (a)(6) of this section are effective on and apply with respect to distributions made after September 25, 2015. However, foundations may continue to rely on the provisions of paragraph (a)(6) of this section as contained in 26 CFR part 53, revised April 1, 2015, with respect to distributions made on or before December 24, 2015 pursuant to a good faith determination made in accordance with such provisions. Also, foundations may continue to rely on the provisions of paragraph (a)(6) of this section as contained in 26 CFR part 53, revised April 1, 2015, with respect to distributions pursuant to a written commitment made on or before September 25, 2015 and pursuant to a good faith determination made on or before such date in accordance with such provisions if the committed amount is distributed within five years of such date.

§ 53.4942(b)–1. Operating foundations.

(a) Operating foundation defined—(1) In general. For purposes of section 4942 and the regulations thereunder, the term "operating foundation" means any private foundation which, in addition to satisfying the assets test, the endowment test or the support test set forth in § 53.4942(b)–2(a), (b) and (c), makes qualifying distributions (within the meaning of § 53.4942(a)–3(a)(2)) directly for the active conduct of activities constituting its charitable, educational, or other similar exempt purpose equal in value to—

(i) For taxable years beginning before January 1, 1982, substantially all of the foundation's adjusted net income (as defined in § 53.4942(a)–2(d)); and

(ii) For taxable years beginning after December 31, 1981, substantially all of the lesser of the foundation's adjusted net income (as defined in § 53.4942(a)–2(d)) or minimum investment return (as defined in § 53.4942(a)–2(c)). If the foundation's qualifying distributions exceed its minimum investment return (but are less than the foundation's adjusted net income) substantially all of such qualifying distributions must be made directly for the active conduct of activities constituting its charitable, educational or other similar exempt purpose. However, if the foundation's minimum investment return is less than its adjusted net income and the foundation's qualifying distributions equal or exceed such adjusted net income, only that portion of the qualifying distributions equal to substantially all of the foundation's adjusted net income must be made directly for the active conduct of activities constituting its charitable, educational or other similar exempt purpose.

* * *

(b) Active conduct of activities constituting the exempt purpose—(1) In general. For purposes of this section, except as provided in subparagraph (2) or (3) of this paragraph, qualifying distributions are not made by a foundation "directly for the active conduct of activities constituting its charitable, educational, or other similar exempt purpose" unless such qualifying distributions are used by the foundation itself, rather than by or through one or more grantee organizations which receive such qualifying distributions directly or indirectly from such foundation. Thus, grants made to other organizations to assist them in conducting activities which help to accomplish their charitable, educational, or other similar exempt purpose are considered an indirect, rather than direct, means of carrying out activities constituting the charitable, educational, or other similar exempt purpose of the grantor foundation, regardless of the fact that the exempt activities of the grantee organization may assist the grantor foundation in carrying out its own exempt activities. However, amounts paid to acquire or maintain assets which are used directly in the conduct of the foundation's exempt activities, such as the operating assets of a museum, public park, or historic site, are considered direct expenditures for the active conduct of the foundation's exempt activities. Likewise, administrative expenses (such as staff salaries and traveling expenses) and other operating costs necessary to conduct the foundation's exempt activities (regardless of whether they are "directly for the active conduct" of such exempt activities) shall be treated as qualifying distributions expended directly for the active conduct of such exempt activities if such expenses and costs are reasonable in amount. Conversely, administrative expenses and operating costs which are not attributable to exempt activities, such as expenses in connection with the production of investment income, are not treated as such qualifying distributions. Expenses attributable to both exempt and nonexempt activities shall be allocated to each such activity on a reasonable and consistently applied basis. Any amount set aside by a foundation for a specific project, such as the acquisition and restoration, or construction, of additional buildings or facilities which are to be used by the foundation directly for the active conduct of the foundation's exempt activities, shall be deemed to be qualifying distributions expended directly for the active conduct of the foundation's exempt activities if the initial setting aside of the funds constitutes a set-aside within the meaning of paragraph (b) of § 53.4942(a)–3.

(2) Payments to individual beneficiaries—(i) In general. If a foundation makes or awards grants, scholarships, or other payments to individual beneficiaries (including program related investments within the meaning of section 4944(c) made to individuals or corporate enterprises) to support active programs conducted to carry out the foundation's charitable, educational, or other similar exempt purpose, such grants, scholarships, or other payments will be treated as qualifying distributions made directly for the active conduct of exempt activities for purposes of paragraph (a) of this section only if the foundation, apart from the making or awarding of the grants, scholarships, or other payments, otherwise maintains some significant involvement (as defined in subdivision (ii) of this subparagraph) in the active programs in support of which such grants, scholarships, or other payments were made or awarded. Whether the making or awarding of grants, scholarships, or other payments constitutes qualifying distributions made directly for the active conduct of the foundation's exempt activities is to be determined on the basis of the facts and circumstances of each particular case. The test applied is a qualitative, rather than a strictly quantitative, one. Therefore, if the foundation maintains a significant involvement (as defined in subdivision (ii) of this subparagraph) it will not fail to meet the general rule of subparagraph (1) of this paragraph solely because more of its funds are devoted to the making or awarding of grants, scholarships, or other payments than to the active programs which such grants, scholarships, or other payments support. However, if a foundation does no more than select, screen, and investigate applicants for grants or scholarships, pursuant to which the recipients perform their work or studies alone or exclusively under the direction of some other organization, such grants or scholarships will not be treated as qualifying distributions made directly for the active conduct of the foundation's exempt activities. The administrative expenses of such screening and investigation (as opposed to the grants or scholarships themselves) may be treated as qualifying distributions made directly for the active conduct of the foundation's exempt activities.

(ii) Definition. For purposes of this subparagraph, a foundation will be considered as maintaining a "significant involvement" in a charitable, educational, or other similar exempt activity in connection with which grants, scholarships, or other payments are made or awarded if—

(A) An exempt purpose of the foundation is the relief of poverty or human distress, and its exempt activities are designed to ameliorate conditions among a poor or distressed class of persons or in an area subject to poverty or national disaster (such as providing food or clothing to indigents or residents of a disaster area), the making or awarding of the grants or other payments to accomplish such exempt purpose is direct and without the assistance of an intervening organization or agency, and the foundation maintains a salaried or voluntary staff of administrators, researchers, or other personnel who supervise and direct the activities described in this subdivision (A) on a continuing basis; or

(B) The foundation has developed some specialized skills, expertise, or involvement in a particular discipline or substantive area (such as scientific or medical research, social work, education, or the social sciences), it maintains a salaried staff of administrators, researchers, or other personnel who supervise or conduct programs or activities which support and advance the foundation's work in its particular area of interest, and, as a part of such programs or activities, the foundation makes or awards grants, scholarships, or other payments to individuals to encourage and further their involvement in the foundation's particular area of interest and in some segment of the programs or activities carried on by the foundation (such as grants under which the recipients, in addition to independent study, attend classes, seminars, or conferences sponsored or conducted by the foundation, or grants to engage in social work or scientific research projects which are under the general direction and supervision of the foundation).

(3) Payment of section 4940 tax. For purposes of section 4942(j)(3)(A) and (B)(ii), payment of the tax imposed upon a foundation under section 4940 shall be considered a qualifying distribution which is made directly for the active conduct of activities constituting the foundation's charitable, educational, or other similar exempt purpose.

(c) Substantially all. For purposes of this section, the term "substantially all" shall mean 85 percent or more. Thus, if a foundation makes qualifying distributions directly for the active conduct of activities constituting its charitable, educational, or other similar exempt purpose in an amount equal to at least 85 percent of its adjusted net income, it will be considered as satisfying the income test described in this section even if it makes grants to organizations or engages in other activities with the remainder of its adjusted net income and with other funds. In determining whether the amount of qualifying distributions made directly for the active conduct of such exempt activities equals at least 85 percent of a foundation's adjusted net income, a foundation is not required to trace the source of such expenditures to determine whether they were derived from income or from contributions.

(d) Examples. The provisions of this section may be illustrated by the following examples. It is assumed that none of the organizations described in these examples is described in section 509(a)(1), (2), or (3).

Example (1). N, an exempt museum described in section 501(c)(3), was founded by the gift of an endowment from a single contributor. N uses 90 percent of its adjusted net income to operate the museum. If N satisfies one of the tests set forth in § 53.4942(b)–2 it may be classified as an operating foundation since substantially all of the qualifying distributions made by N are used directly for the active conduct of N's exempt activities within the meaning of paragraph (b)(1) of this section.

Example (2). M, an exempt organization described in section 501(c)(3), was created to improve conditions in a particular urban ghetto. M receives its funds primarily from a limited number of wealthy contributors interested in helping carry out its exempt purpose. M's program consists of making a survey of the problems of the ghetto to determine the areas in which its funds may be applied most effectively. Approximately 10 percent of M's adjusted net income is used to conduct this survey. The balance of its income is used to make grants to other nonprofit organizations doing work in the ghetto in those areas determined to have the greatest likelihood of resulting in improved conditions. Under these circumstances, since only 10 percent of M's adjusted net income may be considered as constituting qualifying distributions made directly for the active conduct of M's exempt activities, M cannot qualify as an operating foundation.

Example (3). Assume the facts as stated in example (2), except that M uses the remaining 90 percent of its adjusted net income for the following purposes: (1) M maintains a salaried staff of social workers and researchers who analyze its surveys and make recommendations as to methods for improving ghetto conditions; (2) M makes grants to independent social scientists who assist in these analyses and recommendations; (3) M publishes periodic reports indicating the results of its surveys and recommendations; (4) M makes grants to social workers and others who act as advisers to nonprofit organizations, as well as small business enterprises, functioning in the community (these advisers acting under the general direction of M attempt to implement M's recommendations through their advice and assistance to the nonprofit organizations and small business enterprises); and (5) M makes grants to other social scientists who study and report on the success of the various enterprises which attempt to implement M's recommendations. Under these circumstances, M satisfies the requirements of paragraph (b)(2) of this section, and the various grants it makes constitute qualifying distributions made directly for the active conduct of its exempt activities. Thus, if M satisfies one of the tests set forth in § 53.4942(b)–2 it may be classified as an operating foundation.

Example (4). P, an exempt educational organization described in section 501(c)(3), was created for the purpose of training teachers for institutions of higher education. Each year P awards a substantial number of fellowships to students for graduate study leading toward their M.A. or Ph.D. degrees. The applicants for these fellowships are carefully screened by P's staff, and only those applicants who indicate a strong interest in teaching in colleges or universities are chosen. P publishes and circulates various pamphlets encouraging a development of interest in college teaching and describing its fellowships. P also conducts annual summer seminars which are attended by its fellowship recipients, its staff, consultants, and other interested parties. The purpose of these seminars is to foster and encourage the development of college teaching. P publishes a report of the seminar proceedings along with related studies written by those who attended. Despite the fact that a substantial portion of P's adjusted net income is devoted to granting fellowships, its commitment to encouraging individuals to become teachers at institutions of higher learning, its maintenance of a staff and programs designed to further this purpose, and the granting of fellowships to encourage involvement both in its own seminars and in its exempt purpose indicate a significant involvement by P beyond the mere granting of fellowships. Thus, the fellowship grants made by P constitute qualifying distributions made directly for the active conduct of P's exempt activities within the meaning of paragraph (b)(2) of this section.

Example (5). Q, an exempt organization described in section 501(c)(3), is composed of professional organizations interested in different branches of one academic discipline. Q trains its own professional staff, conducts its own program of research, selects research topics, screens and investigates grant recipients, makes grants to those selected, and sets up and conducts conferences and seminars for the grantees. Q has particular knowledge and skill in the given discipline, carries on activities to advance its study of that discipline, and makes grants to individuals to enable them to participate in activities which it conducts in carrying out its exempt purpose. Under these circumstances, Q's grants constitute qualifying distributions made directly for the active conduct of Q's exempt activities within the meaning of paragraph (b)(2) of this section.

Example (6). R, an exempt medical research organization described in section 501(c)(3), was created to study and perform research concerning heart disease. R has its own research center in which it carries on a broad number of research projects in the field of heart disease with its own professional staff. Physicians and scientists who are interested in special projects in this area present the plans for their projects to R. The directors of R study these plans and decide if the project is feasible and will further the work being done by R. If it is, R makes a grant to the individual to enable him to carry out his project, either at R's facilities or elsewhere. Reports of the progress of the project are made periodically to R, and R exercises a certain amount of supervision over the project. The resulting findings of these projects are usually published by R. Under these circumstances, the grants made by R constitute qualifying distributions made directly for the active conduct of R's exempt activities within the meaning of paragraph (b)(2) of this section.

Example (7). S, an exempt organization described in section 501(c)(3), maintains a large library of manuscripts and other historical reference material relating to the history and development of the region in which the collection is located. § makes a limited number of annual grants to enable post-doctoral scholars and doctoral candidates to use its library. Sometimes S obtains the right to publish the scholar's work, although this is not a prerequisite to the receipt of a grant. The primary criterion for selection of grant recipients is the usefulness of the library's resources to the applicant's field of study. Under these circumstances, the grants made by S constitute qualifying distributions made directly for the active conduct of S's exempt activities within the meaning of paragraph (b)(2) of this section.

Example (8). T, an exempt charitable organization described in section 501(c)(3), was created by the members of one family for the purpose of relieving poverty and human suffering. T has a large salaried staff of employees who operate offices in various areas throughout the country. Its employees make gifts of food and clothing to poor persons in the area serviced by each office. On occasion, T also provides temporary relief in the form of food and clothing to persons in areas stricken by natural disasters. If conditions improve in one poverty area, T transfers the resources of the office in that area to another poverty area. Under these circumstances, the gifts of food and clothing made by T constitute qualifying distributions made directly for the active conduct of T's exempt activities within the meaning of paragraph (b)(2) of this section.

Example (9). U, an exempt scientific organization described in section 501(c)(3), was created for the principal purpose of studying the effects of early childhood brain damage. U conducts an active and continuous research program in this area through a salaried staff of scientists and physicians. As part of its research program, U awards scholarships to young people suffering mild brain damage to enable them to attend special schools equipped to handle such problems. The recipients are periodically tested to determine the effect of such schooling upon them. Under these circumstances, the scholarships awarded by U constitute qualifying distributions made directly for the active conduct of U's exempt activities within the meaning of paragraph (b)(2) of this section.

Example (10). O, an exempt charitable organization described in section 501(c)(3), was created for the purpose of giving scholarships to children of the employees of X Corporation who meet the standards set by O. O not only screens and investigates each applicant to make sure that he complies with the academic and financial requirements set for scholarship recipients, but also administers an examination which each applicant must take—90 percent of O's adjusted net income is used in awarding these scholarships to the chosen applicants. O does not conduct any activities of an educational nature on its own. Under these circumstances, O is not using substantially all of its adjusted net income directly for the active conduct of its exempt activities within the meaning of paragraph (b) of this section. Thus, O is not an operating foundation because it fails to satisfy the income test set forth in paragraph (a) of this section.

§ 53.4942(b)–2. Alternative tests.

(a) Assets test—(1) In general. A private foundation will satisfy the assets test under the provisions of this paragraph if substantially more than half of the foundation's assets:

(i) Are devoted directly (A) to the active conduct of activities constituting the foundation's charitable, educational, or other similar exempt purpose, (B) to functionally related businesses (as defined in paragraph (c)(3)(iii) of § 53.4942(a)–2), or (C) to any combination thereof;

(ii) Are stock of a corporation which is controlled by the foundation (within the meaning of section 368(c)) and substantially all the assets of which (within the meaning of paragraph (c) of § 53.4942(b)–1) are so devoted; or

(iii) Are in part assets which are described in subdivision (i) of this subparagraph and in part stock which is described in subdivision (ii) of this subparagraph.

(2) Qualifying assets—(i) In general. For purposes of subparagraph (1) of this paragraph, an asset is "devoted directly to the active conduct of activities constituting the foundation's charitable, educational, or other similar exempt purpose" only if the asset is actually used by the foundation directly for the active conduct of activities constituting its charitable, educational, or other similar exempt purpose. Thus, such assets as real estate, physical facilities or objects (such as museum assets, classroom fixtures and equipment, and research facilities), and intangible assets (such as patents, copyrights, and trademarks) will be considered qualifying assets for purposes of this paragraph to the extent they are used directly for the active conduct of the foundation's exempt activities. However, assets which are held for the production of income, for investment, or for some other similar use (for example, stocks, bonds, interest-bearing notes, endowment funds, or, generally, leased real estate) are not devoted directly to the active conduct of the foundation's exempt activities, even though the income derived from such assets is used to carry out such exempt activities. Whether an asset is held for the production of income, for investment, or for some other similar use rather than being used for the active conduct of the foundation's exempt activities is a question of fact. For example, an office building used for the purpose of providing offices for employees engaged in the management of endowment funds of the foundation is not devoted to the active conduct of the foundation's exempt activities. However, where property is used both for exempt purposes and for other purposes, if such exempt use represents 95 percent or more of the total use, such property shall be considered to be used exclusively for an exempt purpose. Property acquired by a foundation to be used in carrying out the foundation's exempt purpose may be considered as devoted directly to the active conduct of such purpose even though the property, in whole or in part, is leased for a limited period of time during which arrangements are made for its conversion to the use for which it was acquired, provided such income-producing use of the property does not exceed a reasonable period of time. Generally, 1 year shall be deemed to be a reasonable period of time for purposes of the immediately preceding sentence. Similarly, where property is leased by a foundation in carrying out its exempt purpose and where the rental income derived from such property by the foundation is less than the amount which would be required to be charged in order to recover the cost of purchase and maintenance of such property (taking into account the deductions permitted by paragraph (d)(4) of § 53.4942(a)–2), such property shall be considered devoted directly to the active conduct of the foundation's exempt activities.

(ii) Limitations. (A) Assets which are held for the purpose of extending credit or making funds available to members of a charitable class (including any interest in a program related-investment, except as provided in paragraph (b)(2) of § 53.4942(b)–1) are not considered assets devoted directly to the active conduct of activities constituting the foundation's charitable, educational, or other similar exempt purpose. For example, assets which are set aside in special reserve accounts to guarantee student loans made by lending institutions will not be considered assets devoted directly to the active conduct of the foundation's exempt activities.

(B) Any amount set aside by a foundation within the meaning of paragraph (b)(1) of § 53.4942(b)–1 shall not be treated as an asset devoted directly to the active conduct of the foundation's exempt activities.

(3) Assets held for less than a taxable year. For purposes of this paragraph, any asset which is held by a foundation for part of a taxable year shall be taken into account for such taxable year by multiplying the fair market value of such asset (as determined pursuant to subparagraph (4) of this paragraph) by a fraction, the numerator of which is the number of days in such taxable year that the foundation held such asset and the denominator of which is the number of days in such taxable year.

(4) Valuation. For purposes of this paragraph, all assets shall be valued at their fair market value. Fair market value shall be determined in accordance with the rules set forth in paragraph (c)(4) of § 53.4942(a)–2, except in the case of assets which are devoted directly to the active conduct of the foundation's exempt activities and for which neither a ready market nor standard valuation methods exist (such as historical objects or buildings, certain works of art, and botanical gardens). In such cases, the historical cost (unadjusted for depreciation) shall be considered equal to fair market value unless the foundation demonstrates that fair market value is other than cost. In any case in which the foundation so demonstrates that the fair market value of an asset is other than historical cost, such substituted valuation may be used for the taxable year for which such new valuation is demonstrated and for each of the succeeding 4 taxable years if the valuation methods and procedures prescribed by paragraph (c)(4)(iv)(B) of § 53.4942(a)–2 are followed.

(5) Substantially more than half. For purposes of this paragraph, the term "substantially more than half" shall mean 65 percent or more.

(6) Examples. The provisions of this paragraph may be illustrated by the following examples. It is assumed that none of the organizations described in these examples is described in section 509(a)(1), (2), or (3).

Example (1). W, an exempt organization described in section 501(c)(3), is devoted to the maintenance and operation of a historic area for the benefit of the general public. W has acquired and erected facilities for lodging and other visitor accommodations in such area, which W operates through a wholly owned, separately incorporated, taxable entity. These facilities comprise substantially all of the subsidiary's assets. The operation of such accommodations constitutes a functionally related business within the meaning of paragraph (c)(3)(iii) of § 53.4942(a)–2. Under these circumstances, the stock of the subsidiary will be considered as part of W's assets which may be taken into account by W in determining whether it satisfies the assets test described in this paragraph.

Example (2). M, an exempt conservation organization described in section 501(c)(3), is devoted to acquiring, preserving, and otherwise making available for public use geographically diversified areas of natural beauty. M has acquired and erected facilities for lodging and other visitor accommodations in national park areas. The operation of such accommodations constitutes a functionally related business within the meaning of paragraph (c)(3)(iii) of § 53.4942(a)–2. Therefore, M's assets which are directly devoted to such visitor accommodations may be taken into account by M in determining whether it satisfies the assets test described in this paragraph.

Example (3). P, an exempt organization described in section 501(c)(3), is devoted to acquiring and restoring historic houses. To insure that the restored houses will be kept in the restored condition, and to make the houses more readily available for public display, P rents the houses rather than sells them once they have been restored. The rental income derived by P is substantially less than the amount which would be required to be charged in order to recover the cost of purchase, restoration, and maintenance of such houses. Therefore, such houses may be taken into account by P in determining whether it satisfies the assets test described in this paragraph.

Example (4). Z, an exempt organization described in section 501(c)(3), is devoted to improving the public's understanding of Renaissance art. Z's principal assets are a number of paintings of this period which it circulates on an active and continuing basis to museums and schools for public display. These paintings constitute 80 percent of Z's assets. Under these circumstances, although Z does not have a building in which it displays these paintings, such paintings are devoted directly to the active conduct of activities constituting Z's exempt purpose. Therefore, Z has satisfied the assets test described in this paragraph.

(b) Endowment test—(1) In general. A foundation will satisfy the endowment test under the provisions of this paragraph if it normally makes qualifying distributions (within the meaning of paragraph (a)(2) of § 53.4942(a)–3) directly for the active conduct of activities constituting its charitable, educational, or other similar exempt purpose in an amount not less than two-thirds of its minimum investment return (as defined in paragraph (c) of § 53.4942(a)–2). In determining whether the amount of such qualifying distributions is not less than an amount equal to two-thirds of the foundation's minimum investment return, the foundation is not required to trace the source of such expenditures to determine whether they were derived from investment income or from contributions.

(2) Definitions. For purposes of this paragraph, the phrase "directly for the active conduct of activities constituting the foundation's charitable, educational, or other similar exempt purpose" shall have the same meaning as in paragraph (b) of § 53.4942(b)–1.

(3) Example. This paragraph may be illustrated by the following example:

Example. X, an exempt organization described in section 501(c)(3) and not described in section 509(a)(1), (2), or (3), was created on July 15, 1970. X uses the cash receipts and disbursements method of accounting. For 1971, the fair market value of X's assets not described in paragraph (c)(2) or (3) of § 53.4942(a)–2 is $400,000. X makes qualifying distributions for 1971 directly for the active conduct of its exempt activities of $17,000. For 1971 two-thirds of X's minimum investment return is $16,000 (6 percent x $400,000 = $24,000; 2/3 x $24,000 = $16,000). Under these circumstances, X has satisfied the endowment test described in this paragraph for 1971. However, if X's qualifying distributions for 1971 directly for the active conduct of its exempt activities were only $15,000, X would not satisfy the endowment test for 1971, unless the fair market value of its assets not described in paragraph (c)(2) or (3) of § 53.4942(a)–2 were no greater than $375,000 (6 percent x $375,000 = $22,500; 2/3 x $22,500 = $15,000).

(c) Support test—(1) In general. A foundation will satisfy the support test under the provisions of this paragraph if:

(i) Substantially all of its support (other than gross investment income as defined in section 509(e)) is normally received from the general public and from five or more exempt organizations which are not described in section 4946(a)(1)(H) with respect to each other or the recipient foundation;

(ii) Not more than 25 percent of its support (other than gross investment income) is normally received from any one such exempt organization; and

(iii) Not more than half of its support is normally received from gross investment income.

(2) Definitions and special rules. For purposes of this paragraph—

(i) Support. The term "support" shall have the same meaning as in section 509(d).

(ii) Substantially all. The term "substantially all" shall have the same meaning as in paragraph (c) of § 53.4942(b)–1.

(iii) Support from exempt organizations. The support received from any one exempt organization may be counted towards satisfaction of the support test described in this paragraph only if the foundation receives support from no fewer than five exempt organizations. For example, a foundation which normally receives 20 percent of its support (other than gross investment income) from each of five exempt organizations may qualify under this paragraph even though it receives no support from the general public. However, if a foundation normally received 10 percent of its support from each of three exempt organizations and the balance of its support from sources other than exempt organizations, such support could not be taken into account in determining whether the foundation had satisfied the support test set forth in this paragraph.

(iv) Support from the general public. "Support" received from an individual, or from a trust or corporation (other than an exempt organization), shall be taken into account as support from the general public only to the extent that the total amount of the support received from any such individual, trust, or corporation during the period for determining the normal sources of the foundation's support (as set forth in § 53.4942(b)–3) does not exceed 1 percent of the foundation's total support (other than gross investment income) for such period. In applying this 1-percent limitation, all support received by the foundation from any person and from any other person or persons standing in a relationship to such person which is described in section 4946(a)(1)(C) through (G) and the regulations thereunder shall be treated as received from one person. For purposes of this paragraph, support received from a governmental unit described in section 170(c)(1) shall be treated as support received from the general public, but shall not be subject to the 1-percent limitation.

§ 53.4942(b)–3. Determination of compliance with operating foundation tests.

(a) In general. A foundation may satisfy the income test and either the assets, endowment, or support test by satisfying such tests for any 3 taxable years during a 4-year period consisting of the taxable year in question and the three immediately preceding taxable years or on the basis of an aggregation of all pertinent amounts of income or assets held, received, or distributed during such 4-year period. A foundation may not use one method for satisfying the income test described in paragraph (a) of § 53.4942(b)–1 and another for satisfying either the assets, endowment, or support test described in § 53.4942(b)–2. Thus, if a foundation satisfies the income test on the 3-out-of-4-year basis for a particular taxable year, it may not use the aggregation method for satisfying either the assets, endowment, or support test for such particular taxable year. However, the fact that a foundation has chosen one method for satisfying the tests under ss 53.4942(b)–1 and 53.4942(b)–2 for 1 taxable year will not preclude it from satisfying such tests for a subsequent taxable year by the alternate method. If a foundation fails to satisfy the income test and either the assets, endowment, or support test for a particular taxable year under either the 3-out-of–4-year method or the aggregation method, it shall be treated as a nonoperating foundation for such taxable year and for all subsequent taxable years until it satisfies the tests set forth in ss 53.4942(b)–1 and 53.4942(b)–2 for a taxable year occurring after the taxable year in which it was treated as a nonoperating foundation.

(b) New organizations—(1) In general. Except as provided in subparagraph (2) of this paragraph, an organization organized after December 31, 1969, will be treated as an operating foundation only if it has satisfied the tests set forth in ss 53.4942(b)–1 and 53.4942(b)–2 for its first taxable year of existence. If an organization satisfies such tests for its 1st taxable year, it will be treated as an operating foundation from the beginning of such taxable year. If such is the case, the organization will be treated as an operating foundation for its 2d and 3d taxable years of existence only if it satisfies the tests set forth in ss 53.4942(b)–1 and 53.4942(b)–2 by the aggregation method for all such taxable years that it has been in existence.

(2) Special rule. An organization organized after December 31, 1969, will be treated as an operating foundation prior to the end of its 1st taxable year if such organization has made a good faith determination that it is likely to satisfy the income test set forth in paragraph (a) of § 53.4942(b)–1 and one of the tests set forth in § 53.4942(b)–2 for such 1st taxable year pursuant to subparagraph (1) of this paragraph. Such a "good faith determination" ordinarily will be considered as made where the determination is based on an affidavit or opinion of counsel of such organization that such requirements will be satisfied. Such an affidavit or opinion must set forth sufficient facts concerning the operations and support of such organization for the Commissioner to be able to determine that such organization is likely to satisfy such requirements. An organization which, pursuant to this subparagraph, has been treated as an operating foundation for its 1st taxable year, but actually fails to qualify as an operating foundation under subparagraph (1) of this paragraph for such taxable year, will be treated as a private foundation which is not an operating foundation as of the 1st day of its 2d taxable year for purposes of making any determination under the internal revenue laws with respect to such organization. The preceding sentence shall not apply if such organization establishes to the satisfaction of the Commissioner that it is likely to qualify as an operating foundation on the basis of its 2d, 3d, and 4th taxable years. Thus, if such an organization fails to qualify as an operating foundation in its 2d, 3d, or 4th taxable year after having failed in its 1st taxable year, it will be treated as a private foundation which is not an operating foundation as of the 1st day of such 2d, 3d, or 4th taxable year in which it fails to qualify as an operating foundation, except as otherwise provided by paragraph (d) of this section. Such status as a private foundation which is not an operating foundation will continue until such time as the organization is able to satisfy the tests set forth in ss 53.4942(b)–1 and 53.4942(b)–2 by either the 3-out-of–4-year method or the aggregation method. For the status of grants or contributions made to such an organization with respect to sections 170 and 4942, see paragraph (d) of this section.

* * *

(d) Treatment of contributions—(1) In general. The status of grants or contributions made to an operating foundation with respect to sections 170 and 4942 will not be affected until notice of change of status of such organization is made to the public (such as by publication in the Internal Revenue Bulletin), unless the grant or contribution was made after:

(i) The act or failure to act that resulted in the organization's inability to satisfy the requirements of ss 53.4942(b)–1 and 53.4942(b)–2, and the grantor or contributor was responsible for, or was aware of, such act or failure to act, or

(ii) The grantor or contributor acquired knowledge that the Commissioner has given notice to such organization that it would be deleted from classification as an operating foundation.

(2) Exception. For purposes of subparagraph (1)(i) of this paragraph, a grantor or contributor will not be considered to be responsible for, or aware of, the act or failure to act that resulted in the grantee organization's inability to satisfy the requirements of §§ 53.4942(b)–1 and 53.4942(b)–2 if such grantor or contributor has made his grant or contribution in reliance upon a written statement by the grantee organization that such grant or contribution would not result in the inability of such grantee organization to qualify as an operating foundation. Such a statement must be signed by a foundation manager (as defined in section 4946(b)) of the grantee organization and must set forth sufficient facts concerning the operations and support of such grantee organization to assure a reasonably prudent man that his grant or contribution will not result in the grantee organization's inability to qualify as an operating foundation.

§ 53.4943–1. General rule; purpose.

Generally, under section 4943, the combined holdings of a private foundation and all disqualified persons (as defined in section 4946(a)) in any corporation conducting a business which is not substantially related (aside from the need of the foundation for income or funds or the use it makes of the profits derived) to the exempt purposes of the foundation are limited to 20 percent of the voting stock in such corporation. In addition, the combined holdings of a private foundation and all disqualified persons in any unincorporated business (other than a sole proprietorship) which is not substantially related (aside from the need of the foundation for income or funds or the use it makes of the profits derived) to the exempt purposes of such foundation are limited to 20 percent of the beneficial or profits interest in such business. In the case of a sole proprietorship which is not substantially related (within the meaning of the preceding sentence), section 4943 provides that a private foundation shall have no permitted holdings. These general provisions are subject to a number of exceptions and special provisions which will be described in following sections.

§ 53.4943-2. Imposition of tax on excess business holdings of private foundations.

(a) Imposition of initial tax—(1) In general—(i) Initial tax. Section 4943(a)(1) imposes an initial excise tax (the "initial tax") on the excess business holdings of a private foundation for each taxable year of the foundation which ends during the taxable period defined in section 4943(d)(2). The amount of such tax is equal to 5 percent of the total value of all the private foundation's excess business holdings in each of its business enterprises. In determining the value of the excess business holdings of the foundation subject to tax under section 4943, the rules set forth in ss 20.2031-1 through 20.2031-3 of this chapter (Estate Tax Regulations) shall apply.

(ii) Disposition of certain excess business holdings within ninety days. In any case in which a private foundation acquires excess business holdings, other than as a result of a purchase by the foundation, the foundation shall not be subject to the taxes imposed by section 4943, but only if it disposes of an amount of its holdings so that it no longer has such excess business holdings within 90 days from the date on which it knows, or has reason to know, of the event which caused it to have such excess business holdings. Similarly, a private foundation shall not be subject to the taxes imposed by section 4943 because of its purchase of holdings where it did not know, or have reason to know of prior acquisitions by disqualified persons, but only if the foundation disposes of its excess holdings within the 90-day period described previously, and its purchase would not have created excess business holding but for such prior acquisitions by disqualified persons. In determining whether for purposes of this (ii) the foundation has disposed of such excess business holdings during such 90-day period, any disposition of holdings, by a disqualified person during such period shall be disregarded.

(iii) Extension of ninety day period. The period described in paragraph (a)(1)(ii) of this section, during which no tax shall be imposed under section 4943, shall be extended to include the period during which a foundation is prevented by federal or state securities laws from disposing of such excess business holdings.

(iv) Effect of disposition subject to material restrictions. If a private foundation disposes of an interest in a business enterprise but imposes any material restrictions or conditions that prevent the transferee from freely and effectively using or disposing of the transferred interest, then the transferor foundation will be treated as owning such interest until all such restrictions or conditions are eliminated (regardless of whether the transferee is treated for other purposes of the Code as owning such interest from the date of the transfer). However, a restriction or condition imposed in compliance with federal or state securities laws, or in accordance with the terms or conditions of the gift or bequest through which such interest was acquired by the foundation, shall not be considered a material restriction or condition imposed by a private foundation.

(v) Foundation knowledge of acquisitions made by disqualified persons. (A) For purposes of paragraph (a)(1)(ii) of this section, whether a private foundation will be treated as knowing, or having reason to know, of the acquisition of holdings by a disqualified person will depend on the facts and circumstances of each case. Factors which will be considered relevant to a determination that a private foundation did not know or had no reason to know of an acquisition are: the fact that it did not discover acquisitions made by disqualified persons through the use of procedures reasonably calculated to discover such holdings; the diversity of foundation holdings; and the existence of large numbers of disqualified persons who have little or no contact with the foundation or its managers.

(B) The provisions of paragraph (a)(1)(v)(A) of this section may be illustrated by the following example:

Example. By the fifteenth day of the fifth month after the close of each taxable year, the F Foundation sends to each foundation manager, substantial contributor, person holding more than a 20% interest (as described in section 4946(a)(1)(C)) in a substantial contributor, and foundation described in section 4946(a)(1)(H), a questionnaire asking such persons to list all holdings, actual or constructive, in each business enterprise in which F had holdings during the taxable year in excess of those permitted by the 2 percent de minimis rule of section 4943(c)(2)(C). In preparing the list of such enterprises, F takes into account its constructive holdings only if, during the taxable year, F (along with all related foundations described in section 4946(a)(1)(H)) owned over 2% of the voting stock, profits interest or beneficial interest in the entity actually owning the holdings constructively held by F. The questionnaire asks each such person to list the holdings in such enterprises of any persons who, because of their relationship to such disqualified person, were themselves disqualified persons (i.e., members of the family (as defined in section 4946(d)), and any corporations, partnerships, trusts and estates described in section 4946(a)(1)(E) through (G) in which such person, or members of his family, had an interest). The questionnaire asks that constructive holdings be listed only if, during the taxable year, the disqualified person owned over 2% of the voting stock, profits interest or beneficial interest in the entity actually owning the holdings constructively held by such person. (Thus a disqualified person owning less than 2% of a mutual fund is not required to list his attributed share of all the securities in the portfolio of the fund.) If no response to the questionnaire is received, the foundation seeks the information requested by the questionnaire by mailing a second (but not a third) questionnaire. If a questionnaire which is returned to the foundation indicates that certain information was unavailable to the person completing the questionnaire, the foundation seeks that information directly. For example, if a disqualified person indicates that he could not find out whether a corporation described in section 4946(a)(1)(E) had holdings in the enterprise listed in the questionnaire, the foundation seeks to obtain this information directly from the corporation by mailing it a questionnaire. In such a case F may be found not to have reason to know of the acquisition of holdings by a disqualified person.

(vi) Holdings acquired other than by purchases. See section 4943(c)(6) and § 53.4943–6 for rules relating to the acquisition of certain holdings other than by purchase by the foundation or a disqualified person.

(2) Special rules. In applying subparagraph (1) of this paragraph, the tax imposed by section 4943(a)(1)—

(i) Shall be imposed on the last day of the private foundation's taxable year, but

(ii) The amount of such tax and the value of the excess business holdings subject to such tax shall be determined with respect to the foundation's holdings (based upon voting power, profits or beneficial interest, or value, whichever is applicable) in any business enterprise as of that day during the foundation's taxable year when the foundation's excess holdings in such enterprise were the greatest.

In applying subdivision (ii) of this subparagraph, if a foundation's excess business holdings in a business enterprise which constitute such foundation's greatest excess holdings in such enterprise for any taxable year are maintained for 2 or more days during such taxable year, the value of such excess holdings which is subject to tax under section 4943(a)(1) shall be the greatest value of such excess holdings in such enterprise as of any day on which such greatest excess holdings are maintained during such taxable year.

(3) Examples. The provisions of this paragraph may be illustrated by the following examples:

Example (1). Y is a private foundation reporting on a calendar year basis. On January 1, 1973, Y has 20 shares of common stock in corporation N, of which five shares constitute excess business holdings. On June 1, 1973, Y disposes of such five shares; however, because of additional acquisitions of N common stock on such date by disqualified persons with respect to Y, the remaining 15 shares of N common stock held by Y now constitute excess business holdings. There are no further acquisitions or dispositions of N common stock during 1973 by Y or its disqualified persons. Although Y's greatest holdings in N during 1973 are held between January 1, 1973, and May 31, 1973, Y's greatest excess holdings in N during 1973 are held between June 1, 1973, and December 31, 1973. Therefore, the tax specified in section 4943(a)(1) shall be computed on the basis of the greatest value of such greatest excess holdings as of any day between June 1 and December 31, 1973.

Example (2). X is a private foundation reporting on a calendar year basis. On January 1, 1972, X has 100 shares of common stock in M corporation which are excess business holdings. On such date each share of M common stock has a fair market value of $100. On February 28, 1972, in an effort to dispose of such excess business holdings, X sells 70 shares of M common stock for $120 per share (the fair market value of each share on such date) to A, an individual who is not a disqualified person within the meaning of section 4946(a). The value of $120 per share is the highest fair market value between January 1 and February 28, 1972. X disposes of no more stock in M for the remainder of calendar year 1972. On December 31, 1972, the fair market value of each share of M common stock is $80. X calculates its tax on its excess business holdings in M for 1972 as follows:

100 shares of M common stock times $120 fair market value per share as of Feb. 28, 1972	$12,000
$12,000 multiplied by rate of tax (percent)	5%
Amount of tax on X foundation's excess bus. holdings for 1972	$600

Example (3). Assume the same facts as in Example (2) except that the sale of X to A occurs on January 7, 1973, when the fair market value of each share of M corporation common stock equals $70. A value of $100 per share is the highest fair market value of the M common stock between January 1 and January 7, 1973. On May 9, 1973, X for the first time has excess business holdings in N corporation in the form of 200 shares of N common stock. The value per share of N common stock on May 9, 1973, equals $200. X makes no disposition of the N common stock during 1973, and the value of each share of N common stock as of December 31, 1973 equals $250 (the highest value of N common stock during 1973). X calculates its tax on its excess business holdings in both M and N for 1973 as follows:

100 shares of M common stock times $100 f.m.v. per share	$10,000
$250 fair market value per share...............	$50,000
Total...	$60,000
$60,000 multiplied by rate of tax	5%
Amount of tax on X fdn.'s excess bus. holdings for 1973....................................	$3,000

(b) Additional tax. In any case in which the initial tax is imposed under section 4943(a) with respect to the holdings of a private foundation in any business enterprise, if, at the close of the taxable period (as defined in section 4943(d)(2) and § 53.4943–9) with respect to such holdings the foundation still has excess business holdings in such enterprise, there is imposed a tax under section 4943(b) equal to 200 percent of the value of such excess holdings as of the last day of the taxable period.

§ 53.4943–3. Determination of excess business holdings.

(a) Excess business holdings—(1) In general. For purposes of section 4943, the term "excess business holdings" means, with respect to the holdings of any private foundation in any business enterprise (as described in section 4943(d)(4)), the amount of stock or other interest in the enterprise which, except as provided in § 53.4943–2(a)(1), the foundation, or a disqualified person, would have to dispose of, or cause the disposition of, to a person other than a disqualified person (as defined in section 4946(a)) in order for the remaining holdings of the foundation in such enterprise to be permitted holdings (as defined in paragraphs (b) and (c) of this section). If a private foundation is required by section 4943 and the regulations thereunder to dispose of certain shares of a class of stock in a particular period of time and other shares of the same class of stock in a shorter period of time, any stock disposed of shall be charged first against those dispositions which must be made in such shorter period.

(2) Example. The provisions of this paragraph may be illustrated by the following example:

Example. Corporation X has outstanding 100 shares of voting stock, with each share entitling the holder thereof to one vote. F, a private foundation, possesses 20 shares of X voting stock representing 20 percent of the voting power in X. Assume that the permitted holdings of F in X under paragraph (b)(1) of this section are 11 percent of the voting stock in X. F, therefore, possesses voting stock in X representing a percentage of voting stock in excess of the percentage permitted by such paragraph. Such excess percentage is 9 percent of the voting stock in X, determined by subtracting the percentage of voting stock representing the permitted holdings of F in X (i.e., 11 percent) from the percentage of voting stock held by F in X (i.e., 20 percent). (20% - 11=9%). The excess business holdings of F in X are an amount of voting stock representing such excess percentage, or 9 shares of X voting stock (9 percent of 100).

(b) Permitted holdings in an incorporated business enterprise—(1) In general—(i) Permitted holdings defined. Except as otherwise provided in section 4943(c)(2) and (4), the permitted holdings of any private foundation in an incorporated business enterprise (including a real estate investment trust, as defined in section 856) are—

(A) 20 percent of the voting stock in such enterprise reduced (but not below zero) by

(B) The percentage of voting stock in such enterprise actually or constructively owned by all disqualified persons.

(ii) Voting stock. For purposes of this section, the percentage of voting stock held by any person in a corporation is normally determined by reference to the power of stock to vote for the election of directors, with treasury stock and stock which is authorized but unissued being disregarded. Thus, for example, if a private foundation holds 20 percent of the shares of one class of stock in a corporation, which class is entitled to elect three directors, and such foundation holds no stock in the other class of stock, which is entitled to elect five directors, such foundation shall be treated as holding 7.5 percent of the voting stock because the class of stock it holds has 37.5 percent of such voting power, by reason of being able to elect three of the eight directors, and the foundation holds one-fifth of the shares of such class (20 percent of 37.5 percent is 7.5 percent). The fact that extraordinary corporate action (e.g., charter or by-law amendments) by a corporation may require the favorable vote of more than a majority of the directors, or of the outstanding voting stock, of such corporation shall not alter the determination of voting power of stock in such corporation in accordance with the two preceding sentences.

(2) Nonvoting stock as permitted holdings—(i) In general. In addition to those holdings permitted by paragraph (b)(1) of this section, the permitted holdings of a private foundation in an incorporated business enterprise shall include any share of nonvoting stock in such enterprise held by the foundation in any case in which all disqualified persons hold, actually or constructively, no more than 20 percent (35 percent where third persons have effective control as defined in paragraph (b)(3)(ii) of this section) of the voting stock in such enterprise. All equity interests which do not have voting power attributable to them shall, for purposes of section 4943, be classified as nonvoting stock. For this purpose, evidences of indebtedness (including convertible indebtedness), and warrants and other options or rights to acquire stock shall not be considered equity interests.

(ii) Stock with contingent voting rights and convertible nonvoting stock. Stock carrying voting rights which will vest only when conditions, the occurrence of which are indeterminate, have been met, such as preferred stock which gains such voting rights only if no dividends are paid thereon, will be treated as nonvoting stock until the conditions have occurred which cause the voting rights to vest. When such rights vest, the stock will be treated as voting stock that was acquired other than by purchase, but only if the private foundation or disqualified persons had no control over whether the conditions would occur. Similarly, nonvoting stock which may be converted into voting stock will not be treated as voting stock until such conversion occurs. For special rules where stock is acquired other than by purchase, see section 4943(c)(6) and the regulations thereunder.

(iii) Example. The provisions of this paragraph (2) may be illustrated by the following example:

Example. Assume that F, a private foundation, holds 10 percent of the single class of voting stock of corporation X, and owns 20 shares of nonvoting stock in X. Assume further that A and B, the only disqualified persons with respect to F, hold 10 percent of the voting stock of X. Under the provisions of paragraph (b)(1) of this section the 10 percent of X voting stock held by F will be classified as permitted holdings of F in X since 20 percent less the percentage of voting stock held by A and B in X is 10 percent. In addition, under the provisions of this (2), the 20 shares of X nonvoting stock will qualify as permitted holdings of F in X since the percentage of voting stock held by A and B in X is no greater than 20 percent.

(3) Thirty-five-percent rule where third person has effective control of enterprise—(i) In general. Except as provided in section 4943(c)(4), paragraph (b)(1) of this section shall be applied by substituting 35 percent for 20 percent if—

(A) The private foundation and all disqualified persons together do not hold, actually or constructively, more than 35 percent of the voting stock in the business enterprise, and

(B) The foundation establishes to the satisfaction of the Commissioner that effective control (as defined in paragraph (b)(3)(ii) of this section) of the business enterprise is in one or more persons (other than the foundation itself) who are not disqualified persons.

(ii) "Effective control" defined. For purposes of this subparagraph, the term "effective control" means the possession, directly or indirectly, of the power to direct or cause the direction of the management and policies of a business enterprise, whether through the ownership of voting stock, the use of voting trusts, or contractual arrangements, or otherwise. It is the reality of control which is decisive and not its form or the means by which it is exercisable. Thus, where a minority interest held by individuals who are not disqualified persons has historically elected the majority of a corporation's directors, effective control is in the hands of those individuals.

(4) Two percent de minimis rule—(i) In general. Under section 4943(c)(2)(C), a private foundation is not treated as having excess business holdings in any incorporated business enterprise in which it (together with all other private foundations (including trusts described in section 4947(a)(2)) which are described in section 4946(a)(1)(H)) actually or constructively owns not more than 2 percent of the voting stock and not more than 2 percent in value of all outstanding shares of all classes of stock. If, however, the private foundation, together with all other private foundations which are described in section 4946(a)(1)(H), actually or constructively owns more than 2 percent of either the voting stock or the value of the outstanding shares of all classes of stock in any incorporated business enterprise, all the stock in such business enterprise classified as excess business holding under section 4943 is treated as excess business holdings. For purposes of this paragraph, any stock owned by a private foundation which is treated as held by a disqualified person under section 4943(c)(4)(B), (5), or (6) shall be treated as actually owned by the private foundation. See paragraph (b)(1) of § 53.4941(d)–4 for the determination of excess business holdings without regard to section 4943(c)(2)(C) for purposes of applying section 101(C)(2)(B) of the Tax Reform Act of 1969 (83 Stat. 533).

(ii) Examples. The provisions of this subparagraph may be illustrated by the following examples:

Example (1). F, a private foundation, owns 1 percent of the single class of voting stock and 1 percent in value of all the outstanding shares of all classes of stock in X corporation. No other private foundation described in section 4946(a)(1)(H) owns any stock in X. All of the stock owned by F in X would be excess business holdings under section 4943(c)(1) if section 4943(c)(2)(C) were inapplicable. F owns no other shares of stock in X. Since F owns more than 2 percent of the voting stock and no more than 2 percent in value of all outstanding shares of all classes of stock in X, under section 4943(c)(2)(C) none of the stock in X owned by F is treated as excess business holdings.

Example (2). Assume the facts as stated in Example (1), except that F and T, a controlled private foundation under section 4946(a)(1)(H), together own 1 percent of all the voting stock and 1 percent in value of all the outstanding shares of all classes of stock in X. All of the stock in X owned by F and T would be excess business holdings under section 4943(c)(1) if section 4943(c)(2)(C) were inapplicable. Since F and T together owned no more than 2 percent of the voting stock and no more than 2 percent in value of all outstanding shares of all classes of stock in X, under section 4943(c)(2)(C) none of the stock in X owned by either F or T is treated as excess business holdings.

Example (3). Assume the facts as stated in Example (1), except that F owns 3 percent of the voting stock in X, 2 percent of which is treated as held by P, a disqualified person of F, under section 4943(c)(4)(B). Under subdivision (i) of this subparagraph, the 2 percent of the stock in X owned by F which is treated as held by P under section 4943(c)(4)(B) is treated as actually owned by F for purposes of section 4943(c)(2)(C). Consequently, all of the X stock owned by F is treated as excess business holdings under section 4943(c)(2)(C). However, only 1 percent of the stock in X is subject to tax under section 4943(a), since the other 2 percent is treated as owned by a disqualified person under section 4943(c)(4)(B) for purposes of determining the tax upon F under section 4943(a).

(c) Permitted holdings in an unincorporated business enterprise—(1) In general. The permitted holdings of a private foundation in any business enterprise which is not incorporated shall, subject to the provisions of subparagraphs (2), (3), and (4) of this paragraph, be determined under the principles of paragraph (b) of this section.

(2) Partnership or joint venture. In the case of a partnership (including a limited partnership) or joint venture. The terms "profits interest" and "capital interest" shall be substituted for "voting stock" and "nonvoting stock," respectively, wherever those terms appear in paragraph (b) of this section. The interest in profits of such foundation (or such disqualified person) shall be determined in the same manner as its distributive share of partnership taxable income. See section 704(b) (relating to the determination of the distributive share by the income or loss ratio) and the regulations thereunder. In the absence of a provision in the partnership agreement, the capital interest of such foundation (or such disqualified person) in a partnership shall be determined on the basis of its interest in the assets of the partnership which would be distributable to such foundation (or such disqualified person) upon its withdrawal from the partnership, or upon liquidation of the partnership, whichever is the greater.

(3) Sole proprietorship. For purposes of section 4943, a private foundation shall have no permitted holdings in a sole proprietorship. In the case of a transfer by a private foundation of a portion of a sole proprietorship, see paragraph (c)(2) of this section (relating to permitted holdings in partnerships). For the treatment of a private foundation's ownership of a sole proprietorship prior to May 26, 1969, see § 53.4943–4.

(4) Trusts and other unincorporated business enterprises—(i) In general. In the case of any unincorporated business enterprise which is not described in paragraph (c)(2) or (3) of this section, the term "beneficial interest" shall be substituted for "voting stock" wherever the term appears in paragraph (b) of this section. Any and all references to nonvoting stock in paragraph (b) of this section shall be inapplicable with respect to any unincorporated business enterprise described in this subparagraph.

(ii) Trusts. For purposes of section 4943, the beneficial interest of a private foundation or any disqualified person in a trust shall be the beneficial remainder interest of such foundation or person determined as provided in paragraph (b) of § 53.4943–8.

(iii) Other unincorporated business enterprises. For purposes of section 4943, the beneficial interest of a private foundation or any disqualified person in an unincorporated business enterprise (other than a trust or an enterprise described in paragraph (c)(2) or (3) of this section) includes any right to receive a portion of distributions of profits of such enterprise, and, if the portion of distributions is not fixed by an agreement among the participants, any right to receive a portion of the assets (if any) upon liquidation of the enterprise, except as a creditor or employee. For purposes of this subparagraph, a right to receive distributions of profits includes a right to receive any amount from such profits (other than as a creditor or employee), whether as a sum certain or as a portion of profits realized by the enterprise. Where there is no agreement fixing the rights of the participants in such enterprise, the interest of such foundation (or such disqualified person) in such enterprise shall be determined by dividing the amount of all equity investments or contributions to the capital of the enterprise made or obligated to be made by such foundation (or such disqualified person) by the amount of all equity investments or contributions to capital made or obligated to be made by all participants in the enterprise.

* * *

§ 53.4943–6. Five-year period to dispose of gifts, bequests, etc.

(a) In general—(1) Application. (i) Paragraph (6) of section 4943(c) prescribes transition rules for a private foundation, which, but for such paragraph, would have excess business holdings as a result of a change in the holdings in a business enterprise after May 26, 1969 (other than by purchase by such private foundation or by a disqualified person) to the extent that section 4943(c)(5) (relating to certain holdings acquired under a pre-May 27, 1969, will on trust) does not apply.

(ii) Subparagraph (A) of section 4943(c)(6) applies where, immediately prior to a change in holdings described in paragraph (a)(1)(i) of this section, the foundation has no excess business holdings in such enterprise (determined without regard to section 4943(c)(4), (5), or (6)). In such a case, the entire interest of the foundation in such enterprise (immediately after such change) shall (while held by the foundation) be treated as held by a disqualified person (rather than by the foundation) during the five-year period beginning on the date of such change.

(iii) Subparagraph (B) of section 4943(c)(6) applies where the foundation has excess business holdings in such enterprise (determined without regard to section 4943(c)(4), (5), or (6)) immediately prior to a change in holdings described in paragraph (a)(1)(i) of this section. In such a case, the interest of the foundation in such enterprise (immediately after such change) shall (while held by the foundation) be treated as held by a disqualified person (rather than the foundation) during the five-year period beginning on the date of such change, except that if and as soon as any holdings in such enterprise become excess business holdings during such period (determined without regard to such change (and the resulting application of section 4943(c)(6) to the foundation's interest in such enterprise)), such holdings shall no longer be treated as held by a disqualified person under this section, but shall constitute excess business holdings subject to the initial tax. In applying the preceding sentence, if holdings of the foundation which (but for such change in holdings (and the resulting application of section 4943(c)(6) to the foundation's interest in such enterprise)) would be subject to the 25 percent limit prescribed by section 4943(c)(4)(D) after the expiration of the first phase, such holdings shall be treated as subject to such percentage limitation for purposes of determining excess business holdings. For example, if a private foundation in 1978 has present holdings of 28 percent in a business enterprise to which section 4943(c)(4) applies, and such holdings would exceed the 25 percent limit of section 4943(c)(4)(D)(i) on May 26, 1979, a gift of 5 percent to the foundation in 1978 of an interest in such enterprise shall not prevent the 3 percent (28%–25%) excess over the 25 percent limit from constituting excess business holdings on May 26, 1979, if on such date disqualified persons hold more than a 2 percent interest in such enterprise (and no other transaction has taken place).

(2) Acquisitions that are not purchases. Section 4943(c)(6) does not apply if a change in holdings in a business enterprise is the result of a purchase by the private foundation or a disqualified person. For purposes of subparagraph (a) of this paragraph, the term "purchase" shall not include any acquisition by gift, devise, bequest, legacy, or interstate succession. Paragraph (d) of this section provides rules for the treatment of increases in holdings received in a readjustment (as defined in § 53.4943–7(d)(1)).

* * *

(b) Special rules for acquisitions by will or trust—(1) In general. In the case of an acquisition of holdings in a business enterprise by a private foundation pursuant to the terms of a will or trust, the five-year period described in section 4943(c)(6) and in this section shall not commence until the date on which the distribution of such holdings from the estate or trust to the foundation occurs. See § 53.4943–5(b)(1) for rules relating to the determination of the date of distribution under the terms of a will or trust. For purposes of this subparagraph, holdings in a business enterprise will not be treated as acquired by a private foundation pursuant to the terms of a will where the holdings in the business enterprise were not held by the decedent. Thus, in the case of after-acquired property, this subparagraph shall not apply, the five-year period described in section 4943(c)(6) and this section shall commence on the date of acquisition of such holdings by the estate, and such five-year period may expire prior to the date of distribution of such holdings from the estate. To the extent that an interest to which section 4943(c)(6) and this paragraph (b)(1) apply is constructively held by a private foundation under section 4943(d)(1) and § 53.4943–8 prior to the date of distribution, it shall be treated as held by a disqualified person prior to such date by reason of section 4943(c)(6). See § 53.4943–8 for rules relating to constructive holdings held in an estate or trust for the benefit of the foundation.

(2) Special rule for section 4943(c)(5) interests acquired from a nondisqualified person. (i) In the case of holdings of a private foundation in a business enterprise to which section 4943(c)(5) (relating to certain holdings acquired under a pre-May 27, 1969, will or trust) applies which are acquired from a nondisqualified person, the interest of the foundation in such enterprise (immediately after such acquisition) shall (while held by the foundation) be treated as held by a disqualified person (rather than the foundation) under section 4943(c)(6)(B) and paragraph (a)(1)(iii) of this section from the date of acquisition until the end of the fifth year following the date of distribution of such holdings. Thereafter, only the holdings to which section 4943(c)(5) and § 53.4943–5(a)(1) apply shall continue to be treated as held by a disqualified person until the end of the first phase with respect thereto.

* * *

(c) Exceptions. (1) Section 4943(c)(6) and this section shall not apply to any transfer of holdings in a business enterprise by one private foundation to another private foundation which is related to the first foundation within the meaning of section 4946(a)(1)(H).

(2) Section 4943(c)(6) and this section shall not apply to an increase in the holdings of a private foundation in a business enterprise that is part of a plan whereby disqualified persons will purchase additional holdings in the same enterprise during the five-year period beginning on the date of such change, e.g., to maintain control of such enterprise, since such increase shall be treated as caused in part by the purchase of such additional holdings.

(3) The purchase of holdings by an entity whose holdings are treated as constructively owned by a foundation, its disqualified persons, or both, under section 4943(d)(1) shall be treated as a purchase by a disqualified person if the foundation, its disqualified persons, or both, have effective control of the entity or otherwise can control the purchase. For example, if a foundation is the beneficiary of a specific bequest of $20,000 and its consent is required for the estate to make a purchase using such cash, then a purchase by the estate using such cash would be treated as a purchase by a disqualified person. Similarly, if an executor of an estate is a disqualified person with respect to a private foundation, any purchase by the estate would be treated as a purchase by a disqualified person.

(4) If a private foundation, its disqualified persons, or both, hold an interest in specific property under the terms of a will or trust, and if the private foundation, its disqualified persons, or both, consent or otherwise agree to the substitution of holdings in a business enterprise for such specific property, such holdings shall be treated as acquired by purchase by a disqualified person. For example, if a private foundation is the beneficiary of a specific bequest of $20,000 and the private foundation agrees to accept certain of the estate's holdings in a business enterprise in satisfaction of such specific bequest, such holdings will be treated as acquired by purchase by a disqualified person even if such holdings were held by the decedent.

(d) Readjustments and distributions—(1) General rule. Except as otherwise provided in subparagraph (2) of this paragraph, any increase in holdings in a business enterprise that is the result of a readjustment (as defined in § 53.4943–7(d)(1)) shall be treated as acquired other than by purchase. However, holdings that are attributable to holdings owned by the private foundation that would have been excess business holdings except for the fact that such holdings were treated as held by a disqualified person prior to the readjustment shall in no event be treated as held by a disqualified person after the date on which the holdings to which the change is attributable would have ceased to be treated as held by a disqualified person.

(2) Exceptions. Any increase in holdings in a business enterprise that is the result of a readjustment (as defined in § 53.4943–7(d)(1)), including any change resulting from application of the rule in § 53.4943–8(c)(3), shall be treated as occurring by purchase by a disqualified person:

(i) To the extent the increase is attributable to holdings that were excess business holdings prior to the readjustment, and separately.

(ii) To the full extent of the increase if the readjustment includes a prohibited transaction, unless the foundation establishes to the satisfaction of the Commissioner that effective control of all parties to the transaction was, at the time of the transaction, in one or more persons (other than the foundation) who are not disqualified persons with respect to the foundation. See § 53.4943–7(d)(2) for the definition of prohibited transaction.

(3) Section 4943(c)(6) holdings. If, immediately prior to a readjustment (as defined in § 53.4943–7(d)(1)), a private foundation has holdings in a business enterprise that are treated under section 4943(c)(6) as held by a disqualified person, then any holdings in a business enterprise that are received in the readjustment in exchange for such section 4943(c)(6) holdings shall be treated as the holdings surrendered in the exchange to the same extent as provided in § 53.4943–7 with respect to exchanges involving holdings to which section 4943(c)(4) or (5) applies. Rules similar to those in § 53.4943–7(a)(2) shall be applied to determine when holdings are treated as surrendered or received in a readjustment for purposes of this paragraph.

(4) Redemption by a corporation that is a disqualified person. If a foundation holds an interest in a corporation that is a disqualified person, an increase in the holdings of the private foundation, its disqualified person, or both, as a result of a redemption or a purchase of stock of the disqualified person corporation by such corporation shall not be treated as acquired by purchase by a disqualified person based solely on the status of the corporation as a disqualified person.

(5) One percent rule for redemptions. If the holdings of a foundation, its disqualified persons, or both, in a business enterprise are increased as a result of one or more redemptions during any taxable year then, unless the aggregate of such increases equals or exceeds one percent of the outstanding voting stock or one percent of the value of all outstanding shares of all classes of stock, the determination of whether such increases cause the foundation to have excess business holdings shall be made only at the close of the private foundation's taxable year. The five-year period described in section 4943(c)(6) or the 90-day period described in § 53.4943–2(a)(1)(ii), whichever is applicable, shall begin on the last day of such taxable year. If, however, the aggregate of such increases equals or exceeds one percent of the outstanding voting stock or one percent of the value of all outstanding shares of all classes of stock, the determination of whether such increases cause the foundation to have excess business holdings shall be made, and the applicable five-year or 90-day period shall begin, as of the date the increases, in the aggregate, equal or exceed one percent.

(6) Examples. The provisions of this paragraph are illustrated in § 53.4943–7(f) and by the following examples:

Example (1). (i) F, a private foundation, holds 20% of the voting stock of X corporation, an active business enterprise. No disqualified person with respect to F holds any X stock. In 1980, X redeems 10% of its outstanding shares, increasing F's holdings to 22% of the X stock. Assume the redemption by X is not a prohibited transaction.

(ii) All of F's holdings before the redemption are permitted holdings under section 4943(c)(2). There is no effective control of X by third parties so the 35% permitted holdings rule is inapplicable. F's holdings after the redemption exceed the permitted holdings under section 4943(c)(2) (20%). Because the increase is attributable to stock that was permitted holdings prior to the readjustment, and the readjustment does not involve a prohibited transaction, the 2% increase in F's holdings of X stock is treated as acquired other than by purchase. Therefore, under section 4943(c)(6) and this section, F will have 5 years from the date of the redemption to dispose of the 2% excess.

Example (2). (i) Assume the same facts as in Example (1) except that the 20% of X stock held by F was donated by X corporation, was worth more than $5,000 and represented 20% of the contributions received by the foundation through the end of the taxable year in which the gift of stock was made.

(ii) X corporation is a disqualified person with respect to F under section 4946(a)(1)(A). Under subparagraph (4), the redemption of X stock is not treated as a purchase by a disqualified person merely because X is a disqualified person with respect to F. Therefore the rules of this paragraph apply as if the redemption were made by a corporation which is not a disqualified person. The analysis and result are the same as in Example (1).

Example (3). (i) On May 1, 1990, F, a private foundation, received a donation of 40% of the stock of X corporation, a business enterprise. Neither F nor any disqualified person with respect to F holds any other interest in X. On June 1, 1992, the X corporation redeemed F's 40% interest in exchange for 100% of the stock of Y corporation, a wholly-owned subsidiary of X. Assume the redemption by X is not a prohibited transaction.

(ii) Under section 4943(c)(6), the X stock acquired by gift is treated as held by disqualified persons through April 30, 1995. Under subparagraph (3) of this paragraph (d), 40% of the 100% interest in Y received in exchange for F's 40% interest in X is treated as F's 40% interest in X and is therefore treated as held by disqualified persons through April 30, 1995. In addition, under subparagraph (1) of this paragraph (d), the 60% interest in Y that represents an increase in holdings above the 40% held before the readjustment will be treated as acquired other than by purchase. However, F's 20% interest in X in excess of 20% permitted holdings under section 4943(c)(2) would have been excess business holdings if such interest had not been treated as held by a disqualified person on June 1, 1992. Therefore, to the extent of a

30% interest in Y, (i.e., the portion of the increased holdings in Y attributable to F's 20% holdings in X) the increased holdings will be treated as held by disqualified person only through April 30, 1995, since this is the latest date on which F's original 40% interest in X would have been treated as held by disqualified persons. The remaining 30% interest in Y will be treated as held by disqualified persons for five years from the date of the exchange (through May 31, 1997).

(e) Constructive holdings. Any change in holdings in a business enterprise that occurs because a corporation ceases to be actively engaged in a trade or business, thus causing its holdings to be constructively owned by its shareholders, shall be treated as acquired other than by purchase.

(f) Certain transactions treated as purchases; cross references. For the application of section 4943(c)(6) to holdings that were not an interest in a business enterprise when acquired but that subsequently became holdings in a business enterprise, see § 53.4943–10(d)(2).

§ 53.4943–8. Business holdings; constructive ownership.

(a) Constructive ownership—(1) In general. For purposes of section 4943, in computing the holdings in a business enterprise of a private foundation, or a disqualified person (as defined in section 4946), any stock or other interest owned, directly or indirectly, by or for a corporation, partnership, estate or trust shall be considered as being owned proportionately by or for its shareholders, partners, or beneficiaries except as otherwise provided by paragraphs (b), (c) and (d) of this section. Any interest in a business enterprise actually or constructively owned by a shareholder of a corporation, a partner of a partnership, or beneficiary of an estate or trust shall not be considered as constructively held by the corporation, partnership, trust or estate. Further, if any corporation, partnership, estate or trust has a warrant or other option to acquire an interest in a business enterprise, such interest is not deemed to be constructively owned by such entity until the option is exercised. (See paragraph (b)(2) of § 53.4943–3 for rules that options are not stock for purposes of determining excess business holdings.)

(2) Powers of appointment. Any interest in business enterprise over which a foundation or a disqualified person has a power of appointment exercisable in favor of the foundation or a disqualified person shall be considered owned by the foundation or disqualified person holding such power of appointment.

(3) Determination of extent of constructive ownership. If an interest in a business enterprise owned by a corporation is constructively owned by a shareholder, each shareholder's proportion of ownership is generally computed on the basis of the voting stock each shareholder has in the corporation. In determining holdings permitted under section 4943(c)(4) and (5), each shareholder's proportion of ownership in the business enterprise shall also be computed on the basis of value, taking into account both voting and nonvoting stock held by the shareholder.

(4) Nonvoting stock. If a private foundation, its disqualified persons, or both, own (directly or constructively) nonvoting stock of a parent corporation the holdings of which are treated as constructively owned by its shareholders by reason of section 4943(d)(1) and this section, such nonvoting stock shall be treated as nonvoting stock of any corporation in which the parent corporation holds an interest for purposes of the limitation on the holding of nonvoting stock under section 4943(c)(2)(A) and § 53.4943–3(b)(2).

(5) Interests held by certain disqualified persons. In the case of an entity that is a disqualified person (other than an entity described in section 4946(a)(1)(H)), the holdings of which are treated as constructively owned by its shareholders, partners, or beneficiaries, for purposes of determining the total holdings of disqualified persons the holdings of the entity shall be considered held by a disqualified person only to the extent such holdings are treated as constructively owned by disqualified persons who are shareholders, partners, or beneficiaries of the entity. In the case of an entity described in section 4946(a)(1)(H) or an entity, the holdings of which are not treated as constructively owned by its shareholders, partners, or beneficiaries, all holdings of such entity shall be treated as held by a disqualified person if and only if the entity itself is a disqualified person.

(b) Estates and trusts—(1) In general. Any interest actually or constructively owned by an estate or trust is deemed constructively owned, in the case of an estate, by its beneficiaries or, in the case of a trust, by its remainder beneficiaries except as provided in paragraphs (b)(2), (3) and (4) of this section (relating to certain split-interest trusts described in section 4947(a)(2), to trusts of qualified pension, profit-sharing, and stock bonus plans described in section 401(a) and to revocable trusts). Thus, if a trust owns 100 percent of the stock of a corporation A, and if, on an actuarial basis, W's life interest in the trust is 15 percent, Y's life interest is 25 percent, and Z's remainder interest is 60 percent, under this paragraph (b), Z will be considered to be the owner of 100 percent of the stock of corporation A. See § 53.4943–4, § 53.4943–5 and § 53.4943–6 for rules relating to certain actual or constructive holdings of a foundation being treated as held by a disqualified person. For the treatment of certain property acquired by an estate or trust after May 26, 1969, see paragraph (a)(2) of § 53.4943–5.

(2) Split-interest trusts—(i) Amounts transferred in trust after May 26, 1969. In the case of an interest in a business enterprise which was transferred to a trust described in section 4947(a)(2) after May 26, 1969, for the benefit of a private foundation, no portion of such interest shall be considered as owned by the private foundation—

(A) If the foundation holds only an income interest in the trust, or

(B) If the foundation holds only a remainder interest in the trust (unless the foundation can exercise primary investment discretion with respect to such interest)

until such trust ceases to be so described. See section 4947(a)(2) and (b)(3) and the regulations thereunder for rules relating to such trusts. See also sections 4946(a)(1)(G) and (H) and the regulations thereunder for rules relating to when a trust described in this paragraph (b)(2) is itself a disqualified person.

* * *

(4) Revocable trusts. An interest in a business enterprise owned by a revocable trust shall be treated as owned by the grantor of such trust.

(5) Estates. For purposes of applying section 4943(d)(1) to estates, the term "beneficiary" includes any person (including a private foundation) entitled to receive property of a decedent pursuant to a will or pursuant to laws of descent and distribution. However, a person shall no longer be considered a beneficiary of an estate when all the property to which he is entitled has been received by him, when he no longer has a claim against the estate and when there is only a remote possibility that it will be necessary for the estate to seek the return of property or to seek payment from him by contribution or otherwise to satisfy claims against the estate or expenses of administration. When pursuant to the preceding sentence, a person (including a private foundation) ceases to be a beneficiary, stock or another interest in a business enterprise owned by the estate shall not thereafter be considered owned by such person. If any person is the constructive owner of an interest in a business enterprise actually held by an estate, the date of death of the testator or decedent intestate shall be the first day on which such person shall be considered a constructive owner of such interest. See § 53.4943–5 for rules relating to wills executed on or before May 26, 1969.

(c) Corporation actively engaged in a trade or business—(1) In general. Except as provided in paragraphs (c)(2) and (3) of this section, any interest (whether or not in a separate entity) owned by a corporation which is actively engaged in a trade or business shall not be deemed to be constructively owned by such corporation's shareholders.

(2) Actively engaged in a trade or business. For purposes of paragraph (c)(1) of this section—

(i) A corporation shall not be considered to be actively engaged in a trade or business if the corporation is not a business enterprise by reason of section 4943(d)(3)(A) or (B) and § 53.4943–10(b) or (c);

(ii) In the case of a corporation which owns passive holdings and is actively engaged in a trade or business, such corporation shall not be considered to be actively engaged in a trade or business if the net assets used in such trade or business are insubstantial when compared to passive holdings.

(3) Exceptions. If a corporation has been involved in a prohibited transaction, any interest in a business enterprise owned by such corporation shall be treated as constructively owned by its shareholders, whether or not such corporation is actively engaged in a trade or business. For a definition of prohibited transaction, see § 53.4943–7(d)(2).

* * *

(d) Partnerships. Any interest in a business enterprise which is owned by a partnership shall be deemed to be constructively owned by the partners in such partnerships.

(e) Examples. The provisions of this section are illustrated by the following examples.

Example (1). F, a private foundation, directly owns voting stock of X, a holding company described in section 4943(d)(3)(B). That stock represents 40% of the voting power in X and 20% of the value of all outstanding shares of all classes of stock in X. F also owns nonvoting stock in X that represents 10% of the value of all outstanding shares of all classes of stock in X. D, a disqualified person, owns voting stock of X that represents 40% of the voting power in X and 20% of the value. D does not own any nonvoting stock in X. X corporation's only holding is stock of Y corporation. The Y voting stock held by X represents 50% of the voting power in Y and 25% of the value of all outstanding shares of all classes of stock in Y. X also owns nonvoting stock in Y that represents 25% of the value of all outstanding shares of all classes of stock in Y. Under paragraph (a)(3) of this section, F and D each constructively owns 20% of the voting power in Y through their voting interest in X (40% of X's 50% of Y). F also constructively owns 15% of the value of all outstanding shares of all classes of stock in Y through F's interest in X (F's 30% of the value of X multiplied by X's 50% of the value of Y). While D constructively owns 10% of the value of Y (D's 20% of the value of X multiplied by X's 50% of the value of Y).

Example (2). (i) F, a private foundation, owns 50% of the one class of nonvoting stock of X corporation, a corporation described in section 4943(d)(3)(B) and paragraph (c)(2)(i) above. D, a disqualified person with respect to F as described in section 4946(a)(1)(A), owns 40% of the one class of voting stock of X. X corporation is a disqualified person with respect to F because D owns more than 35% of the voting of X. (See section 4946(a)(1)(E)). On January 1, 1980, X purchases for cash 40% of the only class of stock of Y corporation, a retail clothing store, from unrelated third parties.

(ii) Under paragraph (a)(4) of this section, F is treated as owning nonvoting stock of Y. Although X is a disqualified person, its holdings are not treated as held by disqualified persons except as constructive holdings. Therefore, the "deemed" nonvoting stock in Y is a permitted holding because D, a disqualified person with respect to F, constructively owns only 16% of the voting stock of Y (less than 20% permitted under section 4943(c)(2)).

Example (3). (i) The facts are the same as in Example (2), except that X purchases 100% of this stock of Y corporation. Under paragraph (a)(4) of this section, F is treated as owning nonvoting stock of Y. The "deemed" nonvoting stock in Y is not a permitted holdings because D, a disqualified person with respect to F, constructively owns 40% of the voting stock of Y.

Example (4). (i) D, a disqualified person with respect to F, owns 40% of the one class of stock in X corporation, an active business. X is a disqualified person with respect to F, X acquires 40% of the voting stock in Y corporation. Under paragraph (a)(5) of this section, the holdings of X in Y are treated as held by a disqualified person. F cannot hold any Y stock, voting or nonvoting.

§ 53.4943–9. Business holdings; certain periods.

(a) Taxable period—(1) In general. For purposes of section 4943, the term "taxable period" means, with respect to any excess business holdings of a private foundation in a business enterprise, the period beginning with the first day on which there are such excess business holdings and ending on the earliest of:

(i) The date of mailing of a notice of deficiency under section 6212 with respect to the tax imposed on the holdings by the section 4943(a);

(ii) The date on which the excess is eliminated; or

(iii) The date on which the tax imposed by section 4943(a) is assessed.

For example, M, a private foundation, first has excess business holdings in X, a corporation, on February 5, 1972. A notice of deficiency is mailed under section 6212 to M on June 1, 1974. With respect to M's excess business holdings in X, the taxable period begins on February 5, 1972, and ends on June 1, 1974.

(2) Special rule. Where a notice of deficiency referred to in subparagraph (1)(i) of this paragraph is not mailed because there is a waiver of the restrictions on assessment and collection of a deficiency, or because the deficiency is paid, the date of filing of the waiver or the date of such payment, respectively, shall be treated as the end of the taxable period.

(3) Suspension of taxable period for 90 days. In any case in which a private foundation has excess business holdings solely because of the acquisition of an interest in a business enterprise to which paragraph (a)(1)(ii) or (iii) of § 53.4943–2 applies, the taxable period described in paragraph (a) of this section shall be suspended for the 90-day period (as extended) starting with the date on which the foundation knows or has reason to know of the acquisition, provided that at the end of such period the foundation has disposed of such excess holdings.

(b) Cross reference. For rules relating to taxable events that are corrected within the correction period, defined in section 4863(e), see section 4861(a) and the regulations thereunder.

(c) Correction. For purposes of section 4943, correction shall be considered as made when no interest in the enterprise held by the foundation is classified as an excess business holdings under section 4943(c)(1). In any case where the private foundation has excess business holdings which are constructively held for it under section 4943(c)(1), correction shall be considered made when either a corporation, partnership, estate, or trust in which holdings in such enterprise are constructively held for the foundation or a disqualified person; the foundation itself; or a disqualified person disposes of a sufficient interest in the enterprise so that no interest in the enterprise held by the foundation is classified as excess business holdings under section 4943(c)(1).

§ 53.4943–10. Business enterprise; definition.

(a) In general. (1) Except as provided in paragraph (b) or (c) of this section under section 4943(d)(4) the term "business enterprise" includes the active conduct of a trade or business, including any activity which is regularly carried on for the production of income from the sale of goods or the performance of services and which constitutes an unrelated trade or business under section 513. For purposes of the preceding sentence, where an activity carried on for profit constitutes an unrelated trade or business, no part of such trade or business shall be excluded from the classification of a business enterprise merely because it does not result in a profit.

(2) Notwithstanding paragraph (a)(1) of this section, a bond or other evidence of indebtedness does not constitute a holding in a business enterprise unless such bond or evidence of indebtedness is otherwise determined to be an equitable interest in such enterprise. Similarly, a lease-hold interest in real property does not constitute an interest in a business enterprise, even though rent payable under such lease is dependent, in whole or in part, upon the income or profits derived by another from such property, unless such leasehold interest constitutes an interest in the income or profits of an unrelated trade or business under section 513.

(b) Certain program-related activities. For purposes of section 4943(d)(4) the term "business enterprise" does not include a functionally related business as defined in section 4942(j)(5). See § 53.4942(a)–2(c)(3)(iii). In addition, business holdings do not include program-related investments (such as investments in small businesses in central cities or in corporations to assist in neighborhood renovation) as defined in section 4944(c) and the regulations thereunder.

(c) Income derived from passive sources—(1) In general. For purposes of section 4943(d)(4), the term "business enterprise" does not include a trade or business at least 95 percent of the gross income of which is derived from passive sources; except that if in the taxable year in question less than 95 percent of the income of a trade or business is from passive sources, the foundation may, in applying this 95 percent test, substitute for the passive source gross income in such taxable year the average gross income from passive sources for the 10 taxable years immediately preceding the taxable year in question (or for such shorter period as the entity has been in existence). Thus, stock in a passive holding company is not to be considered a holding in a business enterprise even if the company is controlled by the foundation. Instead, the foundation is treated as owning its proportionate share of any interests in a business enterprise held by such company under section 4943(d)(1).

(2) Gross income from passive sources. Gross income from passive sources, for purposes of this paragraph, includes the items excluded by section 512(b)(1) (relating to dividends, interest, and annuities), 512(b)(2) (relating to royalties), 512(b)(3) (relating to rent) and 512(b)(5) (relating to gains or losses from the disposition of certain property). Any income classified as passive under this paragraph does not lose its character merely because section 512(b)(4) or 514 (relating to unrelated debt-financed income) applies to such income. In addition, income from passive sources includes income from the sale of goods (including charges or costs passed on at cost to purchasers of such goods or income received in settlement of a dispute concerning or in lieu of the exercise of the right to sell such goods) if the seller does not manufacture, produce, physically receive or deliver, negotiate sales of, or maintain inventories in such goods. Thus, for example, where a corporation purchases a product under a contract with the manufacturer, resells it under contract at a uniform markup in price, and does not physically handle the product, the income derived from that markup meets the definition of passive income for purposes of this paragraph. On the other hand, income from individually negotiated sales, such as those made by a broker, would not meet such definition even if the broker did not physically handle the goods.

* * *

(d) Application of section 4943(c)(6)—(1) Program related activities. If a private foundation holds an interest which is not an interest in a business enterprise because of paragraph (b) of this section (relating to program related activities), and such interest later becomes an interest in a business enterprise solely by reason of failing to meet the requirements of such paragraph (b), such interest will then be subject to section (regardless of when it was originally acquired) and will be treated as having been acquired other than by purchase for purposes of section 4943(c)(6).

(2) Passive holdings, etc. (i) Except as provided in subdivision (ii), if a private foundation holds an interest that is not an interest in a business enterprise, and the interest later becomes an interest in a business enterprise (other than by reason of a readjustment as defined in § 53.4943–7(d)(1)), the interest will be treated as having been acquired by purchase by a disqualified person at the time the interest becomes an interest in a business enterprise. The treatment of an interest that becomes an interest in a business enterprise by reason of a readjustment shall be determined under § 53.4943–6 and § 53.4943–7.

(ii) If a private foundation establishes that the events which caused an interest not originally a business enterprise to become a business enterprise were not effectively controlled by the private foundation, then such interest shall be treated as acquired other than by purchase from the time of the change for purposes of section 4943(c)(6).

(iii) See § 53.4943–3(b)(3)(ii) for the definition of effective control.

(e) Sole Proprietorship. For purposes of section 4943 and the regulations thereunder, the term "sole proprietorship" means any business enterprise (as defined in paragraphs (a), (b), and (c)) of this section—

(1) Which is actually and directly owned by a private foundation,

(2) In which the foundation has a 100 percent equity interest, and

(3) Which is not held by a corporation, trust, or other business entity for such foundation.

A foundation may be considered to own a sole proprietorship even though the foundation is itself a corporation or a trust. However, a sole proprietorship which is owned by a foundation shall cease to be treated as a sole proprietorship when the foundation no longer has a 100-percent interest in the equity of the business enterprise. Thus, if and when a foundation sells a 10-percent interest in a sole proprietorship, such business enterprise shall be treated as a partnership under section 4943 and the regulations thereunder.

§ 53.4944–1. Initial taxes.

(a) On the private foundation—(1) In general. If a private foundation (as defined in section 509) invests any amount in such a manner as to jeopardize the carrying out of any of its exempt purposes, section 4944(a)(1) of the Code imposes an excise tax on the making of such investment. This tax is to be paid by the private foundation and is at the rate of 5 percent of the amount so invested for each taxable year (or part thereof) in the taxable period (as defined in section 4944(e)(1)). The tax imposed by section 4944(a)(1) and this paragraph shall apply to investments of either income or principal.

(2) Jeopardizing investments. (i) Except as provided in section 4944(c), § 53.4944–3, § 53.4944–6(a), and subdivision (ii) of this subparagraph, an investment shall be considered to jeopardize the carrying out of the exempt purposes of a private foundation if it is determined that the foundation managers, in making such investment, have failed to exercise ordinary business care and prudence, under the facts and circumstances prevailing at the time of making the investment, in providing for the long- and short-term financial needs of the foundation to carry out its exempt purposes. In the exercise of the requisite standard of care and prudence the foundation managers may take into account the expected return (including both income and appreciation of capital), the risks of rising and falling price levels, and the need for diversification within the investment portfolio (for example, with respect to type of security, type of industry, maturity of company, degree of risk and potential for return). The determination whether the investment of a particular amount jeopardizes the carrying out of the exempt purposes of a foundation shall be made on an investment by investment basis, in each case taking into account the foundation's portfolio as a whole. No category of investments shall be treated as a per se violation of section 4944. However, the following are examples of types or methods of investment which will be closely scrutinized to determine whether the foundation managers have met the requisite standard of care and prudence: Trading in securities on margin, trading in commodity futures, investments in working interests in oil and gas wells, the purchase of "puts," "calls," and "straddles," the purchase of warrants, and selling short. The determination whether the investment of any amount jeopardizes the carrying out of a foundation's exempt purposes is to be made as of the time that the foundation makes the investment and not subsequently on the basis of hindsight. Therefore, once it has been ascertained that an investment does not jeopardize the carrying out of a foundation's exempt purposes, the investment shall never be considered to jeopardize the carrying out of such purposes, even though, as a result of such investment, the foundation subsequently realizes a loss. The provisions of section 4944 and the regulations thereunder shall not exempt or relieve any person from compliance with any Federal or State law imposing any obligation, duty, responsibility, or other standard of conduct with respect to the operation or administration of an organization or trust to which section 4944 applies. Nor shall any State law exempt or relieve any person from any obligation, duty, responsibility, or other standard of conduct provided in section 4944 and the regulations thereunder.

(ii)(*a*) Section 4944 shall not apply to an investment made by any person which is later gratuitously transferred to a private foundation. If such foundation furnishes any consideration to such person upon the transfer, the foundation will be treated as having made an investment (within the meaning of section 4944(a)(1)) in the amount of such consideration.

(b) Section 4944 shall not apply to an investment which is acquired by a private foundation solely as a result of a corporate reorganization within the meaning of section 368(a).

(iii) For purposes of section 4944, a private foundation which, after December 31, 1969, changes the form or terms of an investment (regardless of whether subdivision (ii) of this subparagraph applies to such investment), will be considered to have entered into a new investment on the date of such change, except as provided in subdivision (ii)(b) of this subparagraph. Accordingly, a determination, under subdivision (i) of this subparagraph, whether such change in the investment jeopardizes the carrying out of the foundation's exempt purposes shall be made at such time.

(iv) It is not intended that the taxes imposed under chapter 42 be exclusive. For example, if a foundation purchases a sole proprietorship in a business enterprise within the meaning of section 4943(d)(4), in addition to tax under section 4943, the foundation may be liable for tax under section 4944 if the investment jeopardizes the carrying out of any of its exempt purposes.

(b) On the management—(1) In general. In any case in which a tax is imposed by section 4944(a)(1) and paragraph (a) of this section, section 4944(a)(2) of the Code imposes on the participation of any foundation manager in the making of the investment, knowing that it is jeopardizing the carrying out of any of the foundation's exempt purposes, a tax equal to 5 percent of the amount so invested for each taxable year of the foundation (or part thereof) in the taxable period (as defined in section 4944(e)(1)), subject to the provisions of section 4944(d) and § 53.4944–4, unless such participation is not willful and is due to reasonable cause. The tax imposed under section 4944(a)(2) shall be paid by the foundation manager.

(2) Definitions and special rules—(i) Knowing. For purposes of section 4944, a foundation manager shall be considered to have participated in the making of an investment "knowing" that it is jeopardizing the carrying out of any of the foundation's exempt purposes only if—

(a) He has actual knowledge of sufficient facts so that, based solely upon such facts, such investment would be a jeopardizing investment under paragraph (a)(2) of this section,

(b) He is aware that such an investment under these circumstances may violate the provisions of federal tax law governing jeopardizing investments, and

(c) He negligently fails to make reasonable attempts to ascertain whether the investment is a jeopardizing investment, or he is in fact aware that it is such an investment.

For purposes of this part and chapter 42, the term "knowing" does not mean "having reason to know". However, evidence tending to show that a foundation manager has reason to know of a particular fact or particular rule is relevant in determining whether he had actual knowledge of such fact or rule. Thus, for example, evidence tending to show that a foundation manager has reason to know of sufficient facts so that, based solely upon such facts, an investment would be a jeopardizing investment is relevant in determining whether he has actual knowledge of such facts.

(ii) Willful. A foundation manager's participation in a jeopardizing investment is willful if it is voluntary, conscious, and intentional. No motive to avoid the restrictions of the law or the incurrence of any tax is necessary to make such participation willful. However, a foundation manager's participation in a jeopardizing investment is not willful if he does not know that it is a jeopardizing investment under paragraph (a)(2) of this section.

(iii) Due to reasonable cause. A foundation manager's actions are due to reasonable cause if he has exercised his responsibility on behalf of the foundation with ordinary business care and prudence.

(iv) Participation. The participation of any foundation manager in the making of an investment shall consist of any manifestation of approval of the investment.

(v) Advice of counsel. If a foundation manager, after full disclosure of the factual situation to legal counsel (including house counsel), relies on the advice of such counsel expressed in a reasoned written legal opinion that a particular investment would not jeopardize the carrying out of any of the foundation's exempt purposes (because, as a matter of law, the investment is excepted from such classification, for example, as a program-related investment under section 4944(c)), then although such investment is subsequently held to be a jeopardizing investment under paragraph (a)(2) of this section, the foundation manager's participation in such investment will ordinarily not be considered "knowing" or "willful" and will ordinarily be considered "due to reasonable cause" within the meaning of section 4944(a)(2). In addition, if a foundation manager, after full disclosure of the factual situation to qualified investment counsel, relies on the advice of such counsel, such advice being derived in a manner consistent with generally accepted practices of persons who are such a qualified investment counsel and being expressed in writing that a particular investment will provide for the long and short term financial needs of the foundation under paragraph (a)(2) of this section, then although such investment is subsequently held not to provide for such long and short term financial needs, the foundation manager's participation in failing to provide for such long and short term financial needs will ordinarily not be considered "knowing" or "willful" and will ordinarily be considered "due to reasonable cause" within the meaning of section 4944(a)(2). For purposes of this subdivision, a written legal opinion will be considered "reasoned" even if it reaches a conclusion which is subsequently determined to be incorrect so long as such opinion addresses itself to the facts and applicable law. However, a written legal opinion will not be considered "reasoned" if it does nothing more than recite the facts and express a conclusion. However, the absence of advice of legal counsel or qualified investment counsel with respect to the investment shall not, by itself, give rise to any inference that a foundation manager participated in such investment knowingly, willfully, or without reasonable cause.

(vi) Cross reference. For provisions relating to the burden of proof in cases involving the issue whether a foundation manager has knowingly participated in the making of a jeopardizing investment, see section 7454(b).

(c) Examples. The provisions of this section may be illustrated by the following examples:

Example (1). A is a foundation manager of B, a private foundation with assets of $100,000. A approves the following three investments by B after taking into account with respect to each of them B's portfolio as a whole: (1) An investment of $5,000 in the common stock of corporation X; (2) an investment of $10,000 in the common stock of corporation Y; and (3) an investment of $8,000 in the common stock of corporation Z. Corporation X has been in business a considerable time, its record of earnings is good and there is no reason to anticipate a diminution of its earnings. Corporation Y has a promising product, has had earnings in some years and substantial losses in others, has never paid a dividend, and is widely reported in investment advisory services as seriously undercapitalized. Corporation Z has been in business a short period of time and manufactures a product that is new, is not sold by others, and must compete with a well-established alternative product that serves the same purpose. Z's stock is classified as a high-risk investment by most investment advisory services with the possibility of substantial long-term appreciation but with little prospect of a current return. A has studied the records of the three corporations and knows the foregoing facts. In each case the price per share of common stock purchased by B is favorable to B. Under the standards of paragraph (a)(2)(i) of this section, the investment of $10,000 in the common stock of Y and the investment of $8,000 in the common stock of Z may be classified as jeopardizing investments, while the investment of $5,000 in the common stock of X will not be so classified. B would then be liable for an initial tax of $500 (i.e., 5 percent of $10,000) for each year (or part thereof) in the taxable period for the investment in Y, and an initial tax of $400 (i.e., 5 percent of $8,000) for each year (or part thereof) in the taxable period for the investment in Z. Further, since A had actual knowledge that the investments in the common stock of Y and Z were jeopardizing investments, A would then be liable for the same amount of initial taxes as B.

Example (2). Assume the facts as stated in Example (1), except that: (1) In the case of corporation Y, B's investment will be made for new stock to be issued by Y and there is reason to anticipate that B's investment, together with investments required by B to be made concurrently with its own, will satisfy the capital needs of corporation Y and will thereby overcome the difficulties that have resulted in Y's uneven earnings record; and (2) in the case of corporation Z, the management has a demonstrated capacity for getting new businesses started successfully and Z has received substantial orders for its new product. Under the standards of paragraph (a)(2)(i) of this section, neither the investment in Y nor the investment in Z will be classified as a jeopardizing investment and neither A nor B will be liable for an initial tax on either of such investments.

Example (3). D is a foundation manager of E, a private foundation with assets of $200,000. D was hired by E to manage E's investments after a careful review of D's training, experience and record in the field of investment management and advice indicated to E that D was well qualified to provide professional investment advice in the management of E's investment assets. D, after careful research into how best to diversify E's investments, provide for E's long-term financial needs, and protect against the effects of long-term inflation, decides to allocate a portion of E's investment assets to unimproved real estate in selected areas of the country where population patterns and economic factors strongly indicate continuing growth at a rapid rate. D determines that the short-term financial needs of E can be met through E's other investments. Under the standards of paragraph (a)(2)(i) of this section, the investment of a portion of E's investment assets in unimproved real estate will not be classified as a jeopardizing investment and neither D nor E will be liable for an initial tax on such investment.

§ 53.4944–2. Additional taxes.

(a) On the private foundation. Section 4944(b)(1) of the Code imposes an excise tax in any case in which an initial tax is imposed by section 4944(a)(1) and § 53.4944–1(a) on the making of a jeopardizing investment by a private foundation and such investment is not removed from jeopardy within the taxable period (as defined in section 4944(e)(1)). The tax imposed under section 4944(b)(1) is to be paid by the private foundation and is at the rate of 25 percent of the amount of the investment. This tax shall be imposed upon the portion of the investment which has not been removed from jeopardy within the taxable period.

(b) On the management. Section 4944(b)(2) of the Code imposes an excise tax in any case in which an additional tax is imposed by section 4944(b)(1) and paragraph (a) of this section and a foundation manager has refused to agree to part or all of the removal of the investment from jeopardy. The tax imposed under section 4944(b)(2) is at the rate of 5 percent of the amount of the investment, subject to the provisions of section 4944(d) and § 53.4944–4. This tax is to be paid by any foundation manager who has refused to agree to the removal of part or all of the investment from jeopardy, and shall be imposed upon the portion of the investment which has not been removed from jeopardy within the taxable period.

(c) Examples. The provisions of this section may be illustrated by the following examples:

Example (1). X is a foundation manager of Y, a private foundation. On the advice of X, Y invests $5,000 in the common stock of corporation M. Assume that both X and Y are liable for the taxes imposed by section 4944(a) on the making of the investment. Assume further that no part of the investment is removed from jeopardy within the taxable period and that X refused to agree to such removal. Y will be liable for an additional tax of $1,250 (i.e., $5,000 x 25%). X will be liable for an additional tax of $250 (i.e., $5,000 x 5%).

Example (2). Assume the facts as stated in Example (1), except that X is not liable for the tax imposed by section 4944(a)(2) for his participation in the making of the investment, because such participation was not willful and was due to reasonable cause. X will nonetheless be liable for the tax of $250 imposed by section 4944(b)(2) since an additional tax has been imposed upon Y and since X refused to agree to the removal of the investment from jeopardy.

Example (3). Assume the facts as stated in Example (1), except that Y removes $2,000 of the investment from jeopardy within the taxable period, with X refusing to agree to the removal from jeopardy of the remaining $3,000 of such investment. Y will be liable for an additional tax of $750, imposed upon the portion of the investment which has not been removed from jeopardy within the taxable period (i.e., $3,000 x 25%). Further X will be liable for an additional tax of $150, also imposed upon the same portion of the investment (i.e., $3,000 x 5%).

§ 53.4944–3. Exception for program-related investments.

(a) In general. (1) For purposes of section 4944 and ss 53.4944–1 through 53.4944–6, a "program-related investment" shall not be classified as an investment which jeopardizes the carrying out of the exempt purposes of a private foundation. A "program-related investment" is an investment which possesses the following characteristics:

(i) The primary purpose of the investment is to accomplish one or more of the purposes described in section 170(c)(2)(B);

(ii) No significant purpose of the investment is the production of income or the appreciation of property; and

(iii) No purpose of the investment is to accomplish one or more of the purposes described in section 170(c)(2)(D).

(2)(i) An investment shall be considered as made primarily to accomplish one or more of the purposes described in section 170(c)(2)(B) if it significantly furthers the accomplishment of the private foundation's exempt activities and if the investment would not have been made but for such relationship between the investment and the accomplishment of the foundation's exempt activities. For purposes of section 4944 and ss 53.4944–1 through 53.4944–6, the term "purposes described in section 170(c)(2)(B)" shall be treated as including purposes described in section

170(c)(2)(B) whether or not carried out by organizations described in section 170(c).

(ii) An investment in an activity described in section 4942(j)(5)(B) and the regulations thereunder shall be considered, for purposes of this paragraph, as made primarily to accomplish one or more of the purposes described in section 170(c)(2)(B).

(iii) In determining whether a significant purpose of an investment is the production of income or the appreciation of property, it shall be relevant whether investors solely engaged in the investment for profit would be likely to make the investment on the same terms as the private foundation. However, the fact that an investment produces significant income or capital appreciation shall not, in the absence of other factors, be conclusive evidence of a significant purpose involving the production of income or the appreciation of property.

(iv) An investment shall not be considered as made to accomplish one or more of the purposes described in section 170(c)(2)(D) if the recipient of the investment appears before, or communicates to, any legislative body with respect to legislation or proposed legislation of direct interest to such recipient, provided that the expense of engaging in such activities would qualify as a deduction under section 162.

(3)(i) Once it has been determined that an investment is "program-related" it shall not cease to qualify as a "program-related investment" provided that changes, if any, in the form or terms of the investment are made primarily for exempt purposes and not for any significant purpose involving the production of income or the appreciation of property. A change made in the form or terms of a program-related investment for the prudent protection of the foundation's investment shall not ordinarily cause the investment to cease to qualify as program-related. Under certain conditions, a program-related investment may cease to be program-related because of a critical change in circumstances, as, for example, where it is serving an illegal purpose or the private purpose of the foundation or its managers. For purposes of the preceding sentence, an investment which ceases to be program-related because of a critical change in circumstances shall in no event subject the foundation making the investment to the tax imposed by section 4944(a)(1) before the 30th day after the date on which such foundation (or any of its managers) has actual knowledge of such critical change in circumstances.

(ii) If a private foundation changes the form or terms of an investment, and if, as a result of the application of subdivision (i) of this subparagraph, such investment no longer qualifies as program-related, the determination whether the investment jeopardizes the carrying out of exempt purposes shall be made pursuant to the provisions of § 53.4944–1(a)(2).

(b) Examples. The provisions of this section may be illustrated by the following examples:

Example (1). X is a small business enterprise located in a deteriorated urban area and owned by members of an economically disadvantaged minority group. Conventional sources of funds are unwilling or unable to provide funds to X on terms it considers economically feasible. Y, a private foundation, makes a loan to X bearing interest below the market rate for commercial loans of comparable risk. Y's primary purpose for making the loan is to encourage the economic development of such minority groups. The loan has no significant purpose involving the production of income or the appreciation of property. The loan significantly furthers the accomplishment of Y's exempt activities and would not have been made but for such relationship between the loan and Y's exempt activities. Accordingly, the loan is a program-related investment even though Y may earn income from the investment in an amount comparable to or higher than earnings from conventional portfolio investments.

Example (2). Assume the facts as stated in Example (1), except that after the date of execution of the loan Y extends the due date of the loan. The extension is granted in order to permit X to achieve greater financial stability before it is required to repay the loan. Since the change in the terms of the loan is made primarily for exempt purposes and not for any significant purpose involving the production of income or the appreciation of property, the loan shall continue to qualify as a program-related investment.

Example (3). X is a small business enterprise located in a deteriorated urban area and owned by members of an economically disadvantaged minority group. Conventional sources of funds are unwilling to provide funds to X at reasonable interest rates unless it increases the amount of its equity capital. Consequently, Y, a private foundation, purchases shares of X's common stock. Y's primary purpose in purchasing the stock is to encourage the economic development of such minority group, and no significant purpose involves the production of income or the appreciation of property. The investment significantly furthers the accomplishment of Y's exempt activities and would not have been made but for such relationship between the investment and Y's exempt activities. Accordingly, the purchase of the common stock is a program-related investment, even though Y may realize a profit if X is successful and the common stock appreciates in value.

Example (4). X is a business enterprise which is not owned by low-income persons or minority group members, but the continued operation of X is important to the economic well-being of a deteriorated urban area because X employs a substantial number of low-income persons from such area. Conventional sources of funds are unwilling or unable to provide funds to X at reasonable interest rates. Y, a private foundation, makes a loan to X at an interest rate below the market rate for commercial loans of comparable risk. The loan is made pursuant to a program run by Y to assist low-income persons by providing increased economic opportunities and to prevent community deterioration. No significant purpose of the loan involves the production of income or the appreciation of property. The investment significantly furthers the accomplishment of Y's exempt activities and would not have been made but for such relationship between the loan and Y's exempt activities. Accordingly, the loan is a program-related investment.

Example (5). X is a business enterprise which is financially secure and the stock of which is listed and traded on a national exchange. Y, a private foundation, makes a loan to X at an interest rate below the market rate in order to induce X to establish a new plant in a deteriorated urban area which, because of the high risks involved, X would be unwilling to establish absent such inducement. The loan is made pursuant to a program run by Y to enhance the economic development of the area by, for example, providing employment opportunities for low-income persons at the new plant, and no significant purpose involves the production of income or the appreciation of property. The loan significantly furthers the accomplishment of Y's exempt activities and would not have been made but for such relationship between the loan and Y's exempt activities. Accordingly, even though X is large and established, the investment is program-related.

Example (6). X is a business enterprise which is owned by a nonprofit community development corporation. When fully operational, X will market agricultural products, thereby providing a marketing outlet for low-income farmers in a depressed rural area. Y, a private foundation, makes a loan to X bearing interest at a rate less than the rate charged by financial institutions which have agreed to lend funds to X if Y makes the loan. The loan is made pursuant to a program run by Y to encourage economic redevelopment of depressed areas, and no significant purpose involves the production of income or the appreciation of property. The loan significantly furthers the accomplishment of Y's exempt activities and would not have been made but for such relationship between the loan and Y's exempt activities. Accordingly, the loan is a program-related investment.

Example (7). X, a private foundation, invests $100,000 in the common stock of corporation M. The dividends received from such investment are later applied by X in furtherance of its exempt purposes. Although there is a relationship between the return on the investment and the accomplishment of X's exempt activities, there is no relationship between the investment per se and such accomplishment. Therefore, the investment cannot be considered as made primarily to accomplish one or more of the purposes described in section 170(c)(2)(B) and cannot qualify as program-related.

Example (8). S, a private foundation, makes an investment in T, a business corporation, which qualifies as a program-related investment under section 4944(c) at the time that it is made. All of T's voting stock is owned by S. T experiences financial and management problems which, in the judgment of the foundation, require changes in management, in financial structure or in the form of the investment. The following three methods of resolving the problems appear feasible to S, but each of the three methods would result in reduction of the exempt purposes for which the program-related investment was initially made:

(a) Sale of stock or assets. The foundation sells its stock to an unrelated person. Payment is made in part at the time of sale; the balance is payable over an extended term of years with interest on the amount outstanding. The foundation receives a purchase-money mortgage.

(b) Lease. The corporation leases its assets for a term of years to an unrelated person, with an option in the lessee to buy the assets. If the option is exercised, the terms of payment are to be similar to those described in (a) of this example.

(c) Management contract. The corporation enters into a management contract which gives broad operating authority to one or more unrelated persons for a term of years. The foundation and the unrelated persons are obligated to contribute toward working capital requirements. The unrelated persons will be compensated by a fixed fee or a share of profits, and they will receive an option to buy the stock held by S or the assets of the corporation. If the option is exercised, the terms of payment are to be similar to those described in (a) of this example.

Each of the three methods involves a change in the form or terms of a program-related investment for the prudent protection of the foundation's investment. Thus, under § 53.4944–3(a)(3)(i), none of the three transactions (nor any debt instruments or other obligations held by § as a result of engaging in one of these transactions) would cause the investment to cease to qualify as program-related.

Example (9). X is a socially and economically disadvantaged individual. Y, a private foundation, makes an interest-free loan to X for the primary purpose of enabling X to attend college. The loan has no significant purpose involving the production of income or the appreciation of property. The loan significantly furthers the accomplishment of Y's exempt activities and would not have been made but for such relationship between the loan and Y's exempt activities. Accordingly, the loan is a program-related investment.

Example (10). Y, a private foundation, makes a high-risk investment in low-income housing, the indebtedness with respect to which is insured by the Federal Housing Administration. Y's primary purpose in making the investment is to finance the purchase, rehabilitation, and construction of housing for low-income persons. The investment has no significant purpose involving the production of income or the appreciation of property. The investment significantly furthers the accomplishment of Y's exempt activities and would not have been made but for such relationship between the investment and Y's exempt activities. Accordingly, the investment is program-related.

Example (11). X is a business enterprise that researches and develops new drugs. X's research demonstrates that a vaccine can be developed within ten years to prevent a disease that predominantly affects poor individuals in developing countries. However, neither X nor other commercial enterprises like X will devote their resources to develop the vaccine because the potential return on investment is significantly less than required by X or other commercial enterprises to undertake a project to develop new drugs. Y, a private foundation, enters into an investment agreement with X in order to induce X to develop the vaccine. Pursuant to the investment agreement, Y purchases shares of the common stock of S, a subsidiary corporation that X establishes to research and develop the vaccine. The agreement requires S to distribute the vaccine to poor individuals in developing countries at a price that is affordable to the affected population, although, the agreement does not preclude S from selling the vaccine to other individuals at a market rate. The agreement also requires S to publish the research results, disclosing substantially all information about the results that would be useful to the interested public. S agrees that the publication of its research results will be made as promptly after the completion of the research as is reasonably possible without jeopardizing S's right to secure patents necessary to protect its ownership or control of the results of the research. The expected rate of return on Y's investment in S is less than the expected market rate of return for an investment of similar risk. Y's primary purpose in making the investment is to fund scientific research in the public interest. No significant purpose of the investment involves the production of income or the appreciation of property. The investment significantly furthers the accomplishment of Y's exempt activities and would not have been made but for such relationship between the investment and Y's exempt activities. Accordingly, Y's purchase of the common stock of S is a program-related investment.

Example (12). Q, a developing country, produces a substantial amount of recyclable solid waste materials that are currently disposed of in landfills and by incineration, contributing significantly to environmental deterioration in Q. X is a new business enterprise located in Q. X's only activity will be collecting recyclable solid waste materials in Q and delivering those materials to recycling centers that are inaccessible to a majority of the population. If successful, the recycling collection business would prevent pollution in Q caused by the usual disposition of solid waste materials. X has obtained funding from only a few commercial investors who are concerned about the environmental impact of solid waste disposal. Although X made substantial efforts to procure additional funding, X has not been able to obtain sufficient funding because the expected rate of return is significantly less than the acceptable rate of return on an investment of this type. Because X has been unable to attract additional investors on the same terms as the initial investors, Y, a private foundation, enters into an investment agreement with X to purchase shares of X's common stock on the same terms as X's initial investors. Although there is a high risk associated with the investment in X, there is also the potential for a high rate of return if X is successful in the recycling business in Q. Y's primary purpose in making the investment is to combat environmental deterioration. No significant purpose of the investment involves the production of income or the appreciation of property. The investment significantly furthers the accomplishment of Y's exempt activities and would not have been made but for such relationship between the investment and Y's exempt activities. Accordingly, Y's purchase of the X common stock is a program-related investment.

Example (13). Assume the facts as stated in Example 12, except that X offers Y shares of X's common stock in order to induce Y to make a below-market rate loan to X. X previously made the same offer to a number of commercial investors. These investors were unwilling to provide loans to X on such terms because the expected return on the combined package of stock and debt was below the expected market return for such a package based on the level of risk involved, and they were also unwilling to provide loans on other terms X considers economically feasible. Y accepts the stock and makes the loan on the same terms that X offered to the commercial investors. Y's primary purpose in making the investment is to combat environmental deterioration. No significant purpose of the investment involves the production of income or the appreciation of property. The investment significantly furthers the accomplishment of Y's exempt activities and would not have been made but for such relationship between the investment and Y's exempt activities. Accordingly, the loan accompanied by the acceptance of common stock is a program-related investment.

Example (14). X is a business enterprise located in V, a rural area in State Z. X employs a large number of poor individuals in V. A natural disaster occurs in V, causing significant damage to the area. The business operations of X are harmed because of damage to X's equipment and buildings. X has insufficient funds to continue its business operations and conventional sources of funds are unwilling or unable to provide loans to X on terms it considers economically feasible. In order to enable X to continue its business operations, Y, a private foundation, makes a loan to X bearing interest below the market rate for commercial loans of comparable risk. Y's primary purpose in making the loan is to provide relief to the poor and distressed. No significant purpose of the loan involves the production of income or the appreciation of property. The loan significantly furthers the accomplishment of Y's exempt activities and would not have been made but for such relationship between the loan and Y's exempt activities. Accordingly, the loan is a program-related investment.

Example (15). Y, a private foundation, makes loans bearing interest below the market rate for commercial loans of comparable risk to poor individuals who live in W, a developing country, to enable them to start small businesses such as a roadside fruit stand. Conventional sources of funds were unwilling or unable to provide such loans on terms they consider economically feasible. Y's primary purpose in making the loans is to provide relief to the poor and distressed. No significant purpose of the loans involves the production of income or the appreciation of property. The loans significantly further the accomplishment of Y's exempt activities and would not have been made but for such relationship between the loans and Y's exempt activities. Accordingly, the loans to the poor individuals who live in W are program-related investments.

Example (16). X is a limited liability company treated as a partnership for federal income tax purposes. X purchases coffee from poor farmers residing in a developing country, either directly or through farmer-owned cooperatives. To fund the provision of efficient water management, crop cultivation, pest management, and farm management training to the poor farmers by X, Y, a private foundation, makes a loan to X bearing interest below the market rate for commercial loans of comparable risk. The loan agreement requires X to use the proceeds from the loan to provide the training to the poor farmers. X would not provide such training to the poor farmers absent the loan. Y's primary purpose in making the loan is to educate poor farmers about advanced agricultural methods. No significant purpose of the loan involves the production of income or the appreciation of property. The loan significantly furthers the accomplishment of Y's exempt activities and would not have been made but for such relationship between the loan and Y's exempt activities. Accordingly, the loan is a program-related investment.

Example (17). X is a social welfare organization that is recognized as an organization described in section 501(c)(4). X was formed to develop and encourage interest in painting, sculpture, and other art forms by, among other things, conducting weekly community art exhibits. X needs to purchase a large exhibition space to accommodate the demand for exhibition space within the community. Conventional sources of funds are unwilling or unable to provide funds to X on terms it considers economically feasible. Y, a private foundation, makes a loan to X at an interest rate below the market rate for commercial loans of comparable risk to fund the purchase of the new space. Y's primary purpose in making the loan is to promote the arts. No significant purpose of the loan involves the production of income or the appreciation of property. The loan significantly furthers the accomplishment of Y's exempt activities and would not have been made but for such relationship between the loan and Y's exempt activities. Accordingly, the loan is a program-related investment.

Example (18). X is a non-profit corporation that provides child care services in a low-income neighborhood, enabling many residents of the neighborhood to be gainfully employed. X meets the requirements of section 501(k) and is recognized as an organization described in section 501(c)(3). X's current child care facility has reached capacity and has a long waiting list. X has determined that the demand for its services warrants the construction of a new child care facility in the same neighborhood. X is unable to obtain a loan from conventional sources of funds including B, a commercial bank because of X's credit record. Pursuant to a deposit agreement, Y, a private foundation, deposits $h in B, and B lends an identical amount to X to construct the new child care facility. The deposit agreement requires Y to keep $h on deposit with B during the term of X's loan and provides that if X defaults on the loan, B may deduct the amount of the default from the deposit. To facilitate B's access to the funds in the event of default, the agreement requires that the funds be invested in instruments that allow B to access them readily. The deposit agreement also provides that Y will earn interest at a rate of t% on the deposit. The t% rate is substantially less than Y could otherwise earn on this sum of money, if Y invested it elsewhere. The loan agreement between B and X requires X to use the proceeds from the loan to construct the new child care facility. Y's primary purpose in making the deposit is to further its educational purposes by enabling X to provide child care services within the meaning of section 501(k). No significant purpose of the deposit involves the production of income or the appreciation of property. The deposit significantly furthers the accomplishment of Y's exempt activities and would not have been made but for such relationship between the deposit and Y's exempt activities. Accordingly, the deposit is a program-related investment.

Example (19). Assume the same facts as stated in Example 18, except that instead of making a deposit of $h into B, Y enters into a guarantee agreement with B. The guarantee agreement provides that if X defaults on the loan, Y will repay the balance due on the loan to B. B was unwilling to make the loan to X in the absence of Y's guarantee. X must use the proceeds from the loan to construct the new child care facility. At the same time, X and Y enter into a reimbursement agreement whereby X agrees to reimburse Y for any and all amounts paid to B under the guarantee agreement. The signed guarantee and reimbursement agreements together constitute a "guarantee and reimbursement arrangement." Y's primary purpose in entering into the guarantee and reimbursement arrangement is to further Y's educational purposes. No significant purpose of the guarantee and reimbursement arrangement involves the production of income or the appreciation of property. The guarantee and reimbursement arrangement significantly furthers the accomplishment of Y's exempt activities and would not have been made but for such relationship between the guarantee and reimbursement arrangement and Y's exempt activities. Accordingly, the guarantee and reimbursement arrangement is a program-related investment.

§ 53.4944–4. Special rules.

(a) Joint and several liability. In any case where more than one foundation manager is liable for the tax imposed under section 4944(a)(2) or (b)(2) with respect to any one jeopardizing investment, all such foundation managers shall be jointly and severally liable for the tax imposed under each such paragraph with respect to such investment.

(b) Limits on liability for management. With respect to anyone jeopardizing investment, the maximum aggregate amount of tax collectible under section 4944(a)(2) from all foundation managers shall not exceed $5,000, and the maximum aggregate amount of tax collectible under section 4944(b)(2) from all foundation managers shall not exceed $10,000.

(c) Examples. The provisions of this section may be illustrated by the following examples:

Example (1). A, B, and C are foundation managers of X, a private foundation. Assume that A, B, and C are liable for both initial and additional taxes under sections 4944(a)(2) and 4944(b)(2), respectively, for the following investments by X: an investment of $5,000 in the common stock of corporation M, and an investment of $10,000 in the common stock of corporation N. A, B, and C will be jointly and severally liable for the following initial taxes under section 4944(a)(2): a tax of $250 (i.e., 5 percent of $5,000) for each year (or part thereof) in the taxable period (as defined in section 4944(e)(1)) for the investment in M, and a tax of $500 (i.e., 5 percent of $10,000) for each year (or part thereof) in the taxable period for the investment in N. Further, A, B, and C will be jointly and severally liable for the following additional taxes under section 4944(b)(2): a tax of $250 (i.e., 5 percent of $5,000) for the investment in M, and a tax of $500 (i.e., 5 percent of $10,000) for the investment in N.

Example (2). Assume the facts as stated in Example (1), except that X has invested $500,000 in the common stock of M, and $1 million in the common stock of N. A, B, and C will be jointly and severally liable for the following initial taxes under section 4944(a)(2): a tax of $5,000 for the investment in M, and a tax of $5,000 for the investment in N. Further, A, B, and C will be jointly and severally liable for the following additional taxes under section 4944(b)(2): a tax of $10,000 for the investment in M, and a tax of $10,000 for the investment in N.

§ 53.4944-5. Definitions.

(a) Taxable period—(1) In general. For purposes of section 4944, the term "taxable period" means, with respect to any investment which jeopardizes the carrying out of a private foundation's exempt purposes, the period beginning with the date on which the amount is invested and ending on the earliest of:

(i) The date of mailing of a notice of deficiency under section 6212 with respect to the tax imposed on the making of the investment by section 4944(a)(1);

(ii) The date on which the amount invested is removed from jeopardy; or

(iii) The date on which the tax imposed by section 4944(a)(1) is assessed.

(2) Special rule. Where a notice of deficiency referred to in subparagraph (1)(i) of this paragraph is not mailed because there is a waiver of the restrictions on assessment and collection of a deficiency, or because the deficiency is paid, the date of filing of the waiver or the date of such payment, respectively, shall be treated as the end of the taxable period.

(b) Removal from jeopardy. An investment which jeopardizes the carrying out of a private foundation's exempt purposes shall be considered to be removed from jeopardy when—

(1) The foundation sells or otherwise disposes of the investment, and

(2) The proceeds of such sale or other disposition are not themselves investments which jeopardize the carrying out of such foundation's exempt purposes.

A change by a private foundation in the form or terms of a jeopardizing investment shall result in the removal of the investment from jeopardy if, after such change, the investment no longer jeopardizes the carrying out of such foundation's exempt purposes. For purposes of section 4944, the making by a private foundation of one jeopardizing investment and a subsequent exchange by the foundation of such investment for another jeopardizing investment will be treated as only one jeopardizing investment, except as provided in § 53.4944-6(b) and (c). For the treatment of a jeopardizing investment which is removed from jeopardy or otherwise transferred by a private foundation by the making of a grant or by bargain-sale, see sections 4941 and 4945 and the regulations thereunder. A jeopardizing investment cannot be removed from jeopardy by a transfer from a private foundation to another private foundation which is related to the transferor foundation within the meaning of section 4946(a)(1)(H)(i) or (ii), unless the investment is a program-related investment in the hands of the transferee foundation.

(c) Examples. The provisions of this section may be illustrated by the following examples:

Example (1). X, a private foundation on the calendar year basis, makes a $1,000 jeopardizing investment on January 1, 1970. X thereafter sells the investment for $1,000 on January 3, 1971. The taxable period is from January 1, 1970, to January 3, 1971. X will be liable for an initial tax of $100, that is, a tax of 5 percent of the amount of the investment for each year (or part thereof) in the taxable period.

Example (2). Assume that both C and D are investments which jeopardize exempt purposes. X, a private foundation, purchases C in 1971 and later exchanges C for D. Such exchange does not constitute a removal of C from jeopardy. In addition, no new taxable period will arise with respect to D, since, for purposes of section 4944, only one jeopardizing investment has been made.

Example (3). Assume the facts as stated in Example (2), except that X sells C for cash and later reinvests such cash in D. Two separate investments jeopardizing exempt purposes have resulted. Since the cash received in the interim is not of a jeopardizing nature, the amount invested in C has been removed from jeopardy and, thus, the taxable period with respect to C has been terminated. The subsequent reinvestment of such cash in D gives rise to a new taxable period with respect to D.

(d) Cross reference. For rules relating to taxable events that are corrected within the correction period, defined in section 4963(e), see section 4961(a) and the regulations thereunder.

§ 53.4945–1. Taxes on taxable expenditures.

(a) Imposition of initial taxes—(1) Tax on private foundation. Section 4945(a)(1) of the Code imposes an excise tax on each taxable expenditure (as defined in section 4945(d)) of a private foundation. This tax is to be paid by the private foundation and is at the rate of 10 percent of the amount of each taxable expenditure.

(2) Tax on foundation manager—(i) In general. Section 4945(a)(2) of the Code imposes, under certain circumstances, an excise tax on the agreement of any foundation manager to the making of a taxable expenditure by a private foundation. This tax is imposed only in cases in which the following circumstances are present:

(a) A tax is imposed by section 4945(a)(1);

(b) Such foundation manager knows that the expenditure to which he agrees is a taxable expenditure, and

(c) Such agreement is willful and is not due to reasonable cause.

However, the tax with respect to any particular expenditure applies only to the agreement of those foundation managers who are authorized to approve, or to exercise discretion in recommending approval of, the making of the expenditure by the foundation and to those foundation managers who are members of a group (such as the foundation's board of directors or trustees) which is so authorized. For the definition of the term "foundation manager," see section 4946(b) and the regulations thereunder.

(ii) Agreement. The agreement of any foundation manager to the making of a taxable expenditure shall consist of any manifestation of approval of the expenditure which is sufficient to constitute an exercise of the foundation manager's authority to approve, or to exercise discretion in recommending approval of, the making of the expenditure by the foundation, whether or not such manifestation of approval is the final or decisive approval on behalf of the foundation.

(iii) Knowing.—For purposes of section 4945, a foundation manager shall be considered to have agreed to an expenditure "knowing" that it is a taxable expenditure only if—

(a) He has actual knowledge of sufficient facts so that, based solely upon such facts, such expenditure would be a taxable expenditure,

(b) He is aware that such an expenditure under these circumstances may violate the provisions of federal tax law governing taxable expenditures, and

(c) He negligently fails to make reasonable attempts to ascertain whether the expenditure is a taxable expenditure, or he is in fact aware that it is such an expenditure.

For purposes of this part and chapter 42, the term "knowing" does not mean "having reason to know". However, evidence tending to show that a foundation manager has reason to know of a particular fact or particular rule is relevant in determining whether he had actual knowledge of such fact or rule. Thus, for example, evidence tending to show that a foundation manager has reason to know of sufficient facts so that, based solely upon such facts, an expenditure would be a taxable expenditure is relevant in determining whether he has actual knowledge of such facts.

(iv) Willful. A foundation manager's agreement to a taxable expenditure is willful if it is voluntary, conscious, and intentional. No motive to avoid the restrictions of the law or the incurrence of any tax is necessary to make an agreement willful. However, a foundation manager's agreement to a taxable expenditure is not willful if he does not know that it is a taxable expenditure.

(v) Due to reasonable cause. A foundation manager's actions are due to reasonable cause if he has exercised his responsibility on behalf of the foundation with ordinary business care and prudence.

(vi) Advice of counsel. If a foundation manager, after full disclosure of the factual situation to legal counsel (including house counsel), relies on the advice of such counsel expressed in a reasoned written legal opinion that an expenditure is not a taxable expenditure under section 4945 (or that expenditures conforming to certain guidelines are not taxable expenditures), although such expenditure is subsequently held to be a taxable expenditure (or that certain proposed reporting procedures with respect to an expenditure will satisfy the tests of section 4945(h), although such procedures are subsequently held not to satisfy such section), the foundation manager's agreement to such expenditure (or to grants made with provision for such reporting procedures which are taxable solely because of such inadequate reporting procedures) will ordinarily not be considered "knowing" or "willful" and will ordinarily be considered "due to reasonable cause" within the meaning of section 4945(a)(2). For purposes of the subdivision, a written legal opinion will be considered "reasoned" even if it reaches a conclusion which is subsequently determined to be incorrect so long as such opinion addresses itself to the facts and applicable law. However, a written legal opinion will not be considered "reasoned" if it does nothing more than recite the facts and express a conclusion. However, the absence of advice of counsel with respect to an expenditure shall not, by itself, give rise to any inference that a foundation manager agreed to the making of the expenditure knowingly, willfully, or without reasonable cause.

(vii) Rate and incidence of tax. The tax imposed under section 4945(a)(2) is at the rate of 2 1/2 percent of the amount of each taxable expenditure to which the foundation manager has agreed. This tax shall be paid by the foundation manager.

(viii) Cross reference. For provisions relating to the burden of proof in cases involving the issue whether a foundation manager has knowingly agreed to the making of a taxable expenditure, see section 7454(b).

(b) Imposition of additional taxes—(1) Tax on private foundation. Section 4945(b)(1) of the Code imposes an excise tax in any case in which an initial tax is imposed under section 4945(a)(1) on a taxable expenditure of a private foundation and the expenditure is not corrected within the taxable period (as defined in section 4945(i)(2)). The tax imposed under section 4945(b)(1) is to be paid by the private foundation and is at the rate of 100 percent of the amount of each taxable expenditure.

(2) Tax on foundation manager. Section 4945(b)(2) of the Code imposes an excise tax in any case in which a tax is imposed under section 4945(b)(1) and a foundation manager has refused to agree to part or all of the correction of the taxable expenditure. The tax imposed under section 4945(b)(2) is at the rate of 50 percent of the amount of the taxable expenditure. This tax is to be paid by any foundation manager who has refused to agree to part or all of the correction of the taxable expenditure.

(c) Special rules—(1) Joint and several liability. In any case where more than one foundation manager is liable for tax imposed under section 4945(a)(2) or (b)(2) with respect to the making of a taxable expenditure, all such foundation managers shall be jointly and severally liable for the tax imposed under such paragraph with respect to such taxable expenditure.

(2) Limits on liability for management. The maximum aggregate amount of tax collectible under section 4945(a)(2) from all foundation managers with respect to any one taxable expenditure shall be $5,000, and the maximum aggregate amount of tax collectible under section 4945(b)(2) from all foundation managers with respect to any one taxable expenditure shall be $10,000.

(3) Examples. The provisions of this paragraph may be illustrated by the following examples:

Example (1). A, B, and C comprise the board of directors of Foundation M. They vote unanimously in favor of a grant of $100,000 to D, a business associate of each of the directors. The grant is to be used by D for travel and educational purposes and is not made in accordance with the requirements of section 4945(g). Each director knows that D was selected as the recipient of the grant solely because of his friendship with the directors and is aware that some grants made for travel, study, or other similar purposes may be taxable expenditures. Also, none of the directors makes any attempt to consult counsel, or to otherwise determine, whether this grant is a taxable expenditure. Initial taxes are imposed under paragraphs (1) and (2) of section 4945(a). The tax to be paid by the foundation is $10,000 (10 percent of $100,000). The tax to be paid by the board of directors is $2,500 (2 1/2 percent of $100,000). A, B, and C are jointly and severally liable for this $2,500 and this sum may be collected by the Service from any one of them.

Example (2). Assume the same facts as in example (1). Further assume that within the taxable period A makes a motion to correct the taxable expenditure at a meeting of the board of directors. The motion is defeated by a two-to-one vote, A voting for the motion and B and C voting against it. In these circumstances an additional tax is imposed on the private foundation in the amount of $100,000 (100 percent of $100,000). The additional tax imposed on B and C is $10,000 (50 percent of $100,000 subject to a maximum of $10,000). B and C are jointly and severally liable for the $10,000, and this sum may be collected by the Service from either of them.

(d) Correction—(1) In general. Except as provided in paragraph (d)(2) or (3) of this paragraph, correction of a taxable expenditure shall be accomplished by recovering part or all of the expenditure to the extent recovery is possible, and, where full recovery cannot be accomplished, by any additional corrective action which the Commissioner may prescribe. Such additional corrective action is to be determined by the circumstances of each particular case and may include the following:

(i) Requiring that any unpaid funds due the grantee be withheld;

(ii) Requiring that no further grants be made to the particular grantee;

(iii) In addition to other reports that are required, requiring periodic (e.g., quarterly) reports from the foundation with respect to all expenditures of the foundation (such reports shall be equivalent in detail to the reports required by section 4945(h)(3) and § 53.4945–5(d));

(iv) Requiring improved methods of exercising expenditure responsibility;

(v) Requiring improved methods of selecting recipients of individual grants; and

(vi) Requiring such other measures as the Commissioner may prescribe in a particular case.

The foundation making the expenditure shall not be under any obligation to attempt to recover the expenditure by legal action if such action would in all probability not result in the satisfaction of execution on a judgment.

(2) Correction for inadequate reporting. If the expenditure is taxable only because of a failure to obtain a full and complete report as required by section 4945(h)(2) or because of a failure to make a full and detailed report as required by section 4945(h)(3), correction may be accomplished by obtaining or making the report in question. In addition, if the expenditure is taxable only because of a failure to obtain a full and complete report as required by section 4945(h)(2) and an investigation indicates that no grant funds have been diverted to any use not in furtherance of a purpose specified in the grant, correction may be accomplished by exerting all reasonable efforts to obtain the report in question and reporting the failure to the Internal Revenue Service, even though the report is not finally obtained.

(3) Correction for failure to obtain advance approval. Where an expenditure is taxable under section 4945(d)(3) only because of a failure to obtain advance approval of procedures with respect to grants as required by section 4945(g), correction may be accomplished by obtaining approval of the grant making procedures and establishing to the satisfaction of the Commissioner that:

(i) No grant funds have been diverted to any use not in furtherance of a purpose specified in the grant;

(ii) The grant making procedures instituted would have been approved if advance approval of such procedures had been properly requested; and

(iii) Where advance approval of grant making procedures is subsequently required, such approval will be properly requested.

(e) Certain periods—(1) Taxable period. For purposes of section 4945, the term "taxable period" means, with respect to any taxable expenditure, the period beginning with the date on which the taxable expenditure occurs and ending on the earlier of:

(i) The date of mailing of a notice of deficiency under section 6212 with respect to the tax imposed on taxable expenditures by section 4945(a)(1); or

(ii) The date on which the tax imposed by section 4945(a)(1) is assessed.

(2) Cross reference. For rules relating to taxable events that are corrected within the correction period, defined in section 4963(e), see section 4961(a) and the regulations thereunder.

§ 53.4945–2. Propaganda influencing legislation.

(a) Propaganda influencing legislation, etc.—(1) In general. Under section 4945(d)(1) the term "taxable expenditure" includes any amount paid or incurred by a private foundation to carry on propaganda, or otherwise to attempt, to influence legislation. An expenditure is an attempt to influence legislation if it is for a direct or grass roots lobbying communication, as defined in § 56.4911–2 (without reference to §§ 56.4911–2(b)(3) and 56.4911–2(c)) and § 56.4911–3. See, however, paragraph (d) of this section for exceptions to the general rule of this paragraph (a)(1).

(2) Expenditures for membership communications. Section 56.4911–5, which provides special rules for electing public charities' communications with their members, does not apply to private foundations. Thus, whether a private foundation's communications with its members (assuming it has any) are lobbying communications is determined solely under § 56.4911–2 and without reference to § 56.4911–5. However, where a private foundation makes a grant to an electing public charity, § 56.4911–5 applies to the electing public charity's communications with its own members. Therefore, in the limited context of determining whether a private foundation's grant to an electing public charity is a taxable expenditure under section 4945, the § 56.4911–5 membership rules apply. For example, if the grant is specifically earmarked for a communication from the electing public charity to its members and the communication is, because of § 56.4911–5, a nonlobbying communication, the grant is not a taxable expenditure under section 4945.

(3) Jointly funded projects. A private foundation will not be treated as having paid or incurred any amount to attempt to influence legislation merely because it makes a grant to another organization upon the condition that the recipient obtain a matching support appropriation from a governmental body. In addition, a private foundation will not be treated as having made taxable expenditures of amounts paid or incurred in carrying on discussions with officials of governmental bodies provided that:

(i) The subject of such discussions is a program which is jointly funded by the foundation and the Government or is a new program which may be jointly funded by the foundation and the Government,

(ii) The discussions are undertaken for the purpose of exchanging data and information on the subject matter of the programs, and

(iii) Such discussions are not undertaken by foundation managers in order to make any direct attempt to persuade governmental officials or employees to take particular positions on specific legislative issues other than such program.

(4) Certain expenditures by recipients of program-related investments. Any amount paid or incurred by a recipient of a program-related investment (as defined in § 53.4944–3) in connection with an appearance before, or communication with, any legislative body with respect to legislation or proposed legislation of direct interest to such recipient shall not be attributed to the investing foundation, if—

(i) The foundation does not earmark its funds to be used for any activities described in section 4945(d)(1) and

(ii) A deduction under section 162 is allowable to the recipient for such amount.

(5) Grants to public organizations—(i) In general. A grant by a private foundation to an organization described in section 509(a)(1), (2) or (3) does not constitute a taxable expenditure by the foundation under section 4945(d), other than under section 4945(d)(1), if the grant by the private foundation is not earmarked to be used for any activity described in section 4945(d)(2) or (5), is not earmarked to be used in a manner which would violate section 4945(d)(3) or (4), and there does not exist an agreement, oral or written, whereby the grantor foundation may cause the grantee to engage in any such prohibited activity or to select the recipient to which the grant is to be devoted. For purposes of this paragraph (a)(5)(i), a grant by a private foundation is earmarked if the grant is given pursuant to an agreement, oral or written, that the grant will be used for specific purposes. For the expenditure respnsibility requirements with respect to organizations other than those described in section 509(a)(1), (2), or (3), see § 53.4945–5. For rules for determining whether grants to public charities are taxable expenditures under section 4945(d)(1), see paragraphs (a)(2), (a)(6) and (a)(7) of this section.

(ii) Certain "public" organizations. For purposes of this section, an organization shall be considered a section 509(a)(1) organization if it is treated as such under subparagraph (4) of § 53.4945–5(a).

(6) Grants to public organizations that attempt to influence legislation—(i) General support grant. A general support grant by a private foundation to he organization described in section 509(a)(1), (2), or (3) (a "public charity" for purposes of paragraphs (a)(6) and (7) of this section) does not constitute a taxable expenditure under section 4945(d)(1) to the extent that the grant is not earmarked, within the meaning of § 53.4945–2(a)(5)(i), to be used in an attempt to influence legislation. The preceding sentence applies without regard to whether the public charity has made the election under section 501(h).

(ii) Specific project grant. A grant, by a private foundation to fund a specific project of a public charity is not a taxable expenditure by the foundation under section 4945(d)(1) to the extent that—

(A) The grant is not earmarked, within the meaning of § 53.4945–2(a)(5)(i), to be used in an attempt to influence legislation, and

(B) The amount of the grant, together with other grants by the same private foundation for the same project for the same year, does not exceed the amount budgeted, for the year of the grant, by the grantee organization for activities of the project that are not attempts to influence legislation. If the grant is for more than one year, the preceding sentence applies to each year of the grant with the amount of the grant measured by the amount actually disbursed by the private foundation in each year or divided equally between years, at the option of the private foundation. The same method of measuring the annual amount must be used in all years of a grant. This paragraph (a)(6)(ii) applies without regard to whether the public charity has made the election under section 501(h).

(iii) Reliance upon grantee's budget. For purposes of determining the amount budgeted by a prospective grantee for specific project activities that are not attempts to influence legislation under paragraph (a)(6)(ii) of this section, a private foundation may rely on budget documents or other sufficient evidence supplied by the grantee organization (such as a signed statement by an authorized officer, director or trustee of such grantee organization) showing the proposed budget of the specific project, unless the private foundation doubts or, in light of all the facts and circumstances, reasonably should doubt the accuracy or reliability of the documents.

(7) Grants to organizations that cease to be described in 501(c)(3)—(i) Not taxable expenditure; conditions. A grant to a public charity (as defined in paragraph (a)(6)(i) of this section) that thereafter ceases to be an organization described in section 501(c)(3) by reason of its attempts to influence legislation is not a taxable expenditure if—

(A) The grant meets the requirements of paragraph (a)(6) of this section,

(B) The recipient organization had received a ruling or determination letter, or an advance ruling or determination letter, that it is described in sections 501(c)(3) and 509(a),

(C) Notice of a change in the recipient organization's status has not been made to the public (such as by publication in the Internal Revenue Bulletin), and the private foundation has not acquired knowledge that the Internal Revenue Service has given notice to the recipient organization that it will be deleted from such status; and

(D) The recipient organization is not controlled directly or indirectly by the private foundation. A recipient organization is controlled by a private foundation for this purpose if the private foundation and disqualified persons (defined in section 4946(a)(1)(A) through (H) with reference to the private foundation, by aggregating their votes or positions of authority, can cause or prevent action on legislative issues by the recipient.

(ii) Examples. The provisions of paragraphs (a)(6) and (a)(7) of this section are illustrated by the following examples:

Example (1). W, a private foundation, makes a general support grant to Z, a public charity described in section 509(a)(1). Z informs W that, as an insubstantial portion of its activities, Z attempts to influence the State legislature with regard to changes in the mental health laws. The use of the grant is not earmarked by W to be used in a manner that would violate section 4945(d)(1). Even if the grant is subsequently devoted by Z to its legislative activities, the grant by W is not a taxable expenditure under section 4945(d).

Example (2). X, a private foundation, makes a specific project grant to Y University for the purpose of conducting research on the potential environmental effects of certain pesticides. X does not earmark the grant for any purpose that would violate section 4945(d)(1) and there is no oral or written agreement or understanding whereby X may cause Y to engage in any activity described in section 4945(d)(1), (2), or (5), or to select any recipient to which the grant may be devoted. Further, X determines, based on budget information supplied by Y, that Y's budget for the project does not contain any amount for attempts to influence legislation. X has no reason to doubt the accuracy or reliability of the budget information. Y uses most of the funds for the research project; however, Y expends a portion of the grant funds to send a representative to testify at Congressional hearings on a specific bill proposing certain pesticide control measures. The portion of the grant funds expended with respect to the Congressional hearings is not treated as a taxable expenditure by X under section 4945(d)(1).

Example (3). M, a private foundation, makes a specific project grant of $150,000 to P, a public charity described in section 509(a)(1). In requesting the grant from M, P stated that the total budgeted cost of the project is $200,000, and that of this amount $20,000 is allocated to attempts to influence legislation related to the project. M relies on the budget figures provided by P in determining the amount P will spend on influencing legislation and M has no reason to doubt the accuracy or reliability of P's budget figures. In making the grant, M did not earmark any of the funds from the grant to be used for attempts to influence legislation. M's grant of $150,000 to P will not constitute a taxable expenditure under section 4945(d)(1) because M did not earmark any of the funds for attempts to influence legislation and because the amount of its grant ($150,000) does not exceed the amount allocated to specific project activities that are not attempts to influence legislation ($200,000-$20,000=$180,000).

Example (4). Assume the same facts as in example (3), except that M's grant letter to P provides that M has the right to renegotiate the terms of the grant if there is a substantial deviation from those terms. This additional fact does not make M's grant a taxable expenditure under section 4945(d)(1).

Example (5). Assume the same facts as in example (3), except that M made a specific project grant of $200,000 to P. Part of M's grant of $200,000 will constitute a taxable expenditure under section 4945(d)(1). The amount of the grant ($200,000) exceeds by $20,000 the amount P allocated to specific project activities that are not attempts to influence legislation ($180,000). M has made a taxable expenditure of $20,000.

Example (6). Assume the same facts as example (3), except that M made a specific project grant of $180,000, and received from P an enforceable commitment that grant funds would not be used in connection with attempts to influence legislation. M's grant is not a taxable expenditure under section 4945(d)(1).

Example (7). Assume the same facts as in example (3) except that M directed P to hire A, an individual, to expend $20,000 from the grant to engage in direct lobbying (within the meaning of § 56.4911–2(b)) and grass roots lobbying (within the meaning of § 56.4911–2(c)). P does not expend any other grant funds for lobbying activities. The $20,000 that is earmarked for direct lobbying and grass roots lobbying is a taxable expenditure under section 4945(d)(1).

Example (8). R, a public charity described in section 509(a)(1), requested N, a private foundation, to make a general purpose grant to it to aid R in carrying out its exempt purpose. In making this request, R notified N that it had elected the expenditure test under section 501(h) and that it expected to attempt to influence legislation in areas related to its exempt purpose. Since its formation, R generally has had exempt purpose expenditures (as defined in § 56.4911–4) in excess of $7,000,000 in each of its taxable years, and has budgeted in excess of $7,000,000 of exempt purpose expenditures for the year of the grant. N made a grant of $200,000 to R. N did not earmark the funds for R's attempt to influence legislation. The general purpose grant by N does not constitute a taxable expenditure under section 4945(d)(1).

Example (9). Assume the same facts as in example (8), except that N learns that R has had excess lobbying expenditures (within the meaning of § 56.4911–1(b)) in some prior years. N also learns that in no year has R's lobbying or grass roots expenditures (within the meaning of § 56.4911–2(a) and (c)) exceeded the corresponding ceiling amount (within the meaning of § 1.501(h)–3(c)(3) and (6)). N then makes the grant to R. After receiving the grant, R spends a large portion of its funds on influencing legislation and, as a consequence, is denied exemption from tax, as an organization described in section 501(c)(3), under section 501(h) and § 1.501(h)–3. No disqualified person with respect to N controlled, in whole or in part, R's attempts to influence legislation. The general purpose grant will not constitute a taxable expenditure under section 4945(d)(1).

Example (10). X, a private foundation, makes a specific project grant to Y, a public charity described in section 509(a). In requesting the grant, Y stated that it planned to use the funds to purchase a computer for purpose of computerizing its research files and that the grant will not be used to influence legislation. Two years after X makes the grant, X discovers that Y has also used the computer for purposes of maintaining and updating the mailing list for Y's lobbying newsletter. Because X did not earmark any of the grant funds to be used for attempts to influence legislation and because X had no reason to doubt the accuracy or reliability of Y's documents representing that the grant would not be used to influence legislation, X's grant is not treated as a taxable expenditure.

Example (11). G, a private foundation, makes a specific project grant of $300,000 to L, a public charity described in section 509(a)(1) for a three-year specific project studying child care problems. L provides budget material indicating that the specific project will expend $200,000 in each of three years. L's budget materials indicate that attempts to influence legislation will amount to $10,000 in the first year, $20,000 in the second year and $100,000 in the third year. G intends to pay its $300,000 grant over three years as follows: $200,000 in the first year, $50,000 in the second year and $50,000 in the third year. The amount of the grant actually disbursed by G in the first year of the grant exceeds the nonlobbying expenditures of L in that year. However, because the amount of the grant in each of the three years, when divided equally among the three years ($100,000 for each year), is not more than the nonlobbying expenditures of L on the specific project for any of the three years, none of the grant is treated as a taxable expenditure under section 4945(d)(1).

Example (12). P, a private foundation, makes a $120,000 specific project grant to C, a public charity described in section 509(a) for a three-year project. P intends to pay its grant to C in three equal annual installments of $40,000. C provides budget material indicating that the specific project will expend $100,000 in each of three years. C's budget materials, which P reasonably does not doubt, indicate that the project's attempts to influence legislation will amount to $50,000 in each of the three years. After P pays the first annual installment to C, but before P pays the second installment to C, reliable information comes to P's attention that C has spent $90,000 of the project's $100,000 first-year budget on attempts to influence legislation. This information causes P to doubt the accuracy and reliability of C's budget materials. Because of the information, P does not pay the second-year installment to C. P's payment of the first installment of $40,000 is not a taxable expenditure under section 4945(d)(1) because the grant in the first year is not more than the nonlobbying expenditures C projected in its budget materials that P reasonably did not doubt.

Example (13). Assume the same facts as in Example (12), except that P pays the second-year installment of $40,000 to C. In the project's second year, C once again spends $90,000 of the project's $100,000 annual budget in attempts to influence legislation. Because P doubts or reasonably should doubt the accuracy or reliability of C's budget materials when P makes the second-year grant payment, P may not rely upon C's budget documents at that time. Accordingly, although none of the $40,000 paid in the first installment is a taxable expenditure, only $10,000 ($100,000 minus $90,000) of the second-year grant payment is not a taxable expenditure. The remaining $30,000 of the second installment is a taxable expenditure within the meaning of section 4945(d)(1).

Example (14). B, a private foundation, makes a specific project grant to C, a public charity described in section 509(a), of $40,000 for the purpose of conducting a study on the effectiveness of seat belts in preventing traffic deaths. B did not earmark any of the grant for attempts to influence legislation. In requesting the grant from B, C submitted a budget of $100,000 for the project. The budget contained expenses for postage and mailing, computer time, advertising, consulting services, salaries, printing, advertising, and similar categories of expenses. C also submitted to B a statement, signed by an officer of C, that 30% of the budgeted funds would be devoted to attempts to influence legislation within the meaning of section 4945. B has no reason to doubt the accuracy of the budget figures or the statement. B may rely on the budget figures and signed statement provided by C in determining the amount C will spend on influencing legislation. B's grant to C will not constitute a taxable expenditure under section 4945(d)(1), because the amount of the grant does not exceed the amount allocated to specific project activities that are not attempts to influence legislation.

(b) to (c) [Reserved]

(d) Exceptions—(1) Nonpartisan analysis, study, or research—(i) In general. A communication is not a lobbying communication, for purposes of § 53.4945–2(a)(1), if the communication constitutes engaging in nonpartisan analysis, study or research and making available to the general public or a segment or members thereof or to governmental bodies, officials, or employees the results of such work. Accordingly, an expenditure for such a communication does not constitute a taxable expenditure under section 4945(d)(1) and § 53.4945–2(a)(1).

(ii) Nonpartisan analysis, study, or research. For purposes of section 4945(e), "nonpartisan analysis, study, or research" means an independent and objective exposition of a particular subject matter, including any activity that is "educational" within the meaning of § 1.501(c)(3)–1(d)(3). Thus, "nonpartisan analysis, study, or research" may advocate a particular position or viewpoint so long as there is a sufficiently full and fair exposition of the pertinent facts to enable the public or an individual to form an independent opinion or conclusion. On the other hand, the mere presentation of unsupported opinion does not qualify as "nonpartisan analysis, study, or research".

(iii) Presentation as part of a series. Normally, whether a publication or broadcast qualifies as "nonpartisan analysis, study, or research" will be determined on a presentation-by-presentation basis. However, if a publication or broadcast is one of a series prepared or supported by a private foundation and the series as a whole meets the standards of subdivision (ii) of this subparagraph, then any individual publication or broadcast within the series will not result in a taxable expenditure even though such individual broadcast or publication does not, by itself, meet the standards of subdivision (ii) of this subparagraph. Whether a broadcast or publication is considered part of a series will ordinarily depend on all the facts and circumstances of each particular situation. However, with respect to broadcast activities, all broadcasts within any period of 6 consecutive months will ordinarily be eligible to be considered as part of a series. If a private foundation times or channels a part of a series which is described in this subdivision in a manner designed to influence the general public or the action of a legislative body with respect to a specific legislative proposal in violation of section 4945(d)(1), the expenses of preparing and distributing such part of the analysis, study, or research will be a taxable expenditure under this section.

(iv) Making available results of analysis, study, or research. A private foundation may choose any suitable means, including oral or written presentations, to distribute the results of its nonpartisan analysis, study, or research, with or without charge. Such means include distribution of reprints of speeches, articles, and reports (including the report required under section 6056); presentation of information through conferences, meetings, and discussions; and dissemination to the news media, including radio, television, and newspapers, and to other public forums. For purposes of this paragraph (d)(1)(iv), such communications may not be limited to, or be directed toward, persons who are interested solely in one side of a particular issue.

(v) Subsequent lobbying use of certain analysis, study, or research—(A) In general. Even though certain analysis, study or research is initially within the exception for nonpartisan analysis, study, or research, subsequent use of that analysis, study or research for grass roots lobbying may cause that analysis, study or research to be treated as a grass roots lobbying communication that is not within the exception for nonpartisan analysis, study, or research. This paragraph (d)(1)(v) of this section does not cause any analysis, study, or research to be considered a direct lobbying communication. For rules regarding when analysis, study, or research is treated as a grass roots lobbying communication that is not within the scope of the exception for nonpartisan analysis, study, or research, see § 56.4911–2(b)(2)(v).

(B) Special rule for grants to public charities. This paragraph (d)(1)(v)(B) of this section applies where a public charity uses a private foundation grant to finance, in whole or in part, a nonlobbying communication that is subsequently used in lobbying, causing the public charity's expenditures for the communication to be treated as lobbying expenditures under the subsequent use. In such a case, the private foundation's grant will ordinarily not be characterized as a lobbying expenditure by virtue of the subsequent use rule. The only situations where the private foundation's grant will be treated as a lobbying expenditure under the subsequent use rule are where the private foundation's primary purpose in making the grant to the public charity was for lobbying or where, at the time of making the grant, the private foundation knows (or in light of all the facts and circumstances reasonably should know) that the public charity's primary purpose in preparing the communication to be funded by the grant is for use in lobbying.

(vi) Directly encouraging action by recipients of a communication. A communication that reflects a view on specific legislation is not within the nonpartisan analysis, study, or research exception of this § 53.4945–2(d)(1) if the communication directly encourages the recipient to take action with respect to such legislation. For purposes of this section, a communication directly encourages the recipient to take action with respect to legislation if the communication is described in one or more of § 56.4911–2(b)(2)(iii)(A) through (C). As described in § 56.4911–2(b)(2)(iv), a communication would encourage the recipient to take action with respect to legislation, but not directly encourage such action, if the communication does no more than specifically identify one or more legislators who will vote on the legislation as: opposing the communication's view with respect to the legislation; being undecided with respect to the legislation; being the recipient's representative in the legislature; or being a member of the legislative committee or subcommittee that will consider the legislation.

(vii) Examples. The provisions of this paragraph may be illustrated by the following examples:

Example (1). M, a private foundation, establishes a research project to collect information for the purpose of showing the dangers of the use of pesticides in raising crops. The information collected includes data with respect to proposed legislation, pending before several State legislatures, which would ban the use of pesticides. The project takes favorable positions on such legislation without producing a sufficiently full and fair exposition of the pertinent facts to enable the public or an individual to form an independent opinion or conclusion on the pros and cons of the use of pesticides. This project is not within the exception for nonpartisan analysis, study, or research because it is designed to present information merely on one side of the legislative controversy.

Example (2). N, a private foundation, establishes a research project to collect information concerning the dangers of the use of pesticides in raising crops for the ostensible purpose of examining and reporting information as to the pros and cons of the use of pesticides in raising crops. The information is collected and distributed in the form of a published report which analyzes the effects and costs of the use and nonuse of various pesticides under various conditions on humans, animals, and crops. The report also presents the advantages, disadvantages, and economic cost of allowing the continued use of pesticides unabated, of controlling the use of pesticides, and of developing alternatives to pesticides. Even if the report sets forth conclusions that the disadvantages as a result of using pesticides are greater than the advantages of using pesticides and that prompt legislative regulation of the use of pesticides is needed, the project is within the exception for nonpartisan analysis, study or research since it is designed to present information on both sides of the legislative controversy and presents a sufficiently full and fair exposition of the pertinent facts to enable the public or an individual to form an independent opinion or conclusion.

Example (3). O, a private foundation, establishes a research project to collect information on the presence or absence of disease in humans from eating food grown with pesticides and the presence or absence of disease in humans from eating food not grown with pesticides. As part of the research project, O hires a consultant who prepares a "fact sheet" which calls for the curtailment of the use of pesticides and which addresses itself to the merits of several specific legislative proposals to curtail the use of pesticides in raising crops which are currently pending before State legislatures. The "fact sheet" presents reports of experimental evidence tending to support its conclusions but omits any reference to reports of experimental evidence tending to dispute its conclusions. O distributes 10,000 copies to citizens' groups. Expenditures by O in connection with this work of the consultant are not within the exception for nonpartisan analysis, study, or research.

Example (4). P publishes a bi-monthly newsletter to collect and report all published materials, ongoing research, and new developments with regard to the use of pesticides in raising crops. The newsletter also includes notices of proposed pesticide legislation with impartial summaries of the provisions and debates on such legislation. The newsletter does not encourage recipients to take action with respect to such legislation, but is designed to present information on both sides of the legislative controversy and does present information fully and fairly. It is within the exception for nonpartisan analysis, study, or research.

Example (5). X is satisfied that A, a member of the faculty of Y University, is exceptionally well qualified to undertake a project involving a comprehensive study of the effects of pesticides on crop yields. Consequently, X makes a grant to A to underwrite the cost of the study and of the preparation of a book on the effect of pesticides on crop yields. X does not take any position on the issues or control the content of A's output. A produces a book which concludes that the use of pesticides often has a favorable effect on crop yields, and on that basis argues against pending bills which would ban the use of pesticides. A's book contains a sufficiently full and fair exposition of the pertinent facts, including known or potential disadvantages of the use of pesticides, to enable the public or an individual to form an independent opinion or conclusion as to whether pesticides should be banned as provided in the pending bills. The book does not directly encourage readers to take action with respect to the pending bills. Consequently, the book is within the exception for nonpartisan analysis, study, or research.

Example (6). Assume the same facts as Example (2), except that, instead of issuing a report, X presents within a period of 6 consecutive months a two-program television series relating to the pesticide issue. The first program contains information, arguments, and conclusions favoring legislation to restrict the use of pesticides. The second program contains information, arguments, and conclusions opposing legislation to restrict the use of pesticides. The programs are broadcast within 6 months of each other during commensurate periods of prime time. X's programs are within the exception for nonpartisan analysis, study, or research. Although neither program individually could be regarded as nonpartisan, the series of two programs constitutes a balanced presentation.

Example (7). Assume the same facts as Example (6), except that X arranged for televising the program favoring legislation to restrict the use of pesticides at 8 p.m. on a Thursday evening and for televising the program opposing such legislation at 7 a.m. on a Sunday morning. X's presentation is not within the exception for nonpartisan analysis, study, or research, since X disseminated its information in a manner prejudicial to one side of the legislative controversy.

Example (8). Organization Z researches, writes, prints and distributes a study on the use and effects of pesticide X. A bill is pending in the U.S. Senate to ban the use of pesticide X. Z's study leads to the conclusion that pesticide X is extremely harmful and that the bill pending in the U.S. Senate is an appropriate and much needed remedy to solve the problems caused by pesticide X. The study contains a sufficiently full and fair exposition of the pertinent facts, including known or potential advantages of the use of pesticide X, to enable the public or an individual to form an independent opinion or conclusion as to whether pesticides should be banned as provided in the pending bills. In its analysis of the pending bill, the study names certain undecided Senators on the Senate committee considering the bill. Although the study meets the three part test for determining whether a communication is a grass roots lobbying communication, the study is within the exception for nonpartisan analysis, study or research, because it does not directly encourage recipients of the communication to urge a legislator to oppose the bill.

Example (9). Assume the same facts as in Example (8), except that, after stating support for the pending bill, the study concludes: "You should write to the undecided committee members to support this crucial bill." The study is not within the exception for nonpartisan analysis, study or research because it directly encourages the recipients to urge a legislator to support a specific piece of legislation.

Example (10). Organization X plans to conduct a lobbying campaign with respect to illegal drug use in the United States. It incurs $5,000 in expenses to conduct research and prepare an extensive report primarily for use in the lobbying campaign. Although the detailed report discusses specific pending legislation and reaches the conclusion that the legislation would reduce illegal drug use, the report contains a sufficiently full and fair exposition of the pertinent facts to enable the public or an individual to form an independent conclusion regarding the effect of the legislation. The report does not encourage readers to contact legislators regarding the legislation. Accordingly, the report does not, in and of itself, constitute a lobbying communication.

Copies of the report are available to the public at X's office, but X does not actively distribute the report or otherwise seek to make the contents of the report available to the general public. Whether or not X's distribution is sufficient to meet the requirement in § 53.4945–2(d)(1)(iv) that a nonpartisan communication be made available, X's distribution is not substantial (for purposes of ss 53.4945–2(D)(1)(v) and 56.4911–2(b)(2)(v)) in light of all of the facts and circumstances, including the normal distribution pattern of similar nonpartisan reports. X then mails copies of the report, along with a letter, to 10,000 individuals on X's mailing list. In the letter, X requests that individuals contact legislators urging passage of the legislation discussed in the report. Because X's research and report were primarily undertaken by X for lobbying purposes and X did not make a substantial distribution of the report (without an accompanying lobbying message) prior to or contemporaneously with the use of the report in lobbying, the report is a grass roots lobbying communication that is not within the exception for nonpartisan analysis, study or research. Thus, the expenditures for preparing and mailing both the report and the letter are taxable expenditures under section 4945.

Example (11). Assume the same facts as in Example (10), except that before using the report in the lobbying campaign, X sends the research and report (without an accompanying lobbying message) to universities and newspapers. At the same time, X also advertises the availability of the report in its newsletter. This distribution is similar in scope to the normal distribution pattern of similar nonpartisan reports. In light of all of the facts and circumstances, X's distribution of the report is substantial. Because of X's substantial distribution of the report, X's primary purpose will be considered to be other than for use in lobbying and the report will not be considered a grass roots lobbying communication. Accordingly, only the expenditures for copying and mailing the report to the 10,000 individuals on X's mailing list, as well as for preparing and mailing the letter, are expenditures for grass roots lobbying communications, and are thus taxable expenditures under section 4945.

Example (12). Organization M pays for a bumper sticker that reads: "STOP ABORTION: Vote NO on Prop. X!" M also pays for a 30-second television advertisement and a billboard that similarly advocate opposition to Prop. X. In light of the limited scope of the communications, none of the communications is within the exception for nonpartisan analysis, study or research. First, none of the communications rises to the level of analysis, study or research. Second, none of the communications is nonpartisan because none contains a sufficiently full and fair exposition of the pertinent facts to enable the public or an individual to form an independent opinion or conclusion. Thus, each communication is a lobbying communication.

(2) Technical advice or assistance—(i) In general. Amounts paid or incurred in connection with providing technical advice or assistance to a governmental body, a governmental committee, or a subdivision of either of the foregoing, in response to a written request by such body, committee, or subdivision do not constitute taxable expenditures for purposes of this section. Under this exception, the request for assistance or advice must be made in the name of the requesting governmental body, committee or subdivision rather than an individual member thereof. Similarly, the response to such request must be available to every member of the requesting body, committee or subdivision. For example, in the case of a written response to a request for technical advice or assistance from a congressional committee, the response will be considered available to every member of the requesting committee if the response is submitted to the person making such request in the name of the committee and it is made clear that the response is for the use of all the members of the committee.

(ii) Nature of technical advice or assistance. "Technical advice or assistance" may be given as a result of knowledge or skill in a given area. Because such assistance or advice may be given only at the express request of a governmental body, committee or subdivision, the oral or written presentation of such assistance or advice need not qualify as nonpartisan analysis, study or research. The offering of opinions or recommendations will ordinarily qualify under this exception only if such opinions or recommendations are specifically requested by the governmental body, committee or subdivision or are directly related to the materials so requested.

(iii) Examples. The provisions of this subparagraph may be illustrated by the following examples:

Example (1). A congressional committee is studying the feasibility of legislation to provide funds for scholarships to U.S. students attending schools abroad. X, a private foundation which has engaged in a private scholarship program of this type, is asked, in writing, by the committee to describe the manner in which it selects candidates for its program. X's response disclosing its methods of selection constitutes technical advice or assistance.

Example (2). Assume the same facts as Example (1), except that X's response not only includes a description of its own grant-making procedures, but also its views regarding the wisdom of adopting such a program. Since such views are directly related to the subject matter of the request for technical advice or assistance, expenditures paid or incurred with respect to the presentation of such views would not constitute taxable expenditures. However, expenditures paid or incurred with respect to a response which is not directly related to the subject matter of the request for technical advice or assistance would constitute taxable expenditures unless the presentation can qualify as the making available of nonpartisan analysis, study or research.

Example (3). Assume the same facts as Example (1), except that X is requested, in addition, to give any views it considers relevant. A response to this request giving opinions which are relevant to the committee's consideration of the scholarship program but which are not necessarily directly related to X's scholarship program, such as discussions of alternative scholarship programs and their relative merits, would qualify as "technical advice or assistance", and expenditures paid or incurred with respect to such response would not constitute taxable expenditures.

Example (4). A, an official of the State Department, makes a written request in his official capacity for information from foundation Y relating to the economic development of country M and for the opinions of Y as to the proper position of the United States in pending negotiations with M concerning a proposed treaty involving a program of economic and technical aid to M. Y's furnishing of such information and opinions constitutes technical advice or assistance.

Example (5). In response to a telephone inquiry from Senator X's staff, organization B sends Senator X a report concluding that the Senate should not advise and consent to the nomination of Z to serve as a Supreme Court Justice. Because the request was not in writing, and also because the request was not from the Senate itself or from a committee or subcommittee, B's report is not within the scope of the exception for responses to requests for technical advice. Accordingly, B's report is a lobbying communication unless the report is within the scope of the exception for nonpartisan analysis, study or research.

Example (6). Assume the same facts as in Example (5), except that B's report is sent in response to a written request that Senator X sends to B. The request from Senator X is a request from the Senator as an individual member of the Senate rather than from the Senate itself or from a committee or subcommittee. Accordingly, B's report is not within the scope of the exception for responses to requests for technical advice and is a lobbying communication unless the report is within the scope of the exception for nonpartisan analysis, study or research.

Example (7). Assume the same facts as in Example (6), except that B's report is sent in response to a written request from the Senate committee that is considering the nomination for an evaluation of the nominee's legal writings and a recommendation as to whether the candidate is or is not qualified to serve on the Supreme Court. The report is within the scope of the exception for responses to requests for technical advice and is not a lobbying communication.

(3) Decisions affecting the powers, duties, etc., of a private foundation—(i) In general. Paragraph (c) of this section does not apply to any amount paid or incurred in connection with an appearance before, or communication with, any legislative body with respect to a possible decision of such body which might affect the existence of the private foundation, its powers and duties, its tax-exempt status, or the deductibility of contributions to such foundation. Under this exception, a foundation may communicate with the entire legislative body, committees or subcommittees of such legislative body, individual congressmen or legislators, members of their staffs, or representatives of the executive branch, who are involved in the legislative process, if such communication is limited to the prescribed subjects. Similarly, the foundation may make expenditures in order to initiate legislation if such legislation concerns only matters which might affect the existence of the private foundation, its powers and duties, its tax-exempt status, or the deductibility of contributions to such foundation.

(ii) Examples. The provisions of this subparagraph may be illustrated by the following examples:

Example (1). A bill is being considered by Congress which would, if enacted, restrict the power of a private foundation to engage in transactions with certain related persons. Under the proposed bill a private foundation would lose its exemption from taxation if it engages in such transactions. W, a private foundation, writes to the congressional committee considering the bill, arguing that the enactment of such a bill would not be advisable, and subsequently appears before such committee to make its arguments. In addition, W requests that the congressional committee consider modification of the 2 percent de minimis rule of section 4943(c)(2)(C). Expenditures paid or incurred with respect to such submissions do not constitute taxable expenditures since they are made with respect to a possible decision of Congress which might affect the existence of the private foundation, its powers and duties, its tax-exempt status, or the deduction of contributions to such foundation.

Example (2). A bill being considered in a State legislature is designed to implement the requirements of section 508(e) of the Internal Revenue Code of 1954. Under such section, a private foundation is required to make certain amendments to its governing instrument. X, a private foundation, makes a submission to the legislature which proposes alternative measures which might be taken in lieu of the proposed bill. X also arranges to have its president contact certain State legislators with regard to this bill. Expenditures paid or incurred in making such submission and in contacting the State legislators do not constitute taxable expenditures since they are made with respect to a possible decision of such State legislature which might affect the existence of the private foundation, its powers and duties, its tax-exempt status, or the deduction of contributions to such foundation.

Example (3). A bill is being considered by a State legislature under which the State would assume certain responsibilities for nursing care of the aged. Y, a private foundation which hitherto has engaged in such activities, appears before the State legislature and contends that such activities can be better performed by privately supported organizations. Expenditures paid or incurred with respect to such appearance are not made with respect to possible decisions of the State legislature which might affect the existence of the private foundation, its powers and duties, its tax-exempt status, or the deduction of contributions to such foundation, but rather merely affect the scope of the private foundation's future activities.

Example (4). A State legislature is considering the annual appropriations bill. Z, a private foundation which had hitherto performed contract research for the State, appears before the appropriations committee in order to attempt to persuade the committee of the advisability of continuing the program. Expenditures paid or incurred with respect to such appearance are not made with respect to possible decisions of the State legislature which might affect the existence of the private foundation, its powers and duties, its tax-exempt status, or the deduction of contributions to such foundation, but rather merely affect the scope of the private foundation's future activities.

(4) Examination and discussions of broad social, economic, and similar problems. Examinations and discussions of broad social, economic, and similar problems are neither direct lobbying communications under § 56.4911–2(b)(1) nor grass roots lobbying communications under § 56.4911–2(b)(2) even if the problems are of the type with which government would be expected to deal ultimately. Thus, under ss 56.4911–2(b)(1) and (2), lobbying communications do not include public discussion, or communications with members of legislative bodies or governmental employees, the general subject of which is also the subject of legislation before a legislative body, so long as such discussion does not address itself to the merits of a specific legislative proposal and so long as such discussion does not directly encourage recipients to take action with respect to legislation. For example, this paragraph (d)(4) excludes from grass roots lobbying under § 56.4911(b)(2) an organization's discussions of problems such as environmental pollution or population growth that are being considered by Congress and various State legislatures, but only where the discussions are not directly addressed to specific legislation being considered, and only where the discussions do not directly encourage recipients of the communication to contact a legislator, an employee of a legislative body, or a government official or employee who may participate in the formulation of legislation.

§ 53.4945–3. Influencing elections and carrying on voter registration drives.

(a) Expenditures to influence elections or carry on voter registration drives—(1) In general. Under section 4945(d)(2), the term "taxable expenditure" includes any amount paid or incurred by a private foundation to influence the outcome of any specific public election or to carry on, directly or indirectly, any voter registration drive, unless such amount is paid or incurred by an organization described in section 4945(f). However, for treatment of nonearmarked grants to public organizations, see § 53.4945–2(a)(5) and for treatment of certain earmarked grants to organizations described in section 4945(f), see paragraph (b)(2) of this section.

(2) Influencing the outcome of a specific public election. For purposes of this section, an organization shall be considered to be influencing the outcome of any specific public election if it participates or intervenes, directly or indirectly, in any political campaign on behalf of or in opposition to any candidate for public office. The term "candidate for public office" means an individual who offers himself, or is proposed by others, as a contestant for an elective public office, whether such office be national, State or local. Activities which constitute participation or intervention in a political campaign on behalf of or in opposition to a candidate include, but are not limited to:

(i) Publishing or distributing written or printed statements or making oral statements on behalf of or in opposition to such a candidate;

(ii) Paying salaries or expenses of campaign workers; and

(iii) Conducting or paying the expenses of conducting a voter-registration drive limited to the geographic area covered by the campaign.

(b) Nonpartisan activities carried on by certain organizations—(1) In general. If an organization meets the requirements described in section 4945(f), an amount paid or incurred by such organization shall not be considered a taxable expenditure even though the use of such amount is otherwise described in section 4945(d)(2). Such requirements are:

(i) The organization is described in section 501(c)(3) and exempt from taxation under section 501(a);

(ii) The activities of the organization are nonpartisan, are not confined to one specific election period, and are carried on in five or more States;

(iii) The organization expends at least 85 percent of its income directly for the active conduct (within the meaning of section 4942(j)(3) and the regulations thereunder) of the activities constituting the purpose or function for which it is organized and operated;

(iv) The organization receives at least 85 percent of its support (other than gross investment income as defined in section 509(e)) from exempt organizations, the general public, governmental units described in section 170(c)(1), or any combination of the foregoing; the organization does not receive more than 25 percent of its support (other than gross investment income) from any one exempt organization (for this purpose treating private foundations which are described in section 4946(a)(1)(H) with respect to each other as one exempt organization); and not more than half of the support of the organization is received from gross investment income; and

(v) Contributions to the organization for voter registration drives are not subject to conditions that they may be used only in specified States, possessions of the United States, or political subdivisions or other areas of any of the foregoing, or the District of Columbia, or that they may be used in only one specific election period.

(2) Grants to section 4945(f) organizations. If a private foundation makes a grant to an organization described in section 4945(f) (whether or not such grantee is a private foundation as defined in section 509(a)), such grant will not be treated as a taxable expenditure under section 4945(d)(2) or (4). Even if a grant to such an organization is earmarked for voter registration purposes generally, such a grant will not be treated as a taxable expenditure under section 4945(d)(2) or (4) as long as such earmarking does not violate section 4945(f)(5).

(3) Period for determining support—(i) In general. The determination whether an organization meets the support test in section 4945(f)(4) for any taxable year is to be made by aggregating all amounts of support received by the organization during the taxable year and the immediately preceding four taxable years. However, the support received in any taxable year which begins before January 1, 1970, shall be excluded.

(ii) New organizations and organizations with no preceding taxable years beginning after December 31, 1969. Except as provided in subparagraph (4) of this paragraph, in the case of a new organization or an organization with no taxable years that begin after December 31, 1969, and immediately precede the taxable year in question, the requirements of the support test in section 4945(f)(4) will be considered as met for the taxable year if such requirements are met by the end of the taxable year.

(iii) Organization with three or fewer preceding taxable years. In the case of an organization which has been in existence for at least 1 but fewer than 4 preceding taxable years beginning after December 31, 1969, the determination whether such organization meets the requirements of the support test in section 4945(f)(4) for the taxable year is to be made by taking into account all the support received by such organization during the taxable year and during each preceding taxable year beginning after December 31, 1969.

(4) Advance rulings. An organization will be given an advance ruling that it is an organization described in section 4945(f) for its first taxable year of operation beginning after October 30, 1972, or for its first taxable year of operation beginning after December 31, 1969, if it submits evidence establishing that it can reasonably be expected to meet the tests under section 4945(f) for such taxable year. An organization which, pursuant to this subparagraph, has been treated as an organization described in section 4945(f) for a taxable year (without withdrawal of such treatment by notification from the Internal Revenue Service during such year), but which actually fails to meet the requirements of section 4945(f) for such taxable year, will not be treated as an organization described in section 4945(f) as of the first day of its next taxable year (for purposes of making any determination under the internal revenue laws with respect to such organization) and until such time as the organization does meet the requirements of section 4945(f). For purposes of section 4945, the status of grants or contributions with respect to grantors or contributors to such organization will not be affected until notice of change of status of such organization is made to the public (such as by publication in the Internal Revenue Bulletin). The preceding sentence shall not apply, however, if the grantor or contributor was responsible for, or was aware of, the fact that the organization did not satisfy section 4945(f) at the end of the taxable year with respect to which the organization had obtained an advance ruling or a determination letter that it was a section 4945(f) organization, or acquired knowledge that the Internal Revenue Service had given notice to such organization that it would be deleted from classification as a section 4945(f) organization.

§ 53.4945-4. Grants to individuals.

(a) Grants to individuals.—(1) In general. Under section 4945(d)(3) the term "taxable expenditure" includes any amount paid or incurred by a private foundation as a grant to an individual for travel, study, or other similar purposes by such individual unless the grant satisfies the requirements of section 4945(g). Grants to individuals which are not taxable expenditures because made in accordance with the requirements of section 4945(g) may result in the imposition of excise taxes under other provisions of chapter 42.

(2) "Grants" defined. For purposes of section 4945, the term "grants" shall include, but is not limited to, such expenditures as scholarships, fellowships, internships, prizes, and awards. Grants shall also include loans for purposes described in section 170(c)(2)(B) and "program related investments" (such as investments in small businesses in central cities or in businesses which assist in neighborhood renovation). Similarly, "grants" include such expenditures as payments to exempt organizations to be used in furtherance of such recipient organizations' exempt purposes whether or not such payments are solicited by such recipient organizations. Conversely, "grants" do not ordinarily include salaries or other compensation to employees. For example, "grants" do not ordinarily include educational payments to employees which are includible in the employees' incomes pursuant to section 61. In addition, "grants" do not ordinarily include payments (including salaries, consultants' fees and reimbursement for travel expenses such as transportation, board, and lodging) to persons (regardless of whether such persons are individuals) for personal services in assisting a foundation in planning, evaluating or developing projects or areas of program activity by consulting, advising, or participating in conferences organized by the foundation.

(3) Requirements for individual grants—(i) Grants for other than section 4945(d)(3) purposes. A grant to an individual for purposes other than those described in section 4945(d)(3) is not a taxable expenditure within the meaning of section 4945(d)(3). For example, if a foundation makes grants to indigent individuals to enable them to purchase furniture, such grants are not taxable expenditures within the meaning of section 4945(d)(3) even if the requirements of section 4945(g) are not met.

(ii) Grants for section 4945(d)(3) purposes. Under section 4945(g), a grant to an individual for travel, study, or other similar purposes is not a "taxable expenditure" only if:

(a) The grant is awarded on an objective and nondiscriminatory basis (within the meaning of paragraph (b) of this section);

(b) The grant is made pursuant to a procedure approved in advance by the Commissioner; and

(c) It is demonstrated to the satisfaction of the Commissioner that:

(1) The grant constitutes a scholarship or fellowship grant which is excluded from gross income under section 117(a) and is to be utilized for study at an educational institution described in section 151(e)(4);

(2) The grant constitutes a prize or award which is excluded from gross income under section 74(b), and the recipient of such prize or award is selected from the general public (within the meaning of section 4941(d)(2)(G)(i) and the regulations thereunder); or

(3) The purpose of the grant is to achieve a specific objective, produce a report or other similar product, or improve or enhance a literary, artistic, musical, scientific, teaching, or other similar capacity, skill, or talent of the grantee.

If a grant is made to an individual for a purpose described in section 4945(g)(3) and such grant otherwise meets the requirements of section 4945(g), such grant shall not be treated as a taxable expenditure even if it is a scholarship or a fellowship grant which is not excludable from income under section 117 or if it is a prize or award which is includible in income under section 74.

(iii) Renewals. A renewal of a grant which satisfied the requirements of subdivision (ii) of this subparagraph shall not be treated as a grant to an individual which is subject to the requirements of this section, if—

(a) The grantor has no information indicating that the original grant is being used for any purpose other than that for which it was made,

(b) Any reports due at the time of the renewal decision pursuant to the terms of the original grant have been furnished, and

(c) Any additional criteria and procedures for renewal are objective and nondiscriminatory.

For purposes of this section, an extension of the period over which a grant is to be paid shall not itself be regarded as a grant or a renewal of a grant.

(4) Certain designated grants—(i) In general. A grant by a private foundation to another organization, which the grantee organization uses to make payments to an individual for purposes described in section 4945(d)(3), shall not be regarded as a grant by the private foundation to the individual grantee if the foundation does not earmark the use of the grant for any named individual and there does not exist an agreement, oral or written, whereby such grantor foundation may cause the selection of the individual grantee by the grantee organization. For purposes of this subparagraph, a grant described herein shall not be regarded as a grant by the foundation to an individual grantee even though such foundation has reason to believe that certain individuals would derive benefits from such grant so long as the grantee organization exercises control, in fact, over the selection process and actually makes the selection completely independently of the private foundation.

(ii) Certain grants to "public charities". A grant by a private foundation to an organization described in section 509(a)(1), (2), or (3), which the grantee organization uses to make payments to an individual for purposes described in section 4945(d)

(3), shall not be regarded as a grant by the private foundation to the individual grantee (regardless of the application of subdivision (i) of this subparagraph) if the grant is made for a project which is to be undertaken under the supervision of the section 509(a)(1), (2), or (3) organization and such grantee organization controls the selection of the individual grantee. This subdivision shall apply regardless of whether the name of the individual grantee was first proposed by the private foundation, but only if there is an objective manifestation of the section 509(a), (1), (2), or (3) organization's control over the selection process, although the selection need not be made completely independently of the private foundation. For purposes of this subdivision, an organization shall be considered a section 509(a)(1) organization if it is treated as such under subparagraph (4) of § 53.4945–5(a).

(iii) Grants to governmental agencies. If a private foundation makes a grant to an organization described in section 170(c)(1) (regardless of whether it is described in section 501(c)(3)) and such grant is earmarked for use by an individual for purposes described in section 4945(d)(3), such grant is not subject to the requirements of section 4945(d)(3) and (g) and this section (regardless of the application of subdivision (i) of this subparagraph) if the section 170(c)(1) organization satisfies the Commissioner in advance that its grant-making program:

(a) Is in furtherance of a purpose described in section 170(c)(2)(B),

(b) Requires that the individual grantee submit reports to it which would satisfy paragraph (c)(3) of this section, and

(c) Requires that the organization investigate jeopardized grants in a manner substantially similar to that described in paragraph (c)(4) of this section.

(iv) Examples. The provisions of this subparagraph may be illustrated by the following examples:

Example (1). M, a university described in section 170(b)(1)(A)(ii), requests that P, a private foundation, grant it $100,000 to enable M to obtain the services of a particular scientist for a research project in a special field of biochemistry in which he has exceptional qualifications and competence. P, after determining that the project deserves support, makes the grant to M to enable it to obtain the services of this scientist. M is authorized to keep the funds even if it is unsuccessful in attempting to employ the scientist. Under these circumstances P will not be treated as having made a grant to the individual scientist for purposes of section 4945(d)(3) and (g), since the requirements of subdivision (i) of this subparagraph have been satisfied. Even if M were not authorized to keep the funds if it is unsuccessful in attempting to employ the scientist, P would not be treated as having made a grant to the individual scientist for purposes of section 4945(d)(3) and (g), since it is clear from the facts and circumstances that the selection of the particular scientist was made by M and thus the requirements of subdivision (ii) of this subparagraph would have been satisfied.

Example (2). Assume the same facts as Example (1), except that there are a number of scientists who are qualified to administer the research project, P suggests the name of the particular scientist to be employed by M, and M is not authorized to keep the funds if it is unsuccessful in attempting to employ the particular scientist. For purposes of section 4945(d)(3) and (g), P will be treated as having made a grant to the individual scientist whose name it suggested, since it is clear from the facts and circumstances that selection of the particular scientist was made by P.

Example (3). X, a private foundation, is aware of the exceptional research facilities at Y University, an organization described in section 170(b)(1)(A)(ii). Officials of X approach officials of Y with an offer to give Y a grant of $100,000 if Y will engage an adequately qualified physicist to conduct a specific research project. Y's officials accept this proposal, and it is agreed that Y will administer the funds. After examining the qualifications of several research physicists, the officials of Y agree that A, whose name was first suggested by officials of X and who first suggested the specific research project to X, is uniquely qualified to conduct the project. X's grant letter provides that X has the right to renegotiate the terms of the grant if there is a substantial deviation from such terms, such as breakdown of Y's research facilities or termination of the conduct of the project by an adequately qualified physicist. Under these circumstances, X will not be treated as having made a grant to A for purposes of section 4945(d)(3) and (g), since the requirements of subdivision (ii) of this subparagraph have been satisfied.

Example (4). Professor A, a scholar employed by University Y, an organization described in section 170(b)(1)(A)(ii), approaches Foundation X to determine the availability of grant funds for a particular research project supervised or conducted by Professor A relevant to the program interests of Foundation X. After learning that Foundation X would be willing to consider the project if University Y were to submit the project to X, Professor A submits his proposal to the appropriate administrator of University Y. After making a determination that it should assume responsibility for the project, that Professor A is qualified to conduct the project, and that his participation would be consistent with his other faculty duties, University Y formally adopts the grant proposal and submits it to Foundation X. The grant is made to University Y which, under the terms of the grant, is responsible for the expenditure of the grant funds and the grant project. In such a case, and even if Foundation X retains the right to renegotiate the terms of the grant if the project ceases to be conducted by Professor A, the grant shall not be regarded as a grant by Foundation X to Professor A since University Y has retained control over the selection process within the meaning of subdivision (ii) of this subparagraph.

(5) Earmarked grants to individuals. A grant by a private foundation to an individual, which meets the requirements of section 4945(d)(3) and (g), is a taxable expenditure by such foundation under section 4945(d) only if:

(i) The grant is earmarked to be used for any activity described in section 4945(d)(1), (2), or (5), or is earmarked to be used in a manner which would violate section 4945(d) (3) or (4),

(ii) There is an agreement, oral or written, whereby such grantor foundation may cause the grantee to engage in any such prohibited activity and such grant is in fact used in a manner which violates section 4945(d), or

(iii) The grant is made for a purpose other than a purpose described in section 170(c) (2)(B).

For purposes of this subparagraph, a grant by a private foundation is earmarked if such grant is given pursuant to an agreement, oral or written, that the grant will be used for specific purposes.

(b) Selection of grantees on "an objective and nondiscriminatory basis"—(1) In general. For purposes of this section, in order for a foundation to establish that its grants to individuals are made on an objective and nondiscriminatory basis, the grants must be awarded in accordance with a program which, if it were a substantial part of the foundation's activities, would be consistent with:

(i) The existence of the foundation's exempt status under section 501(c)(3);

(ii) The allowance of deductions to individuals under section 170 for contributions to the granting foundation; and

(iii) The requirements of subparagraphs (2), (3), and (4) of this paragraph.

(2) Candidates for grants. Ordinarily, selection of grantees on an objective and nondiscriminatory basis requires that the group from which grantees are selected be chosen on the basis of criteria reasonably related to the purposes of the grant. Furthermore, the group must be sufficiently broad so that the giving of grants to members of such group would be considered to fulfill a purpose described in section 170(c)(2)(B). Thus, ordinarily the group must be sufficiently large to constitute a charitable class. However, selection from a group is not necessary where taking into account the purposes of the grant, one or several persons are selected because they are exceptionally qualified to carry out these purposes or it is otherwise evident that the selection is particularly calculated to effectuate the charitable purpose of the grant rather than to benefit particular persons or a particular class of persons. Therefore, consistent with the requirements of this subparagraph, the foundation may impose reasonable restrictions on the group of potential grantees. For example, selection of a qualified research scientist to work on a particular project does not violate the requirements of section 4945(d)(3) merely because the foundation selects him from a group of three scientists who are experts in that field.

(3) Selection from within group of potential grantees. The criteria used in selecting grant recipients from the potential grantees should be related to the purpose of the grant. Thus, for example, proper criteria for selecting scholarship recipients might include (but are not limited to) the following: Prior academic performance; performance on tests designed to measure ability and aptitude for college work; recommendations from instructors; financial need; and the conclusions which the selection committee might draw from a personal interview as to the individual's motivation, character, ability, and potential.

(4) Persons making selections. The person or group of persons who select recipients of grants should not be in a position to derive a private benefit, directly or indirectly, if certain potential grantees are selected over others.

(5) Examples. The provisions of this paragraph may be illustrated by the following examples:

Example (1). X company employs 100,000 people of whom 1,000 are classified by the company as executives. The company has organized the X company foundation which, as its sole activity, provides 100 4-year college scholarships per year for children of the company's employees. Children of all employees (other than disqualified persons with respect to the foundation) who have worked for the X company for at least 2 years are eligible to apply for these scholarships. In previous years, the number of children eligible to apply for such scholarships has averaged 2,000 per year. Selection of scholarship recipients from among the applicants is made by three prominent educators, who have no connection (other than as members of the selection committee) with the company, the foundation or any of the employees of the company. The selections are made on the basis of the applicants' prior academic performance, performance on certain tests designed to measure ability and aptitude for college work, and financial need. No disproportionate number of scholarships has been granted to relatives of executives of X company. Under these circumstances, the operation of the scholarship program by the X company foundation: (1) Is consistent with the existence of the foundation's exempt status under section 501(c)(3) and with the allowance of deductions under section 170 for contributions to the foundation; (2) utilizes objective and nondiscriminatory criteria in selecting scholarship recipients from among the applicants; and (3) utilizes a selection committee which appears likely to make objective and nondiscriminatory selections of grant recipients.

Example (2). Assume the same facts as Example (1), except that the foundation establishes a program to provide 20 college scholarships per year for members of a certain ethnic minority. All members of this minority group (other than disqualified persons with respect to the foundation) living in State Z are eligible to apply for these scholarships. It is estimated that at least 400 persons will be eligible to apply for these scholarships each year. Under these circumstances, the operation of this scholarship program by the foundation: (1) Is consistent with the existence of the foundation's exempt status under section 501(c)(3) and with the allowance of deductions under section 170 for contributions to the foundation; (2) utilizes objective and nondiscriminatory criteria in selecting scholarship recipients from among the applicants; and (3) utilizes a selection committee which appears likely to make objective and nondiscriminatory selections of grant recipients.

(c) Requirements of a proper procedure—(1) In general. Section 4945(g) requires that grants to individuals must be made pursuant to a procedure approved in advance. To secure such approval, a private foundation must demonstrate to the satisfaction of the Commissioner that—

(i) Its grant procedure includes an objective and nondiscriminatory selection process (as described in paragraph (b) of this section);

(ii) Such procedure is reasonably calculated to result in performance by grantees of the activities that the grants are intended to finance; and

(iii) The foundation plans to obtain reports to determine whether the grantees have performed the activities that the grants are intended to finance.

No single procedure or set of procedures is required. Procedures may vary depending upon such factors as the size of the foundation, the amount and purpose of the grants and whether one or more recipients are involved.

(2) Supervision of scholarship and fellowship grants. Except as provided in subparagraph (5) of this paragraph, with respect to any scholarship or fellowship grants, a private foundation must make arrangements to receive a report of the grantee's courses taken (if any) and grades received (if any) in each academic period. Such a report must be verified by the educational institution attended by the grantee and must be obtained at least once a year. In cases of grantees whose study at an educational institution does not involve the taking of courses but only the preparation of research papers or projects, such as the writing of a doctoral thesis, the foundation must receive a brief report on the progress of the paper or project at least once a year. Such a report must be approved by the faculty member supervising the grantee or by another appropriate university official. Upon completion of a grantee's study at an educational institution, a final report must also be obtained.

(3) Grants described in section 4945(g)(3). With respect to a grant made under section 4945(g)(3), the private foundation shall require reports on the use of the funds and the progress made by the grantee toward achieving the purposes for which the grant was made. Such reports must be made at least once a year. Upon completion of the undertaking for which the grant was made, a final report must be made describing the grantee's accomplishments with respect to the grant and accounting for the funds received under such grant.

(4) Investigation of jeopardized grants. (i) Where the reports submitted under this paragraph or other information (including the failure to submit such reports) indicates that all or any part of a grant is not being used in furtherance of the purposes of such grant, the foundation is under a duty to investigate. While conducting its investigation, the foundation must withhold further payments to the extent possible until any delinquent reports required by this paragraph have been submitted and where required by subdivision (ii) or (iii) of this subparagraph.

(ii) In cases in which the grantor foundation determines that any part of a grant has been used for improper purposes and the grantee has not previously diverted grant funds to any use not in furtherance of a purpose specified in the grant, the foundation will not be treated as having made a taxable expenditure solely because of the diversion so long as the foundation—

(a) Is taking all reasonable and appropriate steps either to recover the grant funds or to insure the restoration of the diverted funds and the dedication (consistent with the requirements of (b)(1) and (2) of this subdivision) of other grant funds held by the grantee to the purposes being financed by the grant, and

(b) Withholds any further payments to the grantee after the grantor becomes aware that a diversion may have taken place (hereinafter referred to as "further payments") until it has—

(1) Received the grantee's assurances that future diversions will not occur, and

(2) Required the grantee to take extraordinary precaution to prevent future diversions from occurring.

If a foundation is treated as having made a taxable expenditure under this subparagraph in a case to which this subdivision applies, then unless the foundation meets the requirements of (a) of this subdivision the amount of the taxable expenditure shall be the amount of the diversion plus the amount of any further payments to the same grantee. However, if the foundation complies with the requirements of (a) of this subdivision but not the requirements of (b) of this subdivision, the amount of the taxable expenditure shall be the amount of such further payments.

(iii) In cases where a grantee has previously diverted funds received from a grantor foundation, and the grantor foundation determines that any part of a grant has again been used for improper purposes, the foundation will not be treated as having made a taxable expenditure solely by reason of such diversion so long as the foundation—

(a) Is taking all reasonable and appropriate steps to recover the grant funds or to insure the restoration of the funds and the dedication (consistent with the requirements of (b)(2) and (3) of this subdivision) of other grant funds held by the grantee to the purposes being financed by the grant, and

(b) Withholds further payments until:

(1) Such funds are in fact so recovered or restored,

(2) It has received the grantee's assurances that future diversions will not occur, and

(3) It requires the grantee to take extraordinary precautions to prevent future diversions from occurring.

If a foundation is treated as having made a taxable expenditure under this subparagraph in a case to which this subdivision applies, then unless the foundation meets the requirements of (a) of this subdivision, the amount of the taxable expenditure shall be the amount of the diversion plus the amount of any further payments to the same grantee. However, if the foundation complies with the requirements of (a) of this subdivision, but fails to withhold further payments until the requirements of (b) of this subdivision are met, the amount of the taxable expenditure shall be the amount of such further payments.

(iv) The phrase "all reasonable and appropriate steps" in subdivisions (ii) and (iii) of this subparagraph includes legal action where appropriate but need not include legal action if such action would in all probability not result in the satisfaction of execution on a judgment.

(5) Supervision of certain scholarship and fellowship grants. Subparagraphs (2) and (4) of this paragraph shall be considered satisfied with respect to scholarship or fellowship grants under the following circumstances: (i) The scholarship or fellowship grants are described in section 4945(g)(1); (ii) The grantor foundation pays the scholarship or fellowship grants to an educational institution described in section 151(e)(4); and (iii) Such educational institution agrees to use the grant funds to defray the recipient's expenses or to pay the funds (or a portion thereof) to the recipient only if the recipient is enrolled at such educational institution and his standing at such educational institution is consistent with the purposes and conditions of the grant.

(6) Retention of records. A private foundation shall retain records pertaining to all grants to individuals for purposes described in section 4945(d)(3). Such records shall include:

(i) All information the foundation secures to evaluate the qualification of potential grantees;

(ii) Identification of grantees (including any relationship of any grantee to the foundation sufficient to make such grantee a disqualified person of the private foundation within the meaning of section 4946(a)(1));

(iii) Specification of the amount and purpose of each grant; and

(iv) The follow-up information which the foundation obtains in complying with subparagraphs (2), (3), and (4) of this paragraph.

(7) Example. The provisions of paragraphs (b) and (c) of this section may be illustrated by the following example:

Example. The X foundation grants 10 scholarships each year to graduates of high schools in its area to permit the recipients to attend college. It makes the availability of its scholarships known by oral or written communications each year to the principals of three major high schools in the area. The foundation obtains information from each high school on the academic qualifications, background, and financial need of applicants. It requires that each applicant be recommended by two of his teachers or by the principal of his high school. All application forms are reviewed by the foundation officer responsible for making the awards and scholarships are granted on the basis of the academic qualifications and financial need of the grantees. The foundation obtains annual reports on the academic performance of the scholarship recipient from the college or university which he attends. It maintains a file on each scholarship awarded, including the original application, recommendations, a record of the action taken on the application, and the reports on the recipient from the institution which he attends. The described procedures of the X foundation for the making of grants to individuals qualify for Internal Revenue Service approval under section 4945(g). Furthermore, if the X foundation's scholarship program meets the requirements of subparagraph (5) of this paragraph, X foundation will not have to obtain reports on the academic performance of the scholarship recipients.

(d) Submission of grant procedure—(1) Contents of request for approval of grant procedures. A request for advance approval of a foundation's grant procedures must fully describe the foundation's procedures for awarding grants and for ascertaining that such grants are used for the proper purposes. The approval procedure does not contemplate specific approval of particular grant programs but instead one-time approval of a system of standards, procedures, and follow-up designed to result in grants which meet the requirements of section 4945(g). Thus, such approval shall apply to a subsequent grant program as long as the procedures under which it is conducted do not differ materially from those described in the request to the Commissioner. The request must contain the following items:

(i) A statement describing the selection process. Such statement shall be sufficiently detailed for the Commissioner to determine whether the grants are made on an objective and nondiscriminatory basis under paragraph (b) of this section.

(ii) A description of the terms and conditions under which the foundation ordinarily makes such grants, which is sufficient to enable the Commissioner to determine whether the grants awarded under such procedures would meet the requirements of paragraph (1), (2), or (3) of section 4945(g).

(iii) A detailed description of the private foundation's procedure for exercising supervision over grants, as described in paragraphs (c)(2) and (3) of this section.

(iv) A description of the foundation's procedures for review of grantee reports, for investigation where diversion of grant funds from their proper purposes is indicated, and for recovery of diverted grant funds, as described in paragraph (c)(4) of this section.

(2) Place of submission. Request for approval of grant procedures shall be submitted to the District Director.

(3) Internal Revenue Service action on request for approval of grant procedures. The 45th day after a request for approval of grant procedures has been properly submitted to the Internal Revenue Service, the organization has not been notified that such procedures are not acceptable, such procedures shall be considered as approved from the date of submission until receipt of actual notice from the Internal Revenue Service that such procedures do not meet the requirements of this section. If a grant to an individual for a purpose described in section 4945(d)(3) is made after notification to the organization by the Internal Revenue Service that the procedures under which the grant is made are not acceptable, such grant is a taxable expenditure under this section.

* * *

§ 53.4945–5. Grants to organizations.

(a) Grants to nonpublic organizations—(1) In general. Under section 4945(d)(4) the term "taxable expenditure" includes any amount paid or incurred by a private foundation as a grant to an organization (other than an organization described in section 509(a)(1), (a)(2), or (a)(3) (other than an organization described in section 4942(g)(4)(A)(i) or (ii)) or in section 4940(d)(2)), unless the private foundation exercises expenditure responsibility with respect to such grant in accordance with section 4945(h). However, the granting foundation does not have to exercise expenditure responsibility with respect to amounts granted to organizations described in section 4945(f).

(2) "Grants" described. For a description of the term "grants", see s 53.4945–4(a)(2).

(3) Section 509(a)(1), (2), and (3) organizations. See section 508(b) and the regulations thereunder for rules relating to when a grantor may rely on a potential grantee's characterization of its status as set forth in the notice described in section 508(b).

(4) Certain "public" organizations. For purposes of this section, an organization will be treated as a section 509(a)(1) organization if:

(i) It qualifies as such under paragraph (a) of s 1.509(a)–2 of this chapter;

(ii) It is an organization described in section 170(c)(1) or 511(a)(2)(B), even if it is not described in section 501(c)(3);

(iii) It is a foreign government, or any agency or instrumentality thereof, or an international organization designated as such by Executive Order under 22 U.S.C. 288, even if it is not described in section 501(c)(3). However, any grant to an organization referred to in this subparagraph must be made exclusively for charitable purposes as described in section 170(c)(2)(B).

(5) Certain foreign organizations—(i) In general. If a private foundation makes a grant to a foreign organization, which does not have a ruling or determination letter that it is an organization described in section 509(a)(1), (a)(2), or (a)(3) or in section 4940(d)(2), the grant will nonetheless be treated as a grant made to an organization described in section 509(a)(1), (a)(2), or (a)(3) (other than an organization described in section 4942(g)(4)(A)(i) or (ii)) or in section 4940(d)(2) if the grantor private foundation has made a good faith determination that the grantee organization is an organization described in section 509(a)(1), (a)(2), or (a)(3) (other than an organization described in section 4942(g)(4)(A)(i) or (ii)) or in section 4940(d)(2). A determination ordinarily will be considered a good faith determination if the determination is based on current written advice received from a qualified tax practitioner concluding that the grantee is an organization described in section 509(a)(1), (a)(2), or (a)(3) (other than an organization described in section 4942(g)(4)(A)(i) or (ii)) or in section 4940(d)(2), and if the foundation reasonably relied in good faith on the written advice in accordance with the requirements of § 1.6664-4(c)(1) of this chapter. The written advice must set forth sufficient facts concerning the operations and support of the grantee organization for the Internal Revenue Service to determine that the grantee organization would be likely to qualify as an organization described in section 509(a)(1), (a)(2), or (a)(3) (other than an organization described in section 4942(g)(4)(A)(i) or (ii)) or in section 4940(d)(2) as of the date of the written advice. For purposes of these rules, except as provided in the next sentence, written advice will be considered current if, as of the date of the grant payment, the relevant law on which the advice is based has not changed since the date of the written advice and the factual information on which the advice is based is from the grantee's current or prior taxable year (or annual accounting period if the grantee does not have a taxable year for United States federal tax purposes). Written advice that a grantee met the public support test under section 170(b)(1)(A)(vi) or section 509(a)(2) for a test period of five years will be treated as current for purposes of grant payments to the grantee during the two taxable years (or, as applicable, annual accounting periods) of the grantee immediately following the end of the five-year test period. See paragraphs (b)(5) and (6) of this section for additional rules relating to foreign organizations.

(ii) Definitions. For purposes of this paragraph (a)(5)—

(a) The term "foreign organization" means any organization that is not described in section 170(c)(2)(A).

(b) The term "qualified tax practitioner" means an attorney, a certified public accountant, or an enrolled agent, within the meaning of 31 CFR 10.2 and 10.3, who is subject to the requirements in 31 CFR part 10.

(6) Certain earmarked grants—(i) In general. A grant by a private foundation to a grantee organization which the grantee organization uses to make payments to another organization (the secondary grantee) shall not be regarded as a grant by the private foundation to the secondary grantee if the foundation does not earmark the use of the grant for any named secondary grantee and there does not exist an agreement, oral or written, whereby such grantor foundation may cause the selection of the secondary grantee by the organization to which it has given the grant. For purposes of this subdivision, a grant described herein shall not be regarded as a grant by the foundation to the secondary grantee even though such foundation has reason to believe that certain organizations would derive benefits from such grant so long as the original grantee organization exercises control, in fact, over the selection process and actually makes the selection completely independently of the private foundation.

(ii) To governmental agencies. If a private foundation makes a grant to an organization described in section 170(c)(1) and such grant is earmarked for use by another organization, the granting foundation need not exercise expenditure responsibility with respect to such grant if the section 170(c)(1) organization satisfies the Commissioner in advance that:

(a) Its grant-making program is in furtherance of a purpose described in section 170(c)(2)(B), and

(b) The section 170(c)(1) organization exercises "expenditure responsibility" in a manner that would satisfy this section if it applied to such section 170(c)(1) organization. However, with respect to such grant, the granting foundation must make the reports required by section 4945(h)(3) and paragraph (d) of this section, unless such grant is earmarked for use by an organization described in section 509(a)(1), (a)(2), or (a)(3) (other than an organization described in section 4942(g)(4)(A)(i) or (ii)), or in section 4940(d)(2).

However, with respect to such grant, the granting foundation must make the reports required by section 4945(h)(3) and paragraph (d) of this section, unless such grant is earmarked for use by an organization described in section 509(a)(1), (2), or (3).

(b) Expenditure responsibility—(1) In general. A private foundation is not an insurer of the activity of the organization to which it makes a grant. Thus, satisfaction of the requirements of sections 4945(d)(4) and (h) and of subparagraph (3) or (4) of this paragraph, will ordinarily mean that the grantor foundation will not have violated section 4945(d)(1) or (2). A private foundation will be considered to be exercising "expenditure responsibility" under section 4945(h) as long as it exerts all reasonable efforts and establishes adequate procedures—

(i) To see that the grant is spent solely for the purpose for which made,

(ii) To obtain full and complete reports from the grantee on how the funds are spent, and

(iii) To make full and detailed reports with respect to such expenditures to the Commissioner.

In cases in which pursuant to paragraph (a)(6) of this section a grant is considered made to a secondary grantee rather than the primary grantee, the grantor foundation's obligation to obtain reports from the grantee pursuant to section 4945(h)(2) and this section will be satisfied if appropriate reports are obtained from the secondary grantee. For rules relating to expenditure responsibility with respect to transfers of assets described in section 507(b)(2), see section 507(b)(2) and the regulations thereunder.

(2) Pre-grant inquiry—(i) Before making a grant to an organization with respect to which expenditure responsibility must be exercised under this section, a private foundation should conduct a limited inquiry concerning the potential grantee. Such inquiry should be complete enough to give a reasonable man assurance that the grantee will use the grant for the proper purposes. The inquiry should concern itself with matters such as: (a) The identity, prior history and experience (if any) of the grantee organization and its managers; and (b) any knowledge which the private foundation has (based on prior experience or otherwise) of, or other information which is readily available concerning, the management, activities, and practices of the grantee organization. The scope of the inquiry might be expected to vary from case to case depending upon the size and purpose of the grant, the period over which it is to be paid, and the prior experience which the grantor has had with respect to the capacity of the grantee to use the grant for the proper purposes. For example, if the grantee has made proper use of all prior grants to it by the grantor and filed the required reports substantiating such use, no further pregrant inquiry will ordinarily be necessary. Similarly, in the case of an organization, such as a trust described in section 4947(a)(2), which is required by the terms of its governing instrument to make payments to a specified organization exempt from taxation under section 501(a), a less extensive pregrant inquiry is required than in the case of a private foundation possessing discretion with respect to the distribution of funds.

(ii) The provisions of this subparagraph may be illustrated by the following examples:

Example (1). Officials of M, a newly established organization which is described in section 501(c)(4), request a grant from X foundation to be used for a proposed program to combat drug abuse by establishing neighborhood clinics in certain ghetto areas of a city. Before making a grant to M, X makes an inquiry concerning the identity, prior history and experience of the officials of M. X obtains information pertaining to the officials of M from references supplied by these officials. Since one of the references indicated that A, an official of M, has an arrest record, police records are also checked and A's probation officer is interviewed. The inquiry also shows M has no previous history of administering grants and that the officials of M have had no experience in administering programs of this nature. However, in the opinion of X's managers, M's officials (including A who appears to be fully rehabilitated after having been convicted of a narcotics violation several years ago) are well qualified to conduct this program since they are members of the communities in which the clinics are to be established and are more likely to be trusted by drug users in these communities than are outsiders. Under these circumstances X has complied with the requirements of this subparagraph and a grant to M for its proposed program will not be treated as a taxable expenditure solely because of the operation of this subparagraph.

Example (2). Foundation Y wishes to make a grant to foundation R for use in R's scholarship program. Y has made similar grants to R annually for the last several years and knows that R's managers have observed the terms of the previous grants and have made all requested reports with respect to such grants. No changes in R's management have occurred during the past several years. Under these circumstances, Y has enough information to have such assurance as a reasonable man would require that the grant to R will be used for proper purposes. Consequently, Y is under no obligation to make any further pregrant inquiry pursuant to this subparagraph.

Example (3). S foundation requests a grant from Z foundation for use in S's program of providing medical research fellowships. S has been engaged in this program for several years and has received large numbers of grants from other foundations. Z's managers know that the reputations of S and of S's officials are good. Z's managers also have been advised by managers of W foundation that W had recently made a grant to S and that W's managers were satisfied that such grant has been used for the purposes for which it was made. Under these circumstances Z has enough information to have such assurance as a reasonable man would require that the grant to S will be used for proper purposes. Consequently, Z is under no obligation to make any further pregrant inquiry pursuant to this subparagraph.

(3) Terms of grants. Except as provided in subparagraph (4) of this paragraph, in order to meet the expenditure responsibility requirements of section 4945(h), a private foundation must require that each grant to an organization, with respect to which expenditure responsibility must be exercised under this section, be made subject to a written commitment signed by an appropriate officer, director, or trustee of the grantee organization. Such commitment must include an agreement by the grantee—

(i) To repay any portion of the amount granted which is not used for the purposes of the grant,

(ii) To submit full and complete annual reports on the manner in which the funds are spent and the progress made in accomplishing the purposes of the grant, except as provided in paragraph (c)(2) of this section,

(iii) To maintain records of receipts and expenditures and to make its books and records available to the grantor at reasonable times, and

(iv) Not to use any of the funds—

(a) To carry on propaganda, or otherwise to attempt, to influence legislation (within the meaning of section 4945(d)(1)),

(b) To influence the outcome of any specific public election, or to carry on, directly or indirectly, any voter registration drive (within the meaning of section 4945(d)(2)),

(c) To make any grant which does not comply with the requirements of section 4945(d)(3) or (4), or

(d) To undertake any activity for any purpose other than one specified in section 170(c)(2)(B).

The agreement must also clearly specify the purposes of the grant. Such purposes may include contributing for capital endowment, for the purchase of capital equipment, or for general support provided that neither the grants nor the income therefrom may be used for purposes other than those described in section 170(c)(2)(B).

(4) Terms of program-related investments. In order to meet the expenditure responsibility requirements of section 4945(h), with regard to the making of a program-related investment (as defined in section 4944 and the regulations thereunder), a private foundation must require that each such investment with respect to which expenditure responsibility must be exercised under section 4945(d)(4) and (h) and this section be made subject to a written commitment signed by an appropriate officer, director, or trustee of the recipient organization. Such commitment must specify the purpose of the investment and must include an agreement by the organization—

(i) To use all the funds received from the private foundation (as determined under paragraph (c)(3) of this section) only for the purposes of the investment and to repay any portion not used for such purposes, provided that, with respect to equity investments, such repayment shall be made only to the extent permitted by applicable law concerning distributions to holders of equity interests,

(ii) At least once a year during the existence of the program-related investment, to submit full and complete financial reports of the type ordinarily required by commercial investors under similar circumstances and a statement that it has complied with the terms of the investment,

(iii) To maintain books and records adequate to provide information ordinarily required by commercial investors under similar circumstances and to make such books and records available to the private foundation at reasonable times, and

(iv) Not to use any of the funds—

(a) To carry on propaganda, or otherwise to attempt, to influence legislation (within the meaning of section 4945(d)(1)),

(b) To influence the outcome of any specific public election, or to carry on directly or indirectly, and voter registration drive (within the meaning of section 4945(d)(2)), or

(c) With respect to any recipient which is a private foundation (as defined in section 509(a)), to make any grant which does not comply with the requirements of section 4945(d)(3) or (4).

(5) Certain grants to foreign organizations. With respect to a grant to a foreign organization (other than an organization described in section 509(a)(1), (a)(2), or (a)(3) (other than an organization described in section 4942(g)(4)(A)(i) or (ii)) or in section 4940(d)(2) or treated as so described pursuant to paragraph (a)(4) or (5) of this section), paragraph (b)(3)(iv) or (b)(4)(iv) of this section shall be deemed satisfied if the agreement referred to in paragraph (b)(3) or (4) of this section imposes restrictions on the use of the grant substantially equivalent to the limitations imposed on a domestic private foundation under section 4945(d). Such restrictions may be phrased in appropriate terms under foreign law or custom and ordinarily will be considered sufficient if an affidavit or opinion of counsel (of the grantor or grantee) or written advice of a qualified tax practitioner is obtained stating that, under foreign law or custom, the agreement imposes restrictions on the use of the grant substantially equivalent to the restrictions imposed on a domestic private foundation under paragraph (b)(3) or (4) of this section.

(6) Special rules for grants by foreign private foundations. With respect to activities in jurisdictions other than those described in section 170(c)(2)(A), the failure of a foreign private foundation which is described in section 4948(b) to comply with subparagraph (3) or (4) of this paragraph with respect to a grant to an organization shall not constitute an act or failure to act which is a prohibited transaction (within the meaning of section 4948(c)(2)).

(7) Expenditure responsibility with respect to certain transfers of assets described in section 507—(i) Transfers of assets described in section 507(b)(2). For rules relating to the extent to which the expenditure responsibility rules contained in sections 4945(d)(4) and (h) and this section apply to transfers of assets described in section 507(b)(2), see §§ 1.507–3(a)(7), 1.507–3(a)(8)(ii)(f), and 1.507–3(a)(9) of this chapter.

(ii) Certain other transfers of assets. For rules relating to the extent to which the expenditure responsibility rules contained in sections 4945(d)(4) and (h) and this section apply to certain other transfers of assets described in § 1.507–3(b) of this chapter, see § 1.507–3(b) of this chapter.

(8) Restrictions on grants (other than program-related investments) to organizations not described in section 501(c)(3). For other restrictions on certain grants (other than program-related investments) to organizations which are not described in section 501(c)(3), see § 53.4945–6(c).

(c) Reports from grantees—(1) In general. In the case of grants described in section 4945(d)(4), except as provided in subparagraph (2) of this paragraph, the granting private foundation shall require reports on the use of the funds, compliance with the terms of the grant, and the progress made by the grantee toward achieving the purposes for which the grant was made. The grantee shall make such reports as of the end of its annual accounting period within which the grant or any portion thereof is received and all such subsequent periods until the grant funds are expended in full or the period of the grantee for which such reports shall be furnished to the grantor within a reasonable period of time after the close of the annual accounting period of the grantee for which such reports are made. Within a reasonable period of time after the close of its annual accounting period during which the use of the grant funds is completed, the grantee must make a final report with respect to all expenditures made from such funds (including salaries, travel, and supplies), and indicating the progress made toward the goals of the grant. The grantor need not conduct any independent verification of such reports unless it has reason to doubt their accuracy or reliability.

(2) Capital endowment grants to exempt private foundations. If a private foundation makes a grant described in section 4945(d)(4) to a private foundation which is exempt from taxation under section 501(a) for endowment, for the purchase of capital equipment, or for other capital purposes, the grantor foundation shall require reports from the grantee on the use of the principal and the income (if any) from the grant funds. The grantee shall make such reports annually for its taxable year in which the grant was made and the immediately succeeding 2 taxable years. Only if it is reasonably apparent to the grantor that, before the end of such second succeeding taxable year, neither the principal, the income from the grant funds, nor the equipment purchased with the grant funds has been used for any purpose which would result in liability for tax under section 4945(d), the grantor may then allow such reports to be discontinued.

(3) Grantees' accounting and record-keeping procedures. (i) A private foundation grantee exempt from taxation under section 501(a) (or the recipient of a program-related investment) need not segregate grant funds physically nor separately account for such funds on its books unless the grantor requires such treatment of the grant funds. If such a grantee neither physically segregates grant funds nor establishes separate accounts on its books, grants received within a given taxable year beginning after December 31, 1969, shall be deemed, for purposes of section 4945, to be expended before grants received in a succeeding taxable year. In such case expenditures of grants received within any such taxable year shall be prorated among all such grants. In accounting for grant expenditures, private foundations may make the necessary computations on a cumulative annual basis (or, where appropriate, as of the date for which the computations are made). The rules set forth in the preceding three sentences shall apply to the extent they are consistent with the available records of the grantee and with the grantee's treatment of qualifying distributions under section 4942(h) and the regulations thereunder. The records of expenditures, as well as copies of the reports submitted to the grantor, must be kept for at least 4 years after completion of the use of the grant funds.

(ii) For rules relating to accounting and record-keeping requirements for grantees other than those described in subdivision (i) of this subparagraph, see §§ 53.4945–5(b)(8) and 53.4945–6(c).

(4) Reliance on information supplied by grantee. A private foundation exercising expenditure responsibility with respect to its grants may rely on adequate records or other sufficient evidence supplied by the grantee organization (such as a statement by an appropriate officer, director or trustee of such grantee organization) showing, to the extent applicable, the information which the grantor must report to the Internal Revenue Service in accordance with paragraph (d)(2) of this section.

(d) Reporting to Internal Revenue Service by grantor—(1) In general. To satisfy the report-making requirements of section 4945(h)(3), a granting foundation must provide the required information on its annual information return, required to be filed by section 6033, for each taxable year with respect to each grant made during the taxable year which is subject to the expenditure responsibility requirements of section 4945(h). Such information must also be provided on such return with respect to each grant subject to such requirements upon which any amount or any report is outstanding at any time during the taxable year. However, with respect to any grant made for endowment or other capital purposes, the grantor must provide the required information only for any taxable year for which the grantor must require a report from the grantee under paragraph (c)(2) of this section. The requirements of this subparagraph with respect to any grant may be satisfied by submission with the foundation's information return of a report received from the grantee, if the information required by subparagraph (2) of this paragraph is contained in such report.

(2) Contents of report. The report required by this paragraph shall include the following information:

(i) The name and address of the grantee.

(ii) The date and amount of the grant.

(iii) The purpose of the grant.

(iv) The amounts expended by the grantee (based upon the most recent report received from the grantee).

(v) Whether the grantee has diverted any portion of the funds (or the income therefrom in the case of an endowment grant) from the purpose of the grant (to the knowledge of the grantor).

(vi) The dates of any reports received from the grantee.

(vii) The date and results of any verification of the grantee's reports undertaken pursuant to and to the extent required under paragraph (c)(1) of this section by the grantor or by others at the direction of the grantor.

(3) Record-keeping requirements. In addition to the information included on the information return, a granting foundation shall make available to the Internal Revenue Service at the foundation's principal office each of the following items:

(i) A copy of the agreement covering each "expenditure responsibility" grant made during the taxable year.

(ii) A copy of each report received during the taxable year from each grantee on any "expenditure responsibility" grant, and

(iii) A copy of each report made by the grantor's personnel or independent auditors of any audits or other investigations made during the taxable year with respect to any "expenditure responsibility" grant.

(4) Reports received after the close of grantor's accounting year. Data contained in reports required by this paragraph, which reports are received by a private foundation after the close of its accounting year but before the due date of its information return for that year, need not be reported on such return, but may be reported on the grantor's information return for the year in which such reports are received from the grantee.

(e) Violations of expenditure responsibility requirements—(1) Diversions by grantee. (i) Any diversion of grant funds (including the income therefrom in the case of an endowment grant) by the grantee to any use not in furtherance of a purpose specified in the grant may result in the diverted portion of such grant being treated as a taxable expenditure of the grantor under section 4945(d)(4). However, for purposes of this section, the fact that a grantee does not use any portion of the grant funds as indicated in the original budget projection shall not be treated as a diversion if the use to which the funds are committed is consistent with the purpose of the grant as stated in the grant agreement and does not result in a violation of the terms of such agreement required to be included by paragraph (b)(3) or (b)(4) of this section.

(ii) In any event, a grantor will not be treated as having made a taxable expenditure under section 4945(d)(4) solely by reason of a diversion by the grantee, if the grantor has complied with subdivision (iii)(a) and (b) or (iv)(a) and (b) of this subparagraph, whichever is applicable.

(iii) In cases in which the grantor foundation determines that any part of a grant has been used for improper purposes and the grantee has not previously diverted grant funds, the foundation will not be treated as having made a taxable expenditure solely by reason of the diversion so long as the foundation—

(a) Is taking all reasonable and appropriate steps either to recover the grant funds or to insure the restoration of the diverted funds and the dedication (consistent with the requirements of (b)(1) and (2) of this subdivision) of the other grant funds held by the grantee to the purposes being financed by the grant, and

(b) Withholds any further payments to the grantee after the grantor becomes aware that a diversion may have taken place (hereinafter referred to as "further payments") until it has—

(1) Received the grantee's assurances that future diversions will not occur, and

(2) Required the grantee to take extraordinary precautions to prevent future diversions from occurring.

If a foundation is treated as having made a taxable expenditure under this subparagraph in a case to which this subdivision applies, then unless the foundation meets the requirements of (a) of this subdivision the amount of the taxable expenditure shall be the amount of the diversion (for example, the income diverted in the case of an endowment grant, or the rental value of capital equipment for the period of time for which diverted) plus the amount of any further payments to the same grantee. However, if the foundation complies with the requirements of (a) of this subdivision but not the requirements of (b) of this subdivision, the amount of the taxable expenditure shall be the amount of such further payments.

(iv) In cases where a grantee has previously diverted funds received from a grantor foundation, and the grantor foundation determines that any part of a grant has again been used for improper purposes, the foundation will not be treated as having made a taxable expenditure solely by reason of such diversion so long as the foundation—

(a) Is taking all reasonable and appropriate steps to recover the grant funds or to insure the restoration of the diverted funds and the dedication (consistent with the requirements of (b)(2) and (3) of this subdivision) of other grant funds held by the grantee to the purposes being financed by the grant, except that if, in fact, some or all of the diverted funds are not so restored or recovered, then the foundation must take all reasonable and appropriate steps to recover all of the grant funds, and

(b) Withholds further payments until—

(1) Such funds are in fact so recovered or restored,

(2) It has received the grantee's assurances that future diversions will not occur, and

(3) It requires the grantee to take extraordinary precautions to prevent future diversions from occurring. If a foundation is treated as having made a taxable expenditure under this subparagraph in a case to which this subdivision applies, then unless the foundation meets the requirements of (a) of this subdivision, the amount of the taxable expenditure shall be the amount of the diversion plus the amount of any further payments to the same grantee. However, if the foundation complies with the requirements of (a) of this subdivision, but fails to withhold further payments until the requirements of (b) of this subdivision are met, the amount of the taxable expenditure shall be the amount of such further payments.

(v) The phrase "all reasonable and appropriate steps" (as used in subdivisions (iii) and (iv) of this subparagraph) includes legal action where appropriate but need not include legal action if such action would in all probability not result in the satisfaction of execution on a judgment.

(2) Grantee's failure to make reports. A failure by the grantee to make the reports required by paragraph (c) of this section (or the making of inadequate reports) shall result in the grant's being treated as a taxable expenditure by the grantor unless the grantor:

(i) Has made the grant in accordance with paragraph (b) of this section,

(ii) Has complied with the reporting requirements contained in paragraph (d) of this section,

(iii) Makes a reasonable effort to obtain the required report, and

(iv) Withholds all future payments on this grant and on any other grant to the same grantee until such report is furnished.

(3) Violations by the grantor. In addition to the situations described in subparagraphs (1) and (2) of this paragraph, a grant which is subject to the expenditure responsibility requirements of section 4945(h) will be considered a taxable expenditure of the granting foundation if the grantor—

(i) Fails to make a pregrant inquiry as described in paragraph (b)(2) of this section,

(ii) Fails to make the grant in accordance with a procedure consistent with the requirements of paragraph (b)(3) or (4) of this section, or

(iii) Fails to report to the Internal Revenue Service as provided in paragraph (d) of this section.

* * *

§ 53.4945-6. Expenditures for noncharitable purposes.

(a) In general. Under section 4945(d)(5) the term "taxable expenditure" includes any amount paid or incurred by a private foundation for any purpose other than one specified in section 170(c)(2)(B). Thus, ordinarily only an expenditure for an activity which, if it were a substantial part of the organization's total activities, would cause loss of tax exemption is a taxable expenditure under section 4945(d)(5). For purposes of this section and ss 53.4945-1 through 53.4945-5, the term "purposes described in section 170(c)(2)(B)" shall be treated as including purposes described in section 170(c)(2)(B) whether or not carried out by an organization described in section 170(c).

(b) Particular expenditures. (1) The following types of expenditures ordinarily will not be treated as taxable expenditures under section 4945(d)(5):

(i) Expenditures to acquire investments entered into for the purpose of obtaining income or funds to be used in furtherance of purposes described in section 170(c)(2)(B),

(ii) Reasonable expenses with respect to investments described in subdivision (i) of this subparagraph,

(iii) Payment of taxes,

(iv) Any expenses which qualify as deductions in the computation of unrelated business income tax under section 511,

(v) Any payment which constitutes a qualifying distribution under section 4942(g) or an allowable deduction under section 4940,

(vi) Reasonable expenditures to evaluate, acquire, modify, and dispose of program-related investments, or

(vii) Business expenditures by the recipient of a program-related investment.

(2) Conversely, any expenditures for unreasonable administrative expenses, including compensation, consultant fees, and other fees for services rendered, will ordinarily be taxable expenditures under section 4945(d)(5) unless the foundation can demonstrate that such expenses were paid or incurred in the good faith belief that they were reasonable and that the payment or incurrence of such expenses in such amounts was consistent with ordinary business care and prudence. The determination whether an expenditure is unreasonable shall depend upon the facts and circumstances of the particular case.

(c) Grants to "noncharitable" organizations—(1) In general. Since a private foundation cannot make an expenditure for a purpose other than a purpose described in section 170(c)(2)(B), a private foundation may not make a grant to an organization other than an organization described in section 501(c)(3) unless

(i) The making of the grant itself constitutes a direct charitable act or the making of a program-related investment, or

(ii) Through compliance with the requirements of subparagraph (2) of this paragraph, the grantor is reasonably assured that the grant will be used exclusively for purposes described in section 170(c)(2)(B).

For purposes of this paragraph, an organization treated as a section 509(a)(1) organization under § 53.4945–5(a)(4) shall be treated as an organization described in section 501(c)(3).

(2) Grants other than transfers of assets described in § 1.507–3(c)(1). (i) If a private foundation makes a grant which is not a transfer of assets pursuant to any liquidation, merger, redemption, recapitalization, or other adjustment, organization or reorganization to any organization (other than an organization described in section 501(c)(3) except an organization described in section 509(a)(4)), the grantor is reasonably assured (within the meaning of subparagraph (1)(ii) of this paragraph) that the grant will be used exclusively for purposes described in section 170(c)(2)(B) only if the grantee organization agrees to maintain and, during the period in which any portion of such grant funds remain unexpended, does continuously maintain the grant funds (or other assets transferred) in a separate fund dedicated to one or more purposes described in section 170(c)(2)(B). The grantor of a grant described in this paragraph must also comply with the expenditure responsibility provisions contained in sections 4945(d) and (h) and § 53.4945–5.

(ii) For purposes of this paragraph, a foreign organization which does not have a ruling or determination letter that it is an organization described in section 501(c)(3)(other than section 509(a)(4)) will be treated as an organization described in section 501(c)(3) (other than section 509(a)(4)) if in the reasonable judgment of a foundation manager of the transferor private foundation, the grantee organization is an organization described in section 501(c)(3) (other than section 509(a)(4)). The term "reasonable judgment" shall be given its generally accepted legal sense within the outlines developed by judicial decisions in the law of trusts.

* * *

§ 53.4946–1. Definitions and special rules.

(a) Disqualified person. (1) For purposes of chapter 42 and the regulations thereunder, the following are disqualified persons with respect to a private foundation:

(i) All substantial contributors to the foundation, as defined in section 507(d)(2) and the regulations thereunder.

(ii) All foundation managers of the foundation as defined in section 4946(b)(1) and paragraph (f)(1)(i) of this section,

(iii) An owner of more than 20 percent of:

(a) The total combined voting power of a corporation,

(b) The profits interest of a partnership,

(c) The beneficial interest of a trust or unincorporated enterprise.

which is (during such ownership) a substantial contributor to the foundation, as defined in section 507(d)(2) and the regulations thereunder,

(iv) A member of the family, as defined in section 4946(d) and paragraph (h) of this section, of any of the individuals described in subdivision (i), (ii), or (iii) of this subparagraph,

(v) A corporation of which more than 35 percent of the total combined voting power is owned by persons described in subdivision (i), (ii), (iii), or (iv) of this subparagraph,

(vi) A partnership of which more than 35 percent of the profits interest is owned by persons described in subdivision (i), (ii), (iii), or (iv) of this subparagraph, and

(vii) A trust, estate, or unincorporated enterprise of which more than 35 percent of the beneficial interest is owned by persons described in subdivision (i), (ii), (iii), or (iv) of this subparagraph.

(2) For purposes of subparagraphs (1)(iii)(b) and (vi) of this paragraph, the profits interest of a partner shall be equal to his distributive share of income of the partnership, as determined under section 707(b)(3) and the regulations thereunder as modified by section 4946(a)(4).

(3) For purposes of subparagraphs (1)(iii)(c) and (vii) of this paragraph, the beneficial interest in an unincorporated enterprise (other than a trust or estate) includes any right to receive a portion of distributions from profits of such enterprise, and, if the portion of distributions is not fixed by an agreement among the participants, any right to receive a portion of the assets (if any) upon liquidation of the enterprise, except as a creditor or employee. For purposes of this subparagraph, a right to receive distributions of profits includes a right to receive any amount from such profits other than as a creditor or employee, whether as a sum certain or as a portion of profits realized by the enterprise. Where there is no agreement fixing the rights of the participants in such enterprise, the fraction of the respective interests of each participant in such enterprise shall be determined by dividing the amount of all investments or contributions to the capital of the enterprise made or obligated to be made by such participant by the amount of all investments or contributions to capital made or obligated to be made by all of them.

(4) For purposes of subparagraphs (1)(iii)(c) and (vii) of this paragraph, a person's beneficial interest in a trust shall be determined in proportion to the actuarial interest of such person in the trust.

(5) For purposes of subparagraphs (1)(iii)(a) and (v) of this paragraph, the term "combined voting power" includes voting power represented by holdings of voting stock, actual or constructive (under section 4946(a)(3)), but does not include voting rights held only as a director or trustee.

(6) For purposes of subparagraphs (1)(iii)(a) and (v) of this paragraph, the term "voting power" includes outstanding voting power and does not include voting power obtainable but not obtained, such as, for example, voting power obtainable by converting securities or nonvoting stock into voting stock or by exercising warrants or options to obtain voting stock, and voting power which will vest in preferred stockholders only if and when the corporation has failed to pay preferred dividends for a specified period of time or has otherwise failed to meet specified requirements. Similarly, for purposes of subparagraphs (1)(iii)(b) and (c), (vi), and (vii) of this paragraph, the terms "profits interest" and "beneficial interest" include any such interest that is outstanding, but do not include any such interest that is obtainable but has not been obtained.

(7) For purposes of sections 170(b)(1)(E)(iii), 507(d)(1), 508(d), 509(a)(1) and (3), and Chapter 42, the term "disqualified person" shall not include an organization which is described in section 509(a)(1), (2), or (3), or any other organization which is wholly owned by such section 509(a)(1), (2), or (3) organization.

(8) For purposes of section 4941 only, the term "disqualified person" shall not include any organization which is described in section 501(c)(3) (other than an organization described in section 509(a)(4)).

(b) Section 4943. (1) For purposes of section 4943 only, the term "disqualified person" includes a private foundation:

(i) Which is effectively controlled (within the meaning of § 1.482–1(a)(3) of this chapter), directly or indirectly, by the same person or persons (other than a bank, trust company, or similar organization acting only as a foundation manager) who control the private foundation in question, or

(ii) Substantially all the contributions to which were made, directly or indirectly, by persons described in subdivision (i), (ii), (iii), or (iv) of paragraph (a)(1) of this section who made, directly or indirectly, substantially all of the contributions to the private foundation in question.

(2) For purposes of subparagraph (1)(ii) of this paragraph, one or more persons will be considered to have made substantially all of the contributions to a private foundation, if such persons have contributed or bequeathed at least 85 percent (and each such person has contributed or bequeathed at least 2 percent) of the total contributions and bequests (within the meaning of section 507(d)(2) and the regulations thereunder) which have been received by such private foundation during its entire existence.

(3) Examples. The provisions of this paragraph may be illustrated by the following examples:

Example (1). A, a private foundation, has a board of directors made up of X, Y, Z, M, N, and O.

Foundation B's board of directors is made up of Y, M, N, and O. The board of directors in each case has plenary power to determine the manner in which the foundation is operated. For purposes of section 4943, foundation A is a disqualified person with respect to foundation B, and foundation B, is a disqualified person with respect to foundation A.

Example (2). Private foundation A has received contributions of $100,000 throughout its existence: $35,000 from X, $51,000 from Y (who is X's father), and $14,000 from Z (an unrelated person). Private foundation B has received $100,000 in contributions during its existence: $50,000 from X and $50,000 from W, X's wife.

For purposes of section 4943, private foundation A is a disqualified person with respect to private foundation B, and private foundation B is a disqualified person with respect to private foundation A.

(c) Section 4941. For purposes of section 4941, a government official, as defined in section 4946(c) and paragraph (g) of this section, is a disqualified person.

(d) Attribution of stockholdings. (1) For purposes of paragraph (a)(1)(iii)(a) and (v) of this section, indirect stockholdings shall be taken into account under section 267(c) and the regulations thereunder. However, for purposes of this paragraph:

(i) Section 267(c)(4) shall be treated as though it provided that the members of the family of an individual are the members within the meaning of section 4946(d) and paragraph (h) of this section; and

(ii) Any stockholdings which have been counted once (whether by reason of actual or constructive ownership) in applying section 4946(a)(1)(E) shall not be counted a second time.

For purposes of paragraph (a)(1)(v) of this section, section 267(c) shall be applied without regard to section 267(c)(3), and stock constructively owned by an individual by reason of the application of section 267(c)(2) shall not be treated as owned by him if he is described in section 4946(a)(1)(D) but not also in section 4946(a)(1)(A), (B), or (C).

(2) Examples. The provisions of this paragraph may be illustrated by the following examples:

Example (1). D is a substantial contributor to private foundation Y. D owns 20 percent of the outstanding stock of corporation P. E, D's wife, owns none of the outstanding stock of P. F, E's father, owns 10 percent of the outstanding stock of P. E is treated under section 507(d)(2) as a substantial contributor to Y. E is also treated under section 267(c)(2) as owning both D's 20 percent and F's 10 percent of P, but E is treated as owning nothing for purposes of section 4946(a)(1)(E) because D's 20 percent and F's 10 percent have already been taken into account once (because of their actual ownership of the stock of P) for such purposes. Hence, corporation P is not a disqualified person under section 4946(a)(1)(E) with respect to private foundation Y because persons described in section 4946(a)(1)(A), (B), (C), and (D) own only 30 percent of the stock of P.

Example (2). I, a substantial contributor to private foundation X, is the son of J. I owns 100 percent of the stock of corporation R, which in turn owns 18 percent of the stock of corporation S. J owns 18 percent of the stock of S. I constructively owns 36 percent of the stock of S (J's 18 percent plus R's 18 percent). Both J's actual holdings and R's actual holdings are counted in determining I's constructive holdings because this does not result in counting either of the holdings more than once for purposes of section 4946(a)(1)(E). Therefore, S is a disqualified person with respect to private foundation X, since I, a substantial contributor, constructively owns more than 35 percent of S's stock.

(e) Attribution of profits or beneficial interests. (1) For purposes of paragraph (a)(1)(iii)(b), (iii)(c), (vi), and (vii) of this section, ownership of profits or beneficial interests shall be taken into account as though such ownership related to stockholdings, if such stockholdings would be taken into account under section 267(c) and the regulations thereunder, except that section 267(c)(3) shall not apply to attribute the ownership of one partner to another solely by reason of such partner relationship. However, for purposes of this paragraph:

(i) Section 267(c)(4) shall be treated as though it provided that the members of the family of an individual are the members within the meaning of section 4946(d) and paragraph (h) of this section; and

(ii) Any profits interest or beneficial interest which has been counted once (whether by reason of actual or constructive ownership) in applying section 4946(a)(1)(F) or (G) shall not be counted a second time.

For purposes of paragraphs (a)(1)(vi) and (vii) of this section, profits or beneficial interests constructively owned by an individual by reason of the application of section 267(c)(2) shall not be treated as owned by him if he is described in section 4946(a)(1)(D) but not in section 4946(a)(1)(A), (B) or (C).

(2) Example. The provisions of this paragraph may be illustrated by the following example:

Example. Partnership S is a substantial contributor to private foundation X. Trust T, of which G is sole beneficiary, owns 12 percent of the profits interest of S. G's husband, H, owns 10 percent of the profits interest of S. H is a disqualified person with respect to X (under section 4946(a)(1)(C)) because he is considered to own 22 percent of the profits interest of S (10 percent actual ownership, plus G's 12 percent constructively under section 267(c)(2)). G is a disqualified person with respect to X (under section 4946(a)(1)(C) because she is considered to own 22 percent of the profits interest of S (12 percent constructively by reason of her beneficial interest in trust T, plus 10 percent constructively under section 267(c)(2) by reason of being a member of the family of H).

(f) Foundation manager. (1) For purposes of Chapter 42 and the regulations thereunder, the term "foundation manager" means:

(i) An officer, director, or trustee of a foundation (or a person having powers or responsibilities similar to those of officers, directors, or trustees of the foundation), and

(ii) With respect to any act or failure to act, any employee of the foundation having final authority or responsibility (either officially or effectively) with respect to such act or failure to act.

(2) For purposes of subparagraph (1)(i) of this paragraph, a person shall be considered an officer of a foundation if:

(i) He is specifically so designated under the certificate of incorporation, bylaws, or other constitutive documents of the foundation; or

(ii) He regularly exercises general authority to make administrative or policy decisions on behalf of the foundation.

With respect to any act or failure to act, any person described in subdivision (ii) of this subparagraph who has authority merely to recommend particular administrative or policy decisions, but not to implement them without approval of a superior, is not an officer. Moreover, such independent contractors as attorneys, accountants, and investment managers and advisers, acting in their capacities as such, are not officers within the meaning of subparagraph (1)(i) of this paragraph.

(3) For purposes of subparagraph (1)(ii) of this paragraph, an individual rendering services to a private foundation shall be considered an employee of the foundation only if he is an employee within the meaning of section 3121(d)(2).

(4) Since the definition of the term "disqualified person" contained in section 4946(a)(1)(B) incorporates only so much of the definition of the term "foundation manager" as is found in section 4946(b)(1) and subparagraph (1)(i) of this paragraph, any references, in section 4946 and this section, to "disqualified persons" do not constitute references to persons who are "foundation managers" solely by reason of the definition of that term contained in section 4946(b)(2) and subparagraph (1)(ii) of this paragraph.

(g) Government official—(1) In general. Except as provided in subparagraph (3) of this paragraph, for purposes of section 4941 and paragraph (c) of this section, the term "government official" means, with respect to an act of selfdealing described in section 4941, an individual who, at the time of such act, is described in subdivision (i), (ii), (iii), (iv), or (v) of this subparagraph (other than a "special Government employee" as defined in 18 U.S.C. 202(a)):

(i)(a) An individual who holds an elective public office in the executive or legislative branch of the Government of the United States.

(b) An individual who holds an office in the executive or judicial branch of the Government of the United States, appointment to which was made by the President.

(ii) An individual who holds a position in the executive, legislative or judicial branch of the Government of the United States:

(a) Which is listed in schedule C of rule VI of the Civil Service Rules, or

(b) The compensation for which is equal to or greater than the lowest rate prescribed for GS–16 of the General Schedule under 5 U.S.C. 5332.

(iii) An individual who holds a position under the House of Representatives or the Senate of the United States, as an employee of either of such bodies, who receives gross compensation therefrom at an annual rate of $15,000 or more.

(iv) The holder of an elective or appointive public office in the executive, legislative, or judicial branch of the government of a State, possession of the United States, or political subdivision or other area of any of the foregoing, or of the District of Columbia, for which the gross compensation is at an annual rate of $15,000 or more, who is described in subparagraph (2) of this paragraph.

(v) The holder of a position as personal or executive assistant or secretary to any individual described in subdivision (i), (ii), (iii), or (iv) of this subparagraph.

(2) Public office—(i) Definition. In defining the term "public office" for purposes of section 4946(c)(5) and subparagraph (1)(iv) of this paragraph, such term must be distinguished from mere public employment. Although holding a public office is one form of public employment, not every position in the employ of a State or other governmental subdivision (as described in section 4946(c)(5)) constitutes a "public office". Although a determination whether a public employee holds a public office depends on the facts and circumstances of the case, the essential element is whether a significant part of the activities of a public employee is the independent performance of policymaking functions. In applying this subparagraph, several factors may be considered as indications that a position in the executive, legislative, or judicial branch of the government of a State, possession of the United States, or political subdivision or other area of any of the foregoing, or of the District of Columbia, constitutes a "public office". Among such factors to be considered in addition to that set forth above, are that the office is created by the Congress, a State constitution, or the State legislature, or by a municipality or other governmental body pursuant to authority conferred by the Congress, State constitution, or State legislature, and the powers conferred on the office and the duties to be discharged by such office are defined either directly or indirectly by the Congress, State constitution, or State legislature, or through legislative authority.

(ii) Illustrations. The following are illustrations of positions of public employment which do not involve policymaking functions within the meaning of subdivision (i) of this subparagraph and which are thus not a "public office" for purposes of section 4946(c)(5) and subparagraph (1)(iv) of this paragraph:

(a) The chancellor, president, provost, dean, and other officers of a State university who are appointed, elected, or otherwise hired by a State Board of Regents or equivalent public body and who are subject to the direction and supervision of such body;

(b) Professors, instructors, and other members of the faculty of a State educational institution who are appointed, elected, or otherwise hired by the officers of the institution or by the State Board of Regents or equivalent public body;

(c) The superintendent of public schools and other public school officials who are appointed, elected, or otherwise hired by a Board of Education or equivalent public body and who are subject to the direction and supervision of such body;

(d) Public school teachers who are appointed, elected, or otherwise hired by the superintendent of public schools or by a Board of Education or equivalent public body;

(e) Physicians, nurses, and other professional persons associated with public hospitals and State boards of health who are appointed, elected, or otherwise hired by the governing board or officers of such hospitals or agencies; and

(f) Members of police and fire departments, except for those department heads who, under the facts and circumstances of the case, independently perform policymaking functions as a significant part of their activities.

* * *

(h) Members of the family. For purposes of this section, the members of the family of an individual include only:

(1) His spouse,

(2) His ancestors,

(3) His lineal descendants, and

(4) Spouses of his lineal descendants.

For example, a brother or sister of an individual is not a member of his family for purposes of this section. However, for example, the wife of a grandchild of an individual is a member of his family for such purposes. For purposes of this paragraph, a legally adopted child of an individual shall be treated as a child of such individual by blood.

§ 53.4955–1. Tax on political expenditures.

(a) Relationship between section 4955 excise taxes and substantive standards for exemption under section 501(c)(3). The excise taxes imposed by section 4955 do not affect the substantive standards for tax exemption under section 501(c)(3), under which an organization is described in section 501(c)(3) only if it does not participate or intervene in any political campaign on behalf of any candidate for public office.

(b) Imposition of initial taxes on organization managers—(1) In general. The excise tax under section 4955(a)(2) on the agreement of any organization manager to the making of a political expenditure by a section 501(c)(3) organization is imposed only in cases where—

(i) A tax is imposed by section 4955(a)(1);

(ii) The organization manager knows that the expenditure to which the manager agrees is a political expenditure; and

(iii) The agreement is willful and is not due to reasonable cause.

(2) Type of organization managers covered—(i) In general. The tax under section 4955(a)(2) is imposed only on those organization managers who are authorized to approve, or to exercise discretion in recommending approval of, the making of the expenditure by the organization and on those organization managers who are members of a group (such as the organization's board of directors or trustees) which is so authorized.

(ii) Officer. For purposes of section 4955(f)(2)(A), a person is an officer of an organization if—

(A) That person is specifically so designated under the certificate of incorporation, bylaws, or other constitutive documents of the foundation; or

(B) That person regularly exercises general authority to make administrative or policy decisions on behalf of the organization. Independent contractors, acting in a capacity as attorneys, accountants, and investment managers and advisors, are not officers. With respect to any expenditure, any person described in this paragraph (b)(2)(ii)(B) who has authority merely to recommend particular administrative or policy decisions, but not to implement them without approval of a superior, is not an officer.

(iii) Employee. For purposes of section 4955(f)(2)(B), an individual rendering services to an organization is an employee of the organization only if that individual is an employee within the meaning of section 3121(d)(2). With respect to any expenditure, an employee (other than an officer, director, or trustee of the organization) is described in section 4955(f)(2)(B) only if he or she has final authority or responsibility (either officially or effectively) with respect to such expenditure.

(3) Type of agreement required. An organization manager agrees to the making of a political expenditure if the manager manifests approval of the expenditure which is sufficient to constitute an exercise of the organization manager's authority to approve, or to exercise discretion in recommending approval of, the making of the expenditure by the organization. The manifestation of approval need not be the final or decisive approval on behalf of the organization.

(4) Knowing—(i) General rule. For purposes of section 4955, an organization manager is considered to have agreed to an expenditure knowing that it is a political expenditure only if—

(A) The manager has actual knowledge of sufficient facts so that, based solely upon these facts, the expenditure would be a political expenditure;

(B) The manager is aware that such an expenditure under these circumstances may violate the provisions of federal tax law governing political expenditures; and

(C) The manager negligently fails to make reasonable attempts to ascertain whether the expenditure is a political expenditure, or the manager is aware that it is a political expenditure.

(ii) Amplification of general rule. For purposes of section 4955, knowing does not mean having reason to know. However, evidence tending to show that an organization manager has reason to know of a particular fact or particular rule is relevant in determining whether the manager had actual knowledge of the fact or rule. Thus, for example, evidence tending to show that an organization manager has reason to know of sufficient facts so that, based solely upon those facts, an expenditure would be a political expenditure is relevant in determining whether the manager has actual knowledge of the facts.

(5) Willful. An organization manager's agreement to a political expenditure is willful if it is voluntary, conscious, and intentional. No motive to avoid the restrictions of the law or the incurrence of any tax is necessary to make an agreement willful. However, an organization manager's agreement to a political expenditure is not willful if the manager does not know that it is a political expenditure.

(6) Due to reasonable cause. An organization manager's actions are due to reasonable cause if the manager has exercised his or her responsibility on behalf of the organization with ordinary business care and prudence.

(7) Advice of counsel. An organization manager's agreement to an expenditure is ordinarily not considered knowing or willful and is ordinarily considered due to reasonable cause if the manager, after full disclosure of the factual situation to legal counsel (including house counsel), relies on the advice of counsel expressed in a reasoned written legal opinion that an expenditure is not a political expenditure under section 4955 (or that expenditures conforming to certain guidelines are not political expenditures). For this purpose, a written legal opinion is considered reasoned even if it reaches a conclusion which is subsequently determined to be incorrect, so long as the opinion addresses itself to the facts and applicable law. A written legal opinion is not considered reasoned if it does nothing more than recite the facts and express a conclusion. However, the absence of advice of counsel with respect to an expenditure does not, by itself, give rise to any inference that an organization manager agreed to the making of the expenditure knowingly, willfully, or without reasonable cause.

* * *

(c) Amplification of political expenditure definition—(1) General rule. Any expenditure that would cause an organization that makes the expenditure to be classified as an action organization by reason of § 1.501(c)(3)–1(c)(3)(iii) of this chapter is a political expenditure within the meaning of section 4955(d)(1).

(2) Other political expenditures—(i) For purposes of section 4955(d)(2), an organization is effectively controlled by a candidate or prospective candidate only if the individual has a continuing, substantial involvement in the day-to-day operations or management of the organization. An organization is not effectively controlled by a candidate or a prospective candidate merely because it is affiliated with the candidate, or merely because the candidate knows the directors, officers, or employees of the organization. The effectively controlled test is not met merely because the organization carries on its research, study, or other educational activities with respect to subject matter or issues in which the individual is interested or with which the individual is associated.

(ii) For purposes of section 4955(d)(2), a determination of whether the primary purpose of an organization is promoting the candidacy or prospective candidacy of an individual for public office is made on the basis of all the facts and circumstances. The factors to be considered include whether the surveys, studies, materials, etc. prepared by the organization are made available only to the candidate or are made available to the general public; and whether the organization pays for speeches and travel expenses for only one individual, or for speeches or travel expenses of several persons. The fact that a candidate or prospective candidate utilizes studies, papers, materials, etc., prepared by the organization (such as in a speech by the candidate) is not to be considered as a factor indicating that the organization has a purpose of promoting the candidacy or prospective candidacy of that individual where such studies, papers, materials, etc. are not made available only to that individual.

(iii) Expenditures for voter registration, voter turnout, or voter education constitute other expenses, treated as political expenditures by reason of section 4955(d)(2)(E), only if the expenditures violate the prohibition on political activity provided in section 501(c)(3).

(d) Abatement, refund, or no assessment of initial tax. No initial (first-tier) tax will be imposed under section 4955(a), or the initial tax will be abated or refunded, if the organization or an organization manager establishes to the satisfaction of the IRS that—

(1) The political expenditure was not willful and flagrant; and

(2) The political expenditure was corrected.

(e) Correction—(1) Recovery of Expenditure. For purposes of section 4955(f)(3) and this section, correction of a political expenditure is accomplished by recovering part or all of the expenditure to the extent recovery is possible, and, where full recovery cannot be accomplished, by any additional corrective action which the Commissioner may prescribe. The organization making the political expenditure is not under any obligation to attempt to recover the expenditure by legal action if the action would in all probability not result in the satisfaction of execution on a judgment.

(2) Establishing safeguards. Correction of a political expenditure must also involve the establishment of sufficient safeguards to prevent future political expenditures by the organization. The determination of whether safeguards are sufficient to prevent future political expenditures by the organization is made by the District Director.

* * *

INTERMEDIATE SANCTIONS

§ 53.4958–1. Taxes on excess benefit transactions.

(a) In general. Section 4958 imposes excise taxes on each excess benefit transaction (as defined in section 4958(c) and § 53.4958–4) between an applicable tax-exempt organization (as defined in section 4958(e) and § 53.4958–2) and a disqualified person (as defined in section 4958(f)(1) and § 53.4958–3). A disqualified person who receives an excess benefit from an excess benefit transaction is liable for payment of a section 4958(a)(1) excise tax equal to 25 percent of the excess benefit. If an initial tax is imposed by section 4958(a)(1) on an excess benefit transaction and the transaction is not corrected (as defined in section 4958(f)(6) and § 53.4958–7) within the taxable period (as defined in section 4958(f)(5) and paragraph (c)(2)(ii) of this section), then any disqualified person who received an excess benefit from the excess benefit transaction on which the initial tax was imposed is liable for an additional tax of 200 percent of the excess benefit. An organization manager (as defined in section 4958(f)(2) and paragraph (d) of this section) who participates in an excess benefit transaction, knowing that it was such a transaction, is liable for payment of a section 4958(a)(2) excise tax equal to 10 percent of the excess benefit, unless the participation was not willful and was due to reasonable cause. If an organization manager also receives an excess benefit from an excess benefit transaction, the manager may be liable for both taxes imposed by section 4958(a).

(b) Excess benefit defined. An excess benefit is the amount by which the value of the economic benefit provided by an applicable tax-exempt organization directly or indirectly to or for the use of any disqualified person exceeds the value of the consideration (including the performance of services) received for providing such benefit.

(c) Taxes paid by disqualified person—(1) Initial tax. Section 4958(a)(1) imposes a tax equal to 25 percent of the excess benefit on each excess benefit transaction. The section 4958(a)(1) tax shall be paid by any disqualified person who received an excess benefit from that excess benefit transaction. With respect to any excess benefit transaction, if more than one disqualified person is liable for the tax imposed by section 4958(a)(1), all such persons are jointly and severally liable for that tax.

(2) Additional tax on disqualified person—(i) In general. Section 4958(b) imposes a tax equal to 200 percent of the excess benefit in any case in which section 4958(a)(1) imposes a 25-percent tax on an excess benefit transaction and the transaction is not corrected (as defined in section 4958(f)(6) and § 53.4958–7) within the taxable period (as defined in section 4958(f)(5) and paragraph (c)(2)(ii) of this section). If a disqualified person makes a payment of less than the full correction amount under the rules of § 53.4958–7, the 200-percent tax is imposed only on the unpaid portion of the correction amount (as described in § 53.4958–7(c)). The tax imposed by section 4958(b) is payable by any disqualified person who received an excess benefit from the excess benefit transaction on which the initial tax was imposed by section 4958(a)(1). With respect to any excess benefit transaction, if more than one disqualified person is liable for the tax imposed by section 4958(b), all such persons are jointly and severally liable for that tax.

(ii) Taxable period. Taxable period means, with respect to any excess benefit transaction, the period beginning with the date on which the transaction occurs and ending on the earlier of—

(A) The date of mailing a notice of deficiency under section 6212 with respect to the section 4958(a)(1) tax; or

(B) The date on which the tax imposed by section 4958(a)(1) is assessed.

(iii) Abatement if correction during the correction period. For rules relating to abatement of taxes on excess benefit transactions that are corrected within the correction period, as defined in section 4963(e), see sections 4961(a), 4962(a), and the regulations thereunder. The abatement rules of section 4961 specifically provide for a 90-day correction period after the date of mailing a notice of deficiency under section 6212 with respect to the section 4958(b) 200-percent tax. If the excess benefit is corrected during that correction period, the 200-percent tax imposed shall not be assessed, and if assessed the assessment shall be abated, and if collected shall be credited or refunded as an overpayment. For special rules relating to abatement of the 25-percent tax, see section 4962.

(d) Tax paid by organization managers—(1) In general. In any case in which section 4958(a)(1) imposes a tax, section 4958(a)(2) imposes a tax equal to 10 percent of the excess benefit on the participation of any organization manager who knowingly participated in the excess benefit transaction, unless such participation was not willful and was due to reasonable cause. Any organization manager who so participated in the excess benefit transaction must pay the tax.

(2) Organization manager defined—(i) In general. An organization manager is, with respect to any applicable tax-exempt organization, any officer, director, or trustee of such organization, or any individual having powers or responsibilities similar to those of officers, directors, or trustees of the organization, regardless of title. A person is an officer of an organization if that person—

(A) Is specifically so designated under the certificate of incorporation, by-laws, or other constitutive documents of the organization; or

(B) Regularly exercises general authority to make administrative or policy decisions on behalf of the organization. A contractor who acts solely in a capacity as an attorney, accountant, or investment manager or advisor, is not an officer. For purposes of this paragraph (d)(2)(i)(B), any person who has authority merely to recommend particular administrative or policy decisions, but not to implement them without approval of a superior, is not an officer.

(ii) Special rule for certain committee members. An individual who is not an officer, director, or trustee, yet serves on a committee of the governing body of an applicable tax-exempt organization (or as a designee of the governing body described in § 53.4958–6(c)(1)) that is attempting to invoke the rebuttable presumption of reasonableness described in § 53.4958–6 based on the committee's (or designee's) actions, is an organization manager for purposes of the tax imposed by section 4958(a)(2).

(3) Participation. For purposes of section 4958(a)(2) and this paragraph (d), participation includes silence or inaction on the part of an organization manager where the manager is under a duty to speak or act, as well as any affirmative action by such manager. An organization manager is not considered to have participated in an excess benefit transaction, however, where the manager has opposed the transaction in a manner consistent with the fulfillment of the manager's responsibilities to the applicable tax-exempt organization.

(4) Knowing—(i) In general. For purposes of section 4958(a)(2) and this paragraph (d), a manager participates in a transaction knowingly only if the person—

(A) Has actual knowledge of sufficient facts so that, based solely upon those facts, such transaction would be an excess benefit transaction;

(B) Is aware that such a transaction under these circumstances may violate the provisions of Federal tax law governing excess benefit transactions; and

(C) Negligently fails to make reasonable attempts to ascertain whether the transaction is an excess benefit transaction, or the manager is in fact aware that it is such a transaction.

(ii) Amplification of general rule. Knowing does not mean having reason to know. However, evidence tending to show that a manager has reason to know of a particular fact or particular rule is relevant in determining whether the manager had actual knowledge of such a fact or rule. Thus, for example, evidence tending to show that a manager has reason to know of sufficient facts so that, based solely upon such facts, a transaction would be an excess benefit transaction is relevant in determining whether the manager has actual knowledge of such facts.

(iii) Reliance on professional advice. An organization manager's participation in a transaction is ordinarily not considered knowing within the meaning of section 4958(a)(2), even though the transaction is subsequently held to be an excess benefit transaction, to the extent that, after full disclosure of the factual situation to an appropriate professional, the organization manager relies on a reasoned written opinion of that professional with respect to elements of the transaction within the professional's expertise. For purposes of section 4958(a)(2) and this paragraph (d), a written opinion is reasoned even though it reaches a conclusion that is subsequently determined to be incorrect so long as the opinion addresses itself to the facts and the applicable standards. However, a written opinion is not reasoned if it does nothing more than recite the facts and express a conclusion. The absence of a written opinion of an appropriate professional with respect to a transaction shall not, by itself, however, give rise to any inference that an organization manager participated in the transaction knowingly. For purposes of this paragraph, appropriate professionals on whose written opinion an organization manager may rely, are limited to—

(A) Legal counsel, including in-house counsel;

(B) Certified public accountants or accounting firms with expertise regarding the relevant tax law matters; and

(C) Independent valuation experts who—

(1) Hold themselves out to the public as appraisers or compensation consultants;

(2) Perform the relevant valuations on a regular basis;

(3) Are qualified to make valuations of the type of property or services involved; and

(4) Include in the written opinion a certification that the requirements of paragraphs (d)(4)(iii)(C)(1) through (3) of this section are met.

(iv) Satisfaction of rebuttable presumption of reasonableness. An organization manager's participation in a transaction is ordinarily not considered knowing within the meaning of section 4958(a)(2), even though the transaction is subsequently held to be an excess benefit transaction, if the appropriate authorized body has met the requirements of § 53.4958–6(a) with respect to the transaction.

(5) Willful. For purposes of section 4958(a)(2) and this paragraph (d), participation by an organization manager is willful if it is voluntary, conscious, and intentional. No motive to avoid the restrictions of the law or the incurrence of any tax is necessary to make the participation willful. However, participation by an organization manager is not willful if the manager does not know that the transaction in which the manager is participating is an excess benefit transaction.

(6) Due to reasonable cause. An organization manager's participation is due to reasonable cause if the manager has exercised responsibility on behalf of the organization with ordinary business care and prudence.

(7) Limits on liability for management. The maximum aggregate amount of tax collectible under section 4958(a)(2) and this paragraph (d)from organization managers with respect to any one excess benefit transaction is $10,000.

(8) Joint and several liability. In any case where more than one person is liable for a tax imposed by section 4958(a)(2), all such persons shall be jointly and severally liable for the taxes imposed under section 4958(a)(2) with respect to that excess benefit transaction.

(9) Burden of proof. For provisions relating to the burden of proof in cases involving the issue of whether an organization manager has knowingly participated in an excess benefit transaction, see section 7454(b) and § 301.7454–2 of this chapter. In these cases, the Commissioner bears the burden of proof.

(e) Date of occurrence—(1) In general. Except as otherwise provided, an excess benefit transaction occurs on the date on which the disqualified person receives the economic benefit for Federal income tax purposes. When a single contractual arrangement provides for a series of compensation or other payments to (or for the use of) a disqualified person over the course of the disqualified person's taxable year (or part of a taxable year), any excess benefit transaction with respect to these aggregate payments is deemed to occur on the last day of the taxable year (or if the payments continue for part of the year, the date of the last payment in the series).

(2) Special rules. In the case of benefits provided pursuant to a qualified pension, profit-sharing, or stock bonus plan, the transaction occurs on the date the benefit is vested. In the case of a transfer of property that is subject to a substantial risk of forfeiture or in the case of rights to future compensation or property (including benefits under a nonqualified deferred compensation plan), the transaction occurs on the date the property, or the rights to future compensation or property, is not subject to a substantial risk of forfeiture. However, where the disqualified person elects to include an amount in gross income in the taxable year of transfer pursuant to section 83(b), the general rule of paragraph (e)(1) of this section applies to the property with respect to which the section 83(b) election is made. Any excess benefit transaction with respect to benefits under a deferred compensation plan which vest during any taxable year of the disqualified person is deemed to occur on the last day of such taxable year. For the rules governing the timing of the reasonableness determination for deferred, contingent, and certain other noncash compensation, see § 53.4958–4(b)(2).

(3) Statute of limitations rules. See sections 6501(e)(3) and (*l*) and the regulations thereunder for statute of limitations rules as they apply to section 4958 excise taxes.

(f) Effective date for imposition of taxes—(1) In general. The section 4958 taxes imposed on excess benefit transactions or on participation in excess benefit transactions apply to transactions occurring on or after September 14, 1995.

* * *

§ 53.4958–2. Definition of applicable tax-exempt organization.

(a) Organizations described in section 501(c)(3) or (4) and exempt from tax under section 501(a)—(1) In general. An applicable tax-exempt organization is any organization that, without regard to any excess benefit, would be described in section 501(c)(3) or (4) and exempt from tax under section 501(a). An applicable tax-exempt organization also includes any organization that was described in section 501(c)(3) or (4) and was exempt from tax under section 501(a) at any time during a five-year period ending on the date of an excess benefit transaction (the lookback period).

(2) Exceptions from definition of applicable tax-exempt organization—(i) Private foundation. A private foundation as defined in section 509(a) is not an applicable tax-exempt organization for section 4958 purposes.

(ii) Governmental unit or affiliate. A governmental unit or an affiliate of a governmental unit is not an applicable tax-exempt organization for section 4958 purposes if it is—

(A) Exempt from (or not subject to) taxation without regard to section 501(a); or

(B) Relieved from filing an annual return pursuant to the authority of § 1.6033–2(g)(6).

(3) Organizations described in section 501(c)(3). An organization is described in section 501(c)(3) for purposes of section 4958 only if the organization—

(i) Provides the notice described in section 508; or

(ii) Is described in section 501(c)(3) and specifically is excluded from the requirements of section 508 by that section.

(4) Organizations described in section 501(c)(4). An organization is described in section 501(c)(4) for purposes of section 4958 only if the organization—

(i) Has applied for and received recognition from the Internal Revenue Service as an organization described in section 501(c)(4); or

(ii) Has filed an application for recognition under section 501(c)(4) with the Internal Revenue Service, has filed an annual information return as a section 501(c)(4) organization under the Internal Revenue Code or regulations promulgated thereunder, or has otherwise held itself out as being described in section 501(c)(4) and exempt from tax under section 501(a).

(5) Effect of non-recognition or revocation of exempt status. An organization is not described in paragraph (a)(3) or (4) of this section during any period covered by a final determination or adjudication that the organization is not exempt from tax under section 501(a) as an organization described in section 501(c)(3) or (4), so long as that determination or adjudication is not based upon participation in inurement or one or more excess benefit transactions. However, the organization may be an applicable tax-exempt organization for that period as a result of the five-year lookback period described in paragraph (a)(1) of this section.

(6) Examples. The following examples illustrate the principles of this section, which defines an applicable tax-exempt organization for purposes of section 4958:

Example 1. O is a nonprofit corporation formed under state law. O filed its application for recognition of exemption under section 501(c)(3) within the time prescribed under section 508(a). In its application, O described its plans for purchasing property from some of its directors at prices that would exceed fair market value. After reviewing the application, the IRS determined that because of the proposed property purchase transactions, O failed to establish that it met the requirements for an organization described in section 501(c)(3). Accordingly, the IRS denied O's application. While O's application was pending, O engaged in the purchase transactions described in its application at prices that exceeded the fair market value of the property. Although these transactions would constitute excess benefit transactions under section 4958, because the IRS never recognized O as an organization described in section 501(c)(3), O was never an applicable tax-exempt organization under section 4958. Therefore, these transactions are not subject to the excise taxes provided in section 4958.

Example 2. O is a nonprofit corporation formed under state law. O files its application for recognition of exemption under section 501(c)(3) within the time prescribed under section 508(a). The IRS issues a favorable determination letter in Year 1 that recognizes O as an organization described in section 501(c)(3). Subsequently, in Year 5 of O's operations, O engages in certain transactions that constitute excess benefit transactions under section 4958 and violate the proscription against inurement under section 501(c)(3) and § 1.501(c)(3)–1(c)(2). The IRS examines the Form 990, "Return of Organization Exempt From Income Tax", that O filed for Year 5. After considering all the relevant facts and circumstances in accordance with § 1.501(c)(3)–1(g), the IRS concludes that O is no longer described in section 501(c)(3) effective in Year 5. The IRS does not examine the Forms 990 that O filed for its first four years of operations and, accordingly, does not revoke O's exempt status for those years. Although O's tax-exempt status is revoked effective in Year 5, under the lookback rules in § 53.4958–2(a)(1) and § 53.4958–3(a)(1) of this chapter, for a period of five years prior to the excess benefit transactions that occurred in Year 5, O was an applicable tax-exempt organization and O's directors were disqualified persons as to O. Therefore, the transactions between O and its directors during Year 5 are subject to the appropriate excise taxes provided in section 4958.

(b) Special rules—(1) Transition rule for lookback period. In the case of any excess benefit transaction occurring before September 14, 2000, the lookback period described in paragraph (a)(1) of this section begins on September 14, 1995, and ends on the date of the transaction.

(2) Certain foreign organizations. A foreign organization, recognized by the Internal Revenue Service or by treaty, that receives substantially all of its support (other than gross investment income) from sources outside of the United States is not an organization described in section 501(c)(3) or (4) for purposes of section 4958.

§ 53.4958–3. Definition of disqualified person.

(a) In general—(1) Scope of definition. Section 4958(f)(1) defines disqualified person, with respect to any transaction, as any person who was in a position to exercise substantial influence over the affairs of an applicable tax-exempt organization at any time during the five-year period ending on the date of the transaction (the lookback period). Paragraph (b) of this section describes persons who are defined to be disqualified persons under the statute, including certain family members of an individual in a position to exercise substantial influence, and certain 35-percent controlled entities. Paragraph (c) of this section describes persons in a position to exercise substantial influence over the affairs of an applicable tax-exempt organization by virtue of their powers and responsibilities or certain interests they hold. Paragraph (d) of this section describes persons deemed not to be in a position to exercise substantial influence. Whether any person who is not described in paragraph (b), (c) or (d) of this section is a disqualified person with respect to a transaction for purposes of section 4958 is based on all relevant facts and circumstances, as described in paragraph (e) of this section. Paragraph (f) of this section describes special rules for affiliated organizations. Examples in paragraph (g) of this section illustrate these categories of persons.

(2) Transition rule for lookback period. In the case of any excess benefit transaction occurring before September 14, 2000, the lookback period described in paragraph (a)(1) of this section begins on September 14, 1995, and ends on the date of the transaction.

(b) Statutory categories of disqualified persons—(1) Family members. A person is a disqualified person with respect to any transaction with an applicable tax-exempt organization if the person is a member of the family of a person who is a disqualified person described in paragraph (a) of this section (other than as a result of this paragraph) with respect to any transaction with the same organization. For purposes of the following sentence, a legally adopted child of an individual is treated as a child of such individual by blood. A person's family is limited to—

(i) Spouse;

(ii) Brothers or sisters (by whole or half blood);

(iii) Spouses of brothers or sisters (by whole or half blood);

(iv) Ancestors;

(v) Children;

(vi) Grandchildren;

(vii) Great grandchildren; and

(viii) Spouses of children, grandchildren, and great grandchildren.

(2) Thirty-five percent controlled entities—(i) In general. A person is a disqualified person with respect to any transaction with an applicable tax-exempt organization if the person is a 35-percent controlled entity. A 35-percent controlled entity is—

(A) A corporation in which persons described in this section (except in paragraphs (b)(2) and (d) of this section) own more than 35 percent of the combined voting power;

(B) A partnership in which persons described in this section (except in paragraphs (b)(2) and (d) of this section) own more than 35 percent of the profits interest; or

(C) A trust or estate in which persons described in this section (except in paragraphs (b)(2) and (d) of this section) own more than 35 percent of the beneficial interest.

(ii) Combined voting power. For purposes of this paragraph (b)(2), combined voting power includes voting power represented by holdings of voting stock, direct or indirect, but does not include voting rights held only as a director, trustee, or other fiduciary.

(iii) Constructive ownership rules—(A) Stockholdings. For purposes of section 4958(f)(3) and this paragraph (b)(2), indirect stockholdings are taken into account as under section 267(c), except that in applying section 267(c)(4), the family of an individual shall include the members of the family specified in section 4958(f)(4) and paragraph (b)(1) of this section.

(B) Profits or beneficial interest. For purposes of section 4958(f)(3) and this paragraph (b)(2), the ownership of profits or beneficial interests shall be determined in accordance with the rules for constructive ownership of stock provided in section 267(c) (other than section 267(c)(3)), except that in applying section 267(c)(4), the family of an individual shall include the members of the family specified in section 4958(f)(4) and paragraph (b)(1) of this section.

(c) Persons having substantial influence. A person who holds any of the following powers, responsibilities, or interests is in a position to exercise substantial influence over the affairs of an applicable tax-exempt organization:

(1) Voting members of the governing body. This category includes any individual serving on the governing body of the organization who is entitled to vote on any matter over which the governing body has authority.

(2) Presidents, chief executive officers, or chief operating officers. This category includes any person who, regardless of title, has ultimate responsibility for implementing the decisions of the governing body or for supervising the management, administration, or operation of the organization. A person who serves as president, chief executive officer, or chief operating officer has this ultimate responsibility unless the person demonstrates otherwise. If this ultimate responsibility resides with two or more individuals (e.g., co-presidents), who may exercise such responsibility in concert or individually, then each individual is in a position to exercise substantial influence over the affairs of the organization.

(3) Treasurers and chief financial officers. This category includes any person who, regardless of title, has ultimate responsibility for managing the finances of the organization. A person who serves as treasurer or chief financial officer has this ultimate responsibility unless the person demonstrates otherwise. If this ultimate responsibility resides with two or more individuals who may exercise the responsibility in concert or individually, then each individual is in a position to exercise substantial influence over the affairs of the organization.

(4) Persons with a material financial interest in a provider-sponsored organization. For purposes of section 4958, if a hospital that participates in a provider-sponsored organization (as defined in section 1855(e) of the Social Security Act, 42 U.S.C. 1395w–25) is an applicable tax-exempt organization, then any person with a material financial interest (within the meaning of section 501(*o*)) in the provider-sponsored organization has substantial influence with respect to the hospital.

(d) Persons deemed not to have substantial influence. A person is deemed not to be in a position to exercise substantial influence over the affairs of an applicable tax-exempt organization if that person is described in one of the following categories:

(1) Tax-exempt organizations described in section 501(c)(3). This category includes any organization described in section 501(c)(3) and exempt from tax under section 501(a).

(2) Certain section 501(c)(4) organizations. Only with respect to an applicable tax-exempt organization described in section 501(c)(4) and § 53.4958–2(a)(4), this category includes any other organization so described.

(3) Employees receiving economic benefits of less than a specified amount in a taxable year. This category includes, for the taxable year in which benefits are provided, any full- or part-time employee of the applicable tax-exempt organization who—

(i) Receives economic benefits, directly or indirectly from the organization, of less than the amount referenced for a highly compensated employee in section 414(q)(1)(B)(i);

(ii) Is not described in paragraph (b) or (c) of this section with respect to the organization; and

(iii) Is not a substantial contributor to the organization within the meaning of section 507(d)(2)(A), taking into account only contributions received by the organization during its current taxable year and the four preceding taxable years.

(e) Facts and circumstances govern in all other cases—(1) In general. Whether a person who is not described in paragraph (b), (c) or (d) of this section is a disqualified person depends upon all relevant facts and circumstances.

(2) Facts and circumstances tending to show substantial influence. Facts and circumstances tending to show that a person has substantial influence over the affairs of an organization include, but are not limited to, the following—

(i) The person founded the organization;

(ii) The person is a substantial contributor to the organization (within the meaning of section 507(d)(2)(A)), taking into account only contributions received by the organization during its current taxable year and the four preceding taxable years;

(iii) The person's compensation is primarily based on revenues derived from activities of the organization, or of a particular department or function of the organization, that the person controls;

(iv) The person has or shares authority to control or determine a substantial portion of the organization's capital expenditures, operating budget, or compensation for employees;

(v) The person manages a discrete segment or activity of the organization that represents a substantial portion of the activities, assets, income, or expenses of the organization, as compared to the organization as a whole;

(vi) The person owns a controlling interest (measured by either vote or value) in a corporation, partnership, or trust that is a disqualified person; or

(vii) The person is a non-stock organization controlled, directly or indirectly, by one or more disqualified persons.

(3) Facts and circumstances tending to show no substantial influence. Facts and circumstances tending to show that a person does not have substantial influence over the affairs of an organization include, but are not limited to, the following—

(i) The person has taken a bona fide vow of poverty as an employee, agent, or on behalf, of a religious organization;

(ii) The person is a contractor (such as an attorney, accountant, or investment manager or advisor) whose sole relationship to the organization is providing professional advice (without having decision-making authority) with respect to transactions from which the contractor will not economically benefit either directly or indirectly (aside from customary fees received for the professional advice rendered);

(iii) The direct supervisor of the individual is not a disqualified person;

(iv) The person does not participate in any management decisions affecting the organization as a whole or a discrete segment or activity of the organization that represents a substantial portion of the activities, assets, income, or expenses of the organization, as compared to the organization as a whole; or

(v) Any preferential treatment a person receives based on the size of that person's contribution is also offered to all other donors making a comparable contribution as part of a solicitation intended to attract a substantial number of contributions.

(f) Affiliated organizations. In the case of multiple organizations affiliated by common control or governing documents, the determination of whether a person does or does not have substantial influence shall be made separately for each applicable tax-exempt organization. A person may be a disqualified person with respect to transactions with more than one applicable tax-exempt organization.

(g) Examples. The following examples illustrate the principles of this section. A finding that a person is a disqualified person in the following examples does not indicate that an excess benefit transaction has occurred. If a person is a disqualified person, the rules of section 4958(c) and § 53.4958–4 apply to determine whether an excess benefit transaction has occurred. The examples are as follows:

Example 1. N, an artist by profession, works part-time at R, a local museum. In the first taxable year in which R employs N, R pays N a salary and provides no additional benefits to N except for free admission to the museum, a benefit R provides to all of its employees and volunteers. The total economic benefits N receives from R during the taxable year are less than the amount referenced for a highly compensated employee in section 414(q)(1)(B)(i). The part-time job constitutes N's only relationship with R. N is not related to any other disqualified person with respect to R. N is deemed not to be in a position to exercise substantial influence over the affairs of R. Therefore, N is not a disqualified person with respect to R in that year.

Example 2. The facts are the same as in Example 1, except that in addition to the salary that R pays N for N's services during the taxable year, R also purchases one of N's paintings for $x. The total of N's salary plus $x exceeds the amount referenced for highly compensated employees in section 414(q)(1)(B)(i). Consequently, whether N is in a position to exercise substantial influence over the affairs of R for that taxable year depends upon all of the relevant facts and circumstances.

Example 3. Q is a member of K, a section 501(c)(3) organization with a broad-based public membership. Members of K are entitled to vote only with respect to the annual election of directors and the approval of major organizational transactions such as a merger or dissolution. Q is not related to any other disqualified person of K. Q has no other relationship to K besides being a member of K and occasionally making modest donations to K. Whether Q is a disqualified person is determined by all relevant facts and circumstances. Q's voting rights, which are the same as granted to all members of K, do not place Q in a position to exercise substantial influence over K. Under these facts and circumstances, Q is not a disqualified person with respect [to] K.

Example 4. E is the headmaster of Z, a school that is an applicable tax-exempt organization for purposes of section 4958. E reports to Z's board of trustees and has ultimate responsibility for supervising Z's day-to-day operations. For example, E can hire faculty members and staff, make changes to the school's curriculum and discipline students without specific board approval. Because E has ultimate responsibility for supervising the operation of Z, E is in a position to exercise substantial influence over the affairs of Z. Therefore, E is a disqualified person with respect to Z.

Example 5. Y is an applicable tax-exempt organization for purposes of section 4958 that decides to use bingo games as a method of generating revenue. Y enters into a contract with B, a company that operates bingo games. Under the contract, B manages the promotion and operation of the bingo activity, provides all necessary staff, equipment, and services, and pays Y q percent of the revenue from this activity. B retains the balance of the proceeds. Y provides no goods or services in connection with the bingo operation other than the use of its hall for the bingo games. The annual gross revenue earned from the bingo games represents more than half of Y's total annual revenue. B's compensation is primarily based on revenues from an activity B controls. B also manages a discrete activity of Y that represents a substantial portion of Y's income compared to the organization as a whole. Under these facts and circumstances, B is in a position to exercise substantial influence over the affairs of Y. Therefore, B is a disqualified person with respect to Y.

Example 6. The facts are the same as in Example 5, with the additional fact that P owns a majority of the stock of B and is actively involved in managing B. Because P owns a controlling interest (measured by either vote or value) in and actively manages B, P is also in a position to exercise substantial influence over the affairs of Y. Therefore, under these facts and circumstances, P is a disqualified person with respect to Y.

Example 7. A, an applicable tax-exempt organization for purposes of section 4958, owns and operates one acute care hospital. B, a for-profit corporation, owns and operates a number of hospitals. A and B form C, a limited liability company. In exchange for proportional ownership interests, A contributes its hospital, and B contributes other assets, to C. All of A's assets then consist of its membership interest in C. A continues to be operated for exempt purposes based almost exclusively on the activities it conducts through C. C enters into a management agreement with a management company, M, to provide day to day management services to C. Subject to supervision by C's board, M is given broad discretion to manage C's day to day operation and has ultimate responsibility for supervising the management of the hospital. Because M has ultimate responsibility for supervising the management of the hospital operated by C, A's ownership interest in C is its primary asset, and C's activities form the basis for A's continued exemption as an organization described in section 501(c)(3), M is in a position to exercise substantial influence over the affairs of A. Therefore, M is a disqualified person with respect to A.

Example 8. T is a large university and an applicable tax-exempt organization for purposes of section 4958. L is the dean of the College of Law of T, a substantial source of revenue for T, including contributions from alumni and foundations. L is not related to any other disqualified person of T. L does not serve on T's governing body or have ultimate responsibility for managing the university as whole. However, as dean of the College of Law, L plays a key role in faculty hiring and determines a substantial portion of the capital expenditures and operating budget of the College of Law. L's compensation is greater than the amount referenced for a highly compensated employee in section 414(q)(1)(B)(i) in the year benefits are provided. L's management of a discrete segment of T that represents a substantial portion of the income of T (as compared to T as a whole) places L in a position to exercise substantial influence over the affairs of T. Under these facts and circumstances L is a disqualified person with respect to T.

Example 9. S chairs a small academic department in the College of Arts and Sciences of the same university T described in Example 8. S is not related to any other disqualified person of T. S does not serve on T's governing body or as an officer of T. As department chair, S supervises faculty in the department, approves the course curriculum, and oversees the operating budget for the department. S's compensation is greater than the amount referenced for a highly compensated employee in section 414(q)(1)(B)(i) in the year benefits are provided. Even though S manages the department, that department does not represent a substantial portion of T's activities, assets, income, expenses, or operating budget. Therefore, S does not participate in any management decisions affecting either T as a whole, or a discrete segment or activity of T that represents a substantial portion of its activities, assets, income, or expenses. Under these facts and circumstances, S does not have substantial influence over the affairs of T, and therefore S is not a disqualified person with respect to T.

Example 10. U is a large acute-care hospital that is an applicable tax-exempt organization for purposes of section 4958. U employs X as a radiologist. X gives instructions to staff with respect to the radiology work X conducts, but X does not supervise other U employees or manage any substantial part of U's operations. X's compensation is primarily in the form of a fixed salary. In addition, X is eligible to receive an incentive award based on revenues of the radiology department. X's compensation is greater than the amount referenced for a highly compensated employee in section 414(q)(1)(B)(i) in the year benefits are provided. X is not related to any other disqualified person of U. X does not serve on U's governing body or as an officer of U. Although U participates in a provider-sponsored organization (as defined in section 1855(e) of the Social Security Act), X does not have a material financial interest in that organization. X does not receive compensation primarily based on revenues derived from activities of U that X controls. X does not participate in any management decisions affecting either U as a whole or a discrete segment of U that represents a substantial portion of its activities, assets, income, or expenses. Under these facts and circumstances, X does not have substantial influence over the affairs of U, and therefore X is not a disqualified person with respect to U.

Example 11. W is a cardiologist and head of the cardiology department of the same hospital U described in Example 10. The cardiology department is a major source of patients admitted to U and consequently represents a substantial portion of U's income, as compared to U as a whole. W does not serve on U's governing board or as an officer of U. W does not have a material financial interest in the provider-sponsored organization (as defined in section 1855(e) of the Social Security Act) in which U participates. W receives a salary and retirement and welfare benefits fixed by a three-year renewable employment contract with U. W's compensation is greater than the amount referenced for a highly compensated employee in section 414(q)(1)(B)(i) in the year benefits are provided. As department head, W manages the cardiology department and has authority to allocate the budget for that department, which includes authority to distribute incentive bonuses among cardiologists according to criteria that W has authority to set. W's management of a discrete segment of U that represents a substantial portion of its income and activities (as compared to U as a whole) places W in a position to exercise substantial influence over the affairs of U. Under these facts and circumstances, W is a disqualified person with respect to U.

Example 12. M is a museum that is an applicable tax-exempt organization for purposes of section 4958. D provides accounting services and tax advice to M as a contractor in return for a fee. D has no other relationship with M and is not related to any disqualified person of M. D does not provide professional advice with respect to any transaction from which D might economically benefit either directly or indirectly (aside from fees received for the professional advice rendered). Because D's sole relationship to M is providing professional advice (without having decision-making authority) with respect to transactions from which D will not economically benefit either directly or indirectly (aside from customary fees received for the professional advice rendered), under these facts and circumstances, D is not a disqualified person with respect to M.

Example 13. F is a repertory theater company that is an applicable tax-exempt organization for purposes of section 4958. F holds a fund-raising campaign to pay for the construction of a new theater. J is a regular subscriber to F's productions who has made modest gifts to F in the past. J has no relationship to F other than as a subscriber and contributor. F solicits contributions as part of a broad public campaign intended to attract a large number of donors, including a substantial number of donors making large gifts. In its solicitations for contributions, F promises to invite all contributors giving $z or more to a special opening production and party held at the new theater. These contributors are also given a special number to call in F's office to reserve tickets for performances, make ticket exchanges, and make other special arrangements for their convenience. J makes a contribution of $z to F, which makes J a substantial contributor within the meaning of section 507(d)(2)(A), taking into account only contributions received by F during its current and the four preceding taxable years. J receives the benefits described in F's solicitation. Because F offers the same benefit to all donors of $z or more, the preferential treatment that J receives does not indicate that J is in a position to exercise substantial influence over the affairs of the organization. Therefore, under these facts and circumstances, J is not a disqualified person with respect to F.

§ 53.4958–4. Excess benefit transaction.

(a) Definition of excess benefit transaction—(1) In general. An excess benefit transaction means any transaction in which an economic benefit is provided by an applicable tax-exempt organization directly or indirectly to or for the use of any disqualified person, and the value of the economic benefit provided exceeds the value of the consideration (including the performance of services) received for providing the benefit. Subject to the limitations of paragraph (c) of this section (relating to the treatment of economic benefits as compensation for the performance of services), to determine whether an excess benefit transaction has occurred, all consideration and benefits (except disregarded benefits described in paragraph (a)(4) of this section) exchanged between a disqualified person and the applicable tax-exempt organization and all entities the organization controls (within the meaning of paragraph (a)(2)(ii)(B) of this section) are taken into account. For example, in determining the reasonableness of compensation that is paid (or vests, or is no longer subject to a substantial risk of forfeiture) in one year, services performed in prior years may be taken into account. The rules of this section apply to all transactions with disqualified persons, regardless of whether the amount of the benefit provided is determined, in whole or in part, by the revenues of one or more activities of the organization. For rules regarding valuation standards, see paragraph (b) of this section. For the requirement that an applicable tax-exempt organization clearly indicate its intent to treat a benefit as compensation for services when paid, see paragraph (c) of this section.

(2) Economic benefit provided indirectly—(i) In general. A transaction that would be an excess benefit transaction if the applicable tax-exempt organization engaged in it directly with a disqualified person is likewise an excess benefit transaction when it is accomplished indirectly. An applicable tax-exempt organization may provide an excess benefit indirectly to a disqualified person through a controlled entity or through an intermediary, as described in paragraphs (a)(2)(ii) and (iii) of this section, respectively.

(ii) Through a controlled entity—(A) In general. An applicable tax-exempt organization may provide an excess benefit indirectly through the use of one or more entities it controls. For purposes of section 4958, economic benefits provided by a controlled entity will be treated as provided by the applicable tax-exempt organization.

(B) Definition of control—(1) In general. For purposes of this paragraph, control by an applicable tax-exempt organization means—

(i) In the case of a stock corporation, ownership (by vote or value) of more than 50 percent of the stock in such corporation;

(ii) In the case of a partnership, ownership of more than 50 percent of the profits interests or capital interests in the partnership;

(iii) In the case of a nonstock organization (i.e., an entity in which no person holds a proprietary interest), that at least 50 percent of the directors or trustees of the organization are either representatives (including trustees, directors, agents, or employees) of, or directly or indirectly controlled by, an applicable tax-exempt organization; or

(iv) In the case of any other entity, ownership of more than 50 percent of the beneficial interest in the entity.

(2) Constructive ownership. Section 318 (relating to constructive ownership of stock) shall apply for purposes of determining ownership of stock in a corporation. Similar principles shall apply for purposes of determining ownership of interests in any other entity.

(iii) Through an intermediary. An applicable tax-exempt organization may provide an excess benefit indirectly through an intermediary. An intermediary is any person (including an individual or a taxable or tax-exempt entity) who participates in a transaction with one or more disqualified persons of an applicable tax-exempt organization. For purposes of section 4958, economic benefits provided by an intermediary will be treated as provided by the applicable tax-exempt organization when—

(A) An applicable tax-exempt organization provides an economic benefit to an intermediary; and

(B) In connection with the receipt of the benefit by the intermediary—

(1) There is evidence of an oral or written agreement or understanding that the intermediary will provide economic benefits to or for the use of a disqualified person; or

(2) The intermediary provides economic benefits to or for the use of a disqualified person without a significant business purpose or exempt purpose of its own.

(iv) Examples. The following examples illustrate when economic benefits are provided indirectly under the rules of this paragraph (a)(2):

Example 1. K is an applicable tax-exempt organization for purposes of section 4958. L is a wholly-owned taxable subsidiary of K. J is employed by K, and is a disqualified person with respect to K. K pays J an annual salary of $12m, and reports that amount as compensation during calendar year 2001. Although J only performed services for K for nine months of 2001, J performed equivalent services for L during the remaining three months of 2001. Taking into account all of the economic benefits K provided to J, and all of the services J performed for K and L, $12m does not exceed the fair market value of the services J performed for K and L during 2001. Therefore, under these facts, K does not provide an excess benefit to J directly or indirectly.

Example 2. F is an applicable tax-exempt organization for purposes of section 4958. D is an entity controlled by F within the meaning of paragraph (a)(2)(ii)(B) of this section. T is the chief executive officer (CEO) of F. As CEO, T is responsible for overseeing the activities of F. T's duties as CEO make him a disqualified person with respect to F. T's compensation package with F represents the maximum reasonable compensation for T's services as CEO. Thus, any additional economic benefits that F provides to T without T providing additional consideration constitute an excess benefit. D contracts with T to provide enumerated consulting services to D. However, the contract does not require T to perform any additional services for D that T is not already obligated to perform as F's chief executive officer. Therefore, any payment to T pursuant to the consulting contract with D represents an indirect excess benefit that F provides through a controlled entity, even if F, D, or T treats the additional payment to T as compensation.

Example 3. P is an applicable tax-exempt organization for purposes of section 4958. S is a taxable entity controlled by P within the meaning of paragraph (a)(2)(ii)(B) of this section. V is the chief executive officer of S, for which S pays V $w in salary and benefits. V also serves as a voting member of P's governing body. Consequently, V is a disqualified person with respect to P. P provides V with $x representing compensation for the services V provides P as a member of its governing body. Although $x represents reasonable compensation for the services V provides directly to P as a member of its governing body, the total compensation of $w + $x exceeds reasonable compensation for the services V provides to P and S collectively. Therefore, the portion of total compensation that exceeds reasonable compensation is an excess benefit provided to V.

Example 4. G is an applicable tax-exempt organization for section 4958 purposes. F is a disqualified person who was last employed by G in a position of substantial influence three years ago. H is an entity engaged in scientific research and is unrelated to either F or G. G makes a grant to H to fund a research position. H subsequently advertises for qualified candidates for the research position. F is among several highly qualified candidates who apply for the research position. H hires F. There was no evidence of an oral or written agreement or understanding with G that H will use G's grant to provide economic benefits to or for the use of F. Although G provided economic benefits to H, and in connection with the receipt of such benefits, H will provide economic benefits to or for the use of F, H acted with a significant business purpose or exempt purpose of its own. Under these facts, G did not provide an economic benefit to F indirectly through the use of an intermediary.

(3) Exception for fixed payments made pursuant to an initial contract— (i) In general. Except as provided in paragraph (a)(3)(iv) of this section, section 4958 does not apply to any fixed payment made to a person pursuant to an initial contract.

(ii) Fixed payment—(A) In general. For purposes of paragraph (a)(3)(i) of this section, fixed payment means an amount of cash or other property specified in the contract, or determined by a fixed formula specified in the contract, which is to be paid or transferred in exchange for the provision of specified services or property. A fixed formula may incorporate an amount that depends upon future specified events or contingencies, provided that no person exercises discretion when calculating the amount of a payment or deciding whether to make a payment (such as a bonus). A specified event or contingency may include the amount of revenues generated by (or other objective measure of) one or more activities of the applicable tax-exempt organization. A fixed payment does not include any amount paid to a person under a reimbursement (or similar) arrangement where discretion is exercised by any person with respect to the amount of expenses incurred or reimbursed.

(B) Special rules. Amounts payable pursuant to a qualified pension, profit-sharing, or stock bonus plan under section 401(a), or pursuant to an employee benefit program that is subject to and satisfies coverage and nondiscrimination rules under the Internal Revenue Code (e.g., sections 127 and 137), other than nondiscrimination rules under section 9802, are treated as fixed payments for purposes of this section, regardless of the applicable tax-exempt organization's discretion with respect to the plan or program. The fact that a person contracting with an applicable tax-exempt organization is expressly granted the choice whether to accept or reject any economic benefit is disregarded in determining whether the benefit constitutes a fixed payment for purposes of this paragraph.

(iii) Initial contract. For purposes of paragraph (a)(3)(i) of this section, initial contract means a binding written contract between an applicable tax-exempt organization and a person who was not a disqualified person within the meaning of section 4958(f)(1) and § 53.4958–3 immediately prior to entering into the contract.

(iv) Substantial performance required. Paragraph (a)(3)(i) of this section does not apply to any fixed payment made pursuant to the initial contract during any taxable year of the person contracting with the applicable tax-exempt organization if the person fails to perform substantially the person's obligations under the initial contract during that year.

(v) Treatment as a new contract. A written binding contract that provides that the contract is terminable or subject to cancellation by the applicable tax-exempt organization (other than as a result of a lack of substantial performance by the disqualified person, as described in paragraph (a)(3)(iv) of this section) without the other party's consent and without substantial penalty to the organization is treated as a new contract as of the earliest date that any such termination or cancellation, if made, would be effective. Additionally, if the parties make a material change to a contract, it is treated as a new contract as of the date the material change is effective. A material change includes an extension or renewal of the contract (other than an extension or renewal that results from the person contracting with the applicable tax-exempt organization unilaterally exercising an option expressly granted by the contract), or a more than incidental change to any amount payable under the contract. The new contract is tested under paragraph (a)(3)(iii) of this section to determine whether it is an initial contract for purposes of this section.

(vi) Evaluation of non-fixed payments. Any payment that is not a fixed payment (within the meaning of paragraph (a)(3)(ii) of this section) is evaluated to determine whether it constitutes an excess benefit transaction under section 4958. In making this determination, all payments and consideration exchanged between the parties are taken into account, including any fixed payments made pursuant to an initial contract with respect to which section 4958 does not apply.

(vii) Examples. The following examples illustrate the rules governing fixed payments made pursuant to an initial contract. Unless otherwise stated, assume that the person contracting with the applicable tax-exempt organization has performed substantially the person's obligations under the contract with respect to the payment. The examples are as follows:

Example 1. T is an applicable tax-exempt organization for purposes of section 4958. On January 1, 2002, T hires S as its chief financial officer by entering into a five-year written employment contract with S. S was not a disqualified person within the meaning of section 4958(f)(1) and § 53.4958–3 immediately prior to entering into the January 1, 2002, contract (initial contract). S's duties and responsibilities under the contract make S a disqualified person with respect to T (see § 53.4958–3(c)(3)). Under the initial contract, T agrees to pay S an annual salary of $200,000, payable in monthly installments. The contract provides that, beginning in 2003, S's annual salary will be adjusted by the increase in the Consumer Price Index (CPI) for the prior year. Section 4958 does not apply because S's compensation under the contract is a fixed payment pursuant to an initial contract within the meaning of paragraph (a)(3) of this section. Thus, for section 4958 purposes, it is unnecessary to evaluate whether any portion of the compensation paid to S pursuant to the initial contract is an excess benefit transaction.

Example 2. The facts are the same as in Example 1, except that the initial contract provides that, in addition to a base salary of $200,000, T may pay S an annual performance-based bonus. The contract provides that T's governing body will determine the amount of the annual bonus as of the end of each year during the term of the contract, based on the board's evaluation of S's performance, but the bonus cannot exceed $100,000 per year. Unlike the base salary portion of S's compensation, the bonus portion of S's compensation is not a fixed payment pursuant to an initial contract, because the governing body has discretion over the amount, if any, of the bonus payment. Section 4958 does not apply to payment of the $200,000 base salary (as adjusted for inflation), because it is a fixed payment pursuant to an initial contract within the meaning of paragraph (a)(3) of this section. By contrast, the annual bonuses that may be paid to S under the initial contract are not protected by the initial contract exception. Therefore, each bonus payment will be evaluated under section 4958, taking into account all payments and consideration exchanged between the parties.

Example 3. The facts are the same as in Example 1, except that in 2003, T changes its payroll system, such that T makes biweekly, rather than monthly, salary payments to its employees. Beginning in 2003, T also grants its employees an additional two days of paid vacation each year. Neither change is a material change to S's initial contract within the meaning of paragraph (a)(3)(v)of this section. Therefore, section 4958 does not apply to the base salary payments to S due to the initial contract exception.

Example 4. The facts are the same as in Example 1, except that on January 1, 2003, S becomes the chief executive officer of T and a new chief financial officer is hired. At the same time, T's board of directors approves an increase in S's annual base salary from $200,000 to $240,000, effective on that day. These changes in S's employment relationship constitute material changes of the initial contract within the meaning of paragraph (a)(3)(v) of this section. As a result, S is treated as entering into a new contract with T on January 1, 2003, at which time S is a disqualified person within the meaning of section 4958(f)(1) and § 53.4958–3. T's payments to S made pursuant to the new contract will be evaluated under section 4958, taking into account all payments and consideration exchanged between the parties.

Example 5. J is a performing arts organization and an applicable tax-exempt organization for purposes of section 4958. J hires W to become the chief executive officer of J. W was not a disqualified person within the meaning of section 4958(f)(1) and § 53.4958–3 immediately prior to entering into the employment contract with J. As a result of this employment contract, W's duties and responsibilities make W a disqualified person with respect to J (see § 53.4958–3(c)(2)). Under the contract, J will pay W $x (a specified amount) plus a bonus equal to 2 percent of the total season subscription sales that exceed $100z. The $x base salary is a fixed payment pursuant to an initial contract within the meaning of paragraph (a)(3) of this section. The bonus payment is also a fixed payment pursuant to an initial contract within the meaning of paragraph (a)(3) of this section, because no person exercises discretion when calculating the amount of the bonus payment or deciding whether the bonus will be paid. Therefore, section 4958 does not apply to any of J's payments to W pursuant to the employment contract due to the initial contract exception.

Example 6. Hospital B is an applicable tax-exempt organization for purposes of section 4958. Hospital B hires E as its chief operating officer. E was not a disqualified person within the meaning of section 4958(f)(1) and § 53.4958–3 immediately prior to entering into the employment contract with Hospital B. As a result of this employment contract, E's duties and responsibilities make E a disqualified person with respect to Hospital B (see § 53.4958–3(c)(2)). E's initial employment contract provides that E will have authority to enter into hospital management arrangements on behalf of Hospital B. In E's personal capacity, E owns more than 35 percent of the combined voting power of Company X. Consequently, at the time E becomes a disqualified person with respect to B, Company X also becomes a disqualified person with respect to B (see § 53.4958–3(b)(2)(i)(A)). E, acting on behalf of Hospital B as chief operating officer, enters into a contract with Company X under which Company X will provide billing and collection services to Hospital B. The initial contract exception of paragraph (a)(3)(i) of this section does not apply to the billing and collection services contract, because at the time that this contractual arrangement was entered into, Company X was a disqualified person with respect to Hospital B. Although E's employment contract (which is an initial contract) authorizes E to enter into hospital management arrangements on behalf of Hospital B, the payments made to Company X are not made pursuant to E's employment contract, but rather are made by Hospital B pursuant to a separate contractual arrangement with Company X. Therefore, even if payments made to Company X under the billing and collection services contract are fixed payments (within the meaning of paragraph (a)(3)(ii) of this section), section 4958 nonetheless applies to payments made by Hospital B to Company X because the billing and collection services contract itself does not constitute an initial contract under paragraph (a)(3)(iii) of this section. Accordingly, all payments made to Company X under the billing and collection services contract will be evaluated under section 4958.

Example 7. Hospital C, an applicable tax-exempt organization, enters into a contract with Company Y, under which Company Y will provide a wide range of hospital management services to Hospital C. Upon entering into this contractual arrangement, Company Y becomes a disqualified person with respect to Hospital C. The contract provides that Hospital C will pay Company Y a management fee of x percent of adjusted gross revenue (i.e., gross revenue increased by the cost of charity care provided to indigents) annually for a five-year period. The management services contract specifies the cost accounting system and the standards for indigents to be used in calculating the cost of charity care. The cost accounting system objectively defines the direct and indirect costs of all health care goods and services provided as charity care. Because Company Y was not a disqualified person with respect to Hospital C immediately before entering into the management services contract, that contract is an initial contract within the meaning of paragraph (a)(3)(iii) of this section. The annual management fee paid to Company Y is determined by a fixed formula specified in the contract, and is therefore a fixed payment within the meaning of paragraph (a)(3)(ii) of this section. Accordingly, section 4958 does not apply to the annual management fee due to the initial contract exception.

Example 8. The facts are the same as in Example 7, except that the management services contract also provides that Hospital C will reimburse Company Y on a monthly basis for certain expenses incurred by Company Y that are attributable to management services provided to Hospital C (e.g., legal fees and travel expenses). Although the management fee itself is a fixed payment not subject to section 4958, the reimbursement payments that Hospital C makes to Company Y for the various expenses covered by the contract are not fixed payments within the meaning of paragraph (a)(3)(ii) of this section, because Company Y exercises discretion with respect to the amount of expenses incurred. Therefore, any reimbursement payments that Hospital C pays pursuant to the contract will be evaluated under section 4958.

Example 9. X, an applicable tax-exempt organization for purposes of section 4958, hires C to conduct scientific research. On January 1, 2003, C enters into a three-year written employment contract with X (initial contract). Under the terms of the contract, C is required to work full-time at X's laboratory for a fixed annual salary of $90,000. Immediately prior to entering into the employment contract, C was not a disqualified person within the meaning of section 4958(f)(1) and § 53.4958–3, nor did C become a disqualified person pursuant to the initial contract. However, two years after joining X, C marries D, who is the child of X's president. As D's spouse, C is a disqualified person within the meaning of section 4958(f)(1) and § 53.4958–3 with respect to X. Nonetheless, section 4958 does not apply to X's salary payments to C due to the initial contract exception.

Example 10. The facts are the same as in Example 9, except that the initial contract included a below-market loan provision under which C has the unilateral right to borrow up to a specified dollar amount from X at a specified interest rate for a specified term. After C's marriage to D, C borrows money from X to purchase a home under the terms of the initial contract. Section 4958 does not apply to X's loan to C due to the initial contract exception.

Example 11. The facts are the same as in Example 9, except that after C's marriage to D, C works only sporadically at the laboratory, and performs no other services for X. Notwithstanding that C fails to perform substantially C's obligations under the initial contract, X does not exercise its right to terminate the initial contract for nonperformance and continues to pay full salary to C. Pursuant to paragraph (a)(3)(iv) of this section, the initial contract exception does not apply to any payments made pursuant to the initial contract during any taxable year of C in which C fails to perform substantially C's obligations under the initial contract.

(4) Certain economic benefits disregarded for purposes of section 4958. The following economic benefits are disregarded for purposes of section 4958—

(i) Nontaxable fringe benefits. An economic benefit that is excluded from income under section 132, except any liability insurance premium, payment, or reimbursement that must be taken into account under paragraph (b)(1)(ii)(B)(2) of this section;

(ii) Expense reimbursement payments pursuant to accountable plans. Amounts paid under reimbursement arrangements that meet the requirements of § 1.62–2(c) of this chapter;

(iii) Certain economic benefits provided to a volunteer for the organization. An economic benefit provided to a volunteer for the organization if the benefit is provided to the general public in exchange for a membership fee or contribution of $75 or less per year;

(iv) Certain economic benefits provided to a member of, or donor to, the organization. An economic benefit provided to a member of an organization solely on account of the payment of a membership fee, or to a donor solely on account of a contribution for which a deduction is allowable under section 170 (charitable contribution), regardless of whether the donor is eligible to claim the deduction, if—

(A) Any non-disqualified person paying a membership fee or making a charitable contribution above a specified amount to the organization is given the option of receiving substantially the same economic benefit; and

(B) The disqualified person and a significant number of non-disqualified persons make a payment or charitable contribution of at least the specified amount;

(v) Economic benefits provided to a charitable beneficiary. An economic benefit provided to a person solely because the person is a member of a charitable class that the applicable tax-exempt organization intends to benefit as part of the accomplishment of the organization's exempt purpose; and

(vi) Certain economic benefits provided to a governmental unit. Any transfer of an economic benefit to or for the use of a governmental unit defined in section 170(c)(1), if the transfer is for exclusively public purposes.

(5) Exception for certain payments made pursuant to an exemption granted by the Department of Labor under ERISA. Section 4958 does not apply to any payment made pursuant to, and in accordance with, a final individual prohibited transaction exemption issued by the Department of Labor under section 408(a) of the Employee Retirement Income Security Act of 1974 (88 Stat. 854) (ERISA) with respect to a transaction involving a plan (as defined in section 3(3) of ERISA) that is an applicable tax exempt organization.

(b) Valuation standards—(1) In general. This section provides rules for determining the value of economic benefits for purposes of section 4958.

(i) Fair market value of property. The value of property, including the right to use property, for purposes of section 4958 is the fair market value (i.e., the price at which property or the right to use property would change hands between a willing buyer and a willing seller, neither being under any compulsion to buy, sell or transfer property or the right to use property, and both having reasonable knowledge of relevant facts).

(ii) Reasonable compensation—(A) In general. The value of services is the amount that would ordinarily be paid for like services by like enterprises (whether taxable or tax-exempt) under like circumstances (i.e., reasonable compensation). Section 162 standards apply in determining reasonableness of compensation, taking into account the aggregate benefits (other than any benefits specifically disregarded under paragraph (a)(4) of this section) provided to a person and the rate at which any deferred compensation accrues. The fact that a compensation arrangement is subject to a cap is a relevant factor in determining the reasonableness of compensation. The fact that a State or local legislative or agency body or court has authorized or approved a particular compensation package paid to a disqualified person is not determinative of the reasonableness of compensation for purposes of section 4958.

(B) Items included in determining the value of compensation for purposes of determining reasonableness under section 4958. Except for economic benefits that are disregarded for purposes of section 4958 under paragraph (a)(4) of this section, compensation for purposes of determining reasonableness under section 4958 includes all economic benefits provided by an applicable tax-exempt organization in exchange for the performance of services. These benefits include, but are not limited to—

(1) All forms of cash and noncash compensation, including salary, fees, bonuses, severance payments, and deferred and noncash compensation described in § 53.4958–1(e)(2);

(2) Unless excludable from income as a de minimis fringe benefit pursuant to section 132(a)(4), the payment of liability insurance premiums for, or the payment or reimbursement by the organization of—

(i) Any penalty, tax, or expense of correction owed under section 4958;

(ii) Any expense not reasonably incurred by the person in connection with a civil judicial or civil administrative proceeding arising out of the person's performance of services on behalf of the applicable tax-exempt organization; or

(iii) Any expense resulting from an act or failure to act with respect to which the person has acted willfully and without reasonable cause; and

(3) All other compensatory benefits, whether or not included in gross income for income tax purposes, including payments to welfare benefit plans, such as plans providing medical, dental, life insurance, severance pay, and disability benefits, and both taxable and nontaxable fringe benefits (other than fringe benefits described in section 132), including expense allowances or reimbursements (other than expense reimbursements pursuant to an accountable plan that meets the requirements of § 1.62–2(c)), and the economic benefit of a below-market loan (within the meaning of section 7872(e)(1)). (For this purpose, the economic benefit of a below-market loan is the amount deemed transferred to the disqualified person under section 7872(a) or (b), regardless of whether section 7872 otherwise applies to the loan).

(C) Inclusion in compensation for reasonableness determination does not govern income tax treatment. The determination of whether any item listed in paragraph (b)(1)(ii)(B) of this section is included in the disqualified person's gross income for income tax purposes is made on the basis of the provisions of chapter 1 of Subtitle A of the Internal Revenue Code, without regard to whether the item is taken into account for purposes of determining reasonableness of compensation under section 4958.

(2) Timing of reasonableness determination—(i) In general. The facts and circumstances to be taken into consideration in determining reasonableness of a fixed payment (within the meaning of paragraph (a)(3)(ii) of this section) are those existing on the date the parties enter into the contract pursuant to which the payment is made. However, in the event of substantial non-performance, reasonableness is determined based on all facts and circumstances, up to and including circumstances as of the date of payment. In the case of any payment that is not a fixed payment under a contract, reasonableness is determined based on all facts and circumstances, up to and including circumstances as of the date of payment. In no event shall circumstances existing at the date when the payment is questioned be considered in making a determination of the reasonableness of the payment. These general timing rules also apply to property subject to a substantial risk of forfeiture. Therefore, if the property subject to a substantial risk of forfeiture satisfies the definition of fixed payment (within the meaning of paragraph (a)(3)(ii) of this section), reasonableness is determined at the time the parties enter into the contract providing for the transfer of the property. If the property is not a fixed payment, then reasonableness is determined based on all facts and circumstances up to and including circumstances as of the date of payment.

(ii) Treatment as a new contract. For purposes of paragraph (b)(2)(i) of this section, a written binding contract that provides that the contract is terminable or subject to cancellation by the applicable tax-exempt organization without the other party's consent and without substantial penalty to the organization is treated as a new contract as of the earliest date that any such termination or cancellation, if made, would be effective. Additionally, if the parties make a material change to a contract (within the meaning of paragraph (a)(3)(v) of this section), it is treated as a new contract as of the date the material change is effective.

(iii) Examples. The following examples illustrate the timing of the reasonableness determination under the rules of this paragraph (b)(2):

Example 1. G is an applicable tax-exempt organization for purposes of section 4958. H is an employee of G and a disqualified person with respect to G. H's new multi-year employment contract provides for payment of a salary and provision of specific benefits pursuant to a qualified pension plan under section 401(a) and an accident and health plan that meets the requirements of section 105(h)(2). The contract provides that H's salary will be adjusted by the increase in the Consumer Price Index (CPI) for the prior year. The contributions G makes to the qualified pension plan are equal to the maximum amount G is permitted to contribute under the rules applicable to qualified plans. Under these facts, all items comprising H's total compensation are treated as fixed payments within the meaning of paragraph (a)(3)(ii) of this section. Therefore, the reasonableness of H's compensation is determined based on the circumstances existing at the time G and H enter into the employment contract.

Example 2. The facts are the same as in Example 1, except that the multi-year employment contract provides, in addition, that G will transfer title to a car to H under the condition that if H fails to complete x years of service with G, title to the car will be forfeited back to G. All relevant information about the type of car to be provided (including the make, model, and year) is included in the contract. Although ultimate vesting of title to the car is contingent on H continuing to work for G for x years, the amount of property to be vested (i.e., the type of car) is specified in the contract, and no person exercises discretion regarding the type of property or whether H will retain title to the property at the time of vesting. Under these facts, the car is a fixed payment within the meaning of paragraph (a)(3)(ii) of this section. Therefore, the reasonableness of H's compensation, including the value of the car, is determined based on the circumstances existing at the time G and H enter into the employment contract.

Example 3. N is an applicable tax-exempt organization for purposes of section 4958. On January 2, N's governing body enters into a new one-year employment contract with K, its executive director, who is a disqualified person with respect to N. The contract provides that K will receive a specified amount of salary, contributions to a qualified pension plan under section 401(a), and other benefits pursuant to a section 125 cafeteria plan. In addition, the contract provides that N's governing body may, in its discretion, declare a bonus to be paid to K at any time during the year covered by the contract. K's salary and other specified benefits constitute fixed payments within the meaning of paragraph (a)(3)(ii) of this section. Therefore, the reasonableness of those economic benefits is determined on the date when the contract was made. However, because the bonus payment is not a fixed payment within the meaning of paragraph (a)(3)(ii) of this section, the determination of whether any bonus awarded to N is reasonable must be made based on all facts and circumstances (including all payments and consideration exchanged between the parties), up to and including circumstances as of the date of payment of the bonus.

(c) Establishing intent to treat economic benefit as consideration for the performance of services—(1) In general. An economic benefit is not treated as consideration for the performance of services unless the organization providing the benefit clearly indicates its intent to treat the benefit as compensation when the benefit is paid. Except as provided in paragraph (c)(2) of this section, an applicable tax-exempt organization (or entity controlled by an applicable tax-exempt organization, within the meaning of paragraph (a)(2)(ii)(B) of this section) is treated as clearly indicating its intent to provide an economic benefit as compensation for services only if the organization provides written substantiation that is contemporaneous with the transfer of the economic benefit at issue. If an organization fails to provide this contemporaneous substantiation, any services provided by the disqualified person will not be treated as provided in consideration for the economic benefit for purposes of determining the reasonableness of the transaction. In no event shall an economic benefit that a disqualified person obtains by theft or fraud be treated as consideration for the performance of services.

(2) Nontaxable benefits. For purposes of section 4958(c)(1)(A) and this section, an applicable tax-exempt organization is not required to indicate its intent to provide an economic benefit as compensation for services if the economic benefit is excluded from the disqualified person's gross income for income tax purposes on the basis of the provisions of chapter 1 of Subtitle A of the Internal Revenue Code. Examples of these benefits include, but are not limited to, employer-provided health benefits and contributions to a qualified pension, profit-sharing, or stock bonus plan under section 401(a), and benefits described in sections 127 and 137. However, except for economic benefits that are disregarded for purposes of section 4958 under paragraph (a)(4) of this section, all compensatory benefits (regardless of the Federal income tax treatment) provided by an organization in exchange for the performance of services are taken into account in determining the reasonableness of a person's compensation for purposes of section 4958.

(3) Contemporaneous substantiation—(i) Reporting of benefit—(A) In general. An applicable tax-exempt organization provides contemporaneous written substantiation of its intent to provide an economic benefit as compensation if—

(1) The organization reports the economic benefit as compensation on an original Federal tax information return with respect to the payment (e.g., Form W-2, "Wage and Tax Statement", or Form 1099, "Miscellaneous Income") or with respect to the organization (e.g., Form 990, "Return of Organization Exempt From Income Tax"), or on an amended Federal tax information return filed prior to the commencement of an Internal Revenue Service examination of the applicable tax-exempt organization or the disqualified person for the taxable year in which the transaction occurred (as determined under §§ 53.4958–1(e)); or

(2) The recipient disqualified person reports the benefit as income on the person's original Federal tax return (e.g., Form 1040, "U.S. Individual Income Tax Return"), or on the person's amended Federal tax return filed prior to the earlier of the following dates—

(i) Commencement of an Internal Revenue Service examination described in paragraph (c)(3)(i)(A)(1) of this section; or

(ii) The first documentation in writing by the Internal Revenue Service of a potential excess benefit transaction involving either the applicable tax-exempt organization or the disqualified person.

(B) Failure to report due to reasonable cause. If an applicable tax-exempt organization's failure to report an economic benefit as required under the Internal Revenue Code is due to reasonable cause (within the meaning of § 301.6724–1 of this chapter), then the organization will be treated as having clearly indicated its intent to provide an economic benefit as compensation for services. To show that its failure to report an economic benefit that should have been reported on an information return was due to reasonable cause, an applicable tax-exempt organization must establish that there were significant mitigating factors with respect to its failure to report (as described in § 301.6724–1(b) of this chapter), or the failure arose from events beyond the organization's control (as described in § 301.6724–1(c) of this chapter), and that the organization acted in a responsible manner both before and after the failure occurred (as described in § 301.6724–1(d) of this chapter).

(ii) Other written contemporaneous evidence. In addition, other written contemporaneous evidence may be used to demonstrate that the appropriate decision-making body or an officer authorized to approve compensation approved a transfer as compensation for services in accordance with established procedures, including but not limited to—

(A) An approved written employment contract executed on or before the date of the transfer;

(B) Documentation satisfying the requirements of § 53.4958–6(a)(3) indicating that an authorized body approved the transfer as compensation for services on or before the date of the transfer; or

(C) Written evidence that was in existence on or before the due date of the applicable Federal tax return described in paragraph (c)(3)(i)(A)(1) or (2) of this section (including extensions but not amendments), of a reasonable belief by the applicable tax-exempt organization that a benefit was a nontaxable benefit as defined in paragraph (c)(2) of this section.

(4) Examples. The following examples illustrate the requirement that an organization contemporaneously substantiate its intent to provide an economic benefit as compensation for services, as defined in paragraph (c) of this section:

Example 1. G is an applicable tax-exempt organization for purposes of section 4958. G hires an individual contractor, P, who is also the child of a disqualified person of G, to design a computer program for it. G executes a contract with P for that purpose in accordance with G's established procedures, and pays P $1,000 during the year pursuant to the contract. Before January 31 of the next year, G reports the full amount paid to P under the contract on a Form 1099 filed with the Internal Revenue Service. G will be treated as providing contemporaneous written substantiation of its intent to provide the $1,000 paid to P as compensation for the services P performed under the contract by virtue of either the Form 1099 filed with the Internal Revenue Service reporting the amount, or by virtue of the written contract executed between G and P.

Example 2. G is an applicable tax-exempt organization for purposes of section 4958. D is the chief operating officer of G, and a disqualified person with respect to G. D receives a bonus at the end of the year. G's accounting department determines that the bonus is to be reported on D's Form W-2. Due to events beyond G's control, the bonus is not reflected on D's Form W-2. As a result, D fails to report the bonus on D's individual income tax return. G acts to amend Forms W-2 affected as soon as G is made aware of the error during an Internal Revenue Service examination. G's failure to report the bonus on an information return issued to D arose from events beyond G's control, and G acted in a responsible manner both before and after the failure occurred. Thus, because G had reasonable cause (within the meaning § 301.6724–1 of this chapter) for failing to report D's bonus, G will be treated as providing contemporaneous written substantiation of its intent to provide the bonus as compensation for services when paid.

Example 3. H is an applicable tax-exempt organization and J is a disqualified person with respect to H. J's written employment agreement provides for a fixed salary of $y. J's duties include soliciting funds for various programs of H. H raises a large portion of its funds in a major metropolitan area. Accordingly, H maintains an apartment there in order to provide a place to entertain potential donors. H makes the apartment available exclusively to J to assist in the fundraising. J's written employment contract does not mention the use of the apartment. H obtains the written opinion of a benefits compensation expert that the rental value of the apartment is not includable in J's income by reason of section 119, based on the expectation that the apartment will be used for fundraising activities. Consequently, H does not report the rental value of the apartment on J's Form W-2, which otherwise correctly reports J's taxable compensation. J does not report the rental value of the apartment on J's individual Form 1040. Later, the Internal Revenue Service correctly determines that the requirements of section 119 were not satisfied. Because of the written expert opinion, H has written evidence of its reasonable belief that use of the apartment was a nontaxable benefit as defined in paragraph (c)(2) of this section. That evidence was in existence on or before the due date of the applicable Federal tax return. Therefore, H has demonstrated its intent to treat the use of the apartment as compensation for services performed by J.

§ 53.4958–5. Transaction in which the amount of the economic benefit is determined in whole or in part by the revenues of one or more activities of the organization. [Reserved]

§ 53.4958–6. Rebuttable presumption that a transaction is not an excess benefit transaction.

(a) In general. Payments under a compensation arrangement are presumed to be reasonable, and a transfer of property, or the right to use property, is presumed to be at fair market value, if the following conditions are satisfied—

(1) The compensation arrangement or the terms of the property transfer are approved in advance by an authorized body of the applicable tax-exempt organization (or an entity controlled by the organization with the meaning of § 53.4958–4(a)(2)(ii)(B)) composed entirely of individuals who do not have a conflict of interest (within the meaning of paragraph (c)(1)(iii) of this section) with respect to the compensation arrangement or property transfer, as described in paragraph (c)(1) of this section;

(2) The authorized body obtained and relied upon appropriate data as to comparability prior to making its determination, as described in paragraph (c)(2) of this section; and

(3) The authorized body adequately documented the basis for its determination concurrently with making that determination, as described in paragraph (c)(3) of this section.

(b) Rebutting the presumption. If the three requirements of paragraph (a) of this section are satisfied, then the Internal Revenue Service may rebut the presumption that arises under paragraph (a) of this section only if it develops sufficient contrary evidence to rebut the probative value of the comparability data relied upon by the authorized body. With respect to any fixed payment (within the meaning of § 53.4958–4(a)(3)(ii)), rebuttal evidence is limited to evidence relating to facts and circumstances existing on the date the parties enter into the contract pursuant to which the payment is made (except in the event of substantial nonperformance). With respect to all other payments (including non-fixed payments subject to a cap, as described in paragraph (d)(2) of this section), rebuttal evidence may include facts and circumstances up to and including the date of payment. See § 53.4958–4(b)(2)(i).

(c) Requirements for invoking rebuttable presumption—(1) Approval by an authorized body—(i) In general. An authorized body means—

(A) The governing body (i.e., the board of directors, board of trustees, or equivalent controlling body) of the organization;

(B) A committee of the governing body, which may be composed of any individuals permitted under State law to serve on such a committee, to the extent that the committee is permitted by State law to act on behalf of the governing body; or

(C) To the extent permitted under State law, other parties authorized by the governing body of the organization to act on its behalf by following procedures specified by the governing body in approving compensation arrangements or property transfers.

(ii) Individuals not included on authorized body. For purposes of determining whether the requirements of paragraph (a) of this section have been met with respect to a specific compensation arrangement or property transfer, an individual is not included on the authorized body when it is reviewing a transaction if that individual meets with other members only to answer questions, and otherwise recuses himself or herself from the meeting and is not present during debate and voting on the compensation arrangement or property transfer.

(iii) Absence of conflict of interest. A member of the authorized body does not have a conflict of interest with respect to a compensation arrangement or property transfer only if the member—

(A) Is not a disqualified person participating in or economically benefitting from the compensation arrangement or property transfer, and is not a member of the family of any such disqualified person, as described in section 4958(f)(4) or § 53.4958–3(b)(1);

(B) Is not in an employment relationship subject to the direction or control of any disqualified person participating in or economically benefitting from the compensation arrangement or property transfer;

(C) Does not receive compensation or other payments subject to approval by any disqualified person participating in or economically benefitting from the compensation arrangement or property transfer;

(D) Has no material financial interest affected by the compensation arrangement or property transfer; and

(E) Does not approve a transaction providing economic benefits to any disqualified person participating in the compensation arrangement or property transfer, who in turn has approved or will approve a transaction providing economic benefits to the member.

(2) Appropriate data as to comparability—(i) In general. An authorized body has appropriate data as to comparability if, given the knowledge and expertise of its members, it has information sufficient to determine whether, under the standards set forth in § 53.4958–4(b), the compensation arrangement in its entirety is reasonable or the property transfer is at fair market value. In the case of compensation, relevant information includes, but is not limited to, compensation levels paid by similarly situated organizations, both taxable and tax-exempt, for functionally comparable positions; the availability of similar services in the geographic area of the applicable tax-exempt organization; current compensation surveys compiled by independent firms; and actual written offers from similar institutions competing for the services of the disqualified person. In the case of property, relevant information includes, but is not limited to, current independent appraisals of the value of all property to be transferred; and offers received as part of an open and competitive bidding process.

(ii) Special rule for compensation paid by small organizations. For organizations with annual gross receipts (including contributions) of less than $1 million reviewing compensation arrangements, the authorized body will be considered to have appropriate data as to comparability if it has data on compensation paid by three comparable organizations in the same or similar communities for similar services. No inference is intended with respect to whether circumstances falling outside this safe harbor will meet the requirement with respect to the collection of appropriate data.

(iii) Application of special rule for small organizations. For purposes of determining whether the special rule for small organizations described in paragraph (c)(2)(ii) of this section applies, an organization may calculate its annual gross receipts based on an average of its gross receipts during the three prior taxable years. If any applicable tax-exempt organization is controlled by or controls another entity (as defined in § 53.4958–4(a)(2)(ii)(B)), the annual gross receipts of such organizations must be aggregated to determine applicability of the special rule stated in paragraph (c)(2)(ii) of this section.

(iv) Examples. The following examples illustrate the rules for appropriate data as to comparability for purposes of invoking the rebuttable presumption of reasonableness described in this section. In all examples, compensation refers to the aggregate value of all benefits provided in exchange for services. The examples are as follows:

Example 1. Z is a university that is an applicable tax-exempt organization for purposes of section 4958. Z is negotiating a new contract with Q, its president, because the old contract will expire at the end of the year. In setting Q's compensation for its president at $600x per annum, the executive committee of the Board of Trustees relies solely on a national survey of compensation for university presidents that indicates university presidents receive annual compensation in the range of $100x to $700x; this survey does not divide its data by any criteria, such as the number of students served by the institution, annual revenues, academic ranking, or geographic location. Although many members of the executive committee have significant business experience, none of the members has any particular expertise in higher education compensation matters. Given the failure of the survey to provide information specific to universities comparable to Z, and because no other information was presented, the executive committee's decision with respect to Q's compensation was not based upon appropriate data as to comparability.

Example 2. The facts are the same as Example 1, except that the national compensation survey divides the data regarding compensation for university presidents into categories based on various university-specific factors, including the size of the institution (in terms of the number of students it serves and the amount of its revenues) and geographic area. The survey data shows that university presidents at institutions comparable to and in the same geographic area as Z receive annual compensation in the range of $200x to $300x. The executive committee of the Board of Trustees of Z relies on the survey data and its evaluation of Q's many years of service as a tenured professor and high-ranking university official at Z in setting Q's compensation at $275x annually. The data relied upon by the executive committee constitutes appropriate data as to comparability.

Example 3. X is a tax-exempt hospital that is an applicable tax-exempt organization for purposes of section 4958. Before renewing the contracts of X's chief executive officer and chief financial officer, X's governing board commissioned a customized compensation survey from an independent firm that specializes in consulting on issues related to executive placement and compensation. The survey covered executives with comparable responsibilities at a significant number of taxable and tax-exempt hospitals. The survey data are sorted by a number of different variables, including the size of the hospitals and the nature of the services they provide, the level of experience and specific responsibilities of the executives, and the composition of the annual compensation packages. The board members were provided with the survey results, a detailed written analysis comparing the hospital's executives to those covered by the survey, and an opportunity to ask questions of a member of the firm that prepared the survey. The survey, as prepared and presented to X's board, constitutes appropriate data as to comparability.

Example 4. The facts are the same as Example 3, except that one year later, X is negotiating a new contract with its chief executive officer. The governing board of X obtains information indicating that the relevant market conditions have not changed materially, and possesses no other information indicating that the results of the prior year's survey are no longer valid. Therefore, X may continue to rely on the independent compensation survey prepared for the prior year in setting annual compensation under the new contract.

Example 5. W is a local repertory theater and an applicable tax-exempt organization for purposes of section 4958. W has had annual gross receipts ranging from $400,000 to $800,000 over its past three taxable years. In determining the next year's compensation for W's artistic director, the board of directors of W relies on data compiled from a telephone survey of three other unrelated performing arts organizations of similar size in similar communities. A member of the board drafts a brief written summary of the annual compensation information obtained from this informal survey. The annual compensation information obtained in the telephone survey is appropriate data as to comparability.

(3) Documentation—(i) For a decision to be documented adequately, the written or electronic records of the authorized body must note—

(A) The terms of the transaction that was approved and the date it was approved;

(B) The members of the authorized body who were present during debate on the transaction that was approved and those who voted on it;

(C) The comparability data obtained and relied upon by the authorized body and how the data was obtained; and

(D) Any actions taken with respect to consideration of the transaction by anyone who is otherwise a member of the authorized body but who had a conflict of interest with respect to the transaction.

(ii) If the authorized body determines that reasonable compensation for a specific arrangement or fair market value in a specific property transfer is higher or lower than the range of comparability data obtained, the authorized body must record the basis for its determination. For a decision to be documented concurrently, records must be prepared before the later of the next meeting of the authorized body or 60 days after the final action or actions of the authorized body are taken. Records must be reviewed and approved by the authorized body as reasonable, accurate and complete within a reasonable time period thereafter.

(d) No presumption with respect to non-fixed payments until amounts are determined—(1) In general. Except as provided in paragraph (d)(2) of this section, in the case of a payment that is not a fixed payment (within the meaning of § 53.4958–4(a)(3)(ii)), the rebuttable presumption of this section arises only after the exact amount of the payment is determined, or a fixed formula for calculating the payment is specified, and the three requirements for the presumption under paragraph (a) of this section subsequently are satisfied. See § 53.4958–4(b)(2)(i).

(2) Special rule for certain non-fixed payments subject to a cap. If the authorized body approves an employment contract with a disqualified person that includes a non-fixed payment (such as a discretionary bonus) subject to a specified cap, the authorized body may establish a rebuttable presumption with respect to the non-fixed payment at the time the employment contract is entered into if—

(i) Prior to approving the contract, the authorized body obtains appropriate comparability data indicating that a fixed payment of up to a certain amount to the particular disqualified person would represent reasonable compensation;

(ii) The maximum amount payable under the contract (taking into account both fixed and non-fixed payments) does not exceed the amount referred to in paragraph (d)(2)(i) of this section; and

(iii) The other requirements for the rebuttable presumption of reasonableness under paragraph (a) of this section are satisfied.

(e) No inference from absence of presumption. The fact that a transaction between an applicable tax-exempt organization and a disqualified person is not subject to the presumption described in this section neither creates any inference that the transaction is an excess benefit transaction, nor exempts or relieves any person from compliance with any Federal or state law imposing any obligation, duty, responsibility, or other standard of conduct with respect to the operation or administration of any applicable tax-exempt organization.

(f) Period of reliance on rebuttable presumption. Except as provided in paragraph (d) of this section with respect to non-fixed payments, the rebuttable presumption applies to all payments made or transactions completed in accordance with a contract, provided that the provisions of paragraph (a) of this section were met at the time the parties entered into the contract.

§ 53.4958–7. Correction.

(a) In general. An excess benefit transaction is corrected by undoing the excess benefit to the extent possible, and taking any additional measures necessary to place the applicable tax-exempt organization involved in the excess benefit transaction in a financial position not worse than that in which it would be if the disqualified person were dealing under the highest fiduciary standards. Paragraph (b) of this section describes the acceptable forms of correction. Paragraph (c) of this section defines the correction amount. Paragraph (d) of this section describes correction where a contract has been partially performed. Paragraph (e) of this section describes correction where the applicable tax-exempt organization involved in the transaction has ceased to exist or is no longer tax-exempt. Paragraph (f) of this section provides examples illustrating correction.

(b) Form of correction—(1) Cash or cash equivalents. Except as provided in paragraphs (b)(3) and (4) of this section, a disqualified person corrects an excess benefit only by making a payment in cash or cash equivalents, excluding payment by a promissory note, to the applicable tax-exempt organization equal to the correction amount, as defined in paragraph (c) of this section.

(2) Anti-abuse rule. A disqualified person will not satisfy the requirements of paragraph (b)(1) of this section if the Commissioner determines that the disqualified person engaged in one or more transactions with the applicable tax-exempt organization to circumvent the requirements of this correction section, and as a result, the disqualified person effectively transferred property other than cash or cash equivalents.

(3) Special rule relating to nonqualified deferred compensation. If an excess benefit transaction results, in whole or in part, from the vesting (as described in § 53.4958–1(e)(2)) of benefits provided under a nonqualified deferred compensation plan, then, to the extent that such benefits have not yet been distributed to the disqualified person, the disqualified person may correct the portion of the excess benefit resulting from the undistributed deferred compensation by relinquishing any right to receive the excess portion of the undistributed deferred compensation (including any earnings thereon).

(4) Return of specific property—(i) In general. A disqualified person may, with the agreement of the applicable tax-exempt organization, make a payment by returning specific property previously transferred in the excess benefit transaction. In this case, the disqualified person is treated as making a payment equal to the lesser of—

(A) The fair market value of the property determined on the date the property is returned to the organization; or

(B) The fair market value of the property on the date the excess benefit transaction occurred.

(ii) Payment not equal to correction amount. If the payment described in paragraph (b)(4)(i) of this section is less than the correction amount (as described in paragraph (c) of this section), the disqualified person must make an additional cash payment to the organization equal to the difference. Conversely, if the payment described in paragraph (b)(4)(i) of this section exceeds the correction amount (as described in paragraph (c) of this section), the organization may make a cash payment to the disqualified person equal to the difference.

(iii) Disqualified person may not participate in decision. Any disqualified person who received an excess benefit from the excess benefit transaction may not participate in the applicable tax-exempt organization's decision whether to accept the return of specific property under paragraph (b)(4)(i) of this section.

(c) Correction amount. The correction amount with respect to an excess benefit transaction equals the sum of the excess benefit (as defined in § 53.4958–1(b)) and interest on the excess benefit. The amount of the interest charge for purposes of this section is determined by multiplying the excess benefit by an interest rate, compounded annually, for the period from the date the excess benefit transaction occurred (as defined in § 53.4958–1(e)) to the date of correction. The interest rate used for this purpose must be a rate that equals or exceeds the applicable Federal rate (AFR), compounded annually, for the month in which the transaction occurred. The period from the date the excess benefit transaction occurred to the date of correction is used to determine whether the appropriate AFR is the Federal short-term rate, the Federal mid-term rate, or the Federal long-term rate. See section 1274(d)(1)(A).

(d) Correction where contract has been partially performed. If the excess benefit transaction arises under a contract that has been partially performed, termination of the contractual relationship between the organization and the disqualified person is not required in order to correct. However, the parties may need to modify the terms of any ongoing contract to avoid future excess benefit transactions.

(e) Correction in the case of an applicable tax-exempt organization that has ceased to exist, or is no longer tax-exempt—(1) In general. A disqualified person must correct an excess benefit transaction in accordance with this paragraph where the applicable tax-exempt organization that engaged in the transaction no longer exists or is no longer described in section 501(c)(3) or (4) and exempt from tax under section 501(a).

(2) Section 501(c)(3) organizations. In the case of an excess benefit transaction with a section 501(c)(3) applicable tax-exempt organization, the disqualified person must pay the correction amount, as defined in paragraph(c)of this section, to another organization described in section 501(c)(3) and exempt from tax under section 501(a) in accordance with the dissolution clause contained in the constitutive documents of the applicable tax-exempt organization involved in the excess benefit transaction, provided that—

(i) The organization receiving the correction amount is described in section 170(b)(1)(A) (other than in section 170(b)(1)(A)(vii) and (viii)) and has been in existence and so described for a continuous period of at least 60 calendar months ending on the correction date;

(ii) The disqualified person is not also a disqualified person (as defined in § 53.4958–3) with respect to the organization receiving the correction amount; and

(iii) The organization receiving the correction amount does not allow the disqualified person (or persons described in § 53.4958–3(b) with respect to that person) to make or recommend any grants or distributions by the organization.

(3) Section 501(c)(4) organizations. In the case of an excess benefit transaction with a section 501(c)(4) applicable tax-exempt organization, the disqualified person must pay the correction amount, as defined in paragraph(c)of this section, to a successor section 501(c)(4) organization or, if no tax-exempt successor, to any organization described in section 501(c)(3) or (4) and exempt from tax under section 501(a), provided that the requirements of paragraphs (e)(2)(i) through (iii) of this section are satisfied (except that the requirement that the organization receiving the correction amount is described in section 170(b)(1)(A) (other than in section 170(b)(1)(A)(vii) and (viii)) shall not apply if the organization is described in section 501(c)(4)).

(f) Examples. The following examples illustrate the principles of this section describing the requirements of correction:

Example 1. W is an applicable tax-exempt organization for purposes of section 4958. D is a disqualified person with respect to W. W employed D in 1999 and made payments totaling $12t to D as compensation throughout the taxable year. The fair market value of D's services in 1999 was $7t. Thus, D received excess compensation in the amount of $5t, the excess benefit for purposes of section 4958. In accordance with § 53.4958–1(e)(1), the excess benefit transaction with respect to the series of compensatory payments during 1999 is deemed to occur on December 31, 1999, the last day of D's taxable year. In order to correct the excess benefit transaction on June 30, 2002, D must pay W, in cash or cash equivalents, excluding payment with a promissory note, $5t (the excess benefit) plus interest on $5t for the period from the date the excess benefit transaction occurred to the date of correction (i.e., December 31, 1999, to June 30, 2002). Because this period is not more than three years, the interest rate D must use to determine the interest on the excess benefit must equal or exceed the short-term AFR, compounded annually, for December, 1999 (5.74%, compounded annually).

Example 2. X is an applicable tax-exempt organization for purposes of section 4958. B is a disqualified person with respect to X. On January 1, 2000, B paid X $6v for Property F. Property F had a fair market value of $10v on January 1, 2000. Thus, the sales transaction on that date provided an excess benefit to B in the amount of $4v. In order to correct the excess benefit on July 5, 2005, B pays X, in cash or cash equivalents, excluding payment with a promissory note, $4v (the excess benefit) plus interest on $4v for the period from the date the excess benefit transaction occurred to the date of correction (i.e., January 1, 2000, to July 5, 2005). Because this period is over three but not over nine years, the interest rate B must use to determine the interest on the excess benefit must equal or exceed the mid-term AFR, compounded annually, for January, 2000 (6.21%, compounded annually).

Example 3. The facts are the same as in Example 2, except that B offers to return Property F. X agrees to accept the return of Property F, a decision in which B does not participate. Property F has declined in value since the date of the excess benefit transaction. On July 5, 2005, the property has a fair market value of $9v. For purposes of correction, B's return of Property F to X is treated as a payment of $9v, the fair market value of the property determined on the date the property is returned to the organization. If $9v is greater than the correction amount ($4v plus interest on $4v at a rate that equals or exceeds 6.21%, compounded annually, for the period from January 1, 2000, to July 5, 2005), then X may make a cash payment to B equal to the difference.

Example 4. The facts are the same as in Example 3, except that Property F has increased in value since January 1, 2000, the date the excess benefit transaction occurred, and on July 5, 2005, has a fair market value of $13v. For purposes of correction, B's return of Property F to X is treated as a payment of $10v, the fair market value of the property on the date the excess benefit transaction occurred. If $10v is greater than the correction amount ($4v plus interest on $4v at a rate that equals or exceeds 6.21%, compounded annually, for the period from January 1, 2000, to July 5, 2005), then X may make a cash payment to B equal to the difference.

Example 5. The facts are the same as in Example 2. Assume that the correction amount B paid X in cash on July 5, 2005, was $5.58v. On July 4, 2005, X loaned $5.58v to B, in exchange for a promissory note signed by B in the amount of $5.58v, payable with interest at a future date. These facts indicate that B engaged in the loan transaction to circumvent the requirement of this section that (except as provided in paragraph (b)(3) or (4) of this section), the correction amount must be paid only in cash or cash equivalents. As a result, the Commissioner may determine that B effectively transferred property other than cash or cash equivalents, and therefore did not satisfy the correction requirements of this section.

§ 53.4958–8. Special rules.

(a) Substantive requirements for exemption still apply. Section 4958 does not affect the substantive standards for tax exemption under section 501(c)(3) or (4), including the requirements that the organization be organized and operated exclusively for exempt purposes, and that no part of its net earnings inure to the benefit of any private shareholder or individual. Thus, regardless of whether a particular transaction is subject to excise taxes under section 4958, existing principles and rules may be implicated, such as the limitation on private benefit. For example, transactions that are not subject to section 4958 because of the initial contract exception described in § 53.4958–4(a)(3) may, under certain circumstances, jeopardize the organization's tax-exempt status.

(b) Interaction between section 4958 and section 7611 rules for church tax inquiries and examinations. The procedures of section 7611 will be used in initiating and conducting any inquiry or examination into whether an excess benefit transaction has occurred between a church and a disqualified person. For purposes of this rule, the reasonable belief required to initiate a church tax inquiry is satisfied if there is a reasonable belief that a section 4958 tax is due from a disqualified person with respect to a transaction involving a church. See § 301.7611–1 Q&A 19 of this chapter.

(c) Other substantiation requirements. These regulations, in § 53.4958–4(c)(3), set forth specific substantiation rules. Compliance with the specific substantiation rules of that section does not relieve applicable tax-exempt organizations of other rules and requirements of the Internal Revenue Code, regulations, Revenue Rulings, and other guidance issued by the Internal Revenue Service (including the substantiation rules of sections 162 and 274, or § 1.6001–1(a) and (c) of this chapter).

§ 53.4960–1. Scope and definitions.

(a) Scope. This section provides definitions for purposes of section 4960, this section, and §§ 53.4960–2 through 53.4960–6. Section 53.4960–2 provides definitions and rules for determining the amount of remuneration paid for a taxable year. Section 53.4960–3 provides definitions and rules for determining whether a parachute payment is paid. Section 53.4960–4 provides definitions and rules for calculating the amount of excess remuneration paid for a taxable year, excess parachute payments paid in a taxable year, and liability for the excise tax. Section 53.4960–5 is reserved for rules on the coordination of sections 4960 and 162(m). Section 53.4960–6 provides rules regarding the applicability date for the regulations in §§ 53.4960–1 through 53.4960–5. The rules and definitions provided in this section through § 53.4960–6 apply solely for purposes of section 4960 unless specified otherwise.

(b) Applicable tax-exempt organization—(1) In general. Applicable tax-exempt organization or ATEO means any organization that is one of the following types of organizations:

(i) Section 501(a) organization. The organization is exempt from taxation under section 501(a) (except as provided in paragraph (b)(2) or (b)(3) of this section);

(ii) Section 521 farmers' cooperative. The organization is a farmers' cooperative organization described in section 521(b)(1);

(iii) Section 115(1) organization. The organization has income excluded from taxation under section 115(1); or

(iv) Section 527 political organization. The organization is a political organization described in section 527(e)(1).

(2) Certain foreign organizations. Any foreign organization described in section 4948(b) that either is exempt from tax under section 501(a) or is a taxable private foundation (section 4948(b) organization) is not an ATEO. A foreign organization is an organization not created or organized in the United States or in any possession thereof, or under the law of the United States, any State, the District of Columbia, or any possession of the United States. See section 4948(b) and § 53.4948–1. For purposes of this paragraph (b)(2) and the application of section 4960 to a taxable year, an organization's status as a section 4948(b) organization is determined at the end of its taxable year.

(c) Applicable year—(1) In general. Applicable year means the calendar year ending with or within the ATEO's taxable year. See § 53.4960–4 regarding how an ATEO's applicable year affects the liability of related organizations.

* * *

(d) Covered employee—(1) In general. For each taxable year, covered employee means any individual who is one of the five highest-compensated employees of the ATEO for the taxable year or was a covered employee of the ATEO (or any predecessor) for any preceding taxable year beginning after December 31, 2016.

(2) Five highest-compensated employees—(i) In general. Except as otherwise provided in this paragraph (d)(2), an individual is one of an ATEO's five highest-compensated employees for the taxable year if the individual is among the five employees of the ATEO with the highest amount of remuneration paid during the applicable year, as determined under § 53.4960–2. However, remuneration for which the deduction is disallowed by reason of section 162(m) is taken into account for purposes of determining an ATEO's five highest-compensated employees. The five highest-compensated employees of an ATEO for the taxable year are identified on the basis of the total remuneration paid during the applicable year to the employee for services performed as an employee of the ATEO or any related organization. An ATEO may have fewer than five highest-compensated employees for a taxable year if it has fewer than five employees other than employees who are disregarded under paragraphs (d)(2)(ii) through (iv) of this section. For purposes of this paragraph (d)(2), a grant of a legally binding right (within the meaning of § 1.409A–1(b)) to vested remuneration is considered to be remuneration paid as of the date of grant, as described in § 53.4960–2(c)(2), and a person or governmental entity is considered to grant a legally binding right to nonvested remuneration if the person or governmental entity grants a legally binding right to remuneration that is not vested within the meaning of § 53.4960–2(c)(2). An employee is disregarded for purposes of determining an ATEO's five highest-compensated employees for a taxable year if, during the applicable year, neither the ATEO nor any related organization paid remuneration or granted a legally binding right to nonvested remuneration to the individual for services the individual performed as an employee of the ATEO or any related organization.

(ii) Limited hours exception—(A) In general. An individual is disregarded for purposes of determining an ATEO's five highest-compensated employees for a taxable year if all of the following requirements are met:

(1) Remuneration requirement. Neither the ATEO nor any related ATEO paid remuneration or granted a legally binding right to nonvested remuneration to the individual for services the individual performed as an employee of the ATEO during the applicable year; and

(2) Hours of service requirement. The individual performed services as an employee of the ATEO and all related ATEOs for no more than 10 percent of the total hours the individual worked as an employee of the ATEO and any related organizations during the applicable year. An ATEO may instead make this determination based on the total days the individual worked as an employee of the ATEO and all related ATEOs as a percentage of the total days worked as an employee of the ATEO and all related organizations, provided that for purposes of the calculation, any day that the individual worked at least one hour as an employee of the ATEO or a related ATEO is treated as a day worked as an employee of the ATEO and not for any other organization.

(B) Certain payments disregarded. For purposes of paragraph (d)(2)(ii)(A)(1) of this section, a payment of remuneration made to the individual by a related organization that is an employer of the individual and for which the related organization is neither entitled to reimbursement by the ATEO nor entitled to any other consideration from the ATEO is not considered remuneration paid by the ATEO under § 53.4960-2(b)(1), and a payment of remuneration made to the individual by a related organization is not treated as remuneration paid by the ATEO under § 53.4960-2(b)(2).

(C) Safe harbor. For purposes of paragraph (d)(2)(ii)(A)(2) of this section, an individual is treated as having performed services as an employee of the ATEO and all related ATEOs for no more than 10 percent of the total hours the individual worked as an employee of the ATEO and all related organizations during the applicable year if the employee performed no more than 100 hours of service as an employee of the ATEO and all related ATEOs during the applicable year.

(iii) Nonexempt funds exception—(A) In general. An individual is disregarded for purposes of determining an ATEO's five highest-compensated employees for a taxable year if all the following requirements are met:

(1) Remuneration requirement. Neither the ATEO, nor any related ATEO, nor any taxable related organization controlled by the ATEO, or by one or more related ATEOs, either alone or together with the ATEO, paid remuneration or granted a legally binding right to nonvested remuneration to the individual for services the individual performed as an employee of an ATEO during the applicable year and the preceding applicable year. For this purpose, whether a taxable related organization is controlled by the ATEO (or one or more related ATEOs) is determined without regard to paragraph (i)(2)(vii)(B)(2) of this section and without regard to section 318(a)(3) for purposes of applying paragraph (i)(2)(vii)(A) of this section, so that an interest in a corporation or nonstock entity is not attributed downward in determining control of the corporation or nonstock entity;

(2) Hours of service requirement. The individual performed services as an employee of the ATEO and any related ATEOs for not more than 50 percent of the total hours worked as an employee of the ATEO and any related organizations during the applicable year and the preceding applicable year. An ATEO may instead make this determination based on the total days the individual worked as an employee of the ATEO and all related ATEOs as a percentage of the total days worked as an employee of the ATEO and all related organizations, provided that for purposes of the calculation, any day that the individual worked at least one hour as an employee of the ATEO or a related ATEO is treated as a day worked as an employee of the ATEO and not for any other organization; and

(3) Related organizations requirement. No related organization that paid remuneration or granted a legally binding right to nonvested remuneration to the individual during the applicable year and the preceding applicable year provided services for a fee to the ATEO, to any related ATEO, or to any taxable related organization controlled by the ATEO or by one or more related ATEOs, either alone or together with the ATEO, during the applicable year and the preceding applicable year. For purposes of this paragraph (d)(2)(iii)(A)(3), whether a taxable related organization is controlled by the ATEO (or one or more related ATEOs) is determined without regard to paragraph (i)(2)(vii)(B)(2) of this section and without regard to section 318(a)(3) for purposes of applying paragraph (i)(2)(vii)(A) of this section, so that an interest in a corporation or nonstock entity is not attributed downward in determining control of the corporation or nonstock entity.

(B) Certain payments disregarded. For purposes of paragraph (d)(2)(iii)(A)(1) of this section, a payment of remuneration made to an individual by a related organization that is an employer of the individual and for which the related organization is neither entitled to reimbursement by the ATEO nor entitled to any other consideration from the ATEO is not considered remuneration paid by the ATEO under § 53.4960–2(b)(1) and a payment of remuneration made to the individual by a related organization is not treated as paid by the ATEO under § 53.4960–2(b)(2).

(iv) Limited services exception. An individual is disregarded for purposes of determining an ATEO's five highest-compensated employees for a taxable year even though the ATEO paid remuneration to the individual if, disregarding § 53.4960–2(b)(2), all of the following requirements are met:

(A) Remuneration requirement. The ATEO did not pay 10 percent or more of the individual's total remuneration for services performed as an employee of the ATEO and all related organizations during the applicable year; and

(B) Related ATEO requirement. The ATEO had at least one related ATEO during the applicable year and one of the following conditions applies:

(1) Ten percent remuneration condition. A related ATEO paid at least 10 percent of the remuneration paid by the ATEO and any related organizations during the applicable year; or

(2) Less remuneration condition. No related ATEO paid at least 10 percent of the total remuneration paid by the ATEO and any related organizations and the ATEO paid less remuneration to the individual than at least one related ATEO during the applicable year.

* * *

(e) Employee—(1) In general. Employee means an employee as defined in section 3401(c) and § 31.3401(c)–1. Section 31.3401(c)–1 generally defines an employee as any individual performing services if the relationship between the individual and the person for whom the individual performs services is the legal relationship of employer and employee. As set forth in § 31.3401(c)–1, this includes common law employees, as well as officers and employees of government entities, whether or not elected. An employee generally also includes an officer of a corporation, but an officer of a corporation who as such does not perform any services or performs only minor services and who neither receives, nor is entitled to receive, any remuneration is not considered to be an employee of the corporation solely due to the individual's status as an officer of the corporation. Whether an individual is an employee depends on the facts and circumstances.

(2) Directors. A director of a corporation (or an individual holding a substantially similar position in a corporation or other entity) in the individual's capacity as such is not an employee of the corporation. See § 31.3401(c)–1(f).

(3) Trustees. The principles of paragraph (e)(2) of this section apply by analogy to a trustee of any arrangement classified as a trust for Federal tax purposes in § 301.7701–4(a).

(f) Employer—(1) In general. Employer means an employer within the meaning of section 3401(d), without regard to section 3401(d)(1) or (2), meaning generally the person or governmental entity for whom the services were performed as an employee. Whether a person or governmental entity is the employer depends on the facts and circumstances, but a person does not cease to be the employer through use of a payroll agent under section 3504, a common paymaster under section 3121(s), a person described in section 3401(d)(1) or (2), a certified professional employer organization under section 7705, or any similar arrangement.

(2) Disregarded entities. In the case of a disregarded entity described in § 301.7701–3, § 301.7701–2(c)(2)(iv) does not apply; thus, the sole owner of the disregarded entity is treated as the employer of any individual performing services as an employee of the disregarded entity.

(g) Medical services—(1) Medical and veterinary services—(i) In general. Medical services means services directly performed by a licensed medical professional (as defined in paragraph (g)(2) of this section) for the diagnosis, cure, mitigation, treatment, or prevention of disease in humans or animals; services provided for the purpose of affecting any structure or function of the human or animal body; and other services integral to providing such medical services. For purposes of section 4960, teaching and research services are not medical services except to the extent that they involve the services performed to directly diagnose, cure, mitigate, treat, or prevent disease or affect a structure or function of the body. Administrative services may be integral to directly providing medical services. For example, documenting the care and condition of a patient is integral to providing medical services, as is accompanying another licensed professional as a supervisor while that medical professional provides medical services. However, managing an organization's operations, including scheduling, staffing, appraising employee performance, and other similar functions that may relate to a particular medical professional or professionals who perform medical services, is not integral to providing medical services. See § 53.4960–2(a)(2)(ii) for rules regarding allocating remuneration paid to a medical professional who performs both medical services and other services.

* * *

(2) Definition of licensed medical professional. Licensed medical professional means an individual who is licensed under applicable state or local law to perform medical services, including as a doctor, nurse, nurse practitioner, dentist, veterinarian, or other licensed medical professional.

* * *

(i) Related organization—(1) In general. Related organization means any person or governmental entity, domestic or foreign, that meets any of the following tests:

(i) Controls or controlled by test. The person or governmental entity controls, or is controlled by, the ATEO;

(ii) Controlled by same persons test. The person or governmental entity is controlled by one or more persons that control the ATEO;

(iii) Supported organization test. The person or governmental entity is a supported organization (as defined in section 509(f)(3)) with respect to the ATEO;

(iv) Supporting organization test. The person or governmental entity is a supporting organization described in section 509(a)(3) with respect to the ATEO; or

(v) VEBA test. With regard to an ATEO that is a voluntary employees' beneficiary association (VEBA) described in section 501(c)(9), the person or governmental entity establishes, maintains, or makes contributions to such VEBA.

(2) Control—(i) In general. Control may be direct or indirect. For rules concerning application of the principles of section 318 in applying this paragraph (i)(2), see paragraph (i)(2)(vii) of this section.

(ii) Stock corporation. A person or governmental entity controls a stock corporation if it owns (by vote or value) more than 50 percent of the stock in the stock corporation.

(iii) Partnership. A person or governmental entity controls a partnership if it owns more than 50 percent of the profits interests or capital interests in the partnership, determined in accordance with the rules and principles of § 1.706–1(b)(4)(ii) for a partner's interest in the profits of a partnership and § 1.706–1(b)(4)(iii) for a partner's interest in the capital of a partnership.

(iv) Trust. A person or governmental entity controls a trust if it owns more than 50 percent of the beneficial interests in the trust, determined by actuarial value.

(v) Nonstock organization—(A) In general. A person or governmental entity controls a nonstock organization if more than 50 percent of the trustees or directors of the nonstock organization are either representatives of, or directly or indirectly controlled by, the person or governmental entity. A nonstock organization is a nonprofit organization or other organization without owners and includes a governmental entity.

(B) Control of a trustee or director of a nonstock organization. A person or governmental entity controls a trustee or director of the nonstock organization if the person or governmental entity has the power (either at will or at regular intervals) to remove such trustee or director and designate a new one.

(C) Representatives. Trustees, directors, officers, employees, or agents of a person or governmental entity are deemed representatives of the person or governmental entity. However, an employee of a person or governmental entity (other than a trustee, director, or officer, or an employee who possesses at least the authority commonly exercised by an officer) who is a director or trustee of a nonstock organization (or acting in that capacity) will not be treated as a representative of the person or governmental entity if the employee does not act as a representative of the person or governmental entity and that fact is reported in the form and manner prescribed by the Commissioner in forms and instructions.

(vi) Brother-sister related organizations. Under paragraph (i)(1)(ii) of this section, an organization is a related organization with respect to an ATEO if one or more persons control both the ATEO and the other organization. In the case of control by multiple persons, the control tests described in this paragraph (i)(2) of this section apply to the persons as a group. For example, if 1,000 individuals who are members of both ATEO 1 and ATEO 2 elect a majority of the board members of each organization, then ATEO 1 and ATEO 2 are related to each other because the same group of 1,000 persons controls both ATEO 1 and ATEO 2.

(vii) Section 318 principles—(A) In general. Section 318 (relating to constructive ownership of stock) applies in determining ownership of stock in a corporation. The principles of section 318 also apply for purposes of determining ownership of interests in a partnership or in a trust with beneficial interests. For example, applying the principles of section 318(a)(1)(A), an individual is considered to own the partnership interest or trust interest owned, directly or indirectly, by or for the family members specified in such section.

* * *

§ 53.4960–2. Determination of remuneration paid for a taxable year.

(a) Remuneration—(1) In general. For purposes of section 4960, remuneration means any amount that is wages as defined in section 3401(a), excluding any designated Roth contribution (as defined in section 402A(c)) and including any amount required to be included in gross income under section 457(f). Remuneration includes amounts includible in gross income as compensation for services as an employee pursuant to a below-market loan described in section 7872(c)(1)(B)(i) (compensation-related loans) but does not include amounts excepted by section 7872(c)(3) ($10,000 de minimis exception). For example, see § 1.7872–15(e)(1)(i). Director's fees paid by a corporation to a director of the corporation are not remuneration, provided that if the director is also an employee of the corporation, the director's fees are excluded from remuneration only to the extent that they do not exceed fees paid to a director who is not an employee of the corporation or any related organization or, if there is no such director, they do not exceed reasonable director's fees. Remuneration does not include any amount that vested or was paid by a taxpayer before the start of the taxpayer's first taxable year that began on or after January 1, 2018.

(2) Exclusion of remuneration for medical services—(i) In general. Remuneration does not include the portion of any remuneration paid to a licensed medical professional that is for the performance of medical services by such professional.

(ii) Allocation of remuneration for medical services and non-medical services. If, during an applicable year, an employer pays a covered employee remuneration for providing both medical services and non-medical services, the employer must make a reasonable, good faith allocation between the remuneration for medical services and the remuneration for non-medical services. For example, if a medical doctor receives current remuneration (or vests in remuneration under a deferred compensation plan) for providing medical services and administrative or management services, the employer must make a reasonable, good faith allocation between the remuneration for the medical services and the remuneration for the administrative or management services. For this purpose, if an employment agreement or similar written arrangement sets forth the remuneration to be paid for particular services, that allocation of remuneration applies unless the facts and circumstances demonstrate that the amount allocated to medical services is unreasonable for those services or that the allocation was established for purposes of avoiding application of the excise tax under section 4960. If some or all of the remuneration is not reasonably allocated in an employment agreement or similar arrangement, an employer may use any reasonable allocation method. For example, an employer may use a representative sample of records, such as patient, insurance, and Medicare/Medicaid billing records or internal time reporting mechanisms to determine the time spent providing medical services, and then allocate remuneration to medical services in the proportion such time bears to the total hours the employee worked for the employer (and any related employer) for purposes of making a reasonable allocation of remuneration. Similarly, if some or all of the remuneration is not reasonably allocated in an employment agreement or other similar arrangement, an employer may use salaries or other remuneration paid by the employer or similarly situated employers for duties comparable to those the employee performs (for example, hospital administrator and physician) for purposes of making a reasonable allocation between remuneration for providing medical services and for providing non-medical services.

§ 53.4960–3. Determination of whether there is a parachute payment.

(a) Parachute payment—(1) In general. Except as otherwise provided in paragraph (a)(2) of this section (relating to payments excluded from the definition of a parachute payment), parachute payment means any payment in the nature of compensation made by an ATEO (or a predecessor of the ATEO) or a related organization to (or for the benefit of) a covered employee if the payment is contingent on the employee's separation from employment with the employer, and the aggregate present value of the payments in the nature of compensation to (or for the benefit of) the individual that are contingent on the separation equals or exceeds an amount equal to 3-times the base amount.

(2) Exclusions. The following payments are not parachute payments:

(i) Certain qualified plans. A payment that is a contribution to or a distribution from a plan described in section 401(a) that includes a trust exempt from tax under section 501(a), an annuity plan described in section 403(a), a simplified employee pension (as defined in section 408(k)), or a simple retirement account described in section 408(p);

(ii) Certain annuity contracts. A payment made under or to an annuity contract described in section 403(b) or a plan described in section 457(b);

(iii) Compensation for medical services. A payment made to a licensed medical professional for the performance of medical services performed by such professional; and

(iv) Payments to non-HCEs. A payment made to an individual who is not a highly compensated employee (HCE) as defined in paragraph (a)(3) of this section.

* * *

(b) Payment in the nature of compensation—(1) In general. Any payment—in whatever form—is a payment in the nature of compensation if the payment arises out of an employment relationship, including holding oneself out as available to perform services and refraining from performing services. Thus, for example, a payment made under a covenant not to compete or a similar arrangement is a payment in the nature of compensation. A payment in the nature of compensation includes (but is not limited to) wages and salary, bonuses, severance pay, fringe benefits, life insurance, pension benefits, and other deferred compensation (including any amount characterized by the parties as interest or earnings thereon). A payment in the nature of compensation also includes cash when paid, the value of the right to receive cash, the value of accelerated vesting, or a transfer of property. The vesting of an option, stock appreciation right, or similar form of compensation as a result of a covered employee's separation from employment is a payment in the nature of compensation. However, a payment in the nature of compensation does not include attorney's fees or court costs paid or incurred in connection with the payment of any parachute payment or a reasonable rate of interest accrued on any amount during the period the parties contest whether a parachute payment will be made.

(2) Consideration paid by covered employee. Any payment in the nature of compensation is reduced by the amount of any money or the fair market value of any property (owned by the covered employee without restriction) that is (or will be) transferred by the covered employee in exchange for the payment.

(c) When payment is considered to be made—(1) In general. A payment in the nature of compensation is considered made in the taxable year in which it is includible in the covered employee's gross income or, in the case of fringe benefits and other benefits that are excludable from income, in the taxable year the benefits are received. In the case of taxable non-cash fringe benefits provided in a calendar year, payment is considered made on the date or dates the employer chooses, but no later than December 31 of the calendar year in which the benefits are provided, except that when the fringe benefit is the transfer of personal property (either tangible or intangible) of a kind normally held for investment or the transfer of real property, payment is considered made on the actual date of transfer. If the fringe benefit is neither a transfer of personal property nor a transfer of real property, the employer may, in its discretion, treat the value of the benefit actually provided during the last two months of the calendar year as paid during the subsequent calendar year. However, an employer that treats the value of a benefit paid during the last two months of a calendar year as paid during the subsequent calendar year under this rule must treat the value of that fringe benefit as paid during the subsequent calendar year with respect to all employees who receive it.

(2) Transfers of section 83 property. A transfer of property in connection with the performance of services that is subject to section 83 is considered a payment made in the taxable year in which the property is transferred or would be includible in the gross income of the covered employee under section 83, disregarding any election made by the employee under section 83(b) or (i). Thus, in general, such a payment is considered made at the later of the date the property is transferred (as defined in § 1.83–3(a)) to the covered employee or the date the property becomes substantially vested (as defined in § 1.83–3(b) and (j)). The amount of the payment is the compensation as determined under section 83, disregarding any amount includible in income pursuant to an election made by an employee under section 83(b).

(3) Stock options. An option (including an option to which section 421 applies) is treated as property that is transferred when the option becomes vested (regardless of whether the option has a readily ascertainable fair market value as defined in § 1.83–7(b)). For purposes of determining the timing and amount of any payment related to the option, the principles of § 1.280G–1, Q/A-13 and any method prescribed by the Commissioner in published guidance of general applicability under § 601.601(d)(2) apply.

(d) Payment contingent on an employee's separation from employment—(1) In general. A payment is contingent on an employee's separation from employment if the facts and circumstances indicate that the employer would not make the payment in the absence of the employee's involuntary separation from employment. A payment generally would be made in the absence of the employee's involuntary separation from employment if it is substantially certain at the time of the involuntary separation from employment that the payment would be made whether or not the involuntary separation occurred. A payment the right to which is not subject to a substantial risk of forfeiture within the meaning of section 457(f)(3)(B) at the time of an involuntary separation from employment generally is a payment that would have been made in the absence of an involuntary separation from employment (and is therefore not contingent on a separation from employment), except that the increased value of an accelerated payment of a vested amount described in paragraph (f)(3) of this section resulting from an involuntary separation from employment is not treated as a payment that would have been made in the absence of an involuntary separation from employment. A payment the right to which is no longer subject to a substantial risk of forfeiture within the meaning of section 457(f)(3)(B) as a result of an involuntary separation from employment, including a payment the vesting of which is accelerated due to the separation from employment as described in paragraph (f)(3) of this section, is not treated as a payment that would have been made in the absence of an involuntary separation from employment (and thus is contingent on a separation from employment). A payment does not fail to be contingent on a separation from employment merely because the payment is conditioned upon the execution of a release of claims, noncompetition or nondisclosure provisions, or other similar requirements. See paragraph (d)(3) of this section for the treatment of a payment made pursuant to a covenant not to compete. If, after an involuntary separation from employment, the former employee continues to provide certain services as a nonemployee, payments for services rendered as a nonemployee are not payments that are contingent on a separation from employment to the extent those payments are reasonable and are not made on account of the involuntary separation from employment. Whether services are performed as an employee or nonemployee depends upon all the facts and circumstances. See § 53.4960–1(e). For rules on determining whether payments are reasonable compensation for services, the rules of § 1.280G–1, Q/A-40 through Q/A-42 (excluding Q/A-40(b) and Q/A-42(b)), and Q/A-44 are applied by analogy (substituting involuntary separation from employment for change in ownership or control).

(2) Employment agreements—(i) In general. If a covered employee involuntarily separates from employment before the end of a contract term and is paid damages for breach of contract pursuant to an employment agreement, the payment of damages is treated as a payment that is contingent on a separation from employment. An employment agreement is an agreement between an employee and employer that describes, among other things, the amount of compensation or remuneration payable to the employee for services performed during the term of the agreement.

* * *

§ 53.4960–4. Liability for tax on excess remuneration and excess parachute payments.

(a) Liability, reporting, and payment of excise taxes—(1) Liability. For each taxable year, with respect to each covered employee, the taxpayer is liable for tax at the rate imposed under section 11 on the sum of the excess remuneration allocated to the taxpayer under paragraph (c) of this section and, if the taxpayer is an ATEO, any excess parachute payment paid by the taxpayer or a predecessor during the taxable year.

(2) Reporting and payment. The excise tax imposed by section 4960 is reported as provided in §§ 53.6011–1(b) and 53.6071–1(i) and paid in the form and manner prescribed by the Commissioner.

(3) Arrangements between an ATEO and a related organization. Calculation of, and liability for, the excise tax imposed by section 4960 is separate from, and unaffected by, any arrangement that an ATEO and any related organization may have for bearing the cost of any liability for the excise tax imposed by section 4960.

(4) Certain foreign related organizations. A related organization that is a foreign organization described in section 4948(b) that either is exempt from tax under section 501(a) or is a taxable private foundation (section 4948(b) related organization) is not liable for the excise tax imposed by section 4960. A foreign organization is an organization not created or organized in the United States or in any possession thereof, or under the law of the United States, any State, the District of Columbia, or any possession of the United States. See section 4948(b) and § 53.4948–1.

For purposes of this paragraph (a)(4) and the application of section 4960 to a taxable year, an organization's status as a section 4948(b) related organization is determined at the end of its taxable year. However, remuneration that the section 4948(b) related organization pays to a covered employee of an ATEO must be taken into account by the ATEO and other related organizations for purposes of section 4960 generally, including for purposes of determining the five highest-compensated employees and the total remuneration paid to a covered employee. For example, if an ATEO and its related organization that is a section 4948(b) related organization each paid $600,000 remuneration to a covered employee during the applicable year, then the related organization would not be liable for the tax that would otherwise be allocable to it, and the ATEO would be liable for tax on $100,000 (50 percent of the $200,000 excess remuneration paid to the employee).

(5) [Reserved]

(b) Amounts subject to tax—(1) Excess remuneration—(i) In general. Excess remuneration means the amount of remuneration paid by an ATEO to any covered employee during an applicable year in excess of $1 million, as determined under § 53.4960–2.

(ii) Exclusion for excess parachute payments. Excess remuneration does not include any amount that is an excess parachute payment as defined in paragraph (b)(2) of this section.

(2) Excess parachute payment. Excess parachute payment means an amount equal to the excess (if any) of the amount of any parachute payment paid by an ATEO, a predecessor of the ATEO, or a related organization, or on behalf of any such person, during the taxable year over the portion of the base amount allocated to such payment.

* * *

ABATEMENT

§ 53.4961–1. Abatement of second tier taxes for correction within correction period.

If any taxable event is corrected during the correction period for the event, then any second tier tax imposed with respect to the event shall not be assessed. If the tax has been assessed, it shall be abated. If the tax has been collected, it shall be credited or refunded as an overpayment. For purposes of this section, the tax imposed includes interest, additions to the tax and additional amounts. For definitions of the terms "second tier tax," "taxable event," "correct," and "correction period," see § 53.4963–1.

§ 53.4961–2. Court proceedings to determine liability for second tier tax.

(a) Introduction. Under section 4961(b) and (c), the period of limitations on collection may be suspended and assessment or collection of first or second tier tax may be prohibited during the pendency of administrative and judicial proceedings conducted to determine a taxpayer's liability for second tier tax. This section provides rules relating to the suspension of the limitations period and the prohibitions on assessment and collection. In addition, this section describes the administrative and judicial proceedings to which these rules apply.

(b) Initial proceeding—(1) Defined. For purposes of subpart K, an initial proceeding means a proceeding described in subparagraph (2) or (3).

(2) Tax Court proceeding before assessment. A proceeding is described in this subparagraph (2) if it is a proceeding with respect to the taxpayer's liability for second tier tax and is commenced in accordance with section 6213(a).

(3) Refund proceeding commenced before correction period ends. A proceeding is described in this subparagraph (3) if it is a proceeding commenced under section 7422, in accordance with the provisions of § 53.4963–1(e)(4) and (5) (relating to prerequisites to extension of the correction period during certain refund proceedings), and with respect to the taxpayer's liability for second tier tax.

(c) Supplemental proceeding—(1) Jurisdiction. If a determination in an initial proceeding that a taxpayer is liable for a second tier tax has become final, the court in which the initial proceeding was commenced shall have jurisdiction to conduct any necessary supplemental proceeding to determine whether the taxable event was corrected during the correction period.

(2) Time for beginning proceeding. The time for beginning a supplemental proceeding begins on the day after a determination in an initial proceeding becomes final and ends on the 90th day after the last day of the correction period.

(d) Restriction on assessment during Tax Court proceeding. If a supplemental proceeding described in section 4961(b) and § 53.4961–2(c) is commenced in the Tax Court, the provisions of the second and third sentences of section 6213(a) and the first and third sentences of § 301.6213–1(a)(2) apply with respect to a deficiency in second tier tax until the decision of the Tax Court in the supplemental proceeding is final.

(e) Suspension of period of collection for second tier tax—(1) Scope. Except as provided in subparagraph (6), this paragraph (e) applies to the second tier tax assessed with respect to a taxable event if a claim described in subparagraph (2) is filed.

(2) Claim for refund. A claim for refund is described in this subparagraph (2) if, no later than 90 days after the day on which the second tier tax is assessed with respect to a taxable event, the taxpayer—

(i) Pays the full amount of first tier tax for the taxable period, and

(ii) Files a claim for refund of the amount paid.

(3) Collection prohibited. No levy or proceeding in court for the collection of the second tier tax shall be made, begun, or prosecuted until the end of the collection prohibition period described in subparagraph (5). Notwithstanding section 7421(a), the collection by levy or proceeding may be enjoined during the collection prohibition period by a proceeding in the proper court.

(4) Suspension of running of period of limitations on collection. With respect to a second tier tax to which this paragraph (e) applies, the running of the period of limitations provided in section 6502 (relating to collection of tax by levy or by a proceeding in court) shall be suspended for the collection prohibition period described in subparagraph (5).

(5) Collection prohibition period. The collection prohibition period begins on the day the second tier tax is assessed and ends on the latest of:

(i) The day a decision in a refund proceeding commenced before the 91st day after denial of the claim described in subparagraph (2) of this paragraph (including any supplemental proceeding under § 53.4961–2(c)) becomes final;

(ii) The 90th day after the claim referred to in subparagraph (2) is denied; or

(iii) The 90th day after the second tier tax is assessed.

(6) Jeopardy collection. If the Secretary makes a finding that the collection of the second tier tax is in jeopardy, nothing in this paragraph (e) shall prevent the immediate collection of such tax.

(f) Finality—(1) Tax Court proceeding. For purposes of this subpart K, section 7481 applies in determining when a decision in a Tax Court proceeding becomes final.

(2) Refund proceeding. For purposes of this subpart K, § 301.7422–1 applies in determining when a decision in a refund proceeding becomes final.

§ 53.4963–1. Definitions.

(a) First tier tax. For purposes of this subpart K, the term first tier tax means any tax imposed by subsection (a) of section 4941, 4942, 4943, 4944, 4945, 4951, 4952, 4955, 4958, 4971, or 4975. A first tier tax may also be referred to as an "initial tax" in parts 53 and 54.

(b) Second tier tax. For purposes of this subpart K, the term second tier tax means any tax imposed by subsection (b) of section 4941, 4942, 4943, 4944, 4945, 4951, 4952, 4955, 4958, 4971, or 4975. A second tier tax may also be referred to as an "additional tax" in parts 53 and 54.

(c) Taxable event. For purposes of this subpart K, the term taxable event means any act, or failure to act, giving rise to liability for tax under section 4941, 4942, 4943, 4944, 4945, 4951, 4952, 4955, 4958, 4971, or 4975.

(d) Correct—(1) In general. Except as provided in subparagraph (2), the term correct has the same meaning for purposes of this subpart K as in the section which imposes the second tier tax or the regulations thereunder.

(2) Special rules. The term correct means—

(i) For a second tier tax imposed by section 4942(b), reducing the amount of the undistributed income to zero,

(ii) For a second tier tax imposed by section 4943(b), reducing the amount of the excess business holdings to zero, and

(iii) For a second tier tax imposed by section 4944(b), removing the investment from jeopardy.

(e) Correction period—(1) In general. The correction period with respect to any taxable event shall begin with the date on which the taxable event occurs and shall end 90 days after the date of mailing of a notice of deficiency under section 6212 with respect to the second tier tax imposed with respect to the taxable event.

(2) Extensions of correction period. The correction period referred to in subparagraph (1) of this paragraph shall be extended by any period in which a deficiency cannot be assessed under section 6213(a). In addition, the correction period referred to in subparagraph (1) of this paragraph (e) shall be extended in accordance with subparagraph (3), (4), and (5) of this paragraph except that subparagraph (4), or (5) shall not operate to extend a correction period with respect to which a taxpayer has filed a petition with the United States Tax Court for redetermination of a deficiency within the time prescribed by section 6213(a).

(3) Extensions by Commissioner. The correction period referred to in subparagraph (1) of this paragraph may be extended by any period which the Commissioner determines is reasonable and necessary to bring about correction (including, for taxes imposed by section 4975, equitable relief sought by the Secretary of Labor) of the taxable event. The Commissioner ordinarily will not extend the correction period unless the following factors are present.

(i) The taxpayer on whom the second tier tax is imposed, the Secretary of Labor (for taxes imposed by section 4975), or an appropriate State officer (as defined in section 6104(c)(2)) is actively seeking in good faith to correct the taxable event;

(ii) Adequate corrective action cannot reasonably be expected to result during the unextended correction period;

(iii) For taxes imposed by section 4975, the Secretary of Labor requests the extension because subdivision (ii) applies; and

(iv) For taxes imposed by chapter 42 (other than taxes imposed by section 4940), the taxable event appears to have been an isolated occurrence so that it appears unlikely that similar taxable events will occur in the future.

(4) Extension for payment of first tier tax. If, within the unexpected correction period, the taxpayer pays the full amount of the first tier tax imposed with respect to the taxable event the Commissioner shall extend the correction period to the later of—

(i) Ninety days after the payment of the first tier tax, or

(ii) The last day of the correction period determined without regard to this paragraph.

(5) Extensions for filing claim for refund or refund suit. If prior to the expiration of the correction period (including extensions) a claim for refund is filed with respect to payment of the full amount of the first tier tax imposed with respect to the taxable event, the Commissioner shall extend the correction period during the pendency of the claim plus an additional 90 days. If within that time a suit or proceeding referred to in section 7422(g) with respect to the claim is filed, the Commissioner shall extend the correction period until the determination in the suit for refund (determined without regard to a supplemental proceeding under section 4861(b)) is final, determined under § 301.7422–2(a).

(6) End of correction period if waiver accepted. If the notice of deficiency referred to in paragraph (1) is not mailed because there is a waiver of the restrictions on assessment and collection of the deficiency or because the deficiency is paid, the correction period will end with the end of the collection prohibition period described in § 53.4961–2(e)(5).

(7) Date on which taxable event occurs. For purposes of subparagraph (1), the taxable event shall be treated as occurring—

(i) Under section 4942, on the first day of the taxable year for which there is undistributed income,

(ii) Under section 4943, on the first day on which there are excess business holdings,

(iii) Under section 4971, on the last day of the plan year in which there is an accumulated funding deficiency, and

(iv) In all other cases, the date on which the event occurred.

(f) Effective date. The provisions of this subpart K are effective with respect to second tier taxes assessed after December 24, 1980. The preceding sentence shall not be construed to permit the assessment of a tax in a case to which, on December 24, 1980, the doctrine of res judicata applied.

TAX ON INVESTMENT INCOME

§ 53.4968–1. Excise tax based on investment income of certain private colleges and universities.

(a) Excise tax on the investment income of certain private colleges and universities. For taxable years beginning after December 31, 2017, section 4968 of the Internal Revenue Code (Code) imposes a tax equal to 1.4 percent of the net investment income (as defined in section 4968(c) and § 53.4968–2) of an applicable educational institution (as defined in section 4968(b)(1) and paragraph (b)(1) of this section).

(b) Definitions. The definitions in this paragraph (b) apply for purposes of section 4968 and §§ 53.4968–1 through 53.4968–4.

(1) Applicable educational institution. The term applicable educational institution means any eligible educational institution (as defined in section 25A(f)(2) of the Code and § 1.25A–2(b) of this chapter)—

(i) That had at least 500 tuition-paying students during the preceding taxable year;

(ii) More than 50 percent of whose tuition-paying students are located in the United States;

(iii) That is not described in the first sentence of section 511(a)(2)(B) of the Code (relating to state colleges and universities); and

(iv) The aggregate fair market value of the assets of which at the end of such preceding taxable year (other than those assets that are used directly in carrying out the institution's exempt purpose) is at least $500,000 per student.

(2) Student. The term student means a person who is enrolled and attending a course for academic credit from the institution and who is being charged tuition at a rate that is commensurate with the tuition rate charged to students enrolled for a degree. The number of students of an educational institution (including for purposes of determining the number of students at a particular location) is based on the daily average number of full-time students (with part-time students taken into account on a full-time student equivalent basis). The standards for determining part-time students, full-time students, full-time equivalents, and daily average are determined by each educational institution. However, the standards may not be lower than the minimum applicable standards established by the Department of Education under the Higher Education Act of 1965 (20 U.S.C. 1088), as amended.

(3) Tuition-paying—(i) In general. The term tuition-paying means the payment of any tuition or fees required for the enrollment or attendance of a student for a course of instruction at an educational institution. Tuition and fees do not include payment for supplies or equipment required during a specific course once a student is enrolled in and attending the course, or payment for room and board or other personal living expenses.

(ii) Treatment of a comprehensive or bundled fee. If a student is required to pay a fee (such as a comprehensive fee or a bundled fee) to an educational institution that combines charges for tuition with charges for personal expenses such as room and board, the student is a tuition-paying student.

(iii) Scholarships, grants, and work study programs. Whether a student is tuition-paying is determined after taking into account any scholarships and grants provided directly by the educational institution or by the Federal government or any state or local government, and after application of any work study programs operated directly by the institution. Scholarships and grants provided by non-governmental third parties, even if administered by the institution, are considered payments of tuition on behalf of the student. Accordingly, a student will be considered a tuition-paying student if payment of tuition or a fee is required for the enrollment or attendance of the student for courses of instruction after the application of any scholarships offered directly by the institution, any work study program operated directly by the institution, and any grants and scholarships provided by the Federal government or any state or local government.

(4) Located in the United States. A student is located in the United States if the student resided in the United States for at least a portion of the time the student attended the educational institution during the institution's preceding taxable year. Whether a student resided in the United States in any given year can be determined using any reasonable method, as long as that method is consistently applied.

(5) Assets used directly in carrying out an institution's exempt purpose— (i) In general. Except as provided in paragraph (b)(5)(iv) of this section, an asset is used directly in carrying out an educational institution's exempt purpose only if the asset is actually used directly by the institution in carrying out its exempt purpose. Whether an asset is used directly by the institution to carry out its exempt purpose is determined based on all the facts and circumstances. If property is used for an exempt purpose and for other purposes, and the exempt use represents 95 percent or more of the total use, the property is considered to be used exclusively for an exempt purpose. If the exempt use of such property represents less than 95 percent of the total use, the institution must make a reasonable allocation between such exempt and nonexempt uses.

(ii) Illustrations. Examples of assets that are used directly in carrying out an institution's exempt purpose include, but are not limited to, the following—

(A) Administrative assets, such as office equipment and supplies used by the institution directly in the administration of its exempt activities;

(B) Real estate or the portion of any building used by the institution directly in its exempt activities;

(C) Physical property such as paintings or other works of art owned by the institution that are on public display (or held for public display), fixtures and equipment in classrooms, research facilities and related equipment that under the facts and circumstances serve a useful purpose in the conduct of the institution's exempt activities;

(D) The reasonable cash balance, determined using any reasonable method, necessary to cover current operating and administrative expenses and other normal and current disbursements directly connected with the educational institution's exempt activities. For this purpose, a reasonable method would include calculating an amount equal to three months of operating expenses allocable to program services, calculated by dividing annual functional expenses allocable to program services by four. A larger amount may be a reasonable cash balance for this purpose if, under the facts and circumstances, a larger amount is established to be necessary to cover administrative expenses and other normal disbursements directly connected with the institution's exempt activity.

(E) Any property the educational institution leases to other persons at no cost (or at a nominal rent) to the lessee in furtherance of the institution's exempt purposes; and

(F) Patents, copyrights, and other intellectual property and intangible property to the extent that income from those assets is excluded from net investment income by § 53.4968–2(b)(2)(iii).

(iii) Assets not used directly. The following assets are examples of assets not used directly in carrying out an institution's exempt purpose—

(A) Assets that are held for the production of income or for investment (for example, stocks, bonds, interest-bearing notes, endowment funds, or leased real estate not described in paragraph (b)(5)(ii)(E) of this section), even if the income from such assets is used to carry out such exempt purpose; and

(B) Property (such as offices and equipment) used for the purpose of managing the institution's endowment funds.

(iv) Assets of related organizations. An asset of a related organization that is treated as an asset of an educational institution by section 4968(d) and § 53.4968–3(c) and that is used directly in carrying out an educational institution's exempt purpose, or that is used directly in carrying out the exempt purpose of a related organization that is described in section 501(c)(3), is considered used directly by the educational institution in carrying out its exempt purpose.

(v) Valuation of assets not used directly in carrying out an institution's exempt purpose—(A) In general. The values of assets not used directly in carrying out an educational institution's exempt purpose are determined under the rules of section 4942(e) and § 53.4942(a)–2(c)(4), as modified by paragraph (b)(5)(v)(B) of this section.

(B) Modifications. In applying the rules of § 53.4942(a)–2(c)(4), an educational institution must—

(1) Substitute "educational institution" for "private foundation" or "foundation" every place they appear; and

(2) Make such adjustments as are reasonable and necessary to obtain the fair market value of any and all assets as of the last day of the preceding taxable year, rather than as of any other times permitted or required by § 53.4942(a)–2(c)(4).

§ 53.4968–2. Net investment income.

(a) Net investment income—(1) In general. For taxable years beginning after December 31, 2017, section 4968(a) of the Internal Revenue Code (Code) imposes a 1.4 percent excise tax on the net investment income (as defined in section 4968(c) and this section) of an applicable educational institution and on certain amounts of net investment income of certain related organizations, as described in section 4968(d) and § 53.4968–3. For purposes of this section, net investment income is determined under rules similar to the rules of section 4940(c) of the Code. Thus, net investment income generally is the amount by which the sum of the gross investment income (as defined in paragraph (b) of this section) and the capital gain net income (as defined in paragraph (d) of this section) exceeds the deductions allowed by paragraph (c) of this section. Except to the extent inconsistent with the provisions of this section, net investment income is determined under the principles of subtitle A of the Code.

(2) Tax-exempt income. For purposes of this section, net investment income is determined by applying section 103 of the Code (relating to State and local bonds) and section 265 of the Code (relating to expenses and interest relating to tax-exempt income).

(b) Gross investment income—(1) In general. For purposes of this section and except as provided in paragraph (b)(2) of this section, the term gross investment income means the gross amounts of income from interest, dividends, rents, payments with respect to securities loans (as defined in section 512(a)(5) of the Code), and royalties, but not including any such income to the extent included in computing the tax imposed by section 511 of the Code. Such term also includes income from sources similar to those in the preceding sentence. In general, gross investment income includes the items of investment income described in § 1.512(b)–1(a) of this chapter.

(2) Exceptions. The following items of income are excluded from the definition of gross investment income:

(i) Interest income from a student loan that was made by the applicable educational institution or a related organization to a student of the applicable educational institution in connection with the student's attendance at the institution;

(ii) Rental income from the provision of housing by the applicable educational institution or a related organization to students of the applicable educational institution and from housing for faculty and staff if the housing is provided contingent on their roles as faculty or staff of the applicable educational institution; and

(iii) Royalty income that is derived from patents, copyrights, and other intellectual property and intangible property to the extent those assets resulted from the work of student(s) or faculty member(s) in their capacities as such with the applicable educational institution. However, neither royalty income from trademarks on the institution's logo or name nor royalty income from intellectual property donated or sold to the institution is excluded from gross investment income under this rule.

(c) Deductions—(1) In general. For purposes of computing net investment income—

(i) There is allowed as a deduction from gross investment income all the ordinary and necessary expenses paid or incurred for the production or collection of gross investment income or for the management, conservation, or maintenance of property held for the production of such income, determined with the modifications set forth in paragraph (c)(2) of this section. Taxes paid or incurred under section 4968 are not paid or incurred for the production or collection of gross investment income. Allowable expenses include that portion of an applicable educational institution's operating expenses that is paid or incurred for the production or collection of gross investment income. An applicable educational institution's operating expenses include compensation of officers, other salaries and wages of employees, outside professional fees, interest, and rent and taxes on property used in the applicable educational institution's operations. Where an applicable educational institution's officers or employees engage in activities on behalf of the institution for both activities that generate net investment income and for activities that do not generate net investment income, compensation and salaries paid to such officers or employees must be allocated between the activities that generate net investment income and for activities that do not generate net investment income.

(ii) Where only a portion of property produces, or is held for the production of, income subject to the section 4968 excise tax, and the remainder of the property is used for other purposes, the deductions allowed by this paragraph must be apportioned between the taxable and other uses.

(iii) No amount is allowable as a deduction under this section to the extent it is paid or incurred for purposes other than those described in paragraph (c)(1)(i) of this section. Thus, for example, the charitable deductions prescribed under sections 170 and 642(c) of the Code; the net operating loss deduction prescribed under section 172; and the special deductions prescribed under part VIII of subchapter B of chapter 1 of the Code are not allowable.

(2) Deduction modifications. The following modifications must be made in determining deductions otherwise allowable under this paragraph (c):

(i) The depreciation deduction is allowed, but only on the basis of the straight-line method provided in section 168(b)(3) and without regard to section 168(b)(1) and (2).

(ii) The depletion deduction is allowed, but such deduction is determined without regard to sections 613 and 613A of the Code, relating to percentage depletion.

(iii) The basis to be used for purposes of the deduction allowed for depreciation or depletion is the basis determined under the rules of part II of subchapter O of chapter 1 of the Code (part II of subchapter O), subject to the modifications found in paragraphs (c)(2)(i) and (ii) of this section (relating to depreciation and depletion), and without regard to § 53.4968–2(d)(2) (relating to the basis for determining gain for property held on December 31, 2017, and continuously thereafter to the date of disposition), or section 362(c) of the Code (relating to certain special basis rules regarding contributions of capital to corporations). Thus, an applicable educational institution must reduce the cost or other substituted or transferred basis by an amount equal to the straight-line depreciation or cost depletion, without regard to whether the applicable educational institution deducted such depreciation or depletion during the period prior to its first taxable year beginning after December 31, 2017. However, where an applicable educational institution has previously taken depreciation or depletion deductions in excess of the amount which would have been taken had the straight-line or cost method been employed, such excess depreciation or depletion also is taken into account to reduce basis. If the facts necessary to determine the basis of property in the hands of the donor or the last preceding owner by whom it was not acquired by gift are unknown to the applicable educational institution, then the original basis to the applicable educational institution of such property is determined under the rules of § 1.1015–1(a)(3) of this chapter.

(iv) The deduction for expenses paid or incurred in any taxable year for the production of gross investment income earned as an incident to a charitable function can be no greater than the income earned from such function which is includible as gross investment income for such year. For example, where rental income incidentally is realized in a year from historic buildings held open to the public, deductions for amounts paid or incurred in that year for the production of such income is limited to the amount of rental income includible as gross investment income for the year.

(d) Capital gains and losses—(1) In general. In determining capital gain net income for purposes of the tax imposed by section 4968—

(i) Interaction with section 511. No gain or loss from the sale or other disposition of property is taken into account to the extent that such gain or loss is taken into account for purposes of computing the tax imposed by section 511.

(ii) Sales or other dispositions of exempt use property. To the extent that property is used by the educational institution for its exempt purposes, capital gain from the sale or exchange of the portion of that property that is used by the educational institution for its exempt purposes is disregarded;

(iii) Sales of donated property—(A) In general. Any appreciation in the value of donated property that occurred prior to the date of its donation to the institution is disregarded.

(B) Date of donation. The date of donation is determined under the timing rules of § 1.170A–1(b) of this chapter.

(C) Value on the date of donation. The value of the donated property on the date of donation is determined under the valuation rules of § 1.170A–1(c) of this chapter; and

(iv) Capital losses. Net losses from sales or other dispositions of property by one related organization (or by the applicable educational institution) reduce (but not below zero) net gains from such sales or other dispositions by other related organizations (or by the applicable educational institution). Should overall net losses from sales or other dispositions of property exceed gains from sales or other dispositions of such property during the same taxable year, such excess may not be deducted from gross investment income in any taxable year, nor may such excess be used to reduce gains in prior taxable years. However, capital loss carryovers are allowed and may be deducted from capital gains in a future year.

(2) Basis—(i) For purposes of calculating gain from the sale or other disposition of property other than a partnership interest. Subject to the modifications of paragraphs (c)(2)(i) and (ii) of this section (referring to the modifications relating to deductions against gross investment income) and without regard to section 362(c), the basis for purposes of determining gain from the sale or other disposition of property (other than a partnership interest) for purposes of determining capital gain net income for purposes of the tax imposed by section 4968 is the greater of—

(A) Fair market value on December 31, 2017, plus or minus all adjustments after December 31, 2017, and before the date of disposition under the rules of part II of subchapter O, provided that the property was held by the applicable educational institution on December 31, 2017, and continuously thereafter to the date of disposition, or

(B) Basis as determined under the rules of part II of subchapter O.

(ii) For purposes of determining a distributive share of gain from the sale or other disposition of a partnership asset. For purposes of determining an applicable educational institution's share of gain upon the sale or other disposition of a partnership asset, the applicable educational institution's basis in each such partnership asset generally is determined under the rules of subchapter K of chapter 1 of the Code (subchapter K). However, see paragraph (d)(3) of this section.

(iii) For purposes of determining gain on the sale or other disposition of a partnership interest. For purposes of determining an applicable educational institution's gain upon the sale or other disposition of all or a portion of a partnership interest, the applicable educational institution's basis in such partnership interest is generally determined under the rules of subchapter K, subject to the special rules in paragraph (d)(3) of this section.

(iv) For purposes of calculating loss. Subject to the modifications of paragraphs (c)(2)(i) and (ii) of this section (referring to the modifications relating to deductions against gross investment income) and without regard to section 362(c), basis as determined in paragraph (d)(2)(i)(B) of this section applies for purposes of determining loss. For purposes of determining loss from the sale or other disposition of a partnership interest, basis is determined under the rules of subchapter K.

(3) Special rules regarding partnership interests and partnership assets—(i) Reduction of distributive share of capital gain net income from a partnership. For purposes of computing net investment income, an applicable educational institution reduces the amount of its distributive share of capital gain net income from a partnership by the least of—

(A) The applicable educational institution's share of applicable capital gain (as defined in paragraph (d)(3)(iii)(A) of this section) from such partnership;

(B) One-third of the applicable educational institution's unadjusted step-up (as defined in paragraph (d)(3)(iii)(B) of this section) for such partnership; or

(C) The applicable educational institution's adjusted step-up (as defined in paragraph (d)(3)(iii)(C) of this section) for such partnership.

(ii) Reduction of capital gain net income from a sale or other disposition of all or a portion of a partnership interest. For purposes of computing net investment income, an applicable educational institution reduces the amount of its capital gain net income upon the sale or other disposition of all or a portion of a partnership interest by an amount that bears the same relation to the applicable educational institution's adjusted step-up (as defined in paragraph (d)(3)(iii)(C) of this section) for such partnership as the fair market value of the transferred portion of the interest bears to the fair market value of the applicable educational institution's entire interest in such partnership before the sale or other disposition.

(iii) Definitions. For purposes of this section—

(A) Applicable capital gain. For an applicable educational institution's first taxable year beginning after December 31, 2017, the term applicable capital gain means an applicable educational institution's share of both short-term and long-term capital gains and losses subject to section 4968 from a partnership. For subsequent taxable years, applicable capital gain does not include an applicable educational institution's share of short-term capital gains and losses subject to section 4968 from a partnership. For purposes of this paragraph, applicable capital gain is not less than zero.

(B) Unadjusted step-up. An applicable educational institution computes an unadjusted step-up for each partnership interest it held on December 31, 2017. The unadjusted step-up for a partnership interest equals the excess, if any, of the fair market value of such partnership interest on December 31, 2017, over the adjusted basis of such partnership interest on December 31, 2017.

(C) Adjusted step-up. An applicable educational institution computes an adjusted step-up for each partnership interest it held on December 31, 2017. The adjusted step-up for a partnership interest equals the unadjusted step-up for such partnership, reduced by the amount of any capital gain net income reduction pursuant to paragraphs (d)(3)(i) and (ii) of this section for such partnership.

(4) Examples. The following examples illustrate paragraph (d)(3) of this section. Unless stated otherwise in the examples, partners have no tax items other than those listed in the example. With respect to partnerships, all allocations are in accordance with section 704(b) and the regulations under section 704(b) in part 1 of this chapter (Income Tax Regulations).

(i) Example 1—(A) Facts. University (U), an applicable educational institution, is a partner in partnership PRS. On December 31, 2017, U's PRS interest had a fair market value of $130 and tax basis of $100. In 2018, U's share of capital gain net income from PRS is $5, which is comprised of $20 of gain from the sale of capital asset X and ($15) of loss from the sale of capital asset Y. Further, such $5 of capital gain net income is applicable capital gain (as defined in paragraph (d)(3)(iii)(A) of this section).

(B) Analysis. U has an unadjusted step-up (as defined in paragraph (d)(3)(iii)(B) of this section) for PRS of $30 ($130 fair market value - $100 tax basis on December 31, 2017). Pursuant to paragraph (d)(3)(i) of this section, for purposes of computing its net investment income, U reduces the amount of its capital gain net income from PRS by $5, which is the least of: U's share of applicable capital gain from PRS ($5); or one-third of U's unadjusted step-up for PRS ($10); or U's adjusted step-up for PRS ($30). Thus, U reduces its $5 of capital gain net income allocated from PRS by $5, resulting in U having $0 of capital gain net income in 2018 for purposes of section 4968. As a result, U's adjusted step-up for PRS for subsequent taxable years is reduced to $25 ($30 - $5) pursuant to paragraph (d)(4)(iii)(C) of this section. Pursuant to section 705, the $5 of gain allocated to U increases U's tax basis in its PRS interest to $105.

(ii) Example 2—(A) Facts. The facts are the same as in paragraph (d)(4)(i)(A) of this section (Example 1). In 2019, U sells its entire interest in PRS for $130, which, immediately prior to the sale, had a tax basis of $105. As a result, U has $25 of capital gain from the sale of its PRS interest.

(B) Analysis. Pursuant to paragraph (d)(3)(iii) of this section, for purposes of computing its net investment income, U reduces its capital gain net income resulting from the sale of its entire PRS interest by $25, which is the amount that bears the same relation to U's adjusted step-up for PRS ($25) as the fair market value of the transferred portion of PRS ($130) bears to the fair market value of the U's entire interest in PRS before the sale or other disposition ($130). Thus, U reduces its $25 of capital gain net income from the sale of its PRS interest by $25, resulting in U having $0 of capital gain net income in 2019 for purposes of section 4968.

(iii) Example 3—(A) Facts. The facts are the same as in paragraph (d)(4)(i)(A) of this section (Example 1). In 2019, U's share of capital gain net income from PRS is $15, which is comprised of $15 of gain from the sale of capital asset Z. Further, such $15 of capital gain net income is applicable capital gain (as defined in paragraph (d)(3)(iii)(A) of this section).

(B) Analysis. Pursuant to paragraph (d)(3)(i) of this section, for purposes of computing its net investment income, U reduces the amount of its capital gain net income from PRS by $10, which is the least of: U's share of applicable capital gain from PRS ($15); or one-third of U's unadjusted step-up for PRS ($10); or U's adjusted step-up for PRS ($25, computed as $30 of unadjusted step-up, less $5 of capital gain net income reduced in 2018 pursuant to paragraph (d)(3)(i) of this section). Thus, U reduces its $15 of capital gain net income allocated from PRS by $10, resulting in U having $5 of capital gain net income in 2019 for purposes of section 4968. As a result, U's adjusted step-up for PRS is reduced for subsequent taxable years to $15 ($25 - $10) pursuant to paragraph (d)(3)(iii)(C) of this section. Pursuant to section 705, the $15 of gain allocated to U increases U's tax basis in its PRS interest to $120.

§ 53.4968–3. Related organizations.

(a) Definition of related organization—(1) In general. For purposes of section 4968(d) of the Internal Revenue Code (Code) and §§ 53.4968–1 through 53.4968–4, except as provided in paragraph (a)(2) of this section, the term related organization means, with respect to an educational institution, any organization that—

(i) Controls such institution;

(ii) Is controlled by such institution;

(iii) Is controlled by one or more persons that also control such institution;

(iv) Is a supported organization (as defined in section 509(f)(3) of the Code) with respect to such institution during the taxable year; or

(v) Is a supporting organization (as described in section 509(a)(3)) with respect to such institution during the taxable year.

(2) Organizations not considered related organizations. For purposes of section 4968(d) and §§ 53.4968–1 through 53.4968–4, the term related organization does not include any organization that is—

(i) A taxable corporation;

(ii) A taxable trust, including a non-grantor charitable lead trust (except to the extent the trust is controlled by the educational institution as described in paragraph (b)(2)(ii) of this section);

(iii) A grantor charitable lead trust;

(iv) A charitable remainder trust;

(v) A partnership, S corporation (as defined in section 1361(a)(1) of the Code), or other pass-through entity that is generally not subject to Federal income tax, the income of which is taxable to its partners or other interest holders; or

(vi) A decedent's estate.

(3) Employee benefit plans or arrangements. A trust or similar funding vehicle of an employee benefit plan or arrangement, such as a section 501(a) trust funding a section 401(a) qualified retirement plan, or an annuity contract funding a section 403(b) plan, or a section 419(e) welfare benefit fund (including a voluntary employees' beneficiary association under section 501(c)(9)) funding a welfare benefit plan, will not be treated as a related organization and its assets will not be treated as the assets of the educational institution or of a related organization. A trust or other funding vehicle of an unfunded employee benefit plan of an educational institution or a related organization, such as a grantor trust described in section 671 et seq., used in connection with a section 457(b) plan or an arrangement subject to section 457(f), will be treated as a related organization for purposes of section 4968(d) and its assets will be treated as the assets of the educational institution or of a related organization, but the assets are not considered "used directly in carrying out the institution's exempt purpose" for purposes of section 4968(b)(1)(D). For purposes of determining whether the employee benefit plan of an educational institution is funded or unfunded, the educational institution and all of its related organizations are treated as a single sponsor and payor of the benefits.

(b) Control—(1) Controls such institution. For purposes of section 4968(d) and §§ 53.4968–1 through 53.4968–4, an organization controls an educational institution if—

(i) The organization owns (by vote or value) more than 50 percent of the voting and non-voting stock or membership interest of the educational institution; or

(ii) The organization (or one or more of its managers, directors, officers, trustees, or employees, acting only in those capacities) can—

(A) Appoint or elect (which must include the power to remove and replace) more than 50 percent of the members of the educational institution's governing body (such as directors, officers, or trustees), or otherwise has the ongoing power to appoint or elect more than 50 percent of such members with reasonable frequency;

(B) Require the educational institution to make an expenditure (or prevent the educational institution from making an expenditure); or

(C) Require the educational institution to perform any act that significantly affects its operations (or prevent it from performing such an act).

(2) Is controlled by such institution. For purposes of section 4968(d) and §§ 53.4968–1 through 53.4968–4, an organization is controlled by an educational institution:

(i) Tax-exempt corporation. In the case of a corporation recognized as exempt from income tax under section 501(a), if the educational institution owns (by vote or value) more than 50 percent of the voting and nonvoting stock or membership interest of the corporation.

(ii) Trust—(A) In general. In the case of a trust—

(1) If the educational institution is substantially the sole permissible trust beneficiary or appointee of both income and principal, whether or not the timing of the distribution is subject to the trustee's discretion;

(2) If the trust is a pooled income fund described in sections 642(c)(3) and 642(c)(5);

(3) If, but only to the extent that, the assets of the trust were contributed to the trust by the educational institution (or by a person controlled by the educational institution); or

(4) If, but only to the extent that, the educational institution (or person controlled by the educational institution) has the right to demand (or can otherwise cause) a distribution of principal from the trust to the educational institution (or a person controlled by the educational institution).

(B) Person controlled by the educational organization. For purposes of this paragraph (b)(2)(ii), a person is controlled by an educational institution if the educational institution has the power to remove and replace such person or otherwise controls the person under one of the tests described in § 53.4968–3(b)(2)(i), (ii), or (iii), with similar principles applying for purposes of determining control of any other form of entity.

(iii) Nonstock organization. In the case of a nonstock organization, if the educational institution (or one or more of its managers, directors, officers, trustees, or employees, acting only in those capacities) can—

(A) Appoint or elect (which must include the power to remove and replace) more than 50 percent of the members of the organization's governing body (such as directors, officers, or trustees), or otherwise has an ongoing power to appoint or elect more than 50 percent of such members with reasonable frequency);

(B) Require the organization to make an expenditure (or prevent the organization from making an expenditure); or

(C) Require the organization to perform any act that significantly affects its operations (or prevent it from performing such an act).

(3) Is controlled by one or more persons that also control such institution. For purposes of section 4968(d) and this section, an organization (other than one described in paragraph (a)(2) of this section) is controlled by one or more persons that also control the educational institution if more than 50 percent of the members of the governing body of the other organization are directly or indirectly controlled by persons that comprise more than 50 percent of the members of the governing body of the educational institution.

(4) Constructive ownership. The principles of section 318(a)(2) (relating to ownership attribution from partnerships, estates, trusts, and corporations) apply for purposes of determining ownership of stock in a corporation, and similar principles apply for purposes of determining ownership of an interest in any other entity.

(5) Method of control. Control includes control by aggregating votes or positions of authority (including by veto power), but applies regardless of the method by which the control is exercised or exercisable.

(c) Organization described in section 509(a)(3) during the taxable year with

respect to the educational institution. A section 509(a)(3) organization is a supporting organization with respect to an educational institution only if the supporting organization meets the organizational, operational, and relationship tests of section 509(a)(3)(B) and § 1.509(a)-4 of this chapter with respect to the educational institution.

(d) Assets and net investment income of related organizations—(1) In general. A related organization's assets and net investment income are taken into account both in determining whether an institution is an applicable educational institution and in computing the net investment income of an applicable educational institution. For purposes of determining the aggregate fair market value of the assets and net investment income of an educational institution, the assets and net investment income of all related organizations are treated as the assets and net investment income, respectively, of the institution, unless an exception provided in paragraph (d)(2) of this section or the exception provided in § 53.4968-1(b)(5)(iv) (relating to assets used directly in carrying out an exempt purpose) applies. In cases in which an organization is a related organization with respect to an educational institution under more than one definition of this § 53.4968-3, then the rule that attributes the largest amount of assets and net investment income of the related organization to the educational institution must be applied.

(2) Exceptions. For purposes of section 4968 and this paragraph (d)(2)—

(i) No amount is taken into account with respect to more than one educational institution. In determining the aggregate fair market value of the assets and net investment income of an educational institution, assets and net investment income of a related organization are not taken into account with respect to more than one educational institution. Thus, in any case in which an organization is a related organization with respect to more than one educational institution, the assets and net investment income of the related organization must be allocated between or among the educational institutions as to which the organization is a related organization, subject to paragraph (d)(2)(ii) of this section. The educational institution must make such allocation in a reasonable manner, taking into account all facts and circumstances, that is consistent across all related organizations.

(ii) Assets and net investment income that are not intended or available for the use or benefit of the educational institution—(A) In general. Unless a related organization is controlled by the educational institution or is a supporting organization described in section 509(a)(3) with respect to such institution for the taxable year, assets and net investment income of a related organization that are not intended or available for the use or benefit of the educational institution are not taken into account by that educational institution.

(B) Determining whether assets and net investment income of a related organization are intended or available for the use or benefit of an educational institution. If a related organization controls the educational institution, is controlled by one or more persons that also control such institution (but is not described in section 509(a)(3) with respect to the educational institution for the taxable year), or is a supported organization (as defined in section 509(f)(3)) during the taxable year with respect to the educational institution, then the related organization's assets and net investment income are taken into account as assets and net investment income of the educational institution only to the extent the assets and net investment income are intended or available for the use or benefit of that educational institution. Assets and net investment income of a related organization are intended or available for the use or benefit of an educational institution if such assets and net investment income are specifically earmarked or restricted for the benefit of, or otherwise are fairly attributable to, the educational institution. For example, assets are fairly attributable to the educational institution if they have been affirmatively designated or appropriated for the educational institution or made available for the educational institution to draw upon at will. Conversely, assets and net investment income of a related organization are not intended or available for the use or benefit of an educational institution if such assets and net investment income are specifically earmarked or restricted for another entity or for unrelated purposes or otherwise are not fairly attributable to the educational institution. The assets and net investment income of a related organization must be allocated between those intended or available for the use or benefit of an educational institution and those not intended or not available for the use or benefit of that same educational institution. The educational institution must make such allocation in a reasonable manner, taking into account all facts and circumstances, that is consistent across all related organizations.

(C) Related organizations that are controlled by the educational institution or that are supporting organizations (as described in section 509(a)(3)) with respect to the educational institution during the taxable year—(1) In general. If a related organization is controlled, as defined in paragraph (b)(2) of this section, by an educational institution, or is a supporting organization with respect to the educational institution during the taxable year, as defined in paragraph (c) of this section, the assets and net investment income of the related organization are taken into account as assets and net investment income of the educational institution regardless of whether those assets and net investment income are earmarked or restricted for the benefit of, or otherwise are fairly attributable to, the educational institution and even if they are specifically earmarked or restricted for another entity or for unrelated purposes or otherwise are not fairly attributable to the educational institution, subject to paragraph (d)(2)(ii)(C)(2) of this section. However, see §§ 53.4968–1(b)(2)(ii)(A)(3) and (4) regarding trusts that are controlled related organizations only to the extent assets of the trust were contributed to the trust by the educational institution (or by a person controlled by the educational institution), or only to the extent the educational institution (or person controlled by the educational institution) has the right to demand (or can otherwise cause) a distribution of principal from the trust to the educational institution (or a person controlled by the educational institution). See also § 53.4968–1(b)(5)(iv) for rules relating to when assets of a related organization are deemed to be used directly in carrying out the institution's exempt purpose.

(2) Special rule for Type III supporting organizations with respect to an educational institution as of December 31, 2017. An educational institution with a related organization that was a Type III supporting organization with respect to the educational institution on December 31, 2017, takes into account only the assets and net investment income of such Type III supporting organization that are intended or available for the use or benefit of, or otherwise are fairly attributable to, the educational institution, as described in paragraph (d)(2)(ii)(B) of this section. An educational institution may determine whether the assets and net investment income of such a Type III supporting organization are intended or available for the use or benefit of, or otherwise are fairly attributable to, the educational institution using any reasonable method. A method that attributes to an educational institution assets and net investment income of a supporting organization that specifically are earmarked for the educational institution, are restricted for the benefit of the educational institution, or otherwise are fairly attributable to the educational institution (such as those that have been affirmatively designated or appropriated for the educational institution or made available for the educational institution to draw upon at will) will be deemed to be reasonable.

(3) Determining assets of related organizations. To determine which assets of a related organization are included by an educational institution under section 4968(b)(1)(D) for a particular year, an educational institution determines which organizations are related organizations, as defined in section 4968(d)(2) and § 53.4968-3, as of the end of the educational institution's preceding taxable year, and values the relevant assets on that date.

(4) Determining net investment income of related organizations. To determine the amount of net investment income of a related organization that is included by the applicable educational institution in calculating the tax imposed by section 4968(a) for a particular taxable year, an applicable educational institution determines which organizations are related organizations, as defined in section 4968(d)(2) and § 53.4968-3, as of the end of that taxable year of the applicable educational institution and includes the net investment income from each related organization's taxable year that ends with or within that same taxable year of the applicable educational institution. If an organization became a related organization after the beginning of the applicable educational institution's taxable year, then the applicable educational institution includes the organization's net investment income for the portion of the year that the organization was a related organization, using any reasonable method.

§ 53.4968-4. Applicability date.

The rules of §§ 53.4968-1 through 53.4968-3 apply to taxable years of an educational institution beginning after October 15, 2020.

PROCEDURAL REGULATIONS

TAX RETURNS & DISCLOSURE

§ 1.6033-2. Returns by exempt organizations and returns by certain nonexempt organizations.

(a) In general. (1) Except as provided in section 6033(a)(2) and paragraph (g) of this section, every organization exempt from taxation under section 501(a) shall file an annual information return specifically setting forth its items of gross income, gross receipts and disbursements, and such other information as may be prescribed in the instructions issued with respect to the return. Except as provided in paragraph (d) of this section, such return shall be filed annually regardless of whether such organization is chartered by, or affiliated or associated with, any central, parent, or other organization.

(2)(i) Except as otherwise provided in this paragraph and paragraph (g) of this section, every organization exempt from taxation under section 501(a), and required to file a return under section 6033 and this section (including, for taxable years ending before December 31, 1972, private foundations, as defined in section 509(a)), other than an organization described in section 401(a) or 501(d), shall file its annual return on Form 990. For taxable years ending on or after December 31, 1972, every private foundation shall file Form 990-PF as its annual information return. For taxable years beginning after December 31, 1977, every section 501(c)(21) black lung trust shall file an annual information return on Form 990-BL or any other form prescribed by the Internal Revenue Service for that purpose.

(ii) Subject to paragraph (a)(1) of this section, the information generally required to be furnished by an organization exempt under section 501(a) is:

(A) Its gross income for the year. For this purpose, gross income includes tax-exempt income, but does not include contributions, gifts, grants, and similar amounts received. Whether an item constitutes a contribution, gift, grant, or similar amount depends upon all the surrounding facts and circumstances. The computation of gross income shall be made by subtracting the cost of goods sold from all receipts other than gross contributions, gifts, grants, and similar amounts received and nonincludible dues and assessments from members and affiliates.

(B) To the extent not included in gross income, its dues and assessments from members and affiliates for the year.

(C) Its expenses incurred within the year attributable to gross income.

(D) Its disbursements (including prior years' accumulations) made within the year for the purposes for which it is exempt.

(E) A balance sheet showing its assets, liabilities, and net worth as of the beginning and end of such year. Detailed information relating to the assets, liabilities, and net worth shall be furnished on the schedule provided for this purpose on the return required by this section. Such schedule shall be supplemented by attachments where appropriate.

(F) The total of the contributions, gifts, grants and similar amounts received by it during the taxable year, and, in the case of an organization described in section 501(c)(3), the names and addresses of all persons who contributed, bequeathed, or devised $5,000 or more (in money or other property) during the taxable year. In the case of a private foundation (as defined in section 509(a)), the names and addresses of all persons who became substantial contributors (as defined in section 507(d)(2)) during the taxable year shall be furnished. In addition, for its first taxable year beginning after December 31, 1969, each private foundation shall furnish the names and addresses of all persons who became substantial contributors before such taxable year. For special rules with respect to contributors and donors, see paragraph (a)(2)(iii) of this subparagraph.

(G) The names and addresses of all officers, directors, or trustees (or any person having responsibilities or powers similar to those of officers, directors, or trustees) of the organization, and, in the case of a private foundation, all persons who are foundation managers, within the meaning of section 4946(b)(1). Organizations described in section 501(c)(3) must also attach a schedule showing the names and addresses of the five employees (if any) who received the greatest amount of annual compensation in excess of $30,000; the total number of other employees who received annual compensation in excess of $30,000; the names and addresses of the five independent contractors (if any) who performed personal services of a professional nature for the organization (such as attorneys, accountants, and doctors, whether such services are performed by such persons in their individual capacity or as employees of a professional service corporation) and who received the greatest amount of compensation in excess of $30,000 from the organization for the year for the performance of such services; and the total number of other such independent contractors who received in excess of $30,000 for the year for the performance of such services.

(H) A schedule showing the compensation and other payments made to each person whose name is required to be listed pursuant to paragraph (a)(2)(ii)(G) of this section during the calendar year ending within the organization's annual accounting period, or during such other period as prescribed by publication, form, or instructions.

* * *

(J) In the case of a private foundation liable for tax imposed under Chapter 42, such information as is required by Form 4720.

(K) In the case of an organization described in section 501(c)(3), the respective amounts (if any) of the taxes imposed on the organization, or any organization manager of the organization, during the taxable year under any of the following provisions (and the respective amounts (if any) of reimbursements paid by the organization during the taxable year with respect to taxes imposed on any such organization manager under any of such provisions):

(1) Section 4911 (relating to tax on excess expenditures to influence legislation);

(2) Section 4912 (relating to tax on disqualifying lobbying expenditures of certain organizations); and

(3) Section 4955 (relating to taxes on political expenditures of section 501(c)(3) organizations), except to the extent that, by reason of section 4962, the taxes imposed under such section are not required to be paid or are credited or refunded.

(L) In the case of organizations described in section 501(c)(3), (4), or (29), the respective amounts (if any) of—

(1) The taxes imposed with respect to the organization on any organization manager, or any disqualified person, during the taxable year under section 4958 (relating to taxes on excess benefit transactions); and

(2) Reimbursements paid by the organization during the taxable year with respect to taxes imposed under such section, except to the extent that, by reason of section 4962, the taxes imposed under such section are not required to be paid or are credited or refunded.

(M) Its lobbying expenditures, grass roots expenditures, exempt purpose expenditures, lobbying nontaxable amount, and grass roots nontaxable amount for the taxable year and for prior taxable years that are base years (within the meaning of section 1.501(h)–3(c)(7)), if the organization has an election under section 501(h) in effect for the taxable year. An organization that is a member of an affiliated group of organizations (as defined in section 56.4911–7(e)) but that is not a member of a limited affiliated group (as defined in section 56.4911–10(b)) shall report this information based on the expenditures of all members of the group during the taxable year of the group that ends with or within the member's taxable year and for prior taxable years of the group that are base years (within the meaning of section 56.4911–9(b)). For additional information required to be furnished by members of an affiliated group of organizations, and by controlling members in a limited affiliated group, see sections 56.4911–9(d) and 56.4911–10(f)(1), respectively.

(iii) Special rules. In providing the names and addresses of contributors and donors under paragraph (a)(2)(ii)(F) of this section.

(A) An organization described in section 501(c)(3) which meets the 33 1/3 percent-of-support test of the regulations under section 170(b)(1)(A)(vi) (without regard to whether such organization otherwise qualifies as an organization described in section 170(b)(1)(A)) is required to provide the name and address of a person who contributed, bequeathed, or devised $5,000 or more during the year only if his amount is in excess of 2 percent of the total contributions, bequests and devises received by the organization during the year.

(B) An organization other than a private foundation is required to report only the names and addresses of contributors of whom it has actual knowledge. For instance, an organization need not require an employer who withholds contributions from the compensation of employees and pays over to the organization periodically the total amounts withheld, to specify the amounts paid over with respect to a particular employee. In such case, unless the organization has actual knowledge that a particular employee gave more than $5,000 (and in excess of 2 percent if paragraph (a)(2)(iii)(A) of this section is applicable), the organization need report only the name and address of the employer, and the total amount paid over by him.

(C) Separate and independent gifts made by one person in a particular year need be aggregated to determine if his contributions and bequests exceed $5,000 (and in excess of 2 percent if paragraph (a)(2)(iii)(A) of this section is applicable), only if such gifts are of $1,000 or more.

(D)(1) Organizations described in section 501(c)(8) or (10) that receive contributions or bequests to be used exclusively for purposes described in section 170(c)(4), 2055(a)(3), or 2522(a)(3), must attach a schedule with respect to all gifts which aggregate more than $1,000 from any one person showing the total amount of the contributions or bequests from each such person, the specific purpose for which such amount was received, and the specific use or uses to which such amount was put. In the case of an amount set aside for such purposes, the organization shall indicate the manner in which such amount is held (for instance, whether such amount is commingled with amounts held for other purposes). If the contribution or bequest was transferred to another organization, the schedule must include the name of the transferee organization, a description of the nature of such organization, and a description of the relationship between the transferee and transferor organizations.

(2) For taxable years beginning after December 31, 1970, such organizations must also attach a statement showing the total dollar amount of contributions and bequests received for such purposes which are $1,000 or less.

* * *

(5) Political organizations, as defined by section 527(e)(1), that have gross receipts of $25,000 or more for the taxable year (or in the case of a qualified State or local political organization, as defined in section 527(e)(5), that has gross receipts of $100,000 or more for the taxable year) generally must comply with the requirements of section 6033 and this section in the same manner as organizations exempt from tax under section 501(a), except to the extent that the Commissioner may modify such requirements through forms, instructions to forms, or guidance published in the Internal Revenue Bulletin as appropriate for carrying out the purposes of section 527. For the purposes of this section, all references to organizations exempt from tax under section 501(a) shall include political organizations referred to in section 6033(g), other than those referred to in section 6033(g)(3) and except to the extent the Commissioner exercises discretion under section 6033(g)(4). This discretion may be exercised through forms, instructions to forms, or guidance published in the Internal Revenue Bulletin. In addition to the reporting requirements applicable to organizations exempt under section 501(a), such political organizations generally must report the names and addresses of all persons that contributed, bequeathed, or devised $5,000 or more (in money or other property) during the taxable year.

(6) Each controlling organization (within the meaning of section 512(b)(13)) that is

subject to the requirements of section 6033(a) shall include on its annual return such information required by that return regarding—

(i) Any interest, annuities, royalties, or rents received from each controlled entity (within the meaning of section 512(b)(13));

(ii) Any loans made to each such controlled entity; and

(iii) Any transfers of funds between such controlling organization and each such controlled entity.

(7) Every organization described in section 4966(d)(1) shall, on its annual return for the taxable year—

(i) List the total number of donor advised funds (as defined in section 4966(d)(2)) it owns at the end of such taxable year;

(ii) Report the aggregate value of assets held in such funds at the end of such taxable year; and

(iii) Report the aggregate contributions to and grants made from such funds during such taxable year.

(8) Every organization described in section 509(a)(3) shall, on its annual return—

(i) List the supported organizations (as defined in section 509(f)(3)) with respect to which such organization provides support;

(ii) Specify whether the organization meets the requirements of clause (i), (ii), or (iii) of section 509(a)(3)(B); and

(iii) Certify that the organization meets the requirements of section 509(a)(3)(C).

* * *

(e) Time and place for filing. The annual return required by this section shall be filed on or before the 15th day of the fifth calendar month following the close of the period for which the return is required to be filed. The annual return on Form 1065 required to be filed by a religious or apostolic association or corporation shall be filed on or before the 15th day of the fourth month following the close of the taxable year for which the return is required to be filed. Each such return shall be filed in accordance with the instructions applicable thereto.

(f) Penalties and additions to tax. For penalties and additions to tax for failure to file a return and filing a false or fraudulent return, see sections 6652, 7203, 7206, and 7207.

(g) Organizations not required to file annual returns. (1) Annual returns required by this section are not required to be filed by an organization exempt from taxation under section 501(a) which is:

(i) A church, an interchurch organization of local units of a church, a convention or association of churches, or an integrated auxiliary of a church (as defined in paragraph (h) of this section);

(ii) An exclusively religious activity of any religious order;

(iii) Except as provided in paragraph (g)(1)(viii) of this section, an organization described in section 501(c) (other than a private foundation or a supporting organization described in section 509(a)(3)) the gross receipts of which in each taxable year are normally not more than $50,000 (as described in paragraph (g)(3) of this section);

(iv) A mission society sponsored by or affiliated with one or more churches or church denominations, more than one-half of the activities of which society are conducted in, or directed at persons in foreign countries;

(v) A State institution, the income of which is excluded from gross income under section 115(a);

(vi) An organization described in section 501(c)(1);

(vii) An educational organization (below college level) that is described in section 170(b)(1)(A)(ii), that has a program of a general academic nature, and that is affiliated (within the meaning of paragraph (h)(2) of this section) with a church or operated by a religious order, or

(viii) A foreign organization (described in paragraph (k)(1) of this section) or a United States possession organization (described in paragraph (k)(2) of this section) (other than a private foundation or a supporting organization described in section 509(a)(3))—

(A) The gross receipts of which in each taxable year from sources within the United States (as determined under paragraph (k)(3) of this section) are normally not more than $50,000 (as described in paragraph (g)(3) of this section); and

(B) That has no significant activity (including lobbying and political activity and the operation of a trade or business, but excluding investment activity) in the United States.

(2) The provisions of section 6033(a) relieving certain specified types of organizations exempt from taxation under section 501(a) from filing annual returns do not abridge or impair in any way the powers and authority of district directors or directors of service centers provided for in other provisions of the Code and in regulations thereunder to require the filing of returns or notices by such organizations. See section 6001 and section 1.6001–1.

(3) For purposes of paragraphs (g)(1)(iii) and (viii) of this section, the gross receipts (as defined in paragraph (g)(4) of this section) of an organization are normally not more than $50,000 if:

(i) In the case of an organization that has been in existence for 1 year or less, the organization has received, or donors have pledged to give, gross receipts of $75,000 or less during the first taxable year of the organization;

(ii) In the case of an organization that has been in existence for more than one but less than 3 years, the average of the gross receipts received by the organization in its first 2 taxable years is $60,000 or less; and

(iii) In the case of an organization that has been in existence for 3 years or more, the average of the gross receipts received by the organization in the immediately preceding 3 taxable years, including the year for which the return would be required to be filed, is $50,000 or less.

(4) For purposes of this paragraph and paragraph (a)(2) of this section, "gross receipts" means the gross amount received by the organization during its annual accounting period from all sources without reduction for any costs or expenses including, for example, cost of goods or assets sold, cost of operations, or expenses of earning, raising, or collecting such amounts. Thus "gross receipts" includes, but is not limited to (i) the gross amount received as contributions, gifts, grants, and similar amounts without reduction for the expenses of raising and collecting such amounts, (ii) the gross amount received as dues or assessments from members or affiliated organizations without reduction for expenses attributable to the receipt of such amounts, (iii) gross sales or receipts from business activities (including business activities unrelated to the purpose for which the organization qualifies for exemption, the net income or loss from which may be required to be reported on Form 990-T), (iv) the gross amount received from the sale of assets without reduction for cost or other basis and expenses of sale, and (v) the gross amount received as investment income, such as interest, dividends, rents, and royalties.

(5) An organization that is not required to file an annual return by virtue of paragraphs (g)(1)(iii) and (viii) of this section must submit an annual electronic notification as described in section 6033(i). See § 1.6033–6.

(6) The Commissioner may relieve any organization or class of organizations from filing, in whole or in part, the annual return required by this section where he determines that such returns are not necessary for the efficient administration of the internal revenue laws. This discretion may be exercised through forms, instructions to forms, or guidance published in the Internal Revenue Bulletin.

(h) Integrated auxiliary—(1) In General. For purposes of this title, the term integrated auxiliary of a church means an organization that is—

(i) Described both in sections 501(c)(3) and 509(a)(1), (2), or (3);

(ii) Affiliated with a church or a convention or association of churches; and

(iii) Internally supported.

(2) Affiliation. An organization is affiliated with a church or a convention or association of churches, for purposes of paragraph (h)(1)(ii) of this section, if—

(i) The organization is covered by a group exemption letter issued under applicable administrative procedures, (such as Rev. Proc. 80–27 (1980–1 C.B. 677); See section 601.601(a)(2)(ii)(b)), to a church or a convention or association of churches;

(ii) The organization is operated, supervised, or controlled by or in connection with (as defined in section 1.509(a)–4) a church or a convention or association of churches; or

(iii) Relevant facts and circumstances show that it is so affiliated.

(3) Facts and circumstances. For purposes of paragraph (h)(2)(iii) of this section, relevant facts and circumstances that indicate an organization is affiliated with a church or a convention or association of churches include the following factors. However, the absence of one or more of the following factors does not necessarily preclude classification of an organization as being affiliated with a church or a convention or association of churches—

(i) The organization's enabling instrument (corporate charter, trust instrument, articles of association, constitution or similar document) or by-laws affirm that the organization shares common religious doctrines, principles, disciplines, or practices with a church or a convention or association of churches;

(ii) A church or a convention or association of churches has the authority to appoint or remove, or to control the appointment or removal of, at least one of the organization's officers or directors;

(iii) The corporate name of the organization indicates an institutional relationship with a church or a convention or association of churches;

(iv) The organization reports at least annually on its financial and general operations to a church or a convention or association of churches;

(v) An institutional relationship between the organization and a church or a convention or association of churches is affirmed by the church, or convention or association of churches, or a designee thereof; and

(vi) In the event of dissolution, the organization's assets are required to be distributed to a church or a convention or association of churches, or to an affiliate thereof within the meaning of this paragraph (h).

(4) Internal support. An organization is internally supported, for purposes of paragraph (h)(1)(iii) of this section, unless it both—

(i) Offers admissions, goods, services or facilities for sale, other than on an incidental basis, to the general public (except goods, services, or facilities sold at a nominal charge or for an insubstantial portion of the cost); and

(ii) Normally receives more than 50 percent of its support from a combination of governmental sources, public solicitation of contributions, and receipts from the sale of admissions, goods, performance of services, or furnishing of facilities in activities that are not unrelated trades or businesses.

(5) Special rule. Men's and women's organizations, seminaries, mission societies, and youth groups that satisfy paragraphs (h)(1)(i) and (ii) of this section are integrated auxiliaries of a church regardless of whether such an organization meets the internal support requirement under paragraph (h)(1)(iii) of this section.

(6) Effective date. This paragraph (h) applies for returns filed for taxable years beginning after December 31, 1969. For returns filed for taxable years beginning after December 31, 1969 but beginning before December 20, 1995, the definition for the term integrated auxiliary of a church set forth in section 1.6033–2(g)(5) (as contained in the 26 CFR edition revised as of April 1, 1995) may be used as an alternative definition to such term set forth in this paragraph (h).

(7) Examples of internal support. The internal support test of this paragraph (h) is illustrated by the following examples, in each of which it is assumed that the organization's provision of goods and services does not constitute an unrelated trade or business:

Example 1. Organization A is described in sections 501(c)(3) and 509(a)(2) and is affiliated (within the meaning of this paragraph (h)) with a church. Organization A publishes a weekly newspaper as its only activity. On an incidental basis, some copies of Organization A's publication are sold to nonmembers of the church with which it is affiliated. Organization A advertises for subscriptions at places of worship of the church. Organization A is internally supported, regardless of its sources of financial support, because it does not offer admissions, goods, services, or facilities for sale, other than on an incidental basis, to the general public. Organization A is an integrated auxiliary.

Example 2. Organization B is a retirement home described in sections 501(c)(3) and 509(a)(2). Organization B is affiliated (within the meaning of this paragraph (h)) with a church. Admission to Organization B is open to all members of the community for a fee. Organization B advertises in publications of general distribution appealing to the elderly and maintains its name on non-denominational listings of available retirement homes. Therefore, Organization B offers its services for sale to the general public on more than an incidental basis. Organization B receives a cash contribution of $50,000 annually from the church. Fees received by Organization B from its residents total $100,000 annually. Organization B does not receive any government support or contributions from the general public. Total support is $150,000 ($100,000 + $50,000), and $100,000 of that total is from receipts from the performance of services (66–2/3% of total support). Therefore, Organization B receives more than 50 percent of its support from receipts from the performance of services. Organization B is not internally supported and is not an integrated auxiliary.

Example 3. Organization C is a hospital that is described in sections 501(c)(3) and 509(a)(1). Organization C is affiliated (within the meaning of this paragraph (h)) with a church. Organization C is open to all persons in need of hospital care in the community, although most of Organization C's patients are members of the same denomination as the church with which Organization C is affiliated. Organization C maintains its name on hospital listings used by the general public, and participating doctors are allowed to admit all patients. Therefore, Organization C offers its services for sale to the general public on more than an incidental basis. Organization C annually receives $250,000 in support from the church, $1,000,000 in payments from patients and third party payors (including Medicare, Medicaid and other insurers) for patient care, $100,000 in contributions from the public,§ $100,000 in grants from the federal government (other than Medicare and Medicaid payments) and $50,000 in investment income. Total support is $1,500,000 ($250,000 + $1,000,000 + $100,000 + $100,000 + $50,000), and $1,200,000 ($1,000,000 + $100,000 + $100,000) of that total is support from receipts from the performance of services, government sources, and public contributions (80% of total support). Therefore, Organization C receives more than 50 percent of its support from receipts from the performance of services, government sources, and public contributions. Organization C is not internally supported and is not an integrated auxiliary.

(i) Records, statements, and other returns of tax-exempt organizations. (1) An organization which is exempt from taxation under section 501(a) and is not required to file annually an information return required by this section shall immediately notify in writing the district director for the internal revenue district in which its principal office is located of any changes in its character, operations, or purpose for which it was originally created.

(2) Every organization which is exempt from tax, whether or not it is required to file an annual information return, shall submit such additional information as may be required by the Internal Revenue Service for the purpose of inquiring into its exempt status and administering the provisions of Subchapter F (section 501 and following), Chapter 1 of Subtitle A of the Code, section 6033, and Chapter 42 of Subtitle D of the Code. See section 6001 and section 1.6001–1 with respect to the authority of the district directors or directors of service centers to require such additional information and with respect to the books of account or records to be kept by such organizations.

(3) An organization which has established its exemption from taxation under section 501(a), including an organization which is relieved under section 6033 and this section from filing annual returns of information, is not relieved of the duty of filing other returns of information. See, for example, sections 6041, 6043, 6051, 6057, and 6058 and the regulations thereunder.

(j) Unrelated business tax returns. In addition to the foregoing requirements of this section, certain organizations otherwise exempt from tax under section 501(a) which are subject to tax on unrelated business taxable income are also required to file returns on Form 990-T. See paragraph (e) of section 1.6012–2 and paragraph (a)(5) of section 1.6012–3 for requirements with respect to such returns.

(k) Foreign organizations and United States possession organizations—(1) Foreign organization. For purposes of this section, a foreign organization is any organization not described in section 170(c)(2)(A).

(2) United States possession organization. For purposes of this section, a United States possession organization is any organization created or organized in a possession of the United States.

(3) Source of funds. For purposes of paragraph (g)(1)(viii) of this section, the source of an organization's gross receipts from gifts, grants, contributions or membership fees is determined by applying the rules found in § 53.4948–1(b) of this chapter. For purposes of paragraph (g)(1)(viii) of this section, the source of an organization's gross receipts other than gifts, grants, contributions, and membership fees is determined by applying the rules in sections 861 through 865 and the regulations in this part issued under section 861 through 865. For purposes of applying this paragraph (k)(3) regarding United States possession organizations, a United States person does not include individuals who are bona fide residents of a United States possession.

(*l*) Applicability date—(1) Generally. This section applies to returns filed on or after January 30, 2020. Section 1.6033–2T (as contained in 26 CFR part 1, revised April 2019) applies to returns filed before January 30, 2020.

(2) Paragraphs (a)(2)(ii)(F), (a)(2)(iii)(D)(1), (g)(1)(iii) and (viii), and (g)(3) of this section apply to annual information returns filed after May 28, 2020. Under section 7805(b)(7) an organization may choose to apply the paragraphs listed in this paragraph (*l*)(2) to returns filed after September 6, 2019.

§ 1.6033–3. Additional provisions relating to private foundations.

(a) In general. The foundation managers (as defined in section 4946(b)) of every organization (including a trust described in section 4947(a)(1)) which is (or is treated as) a private foundation (as defined in section 509) the assets of which are at least $5,000 at any time during a taxable year shall include the following information on its annual return in addition to that information required under section 1.6033–2(a):

(1) An itemized statement of its securities and all other assets at the close of the year, showing both book and market value,

(2) An itemized list of all grants and contributions made or approved for future payment during the year, showing the amount of each such grant or contribution, the name and address of the recipient (other than a recipient who is not a disqualified person and who receives, from the foundation, grants to indigent or needy persons that, in the aggregate, do not exceed $1,000 during the year), any relationship between any individual recipient and the foundation's managers or substantial contributors, and a concise statement of the purpose of each such grant or contribution,

(3) The address of the principal office of the foundation and (if different) of the place where its books and records are maintained,

(4) The names and addresses of its foundation managers (within the meaning of section 4946(b)), that are substantial contributors (within the meaning of section 507(d)(2)) or that own 10 percent or more of the stock of any corporation of which the foundation owns 10 percent or more of the stock, or corresponding interests in partnerships or other entities, in which the foundation has a 10 percent or greater interest.

For purposes of subparagraph (2) of this paragraph, the business address of an individual grant recipient or foundation manager may be used by the foundation in its annual return in lieu of the home address of such recipient or manager, and the term "relationship" shall include, but is not limited to, any case in which an individual recipient of a grant or contribution by a private foundation is (i) a member of the family (as defined in section 4946(d)) of a substantial contributor or foundation manager of such foundation, (ii) a partner of such substantial contributor or foundation manager, or (iii) an employee of such substantial contributor or foundation manager or of an organization which is effectively controlled (within the meaning of section 4946(a)(1)(H)(i) and the regulations thereunder), directly or indirectly, by one or more such substantial contributors or foundation managers.

(b) Notice to public of availability of annual return. A copy of the notice required by section 6104(d) (relating to public inspection of private foundations' annual returns), and proof of publication thereof, shall be filed with the annual return required by section 1.6033–2(a). A copy of such notice as published, and a statement signed by a foundation manager stating that such notice was published, setting forth the date of publication and the publication in which it appeared, shall be sufficient proof of publication for purposes of this paragraph.

(c) Special rules—(1) Furnishing of copies to State officers. The foundation managers of a private foundation shall furnish a copy of the annual return required by section 6033 and section 1.6033–2 to the Attorney General of:

(i) Each State which the foundation is required to list on its return pursuant to section 1.6033–2(a)(2)(iv),

(ii) The State in which is located the principal office of the foundation, and

(iii) The State in which the foundation was incorporated or created.

The annual return shall be sent to each Attorney General described in paragraphs (c)(1)(i), (ii), or (iii) of this section at the same time as it is sent to the Internal Revenue Service. Upon request the foundation managers shall also furnish a copy of the annual return to the Attorney General or other appropriate State officer (within the meaning of section 6104(c)(2)) of any State. The foundation managers shall attach to each copy of the annual return sent to State officers under this subparagraph a copy of the Form 4720, if any, filed by the foundation for the year.

(2) Cross-reference. For additional rules with respect to private foundations' returns and the public inspection of such returns, see section 6104(d) and the regulations thereunder.

(d) Special rules for certain foreign organizations. The provisions of paragraphs (b) and (c) of this section shall not apply with respect to an organization described in section 4948(b). The foundation managers of such organizations are not required to publish notice of availability of the annual return for inspection, to make the annual return available at the principal office of the foundation for public inspection under section 6104(d), or to send copies of the annual return to State officers.

(e) Effective date. The provisions of this section shall apply with respect to returns filed for taxable years beginning after December 31, 1980.

DISCLOSURE OF RETURNS

§ 301.6104(d)–1. Public inspection and distribution of applications for tax exemption and annual information returns of tax-exempt organizations.

(a) In general. Except as otherwise provided in this section, if a tax-exempt organization (as defined in paragraph (b)(1) of this section) filed an application for recognition of exemption under section 501, it shall make its application for tax exemption (as defined in paragraph (b)(3) of this section) available for public inspection without charge at its principal, regional and district offices during regular business hours. Except as otherwise provided in this section, a tax-exempt organization shall make its annual information returns (as defined in paragraph (b)(4) of this section) available for public inspection without charge in the same offices during regular business hours. Each annual information return shall be made available for a period of three years beginning on the date the return is required to be filed (determined with regard to any extension of time for filing) or is actually filed, whichever is later. In addition, except as provided in § 301.6104(d)–2 and 301.6104(d)–3, an organization shall provide a copy without charge, other than a reasonable fee for reproduction and actual postage costs, of all or any part of any application or return required to be made available for public inspection under this paragraph to any individual who makes a request for such copy in person or in writing. See paragraph (d)(3) of this section for rules relating to fees for copies.

(b) Definitions. For purposes of applying the provisions of section 6104(d), this section and § 301.6104(d)–2 and 301.6104(d)–3, the following definitions apply:

(1) Tax-exempt organization. The term tax-exempt organization means any organization that is described in section 501(c) or section 501(d) and is exempt from taxation under section 501(a). The term tax-exempt organization also includes any nonexempt charitable trust described in section 4947(a)(1) or nonexempt private foundation that is subject to the reporting requirements of section 6033 pursuant to section 6033(d).

(2) Private foundation. The term private foundation means a private foundation as defined in section 509(a) or a nonexempt charitable trust described in section 4947(a)(1) or a nonexempt private foundation subject to the information reporting requirements of section 6033 pursuant to section 6033(d).

(3) Application for tax exemption—(i) In general. Except as described in paragraph (b)(3)(iii) of this section, the term application for tax exemption includes any prescribed application form (such as Form 1023 or Form 1024), all documents and statements the Internal Revenue Service requires an applicant to file with the form, any statement or other supporting document submitted by an organization in support of its application, and any letter or other document issued by the Internal Revenue Service concerning the application (such as a favorable determination letter or a list of questions from the Internal Revenue Service about the application). For example, a legal brief submitted in support of an application, or a response to questions from the Internal Revenue Service during the application process, is part of an application for tax exemption.

(ii) No prescribed application form. If no form is prescribed for an organization's application for tax exemption, the application for tax exemption includes—

(A) The application letter and copy of the articles of incorporation, declaration of trust, or other similar instrument that sets forth the permitted powers or activities of the organization;

(B) The organization's bylaws or other code of regulations;

(C) The organization's latest financial statements showing assets, liabilities, receipts and disbursements;

(D) Statements describing the character of the organization, the purpose for which it was organized, and its actual activities;

(E) Statements showing the sources of the organization's income and receipts and their disposition; and

(F) Any other statements or documents the Internal Revenue Service required the organization to file with, or that the organization submitted in support of, the application letter.

(iii) Exceptions. The term application for tax exemption does not include—

(A) Any application for tax exemption filed by an organization that the Internal Revenue Service has not yet recognized, on the basis of the application, as exempt from taxation under section 501 for any taxable year;

(B) Any application for tax exemption filed before July 15, 1987, unless the organization filing the application had a copy of the application on July 15, 1987;

(C) In the case of a tax-exempt organization other than a private foundation, the name and address of any contributor to the organization; or

(D) Any material, including the material listed in § 301.6104(a)–1(i) and information that the Secretary would be required to withhold from public inspection, that is not available for public inspection under section 6104.

(iv) Local or subordinate organizations. For rules relating to applications for tax exemption of local or subordinate organizations, see paragraph (f)(1) of this section.

(4) Annual information return—(i) In general. Except as described in paragraph (b)(4)(ii) of this section, the term annual information return includes an exact copy of any return filed by a tax-exempt organization pursuant to section 6033. It also includes any amended return the organization files with the Internal Revenue Service after the date the original return is filed. Returns filed pursuant to section 6033 include Form 990, Return of Organization Exempt From Income Tax, Form 990-PF, Return of Private Foundation, or any other version of Form 990 (such as Forms 990-EZ or 990-BL, except Form 990-T) and Form 1065. Each copy of a return must include all information furnished to the Internal Revenue Service on the return, as well as all schedules, attachments and supporting documents. For example, in the case of a Form 990, the copy must include Schedule A of Form 990 (containing supplementary information on section 501(c)(3) organizations), and those parts of the return that show compensation paid to specific persons (currently, Part V of Form 990 and Parts I and II of Schedule A of Form 990).

(ii) Exceptions. The term annual information return does not include Schedule A of Form 990-BL, Form 990-T, Exempt Organization Business Income Tax Return, Schedule K–1 of Form 1065 or Form 1120-POL, U.S. Income Tax Return For Certain Political Organizations. In the case of a tax-exempt organization other than a private foundation, the term annual information return does not include the name and address of any contributor to the organization.

(iii) Returns more than 3 years old. The term annual information return does not include any return after the expiration of 3 years from the date the return is required to be filed (including any extension of time that has been granted for filing such return) or is actually filed, whichever is later. If an organization files an amended return, however, the amended return must be made available for a period of 3 years beginning on the date it is filed with the Internal Revenue Service.

(iv) Local or subordinate organizations. For rules relating to annual information returns of local or subordinate organizations, see paragraph (f)(2) of this section.

(5) Regional or district offices—(i) In general. A regional or district office is any office of a tax-exempt organization, other than its principal office, that has paid employees, whether part-time or full-time, whose aggregate number of paid hours a week are normally at least 120.

(ii) Site not considered a regional or district office. A site is not considered a regional or district office, however, if—

(A) The only services provided at the site further exempt purposes (such as day care, health care or scientific or medical research); and

(B) The site does not serve as an office for management staff, other than managers who are involved solely in managing the exempt function activities at the site.

(c) Special rules relating to public inspection—(1) Permissible conditions on public inspection. A tax-exempt organization may have an employee present in the room during an inspection. The organization, however, must allow the individual conducting the inspection to take notes freely during the inspection. If the individual provides photocopying equipment at the place of inspection, the organization must allow the individual to photocopy the document at no charge.

(2) Organizations that do not maintain permanent offices. If a tax-exempt organization does not maintain a permanent office, the organization shall comply with the public inspection requirements of paragraph (a) of this section by making its application for tax exemption and its annual information returns, as applicable, available for inspection at a reasonable location of its choice. Such an organization shall permit public inspection within a reasonable amount of time after receiving a request for inspection (normally not more than 2 weeks) and at a reasonable time of day. At the organization's option, it may mail, within 2 weeks of receiving the request, a copy of its application for tax exemption and annual information returns to the requester in lieu of allowing an inspection. The organization may charge the requester for copying and actual postage costs only if the requester consents to the charge. An organization that has a permanent office, but has no office hours or very limited hours during certain times of the year, shall make its documents available during those periods when office hours are limited or not available as though it were an organization without a permanent office.

(d) Special rules relating to copies—(1) Time and place for providing copies in response to requests made in-person—(i) In general. Except as provided in paragraph (d)(1)(iii) of this section, a tax-exempt organization shall provide copies of the documents it is required to provide under section 6104(d) in response to a request made in person at its principal, regional and district offices during regular business hours. Except as provided in paragraph (d)(1)(ii) of this section, an organization shall provide such copies to a requester on the day the request is made.

(ii) Unusual circumstances. In the case of an in-person request, where unusual circumstances exist such that fulfilling the request on the same business day places an unreasonable burden on the tax-exempt organization, the organization must provide the copies no later than the next business day following the day that the unusual circumstances cease to exist or the fifth business day after the date of the request, whichever occurs first. Unusual circumstances include, but are not limited to, receipt of a volume of requests that exceeds the organization's daily capacity to make copies; requests received shortly before the end of regular business hours that require an extensive amount of copying; or requests received on a day when the organization's managerial staff capable of fulfilling the request is conducting special duties, such as student registration or attending an off-site meeting or convention, rather than its regular administrative duties.

(iii) Agents for providing copies. A principal, regional or district office of a tax-exempt organization subject to the requirements of this section may retain a local agent to process requests made in person for copies of its documents. A local agent must be located within reasonable proximity of the applicable office. A local agent that receives a request made in person for copies must provide the copies within the time limits and under the conditions that apply to the organization itself. For example, a local agent generally must provide a copy to a requester on the day the agent receives the request. When a principal, regional or district office of a tax-exempt organization using a local agent receives a request made in person for a copy, it must immediately provide the name, address and telephone number of the local agent to the requester. An organization that provides this information is not required to respond further to the requester. However, the penalty provisions of sections 6652(c)(1)(C), 6652(c)(1)(D), and 6685 continue to apply to the tax-exempt organization if the organization's local agent fails to provide the documents as required under section 6104(d).

(2) Request for copies in writing—(i) In general. A tax-exempt organization must honor a written request for a copy of documents (or the requested part) that the organization is required to provide under section 6104(d) if the request—

(A) Is addressed to, and delivered by mail, electronic mail, facsimile, or a private delivery service as defined in section 7502(f) to a principal, regional or district office of the organization; and

(B) Sets forth the address to which the copy of the documents should be sent.

(ii) Time and manner of fulfilling written requests—(A) In general. A tax-exempt organization receiving a written request for a copy shall mail the copy of the requested documents (or the requested parts of documents) within 30 days from the date it receives the request. However, if a tax-exempt organization requires payment in advance, it is only required to provide the copies within 30 days from the date it receives payment. For rules relating to payment, see paragraph (d)(3) of this section. In the absence of evidence to the contrary, a request or payment that is mailed shall be deemed to be received by an organization 7 days after the date of the postmark. A request that is transmitted to the organization by electronic mail or facsimile shall be deemed received the day the request is transmitted successfully. If an organization requiring payment in advance receives a written request without payment or with an insufficient payment, the organization must, within 7 days from the date it receives the request, notify the requester of its prepayment policy and the amount due. A copy is deemed provided on the date of the postmark or private delivery mark (or if sent by certified or registered mail, the date of registration or the date of the postmark on the sender's receipt). If an individual making a request consents, a tax-exempt organization may provide a copy of the requested document exclusively by electronic mail. In such case, the material is provided on the date the organization successfully transmits the electronic mail.

(B) Request for a copy of parts of document. A tax-exempt organization must fulfill a request for a copy of the organization's entire application for tax exemption or annual information return or any specific part or schedule of its application or return. A request for a copy of less than the entire application or less than the entire return must specifically identify the requested part or schedule.

(C) Agents for providing copies. A tax-exempt organization subject to the requirements of this section may retain an agent to process written requests for copies of its documents. The agent shall provide the copies within the time limits and under the conditions that apply to the organization itself. For example, if the organization received the request first (e.g., before the agent), the deadline for providing a copy in response to a request shall be determined by reference to when the organization received the request, not when the agent received the request. An organization that transfers a request for a copy to such an agent is not required to respond further to the request. If the organization's agent fails to provide the documents as required under section 6104(d), however, the penalty provisions of sections 6652(c)(1)(C), 6652(c)(1)(D), and 6685 continue to apply to the tax-exempt organization.

(3) Fees for copies—(i) In general. A tax-exempt organization may charge a reasonable fee for providing copies. A fee is reasonable only if it is no more than the total of the applicable per-page copying charge prescribed by the fee schedule promulgated pursuant to section (a)(4)(A)(i) of the Freedom of Information Act, 5 U.S.C. 552, by the Commissioner from time to time, and the actual postage costs incurred by the organization to send the copies. The applicable per-page copying charge shall be determined without regard to any applicable fee exclusion provided in the fee schedule for an initial or de minimis number of pages (*e.g.* the first 100 pages). Before the organization provides the documents, it may require that the individual requesting copies of the documents pay the fee. If the organization has provided an individual making a request with notice of the fee, and the individual does not pay the fee within 30 days, or if the individual pays the fee by check and the check does not clear upon deposit, the organization may disregard the request.

(ii) Form of payment—(A) Request made in person. If a tax-exempt organization charges a fee for copying (as permitted under paragraph (d)(3)(i) of this section), it shall accept payment by cash and money order for requests made in person. The organization may accept other forms of payment, such as credit cards and personal checks.

(B) Request made in writing. If a tax-exempt organization charges a fee for copying and postage (as permitted under paragraph (d)(3)(i) of this section), it shall accept payment by certified check, money order, and either personal check or credit card for requests made in writing. The organization may accept other forms of payment.

(iii) Avoidance of unexpected fees. Where a tax-exempt organization does not require prepayment and a requester does not enclose payment with a request, an organization must receive consent from a requester before providing copies for which the fee charged for copying and postage exceeds $20.

(iv) Responding to inquiries of fees charged. In order to facilitate a requester's ability to receive copies promptly, a tax-exempt organization shall respond to any questions from potential requesters concerning its fees for copying and postage. For example, the organization shall inform the requester of its charge for copying and mailing its application for exemption and each annual information return, with and without attachments, so that a requester may include payment with the request for copies.

(e) Documents to be provided by regional and district offices. Except as otherwise provided, a regional or district office of a tax-exempt organization must satisfy the same rules as the principal office with respect to allowing public inspection and providing copies of its application for tax exemption and annual information returns. A regional or district office is not required, however, to make its annual information return available for inspection or to provide copies until 30 days after the date the return is required to be filed (including any extension of time that is granted for filing such return) or is actually filed, whichever is later.

(f) Documents to be provided by local and subordinate organizations—(1) Applications for tax exemption. Except as otherwise provided, a tax-exempt organization that did not file its own application for tax exemption (because it is a local or subordinate organization covered by a group exemption letter referred to in § 1.508–1 of this chapter) must, upon request, make available for public inspection, or provide copies of, the application submitted to the Internal Revenue Service by the central or parent organization to obtain the group exemption letter and those documents which were submitted by the central or parent organization to include the local or subordinate organization in the group exemption letter. However, if the central or parent organization submits to the Internal Revenue Service a list or directory of local or subordinate organizations covered by the group exemption letter, the local or subordinate organization is required to provide only the application for the group exemption ruling and the pages of the list or directory that specifically refer to it. The local or subordinate organization shall permit public inspection, or comply with a request for copies made in person, within a reasonable amount of time (normally not more than 2 weeks) after receiving a request made in person for public inspection or copies and at a reasonable time of day. In a case where the requester seeks inspection, the local or subordinate organization may mail a copy of the applicable documents to the requester within the same time period in lieu of allowing an inspection. In such a case, the organization may charge the requester for copying and actual postage costs only if the requester consents to the charge. If the local or subordinate organization receives a written request for a copy of its application for tax exemption, it must fulfill the request in the time and manner specified in paragraph (d)(2) of this section. The requester has the option of requesting from the central or parent organization, at its principal office, inspection or copies of the application for group exemption and the material submitted by the central or parent organization to include a local or subordinate organization in the group ruling. If the central or parent organization submits to the Internal Revenue Service a list or directory of local or subordinate organizations covered by the group exemption letter, it must make such list or directory available for public inspection, but it is required to provide copies only of those pages of the list or directory that refer to particular local or subordinate organizations specified by the requester. The central or parent organization must fulfill such requests in the time and manner specified in paragraphs (c) and (d) of this section.

(2) Annual information returns. A local or subordinate organization that does not file its own annual information return (because it is affiliated with a central or parent organization that files a group return pursuant to § 1.6033–2(d) of this chapter) must, upon request, make available for public inspection, or provide copies of, the group returns filed by the central or parent organization. However, if the group return includes separate schedules with respect to each local or subordinate organization included in the group return, the local or subordinate organization receiving the request may omit any schedules relating only to other organizations included in the group return. The local or subordinate organization shall permit public inspection, or comply with a request for copies made in person, within a reasonable amount of time (normally not more than 2 weeks) after receiving a request made in person for public inspection or copies and at a reasonable time of day. In a case where the requester seeks inspection, the local or subordinate organization may mail a copy of the applicable documents to the requester within the same time period in lieu of allowing an inspection. In such a case, the organization may charge the requester for copying and actual postage costs only if the requester consents to the charge. If the local or subordinate organization receives a written request for a copy of its annual information return, it must fulfill the request by providing a copy of the group return in the time and manner specified in paragraph (d)(2) of this section. The requester has the option of requesting from the central or parent organization, at its principal office, inspection or copies of group returns filed by the central or parent organization. The central or parent organization must fulfill such requests in the time and manner specified in paragraphs (c) and (d) of this section.

(3) Failure to comply. If an organization fails to comply with the requirements specified in this paragraph, the penalty provisions of sections 6652(c)(1)(C), 6652(c)(1)(D), and 6685 apply.

(g) Failure to comply with public inspection or copying requirements. If a tax-exempt organization denies an individual's request for inspection or a copy of an application for tax exemption or an annual information return as required under this section, and the individual wants to alert the Internal Revenue Service to the possible need for enforcement action, the individual may provide a statement to the district director for the key district in which the applicable tax-exempt organization's principal office is located (or such other person as the Commissioner may designate) that describes the reason why the individual believes the denial was in violation of the requirements of section 6104(d).

(h) Effective date—(1) In general. For a tax-exempt organization, other than a private foundation, this section is applicable June 8, 1999. For a private foundation, this section is applicable (except as provided in paragraph (h)(2) of this section) beginning March 13, 2000.

(2) Private foundation annual information returns. This section does not apply to any private foundation return the due date for which (determined with regard to any extension of time for filing) is before the applicable date for private foundations specified in paragraph (h)(1) of this section.

§ 301.6104(d)–2. Making applications and returns widely available.

(a) In general. A tax-exempt organization is not required to comply with a request for a copy of its application for tax exemption or an annual information return pursuant to § 301.6104(d)–1(a) if the organization has made the requested document widely available in accordance with paragraph (b) of this section. An organization that makes its application for tax exemption and/or annual information return widely available must nevertheless make the document available for public inspection as required under § 301.6104(d)–1(a), as applicable.

(b) Widely available—(1) In general. A tax-exempt organization makes its application for tax exemption and/or an annual information return widely available if the organization complies with the requirements specified in paragraph (b)(2) of this section, and if the organization satisfies the requirements of paragraph (d) of this section.

(2) Internet posting—(i) In general. A tax-exempt organization can make its application for tax exemption and/or an annual information return widely available by posting the document on a World Wide Web page that the tax-exempt organization establishes and maintains or by having the document posted, as part of a database of similar documents of other tax-exempt organizations, on a World Wide Web page established and maintained by another entity. The document will be considered widely available only if—

(A) the World Wide Web page through which it is available clearly informs readers that the document is available and provides instructions for downloading it;

(B) the document is posted in a format that, when accessed, downloaded, viewed and printed in hard copy, exactly reproduces the image of the application for tax exemption or annual information return as it was originally filed with the Internal Revenue Service, except for any information permitted by statute to be withheld from public disclosure. (See section 6104(d)(3) and § 301.6104(d)–3(b)(3) and (4)); and

(C) any individual with access to the Internet can access, download, view and print the document without special computer hardware or software required for that format (other than software that is readily available to members of the public without payment of any fee) and without payment of a fee to the tax-exempt organization or to another entity maintaining the World Wide Web page.

(ii) Transition rule. A tax-exempt organization that posted its application for tax exemption or its annual information returns on a World Wide Web page on or before April 9, 1999 in a manner consistent with regulation project REG–246250–96 (1997 C.B. 627) (See § 601.601(d)(2) of this chapter.) will be treated as satisfying the requirements of paragraphs (b)(2)(i)(B) & (C) of this section until June 8, 2000 provided that an individual can access, download, view and print the document without payment of a fee to the tax-exempt organization or to another entity maintaining the World Wide Web page.

(iii) Reliability and accuracy. In order for the document to be widely available through an Internet posting, the entity maintaining the World Wide Web page must have procedures for ensuring the reliability and accuracy of the document that it posts on the page and must take reasonable precautions to prevent alteration, destruction or accidental loss of the document when posted on its page. In the event that a posted document is altered, destroyed or lost, the entity must correct or replace the document.

(c) Discretion to prescribe other methods for making documents widely available. The Commissioner, from time to time, may prescribe additional methods, other than an Internet posting meeting the requirements of paragraph (b)(2) of this section, that a tax-exempt organization may use to make its documents widely available.

(d) Notice requirement. If a tax-exempt organization has made its application for tax exemption and/or an annual information return widely available it must notify any individual requesting a copy where the documents are available (including the address on the World Wide Web, if applicable). If the request is made in person, the organization shall provide such notice to the individual immediately. If the request is made in writing, the notice shall be provided within 7 days of receiving the request.

(e) Effective date. For a tax-exempt organization, other than a private foundation, this section is applicable June 8, 1999. For a private foundation, this section is applicable beginning March 13, 2000.

§ 301.6104(d)–3. Tax-exempt organization subject to harassment campaign.

(a) In general. If the district director for the key district in which the organization's principal office is located (or such other person as the Commissioner may designate) determines that the organization is the subject of a harassment campaign and compliance with the requests that are part of the harassment campaign would not be in the public interest, a tax-exempt organization is not required to fulfill a request for a copy (as otherwise required by § 301.6104(d)–1(a)) that it reasonably believes is part of the campaign.

(b) Harassment. A group of requests for an organization's application for tax exemption or annual information returns is indicative of a harassment campaign if the requests are part of a single coordinated effort to disrupt the operations of a tax-exempt organization, rather than to collect information about the organization. Whether a group of requests constitutes such a harassment campaign depends on the relevant facts and circumstances. Facts and circumstances that indicate the organization is the subject of a harassment campaign include: a sudden increase in the number of requests; an extraordinary number of requests made through form letters or similarly worded correspondence; evidence of a purpose to deter significantly the organization's employees or volunteers from pursuing the organization's exempt purpose; requests that contain language hostile to the organization; direct evidence of bad faith by organizers of the purported harassment campaign; evidence that the organization has already provided the requested documents to a member of the purported harassing group; and a demonstration by the tax-exempt organization that it routinely provides copies of its documents upon request.

(c) Special rule for multiple requests from a single individual or address. A tax-exempt organization may disregard any request for copies of all or part of any document beyond the first two received within any 30-day period or the first four received within any one-year period from the same individual or the same address, regardless of whether the district director for the applicable key district (or such other person as the Commissioner may designate) has determined that the organization is subject to a harassment campaign.

(d) Harassment determination procedure. A tax-exempt organization may apply for a determination that it is the subject of a harassment campaign and that compliance with requests that are part of the campaign would not be in the public interest by submitting a signed application to the district director for the key district where the organization's principal office is located (or such other person as the Commissioner may designate). The application shall consist of a written statement giving the organization's name, address, employer identification number, and the name, address and telephone number of the person to contact regarding the application. The application must describe in detail the facts and circumstances that the organization believes support a determination that the organization is subject to a harassment campaign. The organization may suspend compliance with respect to any request for a copy of its documents based on its reasonable belief that such request is part of a harassment campaign, provided that the organization files an application for a determination within 10 business days from the day the organization first suspends compliance with respect to a request that is part of the alleged campaign. In addition, the organization may suspend compliance with any request it reasonably believes to be part of the harassment campaign until it receives a response to its application for a harassment campaign determination.

(e) Effect of a harassment determination. If the appropriate district director (or such other person as the Commissioner may designate) determines that a tax-exempt organization is the subject of a harassment campaign and it is not in the public interest to comply with requests that are part of the campaign, such organization is not required to comply with any request for copies that it reasonably believes is part of the campaign.

This determination may be subject to other terms and conditions set forth by the district director (or such other person as the Commissioner may designate). A person (as defined in section 6652(c)(4)(C)) shall not be liable for any penalty under sections 6652(c)(1)(C), 6652(c)(1)(D) or 6685 for failing to timely provide a copy of documents in response to a request covered in a request for a harassment determination if the organization fulfills the request within 30 days of receiving a determination from the district director (or such other person as the Commissioner may designate) that the organization is not subject to a harassment campaign. Notwithstanding the preceding sentence, if the district director (or such other person as the Commissioner may designate) further determines that the organization did not have a reasonable basis for requesting a determination that it was subject to a harassment campaign or reasonable belief that a request was part of the campaign, the person (as defined in section 6652(c)(4)(C)) remains liable for any penalties that result from not providing the copies in a timely fashion.

(f) Examples. The provisions of this section are illustrated by the following examples:

Example 1. V, a tax-exempt organization, receives an average of 25 requests per month for copies of its three most recent information returns. In the last week of May, V is mentioned in a national news magazine story that discusses information contained in V's 1996 information return. From June 1 through June 30, 1997 V receives 200 requests for a copy of its documents. Other than the sudden increase in the number of requests for copies, there is no other evidence to suggest that the requests are part of an organized campaign to disrupt V's operations. Although fulfilling the requests will place a burden on V, the facts and circumstances do not show that V is subject to a harassment campaign. Therefore, V must respond timely to each of the 200 requests it receives in June.

Example 2. Y is a tax-exempt organization that receives an average of 10 requests a month for copies of its annual information returns. From March 1, 1997 to March 31, 1997, Y receives 25 requests for copies of its documents. Fifteen of the requests come from individuals Y knows to be active members of the board of organization X. In the past X has opposed most of the positions and policies that Y advocates. None of the requesters have asked for copies of documents from Y during the past year. Y has no other information about the requesters. Although the facts and circumstances show that some of the individuals making requests are hostile to Y, they do not show that the individuals have organized a campaign that will place enough of a burden on Y to disrupt its activities. Therefore, Y must respond to each of the 25 requests it receives in March.

Example 3. The facts are the same as in Example 2, except that during March 1997, Y receives 100 requests. In addition to the fifteen requests from members of organization X's board, 75 of the requests are similarly worded form letters. Y discovers that several individuals associated with X have urged the X's members and supporters, via the Internet, to submit as many requests for a copy of Y's annual information returns as they can. The message circulated on the Internet provides a form letter that can be used to make the request. Both the appeal via the Internet and the requests for copies received by Y contain hostile language. During the same year but before the 100 requests were received, Y provided copies of its annual information returns to the headquarters of X. The facts and circumstances show that the 75 form letter requests are coordinated for the purpose of disrupting Y's operations, and not to collect information that has already been provided to an association representing the requesters' interests. Thus, the fact and circumstances show that Y is the subject of an organized harassment campaign. To confirm that it may disregard the 90 requests that constitute the harassment campaign, Y must apply to the applicable district director (or such other person as the Commissioner may designate) for a determination. Y may disregard the 90 requests while the application is pending and after the determination is received. However, it must respond within the applicable time limits to the 10 requests it received in March that were not part of the harassment campaign.

Example 4. The facts are the same as in Example 3, except that Y receives 5 additional requests from 5 different representatives of the news media who in the past have published articles about Y. Some of these articles were hostile to Y. Normally, the Internal Revenue Service will not consider a tax-exempt organization to have a reasonable belief that a request from a member of the news media is part of a harassment campaign absent additional facts that demonstrate that the organization could reasonably believe the particular requests from the news media to be part of a harassment campaign. Thus, absent such additional facts, Y must respond within the applicable time limits to the 5 requests that it received from representatives of the news media.

(g) Effective date. For a tax-exempt organization, other than a private foundation, this section is applicable June 8, 1999. For a private foundation, this section is applicable beginning March 13, 2000.

§ 1.6115–1. Disclosure requirements for quid pro quo contributions.

(a) Good faith estimate defined—(1) In general. A good faith estimate of the value of goods or services provided by an organization described in section 170(c) in consideration for a taxpayer's payment to that organization is an estimate of the fair market value, within the meaning of section 1.170A–1(c)(2), of the goods or services. The organization may use any reasonable methodology in making a good faith estimate, provided it applies the methodology in good faith. If the organization fails to apply the methodology in good faith, the organization will be treated as not having met the requirements of section 6115. See section 6714 for the penalties that apply for failure to meet the requirements of section 6115.

(2) Good faith estimate for goods or services that are not commercially available. A good faith estimate of the value of goods or services that are not generally available in a commercial transaction may be determined by reference to the fair market value of similar or comparable goods or services. Goods or services may be similar or comparable even though they do not have the unique qualities of the goods or services that are being valued.

(3) Examples. The following examples illustrate the rules of this paragraph (a).

Example 1. *Facility not available on a commercial basis.* Museum M, an organization described in section 170(c), is located in Community N. In return for a payment of $50,000 or more, M allows a donor to hold a private event in a room located in M. Private events other than those held by such donors are not permitted to be held in M. In Community N, there are four hotels, O, P, Q, and R, that have ballrooms with the same capacity as the room in M. Of these hotels, only O and P have ballrooms that offer amenities and atmosphere that are similar to the amenities and atmosphere of the room in M (although O and P lack the unique collection of art that is displayed in the room in M). Because the capacity, amenities, and atmosphere of ballrooms in O and P are comparable to the capacity, amenities, and atmosphere of the room in M, a good faith estimate of the benefits received from M may be determined by reference to the cost of renting either the ballroom in O or the ballroom in P. The cost of renting the ballroom in O is $2500 and, therefore, a good faith estimate of the fair market value of the right to host a private event in the room at M is $2500. In this example, the ballrooms in O and P are considered similar and comparable facilities to the room in M for valuation purposes, notwithstanding the fact that the room in M displays a unique collection of art.

Example 2. *Services available on a commercial basis.* Charity S is an organization described in section 170(c). S offers to provide a one-hour tennis lesson with Tennis Professional T in return for the first payment of $500 or more that it receives. T provides one-hour tennis lessons on a commercial basis for $100. Taxpayer pays $500 to S and in return receives the tennis lesson with T. A good faith estimate of the fair market value of the lesson provided in exchange for Taxpayer's payment is $100.

Example 3. *Celebrity presence.* Charity U is an organization described in section 170(c). In return for the first payment of $1000 or more that it receives, U will provide a dinner for two followed by an evening tour of Museum V conducted by Artist W, whose most recent works are on display at V. W does not provide tours of V on a commercial basis. Typically, tours of V are free to the public. Taxpayer pays $1000 to U and in return receives a dinner valued at $100 and an evening tour of V conducted by W. Because tours of V are typically free to the public, a good faith estimate of the value of the evening tour conducted by W is $0. In this example, the fact that Taxpayer's tour of V is conducted by W rather than V's regular tour guides does not render the tours dissimilar or incomparable for valuation purposes.

(b) Certain goods or services disregarded. For purposes of section 6115, an organization described in section 170(c) may disregard goods or services described in section 1.170A–13(f)(8)(i).

(c) Value of the right to purchase tickets to a college or university athletic event. For purposes of section 6115, the right to purchase tickets for seating at an athletic event in exchange for a payment described in section 170(*l*) is treated as having a value equal to twenty percent of such payment.

(d) Goods or services provided to employees or partners of donor—(1) Certain goods or services disregarded. For purposes of section 6115, goods or services provided by an organization described in section 170(c) to employees of a donor or to partners of a partnership that is a donor in return for a payment to the donee organization may be disregarded to the extent that the goods or services provided to each employee or partner are the same as those described in section 1.170A–13(f)(8)(i).

(2) Description permitted in lieu of good faith estimate for other goods or services. The written disclosure statement required by section 6115 may include a description of goods or services, in lieu of a good faith estimate of their value, if the donor is—

(i) An employer and, in return for the donor's quid pro quo contribution, an organization described in section 170(c) provides the donor's employees with goods or services other than those described in paragraph (d)(1) of this section; or

(ii) A partnership and, in return for its quid pro quo contribution, the organization provides partners in the partnership with goods or services other than those described in paragraph (d)(1) of this section.

(e) Effective date. This section applies to contributions made on or after December 16, 1996. However, taxpayers may rely on the rules of this section for contributions made on or after January 1, 1994.

CHURCH TAX INQUIRIES

§ 301.7611-1. Questions and answers relating to church tax inquiries and examinations.

CHURCH TAX INQUIRY

Q-1: When may the Internal Revenue Service begin an inquiry of a church's tax liability?

A-1: Under section 7611 of the Internal Revenue Code, the Internal Revenue Service may begin a church tax inquiry only when the appropriate Regional Commissioner (or higher Treasury official) reasonably believes, on the basis of facts and circumstances recorded in writing, that the organization (1) may not qualify for tax exemption as a church; (2) may be carrying on an unrelated trade or business (within the meaning of section 513); or (3) may be otherwise engaged in activities subject to tax. Information received by the Internal Revenue Service at its request may not be used to form the basis of a reasonable belief to begin a church tax inquiry, unless the Service's request is made within the procedures of section 7611, is a request permitted by these questions and answers to be made without application of the procedures of section 7611, or is a request to which the procedures of section 7611 do not apply.

Q-2: What is a church tax inquiry within the meaning of section 7611?

A-2: A church tax inquiry is any inquiry to a church (other than a routine request described in Q and A-4, an inquiry described in Q and A-5, an investigation described in Q and A-6 or an examination described in Qs and As 10 and 14), to serve as a basis for determining whether the organization qualifies for tax exemption as a church or whether it is carrying on an unrelated trade or business or is otherwise engaged in activities subject to tax. An inquiry is considered to commence when the Internal Revenue Service requests information or materials from a church of a type contained in church records. The term "church tax inquiry" does not include routine requests for information or inquiries regarding matters which do not primarily concern the tax status or liability of the church itself. See Q and A-4 with respect to routine requests regarding, among other things, withholding responsibilities for income tax or FICA (social security) tax liabilities. See Q and A-6 with respect to the types of investigations, other than routine requests, that are outside the scope of the procedures of section 7611. See Q and A-5 with respect to requests for third party records that are outside the scope of the procedures of section 7611.

Q-3: What is a "church" for purposes of the church tax inquiry and examination procedures of section 7611?

A-3: Solely for purposes of applying the procedures of section 7611, and as used in these questions and answers, the term "church" includes any organization claiming to be a church and any convention or association of churches. For purposes of the procedures of section 7611 and these questions and answers a church does not include separately incorporated church-supported schools or other organizations incorporated separately from the church.

ROUTINE REQUESTS

Q-4: What is a routine request to a church that is outside the scope of and does not necessitate application of the procedures set forth in section 7611?

A-4: Routine requests to a church will not be considered to commence a church tax inquiry and will not necessitate application of the procedures set forth in section 7611. Routine requests for this purpose include (but are not limited to) questions regarding (1) the filing or failure to file any tax return or information return by the church; (2) compliance with income tax or FICA (social security) tax withholding responsibilities by the church; (3) any supplemental information needed to complete the mechanical processing of any incomplete or incorrect return filed by the church; (4) information necessary to process applications for exempt status and letter ruling requests; (5) information necessary to process and update periodically a church's (i) registrations for tax-free transactions (excise tax), (ii) elections for exemption from windfall profit tax, or (iii) employment tax exemption requests; (6) information identifying a church that is used to update the Cumulative List of Tax Exempt Organizations (Publication No. 78) and other computer files; and

(7) confirmation that a specific business is or is not owned or operated by a church.

THIRD PARTY RECORDS

Q-5: To what extent may the Internal Revenue Service gain access to third party records?

A-5: The Internal Revenue Service may request a church to provide information necessary to locate third-party records (for instance, bank records), including information regarding the church's chartered name, state and year of incorporation, and location of checking and savings accounts, without application of the procedures of section 7611.

Records (for instance, cancelled checks or other records in the possession of a bank) held by third party recordkeepers, as defined in section 7609, are not considered church records. Thus, subject to the provisions set forth in section 7609 regarding third party summonses, access is permitted to such records without regard to the requirements of the procedures set forth in section 7611. The Internal Revenue Service is generally required, under other rules, to inform a church of any Internal Revenue Service requests for materials.

Third party materials may be acquired without application of the procedures of section 7611; however, a determination that a church is not entitled to an exemption, or an assessment of tax for unrelated business income against a church, may not be made solely on the basis of third party records, without first complying with the requirements of two notices and offering of a conference (see Qs and As 9 and 10) pursuant to the procedures set forth in section 7611. This limitation does not apply to assessments of tax other than income tax resulting from loss of exemption or for unrelated business income (for instance, assessments of social security or other employment taxes). Third party bank records will not be used in a manner inconsistent with the procedures set forth in section 7611 or in these questions and answers.

SCOPE OF SECTION 7611

Q-6: What types of investigations, other than routine requests and requests for information necessary to locate and examine third party records, and examination of those records, are outside the scope of the procedures of section 7611?

A-6: The church inquiry and examination procedures described in section 7611 do not apply to (1) any inquiry or examination relating to the tax liability of any person other than a church; (2) any termination assessment under section 6851 or 6852, or jeopardy assessment under section 6861; or (3) any case involving a knowing failure to file a return or a willful attempt to defeat or evade tax (including but not limited to any case involving a failure by the church to withhold or pay social security or other employment taxes or income tax required to be withheld from wages). Additionally, the church inquiry and examination procedures do not apply to any criminal investigations.

The church tax inquiry and examination procedures also do not apply to inquiries or examinations which relate primarily to the tax status (including, but not limited to, social security or self-employment tax or income tax required to be withheld from wages) or liability of persons other than the church (including, but not limited to, the tax status or liability of a contributor or contributors to the church), rather than the tax status or liability of the church itself. These may include, but are not limited to: (1) inquiries or examinations regarding the inurement of church funds to a particular individual or individuals or to another organization, which may result in the denial of all or part of such individual's or organization's deduction for charitable contributions to a church; (2) inquiries or examinations regarding the assignment of income or services or contributions to a church; and (3) inquiries or examinations regarding a vow of poverty by an individual or individuals followed by a transfer of property or an assignment of income or services to a church. Inquiries may be made to a church regarding these matters without being considered to have commenced a church tax inquiry under section 7611, and an examination of church records may be made relating to these issues (including enforcement of a summons for access to such records) without application of the requirements contained in section 7611 applicable to church tax inquiries and examinations. Such examinations are subject to the general rules regarding examinations of taxpayer books and records.

Q-7: What action may be taken if the church or its agents fail to respond to routine requests, or questions regarding other individuals' or organizations' tax liabilities?

A-7: Repeated (two or more) failures by a church or its agents to reply to routine requests (see Q and A-4) will be considered by the appropriate Internal Revenue Service Regional Commissioner to be a reasonable basis for commencement of a church tax inquiry under the church tax inquiry and examination procedures of section 7611. The failure of a church to respond to repeated requests for information regarding individuals' or other organizations' tax liabilities (see Q and A-6) will be considered a reasonable basis for commencement of a church tax inquiry. Failure by a church to provide information necessary to locate third-party records (see Q and A-5) will be a factor, but not a conclusive factor, in determining if there is reasonable cause for commencing a church tax inquiry. For this purpose, a failure to respond to a request means either that no response has been made or that the response does not make a reasonable attempt to submit the information called for by the specific language of the request.

Q-8: Where an inquiry or examination is outside the scope of and does not necessitate application of the procedures of section 7611, what are the limitations on the Internal Revenue Service's actions?

A-8: Inquiries or examinations which are outside the scope of the procedures of section 7611 and therefore are conducted without application of the procedures of section 7611 (for instance, those addressed in Q and A-6) will be limited to the determination of facts and circumstances specifically relating to the tax liabilities of the individuals or other organizations in question. For example, in a case against an individual or other organization, information may be requested or church records examined, if pertinent, regarding amounts of money, property, or services transferred to the individual or individuals in question (including, but not limited to wages, loans, or noncontractual transfers), the use of church funds for personal expenses, or other similar matters, without having to follow the church tax inquiry and examination procedures. As one example, in an assignment of income case against an individual or other organization, information could be requested or church records examined if relevant to an individual's assignment of particular income, donation of property, or transfer of a business to a church. However, without following the church tax inquiry and examination procedures, no examination of a contributor or membership list in the possession of the church will be made, other than under the applicable procedures of section 7611, for the purpose of determining the overall financial structure of the church, merely because such structure was relevant to the church's qualification as a tax-exempt entity and therefore indirectly relevant to the validity of contributors' deductions in general. Inquiries or examinations regarding individuals' or other organizations' tax liabilities will not be used in a manner inconsistent with the procedures set forth in section 7611 or in these questions and answers.

NOTICE REQUIREMENTS

Q-9: What satisfies the inquiry notice requirement (first notice) upon commencement of a church tax inquiry?

A-9: Upon commencing a church tax inquiry, the appropriate Regional Commissioner is required to provide written notice to the church of the beginning of the inquiry. This notice will include (1) an explanation of the concerns which gave rise to the inquiry and the general subject matter of the inquiry, which is sufficiently specific to allow the church to understand the particular area of church activities or behavior which is at issue; (2) a general explanation of the provisions of the Internal Revenue Code which authorize the inquiry or which may otherwise be involved in the inquiry; and (3) a general explanation of applicable administrative and constitutional provisions with respect to the inquiry, including the right to a conference with the Internal Revenue Service before an examination of church records is commenced. The inquiry notice (first notice) will generally request information in an effort to alleviate the concerns which gave rise to the inquiry.

However, the Internal Revenue Service is not precluded from expanding its inquiry beyond the concerns expressed in the inquiry notice (first notice) as a result of facts and circumstances which subsequently comes to its attention (including, where appropriate, an expansion of an unrelated business income inquiry to include questions of tax-exempt status, and vice-versa).

The inquiry notice requirement (first notice) does not require the Internal Revenue Service to share particular items of evidence with the church, or to identify its sources of information regarding church activities, if providing such information would be damaging to the inquiry or to the sources of information. For example, in an inquiry regarding unrelated business income, the Internal Revenue Service might state that its inquiry was prompted by a local newspaper advertisement regarding a church-owned business. However, the Internal Revenue Service would not be required to reveal the existence or identity of any so-called "informers" within a church (including present or former employees).

Q-10: What must be done to satisfy the examination notice requirement (second notice) before commencing an examination of church records or religious activities with respect to an examination conducted under section 7611?

A-10: Where an examination is conducted under section 7611, church records or religious activities of a church may be examined only if, at least 15 days prior to the examination, written notice of the proposed examination is provided to the church and to the appropriate Regional Counsel. This notice is in addition to the notice of commencement of inquiry (first notice) previously provided to the church.

The notice of examination (second notice) is required to include (1) a copy of the church tax inquiry notice (first notice) previously provided to the church; (2) a description of the church records and activities sought to be examined; and (3) a copy of all documents which were collected or prepared by the Internal Revenue Service for use in the examination, and which are required to be disclosed under the Freedom of Information Act (5 U.S.C. 552) as supplemented by section 6103 of the Code (relating to disclosure and confidentiality of tax return information). The documents to be supplied under this provision will be limited to documents specifically concerning the church whose records are to be examined and will not include documents relating to other inquiries or examinations or to Internal Revenue Service practices and procedures in general. Disclosure to the church will be subject to restrictions regarding the disclosure of the existence or identity of informants. Although a description of materials to be examined will be provided in the notice of examination (second notice), the description does not restrict the ability of the Internal Revenue Service to examine church records or religious activities which are not specifically mentioned in the notice of examination (second notice) but which are properly within the scope of the examination. Thus, the Internal Revenue Service is not precluded from expanding its inquiry beyond the concerns expressed in the examination notice (second notice) as a result of facts and circumstances which subsequently come to its attention (including, where appropriate, an expansion of an unrelated business income examination to include questions of tax-exempt status, and vice versa).

At the time the notice of examination (second notice) is provided to the church, a copy of the same notice will be provided to the appropriate Regional Counsel. The Regional Counsel is then allowed 15 days from issuance of the second notice in which to file an advisory objection to the examination. (This is concurrent with the 15-day period during which an examination of church records is prohibited pending a request for a conference.)

As part of the notice of examination (second notice), the church will be offered an opportunity to meet with an Internal Revenue Service official to discuss the concerns which gave rise to the inquiry and the general subject matter of the inquiry. An examination will not begin until 15 days after the mailing of the notice of examination (second notice). The organization may request a conference at any time prior to beginning of the examination and a conference so requested will be scheduled within a reasonable time after the request is made.

The purpose of the conference is to remind the church, in general terms, of the stages of the church tax inquiry and examination procedures and to discuss the relevant issues that may arise as part of the inquiry, in an effort to resolve the issues of tax exemption or liability without the necessity of an examination of church records or activities. Information properly excludable from a written notice of examination (second notice) (including information regarding the identity of third-party witnesses or evidence provided by such witnesses) is not a subject for discussion at, and will not be revealed during, a conference.

Once a conference request is timely made, an examination will begin only following the conference. The conference requirement may not be utilized to delay an examination beyond the time reasonably necessary to prepare for and hold the conference. The holding of one conference with the church will be sufficient to satisfy the requirements of section 7611 and these questions and answers.

ACTION AFTER ISSUANCE OF NOTICE

Q-11: What action may be taken after issuance of the examination notice (second notice)?

A-11: After the examination notice (second notice) is issued, the organization may request a conference as described in Q and A-10 (see Q and A-12 with respect to time for issuance of examination notice). If the matters of concern which gave rise to the issuance of the examination notice (second notice) are resolved at the conference, it may be determined that an examination is not necessary. If the matters of concern are not resolved at the conference, or if the organization does not request a conference, the examination will ordinarily begin.

The examination will be conducted under the Internal Revenue Service's general examination procedures and the procedures of section 7611. The outcome of such an examination will ordinarily be: (1) No change in tax-exempt status or tax liability; (2) no change in such status or liability, conditioned on compliance with a request to modify in future tax periods matters such as internal accounting practices and procedures or coupled with a caution to refrain from increasing certain activities limited by the Internal Revenue Code, such as lobbying programs aimed at influencing legislation; (3) a proposal to revoke tax-exempt status; (4) a proposal asserting unrelated business income tax liability; or (5) a proposal asserting liability for other taxes.

In certain exceptional circumstances the Internal Revenue Service may, in lieu of an examination, propose to revoke the organization's exemption based upon the facts and circumstances which form the basis for a reasonable belief to commence an inquiry under section 7611 and any other appropriate information that becomes apparent as a result of the inquiry, the conference, or both.

Pursuant to section 7611(d), the Regional Counsel is required to approve, in writing, certain final determinations that are within the scope of section 7611 and adversely affect tax-exempt status or increase any tax liability. The Regional Counsel will review and approve (1) a determination that an organization is not entitled to tax-exempt status; (2) a determination that an organization is not entitled to receive tax-deductible contributions; or (3) the issuance of a notice of tax deficiency to a church arising out of an inquiry or examination or, in cases where deficiency procedures are inapplicable, the assessment of any underpayment of tax by the church arising out of an inquiry or examination. The Regional Counsel will also state in writing that there has been substantial compliance with section 7611, when applicable.

PROCEDURAL TIME LIMITATIONS

Q-12: When may the notice of examination (second notice) be sent?

A-12: The notice of examination (second notice) may be mailed to a church not less than 15 days after the notice of commencement of a church tax inquiry (first notice). Thus, at least 30 days must pass between the first notice and the actual examination of church records since an examination may not begin until 15 days after the notice of examination (second notice). For example, if notice of commencement of an inquiry is mailed to a church on March 1st, the notice of proposed examination may be mailed to the church no earlier than the 15th day after the date of the inquiry notice, or March 16th. If the notice of examination (second notice) was mailed March 16th, no examination of church records may be made prior to day 30; thus, the earliest date the examination may commence is March 31st. If an organization does not request a conference prior to day 30, the Internal Revenue Service may proceed to examine church records and complete its investigation or make a determination based on the information already in its possession.

Q-13: What is the limitation on the amount of time the Internal Revenue Service has to complete inquiries and examinations?

A-13: The Internal Revenue Service is required to complete any church inquiry or examination, and to make a final determination with respect thereto, not later than two years after the date on which the notice of examination (second notice) is mailed to the church. The running of this two-year period is suspended for any period during which (1) a judicial proceeding brought by the church or its officials or agents against the Internal Revenue Service with respect to the church tax inquiry or examination is pending or being appealed (even though section 7611(e)(2) describes the exclusive remedy for a violation of the church tax inquiry and examination procedures; see Q and A-17); (2) a judicial proceeding brought by the Internal Revenue Service against the church (or any official or agent thereof) to compel compliance with any reasonable request for examination of church records or religious activities is pending or being appealed; or (3) the Internal Revenue Service is unable to take actions with respect to the church tax inquiry or examination by reason of an order issued in a suit under section 7609 involving access to records held by third-party recordkeepers. The two-year period is also suspended for any period in excess of 20 days (but not in excess of 6 months) in which the church or its agents fail to comply with any reasonable request for church records or other information. The two-year period may be extended by mutual agreement of the church and the Internal Revenue Service.

In cases where the inquiry is not followed by an examination notice (second notice), the inquiry must be concluded and a final determination made within 90 days of the date of the notice of inquiry (first notice). This 90-day period is suspended during any period for which the two year period for duration of a church examination would be suspended; except that the 90-day period will not be suspended because of the church's failure to comply with requests for information made prior to the notice of examination (second notice).

Q-13a: When do the church tax inquiry and church tax examination periods commence and conclude?

A-13a: A church tax inquiry commences when the church tax inquiry notice (first notice) is mailed. A church tax inquiry must be concluded not later than 90 days after the church tax inquiry notice (first notice) date. The period is counted from the day after the inquiry notice (first notice) is mailed. A church tax inquiry is concluded when the results of the inquiry or the notice of examination, as appropriate, is mailed. For example, if the inquiry notice (first notice) is mailed on November 1, 1985, the church tax inquiry must be concluded, in the absence of a permissible suspension of the period (see Q and A-13), on or before January 30, 1986.

A church tax examination commences when the church tax examination notice (second notice) is mailed. A church tax examination must be concluded not later than the date which is 2 years after the examination notice (second notice) date. The period is counted from the day after the examination notice (second notice) is mailed. A church tax examination is concluded when the final determination is mailed. For example, if the examination notice is mailed November 16, 1985, the final determination must be made, in the absence of a permissible suspension of the period (see Q and A-13), on or before November 16, 1987.

EXAMINATION OF RECORDS OR RELIGIOUS ACTIVITIES

Q-14: To what extent may church records or religious activities of a church be examined?

A-14: In cases conducted under section 7611, an examination of church records may be made only after complying with the notice provisions of section 7611 (see Qs and As 9, 10 and 12) unless the church files a written waiver of the provisions of section 7611 or a part thereof. In cases conducted under section 7611 where no written waiver has been filed, church records may be examined only to the extent necessary to determine the liability for, and the amount of, any Federal tax. This includes examinations (1) to determine the initial or continuing qualification of the organization whose records are being examined as a tax-exempt church under section 501(c)(3); (2) to determine whether the organization qualifies to receive tax-deductible contributions under section 170(c); or (3) to determine the amount of tax (including unrelated business income tax), if any, which is to be imposed on the organization.

Church records include all regularly kept church corporate and financial records including (but not limited to) corporate minute books, contributor or membership lists, and any materials which qualified as church books of account under section 7605(c), as in effect on December 31, 1984. Church records include private correspondence between a church and its members that is in the possession of the church. However, church records do not include records previously filed with a public official or newspapers or newsletters distributed generally to church members.

The religious activities of an organization claiming to be a church (see Q and A-3 for a definition of the term "church" as used in section 7611 and in these questions and answers) may be examined only to the extent necessary to determine if the organization actually is a church exempt from tax. This includes a determination of the organization's qualification as a church for any period.

LIMITATIONS ON PERIOD OF ASSESSMENT OR PROCEEDINGS FOR COLLECTION WITHOUT ASSESSMENT

Q-15: What are the special limitations on the period of assessment or proceedings for collection without assessment?

A-15: The special limitation periods for church tax liabilities are described below and are not to be construed to increase an otherwise applicable limitation period. Thus, a three-year limitation period would apply where a church filed a tax return before an examination was held and did not substantially understate income. No limitation period is to apply in any case of fraud, willful tax evasion, or knowing failure to file a return which should have been filed.

In the case of any church tax examination with respect to the revocation of tax-exempt status under section 501(a), any tax imposed by chapter 1 (other than section 511) may be assessed, or a proceeding in court for collection of such tax may be begun without assessment, only for the three most recently completed taxable years preceding the examination notice date (*i.e.*, the date the notice of examination is mailed to the church). If an organization is not a church exempt from tax under section 501(a) for any of the three years described in the preceding sentence, then the period of assessment will apply to the six most recently completed taxable years ending before the examination notice date.

For examinations concerning qualification for tax-exempt status, the examination is limited initially to an examination of church records which are relevant to a determination of tax status or liability for the three most recently completed taxable years ending before the examination notice date. If it is determined that an organization is not a church exempt from tax for one or more of the three most recently completed taxable years and no return has been filed for the three years ending before the three most recently completed taxable years, an examination of relevant records may be made, as part of the same examination, for the six most recently completed taxable years ending before the examination notice date. (This assumes that no returns were filed for any of the three years to which the examination is to be extended. If a return was timely filed for any such year, the filing of that return determines the applicable statute of limitations for that year in the absence of other factors, for example, fraud, willful tax evasion or substantial understatement, which ordinarily would extend the statute of limitations.)

For purposes of section 7611(d)(2)(A) and this question and answer, an organization is determined not to be a church exempt from tax for one or more of the three most recently completed taxable years ending before the examination notice date, when the appropriate Regional Commissioner approves, in writing, the completed findings of the examining agent that the organization is not a church exempt from tax for one or more of such years. Such approval may not be delegated by the Regional Commissioner to a subordinate official. The completed findings of the examining agent, as approved by the appropriate Regional Commissioner for this purpose, do not constitute a final revenue agent's report under section 7611(g).

Church records of a year earlier than the third or sixth completed taxable year, as applicable, may be examined if material to a determination of tax-exempt status during the applicable three or six year period.

For examinations concerning unrelated business taxable income, where no return has been filed by the church, tax may be assessed or collected for the six most recently completed taxable years ending before the examination notice date. Church records of a year earlier than the sixth year may be examined if material to a determination of unrelated business income tax liability during the six year period.

For examinations involving issues other than revocation of exempt status or unrelated business income (e.g., examinations relating to social security or other employment taxes), no limitation period is to apply if no return has been filed.

The applicable limitation period may be extended by mutual agreement of the church and the Internal Revenue Service.

MULTIPLE EXAMINATIONS

Q-16: What are the special multiple examination rules applicable to churches?

A-16: The Assistant Commissioner (Employee Plans and Exempt Organizations) is required to approve, in writing, any second inquiry or examination of a church, if the second inquiry or examination is to be undertaken within five years of an earlier inquiry or examination and if the earlier inquiry or examination did not result in either (1) revocation of tax exemption, notice of deficiency or an assessment of tax, or (2) a request for any significant changes in church operational practices (including the adequacy or sufficiency of records maintained to reflect income). The Assistant Commissioner's approval is required only if the second inquiry or examination involves the same or similar issues as the earlier inquiry or examination. The 5-year period is counted from the examination notice date of the earlier examination or, if no notice of examination was mailed, the inquiry notice date of the earlier examination. This 5-year period is to be suspended for periods during which the two-year period for completion of an examination is suspended (as described in Q and A-13) unless the prior examination was actually concluded within 2 years of the notice of examination.

In determining whether the second church tax inquiry or examination involves the same or similar issues as the preceding inquiry or examination, the substantive factual issues involved in the two examinations, rather than legal classifications, will govern. For example, where a prior examination and a current examination of unrelated business income involve income from different sources, the current examination involves different issues than the prior examination and the approval of the Assistant Commissioner (Employee Plans and Exempt Organizations) is not necessary.

Remedy for Violations of Section 7611

Q-17: What remedy is available for a violation of the church inquiry and examination procedures?

A-17: The exclusive remedy for any Internal Revenue Service violation of the church tax inquiry and examination procedures is as follows: Failure to comply substantially with the requirements that (1) two notices be sent to the church; (2) the Regional Commissioner approve the commencement of a church tax inquiry; or (3) an offer of a conference with the church be made (and a conference held if timely requested), will result in a stay of proceedings in a summons proceeding to gain access to church records (but not in dismissal of such proceeding), until these requirements are satisfied. The two-year limitation on duration of a church tax examination will not be suspended during stays of summons proceedings resulting from violations described above; however, violations may be corrected without regard to the otherwise applicable time limits prescribed under the procedures of section 7611. In determining whether a stay is necessary, a court must consider the good faith effort of the Internal Revenue Service and the effect of any violation of the proper examination procedures.

Section 7611(e)(2) provides that no suit may be maintained and no defense may be raised, other than a stay in a summons enforcement proceeding, by reason of any noncompliance with the requirements of section 7611. Thus, failure to comply with any of these requirements may not be raised as a defense or affirmative ground for relief in any judicial proceeding including, but not limited to, a summons proceeding to gain access to church records; a declaratory judgment proceeding involving a determination of tax-exempt status under section 7428; a proceeding to collect unpaid tax; or a deficiency or refund proceeding. Additionally, failure to substantially comply with the requirements that two notices be sent, that the Regional Commissioner approve an inquiry, and that a conference be offered (and the conference held if requested) may not be raised as a defense or as an affirmative ground for relief in a summons proceeding or any other judicial proceeding other than as specifically set forth above. Therefore, a church or its representatives will not be able to litigate the issue of the reasonableness of the appropriate Regional Commissioner's belief in approving the commencement of a church tax inquiry (*i.e.*, that the church may not be tax-exempt or may be engaged in taxable activities) in a summons proceeding or any other judicial proceeding. The church retains the right to raise any substantive or procedural argument which would be available to taxpayers generally in an appropriate proceeding.

EFFECTIVE DATE

Q-18: What is the effective date of the church examination procedures?

A-18: The procedures set forth in section 7611 apply to all tax inquiries and examinations beginning after December 31, 1984. The procedures of section 7605 will apply to any examination commenced before January 1, 1985. Any activities commenced after December 31, 1984, that would constitute a new inquiry or new examination must comply with the procedures of section 7611.

APPLICATION TO SECTION 4958

Q-19: When do the church tax inquiry and examination procedures described in section 7611 apply to a determination of whether there was an excess benefit transaction described in section 4958?

A-19: See § 53.4958–8(b) of this chapter for rules governing the interaction between section 4958 excise taxes on excess benefit transactions and section 7611 church tax inquiry and examination procedures.

FORMS AND OTHER MATERIALS

APPENDIX

SAMPLE ARTICLES OF ORGANIZATION

Department of the Treasury, Internal Revenue Service, Publication 557
Tax Exempt Status for Your Organization

The following are examples of Articles of Incorporation and a declaration of trust that contain the required information as to purposes and powers of an organization and disposition of its assets upon dissolution. You should bear in mind that requirements for these instruments may vary under applicable state law.

See *Private Foundations and Public Charities*, for the special provisions required in a private foundation's governing instrument in order for it to qualify for exemption.

Articles of Incorporation of the undersigned, a majority of whom are citizens of the United States, desiring to form a Non-Profit Corporation under the Non-Profit Corporation Law of ________, do hereby certify:

First: The name of the Corporation shall be _________.

Second: The place in this state where the principal office of the Corporation is to be located is the City of ____________, ______________ County.

Third: Said corporation is organized exclusively for charitable, religious, educational, and scientific purposes, including, for such purposes, the making of distributions to organizations that qualify as exempt organizations under section 501(c)(3) of the Internal Revenue Code, or the corresponding section of any future federal tax code.

Fourth: The names and addresses of the persons who are the initial trustees of the corporation are as follows:

Name______________ Address__________________________

Fifth: No part of the net earnings of the corporation shall inure to the benefit of, or be distributable to its members, trustees, officers, or other private persons, except that the corporation shall be authorized and empowered to pay reasonable compensation for services rendered and to make payments and distributions in furtherance of the purposes set forth in Article Third hereof. No substantial part of the activities of the corporation shall be the carrying on of propaganda, or otherwise attempting to influence legislation, and the corporation shall not participate in, or intervene in (including the publishing or distribution of statements) any political campaign on behalf of or in opposition to any candidate for public office. Notwithstanding any other provision of these articles, the corporation shall not carry on any other activities not permitted to be carried on (a) by a corporation exempt from federal income tax under section 501(c)(3) of the Internal Revenue Code, or the corresponding section of any future federal tax code, or (b) by a corporation, contributions to which are deductible under section 170(c)(2) of the Internal Revenue Code, or the corresponding section of any future federal tax code.

[If reference to federal law in articles of incorporation imposes a limitation that is invalid in your state, you may wish to substitute the following for the last sentence of the preceding paragraph:

> "Notwithstanding any other provision of these articles, this corporation shall not, except to an insubstantial degree, engage in any activities or exercise any powers that are not in furtherance of the purposes of this corporation."]

Sixth: Upon the dissolution of the corporation, assets shall be distributed for one or more exempt purposes within the meaning of section 501(c)(3) of the Internal Revenue Code, or the corresponding section of any future federal tax code, or shall be distributed to the federal government, or to a state or local government, for a public purposes. Any such assets not so disposed of shall be disposed of by a Court of Competent Jurisdiction of the county in which the principal office of the corporation is then located, exclusively for such purposes or to such organization or organizations, as said Court shall determine, which are organized and operated exclusively for such purposes.

In witness whereof, we have hereunto subscribed our names this ___ day of 20______.

SAMPLE BYLAWS

BY-LAWS OF XYZ, INC.

ARTICLE I
Members

The corporation shall have no members.

ARTICLE II
Board of Directors

Section 1. Powers and Number. The Board of Directors shall have general power to control and manage the affairs and property of the Corporation in accordance with the purposes and limitations set forth in the Certificate of Incorporation. The number of Directors constituting the entire Board after the first annual meeting of the Board of Directors shall be [odd number], but in no event shall the entire Board consist of less than three (3) Directors. Each Director shall be at least eighteen (18) years of age.

Section 2. Election and Term of Office. The initial directors shall be the persons named in the Certificate of Incorporation. The Directors shall hold office for one-year terms, and shall serve until the first annual meeting of the Board of Directors; provided, however, that any Director elected to fill an unexpired term (whether resulting from the death, resignation or removal or created by an increase in the number of Directors) shall hold office until the next election of Directors. Directors may be elected to any number of consecutive terms. To become a Director, a person shall be nominated by a then existing Director and elected by a majority of the Board.

Section 3. Removal. Any Director may be removed at any time for cause by a vote of a majority of the entire Board at any special meeting of the Board called for that purpose, provided that at least one week's notice of the proposed action shall have been given to the entire Board of Directors then in office. A Director who misses three consecutive meetings shall be automatically removed, but may be reinstated by a vote of a majority of the entire Board for good cause shown.

Section 4. Resignation. Any Director may resign from office at any time. Such resignation shall be made in writing, and shall take effect at the time specified therein, and if no time be specified, at the time of its receipt by the Corporation or its Chairperson. The acceptance of a resignation by the Board of Directors shall not be necessary to make it effective, but no resignations shall discharge any accrued obligation or duty of a Director.

Section 5. Vacancies and Newly Created Directorships. Any newly created directorships and any vacancies on the Board of Directors arising at any time and from any cause may be filled at any meeting of the Board of Directors by a majority of the Directors then in office, regardless of their number, and the Directors so elected shall serve until the next annual meeting.

Section 6. Meetings. Meetings of the Board may be held at any place within or without the State of New York as the Board may from time to time fix, or as shall be specified in the notice or waivers of notice thereof. The annual meeting of the Board shall be held in [month] of each year at a time and place fixed by the Board. Other regular meetings of the Board shall be held no less than [ ] times during the year. Special meetings of the Board shall be held whenever called by a majority of the Board of Directors, the Chairperson of the Board, or the Executive Director, in each case at such time and place as shall be fixed by the person or persons calling the meeting.

Section 7. Notice of Meetings. Notice of the time and place of each regular or special meeting of the Board, together with a written agenda stating all matters upon which action is proposed to be taken and, to the extent possible, copies of all documents on which action is proposed to be taken, shall be mailed to each Director, postage prepaid, addressed to him or her at his or her residence or usual place of business (or at such other address as he or she may have designated in a written request filed with the Secretary), at least seven days before the day on which the meeting is to be held; provided, however, that notice of special meetings to discuss matters requiring prompt action may be sent to him or her at such address by telegram or cablegram or given personally or by telephone, no less than forty-eight hours before the time at which such meeting is to be held, unless the meeting must be held within forty-eight hours. Notice of a meeting need not be given to any Director who submits a signed waiver of notice whether before or after the meeting, or who attends the meeting without protesting, prior thereto or at its commencement, the lack of notice to him or her. No notice need be given of any adjourned meeting.

Section 8. Quorum and Voting. Unless greater proportion is required by law, a majority of the entire Board shall constitute a quorum for the transaction of business or of any specified item of business. Except as otherwise provided by statue or by these by-laws, the vote of a majority of the Directors present at the time of the vote, if a quorum is present at such time, shall be the act of the Board. If at any meeting of the Board there shall be less than a quorum present, the Directors present may adjourn the meeting until a quorum is obtained.

Section 9. Action by the Board. Any action required or permitted to be taken by the Board or by any committee thereof may be taken without a meeting if all members of the Board or the committee consent in writing to the adoption of a resolution authorizing the action. The resolution and the written consents thereto by the members of the Board or committee shall be filed with the minutes of the proceedings of the Board or committee. Any one or more members of the Board or any committee thereof may participate in a meeting of the Board or committee by means of a conference telephone or similar communications equipment by means of which all persons participating in the meeting can hear each other at the same time. Participation by such means shall constitute presence in person at a meeting.

Section 10. Compensation. Any Director of the Corporation is authorized to receive a reasonable salary or other reasonable compensation for services rendered to the Corporation when authorized by two-thirds of the Board of Directors and only when so authorized. [No compensation shall be paid to Directors]

ARTICLE III

Officers Employees and Agents

Section 1. Officers. The Officers of the Corporation shall be a Chairperson, a Secretary, a Treasurer, and such other Officers, including one or more Vice Chairpersons, as the Board of Directors may from time to time appoint. One person may hold more than one office in the Corporation except that no one person may hold the offices of Chairperson and Secretary. The Chairperson shall be a member of the Board of Directors. The other officers may, but need not, be members of the Board of Directors. No instrument required to be signed by more than one officer may be signed by one person in more than one capacity.

Section 2. Election, Term of Office and Removal. The Officers of the Corporation shall be elected for a one year term at the annual meeting of the Board of Directors immediately following the election of Directors, and each shall continue in office until his or her successor shall have been elected and qualified, or until his or her death, resignation or removal. Any officer of the Corporation may be removed, with or without cause, by a vote of a majority of the entire Board.

Section 3. Other Agents and Employees. The Board of Directors may from time to time appoint such agents and employees as it shall deem necessary, each of whom shall hold office during the pleasure of the Board of Directors, and shall have such authority, perform such duties [and receive such reasonable compensation], if any, as a majority of the Board of Directors may from time to time determine. No such other Officer or agent need be a Director of the Corporation. To the full extent allowed by law, the Board of Directors may delegate to any Officer or agent any powers possessed by the Board of Directors and may prescribe their respective title, terms of office, authorities and duties.

Section 4. Removal. Any Officer, employee or agent of the Corporation may be removed with or without cause by a vote of the majority of the entire Board of Directors.

Section 5. Vacancies. In case of any vacancy in any office, a successor to fill the unexpired portion of the term may be elected by the Board of Directors.

Section 6. Chairperson: Powers and Duties. The Chairperson shall preside at all meetings of the Board of Directors. The Chairperson shall have general supervision over the affairs of the Corporation, and shall keep the Board of Directors fully informed about the activities of the Corporation. He or she shall have the power to sign and execute alone in the name of the Corporation all contracts authorized either generally or specifically by the Board, unless the Board shall specifically require an additional signature. The Chairperson shall perform all the duties incident to the office of the Chairperson, and shall perform such other duties as from time to time may be assigned by the Board of Directors.

Section 7. Vice Chairperson: Powers and Duties. A Vice Chairperson shall have such powers and duties as may be assigned to them by the Board of Directors. In the absence of the Chairperson, the Vice Chairperson(s), in the order designated by the Board of Directors, shall perform the duties of the Chairperson.

Section 8. Secretary: Powers and Duties of the Secretary. The Secretary shall keep the minutes of the Annual Meeting and all meetings of the Board of Directors in books provided for that purpose. He or she shall be responsible for the giving and serving of all notices of the Corporation, and shall perform all the duties customarily incident to the office of Secretary, subject to the control of the Board of Directors, and shall perform such other duties as shall from time to time be assigned to him or her by the Board of Directors.

Section 9. Treasurer: Powers and Duties. The Treasurer shall keep or cause to be kept full and accurate accounts of receipts and disbursements of the Corporation, and shall deposit or cause to be deposited all moneys, evidences of indebtedness and other valuable documents of the Corporation in the name and to the credit of the Corporation in such banks or depositories as the Board of Directors may designate. At the annual meeting and whenever else required by the Board of Directors, he or she shall render a statement of the Corporation's accounts. He or she shall at all reasonable times exhibit the Corporation's books and accounts to any Officer or Director of the Corporation, and shall perform all duties incident to the position of Treasurer, subject to the control of the Board of Directors, and shall when required, give such security for the faithful performance of this or her duties as the Board of Directors may determine.

Section 10. Compensation. Any Officer, employee or agent of the Corporation is authorized to receive a reasonable salary or other reasonable compensation for services rendered to the Corporation when authorized by a majority of the Board of Directors, and only when so authorized.

ARTICLE IV
Committees

Section 1. Committees of the Board. The Board may, by resolution adopted by a majority of the entire Board, establish and appoint an executive and other standing committees. The Chairperson of the Board of Directors shall appoint the Chairperson of each committee. Each committee so appointed shall consist of three or more directors and, to the extent provided in the resolution establishing it, shall have all the authority of the Board except as to the following matters:

1. the filling of vacancies on the Board or on any committee;

2. the amendment or repeal of the by-laws or the adoption of new by-laws;

3. the amendment or repeal of any resolution of the Board which by its terms shall not be so amendable or repealable;

4. the fixing of compensation of the directors for serving on the Board or any committee.

Special Committees may be appointed by the Chairperson with the consent of the Board and shall have only the powers specifically delegated to them by the Board.

ARTICLE V
Contracts, Checks, Bank Accounts and Investments

Section 1. Checks. Notes and Contracts. The Board of Directors is authorized to select the banks or depositories it deems proper for the funds of the Corporation and shall determine who shall be authorized in the Corporation's behalf to sign bills, notes, receipts, acceptances, endorsements, checks, releases, contracts and documents.

Section 2. Investments. The funds of the Corporation may be retained in whole or in part in cash or be invested and reinvested from time to time in such property, real, personal or otherwise, including stocks, bonds or other securities, as the Board of Directors may deem desirable.

ARTICLE VI
Office and Books

Section 1. Office. The office of the Corporation shall be located at such place as the Board of Directors may from time to time determine.

Section 2. Books. There shall be kept at the office of the Corporation correct books of account of the activities and transactions of the Corporation including a minute book, which shall contain a copy of the certificate of incorporation, a copy of these by-laws, and all minutes of meetings of the Board of Directors.

ARTICLE VII
Fiscal Year

The fiscal year of the Corporation shall be determined by the Board of Directors.

ARTICLE VIII
Indemnification

The Corporation may, to the fullest extent now or hereafter permitted by and in accordance with the standards and procedures provided for by applicable law and any amendments thereto, indemnify any person made, or threatened to be made, a party to any action or proceeding by reason of the fact that he, his testator or intestate was a director, officer, employee or agent of the Corporation, against judgments, fines, amounts paid in settlement and reasonable expenses, including attorneys' fees.

ARTICLE IX
Amendments

These by-laws may be amended or repealed by the affirmative vote of the majority of the entire Board at any meeting of the Board of Directors.

SAMPLE FORM OF CHARITABLE TRUST

Department of the Treasury, Internal Revenue Service, Publication 557
Tax-Exempt Status for Your Organization

The ______ Charitable Trust. Declaration of Trust made as of the __ day of ______, 20__, by of ________, and ________, of ________, who hereby declare and agree that they have received this day from, as Donor, the sum of Ten Dollars ($10) and that they will hold and manage the same, and any additions to it, in trust, as follows:

First: This trust shall be called "The ________ Charitable Trust."

Second: The trustees may receive and accept property, whether real, personal, or mixed, by way of gift, bequest, or devise, from any person, firm, trust, or corporation, to be held, administered, and disposed of in accordance with and pursuant to the provisions of this Declaration of Trust; but no gift, bequest or devise of any such property shall be received and accepted if it is conditioned or limited in such manner as to require the disposition of the income or its principal to any person or organization other than a "charitable organization" or for other than "charitable purposes" within the meaning of such terms as defined in Article Third of this Declaration of Trust, or as shall in the opinion of the trustees, jeopardize the federal income tax exemption of this trust pursuant to section 501 (c)(3) of the Internal Revenue Code or the corresponding section of any future federal tax code.

Third: A. The principal and income of all property received and accepted by the trustees to be administered under this Declaration of Trust shall be held in trust by them, and the trustees may make payments or distributions from income or principal, or both, to or for the use of such charitable organizations, within the meaning of that term as defined in paragraph C, in such amounts and for such charitable purposes of the trust as the trustees shall from time to time select and determine; and the trustees may make payments or distributions from income or principal, or both, directly for such charitable purposes, within the meaning of that term as defined in paragraph D, in such amounts as the trustees shall from time to time select and determine without making use of any other charitable organization. The trustees may also make payments or distributions of all or any part of the income or principal to states, territories, or possessions of the United States, any political subdivision of any of the foregoing, or to the United States or the District of Columbia but only for charitable purposes within the meaning of that term as defined in paragraph D. Income or principal derived from contributions by corporations shall be distributed by the trustees for use solely within the United States or its possessions. No part of the net earnings of this trust shall inure or be payable to or for the benefit of any private shareholder or individual, and no substantial part of the activities of this trust shall be the carrying on of propaganda, or otherwise attempting, to influence legislation. No part of the activities of this trust shall be the participation in, or intervention in (including the publishing or distributing of statements), any political campaign on behalf of or in opposition to any candidate for public office.

B. The trust shall continue forever unless the trustees terminate it and distribute all of the principal and income, which action may be taken by the trustees in their discretion at any time. On such termination, assets shall be distributed for one or more exempt purposes within the meaning of section 501(c)(3) of the Internal Revenue Code, or the corresponding section of any future federal tax code, or shall be distributed to the federal government, or to a state or local government, for a public purpose. The donor authorizes and empowers the trustees to form and organize a nonprofit corporation limited to the uses and purposes provided for in this Declaration of Trust, such corporation to be organized under the laws of any state or under the laws of the United States as may be determined by the trustees; such corporation when organized to have power to administer and control the affairs and properly and to carry out the uses, objects, and purposes of this trust. Upon the creation and organization of such corporation, the trustees are authorized and empowered to convey, transfer, and deliver to such corporation all the property and assets to which this trust may be or become entitled. The charter, bylaws, and other provisions for the organization and management of such corporation and its affairs and property shall be such as the trustees shall determine, consistent with the provisions of this paragraph.

C. In this Declaration of Trust and in any amendments to it, references to "charitable organizations" or "charitable organization" mean corporations, trusts, funds, foundations, or community chests created or organized in the United States or in any of its possessions, whether under the laws of the United States, any state or territory, the District of Columbia, or any possession of the United States, organized and operated exclusively for charitable purposes, no part of the net earnings of which inures or is payable to or for the benefit of any private shareholder or individual, and no substantial part of the activities of which is carrying on propaganda, or otherwise attempting, to influence legislation, and which do not participate in or intervene in (including the publishing or distributing of statements), any political campaign on behalf of or in opposition to any candidate for public office. It is intended that the organization described in this paragraph C shall be entitled to exemption from federal income tax under section 501(c)(3) of the Internal Revenue Code, or the corresponding section of any future federal tax code.

D. In this Declaration of Trust and in any amendments to it, the term "charitable purposes" shall be limited to and shall include only religious charitable, scientific, literary, or educational purposes within the meaning of those terms as used in section 501(c)(3) of the Internal Revenue Code, or the corresponding section of any future federal tax code, but only such purposes as also constitute public charitable purposes under the law of trusts of the State of ________________.

Fourth: This Declaration of Trust may be amended at any time or times by written instrument or instruments signed and sealed by the trustees, and acknowledged by any of the trustees, provided that no amendment shall authorize the trustees to conduct the affairs of this trust in any manner or for any purpose contrary to the provisions of section 501 (c)(3) of the Internal Revenue Code, or the corresponding section of any future federal tax code. An amendment of the provisions of this Article Fourth (or any amendment to it) shall be valid only if and to the extent that such amendment further restricts the trustees' amending power. All instruments amending this Declaration of Trust shall be noted upon or kept attached to the executed original of this Declaration of Trust held by the trustees.

Fifth: Any trustee under this Declaration of Trust may, by written instrument, signed and acknowledged, resign his office. The number of trustees shall be at all times not less than two, and whenever for any reason the number is reduced to one, there shall be, and at any other time there may be, appointed one or more additional trustees. Appointments shall be made by the trustee or trustees for the time in office by written instruments signed and acknowledged. Any succeeding or additional trustee shall, upon his acceptance of the office by written instrument signed and acknowledged, have the same powers, rights and duties, and the same title to the trust estate jointly with the surviving or remaining trustee or trustees as if originally appointed.

None of the trustees shall be required to furnish any bond or surety. None of them shall be responsible or liable for the acts of omissions of any other of the trustees or of any predecessor or of a custodian, agent, depositary or counsel selected with reasonable care.

The one or more trustees, whether original or successor, for the time being in office, shall have full authority to act even though one or more vacancies may exist. A trustee may, by appropriate written instrument, delegate all or any part of his powers to another or others of the trustees for such periods and subject to such conditions as such delegating trustee may determine.

The trustees serving under this Declaration of Trust are authorized to pay to themselves amounts for reasonable expenses incurred and reasonable compensation for services rendered in the administration of this trust, but in no event shall any trustee who has made a contribution to this trust ever receive any compensation thereafter.

Sixth: In extension and not in limitation of the common law and statutory powers of trustees and other powers granted in this Declaration of Trust, the trustees shall have the following discretionary powers:

a) To invest and reinvest the principal and income of the trust in such property, real, personal or mixed, and in such manner as they shall deem proper, and from time to time to change investments as they shall deem advisable, to invest in or retain any stocks, shares, bonds, notes, obligations, or personal or real property (including without limitation any interests in or obligations of any corporation, association, business trust, investment trust, common trust fund, or investment company) although some or all of the property so acquired or retained is of a kind or size which but for this express authority would not be considered proper and although all of the trust funds are invested in the securities of one company. No principal or income, however, shall be loaned, directly or indirectly, to any trustee or to anyone else, corporate or otherwise, who has at any time made a contribution to this trust, nor to anyone except on the basis of an adequate interest charge and with adequate security.

b) To sell, lease, or exchange any personal, mixed, or real property, at public auction or by private contract, for such consideration and on such terms as to credit or otherwise, and to make such contracts and enter into such undertakings relating to the trust property, as they consider advisable, whether or not such leases or contracts may extend beyond the duration of the trust.

c) To borrow money for such periods, at such rates of interest, and upon such terms as the trustees consider advisable, and as security for such loans to mortgage or pledge any real or personal property with or without power of sale; to acquire or hold any real or personal property, subject to any mortgage or pledge on or of property acquired or held by this trust.

d) To execute and deliver deeds, assignments, transfers, mortgages, pledges, leases, covenants contracts, promissory notes, releases, and other instruments, sealed or unsealed, incident to any transaction in which they engage.

e) To vote, to give proxies, to participate in the reorganization, merger or consolidation of any concern, or in the sale, lease, disposition, or distribution of its assets; to join with other security holders in acting through a committee, depositary, voting trustees, or otherwise, and in this connection to delegate authority to such committee, depositary, or trustees and to deposit securities with them or transfer securities to them to pay assessments levied on securities or to exercise subscription rights in respect of securities.

f) To employ a bank or trust company as custodian of any funds or securities and to delegate to it such powers as they deem appropriate; to hold trust property without indication of fiduciary capacity but only in the name of a registered nominee, provided the trust property is at all times identified as such on the books of the trust; to keep any or all of the trust property or funds in any place or places in the United States of America; to employ clerks, accountants, investment counsel, investment agents, and any special services, and to pay the reasonable compensation and expenses of all such services in addition to the compensation of the trustees.

Seventh: The trustees' powers are exercisable solely in the fiduciary capacity consistent with and in furtherance of the charitable purposes of this trust as specified in Article Third and not otherwise.

Eighth: In this Declaration of Trust and in any amendment to it, references to "trustees" mean the one or more trustees, whether original or successor, for the time being in office.

Ninth: Any person may rely on a copy, certified by a notary public, of the executed original of this Declaration of Trust held by the trustees, and of any of the notations on it and writings attached to it, as fully as he might rely on the original documents themselves. Any such person may rely fully on any statements of fact certified by anyone who appears from such original documents or from such certified copy to be a trustee under this Declaration of Trust. No one dealing with the trustees need inquire concerning the validity of anything the trustees purport to do. No one dealing with the trustees need see to the application of anything paid or transferred to or upon the order of the trustees of the trust.

Tenth: This Declaration of Trust is to be governed in all respects by the laws of the State of ______________.

Trustee—

Trustee—

SAMPLE CONFLICT OF INTEREST POLICY

Article I. Explanation

This conflict of interest policy is designed to help directors, officers, advisors and employees of [insert name of public charity ("Charity")] identify situations that present potential conflicts of interest and to provide Charity with a procedure which, if observed, will allow Charity to enter into a transaction even though a director, officer or employee has or may have a conflict of interest with respect to the transaction

Article II. Definitions

A "Conflict of Interest" is any circumstance described in Article III of this Policy.An "Interested Person" is any person serving as a director, officer, member of the Board, employee, or member of a committee with Board-delegated powers of Charity.

A "Family Member" is a spouse, ancestor, child, grandchild, great grandchild, brother, sister, or spouse of a child, grandchild, great grandchild, brother or sister, of an Interested Person.

A "Financial Interest" in an entity is a financial interest of any kind, which, in view of all the circumstances, would, or reasonably could, affect an Interested Person's or Family Member's judgment with respect to transactions to which the entity is a party.

Article III. Conflict of Interest Defined

A Conflict of Interest exists where the personal interests of an Interested Person are or may be inconsistent with the best interests of Charity. For purposes of this Policy, the following circumstances shall be deemed to create a Conflict of Interest:

A contract or transaction between Charity and an Interested Person or Family Member (e.g., Charity contracts for services to be provided by a director's child).

A contract or transaction between Charity and an entity in which an Interested Person or Family Member has a Financial Interest or with which such person has a relationship, for example as a director, officer, trustee, or guardian (e.g., Charity makes a grant to a university where a member of Charity's board of advisors serves on the board of trustees).

A compensation arrangement between any entity or individual with which Charity has a contract or transaction and an Interested Person or Family Member (e.g., Charity makes a grant to a university where a director's sister is employed).

A compensation arrangement between any entity or individual with which Charity has a contract or transaction and an entity in which an Interested Person or Family Member has a Financial Interest or with which such person has a relationship, for example as a director, officer, trustee, or guardian (*e.g.,* Charity makes a grant to a university which is performing research, for a fee, for a company owned by one of Charity's directors).

An Interested Person competing with Charity in the rendering of services or in any other contract or transaction with a third party (e.g., one of Charity's employees seeks a research grant to write a paper on international energy issues from a foundation to which Charity has applied for funding).An Interested Person having a Financial Interest in, or maintaining a relationship with (for example, as director, officer, trustee or guardian), an entity or individual that competes with Charity in the provision of services or in any other contract or transaction (e.g., one of Charity's employees serves as director of a new charity with a mission similar to Charity's).

An Interested Person accepting gifts, entertainment or other favors from any individual or entity that (i) does or is seeking to do business with, or is a competitor of, Charity or (ii) has received, is receiving or is seeking to receive a loan or grant, or to secure other financial commitments from Charity, in both cases under circumstances where it might be inferred that such action was intended to influence or might influence the Interested Person in the performance of his or her duties (e.g., a potential grantee offers one of Charity's employees free tickets to the World Series).

Article IV. Procedures

1. An Interested Person must disclose orally or in writing all material facts related to an actual or potential Conflict of Interest to directors and/or members of committees considering a proposed contract or transaction to which the Conflict of Interest relates. If a contract or transaction is not being considered by the Board or a committee, the required disclosure must be made to the President or the President's designee. Until a Conflict of Interest has been voted upon by the Board or a committee in accordance with this Policy, an Interested Person shall refrain from any action that might affect Charity's participation in any contract or transaction affected by a Conflict of Interest.

2. After disclosure of the Conflict of Interest and all material facts, and after the Interested Person responds to any questions that the Board or committee may have regarding the Conflict of Interest, the Interested Person shall leave the Board or committee meeting while the Conflict of Interest is discussed and voted upon in accordance with the procedures set forth in 3 below. An Interested Person may not vote on the contract or transaction to which the Conflict of Interest relates, but may be counted in determining the presence of a quorum for purposes of the vote.

3. The Board or committee shall determine by a majority vote of the disinterested directors whether a Conflict of Interest exists and, if so, whether Charity should nonetheless enter into the contract or transaction because it is in Charity's best interest. If appropriate, the President may appoint a disinterested person or committee to investigate alternatives to a proposed contract or transaction.

4. The minutes of the Board or committee meeting shall reflect (a) that the Conflict of Interest was disclosed, (b) the Board or committee's decision regarding the Conflict of

Interest, including a statement that the Interested Person was not present during the final discussion and vote, and (c) that the Interested Person abstained from voting.

Article V. Violations of the Conflict of Interest Policy

1. If the Board or committee believes that an Interested Person has failed to disclose an actual or potential Conflict of Interest, it shall inform the Interested Person of the basis for such belief and afford the Interested Person an opportunity to explain the alleged failure to disclose.

2. If, after hearing the response of the Interested Person and making any further investigation as may be warranted in the circumstances, the Board or committee determines that the member has in fact failed to disclose an actual or potential Conflict of Interest, it shall take appropriate disciplinary and corrective action, which might include removal of a director from a committee or termination of an employee's employment.

Article VI. Annual Statements

Each Interested Person shall annually sign a statement which affirms that such person has received a copy of the Conflict of Interest Policy, has read and understands the Policy, and has agreed to comply with the Policy. In addition, each Interested Person shall disclose on the annual statement any relationships, circumstances or positions in which the Interested Person or a Family Member is involved that he or she believes could contribute to a Conflict of Interest arising. Any such information regarding an Interested Person or a Family Member shall be treated as confidential and shall generally be made available only to the President, the Executive Director, and any committee appointed to address Conflicts of Interest, except to the extent additional disclosure is necessary in connection with the implementation of the Policy.

Article VII. Review of Policy

This Policy shall be reviewed annually by the Board of Directors. Any changes to this policy shall be communicated immediately to all Interested Persons.

Attachment: Annual Conflict of Interest Disclosure Statement

ANNUAL CONFLICT OF INTEREST DISCLOSURE STATEMENT

FOR FISCAL YEAR _____

Name:____________________

Title:____________________

Please describe below any relationships, positions, or circumstances in which you or a Family Member (as defined in the Conflict of Interest Policy) are involved that you believe might constitute or lead to a conflict of interest:

I hereby certify that I have received a copy of the current Conflict of Interest Policy, have read and understand the Policy, and agree to abide by it. I further certify that the information set forth above is true and complete to the best of my knowledge.

Signature:___________________

Date:______________________

CONFIDENTIALITY STATEMENT

Name:______________________

Title:____________________

I hereby agree that all knowledge and information not within the public domain which I may acquire from Charity or its directors, officers, employees or other contractors, or by virtue of the performance of my duties as a director, officer, member of the Board of Advisors, or employee of Charity, shall for all time and for all purposes be regarded by me as strictly confidential and held by me in confidence, and solely for use in connection with my Charity-related duties, and shall not be directly or indirectly disclosed by me to any person or entity whatsoever except with Charity's prior written permission.

Signature: ____________________

Date: _____________

THE CHARLESTON PRINCIPLES: GUIDELINES ON CHARITABLE SOLICITATIONS USING THE INTERNET

National Association of State Charity Officials

Approved by NASCO Board as Advisory Guidelines
March 14, 2001

WHEREAS:

1. Most charitable organizations provide valuable services to society—services that are not provided by government or the private for-profit sector. At the same time, deceptive charitable solicitations, including fraud and misuse of charitable contributions, are significant problems in our country. Reasonable state oversight of charitable organizations and professional fundraisers can remedy or minimize such abuses while facilitating the charitable missions of those who provide needed services to our nation and communities, and by providing information and education to donors;

2. Registration and financial reporting by charitable organizations and their internal fundraisers, their external commercial fundraisers and, where applicable, their fundraising counsel and commercial coventurers is critical to (a) providing information to the public in order to increase donor confidence in those who solicit their support and (b) providing information to law enforcers to enable them to fight deception and misuse of contributions;

3. Existing registration statutes generally, of their own terms, encompass and apply to Internet solicitations. The application of those statutes beyond more established fundraising techniques, such as telephone, direct mail, and in-person solicitations, raises a number of issues that state charity officials are often called upon to address;

4. The proliferation of web site solicitations compels state charity officials to address the issue of who has to register where;

5. State charity officials consistently gain valuable insights when the views of the regulated communities are sought;

6. Consistent guidelines addressing online charitable solicitations will assist state charity officials, as well as donors, charities, and online entrepreneurs, throughout the nation. These Principles have been adopted as guidance to state charity officials, but with the express intention of both creating a climate in which creativity and enterprise in the use of the Internet to support charitable activities is encouraged and in which the public interest is vigorously protected; and

7. Therefore, state charity officials discussed the formation of these Principles while gathered at the National Association of Attorneys General/National Association of State Charity Officials ("NAAG/NASCO") Conference in Charleston, South Carolina in October 1999. During the public portion of that conference, which was devoted to the subject of Internet solicitations, state charity officials began a dialogue with invited guests on this topic.

THEREFORE WE, THE BOARD OF DIRECTORS OF NASCO, OFFER THE FOLLOWING PRINCIPLES:

I. General Principles

A. These Principles are offered as a guide to states as to when charities, and their fundraisers,fundraising counsel and commercial co-venturers may be required to register, or may be subject to enforcement action, and in what jurisdictions, with regard to charitable solicitations via the Internet. States are encouraged to use these Principles to develop common policies to implement their specific state laws, but these Principles are not necessarily the views of any particular individual, office, or state, nor do they state an official policy position of NASCO. These Principles recognize that the laws of individual states vary, and that implementation of these Principles may also vary.

B. These Principles are necessarily dynamic, and may change as laws, technology and business models change. Further discussions among states and between states and the regulated community are desirable.

C. The Internet can be a valuable and efficient forum for conducting charitable solicitations. State charity officials do not desire to discourage or limit its use.

D. The basic premise of these Principles is this: Although existing state laws govern charitable solicitations on the Internet, in many instances the use of the Internet raises new questions that state charity officials must answer in order to effectively carry out their statutory missions. Therefore, state charity officials should require registration of those over whom their state courts could constitutionally assert personal jurisdiction to enforce a registration requirement. State charity officials and those who solicit contributions using the Internet should note that in actions to enforce state laws against deceptive charitable solicitations, including fraud and misuse of charitable funds, jurisdiction typically exists over some organizations not required to register in the state.

E. Nothing in these Principles is intended to limit jurisdiction available under common law. The traditional jurisprudence analysis for jurisdiction is the appropriate rule with which states need to comply.

II. Actions to Enforce State Laws Against Charitable Solicitation Fraud

States will enforce the law against any entity whose Internet solicitations mislead or defraud persons physically located within a particular state, without regard to whether that entity is domiciled in the state or is required to register in that state pursuant to these Principles.

III. Application of Registration Requirements to Internet Solicitation

A. Entities That Are Domiciled Within the State

1. An entity that is domiciled within a state and uses the Internet to conduct charitable solicitations in that state must register in that state. This is true without regard to whether the Internet solicitation methods it uses are passive or interactive, maintained by itself or another entity with which it contracts, or whether it conducts solicitations in any other manner.

2. An entity is domiciled within a particular state if its principal place of business is in that state.

B. Entities That Are Domiciled Outside the State

1. An entity that is not domiciled within a state must register in accordance with the law of that state if:

    a. Its non-Internet activities alone would be sufficient to require registration;

    b. (1) The entity solicits contributions through an interactive web site; and

    (2) Either the entity:

    i. Specifically targets persons physically located in the state for solicitation, or

    ii. Receives contributions from the state on a repeated and ongoing basis or a substantial basis through its web site.; or

    c. (1) The entity solicits contributions through a site that is not interactive, but either specifically invites further offline activity to complete a contribution, or establishes other contacts with that state, such as sending e-mail messages or other communications that promote the web site; and

    (2) The entity satisfies Principle III(B)(1)(b)(2).

2. For purposes of these Principles, each of the following terms shall have the following meanings:

a An interactive web site is a web site that permits a contributor to make a contribution, or purchase a product in connection with a charitable solicitation, by electronically completing the transaction, such as by submitting credit card information or authorizing an electronic funds transfer. Interactive sites include sites through which a donor may complete a transaction online through any online mechanism processing a financial transaction even if completion requires the use of linked or redirected sites. A web site is interactive if it has this capacity, regardless of whether donors actually use it.

b. To specifically target persons physically located in the state for solicitation means to either (i) include on its web site an express or implied reference to soliciting contributions from that state; or (ii) to otherwise affirmatively appeal to residents of the state, such as by advertising or sending messages to persons located in the state (electronically or otherwise) when the entity knows or reasonably should know the recipient is physically located in the state. Charities operating on a purely local basis, or within a limited geographic area, do not target states outside their operating area, if their web site makes clear in context that their fundraising focus is limited to that area even if they receive contributions from outside that area on less than a repeated and ongoing basis or on a substantial basis.

c. To receive contributions from the state on a repeated and ongoing basis or a substantial basis means receiving contributions within the entity's fiscal year, or relevant portion of a fiscal year, that are of sufficient volume to establish the regular or significant (as opposed to rare, isolated, or insubstantial) nature of those contributions. States should set, and communicate to the regulated Entities, numerical levels at which it will regard this criterion as satisfied. Such numerical levels should define "repeated and ongoing" in terms of a number of contributors and "substantial" in terms of a total dollar amount of contributions or percentage of total contributions received by or on behalf of the charity. Meeting any threshold would give rise to a registration requirement but would not limit an enforcement action for deceptive solicitations. For example, a state might explain that an entity receives contributions on a repeated and ongoing basis if it receives at least one hundred online contributions at any time in a year and that it receives substantial contributions if it receives $25,000, or a stated percentage of its total contributions, in online contributions in a year.

3. An entity that solicits via e-mail into a particular state shall be treated the same as one that solicits via telephone or direct mail, if the soliciting party knew or reasonably should have known that the recipient was a resident of or was physically located in that state.

4. Questions may arise as to whether individual charities are required to register in a particular state when the operator of a web site through which contributions for that charity are solicited or received is required to register, but the charity itself would not independently satisfy the criteria of Principle III(B)(1)(b). As to such charities:

a. If the law of the state does not universally require the registration of all charities on whose behalf contributions are solicited or received through a commercial fundraiser, commercial co-venturer, or fundraising counsel who is required to register, then states should independently apply the criteria of Principle III(B)(1)(b) to each charity and require registration only by charities that independently meet those tests; but

b. If the law of the state universally requires registration of all charities under such circumstances, states should consider whether, as a matter of prosecutorial discretion, public policy, and the prioritized use of limited resources, it would take action to enforce registration requirements as to charities who do not independently meet the criteria of Principle III(B)(1)(b); and

c. For purposes of this Principle, a charity satisfies the interactivity criterion of Principle III(B)(1)(b)(i) if (i) any web site through which contributions are solicited or received for that charity satisfies that requirement, and (ii) that web site is operated by an entity with whom the charity contracts. This paragraph does not define the concept of interactivity, but merely addresses the application of that concept in this specific context.

5. Solicitations for the sale of a product or service that include a representation that some portion of the price shall be devoted to a charitable organization or charitable purpose (often referred to as "commercial coventuring" or "cause marketing") shall be governed by the same standards as otherwise set out in these Principles governing charitable solicitations. Registration is therefore required in those states that require registration for such activities, by charitable organizations and their internal fundraisers, their external commercial fundraisers as applicable.

C. General Exclusions from Registration

1. Maintaining or operating a web site that does not contain a solicitation of contributions but merely provides program services via the Internet—such as through a public information web site—does not, by itself, invoke a registration requirement. This is true even if unsolicited donations are received.

2. Entities that provide solely administrative, supportive or technical services to charities without providing substantive content, or advice concerning substantive content, are not required to register. Such service providers (a) include Internet service providers and entities that do nothing more than process online transactions for a separate firm that operates a web site or provide similar services, but (b) do not include commercial fundraisers, commercial co-venturers, or fundraising counsel. Administrative, supportive, or technical service providers may be required to register if they do more than simply provide such technical services and actually solicit, promote a web site or engage in other conduct that requires registration. Compensation for services based on the amount of

funds raised may be a strong indication the entity is doing more than simply providing technical services.

IV. Principles Related to Minimizing Regulatory Responsibilities for Multi-State Filers

A. State charity officials recognize that the burden of compliance by charitable organizations and their agents, professional fundraisers, commercial co-venturers and/or professional fundraising counsel should be kept reasonable in relation to the benefits to the public achieved by registration. The acceptance and use of the Unified Registration Statement for charitable organizations by state charity offices and the development and acceptance of other related projects to create such common forms are strongly encouraged.

B. State charity officials recognize the power of the Internet to assist in the registration of charitable organizations and their agents. State charity offices are strongly encouraged to publish their registration and reporting forms, their laws and regulations and other related information on the Internet to facilitate registration and reporting by charitable organizations and their agents while assuring proper public accountability by regulated entities.

C. State charity officials, charitable organizations and their agents, professional fundraisers, commercial co-venturers and/or professional fundraising counsel have a mutual interest in exploring how to develop the information technology infrastructure so that registration and reporting can be accomplished electronically in the future. Collaboration on this project between state charity officials and these entities, where appropriate, will advance the timeframe for establishing electronic filing. This collaboration may include discussion of the types of information that entities soliciting through the Internet should be required to retain, so that these Principles can be applied to a particular web site. This would include information sufficient to determine, within the scope of the law and relevant donor privacy concerns, whether an entity's ties to a particular state are sufficient to give rise to a registration requirement.

D. Because disclosure to the public promotes informed giving, charitable organizations are encouraged to satisfy the IRS "widely available" standard by posting, without charge, their current Unified Registration Statement, their last three IRS Forms 990, and their complete IRS Form 1023 or 1024 application and resulting determination letter on their web pages. Links to other sites that provide such information, including any relevant state agency, or other web sites, are also encouraged. Such postings, however, do not currently fulfill any applicable registration requirements.

Form **990**

Department of the Treasury
Internal Revenue Service

Return of Organization Exempt From Income Tax

Under section 501(c), 527, or 4947(a)(1) of the Internal Revenue Code (except private foundations)

Do not enter social security numbers on this form as it may be made public.

Go to *www.irs.gov/Form990* for instructions and the latest information.

OMB No. 1545-0047

2025

Open to Public Inspection

A For the 2025 calendar year, or tax year beginning , 2025, and ending , 20

B Check if applicable:
- ☐ Address change
- ☐ Name change
- ☐ Initial return
- ☐ Final return/terminated
- ☐ Amended return
- ☐ Application pending

C Name of organization

Doing business as

Number and street (or P.O. box if mail is not delivered to street address) | Room/suite

City or town, state or province, country, and ZIP or foreign postal code

D Employer identification number

E Telephone number

G Gross receipts $

F Name and address of principal officer:

H(a) Is this a group return for subordinates? ☐ **Yes** ☐ **No**

H(b) Are all subordinates included? ☐ **Yes** ☐ **No**

If "No," attach a list. See instructions.

I Tax-exempt status: ☐ 501(c)(3) ☐ 501(c) ( ) (insert no.) ☐ 4947(a)(1) or ☐ 527

J **Website:**

H(c) Group exemption number

K Form of organization: ☐ Corporation ☐ Trust ☐ Association ☐ Other | **L** Year of formation: | **M** State of legal domicile:

Part I Summary

Activities & Governance

1 Briefly describe the organization's mission or most significant activities:

2 Check this box ☐ if the organization discontinued its operations or disposed of more than 25% of its net assets.

3	Number of voting members of the governing body (Part VI, line 1a)	3	
4	Number of independent voting members of the governing body (Part VI, line 1b)	4	
5	Total number of individuals employed in calendar year 2025 (Part V, line 2a)	5	
6	Total number of volunteers (estimate if necessary)	6	
7a	Total unrelated business revenue from Part VIII, column (C), line 12	7a	
b	Net unrelated business taxable income from Form 990-T, Part I, line 11	7b	

			Prior Year	**Current Year**
Revenue	8	Contributions and grants (Part VIII, line 1h)		
	9	Program service revenue (Part VIII, line 2g)		
	10	Investment income (Part VIII, column (A), lines 3, 4, and 7d)		
	11	Other revenue (Part VIII, column (A), lines 5, 6d, 8c, 9c, 10c, and 11e)		
	12	Total revenue—add lines 8 through 11 (must equal Part VIII, column (A), line 12)		
Expenses	13	Grants and similar amounts paid (Part IX, column (A), lines 1–3)		
	14	Benefits paid to or for members (Part IX, column (A), line 4)		
	15	Salaries, other compensation, employee benefits (Part IX, column (A), lines 5–10)		
	16a	Professional fundraising fees (Part IX, column (A), line 11e)		
	b	Total fundraising expenses (Part IX, column (D), line 25)		
	17	Other expenses (Part IX, column (A), lines 11a–11d, 11f–24e)		
	18	Total expenses. Add lines 13–17 (must equal Part IX, column (A), line 25)		
	19	Revenue less expenses. Subtract line 18 from line 12		
			Beginning of Current Year	**End of Year**
Net Assets or Fund Balances	20	Total assets (Part X, line 16)		
	21	Total liabilities (Part X, line 26)		
	22	Net assets or fund balances. Subtract line 21 from line 20		

Part II Signature Block

Under penalties of perjury, I declare that I have examined this return, including accompanying schedules and statements, and to the best of my knowledge and belief, it is true, correct, and complete. Declaration of preparer (other than officer) is based on all information of which preparer has any knowledge.

Sign Here

Signature of officer | Date

Type or print name and title

Paid Preparer Use Only

Preparer's name	Preparer's signature	Date	Check ☐ if self-employed	PTIN
Firm's name			Firm's EIN	
Firm's address			Phone no.	

May the IRS discuss this return with the preparer shown above? See instructions ☐ **Yes** ☐ **No**

For Paperwork Reduction Act Notice, see the separate instructions. Cat. No. 11282Y Form **990** (2025) Created 4/30/25

Form 990 (2025) Page 2

Part III **Statement of Program Service Accomplishments**

Check if Schedule O contains a response or note to any line in this Part III . . . . ☐

1 Briefly describe the organization's mission:

2 Did the organization undertake any significant program services during the year which were not listed on the prior Form 990 or 990-EZ? . . . . ☐ **Yes** ☐ **No**

If "Yes," describe these new services on Schedule O.

3 Did the organization cease conducting, or make significant changes in how it conducts, any program services? . . . . ☐ **Yes** ☐ **No**

If "Yes," describe these changes on Schedule O.

4 Describe the organization's program service accomplishments for each of its three largest program services, as measured by expenses. Section 501(c)(3) and 501(c)(4) organizations are required to report the amount of grants and allocations to others, the total expenses, and revenue, if any, for each program service reported.

4a (Code: ______) (Expenses $ ______ including grants of $ ______) (Revenue $ ______)

4b (Code: ______) (Expenses $ ______ including grants of $ ______) (Revenue $ ______)

4c (Code: ______) (Expenses $ ______ including grants of $ ______) (Revenue $ ______)

4d Other program services (Describe on Schedule O.)
(Expenses $ including grants of $) (Revenue $)

4e Total program service expenses

Form **990** (2025)

Part IV Checklist of Required Schedules

			Yes	No
1	Is the organization described in section 501(c)(3) or 4947(a)(1) (other than a private foundation)? *If "Yes," complete Schedule A*	1		
2	Is the organization required to complete Schedule B, Schedule of Contributors? See instructions	2		
3	Did the organization engage in direct or indirect political campaign activities on behalf of or in opposition to candidates for public office? *If "Yes," complete Schedule C, Part I*	3		
4	**Section 501(c)(3) organizations.** Did the organization engage in lobbying activities, or have a section 501(h) election in effect during the tax year? *If "Yes," complete Schedule C, Part II*	4		
5	Is the organization a section 501(c)(4), 501(c)(5), or 501(c)(6) organization that receives membership dues, assessments, or similar amounts as defined in Rev. Proc. 98-19? *If "Yes," complete Schedule C, Part III*	5		
6	Did the organization maintain any donor advised funds or any similar funds or accounts for which donors have the right to provide advice on the distribution or investment of amounts in such funds or accounts? *If "Yes," complete Schedule D, Part I*	6		
7	Did the organization receive or hold a conservation easement, including easements to preserve open space, the environment, historic land areas, or historic structures? *If "Yes," complete Schedule D, Part II*	7		
8	Did the organization maintain collections of works of art, historical treasures, or other similar assets? *If "Yes," complete Schedule D, Part III*	8		
9	Did the organization report an amount in Part X, line 21, for escrow or custodial account liability; serve as a custodian for amounts not listed in Part X; or provide credit counseling, debt management, credit repair, or debt negotiation services? *If "Yes," complete Schedule D, Part IV*	9		
10	Did the organization, directly or through a related organization, hold assets in donor-restricted endowments or in quasi-endowments? *If "Yes," complete Schedule D, Part V*	10		
11	If the organization's answer to any of the following questions is "Yes," then complete Schedule D, Parts VI, VII, VIII, IX, or X, as applicable.			
a	Did the organization report an amount for land, buildings, and equipment in Part X, line 10? *If "Yes," complete Schedule D, Part VI*	11a		
b	Did the organization report an amount for investments—other securities in Part X, line 12, that is 5% or more of its total assets reported in Part X, line 16? *If "Yes," complete Schedule D, Part VII*	11b		
c	Did the organization report an amount for investments—program related in Part X, line 13, that is 5% or more of its total assets reported in Part X, line 16? *If "Yes," complete Schedule D, Part VIII*	11c		
d	Did the organization report an amount for other assets in Part X, line 15, that is 5% or more of its total assets reported in Part X, line 16? *If "Yes," complete Schedule D, Part IX*	11d		
e	Did the organization report an amount for other liabilities in Part X, line 25? *If "Yes," complete Schedule D, Part X*	11e		
f	Did the organization's separate or consolidated financial statements for the tax year include a footnote that addresses the organization's liability for uncertain tax positions under FIN 48 (ASC 740)? *If "Yes," complete Schedule D, Part X*	11f		
12a	Did the organization obtain separate, independent audited financial statements for the tax year? *If "Yes," complete Schedule D, Parts XI and XII*	12a		
b	Was the organization included in consolidated, independent audited financial statements for the tax year? *If "Yes," and if the organization answered "No" to line 12a, then completing Schedule D, Parts XI and XII is optional*	12b		
13	Is the organization a school described in section 170(b)(1)(A)(ii)? *If "Yes," complete Schedule E*	13		
14a	Did the organization maintain an office, employees, or agents outside of the United States?	14a		
b	Did the organization have aggregate revenues or expenses of more than $10,000 from grantmaking, fundraising, business, investment, and program service activities outside the United States, or aggregate foreign investments valued at $100,000 or more? *If "Yes," complete Schedule F, Parts I and IV*	14b		
15	Did the organization report on Part IX, column (A), line 3, more than $5,000 of grants or other assistance to or for any foreign organization? *If "Yes," complete Schedule F, Parts II and IV*	15		
16	Did the organization report on Part IX, column (A), line 3, more than $5,000 of aggregate grants or other assistance to or for foreign individuals? *If "Yes," complete Schedule F, Parts III and IV.*	16		
17	Did the organization report a total of more than $15,000 of expenses for professional fundraising services on Part IX, column (A), lines 6 and 11e? *If "Yes," complete Schedule G, Part I.* See instructions	17		
18	Did the organization report more than $15,000 total of fundraising event gross income and contributions on Part VIII, lines 1c and 8a? *If "Yes," complete Schedule G, Part II*	18		
19	Did the organization report more than $15,000 of gross income from gaming activities on Part VIII, line 9a? *If "Yes," complete Schedule G, Part III*	19		
20a	Did the organization operate one or more hospital facilities? *If "Yes," complete Schedule H*	20a		
b	If "Yes" to line 20a, did the organization attach a copy of its audited financial statements to this return?	20b		
21	Did the organization report more than $5,000 of grants or other assistance to any domestic organization or domestic government on Part IX, column (A), line 1? *If "Yes," complete Schedule I, Parts I and II*	21		

Form **990** (2025)

Form 990 (2025) Page 4

Part IV Checklist of Required Schedules *(continued)*

			Yes	No
22	Did the organization report more than $5,000 of grants or other assistance to or for domestic individuals on Part IX, column (A), line 2? *If "Yes," complete Schedule I, Parts I and III*	22		
23	Did the organization answer "Yes" to Part VII, Section A, line 3, 4, or 5, about compensation of the organization's current and former officers, directors, trustees, key employees, and highest compensated employees? *If "Yes," complete Schedule J*	23		
24a	Did the organization have a tax-exempt bond issue with an outstanding principal amount of more than $100,000 as of the last day of the year, that was issued after December 31, 2002? *If "Yes," answer lines 24b through 24d and complete Schedule K. If "No," go to line 25a*	24a		
b	Did the organization invest any proceeds of tax-exempt bonds beyond a temporary period exception?	24b		
c	Did the organization maintain an escrow account other than a refunding escrow at any time during the year to defease any tax-exempt bonds?	24c		
d	Did the organization act as an "on behalf of" issuer for bonds outstanding at any time during the year?	24d		
25a	**Section 501(c)(3), 501(c)(4), and 501(c)(29) organizations.** Did the organization engage in an excess benefit transaction with a disqualified person during the year? *If "Yes," complete Schedule L, Part I*	25a		
b	Is the organization aware that it engaged in an excess benefit transaction with a disqualified person in a prior year, and that the transaction has not been reported on any of the organization's prior Forms 990 or 990-EZ? *If "Yes," complete Schedule L, Part I*	25b		
26	Did the organization report any amount on Part X, line 5 or 22, for receivables from or payables to any current or former officer, director, trustee, key employee, creator or founder, substantial contributor, or 35% controlled entity or family member of any of these persons? *If "Yes," complete Schedule L, Part II*	26		
27	Did the organization provide a grant or other assistance to any current or former officer, director, trustee, key employee, creator or founder, substantial contributor or employee thereof, a grant selection committee member, or to a 35% controlled entity (including an employee thereof) or family member of any of these persons? *If "Yes," complete Schedule L, Part III*	27		
28	Was the organization a party to a business transaction with one of the following parties? (See the Schedule L, Part IV, instructions for applicable filing thresholds, conditions, and exceptions).			
a	A current or former officer, director, trustee, key employee, creator or founder, or substantial contributor? *If "Yes," complete Schedule L, Part IV*	28a		
b	A family member of any individual described in line 28a? *If "Yes," complete Schedule L, Part IV*	28b		
c	A 35% controlled entity of one or more individuals and/or organizations described in line 28a or 28b? *If "Yes," complete Schedule L, Part IV*	28c		
29	Did the organization receive more than $25,000 in noncash contributions? *If "Yes," complete Schedule M*	29		
30	Did the organization receive contributions of art, historical treasures, or other similar assets, or qualified conservation contributions? *If "Yes," complete Schedule M*	30		
31	Did the organization liquidate, terminate, or dissolve and cease operations? *If "Yes," complete Schedule N, Part I*	31		
32	Did the organization sell, exchange, dispose of, or transfer more than 25% of its net assets? *If "Yes," complete Schedule N, Part II*	32		
33	Did the organization own 100% of an entity disregarded as separate from the organization under Regulations sections 301.7701-2 and 301.7701-3? *If "Yes," complete Schedule R, Part I*	33		
34	Was the organization related to any tax-exempt or taxable entity? *If "Yes," complete Schedule R, Part II, III, or IV, and Part V, line 1*	34		
35a	Did the organization have a controlled entity within the meaning of section 512(b)(13)?	35a		
b	If "Yes" to line 35a, did the organization receive any payment from or engage in any transaction with a controlled entity within the meaning of section 512(b)(13)? *If "Yes," complete Schedule R, Part V, line 2*	35b		
36	**Section 501(c)(3) organizations.** Did the organization make any transfers to an exempt non-charitable related organization? *If "Yes," complete Schedule R, Part V, line 2*	36		
37	Did the organization conduct more than 5% of its activities through an entity that is not a related organization and that is treated as a partnership for federal income tax purposes? *If "Yes," complete Schedule R, Part VI*	37		
38	Did the organization complete Schedule O and provide explanations on Schedule O for Part VI, lines 11b and 19? **Note:** All Form 990 filers are required to complete Schedule O	38		

Part V Statements Regarding Other IRS Filings and Tax Compliance

Check if Schedule O contains a response or note to any line in this Part V ☐

					Yes	No
1a	Enter the number reported in box 3 of Form 1096. Enter -0- if not applicable	1a				
b	Enter the number of Forms W-2G included on line 1a. Enter -0- if not applicable	1b				
c	Did the organization comply with backup withholding rules for reportable payments to vendors and reportable gaming (gambling) winnings to prize winners?			1c		

Form **990** (2025)

Form 990 (2025) Page 5

Part V	Statements Regarding Other IRS Filings and Tax Compliance *(continued)*		Yes	No
2a	Enter the number of employees reported on Form W-3, Transmittal of Wage and Tax Statements, filed for the calendar year ending with or within the year covered by this return **2a**			
b	If at least one is reported on line 2a, did the organization file all required federal employment tax returns?	2b		
3a	Did the organization have unrelated business gross income of $1,000 or more during the year?	3a		
b	If "Yes," has it filed a Form 990-T for this year? *If "No" to line 3b, provide an explanation on Schedule O*	3b		
4a	At any time during the calendar year, did the organization have an interest in, or a signature or other authority over, a financial account in a foreign country (such as a bank account, securities account, or other financial account)?	4a		
b	If "Yes," enter the name of the foreign country ________ See instructions for filing requirements for FinCEN Form 114, Report of Foreign Bank and Financial Accounts (FBAR).			
5a	Was the organization a party to a prohibited tax shelter transaction at any time during the tax year?	5a		
b	Did any taxable party notify the organization that it was or is a party to a prohibited tax shelter transaction?	5b		
c	If "Yes" to line 5a or 5b, did the organization file Form 8886-T?	5c		
6a	Does the organization have annual gross receipts that are normally greater than $100,000, and did the organization solicit any contributions that were not tax deductible as charitable contributions?	6a		
b	If "Yes," did the organization include with every solicitation an express statement that such contributions or gifts were not tax deductible?	6b		
7	**Organizations that may receive deductible contributions under section 170(c).**			
a	Did the organization receive a payment in excess of $75 made partly as a contribution and partly for goods and services provided to the payor?	7a		
b	If "Yes," did the organization notify the donor of the value of the goods or services provided?	7b		
c	Did the organization sell, exchange, or otherwise dispose of tangible personal property for which it was required to file Form 8282?	7c		
d	If "Yes," indicate the number of Forms 8282 filed during the year **7d**			
e	Did the organization receive any funds, directly or indirectly, to pay premiums on a personal benefit contract?	7e		
f	Did the organization, during the year, pay premiums, directly or indirectly, on a personal benefit contract?	7f		
g	If the organization received a contribution of qualified intellectual property, did the organization file Form 8899 as required?	7g		
h	If the organization received a contribution of cars, boats, airplanes, or other vehicles, did the organization file a Form 1098-C?	7h		
8	**Sponsoring organizations maintaining donor advised funds.** Did a donor advised fund maintained by the sponsoring organization have excess business holdings at any time during the year?	8		
9	**Sponsoring organizations maintaining donor advised funds.**			
a	Did the sponsoring organization make any taxable distributions under section 4966?	9a		
b	Did the sponsoring organization make a distribution to a donor, donor advisor, or related person?	9b		
10	**Section 501(c)(7) organizations.** Enter:			
a	Initiation fees and capital contributions included on Part VIII, line 12 **10a**			
b	Gross receipts, included on Form 990, Part VIII, line 12, for public use of club facilities **10b**			
11	**Section 501(c)(12) organizations.** Enter:			
a	Gross income from members or shareholders **11a**			
b	Gross income from other sources. (Do not net amounts due or paid to other sources against amounts due or received from them.) **11b**			
12a	**Section 4947(a)(1) non-exempt charitable trusts.** Is the organization filing Form 990 in lieu of Form 1041?	12a		
b	If "Yes," enter the amount of tax-exempt interest received or accrued during the year **12b**			
13	**Section 501(c)(29) qualified nonprofit health insurance issuers.**			
a	Is the organization licensed to issue qualified health plans in more than one state? **Note:** See the instructions for additional information the organization must report on Schedule O.	13a		
b	Enter the amount of reserves the organization is required to maintain by the states in which the organization is licensed to issue qualified health plans **13b**			
c	Enter the amount of reserves on hand **13c**			
14a	Did the organization receive any payments for indoor tanning services during the tax year?	14a		
b	If "Yes," has it filed a Form 720 to report these payments? *If "No," provide an explanation on Schedule O*	14b		
15	Is the organization subject to the section 4960 tax on payment(s) of more than $1,000,000 in remuneration or excess parachute payment(s) during the year? If "Yes," see the instructions and file Form 4720, Schedule N.	15		
16	Is the organization an educational institution subject to the section 4968 excise tax on net investment income? If "Yes," complete Form 4720, Schedule O.	16		
17	**Section 501(c)(21) organizations.** Did the trust, or any disqualified or other person, engage in any activities that would result in the imposition of an excise tax under section 4951, 4952, or 4953? If "Yes," complete Form 6069.	17		

Form **990** (2025)

Form 990 (2025) Page 6

Part VI **Governance, Management, and Disclosure.** *For each "Yes" response to lines 2 through 7b below, and for a "No" response to line 8a, 8b, or 10b below, describe the circumstances, processes, or changes on Schedule O. See instructions.*

Check if Schedule O contains a response or note to any line in this Part VI . . . . ☐

Section A. Governing Body and Management

				Yes	No
1a	Enter the number of voting members of the governing body at the end of the tax year. .	1a			
	If there are material differences in voting rights among members of the governing body, or if the governing body delegated broad authority to an executive committee or similar committee, explain on Schedule O.				
b	Enter the number of voting members included on line 1a, above, who are independent .	1b			
2	Did any officer, director, trustee, or key employee have a family relationship or a business relationship with any other officer, director, trustee, or key employee?		2		
3	Did the organization delegate control over management duties customarily performed by or under the direct supervision of officers, directors, trustees, or key employees to a management company or other person? .		3		
4	Did the organization make any significant changes to its governing documents since the prior Form 990 was filed?		4		
5	Did the organization become aware during the year of a significant diversion of the organization's assets? .		5		
6	Did the organization have members or stockholders?		6		
7a	Did the organization have members, stockholders, or other persons who had the power to elect or appoint one or more members of the governing body?		7a		
b	Are any governance decisions of the organization reserved to (or subject to approval by) members, stockholders, or persons other than the governing body?		7b		
8	Did the organization contemporaneously document the meetings held or written actions undertaken during the year by the following:				
a	The governing body?		8a		
b	Each committee with authority to act on behalf of the governing body?		8b		
9	Is there any officer, director, trustee, or key employee listed in Part VII, Section A, who cannot be reached at the organization's mailing address? *If "Yes," provide the names and addresses on Schedule O*		9		

Section B. Policies *(This Section B requests information about policies not required by the Internal Revenue Code.)*

			Yes	No
10a	Did the organization have local chapters, branches, or affiliates?	10a		
b	If "Yes," did the organization have written policies and procedures governing the activities of such chapters, affiliates, and branches to ensure their operations are consistent with the organization's exempt purposes?	10b		
11a	Has the organization provided a complete copy of this Form 990 to all members of its governing body before filing the form?	11a		
b	Describe on Schedule O the process, if any, used by the organization to review this Form 990.			
12a	Did the organization have a written conflict of interest policy? *If "No," go to line 13*	12a		
b	Were officers, directors, or trustees, and key employees required to disclose annually interests that could give rise to conflicts?	12b		
c	Did the organization regularly and consistently monitor and enforce compliance with the policy? *If "Yes," describe on Schedule O how this was done*	12c		
13	Did the organization have a written whistleblower policy?	13		
14	Did the organization have a written document retention and destruction policy?	14		
15	Did the process for determining compensation of the following persons include a review and approval by independent persons, comparability data, and contemporaneous substantiation of the deliberation and decision?			
a	The organization's CEO, Executive Director, or top management official	15a		
b	Other officers or key employees of the organization	15b		
	If "Yes" to line 15a or 15b, describe the process on Schedule O. See instructions.			
16a	Did the organization invest in, contribute assets to, or participate in a joint venture or similar arrangement with a taxable entity during the year?	16a		
b	If "Yes," did the organization follow a written policy or procedure requiring the organization to evaluate its participation in joint venture arrangements under applicable federal tax law, and take steps to safeguard the organization's exempt status with respect to such arrangements?	16b		

Section C. Disclosure

17 List the states with which a copy of this Form 990 is required to be filed ____________

18 Section 6104 requires an organization to make its Forms 1023 (1024 or 1024-A, if applicable), 990, and 990-T (section 501(c)(3)s only) available for public inspection. Indicate how you made these available. Check all that apply.

☐ Own website ☐ Another's website ☐ Upon request ☐ Other *(explain on Schedule O)*

19 Describe on Schedule O whether (and if so, how) the organization made its governing documents, conflict of interest policy, and financial statements available to the public during the tax year.

20 State the name, address, and telephone number of the person who possesses the organization's books and records.

Form **990** (2025)

Part VII Compensation of Officers, Directors, Trustees, Key Employees, Highest Compensated Employees, and Independent Contractors

Check if Schedule O contains a response or note to any line in this Part VII . . . . ☐

Section A. Officers, Directors, Trustees, Key Employees, and Highest Compensated Employees

1a Complete this table for all persons required to be listed. Report compensation for the calendar year ending with or within the organization's tax year.

- List all of the organization's **current** officers, directors, trustees (whether individuals or organizations), regardless of amount of compensation. Enter -0- in columns (D), (E), and (F) if no compensation was paid.
- List all of the organization's **current** key employees, if any. See the instructions for definition of "key employee."
- List the organization's five **current** highest compensated employees (other than an officer, director, trustee, or key employee) who received reportable compensation (box 5 of Form W-2, box 6 of Form 1099-MISC, and/or box 1 of Form 1099-NEC) of more than $100,000 from the organization and any related organizations.
- List all of the organization's **former** officers, key employees, and highest compensated employees who received more than $100,000 of reportable compensation from the organization and any related organizations.
- List all of the organization's **former directors or trustees** that received, in the capacity as a former director or trustee of the organization, more than $10,000 of reportable compensation from the organization and any related organizations.

See the instructions for the order in which to list the persons above.

☐ Check this box if neither the organization nor any related organization compensated any current officer, director, or trustee.

(A) Name and title	(B) Average hours per week (list any hours for related organizations below dotted line)	(C) Position (do not check more than one box, unless person is both an officer and a director/trustee)						(D) Reportable compensation from the organization (W-2/ 1099-MISC/ 1099-NEC)	(E) Reportable compensation from related organizations (W-2/ 1099-MISC/ 1099-NEC)	(F) Estimated amount of other compensation from the organization and related organizations
		Individual trustee or director	Institutional trustee	Officer	Key employee	Highest compensated employee	Former			
(1)										
(2)										
(3)										
(4)										
(5)										
(6)										
(7)										
(8)										
(9)										
(10)										
(11)										
(12)										
(13)										
(14)										

Form 990 (2025) Page 8

Part VII **Section A. Officers, Directors, Trustees, Key Employees, and Highest Compensated Employees** *(continued)*

(A) Name and title	(B) Average hours per week (list any hours for related organizations below dotted line)	(C) Position (do not check more than one box, unless person is both an officer and a director/trustee): Individual trustee or director	Institutional trustee	Officer	Key employee	Highest compensated employee	Former	(D) Reportable compensation from the organization (W-2/ 1099-MISC/ 1099-NEC)	(E) Reportable compensation from related organizations (W-2/ 1099-MISC/ 1099-NEC)	(F) Estimated amount of other compensation from the organization and related organizations
(15)										
(16)										
(17)										
(18)										
(19)										
(20)										
(21)										
(22)										
(23)										
(24)										
(25)										

1b	**Subtotal**			
c	**Total from continuation sheets to Part VII, Section A**			
d	**Total (add lines 1b and 1c)**			

2 Total number of individuals (including but not limited to those listed above) who received more than $100,000 of reportable compensation from the organization

			Yes	No
3	Did the organization list any **former** officer, director, trustee, key employee, or highest compensated employee on line 1a? *If "Yes," complete Schedule J for such individual*	3		
4	For any individual listed on line 1a, is the sum of reportable compensation and other compensation from the organization and related organizations greater than $150,000? *If "Yes," complete Schedule J for such individual*	4		
5	Did any person listed on line 1a receive or accrue compensation from any unrelated organization or individual for services rendered to the organization? *If "Yes," complete Schedule J for such person*	5		

Section B. Independent Contractors

1 Complete this table for your five highest compensated independent contractors that received more than $100,000 of compensation from the organization. Report compensation for the calendar year ending with or within the organization's tax year.

(A) Name and business address	(B) Description of services	(C) Compensation

2 Total number of independent contractors (including but not limited to those listed above) who received more than $100,000 of compensation from the organization

Form **990** (2025)

Form 990 (2025) Page 9

Part VIII Statement of Revenue

Check if Schedule O contains a response or note to any line in this Part VIII . . . . ☐

					(A) Total revenue	(B) Related or exempt function revenue	(C) Unrelated business revenue	(D) Revenue excluded from tax under sections 512–514
Contributions, Gifts, Grants, and Other Similar Amounts	1a	Federated campaigns	1a					
	b	Membership dues	1b					
	c	Fundraising events	1c					
	d	Related organizations	1d					
	e	Government grants (contributions)	1e					
	f	All other contributions, gifts, grants, and similar amounts not included above	1f					
	g	Noncash contributions included in lines 1a–1f	1g	$				
	h	**Total.** Add lines 1a–1f						
Program Service Revenue				Business Code				
	2a							
	b							
	c							
	d							
	e							
	f	All other program service revenue . .						
	g	**Total.** Add lines 2a–2f						
Other Revenue	3	Investment income (including dividends, interest, and other similar amounts)						
	4	Income from investment of tax-exempt bond proceeds						
	5	Royalties						
				(i) Real	(ii) Personal			
	6a	Gross rents . .	6a					
	b	Less: rental expenses	6b					
	c	Rental income or (loss)	6c					
	d	Net rental income or (loss)						
				(i) Securities	(ii) Other			
	7a	Gross amount from sales of assets other than inventory	7a					
	b	Less: cost or other basis and sales expenses .	7b					
	c	Gain or (loss) . .	7c					
	d	Net gain or (loss)						
	8a	Gross income from fundraising events (not including $ ______ of contributions reported on line 1c). See Part IV, line 18 . . .	8a					
	b	Less: direct expenses	8b					
	c	Net income or (loss) from fundraising events . . .						
	9a	Gross income from gaming activities. See Part IV, line 19 .	9a					
	b	Less: direct expenses	9b					
	c	Net income or (loss) from gaming activities						
	10a	Gross sales of inventory, less returns and allowances . . .	10a					
	b	Less: cost of goods sold . . .	10b					
	c	Net income or (loss) from sales of inventory						
Miscellaneous Revenue				Business Code				
	11a							
	b							
	c							
	d	All other revenue						
	e	**Total.** Add lines 11a–11d						
	12	**Total revenue.** See instructions						

Form **990** (2025)

Form 990 (2025) Page **10**

Part IX Statement of Functional Expenses

Section 501(c)(3) and 501(c)(4) organizations must complete all columns. All other organizations must complete column (A).

Check if Schedule O contains a response or note to any line in this Part IX . . . . ☐

Do not include amounts reported on lines 6b, 7b, 8b, 9b, and 10b of Part VIII.	(A) Total expenses	(B) Program service expenses	(C) Management and general expenses	(D) Fundraising expenses
1 Grants and other assistance to domestic organizations and domestic governments. See Part IV, line 21				
2 Grants and other assistance to domestic individuals. See Part IV, line 22				
3 Grants and other assistance to foreign organizations, foreign governments, and foreign individuals. See Part IV, lines 15 and 16				
4 Benefits paid to or for members				
5 Compensation of current officers, directors, trustees, and key employees				
6 Compensation not included above to disqualified persons (as defined under section 4958(f)(1)) and persons described in section 4958(c)(3)(B)				
7 Other salaries and wages				
8 Pension plan accruals and contributions (include section 401(k) and 403(b) employer contributions)				
9 Other employee benefits				
10 Payroll taxes				
11 Fees for services (nonemployees):				
a Management				
b Legal				
c Accounting				
d Lobbying				
e Professional fundraising services. See Part IV, line 17				
f Investment management fees				
g Other. (If line 11g amount exceeds 10% of line 25, column (A), amount, list line 11g expenses on Schedule O.)				
12 Advertising and promotion				
13 Office expenses				
14 Information technology				
15 Royalties				
16 Occupancy				
17 Travel				
18 Payments of travel or entertainment expenses for any federal, state, or local public officials				
19 Conferences, conventions, and meetings				
20 Interest				
21 Payments to affiliates				
22 Depreciation, depletion, and amortization				
23 Insurance				
24 Other expenses. Itemize expenses not covered above. (List miscellaneous expenses on line 24e. If line 24e amount exceeds 10% of line 25, column (A), amount, list line 24e expenses on Schedule O.)				
a				
b				
c				
d				
e All other expenses				
25 **Total functional expenses.** Add lines 1 through 24e				
26 **Joint costs.** Complete this line only if the organization reported in column (B) joint costs from a combined educational campaign and fundraising solicitation. Check here ☐ if following SOP 98-2 (ASC 958-720)				

Form **990** (2025)

Form 990 (2025) Page **11**

Part X **Balance Sheet**

Check if Schedule O contains a response or note to any line in this Part X . . . . ☐

				(A) Beginning of year		(B) End of year
Assets	1	Cash—non-interest-bearing			1	
	2	Savings and temporary cash investments			2	
	3	Pledges and grants receivable, net			3	
	4	Accounts receivable, net			4	
	5	Loans and other receivables from any current or former officer, director, trustee, key employee, creator or founder, substantial contributor, or 35% controlled entity or family member of any of these persons			5	
	6	Loans and other receivables from other disqualified persons (as defined under section 4958(f)(1)), and persons described in section 4958(c)(3)(B)			6	
	7	Notes and loans receivable, net			7	
	8	Inventories for sale or use			8	
	9	Prepaid expenses and deferred charges			9	
	10a	Land, buildings, and equipment: cost or other basis. Complete Part VI of Schedule D	10a			
	b	Less: accumulated depreciation	10b		10c	
	11	Investments—publicly traded securities			11	
	12	Investments—other securities. See Part IV, line 11			12	
	13	Investments—program-related. See Part IV, line 11			13	
	14	Intangible assets			14	
	15	Other assets. See Part IV, line 11			15	
	16	**Total assets.** Add lines 1 through 15 (must equal line 33)			16	
Liabilities	17	Accounts payable and accrued expenses			17	
	18	Grants payable			18	
	19	Deferred revenue			19	
	20	Tax-exempt bond liabilities			20	
	21	Escrow or custodial account liability. Complete Part IV of Schedule D			21	
	22	Loans and other payables to any current or former officer, director, trustee, key employee, creator or founder, substantial contributor, or 35% controlled entity or family member of any of these persons			22	
	23	Secured mortgages and notes payable to unrelated third parties			23	
	24	Unsecured notes and loans payable to unrelated third parties			24	
	25	Other liabilities (including federal income tax, payables to related third parties, and other liabilities not included on lines 17–24). Complete Part X of Schedule D			25	
	26	**Total liabilities.** Add lines 17 through 25			26	
Net Assets or Fund Balances		**Organizations that follow FASB ASC 958, check here ☐ and complete lines 27, 28, 32, and 33.**				
	27	Net assets without donor restrictions			27	
	28	Net assets with donor restrictions			28	
		Organizations that do not follow FASB ASC 958, check here ☐ and complete lines 29 through 33.				
	29	Capital stock or trust principal, or current funds			29	
	30	Paid-in or capital surplus, or land, building, or equipment fund			30	
	31	Retained earnings, endowment, accumulated income, or other funds			31	
	32	Total net assets or fund balances			32	
	33	Total liabilities and net assets/fund balances			33	

Form **990** (2025)

Form 990 (2025) Page 12

Part XI Reconciliation of Net Assets

Check if Schedule O contains a response or note to any line in this Part XI . . . . ☐

1	Total revenue (must equal Part VIII, column (A), line 12)	1	
2	Total expenses (must equal Part IX, column (A), line 25)	2	
3	Revenue less expenses. Subtract line 2 from line 1	3	
4	Net assets or fund balances at beginning of year (must equal Part X, line 32, column (A))	4	
5	Net unrealized gains (losses) on investments	5	
6	Donated services and use of facilities	6	
7	Investment expenses	7	
8	Prior period adjustments	8	
9	Other changes in net assets or fund balances (explain on Schedule O)	9	
10	Net assets or fund balances at end of year. Combine lines 3 through 9 (must equal Part X, line 32, column (B))	10	

Part XII Financial Statements and Reporting

Check if Schedule O contains a response or note to any line in this Part XII . . . . ☐

			Yes	No
1	Accounting method used to prepare the Form 990: ☐ Cash ☐ Accrual ☐ Other ______ If the organization changed its method of accounting from a prior year or checked "Other," explain on Schedule O.			
2a	Were the organization's financial statements compiled or reviewed by an independent accountant?	2a		
	If "Yes," check a box below to indicate whether the financial statements for the year were compiled or reviewed on a separate basis, consolidated basis, or both. ☐ Separate basis ☐ Consolidated basis ☐ Both consolidated and separate basis			
b	Were the organization's financial statements audited by an independent accountant?	2b		
	If "Yes," check a box below to indicate whether the financial statements for the year were audited on a separate basis, consolidated basis, or both. ☐ Separate basis ☐ Consolidated basis ☐ Both consolidated and separate basis			
c	If "Yes" to line 2a or 2b, does the organization have a committee that assumes responsibility for oversight of the audit, review, or compilation of its financial statements and selection of an independent accountant?	2c		
	If the organization changed either its oversight process or selection process during the tax year, explain on Schedule O.			
3a	As a result of a federal award, was the organization required to undergo an audit or audits as set forth in the Uniform Guidance, 2 C.F.R. Part 200, Subpart F?	3a		
b	If "Yes," did the organization undergo the required audit or audits? If the organization did not undergo the required audit or audits, explain why on Schedule O and describe any steps taken to undergo such audits	3b		

Form **990** (2025)

SCHEDULE A (Form 990)

Department of the Treasury
Internal Revenue Service

Public Charity Status and Public Support

Complete if the organization is a section 501(c)(3) organization or a section 4947(a)(1) nonexempt charitable trust.
Attach to Form 990 or Form 990-EZ.
Go to *www.irs.gov/Form990* for instructions and the latest information.

OMB No. 1545-0047
2025
Open to Public Inspection

Name of the organization | **Employer identification number**

Part I **Reason for Public Charity Status.** (All organizations must complete this part.) See instructions.

The organization is not a private foundation because it is: (For lines 1 through 12, check only one box.)

1 ☐ A church, convention of churches, or association of churches described in **section 170(b)(1)(A)(i)**.
2 ☐ A school described in **section 170(b)(1)(A)(ii)**. (Attach Schedule E (Form 990).)
3 ☐ A hospital or a cooperative hospital service organization described in **section 170(b)(1)(A)(iii)**.
4 ☐ A medical research organization operated in conjunction with a hospital described in **section 170(b)(1)(A)(iii)**. Enter the hospital's name, city, and state: ____________
5 ☐ An organization operated for the benefit of a college or university owned or operated by a governmental unit described in **section 170(b)(1)(A)(iv)**. (Complete Part II.)
6 ☐ A federal, state, or local government or governmental unit described in **section 170(b)(1)(A)(v)**.
7 ☐ An organization that normally receives a substantial part of its support from a governmental unit or from the general public described in **section 170(b)(1)(A)(vi)**. (Complete Part II.)
8 ☐ A community trust described in **section 170(b)(1)(A)(vi)**. (Complete Part II.)
9 ☐ An agricultural research organization described in **section 170(b)(1)(A)(ix)** operated in conjunction with a land-grant college or university or a non-land-grant college of agriculture (see instructions). Enter the name, city, and state of the college or university: ____________
10 ☐ An organization that normally receives (1) more than 33⅓% of its support from contributions, membership fees, and gross receipts from activities related to its exempt functions, subject to certain exceptions; and (2) no more than 33⅓% of its support from gross investment income and unrelated business taxable income (less section 511 tax) from businesses acquired by the organization after June 30, 1975. See **section 509(a)(2)**. (Complete Part III.)
11 ☐ An organization organized and operated exclusively to test for public safety. See **section 509(a)(4)**.
12 ☐ An organization organized and operated exclusively for the benefit of, to perform the functions of, or to carry out the purposes of one or more publicly supported organizations described in **section 509(a)(1)** or **section 509(a)(2)**. See **section 509(a)(3)**. Check the box on lines 12a through 12d that describes the type of supporting organization and complete lines 12e, 12f, and 12g.

a ☐ **Type I.** A supporting organization operated, supervised, or controlled by its supported organization(s), typically by giving the supported organization(s) the power to regularly appoint or elect a majority of the directors or trustees of the supporting organization. **You must complete Part IV, Sections A and B.**

b ☐ **Type II.** A supporting organization supervised or controlled in connection with its supported organization(s), by having control or management of the supporting organization vested in the same persons that control or manage the supported organization(s). **You must complete Part IV, Sections A and C.**

c ☐ **Type III functionally integrated.** A supporting organization operated in connection with, and functionally integrated with, its supported organization(s) (see instructions). **You must complete Part IV, Sections A, D, and E.**

d ☐ **Type III non-functionally integrated.** A supporting organization operated in connection with its supported organization(s) that is not functionally integrated. The organization must generally satisfy a distribution requirement and an attentiveness requirement (see instructions). **You must complete Part IV, Sections A and D, and Part V.**

e ☐ Check this box if the organization received a written determination from the IRS that it is a Type I, Type II, Type III functionally integrated, or Type III non-functionally integrated supporting organization.

f Enter the number of supported organizations . . . . ☐

g Provide the following information about the supported organization(s).

	(i) Name of supported organization	(ii) EIN	(iii) Type of organization (described on lines 1–10 above (see instructions))	(iv) Is the organization listed in your governing document? Yes	No	(v) Amount of monetary support (see instructions)	(vi) Amount of other support (see instructions)
(A)							
(B)							
(C)							
(D)							
(E)							
Total							

For Paperwork Reduction Act Notice, see the Instructions for Form 990 or 990-EZ. Cat. No. 11285F **Schedule A (Form 990) 2025** Created 4/11/25

Schedule A (Form 990) 2025 Page **2**

Part II **Support Schedule for Organizations Described in Sections 170(b)(1)(A)(iv) and 170(b)(1)(A)(vi)**
(Complete only if you checked the box on line 5, 7, or 8 of Part I or if the organization failed to qualify under Part III. If the organization fails to qualify under the tests listed below, please complete Part III.)

Section A. Public Support

Calendar year (or fiscal year beginning in)	**(a)** 2021	**(b)** 2022	**(c)** 2023	**(d)** 2024	**(e)** 2025	**(f)** Total
1 Gifts, grants, contributions, and membership fees received. (Do not include any "unusual grants.")						
2 Tax revenues levied for the organization's benefit and either paid to or expended on its behalf						
3 The value of services or facilities furnished by a governmental unit to the organization without charge						
4 **Total.** Add lines 1 through 3						
5 The portion of total contributions by each person (other than a governmental unit or publicly supported organization) included on line 1 that exceeds 2% of the amount shown on line 11, column (f)						
6 **Public support.** Subtract line 5 from line 4						

Section B. Total Support

Calendar year (or fiscal year beginning in)	**(a)** 2021	**(b)** 2022	**(c)** 2023	**(d)** 2024	**(e)** 2025	**(f)** Total
7 Amounts from line 4						
8 Gross income from interest, dividends, payments received on securities loans, rents, royalties, and income from similar sources						
9 Net income from unrelated business activities, whether or not the business is regularly carried on						
10 Other income. Do not include gain or loss from the sale of capital assets (Explain in Part VI.)						
11 **Total support.** Add lines 7 through 10						

12 Gross receipts from related activities, etc. (see instructions) . . . **12**

13 **First 5 years.** If the Form 990 is for the organization's first, second, third, fourth, or fifth tax year as a section 501(c)(3) organization, check this box and **stop here** . . . ☐

Section C. Computation of Public Support Percentage

14 Public support percentage for 2025 (line 6, column (f), divided by line 11, column (f)) . . . **14** %

15 Public support percentage from 2024 Schedule A, Part II, line 14 . . . **15** %

16a **33⅓% support test—2025.** If the organization did not check the box on line 13, and line 14 is 33⅓% or more, check this box and **stop here.** The organization qualifies as a publicly supported organization . . . ☐

b **33⅓% support test—2024.** If the organization did not check a box on line 13 or 16a, and line 15 is 33⅓% or more, check this box and **stop here.** The organization qualifies as a publicly supported organization . . . ☐

17a **10%-facts-and-circumstances test—2025.** If the organization did not check a box on line 13, 16a, or 16b, and line 14 is 10% or more, and if the organization meets the facts-and-circumstances test, check this box and **stop here.** Explain in Part VI how the organization meets the facts-and-circumstances test. The organization qualifies as a publicly supported organization . . . ☐

b **10%-facts-and-circumstances test—2024.** If the organization did not check a box on line 13, 16a, 16b, or 17a, and line 15 is 10% or more, and if the organization meets the facts-and-circumstances test, check this box and **stop here.** Explain in Part VI how the organization meets the facts-and-circumstances test. The organization qualifies as a publicly supported organization . . . ☐

18 **Private foundation.** If the organization did not check a box on line 13, 16a, 16b, 17a, or 17b, check this box and see instructions . . . ☐

Schedule A (Form 990) 2025

Schedule A (Form 990) 2025 Page 3

Part III **Support Schedule for Organizations Described in Section 509(a)(2)**
(Complete only if you checked the box on line 10 of Part I or if the organization failed to qualify under Part II. If the organization fails to qualify under the tests listed below, please complete Part II.)

Section A. Public Support

Calendar year (or fiscal year beginning in)	(a) 2021	(b) 2022	(c) 2023	(d) 2024	(e) 2025	(f) Total
1 Gifts, grants, contributions, and membership fees received. (Do not include any "unusual grants.")						
2 Gross receipts from admissions, merchandise sold or services performed, or facilities furnished in any activity that is related to the organization's tax-exempt purpose						
3 Gross receipts from activities that are not an unrelated trade or business under section 513						
4 Tax revenues levied for the organization's benefit and either paid to or expended on its behalf						
5 The value of services or facilities furnished by a governmental unit to the organization without charge						
6 **Total.** Add lines 1 through 5						
7a Amounts included on lines 1, 2, and 3 received from disqualified persons						
b Amounts included on lines 2 and 3 received from other than disqualified persons that exceed the greater of $5,000 or 1% of the amount on line 13 for the year						
c Add lines 7a and 7b						
8 **Public support.** (Subtract line 7c from line 6.)						

Section B. Total Support

Calendar year (or fiscal year beginning in)	(a) 2021	(b) 2022	(c) 2023	(d) 2024	(e) 2025	(f) Total
9 Amounts from line 6						
10a Gross income from interest, dividends, payments received on securities loans, rents, royalties, and income from similar sources						
b Unrelated business taxable income (less section 511 taxes) from businesses acquired after June 30, 1975						
c Add lines 10a and 10b						
11 Net income from unrelated business activities not included on line 10b, whether or not the business is regularly carried on						
12 Other income. Do not include gain or loss from the sale of capital assets (Explain in Part VI.)						
13 **Total support.** (Add lines 9, 10c, 11, and 12.)						

14 **First 5 years.** If the Form 990 is for the organization's first, second, third, fourth, or fifth tax year as a section 501(c)(3) organization, check this box and **stop here** ☐

Section C. Computation of Public Support Percentage

15	Public support percentage for 2025 (line 8, column (f), divided by line 13, column (f))	15	%
16	Public support percentage from 2024 Schedule A, Part III, line 15	16	%

Section D. Computation of Investment Income Percentage

17	Investment income percentage for **2025** (line 10c, column (f), divided by line 13, column (f))	17	%
18	Investment income percentage from **2024** Schedule A, Part III, line 17	18	%

19a **33⅓% support tests—2025.** If the organization did not check the box on line 14, and line 15 is more than 33⅓%, and line 17 is not more than 33⅓%, check this box and **stop here.** The organization qualifies as a publicly supported organization ☐

b **33⅓% support tests—2024.** If the organization did not check a box on line 14 or line 19a, and line 16 is more than 33⅓%, and line 18 is not more than 33⅓%, check this box and **stop here.** The organization qualifies as a publicly supported organization ☐

20 **Private foundation.** If the organization did not check a box on line 14, 19a, or 19b, check this box and see instructions ☐

Schedule A (Form 990) 2025

Schedule A (Form 990) 2025 Page **4**

Part IV **Supporting Organizations**

(Complete only if you checked a box on line 12 of Part I. If you checked box 12a, Part I, complete Sections A and B. If you checked box 12b, Part I, complete Sections A and C. If you checked box 12c, Part I, complete Sections A, D, and E. If you checked box 12d, Part I, complete Sections A and D, and complete Part V.)

Section A. All Supporting Organizations

			Yes	No
1	Are all of the organization's supported organizations listed by name in the organization's governing documents? *If "No," describe in* ***Part VI*** *how the supported organizations are designated. If designated by class or purpose, describe the designation. If historic and continuing relationship, explain.*	1		
2	Did the organization have any supported organization that does not have an IRS determination of status under section 509(a)(1) or (2)? *If "Yes," explain in* ***Part VI*** *how the organization determined that the supported organization was described in section 509(a)(1) or (2).*	2		
3a	Did the organization have a supported organization described in section 501(c)(4), (5), or (6)? *If "Yes," answer lines 3b and 3c below.*	3a		
b	Did the organization confirm that each supported organization qualified under section 501(c)(4), (5), or (6) and satisfied the public support tests under section 509(a)(2)? *If "Yes," describe in* ***Part VI*** *when and how the organization made the determination.*	3b		
c	Did the organization ensure that all support to such organizations was used exclusively for section 170(c)(2)(B) purposes? *If "Yes," explain in* ***Part VI*** *what controls the organization put in place to ensure such use.*	3c		
4a	Was any supported organization not organized in the United States ("foreign supported organization")? *If "Yes," and if you checked box 12a or 12b in Part I, answer lines 4b and 4c below.*	4a		
b	Did the organization have ultimate control and discretion in deciding whether to make grants to the foreign supported organization? *If "Yes," describe in* ***Part VI*** *how the organization had such control and discretion despite being controlled or supervised by or in connection with its supported organizations.*	4b		
c	Did the organization support any foreign supported organization that does not have an IRS determination under sections 501(c)(3) and 509(a)(1) or (2)? *If "Yes," explain in* ***Part VI*** *what controls the organization used to ensure that all support to the foreign supported organization was used exclusively for section 170(c)(2)(B) purposes.*	4c		
5a	Did the organization add, substitute, or remove any supported organizations during the tax year? *If "Yes," answer lines 5b and 5c below (if applicable). Also, provide detail in* ***Part VI****, including (i) the names and EIN numbers of the supported organizations added, substituted, or removed; (ii) the reasons for each such action; (iii) the authority under the organization's organizing document authorizing such action; and (iv) how the action was accomplished (such as by amendment to the organizing document).*	5a		
b	**Type I or Type II only.** Was any added or substituted supported organization part of a class already designated in the organization's organizing document?	5b		
c	**Substitutions only.** Was the substitution the result of an event beyond the organization's control?	5c		
6	Did the organization provide support (whether in the form of grants or the provision of services or facilities) to anyone other than (i) its supported organizations, (ii) individuals that are part of the charitable class benefited by one or more of its supported organizations, or (iii) other supporting organizations that also support or benefit one or more of the filing organization's supported organizations? *If "Yes," provide detail in* ***Part VI.***	6		
7	Did the organization provide a grant, loan, compensation, or other similar payment to a substantial contributor (as defined in section 4958(c)(3)(C)), a family member of a substantial contributor, or a 35% controlled entity with regard to a substantial contributor? *If "Yes," complete Part I of Schedule L (Form 990).*	7		
8	Did the organization make a loan to a disqualified person (as defined in section 4958) not described on line 7? *If "Yes," complete Part I of Schedule L (Form 990).*	8		
9a	Was the organization controlled directly or indirectly at any time during the tax year by one or more disqualified persons, as defined in section 4946 (other than foundation managers and organizations described in section 509(a)(1) or (2))? *If "Yes," provide detail in* ***Part VI.***	9a		
b	Did one or more disqualified persons (as defined on line 9a) hold a controlling interest in any entity in which the supporting organization had an interest? *If "Yes," provide detail in* ***Part VI.***	9b		
c	Did a disqualified person (as defined on line 9a) have an ownership interest in, or derive any personal benefit from, assets in which the supporting organization also had an interest? *If "Yes," provide detail in* ***Part VI.***	9c		
10a	Was the organization subject to the excess business holdings rules of section 4943 because of section 4943(f) (regarding certain Type II supporting organizations, and all Type III non-functionally integrated supporting organizations)? *If "Yes," answer line 10b below.*	10a		
b	Did the organization have any excess business holdings in the tax year? *(Use Schedule C, Form 4720, to determine whether the organization had excess business holdings.)*	10b		

Schedule A (Form 990) 2025

Part IV Supporting Organizations *(continued)*

			Yes	No
11	Has the organization accepted a gift or contribution from any of the following persons?			
a	A person who directly or indirectly controls, either alone or together with persons described on lines 11b and 11c below, the governing body of a supported organization?	11a		
b	A family member of a person described on line 11a above?	11b		
c	A 35% controlled entity of a person described on line 11a or 11b above? *If "Yes" to line 11a, 11b, or 11c, provide detail in* ***Part VI.***	11c		

Section B. Type I Supporting Organizations

			Yes	No
1	Did the governing body, members of the governing body, officers acting in their official capacity, or membership of one or more supported organizations have the power to regularly appoint or elect at least a majority of the organization's officers, directors, or trustees at all times during the tax year? *If "No," describe in* ***Part VI*** *how the supported organization(s) effectively operated, supervised, or controlled the organization's activities. If the organization had more than one supported organization, describe how the powers to appoint and/or remove officers, directors, or trustees were allocated among the supported organizations and what conditions or restrictions, if any, applied to such powers during the tax year.*	1		
2	Did the organization operate for the benefit of any supported organization other than the supported organization(s) that operated, supervised, or controlled the supporting organization? *If "Yes," explain in* ***Part VI*** *how providing such benefit carried out the purposes of the supported organization(s) that operated, supervised, or controlled the supporting organization.*	2		

Section C. Type II Supporting Organizations

			Yes	No
1	Were a majority of the organization's directors or trustees during the tax year also a majority of the directors or trustees of each of the organization's supported organization(s)? *If "No," describe in* ***Part VI*** *how control or management of the supporting organization was vested in the same persons that controlled or managed the supported organization(s).*	1		

Section D. All Type III Supporting Organizations

			Yes	No
1	Did the organization provide to each of its supported organizations, by the last day of the fifth month of the organization's tax year, (i) a written notice describing the type and amount of support provided during the prior tax year, (ii) a copy of the Form 990 that was most recently filed as of the date of notification, and (iii) copies of the organization's governing documents in effect on the date of notification, to the extent not previously provided?	1		
2	Were any of the organization's officers, directors, or trustees either (i) appointed or elected by the supported organization(s), or (ii) serving on the governing body of a supported organization? *If "No," explain in* ***Part VI*** *how the organization maintained a close and continuous working relationship with the supported organization(s).*	2		
3	By reason of the relationship described on line 2, above, did the organization's supported organizations have a significant voice in the organization's investment policies and in directing the use of the organization's income or assets at all times during the tax year? *If "Yes," describe in* ***Part VI*** *the role the organization's supported organizations played in this regard.*	3		

Section E. Type III Functionally Integrated Supporting Organizations

1 *Check the box next to the method that the organization used to satisfy the Integral Part Test during the year* ***(see instructions).***

a ☐ The organization satisfied the Activities Test. *Complete* ***line 2*** *below.*

b ☐ The organization is the parent of each of its supported organizations. *Complete* ***line 3*** *below.*

c ☐ The organization supported a governmental supported organization. *Describe in* ***Part VI*** *how you supported a governmental supported organization (see instructions).*

			Yes	No
2	Activities Test. ***Answer lines 2a and 2b below.***			
a	Did substantially all of the organization's activities during the tax year directly further the exempt purposes of its supported organization(s)? *If "Yes," then in* ***Part VI identify those supported organizations and explain*** *how these activities directly furthered their exempt purposes, how the organization was responsive to each of its supported organizations, and how the organization determined that these activities constituted substantially all of its activities.*	2a		
b	Did the activities described on line 2a, above, constitute activities that, but for the organization's involvement, one or more of the organization's supported organization(s) would have been engaged in? *If "Yes," explain in* ***Part VI*** *the reasons for the organization's position that its supported organization(s) would have engaged in these activities but for the organization's involvement.*	2b		
3	Parent of Supported Organizations. ***Answer lines 3a, 3b, and 3c below.***			
a	Are the organization and its supported organization(s) part of an integrated system (for example, a hospital system)? *If "Yes," provide details in* ***Part VI.***	3a		
b	Did the organization direct the policies, programs, and activities of each of its supported organizations? *If "Yes," describe in* ***Part VI*** *the role played by the organization in this regard.*	3b		
c	Did the organization have the power to regularly appoint or elect (and remove) a majority of the officers, directors, or trustees of each of the supported organizations? *If "Yes" or "No," provide details in* ***Part VI.***	3c		

Schedule A (Form 990) 2025 Page **6**

Part V Type III Non-Functionally Integrated 509(a)(3) Supporting Organizations

1 ☐ Check here if the organization satisfied the Integral Part Test as a qualifying trust on Nov. 20, 1970 (*explain in **Part VI***). **See instructions.** All other Type III non-functionally integrated supporting organizations must complete Sections A through E.

Section A—Adjusted Net Income			(A) Prior Year	(B) Current Year (optional)
1	Net short-term capital gain	1		
2	Recoveries of prior-year distributions	2		
3	Other gross income (see instructions)	3		
4	Add lines 1 through 3.	4		
5	Depreciation and depletion	5		
6	Portion of operating expenses paid or incurred for production or collection of gross income or for management, conservation, or maintenance of property held for production of income (see instructions)	6		
7	Other expenses (see instructions)	7		
8	**Adjusted Net Income** (subtract lines 5, 6, and 7 from line 4)	8		

Section B—Minimum Asset Amount			(A) Prior Year	(B) Current Year (optional)
1	Aggregate fair market value of all non-exempt-use assets (see instructions for short tax year or assets held for part of year):			
a	Average monthly value of securities	1a		
b	Average monthly cash balances	1b		
c	Fair market value of other non-exempt-use assets	1c		
d	**Total** (add lines 1a, 1b, and 1c)	1d		
e	**Discount** claimed for blockage or other factors (*explain in detail in **Part VI***):			
2	Acquisition indebtedness applicable to non-exempt-use assets	2		
3	Subtract line 2 from line 1d.	3		
4	Cash deemed held for exempt use. Enter 0.015 of line 3 (for greater amount, see instructions).	4		
5	Net value of non-exempt-use assets (subtract line 4 from line 3)	5		
6	Multiply line 5 by 0.035.	6		
7	Recoveries of prior-year distributions	7		
8	**Minimum Asset Amount** (add line 7 to line 6)	8		

Section C—Distributable Amount				Current Year
1	Adjusted net income for prior year (from Section A, line 8, column A)	1		
2	Enter 0.85 of line 1.	2		
3	Minimum asset amount for prior year (from Section B, line 8, column A)	3		
4	Enter greater of line 2 or line 3.	4		
5	Income tax imposed in prior year	5		
6	**Distributable Amount.** Subtract line 5 from line 4, unless subject to emergency temporary reduction (see instructions).	6		

7 ☐ Check here if the current year is the organization's first as a non-functionally integrated Type III supporting organization (see instructions).

Schedule A (Form 990) 2025

Part V **Type III Non-Functionally Integrated 509(a)(3) Supporting Organizations** *(continued)*

Section D—Distributions			**Current Year**
1	Amounts paid to supported organizations to accomplish exempt purposes	1	
2	Amounts paid to perform activity that directly furthers exempt purposes of supported organizations, in excess of income from activity	2	
3	Administrative expenses paid to accomplish exempt purposes of supported organizations	3	
4	Amounts paid to acquire exempt-use assets	4	
5	Qualified set-aside amounts (prior IRS approval required—*provide details in* ***Part VI***)	5	
6	**Total annual distributions.** Add lines 1 through 5.	6	
7	Distributions to attentive supported organizations to which the organization is responsive (*provide details in* ***Part VI***). See instructions.	7	
8	Distributable amount for 2025 from Section C, line 6	8	
9	Line 7 amount divided by line 8 amount	9	

	Section E—Distribution Allocations (see instructions)	**(i)** **Excess Distributions**	**(ii)** **Underdistributions Pre-2025**	**(iii)** **Distributable Amount for 2025**
1	Distributable amount for 2025 from Section C, line 6			
2	Underdistributions, if any, for years prior to 2025 (reasonable cause required—*explain in* ***Part VI***). See instructions.			
3	Excess distributions carryover, if any, to 2025			
a	From 2020			
b	From 2021			
c	From 2022			
d	From 2023			
e	From 2024			
f	**Total** of lines 3a through 3e			
g	Applied to underdistributions of prior years			
h	Applied to 2025 distributable amount			
i	Carryover from 2020 not applied (see instructions)			
j	Remainder. Subtract lines 3g, 3h, and 3i from line 3f.			
4	Distributions for 2025 from Section D, line 6: $			
a	Applied to underdistributions of prior years			
b	Applied to 2025 distributable amount			
c	Remainder. Subtract lines 4a and 4b from line 4.			
5	Remaining underdistributions for years prior to 2025, if any. Subtract lines 3g and 4a from line 2. For result greater than zero, *explain in* ***Part VI***. See instructions.			
6	Remaining underdistributions for 2025. Subtract lines 3h and 4b from line 1. For result greater than zero, *explain in* ***Part VI***. See instructions.			
7	**Excess distributions carryover to 2026.** Add lines 3j and 4c.			
8	Breakdown of line 7:			
a	Excess from 2021 . . .			
b	Excess from 2022 . . .			
c	Excess from 2023 . . .			
d	Excess from 2024 . . .			
e	Excess from 2025 . . .			

Schedule A (Form 990) 2025 Page 8

Part VI **Supplemental Information.** Provide the explanations required by Part II, line 10; Part II, line 17a or 17b; Part III, line 12; Part IV, Section A, lines 1, 2, 3b, 3c, 4b, 4c, 5a, 6, 9a, 9b, 9c, 11a, 11b, and 11c; Part IV, Section B, lines 1 and 2; Part IV, Section C, line 1; Part IV, Section D, lines 2 and 3; Part IV, Section E, lines 1c, 2a, 2b, 3a, 3b, and 3c; Part V, line 1; Part V, Section B, line 1e; Part V, Section D, lines 5 and 7; and Part V, Section E, lines 2, 5, and 6. Also complete this part for any additional information. (See instructions.)

Schedule A (Form 990) 2025

Schedule B (Form 990)
(Rev. December 2024)
Department of the Treasury
Internal Revenue Service

Schedule of Contributors

Attach to Form 990, 990-EZ, or 990-PF.
Go to *www.irs.gov/Form990* for the latest information.

OMB No. 1545-0047

Name of the organization	**Employer identification number**

Organization type (check one):

Filers of:	**Section:**
Form 990 or 990-EZ	☐ 501(c)( ) (enter number) organization
	☐ 4947(a)(1) nonexempt charitable trust **not** treated as a private foundation
	☐ 527 political organization
Form 990-PF	☐ 501(c)(3) exempt private foundation
	☐ 4947(a)(1) nonexempt charitable trust treated as a private foundation
	☐ 501(c)(3) taxable private foundation

Check if your organization is covered by the **General Rule** or a **Special Rule**.
Note: Only a section 501(c)(7), (8), or (10) organization can check boxes for both the General Rule and a Special Rule. See instructions.

General Rule

☐ For an organization filing Form 990, 990-EZ, or 990-PF that received, during the year, contributions totaling $5,000 or more (in money or property) from any one contributor. Complete Parts I and II. See instructions for determining a contributor's total contributions.

Special Rules

☐ For an organization described in section 501(c)(3) filing Form 990 or 990-EZ that met the 33$^{1}/_{3}$% support test of the regulations under sections 509(a)(1) and 170(b)(1)(A)(vi), that checked Schedule A (Form 990), Part II, line 13, 16a, or 16b, and that received from any one contributor, during the year, total contributions of the greater of (**1**) $5,000; or (**2**) 2% of the amount on (i) Form 990, Part VIII, line 1h; or (ii) Form 990-EZ, line 1. Complete Parts I and II.

☐ For an organization described in section 501(c)(7), (8), or (10) filing Form 990 or 990-EZ that received from any one contributor, during the year, total contributions of more than $1,000 *exclusively* for religious, charitable, scientific, literary, or educational purposes, or for the prevention of cruelty to children or animals. Complete Parts I (entering "N/A" in column (b) instead of the contributor name and address), II, and III.

☐ For an organization described in section 501(c)(7), (8), or (10) filing Form 990 or 990-EZ that received from any one contributor, during the year, contributions *exclusively* for religious, charitable, etc., purposes, but no such contributions totaled more than $1,000. If this box is checked, enter here the total contributions that were received during the year for an *exclusively* religious, charitable, etc., purpose. Don't complete any of the parts unless the **General Rule** applies to this organization because it received *nonexclusively* religious, charitable, etc., contributions totaling $5,000 or more during the year . . . . $ ______________

Caution: An organization that isn't covered by the General Rule and/or the Special Rules doesn't file Schedule B (Form 990), but it **must** answer "No" on Part IV, line 2, of its Form 990; or check the box on line H of its Form 990-EZ or on its Form 990-PF, Part I, line 2, to certify that it doesn't meet the filing requirements of Schedule B (Form 990).

For Paperwork Reduction Act Notice, see the instructions for Form 990, 990-EZ, or 990-PF. Cat. No. 30613X **Schedule B (Form 990) (Rev. 12-2024)**

Schedule B (Form 990) (Rev. 12-2024) Page 2

Name of organization	Employer identification number

Part I **Contributors** (see instructions). Use duplicate copies of Part I if additional space is needed.

(a) No.	(b) Name, address, and ZIP + 4	(c) Total contributions	(d) Type of contribution
		$	Person ☐ Payroll ☐ Noncash ☐ (Complete Part II for noncash contributions.)

(a) No.	(b) Name, address, and ZIP + 4	(c) Total contributions	(d) Type of contribution
		$	Person ☐ Payroll ☐ Noncash ☐ (Complete Part II for noncash contributions.)

(a) No.	(b) Name, address, and ZIP + 4	(c) Total contributions	(d) Type of contribution
		$	Person ☐ Payroll ☐ Noncash ☐ (Complete Part II for noncash contributions.)

(a) No.	(b) Name, address, and ZIP + 4	(c) Total contributions	(d) Type of contribution
		$	Person ☐ Payroll ☐ Noncash ☐ (Complete Part II for noncash contributions.)

(a) No.	(b) Name, address, and ZIP + 4	(c) Total contributions	(d) Type of contribution
		$	Person ☐ Payroll ☐ Noncash ☐ (Complete Part II for noncash contributions.)

(a) No.	(b) Name, address, and ZIP + 4	(c) Total contributions	(d) Type of contribution
		$	Person ☐ Payroll ☐ Noncash ☐ (Complete Part II for noncash contributions.)

Schedule B (Form 990) (Rev. 12-2024)

Schedule B (Form 990) (Rev. 12-2024) Page **3**

Name of organization	Employer identification number

Part II **Noncash Property** (see instructions). Use duplicate copies of Part II if additional space is needed.

(a) No. from Part I	(b) Description of noncash property given	(c) FMV (or estimate) (See instructions.)	(d) Date received
		$	

(a) No. from Part I	(b) Description of noncash property given	(c) FMV (or estimate) (See instructions.)	(d) Date received
		$	

(a) No. from Part I	(b) Description of noncash property given	(c) FMV (or estimate) (See instructions.)	(d) Date received
		$	

(a) No. from Part I	(b) Description of noncash property given	(c) FMV (or estimate) (See instructions.)	(d) Date received
		$	

(a) No. from Part I	(b) Description of noncash property given	(c) FMV (or estimate) (See instructions.)	(d) Date received
		$	

(a) No. from Part I	(b) Description of noncash property given	(c) FMV (or estimate) (See instructions.)	(d) Date received
		$	

Schedule B (Form 990) (Rev. 12-2024)

Schedule B (Form 990) (Rev. 12-2024) Page **4**

Name of organization | **Employer identification number**

Part III ***Exclusively* religious, charitable, etc., contributions to organizations described in section 501(c)(7), (8), or (10) that total more than $1,000 for the year from any one contributor.** Complete columns **(a)** through **(e) and** the following line entry. For organizations completing Part III, enter the total of *exclusively* religious, charitable, etc., contributions of **$1,000 or less** for the year. (Enter this information once. See instructions.) $ ____________
Use duplicate copies of Part III if additional space is needed.

(a) No. from Part I	(b) Purpose of gift	(c) Use of gift	(d) Description of how gift is held

(e) Transfer of gift

Transferee's name, address, and ZIP + 4	Relationship of transferor to transferee

(a) No. from Part I	(b) Purpose of gift	(c) Use of gift	(d) Description of how gift is held

(e) Transfer of gift

Transferee's name, address, and ZIP + 4	Relationship of transferor to transferee

(a) No. from Part I	(b) Purpose of gift	(c) Use of gift	(d) Description of how gift is held

(e) Transfer of gift

Transferee's name, address, and ZIP + 4	Relationship of transferor to transferee

(a) No. from Part I	(b) Purpose of gift	(c) Use of gift	(d) Description of how gift is held

(e) Transfer of gift

Transferee's name, address, and ZIP + 4	Relationship of transferor to transferee

Schedule B (Form 990) (Rev. 12-2024)

SCHEDULE C (Form 990)

Department of the Treasury
Internal Revenue Service

Political Campaign and Lobbying Activities

For Organizations Exempt From Income Tax Under Section 501(c) and Section 527

Complete if the organization is described below. Attach to Form 990 or Form 990-EZ.
Go to *www.irs.gov/Form990* for instructions and the latest information.

OMB No. 1545-0047

2025

Open to Public Inspection

If the organization answered "Yes" on Form 990, Part IV, line 3, or Form 990-EZ, Part V, line 46 (Political Campaign Activities), then:

- Section 501(c)(3) organizations: Complete Parts I-A and I-B. Do not complete Part I-C.
- Section 501(c) (other than section 501(c)(3)) organizations: Complete Parts I-A and I-C below. Do not complete Part I-B.
- Section 527 organizations: Complete Part I-A only.

If the organization answered "Yes" on Form 990, Part IV, line 4, or Form 990-EZ, Part VI, line 47 (Lobbying Activities), then:

- Section 501(c)(3) organizations that have filed Form 5768 (election under section 501(h)): Complete Part II-A. Do not complete Part II-B.
- Section 501(c)(3) organizations that have NOT filed Form 5768 (election under section 501(h)): Complete Part II-B. Do not complete Part II-A.

If the organization answered "Yes" on Form 990, Part IV, line 5 (Proxy Tax) (see separate instructions), or Form 990-EZ, Part V, line 35c (Proxy Tax) (see separate instructions), then:

- Section 501(c)(4), (5), or (6) organizations: Complete Part III.

Name of organization	**Employer identification number (EIN)**

Part I-A Complete if the organization is exempt under section 501(c) or is a section 527 organization.

1 Provide a description of the organization's direct and indirect political campaign activities in Part IV. See instructions for definition of "political campaign activities."

2 Political campaign activity expenditures. See instructions . . . . $

3 Volunteer hours for political campaign activities. See instructions . . . .

Part I-B Complete if the organization is exempt under section 501(c)(3).

1 Enter the amount of any excise tax incurred by the organization under section 4955 . . . . . . $

2 Enter the amount of any excise tax incurred by organization managers under section 4955 . . . $

3 If the organization incurred a section 4955 tax, did it file Form 4720 for this year? . . . . ☐ **Yes** ☐ **No**

4a Was a correction made? . . . . ☐ **Yes** ☐ **No**

b If "Yes," describe in Part IV.

Part I-C Complete if the organization is exempt under section 501(c), except section 501(c)(3).

1 Enter the amount directly expended by the filing organization for section 527 exempt function activities . . . . $

2 Enter the amount of the filing organization's funds contributed to other organizations for section 527 exempt function activities . . . . $

3 Total exempt function expenditures. Add lines 1 and 2. Enter here and on Form 1120-POL, line 17b . . . . $

4 Did the filing organization file **Form 1120-POL** for this year? . . . . ☐ **Yes** ☐ **No**

5 Enter the names, addresses, and EINs of all section 527 political organizations to which the filing organization made payments. For each organization listed, enter the amount paid from the filing organization's funds. Also enter the amount of political contributions received that were promptly and directly delivered to a separate political organization, such as a separate segregated fund or a political action committee (PAC). If additional space is needed, provide information in Part IV.

	(a) Name	**(b)** Address	**(c)** EIN	**(d)** Amount paid from filing organization's funds. If none, enter -0-.	**(e)** Amount of political contributions received and promptly and directly delivered to a separate political organization. If none, enter -0-.
(1)					
(2)					
(3)					
(4)					
(5)					
(6)					

For Paperwork Reduction Act Notice, see the Instructions for Form 990 or 990-EZ. Cat. No. 50084S **Schedule C (Form 990) 2025** Created 7/1/25

Schedule C (Form 990) 2025 Page 2

Part II-A Complete if the organization is exempt under section 501(c)(3) and filed Form 5768 (election under section 501(h)).

A Check ☐ if the filing organization belongs to an affiliated group (and list in Part IV each affiliated group member's name, address, EIN, expenses, and share of excess lobbying expenditures).

B Check ☐ if the filing organization checked box A and "limited control" provisions apply.

	Limits on Lobbying Expenditures (The term "expenditures" means amounts paid or incurred.)	**(a)** Filing organization's totals	**(b)** Affiliated group totals
1a	Total lobbying expenditures to influence public opinion (grassroots lobbying)		
b	Total lobbying expenditures to influence a legislative body (direct lobbying)		
c	Total lobbying expenditures (add lines 1a and 1b)		
d	Other exempt purpose expenditures		
e	Total exempt purpose expenditures (add lines 1c and 1d)		
f	Lobbying nontaxable amount. Enter the amount from the following table in both columns		

IF the amount on line 1e, column (a) or (b), is:	THEN the lobbying nontaxable amount is:
not over $500,000	20% of the amount on line 1e.
over $500,000 but not over $1,000,000	$100,000 plus 15% of the excess over $500,000.
over $1,000,000 but not over $1,500,000	$175,000 plus 10% of the excess over $1,000,000.
over $1,500,000 but not over $17,000,000	$225,000 plus 5% of the excess over $1,500,000.
over $17,000,000	$1,000,000.

		(a)	(b)
g	Grassroots nontaxable amount (enter 25% of line 1f)		
h	Subtract line 1g from line 1a. If zero or less, enter -0-		
i	Subtract line 1f from line 1c. If zero or less, enter -0-		

j If there is an amount other than zero on either line 1h or line 1i, did the organization file Form 4720 reporting section 4911 tax for this year? ☐ **Yes** ☐ **No**

4-Year Averaging Period Under Section 501(h)
(Some organizations that made a section 501(h) election do not have to complete all of the five columns below. See the separate instructions for lines 2a through 2f.)

Lobbying Expenditures During 4-Year Averaging Period

	Calendar year (or fiscal year beginning in)	**(a)** 2022	**(b)** 2023	**(c)** 2024	**(d)** 2025	**(e)** Total
2a	Lobbying nontaxable amount					
b	Lobbying ceiling amount (150% of line 2a, column (e))					
c	Total lobbying expenditures					
d	Grassroots nontaxable amount					
e	Grassroots ceiling amount (150% of line 2d, column (e))					
f	Grassroots lobbying expenditures					

Schedule C (Form 990) 2025

Schedule C (Form 990) 2025 Page 3

Part II-B Complete if the organization is exempt under section 501(c)(3) and has NOT filed Form 5768 (election under section 501(h)).

For each "Yes" response on lines 1a through 1i below, provide in Part IV a detailed description of the lobbying activity.		(a) Yes	(a) No	(b) Amount
1	During the year, did the filing organization attempt to influence foreign, national, state, or local legislation, including any attempt to influence public opinion on a legislative matter or referendum, through the use of:			
a	Volunteers?			
b	Paid staff or management (include compensation in expenses reported on lines 1c through 1i)?			
c	Media advertisements?			
d	Mailings to members, legislators, or the public?			
e	Publications, or published or broadcast statements?			
f	Grants to other organizations for lobbying purposes?			
g	Direct contact with legislators, their staffs, government officials, or a legislative body?			
h	Rallies, demonstrations, seminars, conventions, speeches, lectures, or any similar means?			
i	Other activities?			
j	Total. Add lines 1c through 1i			
2a	Did the activities in line 1 cause the organization to not be described in section 501(c)(3)?			
b	If "Yes," enter the amount of any tax incurred under section 4912			
c	If "Yes," enter the amount of any tax incurred by organization managers under section 4912			
d	If the filing organization incurred a section 4912 tax, did it file Form 4720 for this year?			

Part III-A Complete if the organization is exempt under section 501(c)(4), section 501(c)(5), or section 501(c)(6).

			Yes	No
1	Were substantially all (90% or more) dues received nondeductible by members?	1		
2	Did the organization make only in-house lobbying expenditures of $2,000 or less?	2		
3	Did the organization agree to carry over lobbying and political campaign activity expenditures from the prior year?	3		

Part III-B Complete if the organization is exempt under section 501(c)(4), section 501(c)(5), or section 501(c)(6) and if either (a) BOTH Part III-A, lines 1 and 2, are answered "No;" OR (b) Part III-A, line 3, is answered "Yes."

1	Dues, assessments, and similar amounts from members	1	
2	Section 162(e) nondeductible lobbying and political expenditures **(do not include amounts of political expenses for which the section 527(f) tax was paid)**:		
a	Current year	2a	
b	Carryover from last year	2b	
c	Total	2c	
3	Aggregate amount reported in section 6033(e)(1)(A) notices of nondeductible section 162(e) dues	3	
4	If notices were sent and the amount on line 2c exceeds the amount on line 3, what portion of the excess does the organization agree to carry over to the reasonable estimate of nondeductible lobbying and political expenditures next year?	4	
5	Taxable amount of lobbying and political expenditures. See instructions	5	

Part IV Supplemental Information

Provide the descriptions required for Part I-A, line 1; Part I-B, line 4; Part I-C, line 5; Part II-A (affiliated group list); Part II-A, lines 1 and 2 (see instructions); and Part II-B, line 1. Also, complete this part for any additional information.

Schedule C (Form 990) 2025

Schedule C (Form 990) 2025 Page **4**

Part IV **Supplemental Information** *(continued)*

Schedule C (Form 990) 2025

SCHEDULE D (Form 990)
(Rev. December 2024)
Department of the Treasury
Internal Revenue Service

Supplemental Financial Statements

Complete if the organization answered "Yes" on Form 990, Part IV, line 6, 7, 8, 9, 10, 11a, 11b, 11c, 11d, 11e, 11f, 12a, or 12b.
Attach to Form 990.
Go to *www.irs.gov/Form990* for instructions and the latest information.

OMB No. 1545-0047

Open to Public Inspection

Name of the organization	**Employer identification number**

Part I Organizations Maintaining Donor Advised Funds or Other Similar Funds or Accounts

Complete if the organization answered "Yes" on Form 990, Part IV, line 6.

		(a) Donor advised funds	(b) Funds and other accounts
1	Total number at end of year		
2	Aggregate value of contributions to (during year)		
3	Aggregate value of grants from (during year)		
4	Aggregate value at end of year		

5 Did the organization inform all donors and donor advisors in writing that the assets held in donor advised funds are the organization's property, subject to the organization's exclusive legal control? ☐ Yes ☐ No

6 Did the organization inform all grantees, donors, and donor advisors in writing that grant funds can be used only for charitable purposes and not for the benefit of the donor or donor advisor, or for any other purpose conferring impermissible private benefit? ☐ Yes ☐ No

Part II Conservation Easements

Complete if the organization answered "Yes" on Form 990, Part IV, line 7.

1 Purpose(s) of conservation easements held by the organization (check all that apply).
☐ Preservation of land for public use (for example, recreation or education)
☐ Preservation of a historically important land area
☐ Protection of natural habitat
☐ Preservation of a certified historic structure
☐ Preservation of open space

2 Complete lines 2a through 2d if the organization held a qualified conservation contribution in the form of a conservation easement on the last day of the tax year.

			Held at the End of the Tax Year
a	Total number of conservation easements	2a	
b	Total acreage restricted by conservation easements	2b	
c	Number of conservation easements on a certified historic structure included on line 2a	2c	
d	Number of conservation easements included on line 2c acquired after July 25, 2006, and not on a historic structure listed in the National Register	2d	

3 Number of conservation easements modified, transferred, released, extinguished, or terminated by the organization during the tax year ________

4 Number of states where property subject to conservation easement is located ________

5 Does the organization have a written policy regarding the periodic monitoring, inspection, handling of violations, and enforcement of the conservation easements it holds? ☐ Yes ☐ No

6 Staff and volunteer hours devoted to monitoring, inspecting, handling of violations, and enforcing conservation easements during the year ________

7 Amount of expenses incurred in monitoring, inspecting, handling of violations, and enforcing conservation easements during the year $________

8 Does each conservation easement reported on line 2d above satisfy the requirements of section 170(h)(4)(B)(i) and section 170(h)(4)(B)(ii)? ☐ Yes ☐ No

9 In Part XIII, describe how the organization reports conservation easements in its revenue and expense statement and balance sheet, and include, if applicable, the text of the footnote to the organization's financial statements that describes the organization's accounting for conservation easements.

Part III Organizations Maintaining Collections of Art, Historical Treasures, or Other Similar Assets

Complete if the organization answered "Yes" on Form 990, Part IV, line 8.

1a If the organization elected, as permitted under FASB ASC 958, not to report in its revenue statement and balance sheet works of art, historical treasures, or other similar assets held for public exhibition, education, or research in furtherance of public service, provide in Part XIII the text of the footnote to its financial statements that describes these items.

b If the organization elected, as permitted under FASB ASC 958, to report in its revenue statement and balance sheet works of art, historical treasures, or other similar assets held for public exhibition, education, or research in furtherance of public service, provide the following amounts relating to these items.

(i) Revenue included on Form 990, Part VIII, line 1 $________

(ii) Assets included in Form 990, Part X $________

2 If the organization received or held works of art, historical treasures, or other similar assets for financial gain, provide the following amounts required to be reported under FASB ASC 958 relating to these items.

a Revenue included on Form 990, Part VIII, line 1 $________

b Assets included in Form 990, Part X $________

For Paperwork Reduction Act Notice, see the Instructions for Form 990. Cat. No. 52283D **Schedule D (Form 990) (Rev. 12-2024)**

Schedule D (Form 990) (Rev. 12-2024) Page **2**

Part III Organizations Maintaining Collections of Art, Historical Treasures, or Other Similar Assets *(continued)*

3 Using the organization's acquisition, accession, and other records, check any of the following that make significant use of its collection items (check all that apply).

a ☐ Public exhibition
b ☐ Scholarly research
c ☐ Preservation for future generations
d ☐ Loan or exchange program
e ☐ Other ____________

4 Provide a description of the organization's collections and explain how they further the organization's exempt purpose in Part XIII.

5 During the year, did the organization solicit or receive donations of art, historical treasures, or other similar assets to be sold to raise funds rather than to be maintained as part of the organization's collection? . . ☐ **Yes** ☐ **No**

Part IV Escrow and Custodial Arrangements

Complete if the organization answered "Yes" on Form 990, Part IV, line 9, or reported an amount on Form 990, Part X, line 21.

1a Is the organization an agent, trustee, custodian, or other intermediary for contributions or other assets not included on Form 990, Part X? . . . . ☐ **Yes** ☐ **No**

b If "Yes," explain the arrangement in Part XIII and complete the following table.

			Amount
c	Beginning balance	**1c**	
d	Additions during the year	**1d**	
e	Distributions during the year	**1e**	
f	Ending balance	**1f**	

2a Did the organization include an amount on Form 990, Part X, line 21, for escrow or custodial account liability? ☐ **Yes** ☐ **No**

b If "Yes," explain the arrangement in Part XIII. Check here if the explanation has been provided in Part XIII . . . . ☐

Part V Endowment Funds

Complete if the organization answered "Yes" on Form 990, Part IV, line 10.

		(a) Current year	**(b)** Prior year	**(c)** Two years back	**(d)** Three years back	**(e)** Four years back
1a	Beginning of year balance					
b	Contributions					
c	Net investment earnings, gains, and losses					
d	Grants or scholarships					
e	Other expenditures for facilities and programs					
f	Administrative expenses					
g	End of year balance					

2 Provide the estimated percentage of the current year end balance (line 1g, column (a)) held as:

a Board designated or quasi-endowment ________ %

b Permanent endowment ________ %

c Term endowment ________ %

The percentages on lines 2a, 2b, and 2c should equal 100%.

3a Are there endowment funds not in the possession of the organization that are held and administered for the organization by:

			Yes	No
	(i) Unrelated organizations?	**3a(i)**		
	(ii) Related organizations?	**3a(ii)**		
b	If "Yes" on line 3a(ii), are the related organizations listed as required on Schedule R?	**3b**		

4 Describe in Part XIII the intended uses of the organization's endowment funds.

Part VI Land, Buildings, and Equipment

Complete if the organization answered "Yes" on Form 990, Part IV, line 11a. See Form 990, Part X, line 10.

	Description of property	**(a)** Cost or other basis (investment)	**(b)** Cost or other basis (other)	**(c)** Accumulated depreciation	**(d)** Book value
1a	Land				
b	Buildings				
c	Leasehold improvements				
d	Equipment				
e	Other				
Total.	Add lines 1a through 1e. *(Column (d) must equal Form 990, Part X, line 10c, column (B))*				

Schedule D (Form 990) (Rev. 12-2024)

Part VII Investments—Other Securities

Complete if the organization answered "Yes" on Form 990, Part IV, line 11b. See Form 990, Part X, line 12.

(a) Description of security or category (including name of security)	(b) Book value	(c) Method of valuation: Cost or end-of-year market value
(1) Financial derivatives		
(2) Closely held equity interests		
(3) Other		
(A)		
(B)		
(C)		
(D)		
(E)		
(F)		
(G)		
(H)		
Total. *(Column (b) must equal Form 990, Part X, line 12, col. (B))*		

Part VIII Investments—Program Related

Complete if the organization answered "Yes" on Form 990, Part IV, line 11c. See Form 990, Part X, line 13.

(a) Description of investment	(b) Book value	(c) Method of valuation: Cost or end-of-year market value
(1)		
(2)		
(3)		
(4)		
(5)		
(6)		
(7)		
(8)		
(9)		
Total. *(Column (b) must equal Form 990, Part X, line 13, col. (B))*		

Part IX Other Assets

Complete if the organization answered "Yes" on Form 990, Part IV, line 11d. See Form 990, Part X, line 15.

(a) Description	(b) Book value
(1)	
(2)	
(3)	
(4)	
(5)	
(6)	
(7)	
(8)	
(9)	
Total. *(Column (b) must equal Form 990, Part X, line 15, col. (B))*	

Part X Other Liabilities

Complete if the organization answered "Yes" on Form 990, Part IV, line 11e or 11f. See Form 990, Part X, line 25.

1. (a) Description of liability	(b) Book value
(1) Federal income taxes	
(2)	
(3)	
(4)	
(5)	
(6)	
(7)	
(8)	
(9)	
Total. *(Column (b) must equal Form 990, Part X, line 25, col. (B))*	

2. Liability for uncertain tax positions. In Part XIII, provide the text of the footnote to the organization's financial statements that reports the organization's liability for uncertain tax positions under FASB ASC 740. Check here if the text of the footnote has been provided in Part XIII . ☐

Schedule D (Form 990) (Rev. 12-2024) Page 4

Part XI Reconciliation of Revenue per Audited Financial Statements With Revenue per Return
Complete if the organization answered "Yes" on Form 990, Part IV, line 12a.

1	Total revenue, gains, and other support per audited financial statements			1	
2	Amounts included on line 1 but not on Form 990, Part VIII, line 12:				
a	Net unrealized gains (losses) on investments	2a			
b	Donated services and use of facilities	2b			
c	Recoveries of prior year grants	2c			
d	Other (Describe in Part XIII.)	2d			
e	Add lines 2a through 2d			2e	
3	Subtract line 2e from line 1			3	
4	Amounts included on Form 990, Part VIII, line 12, but not on line 1:				
a	Investment expenses not included on Form 990, Part VIII, line 7b	4a			
b	Other (Describe in Part XIII.)	4b			
c	Add lines 4a and 4b			4c	
5	Total revenue. Add lines 3 and 4c. *(This must equal Form 990, Part I, line 12.)*			5	

Part XII Reconciliation of Expenses per Audited Financial Statements With Expenses per Return
Complete if the organization answered "Yes" on Form 990, Part IV, line 12a.

1	Total expenses and losses per audited financial statements			1	
2	Amounts included on line 1 but not on Form 990, Part IX, line 25:				
a	Donated services and use of facilities	2a			
b	Prior year adjustments	2b			
c	Other losses	2c			
d	Other (Describe in Part XIII.)	2d			
e	Add lines 2a through 2d			2e	
3	Subtract line 2e from line 1			3	
4	Amounts included on Form 990, Part IX, line 25, but not on line 1:				
a	Investment expenses not included on Form 990, Part VIII, line 7b	4a			
b	Other (Describe in Part XIII.)	4b			
c	Add lines 4a and 4b			4c	
5	Total expenses. Add lines 3 and 4c. *(This must equal Form 990, Part I, line 18.)*			5	

Part XIII Supplemental Information

Provide the descriptions required for Part II, lines 3, 5, and 9; Part III, lines 1a and 4; Part IV, lines 1b and 2b; Part V, line 4; Part X, line 2; Part XI, lines 2d and 4b; and Part XII, lines 2d and 4b. Also complete this part to provide any additional information.

Schedule D (Form 990) (Rev. 12-2024)

Schedule D (Form 990) (Rev. 12-2024) Page 5

Part XIII **Supplemental Information** *(continued)*

Schedule D (Form 990) (Rev. 12-2024)

SCHEDULE E (Form 990)
(Rev. December 2024)
Department of the Treasury
Internal Revenue Service

Schools

Complete if the organization answered "Yes" on Form 990, Part IV, line 13, or Form 990-EZ, Part VI, line 48.
Attach to Form 990 or Form 990-EZ.
Go to *www.irs.gov/Form990* for instructions and the latest information.

OMB No. 1545-0047

Open to Public Inspection

Name of the organization | **Employer identification number**

Part I

			YES	NO
1	Does the organization have a racially nondiscriminatory policy toward students by statement in its charter, bylaws, other governing instrument, or in a resolution of its governing body?	1		
2	Does the organization include a statement of its racially nondiscriminatory policy toward students in all its brochures, catalogues, and other written communications with the public dealing with student admissions, programs, and scholarships?	2		
3	Has the organization publicized its racially nondiscriminatory policy on its primary publicly accessible Internet homepage at all times during its tax year in a manner reasonably expected to be noticed by visitors to the homepage, or through newspaper or broadcast media during the period of solicitation for students, or during the registration period if it has no solicitation program, in a way that makes the policy known to all parts of the general community it serves? If "Yes," please describe. If "No," please explain. If you need more space, use Part II	3		
4	Does the organization maintain the following:			
a	Records indicating the racial composition of the student body, faculty, and administrative staff?	4a		
b	Records documenting that scholarships and other financial assistance are awarded on a racially nondiscriminatory basis?	4b		
c	Copies of all catalogues, brochures, announcements, and other written communications to the public dealing with student admissions, programs, and scholarships?	4c		
d	Copies of all material used by the organization or on its behalf to solicit contributions?	4d		
	If you answered "No" to any of the above, please explain. If you need more space, use Part II.			
5	Does the organization discriminate by race in any way with respect to:			
a	Students' rights or privileges?	5a		
b	Admissions policies?	5b		
c	Employment of faculty or administrative staff?	5c		
d	Scholarships or other financial assistance?	5d		
e	Educational policies?	5e		
f	Use of facilities?	5f		
g	Athletic programs?	5g		
h	Other extracurricular activities?	5h		
	If you answered "Yes" to any of the above, please explain. If you need more space, use Part II.			
6a	Does the organization receive any financial aid or assistance from a governmental agency?	6a		
b	Has the organization's right to such aid ever been revoked or suspended?	6b		
	If you answered "Yes" on either line 6a or line 6b, explain in Part II.			
7	Does the organization certify that it has complied with the applicable requirements of sections 4.01 through 4.05 of Rev. Proc. 75-50, 1975-2 C.B. 587, as modified by Rev. Proc. 2019-22, 2019-22 I.R.B. 1260, covering racial nondiscrimination? If "No," explain in Part II	7		

For Paperwork Reduction Act Notice, see the Instructions for Form 990 or 990-EZ. Cat. No. 50085D **Schedule E (Form 990) (Rev. 12-2024)**

Schedule E (Form 990) (Rev. 12-2024) Page **2**

Part II **Supplemental Information.** Provide the explanations required by Part I, lines 3, 4d, 5h, 6b, and 7, as applicable. Also provide any other additional information. See instructions.

Schedule E (Form 990) (Rev. 12-2024)

SCHEDULE F (Form 990) (Rev. December 2024) Department of the Treasury Internal Revenue Service	**Statement of Activities Outside the United States** Complete if the organization answered "Yes" on Form 990, Part IV, line 14b, 15, or 16. Attach to Form 990. Go to *www.irs.gov/Form990* for instructions and the latest information.	OMB No. 1545-0047 Open to Public Inspection

Name of the organization | Employer identification number

Part I **General Information on Activities Outside the United States.** Complete if the organization answered "Yes" on Form 990, Part IV, line 14b.

1 **For grantmakers.** Does the organization maintain records to substantiate the amount of its grants and other assistance, the grantees' eligibility for the grants or assistance, and the selection criteria used to award the grants or assistance? . . . . ☐ **Yes** ☐ **No**

2 **For grantmakers.** Describe in Part V the organization's procedures for monitoring the use of its grants and other assistance outside the United States.

3 Activities per Region. (The following Part I, line 3 table can be duplicated if additional space is needed.)

(a) Region	**(b)** Number of offices in the region	**(c)** Number of employees, agents, and independent contractors in the region	**(d)** Activities conducted in the region (by type) (such as, fundraising, program services, investments, grants to recipients located in the region)	**(e)** If activity listed in (d) is a program service, describe specific type of service(s) in the region	**(f)** Total expenditures for and investments in the region
(1)					
(2)					
(3)					
(4)					
(5)					
(6)					
(7)					
(8)					
(9)					
(10)					
(11)					
(12)					
(13)					
(14)					
(15)					
(16)					
(17)					
3a Subtotal					
b Total from continuation sheets to Part I					
c **Totals** (add lines 3a and 3b)					

For Paperwork Reduction Act Notice, see the Instructions for Form 990. Cat. No. 50082W **Schedule F (Form 990) (Rev. 12-2024)**

Schedule F (Form 990) (Rev. 12-2024) Page 2

Part II **Grants and Other Assistance to Organizations or Entities Outside the United States.** Complete if the organization answered "Yes" on Form 990, Part IV, line 15, for any recipient who received more than $5,000. Part II can be duplicated if additional space is needed.

1	(a) Name of organization	(b) IRS code section and EIN (if applicable)	(c) Region	(d) Purpose of grant	(e) Amount of cash grant	(f) Manner of cash disbursement	(g) Amount of noncash assistance	(h) Description of noncash assistance	(i) Method of valuation (book, FMV, appraisal, other)
(1)									
(2)									
(3)									
(4)									
(5)									
(6)									
(7)									
(8)									
(9)									
(10)									
(11)									
(12)									
(13)									
(14)									
(15)									
(16)									

2 Enter total number of recipient organizations listed above that are recognized as charities by the foreign country, recognized as a tax exempt 501(c)(3) organization by the IRS, or for which the grantee or counsel has provided a section 501(c)(3) equivalency letter . . .

3 Enter total number of other organizations or entities . . . .

Schedule F (Form 990) (Rev. 12-2024)

Schedule F (Form 990) (Rev. 12-2024) Page 3

Part III **Grants and Other Assistance to Individuals Outside the United States.** Complete if the organization answered "Yes" on Form 990, Part IV, line 16. Part III can be duplicated if additional space is needed.

(a) Type of grant or assistance	**(b)** Region	**(c)** Number of recipients	**(d)** Amount of cash grant	**(e)** Manner of cash disbursement	**(f)** Amount of noncash assistance	**(g)** Description of noncash assistance	**(h)** Method of valuation (book, FMV, appraisal, other)
(1)							
(2)							
(3)							
(4)							
(5)							
(6)							
(7)							
(8)							
(9)							
(10)							
(11)							
(12)							
(13)							
(14)							
(15)							
(16)							
(17)							
(18)							

Schedule F (Form 990) (Rev. 12-2024)

Schedule F (Form 990) (Rev. 12-2024) Page 4

Part IV **Foreign Forms**

1 Was the organization a U.S. transferor of property to a foreign corporation during the tax year? *If "Yes," the organization may be required to file Form 926, Return by a U.S. Transferor of Property to a Foreign Corporation (see the Instructions for Form 926)* . . . . ☐ Yes ☐ No

2 Did the organization have an interest in a foreign trust during the tax year? *If "Yes," the organization may be required to separately file Form 3520, Annual Return To Report Transactions With Foreign Trusts and Receipt of Certain Foreign Gifts, and/or Form 3520-A, Annual Information Return of Foreign Trust With a U.S. Owner (see the Instructions for Forms 3520 and 3520-A; don't file with Form 990)* . . . . ☐ Yes ☐ No

3 Did the organization have an ownership interest in a foreign corporation during the tax year? *If "Yes," the organization may be required to file Form 5471, Information Return of U.S. Persons With Respect to Certain Foreign Corporations (see the Instructions for Form 5471)* . . . . ☐ Yes ☐ No

4 Was the organization a direct or indirect shareholder of a passive foreign investment company or a qualified electing fund during the tax year? *If "Yes," the organization may be required to file Form 8621, Information Return by a Shareholder of a Passive Foreign Investment Company or Qualified Electing Fund (see the Instructions for Form 8621)* . . . . ☐ Yes ☐ No

5 Did the organization have an ownership interest in a foreign partnership during the tax year? *If "Yes," the organization may be required to file Form 8865, Return of U.S. Persons With Respect to Certain Foreign Partnerships (see the Instructions for Form 8865)* . . . . ☐ Yes ☐ No

6 Did the organization have any operations in or related to any boycotting countries during the tax year? *If "Yes," the organization may be required to separately file Form 5713, International Boycott Report (see the Instructions for Form 5713; don't file with Form 990)* . . . . ☐ Yes ☐ No

Schedule F (Form 990) (Rev. 12-2024)

Schedule F (Form 990) (Rev. 12-2024) Page 5

Part V **Supplemental Information**

Provide the information required by Part I, line 2 (monitoring of funds); Part I, line 3, column (f) (accounting method; amounts of investments vs. expenditures per region); Part II, line 1 (accounting method); Part III (accounting method); and Part III, column (c) (estimated number of recipients), as applicable. Also complete this part to provide any additional information. See instructions.

Schedule F (Form 990) (Rev. 12-2024)

SCHEDULE G (Form 990)
(Rev. December 2024)
Department of the Treasury
Internal Revenue Service

Supplemental Information Regarding Fundraising or Gaming Activities

Complete if the organization answered "Yes" on Form 990, Part IV, line 17, 18, or 19; or if the organization entered more than $15,000 on Form 990-EZ, line 6a.
Attach to Form 990 or Form 990-EZ.
Go to *www.irs.gov/Form990* for instructions and the latest information.

OMB No. 1545-0047

Open to Public Inspection

Name of the organization | **Employer identification number**

Part I **Fundraising Activities.** Complete if the organization answered "Yes" on Form 990, Part IV, line 17. Form 990-EZ filers are not required to complete this part.

1 Indicate whether the organization raised funds through any of the following activities. Check all that apply.

a ☐ Mail solicitations
b ☐ Internet and email solicitations
c ☐ Phone solicitations
d ☐ In-person solicitations
e ☐ Solicitation of nongovernment grants
f ☐ Solicitation of government grants
g ☐ Special fundraising events

2a Did the organization have a written or oral agreement with any individual (including officers, directors, trustees, or key employees listed in Form 990, Part VII) or entity in connection with professional fundraising services? ☐ **Yes** ☐ **No**

b If "Yes," list the 10 highest paid individuals or entities (fundraisers) pursuant to agreements under which the fundraiser is to be compensated at least $5,000 by the organization.

(i) Name and address of individual or entity (fundraiser)	(ii) Activity	(iii) Did fundraiser have custody or control of contributions?		(iv) Gross receipts from activity	(v) Amount paid to (or retained by) fundraiser listed in col. (i)	(vi) Amount paid to (or retained by) organization
		Yes	No			
1						
2						
3						
4						
5						
6						
7						
8						
9						
10						
Total						

3 List all states in which the organization is registered or licensed to solicit contributions or has been notified it is exempt from registration or licensing.

For Paperwork Reduction Act Notice, see the Instructions for Form 990 or 990-EZ. Cat. No. 50083H **Schedule G (Form 990) (Rev. 12-2024)**

Schedule G (Form 990) (Rev. 12-2024) Page **2**

Part II **Fundraising Events.** Complete if the organization answered "Yes" on Form 990, Part IV, line 18, or reported more than $15,000 of fundraising event contributions and gross income on Form 990-EZ, lines 1 and 6b. List events with gross receipts greater than $5,000.

			(a) Event #1 (event type)	(b) Event #2 (event type)	(c) Other events (total number)	(d) Total events (add col. (a) through col. (c))
Revenue	1	Gross receipts				
	2	Less: Contributions				
	3	Gross income (line 1 minus line 2)				
Direct Expenses	4	Cash prizes				
	5	Noncash prizes				
	6	Rent/facility costs				
	7	Food and beverages				
	8	Entertainment				
	9	Other direct expenses				
	10	Direct expense summary. Add lines 4 through 9 in column (d)				
	11	Net income summary. Subtract line 10 from line 3, column (d)				

Part III **Gaming.** Complete if the organization answered "Yes" on Form 990, Part IV, line 19, or reported more than $15,000 on Form 990-EZ, line 6a.

			(a) Bingo	(b) Pull tabs/instant bingo/progressive bingo	(c) Other gaming	(d) Total gaming (add col. (a) through col. (c))
Revenue	1	Gross revenue				
Direct Expenses	2	Cash prizes				
	3	Noncash prizes				
	4	Rent/facility costs				
	5	Other direct expenses				
	6	Volunteer labor	☐ Yes ____ % ☐ No	☐ Yes ____ % ☐ No	☐ Yes ____ % ☐ No	
	7	Direct expense summary. Add lines 2 through 5 in column (d)				
	8	Net gaming income summary. Subtract line 7 from line 1, column (d)				

9 Enter the state(s) in which the organization conducts gaming activities: ____________

a Is the organization licensed to conduct gaming activities in each of these states? ☐ Yes ☐ No

b If "No," explain: ____________

10a Were any of the organization's gaming licenses revoked, suspended, or terminated during the tax year? ☐ Yes ☐ No

b If "Yes," explain: ____________

Schedule G (Form 990) (Rev. 12-2024)

11 Does the organization conduct gaming activities with nonmembers? . . . . ☐ **Yes** ☐ **No**

12 Is the organization a grantor, beneficiary, or trustee of a trust; or a member of a partnership or other entity formed to administer charitable gaming? . . . . ☐ **Yes** ☐ **No**

13 Indicate the percentage of gaming activity conducted in:

a	The organization's facility	**13a**	%
b	An outside facility	**13b**	%

14 Enter the name and address of the person who prepares the organization's gaming/special events books and records:

Name ______________________________

Address ______________________________

15a Does the organization have a contract with a third party from whom the organization receives gaming revenue? . . . . ☐ **Yes** ☐ **No**

b If "Yes," enter the amount of gaming revenue received by the organization $ ____________ and the amount of gaming revenue retained by the third party $ ____________

c If "Yes," enter the name and address of the third party:

Name ______________________________

Address ______________________________

16 Gaming manager information:

Name ______________________________

Gaming manager compensation $ ____________

Description of services provided ______________________________

☐ Director/officer ☐ Employee ☐ Independent contractor

17 Mandatory distributions:

a Is the organization required under state law to make charitable distributions from the gaming proceeds to retain the state gaming license? . . . . ☐ **Yes** ☐ **No**

b Enter the amount of distributions required under state law to be distributed to other exempt organizations or spent in the organization's own exempt activities during the tax year . . . . . . $

Part IV **Supplemental Information.** Provide the explanations required by Part I, line 2b, columns (iii) and (v); and Part III, lines 9, 9b, 10b, 15b, 15c, 16, and 17b, as applicable. Also provide any additional information. See instructions.

SCHEDULE H (Form 990)

Department of the Treasury
Internal Revenue Service

Hospitals

Complete if the organization answered "Yes" on Form 990, Part IV, question 20a.
Attach to Form 990.
Go to *www.irs.gov/Form990* for instructions and the latest information.

OMB No. 1545-0047
2025
Open to Public Inspection

Name of the organization | **Employer identification number**

Part I **Financial Assistance and Certain Other Community Benefits at Cost**

			Yes	No
1a	Did the organization have a financial assistance policy (FAP) during the tax year? If "No," skip to question 6a	1a		
b	If "Yes," was it a written policy?	1b		
2	If the organization had multiple hospital facilities, indicate which of the following best describes application of the FAP to its various hospital facilities during the tax year. ☐ Applied uniformly to all hospital facilities ☐ Applied uniformly to most hospital facilities ☐ Generally tailored to individual hospital facilities			
3	Answer the following based on the financial assistance eligibility criteria that applied to the largest number of the organization's patients during the tax year.			
a	Did the organization use federal poverty guidelines (FPG) as a factor in determining eligibility for providing *free* care? If "Yes," indicate which of the following was the FPG family income limit for eligibility for free care:	3a		
	☐ 100% ☐ 150% ☐ 200% ☐ Other ______ %			
b	Did the organization use FPG as a factor in determining eligibility for providing *discounted* care? If "Yes," indicate which of the following was the family income limit for eligibility for discounted care:	3b		
	☐ 200% ☐ 250% ☐ 300% ☐ 350% ☐ 400% ☐ Other ______ %			
c	If the organization used factors other than FPG in determining eligibility, describe in Part VI the criteria used for determining eligibility for free or discounted care. Include in the description whether the organization used an asset test or other threshold, regardless of income, as a factor in determining eligibility for free or discounted care.			
4	Did the organization's FAP that applied to the largest number of its patients during the tax year provide for free or discounted care to the "medically indigent"?	4		
5a	Did the organization budget amounts for free or discounted care provided under its FAP during the tax year?	5a		
b	If "Yes," did the organization's financial assistance expenses exceed the budgeted amount?	5b		
c	If "Yes" to line 5b, as a result of budget considerations, was the organization unable to provide free or discounted care to a patient who was eligible for free or discounted care?	5c		
6a	Did the organization prepare a community benefit report during the tax year?	6a		
b	If "Yes," did the organization make it available to the public?	6b		
	Complete the following table using the worksheets provided in the Schedule H instructions. Do not submit these worksheets with the Schedule H.			

7 Financial Assistance and Certain Other Community Benefits at Cost

	Financial Assistance and Means-Tested Government Programs	(a) Number of activities or programs (optional)	(b) Persons served (optional)	(c) Total community benefit expense	(d) Direct offsetting revenue	(e) Net community benefit expense	(f) Percent of total expense
a	Financial assistance at cost (from Worksheet 1)						
b	Medicaid (from Worksheet 3, column a)						
c	Costs of other means-tested government programs (from Worksheet 3, column b)						
d	**Total.** Financial assistance and means-tested government programs						
	Other Benefits						
e	Community health improvement services and community benefit operations (from Worksheet 4)						
f	Health professions education (from Worksheet 5)						
g	Subsidized health services (from Worksheet 6)						
h	Research (from Worksheet 7)						
i	Cash and in-kind contributions for community benefit (from Worksheet 8)						
j	**Total.** Other benefits						
k	**Total.** Add lines 7d and 7j						

For Paperwork Reduction Act Notice, see the Instructions for Form 990. Cat. No. 50192T **Schedule H (Form 990) 2025** Created 8/13/25

Part II **Community Building Activities.** Complete this table if the organization conducted any community building activities during the tax year and describe in Part VI how its community building activities promoted the health of the communities it serves.

		(a) Number of activities or programs (optional)	(b) Persons served (optional)	(c) Total community building expense	(d) Direct offsetting revenue	(e) Net community building expense	(f) Percent of total expense
1	Physical improvements and housing						
2	Economic development						
3	Community support						
4	Environmental improvements						
5	Leadership development and training for community members						
6	Coalition building						
7	Community health improvement advocacy						
8	Workforce development						
9	Other						
10	**Total**						

Part III **Bad Debt, Medicare, & Collection Practices**

Section A. Bad Debt Expense

				Yes	No
1	Did the organization report bad debt expense in accordance with Healthcare Financial Management Association Statement No. 15?		1		
2	Enter the amount of the organization's bad debt expense. Explain in Part VI the methodology used by the organization to estimate this amount	2			
3	Enter the estimated amount of the organization's bad debt expense attributable to patients eligible under the organization's FAP. Explain in Part VI the methodology used by the organization to estimate this amount and the rationale, if any, for including this portion of bad debt as community benefit	3			
4	Provide in Part VI the text of the footnote to the organization's financial statements that describes bad debt expense or the page number on which this footnote is contained in the attached financial statements.				

Section B. Medicare

				Yes	No
5	Enter total revenue received from Medicare (including DSH and IME)	5			
6	Enter Medicare allowable costs of care relating to payments on line 5	6			
7	Subtract line 6 from line 5. This is the surplus (or shortfall)	7			
8	Describe in Part VI the extent to which any shortfall reported on line 7 should be treated as community benefit. Also describe in Part VI the costing methodology or source used to determine the amount reported on line 6. Check the box that describes the method used: ☐ Cost accounting system ☐ Cost to charge ratio ☐ Other				

Section C. Collection Practices

			Yes	No
9a	Did the organization have a written debt collection policy during the tax year?	9a		
b	If "Yes," did the organization's collection policy that applied to the largest number of its patients during the tax year contain provisions on the collection practices to be followed for patients who are known to qualify for financial assistance? Describe in Part VI	9b		

Part IV **Management Companies and Joint Ventures** (owned 10% or more by officers, directors, trustees, key employees, and physicians—see instructions)

	(a) Name of entity	(b) Description of primary activity of entity	(c) Organization's profit % or stock ownership %	(d) Officers', directors', trustees', or key employees' profit % or stock ownership %	(e) Physicians' profit % or stock ownership %
1					
2					
3					
4					
5					
6					
7					
8					
9					
10					
11					
12					
13					

Schedule H (Form 990) 2025 Page **3**

Part V Facility Information

Section A. Hospital Facilities (list in order of size, from largest to smallest—see instructions) How many hospital facilities did the organization operate during the tax year? ________ Name, address, primary website address, and state license number (and if a group return, the name and EIN of the subordinate hospital organization that operates the hospital facility):	Licensed hospital	General medical & surgical	Children's hospital	Teaching hospital	Critical access hospital	Research facility	ER-24 hours	ER-other	Other (describe)	Facility reporting group
1										
2										
3										
4										
5										
6										
7										
8										
9										
10										

Schedule H (Form 990) 2025

Part V **Facility Information** *(continued)*

Section B. Facility Policies and Practices

(complete a separate Section B for each of the hospital facilities or facility reporting groups listed in Part V, Section A)

Name of hospital facility or letter of facility reporting group: ______________________

Line number of hospital facility or line numbers of hospital facilities in a facility reporting group (from Part V, Section A): ______________

				Yes	No
Community Health Needs Assessment (CHNA)					
1		Was the hospital facility first licensed, registered, or similarly recognized by a state as a hospital facility in the current tax year or the immediately preceding tax year?	1		
2		Was the hospital facility acquired or placed into service as a tax-exempt hospital in the current tax year or the immediately preceding tax year? If "Yes," provide details of the acquisition in Section C	2		
3		During the tax year or either of the 2 immediately preceding tax years, did the hospital facility conduct a CHNA? If "No," skip to line 12	3		
		If "Yes," indicate what the CHNA report describes (check all that apply):			
a	☐	A definition of the community served by the hospital facility			
b	☐	Demographics of the community			
c	☐	Existing health care facilities and resources within the community that are available to respond to the health needs of the community			
d	☐	How data was obtained			
e	☐	The significant health needs of the community			
f	☐	Primary and chronic disease needs and other health issues of uninsured persons, low-income persons, and minority groups			
g	☐	The process for identifying and prioritizing community health needs and services to meet the community health needs			
h	☐	The process for consulting with persons representing the community's interests			
i	☐	The impact of any actions taken to address the significant health needs identified in the hospital facility's prior CHNA			
j	☐	Other (describe in Section C)			
4		Indicate the tax year the hospital facility last conducted a CHNA: 20 ____			
5		In conducting its most recent CHNA, did the hospital facility take into account input from persons who represent the broad interests of the community served by the hospital facility, including those with special knowledge of or expertise in public health? If "Yes," describe in Section C how the hospital facility took into account input from persons who represent the community, and identify the persons the hospital facility consulted	5		
6a		Was the hospital facility's CHNA conducted with one or more other hospital facilities? If "Yes," list the other hospital facilities in Section C	6a		
b		Was the hospital facility's CHNA conducted with one or more organizations other than hospital facilities? If "Yes," list the other organizations in Section C	6b		
7		Did the hospital facility make its CHNA report widely available to the public?	7		
		If "Yes," indicate how the CHNA report was made widely available (check all that apply):			
a	☐	Hospital facility's website (list url): ______________________			
b	☐	Other website (list url): ______________________			
c	☐	Made a paper copy available for public inspection without charge at the hospital facility			
d	☐	Other (describe in Section C)			
8		Did the hospital facility adopt an implementation strategy to meet the significant community health needs identified through its most recently conducted CHNA? If "No," skip to line 11	8		
9		Indicate the tax year the hospital facility last adopted an implementation strategy: 20 ____			
10		Is the hospital facility's most recently adopted implementation strategy posted on a website?	10		
a		If "Yes," list url: ______________________			
b		If "No," is the hospital facility's most recently adopted implementation strategy attached to this return?	10b		
11		Describe in Section C how the hospital facility is addressing the significant needs identified in its most recently conducted CHNA and any such needs that are not being addressed together with the reasons why such needs are not being addressed.			
12a		Did the organization incur an excise tax under section 4959 for the hospital facility's failure to conduct a CHNA as required by section 501(r)(3)?	12a		
b		If "Yes" to line 12a, did the organization file Form 4720 to report the section 4959 excise tax?	12b		
c		If "Yes" to line 12b, what is the total amount of section 4959 excise tax the organization reported on Form 4720 for all of its hospital facilities? $ ______________			

Schedule H (Form 990) 2025 Page **5**

Part V **Facility Information** *(continued)*

Financial Assistance Policy (FAP)

Name of hospital facility or letter of facility reporting group: ____________

				Yes	No
		Did the hospital facility have in place during the tax year a written FAP that:			
13		Explained eligibility criteria for financial assistance and whether such assistance included free or discounted care?	13		
		If "Yes," indicate the eligibility criteria explained in the FAP:			
a	☐	FPG, with FPG family income limit for eligibility for free care of _ _ _ % and FPG family income limit for eligibility for discounted care of _ _ _ %			
b	☐	Income level other than FPG (describe in Section C)			
c	☐	Asset level			
d	☐	Medical indigency			
e	☐	Insurance status			
f	☐	Underinsurance status			
g	☐	Residency			
h	☐	Other (describe in Section C)			
14		Explained the basis for calculating amounts charged to patients?	14		
15		Explained the method for applying for financial assistance?	15		
		If "Yes," indicate how the hospital facility's FAP or FAP application form (including accompanying instructions) explained the method for applying for financial assistance (check all that apply):			
a	☐	Described the information the hospital facility may require an individual to provide as part of their application			
b	☐	Described the supporting documentation the hospital facility may require an individual to submit as part of their application			
c	☐	Provided the contact information of hospital facility staff who can provide an individual with information about the FAP and FAP application process			
d	☐	Provided the contact information of nonprofit organizations or government agencies that may be sources of assistance with FAP applications			
e	☐	Other (describe in Section C)			
16		Was widely publicized within the community served by the hospital facility?	16		
		If "Yes," indicate how the hospital facility publicized the policy (check all that apply):			
a	☐	The FAP was widely available on a website (list url): ____________			
b	☐	The FAP application form was widely available on a website (list url): ____________			
c	☐	A plain language summary of the FAP was widely available on a website (list url): ____________			
d	☐	The FAP was available upon request and without charge (in public locations in the hospital facility and by mail)			
e	☐	The FAP application form was available upon request and without charge (in public locations in the hospital facility and by mail)			
f	☐	A plain language summary of the FAP was available upon request and without charge (in public locations in the hospital facility and by mail)			
g	☐	Individuals were notified about the FAP by being offered a paper copy of the plain language summary of the FAP, by receiving a conspicuous written notice about the FAP on their billing statements, and via conspicuous public displays or other measures reasonably calculated to attract patients' attention			
h	☐	Notified members of the community who are most likely to require financial assistance about availability of the FAP			
i	☐	The FAP, FAP application form, and plain language summary of the FAP were translated into the primary language(s) spoken by limited-English proficiency (LEP) populations			
j	☐	Other (describe in Section C)			

Schedule H (Form 990) 2025

Part V Facility Information *(continued)*

Billing and Collections

Name of hospital facility or letter of facility reporting group: ____________

				Yes	No
17	Did the hospital facility have in place during the tax year a separate billing and collections policy, or a written FAP that explained all of the actions the hospital facility or other authorized party may take upon nonpayment?		**17**		
18	Check all of the following actions against an individual that were permitted under the hospital facility's policies during the tax year before making reasonable efforts to determine the individual's eligibility under the facility's FAP:				
a	☐ Reporting to credit agency(ies)				
b	☐ Selling an individual's debt to another party				
c	☐ Deferring, denying, or requiring a payment before providing medically necessary care due to nonpayment of a previous bill for care covered under the hospital facility's FAP				
d	☐ Actions that require a legal or judicial process				
e	☐ Other similar actions (describe in Section C)				
f	☐ None of these actions or other similar actions were permitted				
19	Did the hospital facility or other authorized party perform any of the following actions during the tax year before making reasonable efforts to determine the individual's eligibility under the facility's FAP?		**19**		
	If "Yes," check all actions in which the hospital facility or a third party engaged:				
a	☐ Reporting to credit agency(ies)				
b	☐ Selling an individual's debt to another party				
c	☐ Deferring, denying, or requiring a payment before providing medically necessary care due to nonpayment of a previous bill for care covered under the hospital facility's FAP				
d	☐ Actions that require a legal or judicial process				
e	☐ Other similar actions (describe in Section C)				

20 Indicate which efforts the hospital facility or other authorized party made before initiating any of the actions listed (whether or not checked) on line 19 (check all that apply):

- **a** ☐ Provided a written notice about upcoming extraordinary collection actions (ECAs) and a plain language summary of the FAP at least 30 days before initiating those ECAs (if not, describe in Section C)
- **b** ☐ Made a reasonable effort to orally notify individuals about the FAP and FAP application process (if not, describe in Section C)
- **c** ☐ Processed incomplete and complete FAP applications (if not, describe in Section C)
- **d** ☐ Made presumptive eligibility determinations (if not, describe in Section C)
- **e** ☐ Other (describe in Section C)
- **f** ☐ None of these efforts were made

Policy Relating to Emergency Medical Care

				Yes	No
21	Did the hospital facility have in place during the tax year a written policy relating to emergency medical care that required the hospital facility to provide, without discrimination, care for emergency medical conditions to individuals regardless of their eligibility under the hospital facility's FAP?		**21**		
	If "No," indicate why:				
a	☐ The hospital facility did not provide care for any emergency medical conditions				
b	☐ The hospital facility's policy was not in writing				
c	☐ The hospital facility limited who was eligible to receive care for emergency medical conditions (describe in Section C)				
d	☐ Other (describe in Section C)				

Schedule H (Form 990) 2025 Page **7**

Part V **Facility Information** *(continued)*

Charges to Individuals Eligible for Assistance Under the FAP (FAP-Eligible Individuals)

Name of hospital facility or letter of facility reporting group: ____________________

			Yes	No
22	Indicate how the hospital facility determined, during the tax year, the maximum amounts that can be charged to FAP-eligible individuals for emergency or other medically necessary care:			
a	☐ The hospital facility used a look-back method based on claims allowed by Medicare fee-for-service during a prior 12-month period			
b	☐ The hospital facility used a look-back method based on claims allowed by Medicare fee-for-service and all private health insurers that pay claims to the hospital facility during a prior 12-month period			
c	☐ The hospital facility used a look-back method based on claims allowed by Medicaid, either alone or in combination with Medicare fee-for-service and all private health insurers that pay claims to the hospital facility during a prior 12-month period			
d	☐ The hospital facility used a prospective Medicare or Medicaid method			
23	During the tax year, did the hospital facility charge any FAP-eligible individual to whom the hospital facility provided emergency or other medically necessary services more than the amounts generally billed to individuals who had insurance covering such care?	**23**		
	If "Yes," explain in Section C.			
24	During the tax year, did the hospital facility charge any FAP-eligible individual an amount equal to the gross charge for any service provided to that individual?	**24**		
	If "Yes," explain in Section C.			

Schedule H (Form 990) 2025

Part V **Facility Information** *(continued)*

Section C. Supplemental Information for Part V, Section B. Provide descriptions required for Part V, Section B, lines 2, 3j, 5, 6a, 6b, 7d, 11, 13b, 13h, 15e, 16j, 18e, 19e, 20a, 20b, 20c, 20d, 20e, 21c, 21d, 23, and 24. If applicable, provide separate descriptions for each hospital facility in a facility reporting group, designated by facility reporting group letter and hospital facility line number from Part V, Section A ("A, 1," "A, 4," "B, 2," "B, 3," etc.) and name of hospital facility.

Schedule H (Form 990) 2025 Page 9

Part V **Facility Information** *(continued)*

Section D. Other Health Care Facilities That Are Not Licensed, Registered, or Similarly Recognized as a Hospital Facility
(list in order of size, from largest to smallest)

How many non-hospital health care facilities did the organization operate during the tax year? ______________

Name and address	Type of facility (describe)
1	
2	
3	
4	
5	
6	
7	
8	
9	
10	

Schedule H (Form 990) 2025

Part VI Supplemental Information

Provide the following information.

1 **Required descriptions.** Provide the descriptions required for Part I, lines 3c, 6a, and 7; Part II, and Part III, lines 2, 3, 4, 8, and 9b.

2 **Needs assessment.** Describe how the organization assesses the health care needs of the communities it serves, in addition to any CHNAs reported in Part V, Section B.

3 **Patient education of eligibility for assistance.** Describe how the organization informs and educates patients and persons who may be billed for patient care about their eligibility for assistance under federal, state, or local government programs or under the organization's FAP.

4 **Community information.** Describe the community the organization serves, taking into account the geographic area and demographic constituents it serves.

5 **Promotion of community health.** Provide any other information important to describing how the organization's hospital facilities or other health care facilities further its exempt purpose by promoting the health of the community (for example, open medical staff, community board, use of surplus funds, etc.).

6 **Affiliated health care system.** If the organization is part of an affiliated health care system, describe the respective roles of the organization and its affiliates in promoting the health of the communities served.

7 **State filing of community benefit report.** If applicable, identify all states with which the organization, or a related organization, files a community benefit report.

SCHEDULE I (Form 990)

(Rev. December 2024)

Department of the Treasury
Internal Revenue Service

Grants and Other Assistance to Organizations, Governments, and Individuals in the United States

Complete if the organization answered "Yes" on Form 990, Part IV, line 21 or 22.

Attach to Form 990.

Go to *www.irs.gov/Form990* for instructions and the latest information.

OMB No. 1545-0047

Open to Public Inspection

Name of the organization | **Employer identification number**

Part I — General Information on Grants and Assistance

1 Does the organization maintain records to substantiate the amount of the grants or assistance, the grantees' eligibility for the grants or assistance, and the selection criteria used to award the grants or assistance? . . . . ☐ **Yes** ☐ **No**

2 Describe in Part IV the organization's procedures for monitoring the use of grant funds in the United States.

Part II — Grants and Other Assistance to Domestic Organizations and Domestic Governments. Complete if the organization answered "Yes" on Form 990, Part IV, line 21, for any recipient that received more than $5,000. Part II can be duplicated if additional space is needed.

1 (a) Name and address of organization or government	(b) EIN	(c) IRC section (if applicable)	(d) Amount of cash grant	(e) Amount of noncash assistance	(f) Method of valuation (book, FMV, appraisal, other)	(g) Description of noncash assistance	(h) Purpose of grant or assistance
(1)							
(2)							
(3)							
(4)							
(5)							
(6)							
(7)							
(8)							
(9)							
(10)							
(11)							
(12)							

2 Enter total number of section 501(c)(3) and government organizations listed in the line 1 table . . . .

3 Enter total number of other organizations listed in the line 1 table . . . .

For Paperwork Reduction Act Notice, see the Instructions for Form 990. Cat. No. 50055P **Schedule I (Form 990) (Rev. 12-2024)**

Part III **Grants and Other Assistance to Domestic Individuals.** Complete if the organization answered "Yes" on Form 990, Part IV, line 22. Part III can be duplicated if additional space is needed.

	(a) Type of grant or assistance	(b) Number of recipients	(c) Amount of cash grant	(d) Amount of noncash assistance	(e) Method of valuation (book, FMV, appraisal, other)	(f) Description of noncash assistance
1						
2						
3						
4						
5						
6						
7						

Part IV **Supplemental Information.** Provide the information required in Part I, line 2; Part III, column (b); and any other additional information.

SCHEDULE J
(Form 990)
(Rev. December 2024)
Department of the Treasury
Internal Revenue Service

Compensation Information

For certain Officers, Directors, Trustees, Key Employees, and Highest Compensated Employees
Complete if the organization answered "Yes" on Form 990, Part IV, line 23.
Attach to Form 990.
Go to *www.irs.gov/Form990* for instructions and the latest information.

OMB No. 1545-0047

Open to Public Inspection

Name of the organization | **Employer identification number**

Part I Questions Regarding Compensation

			Yes	No
1a	Check the appropriate box(es) if the organization provided any of the following to or for a person listed on Form 990, Part VII, Section A, line 1a. Complete Part III to provide any relevant information regarding these items. ☐ First-class or charter travel ☐ Housing allowance or residence for personal use ☐ Travel for companions ☐ Payments for business use of personal residence ☐ Tax indemnification and gross-up payments ☐ Health or social club dues or initiation fees ☐ Discretionary spending account ☐ Personal services (such as maid, chauffeur, chef)			
b	If any of the boxes on line 1a are checked, did the organization follow a written policy regarding payment or reimbursement or provision of all of the expenses described above? If "No," complete Part III to explain . . .	**1b**		
2	Did the organization require substantiation prior to reimbursing or allowing expenses incurred by all directors, trustees, and officers, including the CEO/Executive Director, regarding the items checked on line 1a? . . .	**2**		
3	Indicate which, if any, of the following the organization used to establish the compensation of the organization's CEO/Executive Director. Check all that apply. Do not check any boxes for methods used by a related organization to establish compensation of the CEO/Executive Director, but explain in Part III. ☐ Compensation committee ☐ Written employment contract ☐ Independent compensation consultant ☐ Compensation survey or study ☐ Form 990 of other organizations ☐ Approval by the board or compensation committee			
4	During the year, did any person listed on Form 990, Part VII, Section A, line 1a, with respect to the filing organization or a related organization:			
a	Receive a severance payment or change-of-control payment? . . .	**4a**		
b	Participate in or receive payment from a supplemental nonqualified retirement plan? . . .	**4b**		
c	Participate in or receive payment from an equity-based compensation arrangement? . . . If "Yes" to any of lines 4a–c, list the persons and provide the applicable amounts for each item in Part III.	**4c**		
	Only section 501(c)(3), 501(c)(4), and 501(c)(29) organizations must complete lines 5–9.			
5	For persons listed on Form 990, Part VII, Section A, line 1a, did the organization pay or accrue any compensation contingent on the revenues of:			
a	The organization? . . .	**5a**		
b	Any related organization? . . . If "Yes" on line 5a or 5b, describe in Part III.	**5b**		
6	For persons listed on Form 990, Part VII, Section A, line 1a, did the organization pay or accrue any compensation contingent on the net earnings of:			
a	The organization? . . .	**6a**		
b	Any related organization? . . . If "Yes" on line 6a or 6b, describe in Part III.	**6b**		
7	For persons listed on Form 990, Part VII, Section A, line 1a, did the organization provide any nonfixed payments not described on lines 5 and 6? If "Yes," describe in Part III . . .	**7**		
8	Were any amounts reported on Form 990, Part VII, paid or accrued pursuant to a contract that was subject to the initial contract exception described in Regulations section 53.4958-4(a)(3)? If "Yes," describe in Part III . . .	**8**		
9	If "Yes" on line 8, did the organization also follow the rebuttable presumption procedure described in Regulations section 53.4958-6(c)? . . .	**9**		

For Paperwork Reduction Act Notice, see the Instructions for Form 990. Cat. No. 50053T **Schedule J (Form 990) (Rev. 12-2024)**

Part II Officers, Directors, Trustees, Key Employees, and Highest Compensated Employees. Use duplicate copies if additional space is needed.

For each individual whose compensation must be reported on Schedule J, report compensation from the organization on row (i) and from related organizations, described in the instructions, on row (ii). Do not list any individuals that aren't listed on Form 990, Part VII.

Note: The sum of columns (B)(i)–(iii) for each listed individual must equal the total amount of Form 990, Part VII, Section A, line 1a, applicable column (D) and (E) amounts for that individual.

(A) Name and Title		(B) Breakdown of W-2 and/or 1099-MISC and/or 1099-NEC compensation			(C) Retirement and other deferred compensation	(D) Nontaxable benefits	(E) Total of columns (B)(i)–(D)	(F) Compensation in column (B) reported as deferred on prior Form 990
		(i) Base compensation	(ii) Bonus & incentive compensation	(iii) Other reportable compensation				
1	(i)							
	(ii)							
2	(i)							
	(ii)							
3	(i)							
	(ii)							
4	(i)							
	(ii)							
5	(i)							
	(ii)							
6	(i)							
	(ii)							
7	(i)							
	(ii)							
8	(i)							
	(ii)							
9	(i)							
	(ii)							
10	(i)							
	(ii)							
11	(i)							
	(ii)							
12	(i)							
	(ii)							
13	(i)							
	(ii)							
14	(i)							
	(ii)							
15	(i)							
	(ii)							
16	(i)							
	(ii)							

Part III **Supplemental Information**

Provide the information, explanation, or descriptions required for Part I, lines 1a, 1b, 3, 4a, 4b, 4c, 5a, 5b, 6a, 6b, 7, and 8, and for Part II. Also complete this part for any additional information.

SCHEDULE K (Form 990)
(Rev. December 2024)
Department of the Treasury Internal Revenue Service

Supplemental Information on Tax-Exempt Bonds

Complete if the organization answered "Yes" on Form 990, Part IV, line 24a. Provide descriptions, explanations, and any additional information in Part VI.
Attach to Form 990.
Go to *www.irs.gov/Form990* for instructions and the latest information.

OMB No. 1545-0047
Open to Public Inspection

Name of the organization	Employer identification number

Part I Bond Issues

	(a) Issuer name	(b) Issuer EIN	(c) CUSIP #	(d) Date issued	(e) Issue price	(f) Description of purpose	(g) Defeased		(h) On behalf of issuer		(i) Pooled financing	
							Yes	No	Yes	No	Yes	No
A												
B												
C												
D												

Part II Proceeds

		A	B	C	D
1	Amount of bonds retired				
2	Amount of bonds legally defeased				
3	Total proceeds of issue				
4	Gross proceeds in reserve funds				
5	Capitalized interest from proceeds				
6	Proceeds in refunding escrows				
7	Issuance costs from proceeds				
8	Credit enhancement from proceeds				
9	Working capital expenditures from proceeds				
10	Capital expenditures from proceeds				
11	Other spent proceeds				
12	Other unspent proceeds				
13	Year of substantial completion				

		A Yes	A No	B Yes	B No	C Yes	C No	D Yes	D No
14	Were the bonds issued as part of a refunding issue of tax-exempt bonds (or, if issued prior to 2018, a current refunding issue)?								
15	Were the bonds issued as part of a refunding issue of taxable bonds (or, if issued prior to 2018, an advance refunding issue)?								
16	Has the final allocation of proceeds been made?								
17	Does the organization maintain adequate books and records to support the final allocation of proceeds?								

For Paperwork Reduction Act Notice, see the Instructions for Form 990. Cat. No. 50193E **Schedule K (Form 990) (Rev. 12-2024)**

Schedule K (Form 990) (Rev. 12-2024) Page 2

Part III Private Business Use

		A		B		C		D	
		Yes	No	Yes	No	Yes	No	Yes	No
1	Was the organization a partner in a partnership, or a member of an LLC, which owned property financed by tax-exempt bonds?								
2	Are there any lease arrangements that may result in private business use of bond-financed property?								
3a	Are there any management or service contracts that may result in private business use of bond-financed property?								
b	If "Yes" to line 3a, does the organization routinely engage bond counsel or other outside counsel to review any management or service contracts relating to the financed property?								
c	Are there any research agreements that may result in private business use of bond-financed property?								
d	If "Yes" to line 3c, does the organization routinely engage bond counsel or other outside counsel to review any research agreements relating to the financed property?								
4	Enter the percentage of financed property used in a private business use by entities other than a section 501(c)(3) organization or a state or local government		%		%		%		%
5	Enter the percentage of financed property used in a private business use as a result of unrelated trade or business activity carried on by your organization, another section 501(c)(3) organization, or a state or local government		%		%		%		%
6	Total of lines 4 and 5		%		%		%		%
7	Does the bond issue meet the private security or payment test?								
8a	Has there been a sale or disposition of any of the bond-financed property to a nongovernmental person other than a 501(c)(3) organization since the bonds were issued?								
b	If "Yes" to line 8a, enter the percentage of bond-financed property sold or disposed of		%		%		%		%
c	If "Yes" to line 8a, was any remedial action taken pursuant to Regulations sections 1.141-12 and 1.145-2?								
9	Has the organization established written procedures to ensure that all nonqualified bonds of the issue are remediated in accordance with the requirements under Regulations sections 1.141-12 and 1.145-2?								

Part IV Arbitrage

		A		B		C		D	
		Yes	No	Yes	No	Yes	No	Yes	No
1	Has the issuer filed Form 8038-T, Arbitrage Rebate, Yield Reduction and Penalty in Lieu of Arbitrage Rebate?								
2	If "No" to line 1, did the following apply?								
a	Rebate not due yet?								
b	Exception to rebate?								
c	No rebate due?								
	If "Yes" to line 2c, provide in Part VI the date the rebate computation was performed								
3	Is the bond issue a variable rate issue?								

Schedule K (Form 990) (Rev. 12-2024)

Part IV Arbitrage *(continued)*

		A		B		C		D	
		Yes	No	Yes	No	Yes	No	Yes	No
4a	Has the organization or the governmental issuer entered into a qualified hedge with respect to the bond issue?								
b	Name of provider								
c	Term of hedge								
d	Was the hedge superintegrated?								
e	Was the hedge terminated?								
5a	Were gross proceeds invested in a guaranteed investment contract (GIC)?								
b	Name of provider								
c	Term of GIC								
d	Was the regulatory safe harbor for establishing the fair market value of the GIC satisfied?								
6	Were any gross proceeds invested beyond an available temporary period?								
7	Has the organization established written procedures to monitor the requirements of section 148?								

Part V Procedures To Undertake Corrective Action

	A		B		C		D	
	Yes	No	Yes	No	Yes	No	Yes	No
Has the organization established written procedures to ensure that violations of federal tax requirements are timely identified and corrected through the voluntary closing agreement program if self-remediation isn't available under applicable regulations?								

Part VI Supplemental Information. Provide additional information for responses to questions on Schedule K. See instructions.

Schedule K (Form 990) (Rev. 12-2024) Page **4**

Part VI **Supplemental Information.** Provide additional information for responses to questions on Schedule K. See instructions. *(continued)*

Schedule K (Form 990) (Rev. 12-2024)

SCHEDULE L (Form 990)
(Rev. December 2024)
Department of the Treasury
Internal Revenue Service

Transactions With Interested Persons

Complete if the organization answered "Yes" on Form 990, Part IV, line 25a, 25b, 26, 27, 28a, 28b, or 28c; or Form 990-EZ, Part V, line 38a or 40b.
Attach to Form 990 or Form 990-EZ.
Go to *www.irs.gov/Form990* for instructions and the latest information.

OMB No. 1545-0047

Open to Public Inspection

Name of the organization | **Employer identification number**

Part I **Excess Benefit Transactions** (section 501(c)(3), section 501(c)(4), and section 501(c)(29) organizations only)
Complete if the organization answered "Yes" on Form 990, Part IV, line 25a or 25b; or Form 990-EZ, Part V, line 40b.

1	**(a)** Name of disqualified person	**(b)** Relationship between disqualified person and organization	**(c)** Description of transaction	**(d)** Corrected?	
				Yes	**No**
(1)					
(2)					
(3)					
(4)					
(5)					
(6)					

2 Enter the amount of tax incurred by the organization managers or disqualified persons during the year under section 4958 . . . . . $______

3 Enter the amount of tax, if any, on line 2, above, reimbursed by the organization . . . . . $______

Part II **Loans to and/or From Interested Persons**
Complete if the organization answered "Yes" on Form 990-EZ, Part V, line 38a, or Form 990, Part IV, line 26; or if the organization reported an amount on Form 990, Part X, line 5, 6, or 22.

	(a) Name of interested person	**(b)** Relationship with organization	**(c)** Purpose of loan	**(d)** Loan to or from the organization?		**(e)** Original principal amount	**(f)** Balance due	**(g)** In default?		**(h)** Approved by board or committee?		**(i)** Written agreement?	
				To	From			**Yes**	**No**	**Yes**	**No**	**Yes**	**No**
(1)													
(2)													
(3)													
(4)													
(5)													
(6)													
(7)													
(8)													
(9)													
(10)													
Total							$						

Part III **Grants or Assistance Benefiting Interested Persons**
Complete if the organization answered "Yes" on Form 990, Part IV, line 27.

	(a) Name of interested person	**(b)** Relationship between interested person and the organization	**(c)** Amount of assistance	**(d)** Type of assistance	**(e)** Purpose of assistance
(1)					
(2)					
(3)					
(4)					
(5)					
(6)					
(7)					
(8)					
(9)					
(10)					

For Paperwork Reduction Act Notice, see the instructions for Form 990 or 990-EZ. Cat. No. 50056A **Schedule L (Form 990) (Rev. 12-2024)**

Schedule L (Form 990) (Rev. 12-2024) Page 2

Part IV **Business Transactions Involving Interested Persons**
Complete if the organization answered "Yes" on Form 990, Part IV, line 28a, 28b, or 28c.

	(a) Name of interested person	(b) Relationship between interested person and the organization	(c) Amount of transaction	(d) Description of transaction	(e) Sharing of organization's revenues? Yes	No
(1)						
(2)						
(3)						
(4)						
(5)						
(6)						
(7)						
(8)						
(9)						
(10)						

Part V **Supplemental Information**
Provide additional information for responses to questions on Schedule L. See instructions.

Schedule L (Form 990) (Rev. 12-2024)

SCHEDULE M (Form 990)

Department of the Treasury
Internal Revenue Service

Noncash Contributions

Complete if the organizations answered "Yes" on Form 990, Part IV, line 29 or 30.
Attach to Form 990.
Go to *www.irs.gov/Form990* for instructions and the latest information.

OMB No. 1545-0047

2025

Open to Public Inspection

Name of the organization | **Employer identification number**

Part I Types of Property

		(a) Check if applicable	(b) Number of contributions or items contributed	(c) Noncash contribution amounts reported on Form 990, Part VIII, line 1g	(d) Method of determining noncash contribution amounts
1	Art—Works of art				
2	Art—Historical treasures				
3	Art—Fractional interests				
4	Books and publications				
5	Clothing and household goods				
6	Cars and other vehicles				
7	Boats and planes				
8	Intellectual property				
9	Securities—Publicly traded				
10	Securities—Closely held stock				
11	Securities—Partnership, LLC, or trust interests				
12	Securities—Miscellaneous				
13	Qualified conservation contribution—Historic structures				
14	Qualified conservation contribution—Other				
15	Real estate—Residential				
16	Real estate—Commercial				
17	Real estate—Other				
18	Collectibles				
19	Food inventory				
20	Drugs and medical supplies				
21	Taxidermy				
22	Historical artifacts				
23	Scientific specimens				
24	Archeological artifacts				
25	Other ( )				
26	Other ( )				
27	Other ( )				
28	Other ( )				

			Yes	No
29	Number of Forms 8283 received by the organization during the tax year for contributions for which the organization completed Form 8283, Part V, Donee Acknowledgment	29		
30a	During the year, did the organization receive by contribution any property reported in Part I, lines 1 through 28, that it must hold for at least 3 years from the date of the initial contribution, and which isn't required to be used for exempt purposes for the entire holding period?	30a		
b	If "Yes," describe the arrangement in Part II.			
31	Does the organization have a gift acceptance policy that requires the review of any nonstandard contributions?	31		
32a	Does the organization hire or use third parties or related organizations to solicit, process, or sell noncash contributions?	32a		
b	If "Yes," describe in Part II.			
33	If the organization didn't report an amount in column (c) for a type of property for which column (a) is checked, describe in Part II.			

For Paperwork Reduction Act Notice, see the Instructions for Form 990. Cat. No. 51227J **Schedule M (Form 990) 2025** Created 12/29/25

Schedule M (Form 990) 2025 Page **2**

Part II **Supplemental Information.** Provide the information required by Part I, lines 30b, 32b, and 33, and whether the organization is reporting in Part I, column (b), the number of contributions, the number of items received, or a combination of both. Also, complete this part for any additional information.

Schedule M (Form 990) 2025

General Instructions

Section references are to the Internal Revenue Code unless otherwise noted.

Future developments. For the latest information about developments related to Schedule M (Form 990), such as legislation enacted after the schedule and its instructions were published, go to *www.irs.gov/Form990*.

Note: Terms in **bold** are defined in the *Glossary* of the Instructions for Form 990.

Purpose of Schedule

Schedule M (Form 990) is used by an organization that files Form 990 to report the types of **noncash contributions** received during the year by the organization and certain information regarding such **contributions**. The schedule requires reporting of the quantity and the reported financial statement amount of noncash contributions received by type of property. Report noncash donated items even if sold immediately after received. Don't report noncash contributions received by the organization in a prior year. Don't report donations of services or the donated use of facilities, equipment, or materials donated.

Who Must File

An organization that answered "Yes" to Form 990, Part IV, line 29 or 30, must complete Schedule M (Form 990) and attach it to Form 990. This means an organization that reported more than $25,000 of aggregate **noncash contributions** on Form 990, Part VIII, line 1g, or that during the year received **contributions** of **art, historical treasures**, or other similar assets, or **qualified conservation contributions**, regardless of whether it reported any revenues for such contributions in Part VIII.

If an organization isn't required to file Form 990 but chooses to do so, it must file a complete return and provide all of the information requested, including the required schedules.

Specific Instructions

Part I. Types of Property

Column (a). Check the box if during the year the organization received any contributions of the property type identified.

Column (b). For each type of property received during the year, enter the number of **contributions** or the number of items contributed, determined in accordance with the organization's recordkeeping practices. Explain in Part II of this schedule whether the organization is reporting the number of contributions or the number of items received, or a combination of both methods. As described below, for contributions of securities, such as publicly traded stock, treat each separate gift (rather than each share received) as an item for this purpose.

Organizations that receive contributions of books, publications, clothing, and household goods aren't required to complete column (b) for those items reported on lines 4 and 5.

Columns (c)–(d). In column (c), enter the revenues reported on Form 990, Part VIII, line 1g, for the appropriate property type. If none were reported, enter "-0-."

In column (d), describe the method used to determine the amount reported on Form 990, Part VIII, line 1g (for example, cost or selling price of the donated property, sale of comparable properties, replacement cost, opinions of experts, etc.). See Pub. 561, Determining the Value of Donated Property, for more information.

Example 1. A used car in poor condition is donated to a local high school for use by students studying car repair. A used car guide shows the dealer retail value for this type of car in poor condition is $1,600. However, the guide shows the price for a private party sale of the car is only $750. The fair market value of the car is considered to be $750, which is the amount the organization reported on Form 990, Part VIII, line 1g. In column (c), the organization should enter $750. In column (d), the organization should enter "sale of comparable properties and/or opinion of expert" as the method used to determine fair market value.

Example 2. An organization primarily receives bulk donations of clothing, household goods, and other similar items, intended for resale. Under its permitted financial reporting practices, it doesn't recognize or record revenue at the time of receipt of the contribution, but instead records such items in inventory and reports contribution revenues at the time of sale based on prior inventory turnover experience. In column (c), the organization can enter the amount that represents the total estimated amount of annual sales revenue for each type of property received under its permitted financial reporting method, and in column (d), enter "resale value or annual sales revenue" as the method of determining revenue.

Museums and other organizations that don't report contributions of **art**, **historical treasures**, and other similar items as revenue, as permitted under generally accepted accounting principles, enter "-0-" in column (c) and leave column (d) blank. The organization can explain in Part II that a zero amount was reported on Form 990, Part VIII, line 1g, because the museum did not capitalize its collections, as allowed under Financial Accounting Standards Board Accounting Standards Codification 958-360-25 (ASC 958-360-25).

An organization that received **qualified conservation contributions** or **conservation easements** must report column (c) revenue consistent with how it reports revenue from such contributions in its books, records, and financial statements. The organization must also report revenue from such qualified conservation contributions and conservation easements consistently with how it reports such revenue in Form 990, Part VIII.

Line 1. Works of art include paintings, sculptures, prints, drawings, ceramics, antiques, decorative arts, textiles, carpets, silver, photography, film, video, installation and multimedia arts, rare books and manuscripts, historical memorabilia, and other similar objects. Works of art don't include **collectibles** reported on line 18 or taxidermy reported on line 21.

Line 2. An **historical treasure** is a building, structure, area, or property with recognized cultural, aesthetic, or historical value that is significant in the history, architecture, archeology, or culture of a country, state, or city.

Line 3. A **contribution** of a fractional interest in art is a contribution, not in trust, of an undivided portion of a donor's entire interest in a **work of art**. A contribution of the donor's entire interest must consist of a part of each substantial interest or right the donor owns in such work of art and must extend over the entire term of the donor's interest in the property. A gift generally is treated as a gift of an undivided portion of a donor's entire interest in property if the donee is given the right, as a tenant in common with the donor, to possession, dominion, and control of the property for a portion of each year appropriate to its interest in such property. For each work of art or item, report in column (b) the fractional interest for each year an interest in the property is received for the underlying work of art or item. See section 170(o) for special rules for fractional gifts.

Line 4. Enter information about **contributions** of all books and publications. Don't include rare books and manuscripts reported on line 1, **collectibles** reported on line 18, and archival records reported on lines 25 through 28.

Line 5. Enter information about clothing items and **household goods** that were in good used condition or better. Clothing items and household goods that weren't in good used condition or better are to be reported as a separate type in "Other" beginning with line 25.

Lines 6–7. On line 6, include only **contributions** of motor vehicles manufactured primarily for use on public streets, roads, and highways. Don't include on line 6 or 7 contributions of the donor's stock in trade or property held by the donor primarily for sale to customers in the ordinary course of a trade or business. The organization is required to furnish to the donor and file with the IRS Form 1098-C, Contributions of Motor Vehicles, Boats, and Airplanes, for contributions reported on these lines. See Form 990, Part V, line 7h.

Line 8. Intellectual property is any patent, copyright (other than a copyright described in section 1221(a)(3) or 1231(b)(1)(C)), trademark, trade name, trade secret, know-how, software (other than software described in section 197(e)(3)(A)(i)), or similar property. The organization is required to furnish to the donor and file with the IRS Form 8899, Notice of Income From Donated Intellectual Property, for certain contributions on this line. See Form 990, Part V, line 7g.

Line 9. Publicly traded securities means **securities** for which (as of the date of the contribution) market quotations are readily available on an established securities market. For each **security**, treat each separate gift (rather than each share received) as a **contribution** for this purpose. Include on this line interests in publicly traded partnerships, limited liability companies or trusts, and publicly traded corporations.

Line 10. Closely held stock means shares of stock issued by a corporation that isn't publicly traded. For each **security**, treat each separate gift (rather than each share received) as a **contribution** for this purpose.

Line 11. Enter information about **contributions** of interests in a partnership, limited liability company, or trust that isn't publicly traded. For each **security**, treat each separate gift (rather than each share received) as a contribution for this purpose.

Line 12. Enter information about **contributions** of **securities** that aren't reported on lines 9 through 11. For each **security**, treat each separate gift (rather than each share received) as a contribution for this purpose.

Lines 13–14. A **qualified conservation contribution** is a contribution of a qualified real property interest to a qualified organization exclusively for conservation purposes. A qualified real property interest means any of the following interests in real property.

1. The entire interest of the donor.

2. A remainder interest.

3. A restriction (an easement), granted in perpetuity, on the use that may be made of the real property.

A **qualified organization** means an organization that is:

1. A **governmental unit** described in section 170(c)(1);

2. A publicly supported charitable organization described in sections 501(c)(3) and 170(b)(1)(A)(vi) or section 509(a)(2) (see the instructions for Parts II and III of Schedule A (Form 990)), or

3. A **supporting organization** described in sections 501(c)(3) and 509(a)(3) that is controlled by a governmental unit or a publicly supported charitable organization.

In addition, a qualified organization must have a commitment to protect the conservation purposes of a qualified conservation contribution, and have the resources to enforce those restrictions.

A **conservation purpose** means:

1. The preservation of land areas for outdoor recreation used by, or for the education of, the general public;

2. The protection of a relatively natural habitat of fish, wildlife, plants, or similar ecosystems;

3. The preservation of open space (including farmland and forest land) where such preservation is for the scenic enjoyment of the general public or pursuant to a clearly delineated federal, state, or local governmental conservation policy; or

4. The preservation of an historically important land area or a certified historic structure.

See section 170(h) for additional information, including special rules for the conservation purpose requirement for buildings in registered historic districts.

On line 13, enter information about contributions of a qualified real property interest that is a restriction for the exterior of a certified historic structure. A **certified historic structure** is any building or structure listed on the National Register of Historic Places as well as any building certified as being of historic significance to a registered historic district. See section 170(h)(4)(B) for special rules that apply to contributions made after August 17, 2006.

On line 14, enter information about qualified conservation contributions other than those entered on line 13. This includes **conservation easements** to preserve land areas for outdoor recreation used by, or for the education of, the general public; to protect a relatively natural habitat or ecosystem; to preserve open space; or to preserve an historically important land area.

Line 15. Enter information about **contributions** of residential real estate. Include information about contributions (not in trust) of a remainder interest in a personal residence that wasn't the donor's entire interest in the property. The term "personal residence" includes any property used by the donor as a personal residence but isn't limited to the donor's principal residence. The term "personal residence" also includes stock owned by the donor as a tenant-stockholder in a cooperative housing corporation if the dwelling the donor is entitled to occupy as a tenant-stockholder is used by the donor as a personal residence. Don't enter information about contributions of the use of facilities or property, as such contributions aren't reportable on Form 990, Part VIII.

Line 16. Enter information about **contributions** of commercial real estate, such as a commercial office building. Include information about contributions (not in trust) of a remainder interest in a farm that wasn't the donor's entire interest in the property. The term "farm" refers to land used for the production of crops, fruits, or other agricultural products, or for the maintenance of livestock. A farm includes the improvements located on the farm property.

Line 17. Enter information about real estate interests not reported on line 15 or 16.

Line 18. Collectibles include autographs, sports memorabilia, dolls, stamps, coins, books (other than books and publications reported on line 4), gems, and jewelry (other than costume jewelry reported on line 5), but not art reported on lines 1 through 3, or historical artifacts or scientific specimens reported on line 22 or 23.

Line 19. Enter information about food items, including food inventory contributed by corporations and other businesses.

Line 20. Enter information about drugs, medical supplies, and similar items contributed by corporations and other businesses that manufactured or distributed such items.

Line 21. "Taxidermy" property means any work of art that is the reproduction or preservation of an animal, in whole or in part; is prepared, stuffed, or mounted to recreate one or more characteristics of the animal; and contains a part of the body of the dead animal.

Line 22. Enter information about historical artifacts such as furniture, fixtures, textiles, and household items of an historic nature. Don't include **Art** reported on lines 1 through 3, or any archeological artifacts reported on line 24.

Line 23. Scientific specimens include living plant and animal specimens, natural and physical sciences specimens (such as rocks and minerals), and objects or materials that relate to, or exhibit, the methods or principles of science.

Line 24. Enter information about archeological and ethnographical artifacts, other than **Art** reported on lines 1 through 3, and historical artifacts reported on line 22. An archaeological artifact is any object over 250 years old and is normally discovered as a result of scientific excavation, clandestine or accidental digging for exploration on land, or under water. Ethnological artifacts are objects that are the product of a tribal or nonindustrial society, and important to the cultural heritage of a people because of its distinctive characteristics, comparative rarity, or its contribution to the knowledge of the origins, development, or history of that people.

Lines 25–28. Use lines 25 through 28 to separately report other types of property not described above or reported on previous lines. These include items that didn't satisfy specific charitable deduction requirements applicable to the **contribution** of such type of property, but that were contributed to the organization, such as clothing and **household goods** that weren't in good used or better condition, and **conservation easements** that the organization knows don't constitute **qualified conservation contributions**.

Self-created items, such as personal papers and manuscripts, including archival records, are to be listed separately as a type. Archival records are materials of any kind created or received by any person, family, or organization in the conduct of their affairs that are preserved because of the enduring value of the information they contain or as evidence of the functions and responsibilities of their creator.

Donations of items used by the organization at a charitable auction (other than goods sold by the charity at the auction, which should be reported on lines 1 through 24, as appropriate), such as food served at the event or floral centerpieces, can be reported separately on lines 25 through 28. **Noncash contributions** don't include donations of services or donated use of materials, equipment, or facilities, which may be reported in the narrative section of Form 990, Part III, line 4.

Line 29. Enter the number of Forms 8283, Noncash Charitable Contributions, received by the organization during the year for **contributions** for which the organization completed Form 8283, Part V.

Lines 30a–30b. Answer "Yes" to line 30a if the organization received during the year a **noncash contribution** reportable on lines 1 through 28 for which the organization is required, by the terms of the gift or otherwise, to hold the property for at least 3 years from the date of the **contribution** and which property is not required to be used for exempt purposes for the entire holding period. An organization that answers "Yes" to line 30a must describe the arrangement in Part II.

Line 31. Answer "Yes" if the organization has a gift acceptance policy that requires the review of any nonstandard contributions. A non-standard contribution includes a contribution of an item that isn't reasonably expected to be used to satisfy or further the organization's exempt purposes (aside from the need of such organization for income or funds) and for which (a) there is no ready market to which the organization can go to liquidate the contribution and convert it to cash, and (b) the value of the item is highly speculative or difficult to ascertain. For example, the contribution of a taxpayer's successor member interest of the type described in Notice 2007-72, 2007-36 I.R.B. 544, available at *www.irs.gov/pub/irs-irbs/irb07-36.pdf*, is a nonstandard contribution for this purpose.

Lines 32a–32b. Answer "Yes" to line 32a if the organization hires or uses third parties or related organizations to solicit, process, or sell **noncash contributions**. Answer "No" if the only third party used by the organization to solicit, process, or sell noncash contributions is a broker who sells publicly traded securities received by the organization as a gift. An organization that answers "Yes" to line 32a must describe these arrangements in Part II.

Line 33. If applicable, describe in Part II why the organization didn't report revenue in column (c) for a type of property for which column (a) is checked.

Part II. Supplemental Information

Use Part II to provide narrative information required in Part I, column (b); and Part I, lines 30b, 32b, and 33, and whether the organization is reporting in Part I, column (b), the number of contributions, the number of items received, or a combination of both. Also use Part II to provide other narrative explanations and descriptions, as needed. Identify the specific line number that the response supports. Part II can be duplicated if more space is needed.

SCHEDULE R
(Form 990)
(Rev. December 2024)
Department of the Treasury
Internal Revenue Service

Related Organizations and Unrelated Partnerships

Complete if the organization answered "Yes" on Form 990, Part IV, line 33, 34, 35b, 36, or 37.
Attach to Form 990.
Go to *www.irs.gov/Form990* for instructions and the latest information.

OMB No. 1545-0047

Open to Public Inspection

Name of the organization	Employer identification number

Part I **Identification of Disregarded Entities.** Complete if the organization answered "Yes" on Form 990, Part IV, line 33.

(a) Name, address, and EIN (if applicable) of disregarded entity	(b) Primary activity	(c) Legal domicile (state or foreign country)	(d) Total income	(e) End-of-year assets	(f) Direct controlling entity
(1)					
(2)					
(3)					
(4)					
(5)					
(6)					

Part II **Identification of Related Tax-Exempt Organizations.** Complete if the organization answered "Yes" on Form 990, Part IV, line 34, because it had one or more related tax-exempt organizations during the tax year.

(a) Name, address, and EIN of related organization	(b) Primary activity	(c) Legal domicile (state or foreign country)	(d) Exempt Code section	(e) Public charity status (if section 501(c)(3))	(f) Direct controlling entity	(g) Section 512(b)(13) controlled entity?	
						Yes	No
(1)							
(2)							
(3)							
(4)							
(5)							
(6)							
(7)							

For Paperwork Reduction Act Notice, see the Instructions for Form 990. Cat. No. 50135Y **Schedule R (Form 990) (Rev. 12-2024)**

Part III **Identification of Related Organizations Taxable as a Partnership.** Complete if the organization answered "Yes" on Form 990, Part IV, line 34, because it had one or more related organizations treated as a partnership during the tax year.

(a) Name, address, and EIN of related organization	(b) Primary activity	(c) Legal domicile (state or foreign country)	(d) Direct controlling entity	(e) Predominant income (related, unrelated, excluded from tax under sections 512–514)	(f) Share of total income	(g) Share of end-of-year assets	(h) Disproportionate allocations?		(i) Code V—UBI amount in box 20 of Schedule K-1 (Form 1065)	(j) General or managing partner?		(k) Percentage ownership
							Yes	No		Yes	No	
(1)												
(2)												
(3)												
(4)												
(5)												
(6)												
(7)												

Part IV **Identification of Related Organizations Taxable as a Corporation or Trust.** Complete if the organization answered "Yes" on Form 990, Part IV, line 34, because it had one or more related organizations treated as a corporation or trust during the tax year.

(a) Name, address, and EIN of related organization	(b) Primary activity	(c) Legal domicile (state or foreign country)	(d) Direct controlling entity	(e) Type of entity (C corp, S corp, or trust)	(f) Share of total income	(g) Share of end-of-year assets	(h) Percentage ownership	(i) Section 512(b)(13) controlled entity?	
								Yes	No
(1)									
(2)									
(3)									
(4)									
(5)									
(6)									
(7)									

Schedule R (Form 990) (Rev. 12-2024) Page 3

Part V **Transactions With Related Organizations.** Complete if the organization answered "Yes" on Form 990, Part IV, line 34, 35b, or 36.

				Yes	No
Note: Complete line 1 if any entity is listed in Parts II, III, or IV of this schedule.					
1		During the tax year, did the organization engage in any of the following transactions with one or more related organizations listed in Parts II–IV?			
	a	Receipt of **(i)** interest, **(ii)** annuities, **(iii)** royalties, or **(iv)** rent from a controlled entity	**1a**		
	b	Gift, grant, or capital contribution to related organization(s)	**1b**		
	c	Gift, grant, or capital contribution from related organization(s)	**1c**		
	d	Loans or loan guarantees to or for related organization(s)	**1d**		
	e	Loans or loan guarantees by related organization(s)	**1e**		
	f	Dividends from related organization(s)	**1f**		
	g	Sale of assets to related organization(s)	**1g**		
	h	Purchase of assets from related organization(s)	**1h**		
	i	Exchange of assets with related organization(s)	**1i**		
	j	Lease of facilities, equipment, or other assets to related organization(s)	**1j**		
	k	Lease of facilities, equipment, or other assets from related organization(s)	**1k**		
	l	Performance of services or membership or fundraising solicitations for related organization(s)	**1l**		
	m	Performance of services or membership or fundraising solicitations by related organization(s)	**1m**		
	n	Sharing of facilities, equipment, mailing lists, or other assets with related organization(s)	**1n**		
	o	Sharing of paid employees with related organization(s)	**1o**		
	p	Reimbursement paid to related organization(s) for expenses	**1p**		
	q	Reimbursement paid by related organization(s) for expenses	**1q**		
	r	Other transfer of cash or property to related organization(s)	**1r**		
	s	Other transfer of cash or property from related organization(s)	**1s**		

2 If the answer to any of the above is "Yes," see the instructions for information on who must complete this line, including covered relationships and transaction thresholds.

	(a) Name of related organization	**(b)** Transaction type (a–s)	**(c)** Amount involved	**(d)** Method of determining amount involved
(1)				
(2)				
(3)				
(4)				
(5)				
(6)				

Schedule R (Form 990) (Rev. 12-2024)

Part VI **Unrelated Organizations Taxable as a Partnership.** Complete if the organization answered "Yes" on Form 990, Part IV, line 37.

Provide the following information for each entity taxed as a partnership through which the organization conducted more than five percent of its activities (measured by total assets or gross revenue) that was not a related organization. See instructions regarding exclusion for certain investment partnerships.

(a) Name, address, and EIN of entity	(b) Primary activity	(c) Legal domicile (state or foreign country)	(d) Predominant income (related, unrelated, excluded from tax under sections 512–514)	(e) Are all partners section 501(c)(3) organizations?		(f) Share of total income	(g) Share of end-of-year assets	(h) Disproportionate allocations?		(i) Code V—UBI amount in box 20 of Schedule K-1 (Form 1065)	(j) General or managing partner?		(k) Percentage ownership
				Yes	No			Yes	No		Yes	No	
(1)													
(2)													
(3)													
(4)													
(5)													
(6)													
(7)													
(8)													
(9)													
(10)													
(11)													
(12)													
(13)													
(14)													
(15)													
(16)													

Schedule R (Form 990) (Rev. 12-2024) Page **5**

Part VII **Supplemental Information**
Provide additional information for responses to questions on Schedule R. See instructions.

Schedule R (Form 990) (Rev. 12-2024)

Form **990-T**

Department of the Treasury
Internal Revenue Service

Exempt Organization Business Income Tax Return
(and proxy tax under section 6033(e))

For calendar year 2025 or other tax year beginning ________, 2025, and ending ________, 20____

Go to *www.irs.gov/Form990T* for instructions and the latest information.
Do not enter SSNs on this form as it may be made public if your organization is a 501(c)(3).

OMB No. 1545-0047

2025

Open to Public Inspection for 501(c)(3) Organizations Only

A ☐ Check box if address changed.

Name of organization (☐ Check box if name changed and see instructions.)

D Employer identification number

B Exempt under section
☐ 501( )( )
☐ 408(e) ☐ 220(e)
☐ 408A ☐ 530(a)
☐ 529(a) ☐ 529A

Number and street. If a P.O. box, see instructions. | Room or suite no.

E Group exemption number (see instructions)

City or town | State or province | Country | ZIP or foreign postal code

F ☐ Check box if an amended return.

C Book value of all assets at end of year . . . .

G Check organization type ☐ 501(c) corporation ☐ 501(c) trust ☐ 401(a) trust ☐ Other trust ☐ State college/university ☐ 6417(d)(1)(A) Applicable entity

H Check if filing only to claim ☐ Credit from Form 8941 ☐ Refund shown on Form 2439 ☐ Elective payment amount from Form 3800

I Check if a 501(c)(3) organization filing a consolidated return with a 501(c)(2) titleholding corporation . . . . ☐

J Enter the number of attached Schedules A (Form 990-T) . . . .

K During the tax year, was the corporation a subsidiary in an affiliated group or a parent-subsidiary controlled group? ☐ **Yes** ☐ **No**
If "Yes," enter the name and identifying number of the parent corporation

L The books are in care of Telephone number

Part I Total Unrelated Business Taxable Income

1	Total of unrelated business taxable income computed from all unrelated trades or businesses (see instructions)	1	
2	Reserved for future use	2	
3	Add lines 1 and 2	3	
4	Charitable contributions (see instructions for limitation rules)	4	
5	Total unrelated business taxable income before net operating losses. Subtract line 4 from line 3 . .	5	
6	Deduction for net operating loss. See instructions	6	
7	Total of unrelated business taxable income before specific deduction and section 199A deduction. Subtract line 6 from line 5	7	
8	Specific deduction (generally $1,000, but see instructions for exceptions)	8	
9	**Trusts.** Section 199A deduction. See instructions	9	
10	**Total deductions.** Add lines 8 and 9	10	
11	**Unrelated business taxable income.** Subtract line 10 from line 7. If line 10 is greater than line 7, enter zero	11	

Part II Tax Computation

1	**Organizations taxable as corporations.** Multiply Part I, line 11, by 21% (0.21)	1	
2	**Trusts taxable at trust rates.** See instructions for tax computation. Income tax on the amount on Part I, line 11, from: ☐ Tax rate schedule or ☐ Schedule D (Form 1041)	2	
3	**Proxy tax.** See instructions	3	
4a	Amount from Form 4255, Part I, line 3, column (q).	4a	
b	Other tax amounts. See instructions	4b	
5	Alternative minimum tax	5	
6	**Tax on noncompliant facility income.** See instructions	6	
7	**Total.** Add lines 3 through 6 to line 1 or 2, whichever applies	7	

Part III Tax and Payments

1a	Foreign tax credit (corporations attach Form 1118; trusts attach Form 1116) .	1a			
b	Other credits (see instructions)	1b			
c	General business credit. Attach Form 3800 (see instructions)	1c			
d	Credit for prior-year minimum tax (attach Form 8801 or 8827)	1d			
e	**Total credits.** Add lines 1a through 1d			1e	
2	Subtract line 1e from Part II, line 7			2	
3a	Amount from Form 4255, Part I, line 3, column (r) (see instructions)	3a			
b	Amount due from Form 8611	3b			
c	Amount due from Form 8697	3c			
d	Amount due from Form 8866	3d			
e	Other amounts due (see instructions)	3e			
f	Total amounts due. Add lines 3a through 3e			3f	
4	**Total tax.** Add lines 2 and 3f (see instructions). ☐ Check if includes tax previously deferred under section 1294. Enter tax amount here			4	

For Paperwork Reduction Act Notice, see instructions. Cat. No. 11291J Form **990-T** (2025) Created 1/12/26

Form 990-T (2025) Page **2**

Part III Tax and Payments *(continued)*

5a	Current net 965 tax liability paid from Form 965-A, Part II, column (k)			**5a**	
b	First installment of section 1062 applicable net tax liability. Enter amount from Form 1062, line 15			**5b**	
6a	Payments: Preceding year's overpayment credited to the current year	**6a**			
b	Current year's estimated tax payments. Check if section 643(g) election applies ☐	**6b**			
c	Tax deposited with Form 8868	**6c**			
d	Foreign organizations: Tax paid or withheld at source (see instructions)	**6d**			
e	Backup withholding (see instructions)	**6e**			
f	Credit for small employer health insurance premiums (attach Form 8941)	**6f**			
g	Elective payment election amount from Form 3800	**6g**			
h	Payment from Form 2439	**6h**			
i	Credit from Form 4136	**6i**			
j	Other (see instructions)	**6j**			
k	Section 1062 applicable net tax liability. Enter amount from Form 1062, line 14	**6k**			
7	**Total payments and section 1062 applicable net tax liability.** Add lines 6a through 6k			**7**	
8	Estimated tax penalty (see instructions). Check if Form 2220 is attached ☐			**8**	
9	**Tax due.** If line 7 is smaller than the total of lines 4, 5a, 5b, and 8, enter amount owed			**9**	
10	**Overpayment.** If line 7 is larger than the total of lines 4, 5a, 5b, and 8, enter amount overpaid			**10**	
11	Enter the amount of line 10 you want: **Credited to 2026 estimated tax** ______ **Refunded**			**11**	
	For Refunded amount, also complete and attach Form 8050. See instructions.				

Part IV Statements Regarding Certain Activities and Other Information (see instructions)

		Yes	No
1	At any time during the 2025 calendar year, did the organization have an interest in or a signature or other authority over a financial account (bank, securities, or other) in a foreign country? If "Yes," the organization may have to file FinCEN Form 114, Report of Foreign Bank and Financial Accounts. If "Yes," enter the name of the foreign country here ______		
2	During the tax year, did the organization receive a distribution from or was it the grantor of or transferor to a foreign trust? If "Yes," see instructions for other forms the organization may have to file.		
3	Enter the amount of tax-exempt interest received or accrued during the tax year $ ______		
4	Enter available pre-2018 NOL carryovers here $ ______. Do not include any post-2017 NOL carryover shown on Schedule A (Form 990-T). Don't reduce the NOL carryover shown here by any deduction reported on Part I, line 6.		
5	Post-2017 NOL carryovers. Enter the Business Activity Code and available post-2017 NOL carryovers. Don't reduce the amounts shown below by any NOL claimed on any Schedule A, Part II, line 17, for the tax year. See instructions.		
6a	Reserved for future use		
b	Reserved for future use		

Business Activity Code	Available post-2017 NOL carryover
	$
	$
	$
	$

Part V Supplemental Information

Provide any additional information. See instructions.

Sign Here

Under penalties of perjury, I declare that I have examined this return, including accompanying schedules and statements, and to the best of my knowledge and belief, it is true, correct, and complete. Declaration of preparer (other than taxpayer) is based on all information of which preparer has any knowledge.

Signature of officer | Date | Title

May the IRS discuss this return with the preparer shown below (see instructions)? ☐Yes ☐No

Paid Preparer Use Only

Enter preparer's name	Preparer's signature	Date	Check ☐ if self-employed	PTIN
Firm's name			Firm's EIN	
Firm's address			Phone no.	

Form **990-T** (2025)

Form **1023** (Rev. January 2020) Department of the Treasury Internal Revenue Service	**Application for Recognition of Exemption Under Section 501(c)(3) of the Internal Revenue Code** Do not enter social security numbers on this form as it may be made public. Go to www.irs.gov/Form1023 for instructions and the latest information.	OMB No. 1545-0047 **Note:** *If exempt status is approved, this application will be open for public inspection.*

Form 1023 must be filled and submitted online, this PDF copy is for reference only! Please go to https://form1023.org for complete instructions, tips and help to complete the form 1023.

Part I **Identification of Applicant**

1a Full Name of Organization (exactly as it appears in your organizing document)		**b** Care of Name (if applicable)	
c Mailing Address (Number, street and room/suite)	**d** City	**e** Country UNITED STATES	
f State	**g** Zip Code + 4	**h** Foreign Province (or State)	**i** Foreign Postal Code
2 Employer Identification Number	**3** Month Tax Year Ends	**4** Person to Contact if More Information is Needed (officer, director, trustee, or authorized representative)	
5 Contact Telephone Number	**6** Fax Number (optional)	**7** User Fee Submitted $600.00	

8 Organization's Website (if available):

9 List the names, titles, and mailing addresses of your officers, directors, and/or trustees.

First Name:	Last Name:	Title:
Mailing Address:	City:	
State (or Province):	Zip Code (or Foreign Postal Code):	
First Name:	Last Name:	Title:
Mailing Address:	City:	
State (or Province):	Zip Code (or Foreign Postal Code):	
First Name:	Last Name:	Title:
Mailing Address:	City:	
State (or Province):	Zip Code (or Foreign Postal Code):	
First Name:	Last Name:	Title:
Mailing Address:	City:	
State (or Province):	Zip Code (or Foreign Postal Code):	
First Name:	Last Name:	Title:
Mailing Address:	City:	
State (or Province):	Zip Code (or Foreign Postal Code):	

☐ Check here to add more officers, directors, and/or trustees.

Part II Organizational Structure

1 You must be a corporation, limited liability company (LLC), unincorporated association, or trust to be tax exempt.

Select your type of organization.

◯ Corporation

At the end of this form, you must upload a copy of your articles of incorporation (and any amendments) that shows proof of filing with the appropriate state agency.

◯ Limited Liability Company (LLC)

At the end of this form, you must upload a copy of your articles of organization (and any amendments) that shows proof of filing with the appropriate state agency. Also, if you adopted an operating agreement, upload a copy, along with any amendments.

◯ Unincorporated Association

At the end of this form, you must upload a copy of your articles of association, constitution, or other similar organizing document that is dated and includes at least two signatures. Include signed and dated copies of any amendments.

◯ Trust

At the end of this form, you must upload a signed and dated copy of your trust agreement. Include signed and dated copies of any amendments.

2 Enter the date you formed. (MM/DD/YYYY)

3 Select your state (or U.S. territory) of incorporation or other formation. If you were formed under the laws of a foreign country, select Foreign Country.

4 Have you adopted bylaws? If "Yes," at the end of this form, upload a current copy showing the date of adoption. If "No," explain how you select your officers, directors, or trustees. ◯ Yes ◯ No

5 Are you a successor to another organization? ◯ Yes ◯ No

Answer "Yes" if you have taken or will take over the activities of another organization, you took over 25% or more of the fair market value of the net assets of another organization, or you were established upon the conversion of an organization from for-profit to nonprofit status. If "Yes," complete Schedule G.

Part III **Required Provisions in Your Organizing Document**

Part III helps ensure that, when you submit this application, your organizing document contains the required provisions to meet the organizational test under section 501(c)(3).

If you cannot check "Yes" in both Lines 1 and 2, your organizing document does not meet the organizational test. DO NOT file this application until you have amended your organizing document. Remember to upload your original and amended organizing documents at the end of this form.

1 Section 501(c)(3) requires that your organizing document limit your purposes to one or more exempt purposes within section 501(c)(3), such as charitable, religious, educational, and/or scientific purposes.

The following is an example of an acceptable purpose clause: The organization is organized exclusively for charitable, religious, educational, and scientific purposes under section 501(c)(3) of the Internal Revenue Code, or corresponding section of any future federal tax code.

Does your organizing document meet this requirement? ◯ Yes ◯ No

1a State specifically where your organizing document meets this requirement, such as a reference to a particular article or section in your organizing document (Page/Article/Paragraph):

2 Section 501(c)(3) requires that your organizing document provide that upon dissolution, your remaining assets be used exclusively for section 501(c)(3) exempt purposes, such as charitable, religious, educational, and/or scientific purposes. Depending on your entity type and the state in which you are formed, this requirement may be satisfied by operation of state law.

The following is an example of an acceptable dissolution clause: Upon the dissolution of this organization, assets shall be distributed for one or more exempt purposes within the meaning of section 501(c)(3) of the Internal Revenue Code, or corresponding section of any future federal tax code, or shall be distributed to the federal government, or to a state or local government, for a public purpose.

Does your organizing document meet this requirement? ◯ Yes ◯ No

2a State specifically where your organizing document meets this requirement, such as a reference to a particular article or section in your organizing document (Page/Article/Paragraph) or indicate that you rely on state law.

Form 1023 (Rev. 01-2020) Name: EIN: Page **4**

Part IV **Your Activities**

1 Describe completely and in detail your past, present, and planned activities. Do not refer to or repeat the purposes in your organizing document. For each past, present, or planned activity, include information that answers the following questions:

a. What is the activity?
b. Who conducts the activity?
c. Where is the activity conducted?
d. What percentage of your total time is allocated to the activity?
e. How is the activity funded (for example, donations, fees, etc.) and what percentage of your overall expenses is allocated to this activity?
f. How does the activity further your exempt purposes?

Form **1023** (Rev. 01-2020)

Part IV **Your Activities** *(continued)*

2 Enter the 3-character NTEE Code that best describes your activities. [ ]

Or check here if you want the IRS to select the NTEE Code that best describes your activities. ☐

3 Do any of your programs limit the provision of goods, services, or funds to a specific individual or group of specific individuals? For example, answer "Yes" if goods, services, or funds are provided only for a particular individual, your members, individuals who work for a particular employer, or graduates of a particular school. If "Yes," explain the limitation and how recipients are selected for each program. ◯ Yes ◯ No

4 Do any individuals who receive goods, services, or funds through your programs have a family or business relationship with any officer, director, trustee, or with any of your highest compensated employees or highest compensated independent contractors? If "Yes," explain how these related individuals are eligible for goods, services, or funds. ◯ Yes ◯ No

5 Do you or will you support or oppose candidates in political campaigns in any way? If "Yes," explain. ◯ Yes ◯ No

6 Do you or will you attempt to influence legislation? If "Yes," explain how you attempt to influence legislation. ◯ Yes ◯ No

Form 1023 (Rev. 01-2020) Name: EIN: Page **6**

Part IV **Your Activities** *(continued)*

6a Did you or will you make an election to have your legislative activities measured by expenditures by filing Form 5768? If "No," describe whether your attempts to influence legislation are a substantial part of your activities. Include the time and money spent on your attempts to influence legislation as compared to your total activities. ◯ Yes ◯ No

7 Do you or will you publish, own, or have rights in music, literature, tapes, artworks, choreography, scientific discoveries, or other intellectual property? If "Yes," describe who owns or will own any copyrights, patents, or trademarks, whether fees are or will be charged, how the fees are determined, and how any items are or will be produced, distributed, and marketed. ◯ Yes ◯ No

8 Do you or will you provide educational information to the general public on budgeting, personal finance, financial literacy, saving and spending practices, the sound use of consumer credit, and/or assist individuals and families with financial problems such as credit card debt and foreclosure by providing them with counseling? If "Yes," explain. ◯ Yes ◯ No

9 Do you or will you make grants, loans, or other distributions to organizations? If "Yes," describe the type and purpose of the grants, loans, or distributions, how you select your recipients including submission requirements (such as grant proposals or application forms), and the criteria you use or will use to select recipients. Also describe how you ensure the grants, loans, and other distributions are or will be used for their intended purposes (including whether you require periodic or final reports on the use of funds and any procedures you have if you identify that funds are not being used for their intended purposes). Finally, describe the records you keep with respect to grants, loans, or other distributions you make and identify any recipient organizations and any relationships between you and the recipients. If "No," continue to Line 10. ◯ Yes ◯ No

Form **1023** (Rev. 01-2020)

Part IV **Your Activities** *(continued)*

9a Do you or will you make grants, loans, or other distributions to organizations that are not recognized by the IRS as tax exempt under section 501(c)(3)? If "Yes," name and/or describe the non-section 501(c)(3) organizations to whom you do or will make distributions and explain how these distributions further your exempt purposes. ◯ Yes ◯ No

9b Do you or will you make grants, loans, or other distributions to foreign organizations? If "Yes," name each foreign organization (if not already provided), the country and region within each country in which each foreign organization operates, any relationship you have with each foreign organization, and whether the foreign organization accepts contributions earmarked for a specific country or organization (if so, specify which countries or organizations). If "No," continue to Line 10. ◯ Yes ◯ No

9c Do your contributors know that you have ultimate authority to use contributions made to you at your discretion for purposes consistent with your exempt purposes? If "Yes," describe how you relay this information to contributors. ◯ Yes ◯ No

9d Do you or will you make pre-grant inquiries about the recipient organization? If "Yes," describe these inquiries, including whether you inquire about the recipient's financial status, its tax-exempt status under the Internal Revenue Code, its ability to accomplish the purpose for which the resources are provided, and other relevant information. ◯ Yes ◯ No

9e Do you or will you use any additional procedures to ensure that your distributions to foreign organizations are used in furtherance of your exempt purposes? If "Yes," describe these procedures, including periodic reporting requirements, auditing grantees, site visits by your employees or compliance checks by impartial experts, etc., to verify that grant funds are being used appropriately. ◯ Yes ◯ No

Form 1023 (Rev. 01-2020) Name: EIN: Page **8**

Part IV **Your Activities** *(continued)*

9f Do you share board members or other key personnel with the recipient organization(s)? If "Yes," identify the relationships. ◯ Yes ◯ No

9g When you make grants, loans, or other distributions to foreign organizations, will you check the OFAC List of Specially Designated Nationals and Blocked Persons for names of individuals and entities with whom you are dealing to determine if they are included on the list? Describe any other practices you will engage in to ensure that foreign expenditures or grants are not diverted to support terrorism or other non-charitable activities. ◯ Yes ◯ No

9h Will you comply with all United States statutes, executive orders, and regulations that restrict or prohibit U.S. persons from engaging in transactions and dealings with designated countries, entities, or individuals, or otherwise engaging in activities in violation of economic sanctions administered by OFAC? ◯ Yes ◯ No

9i Will you acquire from OFAC the appropriate license and registration where necessary? ◯ Yes ◯ No

10 Do you or will you operate in a foreign country or countries? If "Yes," name each foreign country and region within each country in which you do or will operate and describe your operations in each one. If "No," continue to Line 11. ◯ Yes ◯ No

10a When you conduct activities in foreign countries, will you check the OFAC List of Specially Designated Nationals and Blocked Persons for names of individuals and entities with whom you are dealing to determine if they are included on the list? Describe any other practices you will engage in to ensure that foreign expenditures or grants are not diverted to support terrorism or other non-charitable activities. ◯ Yes ◯ No

10b Will you comply with all United States statutes, executive orders, and regulations that restrict or prohibit U.S. persons from engaging in transactions and dealings with designated countries, entities, or individuals, or otherwise engaging in activities in violation of economic sanctions administered by OFAC? ◯ Yes ◯ No

10c Will you acquire from OFAC the appropriate license and registration where necessary? ◯ Yes ◯ No

Form **1023** (Rev. 01-2020)

Part IV **Your Activities** *(continued)*

11 Are you a sponsoring organization that maintains one or more donor advised funds? If yes, please provide a complete description of your program, including the specific advice that such donors may provide. Describe in detail the control you maintain (or will maintain) over the use of the funds. ◯ Yes ◯ No

12 Do you or will you operate a school? ◯ Yes ◯ No
If "Yes," complete Schedule B.

13 Is your principal purpose or function to provide hospital or medical care? ◯ Yes ◯ No
If "Yes," complete Schedule C.

14 Do you or will you provide low-income housing? ◯ Yes ◯ No
If "Yes," complete Schedule F.

15 Do you or will you provide scholarships, fellowships, educational loans, or other educational grants to individuals, including grants for travel, study, or other similar purposes? ◯ Yes ◯ No
If "Yes," complete Schedule H - Section I.

16 Check any of the following fundraising activities that you will undertake (check all that apply):

- ☐ Website, mail, email, personal, and/or phone solicitations
- ☐ Foundation grant solicitations
- ☐ Receive donations from another organization's website
- ☐ Government grant solicitations
- ☐ Bingo
- ☐ Other (non-bingo) gaming activities
- ☐ Other (describe)
- ☐ We will not engage in fundraising activities.

17 Do you or will you engage in fundraising activities for other organizations? If "Yes," describe these arrangements, including the names or descriptions of the organizations for which you raise funds. ◯ Yes ◯ No

Form 1023 (Rev. 01-2020) Name: EIN: Page **10**

Part V **Compensation and Other Financial Arrangements**

1 Do you or will you compensate officers, directors, or trustees, or do or will you have highest compensated employees, or highest compensated independent contractors? If "No," continue to Line 2. ◯ Yes ◯ No

In establishing compensation for your officers, directors, trustees, highest compensated employees, and highest compensated independent contractors:

1a Do or will the individuals that approve compensation arrangements follow a conflict of interest policy? ◯ Yes ◯ No

1b Do or will you approve compensation arrangements in advance of paying compensation? ◯ Yes ◯ No

1c Do or will you document in writing the date and terms of approved compensation arrangements? ◯ Yes ◯ No

1d Do or will you record in writing the decision made by each individual who decided or voted on compensation arrangements? ◯ Yes ◯ No

1e Do or will you approve compensation arrangements based on information about compensation paid by similarly situated taxable or tax-exempt organizations for similar services, current compensation surveys compiled by independent firms, or actual written offers from similarly situated organizations? ◯ Yes ◯ No

1f Do or will you record in writing both the information on which you relied to base your decision and its source? ◯ Yes ◯ No

1g Do or will you have any other practices you use to set reasonable compensation? If "Yes," describe these practices. ◯ Yes ◯ No

2 Have you adopted a conflict of interest policy consistent with the sample conflict of interest policy in Appendix A to the instructions? If you are a hospital, answer "Yes" if your conflict of interest policy includes provisions consistent with the additional healthcare related provisions in the sample document. If "No," describe the procedures you will follow to ensure that persons who have a conflict of interest will not have influence over setting their own compensation or regarding business deals with themselves. ◯ Yes ◯ No

3 Do you or will you compensate any of your officers, directors, trustees, highest compensated employees, and highest compensated independent contractors through non-fixed payments, such as discretionary bonuses or revenue-based payments? If "Yes," describe all non-fixed compensation arrangements, including how the amounts are determined, who is eligible for such arrangements, whether you place a limitation on total compensation, and how you determine or will determine that you pay no more than reasonable compensation for services. ◯ Yes ◯ No

Form **1023** (Rev. 01-2020)

Part V Compensation and Other Financial Arrangements *(continued)*

4 Do you or will you purchase or sell any goods, services, or assets from or to: (i) any of your officers, directors, or trustees; (ii) any family of any of your officers, directors, or trustees; (iii) any organizations in which any of your officers, directors, or trustees are also officers, directors, or trustees, or in which any individual officer, director, or trustee owns more than a 35% interest; (iv) your highest compensated employees; or (v) your highest compensated independent contractors? If "Yes," describe any such transactions that you made or intend to make, with whom you make or will make such transactions, how the terms are or will be negotiated at arm's length, and how you determine you pay no more than fair market value or you are paid at least fair market value. ◯ Yes ◯ No

5 Do you or will you have any leases, contracts, loans, or other agreements with: (i) your officers, directors, or trustees; (ii) any family of any of your officers, directors, or trustees; (iii) any organizations in which any of your officers, directors, or trustees are also officers, directors, or trustees, or in which any individual officer, director, or trustee owns more than a 35% interest; (iv) your highest compensated employees; or (v) your highest compensated independent contractors? If "Yes," describe any written or oral arrangements that you made or intend to make, with whom you have or will have such arrangements, how the terms are or will be negotiated at arm's length, and how you determine you pay no more than fair market value or you are paid at least fair market value. ◯ Yes ◯ No

6 Do you or will you contract with another organization to develop, build, market, or finance your facilities? If "Yes," describe each facility, the role of the other organization, and any business or family relationship between the organization and your officers, directors, or trustees. Explain how that entity is selected, how the terms of any contract(s) are negotiated at arm's length, and how you determine you will pay no more than fair market value for services. ◯ Yes ◯ No

Part V Compensation and Other Financial Arrangements *(continued)*

7 Does or will someone other than your own employees or volunteers manage your activities or facilities? ◯ Yes ◯ No
If "Yes," describe the activities or facilities that will be managed by others, the names of the persons or organizations that manage or will manage your activities or facilities, and any business or family relationship between the organization and your officers, directors, or trustees. Explain how these managers were or will be selected, how the terms of any contracts or other agreements were or will be negotiated, and how you determine you will pay no more than fair market value for services.

8 Do you participate in any joint ventures, including partnerships or limited liability companies treated as partnerships, in which you share profits and losses with partners? If "Yes," state your ownership percentage in each joint venture, list your investment in each joint venture, describe the tax status of other participants in each joint venture (including whether they are section 501(c)(3) organizations), describe the activities of each joint venture, describe how you exercise control over the activities of each joint venture, and describe how each joint venture furthers your exempt purposes. ◯ Yes ◯ No

Part VI Financial Data

1 Select the option that best describes you to determine the years of revenues and expenses you need to provide.

◯ You completed less than one tax year.

Provide a total of three years of financial information (including the current year and two future years of reasonable and good faith projections of your future finances) in the following Statement of Revenues and Expenses.

◯ You completed at least one tax year but fewer than five.

Provide a total of four years financial information (including the current year and three years of actual financial information or reasonable and good faith projections of your future finances) in the following Statement of Revenues and Expenses.

◯ You completed five or more tax years.

Provide financial information for your five most recent tax years (including the current year) in the following Statement of Revenues and Expenses.

Part VI Financial Data *(continued)*

A. Statement of Revenues and Expenses

Type of revenue	Current tax year	4 prior tax years or 2 succeeding tax years			
	From: To:	From: To:	From: To:	From: To:	From: To:
1 Gifts, grants, and contributions received (do not include unusual grants)					
2 Membership fees received					
3 Gross investment income					
4 Net unrelated business income					
5 Taxes levied for your benefit					
6 Value of services or facilities furnished by a governmental unit without charge (not including the value of services generally furnished to the public without charge)					
7 Any revenue not otherwise listed above or in lines 9 - 12 below (provide an itemized list below)					
8 Total of lines 1 through 7					
9 Gross receipts from admissions, merchandise sold or services performed, or furnishing of facilities in any activity that is related to your exempt purposes (provide an itemized list below)					
10 Total of lines 8 and 9					
11 Net gain or loss on sale of capital assets (provide an itemized list below)					
12 Unusual grants (provide an itemized list below)					
13 Total Revenue (add lines 10 through 12)					
Type of expense	**Current tax year**	**4 prior tax years or 2 succeeding tax years**			
14 Fundraising expenses					
15 Contributions, gifts, grants, and similar amounts paid out (provide an itemized list below)					
16 Disbursements to or for the benefit of members (provide an itemized list below)					
17 Compensation of officers, directors, and trustees					
18 Other salaries and wages					
19 Interest expense					
20 Occupancy (rent, utilities, etc.)					
21 Depreciation and depletion					
22 Professional fees					
23 Any expense not otherwise classified, such as program services (provide an itemized list below)					
24 Total Expenses (add lines 14 through 23)					

25 Itemized financial data

Form 1023 (Rev. 01-2020) Name: EIN: Page **14**

Part VI **Financial Data** *(continued)*

B. Balance Sheet (for your most recently completed tax year)	Year End:
Assets	
1 Cash	
2 Accounts receivable, net	
3 Inventories	
4 Bonds and notes receivable (provide an itemized list below)	
5 Corporate stocks (provide an itemized list below)	
6 Loans receivable (provide an itemized list below)	
7 Other investments (provide an itemized list below)	
8 Depreciable assets (provide an itemized list below)	
9 Land	
10 Other assets (provide an itemized list below)	
11 Total Assets (add lines 1 through 10)	
Liabilities	
12 Accounts payable	
13 Contributions, gifts, grants, etc. payable	
14 Mortgages and notes payable (provide an itemized list below)	
15 Other liabilities (provide an itemized list below)	
16 Total Liabilities (add lines 12 through 15)	
Fund Balances or Net Assets	
17 Total fund balances or net assets	
18 Total Liabilities and Fund Balances or Net Assets (add lines 16 and 17)	

19 Itemized financial data

Form **1023** (Rev. 01-2020)

Part VII Foundation Classification

Part VII is designed to classify you as an organization that is either a private foundation or a public charity. Public charity classification is a more favorable tax status than private foundation classification. If you are a private foundation, this part will further determine whether you are a private operating foundation.

1 Select the foundation classification you are requesting from the list below.

- ◯ You are described in 509(a)(1) and 170(b)(1)(A)(vi) as an organization that receives a substantial part of its financial support in the form of contributions from publicly supported organizations, from a governmental unit, or from the general public.
- ◯ You are described in 509(a)(2) as an organization that normally receives not more than one-third of its financial support from gross investment income and receives more than one-third of its financial support from contributions, membership fees, and gross receipts from activities related to its exempt functions (subject to certain exceptions).
- ◯ You are described in 509(a)(1) and 170(b)(1)(A)(i) as a church or a convention or association of churches. Complete Schedule A.
- ◯ You are described in 509(a)(1) and 170(b)(1)(A)(ii) as a school. Complete Schedule B.
- ◯ You are described in 509(a)(1) and 170(b)(1)(A)(iii) as a hospital, a cooperative hospital service organization, or a medical research organization operated in conjunction with a hospital. Complete Schedule C.
- ◯ You are described in 509(a)(1) and 170(b)(1)(A)(iv) as an organization operated for the benefit of a college or university that is owned or operated by a governmental unit.
- ◯ You are described in 509(a)(1) and 170(b)(1)(A)(ix) as an agricultural research organization directly engaged in the continuous active conduct of agricultural research in conjunction with a college or university.
- ◯ You are described in 509(a)(3) as an organization supporting either one or more organizations described in 509(a)(1) or 509(a)(2) or a publicly supported section 501(c)(4), (5), or (6) organization. Complete Schedule D.
- ◯ You are described in 509(a)(4) as an organization organized and operated exclusively for testing for public safety.
- ◯ You are a publicly supported organization and would like the IRS to decide your correct classification.
- ◯ You are a private foundation.

1a As a private foundation, section 508(e) requires special provisions in your organizing document in addition to those that apply to all organizations described in section 501(c)(3). Check this box to confirm that your organizing document includes these provisions or you rely on state law. ☐

State specifically where your organizing document meets this requirement, such as a reference to a particular article or section in your organizing document (Page/Article/Paragraph) or state that you rely on state law.

1b Do you or will you provide scholarships, fellowships, educational loans, or other educational grants to individuals, including grants for travel, study, or other similar purposes? ◯ Yes ◯ No
If "Yes," complete Schedule H - Section II.

1c Are you a private operating foundation? ◯ Yes ◯ No

To be a private operating foundation you must engage directly in the active conduct of charitable, religious, educational, and similar activities, as opposed to indirectly carrying out these activities by providing grants to individuals or other organizations.

Form 1023 (Rev. 01-2020) Name: EIN: Page **16**

Part VII **Foundation Classification** *(continued)*

1d Describe how you meet the requirements for private operating foundation status, including how you meet the income test and either the assets test, the endowment test, or the support test. If you've been in existence for less than one year, describe how you are likely to satisfy the requirements for private operating foundation status.

2 If you have been in existence more than 5 years, you must confirm your public support status. To confirm your qualification as a public charity described in 509(a)(1) and 170(b)(1)(A)(vi) in existence for five or more tax years, you must have received one-third or more of your total support from governmental agencies, contributions from the general public, and contributions or grants from other public charities; or 10% or more of your total support from governmental agencies, contributions from the general public, and contributions or grants from other public charities and the facts and circumstances indicate you are a publicly supported organization. Calculate whether you meet this support test for your most recent five-year period.

i. Did you receive contributions from any person, company, or organization whose gifts totaled more than the 2% amount of line 8 in Part VI-A? ◯ Yes ◯ No

If "Yes," identify each person, company, or organization by letter (A, B, C, etc.) and indicate the amount contributed by each. Keep a list showing the name of and amount contributed by each of these donors for your records.

ii. Based on your calculations, did you receive at least one-third of your support from public sources or did you normally receive at least 10 percent of your support from public sources and you have other characteristics of a publicly supported organization? ◯ Yes ◯ No

2a If you have been in existence more than 5 years, you must confirm your public support status. To confirm your qualification as a public charity described in 509(a)(2) in existence for five or more tax years, you must have normally received more than one-third of your support from contributions, membership fees, and gross receipts from activities related to your exempt functions, or a combination of these sources, and not more than one-third of your support from gross investment income and net unrelated business income. Calculate whether you meet this support test for your most recent five-year period.

i. Did you receive amounts from any disqualified persons? ◯ Yes ◯ No

If "Yes," identify each disqualified person by letter (A, B, C, etc.) and indicate the amount contributed by each. Keep a list showing the name of and amount contributed by each of these donors for your records.

ii. Did you receive amounts from individuals or organizations other than disqualified persons that exceeded the greater of $5,000 or 1% of the amount on line 10 of Part VI-A Statement of Revenues and Expenses? ◯ Yes ◯ No

If "Yes," identify each individual or organization by letter (A, B, C, etc.) and indicate the amount contributed by each. Keep a list showing the name of and amount contributed by each of these donors for your records.

iii. Based on your calculations, did you normally receive more than one-third of your support from a combination of gifts, grants, contributions, membership fees, and gross receipts (from permitted sources) from activities related to your exempt functions and normally receive not more than one-third of your support from investment income and unrelated business taxable income? ◯ Yes ◯ No

Form **1023** (Rev. 01-2020)

Part VIII Effective Date

In general, a determination letter recognizing exemption of an organization described in section 501(c)(3) is effective as of the date of formation of an organization if: (1) its purposes and activities prior to the date of the determination letter have been consistent with the requirements for exemption; and (2) it has filed an application for recognition of exemption within 27 months from the end of the month in which it was organized.

1 Are you submitting this application within 27 months of the end of the month in which you were legally formed? ◯ Yes ◯ No

If "No," complete Schedule E.

Part IX Annual Filing Requirements

If you fail to file a required information return or notice for three consecutive years, your exempt status will be automatically revoked.

1 Certain organizations are not required to file annual information returns or notices (Form 990, Form 990-EZ, or Form 990-N, e-Postcard). If you are granted tax-exemption, are you claiming to be excused from filing Form 990, Form 990-EZ, or Form 990-N? ◯ Yes ◯ No

If "Yes," are you claiming you are excepted from filing because you are:

◯ A church or association of churches

◯ An integrated auxiliary (such as a men's or women's organization, religious school, mission society, or religious group)

◯ A church-affiliated organization (other than a section 509(a)(3) organization) that is exclusively engaged in managing funds or maintaining retirement programs and is described in Revenue Procedure 96-10, 1996-1 C.B. 577

◯ A school below college level affiliated with a church or operated by a religious order

◯ A mission society (other than a section 509(a)(3) supporting organization) sponsored by, or affiliated with, one or more churches or church denominations, if more than half of the society's activities are conducted in, or directed at, persons in foreign countries

◯ An affiliate of a governmental unit that meets the requirements of Revenue Procedure 95-48, 1995-2 C.B. 418 (other than a section 509(a)(3) supporting organization)

◯ Other (describe)

Part X Signature

☐ I declare under the penalties of perjury that I am authorized to sign this application on behalf of the above organization and that I have examined this application, and to the best of my knowledge it is true, correct, and complete.

(Type name of signer)

(Type title or authority of signer)

05/13/2020

(Date)

Upload checklist:

- ☐ Organizing document (and any amendments)
- ☐ Bylaws, if adopted
- ☐ Form 2848, Power of Attorney and Declaration of Representative (if applicable)
- ☐ Form 8821, Tax Information Authorization (if applicable)
- ☐ Supplemental responses (if applicable)
- ☐ Expedited handling request (if applicable)

Schedule A. Churches

1 Do you have a written creed, statement of faith, or summary of beliefs? If "Yes," describe your written creed, statement of faith, or summary of beliefs. ◯ Yes ◯ No

2 Do you have a literature of your own? If "Yes," describe your literature. ◯ Yes ◯ No

3 Do you have a formal code of doctrine and discipline? If "Yes," describe your code of doctrine and discipline. ◯ Yes ◯ No

4 Describe your religious hierarchy or ecclesiastical government.

5 Are you part of a group of churches with similar beliefs and structures? If "Yes," explain. ◯ Yes ◯ No

6 Do you have a form of worship? If "Yes," describe your form of worship. ◯ Yes ◯ No

7 Do you have regularly scheduled religious services? If "Yes," describe the nature of the services. ◯ Yes ◯ No

7a What is the average attendance at your regularly scheduled religious services?

8 Do you have an established place of worship? If "Yes," describe your established place of worship or where you meet to hold regularly scheduled religious services. ◯ Yes ◯ No

Schedule A. Churches *(continued)*

9	Do you have an established congregation or other regular membership group? If "No," continue to Line 10.	◯ Yes	◯ No
9a	How many members do you have?		
9b	Do you have a process by which an individual becomes a member? If "Yes," describe the process.	◯ Yes	◯ No
9c	Do your members have voting rights, rights to participate in religious functions, or other rights? If "Yes," describe the rights your members have.	◯ Yes	◯ No
9d	May your members be associated with another denomination or church?	◯ Yes	◯ No
9e	Are all of your members part of the same family?	◯ Yes	◯ No
10	Do you conduct baptisms, weddings, funerals, or other religious rites?	◯ Yes	◯ No
11	Do you have a school for the religious instruction of the young?	◯ Yes	◯ No
12	Do you have ministers or religious leaders? If "Yes," describe these roles and explain whether the ministers or religious leaders are ordained, commissioned, or licensed after a prescribed course of study.	◯ Yes	◯ No
13	Do you have schools for the preparation of your ordained ministers or religious leaders?	◯ Yes	◯ No
14	Do you ordain, commission, or license ministers or religious leaders? If "Yes," describe the requirements for ordination, commission, or licensure.	◯ Yes	◯ No
15	Do you have other information you believe should be considered regarding your status as a church? If "Yes," explain.	◯ Yes	◯ No

Schedule B. Schools, Colleges, and Universities

1 Do you normally have a regularly scheduled curriculum, a regular faculty of qualified teachers, a regularly enrolled student body, and facilities where your educational activities are regularly carried on? ◯ Yes ◯ No

2 Is the primary function of your school the presentation of formal instruction? If "No," continue to Line 3. ◯ Yes ◯ No

2a Select the best description(s) of your school:

☐ Elementary school

☐ Secondary school

☐ Charter school

☐ College or university

☐ Technical school

☐ Other school (describe)

3 Are you a public school because you are operated by a state or subdivision of a state or operated wholly or predominantly from government funds or property? If "Yes," explain how you are operated by a state or subdivision of a state. Do not complete the remainder of Schedule B. ◯ Yes ◯ No

4 Were you formed or substantially expanded at the time of public school desegregation in the school district or county in which you are located? ◯ Yes ◯ No

5 Has a state or federal administrative agency or judicial body ever determined that you are racially discriminatory? If "Yes," explain. ◯ Yes ◯ No

6 Has your right to receive financial aid or assistance from a governmental agency ever been revoked or suspended? If "Yes," explain. ◯ Yes ◯ No

Information Required by Revenue Procedure 75-50 as Modified by Revenue Procedure 2019-22

7 Have you adopted a racially nondiscriminatory policy as to students in your organizing document, bylaws, or by resolution of your governing body? ◯ Yes ◯ No

State where the policy is located or if adopted by resolution of your governing body.

8 Do your brochures, application forms, advertisements, and catalogues dealing with student admissions, programs, and scholarships contain a statement of your racially nondiscriminatory policy? If "Yes," continue to Line 9. ◯ Yes ◯ No

8a ☐ By checking this box, you agree that all future printed materials, including website content, will contain the required nondiscriminatory policy statement.

Schedule B. Schools, Colleges, and Universities *(continued)*

9 Have you made your racially nondiscriminatory policy known to all segments of the general community you serve by: a) publishing a notice of your policy in a newspaper of general circulation that serves all racial segments of the community; b) publicizing your policy over broadcast media in a way that is reasonably expected to be effective; or c) displaying a notice of your policy at all times on your primary, publicly accessible internet home page in a manner reasonably expected to be noticed by visitors to the homepage? If "Yes," continue to Line 10. ◯ Yes ◯ No

9a

☐ By checking this box, you agree that you will publicize your nondiscriminatory policy in a way that meets the requirements of Revenue Procedure 75-50, 1975-2 C.B. 587, as modified by Revenue Procedure 2019-22, I.R.B. 1260.

10 Do or will you (or any department or division of your organization) discriminate in any way on the basis of race with respect to admissions, use of facilities or exercise of student privileges, faculty or administrative staff, or scholarship or loan programs? If "Yes," for any of the above, explain fully. ◯ Yes ◯ No

11 Complete the table below to show the racial composition for the current academic year and projected for the next academic year. If you are not operational, submit an estimate based on the best information available (such as the racial composition of the community you serve).

For each racial category, enter the number of (a) students, (b) faculty, and (c) administrative staff. Provide actual numbers rather than percentages for each racial category.

Racial Category	**(a) Student Body**		**(b) Faculty**		**(c) Administrative Staff**	
	Current Year	Next Year	Current Year	Next Year	Current Year	Next Year
Total						

12 In the table below, enter the number and amount of loans and scholarships awarded to enrolled students by racial categories. Provide actual numbers rather than percentages for each racial category.

☐ Check here if you will not provide any loans or scholarships to students.

Racial Category	**Number of Loans**		**Amount of Loans**		**Number of Scholarships**		**Amount of Scholarships**	
	Current Year	Next Year	Current Year	Next Year	Current Year	Next Year	Current Year	Next Year
Total								

Schedule B. Schools, Colleges, and Universities *(continued)*

13 List your incorporators, founders, board members, and donors of land or buildings, whether individuals or organizations.

14 Do any of your incorporators, founders, board members, and donors of land or buildings, whether individuals or organizations, have an objective to maintain segregated public or private school education? If "Yes," explain. ◯ Yes ◯ No

15 Will you maintain records according to the nondiscrimination provisions contained in Revenue Procedure 75-50? If "No," explain. ◯ Yes ◯ No

Schedule C. Hospitals and Medical Research Organizations

1 Are you a medical research organization (an organization whose principal purpose or function is medical research and which is directly engaged in the continuous active conduct of medical research) operated in conjunction with a hospital? If "No," continue to Line 2. ◯ Yes ◯ No

1a Name the hospitals with which you have a relationship and describe the relationship.

1b List your assets showing their fair market value and the portion of your assets directly devoted to medical research.

Do not complete the remainder of Schedule C.

2 Are you applying for exemption as a cooperative hospital service organization described in section 501(e)? If "Yes," explain. ◯ Yes ◯ No

Do not complete the remainder of Schedule C.

3 Are all the doctors in the community eligible for staff privileges? If "No," give the reasons why and explain how the medical staff is selected. ◯ Yes ◯ No

Schedule C. Hospitals and Medical Research Organizations *(continued)*

4	Do or will you provide medical services to all individuals in your community who can pay for themselves or are able to pay through some form of insurance? If "No," explain.	◯ Yes	◯ No
5	Do you or will you maintain a full-time emergency room? If "Yes," continue to Line 6.	◯ Yes	◯ No
5a	Are you a specialty hospital or would emergency services be duplicative based on your region or locality?	◯ Yes	◯ No
6	Do you provide free or below cost services? If "Yes," describe your policy for determining when and to whom you provide these services and how these services promote the organization's benefit to the community.	◯ Yes	◯ No
7	Do you or will you carry on a formal program of medical training or medical research? If "Yes," describe such programs, including the type of programs offered, the scope of such programs, and affiliations with other hospitals or medical care providers with which you carry on the medical training or research programs.	◯ Yes	◯ No
8	Do you or will you carry on a formal program of community education? If "Yes," describe such programs, including the type of programs offered, the scope of such programs, and affiliation with other hospitals or medical care providers with which you offer community education programs.	◯ Yes	◯ No

Schedule C. Hospitals and Medical Research Organizations *(continued)*

9 Is your board of directors composed of a majority of individuals who are representative of the community you serve, or do you operate under a parent organization whose board of directors is composed of a majority of individuals who are representative of the community you serve? If "Yes," continue to Line 10. ◯ Yes ◯ No

9a List each board member's name and business, financial, or professional relationship with the hospital. Also, identify each board member who is representative of the community and describe how that individual is a community representative. If you operate under a parent organization whose board of directors is not composed of a majority of individuals who are representative of the community you serve, provide the requested information for your parent's board of directors as well.

10 Do you operate a facility which is required by a state to be licensed, registered, or similarly recognized as a hospital? If "No," do not complete the rest of Schedule C. ◯ Yes ◯ No

10a Do you conduct a community health needs assessment (CHNA) at least once every three years and adopt an implementation strategy to meet the community health needs identified in the assessment as required by section 501(r)(3)? If "No," explain. ◯ Yes ◯ No

10b Do you have a written financial assistance policy (FAP) and a written policy relating to emergency medical care as required by section 501(r)(4)? If "No," explain. ◯ Yes ◯ No

Schedule C. Hospitals and Medical Research Organizations *(continued)*

10c Do you both (1) limit amounts charged for emergency or other medically necessary care provided to individuals eligible for assistance under your FAP to not more than amounts generally billed to individuals who have insurance covering such care, and (2) prohibit use of gross charges as required by section 501(r)(5)? If "No," explain. ◯ Yes ◯ No

10d Do you make reasonable efforts to determine whether an individual is FAP-eligible before engaging in extraordinary collection actions as required by section 501(r)(6)? If "No," explain. ◯ Yes ◯ No

Form 1023 (Rev. 01-2020) Name: EIN: Page **28**

Schedule D. Section 509(a)(3) Supporting Organizations

1 List the names, addresses, and EINs of the organizations you support.

2 Are all your supported organizations public charities under section 509(a)(1) or (2)? If "Yes," continue to Line 3. ◯ Yes ◯ No

2a Are your supported organizations tax exempt under section 501(c)(4), 501(c)(5), or 501(c)(6) and do your supported organizations meet the public support test under section 509(a)(2)? If "No," explain how each organization you support is a public charity under section 509(a)(1) or 509(a)(2). ◯ Yes ◯ No

3 Which of the following describes your relationship with your supported organization(s)?

◯ A majority of your governing board or officers are elected or appointed by your supported organization(s). (Type I supporting organization)

◯ Your control or management is vested in the same persons who control or manage your supported organization(s). (Type II supporting organization)

◯ One or more of your officers, directors, or trustees are elected or appointed by the officers, directors, trustees, or membership of your supported organization(s), or one or more of your officers, directors, trustees, or other important office holders, are also members of the governing body of your supported organization(s), or your officers, directors, or trustees maintain a close and continuous working relationship with the officers, directors, or trustees of your supported organization(s). (Type III supporting organization)

4 Describe how your governing board and officers are selected. If you are a Type III organization, also describe how your officers, directors, or trustees maintain a close and continuous working relationship with the officers, directors, or trustees of your supported organization(s).

Form **1023** (Rev. 01-2020)

Schedule D. Section 509(a)(3) Supporting Organizations *(continued)*

5 Do any persons who are disqualified persons (except individuals who are disqualified persons only because they are foundation managers) with respect to you or persons who have a family or business relationship with any disqualified persons appoint any of your foundation managers? If "Yes," (1) describe the process by which disqualified persons appoint any of your foundation managers, (2) provide the names of these disqualified persons and the foundation managers they appoint, and (3) explain how control is vested over your operations (including assets and activities) by persons other than disqualified persons. ◯ Yes ◯ No

6 Do any persons who are disqualified persons (except individuals who are disqualified persons only because they are foundation managers) have any influence regarding your operations, including your assets or activities? If "Yes," (1) provide the names of these disqualified persons, (2) explain how influence is exerted over your operations (including assets and activities), and (3) explain how control is vested over your operations (including assets and activities) by individuals other than disqualified persons. ◯ Yes ◯ No

7 Does your organizing document specify your supported organization(s) by name? ◯ Yes ◯ No
If "Yes" and you selected Type I above, continue to Line 8.
If "Yes," and you selected Type II, do not complete the rest of Schedule D.
If "No" and you selected Type III above, amend your organizing document to specify your supported organization(s) by name or you will not meet the organizational test and need to reconsider your requested public charity classification; then continue to Line 8.

7a Does your organizing document name a similar purpose or charitable class of beneficiaries as to your supported organization(s)? If "No," amend your organizing document to specify your supported organization(s) by name, purpose, or class or you will not meet the organizational test and need to reconsider your requested public charity classification. ◯ Yes ◯ No

If you selected Type II above, do not complete the rest of Schedule D.

8 Do you or will you receive contributions from any person who alone, or combined with family members or an entity at least 35% controlled by that person, controls any of your supported organizations, or will you receive contributions from any family member of, or an entity at least 35% controlled by, any person who controls any of your supported organizations? If "Yes," explain. ◯ Yes ◯ No

If you selected Type I above, do not complete the rest of Schedule D.

Schedule D. Section 509(a)(3) Supporting Organizations *(continued)*

9 Do the officers, directors, or trustees of your supported organization have a significant voice in your investment policies, the timing and making of grants, the selection of grant recipients, and in otherwise directing the use of your income or assets? If "Yes," explain. ◯ Yes ◯ No

10 In each taxable year, do you or will you provide each of your supported organizations with (a) a written notice addressed to a principal officer of the supported organization describing the type and amount of all of the support you provided to the supported organization during the immediately preceding taxable year, (b) a copy of your most recently filed Form 990-series return or notice, and (c) a copy of your governing documents? If 'No,' explain. ◯ Yes ◯ No

11 Do you exercise a substantial degree of direction over the policies, programs, and activities of your supported organization(s) and appoint or elect (directly or indirectly) a majority of the officers, directors, or trustees of your supported organization(s)? If "Yes," explain. ◯ Yes ◯ No

12 Do substantially all of your activities directly further the exempt purposes of one or more supported organizations to which you are responsive by performing the functions of, or carrying out the purposes of, such supported organization(s) and but for your involvement would normally be engaged in by such supported organization(s). If "Yes," explain and do not complete the rest of Schedule D. ◯ Yes ◯ No

Schedule D. Section 509(a)(3) Supporting Organizations *(continued)*

13 Do you distribute at least 85% of your annual net income or 3.5% of the aggregate fair market value of all of your non-exempt-use assets (whichever is greater) to your supported organization(s)? If "No," explain. ◯ Yes ◯ No

13a How much do you contribute annually to each supported organization?

13b What is the total annual revenue of each supported organization?

13c Do you or the supported organization(s) earmark your funds for support of a particular program or activity? If "Yes," explain. ◯ Yes ◯ No

Form 1023 (Rev. 01-2020) Name: EIN: Page **32**

Schedule E. Effective Date

1 Are you applying for reinstatement of exemption after being automatically revoked for failure to file required returns or notices for three consecutive years? If "No," continue to Line 2. ◯ Yes ◯ No

1a Revenue Procedure 2014-11, 2014-1 C.B. 411, provides procedures for reinstating your tax-exempt status. Select the section of Revenue Procedure 2014-11 under which you want us to consider your reinstatement request.

◯ Section 4. You are seeking retroactive reinstatement under section 4 of Revenue Procedure 2014-11. By selecting this line, you attest that you meet the specified requirements of section 4, that your failure to file was not intentional, and that you have put in place procedures to file required returns or notices in the future. Do not complete the rest of Schedule E.

◯ Section 5. You are seeking retroactive reinstatement under section 5 of Revenue Procedure 2014-11. By selecting this line, you attest that you meet the specified requirements of section 5, that you have filed required annual returns, that your failure to file was not intentional, and that you have put in place procedures to file required returns or notices in the future.

Describe how you exercised ordinary business care and prudence in determining and attempting to comply with your filing requirements in at least one of the three years of revocation and the steps you have taken or will take to avoid or mitigate future failures to file timely returns or notices. Do not complete the rest of Schedule E.

◯ Section 6. You are seeking retroactive reinstatement under section 6 of Revenue Procedure 2014-11. By selecting this line, you attest that you meet the specified requirements of section 6, that you have filed required annual returns, that your failure to file was not intentional, and that you have put in place procedures to file required returns or notices in the future.

Describe how you exercised ordinary business care and prudence in determining and attempting to comply with your filing requirements in each of the three years of revocation and the steps you have taken or will take to avoid or mitigate future failures to file timely returns or notices. Do not complete the rest of Schedule E.

◯ Section 7. You are seeking reinstatement under section 7 of Revenue Procedure 2014-11, effective the date you are filling this application. Do not complete the rest of Schedule E.

2 Generally, if you did not file Form 1023 within 27 months of formation, the effective date of your exempt status will be the date you filed Form 1023 (submission date). Requests for an earlier effective date may be granted when there is evidence to establish you acted reasonably and in good faith and the grant of relief will not prejudice the interests of the government.

◯ Check this box if you accept the submission date as the effective date of your exempt status. Do not complete the rest of Schedule E.

◯ Check this box if you are requesting an earlier effective date than the submission date.

2a Explain why you did not file Form 1023 within 27 months of formation, how you acted reasonably and in good faith, and how granting an earlier effective date will not prejudice the interests of the Government.

You may want to include the events that led to the failure to timely file Form 1023 and to the discovery of the failure, any reliance on the advice of a qualified tax professional and a description of the engagement and responsibilities of the professional as well as the extent to which you relied on the professional, a comparison of (1) what your aggregate tax liability would be if you had filed this application within the 27-month period with (2) what your aggregate liability would be if you were exempt as of your formation date, or any other information you believe will support your request for relief.

Form **1023** (Rev. 01-2020)

Schedule F. Low-Income Housing

1 Describe each facility including the type of facility, whether you own or lease the facility, how many residents it can accommodate, the current number of residents, and whether the residents purchase or rent housing from you.

2 Describe who qualifies for your housing in terms of income levels or other criteria and explain how you select residents.

3 Do you meet the safe harbor requirements outlined in Revenue Procedure 96-32, 1996-1 C.B. 717, which provides guidelines for providing low-income housing that will be treated as charitable, including for each project that (a) at least 75 percent of the units are occupied by residents that qualify as low-income and (b) either at least 20 percent of the units are occupied by residents that also meet the very low-income limit for the area or 40 percent of the units are occupied by residents that also do not exceed 120 percent of the area's very low-income limit, and less than 25 percent of the units are provided at market rates to persons who have incomes in excess of the low-income limit? ◯ Yes ◯ No

4 Is your housing affordable to low-income residents? If "Yes," describe how your housing is made affordable to low-income residents. ◯ Yes ◯ No

5 Do you impose any restrictions to make sure that your housing remains affordable to low-income residents? If "Yes," describe these restrictions. ◯ Yes ◯ No

Schedule F. Low-Income Housing *(continued)*

6 In addition to rent or mortgage payments, do residents pay periodic fees or maintenance charges? If "Yes," describe what these charges cover and how they are determined. ◯ Yes ◯ No

7 Do you provide social services to residents? If "Yes," describe these services. ◯ Yes ◯ No

8 Do you participate in any government housing programs? If "Yes," describe these programs. ◯ Yes ◯ No

Schedule G. Successors to Other Organizations

1 List the name, last address, and EIN of your predecessor organization and describe its activities.

2 List the owners, partners, principal stockholders, officers, and governing board members of your predecessor organization. Include their names, addresses, and share/interest in the predecessor organization (if for-profit).

3 Are you a successor to a for-profit organization? If "Yes," explain your relationship with the predecessor organization that resulted in your creation and explain why you took over the activities or assets of a for-profit organization or converted from for-profit to nonprofit status; continue to Line 4. ◯ Yes ◯ No

3a Explain your relationship with the other organization that resulted in your creation and why you took over the activities or assets of another organization.

Schedule G. Successors to Other Organizations *(continued)*

4 Do or will you maintain a working relationship with any of the persons listed in question 2 or with any for-profit organization in which these persons own more than a 35% interest? If "Yes," describe the relationship. ◯ Yes ◯ No

5 Were any assets transferred, whether by gift or sale, from the predecessor organization to you? If "Yes," provide a list of assets, indicate the value of each asset, explain how the value was determined, and attach an appraisal, if available. For each asset listed, also explain if the transfer was by gift, sale, or combination thereof and describe any restrictions that were placed on the use or sale of the assets. ◯ Yes ◯ No

6 Were any debts or liabilities transferred from the predecessor for-profit organization to you? If "Yes," provide a list of the debts or liabilities that were transferred to you, indicating the amount of each, how the amount was determined, and the name of the person to whom the debt or liability is owed. ◯ Yes ◯ No

7 Will you lease or rent any property or equipment to or from the predecessor organization or any persons listed in Line 2 or a for-profit organization in which these persons own more than a 35% interest? If "Yes," describe the arrangement(s) including how the lease or rental value was determined. ◯ Yes ◯ No

Schedule H. Organizations Providing Scholarships, Fellowships, Educational Loans, or Other Educational Grants to Individuals and Private Foundations Requesting Advance Approval of Individual Grant Procedures

Section I **Public charities and private foundations complete lines 1 through 8 of this section.**

1 Describe the types of educational grants you provide to individuals, such as scholarships, fellowships, loans, etc., including the purpose, number and amount(s) of grants, how the program is publicized, and if you award educational loans, the terms of the loans.

2 Do you maintain case histories showing recipients of your scholarships, fellowships, educational loans, or other educational grants, including names, addresses, purposes of awards, amount of each grant, manner of selection, and relationship (if any) to officers, trustees, or donors of funds to you? If "No," explain. ◯ Yes ◯ No

3 Describe the specific criteria you use to determine who is eligible for your program (for example, eligibility selection criteria could consist of graduating high school students from a particular high school who will attend college, writers of scholarly works about American history, etc.).

4 Describe the specific criteria you use to select recipients (for example, specific selection criteria could consist of prior academic performance, financial need, etc.).

Form 1023 (Rev. 01-2020) Name: EIN: Page **38**

Schedule H. Organizations Providing Scholarships, Fellowships, Educational Loans, or Other Educational Grants to Individuals and Private Foundations Requesting Advance Approval of Individual Grant Procedures *(continued)*

5 Describe any requirement or condition you impose on recipients to obtain, maintain, or qualify for renewal of a grant (for example, specific requirements or conditions could consist of attendance at a four-year college, maintaining a certain grade point average, teaching in public school after graduation from college, etc.).

6 Describe your procedures for supervising the scholarships, fellowships, educational loans, or other educational grants. Explain whether you obtain reports and grade transcripts from recipients, or you pay grants directly to a school under an arrangement whereby the school will apply the grant funds only for enrolled students who are in good standing. Also, describe your procedures for taking action if the terms of the award are violated.

7 How do you determine who is on the selection committee for the awards made under your program?

8 Are relatives of members of the selection committee, or of your officers, directors, or substantial contributors eligible for awards made under your program? If "Yes," what measures do you take to ensure unbiased selections? ◯ Yes ◯ No

Do not complete the rest of Schedule H. If you are a private foundation, you will be directed to complete Section II of Schedule H later in the application.

Form **1023** (Rev. 01-2020)

Schedule H. Organizations Providing Scholarships, Fellowships, Educational Loans, or Other Educational Grants to Individuals and Private Foundations Requesting Advance Approval of Individual Grant Procedures *(continued)*

Section II **Private foundations complete lines 1 through 7 of this section. Public charities do not complete this section.**

1 As a private foundation, do you want this application to be considered as a request for advance approval of grant making procedures? ◯ Yes ◯ No

If "No," do not complete the rest of Schedule H.

1a Check the box(es) indicating under which section(s) you want your grant making procedures to be considered.

☐ 4945(g)(1) - Scholarship or fellowship grant to an individual for study at an educational institution

☐ 4945(g)(3) - Other grants, including loans, to an individual for travel, study, or other similar purposes, to enhance a particular skill of the grantee or to produce a specific product

2 Do you represent that you will (1) arrange to receive and review grantee reports annually and upon completion of the purpose for which the grant was awarded, (2) investigate diversions of funds from their intended purposes, and (3) take all reasonable and appropriate steps to recover diverted funds, ensure other grant funds held by a grantee are used for their intended purposes, and withhold further payments to grantees until you obtain grantees' assurances that future diversions will not occur and that grantees will take extraordinary precautions to prevent future diversions from occurring? ◯ Yes ◯ No

3 Do you represent that you will maintain all records relating to individual grants, including information obtained to evaluate grantees, identify whether a grantee is a disqualified person, establish the amount and purpose of each grant, and establish that you undertook the supervision and investigation of grants described in Line 2? ◯ Yes ◯ No

4 Do you or will you award scholarships, fellowships, and educational loans to attend an educational institution based on the status of an individual being an employee of a particular employer? ◯ Yes ◯ No

If "No," do not complete the rest of Schedule H.

5 Will you comply with the seven conditions and either the percentage tests or facts and circumstances test for scholarships, fellowships, and educational loans to attend an educational institution as set forth in Revenue Procedures 76-47, 1976-2 C.B. 670, and 80-39, 1980-2 C.B. 772, which apply to inducement, selection committee, eligibility requirements, objective basis of selection, employment, course of study, and other objectives? ◯ Yes ◯ No

6 Do you or will you provide scholarships, fellowships, or educational loans to attend an educational institution to employees of a particular employer? If "No," continue to Line 7. ◯ Yes ◯ No

6a Will you award grants to 10% or fewer of the eligible applicants who were actually considered by the selection committee in selecting recipients of grants in that year as provided by Revenue Procedures 76-47 and 80-39? ◯ Yes ◯ No

7 Do you provide scholarships, fellowships, or educational loans to attend an educational institution to children of employees of a particular employer? ◯ Yes ◯ No

If "No," do not complete the rest of Schedule H.

7a Will you award grants to 25% or fewer of the eligible applicants who were actually considered by the selection committee in selecting recipients of grants in that year as provided by Revenue Procedures 76-47 and 80-39? ◯ Yes ◯ No

If "Yes," do not complete the rest of Schedule H.

Form 1023 (Rev. 01-2020) Name: EIN: Page **40**

Schedule H. Organizations Providing Scholarships, Fellowships, Educational Loans, or Other Educational Grants to Individuals and Private Foundations Requesting Advance Approval of Individual Grant Procedures *(continued)*

7b Will you award grants to 10% or fewer of the number of employees' children who can be shown to be eligible for grants (whether or not they submitted an application) in that year, as provided by Revenue Procedures 76-47 and 80-39? If "Yes," describe how you will determine who can be shown to be eligible for grants without submitting an application, such as by obtaining written statements or other information about the expectations of employees' children to attend an educational institution; do not complete the rest of Schedule H. ◯ Yes ◯ No

7c Will you award grants based on facts and circumstances that demonstrate that the grants will not be considered compensation for past, present, or future services or otherwise provide a significant benefit to the particular employer? If "Yes," describe the facts and circumstances you believe will demonstrate that the grants are neither compensatory nor a significant benefit to the particular employer. In your explanation, describe why you cannot satisfy either the 25% test or the 10% test in questions 7a and 7b. ◯ Yes ◯ No

Form **1023** (Rev. 01-2020)

Form **1023-EZ** (Rev. April 2021) Department of the Treasury Internal Revenue Service

Streamlined Application for Recognition of Exemption Under Section 501(c)(3) of the Internal Revenue Code

Do not enter Social Security numbers on this form as it will be made public.

Information about Form 1023-EZ and its separate instructions is at www.irs.gov/form1023ez

OMB No. 1545-0047

Note: *If exempt status is approved, this application will be open for public inspection.*

☐ **Check this box to attest that you have completed the Form 1023-EZ Eligibility Worksheet in the current instructions, are eligible to apply for exemption using Form 1023-EZ, and have read and understand the requirements to be exempt under section 501(c)(3).**

Have your annual gross receipts exceeded $50,000 in any of the past 3 years and/or do you project that your annual gross receipts will exceed $50,000 in any of the next 3 years? If yes, stop. Do not file Form 1023-EZ. See Instructions. ○ Yes ○ No

Do you have total assets the fair market value of which is in excess of $250,000? If yes, stop. Do not file Form 1023-EZ. See Instructions. ○ Yes ○ No

Part I Identification of Applicant

1a Full Name of Organization	**b** Care Of Name (if applicable)

c Mailing Address (number, street, and room/suite). If a P.O. box, see instructions.	**d** City	**e** State	**f** Zip code + 4

2 Employer Identification Number	**3** Month Tax Year Ends (MM)	**4** Person to Contact If More Information is Needed

5 Contact Telephone Number	**6** Fax Number (optional)	**7** User Fee Submitted $275.00

8 List the names, titles, and mailing addresses of your officers, directors, and/or trustees. (If you have more than five, see instructions.)

First Name:	Last Name:	Title:	
Street Address:	City:	State:	Zip code + 4:
First Name:	Last Name:	Title:	
Street Address:	City:	State:	Zip code + 4:
First Name:	Last Name:	Title:	
Street Address:	City:	State:	Zip code + 4:
First Name:	Last Name:	Title:	
Street Address:	City:	State:	Zip code + 4:
First Name:	Last Name:	Title:	
Street Address:	City:	State:	Zip code + 4:

9a Organization's Website (if available):

b Organization's Email (optional):

Part II Organizational Structure

1 To file this form, you must be a corporation, an unincorporated association, or a trust. **Select the box** for the type of organization.

☐ Corporation ☐ Unincorporated association ☐ Trust

2 ☐ **Check this box** to attest that you have the organizing document necessary for the organizational structure indicated above. (See the instructions for an explanation of **necessary organizing documents.**)

3 Date incorporated if a corporation, or formed if other than a corporation (MMDDYYYY): ____________

4 State of incorporation or other formation: undefined

5 Section 501(c)(3) requires that your organizing document must limit your purposes to one or more exempt purposes within section 501(c)(3).

☐ **Check this box** to attest that your organizing document contains this limitation.

6 Section 501(c)(3) requires that your organizing document must not expressly empower you to engage, otherwise than as an insubstantial part of your activities, in activities that in themselves are not in furtherance of one or more exempt purposes.

☐ **Check this box** to attest that your organizing document does not expressly empower you to engage, otherwise than as an insubstantial part of your activities, in activities that in themselves are not in furtherance of one or more exempt purposes.

7 Section 501(c)(3) requires that your organizing document must provide that upon dissolution, your remaining assets be used exclusively for section 501(c)(3) exempt purposes. Depending on your entity type and the state in which you are formed, this requirement may be satisfied by operation of state law.

☐ **Check this box** to attest that your organizing document contains the dissolution provision required under section 501(c)(3) or that you do not need an express dissolution provision in your organizing document because you rely on the operation of state law in the state in which you are formed for your dissolution provision.

For Paperwork Reduction Act Notice, see the instructions Catalog No. 66267N Form **1023-EZ** (Rev 4-2021)

Form 1023-EZ (Rev. 4-2021) Page **2**

Part III **Your Specific Activities**

1 Briefly describe the organization's mission or most significant activities (limit 250 characters)

2 Enter the appropriate 3-character NTEE Code that best describes your activities (See the instructions): ________

3 To qualify for exemption as a section 501(c)(3) organization, you must be organized and operated exclusively to further one or more of the following purposes. By checking the box or boxes below, you attest that you are organized and operated exclusively to further the purposes indicated. **Check all that apply.**

☐ Charitable ☐ Religious ☐ Educational

☐ Scientific ☐ Literary ☐ Testing for public safety

☐ To foster national or international amateur sports competition ☐ Prevention of cruelty to children or animals

4 To qualify for exemption as a section 501(c)(3) organization, you must:

- Refrain from supporting or opposing candidates in political campaigns in any way.
- Ensure that your net earnings do not inure in whole or in part to the benefit of private shareholders or individuals (that is, board members, officers, key management employees, or other insiders).
- Not further non-exempt purposes (such as purposes that benefit private interests) more than insubstantially.
- Not be organized or operated for the primary purpose of conducting a trade or business that is not related to your exempt purpose(s).
- Not devote more than an insubstantial part of your activities attempting to influence legislation or, if you made a section 501(h) election, not normally make expenditures in excess of expenditure limitations outlined in section 501(h).
- Not provide commercial-type insurance as a substantial part of your activities.

☐ **Check this box** to attest that you have not conducted and will not conduct activities that violate these prohibitions and restrictions.

5 Do you or will you attempt to influence legislation? (If yes, consider filing Form 5768. See the instructions for more details.) ○ Yes ○ No

6 Do you or will you pay compensation to any of your officers, directors, or trustees? (Refer to the instructions for a definition of **compensation.**) ○ Yes ○ No

7 Do you or will you donate funds to or pay expenses for individual(s)? ○ Yes ○ No

8 Do you or will you conduct activities or provide grants or other assistance to individual(s) or organization(s) outside the United States? ○ Yes ○ No

9 Do you or will you engage in financial transactions (for example, loans, payments, rents, etc.) with any of your officers, directors, or trustees, or any entities they own or control? ○ Yes ○ No

10 Do you or will you have unrelated business gross income of $1,000 or more during a tax year? ○ Yes ○ No

11 Do you or will you operate bingo or other gaming activities? ○ Yes ○ No

12 Do you or will you provide disaster relief? ○ Yes ○ No

Part IV **Foundation Classification**

Part IV is designed to classify you as an organization that is either a private foundation or a public charity. Public charity status is a more favorable tax status than private foundation status.

1 Are you applying for recognition as a church, school, or hospital (described in section 170(b)(1)(A)(i), (ii), or (iii) of the Internal Revenue Code)? If yes, stop. Do not file Form 1023-EZ. See Instructions ○ Yes ○ No

2 If you qualify for public charity status, check the appropriate box (**2a - 2c** below) and skip to **Part V** below.

a ○ **Select this box** to attest that you normally receive at least one-third of your support from public sources or you normally receive at least 10 percent of your support from public sources and you have other characteristics of a publicly supported organization. **Sections 509(a)(1) and 170(b)(1)(A)(vi).**

b ○ **Select this box** to attest that you normally receive more than one-third of your support from a combination of gifts, grants, contributions, membership fees, and gross receipts (from permitted sources) from activities related to your exempt functions and normally receive not more than one-third of your support from investment income and unrelated business taxable income. **Section 509(a)(2).**

c ○ **Select this box** to attest that you are operated for the benefit of a college or university that is owned or operated by a governmental unit. **Sections 509(a)(1) and 170(b)(1)(A)(iv).**

3 If you are not described in items **2a - 2c** above, you are a private foundation. As a private foundation, you are required by section 508(e) to have specific provisions in your organizing document, unless you rely on the operation of state law in the state in which you were formed to meet these requirements. These specific provisions require that you operate to avoid liability for private foundation excise taxes under sections 4941-4945.

○ **Select this box** to attest that your organizing document contains the provisions required by section 508(e) or that your organizing document does not need to include the provisions required by section 508(e) because you rely on the operation of state law in your particular state to meet the requirements of section 508(e). (See the instructions for explanation of the section 508(e) requirements.)

Form **1023-EZ** (Rev. 4-2021)

Form 1023-EZ (Rev. 4-2021) Page **3**

Part V **Reinstatement After Automatic Revocation**

Complete this section only if you are applying for reinstatement of exemption after being automatically revoked for failure to file required annual returns or notices for three consecutive years, and you are applying for reinstatement under section 4 or 7 of Revenue Procedure 2014-11. (Check only one box.)

1 ☐ **Check this box** if you are seeking retroactive reinstatement under section 4 of Revenue Procedure 2014-11. By checking this box, you attest that you meet the specified requirements of section 4, that your failure to file was not intentional, and that you have put in place procedures to file required returns or notices in the future. (See the instructions for requirements.)

2 ☐ **Check this box** if you are seeking reinstatement under section 7 of Revenue Procedure 2014-11, effective the date you are filing this application.

Part VI **Signature**

☐ **I declare under the penalties of perjury that I am authorized to sign this application on behalf of the above organization and that I have examined this application, and to the best of my knowledge it is true, correct, and complete.**

(Type name of signer) (Type title or authority of signer)

02152026
(Date)

Form **1023-EZ** (Rev. 4-2021)

Form **5768**

(Rev. September 2016)

Department of the Treasury
Internal Revenue Service

Election/Revocation of Election by an Eligible Section 501(c)(3) Organization To Make Expenditures To Influence Legislation

(Under Section 501(h) of the Internal Revenue Code)

► Information about Form 5768 and its instructions is at *www.irs.gov/form5768*.

For IRS Use Only ►

Name of organization	Employer identification number
Number and street (or P.O. box no., if mail is not delivered to street address)	Room/suite
City, town or post office, and state	ZIP + 4

1 **Election—** As an eligible organization, we hereby elect to have the provisions of section 501(h) of the Code, relating to expenditures to influence legislation, apply to our tax year ending ______________ (Month, day, and year) and all subsequent tax years until revoked.

Note: This election must be signed and postmarked within the first taxable year to which it applies.

2 **Revocation—** As an eligible organization, we hereby revoke our election to have the provisions of section 501(h) of the Code, relating to expenditures to influence legislation, apply to our tax year ending ______________ (Month, day, and year) and all subsequent tax years *(until a new election is made)*.

Note: This revocation must be signed and postmarked before the first day of the tax year to which it applies.

Under penalties of perjury, I declare that I am authorized to make this (check applicable box) ► ☐ election ☐ revocation on behalf of the above named organization.

(Signature of officer or trustee)	(Type or print name and title)	(Date)

General Instructions

Section references are to the Internal Revenue Code.

Section 501(c)(3) states that an organization exempt under that section will lose its tax-exempt status and its qualification to receive deductible charitable contributions if a substantial part of its activities are carried on to influence legislation. Section 501(h), however, permits certain eligible section 501(c)(3) organizations to elect to make limited expenditures to influence legislation. An organization making the election will, however, be subject to an excise tax under section 4911 if it spends more than the amounts permitted by that section. Also, the organization may lose its exempt status if its lobbying expenditures exceed the permitted amounts by more than 50% over a 4-year period. For any tax year in which an election under section 501(h) is in effect, an electing organization must report the actual and permitted amounts of its lobbying expenditures and grass roots expenditures (as defined in section 4911(c)) on its annual return required under section 6033. See Part II-A of Schedule C (Form 990 or Form 990-EZ). Each electing member of an affiliated group must report these amounts for both itself and the affiliated group as a whole.

To make or revoke the election, enter the ending date of the tax year to which the election or revocation applies in item **1** or **2**, as applicable, and sign and date the form in the spaces provided.

Eligible organizations. A section 501(c)(3) organization is permitted to make the election if it is not a disqualified organization (see below) and is described in:

1. Section 170(b)(1)(A)(ii) (relating to educational institutions),
2. Section 170(b)(1)(A)(iii) (relating to hospitals and medical research organizations),
3. Section 170(b)(1)(A)(iv) (relating to organizations supporting government schools),
4. Section 170(b)(1)(A)(vi) (relating to organizations publicly supported by charitable contributions),
5. Section 170(b)(1)(A)(ix) (relating to agricultural research organizations),
6. Section 509(a)(2) (relating to organizations publicly supported by admissions, sales, etc.), or
7. Section 509(a)(3) (relating to organizations supporting certain types of public charities other than those section 509(a)(3) organizations that support section 501(c)(4), (5), or (6) organizations).

Disqualified organizations. The following types of organizations are not permitted to make the election:

a. Section 170(b)(1)(A)(i) organizations (relating to churches),

b. An integrated auxiliary of a church or of a convention or association of churches, or

c. A member of an affiliated group of organizations if one or more members of such group is described in **a** or **b** of this paragraph.

Affiliated organizations. Organizations are members of an affiliated group of organizations only if (1) the governing instrument of one such organization requires it to be bound by the decisions of the other organization on legislative issues, or (2) the governing board of one such organization includes persons (i) who are specifically designated representatives of another such organization or are members of the governing board, officers, or paid executive staff members of such other organization, and (ii) who, by aggregating their votes, have sufficient voting power to cause or prevent action on legislative issues by the first such organization.

For more details, see section 4911 and section 501(h).

Note: A private foundation (including a private operating foundation) is not an eligible organization.

Where to file. Mail Form 5768 to:

Department of the Treasury
Internal Revenue Service Center
Ogden, UT 84201-0027

Cat. No. 12125M

Form **5768** (Rev. 9-2016)

Form **8282** (Rev. October 2021) Department of the Treasury Internal Revenue Service

Donee Information Return

(Sale, Exchange, or Other Disposition of Donated Property)

► **Go to *www.irs.gov/Form8282* for latest information.**

OMB No. 1545-0047

Give a Copy to Donor

Parts To Complete

- If the organization is an **original donee,** complete *Identifying Information,* Part I (lines 1a–1d and, if applicable, lines 2a–2d), and Part III.
- If the organization is a **successor donee,** complete *Identifying Information,* Part I, Part II, and Part III.

Identifying Information

Print or Type	Name of charitable organization (donee)	**Employer identification number**
	Address (number, street, and room or suite no.) (or P.O. box no. if mail is not delivered to the street address)	
	City or town, state, and ZIP code	

Part I **Information on ORIGINAL DONOR and SUCCESSOR DONEE Receiving the Property**

1a Name of original donor of the property	**1b Identifying number(s)**
1c Address (number, street, and room or suite no.) (P.O. box no. if mail is not delivered to the street address)	
1d City or town, state, and ZIP code	

Note. Complete lines 2a–2d only if the organization gave this property to another charitable organization (successor donee).

2a Name of charitable organization	**2b Employer identification number**
2c Address (number, street, and room or suite no.) (or P.O. box no. if mail is not delivered to the street address)	
2d City or town, state, and ZIP code	

Part II **Information on PREVIOUS DONEES. Complete this part only if the organization was not the first donee to receive the property.** See the instructions before completing lines 3a through 4d.

3a Name of original donee	**3b Employer identification number**
3c Address (number, street, and room or suite no.) (or P.O. box no. if mail is not delivered to the street address)	
3d City or town, state, and ZIP code	
4a Name of preceding donee	**4b Employer identification number**
4c Address (number, street, and room or suite no.) (or P.O. box no. if mail is not delivered to the street address)	
4d City or town, state, and ZIP code	

For Paperwork Reduction Act Notice, see Instructions for Form 990. Cat. No. 62307Y Form **8282** (Rev. 10-2021)

Form 8282 (Rev. 10-2021) Page **2**

Part III Information on DONATED PROPERTY

	1. Description of the donated property sold, exchanged, or otherwise disposed of and how the organization used the property. (If you need more space, attach a separate statement.)	2. Did the disposition involve the organization's entire interest in the property? Yes	No	3. Was the use related to the organization's exempt purpose or function? Yes	No	4. Information on use of property. • If you answered "Yes" to question 3 and the property was tangible personal property, describe how the organization's use of the property furthered its exempt purpose or function. Also complete Part IV below. • If you answered "No" to question 3 and the property was tangible personal property, describe the organization's intended use (if any) at the time of the contribution. Also complete Part IV below, if the intended use at the time of the contribution was related to the organization's exempt purpose or function and it became impossible or infeasible to implement.
A						
B						
C						
D						

		Donated Property			
		A	B	C	D
5	Date the organization received the donated property (MM/DD/YY)	/ /	/ /	/ /	/ /
6	Date the original donee received the property (MM/DD/YY)	/ /	/ /	/ /	/ /
7	Date the property was sold, exchanged, or otherwise disposed of (MM/DD/YY)	/ /	/ /	/ /	/ /
8	Amount received upon disposition	$	$	$	$

Part IV Certification

You must sign the certification below if any property described in Part III above is tangible personal property and:

- You answered "Yes" to question 3 above, or
- You answered "No" to question 3 above and the intended use of the property became impossible or infeasible to implement.

Under penalties of perjury and the penalty under section 6720B, I certify that either: (1) the use of the property that meets the above requirements, and is described above in Part III, was substantial and related to the donee organization's exempt purpose or function; or (2) the donee organization intended to use the property for its exempt purpose or function, but the intended use has become impossible or infeasible to implement.

Signature of officer | Title | Date

Sign Here

Under penalties of perjury, I declare that I have examined this return, including accompanying schedules and statements, and to the best of my knowledge and belief, it is true, correct, and complete.

Signature of officer | Title | Date

Type or print name

Form **8282** (Rev. 10-2021)

General Instructions

Section references are to the Internal Revenue Code.

Future developments. For the latest information about developments related to Form 8282 and its instructions, such as legislation enacted after they were published, go to *www.irs.gov/Form8282*.

Purpose of Form

Donee organizations use Form 8282 to report information to the IRS and donors about dispositions of certain charitable deduction property made within 3 years after the donor contributed the property.

Definitions

CAUTION *For Form 8282 and these instructions, the term "donee" includes all donees, unless specific reference is made to "original" or "successor" donees.*

Original donee. The first donee to or for which the donor gave the property. The original donee is required to sign Form 8283, Noncash Charitable Contributions, *Section B. Donated Property Over $5,000 (Except Certain Publicly Traded Securities)*, presented by the donor for charitable deduction property.

Successor donee. Any donee of property other than the original donee.

Charitable deduction property. Any donated property (other than money and publicly traded securities) if the claimed value exceeds $5,000 per item or group of similar items donated by the donor to one or more donee organizations. This is the property listed in Section B on Form 8283.

Who Must File

Original and successor donee organizations must file Form 8282 if they sell, exchange, consume, or otherwise dispose of (with or without consideration) charitable deduction property (or any portion) within 3 years after the date the original donee received the property. See *Charitable deduction property* above.

If the organization sold, exchanged, or otherwise disposed of motor vehicles, airplanes, or boats, see Pub. 526, Charitable Contributions.

Exceptions. There are two situations where Form 8282 does not have to be filed.

1. Items valued at $500 or less. The organization does not have to file Form 8282 if, at the time the original donee signed Section B of Form 8283, the donor had signed a statement on Form 8283 that the appraised value of the specific item was not more than $500. If Form 8283 contains more than one item, this exception applies only to those items that are clearly identified as having a value of $500 or less. However, for purposes of the donor's determination of whether the appraised value of the item exceeds $500, all shares of nonpublicly traded stock, or items that form a set, are considered one item. For example, a collection of books written by the same author, components of a stereo system, or six place settings of a pattern of silverware are considered one item.

2. Items consumed or distributed for charitable purpose. The organization does not have to file Form 8282 if an item is consumed or distributed, without consideration, in fulfilling your purpose or function as a tax-exempt organization. For example, no reporting is required for medical supplies consumed or distributed by a tax-exempt relief organization in aiding disaster victims.

When To File

If the organization disposes of charitable deduction property within 3 years of the date the original donee received it and the organization does not meet exception 1 or 2 above, the organization must file Form 8282 within 125 days after the date of disposition.

Exception. If the organization did not file because it had no reason to believe the substantiation requirements applied to the donor, but the organization later becomes aware that the substantiation requirements did apply, the organization must file Form 8282 within 60 days after the date it becomes aware it was liable. For example, this exception would apply where Section B of Form 8283 is furnished to a successor donee after the date that donee disposes of the charitable deduction property.

Missing information. If Form 8282 is filed by the due date, enter the organization's name, address, and employer identification number (EIN) and complete at least Part III, columns 1, 2, 3, and 4; and Part IV. The organization does not have to complete the remaining items if the information is not available. For example, the organization may not have the information necessary to complete all entries if the donor did not make Section B of Form 8283 available.

Where To File

Send Form 8282 to the Department of Treasury, Internal Revenue Service Center, Ogden, UT 84201-0027.

Other Requirements

Information the organization must give a successor donee. If the property is transferred to another charitable organization within the 3-year period discussed earlier, the organization must give the successor donee all of the following information.

1. The name, address, and EIN of the organization.

2. A copy of Section B of Form 8283 that the organization received from the donor or a preceding donee. The preceding donee is the one who gave the organization the property.

3. A copy of this Form 8282, within 15 days after the organization files it.

The organization must furnish items 1 and 2 above within 15 days after the latest of the date:

- The organization transferred the property,
- The original donee signed Section B of Form 8283, or
- The organization received a copy of Section B of Form 8283 from the preceding donee if the organization is also a successor donee.

Information the successor donee must give the organization. The successor donee organization to whom the organization transferred this property is required to give the organization its name, address, and EIN within 15 days after the later of:

- The date the organization transferred the property, or
- The date the successor donee received a copy of Section B of Form 8283.

Information the organization must give the donor. The organization must give a copy of Form 8282 to the original donor of the property.

Recordkeeping. The organization must keep a copy of Section B of Form 8283 in its records.

Penalties

Failure to file penalty. The organization may be subject to a penalty if it fails to file this form by the due date, fails to include all of the information required to be shown on the filed form, or includes incorrect information on the filed form. The penalty is generally $50 per form. For more details, see sections 6721 and 6724.

Fraudulent identification of exempt use property. A $10,000 penalty may apply to any person who identifies in Part III tangible personal property the organization sold, exchanged, or otherwise disposed of, as having a use that is related to a purpose or function knowing that such property was not intended for such a use. For more details, see section 6720B.

Specific Instructions

Part I

Line 1a. Enter the name of the original donor.

Line 1b. The donor's identifying number may be either an employer identification number or a social security number, and should be the same number provided on page 2 of Form 8283.

Line 1c and 1d. Enter the last known address of the original donor.

Lines 2a–2d. Complete these lines if the organization gave the property to another charitable organization successor donee (defined earlier). If the organization is an original donee, skip Part II and go to Part III.

Part II

Complete Part II only if the organization is a successor donee. If the organization is the original donee, do not complete any lines in Part II; go directly to Part III.

If the organization is the **second donee**, complete lines 3a through 3d. If the organization is the **third or later donee,** complete lines 3a through 4d. On lines 4a through 4d, give information on the preceding donee.

Part III

Column 1. For charitable deduction property that the organization sold, exchanged, or otherwise disposed of within 3 years of the original contribution, describe each item in detail. For a motor vehicle, include the vehicle identification number. For a boat, include the hull identification number. For an airplane, include the aircraft identification number. Additionally, for the period of time the organization owned the property, explain how it was used. If additional space is needed, attach a statement.

Column 3. Check "Yes" if the organization's use of the charitable deduction property was related to its exempt purpose or function. Check "No" if the organization sold, exchanged, or otherwise disposed of the property without using it.

Part IV

Certification. Sign and date the certification if any property described in Part III is tangible personal property and you answered "Yes" to Part III, question 3, or you answered "No" to Part III, question 3 and the intended use of the property became impossible or infeasible to implement.

Signature

Form 8282 is not valid unless it is signed by an officer of the organization. Be sure to include the title of the person signing the form and the date the form was signed.

How To Get Tax Help

Internet

You can access the IRS website 24 hours a day, 7 days a week, at *www.IRS.gov* to:

- Download forms and publications.
- Order IRS products online.
- Research your tax questions online.
- Search publications online by topic or keyword.
- Use the online Internal Revenue Code (IRC), Regulations, or other official guidance.
- View Internal Revenue Bulletins (IRBs) published in the last few years.
- Sign up to receive local and national tax news by email. To subscribe, visit *www.irs.gov/Charities*.

Ordering Forms and Publications

Visit *www.irs.gov/Formspubs* to download forms and publications. Otherwise, you can go to *www.irs.gov/OrderForms* to order current and prior-year forms and instructions. Your order should arrive within 10 business days.

Phone Help

If you have questions and/or need help completing this form, please call 877-829-5500. This toll-free telephone service is available Monday through Friday.

Form **8283**

(Rev. December 2025)

Department of the Treasury Internal Revenue Service

Noncash Charitable Contributions

Attach one or more Forms 8283 to your tax return if you claimed a total deduction of over $500 for all contributed property.

Go to *www.irs.gov/Form8283* for instructions and the latest information.

OMB No. 1545-0074

Attachment Sequence No. **36**

Name(s) shown on your income tax return | **Identifying number**

Enter the entity name and identifying number from the tax return where the noncash charitable contribution was originally reported, if different from above.

Name: ______ Identifying number: ______

Check this box if a family pass-through entity made the non-cash charitable contribution. See instructions . . . . ☐

Note: Figure the amount of your contribution deduction before completing this form. See your tax return instructions.

Section A. Donated Property of $5,000 or Less and Publicly Traded Securities—List in this section **only** an item (or a group of similar items) for which you claimed a deduction of $5,000 or less. Also list publicly traded securities and certain other property even if the deduction is more than $5,000. If you need more space, attach a statement. See instructions.

1	**(a)** Name and address of the donee organization	**(b)** If donated property is a vehicle (see instructions), check the box. Also enter the vehicle identification number (unless Form 1098-C is attached).	**(c)** Description and condition of donated property (For a vehicle, enter the year, make, model, and mileage. For securities and other property, see instructions.)
A		☐	
B		☐	
C		☐	
D		☐	

Note: If the amount you claimed as a deduction for an item is $500 or less, you do not have to complete columns (e), (f), and (g).

	(d) Date of the contribution	**(e)** Date acquired by donor (mo., yr.)	**(f)** How acquired by donor	**(g)** Donor's cost or adjusted basis	**(h)** Fair market value (see instructions)	**(i)** Method used to determine the fair market value
A						
B						
C						
D						

Section B. Donated Property Over $5,000 (Except Publicly Traded Securities, Vehicles, Intellectual Property or Inventory Reportable in Section A)—Complete this section for one item (or a group of similar items) for which you claimed a deduction of more than $5,000 per item or group (except contributions reportable in Section A). Provide a separate form for each item donated unless it is part of a group of similar items. A qualified appraisal is required for items reportable in Section B and in certain cases must be attached. See instructions.

Part I **Information on Donated Property**

2 Check the box that describes the type of property donated. See instructions for definitions.

- **a** ☐ Art (contribution of $20,000 or more)
- **b** ☐ Qualified conservation contribution
- **b(1)** ☐ Certified historic structure
  NPS # ______
- **c** ☐ Art (contribution of less than $20,000)
- **d** ☐ Other real estate
- **e** ☐ Equipment
- **f** ☐ Securities
- **g** ☐ Collectibles
- **h** ☐ Intellectual property
- **i** ☐ Vehicles
- **j** ☐ Clothing and household items
- **k** ☐ Digital assets
- **l** ☐ Other

3	**(a)** Description of donated property (if you need more space, attach a separate statement)	**(b)** If any tangible personal property or real property was donated, give a brief summary of the overall physical condition of the property at the time of the gift.	**(c)** Appraised fair market value
A			
B			
C			

	(d) Date acquired by donor (mo., yr.)	**(e)** How acquired by donor	**(f)** Donor's cost or adjusted basis	**(g)** For bargain sales, enter amount received	**(h)** Qualified conservation contribution relevant basis (see instructions)	**(i)** Amount claimed as a deduction (see instructions)
A						
B						
C						

For Paperwork Reduction Act Notice, see separate instructions. Cat. No. 62299J Form **8283** (Rev. 12-2025) Created 7/1/25

Form 8283 (Rev. 12-2025) Page **2**

Name(s) shown on your income tax return	**Identifying number**

Part II **Partial Interests and Restricted Use Property (Other Than Qualified Conservation Contributions)—** Complete lines 4a through 4e if you gave less than an entire interest in a property listed in Section B, Part I. Complete lines 5a through 5c if conditions were placed on a contribution listed in Section B, Part I; also attach the required statement. See instructions.

4a Enter the letter from Section B, Part I that identifies the property for which you gave less than an entire interest ____________
If Section B, Part II applies to more than one property, attach a separate statement.

b Total amount claimed as a deduction for the property listed in Section B, Part I: **(1)** For this tax year . . ____________
(2) For any prior tax years ____________

c Name and address of each organization to which any such contribution was made in a prior year (complete only if different from the donee organization in Section B, Part V, below):

Name of charitable organization (donee)

Address (number, street, and room or suite no.)	City or town, state, and ZIP code

d For tangible property, enter the place where the property is located or kept ____________

e Name of any person, other than the donee organization, having actual possession of the property ____________

		Yes	No
5a	Is there a restriction, either temporary or permanent, on the donee's right to use or dispose of the donated property?		
b	Did you give to anyone (other than the donee organization or another organization participating with the donee organization in cooperative fundraising) the right to the income from the donated property or to the possession of the property, including the right to vote donated securities, to acquire the property by purchase or otherwise, or to designate the person having such income, possession, or right to acquire?		
c	Is there a restriction limiting the donated property for a particular use?		

Part III **Taxpayer (Donor) Statement—**List each item included in Section B, Part I above that the appraisal identifies as having a value of $500 or less. See instructions.

I declare that the following item(s) included in Section B, Part I above has to the best of my knowledge and belief an appraised value of not more than $500 (per item). Enter identifying letter from Section B, Part I and describe the specific item. See instructions.

Signature of taxpayer (donor) Date

Part IV **Declaration of Appraiser—**See instructions.

I declare that I am not the donor, the donee, a party to the transaction in which the donor acquired the property, employed by, or related to any of the foregoing persons, or married to any person who is related to any of the foregoing persons. And, if regularly used by the donor, donee, or party to the transaction, I performed the majority of my appraisals during my tax year for other persons.

Also, I declare that I perform appraisals on a regular basis; and that because of my qualifications as described in the appraisal, I am qualified to make appraisals of the type of property being valued. I certify that the appraisal fees were not based on a percentage of the appraised property value. Furthermore, I understand that a false or fraudulent overstatement of the property value as described in the qualified appraisal or this Form 8283 may subject me to the penalty under section 6701(a) (aiding and abetting the understatement of tax liability). I understand that my appraisal will be used in connection with a return or claim for refund. I also understand that, if there is a substantial or gross valuation misstatement of the value of the property claimed on the return or claim for refund that is based on my appraisal, I may be subject to a penalty under section 6695A of the Internal Revenue Code, as well as other applicable penalties. I affirm that I have not been at any time in the three-year period ending on the date of the appraisal barred from presenting evidence or testimony before the Department of the Treasury or the Internal Revenue Service pursuant to 31 U.S.C. 330(c).

Sign Here	Appraiser signature		Date
	Appraiser name	Title	

Business address (including room or suite no.)	**Identifying number**
City or town, state, and ZIP code	

Part V **Donee Acknowledgment—**See instructions.

This charitable organization acknowledges that it is a qualified organization under section 170(c) and that it received the donated property as described in Section B, Part I, above on the following date ____________

Furthermore, this organization affirms that in the event it sells, exchanges, or otherwise disposes of the property described in Section B, Part I (or any portion thereof) within 3 years after the date of receipt, it will file **Form 8282**, Donee Information Return, with the IRS and give the donor a copy of that form. This acknowledgment does not represent agreement with the claimed fair market value.

Does the organization intend to use the property for an unrelated use? . . . . ☐ **Yes** ☐ **No**

Name of charitable organization (donee)	**Employer identification number**	
Address (number, street, and room or suite no.)	City or town, state, and ZIP code	
Authorized signature	Title	Date

Form **8283** (Rev. 12-2025)

APPENDIX

SELECTED NONPROFIT INTERNET RESOURCES

Academic and Public Policy Centers

Association for Research on Nonprofit Organizations and Voluntary Action—international membership organization dedicated to fostering through research an understanding of the nonprofit sector, philanthropy and volunteerism.
www.arnova.org

Indiana University Lilly Family School of Philanthropy—works to increase the understanding of philanthropy and improve its practice through research, teaching, and public service.
philanthropy.iupui.edu/

International Charity Law Network— association of charity law scholars involved in international and comparative work and including a database of more than 700 international and comparative publications relating to charity law.
charitylaw.nd.edu

International Society for Third-Sector Research—international membership organization dedicated to rigorous interdisciplinary approaches in third-sector research.
www.istr.org

Johns Hopkins Center for Civil Society Studies—archival research relating to the nonprofit sector.
ccss.jhu.edu/publications-findings/

Lowell Milken Center for Philanthropy and Nonprofits—academic center devoted to deepening the understanding of the nonprofit sector.
www.nonprofits.law.ucla.edu/

National Center on Philanthropy and the Law, New York University School of Law—major legal academic center; website contains a comprehensive bibliography of resources pertaining to nonprofit organization law and papers from annual conferences.
ncpl.law.nyu.edu/

Nonprofit Academic Centers Council—membership organization for nonprofit academic programs.
www.nonprofit-academic-centers-council.org

Urban Institute/National Center for Charitable Statistics—economic and social policy research organization; co-sponsors of project to compile and report statistical information on nonprofit organizations.
www.urban.org and nccs.urban.org

Blogs

Nonprofit Law Blog—includes nonprofit law "essentials," news and other resources.
nonprofitlawprofblog.com

Nonprofit Law Prof Blog—includes news and commentary about nonprofit sector developments edited by law professors who specialize in the field.
lawprofessors.typepad.com/nonprofit/

Government

Federal

Internal Revenue Service—the IRS web site includes a portal dedicated to charities and other nonprofit organizations.
www.irs.gov/charities-and-nonprofits

State

National Association of State Charity Officials—an association of state officials (attorneys general, secretaries of state, and others) charged with the regulation and oversight of charitable organizations and charitable solicitation.
nasconet.org

Selected States

Note: These state web sites include links to many other useful state resources and nonprofit sector web sites.

California Department of Justice, Registry of Charitable Trusts
oag.ca.gov/charities

Massachusetts Attorney General, Non-Profit Organizations/Public Charities Division
www.mass.gov/orgs/the-attorney-generals-non-profit-organizationspublic-charities-division

New York State Attorney General's Office, Charities, Nonprofits & Fundraisers Bureau
ag.ny.gov/resources/government-organizations/charities-nonprofits-fundraisers

Ohio Attorney General's Office, Charitable Law Section
charitable.ohioago.gov

Nonprofit Sector

National and International Organizations

BoardSource—mission is to strengthen effectiveness of nonprofit boards of directors.
boardsource.org

Candid (formerly GuideStar and Foundation Center)—a preeminent source of online information on nonprofit organizations; includes complete copies of recent Form 990's and 990-PFs for virtually all U.S. charities.
candid.org

Independent Sector—the major national association for nonprofit organizations; works to encourage philanthropy, volunteering, and citizen action.
www.independentsector.org

International Center for Not-for-Profit Law—gathers information about and promotes reforms relating to the legal environment for nonprofit organizations globally
www.icnl.org

National Center on Nonprofit Enterprise—mission is to help nonprofit managers and leaders make wise economic decisions.
nationalcne.org

National Council of Nonprofits—network of national and regional nonprofit associations.
www.councilofnonprofits.org

Nonprofit Explorer, a project of ProPublica—an online database of Form 990s and other financial information about tax-exempt organizations.
projects.propublica.org/nonprofits/

Selected State and Local Organizations

Lawyers Alliance for New York—provider of affordable business and transactional legal services for nonprofit organizations in New York City.
lawyersalliance.org

Minnesota Council of Nonprofits—web site includes a useful guide on best practices.
www.minnesotanonprofits.org

Nonprofit New York—information source for New York nonprofit organizations; includes useful resource on "How to Read Form 990."
www.nonprofitnewyork.org

Pennsylvania Association of Nonprofit Organizations—advocacy, education and services to Pennsylvania nonprofit organizations.
pano.org

Private Foundations

Council on Foundations—nonprofit membership association of grantmaking foundations and corporations.
cof.org

Exponent Philanthropy (formerly Association of Small Foundations)—provides programs, products and services to foundations with small or no staff.
exponentphilanthropy.org

Investment Fund for Foundations—provides customized investment vehicles and education for private foundations and other § 501(c)(3) organizations.
tiff.org

Grantmaking

The United Philanthropy Forum—national service association for philanthropy.
www.unitedphilforum.org/

Advocacy and Lobbying

Alliance for Justice—national association of advocacy organizations that works to strengthen the public interest community's ability to influence public policy.
afj.org

Media

Chronicle of Philanthropy
www.philanthropy.com

Philanthropy and Fundraising

Association of Fundraising Professionals—professional association for individuals responsible for generating philanthropic support for a wide variety of charitable organizations.
afpglobal.org

Center for Effective Philanthropy—an organization focused on developing data and insight to enable funders to be more effective.
cep.org

Give.org—an alliance of the Better Business Bureau and the National Charities Information Bureau; designed to help donors make informed giving decisions.
www.give.org

The Giving Institute—promotes need for professional and ethical standards of practice; influences laws governing philanthropy.
givinginstitute.org

National Center for Family Philanthropy—national resource center focusing on matters of importance to families engaged in philanthropy and their effective giving.
www.ncfp.org

National Center for Responsive Philanthropy—advocacy organization that seeks to promote philanthropy that is responsive to communities and people with the least wealth and opportunity.
ncrp.org

The Philanthropic Initiative—organization offering philanthropic design and management services to corporations, foundations, individuals and families.
tpi.org

The Philanthropy Roundtable—organization dedicated to fostering excellence in philanthropy and protect philanthropic freedom.
www.philanthropyroundtable.org

SELECTED SECTIONS
NONPROFIT ORGANIZATIONS
STATUTES, REGULATIONS, AND FORMS
2026 Edition

Selected and edited by

JAMES J. FISHMAN
Professor of Law Emeritus
Elisabeth Haub School of Law at Pace University

STEPHEN SCHWARZ
Professor of Law Emeritus
University of California College of the Law, San Francisco

LLOYD HITOSHI MAYER
Professor of Law
University of Notre Dame Law School

ROGER COLINVAUX
Professor of Law
The Catholic University of America, Columbus School of Law

FOUNDATION PRESS

The publisher is not engaged in rendering legal or other professional advice, and this publication is not a substitute for the advice of an attorney. If you require legal or other expert advice, you should seek the services of a competent attorney or other professional.

860 Blue Gentian Road, Suite 350
Eagan, MN 55121
1-877-888-1330

Published in the United States of America

ISBN: 979-8-31770-155-0